I0759518

MURTY CLASSICAL
LIBRARY OF INDIA

THE QUESTIONS OF MILINDA

MCLI 39

THE QUESTIONS OF MILINDA

Translated by
MARIA HEIM

MURTY CLASSICAL LIBRARY OF INDIA
HARVARD UNIVERSITY PRESS
Cambridge, Massachusetts
London, England
2025

Printed in the United States of America
First printing

SERIES DESIGN BY M9DESIGN

Library of Congress Cataloging-in-Publication Data

Names: Heim, Maria, 1969- translator.
Title: The Questions of Milinda / translated by Maria Heim.
Other titles: Milindapañhā. | Murty classical library of India ; 39.
Description: Cambridge, Massachusetts ; London, England : Harvard University Press, 2025. | Series: Murty classical library of India ; 39 | Includes bibliographical references and index. |
Pali (romanized) with English translation.
Identifiers: LCCN 2024003685 | ISBN 9780674295773 (cloth)
Subjects: LCSH: Menander, Indo-Greek king, active 2nd century B.C. | Nag Sen, active 4th century. | Milindapañhā. |
Milindapañhā--Translations into English. |
Buddhism--Early works to 1800.
Classification: LCC BQ2612.E5 Q47 2025 |
DDC 294.3/42041--dc23/eng/20240328
LC record available at https://lccn.loc.gov/2024003685

CONTENTS

INTRODUCTION

For at least two millennia people have been captivated by the story of a Greek king and a Buddhist monk meeting in the northwestern part of the Indian subcontinent and engaging in philosophical discussion. Perhaps the story is based on an actual encounter between a monk called Nagasena and a king ruling a Greek satrapy in the aftermath of Alexander's campaign into the region around 327 B.C.E. Scholars have tentatively identified the possible historical king as Menander, the most prominent of the Greek kings of Bactria (which reached from today's northern Afghanistan into Central Asia); his visage is recalled on the many coins with his name found in the region. Or perhaps the story is a legend, a literary conceit that represents not so much what actually happened as what might have happened sometime during the rich intellectual and cultural exchange forged in the Buddhist lands of the cosmopolitan Indo-Greek civilization in the early centuries before the Common Era. The present volume translates the longest and most substantial version of the story still extant, *The Questions of Milinda* (*Milindapañha*). This telling was preserved in a language called Pali and treasured for centuries by the Theravada school of Buddhism.

The History

Archaeological evidence confirms a Buddhist presence in the region referred to as greater Gandhara from at least the middle of the third century B.C.E. The Indian emperor Ashoka (r. 268–232 B.C.E.) had edicts chiseled on rock faces proclaiming his adherence to Buddhist values, at sites in Mansehra, Shahbazgaṛhi, and Kandahar. Subsequent centuries yield more material evidence of Buddhism in the form of Greek coins bearing Buddhist symbols, and then the development of Gandharan Buddhist sculpture in the early centuries of the Common Era. When Menander I reigned in the middle of the first century B.C.E. from his capital at Sagala (thought to be present-day Sialkot in Pakistan), Buddhism was present throughout the region.

Although Menander (if indeed he is the same king referred to as Milinda in the Pali tradition) is remembered fondly in later Buddhist sources, evidence outside of the text that he may have converted to Buddhism is suggestive but not definitive. His coins hint at possible Buddhist symbols, such as the eight-spoked wheel, though this could easily be associated with a more general symbol of the Indian ideal of the "wheel-turning emperor." On the Greek side, Plutarch recounts that Menander was a "good king" and that at his funeral various claimants to his ashes were instructed to divide the remains among themselves and go to their many cities to erect monuments to him.[1] This detail echoes events following the Buddha's own death as we know them from the early scriptures, when rival kings vied for his relics before they were distributed and established in monuments. Much later Indian, Chinese, and Tibetan sources celebrate Menander as a convert to Buddhism, and he is the only Indo-Greek king named in classical Indian literature.[2]

It is also possible that the king known to the text as Milinda was not in fact Menander; he might be a literary invention entirely. Of the figure of the monk Nagasena, we have no trace besides his presence in the Milinda-Nagasena corpus itself.

The Pali version of the story is likely based on an earlier text in a northwestern Indian language, probably a Prakrit called Gandhari. (Pali was not a language used in the region; it is the scriptural language used exclusively by Theravada Buddhists, historically prevalent in Sri Lanka and mainland Southeast Asia.) We also have a Chinese work preserved in two surviving recensions that differs substantially from the Pali text. The posited original text from which these and perhaps other versions sprang is unfortunately lost.[3] The Pali *Milindapañha* adds significant material not attested in the Chinese versions and is thought to be a composite of several distinct layers added to an earlier core in the first few centuries C.E. At no time is an author's name attached to any of these versions.

The *Questions of Milinda* has enjoyed high standing in the Theravada tradition from at least the fifth century, when the great translator and commentator Buddhaghosa helped systematize Pali Buddhist doctrine. It is the only noncanonical text that he quotes frequently (although in some instances he seems to have had a slightly different text in front of him than what has come down to us). In subsequent Theravada Buddhism the work came to be considered canonical by the Burmese monastic establishment, and it is highly esteemed and widely discussed in other branches of the Theravada.

In the modern global context, the *Milindapañha*—suggesting as it does one of the earliest encounters between East and West—was among the very first Buddhist texts translated into European languages. By now it has been translated into English, French, Italian, German, Japanese, Russian, Newari, Sinhala, Chinese, Thai, and Khmer, and is one of the most famous Buddhist texts in the world.[4] The work has naturally attracted scholars interested in questions of influence, and there has been over a century of debate on this issue. Does the *Milindapañha* indicate Greek philosophical influence on India or the other way around? While not discounting any Greek elements in the text, the weight of scholarly opinion leans in the direction of seeing it as largely a product of Indian ideas and intellectual practices. How deeply Indian influences impacted the Hellenistic world continues to be discussed.[5] The debate remains lively, and the text invites further investigation on this question.

The Story

Buddhist texts typically offer some sort of frame story that sets the stage for the rest of the work. The discussion between King Milinda and the scholarly monk Nagasena is framed in the first chapter, "Former Connections," with a backstory (*bāhirakathā*) that extends to an earlier encounter many lifetimes before. This distant incident serves as impetus for their present encounter. Timescapes are huge in the Indian thought world. Here the incident in question occurred at the time of a previous buddha, called Kassapa, who lived and taught the Dhamma millions of eons prior to the current dispensation of the buddha of our time, Gotama. The backstory provides a rather humorous account of the two protagonists falling out over a trifle, then vowing to meet in debate in a future encounter.

The novice monk in that distant time fails to sweep up and toss away the monastery's rubbish and is scolded and struck with a broomstick by a senior monk. He complies and removes the rubbish, and then, on the basis of the good he did in tidying up the place, makes this aspiration as he watches the tossing waves of the Ganga River: "May I in birth after birth until I attain nibbana always have a ready wit and unfailing speech like these tossing waves!"[6] The senior monk overhears this and reasons that if such a meager act of merit can yield such blessings in the future, he should attempt an aspiration himself: "May I too in birth after birth until I attain nibbana always have unfailing speech like these tossing waves of the Ganga, and may I be able to either provide answers or unravel questions in whatever ways they are asked by him!"[7]

We are then told that the two are reborn as gods and humans numerous times in the long era between buddhas, until they reach the present time, five hundred years after the passing away of Gotama Buddha. But while he was still alive, Gotama Buddha predicted their encounter (which itself authorizes the value and authenticity of the text): "These two will be reborn five hundred years after my final nibbana, and they will provide analyses of the areas of the Dhamma and the *vinaya,* which I have taught but made subtle, disentangling them and making them clear by asking questions and applying analogies." The stage is then set for this clarification of the Buddha's teaching through a question-and-answer format by one of ready wit, on the one side, and one capable of unraveling all knotty dilemmas, on the other.

The present story then shifts into high drama as King Milinda, the former novice, at the height of his intellectual hubris (to import an appropriately Greek idea), publicly bemoans the lack of worthy philosophical interlocutors in his realm. The trope of the intellectually perspicacious king seeking to engage wise sages of all sectarian persuasions for debate is an ancient Indian ideal reaching back at least to the Upanishads. Finding none worthy to engage with his own formidable intellect, he declares that India is "empty and sheer nonsense"—a humiliating charge coming from this cosmopolitan Greek figure.

Buddhist texts often proceed by way of pastiche, borrowing tropes and elements from other texts that echo the Buddha's own story and teachings. Milinda's story picks up trace elements of the canonical books, most evidently in a story of a king in the Buddha's own day, Ajatasattu, who seeks out various holy men and teachers on a lovely moonlit night to answer his questions and settle his doubts. He is presented with six—Ancient Kassapa, Makkhali of the Cow Pen (an Ajivaka, a fatalist), the Jain Nataputta, Sanjaya son of Belattha (a skeptic), Ajita of the Hair Shirt (a materialist), and Pakudha Kaccayana—and finds them spectacularly inadequate to the task. He must turn to the Buddha, who alone is able to handle his questions. That these same figures pop up in a parallel fashion for Milinda only reaffirms the perennial sectarian claims of the uniqueness of the Buddha's teaching for offering genuine intellectual and spiritual solace.

While Milinda is vainly searching for philosophers, the Buddhist monks in the region quietly retreat to the Himalayas, unable to supply one of their own to handle the king's questions. They realize that the wisest among them is actually a god in heaven who must be induced (rather against his preference to avoid the troubled nature of the human realm) to take birth as a human called Nagasena, come of age, enter the monastic order, and eventually debate King Milinda. By the time the two meet, as the chapter "Former Connections" draws to a close, we are primed for a public contest. Milinda is flanked by five hundred Yonakas ("Ionians," the Indo-Greeks), and Nagasena arrives with a retinue of eighty thousand monks. The chapter ends with Milinda suddenly apprehensive, "his mind in turmoil and his thoughts awhirl," as he begins to take the measure of his opponent, a young monk sitting in perfect composure waiting for the discussion to commence.

The debate begins in chapter 2 with perhaps the most celebrated metaphor in Buddhism, the analogy of the chariot (standardly featured in undergraduate classrooms and textbooks today). Nagasena introduces himself by denying himself. He insists that though he has the name Nagasena, "there is no person found here." With this he goes straight to the heart of one of Buddhism's most central teachings.

Despite a strong intuitive sense of having a "self" or "soul," that is, an enduring identity, personhood, or essence, humans are in fact composed of many changing and causally interconnected phenomena, much like the chariot the king took to the debate. As a chariot is a conventional designation or name we give to a collection of interworking parts, none of which is the "self" or "essence" of the chariot, Nagasena is a name we give to a collection of interworking bodily and mental experiences, none of which is an essence, and together the parts do not add up to an essence. We thus begin with the foundational antiessentialism at the heart of all Buddhist philosophy.

Before the debate goes much further, Nagasena seeks an assurance. He will discuss philosophy only if Milinda agrees to converse not as kings converse, but as scholars converse. Milinda asks the difference and is told:

> "In the debates of scholars, great king, there are entangling and unraveling, refuting and countering, and agreeing and disagreeing, but scholars do not get angry. This is how scholars converse."
>
> "How do kings converse, sir?"
>
> "Great king, when kings debate, one account is approved and whoever disputes it invites punishment—'Have him punished!' This is how kings converse."[8]

Milinda agrees to the open and civil norms of scholarly conversation, where debate and the exchange of ideas may get spirited but no one loses his head.

The text then shifts from the narrative details of their exchange to focus largely on the questions and dilemmas discussed. But before we turn to the philosophical exchange, a few more tantalizing details of the circumstances of their meetings over the arc of the book draw attention. At this point in the narrative, the king and the monk move from the public arena to a smaller setting, meeting the next day with a group of ten monks accompanying Nagasena in the king's inner apartments. A long day ensues and they talk deep into the night. After they have parted, each retires to his own quarters and worries to himself about his performance, Milinda wondering if his questions were apt and Nagasena wondering if his replies were adequate. Very beautifully and humanely, chapter 2 ends with their meeting again the next morning and Milinda volunteering that he would not have Nagasena suppose that he spent the night exulting in his own performance the day before. Rather, he reports that he spent the whole night mulling over the discussion before concluding that each party had acquitted himself well. The monk hastens to assure the king of his similar night mulling over the discussion and his conclusion that both had done admirably. We now understand that these two men trust and admire each other, and the conversation can go even deeper.

We do not know exactly over how many days and evenings the conversation took place. At the start of chapter 3, Milinda goes into a week of retreat, stepping away from the cares of state and living in ascetic seclusion and moral discipline. At the end of this, he approaches Nagasena for consultation in an even more private setting, and the two together enter the woods. Though vital philosophical discussion has always taken place at court and in the public arena in India, the forest may be the setting for the deepest philosophical conversations. The rest of the text continues their dialogue, with Milinda posing a question, dilemma, or challenge and Nagasena answering, sometimes with further challenges by Milinda, until the king is satisfied with each, as he always is, before turning to another. Milinda gradually converts to Nagasena's ways of thinking, indicated both overtly—he regularly praises Nagasena's wisdom and intellectual excellence and becomes his student—and subtly, indicated by his gradually ceasing to refer to the Buddha as "the Buddha" and increasingly referring to him, as Nagasena has done throughout, as the "Bhagavan." ("Bhagavan" is a hard epithet to translate, meaning something like "Lord," or "Blessed One," and indicating a degree of commitment.) The text ends with Milinda casting away the pride in his heart and finding immense joy in the discussion; he converts to Buddhism as a layperson at first, building and dedicating a monastery to Nagasena. His final act is to hand the kingdom over to his son and take monastic robes himself.

The Philosophy

The entire text is composed of questions and answers, but as it progresses it uses different styles of dialogic engagement. These indicate different styles of philosophy that may be usefully sketched here.

Chapter 2 starts with a style of Buddhist philosophy known as *abhidhamma,* a kind of fine-grained analysis of experience.

The *abhidhamma* is one of the three genres of Pali scripture (the other two are the *suttas,* the Buddha's sermons, and the *vinaya,* the monastic rules). The *Milindapañha* holds the *abhidhamma* in very high regard. Nagasena has been well trained in it and has had the opportunity to teach it on several previous occasions, to great effect.

The *abhidhamma* consists of seven canonical books, but it also refers to a style of teaching that analyzes, through precise definitions and various classificatory schemas, the causally interactive phenomena that human experience comprises. A metaphor from the text itself may be the most helpful way to understand what it attempts. Nagasena points out that the Bhagavan did a "difficult thing" when he discovered and taught the *abhidhamma.* Suppose a person at sea scoops up a handful of ocean water and tastes it, and then, with an unusually refined palate, is able to identify which droplets come from which rivers. In a similar way, the Bhagavan can examine and disaggregate a brief moment of experience and identify each phenomenon in it and where it comes from.[9] Each fleeting moment of experience contains elements of feeling, intention, perception, and other phenomena that Buddhist psychology has identified with exacting precision.

The key term here is "phenomena," a specialized meaning of the word dhamma that I translate in these contexts as "phenomenal state." These are ephemeral and mutually conditioning events that can be identified and defined through the sort of deep introspection the Buddha mastered. The first part of chapter 2 provides definitions and lists of the key characteristics and functional operations of phenomenal states considered to be valuable for the moral and religious aims of Buddhist practice. The listings are part of the classificatory practices defining and illustrating how these constituents of experience interact. (These items are also defined in the Glossary.)

The key philosophical device that Nagasena engages to explain *abhidhamma* phenomena is *opamma,* analogy, simile, metaphor, or illustration. *Opamma* does essential philosophical and literary work throughout the entire text. In the *abhidhamma* sections, *opamma* makes rarified and abstract ideas understandable. We have already encountered the metaphor of the chariot used to explain the essencelessness of a person, and the metaphor of tasting seawater to explain the practices of disaggregating and identifying the components of experience. These illustrations do the heavy lifting of philosophical explanation. We come to understand the workings of attention, to enlist a further example, as the mind's grabbing hold of an object, much as a barley reaper grabs a bunch of barley before slicing through it. And the important work of understanding (*paññā*) is like the sickle that slices through the bunch of barley, as the mind cuts through confusion to discern the phenomena in experience.[10] Understanding is also represented as the illumination of a lamp entering a dark room suddenly making everything visible.[11]

As philosopher Iris Murdoch saw clearly, "metaphors are not merely peripheral decorations or even useful models, they are fundamental forms of our awareness of our condition." She suggests that it may be impossible to discuss certain types of concepts "without resort to metaphor, since the concepts are themselves metaphorical and cannot be analyzed into non-metaphorical components without a loss of substance."[12] They may be particularly indispensable when we analyze consciousness. The analogies on nearly every page of the *Milindapañha* render difficult psychological terminology visible and interpretable.

Analogy and illustration also play an essential role in Indian systems of logic and epistemology. In Indian logic, an analogy is a formal part of the logical syllogism: *There is fire on the hill because there is smoke there. Wherever there is smoke, there is fire, as, for example, in a kitchen. The hill has smoke that is pervaded with fire. Therefore, there is fire on the hill.* The analogy (Sanskrit, *udāharaṇa*) "*as, for example, in a kitchen*" is considered an indispensable part of the syllogism. And in epistemology, comparison (Sanskrit, *upamāna*) is considered by certain philosophical schools to be a valid means of knowledge (Sanskrit, *pramāṇa*) in its own right. For example, suppose a friend were to describe a new kind of fruit you had never tasted before; the friend suggests that it is somewhat similar to, as well as somewhat different from, fruits and tastes with which you are familiar, giving you a sense of what the new fruit is like. This can convey a type of valid knowledge secured in a different way than from direct perception or logical inference. Andrew Schumann has argued that the *Milindapañha,* although it did not flesh out the mature systems of Sanskrit logic and epistemology just described, was a precursor to these developments that later took form in the philosophical school known as Nyaya. He suggests that "the *Milindapañha* is a unique Pāli text close to the true original point of logic's emergence in India."[13]

Whatever the truth of the historical development of Indian logic, we know from the text itself that *opamma* is central to Nagasena's pedagogical practice. The work opens with the claim that "the brilliant talk of Nagasena, with its analogies and methods, penetrated the heart of the *abhidhamma* and the *vinaya,* and unraveled the net of *suttas.*"[14] At a particularly thorny question deep in their discussions, Milinda presses Nagasena to "convince me with reasons and explain with analogies."[15] He seldom permits Nagasena to simply state doctrine and at every turn requires reason and explanation, in the form of down-to-earth analogies and illustrations.

While also making ample use of analogical reasoning, chapters 3 and 5 on "Ram Horn Dilemmas" move from *abhidhamma*-style philosophy into dilemmatic forms of argument, whether concerning apparent logical contradictions or seeming conflicts in the Buddha's statements. While the association of these questions with the ram (*meṇḍa*) is not entirely clear, the dilemmas are referred to in the work as "two-pronged" questions in which one is caught between two horns, perhaps sharp and twisty ones like those of a ram. V. Trenckner, editor of the Pali Text Society's edition of the text, suggested that the puzzles were likened to a *jātaka* story about a ram, where a perplexing friendship between a ram and a dog—animals not normally associated together—requires solving. More persuasively, Ooi, Schumann, and Sirisawad have argued that a certain kind of fallacious dilemma in ancient Greek philosophy was referred to as "being horned," and that *meṇḍaka* may be a direct translation of the Greek idea.[16]

In any case, the "Ram Horn Dilemmas" form the longest section of the book and perhaps the liveliest, in that Milinda confronts Nagasena with seeming contradictions and Nagasena must somehow, often very creatively, provide explanations that straighten out apparent inconsistencies. Along the way, many intriguing questions emerge. Some concern the extraordinary person of the Buddha: What does it actually mean that the Buddha is omniscient? Can worship at a shrine to the Buddha be helpful when in fact the Buddha has attained "final nibbana" and is no longer with us? Why would the Buddha have ordained Devadatta, his archrival, if he was omniscient and knew in advance that Devadatta would try to split the community (*saṅgha*)? Perhaps most pointedly, Milinda interrogates Nagasena on the ethical dilemmas surrounding the gift of the children in the heart-wrenching story of Vessantara, when our Buddha in a previous life gave away his children in his quest for spiritual perfection.

In other cases, Milinda wonders if becoming a monastic is necessary for nibbana, whether children can attain nibbana, whether nibbana is only pure happiness or if suffering can be present, and indeed, whether nibbana is even real. On several occasions he somewhat tactlessly presses Nagasena on whether Nagasena will be reborn. (Nagasena deftly sidesteps the question.) But the queries are not limited to Buddhist doctrine. Milinda asks time-honored questions concerning the natural world, about how conception occurs, what time is, how we may understand space, whether trees can think, why the sun seems to burn softly sometimes and fiercely at others, whether fire and water are alive. Often he asks questions concerning his own domain, statecraft, such as whether there are constraints on kings when it comes to violent punishment. In all of these cases, Nagasena patiently provides answers, always grounding his explanations with vivid analogies.

Chapter 4 returns to questions of Indian epistemology and logic because of its explicit development of an argument by inference (*anumāna*). As Indian epistemology developed, philosophers debated the sources of valid knowledge, with Buddhist thinkers in the early centuries of the Common Era settling on two: direct perception and inference. Various Hindu schools admitted further sources, with the system of Nyaya eventually including, as noted earlier, comparison as well as testimony, whether of scripture or of reliable others. In chapter 4, "A Question Resolved by Inference," an elaborate illustrative inference establishes the existence of the Buddha, which Milinda has called into doubt. Although we must proceed with all due caution against anachronism in importing later developments back into this early text, the text grounds the existence of the Buddha in inferential reasoning rather than in an appeal to scriptural authority.

It is also notable that the inference in question is an elaborate simile. Just as a great urban architect who designed a well-planned city is known to have existed owing to the splendid city he left behind, we can infer that the Buddha did exist from the splendid teaching he designed. The city metaphor is then lavishly elaborated. The city built by the celebrated architect offers a glimpse of a cosmopolitan ideal of an early Indo-Greek entrepôt, with all sorts of people welcomed from all over the subcontinent and beyond, and boasting magnificent shops, goods, merchants, craftspeople plying their trades, and religious and philosophical sages and seekers.[17] Dhamma City, the city constructed by the teachings of the Buddha, has "the moral precepts as its moats, a sense of shame as its ramparts, knowledge as its gates and gatehouses, exertion as its watchtower, faith as its pillars, mindfulness as its gatekeepers, understanding as its palace, the *suttas* as its crossroads, the *abhidhamma* as its plazas, the *vinaya* as its law court, and the foundations of mindfulness as its city streets."[18] Its bazaars and shops burst with the fine goods of the religious path, meticulously described over many pages in the chapter. To learn the streets and avenues of Dhamma City is not only to come to know that a great architect built it but also to inhabit it and make it one's own well-traversed locality.

By the book's sixth and final chapter, "Questions and Discussions of Analogies," the vigor of debate and the probing questions characterizing earlier sections of the text have settled into a catechism of religious doctrine. The marked difference in the sections is a reminder that the text as we have it is a composite of different layers. Milinda continues to ask questions, but in this chapter they are very specific and formulaic in nature, inquiring into the qualities of various animals, features of the natural world, and artifacts made by humans that are similar to the ideal qualities of the yogi, that is, the earnest disciple undertaking the disciplinary practices of seclusion and asceticism. The text uses the terms "yoga" and "yogi" frequently. Although nowadays yoga is largely associated with Hinduism, Buddhists and Jains also used it to refer generally to the ascetic discipline practiced by renouncers.

The Literary Qualities

The *Milindapañha* is a celebrated literary classic that has brought pleasure and beauty to countless readers through the centuries. The first translator of the text into English, T. W. Rhys Davids, was moved to describe the work as "the masterpiece of Indian prose" and "the best book of its class, from a literary point of view, that had then been produced in any country."[19] Bhikkhu Bodhi has referred to it as a "gem of classical Pali literature" and "a literary monument exhibiting intellectual acuity, subtle humor, inspirational fervor and bold imagination."[20] In its opening verses, the work itself promises to "stir the heart, please the ear, and send shivers down the spine."

We have already had occasion to suggest that the philosophical discussion is enabled by its use of narrative, illustration, and simile. The work also deploys its illustrative and analogical features for aesthetic impact. India has a long history of reflection on simile (Sanskrit, *upamā*). As far back as the ancient Vedic texts, thinkers noticed it as a figure used in language, and the great grammarian Panini offered a technical analysis.[21] The Buddha himself made frequent use of similes and noted both their heuristic and literary power: "I will make a simile for you, friend, for some intelligent people here grasp the meaning of what is said by means of similes." His similes are also said to "please and delight" his audiences.[22] And although it is likely more recent than the *Milindapañha,* the earliest text on Indian aesthetics, Bharata's *Nāṭyaśāstra,* discusses similes, metaphors, and other literary figures. It is fascinating to consider the possibility that the *Milindapañha's* extensive use of *opamma* as a literary figure and self-aware reflecting on the importance of simile might prefigure features of this tradition.

Literary figures enhance perception and invite us to see the world in new and heightened ways. When Nagasena advises the king to observe closely the habits of an elderly jackal to discern the qualities of an aspiring yogi, he would have him notice how the old critter seldom finds food but eats what he does find without discrimination or disgust. As elephants plunge into lovely lotus ponds of "pure, clear, and cool water covered with lilies" to play wonderful elephant games, so too, the yogi should "plunge into the lotus pond of the great foundations of mindfulness filled with the wonderful water of the flawless Dhamma, pure, clear, and limpid," where he may slough off the impurities of moral defilement. And just as an elephant steps mindfully and deliberately, softly placing each foot down in turn, the yogi should only ever tread upon the earth with mindfulness and deliberation. The imagery and literary qualities of language do not just aid conceptual understanding, they also add poignancy and depth to perception to help us see things more clearly. Literary figures help us to *see as,* where the world around the forest yogi comes to reflect back at him the values he is trying to embody—the peaceful contentment and freedom of quiet seclusion away from the crowd and the noise.

The Religious Ideals

While the earliest kernel of the story, the presumed original Gandhari version, likely reflected the doctrines of the Buddhism influential in the region (chiefly the Sarvastivada school), the Pali version conforms, in large measure, to Theravada orthodoxy. Given that the Pali version is substantially different and significantly longer than the extant Chinese recensions, scholars have generally assumed that the Pali version is the result of alterations and supplements as it came to be incorporated in the Theravada corpus. Certain quoted material in the *Milindapañha* is not traceable to the Pali canon, and certain issues discussed may suggest Sarvastivada influence, but the text largely reflects Theravada doctrine.[23]

Buddhists from across the doctrinal spectrum, including later Mahayana traditions, share many of the basic Buddhist assumptions and perspectives articulated by Nagasena. These include views concerning samsara, the round of rebirths marked by suffering and loss propelled endlessly by karma, our ethical actions and their effects. Constant rebirth in samsara can only be brought to a halt by achieving nibbana (Sanskrit, *nirvāṇa*). Although Buddhists have disagreed on the details of what exactly this "awakening" is and how it is to be achieved, all agree that greed, hatred, and delusion come to a full stop in an awakened person (*arhat*), who is thus released from future births. In this sense, nibbana is complete liberation, and the Buddhist path is conceived as a quest, above all, for freedom.

Buddhists also largely concur that the monastic life of discipline, requiring vows taken by the community of monks and nuns and articulated in the *vinaya* texts, provides the best means to practice the spiritual and moral development necessary to achieve this ambitious goal. The *Questions of Milinda* extols the freedom found in ascetic detachment from the treadmill of endless desires and the hustle of worldly affairs. Still, Buddhists have always recognized the importance of laypeople who support Buddhism and its highest ideals while living life ethically in the world. In this respect, and insofar as the ideal Buddhist king has often been regarded as representing the paradigmatic layperson, in the persons of King Milinda and the monk Nagasena the *Milindapañha* reflects two different but mutually compatible ways of being Buddhist.

Still, the *Milindapañha* assumes mainstream Buddhist conceptions of time, space, and cosmos. Samsara teems with realms seen and unseen, with heavens, hells, and ghost realms, as well as the visible world of humans and animals. All beings have cycled through all of these realms in the long sweep of beginningless time. In this framework, time is eternal in both directions, and our era is just one in an infinite sequence. Gotama Buddha is the latest in a long line of buddhas, many of whom are named and known in the texts (such as Kassapa Buddha). Gotama Buddha is important to our time because the memory and institutions of his dispensation (*sāsana*) are still present. As discussed in the *Milindapañha* itself, the dispensation, like all things, is perishable and will eventually be forgotten. In time, another figure will rediscover the truths of Buddhism (the Dhamma), become a buddha, and teach the Dhamma again.

The journey of all buddhas begins many lifetimes before they are spiritually and morally ready to discover the Dhamma, and the time spans in question are mind-blowingly large. Time is reckoned in "eons" and "incalculables" that themselves must be understood metaphorically: an eon is the time it would take a steel mountain the size of Mount Everest to erode to sea level by the action of a bird lightly brushing its peak with a silk scarf once a century; an "incalculable" is something like a "gazillion" eons. The journey of our Buddha began in a distant previous life "four incalculables and a hundred thousand eons" ago when he encountered a certain buddha living at that time, performed an act of great devotion, received a prediction of future buddhahood, and made the aspiration to practice a series of moral excellences that lay the foundation for the "perfect awakening" of a buddha. While on this long quest he is called a "bodhisatta" (*bodhisattva* in Sanskrit), which can be translated as a "buddha-to-be," and the stories of some of these past lives are collected in the anthology of "birth stories" known as the *Jātakas,* frequently referred to in our text. In his final life, a bodhisatta attains nibbana under an "awakening tree"—the Bodhi tree—and teaches the Dhamma, reintroducing the world to its truths. His teaching of the perennial Dhamma is known as "turning the wheel of the Dhamma," as he gets the teachings also taught by previous buddhas rolling once again. At this point, he comes to be known by various sublime epithets: the Tathagata (one who is "Thus-Gone," an epithet of uncertain meaning), the Victor (one who has conquered samsara), the Bhagavan, and simply the Buddha. Although, strictly speaking, he is not a "god" (since gods are still subject to samsara), the *Milindapañha* regularly calls him "god above gods" (*devātideva*). Upon his death, an event known as the "final nibbana," he transcends the reach of space, time, and ordinary human comprehension.

The *Milindapañha* is, of course, a conversion narrative. While it celebrates and develops the intellectual side of Buddhism, it also depicts the gradual spiritual reorientation of a man from curious seeker and skeptic to confirmed Buddhist believer, with doubts and perplexity eradicated. Part of Nagasena's success in aiding this transformation is his repeated emphasis on the peace to be found in the life of seclusion in the forest. Chapter 5, subtitled "Discussions About Yogis," though in form part of the "Ram Horn Dilemmas," follows the other dilemmas and chapter 4. It foregrounds questions concerning the forest austerities and affirms their indispensability to the path of spiritual freedom. The forest austerities (*dhutanga*s) are thirteen penances and mortifications more exacting than the strictures of ordinary monks and nuns (listed at *Miln* 5.26). With higher austerity comes greater freedom and detachment, and with these, peace.

The final chapter involves elaborating the many qualities of the forest yogi, who embodies the romantic ideal of wandering untethered from the trappings and perils of social life. The ideal clearly appealed to the king, harried and hemmed in at the court. A hint of Milinda's yearning for a freer and more peaceful life is a moment early in the discussions when he admits to feeling like a lion in a golden cage who sits looking outward.[24] King of beasts the lion may be, but even in a golden cage he has nothing to do but gaze longingly at the freedom beyond its bars. As a householder with many cares, the king too can do nothing but gaze longingly at the freedom beyond the palace walls.

Acknowledgements

This translation would not have been imagined save for Sheldon Pollock's invitation to translate this beautiful text, and for his kind, generous, and meticulous editorial support at every step of the way. What an extraordinary gift he has given the world as the founding general editor of the Murty Classical Library of India.

I am grateful also to David Shulman for his early encouragement, and to the other editors on the editorial board —Archana Venkatesan, Francesca Orsini, Whitney Cox, and Rajeev Kinra—for their friendship, hard work, and deep commitment to the Murty Classical Library. Thanks also to Heather Hughes and Sam Mateo for their dedicated and scrupulous work on this volume, and to Beatrice Chrystall for her thorough Pali editing.

I am ever grateful to Charles Hallisey, who called me up one evening the day before classes began early in my graduate career and insisted that I take Pali. He has been a caring and wise teacher ever since, with an ethic of teaching that calls to mind the *Milindapañha*'s own high standards for a teacher.[25] And thanks too to Steve, Soren, and Zack, as ever.

Dedicated to Sheldon Pollock,
true friend of the Indian classics

NOTES

1 The well-known Shinkot reliquary has a broken stone lid bearing a fragmentary inscription that mentions the dedication of Buddhist relics during Menander's reign (Salomon 2018: 27). Besides Salomon (24–28), see also Stoneman 2019: 365 and Bopearachchi 2020: 22–23 on the archaeological evidence.

2 A trace of a discussion of Nagasena and "the king of Kalinga" is recalled in a fourth-century Sanskrit text composed by Vasubandhu, but the remembered discussion is not identical to any passage in any versions that we have (Skilling 1998, on Vasubandhu's *Abhidharmakośabhāṣya,* 4.1332-1333). Eleventh-century Kashmiri Kshemendra mentions King "Milindra" in his *Avadānakalpalatā* (chapter 57, v.15, as cited in Lamotte 1988: 426; see also Kubica 2021). A medieval Sinhala story collection tells the story of Nagasena and Milinda, though it is likely drawing on the Pali text (Obeyesekere 1991: 53–84). Tibetan historian Taranatha (1575–1634) mentions a king thought to be Menander (cited in Stoneman 2019: 365–366).

3 With the possible exception of recently discovered fragments of a Gandhari text mentioning Nagasena (Salomon 2018: 26). See Demiéville 1924 for a meticulous comparison of the Milinda-Nagasena corpus, and Levman 2021 for a recent comparison of the Pali and Chinese versions and a discussion of the scholarship on the question.

4 See Skilling 2010 for bibliographical information on editions and translations of the *Milindapañha.*

5 See Tarn 1938 and Gonda 1949b for opposing views on questions of influence. See also Vasil'kov 1993, Halkias 2014, Stoneman 2019, Baums 2018, and Kubica 2014.

6 *Miln* 2.4.

7 *Miln* 2.5.

8 *Miln* 2.9–10.

9 *Miln* 2.169-170.

10 *Miln* 2.20.

11 *Miln* 2.38.

12 Murdoch 2010: 75.

13 Schumann 2019: 358.

14 *Miln* 1.2.

15 *Miln* 3.520.

16 Trenckner 1890: 422–423; Ooi, Schumann, and Sirisawad 2023.

17 See Schmiedchen 2017: 61–68 on this ideal city and its occupants, as well as her discussion of the account, given at the start of the *Milindapañha,* of Milinda's capital, Sāgala (*Miln* 1.1-2).

18 *Miln* 4.9.

19 Rhys Davids 1890: xlviii.

20 Bodhi in Mendis 2001: 1, 13.

21 See Gonda 1949a: 2 and Gerow 1977: 221 on the treatments of *upamā* in the *Nirukta* of Yaska (3, 13) and Panini's *Aṣṭādhyāyī* 2.1.55–56; 2, 3, 72. Panini analyzes simile according to its four elements: the subject of comparison, the thing with which it is compared, the property or standard of similitude, and the adverbial or grammatical indicator of comparison (Gerow 1977: 221).

22 *Saṃyuttanikāya* 1.114; *Majjhimanikāya* 1.378.

23 The introduction to Horner (2015) discusses the possible Sarvastivada influences, or at least elements in the text that do not match Theravada orthodoxy as we know it from the surviving Pali canon.

24 *Miln* 2.173.

25 *Miln* 3.16.

NOTE ON THE TEXT AND TRANSLATION

The text of the *Milindapañha* presented here is based on V. Trenckner's, first published by the Pali Text Society in 1890 (cited as T in Notes to the Text). It was digitized by the Dhammakaya Foundation and made available for public use on the Göttingen Register of Electronic Texts in Indian Languages (GRETIL), © 2015 by the Pali Text Society and the Dhammakaya Foundation, licensed under a Creative Commons Attribution-ShareAlike 4.0 International License (CC BY-NC 4.0). In preparing the text for the Murty Classical Library of India, I consulted two other editions, that of the Sri Lanka Tripitaka Project (S), also available on GRETIL, and the Chaṭṭha Saṅgāyana Tipiṭaka edition produced by the Vipassana Research Institute (C). I have adopted variant readings (departures from T) only rarely.

A substantial number of manuscripts of the *Milindapañha* from Thailand have come to light in the past several decades as they have been catalogued and digitized, and there are other editions in Khmer, Sinhala, Nagari, and Bengali scripts.[1] A complete study of the different recensions and versions of the Pali text remains a desideratum.

I have aimed to translate this ancient text into a contemporary idiom, although one that I hope is enduring. I follow English rather than Pali syntax, and, in keeping with MCLI style, I have aimed for fidelity rather than literalness.

The *Milindapañha* is a dialogue that begins as a public debate between an esteemed monk and a great king. Over the course of their long discussion, it softens into a private conversation between two men searching together for the truth. Pali dialogue is marked with much more pervasive use of the vocative than contemporary English. While retaining many vocatives and honorifics to indicate the formal nature of the discussion and the high regard in which the two participants hold each other, I have reduced their number in my translation.

The *Milindapañha* quotes extensively from Pali canonical materials. Previous translators cite the sources of these quotations and note the instances in which quoted passages have not been traced. So as not to duplicate their efforts and to keep the apparatus of this translation lean, I have not done this. Interested scholars may consult the English translations by Rhys Davids (1890) and Horner (2015; originally 1963) for such material.

Certain portions of the *Milindapañha* have a technical character in which psychological phenomena and elements of the Buddhist path are defined, listed, and classified. I have translated nearly all of these terms. The first mention of a recurring technical term is given an endnote that defines the term and provides the Pali. Following MCLI style, Pali terms are defined in the Glossary.

Finally, a word on the structure of the text. Early in its introduction, the text lists its contents as having six main sections, and it references its six parts again at the very end of the book. However, the actual sequence of these sections unfolds slightly differently in the text itself. I have followed that structure, while giving chapter names based on the outline given on *Milindapañha* 1.3 . The longest chapter, "Ram Horn Dilemmas," for example, is said to have two divisions. First is "The Great Chapter," which has eight sections; it is my chapter 3. The second division is a ninth section of dilemmas, but it occurs later in the text following chapter 4, so I call it chapter 5, with the subtitle "Questions and Discussions About Yogis," as it concerns the forest practices of wandering ascetics. The final chapter, "Questions and Discussions of Analogies," seems to be cut off midway through in the editions I used, in that an outline of analogies given at the start of the chapter has not received full elaboration. Scholars do not know if part of the original text was lost or the author just got exhausted making similes. However, the text as we have it wraps up the book at this point by supplying a brief epilogue to the narrative of King Milinda and Elder Nagasena.

NOTES

1 Ooi 2021; Skilling 2010.

CHAPTER 1

Former Connections

1 namo tassa bhagavato arahato sammāsambuddhassa.

milindo nāma so rājā sāgalāyam-puruttame
upagañchi nāgasenaṃ, gaṅgāva yatha sāgaraṃ.
asajja rājā citrakathiṃ ukkādhāraṃ tamonudaṃ
apucchi nipuṇe pañhe ṭhānāṭhānagate puthū.
pucchāvissajjanā c' eva gambhīratthūpanissitā
hadayaṅgamā kaṇṇasukhā abbhutā lomahaṃsanā.
abhidhammavinayogāḷhā suttajālasamatthitā
nāgasenakathā citrā opammehi nayehi ca.
tattha ñāṇaṃ paṇidhāya hāsayitvāna mānasaṃ
suṇotha nipuṇe pañhe kaṅkhāṭhānavidālane ti.

2 taṃyathā 'nusūyate. atthi yonakānaṃ nānāpuṭabhedanaṃ sāgalan-nāma nagaram nadī-pabbata-sobhitaṃ ramaṇīya-bhūmippadesabhāgaṃ ārāmuyyānopavana-taḷāka-pokkha-raṇī-sampannaṃ nadī-pabbata-vana-rāmaṇeyyakaṃ sutavantanimmitaṃ nihata-paccatthika-paccāmittaṃ anu-papīḷitaṃ vividha-vicitra-daḷha-m-aṭṭāla-koṭṭakaṃ varapavara-gopuratoraṇaṃ gambhīraparikhā-paṇḍara-pākāra-parikkhittantepuraṃ suvibhatta-vīthi-caccara-

Homage to the Bhagavan, the Enlightened One, the Perfectly 1
Awakened Buddha.

A king named Milinda approached Nagasena in that
best of cities, Sagala, much as the Ganga draws
near the ocean.
The king advanced and put to that brilliant orator, a
torchbearer dispelling darkness, numerous subtle
questions on possibilities and impossibilities.
The marvelous questions and answers pertain to
matters of profound significance, as they stir the
heart, please the ear, and send shivers down the
spine.
The brilliant talk of Nagasena, with its analogies
and methods, penetrated the heart of the
abhidhamma and the *vinaya,* and unraveled the
net of *suttas.*[1]
So seek knowledge here and cheer the mind
as you listen to these subtle questions that resolve all
points of uncertainty.

This is the account that has been handed down by tradition. 2
The city called Sagala was a center of trade for the Yonakas, part of a lovely region of earth, resplendent with rivers and mountains and abounding in parks, gardens, woods, lakes, and lotus pools. It was a city founded by learned people and delightful for its rivers, hills, and woods. Its enemies vanquished, it was free of oppression by adversaries. It boasted diverse and formidable watchtowers and gates, excellent and noble arches mounted over the city portals, and encircling white walls and deep moats around the palace.

catukka-siṅghāṭakaṃ suppasāritānekavidha-vara-bhaṇḍa-paripūritantarāpaṇaṃ vividha-dānagga-sata-samupasobhitaṃ himagirisikharasaṅkāsa-varabhavansatasahassa-patimaṇḍitaṃ gaja-haya-ratha-pattisamākulaṃ abhirūpa-naranāri-gaṇānucaritaṃ ākiṇṇa-janamanussaṃ puthu-khattiya-brāhmaṇa-vessa-suddaṃ vividha-samaṇabrāhmaṇasabhājana-saṅghaṭitaṃ bahuvidhavijjāvanta-naravīra-nisevitaṃ kāsika-koṭumbarakādi-nānāvidha-vatthāpaṇa-sampannaṃ suppasārita-rucira-bahuvidha-pupphagandhāpaṇagandhagandhitaṃ āsiṃsaniya-bahuratana-paripūritaṃ disāmukha-suppasāritāpaṇa-siṅgāravāṇijagaṇānucaritaṃ kahāpaṇa-rajata-suvaṇṇa-kaṃsa-patthara-paripūraṃ pajjotamāna-nidhi-niketaṃ pahūta-dhanadhañña-vittūpakaraṇaṃ paripuṇṇa-kosa-koṭṭhāgāraṃ bahv-annapānaṃ bahu-vidha-khajja-bhojja-leyya-peyya-sāyaniyaṃ uttarakurusaṅkāsaṃ sampanna-sassaṃ aḷakamandā viya devapuraṃ.

3 ettha ṭhatvā tesaṃ pubbakammaṃ kathetabbaṃ, kathentena ca chaddhā vibhajitvā kathetabbaṃ, seyyathīdaṃ: pubbayogo, milindapañhaṃ, lakkhaṇapañhaṃ, meṇḍakapañhaṃ, anumānapañhaṃ, opammakathāpañhan ti.

Its streets, squares, and intersections were well planned, and the interiors of its shops were stocked with many varieties of fine goods exquisitely displayed. It was graced with hundreds of diverse alms halls and embellished with hundreds of thousands of fine houses resembling Himalayan peaks.

The city teemed with elephants, horses, chariots, and infantry. It was crowded with the multitudes of humanity, including throngs of handsome men and women and numerous Kshatriyas, Brahmans, Vaishyas, and Shudras. It resounded with cries of welcome to various renouncers and Brahmans and became the resort of many types of educated and heroic men. Fragrant with scents, the city's bazaars were packed with stores of various cloths, including Kasi and Kotumbara textiles, and emporia displaying numerous exquisite flowers and perfumes. Its shops were arrayed in all directions and boasted many prized jewels. The city was the home of glittering treasure, full of merchant guilds trading in finery, bursting with copper, silver, gold, bronze, and stoneware, a place of lavish riches, good fortune, and luxury. Its treasuries and granaries were stuffed; there was plentiful food and drink of choice fare, cuisines, sauces, beverages, and savories, and crops so successful that the city resembled Uttarakuru and the heavenly city Alakamanda.[2]

The setting thus established, the previous deeds of 3
Milinda and Nagasena should be described, in addition to relating their conversation, divided into six thusly: "Former Connections," "Questions of Milinda," "Questions on Defining Characteristics," "Ram Horn Dilemmas," "A Question Resolved by Inference," and "Questions and Discussions of Analogies."

tattha milindapañho: lakkhaṇapañho vimaticchedanapañho ti duvidho; meṇḍakapañho pi: mahāvaggo yogikathāpañho ti duvidho.

bāhirakathā.

4 pubbayogo ti tesaṃ pubbakammaṃ. atīte kira kassapassa bhagavato sāsane vattamāne gaṅgāya samīpe ekasmiṃ āvāse mahābhikkhusaṅgho paṭivasati. tattha vattasīlasampannā bhikkhū pātova uṭṭhāya yaṭṭhisammuñjaniyo ādāya buddhaguṇe āvajjentā aṅgaṇaṃ sammajjitvā kacavaraṃ byūhaṃ karonti. atheko bhikkhu ekaṃ sāmaṇeraṃ: ehi sāmaṇera, imaṃ kacavaraṃ chaḍḍehīti āha; so asuṇanto viya gacchati. so dutiyam-pi tatiyam-pi āmantiyamāno asuṇanto viya gacchateva. tato so bhikkhu: dubbaco ayaṃ sāmaṇero ti kuddho sammuñjanidaṇḍena pahāraṃ adāsi. tato so rodanto bhayena kacavaraṃ chaḍḍento: iminā 'haṃ kacavarachaḍḍanapuññakammena yāvāhaṃ nibbānaṃ pāpuṇāmi etthantare nibbattanibbattaṭṭhāne majjhantikasuriyo viya mahesakkho mahātejo bhaveyyan-ti paṭhamapatthanaṃ paṭṭhapesi. kacavaraṃ chaḍḍetvā nahānatthāya gaṅgātitthaṃ gato gaṅgāya ūmivegaṃ gaggarāyamānaṃ disvā: yāvāhaṃ nibbānaṃ pāpuṇāmi etthantare nibbattanibbattaṭṭhāne ayaṃ ūmivego viya ṭhānuppattikapaṭibhāno

And within that, the "Questions of Milinda" has two parts: "Questions on Defining Characteristics" and "Questions for Resolving Doubt." And further, "Ram Horn Dilemmas" is twofold: the "Great Chapter" and "Questions and Discussions About Yogis."

The Backstory

This section, on former connections, deals with past karma. 4
A long time ago during the dispensation of the Bhagavan Kassapa,* there lived a large community of monks in a single residence near the Ganga. There the monks completed the observances and the moral discipline, and they rose early, took up their brooms, and swept up the place by brushing the rubbish into a heap, all the while contemplating the Buddha's qualities.[3] Once a monk told a novice, "Come here, novice, and throw out this rubbish," but the novice went on his way, not listening. And this happened a second time and a third in which, though addressed, he did not listen and just carried on. So the monk got angry, thinking the novice incorrigible, and gave him a blow with a broomstick.

At this the novice cried out with fear and threw out the rubbish, while making his first aspiration: "By this meritorious karma of throwing out the rubbish, may I in birth after birth until I attain nibbana always be born splendid and powerful like the noonday sun!"[4]

Then, having thrown out the rubbish, he went to the bank of the Ganga to bathe and saw the tossing waves roaring in

*The buddha before Gotama Buddha.

bhaveyyaṃ akkhayapaṭibhāno ti dutiyam-pi patthanaṃ paṭṭhapesi.

5 so pi bhikkhu sammuñjanisālāya sammuñjaniṃ ṭhapetvā nahānatthāya gaṅgātitthaṃ gacchanto sāmaṇerassa patthanaṃ sutvā: esa mayā payojito pi tāva evaṃ pattheti, mayhaṃ kiṃ na samijjhissatīti cintetvā: yāvāhaṃ nibbānaṃ pāpuṇāmi etth' antare nibbattanibbattaṭṭhāne ayaṃ gaṅgāūmivego viya akkhayapaṭibhāno bhaveyyaṃ, iminā pucchitapucchitaṃ sabbaṃ pañhapaṭibhānaṃ vijaṭetuṃ nibbeṭhetuṃ samattho bhaveyyan-ti patthanaṃ paṭṭhapesi.

6 te ubho pi devesu ca manussesu ca saṃsarantā ekaṃ buddhantaraṃ khepesuṃ. atha amhākaṃ bhagavatā pi yathā moggaliputta-tissatthero dissati evam-ete pi dissanti: mama parinibbānato pañcavassasate atikkante ete uppajjissanti, yaṃ mayā sukhumaṃ katvā desitaṃ dhammavinayaṃ taṃ ete pañhapucchana-opammayutti-vasena nijjaṭaṃ niggumbaṃ katvā vibhajissantīti niddiṭṭhā.

7 tesu sāmaṇero jambudīpe sāgalanagare milindo nāma rājā ahosi, paṇḍito byatto medhāvī paṭibalo, atītānāgata-paccuppannānaṃ samanta[1]yogavidhānakiriyānaṃ karaṇakāle nisammakārī hoti; bahūni cassa satthāni uggahitāni honti, seyyathīdaṃ: suti sammuti sankhyā yogā nīti visesikā gaṇikā

the Ganga. At this he made a second aspiration: “May I in birth after birth until I attain nibbana always have a ready wit and unfailing speech like these tossing waves!”

Meanwhile, the monk had put away the broom in the 5
broom closet and gone to the bank of the Ganga to bathe as well. He overheard the novice’s aspiration and thought, *If he can aspire to this just by doing something I forced him to do, then how might I succeed?* So he too made an aspiration: “May I too in birth after birth until I attain nibbana always have unfailing speech like these tossing waves of the Ganga, and may I be able either to provide answers or unravel questions in whatever ways they are asked by him!”

They both then spent an entire era between buddhas being 6
reborn among gods and humans. And then our Bhagavan recognized them, much as he had recognized the elder Tissa, son of Moggali, and he made a prediction: “These two will be reborn five hundred years after my final nibbana, and they will provide analyses of the Dhamma and the *vinaya,* which I have taught but made subtle, disentangling them and making them clear by asking questions and applying analogies.”[5]

In due course, the novice was born in Jambudipa* in the 7
city of Sagala as a king called Milinda. He was learned, experienced, intelligent, and able, and he observed at the proper time all the duties, ceremonies, yogic practices, and mantras related to the past, present, and future. He mastered the many areas of learning—the revealed texts, the moral codes, Sankhya, Yoga, political philosophy, Vaisheshika,

*India.

gandhabbā tikicchā cātubbedā purāṇā itihāsā jotisā māyā hetu mantaṇā yuddhā chandasā muddā, vacanena ekūnavīsati; vādī durāsado duppasaho, puthutitthakarānaṃ aggam-akkhāyati; sakala-jambudīpe milindena raññā samo koci nāhosi, yad-idaṃ thāmena javena sūriyena paññāya, aḍḍho mahaddhano mahābhogo anantabalavāhano.

8 athekadivasaṃ milindo rājā anantabalavāhanaṃ caturaṅginiṃ balaggasenābyūhaṃ dassanakamyatāya nagarā nikkhamitvā bahinagare senāgaṇanaṃ kāretvā so rājā bhassappavādako lokāyata-vitaṇḍa-janasallāpa-ppavattakotūhalo suriyaṃ oloketvā amacce āmantesi: bahu tāva divasāvaseso, kiṃ karissāma idān' eva nagaraṃ pavisitvā; atthi koci paṇḍito samaṇo vā brāhmaṇo vā saṅghī gaṇī gaṇācariyo, api arahantaṃ sammāsambuddhaṃ paṭijānamāno, yo mayā saddhiṃ sallapituṃ sakkoti kaṅkhaṃ paṭivinetun-ti.

9 evaṃ vutte pañcasatā yonakā rājānaṃ milindaṃ etad-avocuṃ: atthi mahārāja cha satthāro: pūraṇo kassapo, makkhali gosālo, nigaṇṭho nātaputto, sañjayo belaṭṭhaputto, ajito kesakambalī, pakudho kaccāyano, te saṅghino gaṇino gaṇācariyakā ñātā yasassino titthakarā sādhusammatā

arithmetic, music, medicine, archery, the Puranas, the histories, astrology, the art of deception, the art of discernment,* the art of counsel, the art of war, the Vedic meters, and the art of hand gestures—that is to say, the nineteen arts.[6] As a speaker he was hard to approach and hard to defeat, and he came to be recognized as the best among the various exalted teachers of the day. This king Milinda simply had no equal in all of Jambudipa in fortitude, quickness, valor, and understanding. He was also very rich and enjoyed a vast treasury, great prosperity, and limitless armed forces.

Now one day, King Milinda set out from the city desiring 8
to survey his limitless armed forces with the four branches† of the army, troops mustered and in battle array. When he had finished counting the troops, and while still outside the city, the king, who loved debate and discussion and was eager to converse with materialists, sophists, and other such persons, noted the position of the sun and addressed his companions: "Much of the day still remains. What would be the point of returning to the city now? Surely here there is some learned person, renouncer, Brahman, head of an order, teacher with a large following, or prominent professor, even one who approves of the Arhat, the Perfectly Awakened Buddha, who is able to converse with me and dispel my uncertainties."

When addressed thus, the five hundred Yonakas replied to 9
King Milinda, "Great king, there are six teachers—Ancient Kassapa, Makkhali of the Cow Pen, the Jain Nataputta, Sanjaya son of Belattha, Ajita of the Hair Shirt, and Pakudha Kaccayana—who are prominent professors, heads of orders,

* *Ketu*, which could also be reading omens.

† Infantry, cavalry, chariots, and elephants.

bahujanassa, gaccha tvaṃ mahārāja, te pañhaṃ pucchassu kaṅkhaṃ paṭivinayassūti.

10 atha kho milindo rājā pañcahi yonakasatehi parivuto bhadravāhanaṃ rathavaram-āruyha yena pūraṇo kassapo ten' upasaṅkami, upasaṅkamitvā pūraṇena kassapena saddhiṃ sammodi, sammodanīyaṃ kathaṃ sārāṇīyaṃ vītisāretvā ekamantaṃ nisīdi. ekamantaṃ nisinno kho milindo rājā pūraṇaṃ kassapaṃ etad-avoca: ko bhante kassapa lokaṃ pāletīti. paṭhavī mahārāja lokaṃ pāletīti. yadi bhante kassapa paṭhavī lokaṃ pāleti atha kasmā avīci-nirayaṃ gacchantā sattā paṭhaviṃ atikkamitvā gacchantīti.

11 evaṃ vutte pūraṇo kassapo n'eva sakkhi ogilituṃ n'eva sakkhi uggilituṃ, pattakkhandho tuṇhībhūto pajjhāyanto[2] nisīdi. atha kho milindo rājā makkhali-gosālaṃ etad-avoca: atthi bhante gosāla kusalākusalāni kammāni, atthi sukaṭa-dukkaṭānaṃ kammānaṃ phalaṃ vipāko ti. natthi mahārāja kusalākusalāni kammāni, natthi sukaṭa-dukkaṭā-naṃ kammānaṃ phalaṃ vipāko, ye te mahārāja idhaloke khattiyā te paralokaṃ gantvā pi puna khattiyāva bhavissanti, ye te brāhmaṇā vessā suddā caṇḍālā pukkusā te paralokaṃ gantvā pi puna brāhmaṇā vessā suddā caṇḍālā pukkusā va bhavissanti, kiṃ kusalākusalehi kammehīti. yadi bhante gosāla idhaloke khattiyā brāhmaṇā vessā suddā caṇḍālā

and teachers with large followings, renowned and famous ford crossers,* celebrated by many people. You should go to them, great king, to ask them questions and dispel your uncertainties."

And so King Milinda, surrounded by the five hundred 10
Yonakas, mounted his finest royal chariot and proceeded to Ancient Kassapa. Approaching him, he addressed Ancient Kassapa cordially, exchanging polite and friendly greetings, and sat down to one side. As he sat to the side, King Milinda said, "Kassapa, sir, who keeps the world going?"

"The earth, great king, keeps the world going."

"But, Kassapa, if the earth keeps the world going, then how can beings going to the Avici hell travel there, since it extends beyond the earth?"

At this reply, Ancient Kassapa could neither swallow nor 11
sputter, and sat there with his shoulders slumped, crestfallen and silent.

So then King Milinda went to Makkhali of the Cow Pen: "Cow Pen, sir, is there good and bad karma, and are there effects that are the fruit of karma, whether virtue or vice?"

"No, great king, there is no such thing as good and bad karma, nor any effects that are the fruit of karma, whether virtue or vice. Whoever is a Kshatriya in this world will go to the next and be a Kshatriya there. Whoever is a Brahman, Vaishya, Shudra, outcaste, or sweeper will go to the next world and become likewise. What is the point of good and bad karma?"

---

*Spiritual teachers who help others cross the cycle of samsara.

pukkusā paralokaṃ gantvā pi puna khattiyā brāhmaṇā vessā suddā caṇḍālā pukkusāva bhavissanti, natthi kusalākusalehi kammehi karaṇīyaṃ; tena hi bhante gosāla ye te idhaloke hatthacchinnā te paralokaṃ gantvā pi puna hatthacchinnāva bhavissanti, ye pādacchinnā te pādacchinnāva bhavissanti, ye kaṇṇanāsacchinnā te kaṇṇanāsacchinnāva bhavissantīti. evaṃ vutte gosālo tuṇhī ahosi.

12 atha kho milindassa rañño etad-ahosi: tuccho vata bho jambudīpo, palāpo vata bho jambudīpo, natthi koci samaṇo vā brāhmaṇo vā yo mayā saddhiṃ sallapituṃ sakkoti kaṅkhaṃ paṭivinetun-ti. atha kho milindo rājā amacce āmantesi: ramaṇīyā vata bho dosinā ratti, kan-nu khv-ajja samaṇaṃ vā brāhmaṇaṃ vā upasaṅkameyyāma pañhaṃ pucchituṃ, ko mayā saddhiṃ sallapituṃ sakkoti kaṅkhaṃ paṭivinetun-ti. evaṃ vutte amaccā tuṇhībhūtā rañño mukhaṃ olokayamānā aṭṭhaṃsu.

13 tena kho pana samayena sāgalanagaraṃ dvādasa vassāni suññaṃ ahosi samaṇa-brāhmaṇa-gahapati-paṇḍitehi; yattha samaṇa-brāhmaṇa-gahapati-paṇḍitā paṭivasantīti suṇāti tattha gantvā rājā te pañhaṃ pucchati; te sabbe pi pañhavissajjanena rājānaṃ ārādhetuṃ asakkontā yena vā tena vā pakkamanti, ye aññaṃ disaṃ na pakkamanti te sabbe tuṇhībhūta acchanti. bhikkhū pana yebhuyyena himavantam-eva gacchanti.

14 tena kho pana samayena koṭisatā arahanto himavante pabbate rakkhitatale paṭivasanti. atha kho āyasmā assagutto dibbāya sotadhātuyā milindassa rañño vacanaṃ sutvā yugandharamatthake bhikkhusaṅghaṃ sannipātetvā

"But, Cow Pen, if Kshatriyas, Brahmans, Vaishyas, Shudras, outcastes, and sweepers in this world go to the next and become Kshatriyas, Brahmans, Vaishyas, Shudras, outcastes, and sweepers there, and good and bad karma are irrelevant, then is it also the case, Cow Pen, that people in this world with their hands cut off find themselves with hands cut off in the next? And what about those with feet cut off, or ears and noses cut off? Are they born like this in the next life too?" At this reply, Cow Pen fell silent.

King Milinda exclaimed: "Jambudipa is simply empty, 12
Jambudipa is sheer nonsense, for nowhere is there a renouncer or Brahman who can converse with me and dispel my uncertainties!" But he turned to his companions and tried once more. "It is a lovely moonlit night. Which renouncer or Brahman may we approach tonight to ask questions? Who is able to converse with me and to dispel my uncertainties?"

In response the companions just stood there staring silently into the king's face.

Now, at that time the city of Sagala had been empty of 13
learned renouncers, Brahmans, and householders for twelve years. So whenever the king heard of learned renouncers, Brahmans, or householders living elsewhere, he repaired to them and asked them questions. But none of these was ever able to please him; they either remained silent or else tried to slink away to another place.

For their part, the monks usually just went to the Himalayas.

Now, at that time there were hundreds of millions of arhats 14
living on Sheltered Mesa in the Himalayan mountains. The revered monk Assagutta heard with his clairaudience

bhikkhū pucchi: atth' āvuso koci bhikkhu paṭibalo milindena raññā saddhiṃ sallapituṃ kaṅkhaṃ paṭivinetun-ti. evaṃ vutte koṭisatā arahanto tuṇhī ahesuṃ. dutiyam-pi kho tatiyam-pi kho puṭṭhā tuṇhī ahesuṃ. atha kho āyasmā assagutto bhikkhusaṅghaṃ etad-avoca:

15 atth' āvuso tāvatiṃsabhavane vejayantassa pācīnato ketumatī nāma vimānaṃ, tattha mahāseno nāma devaputto paṭivasati, so paṭibalo tena milindena raññā saddhiṃ sallapituṃ kaṅkhaṃ paṭivinetun-ti. atha kho koṭisatā arahanto yugandharapabbate antarahitā tāvatiṃsabhavane pāturahesuṃ.

16 addasā kho sakko devānam-indo te bhikkhū dūratova āgacchante, disvāna yen' āyasmā assagutto ten' upasaṅkami, upasaṅkamitvā āyasmantaṃ assaguttaṃ abhivādetvā ekamantaṃ aṭṭhāsi. ekamantaṃ ṭhito kho sakko devānam-indo āyasmantaṃ assaguttaṃ etadavoca: mahā kho bhante bhikkhusaṅgho anuppatto, ahaṃ saṅghassa ārāmiko, ken' attho, kiṃ mayā karaṇīyan-ti.

17 atha kho āyasmā assagutto sakkaṃ devānaṃ indaṃ etad avoca: ayaṃ kho mahārāja jambudīpe sāgalanagare milindo nāma rājā, vādī durāsado duppasaho, puthutitthakarānaṃ aggam-akkhāyati, so bhikkhusaṅghaṃ upasaṅkamitvā diṭṭhivādena pañhaṃ pucchitvā bhikkhusaṅghaṃ viheṭhetīti. atha kho sakko devānam-indo āyasmantaṃ assaguttaṃ etad-avoca: ayaṃ kho bhante milindo rājā ito cuto manussesu uppanno; eso kho bhante ketumatīvimāne mahāseno

the words of King Milinda and convened the community of monks at the summit of Mount Yugandhara. He asked the monks: "Friends, is there anyone here competent to converse with King Milinda and dispel his uncertainties?"

At this, the hundreds of millions of arhats remained silent. He put the question to them a second time and a third time, but each time they remained silent. And so the revered Assagutta announced to the community of monks:

"Friends, in the Heaven of the Thirty-Three Gods there 15
is a mansion to the east of Vejayanta known as Ketumati. It is there that a god named Mahasena lives. He is competent to converse with King Milinda and dispel his uncertainties." At that, the hundreds of millions of arhats vanished from Mount Yugandhara and appeared in the Heaven of the Thirty-Three.

Sakka, the king of the gods, saw the monks arriving from 16
afar, and while still observing them he approached the revered Assagutta. Prepared to address him, he drew near and then stood to one side. And then the king of the gods stood there and said to the revered Assagutta: "It is a large community of monks that has come. I put myself at the service of the order. What is your purpose and how may I help?"

The revered Assagutta replied to Sakka, king of the gods: 17
"In Jambudipa in the city of Sagala there is a great king called Milinda. As a speaker he is hard to approach, hard to beat, and widely recognized as the best among the various exalted teachers of the day. He comes to the community of monks, lobs questions based on wrong views and doctrines, and harasses us."

nāma devaputto paṭivasati, so tena milindena raññā saddhiṃ paṭibalo sallapituṃ kaṅkhaṃ paṭivinetuṃ, taṃ devaputtaṃ yācissāma manussalokūpapattiyā ti.

18 atha kho sakko devānam-indo bhikkhusaṅghaṃ purakkhatvā ketumatīvimānaṃ pavisitvā mahāsenaṃ devaputtaṃ āliṅgitvā etad-avoca: yācati taṃ mārisa bhikkhusaṅgho manussalokūpapattiyā ti. na me bhante manussaloken' attho kammabahulena, tibbo manussaloko, idh' evāhaṃ bhante devaloke uparūparuppattiko hutvā parinibbāyissāmīti. dutiyam-pi kho tatiyam-pi kho sakke devānam-inde yācante mahāseno devaputto evam āha: na me bhante manussaloken' attho kammabahulena, tibbo manussaloko, idh' evāhaṃ bhante devaloke uparūparuppattiko hutvā parinibbāyissāmīti. atha kho āyasmā assagutto mahāsenaṃ devaputtaṃ etad-avoca: idha mayaṃ mārisa sadevakaṃ lokaṃ anuvilokayamānā aññatra tayā milindassa rañño vādaṃ bhinditvā sāsanaṃ paggahetuṃ samatthaṃ aññaṃ kañci na passāma, yācati taṃ mārisa bhikkhusaṅgho: sādhu sappurisa, manussaloke nibbattitvā dasabalassa sāsanaṃ paggaṇhitvā dehīti.

19 evaṃ vutte mahāseno devaputto: ahaṃ kira milindassa rañño vādaṃ bhinditvā sāsanaṃ paggahetuṃ samattho

Sakka, king of the gods, replied to Assagutta: "Sir, this King Milinda came from here and was born among humans. However, there is a god named Mahasena living in the Ketumati mansion who is competent to converse with him and dispel his uncertainties. Let us ask this god to take birth in the human realm."

And so Sakka, king of the gods, paid his respects to the 18
community of monks and then paid a visit to the Ketumati mansion and embraced this god, saying, "The community of monks respectfully requests that you take birth in the human realm."

"No, thank you, sir. For the human realm is riddled with karma and the human realm is dark. I prefer to stay here in the realm of gods, being born higher and higher until I attain nibbana." A second time and then a third time Sakka asked the god Mahasena, and each time he repeated, "No, thank you, sir. For the human realm is riddled with karma and the human realm is dark. I prefer to stay here in the realm of gods, being born higher and higher until I attain nibbana."

At this, the revered Assagutta addressed the god Mahasena: "With all due respect, sir, surveying the divine realm here, we do not see anyone else able to uphold the Buddhist dispensation by dismantling the arguments of King Milinda. And so the community of monks requests this of you. Dear sir, please, permit yourself to be reborn in the human realm and make every effort on behalf of the dispensation of the Ten-Powered Buddha."

Thus addressed, the god Mahasena began to think, *Perhaps* 19
I just might be able to uphold the dispensation by dismantling

bhavissāmīti haṭṭhatuṭṭho udaggudaggo hutvā: sadhu bhante, manussaloke uppajjissāmīti paṭiññaṃ adāsi. atha kho te bhikkhū devaloke taṃ karaṇīyaṃ tīretvā devesu tāvatiṃsesu antarahitā himavante pabbate rakkhitatale pāturahesuṃ. atha kho āyasmā assagutto bhikkhusaṅghaṃ etadavoca: atth' āvuso imasmiṃ bhikkhusaṅghe koci bhikkhu sannipātaṃ anāgato ti. evaṃ vutte aññataro bhikkhu āyasmantaṃ assaguttaṃ etad avoca: atthi bhante, āyasmā rohaṇo ito sattame divase himavantaṃ pabbataṃ pavisitvā nirodhaṃ samāpanno, tassa santike dūtaṃ pāhethāti.

20 āyasmā pi rohaṇo taṃ khaṇaññeva nirodhā vuṭṭhāya: saṅgho maṃ patimānetīti himavante pabbate antarahito rakkhitatale koṭisatānaṃ arahantānaṃ purato pāturahosi. atha kho āyasmā assagutto āyasmantaṃ rohaṇaṃ etadavoca: kin-nu kho āvuso rohaṇa buddhasāsane palujjante na passasi saṅghassa karaṇīyānīti. amanasikāro me bhante ahosīti. tena h' āvuso rohaṇa daṇḍakammaṃ karohīti. kiṃ bhante karomīti. atth' āvuso rohaṇa himavantapabbatapasse kajaṅgalannāma brāhmaṇagāmo, tattha soṇuttaro nāma brāhmaṇo paṭivasati, tassa putto uppajjissati nāgaseno nāma dārako; tena hi tvaṃ āvuso rohaṇa dasamāsādhikāni satta vassāni taṃ kulaṃ piṇḍāya pavisa, piṇḍāya pavisitvā nāgasenaṃ dārakaṃ nīharitvā pabbājehi, pabbajite ca tasmiṃ daṇḍakammato muccissasīti āha. āyasmā pi kho rohaṇo: sādhūti sampaṭicchi.

the arguments of King Milinda. And he got very excited and his hair stood on end. So he promised: "Very well then, sir, I will take rebirth in the human realm."

With their mission in the divine realm complete, the monks vanished from the Heaven of the Thirty-Three and appeared back at Sheltered Mesa in the Himalayan mountains. The revered Assagutta addressed the community of monks: "Now, friends, are there any monks who have not come to this assembly of the community?" In reply a certain monk told Assagutta, "Sir, the revered Rohana has been visiting another Himalayan mountain for the past seven days, where he has attained the spiritual achievement called 'stopping.'[7] Send a messenger."

Just at that very moment the revered Rohana came out 20
of this stopping, and realizing, *The community is looking for me*, he vanished from his Himalayan mountain and appeared before the many hundred arhats at Sheltered Mesa. At this, Assagutta spoke to Rohana: "Friend Rohana, how is it that at the ruin of the Buddha's dispensation you do not see what needs to be done?" "I was inattentive, sir." "Then there should be a punishment, Rohana." "What should I do, sir?"

"Go to a Brahman village called Kajangala on the slope of the Himalayan mountain where a Brahman named Sonuttara lives. He will have a son, a youth called Nagasena. Friend, you are to live there seeking alms from this family for seven years and ten months. While visiting for alms, draw the boy Nagasena away and ordain him. When he is ordained, you will be released from this punishment."

"Very well," assented Rohana.

21 mahāseno pi kho devaputto devalokā cavitvā soṇuttarabrāhmaṇassa bhariyāya kucchismiṃ paṭisandhiṃ aggahesi. saha paṭisandhigahaṇā tayo acchariyā abbhutā dhammā pāturahesuṃ: āvudhabhaṇḍāni pajjaliṃsu, aggasassaṃ abhinipphannaṃ, mahāmegho abhippavassi. āyasmā pi kho rohaṇo tassa paṭisandhigahaṇato paṭṭhāya dasamāsādhikāni satta vassāni taṃ kulaṃ piṇḍāya pavisanto ekadivasam-pi kaṭacchumattaṃ bhattaṃ vā uḷuṅkamattaṃ yāguṃ vā abhivādanaṃ vā añjalikammaṃ vā sāmīcikammaṃ vā nālattha, atha kho akkosañ-ñeva paribhāsaññeva paṭilabhati, aticchatha bhante ti vacanamattam-pi vattā nāma nāhosi. dasamāsādhikānaṃ pana sattannaṃ vassānaṃ accayena ekadivasaṃ aticchatha bhante ti vacanamattaṃ alattha.

22 taṃ divasam-eva ca brāhmaṇo pi bahikammantā āgacchanto paṭipathe theraṃ disvā: kiṃ bho pabbajita amhākaṃ geham-agamatthāti āha: āma brāhmaṇa, agamamhāti. api kiñci labhitthāti. āma brāhmaṇa, labhimhāti. so anattamano gehaṃ gantvā pucchi: tassa pabbajitassa kiñci adatthāti. na kiñci adamhāti. brāhmaṇo dutiyadivase gharadvāre yeva nisīdi: ajja pabbajitaṃ musāvādena niggahessāmīti. thero dutiyadivase brāhmaṇassa gharadvāraṃ sampatto; brāhmaṇo theraṃ disvā va evam-āha: tumhe hiyyo amhā-

Meanwhile, the god Mahasena had fallen from the divine realm and taken rebirth in the womb of the wife of the Brahman Sonuttara. At the precise moment of his conception three wonderful and marvelous things occurred: stocks of weapons burst into flames, the first crops came to harvest, and a great cloud shed rain. As for the revered Rohana, he lived there from the time of this conception and sought alms from this family for seven years and ten months. But he never once obtained food there, even so much as a spoonful of rice or a ladle of gruel, or, for that matter, even a greeting, sign of respect, or any appropriate acknowledgment. Far from it. He received only insults and abuse, and these people could not even bring themselves to ask him to just move along. But one day, after seven years and ten months had elapsed, he did get at least this much: "Move along, sir." 21

That very day the Brahman was returning from doing business away and saw the elder coming the other way on the road. He called out, "Hey, renouncer, have you just come from my house?" "Yes, Brahman, I have just come from there." "Did you actually get anything?" "Yes, Brahman, I did receive something." 22

At this the Brahman was disgruntled and went home and asked, "What did you give to that renouncer?" "But we gave him nothing."

The next day the Brahman sat at the door of the house thinking, *Today I will harangue that renouncer for telling a lie.* On the second day the elder reached the door to the house of the Brahman. When the Brahman saw the elder he said: "Yesterday you got nothing from our house, and yet you said

kaṃ gehe kiñci alabhitvā yeya labhimhāti avocuttha, vaṭṭati nu kho tumhākaṃ musāvādo ti.

23 thero āha: mayaṃ brāhmaṇa tumhākaṃ gehe dasamāsādhikāni satta vassāni aticchathāti vacanamattam-pi alabhitvā hiyyo aticchathāti vacanamattaṃ alabhimha, ath' etaṃ vacīpaṭisanthāraṃ upādāya evam-avocumhāti. brāhmaṇo cintesi: ime vācāpaṭisanthāramattam-pi labhitvā janamajjhe labhimhāti pasaṃsanti, aññaṃ kiñci khādaniyaṃ vā bhojaniyaṃ vā labhitvā kasmā na-ppasaṃsantīti pasīditvā attano atthāya paṭiyāditabhattato kaṭacchubhikkhaṃ tadūpiyañ-ca byañjanaṃ dāpetvā: imaṃ bhikkhaṃ sabbakālaṃ tumhe labhissathāti āha. so punadivasato-ppabhuti upasaṅkamantassa therassa upasamaṃ disvā bhiyyo somattāya pasīditvā theraṃ niccakālaṃ attano ghare bhattavissaggakaraṇatthāya yāci. thero tuṇhībhāvena adhivāsetvā divase divase bhattakiccaṃ katvā gacchanto thokaṃ thokaṃ buddhavacanaṃ kathetvā gacchati.

24 sā pi kho brāhmaṇī dasamāsaccayena puttaṃ vijāyi, nāgaseno ti 'ssa nāmaṃ ahosi. so anukkamena vaḍḍhanto sattavassiko jāto. atha kho nāgasenassa dārakassa pitā nāgasenaṃ dārakaṃ etad-avoca: imasmiṃ kho tāta nāgasena brāhmaṇakule sikkhāni sikkheyyāsīti. katamāni tāta imasmiṃ brāhmaṇakule sikkhāni nāmāti. tayo kho tāta nāgasena vedā sikkhāni nāma, avasesāni sippāni sippaṃ nāmāti. tena hi tāta sikkhissāmīti.

that you had received something. It is not right for you to tell a lie."

The elder said, "Brahman, for seven years and ten months 23
I have come to your house and never received so much as a 'Move along, sir.' But yesterday I was told, 'Move along, sir,' and it was regarding this act of verbal goodwill that I spoke."

The Brahman considered this. *These monks make it known among the public that they have received something. But this one got only a verbal kindness! Think of how they will sing our praises should they actually get substantial or fine food.* He became very pleased at this and gave the monk ladles of alms from his own prepared rice, along with curries. And he announced that henceforth the elder would receive such alms every time. From that day forward he observed the elder's calm composure as he arrived, and his faith greatly increased. He asked the elder to take his main meal in his own home in perpetuity. The elder consented with dignified silence, and daily, after the meal, bit by bit, he would preach the Buddha's words before departing.

Now, the Brahman's wife had given birth to a son after 24
ten months following the conception, and they gave him the name Nagasena. He had gradually grown up and reached seven years. The father of this youth Nagasena asked him: "Nagasena, son, would you like to study the branches of knowledge in a Brahman family?" "What are the branches of knowledge in the Brahman family called, Father?" "The branches of knowledge are called the three Vedas, Nagasena, and the remaining arts are called the arts." "I will study them, Father."

25 atha kho soṇuttaro brāhmaṇo ācariyabrāhmaṇassa ācariyabhāgaṃ sahassaṃ datvā antopāsāde ekasmiṃ gabbhe ekato mañcakaṃ paññāpetvā ācariyabrāhmaṇaṃ etad avoca: sajjhāyāpehi kho tvaṃ brāhmaṇa imaṃ dārakaṃ mantānīti. tena hi tāta dāraka uggaṇhāhi mantānīti ācariyabrāhmaṇo sajjhāyati.

26 nāgasenassa dārakassa eken'eva uddesena tayo vedā hadayaṅgatā vācuggatā sūpadhāritā suvavatthāpitā sumanasikatā ahesuṃ, sakim-eva cakkhuṃ udapādi tīsu vedesu sa-nighaṇḍu-keṭubhesu sākkharappabhedesu itihāsapañcamesu, padako veyyākaraṇo lokāyata-mahāpurisalakkhaṇesu anavayo ahosi. atha kho nāgaseno dārako pitaraṃ etad-avoca: atthi nu kho tāta imasmiṃ brāhmaṇakule ito uttarim-pi sikkhitabbāni, udāhu ettakān'evāti. natthi tāta nāgasena imasmiṃ brāhmaṇakule ito uttariṃ sikkhitabbāni, ettakān' eva sikkhitabbānīti.

27 atha kho nāgaseno dārako ācariyassa anuyogaṃ datvā pāsādā oruyha pubbavāsanāya coditahadayo rahogato patisallīno attano sippassa ādi-majjha-pariyosānaṃ olokento ādimhi vā majjhe vā pariyosāne vā appamattakam-pi sāraṃ adisvā: tucchā vata bho ime vedā, palāpā vata bho ime vedā, asārā nissārā ti vippaṭisārī anattamano ahosi.

28 tena kho pana samayena āyasmā rohaṇo vattaniye senāsane nisinno nāgasenassa dārakassa cetasā cetoparivitakkam-aññāya nivāsetvā pattacīvaram-ādāya vatta-

And so the Brahman Sonuttara gave a thousand for the teacher's fee to a Brahman teacher, spread out a bed on one side of a room inside his house, and told the Brahman teacher, "Brahman, you are to teach this boy the mantras." And so the Brahman teacher instructed him, "Boy, master the mantras." 25

With but a single recitation the youth Nagasena learned the three Vedas by heart, and they were well voiced, well put, properly arranged, and given his full attention. At once he achieved insight into the three Vedas, lexicography, ritual science, phonology, etymology, and history, which is the fifth; his knowledge of the words, grammar, materialist philosophy, and the marks of a great person was completed.[8] So then the youth Nagasena reported to his father: "Father, is there anything further to be learned in the house of this Brahman, or is this it?" 26

"No, Nagasena, there is nothing more to be learned in the house of the Brahman. Only this much is to be mastered."

So the boy sat for his final examination by the teacher, came away from his house, and, with a heart questioning as a result of past karmic impressions, sought privacy and solitude to contemplate the beginning, middle, and end of his learning. Finding no substance, even as much as a jot, in the beginning, middle, or end, he grew disappointed and full of regret: *These Vedas are simply empty, these Vedas are sheer nonsense, these Vedas are without substance and of no importance.* 27

Now, at that very moment the revered Rohana was sitting in his room at Vattaniya and came to realize the thoughts of the youth Nagasena. He got dressed, picked up his 28

niye senāsane antarahito kajaṅgalabrāhmaṇagāmassa purato pāturahosi. addasā kho nāgaseno dārako attano dvārakoṭṭhake ṭhito āyasmantaṃ rohaṇaṃ dūratova āgacchantaṃ, disvāna attamano udaggo pamudito pītisomanassajāto: app-eva nāmāyaṃ pabbajito kadāci sāraṃ jāneyyāti yen' āyasmā rohaṇo ten' upasankami, upasankamitvā āyasmantaṃ rohaṇaṃ etad-avoca: ko nu kho tvaṃ mārisa, ediso bhaṇḍu kāsāvavasano ti.

29 pabbajito nāmāhaṃ dārakāti. kena tvaṃ mārisa pabbajito nāmāsīti. pāpakānaṃ malānaṃ pabbājetuṃ pabbajito, tasmā'haṃ dāraka pabbajito nāmāti. kiṅkāraṇā mārisa kesā te na yathā aññesanti. soḷas' ime dāraka palibodhe disvā kesamassuṃ ohāretvā pabbajito, katame soḷasa: alaṅkārapalibodho maṇḍanapalibodho telamakkhanapalibodho dhovanapalibodho mālāpalibodho gandhanapalibodho vāsanapalibodho harīṭakapalibodho āmalakapalibodho raṅgapalibodho bandhanapalibodho kocchapalibodho kappakapalibodho vijaṭanapalibodho ūkāpalibodho, kesesu vilūnesu socanti kilamanti paridevanti urattāḷiṃ kandanti sammohamāpajjanti, imesu kho dāraka soḷasapalibodhesu paliguṇṭhitā manussā sabbāni atisukhumāni sippāni nāsentīti.

30 kiṅkāraṇā mārisa vatthāni pi te na yathā aññesan ti. kāmanissitāni kho dāraka vatthāni kamanīyāni gihibyañjanāni, yāni kānici kho bhayāni vatthato uppajjanti tāni kāsāvavasanassa na honti, tasmā vatthāni pi me na yathā aññesan-ti. jānāsi kho tvaṃ mārisa sippāni nāmāti. ama dāraka, jānām' ahaṃ sippāni, yaṃ loke uttamaṃ mantaṃ tam-pi jānāmīti. mayham-pi taṃ mārisa dātuṃ sakkā ti. āma dāraka, sakkā ti. tena hi me dehīti. akālo kho dāraka, antaragharaṃ piṇḍāya

bowl and robe, vanished from his room in Vattaniya, and appeared in front of the Brahman village Kajangala. Standing at the door of the storeroom, the youth Nagasena saw the revered Rohana from afar and watched him arrive. He became pleased, elated, happy, and full of joy and delight. He began to wonder if this renouncer might know something of substance. He approached Rohana and drawing near, asked him: “Tell me, sir, who are you that your head is shaved and you wear a saffron robe?”

“Young man, I am called a renouncer.” “Why are you called 29
a renouncer?” “A renouncer must renounce wicked stains, and so I said, ‘Young man, I am called a renouncer.’” “But why is your hair different from other people’s?”

“Seeing sixteen drawbacks to having hair and beard, a renouncer shaves them off. These are the sixteen drawbacks: one must ornament one’s hair, dress it, put oil on it, wash it, garland it, perfume it, apply fragrance, use myrobalan, use amla, dye it, tie it back, comb it, go to the barber, untangle it, and deal with lice; and then, when they lose their hair, people sorrow, grieve, beat their breasts, lament, and lapse into confusion. Young man, people get entangled in these sixteen drawbacks and they neglect the most subtle arts.”

“But why are your clothes different from other people’s?” 30
“Beautiful clothing worn by householders is the basis of desire, and all sorts of anxieties arise from clothes. But for the one wearing just the saffron robe none of these is known, and so my clothes are different from other people’s.”

“Do you know any arts, sir?” “Yes, young man, I know the arts. In fact, I know the most supreme mantra in the world.” “Can you please give it to me?” “Yes, I can.” “Then give it to

paviṭṭh' amhāti.

31 atha kho nāgaseno dārako āyasmato rohaṇassa hatthato pattaṃ gahetvā gharaṃ pavesetvā paṇītena khādaniyena bhojaniyena sahatthā santappetvā sampavāretvā āyasmantaṃ rohaṇaṃ bhuttāviṃ onītapattapāṇiṃ etad-avoca: dehi me dāni mārisa mantan-ti. yadā kho tvaṃ dāraka nippalibodho hutvā mātāpitaro anujānāpetvā mayā gahitaṃ pabbajitavesaṃ gaṇhissasi tadā dassāmīti āha.

32 atha kho nāgaseno dārako mātāpitaro upasaṅkamitvā āha: amma tāta, ayaṃ pabbajito: yaṃ loke uttamaṃ mantaṃ taṃ jānāmīti vadati, na ca attano santike apabbajitassa deti, ahaṃ etassa santike pabbajitvā taṃ mantaṃ uggaṇhissāmīti. ath'assa mātāpitaro: pabbajitvā pi no putto mantaṃ gaṇhātu, gahetvā punāgacchatīti maññamānā: gaṇha puttāti anujāniṃsu.

33 atha kho āyasmā rohaṇo nāgasenaṃ dārakaṃ ādāya yena vattaniyaṃ senāsanaṃ yena vijambhavatthu tenupasaṅkami, upasaṅkamitvā vijambhavatthusmiṃ senāsane ekarattiṃ vasitvā yena rakkhitatalaṃ ten' upasaṅkami, upasaṅkamitvā koṭisatānaṃ arahantānaṃ majjhe nāgasenaṃ dārakaṃ pabbājesi. pabbajito ca pan' āyasmā nāgaseno āyasmantaṃ rohaṇaṃ etad-avoca: gahito me bhante tava veso, detha me dāni mantan-ti.

34 atha kho āyasmā rohaṇo: kimhi nu kho 'haṃ nāgasenaṃ paṭhamaṃ vineyyaṃ, suttante vā abhidhamme vā ti cintetvā: paṇḍito kho ayaṃ nāgaseno, sakkoti sukhen' eva abhidhammaṃ pariyāpuṇitun-ti paṭhamaṃ abhidhamme

me." "Not right now, boy, as we are just entering the house for alms."

At this the youth Nagasena took the bowl from the revered 31
Rohana's hand, went into the house, and, with his own hand, provided and served him plentiful, substantial, and fine food. And when Rohana had eaten his fill and taken his hand from the bowl, the boy said again: "Please give me the mantra."

"When you are free of the drawbacks, have received your parents' permission, and have procured the robe of a renouncer that I too have taken up, then I will teach you."

At this, the youth Nagasena approached his parents and 32
said: "Mother, Father, the renouncer said that he knows the most supreme mantra in the world, but he will not give it to someone who has not renounced in his own presence. Having renounced in his presence, I am going to acquire that mantra."

His parents thought: *Let our son renounce and acquire the mantra; when he has it, he will come back to us.* So they gave him permission: "Learn it, son."

The revered Rohana received the youth Nagasena and set 33
out to his quarters at Vattaniya at Vijambhavatthu. Upon arrival he ordained the boy in the midst of the hundreds of millions of arhats. Newly ordained, the revered Nagasena said to the revered Rohana: "Now that I have taken up your robe, please give me the mantra."

Rohana pondered what he should teach Nagasena first. 34
The *suttas?* The *abhidhamma?* This Nagasena was quite learned and could surely easily master even the *abhidhamma*. And so he taught him the *abhidhamma* first.

vinesi. āyasmā ca nāgaseno: kusalā dhammā akusalā dhammā abyākatā dhammā ti tika-duka-patimaṇḍitaṃ dhammasaṅgaṇiṃ, khandhavibhaṅgādi-aṭṭhārasavibhaṅga-patimaṇḍitaṃ vibhaṅgappakaraṇaṃ, saṅgaho asaṅgaho ti-ādinā cuddasavidhena vibhattaṃ dhātukathāpakaraṇaṃ, khandhapaññatti-āyatanapaññattīti-ādinā chabbidhena vibhattaṃ puggalapaññattim, sakavāde pañca suttasatāni paravāde pañca suttasatānīti suttasahassaṃ samodhānetvā vibhattaṃ kathāvatthuppakaraṇaṃ, mūlayamakaṃ khandhayamakan-ti-ādinā dasavidhena vibhattaṃ yamakaṃ, hetupaccayo ārammaṇapaccayo ti-ādinā catuvīsatividhena vibhattaṃ paṭṭhānappakaraṇan-ti sabban-taṃ abhidhammapiṭakaṃ eken' eva sajjhāyena paguṇaṃ katvā: tiṭṭhatha bhante, na puna osāretha, ettaken' evāhaṃ sajjhāyissāmīti āha.

35 ath' āyasmā nāgaseno yena koṭisatā arahanto tenupasaṅkami, upasaṅkamitvā koṭisatānaṃ arahantānaṃ etad-avoca: ahaṃ kho bhante kusalā dhammā akusalā dhammā abyākatā

Nagasena learned the entire *abhidhamma* collection by heart with one recitation: first, the *Dhammasangaṇi* (Enumeration of Phenomenal States), which contains pairs and lists of three and begins, "These phenomenal states are good, these phenomenal states are bad, these phenomenal states are indeterminate."[9] Next there is the treatise called the *Vibhaṅga* (Analysis) that contains eighteen analyses, beginning with an analysis of the clusters.[10] Then the treatise called the *Dhātukathā* (Teaching on the Elements), divided into fourteen sections, beginning with inclusions and exclusions. Then the *Puggalapaññatti* (Descriptions of Persons), a sixfold description starting with describing the clusters, the bases of sensory experience, and so on.[11] After that comes the *Kathāvatthu* (Subjects of Discussion), with its thousand collected discourses, divided into five hundred from our own doctrine and five hundred introduced by interlocutors. Then the *Yamaka* (The Pairs), divided into ten pairs, such as the twofold classifications of roots* and then the twofold classification of the clusters, and so on. Finally, there is the treatise known as the *Paṭṭhāna* (Starting Points) with its twenty-four types of conditions, such as the conditions from a cause, the conditions from the starting points, and so forth. "I have mastered all of this, sir, so please stop there and do not explain it further."

Then the revered Nagasena went to the hundreds of 35
millions of arhats, and drawing near to them, announced: "I am ready to explain in detail the *abhidhamma* collection, sirs. And I have rearranged it into three parts: 'These phenome-

*Deeply lodged motivations generating experience.

dhammā ti imesu tīsu padesu pakkhipitvā sabban-taṃ abhidhammapiṭakaṃ vitthārena osāressāmīti. sādhu nāgasena, osārehīti.

36 atha kho āyasmā nāgaseno satta māsāni satta-ppakaraṇe vitthārena osāresi; paṭhavī unnadi, devatā sādhukāram-adaṃsu, brahmāno apphoṭesuṃ, dibbāni candanacuṇṇāni dibbāni ca mandāravapupphāni abhippavassiṃsu. atha kho koṭisatā arahanto āyasmantaṃ nāgasenaṃ paripuṇṇavīsativassaṃ rakkhitatale upasampādesuṃ. upasampanno ca pan' āyasmā nāgaseno tassā rattiyā accayena pubbaṅhasamayaṃ nivāsetvā pattacīvaram ādāya upajjhāyena saddhiṃ gāmaṃ piṇḍāya pavisanto evarūpaṃ parivitakkaṃ uppādesi: tuccho vata me upajjhāyo, bālo vata me upajjhāyo, ṭhapetvā avasesaṃ buddhavacanaṃ paṭhamaṃ maṃ abhidhamme vinesīti.

37 atha kho āyasmā rohaṇo āyasmato nāgasenassa cetasā cetoparivitakkam-aññāya āyasmantaṃ nāgasenaṃ etad-avoca: ananucchaviyaṃ kho nāgasena parivitakkaṃ vitakkesi, na kho pan' etaṃ nāgasena tavānucchaviyan-ti. atha kho āyasmato nāgasenassa etad ahosi: acchariyaṃ vata bho, abbhutaṃ vata bho, yatra hi nāma me upajjhāyo cetasā cetoparivitakkaṃ jānissati, paṇḍito vata me upajjhāyo, yan-nūnāhaṃ upajjhāyaṃ khamāpeyyan-ti. atha kho āyasmā nāgaseno āyasmantaṃ rohaṇaṃ etad-avoca: khamatha me bhante, na puna evarūpaṃ vitakkessāmīti.

38 atha kho āyasmā rohaṇo āyasmantaṃ nāgasenaṃ etad-avoca: na kho tyāhaṃ nāgasena ettāvatā khamāmi, atthi kho nāgasena sāgalaṃ nāma nagaraṃ, tattha milindo nāma rājā

nal states are good, these phenomenal states are bad, these phenomenal states are indeterminate.'"

"Very well, then, Nagasena. Do explain."

Over the next seven months, the revered Nagasena 36
explained in detail the seven treatises. At this, the earth roared. Deities shouted out, "Well done!" Even Brahmans clapped. And divine sandalwood powder and heavenly coral tree blossoms showered down. And later, when the revered Nagasena turned twenty years old, the hundreds of millions of arhats gave him full ordination at Sheltered Mesa.

Now fully ordained, the revered Nagasena got dressed very early one morning—indeed it was really still the wee hours of the night—and taking his robe and bowl, he entered a village with his teacher to seek alms. He began to think: *My teacher was inept; my teacher was foolish when he taught me the* abhidhamma *first and left out the rest of the Buddha's words.*

Now Rohana came to know Nagasena's thoughts through 37
his mental concentration, so he said to him: "Nagasena, it is inappropriate to harbor such thoughts, and it is unbecoming of you."

This struck Nagasena: *It is a marvel and a wonder that the teacher came to know my thoughts through his mental concentration. My teacher is actually quite learned, and I must certainly beg his forgiveness.* And so the revered Nagasena turned to the revered Rohana and said: "Forgive me, sir. Never again will I entertain such thoughts."

Rohana told Nagasena: "I do not fully forgive you, Naga- 38
sena. However, there is a city called Sagala where a king known as Milinda reigns. He lobs questions based on wrong views and doctrines, and harasses the community of monks.

rajjaṃ kāreti, so diṭṭhivādena pañhaṃ pucchitvā bhikkhu-saṅghaṃ viheṭheti, sace tvaṃ tattha gantvā taṃ rājānaṃ dametvā pasādessasi evāhan-taṃ khamissāmīti. tiṭṭhatu bhante eko milindo rājā, sace bhante sakala-jambudīpe sabbe rājāno āgantvā maṃ pañhaṃ puccheyyuṃ sabban-taṃ vissajjetvā sampadālessāmi, khamatha me bhante ti vatvā: na khamāmīti vutte: tena hi bhante imaṃ temāsaṃ kassa santike vasissāmīti āha. ayaṃ kho nāgasena āyasmā assagutto vattaniye senāsane viharati, gaccha tvaṃ nāgasena, yenāyasmā assagutto ten' upasaṅkama, upasaṅkamitvā mama vacanena[3] āyasmato assaguttassa pāde sirasā vanda, evañ-ca naṃ vadehi: upajjhāyo me bhante tumhākaṃ pāde sirasā vandati, appābādhaṃ appātaṅkaṃ lahuṭṭhānaṃ balaṃ phāsuvihāraṃ pucchati, imaṃ temāsaṃ tumhākaṃ santike vasituṃ maṃ pahiṇīti; konāmo te upajjhāyoti ca vutte: rohaṇatthero nāma bhante ti vadeyyāsi; ahaṃ konāmo ti ca vutte evaṃ vadeyyāsi: mama upajjhāyo bhante tumhākaṃ nāmaṃ jānātīti.

39 evaṃ bhante ti kho āyasmā nāgaseno āyasmantaṃ rohaṇaṃ abhivādetvā padakkhiṇaṃ katvā pattacīvaram-ādāya anupubbena cārikaṃ caramāno yena vattaniyaṃ senāsanaṃ yen' āyasmā assagutto ten' upasaṅkami, upasaṅkamitvā āyasmantaṃ assaguttaṃ abhivādetvā ekamantaṃ aṭṭhāsi. ekamantaṃ ṭhito kho āyasmā nāgaseno āyasmantaṃ assaguttaṃ etad avoca: upajjhāyo me bhante tumhākaṃ pāde sirasā vandati, evañ-ca vadeti: appābādhaṃ appātaṅkaṃ lahuṭṭhānaṃ balaṃ phāsuvihāraṃ pucchati, upajjhāyo maṃ bhante imaṃ temāsaṃ tumhākaṃ santike vasituṃ pahiṇīti.

If you go there, tame this king, and make him faithful, I will forgive you."

"Let it be so, sir. In fact, not just this one King Milinda, but if every king in all of Jambudipa were to come and question me, I would answer and cut them down if you would just forgive me." But what he said was, "I do not forgive you."

"Then with whom, sir, should I spend the three months of the rainy season?"

"Nagasena, the revered Assagutta has his quarters at Vattaniya. You should go to him, and when you approach Assagutta with my words, bow with your head to his feet. Tell him: 'My teacher bows with his head to your feet, asks after your comfort, and trusts that you are healthy, free from illness, vigorous, and strong. He has sent me to stay with you for the three-month season.' Should he ask, 'What is your teacher's name?' tell him 'The elder Rohana.' But if he should ask, 'What is my name?' tell him simply: 'My teacher knows your name, sir.'"

"It will be so, sir." The revered Nagasena paid his respects 39
to the revered Rohana by walking reverently around him. He took his bowl and robe and set out on the journey. In time he arrived at the quarters at Vattaniya. He approached the revered Assagutta, greeted him, and stood to one side. As he stood there, he told Assagutta: "My teacher bows with his head to your feet. He asks after your comfort and trusts that you are healthy, free from illness, vigorous, and strong. The teacher has sent me to stay with you for the three-month season."

40 atha kho āyasmā assagutto āyasmantaṃ nāgasenaṃ etadavoca: tvaṃ kinnāmo 'sīti. ahaṃ bhante nāgaseno nāmāti. konāmo te upajjhāyo ti. upajjhāyo me bhante rohaṇatthero nāmāti. ahaṃ konāmo ti. upajjhāyo me bhante tumhākaṃ nāmaṃ jānātīti. sādhu nāgasena, pattacīvaraṃ paṭisāmehīti. sādhu bhante ti pattacīvaraṃ paṭisāmetvā punadivase pariveṇaṃ sammajjitvā mukhodakaṃ dantapoṇaṃ upaṭṭhāpesi. thero sammaṭṭaṭṭhānaṃ paṭisammajji, taṃ udakaṃ chaḍḍetvā aññaṃ udakaṃ āhari, tañca dantakaṭṭhaṃ apanetvā aññaṃ dantakaṭṭhaṃ gaṇhi, na allāpasallāpaṃ akāsi. evaṃ satta divasāni katvā sattame divase puna pucchitvā puna tena tath' eva vutte vassāvāsaṃ anujāni.

41 tena kho pana samayena ekā mahāupāsikā āyasmantaṃ assaguttaṃ tiṃsamattāni vassāni upaṭṭhāsi. atha kho sā mahāupāsikā temāsaccayena yen' āyasmā assagutto ten' upasaṅkami, upasaṅkamitvā āyasmantaṃ assaguttaṃ etadavoca: atthi nu kho tāta tumhākaṃ santike añño bhikkhūti. atthi mahāupāsike amhākaṃ santike nāgaseno nāma bhikkhūti. tena hi tāta assagutta adhivāsehi nāgasenena saddhiṃ svātanāya bhattan-ti. adhivāsesi kho āyasmā assagutto tuṇhībhāvena. atha kho āyasmā assagutto tassā rattiyā accayena pubbaṅhasamayaṃ nivāsetvā pattacīvaram-ādāya āyasmatā nāgasenena saddhiṃ pacchāsamaṇena yena mahāupāsikāya nivesanaṃ ten' upasaṅkami, upasaṅkamitvā paññatte āsane nisīdi. atha kho sā mahāupāsikā āyasmantaṃ assaguttaṃ āyasmantañca nāgasenaṃ paṇītena khādaniyena bhojaniyena sahatthā santappesi sampavāresi. atha kho āyasmā

Assagutta asked Nagasena: “What is your name?” “I am 40
called Nagasena, sir.” “What is the name of your teacher?” “My teacher is known as the elder Rohana.” “And what is my name?” “My teacher knows your name, sir.” “Very well, then, Nagasena, put away your bowl and robe.”

“Very well, sir,” and he put away his bowl and robe. The next day he swept up the cell and put out water for rinsing the mouth and a toothbrush. But the elder swept the clean floor and tossed out the water and replaced it with fresh water. He set aside the tooth stick and used a different tooth stick. And he did not engage in conversation. This went on for seven days, but on the seventh day he queried Nagasena again. Being given the same replies, he permitted him to stay for the rains retreat.

At that time there was a certain eminent laywoman who 41
had attended the revered Assagutta for thirty years. At the end of the three-month season this eminent laywoman approached Assagutta: “Is there another monk staying with you, dear?”

“Yes, eminent laywoman, a monk named Nagasena is staying with me.”

“Then please agree to come for a meal tomorrow, dear, with Nagasena.” Assagutta’s silence indicated his assent. And so at dawn the next morning the revered Assagutta got dressed, took his bowl and robe, and with Nagasena as the junior monk walking behind him, proceeded to the house of the eminent laywoman. He drew near and sat down on the appointed seat. With her own hand, the laywoman provided and served both Assagutta and Nagasena with plentiful food, both substantial and fine. When Assagutta was well fed and

assagutto bhuttāvī onītapattapāṇi āyasmantaṃ nāgasenaṃ etad-avoca: tvaṃ nāgasena mahāupāsikāya anumodanaṃ karohīti. idaṃ vatvā uṭṭhāy' āsanā pakkāmi.

42 atha kho sā mahāupāsikā āyasmantaṃ nāgasenaṃ etad avoca: mahallikā kho 'haṃ tāta nāgasena, gambhīrāya dhammakathāya mayhaṃ anumodanaṃ karohīti. Atha kho āyasmā nāgaseno tassā mahāupāsikāya gambhīrāya abhidhammakathāya lokuttarāya suññatāpaṭisaṃyuttāya anumodanaṃ akāsi. atha kho tassā mahāupāsikāya tasmiṃ yeva āsane virajaṃ vītamalaṃ dhammacakkhuṃ udapādi: yaṃ kiñci samudayadhammaṃ sabban-taṃ nirodhadhamman-ti. āyasmā pi kho nāgaseno tassā mahāupāsikāya anumodanaṃ katvā attanā desitaṃ dhammaṃ paccavekkhanto vipassanaṃ paṭṭhapetvā tasmiṃ yeva āsane nisinno sotāpattiphale patiṭṭhasi.

43 atha kho āyasmā assagutto maṇḍalamāḷe nisinnova dvinnam-pi dhammacakkhupaṭilābhaṃ ñatvā sādhukāraṃ pavattesi: sādhu sādhu nāgasena, ekena kaṇḍappahārena dve mahākāyā padālitā ti. anekāni ca devatāsahassāni sādhukāraṃ pavattesuṃ. atha kho āyasmā nāgaseno uṭṭhāy' āsanā yen' āyasmā assagutto ten' upasaṅkami, upasaṅkamitvā āyasmantaṃ assaguttaṃ abhivādetvā ekamantaṃ nisīdi. ekamantaṃ nisinnaṃ kho āyasmantaṃ nāgasenaṃ āyasmā assagutto etad-avoca: gaccha tvaṃ nāgasena pāṭaliputtaṃ, pāṭaliputtanagare asokārāme āyasmā dhammarakkhito paṭivasati, tassa santike buddhavacanaṃ pariyāpuṇāhīti.

44 kīva dūre bhante ito pāliputtanagaran-ti. yojanasatāni kho nāgasenāti. dūro kho bhante maggo, antarāmagge bhikkhā

had removed his hand from the bowl, he told Nagasena: "Please say the blessing for the eminent laywoman, Nagasena." He himself got up from his seat and departed.

The laywoman turned to Nagasena. "I am an old woman, 42
dear. Please give a blessing from a profound teaching on the Dhamma." And so Nagasena gave the blessing from a profound teaching on the *abhidhamma,* something transcendent and connected with emptiness. As she sat there this great woman attained the following stainless and dustless insight into the Dhamma: *Whatever is subject to arising is invariably subject to ending.*[12] For his part, when he had finished giving the blessing to the laywoman, Nagasena reviewed the Dhamma that he himself had taught, and he became established in insight meditation.[13] In fact, sitting on that very seat, he attained the fruit of stream entry.[14]

All the while, the revered Assagutta was sitting in the 43
circular pavilion, and when he realized that both of them had attained insight into the Dhamma, he cheered: "Well done! This was very well done, Nagasena. By a single shot of an arrow two great bodies are pierced." And many thousands of gods also exclaimed, "Well done!" Nagasena got up from his seat and went to Assagutta, and when he arrived, he greeted him and stood to one side. As he sat there Assagutta told him: "You are to go to Pataliputta, Nagasena. In the city of Pataliputta at the Ashoka monastery lives the revered Dhammarakkhita. You are to study the words of the Buddha with him."

"How far from here is the city of Pataliputta?" "It is a 44
hundred leagues, Nagasena."[15] "That is a long road, sir, and along the way alms will be scarce. How will I go?" "Just go,

dullabhā, kathāhaṃ gamissāmīti. gaccha tvaṃ nāgasena, antarāmagge piṇḍapātaṃ labhissasi, sālīnaṃ odanaṃ vicitakāḷakaṃ anekasūpaṃ anekabyañjanan-ti. evaṃ bhante ti kho āyasmā nāgaseno āyasmantaṃ assaguttaṃ abhivādetvā padakkhiṇaṃ katvā pattacīvaram-ādāya yena pāṭaliputtaṃ tena cārikaṃ pakkāmi.

45 tena kho pana samayena pāṭaliputtako seṭṭhi pañcahi sakaṭasatehi pāṭaliputtagāmimaggaṃ paṭipanno hoti. addasā kho pāṭaliputtako seṭṭhi āyasmantaṃ nāgasenaṃ dūratova āgacchantaṃ, disvāna pañca sakaṭasatāni paṭipaṇāmetvā yen' āyasmā nāgaseno ten' upasaṅkami, upasaṅkamitvā āyasmantaṃ nāgasenaṃ abhivādetvā: kuhiṃ gacchasi tātāti āha. pāṭaliputtaṃ gahapatīti. sādhu tāta, mayam-pi pāṭaliputtaṃ gacchāma, amhehi saddhiṃ sukhaṃ gacchathāti.

46 atha kho pāṭaliputtako seṭṭhi āyasmato nāgasenassa iriyāpathe pasīditvā āyasmantaṃ nāgasenaṃ paṇītena khādaniyena bhojaniyena sahatthā santappetvā sampavāretvā āyasmantaṃ nāgasenaṃ bhuttāviṃ onītapattapāṇiṃ aññataraṃ nīcaṃ āsanaṃ gahetvā ekamantaṃ nisīdi. ekamantaṃ nisinno kho pāṭaliputtako seṭṭhi āyasmantaṃ nāgasenaṃ etad-avoca: kinnāmosi tvaṃ tātāti. ahaṃ gahapati nāgaseno nāmāti. jānāsi kho tvaṃ tāta buddhavacanaṃ nāmāti. jānāmi kho 'haṃ gahapati abhidhammapadānīti. lābhā no tāta, suladdhaṃ no tāta, aham-pi kho tata ābhidhammiko tvam-pi ābhidhammiko, bhaṇa tāta abhidhammapadānīti.

47 atha kho āyasmā nāgaseno pāṭaliputtakassa seṭṭhissa abhidhammaṃ desesi, desente desente yeva pāṭaliputtakassa seṭṭhissa virajaṃ vītamalaṃ dhammacakkhuṃ udapādi: yaṃ

Nagasena. Along the way, you will receive alms of rice, rice gruel, rice separated from black grains, various sauces, and a variety of curries." At this the revered Nagasena took his leave from the revered Assagutta by walking reverently around him. He picked up his bowl and robe and set out on the journey to Pataliputta.

Now at that time a Pataliputta merchant happened to 45
be going along the road, returning to Pataliputta with five hundred wagons. From afar, the Pataliputta merchant saw the revered Nagasena traveling along. As he watched him, he had the five hundred wagons turn off the road, and he approached Nagasena. He greeted him and asked where he was going. "To Pataliputta, householder." "Very well, son. Go with us to Pataliputta. Traveling with us will make it easy."

The merchant was very pleased with Nagasena's deport- 46
ment and so he offered him plentiful food, both substantial and fine, serving him with his own hand. And when Nagasena had removed his hand from his bowl, the merchant took a low seat and sat down to the side. He asked him: "What is your name, son?"

"I am called Nagasena, householder." "Do you know the Buddha's words, son?" "I know the *abhidhamma* section." "This is very fortunate for me, son, what a boon! For I too have studied the *abhidhamma,* and here you are, an *abhidhamma* man also. Please recite a portion of the *abhidhamma.*"

And so the revered Nagasena taught the *abhidhamma* 47
to the Pataliputta merchant, and while he was teaching, the following dustless and stainless insight into the Dhamma arose in the merchant: *Whatever is subject to arising is*

kiñci samudayadhammaṃ sabban-taṃ nirodhadhamman-ti. atha kho pāṭaliputtako seṭṭhi pañcamattāni sakaṭasatāni purato uyyojetvā sayaṃ pacchato gacchanto pāṭaliputtassa avidūre dvedhāpathe ṭhatvā āyasmantaṃ nāgasenaṃ etad-avoca: ayaṃ kho tāta nāgasena asokārāmassa maggo; imaṃ kho tāta mayhaṃ kambalaratanaṃ soḷasahatthaṃ āyāmena aṭṭhahatthaṃ vitthārena, patigaṇhāhi kho tāta imaṃ kambalaratanaṃ anukampaṃ upādāyāti. paṭiggahesi kho āyasmā nāgaseno taṃ kambalaratanaṃ anukampaṃ upādāya. atha kho pāṭaliputtako seṭṭhi attamano udaggo pamuditahadayo pītisomanassajāto āyasmantaṃ nāgasenaṃ abhivādetvā padakkhiṇaṃ katvā pakkāmi.

48 atha kho āyasmā nāgaseno yena asokārāmo yen' āyasmā dhammarakkhito ten' upasaṅkami, upasaṅkamitvā āyasmantaṃ dhammarakkhitaṃ abhivādetvā attano āgatakāraṇaṃ kathetvā āyasmato dhammarakkhitassa santike tepiṭakaṃ buddhavacanaṃ eken' eva uddesena tīhi māsehi byañjanato pariyāpuṇitvā puna tīhi māsehi atthato manasākāsi. atha kho āyasmā dhammarakkhito āyasmantaṃ nāgasenaṃ etad-avoca: seyyathā pi nāgasena gopālako gāvo rakkhati, aññe gorasaṃ paribhuñjanti, evam-eva kho tvaṃ nāgasena tepiṭakaṃ buddhavacanaṃ dhārento pi na bhāgī sāmaññassāti.

49 hotu bhante, alaṃ ettakenāti ten' eva divasabhāgena tena rattibhāgena saha paṭisambhidāhi arahattaṃ pāpuṇi. saha saccapaṭivedhena āyasmato nāgasenassa sabbe devā sādhukāraṃ-adaṃsu, paṭhavī unnadi, brahmāno apphoṭesuṃ, dibbāni candanacuṇṇāni c' eva dibbāni ca mandāravapupphāni abhippavassiṃsu.

invariably subject to ending. At this, the merchant sent his five hundred carts ahead whiie he traveled along behind them, until they reached a fork in the road near Pataliputta. He informed Nagasena: "This is the road to the Ashoka monastery. This excellent woolen cloth measures sixteen cubits in length and eight cubits in width. Out of compassion for me, son, please accept this excellent cloth." Out of compassion for him, Nagasena accepted the cloth, and the Pataliputta merchant became pleased, elated, with a happy heart, and full of joy and delight. He paid his respects to Nagasena, walking reverently around him, and departed.

The revered Nagasena went to the Ashoka monastery, 48
greeted the revered Dhammarakkhita, and explained why he had come. After three months with Dhammarakkhita and with just one recitation of the Three Baskets of scripture, that is, the Buddha's words, he had mastered the phrasing. He pondered the meaning for another three months. But then Dhammarakkhita said to Nagasena: "Just as a herdsman guards the cattle but leaves it to others to enjoy their produce, so too are you one who understands the Three Baskets of the Buddha's words, and yet you do not enjoy the rewards of the religious life."

"Then no more will I settle for only this much, sir." And 49
during the night of the very next day he attained the analytical insights and became an arhat.[16] Immediately following Nagasena's comprehension of the truth, all the gods cheered, "Well done!" The earth roared, and even Brahmans clapped. And divine sandalwood powder and heavenly coral tree blossoms showered down.

50 tena kho pana samayena koṭisatā arahanto himavante pabbate rakkhitatale sannipatitvā āyasmato nāgasenassa santike dūtaṃ pāhesuṃ: āgacchatu nāgaseno, dassanakāmā mayaṃ nāgasenan-ti. atha kho āyasmā nāgaseno dūtassa vacanaṃ sutvā asokārāme antarahito himavante pabbate rakkhitatale koṭisatānaṃ arahantānaṃ purato pāturahosi. atha kho koṭisatā arahanto āyasmantaṃ nāgasenaṃ etad-avocuṃ: eso kho nāgasena milindo rājā bhikkhusaṅghaṃ viheṭheti vādapaṭivādena pañhapucchāya; sādhu nāgasena, gaccha tvaṃ milindaṃ rājānaṃ damehīti.

51 tiṭṭhatu bhante eko milindo rājā, sace bhante sakalajambudīpe rājāno āgantvā maṃ pañhaṃ puccheyyuṃ sabban-taṃ vissajjetvā sampadālessāmi, gacchatha vo bhante asambhītā sāgalanagaran-ti. Atha kho therā bhikkhū sāgalanagaraṃ kāsāvapajjotaṃ isivātaparivātaṃ akaṃsu.

52 tena kho pana samayena āyasmā āyupālo saṅkheyyapariveṇe paṭivasati. atha kho milindo rājā amacce etad-avoca: ramaṇīyā vata bho dosinā ratti, kan-nu khv-ajja samaṇaṃ vā brāhmaṇaṃ vā upasaṅkameyyāma sākacchāya pañhapucchanāya, ko mayā saddhiṃ sallapituṃ ussahati kaṅkhaṃ paṭivinetun-ti. evaṃ vutte pañcasatā yonakā rājānaṃ milindaṃ etad-avocuṃ: atthi mahārāja āyupālo nāma thero tepiṭako bahussuto āgatāgamo, so etarahi saṅkheyyapariveṇe paṭivasati, gaccha tvaṃ mahārāja, āyasmantaṃ āyupālaṃ pañhaṃ pucchassūti. tena hi bhaṇe bhadantassa ārocethāti.

Now at that time the hundreds of millions of arhats had 50
assembled at Sheltered Mesa in the Himalayan mountains, and they sent a messenger to the revered Nagasena: "May Nagasena please come, as we wish to see him." Hearing the words of the messenger, Nagasena vanished from Ashoka monastery and appeared before the hundreds of millions of arhats at Sheltered Mesa in the Himalayan mountains. The hundreds of millions of arhats addressed him: "Nagasena, King Milinda is harassing the community of monks by lobbing questions along with arguments and counterarguments. It would be good if you could go and tame this King Milinda."

"Forget about King Milinda, let kings from all over 51
Jambudipa come and ask questions. In replying to everything, I will cut them down. So please proceed without fear, good sirs, to the city of Sagala." Then the elder monks made the city of Sagala brilliant with their saffron robes and breezy with the wafting fragrance of holy men.

Now, at that time the revered Ayupala lived in the San- 52
kheyya monastery. King Milinda said to his companions: "It is a lovely moonlit night. Which renouncer or Brahman may we approach tonight to ask questions? Who is able to converse with me and to dispel my uncertainties?"

In reply, the five hundred Yonakas said: "Great king, there is an elder called Ayupala who knows the Three Baskets, has heard much, and is well versed in doctrine. He is now staying at Sankheyya monastery. Go to this revered Ayupala and ask him your questions."

"Very well, then. Do inform him."

53 atha kho nemittiko āyasmato āyupālassa santike dūtaṃ pāhesi: rājā bhante milindo āyasmantaṃ āyupālaṃ dassanakāmo ti. āyasmā pi kho āyupālo evam-āha: tena hi āgacchatūti. atha kho milindo rājā pañcamattehi yonakasatehi parivuto rathavaram-āruyha yena saṅkheyyapariveṇaṃ yen' āyasmā āyupālo ten' upasaṅkami, upasaṅkamitvā āyasmatā āyupālena saddhiṃ sammodi, sammodanīyaṃ kathaṃ sārāṇīyaṃ vītisāretvā ekamantaṃ nisīdi. ekamantaṃ nisinno kho milindo rājā āyasmantaṃ āyupālaṃ etad-avoca: kimatthiyā bhante āyupāla tumhākaṃ pabbajjā, ko ca tumhākaṃ paramattho ti.

54 thero āha: dhammacariyasamacariyatthā kho mahārāja pabbajjā ti. atthi pana bhante koci gihī pi dhammacārī samacārī ti. āma mahārāja, atthi gihī pi dhammacārī samacārī. bhagavati kho mahārāja bārāṇasiyaṃ isipatane migadāye dhammacakkaṃ pavattente aṭṭhārasannaṃ brahmakoṭīnaṃ dhammābhisamayo ahosi, devatānaṃ pana dhammābhisamayo gaṇanapathaṃ vītivatto; sabbe te gihibhūtā na pabbajitā. puna ca paraṃ mahārāja bhagavatā mahāsamayasuttante desiyamāne, mahāmaṅgalasuttante desiyamāne, samacittapariyāyasuttante desiyamāne, rāhulovādasuttante desiyamāne, parābhavasuttante desiyamāne gaṇanapatham-atītānaṃ devatānaṃ dhammābhisamayo ahosi; sabbe te gihibhūtā na pabbajitā ti.

55 tena hi bhante āyupāla niratthikā tumhākaṃ pabbajjā, pubbe katassa pāpakammassa nissandena samaṇā sakyaput-

And so a soothsayer sent a messenger to Ayupala who told 53
him that King Milinda wished to see him, and Ayupala replied that the king should indeed come. So King Milinda mounted his finest royal chariot and with his retinue of five hundred Yonakas arrived at Sankheyya monastery and approached Ayupala. He addressed Ayupala cordially, exchanging polite and friendly greetings, and sat down to one side. And as he sat there, he addressed Ayupala: "What is the point of renunciation, Ayupala? What is your highest purpose?"

The monk replied: "Renunciation is a way of living accord- 54
ing to the Dhamma, and it is a way of living that is calming, great king."

"But could a householder live according to the Dhamma and live in this calming way also, sir?"

"Yes, a householder can live according to the Dhamma in this calming way. When the Bhagavan turned the Wheel of the Dhamma at Deer Park in Sarnath near Baranasi, eighteen myriads of Brahma deities grasped the Dhamma, and an unreckoned number of other gods also grasped the Dhamma.[17] All of these were householders, not renouncers. And there is more. In the past when the Bhagavan taught these *suttas*—the *Great Assembly Sutta*, the *Great Auspiciousness Sutta*, the *Sutta Teaching Equanimity*, the *Advice to Rahula Sutta*, and the *Sutta on Destruction*—an unreckoned number of gods grasped the Dhamma, and all of these were householders, not renouncers."

"But then there is no point in your renunciation, Ayupala. 55
Surely it is the result of some wicked karma in the past that

tiyā pabbajanti dhutaṅgāni ca pariharanti. ye kho te bhante āyupāla bhikkhū ekāsanikā nūna te pubbe paresaṃ bhogahārakā corā, te paresaṃ bhoge acchinditvā tassa kammassa nissandena etarahi ekāsanikā bhavanti, na labhanti kālena kālaṃ paribhuñjituṃ, na-tthi tesaṃ sīlaṃ, na-tthi tapo, na-tthi brahmacariyaṃ. Ye kho pana te bhante āyupāla bhikkhū abbhokāsikā nūna te pubbe gāmaghātakā corā, te paresaṃ gehāni vināsetvā tassa kammassa nissandena etarahi abbhokāsikā bhavanti, na labhanti senāsanāni paribhuñjituṃ, na-tthi tesaṃ sīlaṃ, na-tthi tapo, na-tthi brahmacariyaṃ. ye kho pana te bhante āyupāla bhikkhū nesajjikā nūna te pubbe panthadūsakā corā, te panthike jane gahetvā bandhitvā nisīdāpetvā tassa kammassa nissandena etarahi nesajjikā bhavanti, na labhanti seyyaṃ kappetuṃ, na-tthi tesaṃ sīlaṃ, na-tthi tapo, na-tthi brahmacariyan-ti āha.

56 evaṃ vutte āyasmā āyupālo tuṇhī ahosi, na kiñci paṭibhāsi. atha kho pañcasatā yonakā rājānaṃ milindaṃ etad-avocuṃ: paṇḍito mahārāja thero, api ca kho avisārado na kiñci paṭibhāsatīti. atha kho milindo rājā āyasmantaṃ āyupālaṃ tuṇhībhūtaṃ disvā apphoṭetvā ukkuṭṭhiṃ katvā yonake etad-avoca: tuccho vata bho jambudīpo, palāpo vata bho jambudīpo, na-tthi koci samaṇo vā brāhmaṇo vā yo mayā saddhiṃ sallapituṃ ussahati kaṅkhaṃ paṭivinetun-ti. atha kho milindassa rañño sabban-taṃ parisaṃ anuvilokentassa abhīte amaṅkubhūte yonake disvā etad-ahosi: nissaṃsayaṃ atthi maññe añño koci paṇḍito bhikkhu yo mayā saddhiṃ

you renouncers in the lineage of the Sakya* must renounce the world and live by ascetic practices. Perhaps the monks who eat but one meal a day were thieves who stole food from others in a previous life; plundering others' food then, they now eat only one meal a day as a result of that karma, and so they do not receive meals at the right time to enjoy them. It is not a matter of morality, asceticism, or the religious life. And further, Ayupala, those monks who live in the open air were surely thieves who sacked villages in a previous life and destroyed people's homes. They live out in the open now as a result of this karma, and do not receive lodgings that they can enjoy. It is hardly a matter of morality, asceticism, or the religious life. Still more, Ayupala, monks who take up the ascetic practice of sitting still were surely robber thieves in a previous life who seized travelers, bound them, and did not let them sit down. They now practice sitting still and are unable to secure a bed to lie down on because of this karma. It has nothing to do with morality, asceticism, or the religious life."

When this was said the revered Ayupala remained silent, 56
not uttering a word. The five hundred Yonakas said to King Milinda: "Great king, the elder is learned but he is not confident, so he says nothing." But when King Milinda saw Ayupala remain silent he clapped his hands and gave a shout. He exclaimed to the Yonakas: "Jambudipa is simply empty, Jambudipa is sheer nonsense, for nowhere is there a recluse or Brahman who is able to converse with me and dispel my uncertainties." But he surveyed his entire

* The Buddha.

sallapituṃ ussahati, yen' ime yonakā na maṅkubhūtā ti. atha kho milindo rājā yonake etad-avoca: atthi bhaṇe añño koci paṇḍito bhikkhu yo mayā saddhiṃ sallapituṃ ussahati kaṅkhaṃ paṭivinetun-ti.

57 tena kho pana samayena āyasmā nāgaseno samaṇa-gaṇaparivuto saṅghī gaṇī gaṇācariyo ñāto yasassī sādhu-sammato bahujanassa paṇḍito byatto medhāvī nipuṇo viññū vibhāvī vinīto visārado bahussuto tepiṭako vedagū pabhinnabuddhimā āgatāgamo pabhinnapaṭisambhido navaṅgasatthusāsana-pariyattidharo pāramippatto jinava-cane dhammattha-desanā-paṭivedha-kusalo akkhaya-vi-citra-paṭibhāno citrakathī kalyāṇavākkaraṇo durāsado duppasaho duruttaro durāvaraṇo dunnivārayo, sāgaro viya akkhobbho, girirājā viya niccalo, raṇañjaho tamonudo pabhaṅkaro, mahākathī paragaṇigaṇa-mathano paratitthi-ya-maddano, bhikkhūnaṃ bhikkhunīnaṃ upāsakānaṃ upāsikānaṃ rājūnaṃ rājamahāmattānaṃ sakkato garukato mānito pūjito apacito, lābhī cīvara-pindapāta-senāsana-gi-

assembly and saw that the Yonakas were neither afraid nor rattled. *I think there must assuredly be some learned monk who is able to converse with me, because why else would these Yonakas not be rattled?* So he told them: "Look here, surely there is some learned monk who is able to converse with me and dispel my uncertainties."

Now, at that time the revered Nagasena had a following 57
of renouncers and had become the head of the community, a leader, and a celebrated and renowned professor. He was learned and highly regarded by many people, experienced, intelligent, accomplished, clever, wise, and educated. He was confident, for he had heard much; he knew completely the three collections; he had an ever-expanding intellect, was proficient in the scripture, enjoyed ever-expanding skills in analysis, and was an expert in the study of the nine-part teaching of the Buddha.[18] He had attained the perfections and was proficient at analyzing phenomenal states, the meanings, the teaching, and comprehension in relation to the words of the Victor. A brilliant speaker, he had a skill in exposition that was unfailingly eloquent, and his speech was beautiful. He was unapproachable, hard to overcome, hard to best, hard to restrain, and hard to block; he was tranquil as the ocean, still as the king of mountains, and, abandoning impurities, he dispelled darkness and cast light. A great preacher who could perplex the followers of other leaders and crush those of other sects, he was honored, esteemed, respected, adored, and reverenced by monks, nuns, laymen, laywomen, kings, and high royal officials. Because he had achieved such fame, he found it easy to acquire the requisite belongings of a monk, that is, the robe, alms bowl,

lānappaccayabhesajja-parikkhārānaṃ lābhagga-yasaggappatto, buddhānaṃ viññūnaṃ sotāvadhānena samannāgatānaṃ sandassento navaṅgaṃ jinasāsanaratanaṃ, upadisanto dhammamaggaṃ, dhārento dhammappajjotaṃ, ussāpento dhammayūpaṃ, yajanto dhammayāgaṃ, paggaṇhāpento dhammaddhajaṃ, ussāpento dhammaketuṃ, uppaḷāsento dhammasaṅkhaṃ, āhananto dhammabheriṃ, nadanto sīhanādaṃ, gajjanto indagajjitaṃ, madhura-gira-gajjitena ñāṇavaravijjujāla-pariveṭhitena karuṇājala-bharitena mahatā dhammāmata-meghena sakalalokam-abhitappayanto, gāma-nigama-rājadhānīsu cārikaṃ caramāno anupubbena sāgalanagaraṃ anuppatto hoti.

58 tatra sudaṃ āyasmā nāgaseno asītiyā bhikkhusahassehi saddhiṃ saṅkheyyapariveṇe paṭivasati. ten' āhu:

bahussuto citrakathī nipuṇo ca visārado sāmāyiko ca
kusalo paṭibhāne ca kovido.
te ca tepiṭakā bhikkhū pañcanekāyikā pi ca catunekāyikā
c' eva nāgasenaṃ purakkharuṃ.

lodging, and medicines for sickness. To the wise and intelligent followers who turned their ears to him, he taught the ninefold jewel of the Victor's teaching, pointing out the path of the Dhamma, hoisting the lamp of the Dhamma, raising up the pillar of the Dhamma, offering the munificence of the Dhamma, holding up the banner of the Dhamma, raising up the flag of the Dhamma, sounding the conch of the Dhamma, and striking the kettledrum of the Dhamma. Roaring the lion's roar, clapping with Indra's thunder, he gratified the whole world with a huge cloud full of the nectar of the Dhamma. But this was a cloud that was heavy with the waters of compassion, thundering with sweet words, and enveloping people with the glow of the finest flashes of lightning—those that come from knowledge. It was this Nagasena who wandered on his journey through villages, market towns, and capital cities until he gradually reached the city of Sagala.

Once there, he stayed in the Sankheyya monastery with 58
eighty thousand monks. About him they say:

Having heard much, he was a brilliant speaker,
accomplished and educated, seasoned, skillful,
ready of wit, and wise.
Nagasena was at the forefront of all monks learned
in the Three Baskets and the Four Collections,
and even among those who knew all Five
Collections.[19]

gambhīrapañño medhāvī maggāmaggassa kovido
uttamatthaṃ anuppatto nāgaseno visārado.
tehi bhikkhūhi parivuto nipuṇehi saccavādibhi caranto
gāmanigamaṃ sāgalaṃ upasankami.
saṅkheyyapariveṇasmiṃ nāgaseno tadā vasi, katheti so
manussehi pabbate kesarī yathā ti.

59 atha kho devamantiyo rājānaṃ milindaṃ etad-avoca: āgamehi tvaṃ mahārāja, āgamehi tvaṃ mahārāja, atthi mahārāja nāgaseno nāma thero paṇḍito byatto medhāvi vinīto visārado bahussuto citrakathī kalyāṇapaṭibhāno attha-dhamma-nirutti-paṭibhāna-paṭisambhidāsu pārami-ppatto, so etarahi saṅkheyyapariveṇe paṭivasati, gaccha tvaṃ mahārāja, āyasmantaṃ nāgasenaṃ pañhaṃ pucchassu, ussahati so tayā saddhiṃ sallapituṃ kaṅkhaṃ paṭivinetun-ti. atha kho milindassa rañño sahasā nāgaseno ti saddaṃ sutvāva ahud-eva bhayaṃ, ahudeva chambhitattaṃ, ahud-eva lomahaṃso. atha kho milindo rājā devamantiyaṃ etad-avoca: ussahati bho nāgaseno bhikkhu mayā saddhiṃ sallapitun-ti. ussahati mahārāja api inda-yama-varuṇa-ku-vera-pajāpati-suyāma-santusitalokapālehi pitupitāmahena mahābrahmunā pi saddhiṃ sallapituṃ, kimaṅga pana manussabhūtenāti. atha kho milindo rājā devamantiyaṃ etad avoca: tena hi tvaṃ devamantiyabhadantassa santike dūtaṃ pesehīti. evaṃ devāti kho devamantiyo āyasmato

Intelligent and wise in discerning what is and what is not the path, he had an understanding that was profound, and he was so highly educated that he had achieved preeminence.[20]

With a retinue of accomplished and truth-telling monks, Nagasena wandered through the villages and market towns until he reached Sagala.

There he stayed at Sankheyya monastery preaching to the people, like a maned lion atop a mountain.

Then Devamantiya turned to King Milinda and said: 59
"Please wait a bit, great king, just wait. In fact, there is an elder named Nagasena who is learned, experienced, intelligent, educated, and confident because he has heard much. A brilliant speaker, he has a knowledge that is truly beautiful. He has reached perfection in the four kinds of analytical insight—analysis of meaning, analysis of phenomenal states, analysis of language, and analysis of comprehension. And he is staying right here at the Sankheyya monastery. You must go to this revered Nagasena, great king, and question him, for he is able to converse with you and dispel your uncertainties."

At the mere mention of the sound "Nagasena," King Milinda became afraid and stupefied; his hair stood on end. He turned to Devamantiya: "Is this monk Nagasena really able to converse with me?"

"Great king, he can converse with Indra, Yama, Varuna, Kubera, the Lord of Creatures, Suyama, the kings of the pleasure heaven, and the grandfather Great Brahma himself, to say nothing of mere humans." "Then send a messenger to this honored monk, Devamantiya." "Yes, your majesty,"

nāgasenassa santike dūtaṃ pāhesi: rājā bhante milindo āyasmantaṃ dassanakāmo ti.

60 āyasmā pi kho nāgaseno evam-āha: tena hi āgacchatūti. atha kho milindo rājā pañcamattehi yonakasatehi parivuto rathavaram āruyha mahatā balakāyena saddhiṃ yena saṅkheyyapariveṇaṃ yen' āyasmā nāgaseno ten' upasaṅkami. tena kho pana samayena āyasmā nāgaseno asītiyā bhikkhusahassehi saddhiṃ maṇḍalamāḷe nisinno hoti. addasā kho milindo rājā āyasmato nāgasenassa parisaṃ dūratova, disvāna devamantiyaṃ etad-avoca: kass' esā devamantiya mahatī parisā ti. āyasmato kho mahārāja nāgasenassa parisā ti. atha kho milindassa rañño āyasmato nāgasenassa parisaṃ dūratova disvā ahud-eva bhayaṃ, ahud-eva chambhitattaṃ, ahud-eva lomahaṃso. atha kho milindo rājā, khaggaparivārito viya gajo, garuḷaparivārito viya nāgo, ajagaraparivārito viya kotthuko, mahisaparivārito viya accho, nāgānubaddho viya maṇḍūko, saddūlānubaddho viya migo, ahiguṇṭhika-samāgato viya pannago, majjārasamāgato viya unduro, bhūtavejjasamāgato viya pisāco, rāhumukhagato viya cando, pannago viya peḷantaragato, sakuṇo viya pañjarantaragato, maccho viya jālantaragato, vāḷavanam-anuppaviṭṭho viya puriso, vessavaṇāparādhiko viya yakkho, parikkhīṇāyuko viya devaputto, bhīto ubbiggo utrasto saṃviggo lomahaṭṭhajāto vimano dummano bhantacitto vipariṇatamānaso: mā maṃ ayaṃ jano paribhavīti dhitiṃ upaṭṭhapetvā devamantiyaṃ etad-avoca: mā kho tvaṃ devamantiya āyasmantaṃ nāgasenaṃ mayhaṃ ācikkheyyāsi, anakkhātañ-ñevāhaṃ nāgasenaṃ jānissāmīti.

and Devamantiya dispatched a messenger to the revered Nagasena, who said: “Sir, King Milinda wishes to see you.”

Nagasena replied: “Then let him come.” 60

And so King Milinda, surrounded by his five hundred Yonakas, mounted his finest royal chariot and with his great army went to the Sankheyya monastery and approached Nagasena. Nagasena was sitting in the circular pavilion with the eighty thousand monks. Seeing from afar this assembly surrounding Nagasena, Milinda said to Devamantiya: “Whose enormous assembly is this?” Devamantiya replied, “It is the revered Nagasena’s assembly, great king.” Even at a distance, as he took in Nagasena’s assembly, the king became afraid and stupefied, and his hair stood on end. Like an elephant surrounded by rhinoceroses, a serpent by the mythical *garuḷa* eagles, a jackal by snakes, a bear by buffalo; like a frog chased by a snake, a deer fleeing a leopard, a cobra cornered by a snake charmer, a rat captured by a cat, a ghost seized by an exorcist, the moon swallowed by Rahu,[*] a snake in a basket, a bird in a cage, a fish in a net, a man in a scary forest, a *yakkha*[†] who has offended his king, Kubera, and like a god whose death draws near, Milinda was frightened, anxious, terrified, agitated, breaking out in goose bumps, distressed, confused, with his mind in turmoil and his thoughts awhirl, thinking only: *May these people not come to despise me.* But he mustered his courage and turned to Devamantiya: “Do not point Nagasena out to me. I will recognize him even if he is not announced.”

* Demon who causes eclipses by swallowing the moon and the sun.

† Semidivine beings who attend the god of wealth, Kubera.

61 sādhu mahārāja, tvañ-ñeva jānāhīti. tena kho pana samayena āyasmā nāgaseno tassā bhikkhuparisāya purato cattālīsāya bhikkhusahassānaṃ navakataro hoti, pacchato cattālīsāya bhikkhusahassānaṃ vuḍḍhataro. atha kho milindo rājā sabban-taṃ bhikkhusaṅghaṃ purato ca pacchato ca majjhato ca anuvilokento addasā kho āyasmantaṃ nāgasenaṃ dūratova bhikkhusaṅghassa majjhe nisinnaṃ, kesarasīhaṃ viya vigatabhayabheravaṃ vigatalomahaṃsaṃ vigatabhayasārajjaṃ, disvāna ākāren' eva aññāsi: eso kho ettha nāgaseno ti. atha kho milindo rājā devamantiyaṃ etad avoca: eso kho devamantiya āyasmā nāgaseno ti. āma mahārāja, eso kho nāgaseno, suṭṭhu kho tvaṃ mahārāja nāgasenaṃ aññāsīti. tato rājā tuṭṭho ahosi: anakkhātova mayā nāgaseno aññāto ti. atha kho milindassa rañño āyasmantaṃ nāgasenaṃ disvāva ahud eva bhayaṃ, ahud-eva chambhitattaṃ, ahud-eva lomahaṃso. ten' āhu:

62 caraṇena c' eva sampannaṃ, sudantaṃ uttame dame,
disvā rājā nāgasenaṃ idaṃ vacanam abravi:
kathikā mayā bahū diṭṭhā, sākacchā osaṭā bahū, na
tādisaṃ bhayaṃ āsi ajja tāso yathā mama.
nissaṃsayaṃ parājayo mama ajja bhavissati, jayo ca
nāgasenassa, yathā cittaṃ na saṇṭhitan-ti.

63 bāhirakathā niṭṭhitā.

"Very well, then, great king, find him for yourself." 61

Now, the revered Nagasena had at that point been ordained prior to forty thousand newly ordained monks who had gathered at the assembly, but following another forty thousand who were senior to him. And so when King Milinda scanned the front, the rear, and the middle of the community of monks, he saw even at a distance Nagasena sitting in the middle of the community like a maned lion, free of fear and terror, free of horripilation, and utterly undaunted. By these indications he knew: *That one is Nagasena.* He turned to Devamantiya: "That one is the revered Nagasena."

"Yes, great king, he is in fact Nagasena. It is impressive that you recognize him."

The king was pleased with himself. "I managed to recognize Nagasena without having him being pointed out." But still, as he gazed upon him, Milinda became afraid and stupefied, and his hair stood on end. And so they say:

When the king saw Nagasena, endowed with right 62
behavior and disciplined in the supreme discipline,
he uttered these words:
"I have discussed many points of view; I have held
many conversations.
But never have I known the fear and terror that I felt
today.
Without a doubt today will be my defeat and
Nagasena's victory, for my mind is not
composed."

This concludes the backstory. 63

CHAPTER 2

Questions of Milinda

PART 1

1 atha kho milindo rājā yen' āyasmā nāgaseno ten' upasaṅkami, upasaṅkamitvā āyasmatā nāgasenena saddhiṃ sammodi, sammodanīyaṃ kathaṃ sārāṇīyaṃ vītisāretvā ekam antaṃ nisīdi. āyasmā pi kho nāgaseno paṭisammodi, yen' eva rañño milindassa cittaṃ ārādhesi. atha kho milindo rājā āyasmantaṃ nāgasenaṃ etad-avoca: katham-bhadanto ñāyati, kinnāmosi bhante ti. nāgaseno ti kho ahaṃ mahārāja ñāyāmi, nāgaseno ti maṃ mahārāja sabrahmacārī samudācaranti, api ca mātāpitaro nāmaṃ karonti nāgaseno ti vā sūraseno ti vā vīraseno ti vā sīhaseno ti vā, api ca kho mahārāja saṅkhā samaññā paññatti vohāro nāmamattaṃ yad-idaṃ nāgaseno ti, na h'ettha puggalo upalabbhatīti.

2 atha kho milindo rājā evam-āha: suṇantu me bhonto pañcasatā yonakā asītisahassā ca bhikkhū, ayaṃ nāgaseno evam-āha: na h'ettha puggalo upalabbhatīti, kallan-nu kho tad-abhinanditun-ti. atha kho milindo rājā āyasmantaṃ nāgasenaṃ etad-avoca: sace bhante nāgasena puggalo nūpalabbhati, ko carahi tumhākaṃ cīvara-piṇḍapāta-senāsanagilānapaccayabhesajja-parikkhāraṃ deti, ko taṃ paribhuñjati, ko sīlaṃ rakkhati, ko bhāvanam-anuyuñjati, ko magga-phala-nibbānāni sacchikaroti, ko pāṇaṃ hanati, ko adinnaṃ ādiyati, ko kāmesu micchā carati, ko musā bhaṇati, ko majjaṃ pivati, ko pañcānantariyakammaṃ karoti; tasmā na-tthi kusalaṃ, na-tthi akusalaṃ, na-tthi kusalākusalānaṃ kammānaṃ kattā vā kāretā vā, na-tthi sukaṭadukkaṭānaṃ kammānaṃ phalaṃ vipāko, sace bhante nāgasena yo tumhe

PART 1

Questions on Defining Characteristics

Then King Milinda approached the revered Nagasena, and 1
drawing near, addressed him cordially, exchanged polite and friendly greetings, and sat down to one side. Nagasena pleased King Milinda with his cordial greetings in reply. Then King Milinda asked: "How are you known, sir, what is your name?"

"I am known as Nagasena, great king, and my fellow monks call me Nagasena. Parents give names like Nagasena, Surasena, Virasena, or Sihasena, and yet this 'Nagasena' is just a word, an appellation, a designation, a common usage—that is, it is a mere name and no person is found here."

At this King Milinda spoke: "Now listen to me, all five 2
hundred Yonakas and eighty thousand monks. This Nagasena just told me that no person is found here. Can this be right?"

King Milinda turned again to the revered Nagasena. "If, sir, there is no person, then who exactly is it that gives you a robe, alms bowl, lodging, and medicines and remedies for illness? And who uses these? Who protects moral discipline? Who practices meditation? Who realizes the path, its fruits, and nibbana? Who is it that destroys life, takes what is not given, behaves with desire and lust, tells lies, drinks alcohol, or commits the five karmic acts that bring about immediate retribution?[1] If this is so, there cannot be anything good or bad, or anyone who does good and bad actions or causes others to do so, and no fruit or result of virtuous or immoral

māreti na-tthi tassāpi pāṇātipāto, tumhākam-pi bhante nāgasena na-tthi ācariyo na-tthi upajjhāyo na-tthi upasampadā; nāgaseno ti maṃ mahārāja sabrahmacārī samudācarantīti yaṃ vadesi, katamo ettha nāgaseno, kin-nu kho bhante kesā nāgaseno ti.

3 na hi mahārājāti. lomā nāgaseno ti. na hi mahārājāti. nakhā-pe-dantā taco maṃsaṃ nahāru aṭṭhī aṭṭhimiñjā vakkaṃ hadayaṃ yakanaṃ kilomakaṃ pihakaṃ papphāsaṃ antaṃ antaguṇaṃ udariyaṃ karīsaṃ pittaṃ semhaṃ pubbo lohitaṃ sedo medo assu vasā kheḷo siṅghāṇikā lasikā muttaṃ matthake matthaluṅgaṃ nāgaseno ti. na hi mahārājāti. kin-nu kho bhante rūpaṃ nāgaseno ti. na hi mahārājāti. vedanā nāgaseno ti. na hi mahārājāti. Saññā nāgaseno ti. na hi mahārājāti. saṅkhārā nāgaseno ti. na hi mahārājāti. viññāṇaṃ nāgaseno ti. na hi mahārājāti. kim-pana bhante rūpa-vedanā-saññā-saṅkhāra-viññāṇaṃ nāgaseno ti. na hi mahārājāti. kim-pana bhante aññatra rūpa-vedanā-saññā-sankhāra-viññāṇaṃ nāgaseno ti. na hi mahārājāti. tam-ahaṃ bhante pucchanto pucchanto na passāmi nāgasenaṃ, saddo yeva nu kho bhante nāgaseno, ko pan' ettha nāgaseno, alikaṃ tvaṃ bhante bhāsasi musāvādaṃ, na-tthi nāgaseno ti.

4 atha kho āyasmā nāgaseno milindaṃ rājānaṃ etad avoca: tvaṃ khosi mahārāja khattiyasukhumālo accantasukhumālo, tassa te mahārāja majjhantikasamayaṃ tattāya

karma. And, Nagasena, if someone were to kill you, his act would not be considered murder. And how could you have a teacher, master, or ordination? You said, 'Great king, my fellow monks call me Nagasena,' but what here is Nagasena? What, is the hair on your head Nagasena?"

"No, great king." 3

"Is the hair on your body Nagasena?" "No, great king." "The nails, teeth, skin, flesh, sinews, bones, marrow, kidneys, heart, liver, pleura, spleen, lungs, small intestine, large intestine, stomach, excrement, bile, phlegm, pus, blood, sweat, fat, tears, serum, saliva, mucus, synovial fluid, urine, or the brain matter in your skull—are any of these Nagasena?" "No, great king."

"What is it then, sir? Is your form Nagasena?" "No, great king." "Is your feeling Nagasena?" "No." "Is your perception Nagasena?" "No." "Are your habitual patterns Nagasena?" "No." "Is your awareness Nagasena?" "No, great king." "Well then, is Nagasena form, feeling, perception, habitual patterns, *and* awareness?"[2] "No." "Then is Nagasena something *other than* form, feeling, perception, habitual patterns, and awareness?" "No, great king."

"Sir, though questioning you again and again, I do not see Nagasena! So is Nagasena merely a sound? What here is Nagasena? You have spoken a falsehood, a lie, for there is no Nagasena."

In response, the revered Nagasena turned to the king. 4
"Great king, you have been delicately brought up as a Kshatriya and are exceedingly delicate. If you were to set out on foot at midday on the hot ground, on the scorching sand, treading on the sharp gravel, stones, and sand, your

bhūmiyā uṅhāya vālikāya kharā sakkhara-kaṭhala-vālikā madditvā pādena gacchantassa pādā rujanti, kayo kilamati, cittaṃ upahaññati, dukkhasahagataṃ kāyaviññāṇaṃ uppajjati, kin-nu tvaṃ pāden' āgatosi udāhu vāhanenāti. nāhaṃ bhante pāden' āgacchāmi, rathenāhaṃ āgato 'smīti.

5 sace tvaṃ mahārāja rathen' āgatosi rathaṃ me ārocehi, kin-nu kho mahārāja īsā ratho ti. na hi bhante ti. akkho ratho ti. na hi bhante ti. cakkāni ratho ti. na hi bhante ti. rathapañjaraṃ ratho ti. na hi bhante ti. rathadaṇḍako ratho ti. na hi bhante ti. yugaṃ ratho ti. na hi bhante ti. rasmiyo ratho ti. na hi bhante ti. patodalaṭṭhi ratho ti. na hi bhante ti. kin-nu kho mahārāja īsā-akkha-cakka-rathapañjara-rathadaṇḍa-yuga-rasmi-patodaṃ ratho ti. na hi bhante ti. kim-pana mahārāja aññatra īsā-akkha-cakka-rathapañjara-rathadaṇḍa-yuga-rasmi-patodaṃ ratho ti. na hi bhante ti. tam-ahaṃ mahārāja pucchanto pucchanto na passāmi rathaṃ, saddo yeva nu kho mahārāja ratho, ko pan' ettha ratho, alikaṃ tvaṃ mahārāja bhāsasi musāvādaṃ, na-tthi ratho, tvaṃsi mahārāja sakala-jambudīpe aggarājā, kassa pana tvaṃ bhāyitvā musā bhāsasi, suṇantu me bhonto pañcasatā yonakā asītisahassā ca bhikkhū, ayaṃ milindo rājā evam-āha: rathenāhaṃ āgato'smīti: sace tvaṃ mahārāja rathen' āgatosi rathaṃ me ārocehīti vutto samāno rathaṃ na sampādeti, kallan-nu kho tad-abhinanditun-ti.

6 evaṃ vutte pañcasatā yonakā āyasmato nāgasenassa sādhukāraṃ datvā milindaṃ rājānaṃ etad-avocum: idāni kho tvaṃ mahārāja sakkonto bhāsassūti. atha kho milindo rājā āyasmantaṃ nāgasenaṃ etad-avoca: nāhaṃ bhante nāgasena musā bhaṇāmi, īsañ-ca paṭicca akkhañ-ca paṭicca cakkāni ca paṭicca rathapañjarañ-ca paṭicca rathadaṇḍa-

feet would hurt, your body would ache, your mind would be flustered, and there would arise a painful awareness of your body. Surely you did not come on foot, but instead by vehicle?"

"I did not come by foot, but rather, I came by chariot."

"If you came by chariot, then tell me about the chariot. Is 5
the pole the chariot, great king?" "No, sir." "Is the axle the chariot?" "No, sir." "Are the wheels the chariot?" "No." "Is the frame the chariot?" "No." "Is the flagstaff the chariot?" "No." "Is the yoke the chariot?" "No." "Are the reins the chariot?" "No." "Is the goad the chariot?" "No." "Then are the pole, axle, wheels, frame, flagstaff, yoke, reins, and goad the chariot?" "No, sir."

"Then, great king, though questioning you again and again, I do not see a chariot! So is the chariot merely a sound?"

"No, sir."

"What then is the chariot? You have spoken a falsehood, a lie, for there is no chariot. You are the chief king in all of Jambudipa. Of whom are you frightened, that you would utter a falsehood? Please listen to me, all five hundred Yonakas and eighty thousand monks. This King Milinda declared, 'I came by chariot.' But when asked, 'If you came by chariot, then tell me about the chariot,' he does not produce the chariot. Can this be right?"

Addressed in this way, the five hundred Yonakas applauded 6
the revered Nagasena and said to King Milinda: "Now, great king, are you able to reply?"

At this, the king turned to Nagasena. "Nagasena, I am not telling a falsehood, since it is because of a pole, because of an axle, because of the wheels, because of the frame, and

kañ-ca paṭicca ratho ti sankhā samaññā paññatti vohāro nāmaṃ pavattatīti. sādhu kho tvaṃ mahārāja rathaṃ jānāsi, evam-eva kho mahārāja mayhaṃ-pi kese ca paṭicca lome ca paṭicca-pematthaluṅgañ-ca paṭicca rūpañ-ca paṭicca vedanañ-ca paṭicca saññañ-ca paṭicca saṅkhāre ca paṭicca viññāṇañ-ca paṭicca nāgaseno ti saṅkhā samaññā paññatti vohāro nāmamattaṃ pavattati, paramatthato pan' ettha puggalo nūpalabbhati. bhāsitam-p' etaṃ mahārāja vajirāya bhikkhuniyā bhagavato sammukhā: yathā hi aṅgasambhārā hoti saddo ratho iti, evaṃ khandhesu santesu hoti satto ti sammutīti.

7 acchariyaṃ bhante nāgasena, abbhutaṃ bhante nāgasena, aticitrāni pañhapaṭibhānāni vissajjitāni, yadi buddho tiṭṭheyya sādhukāraṃ dadeyya, sādhu sādhu nāgasena, aticitrāni pañhapaṭibhānāni vissajjitāni. kativassosi tvaṃ bhante nāgasenāti. sattavasso 'haṃ mahārājāti. ke te bhante satta, tvaṃ vā sattagaṇanā vā sattāti. tena kho pana samayena milindassa rañño sabbābharaṇapatimaṇḍitassa alankatapaṭiyattassa paṭhaviyaṃ chāyā dissati, udakamaṇike chāyā dissati. atha kho āyasmā nāgaseno milindaṃ rājānaṃ etad-avoca: ayaṃ te mahārāja chāyā paṭhaviyaṃ udakamaṇike ca dissati, kim-pana mahārāja tvaṃ vā rājā chāyā vā rājā ti.

because of the flagstaff that there comes to be the 'chariot,' which is just a word, an appellation, a designation, a common usage, a mere name."

"Well done, great king. You understand the chariot. It is the same with me. It is because of head hair, body hair, and so on all the way up to the brain matter in the skull, and it is because of form, feeling, perception, habitual patterns, and awareness that there comes to be 'Nagasena,' which is just a word, an appellation, a designation, a common usage, a mere name. But in the absolute sense there is no person found here. In reference to this very point, the nun Vajira said this in the presence of the Bhagavan: 'Just as *chariot* is a word used when there is an assemblage of parts, so too it is conventional to say that there is a *being* when there is only a collection of clusters.'"

"Wonderful, Nagasena! Marvelous, Nagasena! The 7
answers in reply to my questions are brilliant, and if the Buddha were standing here he would surely give his approval. Excellent, Nagasena, are these brilliant answers in reply to the questioning.

"How many years, Nagasena, have you been ordained?" "I am seven years in, great king." "How is it that you are seven? Are you seven or is the number seven?"

Now just at that moment, the shadow of King Milinda, dressed up, decked out, and adorned with all his ornaments, was seen on the ground. And his reflection was seen also in a water pot. So then the revered Nagasena turned to the king: "This shadow of yours, great king, is seen on the ground and in a water pot. Now, are you the king, or is the shadow the king?"

8 ahaṃ bhante nāgasena rājā, nāyaṃ chāyā rājā, maṃ pana nissāya chāyā pavattatīti. evam-eva kho mahārāja vassānaṃ gaṇanā sattāti, na panāhaṃ satta, maṃ pana nissāya satta pavattati chāyūpamaṃ mahārājāti. acchariyaṃ bhante nāgasena, abbhutaṃ bhante nāgasena, aticitrāni pañhapaṭibhānāni vissajjitānīti.

9 rājā āha: bhante nāgasena, sallapissasi mayā saddhin-ti. sace tvaṃ mahārāja paṇḍitavādā sallapissasi sallapissāmi, sace pana rājavādā sallapissasi na sallapissāmīti. kathaṃ bhante nāgasena paṇḍitā sallapantīti. paṇḍitānaṃ kho mahārāja sallāpe āveṭhanam-pi kayirati, nibbeṭhanam-pi kayirati, niggaho pi kayirati, paṭikammam-pi kayirati, viseso pi kayirati, paṭiviseso pi kayirati, na ca tena paṇḍitā kuppanti, evaṃ kho mahārāja paṇḍitā sallapantīti. kathaṃ pana bhante rājāno sallapantīti.

10 rājāno kho mahārāja sallāpe ekaṃ vatthuṃ paṭijānanti, yo taṃ vatthuṃ vilometi tassa daṇḍaṃ āṇāpenti: imassa daṇḍaṃ paṇethāti, evaṃ kho mahārāja rājāno sallapantīti. paṇḍitavādā 'haṃ bhante sallapissāmi no rājavadā, vissattho bhadanto sallapatu, yathā bhikkhunā vā sāmaṇerena vā upāsakena vā ārāmikena vā saddhiṃ sallapati evaṃ vissattho bhadanto sallapatu, mā bhāyatūti. suṭṭhu mahārājāti thero abbhanumodi.

11 rājā āha: bhante nāgasena, pucchissāmīti. Puccha mahārājāti. pucchitosi me bhante ti. vissajjitaṃ mahārājāti. kiṃ pana bhante tayā vissajjitan-ti. kiṃ pana mahārāja tayā pucchitan-ti. atha kho milindassa rañño etad-ahosi: paṇḍito kho ayaṃ bhikkhu, paṭibalo mayā saddhiṃ sallapituṃ, bahukāni

"Nagasena, I am the king. The shadow is not the king, for 8
it occurs entirely dependent on me." "Similarly, seven is the number of years. I am not seven, for seven occurs entirely dependent on me, just as in the example of the shadow."

"Wonderful, Nagasena! Marvelous, Nagasena! The answers in reply to the questioning are brilliant."

The king said: "Nagasena, sir, will you converse with me?" 9

"Great king, if you converse with the arguments of scholars, I will converse with you. But if you converse the way kings argue, I will not."

"How, Nagasena, do scholars converse?"

"In the debates of scholars, great king, there are entangling and unraveling, refuting and countering, and agreeing and disagreeing, but scholars do not get angry. This is how scholars converse."

"And how do kings converse, sir?"

"Great king, when kings debate, one account is approved 10
and whoever disputes it invites punishment—'Have him punished!' This is how kings converse."

"I will converse with the arguments of scholars, and not the way kings argue. Please speak freely as though talking with a monk, novice, layman, or attendant, and in this way speak freely and have no fear."

"Very well, then." And the monk was satisfied.

The king said, "Nagasena, sir, I will ask you something." 11
"Please ask, great king." "It has already been asked by me." "Then it has been answered, great king." "But what has been answered by you?" "But what was asked by you?"

It occurred to King Milinda: *This scholarly monk is competent to converse with me, and there will be so many things that*

ca me ṭhānāni pucchitabbāni bhavissanti, yāva apucchitāni yeva tāni ṭhānāni bhavissanti atha suriyo atthaṃ gamissati, yan-nūnāhaṃ sve antepure sallapeyyan-ti. atha kho rājā devamantiyaṃ etad-avoca: tena hi tvaṃ devamantiya-bhadantassa āroceyyāsi: sve antepure raññā saddhiṃ sallāpo bhavissatīti. idaṃ vatvā milindo rājā uṭṭhāy' āsanā theraṃ nāgasenaṃ āpucchitvā assaṃ abhirūhitvā nāgaseno nāgaseno ti sajjhāyaṃ karonto pakkāmi.

12 atha kho devamantiyo āyasmantaṃ nāgasenaṃ etad-avoca: rājā bhante milindo evam-āha: sve antepure sallāpo bhavissatīti. suṭṭhūti thero abbhanumodi. atha kho tassā rattiyā accayena devamantiyo ca anantakāyo ca maṅkuro ca sabbadinno ca yena milindo rājā ten' upasaṅkamiṃsu, upasaṅkamitvā rājānaṃ milindaṃ etad-avocuṃ: āgacchati mahārāja bhadanto nāgasenoti. āma, āgacchatūti. kittakehi bhikkhūhi saddhiṃ āgacchatīti. yattake bhikkhū icchati tattakehi bhikkhūhi saddhiṃ āgacchatūti. atha kho sabbadinno āha: āgacchatu mahārāja dasahi bhikkhūhi saddhin-ti. dutiyam-pi kho rājā āha: yattake bhikkhu icchati tattakehi bhikkhūhi saddhiṃ āgacchatūti. dutiyam-pi kho sabbadinno āha: āgacchatu mahārāja dasahi bhikkhūhi saddhin-ti. tatiyam-pi kho rājā āha: yattake bhikkhū icchati tattakehi bhikkhūhi saddhiṃ āgacchatūti. tatiyam-pi kho sabbadinno āha: āgacchatu mahārāja dasahi bhikkhūhi saddhin-ti.

13 sabbo panāyaṃ sakkāro paṭiyādito, ahaṃ bhaṇāmi: yattake bhikkhū icchati tattakehi bhikkhūhi saddhiṃ āgacchatūti, ayaṃ bhaṇe sabbadinno aññathā bhaṇati, kin-nu mayaṃ na paṭibalā bhikkhūnaṃ bhojanaṃ dātun-ti. evaṃ vutte sabbadinno maṅku ahosi. atha kho devamantiyo ca anantakāyo ca maṅkuro ca yen' āyasmā nāgaseno ten' upasankamiṃsu,

I should ask about. Yet the sun will set before I can ask them, and so let me speak with him in the inner quarters of the palace tomorrow. And so the king said this to Devamantiya. "Devamantiya, inform the elder that tomorrow in the inner quarters of the palace he will converse with the king." Having announced this, King Milinda rose from his seat, took leave of the monk Nagasena, mounted a horse, and rode off, repeating, "Nagasena, Nagasena."[3]

So Devamantiya spoke to the revered Nagasena: "Sir, King 12
Milinda ordered that tomorrow the conversation with the king will be held in the inner quarters of the palace." "Very well, then." And the monk was satisfied.

Later that night Devamantiya, Anantakaya, Mankura, and Sabbadinna approached King Milinda, and drawing near, said: "Great king, is the revered Nagasena going to come?" "Yes, let him come." "How many monks should come with him?" "Let as many monks as he wants come with him." But Sabbadinna said, "Let him come with ten monks," and the king replied for a second time, "Let as many monks as he wants come with him." Yet a second time, Sabbadinna said, "Let him come with ten monks," and the king replied for a third time, "Let as many monks as he wants come with him." Yet a third time, Sabbadinna said, "Let him come with ten monks."

"But all the hospitality is prepared, and so I said, 'Let as 13
many monks as he wants come with him,' and yet Sabbadinna says otherwise. Is it that I cannot give a meal to the monks?" At this, Sabbadinna was abashed.[4]

So then Devamantiya, Anantakaya, and Mankura approached the revered Nagasena, and when they had come

upasaṅkamitvā āyasmantaṃ nāgasenaṃ etad-avocum: rājā bhante milindo evam-āha: yattake bhikkhū icchati tattakehi bhikkhūhí saddhiṃ āgacchatūti. atha kho āyasmā nāgaseno pubbaṅhasamayaṃ nivāsetvā pattacīvaram-ādāya asītiyā bhikkhusahassehi saddhiṃ sāgalaṃ pāvisi.

14 atha kho anantakāyo āyasmantaṃ nāgasenaṃ nissāya gacchanto āyasmantaṃ nāgasenaṃ etad-avoca: bhante nāgasena, yaṃ pan' etaṃ brūmi nāgaseno ti katam' ettha nāgaseno ti. thero āha: ko pan' ettha nāgaseno ti maññasīti. yo so bhante abbhantare-vāyo jīvo pavisati ca nikkhamati ca so nāgaseno ti maññāmīti. yadi pan' eso vāto nikkhamitvā na paviseyya pavisitvā na nikkhameyya jīveyya nu kho so puriso ti. na hi bhante ti. ye pan' ime saṅkhadhamakā saṅkhaṃ dhamenti tesaṃ vāto puna pavisatīti. na hi bhante ti. ye pan' ime vaṃsadhamakā vaṃsaṃ dhamenti tesaṃ vāto puna pavisatīti. na hi bhante ti. ye pan' ime siṅgadhamakā siṅgaṃ dhamenti tesaṃ vāto puna pavisatīti. na hi bhante ti. atha kissa pana te na marantīti. nāhaṃ paṭibalo tayā vādinā saddhiṃ sallapituṃ, sādhu bhante, atthaṃ jappehīti. n' eso jīvo, assāsa-passāsā nām' ete kāyasankhārā ti thero abhidhammakathaṃ akāsi. atha anantakāyo upāsakattaṃ paṭivedesi.

15 atha kho āyasmā nāgaseno yena milindassa rañño nivesanaṃ ten' upasaṅkami, upasaṅkamitvā paññatte āsane nisīdi. atha kho milindo rājā āyasmantaṃ nāgasenaṃ saparisaṃ paṇītena khādaniyena bhojaniyena sahatthā santappetvā sampavāretvā ekamekaṃ bhikkhuṃ ekamekena dussayugena acchādetvā āyasmantaṃ nāgasenaṃ ticīva-

before him, they said: "Sir, King Milinda said, 'Let as many monks as he wants come with him.'"

And so Nagasena, having dressed in the morning and taken up his bowl and robe, entered Sagala with all eighty thousand monks.

Anantakaya approached Nagasena while he was walking 14
along, and asked him: "Nagasena, when I say 'Nagasena,' what here is Nagasena?"

The elder answered: "But what do you think is Nagasena here?"

"I think that Nagasena is the inner breath that is the soul as it comes and goes."

"But when this breath has gone and not reentered, or has entered but not left, is the person still alive?" "No, sir." "When conch blowers blow the conch, does the breath reenter them?" "No, sir." "When bamboo pipe players blow the bamboo, does the breath reenter them?" "No, sir." "When horn players blow the horn, does the breath reenter them?" "No, sir." "But why do they not die by this?"

"I am not able to converse with this kind of talk. Please just tell me what this means."

And so the elder taught him a teaching on the *abhidhamma*, saying, "The inhalation and exhalation are activities of the body, and are not the soul." At this, Anantakaya declared himself a layman.

By then Nagasena had reached the living quarters of King 15
Milinda. He went up to him and sat down on the appointed seat. Then, with his own hand, King Milinda provided and served Nagasena and the assembly plentiful food, both substantial and fine. He presented each monk with a pair of

renaacchādetvā āyasmantaṃ nāgasenaṃ etad-avoca: bhante nāgasena, dasahi bhikkhūhi saddhiṃ idha nisīdatha, avasesā gacchantūti. atha kho milindo rājā āyasmantaṃ nāgasenaṃ bhuttāviṃ onītapattapāṇiṃ viditvā aññataraṃ nīcaṃ āsanaṃ gahetvā ekamantaṃ nisīdi. ekamantaṃ nisinno kho milindo rājā āyasmantaṃ nāgasenaṃ etad-avoca: bhante nāgasena, kimhi hoti kathāsallāpo ti.

16 atthena mayaṃ mahārāja atthikā, atthe hotu kathāsallāpo ti. rājā āha: kimatthiyā bhante nāgasena tumhākaṃ pabbajjā, ko ca tumhākaṃ paramattho ti. thero āha: kin-ti mahārāja idaṃ dukkhaṃ nirujjheyya aññañ-ca dukkhaṃ na uppajjeyyāti etadatthā mahārāja amhākaṃ pabbajjā, anupādā' parinibbānaṃ kho pana amhākaṃ paramattho ti. kim- pana bhante nāgasena sabbe etadatthāya pabbajantīti. na hi mahārāja, keci etadatthāya pabbajanti, keci rājābhinitā pabbajanti, keci corābhinītā pabbajanti, keci iṇaṭṭā pabbajanti, keci ājīvikatthāya pabbajanti; ye pana sammā pabbajanti te etadatthāya pabbajantīti. tvaṃ pana bhante etadatthāya pabbajitosīti.

17 ahaṃ kho mahārāja daharako santo pabbajito, na jānāmi: iman-nām-atthāya pabbajāmīti, api ca kho me evaṃ ahosi: paṇḍitā ime samaṇā sakyaputtiyā, te maṃ sikkhāpessantīti, svāhaṃ tehi sikkhāpito jānāmi ca passāmi ca: imassa nām' atthāya pabbajjā ti. kallosi bhante nāgasenāti.

18 rājā āha: bhante nāgasena, atthi koci mato na paṭisandahatīti. thero āha: koci paṭisandahati, koci na paṭisandahatīti. ko paṭisandahati, ko na paṭisandahatīti. sakkileso mahārāja paṭisandahati, nikkileso na paṭisandahatiti. tvaṃ

cloths and the revered Nagasena with three robes, telling him, "Nagasena, please sit here with ten monks and let the others depart."

Then King Milinda, observing that Nagasena had eaten and removed his hand from his bowl, took a low seat and sat to one side, and sitting there, asked him this: "Nagasena, what shall we talk about?"[5]

"Great king, we seek a purpose, so let us talk about a 16
purpose."

So the king asked: "For what purpose, Nagasena, do you ordain, and what is your highest purpose?" The elder replied: "Why, it is so that suffering is destroyed and further suffering does not arise. This is the purpose of our ordaining, great king, and our highest purpose is final nibbana without attachment." "But do all ordain for this purpose?" "No, some people ordain for this purpose, some ordain because of fear of the king, some ordain because of fear of thieves, some ordain due to debt, and some ordain for the sake of a livelihood. But those who rightly ordain, ordain for this purpose."

"And did you ordain for this purpose?"

"Great king, I was ordained as a youth, and I did not 17
know I was ordaining for this purpose. But I did think that these renouncers in the lineage of the Sakya were learned, and they would train me in the precepts. And so I was trained by them, and now I know and see that ordaining is for this purpose."

"You are wise, Nagasena."

The king said: "Nagasena, is there anyone who, when 18
dead, is not reborn?" The elder replied: "Some are reborn and some are not reborn." "Who is reborn and who is not

pana bhante paṭisandahissasīti. sace mahārāja saupādāno bhavissāmi paṭisandahissāmi, sace anupādāno bhavissāmi na paṭisandahissāmīti. kallosi bhante nāgasenāti.

19 rājā āha: bhante nāgasena, yo na paṭisandahati nanu so yoniso manasikārena na paṭisandahatīti. Yoniso ca mahārāja manasikārena paññāya ca aññehi ca kusalehi dhammehīti. nanu bhante yoniso manasikāro yeva paññā ti. na hi mahārāja, añño manasikāro aññā paññā; imesaṃ kho mahārāja aj-eḷa-ka-go-mahisa-oṭṭha-gadrabhānam-pi manasikāro atthi, paññā pana tesaṃ na-tthīti. kallosi bhante nāgasenāti.

20 rājā āha: kiṃlakkhaṇo bhante manasikāro, kiṃ lakkhaṇā paññā ti. ūhanalakkhaṇo kho mahārāja manasikāro, chedanalakkhaṇā paññā ti. kathaṃ ūhanalakkhaṇo manasikāro, kathaṃ chedanalakkhaṇā paññā opammaṃ karohīti. jānāsi tvaṃ mahārāja yavalāvake ti. āma bhante, jānāmīti. kathaṃ mahārāja yavalāvakā yavaṃ lunantīti. vāmena bhante hatthena yavakalāpaṃ gahetvā dakkhiṇena hatthena dāttaṃ gahetvā dāttena chindantīti. yathā mahārāja yavalāvako vāmena hatthena yavakalāpaṃ gahetvā dakkhiṇena hatthena dāttaṃ gahetvā dāttena chindati, evam-eva kho mahārāja yogāvacaro manasikārena mānasaṃ gahetvā

reborn?” “Those with defilements are reborn, and those free of defilements are not reborn.”

“Are you, Nagasena, going to be reborn?”

“If I still have attachments, great king, I will be reborn, but if I am free of attachments, I will not be reborn.”

“You are wise, Nagasena.”

The king asked: “Nagasena, is it due to careful attention 19
that one is not reborn?” “It is due to careful attention, understanding, and the presence of other good phenomenal states, great king.”[6] “But is not careful attention the same as understanding?” “Not at all, great king. Attention is one thing, understanding something else. Attention is something goats, sheep, oxen, buffalo, camels, and donkeys have, but they do not have understanding.”

“You are wise, Nagasena.”

The king asked: “What is the defining characteristic of 20
attention, sir, and what is the defining characteristic of understanding?” “The defining characteristic of attention is *examining*, great king, and the defining characteristic of understanding is *cutting through*.” “How is attention defined as examining and understanding defined as cutting through? Please give an analogy.”

“Are you familiar, great king, with barley reapers?” “Yes, I know about them.” “How do barley reapers cut barley?” “With the left hand they grab a bunch of barley, and with the right hand they grab the sickle, and they cut it with the sickle.”

“Just like when a barley reaper grabs a bunch of barley with the left hand, grabs the sickle with the right hand, and cuts the barley, an earnest disciple grabs the mind with attention

paññāya kilese chindati. evaṃ kho mahārāja ūhanalakkhaṇo manasikāro, eyaṃ chedanalakkhaṇā paññā ti. kallosi bhante nāgasenāti.

21 rājā āha: bhante nāgasena, yaṃ pan' etaṃ brūsi: aññehi ca kusalehi dhammehīti, katame te kusalā dhammā ti. sīlaṃ mahārāja saddhā viriyaṃ sati samādhi, ime te kusalā dhammā ti. kiṃlakkhaṇaṃ bhante sīlan-ti. patiṭṭhānalakkhaṇaṃ mahārāja sīlaṃ sabbesaṃ kusalānaṃ dhammānaṃ: indriya-bala-bojjhaṅga-magga-sati-paṭṭhāna-sammappadhāna-iddhipāda-jhāna-vimokha-samādhi-samāpattīnaṃ sīlaṃ patiṭṭhā, sīle patiṭṭhitassa kho mahārāja sabbe kusalā dhammā na parihāyantīti. opammaṃ karohīti.

22 yathā mahārāja ye keci bījagāmabhūtagāmā vuddhiṃ virūḷhiṃ vepullaṃ āpajjanti sabbe te paṭhaviṃ nissāya paṭhaviyaṃ patiṭṭhāya evam-ete bījagāma-bhūtagāmā vuddhiṃ virūḷhiṃ vepullaṃ āpajjanti, evam-eva kho mahārāja yogāvacaro sīlaṃ nissāya sīle patiṭṭhāya pañc' indriyāni bhāveti: saddhindriyaṃ viriyindriyaṃ satindriyaṃ samādhindriyaṃ paññindriyan-ti. bhiyyo opammaṃ karohīti. yathā mahārāja ye keci balakaraṇīyā kammantā karīyanti sabbe te paṭhaviṃ nissāya paṭhaviyaṃ patiṭṭhāya evam-ete balakaraṇīyā kammantā karīyanti, evam-eva kho mahārāja yogāvacaro sīlaṃ nissāya sīle patiṭṭhāya pañc' indriyāni

and cuts through the defilements with understanding. And so attention is defined as examining, and understanding is defined as cutting through."[7]

"You are wise, Nagasena."

The king said: "Nagasena, earlier you mentioned 'other good phenomenal states.' What are these good phenomenal states?" "Great king, moral discipline, faith, exertion, mindfulness, and concentration are good phenomenal states."[8] 21

"What is the defining characteristic of moral discipline, sir?" "Moral discipline has as its defining characteristic that it is the *foundation* of all good phenomenal states because moral discipline is the support of the faculties, the powers, the awakening factors, the path,* the foundations of mindfulness, right striving, the bases of supernatural powers, the *jhānas,* the deliverances, concentration, and the attainments.[9] For someone established in moral discipline, great king, the good phenomenal states are not destroyed."

"Please give an analogy."

"Just as when plants and animals exhibit growth, increase, 22
and development, they are all dependent on the earth, and it is on the foundation of the earth that plants and animals grow, increase, and develop. In the same way, the earnest disciple depending on moral discipline and established in moral discipline brings into being the five faculties of faith, exertion, mindfulness, concentration, and understanding."

"Please give another analogy."

"Great king, whenever there is work to be done that requires strength, it always depends on the earth, and one

* The Noble Eightfold Path.

bhāveti: saddhindriyaṃ viriyindriyaṃ satindriyaṃ samādhindriyaṃ paññindriyan-ti. bhiyyo opammaṃ karohīti.

23 yathā mahārāja nagaravaḍḍhaki nagaraṃ māpetukāmo paṭhamaṃ nagaraṭṭhānaṃ sodhāpetvā khāṇukaṇṭakaṃ apakaḍḍhāpetvā samaṃ kārāpetvā tato aparabhāge vīthi-catukka-siṅghāṭakādi-paricchedena vibhajitvā nagaraṃ māpeti, evam-eva kho mahārāja yogāvacaro sīlaṃ nissāya sīle patiṭṭhāya pañc' indriyāni bhāveti: saddhindriyaṃ viriyindriyaṃ satindriyaṃ samādhindriyaṃ paññindriyan-ti. bhiyyo opammaṃ karohīti. yathā mahārāja laṅghako sippaṃ dassetukāmo paṭhaviṃ khaṇāpetvā sakkhara-kaṭhalakaṃ apakaḍḍhāpetvā bhūmiṃ samaṃ kārāpetvā mudukāya bhūmiyā sippaṃ dasseti, evam-eva kho mahārāja yogāvacaro sīlaṃ nissāya sīle patiṭṭhāya pañc' indriyāni bhāveti: saddhindriyaṃ viriyindriyaṃ satindriyaṃ samādhindriyaṃ paññindriyaṃ. bhāsitam-p' etaṃ mahārāja bhagavatā:

24 sīle patiṭṭhāya naro sapañño cittaṃ paññañ-ca bhāvayaṃ
ātāpī nipako bhikkhu so imaṃ vijaṭaye jaṭan-ti.
ayaṃ patiṭṭhā dharaṇīva pāṇinaṃ, idañ-ca mūlaṃ
kusalābhivuddhiyā,

can only get it done with the support of the earth. In just the same way, the earnest disciple depends and rests on moral discipline in order to bring about the five faculties of faith, exertion, mindfulness, concentration, and understanding."

"Please give another analogy."

"Great king, a city planner who wants to build a city first 23
has the site for the city cleared, the stumps and brambles removed, and the ground leveled. He then determines the future intersections and crossroads by measuring them out, and only then has the city built. In just the same way, the earnest disciple depends and rests on moral discipline in order to bring about the five faculties of faith, exertion, mindfulness, concentration, and understanding."

"Please give another analogy."

"An acrobat wishing to perform his act has the ground dug up, the gravel and stones removed, the earth leveled, and the ground made soft, and then performs his act. In just the same way, the earnest disciple depends and rests on moral discipline in order to bring about the five faculties of faith, exertion, mindfulness, concentration, and understanding. For this has been described, great king, by the Bhagavan:

> When a wise man comes to be established in moral discipline 24
> and develops awareness and understanding,
> then that ardent and intelligent monk disentangles the tangle.

mukhañ-c' idaṃ sabbajinānusāsane yo sīlakkhandho
varapātimokkhiyo ti.
kallosi bhante nāgasenāti.

25 rājā āha: bhante nāgasena, kiṃlakkhaṇā saddhā ti. sampasādanalakkhaṇā ca mahārāja saddhā sampakkhandanalakkhaṇā cāti. katham-bhante sampasādanalakkhaṇā saddhā ti. saddhā kho mahārāja uppajjamānā nīvaraṇe vikkhambheti, vinīvaraṇaṃ cittaṃ hoti acchaṃ vippasannaṃ anāvilaṃ, evaṃ kho mahārāja sampasādanalakkhaṇā saddhā ti. opammaṃ karohīti.

26 yathā mahārāja rājā cakkavattī caturanginiyā senāya saddhiṃ addhānamaggapaṭipanno parittaṃ udakaṃ tareyya, taṃ udakaṃ hatthīhi ca assehi ca rathehi ca pattīhi ca khubhitaṃ bhaveyya āvilaṃ luḷitaṃ kalalībhūtaṃ, uttiṇṇo ca rājā cakkavattī manusse āṇāpeyya: pānīyaṃ bhaṇe āharatha, pivissāmīti, rañño udakappasādako maṇi bhaveyya, evaṃ devāti kho te manussā rañño cakkavattissa paṭissutvā taṃ udakappasādakaṃ maṇiṃ udake pakkhipeyyuṃ, tasmiṃ udake pakkhittamatte sankha-sevāla-paṇakaṃ vigaccheyya kaddamo ca sannisīdeyya, accham-bhaveyya udakaṃ vippasannaṃ anāvilaṃ, tato rañño cakkavattissa pānīyaṃ upanāmeyyuṃ: pivatu devo pānīyan-ti.

27 yathā mahārāja udakaṃ evaṃ cittaṃ daṭṭhabbaṃ, yathā te manussā evaṃ yogāvacaro daṭṭhabbo, yathā saṅkha-

The collection of moral discipline, the excellent
monastic rule,
is the foundation that supports life,
the root from which good things grow,
the beginning of the teaching of all the Victors."

"You are wise, Nagasena."

The king asked: "Nagasena, what is the defining charac- 25
teristic of faith?" "Great king, faith has both *composure* and
taking a leap as its defining characteristics." "In what way,
sir, is faith defined as composure?" "Faith, when it arises,
destroys the hindrances.[10] A mind free of the hindrances,
great king, is clear, purified, and unperturbed. This is why
faith has composure as a defining characteristic."

"Please give an analogy."

"Imagine, great king, a wheel-turning emperor with the 26
four branches of his armed forces traveling along a high-
way. When they cross a shallow body of water, the elephants,
horses, chariots, and foot soldiers make it agitated, disturbed,
turbid, and muddy. Still, the wheel-turning emperor, after
crossing it, orders his people, 'Fetch water for me to drink.'
It seems that the king has a water-clearing jewel. 'Yes, Your
Majesty,' his people promise the wheel-turning emperor, and
they put the water-clearing jewel in the water, whereupon
the aquatic plants, mosses, and leaves disappear, the mud
settles, and the water becomes clear, purified, and unperturbed. They then place the water before the world-turning
emperor and say, 'Please drink this water, Your Majesty.'
Great king, the water should be seen as similar to the mind, 27
the people are like the earnest disciple, and the aquatic

sevāla-paṇakaṃ kaddamo ca evaṃ kilesā daṭṭhabbā, yathā udakappasādako maṇi evaṃ saddhā daṭṭhabbā, yathā udakappasādake maṇimhi udake pakkhittamatte saṅkha-sevāla-paṇakaṃ vigaccheyya kaddamo ca sannisīdeyya, accham-bhaveyya udakaṃ vippasannaṃ anāvilaṃ, evam-eva kho mahārāja saddhā uppajjamānā nīvaraṇe vikkhambheti, vinīvaraṇaṃ cittaṃ hoti acchaṃ vippasannaṃ anāvilaṃ. evaṃ kho mahārāja sampasādanalakkhaṇā saddhā ti.

28 katham-bhante sampakkhandanalakkhaṇā saddhā ti. yathā mahārāja yogāvacaro aññesaṃ cittaṃ vimuttaṃ passitvā sotāpattiphale vā sakadāgāmiphale vā anāgāmiphale vā arahatte vā sampakkhandati, yogaṃ karoti appattassa pattiyā anadhigatassa adhigamāya asacchikatassa sacchikiriyāya, evaṃ kho mahārāja sampakkhandanalakkhaṇā saddhā ti. opammaṃ karohīti.

29 yathā mahārāja uparipabbate mahāmegho abhippavasseyya, taṃ udakaṃ yathāninnaṃ pavattanaṃ pabbata-kandara-padara-sākhā paripūretvā nadiṃ paripūreyya, sā ubhato kūlāni saṃvissandantī gaccheyya, atha mahājanakāyo āgantvā tassā nadiyā uttānataṃ vā gambhīrataṃ vā ajānanto bhīto vitthato tire tiṭṭheyya, ath' aññataro puriso āgantvā attano thāmañ-ca balañ-ca sampassanto gāḷhaṃ kacchaṃ bandhitvā pakkhanditvā tareyya, taṃ tiṇṇaṃ passitvā mahājanakāyo pi tareyya, evam-eva kho mahārāja yogāvacaro aññesaṃ cittaṃ vimuttaṃ passitvā sotāpatti phale vā sakadāgāmiphale vā anāgāmiphale vā arahatte vā sampakkhandati, yogaṃ karoti appattassa pattiyā

plants, mosses, leaves, and mud are the defilements. The water-clearing jewel should be seen as similar to faith, for the water is clarified by the jewel when it is simply placed in the water, since the aquatic plants, mosses, and leaves disappear, the mud settles, and the water becomes clear, purified, and unperturbed. It is the same when faith arises; it destroys the hindrances. A mind free of the hindrances is clear, purified, and unperturbed, and so in this way, faith has composure as a defining characteristic."

"And in what way, sir, is faith defined as taking a leap?" 28

"Great king, it is just like how the earnest disciple, seeing the minds of others liberated, leaps toward the fruit of stream entry, the fruit of once return, the fruit of nonreturn, or the state of being an arhat, and practices yoga for attaining what is not yet attained, knowing what is not yet known, and realizing what is not yet realized.[11] In this way, faith has taking a leap as a defining characteristic."

"Please give an analogy."

"Suppose, great king, a huge cloud were to shed water high 29
on a mountain, and the water washed down, flooding the valleys, gullies, and streams, and overflowing the river until it spilled over both banks. A great crowd gathers, but no one knows the extent or depth of the river. Frightened and hesitating, people line the banks. But then another person comes along who recognizes his own strength and power. He tightly binds up his lower garment, leaps in, and crosses. When they see him make it to the other shore, the people cross too. Similarly, the earnest disciple sees the minds of others liberated and then leaps toward the fruits of stream entry, once return, nonreturn, or the state of being an arhat,

anadhigatassa adhigamāya asacchikatassa sacchikiriyāya. evaṃ kho mahārāja sampakkhandanalakkhaṇā saddhā. bhāsitam-p' etaṃ mahārāja bhagavatā saṃyuttanikāyavare: saddhāya tarati oghaṃ, appamādena aṇṇavaṃ, viriyena dukkhaṃ acceti, paññāya parisujjhatīti. kallosi bhante nāgasenāti.

30 rājā āha: bhante nāgasena, kiṃlakkhaṇaṃ viriyan-ti. upatthambhanalakkhaṇaṃ mahārāja viriyaṃ, viriyūpatthambhitā sabbe kusalā dhammā na parihāyantīti. opammaṃ karohīti. yathā mahārāja puriso gehe patante aññena dārunā upatthambheyya, upatthambhitaṃ santaṃ evan-taṃ gehaṃ na pateyya, evam eva kho mahārāja upatthambhanalakkhaṇaṃ viriyaṃ, viriyūpatthambhitā sabbe kusalā dhammā na parihāyantīti. bhiyyo opammaṃ karohīti.

31 yathā mahārāja parittakaṃ senaṃ mahatī senābhañjeyya, tato rājā aññamaññaṃ anusāreyya anupeseyya, tāya saddhiṃ parittakā senā mahatiṃ senaṃ bhañjeyya, evameva kho mahārāja upatthambhanalakkhaṇaṃ viriyaṃ, viriyūpatthambhitā sabbe kusalā dhammā na parihāyanti. bhāsitam p' etaṃ mahārāja bhagavatā: viriyavā kho bhikkhave

and practices yoga for attaining what is not yet attained, knowing what is not yet known, and realizing what is not yet realized. In this way, great king, faith has taking a leap as a defining characteristic. For the Bhagavan said this in the excellent *Saṃyuttanikāya*: 'With faith, one crosses the flood, with diligence, the choppy sea; with exertion, one overcomes suffering, and with understanding, one becomes purified.'"

"You are wise, Nagasena."

The king asked: "Nagasena, what is the defining character- 30
istic of exertion?" "Exertion has *steadfastness* as its defining
characteristic, great king. Good phenomenal states held fast
by exertion never deteriorate."

"Please give an analogy."

"Suppose a house was falling down and a man made it steadfast with further wood, and, fortified with this, the house did not crumble. Like this, exertion has steadfastness as its defining characteristic, for good phenomenal states fortified by exertion never deteriorate."

"Please give another analogy."

"Suppose that a great army was obliterating a small army, 31
but then the routed king would assemble and advance with
an allied army giving his own small army reinforced strength,
and with it, the small army would destroy the big army. Similarly, great king, exertion has for its defining characteristic
steadfastness. Good phenomenal states held fast by exertion never deteriorate, great king. For the Bhagavan said
this: 'Monks, a noble disciple possessing exertion destroys
what is bad and brings about what is good, destroys what is

ariyasāvako akusalaṃ pajahati kusalaṃ bhāveti, sāvajjaṃ pajahati anavajjaṃ bhāveti, suddham-attānaṃ pariharatīti. kallosi bhante nāgasenāti.

32 rājā āha: bhante nāgasena, kiṃlakkhaṇā satīti. apilāpanalakkhaṇā mahārāja sati upagaṇhanalakkhaṇā cāti. katham-bhante apilāpanalakkhaṇā satīti. sati mahārāja uppajjamānā kusalākusala-sāvajjānavajja-hīnappaṇīta-kaṇhasukka-sappaṭibhāga-dhamme apilāpeti: ime cattāro satipaṭṭhānā, ime cattāro sammappadhānā, ime cattāro iddhipādā, imāni pañc' indriyāni, imāni pañca balāni, ime satta bojjhaṅgā, ayaṃ ariyo aṭṭhaṅgiko maggo, ayaṃ samatho, ayaṃ vipassanā, ayaṃ vijjā, ayaṃ vimuttīti, tato yogāvacaro sevitabbe dhamme sevati asevitabbe dhamme na sevati, bhajitabbe dhamme bhajati abhajitabbe dhamme na bhajati. evaṃ kho mahārāja apilāpanalakkhaṇā satīti. opammaṃ karohīti.

33 yathā mahārāja rañño cakkavattissa bhaṇḍāgāriko rājānaṃ cakkavattiṃ sāyapātaṃ yasaṃ sarāpeti: ettakā deva te hatthī, ettakā assā, ettakā rathā, ettakā pattī, ettakaṃ hiraññaṃ, ettakaṃ suvaṇṇaṃ, ettakaṃ sāpateyyaṃ, taṃ

blameworthy and brings about what is blameless—he thus keeps himself pure.'"

"You are wise, Nagasena."

The king asked: "Nagasena, what is the defining charac- 32
teristic of mindfulness?" "The defining characteristics of mindfulness, great king, are *calling to mind* and *taking hold.*" "In what way, sir, is *calling to mind* a defining characteristic of mindfulness?"

"Mindfulness, when it arises, calls to mind the phenomenal states that are good and bad, blameworthy and blameless, base and exalted, dark and bright, together with their counterparts, observing: 'These are the four foundations of mindfulness, these are the four right strivings, these are the four bases of supernatural power, these are the five faculties, these are the five powers, these are the seven awakening factors, these are the eight Noble Path factors, this is calm meditation, this is insight meditation, this is knowledge, this is freedom.'[12] With this, the earnest disciple practices the phenomenal states that should be practiced and does not practice the phenomenal states that should not be practiced. He cultivates the phenomenal states that should be cultivated and does not cultivate the phenomenal states that should not be cultivated. And so, great king, calling to mind is a defining characteristic of mindfulness."

"Please give an analogy."

"The treasurer of a wheel-turning emperor reminds the 33
emperor of his glory morning and evening as he calls to mind the king's property: 'Your Majesty, remember that you have this many elephants, this many horses, this many chariots, this many foot soldiers, this much gold, this much wealth.'

devo saratūti rañño sāpateyyaṃ apilāpeti, evam-eva kho mahārāja sati uppajjamānā kusalākusala-sāvajjānavajja-hīnappaṇīta-kaṇhasukka-sappaṭibhāga-dhamme apilāpeti: ime cattāro satipaṭṭhānā, ime cattāro sammappadhānā, ime cattāro iddhipādā, imāni pañc' indriyāni, imāni pañca balāni, ime satta bojjhangā, ayaṃ ariyo aṭṭhangiko maggo, ayaṃ samatho, ayaṃ vipassanā, ayaṃ vijjā, ayaṃ vimuttīti, tato yogāvacaro sevitabbe dhamme sevati asevitabbe dhamme na sevati, bhajitabbe dhamme bhajati na bhajitabbe dhamme na bhajati. evaṃ kho mahārāja apilāpanalakkhaṇā satīti.

34 katham-bhante upagaṇhanalakkhaṇā satīti. sati mahārāja uppajjamānā hitāhitānaṃ dhammānaṃ gatiyo samannesati: ime dhammā hitā ime dhammā ahitā, ime dhammā upakārā ime dhammā anupakārā ti, tato yogāvacaro ahite dhamme apanudeti hite dhamme upagaṇhāti, anupakāre dhamme apanudeti upakāre dhamme upagaṇhāti. evaṃ kho mahārāja upagaṇhanalakkhaṇā satīti. opammaṃ karohīti. yathā mahārāja rañño cakkavattissa pariṇāyakaratanaṃ rañño hitāhite jānāti: ime rañño hitā ime ahitā, ime upakārā ime anupakārāti, tato ahite apanudeti hite upagaṇhāti, anupakāre apanudeti upakāre upagaṇhāti, evam-eva kho mahārāja

Similarly, mindfulness, when it arises, calls to mind phenomenal states as good and bad, blameworthy and blameless, base and exalted, dark and bright, together with their counterparts: 'These are the four foundations of mindfulness, these are the four right strivings, these are the four bases of supernatural power, these are the five faculties, these are the five powers, these are the seven factors of awakening, these are the eight Noble Path factors, this is calm meditation, this is insight meditation, this is knowledge, this is freedom.' With this, the earnest disciple practices the phenomenal states that should be practiced and does not practice the phenomenal states that should not be practiced. He cultivates the phenomenal states that should be cultivated and does not cultivate the phenomenal states that should not be cultivated. And so, great king, calling to mind is a defining characteristic of mindfulness."

"In what way, sir, is *taking hold* a defining characteristic 34
of mindfulness?"

"Great king, mindfulness, when it arises, examines the trajectories of beneficial and harmful phenomenal states: 'These phenomenal states are beneficial, these phenomenal states are harmful, these phenomenal states are helpful, these phenomenal states are not helpful.' With this, the earnest disciple removes harmful phenomenal states and takes hold of beneficial phenomenal states, removes unhelpful phenomenal states and takes hold of helpful phenomenal states. This is what is meant by taking hold, and in this way, taking hold is a defining characteristic of mindfulness."

"Please give an analogy."

"Great king, consider the treasure that is the prime

sati uppajjamānā hitāhitānaṃ dhammānaṃ gatiyo samannesati ime dhammā hitā ime dhammā ahitā, ime dhammā upakārā ime dhammā anupakārā ti, tato yogāvacaro ahite dhamme apanudeti hite dhamme upagaṇhāti, anupakāre dhamme apanudeti upakāre dhamme upagaṇhāti. evaṃ kho mahārāja upagaṇhanalakkhaṇā sati. bhāsitam-p'etaṃ mahārāja bhagavatā: satiñ-ca kvāham bhikkhave sabbatthikaṃ vadāmīti. kallosi bhante nāgasenāti.

rājā āha: bhante nāgasena, kiṃlakkhaṇo samādhīti. pamukhalakkhaṇo mahārāja samādhi, ye keci kusalā dhammā sabbe te samādhipamukhā honti samādhininnā samādhipoṇa samādhipabbhārā ti. opammaṃ karohīti. yathā mahārāja kūṭāgārassa yā kāci gopānasiyo sabbātā kūṭangamā honti kūṭaninnā kūṭasamosaraṇā, kūṭaṃ tāsaṃ aggam-akkhāyati, evam-eva kho mahārāja ye keci kusalā dhammā sabbe

minister of a wheel-turning emperor.[13] He knows what is beneficial and harmful for the king: ‘This is beneficial for the king, this is harmful for the king, this is helpful for the king, this is unhelpful for the king.’ Therefore, he removes what is harmful and takes hold of what is beneficial. In just this way, great king, mindfulness, when it arises, examines the trajectories of beneficial and harmful phenomenal states: ‘These phenomenal states are beneficial, these phenomenal states are harmful, these phenomenal states are helpful, these phenomenal states are not helpful.’ With this, the earnest disciple removes harmful phenomenal states and takes hold of beneficial phenomenal states, removes unhelpful phenomenal states and takes hold of helpful phenomenal states. In this way, great king, taking hold is a defining characteristic of mindfulness. This was alluded to by the Bhagavan when he said: ‘Monks, I say that mindfulness is valuable in everything.’”

“You are wise, Nagasena.”

The king asked: “Nagasena what is the defining char- 35
acteristic of concentration?” “Great king, the defining characteristic of concentration is that it is the *high point*. This is because good phenomenal states have concentration as their high point: they point toward concentration, incline toward concentration, and slope toward concentration.”

“Please give an analogy.”

“On a building with a peaked roof, all of the rafters point toward the highest beam and come together at the beam, and so the beam is considered to be the high point. Similarly, good phenomenal states have concentration as their high

te samādhipamukhā honti samādhininnā samādhipoṇā samādhipabbhārā ti. bhiyyo opammaṃ karohīti.

36 yathā mahārāja koci rājā caturaṅginiyā senāya saddhiṃ saṅgāmaṃ otareyya, sabbāva senā, hatthī ca assā ca rathā ca pattī ca, tappamukhā bhaveyyuṃ tanninnā tappoṇā tappabbhārā, taṃ yeva anupariyāyeyyuṃ, evam-eva kho mahārāja ye keci kusalā dhammā sabbe te samādhipamukhā samādhininnā samādhipoṇā samādhipabbhārā. evaṃ kho mahārāja pamukhalakkhaṇo samādhi. bhāsitam-p' etaṃ mahārāja bhagavatā: samādhim-bhikkhave bhāvetha, samāhito yathābhūtaṃ pajānātīti. kallosi bhante nāgasenāti.

37 rājā āha: bhante nāgasena, kiṃlakkhaṇā paññā ti. pubbe kho mahārāja mayā vuttaṃ: chedanalakkhaṇā paññā ti, api ca obhāsanalakkhaṇā pi paññā ti. katham-bhante obhāsanalakkhaṇā paññā ti. paññā mahārāja uppajjamānā avijjandhakāraṃ vidhameti, vijjobhāsaṃ janeti, ñāṇālokaṃ vidaṃseti, ariyasaccāni pākaṭāni karoti, tato yogāvacaro aniccan-ti vā dukkhan-ti vā anattā ti vā sammappaññāya passatīti. opammaṃ karohīti.

38 yathā mahārāja puriso andhakāre gehe padīpaṃ paveseyya, paviṭṭho padīpo andhakāraṃ vidhameti, obhāsaṃ janeti, ālokaṃ vidaṃseti, rūpāni pākaṭāni karoti, evam-eva kho mahārāja paññā uppajjamānā avijjandhakāraṃ vidhameti, vijjobhāsaṃ janeti, ñāṇālokaṃ vidaṃseti, ariyasaccāni

point: they point, incline, and slope toward concentration."

"Please give another analogy."

"Great king, suppose a certain king were to go to battle 36
with the four branches of his armed forces, and the entire army—elephants, horses, chariots, and foot soldiers—would be headed by him, point toward him, incline toward him, and slope toward him, until they would encircle him. So too, good phenomenal states have concentration as their high point: they point, incline, and slope toward concentration. And so, concentration is defined as being the high point, for this was said by the Bhagavan: 'Cultivate concentration, monks, for one who is collected understands whatever has arisen.'"

"You are wise, Nagasena."

The king asked: "Nagasena, what is the defining charac- 37
teristic of understanding?" "Great king, earlier I said that *cutting through* is a defining characteristic of understanding, but *illuminating* is also a defining characteristic of understanding." "How is illuminating a defining characteristic of understanding?" "Understanding, when it arises, dispels the darkness of ignorance, produces the light of knowledge, shines the brightness of knowing, and makes the Noble Truths visible. The earnest disciple uses right understanding to see impermanence, suffering, or the lack of self."

"Please give an analogy."

"Great king, suppose a man were to enter a dark house 38
with a lamp. As he enters, the lamp dispels the darkness, produces light, shines brightness, and makes shapes visible. Similarly, when it arises, understanding dispels the darkness of ignorance, produces the light of knowledge, shines the brightness of knowing, and makes the Noble Truths visible.

pākaṭāni karoti, tato yogāvacaro aniccan-ti vā dukkhan-ti vā anattā ti vā sammappaññāya passati. evaṃ kho mahārāja obhāsanalakkhaṇā paññā ti. kallosi bhante nāgasenāti.

39 rājā āha: bhante nāgasena, ime dhammā nānā santā ekaṃ atthaṃ abhinipphādentīti. āma mahārāja, ime dhammā nānā santā ekaṃ atthaṃ abhinipphādenti: kilese hanantīti. katham-bhante ime dhammā nānā santā ekaṃ atthaṃ abhinipphādenti: kilese hananti, opammaṃ karohīti. yathā mahārāja senā nānā santā, hatthī ca assā ca rathā ca pattī ca, ekaṃ atthaṃ abhinipphādenti: saṅgāme parasenaṃ abhivijinanti, evam-eva kho mahārāja ime dhammā nānā santā ekaṃ atthaṃ abhinipphādenti: kilese hanantīti. kallosi bhante nāgasenāti.

paṭhamo vaggo.

The earnest disciple uses right understanding to see impermanence, suffering, or the lack of self. In this way, illuminating is a defining characteristic of understanding."

"You are wise, Nagasena."

The king asked: "Nagasena, do these different phenome- 39
nal states produce the same purpose?" "Yes, great king. The different phenomenal states do produce the same purpose: they destroy the defilements."[14] "How can different states produce the single purpose of destroying the defilements? Please give an analogy." "It is just like how the different parts of an army—the elephants, horses, chariots, and foot soldiers—produce the same purpose: they conquer the enemy army in battle. And so too do these different phenomenal states produce the same purpose and destroy the defilements."

"You are wise, Nagasena."

End of Section One.

40 rājā āha: bhante nāgasena, yo uppajjati so eva so udāhu aññо ti. thero āha: na ca so na ca añño ti. opammaṃ karohīti. taṃ kim-maññasi mahārāja: yadā tvaṃ daharo taruṇo mando uttānaseyyako ahosi so yeva tvaṃ etarahi mahanto ti. na hi bhante, añño so daharo taruṇo mando uttānaseyyako ahosi, añño ahaṃ etarahi mahanto ti. evaṃ sante kho mahārāja mātā ti pi na bhavissati, pitā ti pi na bhavissati, ācariyo ti pi na bhavissati, sippavā ti pi na bhavissati, sīlavā ti pi na bhavissati, paññāvā ti pi na bhavissati, kin-nu kho mahārāja aññā eva kalalassa mātā, aññā abbudassa mātā, aññā pesiyā mātā, aññā ghanassa mātā, aññā khuddakassa mātā, aññā mahantassa mātā, añño sippaṃ sikkhati, añño sikkhito bhava ti, añño pāpakammaṃ karoti, aññassa hatthapādā chijjantīti. na hi bhante, tvaṃ pana bhante evaṃ vutte kiṃ vadeyyāsīti.

41 thero āha: ahañ-ñeva kho mahārāja daharo ahosiṃ taruṇo mando uttānaseyyako, ahañ-ñeva etarahi mahanto, imañ-ñeva kāyaṃ nissāya sabbe te ekasangahītā ti. opammaṃ karohīti. yathā mahārāja kocid-eva puriso padīpaṃ padīpeyya, kiṃ so sabbarattiṃ dīpeyyāti. āma bhante, sabbarattiṃ dīpeyyāti. kin-nu kho mahārāja yā purime yāme acci sā majjhime yāme accīti. na hi bhante ti. yā majjhime yāme acci sā pacchime yāme accīti. na hi bhante ti. kin-nu kho mahārāja añño so ahosi purime yāme padīpo, añño majjhime yāme padīpo, añño pacchime yāme padīpo ti.

The king said: "Nagasena, sir, does the person who is reborn 40
become the same person or someone else?" The elder replied: "Neither the same nor someone else."

"Please give an analogy."

"What do you think, great king? Once you were a tiny infant lying on your back, tender and naïve. Is he the same as you are now, all grown up?" "No, sir, now that I am an adult, I am different than that tiny infant lying on his back, tender and naïve."

"Does this mean, great king, that you have no mother, father, or teacher? And if without them, that you are not instructed in the arts, morality, or understanding? Is the mother a different person in each of the first four weeks of pregnancy? And is she another person still when her child is small? And then another when the child has grown up? What about the person who is becoming educated and the person who is educated? Are they different? Or the person who has committed a crime. Is he different from the one who is punished by getting his hands or feet cut off?" "No, certainly not. But what would you say about this?"

"I would say that there is an 'I' in relation to the tiny infant 41
lying on his back, tender and naïve, and the 'I' of the adult now. There is a single continuity to it all in relation to the body," the elder replied.

"Please give an analogy."

"Think of a person who lights a lamp, great king. Does it burn all night?" "Yes, it could burn all night." "Is the flame the same flame at the beginning of the night as in the middle of the night? And is it the same in the middle of the night as at the end?" "Neither, sir." "All right, but then is the lamp

na hi bhante, taṃ yeva nissāya sabbarattiṃ padīpito ti. evam-eva kho mahārāja dhammasantati sandahati, añño uppajjati añño nirujjhati, apubbaṃ acarimaṃ viya sandahati, tena na ca so na ca añño pacchimaviññāṇasaṅgahaṃ gacchatīti.

42 bhiyyo opammaṃ karohīti. yathā mahārāja khīraṃ duyhamānaṃ kālantarena dadhi parivatteyya, dadhito navanītaṃ, navanītato ghataṃ parivatteyya, yo nu kho mahārāja evaṃ vadeyya: yaṃ yeva khīraṃ taṃ yeva dadhi taṃ yeva navanītaṃ taṃ yeva ghatan-ti, sammā nu kho so mahārāja vadamāno vadeyyāti. na hi bhante, taṃ yeva nissāya sambhūtan-ti. evam-eva kho mahārāja dhammasantati sandahati, añño uppajjati añño nirujjhati, apubbaṃ acarimaṃ viya sandahati, tena na ca so na ca añño pacchimaviññāṇasaṅgahaṃ gacchatīti. kallosi bhante nāgasenāti.

43 rājā āha: bhante nāgasena, yo na paṭisandahati jānāti so: na paṭisandahissāmīti. āma mahārāja, yo na paṭisandahati jānāti so: na paṭisandahissāmīti. katham-bhante jānātīti. yo hetu yo paccayo paṭisandahanāya tassa hetussa tassa paccayassa uparamā jānāti so: na paṭisandahissāmīti. opammaṃ karohīti.

44 yathā mahārāja kassako gahapatiko kasitvā ca vapitvā ca dhaññāgāraṃ paripūreyya, so aparena samayena n'eva kaseyya na vapeyya, yathāsambhatañ-ca dhaññaṃ paribhuñjeyya vā vissajjeyya vā yathāpaccayaṃ vā kareyya, jāneyya so

different at the beginning, the middle, and the end of the night?" "No, because relying on it, the light shines all night." "In the same way, great king, the continuity of phenomenal states is connected: this arises, that ceases; the next thing arises practically simultaneously. Therefore, it is neither this nor something entirely different that goes along as the continuity from the previous moment of awareness."

"Give another analogy, please." 42

"Just as, great king, fresh milk in a little while turns to curds, and from curds into butter, and from butter into ghee. What if someone were to say that the milk, the curds, the butter, and the ghee are the same? Would it be correct to say this?" "No, because each is produced relying on the other." "In the same way, the continuity of phenomenal states is connected: this arises, that ceases; the next thing is connected practically simultaneously. Therefore, it is neither this nor something entirely different that goes along as the continuity from the previous moment of awareness."

"You are wise, Nagasena."

The king asked: "Nagasena, sir, does the person who will 43
not be reborn know, *I will not be reborn?*" "Yes, great king, one who is not going to reborn knows, *I will not be reborn.*" "How does one know this?" "Causes and conditions bring about rebirth. When there is the termination of those causes and conditions, one knows this and so knows, *I will not be reborn.*"

"Please give an analogy."

"It is much like a householder who runs a farm. He plows, 44
sows, and fills up his granary, but then later does not grow crops and replenish it. Instead, he eats up the stored grain,

mahārāja kassako gahapatiko: na me dhaññāgāraṃ paripūrissatīti. āma bhante, jāneyyāti. kathaṃ jāneyyāti. yo hetu yo paccayo dhaññāgārassa paripūraṇāya tassa hetussa tassa paccayassa uparamā jāneyya: na me dhaññāgāraṃ paripūrissatīti. evam-eva kho mahārāja yo hetu yo paccayo paṭisandahanāya tassa hetussa tassa paccayassa uparamā jānāti so: na paṭisandahissāmīti. kallosi bhante nāgasenāti.

45 rājā āha: bhante nāgasena, yassa ñāṇaṃ uppannaṃ tassa paññā uppannā ti. āma mahārāja, yassa ñāṇaṃ uppannaṃ tassa paññā uppannā ti. kim-bhante yañ-ñeva ñāṇaṃ sā yeva paññā ti. āma mahārāja, yañ-ñeva ñāṇaṃ sā yeva paññā ti. yassa pana bhante tañ-ñeva ñāṇaṃ sā yeva paññā uppannā kiṃ sammuyheyya so udāhu na sammuyheyyāti. katthaci mahārāja sammuyheyya, katthaci na sammuyheyyāti. kuhiṃ bhante sammuyheyya, kuhiṃ na sammuyheyyāti. aññātapubbesu vā mahārāja sippaṭṭhānesu agatapubbāya vā disāya assutapubbāya vā nāmapaññattiyā sammuyheyyāti. kuhiṃ na sammuyheyyāti. yaṃ kho pana mahārāja tāya paññāya kataṃ: aniccan-ti vā dukkhan-ti vā anattā ti vā, tahiṃ na sammuyheyyāti.

46 moho pan'assa bhante kuhiṃ gacchatīti. moho kho mahārāja ñāṇe uppannamatte tatth' eva nirujjhatīti. opammaṃ karohīti. yathā mahārāja kocid-eva puriso andhakāro gehe[1] padīpaṃ āropeyya, tato andhakāro nirujjheyya āloko

gives it away, or uses it according to whatever circumstances. Would this farmer know that his granary is not stocked?" "Of course he would know." "But how would he know?" "Filling a granary is a matter of causes and conditions. At the termination of those causes and conditions, he would know that he is not filling his granary." "Similarly, rebirth is a matter of causes and conditions, great king. One who knows that there has been the termination of those causes and conditions most certainly knows, *I will not be reborn.*"

"You are wise, Nagasena."

The king asked: "Nagasena, has a person who has achieved 45
knowledge also achieved understanding?" "Yes, great king, where knowledge arises so does understanding." "Does that mean that whatever is knowledge is also understanding?" "Yes, that is the case." "Then would there be anything that would still be confusing?" "Some things would be confusing and some things not, great king. One would be confused about arts one did not previously know, places not previously visited, or names and terminology previously unheard of." "And what about the things that would no longer be confusing?" "With the achievement of understanding, great king, one would be free of confusion regarding impermanence, suffering, and lack of self."

"But where does delusion go, sir? Please give an analogy." 46

"When knowledge arises, delusion just dissolves."

"Give an analogy, please."

"It is like when a person brings a lamp into a dark house and the darkness dissolves as light floods in. When knowledge arises, delusion dissolves." "But where does understanding go?" "Having done its work, understanding dissolves too.

pātubhaveyya, evam-eva kho mahārāja ñāṇe uppannamatte moho tatth' eva nirujjhatīti. paññā pana bhante kuhiṃ gacchatīti. paññā pi kho mahārāja sakiccayaṃ katvā tatth' eva nirujjhati, yaṃ pana tāya paññāya kataṃ: aniccan-ti vā dukkhan-ti vā anattā ti vā, taṃ na nirujjhatīti. bhante nāgasena, yaṃ pan' etaṃ brūsi: paññā sakiccayaṃ katvā tatth' eva nirujjhati, yaṃ pana tāya paññāya kataṃ: aniccan-ti vā dukkhan-ti vā anattā ti vā, taṃ na nirujjhatīti, tassa opammaṃ karohīti.

47 yathā mahārāja koci puriso rattiṃ lekhaṃ pesetukāmo lekhakaṃ pakkosāpetvā padīpaṃ āropetvā lekhaṃ likhāpeyya, likhite pana lekhe padīpaṃ vijjhāpeyya, vijjhāpite pi padīpe lekhaṃ na vinasseyya, evam eva kho mahārāja paññā sakiccayaṃ katvā tatth' eva nirujjhati, yam-pana tāya paññāya kataṃ: aniccan-ti vā dukkhan-ti vā anattā ti vā, taṃ na nirujjhatīti. Bhiyyo opammaṃ karohīti.

48 yathā mahārāja puratthimesu janapadesu manussā anugharaṃ pañca pañca udakaghaṭakāni ṭhapenti ālimpanaṃ vijjhāpetuṃ, ghare paditte tāni pañca udakaghaṭakāni gharass' upari khipanti, tato aggivijjhāyati, kin-nu kho mahārāja tesaṃ manussānaṃ evaṃ hoti: puna tehi ghaṭehi ghaṭakiccaṃ karissāmāti. Na hi bhante: alaṃ tehi ghaṭehi, kiṃ tehi ghaṭehīti. yathā mahārāja pañca udakaghaṭakāni evaṃ pañc' indriyāni daṭṭhabbāni: saddhindriyaṃ viriyindriyaṃ satindriyaṃ samādhindriyaṃ paññindriyaṃ, yathā te manussā evaṃ yogāvacaro daṭṭhabbo, yathā aggi evaṃ kilesā daṭṭhabbā, yathā pañcahi udakaghaṭakehi aggi vijjhāpīyati evaṃ pañcindriyehi kilesā vijjhāpīyanti, vijjhāpitā pi kilesā na puna sambhavanti, evam-eva kho mahārāja

But it is through the work of understanding that one recognizes impermanence, suffering, and lack of self, and this does not dissolve."

"Sir, you say that understanding, having done its work, just dissolves, but what is achieved by understanding, that is, impermanence, suffering, and lack of self, does not dissolve. Please give an analogy."

"It is just like a man who wants to send a letter at night, 47
great king. He summons a scribe, brings a lamp, and has the letter written. When the letter is finished, he extinguishes the lamp. But just because the lamp is out doesn't mean that the letter is destroyed. Similarly, understanding dissolves when it has done its work. But it is through the work of understanding that one recognizes impermanence, suffering, and lack of self, great king, and this does not dissolve."

"Another analogy, please."

"It seems that people living in the eastern countries place 48
five pots of water behind each house in order to douse fires. Should a house catch on fire, they throw the five pots of water on the house and extinguish the fire. Do you think, great king, that right after the fire is out the people think, *Let's do this same thing again with the water pots?*" "Unlikely. Once the work of the water pots is done, what use are they?" "In fact, great king, the five water pots can be seen as the five faculties—the faculties of faith, exertion, mindfulness, concentration, and understanding; the people can be seen as the earnest disciple; and the fire is like the defilements. The five faculties extinguish the defilements just as the five pots of water extinguish the fire. Once extinguished, the defilements do not come back. Like this, understanding dissolves

paññā sakiccayaṃ katvā tatth' eva nirujjhati, yam-pana tāya paññāya kataṃ: aniccan-ti vā dukkhan-ti vā anattā ti vā, taṃ na nirujjhatīti. bhiyyo opammaṃ karohīti.

49 yathā mahārāja vejjo pañca mūlabhesajjāni gahetvā gilānakaṃ upasankamitvā tāni pañca mūlabhesajjāni piṃsitvā gānakaṃ pāyeyya, tehi ca dosā niddhameyyuṃ, kin-nu kho mahārāja tassa vejjassa evaṃ hoti: puna tehi mūlabhesajjehi bhesajjakiccaṃ karissāmīti. na hi bhante: alan-tehi mūlabhesajjehi, kin-tehi mūlabhesajjehīti. yathā mahārāja pañca mūlabhesajjāni evaṃ pañc' indriyāni daṭṭhabbāni: saddhindriyaṃ viriyindriyaṃ satindriyaṃ samādhindriyaṃ paññindriyaṃ, yathā vejjo evaṃ yogāvacaro daṭṭhabbo, yathā byādhi evaṃ kilesā daṭṭhabbā, yathā byādhito puriso evaṃ putthujjano daṭṭhabbo, yathā pañcamūlabhesajjehi gilānassa dosā niddhantā, dose niddhante gilāno arogo hoti, evaṃ pañcindriyehi kilesā niddhamīyanti, niddhamitā ca kilesā na puna sambhavanti, evam-eva kho mahārāja paññā sakiccayaṃ katvā tatth'eva nirujjhati, yaṃ pana tāya paññāya kataṃ: aniccan-ti vā dukkhan-ti vā anattā ti vā, taṃ na nirujjhatīti. bhiyyo opammaṃ karohīti.

50 yathā mahārāja sangāmāvacaro yodho pañca kaṇḍāni gahetvā sangāmaṃ otareyya parasenaṃ vijetuṃ, so sangāmagato tāni pañcakaṇḍāni khipeyya, tehi ca parasenā bhijjeyya, kin-nu kho mahārāja tassa saṅgāmāvacarassa yodhassa evaṃ hoti: puna tehi kaṇḍehi kaṇḍakiccaṃ karissāmīti. na hi bhante: alan-tehi kaṇḍehi, kin-tehi kaṇḍehīti. yathā mahārāja pañca kaṇḍāni evaṃ pañc' indriyāni daṭṭhabbāni: saddhindriyaṃ viriyindriyaṃ satindriyaṃ samādhindriyaṃ paññindriyaṃ, yathā saṅgāmāvacaro yodho evaṃ yogāvacaro daṭṭhabbo, yathā parasenā evaṃ kilesā daṭṭhabbā, yathā

when it has done its work. But the work understanding does to recognize impermanence, suffering, and lack of self does not dissolve."

"Give another analogy, please."

"Great king, a physician takes five medicinal roots, grinds 49
them to powder, and administers them to the patient by giving this as a drink. With this, the illness goes away. Does the physician then think, *Let me use these medicinal roots as medicine again?*" "No, sir, once the work of the medicinal roots is done, what use are they?" "It is the same way with the five faculties, great king, taking the five roots as the faculties of faith, exertion, mindfulness, concentration, and understanding, the physician as the earnest disciple, the sickness as the defilements, and the patient as an ordinary person. The illness goes away and the sick person becomes healthy. Like this, with the five faculties, the defilements go away and, once gone, do not return. Understanding dissolves when it has done its work. But the work understanding does to recognize impermanence, suffering, and lack of self does not dissolve."

"Another analogy, please."

"Suppose a career soldier takes five arrows and heads into 50
battle to fight the enemy army. When the battle is joined, he lets the five arrows fly and they scatter the enemy. Great king, do you think that the soldier would then plan to use the same arrows again?" "Certainly not, sir. What would be the point?" "We can again apply the analogy to the five faculties, great king, seeing them as the five arrows, the soldier as the earnest disciple, and the enemy army as the defilements. Just as the five arrows scatter the enemy, so too, the

pañcahi kaṇḍehi parasenā bhijjati evaṃ pañcindriyehi kilesā bhijjanti, bhaggā ca kilesā na puna sambhavanti, evam-eva kho mahārāja paññā sakiccayaṃ katvā tatth' eva nirujjhati, yaṃ pana tāya paññāya kataṃ: aniccan-ti vā dukkhan-ti vā anattā ti vā, taṃ na nirujjhatīti. kallosi bhante nāgasenāti.

51 rājā āha: bhante nāgasena, yo na paṭisandahati vedeti so kañci dukkhaṃ vedanan ti. thero āha: kañci vedeti, kañci na vedetīti. kaṃ vedeti, kaṃ na vedetīti. kāyikaṃ mahārāja vedanaṃ vedeti, cetasikaṃ vedanaṃ na vedetīti. katham-bhante kāyikaṃ vedanaṃ vedeti, kathaṃ cetasikaṃ vedanaṃ na vedetīti. yo hetu yo paccayo kāyikāya dukkha-vedanāya uppattiyā tassa hetussa tassa paccayassa anupa-ramā kāyikaṃ dukkhavedanaṃ vedeti, yo hetu yo paccayo cetasikāya dukkhavedanāya uppattiyā tassa hetussa tassa paccayassa uparamā cetasikaṃ dukkhavedanaṃ na vedeti. bhasitam-p' etaṃ mahārāja bhagavatā: so ekaṃ vedanaṃ vedeti: kāyikaṃ, na cetasikan-ti.

52 bhante nāgasena, yo so dukkhavedanaṃ vedeti kasmā so na parinibbāyatīti. na-tthi mahārāja arahato anunayo vā paṭigho vā, na ca arahanto apakkaṃ pātenti, paripākaṃ āgamenti paṇḍitā. bhāsitam-p' etaṃ mahārāja therena sāri-puttena dhammasenāpatinā:

53 nābhinandāmi maranaṃ, nābhinandāmi jīvitaṃ,
kālañ-ca patikaṅkhāmi, nibbisaṃ bhatako yathā.
nābhinandāmi maraṇaṃ, nābhinandāmi jīvitaṃ,
kālañ-ca patikaṅkhāmi sampajāno patissato ti.

kallosi bhante nāgasenāti.

faculties scatter the defilements. Understanding, as one of the faculties, does its work to recognize impermanence, suffering, and lack of self, but then dissolves, while the work that understanding does remains."

"You are wise, Nagasena."

The king asked: "Nagasena, sir, does one who is not going 51
to be reborn feel pain?" The elder replied: "He feels some
kinds of pain, but not others." "Such as?" "He feels bodily
feelings, but not mental feelings." "Why bodily feelings and
not mental feelings?" "Causes and conditions of bodily pain
continue in the body, and unless they desist, the body feels
pain. But if the causes and conditions of mental pain should
arise, they are terminated, and so one does not feel mental
pain. The Bhagavan said exactly this: 'One feels only bodily
pain, not mental pain.'"

"Why is it that so long as one feels such pain, one does not 52
attain final nibbana?"

"For arhats there is no approval or disapproval; they do not make unripe fruit fall but rather, being learned, allow what is fully ripened simply to come. This was said by Elder Sariputta, General of the Dhamma:[15]

I take no delight in dying; I take no delight in living. 53
I wait out my time as a worker awaits his wages.
I take no delight in dying; I take no delight in living.
I wait out my time, fully awake and mindful."

"You are wise, Nagasena."

54 rājā āha: bhante nāgasena, sukhā vedanā kusalā vā akusalā vā abyākatā vā ti. siyā mahārāja kusalā, siyā akusalā, siyā abyākatā ti. yadi bhante kusalā na dukkhā, yadi dukkhā na kusalā, kusalaṃ dukkhan-ti na uppajjatīti. taṃ kim-maññasi mahārāja: idha purisassa hatthe tattaṃ ayoguḷaṃ nikkhipeyya, dutiye hatthe sītaṃ himapiṇḍaṃ nikkhipeyya, kin-nu kho mahārāja ubho pi te daheyyun-ti. āma bhante, ubho pi te daheyyun-ti. kin-nu kho te mahārāja ubho pi uṇhā ti. na hi bhante ti. kim-pana te mahārāja ubho pi sītalā ti. na hi bhante ti. ājānāhi niggahaṃ: yadi tattaṃ dahati, na ca te ubho pi uṇhā, tena na uppajjati, yadi sītalaṃ dahati, na ca te ubho pi sītalā, tena na uppajjati; kissa pana te mahārāja ubho pi dahanti, na ca te ubho pi uṇhā, na ca te ubho pi sītalā, ekaṃ uṇhaṃ ekaṃ sītalaṃ, ubho pi te dahantīti tena na uppajjatīti.

55 nāhaṃ paṭibalo tayā vādinā saddhiṃ sallapituṃ, sādhu, atthaṃ jappehīti. tato thero abhidhamma-saṃyuttāya kathāya rājānaṃ milindaṃ saññāpesi: cha-y-imāni mahārāja gehanissitāni somanassāni cha nekkhammanissitāni somanassāni, cha gehanissitāni domanassāni cha nekkhammanissitāni domanassāni, cha gehanissitā upekhā cha nekkhammanissitā upekhā ti imāni cha chakkāni, atītā pi chattiṃsavidhā vedanā, anāgatā pi chattiṃsavidhā vedanā, paccuppannā pi chattiṃsavidhā vedanā, tad ekajjhaṃ abhisaññūhitvā abhisaṅkhipitvā aṭṭhasataṃ vedanā hontīti. kallosi bhante nāgasenāti.

The king asked: "Is pleasurable feeling good, bad, or indeterminate?" "It could be good, bad, or indeterminate, great king." "So then, if what is good is not painful, and what is painful is not good, then there can be nothing that is both painful and good." 54

"Think about it this way, great king: suppose a man grabs a heated iron ball with one hand, and a freezing snowball in the other. Would both of these hurt?" "Yes, both would be painful." "Is that because both are hot? Or because both are cold?" "Neither, sir."

"Please learn from the problems in your own argument. If it is the heat that burns, but one of them is not hot, then how can heat cause the pain? And if it is the cold that hurts, but one of them is not cold, then how can it be the cold that causes the pain? One is hot and one is cold, and yet both cause pain. But the pain does not come from the same thing."

"I am not competent to debate this with you, so please just 55
explain the meaning."

And so, to persuade King Milinda, the elder gave a teaching in the style of the *abhidhamma*. "Great king, there are six delights connected to the household life and six delights that renouncers feel; there are six distresses felt by householders and six felt by renouncers; there are six kinds of equanimity for householders and six for renouncers. These are the six sets of six. We can also take each of the six sets and list them by past, present, and future. Adding them all together, we would get one hundred and eight different modes of feeling."[16]

"You are wise, Nagasena."

56 rājā āha: bhante nāgasena, ko paṭisandahatīti. thero āha:
nāmarūpaṃ kho mahārāja paṭisandahatīti. kiṃ imaṃ yeva
nāmarūpaṃ paṭisandahatīti. na kho mahārāja imaṃ yeva
nāmarūpaṃ paṭisandahati, iminā pana mahārāja nāmarūpena kammaṃ karoti sobhanaṃ vā pāpakaṃ vā, tena
kammena aññaṃ nāmarūpaṃ paṭisandahatī ti. yadi bhante
na imaṃ yeva nāmarūpaṃ paṭisandahati nanu so mutto
bhavissati pāpakehi kammehīti. thero āha: yadi na paṭisandaheyya mutto bhaveyya pāpakehi kammehi, yasmā
ca kho mahārāja paṭisandahati tasmā na mutto pāpakehi
kammehīti. opammaṃ karohīti.
57 yathā mahārāja kocid-eva puriso aññatarassa purisassa
ambaṃ avahareyya, tam-enaṃ ambasāmiko gahetvā rañño
dasseyya: iminā deva purisena mayhaṃ ambā avahaṭā
ti, so evaṃ vadeyya: nāhaṃ deva imassa ambe avahar-
āmi; aññe te ambā ye iminā ropitā, aññe te ambā ye mayā
avahaṭā, nāhaṃ daṇḍappatto ti, kin-nu kho so mahārāja
puriso daṇḍappatto bhaveyyāti. āma bhante, daṇḍappatto
bhaveyyāti. kena kāraṇenāti. kiñcāpi so evaṃ vadeyya, purimaṃ bhante ambaṃ apaccakkhāya pacchimena ambena so
puriso daṇḍappatto bhaveyyāti. evam-eva kho mahārāja
iminā nāmarūpena kammaṃ karoti sobhanaṃ vā pāpakaṃ
vā, tena kammena aññaṃ nāmarūpaṃ paṭisandahati, tasmā
na mutto pāpakehi kammehīti. bhiyyo opammaṃ karohīti.
58 yathā mahārāja koci puriso aññatarassa purisassa sāliṃ
avahareyya-pe-ucchuṃ avahareyya pe yathā mahārāja koci
puriso hemantike kāle aggiṃ jaletvā visīvetvā avijjhāpetvā

The king asked: "Nagasena, what is reborn?" The elder 56
replied: "Name-and-form is reborn, great king."[17] "But what is this name-and-form that is reborn?" "Actually, name-and-form is not itself reborn, but rather it is because of name-and-form that beautiful and evil karma are created. And then it is by this karma that a different name-and-form is born." "But if the same name-and-form is not reborn, then why wouldn't one be released from one's evil karma?" The elder answered: "That would be the case if there weren't rebirth. But since there is rebirth, there is no release from evil karma."

"Please give an analogy."

"Suppose a man steals mangos from another person, and 57
the mangos' owner takes the matter to the king. 'This man stole my mangos, Your Majesty.' But what if the thief were to respond that it wasn't the same mangos that he took, because the mangos that were planted were different from the ones he took, and so he should not be punished. Wouldn't he still be punished?" "Of course he would be punished." "But on what grounds?" "Regardless of what the man says, the later mangos are only there because of the earlier, now unseen, mangos, and so he should be punished."

"And so it is also, great king, that beautiful and evil karma are brought about by one name-and-form, and then another name-and-form is reborn with that karma, and so one is not released from the evil karma."

"Please give another analogy."

"One could make the same analogy about a person who 58
steals someone's rice or sugarcane. Or consider the man who kindles a fire in the winter to warm himself. But he forgets to

pakkameyya, atha kho so aggi aññatarassa purisassa khettaṃ ḍaheyya, tam-enaṃ khettasāmiko gahetvā rañño dasseyya: iminā deva purisena mayhaṃ khettaṃ daḍḍhan-ti, so evaṃ vadeyya: nāhaṃ devā imassa khettaṃ jhāpemi, añño so aggi yo mayā avijjhāpito, añño so aggi yen' imassa khettaṃ daḍḍhaṃ, nāhaṃ daṇḍappatto ti, kin-nu kho so mahārāja puriso daṇḍappatto bhaveyyāti. āma bhante, daṇḍappatto bhaveyyāti. kena kāraṇenāti. kiñcāpi so evaṃ vadeyya, purimaṃ bhante aggiṃ apaccakkhāya pacchimena agginā so puriso daṇḍappatto bhaveyyāti.

59 evam eva kho mahārāja iminā nāmarūpena kammaṃ karoti sobhanaṃ vā pāpakaṃ vā, tena kammena aññaṃ nāmarūpaṃ paṭisandahati, tasmā na mutto pāpakehi kammehīti. bhiyyo opammaṃ karohīti. yathā mahārāja kocid-eva puriso padīpaṃ ādāya māḷaṃ abhirūhitvā bhuñjeyya, padīpo jhāyamāno tiṇaṃ jhāpeyya, tiṇaṃ jhāyamānaṃ gharaṃ jhāpeyya, gharaṃ jhāyamānaṃ gāmaṃ jhāpeyya, gāmajano taṃ purisaṃ gahetvā evaṃ vadeyya: kissa tvaṃ bho purisa gāmaṃ jhāpesīti, so evaṃ vadeyya: nāhaṃ bho gāmaṃ jhāpemi, añño so padīpaggiyassāhaṃ ālokena bhuñjiṃ, añño so aggi yena gāmo jhāpito ti; te vivadamānā tava santike āgaccheyyuṃ, kassa tvaṃ mahārāja atthaṃ dhāreyyāsīti. gāmajanassa bhante ti. kiṅkāraṇā ti. kiñcāpi so evaṃ vadeyya, api ca tato eva so aggi nibbatto ti.

60 evam-eva kho mahārāja kiñcāpi aññaṃ māraṇantikaṃ nāmarūpaṃ aññaṃ paṭisandhismiṃ nāmarūpaṃ, api ca tato yeva taṃ nibbattaṃ, tasmā na mutto pāpakehi kammehīti.

douse it and goes away. The fire spreads and burns another person's field, and the owner of the field takes the matter to the king. 'This man burned my field.' What if the man were to reply that he did not set fire to the field because he had kindled another fire, not the one that burned the field? And therefore, he should not be punished. Do you think that he should be punished, great king?" "Of course he should be punished." "On what grounds?" "Despite what the man says, he should be punished because of the later fire, which was only there due to the previous fire, now unseen."

"And so it is also that beautiful and evil karma are brought 59
about by one name-and-form, and then another name-and-form is reborn with that karma, and so one is not released from the evil karma."

"Another analogy, please."

"Suppose a man were to take a lamp and hang it up in a pavilion to make use of its light. As it burns, it sets fire to the thatch, and from there, it burns down the building and spreads to the village. The village people seize him and demand, 'Why did you burn the village?' He replies that in fact he did not burn the village but only lit a lamp to make use of its light. The fire that burned the village was an altogether different fire. If this dispute were brought to you, great king, how would you settle the matter?" "In favor of the villagers, sir." "On what grounds?" "Because regardless of what the man says, that fire came from him."

"Similarly, while there is one name-and-form at the time 60
of death, there is another name-and-form at rebirth, and since it comes from the previous one, one is not released from the evil karma."

bhiyyo opammaṃ karohīti. yathā mahārāja kocid-eva puriso dahariṃ dārikaṃ vāretvā sunkaṃ datvā pakkameyya, sā aparena samayena mahatī assa vayappattā,[2] tato añño puriso suṅkaṃ datvā vivāhaṃ kareyya, itaro āgantvā evaṃ vadeyya: kissa pana me tvaṃ ambho purisa bhariyaṃ nesīti, so evaṃ vadeyya: nāhaṃ tava bhariyaṃ nemi, aññā sā dārikā daharī taruṇī ya tayā vāritā ca dinnasuṅkā ca, aññā 'yaṃ dārikā mahatī vayappattā mayā vāritā ca dinnasuṅkā cāti; te vivadamānā tava santike āgaccheyyuṃ, kassa tvaṃ mahārāja atthaṃ dhāreyyāsīti. purimassa bhante ti. kiṅkāraṇā ti. kiñcāpi so evaṃ vadeyya, api ca tato yeva sā mahatī nibbattā ti. evam-eva kho mahārāja kiñcāpi aññaṃ māraṇantikaṃ nāmarūpaṃ aññaṃ paṭisandhismiṃ nāmarūpaṃ, api ca tato yeva taṃ nibbattaṃ, tasmā na parimutto pāpakehi kammehīti. bhiyyo opammaṃ karohīti.

61 yathā mahārāja kocid-eva puriso gopālakassa hatthato khīraghaṭaṃ kiṇitvā tass' eva hatthe nikkhipitvā pakkameyya: sve gahetvā gamissāmīti, taṃ aparajju dadhi sampajjeyya, so āgantvā evaṃ vadeyya: dehi me khīraghaṭan-ti, so dadhiṃ dasseyya, itaro evaṃ vadeyya: nāhaṃ tava hatthato dadhiṃ kiṇāmi, dehi me khīraghaṭan-ti, so evaṃ vadeyya: ajānato te khīraṃ dadhi bhūtan-ti; te vivadamānā tava santike āgaccheyyuṃ, kassa tvaṃ mahārāja atthaṃ dhāreyyāsīti. gopālakassa bhante ti. kiṅkāraṇā ti. kiñcāpi so evaṃ vadeyya, api ca tato yeva taṃ nibbattan-ti.

"Give another analogy."

"Suppose a man asks for a young girl in marriage, gives the bride price, and leaves. In time, she grows up and comes of age. Another man gives the bride price and they get married. But the first man comes back and exclaims, 'You there, fellow, how could you take my wife?' 'But I didn't take your wife. It was another tender young girl who was contracted to you with the bride price you gave. This adult woman has been contracted to me with my bride price.' How would you settle this dispute, great king, if it came before you? And on what grounds?" "In favor of the first man, sir, because whatever the second man might say, the grown woman came from the girl." "Similarly, while there is one name-and-form at the time of death, there is another name-and-form at the rebirth, and since it comes from the previous one, one is not set free from the evil karma."

"Yet another analogy, please."

"Suppose a man were to buy a jar of milk directly from a 61
dairy farmer. He leaves it in his care and goes away, promising that he will come back the next day. By the following day it has turned to curds, and when the man returns, asks for his jar of milk, and sees curds, he claims that he did not buy curds from the hand of the farmer, and that he should be given a jar of milk. He is told that even though he didn't realize it, the milk became curds. Should this matter be brought before you, great king, how would you settle this dispute, and on what grounds?" "In favor of the dairy farmer, sir, because regardless of what the man says, the one came from the other."

evam-eva kho mahārāja kiñcāpi aññaṃ māraṇantikaṃ nāmarūpaṃ aññaṃ paṭisandhismiṃ nāmarūpaṃ, api ca tato yeva taṃ nibbattaṃ, tasmā na parimutto pāpakehi kammehīti. kallosi bhante nāgasenāti.

62 rājā āha: bhante nāgasena, tvaṃ pana paṭisandahissasīti. alaṃ mahārāja, kin-tena pucchitena, nanu mayā paṭigacc'eva akkhātaṃ: sace mahārāja sa-upādāno bhavissāmi paṭisandahissāmi, sace anupādāno bhavissāmi na paṭisandahissāmīti. opammaṃ karohīti. Yathā mahārāja kocid-eva puriso rañño adhikāraṃ kāreyya, rājā tuṭṭho adhikāraṃ dadeyya, so tena adhikārena pañcahi kāmaguṇehi samappito samaṅgibhūto paricareyya, so ce janassa āroceyya: na me rājā kiñci paṭikarotīti, kin-nu kho so mahārāja puriso yuttakārī bhaveyyāti. na hi bhante ti. evam-eva kho mahārāja kin-te etena pucchitena, nanu mayā paṭigacc'eva akkhātaṃ: sace sa-upādāno bhavissāmi paṭisandahissāmi, sace anupādāno bhavissāmi na paṭisandahissāmīti. kallosi bhante nāgasenāti.

63 rājā āha: bhante nāgasena, yam-pan' etaṃ brūsi: nāmarūpan-ti, tattha katamaṃ nāmaṃ katamaṃ rūpan-ti. yaṃ tattha mahārāja oḷārikaṃ etaṃ rūpaṃ, ye tattha sukhumā cittacetasikā dhammā etaṃ nāman-ti. bhante nāgasena, kena kāraṇena nāmaṃ yeva na paṭisandahati rūpaṃ yeva vā ti. aññamaññūpanissitā mahārāja ete dhammā, ekatova uppajjantīti. opammaṃ karohīti.

"It is the same here, great king: there is one name-and-form at the time of death and a different name-and-form at the time of rebirth. Since one comes from the other, the person is not set free from the evil karma."

"You are wise, Nagasena."

The king asked: "Nagasena, are you going to be reborn?" 62

"Enough, great king. Why keep asking this? Did I not already get this one and answer it? If there is attachment I will be reborn, but if there is no attachment I will not be."

"But could you provide an analogy?"

"Suppose a man does a service for the king, and the king is pleased so he gives him an official position. Prosperous and provided with the pleasures of the five senses, he roves about telling people that the king has provided him nothing in compensation. Would this man be doing the right thing?"

"Certainly not."

"This is the same thing, great king, so why keep asking this? Did I not already get this one and answer it? If there is attachment, I will be reborn, but if there is no attachment I will not be."

"You are wise, Nagasena."

The king said: "Nagasena, earlier you mentioned name- 63
and-form. But what is meant by name and what is meant by form?" "Form is material, great king, while name refers to the subtle phenomena of mind and its accompanying mental processes." "For what reason is name not reborn by itself, nor is form?" "These phenomenal states are dependent on one another, great king, and only occur together."

"Give an analogy, please."

64 yathā mahārāja kukkuṭiyā kalalaṃ na bhaveyya, aṇḍam-pi na bhaveyya, yañ-ca tattha kalalaṃ yañca aṇḍaṃubho p' ete aññamaññanissitā, ekatova nesaṃ uppatti hoti, evam-eva kho mahārāja yadi tattha nāmaṃ na bhaveyya rūpam-pi na bhaveyya, yañ-c' eva tattha nāmaṃ yañ-c' eva rūpaṃ ubho p' ete aññamaññanissitā, ekatova nesaṃ uppatti hoti; evam-etaṃ dīgham-addhānaṃ sambhāvitan-ti. kallosi bhante nāgasenāti.

65 rājā āha: bhante nāgasena, yam-pan' etaṃ brūsi: dīgham-addhānan-ti, kim-etaṃ addhānaṃ nāmāti. atīto mahārāja addhā, anāgato addhā, paccuppanno addhā ti. kim-pana bhante addhā atthīti. koci mahārāja addhā atthi, koci na-tthīti. katamo pana bhante atthi, katamo na-tthīti. ye te mahārāja sankhārā atītā vigatā niruddhā vipariṇatā so addhā na-tthi, ye dhamma vipākā ye ca vipākadhamma-dhammā ye ca aññatra paṭisandhiṃ denti, so addhā atthi, ye sattā kālakatā aññatra uppannā so ca addhā atthi, ye sattā kālakatā aññatra anuppannā so addhā na-tthi, ye ca sattā parinibbutā so ca addhā na-tthi parinibbutattā ti. kallosi bhante nāgasenāti.

dutiyo vaggo.

"One does not get just an embryo or just an eggshell from 64
a chicken, but rather the embryo and the eggshell are dependent on each other and they only occur together. Similarly, if name did not occur, then form wouldn't either, and if form did not occur, then neither would name, and so where there is name, there is form. Dependent on each other, they only occur together, and have arisen like this for a very long time, great king."

"You are wise, Nagasena."

The king asked: "You just said 'a very long time.' What 65
is meant by time, sir?" "Time refers to past, present, and future, great king." "Is there such a thing as time, sir?" "In some sense, there is, great king, and in some sense, there is not."

"In what way is there time and in what way is there not?"

"Past habitual patterns are destroyed, vanish, and change, so in this sense, time does not exist. But there are phenomenal states that are effects and phenomenal states that will effect other phenomenal states, and these give a link to rebirth elsewhere. In this sense, there is time. Beings die and are born elsewhere, and in this sense also, there is time. But when beings die and are not born elsewhere, there is no time. It is this way for those who have attained final nibbana: for them, there is no time."

"You are wise, Nagasena."

End of Section Two.

66 rājā āha: bhante nāgasena, atītassa addhānassa kiṃ mūlaṃ, anāgatassa addhānassa kiṃ mūlaṃ, paccuppannassa addhānassa kiṃ mūlan-ti. atītassa ca mahārāja addhānassa anāgatassa ca addhānassa paccuppannassa ca addhānassa avijjā mūlaṃ, avijjāpaccayā saṅkhārā, saṅkhārapaccayā viññāṇaṃ, viññāṇapaccayā nāmarūpaṃ, nāmarūpapaccayā saḷāyatanaṃ, saḷāyatanapaccayā phasso, phassapaccayā vedanā, vedanāpaccayā taṇhā, taṇhāpaccayā upādānaṃ, upādānapaccayā bhavo, bhavapaccayā jāti, jātipaccayā jarā-maraṇaṃ soka-parideva-dukkha-domanass-upāyāsā sambhavanti; evam-etassa kevalassa addhānassa purimā koṭi na paññāyatīti. kallosi bhante nāgasenāti.

67 rājā āha: bhante nāgasena, yam-pan'etaṃ brūsi: purimā koṭi na paññāyatīti, tassa opammaṃ karohīti. yathā mahārāja puriso parittaṃ bījaṃ paṭhaviyaṃ nikkhipeyya, tato aṅkuro uṭṭhahitvā anupubbena vuddhiṃ virūḷhiṃ vepullaṃ āpajjitvā phalaṃ dadeyya, tato pi bījaṃ gahetvā puna ropeyya, tato pi ankuro uṭṭhahitvā anupubbena vuddhiṃ virūḷhiṃ vepullaṃ āpajjitvā phalaṃ dadeyya, evam etissā santatiyā atthi anto ti. na-tthi bhante ti. evam-eva kho mahārāja addhānassāpi purimā koṭi na paññāyatīti. bhiyyo opammaṃ karohīti.

68 yathā mahārāja kukkuṭiyā aṇḍaṃ, aṇḍato kukkuṭī, kukkuṭiyā aṇḍan-ti evam-etissā santatiyā atthi anto ti. na-tthi bhante ti. evam-eva kho mahārāja addhānassāpi purimā koṭi

The king asked: "Nagasena, sir, what is the root of past time, 66
the root of future time, and the root of present time?"

"Ignorance is the root of past, future, and present time, great king. Conditioned by ignorance there are habitual patterns; conditioned by the habitual patterns there is awareness; conditioned by awareness there is name-and-form; conditioned by name-and-form there are the six bases of sensory experience; conditioned by the six bases there is sensory contact;[18] conditioned by sensory contact there is feeling; conditioned by feeling there is craving; conditioned by craving there is attachment; conditioned by attachment there is becoming; conditioned by becoming there is birth; conditioned by birth there is old age and death. And this generates sorrow, grieving, suffering, distress, and trouble. No beginning point of all this time is known, great king."

"You are wise, Nagasena."

The king said: "Nagasena, you just said that no beginning 67
point is known. Please give an analogy."

"Suppose someone plants a tiny seed in the ground, great king, and from it comes a shoot that eventually grows, develops, and matures until it bears fruit. From planting and cultivating a seed from it, another shoot comes up, and it eventually grows, develops, matures, and bears fruit too. Is there an endpoint to this series?" "No, sir." "In just the same way, great king, no beginning point of time is known."

"Please make another analogy."

"The egg comes from the chicken, the chicken from the 68
egg, and the egg from the chicken. Where does the series end? Similarly, no beginning point of time is known."

"Please make another analogy."

na paññāyatīti. bhiyyo opammaṃ karohīti. thero paṭhaviyā cakkaṃ ālikhitvā milindaṃ rājānaṃ etad-avoca: atthi mahārāja imassa cakkassa anto ti. na-tthi bhante ti. evam-eva kho mahārāja imāni cakkāni vuttāni bhagavatā: cakkhuñ-ca paṭicca rūpe ca uppajjati cakkhuviññāṇaṃ, tiṇṇaṃ saṅgati phasso, phassapaccayā vedanā, vedanāpaccayā taṇhā, taṇhāpaccayā kammaṃ, kammato puna cakkhuṃ jāyati, evam-etissā santatiyā atthi anto ti. na-tthi bhante ti.

69 sotañ-ca paṭicca sadde ca-pe-manañ-ca paṭicca dhamme ca uppajjati manoviññāṇaṃ, tiṇṇaṃ saṅgati phasso, phassapaccayā vedanā, vedanāpaccayā taṇhā, taṇhāpaccayā kammaṃ, kammato puna mano jāyati, evam etissā santatiyā atthi anto ti. na-tthi bhante ti. evam-eva kho mahārāja addhānassāpi purimā koṭi na paññāyatīti. kallosi bhante nāgasenāti.

70 rājā āha: bhante nāgasena, yaṃ pan' etaṃ brūsi: purimā koṭi na paññāyatīti, katamā ca sā purimā koṭīti. yo kho mahārāja atīto addhā esā purimā koṭīti. bhante nāgasena, yaṃ pan' etaṃ brūsi: purimā koṭi na paññāyatīti, kim-pana bhante sabbā pi purimā koṭi na paññāyatīti. kāci mahārāja paññāyati, kāci na paññāyatīti. katamā bhante paññāyati, katamā na paññāyatīti. ito pubbe mahārāja sabbena sabbaṃ

The elder drew a circle on the ground and asked King Milinda: "Is there an end of this circle, great king?" "No, sir."

"In the same way, the Bhagavan said this: 'When its conditions, the eye and a visible form, are present, there arises visual awareness; when the three meet, there is sensory contact. Conditioned by sensory contact, there is feeling; conditioned by feeling, there is craving; conditioned by craving, there is karma, and from karma, vision is produced.' Is there an endpoint in this series, great king?" "No, sir."

"It is the same for hearing and the other senses, including 69
the mind sense. When its conditions, the mind and phenomenal states, are present, there arises mental awareness; when the three meet, there is sensory contact; conditioned by contact, there is feeling; conditioned by feeling, there is craving; conditioned by craving, there is karma, and from karma, the mind is produced. Is there an endpoint in the series, great king?" "No, sir."

"Just so, no beginning point in time is known."

"You are wise, Nagasena."

The king said: "Nagasena, you just said that no beginning 70
point in time is known. But which beginning point do you mean?" "A first point in the past, great king." "But when you said that no beginning point in time is known, did you mean that there are no beginning points in time that can be known?" "Some can be known, and some cannot be." "Which ones are known and which ones aren't?"

"Great king, an earliest point in the very beginning, a time in which there was no ignorance anywhere or in any way, cannot be known. Still, when something nonexistent

sabbathā sabbaṃ avijjā nāhosīti esā purimā koṭi na paññāyati, yaṃ ahutvā sambhoti hutvā paṭivigacchati esā purimā koṭi paññāyatīti.

71 bhante nāgasena, yaṃ ahutvā sambhoti hutvā paṭivigacchati nanu taṃ ubhato chinnaṃ atthaṃ gacchatīti. yadi mahārāja ubhato chinnā atthaṃ gacchati ubhato chinnā sakkā vaḍḍhetun-ti. āma, sā pi sakkā vaḍḍhetun-ti. nāhaṃ bhante etaṃ pucchāmi, koṭito sakkā vaḍḍhetun-ti. āma, sakkā vaḍḍhetun-ti. opammaṃ karohīti. thero tassa rukkhūpamaṃ akāsi: khandhā ca kevalassa dukkhakkhandhassa bījānīti. kallosi bhante nāgasenāti.

72 rājā āha: bhante nāgasena, atthi keci saṅkhārā ye jāyantīti. āma mahārāja, atthi saṅkhārā ye jāyantīti. katame te bhante ti. cakkhusmiñ-ca kho mahārāja sati rūpesu ca cakkhuviññāṇaṃ hoti, cakkhuviññāṇe sati cakkhusamphasso hoti, cakkhusamphasse sati vedanā hoti, vedanāya sati taṇhā hoti, taṇhāya sati upādānaṃ hoti, upādāne sati bhavo hoti, bhave sati jāti hoti, jātiyā sati jarā-maraṇaṃ soka-parideva-dukkha-domanass-upāyāsā sambhavanti, evam-etassa kevalassa dukkhakkhandhassa samudayo hoti. cakkhusmiñ-ca kho mahārāja asati rūpesu ca asati cakkhuviññāṇaṃ na hoti, cakkhuviññāṇe asati cakkhusamphasso na hoti, cakkhusamphasse asati vedanā na hoti, vedanāya asati taṇhā na

comes into existence and, having existed, perishes, this kind of beginning point may be understood."

"Nagasena, if what did not exist came into existence and 71
then dispersed again, then, cut off at both ends, wouldn't it disappear?" "It may be that what is cut off at both ends disappears, but couldn't it also be that from both ends there is further growth?" "I suppose they could grow, but that is not my question. How could growth come from an endpoint? Please give an analogy."

"Growth can come from an endpoint, great king. Consider the example of the tree again and apply it to the clusters: the clusters are the seeds of the whole composite that is suffering."

"You are wise, Nagasena."

The king said: "Nagasena, sir, please explain the occur- 72
rence of habitual patterns, and what they are."

"Well, great king, there are habitual patterns that occur. Where an eye and visible forms are present, visual awareness occurs; where visual awareness occurs, there is contact with sense objects by the eye, and where there is contact with the eye, there is feeling. Where there is feeling, there is craving; where craving, attachment; where attachment, becoming; where becoming, birth; and where there is birth, there are old age and death, and with them arise sorrow, grieving, suffering, distress, and trouble. This is the origin of the entire composite that is suffering. However, great king, where the eye and visible forms are not present, there is no visual awareness; where there is no visual awareness, then there is no visual contact; where there is no visual contact, there is no feeling; where there is no feeling, there is no

hoti, taṇhāya asati upādānaṃ na hoti, upādāne asati bhavo na hoti, bhave asati jāti na hoti, jātiyā asati jarāmaraṇaṃ soka-parideva-dukkha-domanass-upāyāsā na honti, evam-etassa kevalassa dukkhakkhandhassa nirodho hotīti. kallosi bhante nāgasenāti.

73 rājā āha: bhante nāgasena, atthi keci saṅkhārā ye abhavantā jāyantīti. na-tthi mahārāja keci saṅkhārā ye abhavantā jāyanti, bhavantā yeva kho mahārāja saṅkhārā jāyantīti. opammaṃ karohīti. taṃ kimmaññasi mahārāja: idaṃ gehaṃ abhavantaṃ jātaṃ yattha tvaṃ nisinnosīti. na-tthi kiñci bhante idha abhavantaṃ jātaṃ, bhavantaṃ yeva jātaṃ, imāni kho bhante dārūni vane ahesuṃ, ayañ-ca mattikā paṭhaviyaṃ ahosi, itthīnañ-ca purisānañ-ca tajjena vāyāmena evam-idaṃ gehaṃ nibbattan-ti. evam-eva kho mahārāja na-tthi keci saṅkhārā ye abhavantā jāyanti, bhavantā yeva sankhārā jāyantīti. bhiyyo opammaṃ karohīti.

74 yathā mahārāja ye keci bījagāma-bhūtagāmā paṭhaviyaṃ nikkhittā anupubbena vuddhiṃ virūḷhiṃ vepullaṃ āpajjamānā pupphāni ca phalāni ca dadeyyuṃ na te rukkhā abhavantā jātā, bhavantā yeva te rukkhā jātā, evam-eva kho mahārāja na-tthi keci saṅkhārā ye abhavantā jāyanti,

craving; where there is no craving, there is no attachment; where there is no attachment, there is no becoming; where there is no becoming, there is no birth; and where there is no birth, there is no old age and death, and so no sorrow, grieving, suffering, distress, and trouble. It is this that is the stopping of the entire composite that is suffering."

"You are wise, Nagasena.

The king said: "Nagasena, are there any habitual patterns 73
that arise without previously existing?" "No, great king, when habitual patterns arise, they continue to come into being, with existing ones giving rise to further habitual patterns."

"Please give an analogy."

"Consider this building where you are sitting, great king. Was it produced from something nonexistent?" "Nothing produced here, sir, was nonexistent; what was produced was already existing. The wood came from the forest and the clay from the earth, and, with work and effort, women and men fashioned them into this building." "In just the same way, habitual patterns are not produced without previously existing, and as they continue to come into being, further habitual patterns occur."

"Another analogy, please."

"Great king, there are all kinds of seeds and plants that, 74
when sown in the earth, gradually grow, develop, and mature until they produce flowers and fruit. Trees do not arise without previously existing, for they are already coming to be as they are produced. Similarly, habitual patterns are not produced without previously existing, and as they continue to come into being, further habitual patterns occur."

bhavantā yevate sankhārā jāyantīti. bhiyyo opammaṃ karohīti.

75 yathā mahārāja kumbhakāro paṭhaviyā mattikaṃ uddharitvā nānābhājanāni karoti, na tāni bhājanāni abhavantāni jātāni, bhavantāni yeva jātāni, evam-eva kho mahārāja na-tthi keci saṅkhārā ye abhavantā jāyanti, bhavantā yeva saṅkhārā jāyantīti. bhiyyo opammaṃ karohīti. yathā mahārāja vīṇāya pattaṃ na siyā, cammaṃ na siyā, doṇi na siyā, daṇḍo na siyā, upavīṇo na siyā, tantiyo na siyuṃ, koṇo na siyā, purisassa ca tajjo vāyāmo na siyā, jāyeyya saddo ti. na hi bhante ti. yato ca kho mahārāja vīṇāya pattaṃ siyā, cammaṃ siyā, doṇi siyā, daṇḍo siyā, upavīṇo siyā, tantiyo siyuṃ, koṇo siyā, purisassa ca tajjo vāyāmo siyā, jāyeyya saddo ti. āma bhante, jāyeyyāti. evam-eva kho mahārāja na-tthi keci saṅkhārā ye abhavantā jāyanti, bhavantā yeva kho saṅkhārā jāyantīti. bhiyyo opammaṃ karo-hīti.

76 yathā mahārāja araṇi na siyā, araṇipotako na siyā, araṇiyottakaṃ na siyā, uttarāraṇi na siyā, coḷakaṃ na siyā, purisassa ca tajjo vāyāmo na siyā, jāyeyya aggīti. na hi bhante ti. yato ca kho mahārāja araṇi siyā, araṇipotako siyā, araṇiyottakaṃ siyā, uttarāraṇi siyā, coḷakaṃ siyā, purisassa ca tajjo vāyāmo siyā, jāyeyya so aggīti. āma bhante, jāyeyyāti. evam-eva kho mahārāja na-tthi keci saṅkhārā ye abhavantā jāyanti, bhavantā yeva kho saṅkhārā jāyantīti. bhiyyo opammaṃ karohīti. yathā mahārāja maṇi na siyā, ātapo na siyā, gomayaṃ na siyā, jāyeyya so aggīti. na hi bhante ti. yato ca kho mahārāja maṇi siyā, ātapo siyā, gomayaṃ siyā, jāyeyya aggīti. āma bhante, jāyeyyāti. evam-eva kho mahārāja na-tthi keci sankhārā ye abhavantā jāyanti, bhavantā yeva kho saṅkhārā jāyantīti. bhiyyo opammaṃ karohīti.

"Make another analogy."

"A potter digs clay from the earth and works it into various 75
vessels. These vessels do not arise without previously existing, for they are already coming to be as they are produced. Similarly, habitual patterns are not produced without previously existing, and as they continue to come into being, further habitual patterns occur."

"Another analogy, please."

"Without the sling, the sounding board, the body, the head, the arm, the strings, the pick, and the effort of the player, the lute would not produce sound. But with all of these components, it can make music." "Agreed, sir." "Similarly, habitual patterns are not produced without previously existing, and as they continue to come into being, further habitual patterns occur."

"Another analogy, please."

"Without kindling, the twirling stick, the cord for the 76
twirling stick, an upper stick, tinder, and effort on the part of a person, fire would not be produced." "Correct, sir." "Similarly, great king, habitual patterns are not produced without previously existing, and as they continue to come into being, further habitual patterns occur."

"Yet another analogy, please."

"Without the heat of the sun, a burning glass, and cow dung for tinder, fire would not be produced. But with these, there could be fire, and it is much the same way with the habitual patterns." "Indeed, sir. But may I get one last analogy on this?"

77 yathā mahārāja ādāso na siyā, ābhā na siyā, mukhaṃ na siyā, jāyeyya attā ti. na hi bhante ti. yato ca kho mahārāja ādāso siyā, ābhā siyā, mukhaṃ siyā, jāyeyya attā ti. āma bhante, jāyeyyāti. evam-eva kho mahārāja na-tthi keci saṅkhārā ye abhavantā jāyanti, bhavantā yeva kho saṅkhārā jāyantīti. kallosi bhante nāgasenāti.

78 rājā āha: bhante nāgasena, vedagū upalabbhatīti. ko pan' esa mahārāja vedagū nāmāti. yo bhante abbhantare jīvo cakkhunā rūpaṃ passati, sotena saddaṃ suṇāti, ghānena gandhaṃ ghāyati, jivhāya rasaṃ sāyati, kāyena phoṭṭhabbaṃ phusati, manasā dhammaṃ vijānāti, yathā mayaṃ idha pāsāde nisinnā yena yena vātapānena iccheyyāma passituṃ tena tena vātapānena passeyyāma, puratthimena pi vātapānena passeyyāma, pacchimena pi vātapānena passeyyāma, uttarena pi vātapānena passeyyāma, dakkhiṇena pi vātapānena passeyyāma, evam-eva kho bhante ayaṃ abbhantare jīvo yena yena dvārena icchati passituṃ tena tena dvārena passatīti.

79 thero āha: pañcadvāraṃ mahārāja bhaṇissāmi, taṃ suṇohi, sādhukaṃ manasikarohi: yadi abbhantare jīvo cakkhunā rūpaṃ passati, yathā mayaṃ idha pāsāde nisinnā yena yena vātapānena iccheyyāma passituṃ tena tena vātapānena rūpaṃ yeva passeyyāma, puratthimena pi vātapānena rūpaṃ yeva passeyyāma, pacchimena pi vātapānena rūpaṃ yeva passeyyāma, uttarena pi vātapānena rūpaṃ yeva passeyyāma, dakkhiṇena pi vātapānena rūpaṃ yeva passeyyāma, evam-etena abbhantare jivena cakkhunā pi rūpaṃ yeva passitabbaṃ, sotena pi rūpaṃ yeva passitabbaṃ, ghānena pi rūpaṃ yeva passitabbaṃ, jivhāya pi rūpaṃ yeva passitabbaṃ, kāyena pi rūpaṃ yeva passi-

"Without a mirror, light, and a face in front of it, there would be no reflection." "True." "But with a mirror, light, and a face in front of it, there would be a reflection, great king. It is the same with the habitual patterns: habitual patterns are not produced without previously existing, and as they continue to come into being, further habitual patterns occur." 77

"You are wise, Nagasena.

"Nagasena, is there such a thing as a knower?" "It depends, great king, on what you mean by 'knower.'" "An inner soul that sees visible forms with the eye, hears sounds with the ear, smells odors with the nose, savors taste with the tongue, feels contact with the body, and perceives phenomenal states with the mind. It would be like us sitting here in this palace looking through any latticed window we like, east, west, north, or south, to see outside. The inner soul would choose this door or that door to see out of." 78

The elder replied: "I will explain the five doorways, great king, so please listen and attend carefully. If there were an inner soul that perceived visible forms with the eyes, much like our sitting here in the palace looking out of whatever window and direction we wished to perceive the world—an eastern window to see a visible form, or a western window, 79

tabbaṃ, manasā pi rūpaṃ yeva passitabbaṃ; cakkhunā pi saddo yeva sotabbo, ghānena pi saddo yeva sotabbo, jivhāya pi saddo yeva sotabbo, kāyena pi saddo yeva sotabbo, manasā pi saddo yeva sotabbo; cakkhunā pi gandho yeva ghāyitabbo, sotena pi gandho yeva ghāyitabbo, jivhāya pi gandho yeva ghāyitabbo, kāyena pi gandho yeva ghāyitabbo, manasā pi gandho yeva ghāyitabbo; cakkhunā pi raso yeva sāyitabbo, sotena pi raso yeva sāyitabbo, ghānena pi raso yeva sāyitabbo, kāyena pi raso yeva sāyitabbo, manasā pi raso yeva sāyitabbo; cakkhunā pi phoṭṭhabbaṃ yeva phusitabbaṃ, sotena pi phoṭṭhabbaṃ yeva phusitabbaṃ, ghānena pi phoṭṭhabbaṃ yeva phusitabbaṃ, jivhāya pi phoṭṭhabbaṃ yeva phusitabbaṃ, manasā pi phoṭṭhabbaṃ yeva phusitabbaṃ; cakkhunā pi dhammaṃ yeva vijānitabbaṃ, sotena pi dhammaṃ yeva vijānitabbaṃ, ghānena pi dhammaṃ yeva vijānitabbaṃ, jivhāya pi dhammaṃ yeva vijānitabbaṃ, kāyena pi dhammaṃ yeva vijānitabban-ti. na hi bhante ti.

80 na kho te mahārāja yujjati purimena vā pacchimaṃ pacchimena vā purimaṃ. yathā vā pana mahārāja mayaṃ idha pāsāde nisinnā imesu jālavātapānesu ugghāṭitesu mahantena ākāsena bahimukhā suṭṭhutaraṃ rūpaṃ passāma, evam-etena abbhantare jīvenāpi cakkhudvāresu ugghāṭitesu mahantena ākāsena suṭṭhutaraṃ rūpaṃ passitabbaṃ, sotesu ugghāṭitesu ghāne ugghāṭite jivhāya ugghāṭitāya kāye ugghāṭite mahantena ākāsena suṭṭhutaraṃ saddo sotabbo, gandho ghāyitabbo, raso sāyitabbo, phoṭṭhabbo phusitabbo ti. na hi bhante ti.

81 na kho te mahārāja yujjati purimena vā pacchimaṃ pacchimena vā purimaṃ. yathā vā pana mahārāja ayaṃ dinno nikkhamitvā bahidvārakoṭṭhake tiṭṭheyya, jānāsi tvaṃ

or northern and southern ones, and so on—then would that mean that it could see a visible form with the ear, or with the nose, tongue, body, or mind? Could sound be heard by the eye, nose, tongue, body, or mind? An odor perceived by the eye, ear, tongue, body, or mind? Could a taste be savored by the eye, ear, nose, body, or mind? Could a tangible thing be felt by the eye, ear, nose, tongue, or mind? And could the phenomenal states be perceived by eye, ear, nose, tongue, or body?" "No, sir."

"Great king, you did not connect correctly an analogy with 80
the case at hand. We are sitting in a palace, but we would see visible forms far better with our faces outside in the great open air, having thrown completely aside the lattice windows. Does this mean that the inner soul would see visible forms better in the open air, having thrown aside the doors of the eyes? And would it hear sound, smell odor, savor taste, and feel touch by throwing aside the windows of the ears, nose, tongue, and body?" "No, sir."

"Then you did not connect correctly your analogy with 81
the case at hand. Take this Dinna here, great king. Suppose he goes out and stands in front of the gateway. Would you know that he had done so?" "Of course I'd know."

mahārāja: ayaṃ dinno nikkhamitvā bahidvārakoṭṭhake hito ti. āma bhante, jānāmīti. yathā vā pana mahārāja ayaṃ dinno anto pavisitvā tava purato tiṭṭheyya, jānāsi tvaṃ mahārāja: ayaṃ dinno anto pavisitvā mama purato ṭhito ti. āma bhante, jānāmīti. evam-eva kho mahārāja abbhantare so jīvo jivhāya rase nikkhitte jāneyya: ambilattaṃ vā lavaṇattaṃ vā tittakattaṃ vā kaṭukattaṃ vā kasāyattaṃ vā madhurattaṃ vā ti. āma bhante, jāneyyāti. te rase anto paviṭṭhe jāneyya: ambilattaṃ vā lavaṇattaṃ vā tittakattaṃ vā kaṭukattaṃ vā kasāyattaṃ vā madhurattaṃ vā ti. na hi bhante ti.

82 na kho te mahārāja yujjati purimena vā pacchimaṃ pacchimena vā purimaṃ. Yathā mahārāja kocid-eva puriso madhughaṭasataṃ āharāpetvā madhudoṇiṃ pūrāpetvā purisassa mukhaṃ pidahitvā madhudoṇiyā pakkhipeyya, jāneyya so mahārāja puriso: madhu sampannaṃ vā na sampannaṃ vā ti. na hi bhante ti. kena kāraṇenāti. na hi tassa bhante mukhe madhu paviṭṭhan-ti. na kho te mahārāja yujjati purimena vā pacchimaṃ pacchimena vā puriman-ti. nāhaṃ paṭibalo tayā vādinā saddhiṃ sallapituṃ; sādhu, atthaṃ jappehīti.

83 thero abhidhammasaṃyuttāya kathāya rājānaṃ milindaṃ saññāpesi: idha mahārāja cakkhuñ-ca paṭicca rūpe ca uppajjati cakkhuviññāṇaṃ, taṃ sahajātā phasso vedanā saññā cetanā ekaggatā jīvitindriyaṃ manasikāro ti evam-ete dhammā paccayato jāyanti, na h' ettha vedagū upalabbhati; sotañca paṭicca sadde ca-pe-manañ-ca paṭicca dhamme ca uppajjati manoviññāṇaṃ, taṃsahajātā phasso vedanā

"But then suppose this Dinna comes back inside and stands in front of you. Would you be aware that *Dinna has reentered and is standing before me?*" "Certainly I'd know." "So then in a similar way, would the inner soul know when a taste was put on the tongue that it is sour, salty, bitter, pungent, astringent, or sweet?"

"Yes, it would know." "But when these tastes had gone deep into the body, would one know that they were sour, salty, bitter, pungent, astringent, or sweet?" "No, sir."

"Then you have incorrectly applied an analogy to the case 82
at hand. Suppose a man were to have a hundred jars of honey
brought and poured into a big tub. Then he seals the mouth
of a person and puts him in the tub of honey. Would that
person know that this was sweet, or not?" "He would not."
"But why not?" "Because the honey did not enter his mouth,
sir." "So you have not correctly connected an analogy with
the case at hand, great king."

"I am not competent to discuss this argument with you, sir. Please explain the meaning."

So the elder taught King Milinda a teaching in the 83
abhidhamma style: "Great king, when the conditions of
the eye and a visible form are present, there arises visual
awareness. Co-arising with it are sensory contact, feeling,
perception, intention, focus, the vital faculty, and attention.
These phenomenal states are produced from such conditions, and there is no 'knower' present among them. So too
with sound being conditioned by the ear, and so on, all the
way up to how mental awareness arises conditioned by the
mind and phenomenal states. Co-arising with each one are
sensory contact, feeling, perception, intention, focus, the

saññā cetanā ekaggatā jīvitindriyaṃ manasikāro ti evam-ete dhammā paccayato jāyanti, na h' ettha vedagū upalabbhatīti. kallosi bhante nāgasenāti.

84 rājā āha: bhante nāgasena, yattha cakkhuviññāṇaṃ uppajjati tattha manoviññāṇam-pi uppajjatīti. Āma mahārāja, yattha cakkhuviññāṇaṃ uppajjati tattha manoviññāṇam-pi uppajjatīti. kin-nu kho bhante nāgasena paṭhamaṃ cakkhuviññāṇaṃ uppajjati pacchā manoviññāṇaṃ, udāhu manoviññāṇaṃ paṭhamaṃ uppajjati pacchā cakkhuviññāṇan-ti. paṭhamaṃ mahārāja cakkhuviññāṇaṃ uppajjati pacchā manoviññāṇan-ti. kin-nu kho bhante nāgasena cakkhuviññāṇaṃ manoviññāṇaṃ āṇāpeti: yatthāhaṃ uppajjāmi tvam-pi tattha uppajjāhīti, udāhu manoviññāṇaṃ cakkhuviññāṇaṃ āṇāpeti: yattha tvaṃ uppajjissasi aham-pi tattha uppajjissāmīti. na hi mahārāja, anallāpo tesaṃ aññamaññehīti. katham-bhante nāgasena yattha cakkhuviññāṇaṃ uppajjati tattha manoviññāṇam-pi uppajjatīti.

85 ninnattā ca mahārāja dvārattā ca ciṇṇattā ca samudācaritattā cāti. katham bhante nāgasena ninnattā yattha cakkhuviññāṇaṃ uppajjati tattha manoviññāṇam-pi uppajjati, opammaṃ karohīti. taṃ kim-maññasi mahārāja: deve vassante katamena udakaṃ gaccheyyāti. yena bhante ninnaṃ tena gaccheyyāti. athāparena samayena devo vasseyya, katamena taṃ udakaṃ gaccheyyāti. yena bhante purimaṃ udakaṃ gataṃ tam-pi tena gaccheyyāti.

vital faculty, and attention. These phenomenal states are produced from such conditions, and there is no need for a 'knower' to be present among them."

"You are wise, Nagasena."

The king asked: "Nagasena, when visual awareness occurs, 84
does mental awareness occur also?" "Yes, great king, when there is a visual awareness, there also occurs a mental awareness." "Then does the visual awareness occur first and the mental awareness later, or is it that the mental awareness occurs first, followed by the visual awareness?" "Visual awareness occurs first, and then the mental awareness."

"Then does the visual awareness instruct the mental awareness: 'I have arisen, so you should too,' or does the mental awareness tell the visual awareness, 'When you occur, then I will arise also'?" "Great king, they don't talk with each other." "Then, Nagasena, how does it happen that when visual awareness occurs, so too does mental awareness?"

"Because it is downstream, because it is at the door, 85
because of being well traveled, and because of practice." "What do you mean that a mental awareness would follow a visual awareness 'because it is downstream'? Please give an analogy."

"Think about it this way, great king. When it is raining in the sky, which way does the water go?" "Sir, it goes downward." "Then on another occasion when it rains in the sky, which way would the water go?" "That water would also go where the first water went." "Does the first water instruct the second water that it should follow it? Or does the later water tell the first water that wherever the first goes, it will

kin-nu-kho mahārāja purimaṃ udakaṃ pacchimaṃ udakaṃ āṇāpeti: yenāhaṃ gacchāmi tvam-pi tena gacchāhīti, pacchimaṃ vā udakaṃ purimaṃ udakaṃ āṇāpeti: yena tvaṃ gacchissasi aham-pi tena gacchissāmīti. na hi bhante, anālāpo tesaṃ aññamaññehi, ninnattā gacchantīti. evam eva kho mahārāja ninnattā yattha cakkhuviññāṇaṃ uppajjati tattha manoviññāṇam-pi uppajjati, na cakkhuviññāṇaṃ manoviññāṇaṃ āṇāpeti: yatthāhaṃ uppajjāmi tvam-pi tattha uppajjāhīti, na pi manoviññāṇaṃ cakkhuviññāṇaṃ āṇāpeti: yattha tvaṃ uppajjissasi aham-pi tattha uppajjissāmīti, anālāpo tesaṃ aññamaññehi, ninnattā uppajjantīti.

86 katham-bhante nāgasena dvārattā yattha cakkhuviññāṇaṃ uppajjati tattha manoviññāṇam-pi uppajjati, opammaṃ karohīti. taṃ kim-maññasi mahārāja: rañño paccantimaṃ nagaraṃ daḷhapākāratoraṇaṃ ekadvāraṃ, tato puriso nikkhamitukāmo bhaveyya, katamena nikkhameyyāti. dvārena bhante nikkhameyyāti. athāparo puriso nikkhamitukāmo bhaveyya, katamena so nikkhameyyāti. yena bhante purimo puriso nikkhanto so pi tena nikkhameyyāti. kin-nu kho mahārāja purimo puriso pacchimaṃ purisaṃ āṇāpeti: yenāhaṃ gacchāmi tvam-pi tena gacchāhīti, pacchimo vā puriso purimaṃ purisaṃ āṇāpeti: yena tvaṃ gacchissasi aham-pi tena gacchissāmīti. na hi bhante, anālāpo tesaṃ aññamaññehi, dvārattā gacchantīti.

87 evam eva kho mahārāja dvārattā yattha cakkhuviññāṇaṃ uppajjati tattha manoviññāṇam-pi uppajjati, na ca cakkhuviññāṇaṃ manoviññāṇaṃ āṇāpeti: yatthāhaṃ uppajjāmi tvam-pi tattha uppajjāhīti, nāpi manoviññāṇaṃ cakkhuviññāṇaṃ āṇāpeti: yattha tvaṃ uppajjissasi aham-pi tattha uppajjissāmīti, anālāpo tesaṃ aññamaññehi, dvārattā uppajj-

follow?" "Of course not, sir. They don't talk with each other. It is because of being downstream that it follows."

"Just so, great king, because where there is a visual awareness downstream, there will follow a mental awareness, and the visual awareness does not tell the mental awareness that it is going to occur so it should too, and the mental awareness does not advise the visual awareness that it plans to follow. They don't chat with each other. It is just because of the first being downstream that the next one follows."

"All right then. But what did you mean when you said that 86
where a visual awareness arises, then a mental awareness occurs 'because it is at the door'? Please give an analogy."

"Think about it this way, great king: a king has a frontier city with a strongly fortified arched gateway that is the only doorway. Suppose that there is a man who wishes to leave. How would he get out?" "He would have to leave by the door, sir." "And if another person wished to leave, great king? How would he do so?" "He would leave by the same way as the first man." "Is it necessary that the first person instruct the second that where he goes, the other should follow? Or that the second man advise the first that he will follow him?" "Of course not, sir. They don't talk with each other. It is because of the door that he follows."

"In just the same way, great king, where a visual aware- 87
ness occurs, it is because of a single doorway that a mental awareness follows it. They do not talk to each other with the visual awareness telling the mental awareness to arise after it does, or the mental awareness telling the visual awareness that it will follow."

"Now explain how it is that 'because of being well traveled'

antīti. katham-bhante nāgasena ciṇṇattā yattha cakkhuviññāṇaṃ uppajjati tattha manoviññāṇam-pi uppajjati, opammaṃ karohīti.

88 taṃ kim-maññasi mahārāja: paṭhamaṃ ekaṃ sakaṭaṃ gaccheyya, atha dutiyaṃ sakaṭaṃ katamena gaccheyyāti. yena bhante purimaṃ sakaṭaṃ gataṃ tam-pi tena gaccheyyāti. kin-nu kho mahārāja purimaṃ sakaṭaṃ pacchimaṃ sakaṭaṃ āṇāpeti: yenāhaṃ gacchāmi tvam-pi tena gacchāhīti, pacchimaṃ vā sakaṭaṃ purimaṃ sakaṭaṃ āṇāpeti: yena tvaṃ gacchissasi aham-pi tena gacchissāmīti. na hi bhante, anālāpo tesaṃ aññamaññehi, ciṇṇattā gacchantīti. evam-eva kho mahārāja ciṇṇattā yattha cakkhuviññāṇaṃ uppajjati tattha manoviññāṇam-pi uppajjati, na ca cakkhuviññāṇaṃ manoviññāṇaṃ āṇāpeti: yatthāhaṃ uppajjāmi tvam-pi tattha uppajjāhīti, nāpi manoviññāṇaṃ cakkhuviññāṇaṃ āṇāpeti: yattha tvaṃ uppajjissasi aham-pi tattha uppajjissāmīti, anālāpo tesaṃ aññamaññehi, ciṇṇattā uppajjantīti.

89 katham-bhante nāgasena samudācaritattā yattha cakkhuviññāṇaṃ uppajjati tattha manoviññāṇam-pi uppajjati, opammaṃ karohīti. yathā mahārāja muddā-gaṇanā-saṅkhā-lekhā-sippaṭṭhānesu ādikammikassa dandhāyanā bhavati, athāparena samayena nisammakiriyāya samudācaritattā adandhāyanā bhavati, evam-eva kho mahārāja samudācaritattā yattha cakkhuviññāṇaṃ uppajjati tattha manoviññāṇaṃ-pi uppajjati, na ca cakkhuviññāṇaṃ manoviññāṇaṃ āṇāpeti: yatthāhaṃ uppajjāmi tvam-pi tattha uppajjāhīti, nāpi manoviññāṇaṃ cakkhuviññāṇaṃ āṇāpeti: yattha tvaṃ uppajjissasi aham-pi tattha uppajjissāmīti, anālāpo tesaṃ aññamaññehi, samudācaritattā uppajjantīti.

the mental awareness follows the visual awareness. And give an analogy."

"Once a first wagon has gone somewhere, great king, how 88
would a second wagon follow?" "It would go the way that the first wagon went, sir." "Would the first wagon have to instruct the second wagon to follow it? Would the second wagon inform the first wagon that it intends to follow it?" "No. There need not be any discussion between them: they go because it is a well-traveled road."

"Similarly, great king, it is because of its being well traveled that a mental awareness follows a visual awareness. They don't chat with each other about the matter, with one offering instruction and the other its plans."

"Finally, sir, how is it 'because of practice' that where a 89
visual awareness occurs, a mental awareness also arises? And of course, please provide an analogy."

"Just like how people first starting the arts of hand gestures, calculating, estimating, or writing are clumsy at first, but with time, carefully working at it, and practice, they become proficient, so too, it is because of practice that when visual awareness occurs, so does mental awareness. Visual awareness does not instruct mental awareness, and mental awareness does not advise visual awareness of its plans. They don't chat, great king. It is just a matter of practice that they arise this way."

90 bhante nāgasena, yattha sotaviññāṇaṃ uppajjati tattha manoviññāṇam-pi uppajjati-pe-yattha ghānaviññāṇaṃ uppajjati, yattha jivhāviññāṇaṃ uppajjati, yattha kāyaviññāṇaṃ uppajjattattha manoviññāṇam-pi uppajjatīti. āma mahārāja, yattha kāyaviññāṇaṃ uppajjati tattha manoviññāṇam-pi uppajjatīti. kin-nu kho bhante nāgasena paṭhamaṃ kāyaviññāṇaṃ uppajjati pacchā manoviññāṇaṃ, udāhu manoviññāṇaṃ paṭhamaṃ uppajjati pacchā kāyaviññāṇan-ti. kāyaviññāṇaṃ mahārāja paṭhamaṃ uppajjati pacchā manoviññāṇan-ti. kin-nu kho bhante nāgasena - pe- anālāpo tesaṃ aññamaññehi, samudācaritattā uppajjantīti. kallosi bhante nāgasenāti.

91 rājā āha: bhante nāgasena, yattha manoviññāṇaṃ uppajjati vedanā pi tattha uppajjatīti. āma mahārāja, yattha manoviññāṇaṃ uppajjati, phasso pi tattha uppajjati, vedanā pi tattha uppajjati, saññā pi tattha uppajjati, cetanā pi tattha uppajjati, vitakko pi tattha uppajjati, vicāro pi tattha uppajjati, sabbe pi phassappamukhā dhammā tattha uppajjantīti. bhante nāgasena, kiṃlakkhaṇo phasso ti. phusanalakkhaṇo mahārāja phasso ti. opammaṃ karohīti.

92 yathā mahārāja dve meṇḍā yujjheyyuṃ, tesu yathā eko meṇḍo evaṃ cakkhu daṭṭhabbaṃ, yathā dutiyo meṇḍo evaṃ rūpaṃ daṭṭhabbaṃ, yathā tesaṃ sannipāto evam phasso daṭṭhabbo ti. bhiyyo opammaṃ karohīti. yathā mahārāja dve pāṇī vajjeyyuṃ, tesu yathā eko pāṇi evaṃ cakkhu

"Is it the same in the case of mental awareness following 90
auditory awareness, and those of the nose, tongue, body, and mind?"

"Yes, great king. It is the same for all of these."

"To be clear, sir: does the bodily awareness arise first and later the mental awareness, or is it that the mental awareness occurs first and the bodily awareness follows later?" "The bodily awareness arises first, and the mental awareness follows, great king."

They went on like this, and in every case, Nagasena taught that these processes do not talk with each other, and that it is by practice and the other means that the one follows the other, until Milinda pronounced: "You are wise, Nagasena."

The king asked: "Nagasena, is it the case that where mental 91
awareness occurs, so does feeling?" "Yes, great king, when mental awareness occurs, there arises sensory contact, and then feeling arises, then perception arises, then intention arises, then initial thought arises, and then deliberation arises. All of these phenomenal states occur following sensory contact."

"What is the defining characteristic of sensory contact?" "The defining characteristic of sensory contact, great king, is *impacting*."

"Give an analogy, please."

"Suppose two rams were to fight. Think of the first ram as 92
the eye and the second as the visible form. When they come together, there is sensory contact."

"Give another example."

"It is like two hands wringing, great king. Think of the first

daṭṭhabbaṃ, yathā dutiyo pāṇi evaṃ rūpaṃ daṭṭhabbaṃ, yathā tesaṃ sannipāto evaṃ phasso daṭṭhabbo ti. bhiyyo opammaṃ karohīti. yathā mahārāja dve sammā vajjeyyuṃ, tesu yathā eko sammo evaṃ cakkhu daṭṭhabbaṃ, yathā dutiyo sammo evaṃ rūpaṃ daṭṭhabbaṃ, yathā tesaṃ sannipāto evaṃ phasso daṭṭhabbo ti. kallosi bhante nāgasenāti.

93 bhante nāgasena, kiṃlakkhaṇā vedanā ti. vedayitalakkhaṇā mahārāja vedanā anubhavanalakkhaṇā cāti. opammaṃ karohīti. yathā mahārāja kocid eva puriso rañño adhikāraṃ kareyya, tassa rājā tuṭṭho adhikāraṃ dadeyya, so tena adhikārena pañcahi kāmaguṇehi samappito samaṅgibhūto paricareyya, tassa evam assa: mayā kho pubbe rañño adhikāro kato, tassa me rājā tuṭṭho adhikāraṃ adāsi, svāhaṃ tato ṅidānaṃ imaṃ evarūpaṃ vedanaṃ vediyāmīti; yathā vā pana mahārāja kocid-eva puriso kusalaṃ kammaṃ katvā kāyassa bhedā param-maraṇā sugatiṃ saggaṃ lokaṃ uppajjeyya, so tattha dibbehi pañcahi kāmaguṇehi samappito samangibhūto paricareyya, tassa evam-assa: ahaṃ kho pubbe kusalaṃ kammaṃ akāsiṃ, so 'haṃ tato ṅidānaṃ imaṃ evarūpaṃ vedanaṃ vediyāmīti; evam-eva kho mahārāja vedayitalakkhaṇā c' eva vedanā anubhavanalakkhaṇā cāti. kallosi bhante nāgasenāti.

94 bhante nāgasena, kiṃlakkhaṇā saññā ti. sañjānanalakkhaṇā mahārāja saññā; kiṃ sañjānāti: nīlam-pi sañjānāti, pītam-pi sañjānāti, lohitam-pi sañjānāti, odātam-pi sañjānāti, mañjeṭṭham-pi sañjānāti; evaṃ kho mahārāja

as the eye and the second as the visible form. When they come together, there is sensory contact."

"Another example, please."

"Think of two cymbals clashing, with one the eye and the other the visible form. When they come together, there is sensory contact."

"You are wise, Nagasena."

The king asked: "What is the defining characteristic of 93
feeling?" "Feeling has as its defining characteristics that *it is felt* and that *it is experienced*, great king."

"Give an analogy."

"Suppose a man does a service for the king, and the king is pleased, so he gives him an official position. The man comes to be prosperous and well provisioned with the pleasures of the five senses, and roves about saying, 'I did a service for the king, and, pleased, he gave me an official position. That is the source of the feelings I am now feeling.' Or say that a certain person creates good karma, so that when his body gives out and he dies, he is reborn in a blissful and heavenly realm. Prosperous and provisioned with the divine pleasures of the five senses there, he goes around saying, 'I created good karma in the past. This is the source of the feelings I am now feeling.' Similarly, great king, feeling is defined as what is felt and what is experienced."

"You are wise, Nagasena.

"Nagasena, sir, what is the defining characteristic of 94
perception?" "The defining characteristic of perception is *the act of perceiving*. What does one perceive? One perceives blue, yellow, brown, white, and red. In this way, perception is defined as the act of perceiving."

sañjānanalakkhaṇā saññā ti. opammaṃ karohīti. yathā mahārāja rañño bhaṇḍāgāriko bhaṇḍāgāraṃ pavisitvā nīla-pīta-lohit-odāta-mañjeṭṭhāni rājabhogāni rūpāni passitvā sañjānāti, evam-eva kho mahārāja sañjānanalakkhaṇā saññā ti. kallosi bhante nāgasenāti.

95 bhante nāgasena, kiṃlakkhaṇā cetanā ti. cetayitalakkhaṇā mahārāja cetanā abhisaṅkharaṇalakkhaṇā cāti. opammaṃ karohīti. yathā mahārāja kocid-eva puriso visaṃ abhisaṅkharitvā attanā ca piveyya pare ca pāyeyya, so attanā pi dukkhito bhaveyya, pare pi dukkhitā bhaveyyuṃ, evam-eva kho mahārāja idh' ekacco puggalo akusalaṃ kammaṃ cetanāya cetayitvā kāyassa bhedā param-maraṇā apāyaṃ duggatiṃ vinipātaṃ nirayaṃ uppajjeyya, ye pi tassa anusikkhanti te pi kāyassa bhedā param-maraṇā apāyaṃ duggatiṃ vinipātaṃ nirayaṃ uppajjanti.

96 yathā vā pana mahārāja kocid-eva puriso sappi-navanīta-tela-madhu-phāṇitaṃ ekajjhaṃ abhisaṅkharitvā attanā ca piveyya pare ca pāyeyya, so attanā pi sukhito bhaveyya, pare pi sukhitā bhaveyyuṃ, evam-eva kho mahārāja idh' ekacco puggalo kusalaṃ kammaṃ cetanāya cetayitvā kāyassa bhedā param-maraṇā sugatiṃ saggaṃ lokaṃ uppajjati, ye pi tassa anusikkhanti te pi kāyassa bhedā param-maraṇā sugatiṃ saggaṃ lokaṃ uppajjanti. evaṃ kho mahārāja cetayitalakkhaṇā cetanā abhisaṅkharaṇalakkhaṇā cāti. kallosi bhante nāgasenāti.

"Give an analogy."

"The surveyor of the royal storeroom enters the storeroom and looks at the beautiful royal possessions, noting that they are blue, yellow, brown, white, and red, and in this way perceives them. Similarly, perception is defined as the act of perceiving."

"You are wise, Nagasena.

"Nagasena, what is the defining characteristic of inten- 95
tion?" "Great king, intention has *what is intended* and *the act of concocting* as its defining characteristics."

"Please give an analogy."

"Just as a man who concocts a poison and makes himself and someone else drink it causes both himself and the other to become afflicted, so it is in this case. Similarly, a person forms an intention to create bad karma; when his body gives out and he dies, he is reborn in a woeful and punishing hell, and those who imitate him also are reborn in a woeful and punishing hell after death.

Or consider a man who concocts ghee, fresh butter, oil, 96
honey, and raw sugar in a single mixture, and drinks it himself and makes another drink it. He takes pleasure in it and causes the other person to enjoy it too. Similarly, a person forms an intention to create good karma, and when his body gives out and he dies, he is reborn in a blissful and heavenly realm; those who imitate him are also reborn in a blissful and heavenly realm after death. In this way, great king, intention is defined as what is intended and the act of concocting."

"You are wise, Nagasena."

97 bhante nāgasena, kiṃlakkhanaṃ viññāṇan-ti. vijānanalakkhaṇaṃ mahārāja viññāṇan-ti. opammaṃ karohīti. yathā mahārāja nagaraguttiko majjhe nagare siṅghāṭake nisinno passeyya puratthimadisato purisaṃ āgacchantaṃ, passeyya dakkhiṇadisato purisaṃ āgacchantaṃ, passeyya pacchimadisato purisaṃ āgacchantaṃ, passeyya uttaradisato purisaṃ āgacchantaṃ, evam-eva kho mahārāja yañ-ca puriso cakkhunā rūpaṃ passati taṃ viññāṇena vijānāti, yañ-ca sotena saddaṃ suṇāti taṃ viññāṇena vijānāti, yañ-ca ghānena gandhaṃ ghāyati taṃ viññāṇena vijānāti, yañ-ca jivhāya rasaṃ sāyati taṃ viññāṇena vijānāti, yañ-ca kāyena phoṭṭhabbaṃ phusati taṃ viññāṇena vijānāti, yañ-ca manasā dhammaṃ vijānāti taṃ viññāṇena vijānāti. evaṃ kho mahārāja vijānanalakkhaṇaṃ viññāṇan-ti. kallosi bhante nāgasenāti.

98 bhante nāgasena, kiṃlakkhaṇo vitakko ti. appanālakkhaṇo mahārāja vitakko ti. opammaṃ karohīti. yathā mahārāja vaḍḍhaki suparikammakataṃ dāruṃ sandhismiṃ appeti, evaṃ kho mahārāja appanālakkhaṇo vitakko ti. kallosi bhante nāgasenāti.

99 bhante nāgasena, kiṃlakkhaṇo vicāro ti. anumajjanalakkhaṇo mahārāja vicāro ti. opammaṃ karo-hīti. yathā mahārāja kaṃsathālaṃ ākoṭitaṃ pacchā anuravati anusandahati;

"Nagasena, what is the defining characteristic of aware- 97
ness?"[19] "Great king, awareness has *the act of being aware* as its defining characteristic."

"Give an analogy."

"A city's security guard sits in the middle of the city square and looks in all four directions for people arriving from the east, south, west, and north. Similarly, great king, a person who sees a visible form with the eye notices it by means of awareness; hearing a sound with the ear, he notices it by means of awareness; smelling an odor with the nose, he notices it by means of awareness; savoring a taste with the tongue, he notices it by means of awareness; feeling touch with the body, he notices it by means of awareness; and apprehending a phenomenal state with the mind, he notices it by means of awareness. In this way, awareness is defined as the act of being aware."

"You are wise, Nagasena.

"Nagasena, what is the defining characteristic of initial 98
thought?" "Initial thought has *fixing the thought on its object* as its defining characteristic, great king."

"Please give an analogy."

"It is just like when a carpenter inserts a well-prepared piece of wood into a socket. Initial thought is defined as fixing the thought on its object."

"You are wise, Nagasena.

"Nagasena, what is the defining characteristic of delib- 99
eration?" "Great king, deliberation has *applying continuous pressure* as its defining characteristic."

"Give an analogy."

yathā mahārāja ākoṭanā evaṃ vitakko daṭṭhabbo, yathā anuravanā evaṃ vicāro daṭṭhabboti. kallosi bhante nāgasenāti.

tatiyo vaggo.

"It is just like how, when a bronze gong is struck, it resonates and reverberates afterward. Like this, great king, the initial thought should be seen as the striking, and deliberation is the resonating."

"You are wise, Nagasena."

End of Section Three.

100 rājā āha: bhante nāgasena, sakkā imesaṃ dhammānaṃ ekatobhāvagatānaṃ vinibbhujitvā vinibbhujitvā nānākaraṇaṃ paññāpetuṃ: ayaṃ phasso, ayaṃ vedanā, ayaṃ saññā, ayaṃ cetanā, idaṃ viññāṇaṃ, ayaṃ vitakko, ayaṃ vicāro ti. na sakkā mahārāja imesaṃ dhammānaṃ ekatobhāvagatānaṃ vinibbhujitvā vinibbhujitvā nānākaraṇaṃ paññāpetuṃ: ayaṃ phasso, ayaṃ vedanā, ayaṃ saññā, ayaṃ cetanā, idaṃ viññāṇaṃ, ayaṃ vitakko, ayaṃ vicāro ti. opammaṃ karohīti.

101 yathā mahārāja rañño sūdo yūsaṃ vā rasaṃ vā kareyya, so tattha dadhim-pi pakkhipeyya, loṇam pi pakkhipeyya, siṅgiveram-pi pakkhipeyya, jīrakam-pi pakkhipeyya, maricam-pi pakkhipeyya, aññāni pi pakārāni pakkhipeyya; tam-enaṃ rājā evaṃ vadeyya: dadhissa me rasaṃ āhara, loṇassa me rasaṃ āhara, siṅgiverassa me rasaṃ āhara, jīrakassa me rasaṃ āhara, maricassa me rasaṃ āhara, sabbesaṃ me pakkhittānaṃ rasaṃ āharāti; sakkā nu kho mahārāja tesaṃ rasānaṃ ekatobhāvaṅ-gatānaṃ vinibbhujitvā vinibbhujitvā rasaṃ āharituṃ ambilattaṃ vā lavaṇattaṃ vā tittattaṃ vā kaṭukattaṃ vā kasāyattaṃ vā madhurattaṃ vā ti.

102 na hi bhante sakkā tesaṃ rasānaṃ ekatobhāvaṅ-gatānaṃ vinibbhujitvā vinibbhujitvā rasaṃ āharituṃ: ambilattaṃ vā lavaṇattaṃ vā tittattaṃ vā kaṭukattaṃ vā kasāyattaṃ vā madhurattaṃ vā, api ca kho pana sakena sakena lakkhaṇena upaṭṭhahantīti. evam-eva kho mahārāja na sakkā imesaṃ dhammānaṃ ekatobhāvagatānaṃ vinibbhujitvā vinibbhujitvā nānākaraṇaṃ paññāpetuṃ: ayaṃ phasso, ayaṃ vedanā,

The king asked: "Nagasena, sir, is it possible to distinguish each of the phenomenal states in the course of their arising together? And then to analyze the differences: this one is sensory contact, this is feeling, this is perception, this is intention, this is awareness, this is initial thought, this is deliberation?" 100

"No, great king, it is not possible in the course of their arising together to distinguish each of the phenomenal states, analyzing the differences: this one is sensory contact, this is feeling, this is perception, this is intention, this is awareness, this is initial thought, this is deliberation."

"Pleases give an analogy."

"It is just like the royal chef who prepares a soup or a savory rasam.* He puts in curds, salt, ginger, cumin, black pepper, and various other ingredients. The king may request: 'Bring me the taste of curds, bring me the taste of salt, bring me the tastes of ginger, cumin, or black pepper, or of everything put into it.' But would we say that the king is able to distinguish each of the tastes in their blending together in a single preparation? Could he detect the sourness, saltiness, bitterness, pungency, astringency, or sweetness?" 101

"No, he wouldn't be able to distinguish each of the tastes in their blending together in the rasam, the sourness, saltiness, bitterness, pungency, astringency, or sweetness, despite how each one puts forth its defining characteristic." 102

"In the same way, great king, it is not possible in the course of their arising together to distinguish each of the phenomenal states, analyzing the differences: This one is sensory

* A thin soup.

ayaṃ saññā, ayaṃ cetanā, idaṃ viññāṇaṃ, ayaṃ vitakko, ayaṃ vicāro ti, api ca kho pana sakena sakena lakkhaṇena upaṭṭhahantīti. kallosi bhante nāgasenāti.

103 thero āha: loṇaṃ mahārāja cakkhuviññeyyan-ti. āma bhante, cakkhuviññeyyan-ti. suṭṭhu kho mahārāja jānāhīti. kim-pana bhante jivhāviññeyyan-ti. āma mahārāja, jivhāviññeyyan-ti. kim-pana bhante sabbaṃ loṇaṃ jivhāya vijānātīti. āma mahārāja, sabbaṃ loṇaṃ jivhāya vijānātīti. yadi bhante sabbaṃ loṇaṃ jivhāya vijānāti, kissa pana taṃ sakaṭehi balivaddā āharanti, nanu loṇam-eva āharitabban-ti. na sakkā mahārāja loṇam-eva āharituṃ, ekatobhāvaṅgatā ete dhammā, gocaranānattaṅ-gatā: loṇaṃ garubhāvo cāti. sakkā pana mahārāja loṇaṃ tulāya tulayitun-ti. āma bhante, sakkā ti. na sakkā mahārāja loṇaṃ tulāya tulayituṃ, garubhāvo tulāya tulīyatīti. kallosi bhante nāgasenāti.

nāgasena-milindarāja-pañhā niṭṭhitā.

contact, this is feeling, this is perception, this is intention, this is awareness, this is initial thought, this is deliberation. Yet it is true that each one puts forth its defining characteristic."

"You are wise, Nagasena."

Then the elder asked: "Great king, is salt to be known by 103
the eye?" "Yes, sir, it is to be known by the eye." "Be careful here as you figure this out, great king."

"Then is it to be known by the tongue?" "Yes, great king, it is to be known by the tongue."

"Is salt known only by the tongue, sir?" "Yes, salt is known only by the tongue."

"But sir, if salt is known only by the tongue, how is it that we can see it being loaded up on ox-driven carts? Is it the actual saltiness that is being loaded up?" "No, great king, it is not the actual saltiness that is being loaded up. It happens that these things go together as one since they occur in a sensory field that has multiple things in it. Salt is also heavy. Does this mean that it is to be perceived by the body, since it is possible to weigh it with a scale?" "Yes, it is possible."

"No, great king, it is not possible to weigh the saltiness with a scale; it is the heaviness that is being weighed with a scale."[20]

"You are wise, Nagasena."

End of Questions of Milinda to Nagasena.

PART 2

104 rājā āha: bhante nāgasena, yān' imāni pañc' āyatanāni kin-nu tāni nānākammehi nibbattāni udāhu ekena kammenāti. nānākammehi mahārāja nibbattāni, na ekena kammenāti. opammaṃ karohīti. taṃ kimmaññasi mahārāja: ekasmiṃ khette pañca bījāni vapeyyuṃ, tesaṃ nānābījānaṃ nānāphalāni nibbatteyyun-ti. āma bhante, nibbatteyyun-ti. evam-eva kho mahārāja yān imāni pañc' āyatanāni tāni nānākammehi nibbattāni, na ekena kammenāti. kallosi bhante nāgasenāti.

105 rājā āha: bhante nāgasena, kena kāraṇena manussā na sabbe samakā, aññe appāyukā aññe dīghāyukā, aññe bahvābādhā aññe appābādhā, aññe dubbaṇṇā aññe vaṇṇavanto, aññe appesakkhā aññe mahesakkhā, aññe appabhogā aññe mahābhogā, aññe nīcakulīnā aññe mahākulīnā, aññe duppaññā aññe paññāvanto ti. thero āha: kissa pana mahārāja rukkhā na sabbe samakā, aññe ambilā aññe lavaṇā aññe tittakā aññe kaṭukā aññe kasāvā aññe madhurā ti. maññāmi bhante bījānaṃ nānākaraṇenāti.

106 evam-eva kho mahārāja kammānaṃ nānākaraṇena manussā na sabbe samakā, aññe appāyukā aññe dīghāyukā, aññe bahvābādhā aññe appābādhā, aññe dubbaṇṇā aññe vaṇṇavanto, aññe appesakkhā aññe mahesakkhā, aññe appabhogā aññe mahābhogā, aññe nīcakulīnā aññe mahākulīnā, aññe duppaññā aññe paññāvanto. bhāsitam-p' etaṃ mahārāja

PART 2

Questions for Resolving Doubt

The king asked: "Revered Nagasena, do the five sensory 104
bases arise from one karma or many?" "Great king, they arise from many karmas, not just one."

"Give an analogy."

"What do you think, great king? Suppose five seeds were planted in a single field. Wouldn't there be many fruits that come from these different seeds?" "Yes, sir." "It is the same for the five sensory bases, great king. They arise from many karmas, not just one."

"You are wise, Nagasena."

The king asked: "Nagasena, why aren't all people the same, 105
instead of some being short-lived, others long-lived; some sickly, others healthy; some ugly, others beautiful; some weak, others powerful; some poor, others rich; some born to low families, others to high families; some stupid, others wise?"

The elder asked in reply: "Why aren't all trees the same, great king, instead of some sour, others salty, some bitter, others pungent, some astringent, others sweet?" "I think, sir, that it is due to a difference in seeds."

"Similarly, it is due to a difference in karma that people 106
are not all the same. Some are short-lived, others long-lived; some are sickly, others healthy; some are ugly, others beautiful; some are weak, others powerful; some are poor, others rich; some are born to low families, others to high families; and some are stupid, while others are wise. For the Bhagavan said this: 'Student, beings have their own karma. They

bhagavatā: kammassakā māṇava sattā, kammadāyādā kammayonī kammabandhū kammapaṭisaraṇā, kammaṃ satte vibhajati, yad-idaṃ hīnappaṇītatāyāti. kallosi bhante nāgasenāti.

107 rājā āha: bhante nāgasena, tumhe bhaṇatha: kin-ti imaṃ dukkhaṃ nirujjheyya aññañ-ca dukkhaṃ na uppajjeyyāti. etadatthā mahārāja amhākaṃ pabbajjā ti. kiṃ paṭigacc' eva vāyamitena, nanu sampatte kāle vāyamitabban-ti. thero āha: sampatte kāle mahārāja vāyāmo akiccakaro bhavati, paṭigacc' eva vāyāmo kiccakaro bhavatīti. opammaṃ karohīti. taṃ kimmaññasi mahārāja: yadā tvaṃ pipāsito bhaveyyāsi tadā tvaṃ udapānaṃ khaṇāpeyyāsi taḷākaṃ khaṇāpeyyāsi: pānīyaṃ pivissāmīti. na hi bhante ti. evam-eva kho mahārāja sampatte kāle vāyāmo akiccakaro bhavati, paṭigacc' eva vāyāmo kiccakaro bhavatīti. bhiyyo opammaṃ karohīti.

108 taṃ kim-maññasi mahārāja: yadā tvaṃ bubhukkhito bhaveyyāsi tadā tvaṃ khettaṃ kasāpeyyāsi sāliṃ ropāpeyyāsi dhaññaṃ atiharāpeyyāsi: bhattaṃ bhuñjissāmīti. na hi bhante ti. evam-eva kho mahārāja sampatte kāle vāyāmo akiccakaro bhavati, paṭigacc' eva vāyāmo kiccakaro bhavatīti. bhiyyo opammaṃ karohīti. taṃ kim-maññasi mahārāja: yadā te saṅgāmo paccupaṭṭhito bhaveyya tadā tvaṃ parikhaṃ khaṇāpeyyāsi pākāraṃ kārāpeyyāsi gopuraṃ kārāpeyyāsi aṭṭālakaṃ kārāpeyyāsi dhaññaṃ atiharāpeyyāsi, tadā tvaṃ hatthismiṃ sikkheyyāsi assasmiṃ sikkheyyāsi rathasmiṃ sikkheyyāsi dhanusmiṃ sikkheyyāsi tharusmiṃ sikkheyyāsīti. na hi bhante ti. evam-eva kho mahārāja sam-

inherit their karma, originate from their karma, are bound to their karma, and have karma as their refuge. It is karma that distinguishes beings as low and high.'"

"You are wise, Nagasena."

The king said: "Nagasena, you say that suffering may be 107
destroyed, and further suffering may not arise." "Yes, great king, this is the purpose for which we ordain."[21]

"But is your renunciation something that is due to previous effort, or does it require effort now?" The elder answered, "At the present time the effort is not a duty; it was when renouncing that the effort was a duty."

"Give an analogy."

"What do you think, great king? When you become thirsty, is it then that you have a well dug or a reservoir put in, so that you can then say, 'Let me take a drink'?" "No, sir." "Just so, the effort is not a duty now; it was when renouncing that the effort was a duty."

"Another analogy, please."

"What do you think, great king? When you get hungry, 108
do you then have the fields tilled, the crops planted, and the grain harvested, so that you can then say, 'Let me have my meal'?" "No, sir." "Likewise, the effort is not a duty now; it was when renouncing that the effort was a duty."

"Give another analogy."

"What do you think, great king? Is it when the battle is imminent that you dig trenches, make a fort, have a gateway put in, erect a watchtower, and harvest the grain? Do you then begin training with elephants, horses, chariots, bows, and swords?" "No, sir." "Similarly, great king, the effort is not a duty now; it was when renouncing

patte kāle vāyāmo akiccakaro bhavati, paṭigacc' eva vāyāmo kiccakaro bhavati. bhāsitam-p'etaṃ mahārāja bhagavatā:
109 paṭigacc' eva taṃ kayirā yaṃ jaññā hitam-attano; na sākaṭikacintāya, mantā' dhīro parakkame.

yathā sākaṭiko nāma samaṃ hitvā mahāpathaṃ visamaṃ
maggam-āruyha akkhacchinnova jhāyati,
evaṃ dhammā apakkamma adhammam-anuvattiya
mando maccumukhaṃ patto akkhacchinnova socatīti.

kallosi bhante nāgasenāti.

110 rājā āha: bhante nāgasena, tumhe bhaṇatha: pākatikāggito nerayiko aggi mahābhitāpataro hoti, khuddako pi pāsāṇo pākatike aggimhi pakkhitto divasam-pi dhamamāno na vilayaṃ gacchati, kūṭāgāramatto pi pāsāṇo nerayikaggimhi pakkhitto khaṇena vilayaṃ gacchatīti; etaṃ vacanaṃ na saddahāmi. evañ-ca pana vadetha: ye ca tattha uppannā sattā te anekāni pi vassasahassāni niraye paccamānā na vilayaṃ gacchantīti; tam-pi vacanaṃ na saddahāmīti.

111 thero āha: taṃ kim-maññasi mahārāja: yā tā santi makariniyo pi suṃsumāriniyo pi kacchapiniyo pi moriniyo pi kapotiniyo pi kin-nu tā kakkhaḷāni pāsāṇāni sakkharāyo ca khādantīti. āma bhante, khādantīti. kim-pana tāni tāsaṃ kucchiyaṃ koṭṭhabbhantaragatāni vilayaṃ gacchantīti. āma bhante, vilayaṃ gacchantīti. yo pana tāsaṃ kucchiyaṃ gabbho so pi vilayaṃ gacchatīti. na hi bhante ti. kena kāraṇenāti. maññāmi bhante kammādhikatena na vilayaṃ gacchatīti.

that the effort was a duty. For the Bhagavan said this:

> Since one expects and knows what is to one's own benefit, one should do it. 109
> Be wise and steadfast in striving, avoiding the worries of the cart driver.
> For just as the cart driver on the level high road frets when he turns onto a bumpy lane and his axle breaks, the dimwit who swerves away from the Dhamma and pursues what is not right arrives at the maw of Death grieving his broken axle."

"You are wise, Nagasena."

The king asked: "Nagasena, you say that the fire of hell 110
is much hotter than ordinary fire, and that even if a small rock were thrown into an ordinary fire and left there all day, it would still not melt. But then, a boulder the size of a two-story house would liquefy in an instant if thrown into the fire of hell. I just can't believe this claim. And then you say that many beings have been born in hell and have roasted there for thousands of years without burning up. I don't believe this assertion either."

The elder replied: "What do you think, great king? Don't 111
female sea monsters, crocodiles, turtles, peahens, and pigeons take in gravel and pebbles?" "Yes, they do consume this." "And doesn't it get burned up in their stomachs and intestines?" "Yes, it gets burned up." "But does the embryo in the creature's womb get burned up too?" "No, sir." "And why is this?" "I think it is because of karma that it is not burned up."

112 evam eva kho mahārāja kammādhikatena nerayikā sattā anekāni pi vassasahassāni niraye paccamānā na vilayaṃ gacchanti bhāsitam-p' etaṃ mahārāja bhagavatā: so na tāva kālaṃ karoti yāva na taṃ pāpaṃ kammaṃ byantihotīti. bhiyyo opammaṃ karohīti. taṃ kim-maññasi mahārāja: yā tā santi sīhiniyo pi byagghiniyo pi dīpiniyo pi kukkuriniyo pi kin-nu tā kakkhaḷāni aṭṭhikāni maṃsāni khādantīti. āma bhante, khādantīti. kim-pana tāni tāsaṃ kucchiyaṃ koṭṭhabbhantaragatāni vilayaṃ gacchantīti. āma bhante, vilayaṃ gacchantīti. yo pana tāsaṃ kucchiyaṃ gabbho so pi vilayaṃ gacchatīti. na hi bhante ti. kena kāraṇenāti. maññāmi bhante kammādhikatena na vilayaṃ gacchatīti.

113 evam-eva kho mahārāja kammādhikatena nerayikā sattā anekāni pi vassasahassāni niraye paccamānā na vilayaṃ gacchantīti. bhiyyo opammaṃ karohīti. taṃ kim-maññasi mahārāja: yā tā santi yonakasukhumāliniyo pi khattiyasukhumāliniyo pi brāhmaṇasukhumāliniyo pi gahapatisukhumāliniyo pi kin-nu tā kakkhaḷāni khajjakāni maṃsāni khādantīti. āma bhante, khādantīti. kim-pana tāni tāsaṃ kucchiyaṃ koṭṭhabbhantaragatāni vilayaṃ gacchantīti. āma bhante, vilayaṃ gacchantīti. Yo pana tāsaṃ kucchiyaṃ gabbho so pi vilayaṃ gacchatīti. na hi bhante ti. kena kāraṇenāti. Maññāmi bhante kammādhikatena na vilayaṃ gacchatīti. evam eva kho marāja kammādhikatena nerayikā sattā anekāni pi vassasahassāni niraye paccamānā na vilayaṃ gacchanti. bhāsitam-p'etaṃ mahārāja bhagavatā: so na tāva kālaṃ karoti yāva na taṃ pāpaṃ kammaṃ byantihotīti. kallosi bhante nāgasenāti.

"Exactly, great king. It is because of their karma that the many beings roasting in hell for thousands of years do not get burned up. For it was said by the Bhagavan: 'No one dies until their evil karma is exhausted.'" 112

"Please give another analogy."

"What do you think, great king? Don't female lions, tigers, leopards, and dogs eat hard bits of bone along with meat?" "They do eat this." "And doesn't it get burned up in their stomachs and intestines?" "Yes, it gets burned up." "But does the embryo in the womb also get burned up?" "No, sir." "And why not?" "I think, sir, that it is due to karma that it does not get burned up."

"Exactly, great king. It is because of their karma that the many beings roasting in hell for thousands of years do not get burned up." 113

"Another analogy, please."

"There are refined women among the Yonakas, the Kshatriyas, the Brahmans, and prominent householders who eat meat and solid food with hard bits." "Indeed they do." "And this gets burned up in their stomachs and intestines." "Yes, of course it does." "And yet their embryos do not get burned up in the womb." "No, sir." "And why not, great king?" "I think that it is because of karma that they are not destroyed."

"So too, it is because of their karma that the many beings roasting in hell for thousands of years do not get burned up. For the Bhagavan said: 'No one dies until their evil karma is exhausted.'"

"You are wise, Nagasena."

114 rājā āha: bhante nāgasena, tumhe bhaṇatha: ayaṃ mahāpaṭhavī udake patiṭṭhitā, udakaṃ vāte patiṭṭhitaṃ, vāto ākāse patiṭṭhito ti; etam-pi vacanaṃ na saddahāmīti. thero dhammakarakena udakaṃ gahetvā rājānaṃ milindaṃ saññāpesi: yathā mahārāja imaṃ udakaṃ vātena ādhāritaṃ evaṃ tam-pi udakaṃ vātena ādhāritan-ti. kallosi bhante nāgasenāti.

115 rājā āha: bhante nāgasena, nirodho nibbānan-ti. āma mahārāja, nirodho nibbānan-ti. katham bhante nāgasena nirodho nibbānan-ti. sabbe bālaputhujjanā kho mahārāja ajjhattika-bāhire āyatane abhinandanti abhivadanti ajjhosāya tiṭṭhanti, te tena sotena vuyhanti, na parimuccanti jātiyā jarāmaraṇena sokena paridevena dukkhehi domanassehi upāyāsehi, na parimuccanti dukkhasmā ti vadāmi. sutavā ca kho mahārāja ariyasāvako ajjhattika-bāhire āyatane nābhinandati nābhivadati nājjhosāya tiṭṭhati, tassa taṃ anabhinandato anabhivadato anajjhosāya tiṭṭhato taṇhā nirujjhati, taṇhānirodhā upādānanirodho, upādānanirodhā bhavanirodho, bhavanirodhā jātinirodho, jātinirodhā jarā-maraṇaṃ soka-parideva-dukkha-domanass-upāyāsā nirujjhanti, evam-etassa kevalassa dukkhakkhandhassa nirodho hoti. evaṃ kho mahārāja nirodho nibbānan-ti. kallosi bhante nāgasenāti.

116 rājā āha: bhante nāgasena, sabbeva labhanti nibbānan-ti. na kho mahārāja sabbeva labhanti nibbānaṃ, api ca kho

The king said: “Nagasena, sir, you say that ‘the great earth 114
rests on water, water rests on air, and air rests on space.’ I don’t believe this claim either.”

The elder picked up some water with a water strainer and turned to King Milinda. “Just as this water is held in place by air, great king, so too that water is held up by air.”[22]

“You are wise, Nagasena.”

The king said: “Nagasena, is nibbana a matter of stop- 115
ping?” “Yes, great king, nibbana is stopping.” “How is nibbana stopping, Nagasena?”

“All foolish ordinary people welcome and take pleasure in internal and external sensory experience, and get attached; they get carried away by the stream and are not free from the sorrow, grieving, suffering, distress, and trouble that are birth, old age, and death. I say that they are not free from suffering. But the noble disciple who has heard this does not welcome and take pleasure in internal and external sensory experience and does not get attached; because of not welcoming, taking pleasure in, or getting attached to this, craving ceases, and from the stopping of craving there is the stopping of clinging; from stopping clinging, there is the stopping of becoming; from stopping becoming, there is the stopping of birth, and when birth is stopped, the sorrow, grieving, suffering, distress, and trouble that are old age and death end. Thus, there is the stopping of the entire composite that is suffering. And so, great king, nibbana is stopping.”

“You are wise, Nagasena.”

The king asked: “Does everyone attain nibbana?” 116

“No, great king, not everyone attains nibbana. But whoever practices rightly knows by experience the phenomenal states

mahārāja yo sammā paṭipanno abhiññeyye dhamme abhijānāti, pariññeyye dhamme parijānāti, pahātabbe dhamme pajahati, bhāvetabbe dhamme bhāveti, sacchikātabbe dhamme sacchikaroti, so labhati nibbānan-ti. kallosi bhante nāgasenāti.

117 rājā āha: bhante nāgasena, yo na labhati nibbānaṃ jānāti so: sukhaṃ nibbānan-ti āma mahārāja, yo na labhati nibbānaṃ jānāti so: sukhaṃ nibbānan-ti. katham-bhante nāgasena alabhanto jānāti: sukhaṃ nibbānan-ti. taṃ kim-maññasi mahārāja: yesaṃ nacchinnā hatthapādā jāneyyuṃ te mahārāja: dukkhaṃ hatthapādacchedanan-ti. āma bhante, jāneyyun-ti. kathaṃ jāneyyun-ti. aññesaṃ bhante chinnahatthapādānaṃ paridevitasaddaṃ sutvā jānanti: dukkhaṃ hatthapādacchedanan-ti. evam-eva kho mahārāja yesaṃ diṭṭhaṃ nibbānaṃ tesaṃ saddaṃ sutvā jānāti: sukhaṃ nibbānan-ti. kallosi bhante nāgasenāti.

catuttho vaggo.

to be known, comprehends the phenomenal states to be comprehended, gives up the phenomenal states to be abandoned, develops the phenomenal states to be developed, and realizes the phenomenal states to be realized does attain nibbana."

"You are wise, Nagasena."

The king asked: "Nagasena, can someone who has not 117
attained nibbana know that nibbana is happiness?" "Yes, great king, one who has not attained nibbana can know that nibbana is happiness." "But how can one know that nibbana is happiness without having attained it?"

"What do you think, great king? Do people who have not had their hands and feet cut off know that getting hands and feet cut off is painful?" "Of course they know this, sir." "But how do they know?"

"They know that this is painful from hearing the wailing of those lamenting having had their hands and feet cut off." "So too, great king, having heard the reports of those who have seen nibbana, one knows that nibbana is happiness."

"You are wise, Nagasena."

End of Section Four.

118 rājā āha: bhante nāgasena, buddho tayā diṭṭho ti. na hi mahārājāti. atha te ācariyehi buddho diṭṭho ti. na hi mahārājāti. tena hi bhante nāgasena na-tthi buddho ti. kim-pana mahārāja himavati ūhānadī tayā diṭṭhā ti. na hi bhante ti. atha te pitarā ūhānadī diṭṭhā ti. na hi bhante ti. tena hi mahārāja na-tthi ūhānadī ti. atthi bhan, kiñcāpi me ūhānadī na diṭṭhā pitarā pi me ūhānadī na diṭṭhā, api ca atthi ūhānadī ti. evam-eva kho mahārāja kiñcāpi mayā bhagavā na diṭṭho ācariyehi pi me bhagavā na diṭṭho, api ca atthi bhagavā ti. kallosi bhante nāgasenāti.

119 rājā āha: bhante nāgasena, buddho anuttaro ti. āma mahārāja, bhagavā anuttaro ti. katham-bhante nāgasena adiṭṭhapubbaṃ jānāsi: buddho anuttaro ti. taṃ kim-maññasi mahārāja: yehi adiṭṭhapubbo mahāsamuddo jāneyyuṃ te mahārāja: mahanto kho mahāsamuddo gambhīro appameyyo duppariyogāho, yatth' imā pañca mahānadiyo satataṃ samitaṃ appenti, seyyathīdaṃ: gangā yamunā aciravatī sarabhū mahī, n' eva tassa ūnattaṃ vā pūrattaṃ vā paññāyatīti. āma bhante, jāneyyun-ti. evam-eva kho mahārāja sāvake mahante parinibbute passitvā jānāmi: bhagavā anuttaro ti. kallosi bhante nāgasenāti.

120 rājā āha: bhante nāgasena, sakkā jānituṃ: buddho anuttaro ti. āma mahārāja, sakkā jānituṃ: bhagavā anuttaro ti. katham-bhante nāgasena sakkā jānituṃ: buddho anuttaro ti.

The king asked: "Nagasena, sir, have you seen the Buddha?" 118
"No, great king." "Have your teachers seen the Buddha?"
"No, great king." "Then there is no Buddha, Nagasena."

"Have you seen the Uha River in the Himalayas?" "No, sir." "Has your father seen the Uha River?" "No, sir." "Then there is no Uha River, great king."

"But the Uha does exist, even though neither my father nor I have seen it."

"Likewise, the Bhagavan exists, even though neither my teachers nor I have seen him."

"You are wise, Nagasena."

The king asked: "Nagasena, is the Buddha incomparable?" 119
"Yes, great king, the Bhagavan is incomparable." "But how do you know that the Buddha is incomparable despite never having seen him?"

"What do you think, great king? Can one know, despite never having seen the ocean, that the ocean is huge, deep, immeasurable, and hard to fathom? One can understand that the five great rivers—the Ganga, the Yamuna, the Achiravati, the Sarabhu, and the Mahi—constantly and continuously flow into it, and yet it never decreases or spills over." "So one would know." "Similarly, when I consider the great disciples who have achieved final nibbana, I know that the Bhagavan is incomparable."

"You are wise, Nagasena."

The king said: "Nagasena, is it possible to know that the 120
Buddha is incomparable?" "Yes, great king, it is possible to know that the Bhagavan is incomparable." "But how is it possible to know that the Buddha is incomparable?"

bhūtapubbaṃ mahārāja tissatthero nāma lekhācariyo ahosi, bahūni vassāni abbhatītāni kālakatassa, kathaṃ so ñāyatīti. lekhena bhante ti. evam-eva kho mahārāja yo dhammaṃ passati so bhagavantaṃ passati, dhammo hi mahārāja bhagavatā desito ti. kallosi bhante nāgasenāti.

121 rājā āha: bhante nāgasena, dhammo tayā diṭṭho ti. buddhanettiyā kho mahārāja buddhapaññattiyā yāvajīvaṃ sāvakehi vattitabban-ti. kallosi bhante nāgasenāti.

122 rājā āha: bhante nāgasena, na ca saṅkamati paṭisandahati cāti. āma mahārāja, na ca saṅkamati paṭisandahati cāti. katham-bhante nāgasena na ca saṅkamati paṭisandahati ca, opammaṃ karohīti. yathā mahārāja kocid-eva puriso padīpato padīpaṃ padīpeyya, kin-nu kho so mahārāja padīpo padīpamhā saṅkanto ti. na hi bhante ti. evam-eva kho mahārāja na ca saṅkamati paṭisandahati cāti. bhiyyo opammaṃ karohīti.

123 abhijānāsi nu tvaṃ mahārāja daharako santo silokācariyassa santike kañci silokaṃ gahitan-ti. āma bhante ti. kin-nu kho mahārāja so siloko ācariyamhā saṅkanto ti. na hi bhante ti. evam-eva kho mahārāja na ca saṅkamati paṭisandahati cāti. kallosi bhante nāgasenāti.

124 rājā āha: bhante nāgasena, vedagū upalabbhatīti. thero āha: paramatthena kho mahārāja vedagū na upalabbhatīti. kallosi bhante nāgasenāti.

"Formerly there was an instructor in writing who was known as the Elder Tissa. Many years have passed since he died, so how is it that he is still known?" "By his writing, sir." "Likewise, great king, whoever sees the Dhamma sees the Bhagavan, for the Dhamma was taught by the Bhagavan."

"You are wise, Nagasena."

The king asked: "Nagasena, sir, have you seen the 121
Dhamma?"

"Disciples must proceed the length of our lives with the Buddha as our guide and under the Buddha's mandate, great king."

"You are wise, Nagasena."

The king asked: "Nagasena, can something be transferred 122
without transmigrating?" "Yes, great king, something can be transferred without transmigrating." "How can this be? Please give an example."

"Suppose someone were to light a lamp from another lamp. Would the lamp transmigrate from the first lamp?" "No, sir." "So there is something that can be transferred without transmigrating."

"Give another example, please."

"Do you recall being a youth and learning a verse from a 123
poetry teacher, great king?" "Yes, sir." "Did the verse transmigrate from the teacher?" "No, sir." "So there is something that can be transferred without transmigrating, great king."

"You are wise, Nagasena."

The king asked: "Nagasena, sir, can a 'knower' be found?" 124

The elder replied: "In the absolute sense, great king, no knower can be found."

"You are wise, Nagasena."

125 rājā āha: bhante nāgasena, atthi koci satto yo imamhā kāyā aññaṃ kāyaṃ saṅkamatīti. na hi mahārājāti. yadi bhante nāgasena imamhā kāyā aññaṃ kāyaṃ saṅkamanto na-tthi, nanu mutto bhavissati pāpakehi kammehīti. āma mahārāja, yadi na paṭisandaheyya mutto bhavissati pāpakehi kammehi; yasmā ca kho mahārāja paṭisandahati, tasmā na parimutto pāpakehi kammehīti. opammaṃ karohīti.

126 yathā mahārāja kocid-eva puriso aññatarassa purisassa ambaṃ avahareyya, kiṃ so daṇḍappatto bhaveyyāti. āma bhante, daṇḍappatto bhaveyyāti. na kho so mahārāja tāni ambāni avahari yāni tena ropitāni, kasmā daṇḍappatto bhaveyyāti. tāni bhante ambāni nissāya jātāni, tasmā daṇḍappatto bhaveyyāti. evam-eva kho mahārāja iminā nāmarūpena kammaṃ karoti sobhanaṃ vā asobhanaṃ vā, tena kammena aññaṃ nāmarūpaṃ paṭisandahati, tasmā na parimutto pāpakehi kammehīti. kallosi bhante nāgasenāti.

127 rājā āha: bhante nāgasena, iminā nāmarūpena kammaṃ kataṃ kusalaṃ vā akusalaṃ vā, kuhiṃ tāni kammāni tiṭṭhantīti. anubandheyyuṃ kho mahārāja tāni kammāni 'chāyāva anapāyinī' ti. sakkā pana bhante tāni kammāni dassetuṃ: idha vā idha vā tāni kammāni tiṭṭhantīti. na sakkā mahārāja tāni kammāni dassetuṃ: idha vā idha vā' tāni kammāni tiṭṭhantīti. opammaṃ karohīti.

128 taṃ kim-maññasi mahārāja: yān' imāni rukkhāni anibbattaphalāni sakkā tesaṃ phalāni dassetuṃ: idha vā idha vā tāni phalāni tiṭṭhantīti. na hi bhante ti. evam-eva kho mahārāja abbocchinnāya santatiyā na sakkā tāni kammāni dassetuṃ:

The king asked: "Is there a living entity that is transferred 125
from one body to another body?" "No, great king." "But sir, if there is nothing transferred from one body to another body, then one must be released from evil karma."

"To be sure, great king, if one is not reborn, then one will be released from evil karma. But as long as one is reborn, one is not fully released from evil karma."

"Give an analogy."

"It is just like the person who steals mangos from another 126
person. Should he be punished?" "Yes, he should be punished." "But if he did not steal the mangos that had been planted by the other person, why should he be punished?" "Because they were produced from his mangos, and so he should be punished."

"It is the same in this case, great king. With this name-and-form one makes beautiful or ugly karma, and by this karma another name-and-form is born. And so one is not fully released from evil karma."

"You are wise, Nagasena."

The king asked: "Say that good or bad karma is created by 127
this name-and-form. Where do these karmas stay?" "These karmas would follow much as a shadow invariably follows, great king." "Is it possible to point out these karmas as staying here or there?" "No, it is not possible to point out karmas as staying here or there."

"Please give an analogy."

"What do you think, great king? Is it possible to point to 128
the fruits of trees that have not yet produced fruit, saying that these fruits stay here or that they stay there?" "No, sir." "Similarly, as long as there is unbroken continuity, it is not

idha vā idha vā tāni kammāni tiṭṭhantīti. kallosi bhante nāgasenāti.

129 rājā āha: bhante nāgasena, yo uppajjati jānāti so: uppajjissāmīti. āma mahārāja, yo uppajjati jānāti so: uppajjissāmīti. opammaṃ karohīti. yathā mahārāja kassako gahapatiko bījāni paṭhaviyaṃ nikkhipitvā sammā deve vassante jānāti: dhaññaṃ nibbattissatīti. Āma bhante, jāneyyāti. evam-eva kho mahārāja yo uppajjati jānāti so: uppajjissāmīti. kallosi bhante nāgasenāti.

130 rājā āha: bhante nāgasena, buddho atthīti. āma mahārāja, bhagavā atthīti. sakkā pana bhante nāgasena buddho nidassetuṃ: idha vā idha vā ti. parinibbuto mahārāja bhagavā anupādisesāya nibbānadhātuyā, na sakkā bhagavā nidassetuṃ: idha vā idha vā ti. opammaṃ karohīti. taṃ kim-maññasi mahārāja: mahato aggikkhandhassa jalamānassa yā acci atthaṅgatā sakkā sā acci dassetuṃ: idha vā idha vā ti. na hi bhante, niruddhā sā acci, appaññattiṃ gatā ti. evam eva kho mahārāja bhagavā anupādisesāya nibbānadhātuyā pari-

possible to point out the karmas, saying that these karmas stay here or there."

"You are wise, Nagasena."

The king said: "Nagasena, does one who is going to be 129
reborn know *I will be reborn?*" "Yes, one knows that one will be reborn, great king."

"Give an analogy."

"Does the farmer who plants seeds in the earth know that when the sky sheds ample rain, the crops will grow?" "Yes, he would know this."

"It is the same for someone being reborn, great king. One knows *I will be reborn.*"

"You are wise, Nagasena."

The king asked: "Does the Buddha exist?" "Yes, great king, 130
the Bhagavan exists." "But can one point to the Buddha as being here or there?"

"Great king, the Bhagavan attained final nibbana, the domain of nibbana where there is no remaining material support, so one cannot point to the Bhagavan as being here or there."

"Please give an analogy."

"What do you think, great king? When the flame from a huge raging fire goes out, can one point to the flame and say that it is here or there?" "No, sir, when a flame has stopped, it cannot be located."

nibbuto, atthaṅgato bhagavā na sakkā nidassetuṃ: idha vā idha vā ti; dhammakāyena pana kho mahārāja sakkā bhagavā nidassetuṃ, dhammo hi mahārāja bhagavatā desito ti. kallosi bhante nāgasenāti.

pañcamo vaggo.

"So it is with the Bhagavan who has attained final nibbana, the domain of nibbana where there is no remaining material support. The Bhagavan has disappeared, and it is not possible to say that he is here or there. However, one can point to the Bhagavan with the body of the Dhamma, because the Dhamma was taught by the Bhagavan."

"You are wise, Nagasena."

End of Section Five.

131 rājā āha: bhante nāgasena, piyo pabbajitānaṃ kayo ti. na kho mahārāja piyo pabbajitānaṃ kāyo ti. atha kissa nu kho bhante kelāyatha mamāyathāti. kim-pana te mahārāja kadāci karahaci saṅgāmagatassa kaṇḍappahāro hotīti. āma bhante, hotīti. kin-nu kho mahārāja so vaṇo ālepena ca ālimpīyati telena ca makkhīyati sukhumena ca coḷapaṭṭena palivеṭhīyatīti. āma bhante, ālepena ca ālimpīyati telena ca makkhīyati sukhumena ca coḷapaṭṭena paliveṭhīyatīti. kin-nu kho mahārāja piyo te vaṇo, yena ālepena ca ālimpīyati telena ca makkhīyati sukhumena ca coḷapaṭṭena paliveṭhīyatīti.

132 na me bhante piyo vaṇo, api ca maṃsassa rūhanatthāya ālepena ca ālimpīyati telena ca makkhīyati sukhumena ca coḷapaṭṭena paliveṭhīyatīti. evam-eva kho mahārāja appiyo pabbajitānaṃ kāyo, atha ca pabbajitā anajjhositā kāyaṃ pariharanti brahmacariyānuggahāya. api ca kho mahārāja vaṇūpamo kāyo vutto bhagavatā, tena pabbajitā vaṇam-iva kāyaṃ pariharanti anajjhositā. bhāsitam-p' etaṃ mahārāja bhagavatā: allacammapaṭicchanno navadvāro mahāvaṇo samantato paggharati asucī pūtigandhiyo ti. kallosi bhante nāgasenāti.

133 rājā āha: bhante nāgasena, buddho sabbaññū sabbadassāvī ti. āma mahārāja, bhagavā sabbaññū sabbadassāvī ti. atha kissa nu kho bhante nāgasena sāvakānaṃ anupubbena sikkhāpadaṃ paññāpesīti. atthi pana te mahārāja koci vejjo yo

The king asked: "Nagasena, sir, does a renouncer cherish 131
the body?" "No, great king, a renouncer does not cherish the body." "But then why do you care for it? And why are you possessive about it?"

"Surely you have at some point incurred an arrow wound in battle?" "Yes, sir, I have." "Surely the wound was tended with salve, daubed with oil, and wrapped with a delicate cloth, great king." "To be sure, it was tended, daubed, and wrapped in just this way, sir." "Does this mean that you cherish the wound? After all, you tend it with salve, daub it with oil, and wrap it in a delicate cloth."

"Of course not, sir. It is only to promote healing that one 132
tends the wound with salve, daubs it with oil, and wraps it in a fine cloth."

"Then it is not that a renouncer cherishes the body, great king. Renouncers take care of their bodies without clinging to them, for the sake of supporting the religious life. Moreover, great king, the Bhagavan actually likened the body to a wound and taught that renouncers are to take care of the body much as they do a wound, without clinging to it. In fact, the Bhagavan referred to the body as 'a huge wound, covered with clammy skin, having nine openings, seeping everywhere, impure, and foul-smelling.'"

"You are wise, Nagasena."

The king asked: "Is the Buddha all-knowing and all- 133
seeing?" "Yes, great king, the Bhagavan is all-knowing and all-seeing." "Then why did he lay down the monastic rules for the monks only gradually?"

"Do you have any doctors who know all the medicines in the world, great king?" "I do, sir." "Does such a doctor

imissaṃ paṭhaviyaṃ sabbabhesajjāni jānātīti. āma bhante, atthīti. kin-nu kho mahārāja so vejjo gilānakaṃ sampatte kale bhesajjaṃ pāyeti udāhu asampatte kāle ti. sampatte kāle bhante gilānakaṃ bhesajjaṃ pāyeti, no asampatte kāle ti. evam-eva kho mahārāja bhagavā sabbaññū sabbadassāvī na akāle sāvakānaṃ sikkhāpadaṃ paññāpeti, sampatte kāle sāvakānaṃ sikkhāpadaṃ paññāpeti yāvajīvaṃ anatikkam-anīyan-ti. kallosi bhante nāgasenāti.

134 rājā āha: bhante nāgasena, buddho dvattiṃsamahāpurisalakkhaṇehi samannāgato asītiyā ca anubyañjanehi parirañjito suvaṇṇavaṇṇo kañcanasannibhattaco byāmappabho ti. āma mahārāja, bhagavā dvattiṃsamahāpurisalakkhaṇehi samannāgato asītiyā ca anubyañjanehi parirañjito suvaṇṇavaṇṇo kañcanasannibhattaco byāmappabho ti. kim-pan' assa bhante mātāpitaro pi dvattiṃsa-mahāpurisalakkhaṇehi samannāgatā asītiyā ca anubyañjanehi parirañjitā suvaṇṇavaṇṇā kañcanasannibhattacā byāmappabhā ti. na hi mahārājāti. evaṃ sante kho bhante nāgasena uppajjati buddho dvattiṃsamahāpurisalakkhaṇehi samannāgato asītiyā ca anubyañjanehi parirañjito suvaṇṇavaṇṇo kañcanasannibhattaco byāmappabho ti; api ca mātusadiso vā putto hoti mātupakkho vā, pitusadiso vā putto hoti pitupakkho vā ti.

135 thero āha: atthi pana mahārāja kiñci padumaṃ satapattan-ti. āma bhante, atthīti. tassa pana kuhiṃ sambhavo ti. kaddame jāyati, udake āsīyatīti. kin-nu kho mahārāja padumaṃ kaddamena sadisaṃ vaṇṇena vā gandhena vā rasena vā ti. na hi bhante ti. atha udakena sadisaṃ vaṇṇena vā gandhena vā rasena vā ti. na hi bhante ti. evam-eva kho mahārāja bhagavā dvattiṃsamahāpurisalakkhanehi samannāgato asītiyā ca anubyañjanehi parirañjito suvaṇṇavaṇṇo

administer medicine when someone falls ill, or when there is no illness present?" "He administers medicine only when someone is ill, and at no other time."

"Just so, the Bhagavan, while all-knowing and all-seeing, did not lay down the monastic rules to the monks at an inappropriate time. Only as the occasion arose did he establish the rules that are not to be transgressed for as long as the monks live."

"You are wise, Nagasena."

The king asked: "Is it actually true that the Buddha was 134
endowed with the thirty-two marks of a great man? And that he had the eighty minor marks too? Did he really have a golden color, skin like gold, and a fathom-long halo?" "Yes, great king, the Bhagavan did have the thirty-two marks of a great man, the eighty minor marks, a golden color, skin like gold, and a fathom-long halo."

"But did his mother and father have all of these features, the thirty-two marks, and so on?" "No, great king." "But it must be that the Buddha was born with the thirty-two marks of a great man, the eighty minor marks, golden color, skin like gold, and a fathom-long halo. And we know that a child takes after the mother, or the mother's side; or it takes after the father, or the father's side."

The elder said: "Great king, is there such a thing as a 135
hundred-petal lotus?" "There is such a lotus, sir." "Where does it come from, great king?" "It is born from the mud and thrives in the water." "Does the lotus take after the mud in color, fragrance, and taste?" "No, sir." "And does the lotus take after the water in color, fragrance, and taste?" "No, sir."

"It is the same for the Bhagavan, great king. He sported

kañcanasannibhattaco byāmappabho, no c' assa mātāpitaro dvattiṃsa-mahāpurisalakkhaṇehi samannāgatā asītiyā ca anubyañjanehi parirañjitā suvaṇṇavaṇṇā kañcanasannibhattacā byāmappabhā ti. kallosi bhante nāgasenāti.

136 rājā āha: bhante nāgasena, buddho brahmacārī ti. āma mahārāja, bhagavā brahmacārī ti. tena hi bhante nāgasena buddho brahmuno sisso ti. atthi pana te mahārāja hatthipāmokkho ti. āma bhante, atthīti. kin-nu kho mahārāja so hatthī kadāci karahaci koñcanādaṃ nadatīti. āma bhante, nadatīti. tena hi mahārāja so hatthī koñcānaṃ sisso ti. na hi bhante ti. kim-pana mahārāja brahmā sabuddhiko abuddhiko ti. sabuddhiko bhante ti. tena hi mahārāja brahmā bhagavato sisso ti. kallosi bhante nāgasenāti.

137 rājā āha: bhante nāgasena, upasampadā sundarā ti. āma mahārāja, upasampadā sundarā ti. atthi pana bhante buddhassa upasampadā udāhu na-tthīti. upasampanno kho mahārāja bhagavā bodhirukkhamūle saha sabbaññutañāṇena, na-tthi bhagavato upasampadā aññehi dinnā yathā sāvakānaṃ mahārāja bhagavā sikkhāpadaṃ paññāpeti yāvajīvaṃ anatikkamanīyan-ti. kallosi bhante nāgasenāti.

138 rājā āha: bhante nāgasena, yo ca mātari matāya rodati, yo ca dhammapemena rodati, ubhinnaṃ tesaṃ rodantānaṃ kassa assu bhesajjaṃ, kassa na bhesajjan-ti. ekassa kho mahārāja assu rāga-dosa-mohehi samalaṃ uṇhaṃ, ekassa

the thirty-two marks of a great man, the eighty minor marks, a golden color, skin like gold, and a fathom-long halo, even though neither his mother nor his father had these features."

"You are wise, Nagasena."

The king asked: "Nagasena, sir, does the Buddha prac- 136
tice the religious life known as the 'conduct of the divine Brahma'?"[23] "Yes, great king, the Bhagavan practices Brahma conduct."

"Then the Buddha must be a student of Brahma."

"Do you have a state elephant, great king?" "Of course I do." "Does the elephant ever trumpet the 'heron's call'?" "Yes, it does trumpet like that." "Then the elephant must be a student of the heron, great king."

"Actually, no, it isn't."

"Is Brahma intelligent or not?" "Intelligent, sir." "Then Brahma is a student of the Bhagavan, great king."

"You are wise, Nagasena."

The king asked: "Nagasena, is ordination a beautiful 137
thing?"

"Yes, great king, ordination is beautiful."

"But was the Buddha ordained or not?"

"The Bhagavan was ordained at the root of the Bodhi Tree by achieving omniscience, great king. It is not that he was given ordination by someone else, for it was he who established the monastic rules for monks to be followed for life and never transgressed."

"You are wise, Nagasena."

The king said: "One weeps at the death of a mother, while 138
another weeps out of love for the Dhamma. For which of these two are the tears a healing medicine?"

pīti-somanassena vimalaṃ sītalaṃ; yaṃ kho mahārāja sītalaṃ taṃ bhesajjaṃ, yaṃ uṇhaṃ taṃ na bhesajjan-ti. kallosi bhante nāgasenāti.

139 rājā āha: bhante nāgasena, kiṃ nānākaranaṃ sarāgassa ca vītarāgassa cāti. eko kho mahārāja ajjhosito, eko anajjhosito ti. kiṃ etaṃ bhante: ajjhosito anajjhosito nāmāti. eko kho mahārāja atthiko, eko anatthiko ti. passām' ahaṃ bhante evarūpaṃ: yo ca sarāgo yo ca vītarāgo sabbo p' eso sobhanaṃ yeva icchati khādaniyaṃ vā bhojaniyaṃ vā, na koci pāpakaṃ icchatīti. avītarāgo kho mahārāja rasapaṭisaṃvedī ca rasarāgapaṭisaṃvedī ca bhojanaṃ bhuñjati, vītarāgo pana rasapaṭisaṃvedī bhojanaṃ bhuñjati, no ca kho rasarāgapaṭisaṃvedī ti. kallosi bhante nāgasenāti.

140 rājā āha: bhante nāgasena, paññā kuhiṃ paṭivasatīti. na katthaci mahārājāti. tena hi bhante nāgasena na-tthi paññā ti. vāto mahārāja kuhiṃ paṭivasatīti. na katthaci bhante ti. tena hi mahārāja natthi vāto ti. kallosi bhante nāgasenāti.

141 rājā āha: bhante nāgasena, yaṃ pan' etaṃ brūsi: saṃsāro ti, katamo so saṃsāro ti. idha mahārāja jāto idh' eva marati, idha mato aññatra uppajjati, tahiṃ jāto tahiṃ yeva marati, tahiṃ mato aññatra uppajjati; evaṃ kho mahārāja saṃsāro

"Great king, the tears of the first are hot and stained with passion, aversion, and delusion, while the tears of the other are cool, stainless, and accompanied by joy and delight. The cool tears are medicine; the hot are not."

"You are wise, Nagasena."

The king asked: "Revered Nagasena, what is the difference 139
between someone full of passion and one free of passion?" "One is attached, and the other is detached." "What does that mean, sir, that one is attached and the other is detached?" "One desires, the other is free of desire, great king."

"As I see it, whether one has passion or is free of it, everyone wants beautiful things, fine food, or substantial meals, and no one wants evil things."

"When eating, great king, one who is not free of passion experiences the taste of the food and feels passion for the taste. But the one free of passion experiences the taste of the food without also having passion for it."

"You are wise, Nagasena."

The king asked: "Nagasena, where does understanding 140
reside?"

"Nowhere, great king."

"Then there is no understanding."

"Where does the wind reside?"

"Nowhere, sir."

"Then there is no wind, great king."

"You are wise, Nagasena."

The king said: "Nagasena, you speak of samsara. But what 141
is samsara?" "One is born here, dies here, and after death is born elsewhere. Born there, one dies there and after death is born elsewhere. This, great king, is samsara."

hotīti. opammaṃ karohīti. yathā mahārāja kocid-eva puriso pakkaṃ ambaṃ khāditvā aṭṭhiṃ ropeyya, tato mahanto ambarukkho nibbattitvā phalāni dadeyya, atha so puriso tato pi pakkaṃ ambaṃ khāditvā aṭṭhiṃ ropeyya, tato pi mahanto ambarukkho nibbattitvā phalāni dadeyya, evam-etesaṃ rukkhānaṃ koṭi na paññāyati; evam-eva kho mahārāja idha jāto idh' eva marati, idha mato aññatra uppajjati, tahiṃ jāto tahiṃ yeva marati, tahiṃ mato aññatra uppajjati; evaṃ kho mahārāja saṃsāro hotīti. kallosi bhante nāgasenāti.

142 rājā āha: bhante nāgasena, kena atītaṃ cirakataṃ saratīti. satiyā mahārājāti. nanu bhante nāgasena cittena sarati, no satiyā ti. abhijānāsi nu tvaṃ mahārāja kiñcid-eva karaṇīyam katvā pamuṭṭhan-ti. āma bhante ti. kin-nu kho tvaṃ mahārāja tasmiṃ samaye acittako ahosīti. na hi bhante, sati tasmiṃ samaye nāhosīti. atha kasmā tvaṃ mahārāja evam āha: cittena sarati, no satiyā ti. kallosi bhante nāgasenāti.

143 rājā āha: bhante nāgasena, sabbā sati abhijānantā uppajjati udāhu kaṭumikā vā satīti. Abhijānantā pi mahārāja sati uppajjati, kaṭumikā pi satīti. evaṃ hi kho bhante nāgasena sabbā sati[3] abhijānanti, natthi kaṭumikā satīti. yadi na-tthi mahārāja kaṭumikā sati na-tthi kiñci sippikānaṃ kammāyatanehi vā sippāyatanehi vā vijjaṭṭhānehi vā karaṇīyaṃ,

"Give an analogy, please."

"Suppose a person eats a ripe mango and plants the pit. Up grows a huge mango tree, and it produces fruit. As this continues, no endpoint can be grasped. So too, great king, one is born here, dies here, and after death is born elsewhere; born there, one dies there and after death is born elsewhere. This is samsara."

"You are wise, Nagasena."

The king asked: "Nagasena, sir, how does one remember 142
what was done in the distant past?" "By memory, great king." "But isn't it remembered with the mind, not memory?"

"Have you ever had the experience of having done something that needed to be done, great king, but then forgotten that you'd done it?" "Yes, sir." "Were you lacking a mind at that time?" "No, sir. But memory was not present then."

"Then, great king, how can you say that one remembers with the mind, not with memory?"

"You are wise, Nagasena."

The king asked: "Nagasena, is every memory that comes 143
about a recognition, or is memory externally caused?" "Great king, memory occurs from recognition, and memory is externally caused."

"But surely, sir, all memory is recognition rather than being externally caused."

"But if memory were never prompted by something external then artisans would not need to study in the fields of business, craftsmanship, or the arts. Teachers would be unnecessary. It is only because memory can be

niratthakā ācariyā; yasmā ca kho mahārāja atthi kaṭumikā sati tasmā atthi kammāyatanehi vā sippāyatanehi vā vijjāyatanehi vā karaṇīyaṃ, attho ca ācariyehīti. kallosi bhante nāgasenāti.

chaṭṭho vaggo.

externally caused that things can be accomplished by learning a business, craftmanship, and the arts, and that teachers are worthwhile, great king."

"You are wise, Nagasena."

End of Section Six.

144 rājā āha: bhante nāgasena, katihi ākārehi sati uppajjatīti. soḷasahi ākārehi mahārāja sati uppajjati, katamehi soḷasahi ākārehi: abhijānato pi mahārāja sati uppajjati, kaṭumikāya pi sati uppajjati, oḷārikaviññāṇato pi sati uppajjati, hitaviññāṇato pi sati uppajjati, ahita-viññāṇato pi sati uppajjati, sabhāganimittato pi sati uppajjati, visabhāganimittato pi sati uppajjati, kathābhiññāṇato pi sati uppajjati, lakkhaṇato pi sati uppajjati, saraṇato pi sati uppajjati, muddāto pi sati uppajjati, gaṇanāto pi sati uppajjati, dhāraṇato pi sati uppajjati, bhāvanāto pi sati uppajjati, potthakanibandhanato pi sati uppajjati, upanikkhepato pi sati uppajjati, anubhūtato pi sati uppajjati.

145 katham abhijānato sati uppajjati: yathā mahārāja āyasmā ca ānando khujjuttarā ca upāsikā ye vā pan'aññe pi keci jātissarā jātiṃ saranti, evaṃ abhijānato sati uppajjati. kathaṃ kaṭumikāya sati uppajjati: yo pakatiyā muṭṭhassatiko pare ca taṃ sarāpanatthaṃ nibandhanti, evaṃ kaṭumikāya sati uppajjati. kathaṃ oḷārikaviññāṇato sati uppajjati: yadā rajje vā abhisitto hoti sotāpattiphalaṃ vā patto hoti, evaṃ oḷārikaviññāṇato sati uppajjati.

146 kathaṃ hitaviññāṇato sati uppajjati: yamhi sukhāpito: amukasmiṃ evaṃ sukhāpito ti sarati, evaṃ hitaviññāṇato sati uppajjati. kathaṃ ahitaviññāṇato sati uppajjati: yamhi

The king asked: "Nagasena, sir, through how many modes does memory occur?" 144

"Memory occurs through sixteen modes,* great king, and these are the sixteen: memory occurs through remembering; through being prompted by something external; through awareness of something monumental; through awareness of something beneficial; through awareness of something not beneficial; through something with similar characteristics; through something with dissimilar characteristics; through hearing talk; through a defining characteristic; through active recall; through counting on fingers; through numbering; through keeping in mind; through mental development; through what is preserved in books; through a pledge; and through previous experience."

"How does memory occur through remembering?" "Great 145
king, this mode of memory occurred when the revered Ananda and the laywoman Khujjuttara, and in fact anyone with the capacity to recall previous births, remembered their previous births." "How does memory occur through external causes?" "This is when someone who is forgetful by nature is pressed by someone else to remember something." "How does memory occur through awareness of something monumental?" "Great king, consider a king getting anointed or someone attaining the fruit of stream entry."

"How does memory occur through awareness of some- 146
thing beneficial?" "When happy, one recalls what brings about the happiness, and so memory occurs through awareness of what is beneficial." "How does memory occur though

* In fact, Nagasena lists and describes seventeen modes.

dukkhāpito: amukasmiṃ evaṃ dukkhāpito ti sarati, evaṃ ahitaviññāṇato sati uppajjati. kathaṃ sabhāganimittato sati uppajjati: sadisaṃ puggalaṃ disvā mātaraṃ vā pitaraṃ vā bhātaraṃ vā bhaginiṃ vā sarati, oṭṭhaṃ vā goṇaṃ vā gadrabhaṃ vā disvā aññaṃ tādisaṃ oṭṭhaṃ vā goṇaṃ vā gadrabhaṃ vā sarati, evaṃ sabhāganimittato sati uppajjati. kathaṃ visabhāganimittato sati uppajjati: asukassa nāma evaṃ vaṇṇo ediso, saddo ediso, gandho ediso, raso ediso, phoṭṭhabbo ediso ti sarati, evaṃ visabhāganimittato sati uppajjati. kathaṃ kathābhiññāṇato sati uppajjati: yo pakatiyā muṭṭhassatiko hoti taṃ pare sarāpenti, tena so sarati, evaṃ kathābhiññāṇato sati uppajjati.

147 kathaṃ lakkhaṇato sati uppajjati: yo balivaddānaṃ aṅkena jānāti lakkhaṇena jānāti, evaṃ lakkhaṇato sati uppajjati. kathaṃ saraṇato sati uppajjati: yo pakatiyā muṭṭhassatiko hoti, yo taṃ: sarāhi bho, sarāhi bho ti punappunaṃ sarāpeti, evaṃ saraṇato sati uppajjati. kathaṃ muddāto sati uppajjati: lipiyā sikkhitattā jānāti: imassa akkharassa anantaraṃ imaṃ akkharaṃ kātabban-ti, evaṃ muddāto sati uppajjati. kathaṃ gaṇanāto sati uppajjati: gaṇanāya sikkhitattā gaṇakā bahum-pi gaṇenti, evaṃ gaṇanāto sati uppajjati. kathaṃ dhāraṇato sati uppajjati: dhāraṇāya sikkhitattā dhāraṇakā bahum-pi dhārenti, evaṃ dhāranato sati uppajjati.

awareness of something not beneficial?” “One feeling pain recalls what brings about the pain, and so memory occurs through awareness of what is not beneficial.”

“How does memory occur through something with similar characteristics?” “One recalls one’s mother, father, brother, or sister when one sees a similar person. Alternatively, one is able to identify a camel, ox, or donkey only because of seeing each of them before.” “How does memory occur through something with dissimilar characteristics?” “One brings to mind the color, sound, scent, taste, or feeling of something specific.” “How does memory occur through hearing talk?” “When others remind someone who is by nature forgetful, and from this the person remembers something, then this mode of memory occurs.”

“How does memory occur through a defining character- 147
istic?” “Someone who identifies a plow ox by its branding recognizes it through a defining characteristic.” “How does memory occur through active recall?” “When someone who is by nature forgetful reminds themselves again and again to remember something, there is memory through active recall.” “How does memory occur through counting on fingers?” “This is similar to learning to write when one learns that there should be nothing between one letter and another letter.”

“How does memory occur through numbering?” “By being trained in numbering, accountants can keep track of even large numbers.” “How does memory occur through keeping in mind?” “By training the memory, one practiced in memorization can retain a great deal.”

148 kathaṃ bhāvanāto sati uppajjati: idha bhikkhu anekavihitaṃ pubbenivāsaṃ anussarati, seyyathīdaṃ: ekam-pi jātiṃ dve pi jātiyo-pe-iti sākāraṃ sa-uddesaṃ pubbenivāsaṃ anussarati, evaṃ bhāvanāto sati uppajjati. kathaṃ potthakanibandhanato sati uppajjati: rājāno anusāsaniyaṃ anussarantā: ekaṃ potthakaṃ āharathāti tena potthakena anussaranti, evaṃ potthakanibandhanato sati uppajjati. kathaṃ upanikkhepato sati uppajjati: upanikkhittaṃ bhaṇḍaṃ disvā sarati, evaṃ upanikkhepato sati uppajjati. kathaṃ anubhūtato sati uppajjati: diṭṭhattā rūpaṃ sarati, sutattā saddaṃ sarati, ghāyitattā gandhaṃ sarati, sāyitattā rasaṃ sarati, phuṭṭhattā phoṭṭhabbaṃ sarati, viññātattā dhammaṃ sarati, evaṃ anubhūtato sati uppajjati. imehi kho mahārāja soḷasahi ākārehi sati uppajjatīti. kallosi bhante nāgasenāti.

149 rājā āha: bhante nāgasena, tumhe evaṃ bhaṇatha: yo vassasataṃ akusalaṃ kareyya maraṇakāle ca ekaṃ buddhagataṃ satiṃ paṭilabheyya so devesu uppajjeyyāti; etaṃ na saddahāmi. evañ-ca pana vadetha: ekena pāṇātipātena niraye uppajjeyyāti; etam-pi na saddahāmīti. taṃ kim-maññasi mahārāja: khuddako pi pāsāṇo vinā nāvāya udake uppilaveyyāti. na hi bhante ti. kin-nu kho mahārāja vāhasatampi pāsāṇānaṃ nāvāya āropitaṃ udake uppilaveyyāti. āma

"How does memory occur through mental development?" 148
"A monk engages the meditations on previous births when he lived in various circumstances, and so he recalls one life and then a second one, each with its features and details."

"How does memory occur through what is preserved in books?" "When kings are trying to recall advice, they order that a certain book be brought. With the book, they remember." "How does memory occur through a pledge?" "When one sees the goods delivered, one remembers the pledge." "How does memory occur through previous experience?" "From what was seen, one remembers a visible form; from what was heard, one remembers a sound; from what was smelled, one remembers a scent; from what was tasted, one remembers a savor; from what was felt, one remembers a tangible object; and from previous awareness, one remembers a phenomenal state. This is memory through previous experience. Memory occurs in these sixteen modes, great king."

"You are wise, Nagasena."

The king said: "Nagasena, sir, you say that even some- 149
one who does bad things for a hundred years can be reborn among the gods if, on his deathbed, he does a single mindfulness meditation on the Buddha. I just don't believe it. Nor can I accept that someone would go to hell for a single act of killing a living creature."

"What do you think, great king? Can a small stone float on the water without a boat?" "No, sir." "But will a hundred cartloads of stones when loaded onto a boat float on water?" "Of course they will float then."

bhante, uppilaveyyāti. yathā mahārāja nāvā evaṃ kusalāni kammāni daṭṭhabbānīti. kallosi bhante nāgasenāti.

150 rājā āha: bhante nāgasena, kiṃ tumhe atītassa dukkhassa pahānāya vāyamathāti. na hi mahārājāti. kim-pana anāgatassa dukkhassa pahānāya vāyamathāti. na hi mahārājāti. kim-pana paccuppannassa dukkhassa pahānāya vāyamathāti. na hi mahārājāti. yadi tumhe na atītassa dukkhassa pahānāya vāyamatha, na anāgatassa dukkhassa pahānāya vāyamatha, na paccuppannassa dukkhassa pahānāya vāyamatha, atha kimatthāya vāyamathāti.

151 thero āha: kin-ti mahārāja idañ-ca dukkhaṃ nirujjheyya aññañ-ca dukkhaṃ na uppajjeyyāti etadatthāya vāyamāmāti. atthi pana bhante nāgasena anāgataṃ dukkhan-ti. na-tthi mahārājāti. tumhe kho bhante nāgasena atipaṇḍitā ye tumhe asantānaṃ dukkhānaṃ pahānāya vāyamathāti. atthi pana te mahārāja keci paṭirājāno paccatthikā paccāmittā paccupaṭṭhitā hontīti. āma bhante, atthīti. kin-nu kho mahārāja tadā tumhe parikhaṃ khaṇāpeyyātha pākāraṃ cināpeyyātha gopuraṃ kārāpeyyātha aṭṭālakaṃ kārāpeyyātha dhaññaṃ atiharāpeyyāthāti. na hi bhante, paṭigacc' eva taṃ paṭiyattaṃ hotīti. kiṃ tumhe mahārāja tadā hatthismiṃ sikkheyyātha assasmiṃ sikkheyyātha rathasmiṃ sikkheyyātha dhanusmiṃ sikkheyyātha tharusmiṃ sikkheyyāthāti. na hi bhante, paṭigacc' eva taṃ sikkhitaṃ hotīti.

152 kiss' atthāyāti. anāgatānaṃ bhante bhayānaṃ paṭibāhanatthāyāti. kin-nu kho mahārāja atthi anāgataṃ bhayan-ti. na-tthi bhante ti. tumhe ca kho mahārāja atipaṇḍitā ye tumhe anāgatānaṃ bhayānaṃ paṭibāhanatthāya paṭiyādethāti. bhiyyo opammaṃ karohīti. taṃ kim-maññasi mahārāja: yadā tvaṃ pipāsito bhaveyyāsi tadā tvaṃ udapānaṃ khaṇāp-

"Then you should see good karma as similar to a boat, great king."

"You are wise, Nagasena."

The king asked: "Nagasena, are you striving to get rid of 150
past suffering?" "No, great king." "Are you striving to get rid of future suffering?" "No, great king." "Are you striving to get rid of present suffering?" "No, great king."

"But if you are not striving to get rid of past, future, or present suffering, then what are you striving for?"

The elder replied: "I strive so that this suffering will 151
dissolve and that no further suffering should occur." "But does future suffering exist now?" "No, great king." "Here you all are very clever, and yet you strive to get rid of suffering that does not exist!"

"Great king, are there any hostile kings, enemies, or adversaries who have risen up against you?" "Certainly there are." "So now you dig trenches, make a fort, have a gateway put in, erect a watchtower, and harvest the soldiers' grain?" "No, as a precaution, all this has already been prepared." "And now you begin training with elephants, horses, chariots, bows, and swords?" "No, again, out of caution, the training is done."

"For what purpose, great king?" 152

"To guard against future threats, sir." "Does a future threat exist now, great king?" "No, sir." "And yet, you are very clever, great king, to guard against future threats in advance."

"Please give another analogy."

"What do you think, great king? Suppose you become thirsty. Do you then have a well, a tank, or a reservoir dug,

eyyāsi pokkharaṇiṃ khaṇāpeyyāsi taḷākaṃ khaṇāpeyyāsi: pānīyaṃ pivissāmīti. na hi bhante, paṭigacc'eva taṃ paṭiyattaṃ hotīti.

153 kiss' atthāyāti. anāgatānaṃ bhante pipāsānaṃ paṭibāhanatthāya paṭiyattaṃ hotīti. atthi pana mahārāja anāgatā pipāsā ti. na-tthi bhante ti. tumhe kho mahārāja atipaṇḍitā ye tumhe anāgatānaṃ pipāsānaṃ paṭibāhanatthāya taṃ paṭiyādethāti. bhiyyo opammaṃ karohīti. taṃ kim-maññasi mahārāja: yadā tvaṃ bubhukkhito bhaveyyāsi tadā tvaṃ khettaṃ kasāpeyyāsi sāliṃ vapāpeyyāsi: bhattaṃ bhuñjissāmīti. na hi bhante, paṭigacc' eva taṃ paṭiyattaṃ hotīti. kiss' atthāyāti. anāgatānaṃ bhante bubhukkhānaṃ paṭibāhanatthāyāti. atthi pana mahārāja anāgatā bubhukkhā ti. na-tthi bhante ti. tumhe kho mahārāja atipaṇḍitā ye tumhe asantānaṃ anāgatānaṃ bubhukkhānaṃ paṭibāhanatthāya paṭiyādethāti. kallosi bhante nāgasenāti.

154 rājā āha: bhante nāgasena, kīva dūro ito brahmaloko ti. dūro kho mahārāja ito brahmaloko, kūṭāgāramattā silā tamhā patitā ahorattena aṭṭhacattālīsa yojanasahassāni bhassamānā catuhi māsehi paṭhaviyaṃ patiṭṭhaheyyāti. bhante nāgasena, tumhe evaṃ bhaṇatha: seyyathā pi balavā puriso sammiñjitaṃ vā bāhaṃ pasāreyya pasāritaṃ vā bāhaṃ sammiñjeyya, evam-eva iddhimā bhikkhu cetovasippatto jambudīpe antarahito brahmaloke pātubhaveyyāti; etaṃ vacanaṃ na saddahāmi, evaṃ atisīghaṃ tāva bahūni yojanasatāni gacchissatīti.

155 thero āha: kuhiṃ pana mahārāja tava jātabhūmīti. atthi bhante alasando nāma dīpo, tatthāhaṃ jāto ti. kīva dūro mahārāja ito alasando hotīti. dumattāni bhante yojanasatānīti. abhijānāsi nu tvaṃ mahārāja tattha kiñcid-eva

so that you can have a drink?" "No, sir, as a precaution, all of this would have already been prepared."

"For what purpose?" "It was prepared to guard against 153
future thirst, sir." "Does future thirst exist now?" "No, sir." "It seems that you are very clever to guard against future thirst in advance."

"Another analogy, please."

"What do you think, great king? Suppose you get hungry. Do you then have the fields tilled and the crops planted so that you can have a meal?" "No, sir, all of this would have been already done." "Why?" "To guard against future hunger." "But does future hunger exist now?" "No, sir." "You are, in fact, very clever to guard against future hunger in advance, great king."

"You are wise, Nagasena."

The king asked: "Nagasena, how far is the Brahma world 154
from here?"

"The Brahma world is quite far, great king. Suppose a boulder the size of a two-story building fell from it and tumbled forty-eight thousand leagues every day and night. It would take four months to hit the earth."

"Nagasena, you say that a monk who had mastered the mind with supernatural powers could vanish from Jambudipa and appear in the Brahma world, just as quickly as it takes a strong man to bend his straight arm or to straighten his bent arm. I don't find it credible that a monk could travel so many hundred leagues so quickly."

The elder replied: "Where is your birthplace, great king?" 155
"I was born on an island called Alexandria."[24] "How far is Alexandria from here?" "Two hundred leagues, sir." "Think

karaṇīyaṃ karitvā saritā ti. āma bhante, sarāmīti. Lahuṃ kho tvaṃ mahārāja gatosi dumattāni yojanasatānīti. kallosi bhante nāgasenāti.

156 rājā āha: bhante nāgasena, yo idha kālakato brahmaloke uppajjeyya yo ca idha kālakato kasmīre uppajjeyya, ko cirataraṃ ko sīghataran-ti. samakaṃ mahārājāti. opammaṃ karohīti. kuhiṃ pana mahārāja tava jātanagaran-ti. atthi bhante kalasigāmo nāma, tatthāhaṃ jāto ti. kīva dūro mahārāja ito kalasigāmo hotīti. dumattāni bhante yojanasatānīti. kīva dūraṃ mahārāja ito kasmīraṃ hotīti. dvādasa bhante yojanānīti. iṅgha tvaṃ mahārāja kalasigāmaṃ cintehīti. cintito bhante ti. iṅgha tvaṃ mahārāja kasmīraṃ cintehīti. cintitaṃ bhante ti.

157 kataman-nu kho mahārāja cirena cintitaṃ katamaṃ sīghataran-ti. samakaṃ bhante ti. evam-eva kho mahārāja yo idha kālakato brahmaloke uppajjeyya yo ca idha kālakato kasmīre uppajjeyya samakaṃ yeva uppajjantīti. bhiyyo opammaṃ karohīti. taṃ kim-maññasi mahārāja: dve sakuṇā ākāsena gaccheyyuṃ, tesu eko ucce rukkhe nisīdeyya eko nīce rukkhe nisīdeyya, tesaṃ samakaṃ patiṭṭhitānaṃ katamassa chāyā paṭhamataraṃ paṭhaviyaṃ patiṭṭhaheyya katamassa chāyā cirena paṭhaviyaṃ patiṭṭhaheyyāti. samakaṃ bhante ti. evam-eva kho mahārāja yo idha kālakato brahmaloke uppajjeyya yo ca idha kālakato kasmīre uppajjeyya samakaṃ yeva uppajjantīti. kallosi bhante nāgasenāti.

back to some important business you did there, and remember it." "All right, I remember it."

"Great king, you just traveled two hundred leagues very quickly."

"You are wise, Nagasena."

The king said: "Nagasena, suppose a person dies and is 156
reborn from here in the Brahma world, while another person dies and is reborn in Kashmir. Which one gets there faster?" "It takes the same amount of time, great king."

"Give an analogy of this."

"Where is your birth city?" "I was born in a village called Kalasi." "How far is Kalasi from here?" "Two hundred leagues. "And how far is Kashmir from here?" "Just twelve leagues, sir."

"Now think about the village of Kalasi, great king. And then think of Kashmir." "All right, I have thought of each of them."

"Thinking of which of the two took longer and which went 157
more quickly?" "It was the same for each."

"So too for people being reborn in either the Brahma world or Kashmir. It takes the same amount of time."

"Another example, please."

"What do you think, great king? Suppose two birds fly through the sky and at exactly the same moment, one lands on a tall tree and the other on a short tree. Which one's shadow would hit the ground first?" "It would be the same for each." "So too for the people born in the Brahma world and in Kashmir, great king."

"You are wise, Nagasena."

158 rājā āha: kati nu kho bhante nāgasena bojjhaṅgā ti. satta kho mahārāja bojjhaṅgā ti. katihi pana bhante bojjhaṅgehi bujjhatīti. ekena kho mahārāja bojjhaṅgena bujjhati: dhammavicayasambojjhaṅgenāti. atha kissa nu kho bhante vuccanti satta bojjhaṅgā ti. taṃ kim-maññasi mahārāja: asi kosiyā pakkhitto aggahito hatthena ussahati chejjaṃ chinditun-ti. na hi bhante ti. evam-eva kho mahārāja dhammavicayasambojjhaṅgena vinā chahi bojjhaṅgehi na bujjhatīti. kallosi bhante nāgasenāti.

159 rājā āha: bhante nāgasena, kataman-nu kho bahutaraṃ, puññaṃ vā apuññaṃ vā ti. puññaṃ kho mahārāja bahutaraṃ, apuññaṃ thokan-ti. kena kāraṇenāti. apuññaṃ kho mahārāja karonto vippaṭisārī hoti: pāpakammaṃ mayā katan-ti; tena pāpaṃ na vaḍḍhati. puññaṃ kho mahārāja karonto avippaṭisārī hoti, avippaṭisārissa pāmojjaṃ jāyati, pamuditassa pīti jāyati, pītimanassa kāyo passambhati, passaddhakāyo sukhaṃ vedeti, sukhino cittaṃ samādhiyati, samāhito yathābhūtaṃ pajānāti, tena kāraṇena puññaṃ vaḍḍhati; puriso kho mahārāja chinnahatthapādo bhagavato ekaṃ uppalahatthaṃ datvā ekanavuti kappāni vinipātaṃ na

The king asked: "Nagasena, how many awakening factors are there?" "There are seven awakening factors, great king." 158

"How many awakening factors does it take to become awakened?"

"One can become awakened with just one factor, that is, with the investigation into phenomenal states." "Then why are seven awakening factors mentioned?"

"What do you think, great king? Without one's hand pulling out a sheathed sword, is it possible to cut anything?" "No, sir."

"Similarly, one is not awakened by the six awakening factors without the factor of the investigation into phenomenal states."[25]

"You are wise, Nagasena."

The king asked: "Nagasena, sir, which is greater, merit or demerit?" "Merit is greater than demerit, great king." "For what reason?" 159

"When one does something unmeritorious one becomes remorseful: 'I have made evil karma.' And because of this, the evil does not increase. But one who has made merit need not become remorseful, and for someone not troubled with remorse, the delight of being free of regrets arises; for one delighted, joy arises; for one feeling joy, the body is calmed; one with a calmed body feels happiness; a happy person's mind can be concentrated; concentrated, one understands what has arisen, and because of this, merit increases. Suppose a person with hands and feet cut off were to give the Bhagavan even a single bunch of lotuses. That person would not go to hell for

gacchissati; iminā pi mahārāja kāraṇena bhaṇāmi: puññaṃ bahutaraṃ, apuññaṃ thokan-ti. kallosi bhante nāgasenāti.

160 rājā āha: bhante nāgasena, yo jānanto pāpakammaṃ karoti yo ca ajānanto pāpakammaṃ karoti, kassa bahutaraṃ apuññan-ti. thero āha: yo kho mahārāja ajānanto pāpakammaṃ karoti tassa bahutaraṃ apuññan-ti. tena hi bhante nāgasena yo amhākaṃ rājaputto vā rājamahāmatto vā ajānanto pāpakammaṃ karoti taṃ mayaṃ diguṇaṃ daṇḍemāti. taṃ kim-maññasi mahārāja: tattaṃ ayoguḷaṃ ādittaṃ sampajjalitaṃ sajotibhūtaṃ eko ajānanto gaṇheyya eko jānanto gaṇheyya, katamo balikataraṃ dayheyyāti. yo kho bhante ajānanto gaṇheyya so balikataraṃ dayheyyāti. evam-eva kho mahārāja yo ajānanto pāpakammaṃ karoti tassa bahutaraṃ apuññan-ti. kallosi bhante nāgasenāti.

161 rājā āha: bhante nāgasena, atthi koci iminā sarīradehena uttarakuruṃ vā gaccheyya brahmalokaṃ vā aññaṃ vā pana dīpan-ti. atthi mahārāja yo iminā cātummahābhūtikena kāyena uttarakuruṃ vā gaccheyya brahmalokaṃ vā aññaṃ vā pana dīpan-ti. katham bhante nāgasena iminā cātummahābhūtikena kāyena uttarakuruṃ vā gaccheyya brahmalokaṃ vā aññaṃ vā pana dīpan-ti. abhijānāsi nu tvaṃ mahārāja imissā paṭhaviyā vidatthiṃ vā rataniṃ vā laṅghitvā ti. āma bhante, abhijānāmi; aham-bhante nāgasena aṭṭha pi

ninety-one eons. This is why I say that merit is greater than demerit."

"You are wise, Nagasena."

The king asked: "Nagasena, which is the greater demerit: 160
when someone knowingly does an evil action or when one does an evil action without knowing it?"

The elder replied: "Great king, the demerit is greater for one who does an evil action unknowingly."

"Then if this is so, we must inflict twice the punishment on our own prince or prime minister who does an evil action unknowingly."

"What do you think, great king? Which one is burned more severely, the person who without realizing it grabs a blazing, fiery, and burning iron ball, or the one who realizes it?" "The one who doesn't realize it is burned more severely, sir." "In the same way, great king, there is more demerit for someone who does an evil action unknowingly."

"You are wise, Nagasena."

The king asked: "Nagasena, is there anyone who can go 161
to the Brahma realm or to Uttarakuru or another continent with the physical body?" "Yes, great king. With the body made of the four great elements, one can go to the Brahma realm, Uttarakuru, or another continent."

"But how could one go to these places with the physical body, sir?"

"Have you ever had the experience of jumping over a span or length of ground?" "Yes, I have done this. In fact, I can jump eight cubits." "How do you manage to jump eight cubits, great king?" "I form the thought, 'I am going to hurtle this far,' and with this thought, my body becomes light."

rataniyo laṅghāmīti. kathaṃ tvaṃ mahārāja aṭṭha pi rataniyo laṅghesīti. ahaṃ hi bhante cittaṃ uppādemi: ettha nipatissāmīti; saha cittuppādena kāyo me lahuko hotīti. evam-eva kho mahārāja iddhimā bhikkhu cetovasippatto kāyaṃ citte samāropetvā cittavasena vehāsaṃ gacchatīti. kallosi bhante nāgasenāti.

162 rājā āha: bhante nāgasena, tumhe evaṃ bhaṇatha: aṭṭhikāni dīghāni yojanasatikānipī'ti; rukkho pi tāva na-tthi yojanasatiko, kuto pana aṭṭhikāni dīghāni yojanasatikāni bhavissantīti. taṃ kim-maññasi mahārāja: sutan-te mahāsamudde pañcayojanasatikā pi macchā atthīti. āma bhante, sutan-ti. nanu mahārāja pañcayojanasatikassa macchassa aṭṭhikāni dīghāni bhavissanti yojanasatikānipī'ti. kallosi bhante nāgasenāti.

163 rājā āha: bhante nāgasena, tumhe evaṃ bhaṇatha: sakkā assāsa-passāse nirodhetun-ti. āma mahārāja, sakkā assāsa-passāse nirodhetun-ti. katham-bhante nāgasena sakkā assāsa-passāse nirodhetun-ti. taṃ kim-maññasi mahārāja: sutapubbo te koci kākacchamāno ti. āma bhante, sutapubbo ti. kin-nu kho mahārāja so saddo kāye namite virameyyāti. āma bhante, virameyyāti. so hi nāma mahārāja saddo abhāvitakāyassa abhāvitasīlassa abhāvitacittassa abhāvitapaññassa kāye namite viramissati, kim-pana bhāvitakāyassa bhāvitasīlassa bhāvitacittassa bhāvitapaññassa catutthajjhānaṃ samāpannassa assāsa-passāsā na nirujjhissantīti. kallosi bhante nāgasenāti.

"Similarly, great king, a monk with psychic powers who has mastered his mind makes his body ascend in his thoughts, and so, just by means of a thought, he flies through the sky."

"You are wise, Nagasena."

The king said: "Nagasena, you say that there are long 162
bones the length of a hundred leagues, but not even a tree can extend a hundred leagues, so how could bones be so long?" "What do you think, great king? Have you heard that there are fish five hundred leagues long in the great ocean?" "I have heard this."

"Then, great king, do not the bones of fish five hundred leagues long extend to at least one hundred leagues?"

"You are wise, Nagasena."

The king said: "Nagasena, you say that inhalation and 163
exhalation can both be stopped." "Yes, great king, both inhalation and exhalation can be stopped." "But how can this be?"

"What do you think, great king? Have you ever heard anyone snore?" "Yes, I have heard that before." "Could the noise be suppressed by adjusting the body?" "Yes, that would stop it."

"Then, great king, if a noise can be stopped just by adjusting the body without having developed the body, moral discipline, awareness, or understanding, then why couldn't inhalation and exhalation be suppressed in one who has achieved the fourth *jhāna,* and whose body, moral discipline, awareness, and understanding are developed?"

"You are wise, Nagasena."

164 rājā āha: bhante nāgasena, samuddo samuddo ti vuccati, kena kāraṇena udakaṃ samuddo ti vuccatīti. thero āha: yattakaṃ mahārāja udakaṃ tattakaṃ loṇaṃ, yattakaṃ loṇaṃ tattakaṃ udakaṃ, tasmā samuddo ti vuccatīti. kallosi bhante nāgasenāti.

165 rājā āha: bhante nāgasena, kena kāraṇena samuddo ekaraso loṇaraso ti. cirasaṇṭhitattā kho mahārāja udakassa samuddo ekaraso loṇaraso ti. kallosi bhante nāgasenāti.

166 rājā āha: bhante nāgasena, sakkā sabbaṃ sukhumaṃ chinditun-ti. āma mahārāja, sakkā sabbaṃ sukhumaṃ chinditun-ti. kim-pana bhante sabbaṃ sukhuman-ti. dhammo kho mahārāja sabbasukhumo, na kho mahārāja dhammā sabbe sukhumā, sukhuman-ti vā thūlan-ti vā mahārāja dhammānam-etam-adhivacanaṃ, yaṃ kiñci chinditabbaṃ sabbaṃ taṃ paññāya chindati, na-tthi dutiyaṃ paññāya chedanan-ti. kallosi bhante nāgasenāti.

167 rājā āha: bhante nāgasena, viññāṇan-ti vā paññā ti vā bhūtasmiṃ jīvo ti vā, ime dhammā nānatthā c' eva nānābyañjanā ca, udāhu ekatthā, byañjanam-eva nānan-ti. vijānanalakkhaṇaṃ mahārāja viññāṇaṃ, pajānanalakkhaṇā paññā, bhūtasmiṃ jīvo na upalabbhatīti. yadi jīvo na upalabbhati,

The king said: "Nagasena, sir, people call this or that an 'ocean.' But why is water called an ocean?" 164

The elder replied: "When water has an equal amount of salt, or salt has an equal amount of water, then it can be called an ocean."[26]

"You are wise, Nagasena."

The king asked: "Nagasena, why does the ocean have but a single taste, the taste of salt?"[27] 165

"Because of its water having been around for so long, the ocean has one taste, the taste of salt, great king."

"You are wise, Nagasena."

The king asked: "Nagasena, sir, can what is completely subtle be cut through?" "Yes, great king, it is possible to cut through something completely subtle." "But what, sir, is the subtlest thing?" 166

"Great king, the Dhamma is the subtlest thing of all. But not all phenomenal states are subtle, and the same word—"dhamma"—can in this way refer to things subtle or gross.[28] Whatever can be completely cut through is cut through by understanding, though there is no further division of understanding."

"You are wise, Nagasena."

The king asked: "Nagasena, sir, are 'awareness,' 'understanding,' and the 'soul inside a being' phenomenal states that are different both in meaning and in phrasing? Or do they denote the same thing, just with different phrasing?" 167

"Great king, the defining characteristic of awareness is *being aware.* The defining characteristic of understanding is *an act of understanding.* And no 'soul inside a being' is known at all."

atha ko carahi cakkhunā rūpaṃ passati, sotena saddaṃ suṇāti, ghānena gandhaṃ ghāyati, jivhāya rasaṃ sāyati, kāyena phoṭṭhabbaṃ phusati, manasā dhammaṃ vijānātīti.

168 thero āha: yadi jīvo cakkhunā rūpaṃ passati-pe-manasā dhammaṃ vijānāti, so jīvo cakkhudvāresu uppāṭitesu mahantena ākāsena bahimukho suṭṭhutaraṃ rūpaṃ passeyya, sotesu uppāṭitesu ghāne uppāṭite jivhāya uppāṭitāya kāye uppāṭite mahantena ākāsena suṭṭhutaraṃ saddaṃ suṇeyya gandhaṃ ghāyeyya rasaṃ sāyeyya phoṭṭhabbaṃ phuseyyāti. na hi bhante ti. tena hi mahārāja bhūtasmiṃ jīvo na upalabbhatīti. kallosi bhante nāgasenāti.

169 thero āha: dukkaraṃ mahārāja bhagavatā katan-ti. kim-pana bhante nāgasena bhagavatā dukkaraṃ katan-ti. dukkaraṃ mahārāja bhagavatā kataṃ: imesaṃ arūpīnaṃ cittacetasikānaṃ dhammānaṃ ekārammaṇe vattamānānaṃ vavatthānaṃ akkhātaṃ: ayaṃ phasso, ayaṃ vedanā, ayaṃ saññā, ayaṃ cetanā, idaṃ cittan-ti. opammaṃ karohīti.

170 yathā mahārāja kocid-eva puriso nāvāya mahāsamuddaṃ ajjhogāhitvā hatthapuṭena udakaṃ gahetvā jivhāya sāyitvā - jāneyya nu kho mahārāja so puriso: idaṃ gaṅgāya udakaṃ, idaṃ yamunāya udakaṃ, idaṃ aciravatiyā udakaṃ, idaṃ sarabhuyā udakaṃ, idaṃ mahiyā udakan-ti. dukkaraṃ bhante jānitun-ti. ato dukkarataraṃ kho mahārāja

"If no soul is known, then how does the eye see a visible form, the ear hear a sound, the nose smell scents, the tongue taste savor, the body feel tangibles, and the mind know phenomenal states?"

The elder replied: "Great king, if it were the soul that saw 168
a visible form by means of the eye, et cetera, then wouldn't the soul perceive visible forms even better through the great space outside if the door to visual perception were torn out? And wouldn't it better hear sounds, smell scents, taste savors, and touch tangible things if the ears, nose, tongue, and body were removed?" "No, sir."

"Therefore, no soul of beings is known, great king."

"You are wise, Nagasena."

The elder stated: "A difficult thing, great king, was done 169
by the Bhagavan." "What was the difficult thing done by the Bhagavan, Nagasena?" "Great king, the Bhagavan did something difficult when he identified the immaterial phenomena, awareness, and accompanying mental phenomena that occur in a single object of experience, and listed them: 'This is contact, this is feeling, this is perception, this is intention, this is awareness.'"

"Give an analogy."

"Suppose someone went to sea on a boat, scooped up a 170
handful of water, and tasted it with the tongue. Would this person be able to know which drops of water came from the Ganga and which came from the Yamuna, Achiravati, Sarabhu, and Mahi rivers?"

"This would be hard to know, sir."

"Even more difficult, great king, is what the Bhagavan did when he identified the incorporeal phenomena of aware-

bhagavatā kataṃ: imesaṃ arūpīnaṃ cittacetasikānaṃ dhammānaṃ ekārammaṇe vattamānānaṃ vavatthānaṃ akkhātaṃ: ayaṃ phasso, ayaṃ vedanā, ayaṃ saññā, ayaṃ cetanā, idaṃ cittan-ti. suṭṭhu bhante ti rājā abbhanumodi.

sattamo vaggo.

ness and its accompanying mental processes that occur in a single object of experience, and listed them: 'This is contact, this is feeling, this is perception, this is intention, this is awareness.'"

The king was greatly pleased and said, "Well done, revered sir."

End of Section Seven.

171 thero āha jānāsi kho mahārāja sampati kā velā ti. āma bhante, jānāmi, sampati paṭhamo yāmo atikkanto, majjhimo yāmo vattati, ukkā padīpiyanti, cattāri paṭākāni āṇattāni, gamissanti bhaṇḍato rājadeyyā ti. yonakā evam-āhaṃsu: kallosi mahārāja, paṇḍito bhikkhūti. āma bhaṇe, paṇḍito thero, ediso ācariyo bhaveyya mādiso ca antevāsī, na cirass' eva paṇḍito dhammaṃ ājāneyyāti.

172 tassa pañhaveyyākaraṇena tuṭṭho rājā theraṃ nāgasenaṃ satasahassagghanakena kambalena acchādetvā: bhante nāgasena, ajjatagge te aṭṭhasataṃ bhattaṃ paññāpemi, yaṃ kiñci antepure kappiyaṃ tena ca pavāremīti āha. alaṃ mahārāja, jīvāmīti. jānāmi bhante nāgasena jīvasi, api ca attānañ-ca rakkha mamañ-ca rakkhāhi; kathaṃ attānaṃ rakkhasi nāgaseno milindaṃ rājānaṃ pasādesi na ca kiñci alabhīti parāpavādo āgaccheyyāti, evaṃ attānaṃ rakkha; kathaṃ mamaṃ rakkhasi: milindo rājā pasanno pasannākāraṃ na karotīti parāpavādo āgaccheyyāti, evaṃ mamaṃ rakkhāhīti. tathā hotu mahārājāti.

The elder said: "Do you know, great king, what time it is now?" 171

"Yes, sir, I do know. The first watch of the night has now passed and the middle one is in progress. The torches are being lit, the four flags have been raised, and royal offerings are about to go out from the treasury."

The Yonakas spoke: "Great king, you are wise, and the monk is learned."

"Yes, indeed, the elder is learned. Should there be another teacher such as he, any student like me would become learned in the Dhamma in no time at all."

The king was so pleased with the answers to his questions 172
that he presented Nagasena with a woolen cloth worth a hundred thousand, and said: "From this day forward, Nagasena, I will have eight hundred meals laid out, and I invite you all to the inner quarters of the palace in whatever way is suitable."

"No, thank you, great king, as I am already getting by."

"I know that you are already getting by, but please protect both yourself and me. How do you protect yourself? People might criticize you, saying that although Nagasena pleases the king, he does not receive anything. So please protect yourself, sir. And please protect me against those who would criticize me, saying that although King Milinda is pleased, he makes no indication of it."

"Very well, then, great king."

173 seyyathā pi bhante sīho migarājā suvaṇṇapañjare pakkhitto pi bahimukho yeva hoti, evam-eva kho 'haṃ bhante kiñcāpi agāraṃ ajjhāvasāmi, bahimukho yeva pana acchāmi, sace 'haṃ bhante agārasmā anagāriyaṃ pabbajeyyaṃ na ciraṃ jīveyyaṃ, bahū me paccatthikā ti. atha kho āyasmā nāgaseno milindassa rañño pañhaṃ vissajjetvā uṭṭhāy' āsanā saṅghārāmaṃ agamāsi. acirapakkante ca āyasmante nāgasene milindassa rañño etad-ahosi: kiṃ mayā pucchitaṃ, kiṃ bhadantena vissajjitan-ti. atha kho milindassa rañño etad-ahosi: sabbaṃ mayā supucchitaṃ, sabbaṃ bhadantena suvissajjitan-ti.

174 āyasmato pi nāgasenassa saṅghārāmaṃ gatassa etad-ahosi: kiṃ milindena raññā pucchitaṃ, kiṃ mayā vissajjitan-ti. atha kho āyasmato nāgasenassa etad-ahosi: sabbaṃ milindena raññā supucchitaṃ, sabbaṃ mayā suvissajjitan-ti. atha kho āyasmā nāgaseno tassā rattiyā accayena pubbaṇhasamayaṃ nivāsetvā pattacīvaram-ādāya yena milindassa rañño nivesanaṃ ten' upasankami, upasankamitvā paññatte āsane nisīdi. atha kho milindo rājā āyasmantaṃ nāgasenaṃ abhivādetvā ekamantaṃ nisīdi, ekamantaṃ nisinno kho milindo rājā āyasmantaṃ nāgasenaṃ etad-avoca: mā kho bhadantassa evaṃ ahosi: nāgaseno mayā pañhaṃ pucchito ti ten'eva somanassena na taṃ rattāvasesaṃ supīti, na te evaṃ daṭṭhabbaṃ; tassa mayhaṃ bhante taṃ rattāvasesaṃ etad-ahosi: kiṃ mayā pucchitaṃ, kiṃ bhadantena vissajjitan-ti; sabbaṃ mayā supucchitaṃ, sabbaṃ bhadantena suvissajjitan-ti.

"Just as a lion, the king of beasts, when locked in a golden 173
cage, sits looking outward, so too do I, while living the household life, sit looking outward. But if I were to leave home as a homeless renouncer, I would not live long, for I have many enemies."

Then the revered Nagasena, having finished answering King Milinda's questions, rose from his seat and returned to the monastery. But a little while after Nagasena left, King Milinda began thinking: *What did I ask, and how did the worthy monk reply?* But then he considered, *I asked only good questions, and the worthy monk's replies were all well done.*

Meanwhile, Nagasena, back at the monastery, reflected, 174
What did King Milinda ask, and how did I answer? But then he too considered, *Everything King Milinda asked was fitting, and all of my replies were well done.*

Then, when the night was over and morning had dawned, the revered Nagasena got dressed and took up his bowl and outer robe. He went to King Milinda and, approaching him, sat down on the appointed seat. King Milinda greeted Nagasena and sat to one side of him, and as he sat there, he began to speak: "Please do not suppose that I was not able to sleep all night out of delight as I thought of the questioning I put to you. Rather, I spent the night mulling over what I had asked and what the worthy monk had answered. I found that everything was well asked by me and well answered by you, sir."

175 thero pi evam-āha: mā kho mahārājassa evaṃ ahosi: milindassa rañño mayā pañho vissajjito ti ten' eva somanassena taṃ rattāvasesaṃ vītināmesīti, na te evaṃ daṭṭhabbaṃ; tassa mayhaṃ mahārāja taṃ rattāvasesaṃ etad-ahosi: kiṃ milindena raññā pucchitaṃ, kiṃ mayā vissajjitan-ti; sabbaṃ milindena raññā supucchitaṃ, sabbaṃ mayā suvissajjitan-ti. iti ha te mahānāgā aññamaññassa subhāsitaṃ samanumodiṃsūti.

milindapañhānaṃ pucchāvissajjanā samattā.

The elder then said this: "May the great king also not 175
suppose that I spent the night with delight as I reviewed my responses to King Milinda's questions. Rather, I spent the night mulling over what the king asked and how I replied, and I too found that everything was well asked by you and well answered by me."

In this way, these two great beings graciously celebrated what had been so well spoken by each other.

This concludes the questioning and answering of the chapter Questions of Milinda.

CHAPTER 3

Ram Horn Dilemmas I
The Great Chapter

PART 1

1 bhassappavedī vetaṇḍī atibuddhi vicakkhaṇo
milindo ñāṇabhedāya nāgasenam-upāgami.
2 vasanto tassa chāyāya paripucchanto punappunaṃ
pabhinnabuddhi hutvāna so pi āsī tipeṭako.
3 navaṅgaṃ anumajjanto rattibhāge rahogato
addakkhi meṇḍake pañhe dunniveṭhe saniggahe:
4 pariyāyabhāsitaṃ atthi, atthi sandhāya bhāsitaṃ,
sabhāvabhāsitaṃ atthi dhammarājassa sāsane.
5 tesaṃ atthaṃ aviññāya meṇḍake jinabhāsite
anāgatamhi addhāne viggaho tattha hessati.
6 handa kathiṃ pasādetvā chejjapessāmi meṇḍake,
tassa nidditthamaggena niddisissanty-anāgate ti.

PART 1

Milinda, fond of debate and discussion, an expert 1
in reasoning, highly intelligent, and attentive,
approached Nagasena for a breakthrough in
knowledge.
He stayed close to him, questioning him again and 2
again
until his understanding developed, and he mastered
the three baskets of scripture.
As he spent his nights in solitude pondering the nine 3
parts,
he discovered "ram horn" dilemmas, that is, queries
subject to refutation and difficult to resolve.
The Dhamma King's dispensation includes some 4
speech that is figurative, some speech that
requires context, and some speech that describes
things as they actually are.
In the future, due to ignorance of the meaning of 5
these,
there will be disputes about the ram horn dilemmas
apparent in the words of the Victor.
Let me now, with serene confidence in the speaker, 6
settle these dilemmas,
so that in the future they will be explained by the path
now demonstrated.

7 atha kho milindo rājā pabhātāya rattiyā uggate aruṇe sīsaṃ nahātvā sirasi añjalim-paggahetvā atītānāgata-paccuppanne sammāsambuddhe anussaritvā aṭṭha vatapadāni samādiyi: ito me anāgatāni satta divasāni aṭṭha guṇe samādiyitvā tapo caritabbo bhavissati, so 'haṃ ciṇṇatapo samāno ācariyaṃ ārādhetvā meṇḍake pañhe pucchissāmīti. atha kho milindo rājā pakatidussayugaṃ apanetvā ābharaṇāni ca omuñcitvā kāsāyaṃ nivāsetvā muṇḍakapaṭisīsakaṃ sīse paṭimuñcitvā munibhāvam-upagantvā aṭṭha guṇe samādiyi: imaṃ sattāhaṃ mayā na rājāttho anusāsitabbo, na rāgūpasaṃhitaṃ cittaṃ uppādetabbaṃ, na dosūpasaṃhitaṃ cittaṃ uppādetabbaṃ, na mohūpasaṃhitaṃ cittaṃ uppādetabbaṃ, dāsakammakara-porisa-jane pi nivātavuttinā bhavitabbaṃ, kāyikaṃ vācasikaṃ anurakkhitabbaṃ, cha pi āyatanāni niravasesato anurakkhitabbāni, mettābhāvanāya mānasaṃ pakkhipitabban-ti.

8 ime aṭṭha guṇe samādiyitvā tesv-eva aṭṭhasu guṇesu mānasaṃ patiṭṭhapetvā bahi anikkhamitvā sattāhaṃ vītināmetvā aṭṭhame divase pabhātāya rattiyā pag-eva pātarāsaṃ katvā okkhittacakkhu mitabhāṇī susaṇṭhitena iriyāpathena avikkhittena cittena haṭṭhena udaggena vippasannena theraṃ nāgasenaṃ upasaṅkamitvā therassa pāde sirasā vanditvā ekamantaṃ ṭhito idam-avoca:

9 atthi me bhante nāgasena koci attho tumhehi saddhiṃ mantayitabbo, na tattha añño koci tatiyo icchitabbo, suññe okāse pavivitte araññe aṭṭhangupāgate samaṇasāruppe tattha so pañho pucchitabbo bhavissati, tattha me guyhaṃ

When the dawn with its brilliance broke through the night, 7
King Milinda bathed his head and reverently placed his hands
together at his forehead. Calling to mind the past, present,
and future perfect buddhas, he took up eight virtuous practices: "For the next seven days I will live as an ascetic and
observe these virtuous practices. Then, as a disciple having
accomplished austerities, I will win over the teacher and ask
questions about the ram horn dilemmas." He set aside his
usual suit of clothing, took off his ornaments, dressed in a
saffron robe, fastened the novice's topknot to his head, and
took up, as a holy man, eight virtuous practices. "For the next
seven days I will not consider matters of state nor give rise to
thoughts of passion, thoughts of hatred, or thoughts of delusion. I shall behave with humility to slaves, workmen, and
servants, guard my body and speech, safeguard completely
my six sense bases, and direct my mind to the development
of loving-kindness."

For seven days he did not go out. He passed the time 8
observing these eight qualities and directing his mind to
these eight virtuous practices. On the eighth day when
the morning light broke through the night, he breakfasted
early and approached Elder Nagasena, keeping his eyes cast
down, his speech measured, his movements composed, and
his mind unperturbed, joyful, elated, and clear. He bowed
his head to the feet of the elder, stood to one side, and said:
"Revered Nagasena, there is something I must discuss with 9
you alone, and I want no one else present. This is a question
to be asked in an empty place, in a secluded forest appropriate for renouncers in eight respects. Once there, nothing
should be held back or kept secret from me. For I am worthy

na kātabbaṃ na rahassakaṃ, arahām' ahaṃ rahassakaṃ suṇituṃ sumantaṇe upagate. upamāya pi so attho upaparikkhitabbo, yathā kiṃ viya: yathā nāma bhante nāgasena mahāpaṭhavī nikkhepaṃ arahati nikkhepe upagate, evameva kho bhante nāgasena arahāmahaṃ rahassakaṃ suṇituṃ sumantaṇe upagate ti.

10 gurunā pi saha pavivittaṃ pavanaṃ pavisitvā idamavoca: bhante nāgasena, idha purisena mantayitukāmena aṭṭha-ṭṭhānāni parivajjayitabbāni bhavanti, na tesu ṭhānesu viññū puriso atthaṃ manteti, mantito pi attho paripaṭati na sambhavati; katamāni aṭṭha-ṭṭhānāni: visamaṭṭhānaṃ parivajjanīyaṃ, sabhayaṃ parivajjaṇīyaṃ, ativātaṭṭhānaṃ parivajjanīyaṃ, paṭicchannaṭṭhānaṃ parivajjanīyaṃ, devaṭṭhānaṃ parivajjanīyaṃ, pantho parivajjanīyo, saṅkamo parivajjanīyo, udakatitthaṃ parivajjanīyaṃ, imāni aṭṭha-ṭṭhānāni parivajjanīyānīti.

11 thero āha: ko doso visamaṭṭhāne sabhaye ativāte paṭicchanne devaṭṭhāne panthe sankame udakatitthe ti. visame bhante nāgasena mantito attho vikirati vidhamati paggharati na sambhavati; sabhaye mano santasati, santasito na sammā atthaṃ samanupassati; ativāte saddo avibhūto hoti; paṭicchanne upassutiṃ tiṭṭhanti; devaṭṭhāne mantito attho garukaṃ pariṇamati; panthe mantito attho tuccho bhavati; saṅkame calācalo bhavati; udakatitthe pākaṭo bhavati. bhavatīha: visamaṃ sabhayaṃ ativāto paṭicchannaṃ devanissitaṃ pantho ca saṅkamo titthaṃ, aṭṭh' ete parivajjayāti.

to hear secret matters when we come together in consultation. My meaning here may be revealed by a simile: Just as the wide earth is worthy of receiving treasure when treasure is at hand, so I am worthy of hearing secret matters when private counsel is at hand."

When he and the teacher entered a secluded wood, he 10
spoke: "Revered Nagasena, there are eight places to be avoided when a person wishes to consult in private. A wise person does not discuss matters in these places, since whatever is discussed would go to ruin and not be realized. What are the eight places? Places that have uneven ground, are frightening or too windy, covered places, shrines to deities, roadways, bridges, and beaches are all to be avoided. These are the eight places best avoided."

The elder asked: "But what is wrong with uneven ground, 11
frightening, windy, and covered places? Or shrines, roadways, bridges, and beaches?"

"On uneven ground, Nagasena, the meaning discussed stumbles and falls, tumbling out before being composed. In a frightening place, the mind is afraid, and when one is frightened one cannot see the matter properly. In a windy place the sound is not clear; in a covered spot people could be listening; and at a deity's shrine the meaning discussed transforms into something ponderous. On a roadway the meaning discussed becomes vacuous, on a bridge it goes back and forth, and on a beach it becomes commonplace. For this has been said: 'Uneven ground; frightening, windy, and covered places; habitations of deities; roadways; bridges; and beaches: these eight are best avoided.'

12 bhante nāgasena, aṭṭh' ime puggalā mantiyamānā mantitaṃ atthaṃ byāpādenti, katame aṭṭha: rāgacarito dosacarito mohacarito mānacarito luddho alaso ekacintī bālo ti, ime aṭṭha puggalā mantitaṃ atthaṃ byāpādentīti. thero āha: tesaṃ ko doso ti. rāgacarito bhante nāgasena rāgavasena mantitaṃ atthaṃ byāpādeti, dosacarito dosavasena mantitaṃ atthaṃ byāpādeti, mohacarito mohavasena mantitaṃ atthaṃ byāpādeti, mānacarito mānavasena mantitaṃ atthaṃ byāpādeti, luddho lobhavasena mantitaṃ atthaṃ byāpādeti, alaso alasatāya mantitaṃ atthaṃ byāpādeti, ekacintī ekacintitāya mantitaṃ atthaṃ byāpādeti, bālo bālatāya mantitaṃ atthaṃ byāpādeti. bhavatīha: ratto duṭṭho ca mūḷho ca mānī luddho tathā 'laso ekacintī ca bālo ca, ete atthavināsakā ti.

13 bhante nāgasena, nav' ime puggalā mantitaṃ guyhaṃ vivaranti na dhārenti, katame nava: rāgacarito dosacarito mohacarito bhīruko āmisagaruko itthī soṇḍo paṇḍako dārako ti. thero āha: tesaṃ ko doso ti. rāgacarito bhante nāgasena rāgavasena mantitaṃ guyhaṃ vivarati na dhāreti, duṭṭho dosavasena mantitaṃ guyhaṃ vivarati na dhāreti, mūḷho mohavasena mantitaṃ guyhaṃ vivarati na dhāreti, bhīruko bhayavasena mantitaṃ guyhaṃ vivarati na dhāreti, āmisagaruko āmisahetu mantitaṃ guyhaṃ vivarati na dhāreti, itthī ittaratāya mantitaṃ guyhaṃ vivarati na dhāreti, soṇḍiko surālolatāya mantitaṃ guyhaṃ vivarati na dhāreti, paṇḍako anekaṃsikatāya mantitaṃ guyhaṃ vivarati na dhāreti, dārako capalatāya mantitaṃ guyhaṃ vivarati na dhāreti.

"And further, Nagasena, sir, there are eight types of people 12
who, when they consult together, spoil the matter discussed. Which eight? Those given to passion, hate, delusion, or pride; the greedy; the idle; the person who thinks of only one thing; and the fool. These eight people spoil the matter discussed."

The elder asked: "What are their faults?"

"Those given to passion spoil the matter under discussion with their passion; those given to hate spoil the matter with hatred; those given to delusion spoil it with delusion; and those given to pride spoil it with their pride. The greedy spoil the matter under discussion with their greed, the idle with their laziness, the person who thinks of only one thing by pressing only a single idea, and a fool spoils the discussion with stupidity. For this has been said: 'These eight destroy the purpose: the impassioned, malevolent, deluded, prideful, greedy, idle, single-minded, and foolish.'

"Additionally, Nagasena, there are nine people who cannot 13
keep a discussion secret and will broadcast it: one given to passion, hate, or delusion; a coward; one who cares only about wealth; a woman; a drunk; a eunuch; and a child."

The elder asked: "What are their faults?"

"Nagasena, sir, the one given to passion reveals and cannot keep a discussion secret because of passion; a malevolent person will reveal a secret because of hatred; a deluded person because of delusion; a coward because of fear; a person who cares only about wealth will reveal a secret for a reward; a woman because of fickleness; a drunk because of being muddled by drink; a eunuch because of vacillating; and a child because of thoughtlessness.

14 bhavatīha: ratto duṭṭho ca mūḷho ca bhīru āmisacakkhuko itthī soṇḍo paṇḍako ca, navamo bhavati dārako: nav' ete puggalā loke ittarā calitā calā; etehi mantitaṃ guyhaṃ khippaṃ bhavati pākaṭanti. bhante nāgasena, aṭṭhahi kāraṇehi buddhi pariṇamati paripākaṃ gacchati, katamehi aṭṭhahi: vayapariṇāmena buddhi pariṇamati paripākaṃ gacchati, yasapariṇāmena buddhi pariṇamati paripākaṃ gacchati, paripucchāya buddhi pariṇamati paripākaṃ gacchati, titthasaṃvāsena buddhi pariṇamati paripākaṃ gacchati, yoniso manasikārena buddhi pariṇamati paripākaṃ gacchati, sākacchāya buddhi pariṇamati paripākaṃ gacchati, snehūpasevanavasena buddhi pariṇamati paripākaṃ gacchati, patirūpadesavāsena buddhi pariṇamati paripākaṃ gacchati.

15 bhavatīha: vayena yasa-pucchāhi titthavāsena yoniso sākacchā' snehasaṃsevā' patirūpavasena ca: etāni aṭṭha ṭhānāni buddhivisadakārakā, yesaṃ etāni sambhonti tesaṃ buddhi pabhijjatīti. bhante nāgasena, ayam bhumibhāgo aṭṭha-mantadosa-vivajjito, ahañ-ca loke paramo mantisahāyo, guyham-anurakkhī cāhaṃ, yāvāhaṃ jīvissāmi tāva guyham-anurakkhissāmi, aṭṭhahi ca me kāraṇehi buddhi pariṇāmaṃ gatā; dullabho etarahi mādiso antevāsī.

16 sammā paṭipanne antevāsike ye ācariyānaṃ pañcavīsati ācariyaguṇā tehi guṇehi ācariyena sammā paṭipajjitabbaṃ. katame pañcavīsati guṇā: idha bhante ācariyena antevāsimhi satataṃ samitaṃ ārakkhā upaṭṭhapetabbā, asevana-sevanā jānitabbā, pamattāppamattatā jānitabbā, seyyāvakāso jānitabbo, gelaññaṃ jānitabbaṃ, bhojanaṃ laddhāladdhaṃ jānitabbaṃ, viseso jānitabbo, pattagataṃ saṃvibhaj-

"For this has been said: 'The impassioned, the malevolent, the deluded, the fearful, the person eyeing riches, a woman, a drunk, the eunuch, and a child makes up nine: these are the nine kinds of people in this world who are fickle, unstable, and confused, and they quickly broadcast a secret discussion.' 14

"Nagasena, intelligence ripens and matures by eight means. What are the eight means? Intelligence ripens and matures by the ripening of age and by the ripening of reputation. Intelligence ripens and matures by asking questions. And it ripens and matures by living with a teacher, by careful attention, conversation, honoring those one loves, and living in an appropriate place.

"For this has been said: 'Intelligence can be clarified by age, reputation, asking questions, a teacher, attention, conversation, honoring those one loves, and living in an appropriate place. Where these eight occur, intelligence develops.' 15

"Nagasena, this spot of ground is free of the eight faults imperiling private consultation, and I am the best friend in the world for consulting since I protect secrets and will guard a secret for as long as I live. My intelligence has matured by the eight means. Accordingly, a student like me is hard to come by.

"When a student is practicing rightly, the teacher should properly adhere to the twenty-five qualities of a teacher. What are the twenty-five qualities? Sir, a teacher should constantly and consistently look after and protect students; make known what is to be pursued and what is not to be pursued; point out negligence and carefulness; give opportunities for rest; and advise about illness. A teacher should 16

itabbaṃ, assāsetabbo: mā bhāyi, attho te abhikkamatīti, iminā puggalena paṭicaratīti paṭicāro jānitabbo, gāme paṭicāro jānitabbo, vihāre paṭicāro jānitabbo, na tena saha sallāpo kātabbo, chiddaṃ disvā adhivāsetabbaṃ, sakkaccakārinā bhavitabbaṃ, akhaṇḍakārinā bhavitabbaṃ, arahassakārinā bhavitabbaṃ, niravasesakārinā bhavitabbaṃ, janem' imaṃ sippesūti janakacittaṃ upaṭṭhapetabbaṃ, kathaṃ ayaṃ na parihāyeyyāti vaḍḍhicittaṃ upaṭṭhapetabbaṃ, balavaṃ imaṃ karomi sikkhābalenāti cittaṃ upaṭṭhapetabbaṃ mettacittaṃ upaṭṭhapetabbaṃ, āpadāsu na vijahitabbaṃ, karaṇīye nappamajjitabbaṃ, khalite dhammena paggahetabbo ti. ime kho bhante pañcavīsati ācariyassa ācariyaguṇā, tehi guṇehi mayi sammā paṭipajjassu.

17 saṃsayo me bhante uppanno, atthi meṇḍakapañhā jinabhāsitā, anāgate addhāne tattha viggaho uppajjissati, anāgate ca addhāne dullabhā bhavissanti tumhādisā buddhimanto, tesu me pañhesu cakkhuṃ dehi paravādānaṃ niggahāyāti.

18 thero sādhūti sampaṭicchitvā dasa upāsakassa upāsakaguṇe paridīpesi: dasa ime mahārāja upāsakassa upāsakaguṇā, katame dasa: idha mahārāja upāsako saṅghena samānasukhadukkho hoti, dhammādhipateyyo hoti, yathābalaṃ saṃvibhāgarato hoti, jinasāsanaparihāniṃ disvā abhivaḍḍhiyā vāyamati, sammādiṭṭhiko hoti, apagatakotūhalamaṅgaliko jīvitahetu pi na aññaṃ satthāraṃ uddisati, kāyikaṃ vācasikañ-c' assa rakkhitaṃ hoti, samaggārāmo hoti samaggarato, anusuyyako hoti, na ca kuhanavasena sāsane carati,

instruct students about receiving and declining food, and about particular foods, and must share what he has received. A teacher consoles a student, saying, 'Don't worry, you will reach your goal.' When the student sets out to visit someone, the teacher advises about the particulars of the visit, the village, the monastery, and topics of conversation to be avoided. Though seeing a flaw, one should be patient. In all doings, a teacher should be thorough, complete, without secrets, and inclusive. A teacher fosters a mind that grows, reflecting on how one should develop in the arts, and how, once the mind has grown, deterioration can be prevented. Thinking about how to produce strength, a teacher fosters a mind with strength in the monastic training and thoughts of loving-kindness. A teacher must not forsake a student in times of calamity; does not shirk obligations; and catches the faltering student with the Dhamma. These, sir, are the twenty-five qualities of a teacher. May you properly adhere to these qualities with respect to me.

"Sir, I have uncertainty. The words of the Victor include 17
the ram horn dilemmas. In the future there will be quarreling about them and intelligent persons like you will be hard to find. Please give me insight into these questions for the sake of restraining those with opposing views."

The elder agreed, "Very well," and then he explained the 18
ten virtues of a layman. "These, great king, are the ten virtues of a layman: a layman shares the happiness and sorrow of the monastic community; he is governed by the Dhamma; he is as generous as he can afford to be; seeing the dispensation of the Victor deteriorating, he strives to develop it; he holds right views; he gives up trusting in superstitions; he does not

buddhaṃ saranaṃ gato hoti, dhammaṃ saraṇaṃ gato hoti, saṅghaṃ saraṇaṃ gato hoti. ime kho mahārāja dasa upāsakassa upāsakaguṇā, te sabbe guṇā tayi saṃvijjanti, taṃ te yuttaṃ pattaṃ anucchavikaṃ patirūpaṃ yaṃ tvaṃ jinasāsanaparihāniṃ disvā abhivaḍḍhiṃ icchasi. karomi te okāsaṃ, puccha maṃ tvaṃ yathāsukhan-ti.

19 atha kho milindo rājā katāvakāso nipacca guruno pāde sirasi añjaliṃ katvā etad-avoca: bhante nāgasena, ime titthiyā evaṃ bhaṇanti: yadi buddho pūjaṃ sādiyati na parinibbuto buddho, saṃyutto lokena antobhaviko lokasmiṃ lokasādhāraṇo, tasmā tassa kato adhikāro vañjho bhavati aphalo; yadi parinibbuto, visaṃyutto lokena nissaṭo sabbabhavehi, tassa pūjā na uppajjati, parinibbuto na kiñci sādiyati, asādiyantassa kato adhikāro vañjho bhavati aphalo ti. ubhatokoṭiko eso pañho, n'eso visayo appattamānasānaṃ, mahantānaṃ yev' eso visayo, bhind' etaṃ diṭṭhijālaṃ, ekaṃse ṭhapaya, tav' eso pañho anuppatto, anāgatānaṃ jinaputtānaṃ cakkhuṃ dehi paravādaniggahāyāti.

20 thero āha: parinibbuto mahārāja bhagavā, na ca bhagavā pūjaṃ sādiyati, bodhimūle yeva tathāgatassa sādiyanā pahīnā, kim-pana anupādisesāya nibbānadhātuyā parinibbutassa. bhāsitam-p' etaṃ mahārāja therena sāriputtena

go to another teacher even for the sake of his livelihood; he guards his body and speech; he delights in harmony, avoids envy, and lives within the dispensation without hypocrisy; and he has taken refuge in the Buddha, the Dhamma, and the community. Great king, these ten lay virtues are all found in you. It is entirely appropriate, fitting, suitable, and pleasing that you, seeing the dispensation of the Victor deteriorating, want to develop it. I give you permission: ask me whatever you want."

On receiving this permission, King Milinda humbly 19
joined his hands together at his forehead, and bowing to the teacher's feet, said: "Nagasena, other teachers say that if the Buddha receives worship then he cannot have achieved final nibbana. He still partakes of worldly things, is in the world, and is still tied to the world. And so service done to him is barren and fruitless. On the other hand, if he has achieved final nibbana, he is disconnected from the world and free of all conditions, and no worship occurs since he does not receive it. Service done to one who does not receive it is also barren and fruitless. This two-pronged dilemma is not within the scope of those whose minds are not realized. It is within the scope only of the great. Cut through this net of wrong views and set it aside. This question has come to you. Please grant insight to the Victor's future descendants for refuting those of opposing views."[1]

The elder replied: "Great king, the Bhagavan has attained 20
final nibbana and he does not receive worship. The Tathagata gave up receiving everything even while at the root of the Bodhi Tree, to say nothing of his final nibbana, the domain of nibbana where there is no remaining material support.[2]

dhammasenāpatinā: pūjiyantā asamasamā sadevamānusehi te na sādiyanti sakkāraṃ, buddhānaṃ esa dhammatā ti.

21 rājā āha: bhante nāgasena, putto vā pituno vaṇṇaṃ bhāsati pitā vā puttassa vaṇṇaṃ bhāsati, na c' etaṃ kāraṇaṃ paravādānaṃ niggahāya, pasādappakāsanaṃ nām' etaṃ, iṅgha me tvaṃ tattha kāraṇaṃ sammā brūhi sakavādassa patiṭṭhāpanāya diṭṭhijālaviniveṭhanāyāti. thero āha: parinibbuto mahārāja bhagavā, na ca bhagavā pūjaṃ sādiyati, asādiyantass' eva tathāgatassa devamanussā dhāturatanaṃ vatthuṃ karitvā tathāgatassa ñāṇaratanārammaṇena sammāpaṭipattiṃ sevantā tisso sampattiyo paṭilabhanti.

22 yathā mahārāja mahatimahāaggikkhandho pajjalitvā nibbāyeyya, api nu kho so mahārāja aggikkhandho sādiyati tiṇakaṭṭhupādānan-ti. jalamāno pi so bhante mahāaggikkhandho tiṇakaṭṭhupādānaṃ na sādiyati, kim-pana nibbuto upasanto acetano sādiyatīti. tasmiṃ pana mahārāja aggikkhandhe uparate upasante loke aggi suñño hotīti. na hi bhante, kaṭṭhaṃ aggissa vatthu hoti upādānaṃ, ye keci manussā aggikāmā te attano thāmabalaviriyena paccattapurisakārena kaṭṭhaṃ manthayitvā aggiṃ nibbattetvā tena agginā aggikaraṇīyāni kammāni karontīti.

For Elder Sariputta, the General of the Dhamma, said this: 'Though worshiped by humans and gods, the incomparable ones do not accept homage. This is the nature of things for buddhas.'"

The king asserted: "Nagasena, a son will praise his father, 21
or a father will praise his son. But this cannot be a basis for
refuting other views. It only expresses one's own confidence.
Come, give me a proper reason for staying with your own
view and for unraveling the net of wrong views."

The elder replied: "Great king, the Bhagavan has achieved
final nibbana and the Bhagavan does not receive worship.
But if gods and humans build a site with a precious relic of
the Tathagata and practice the proper method with it as a
basis for meditating on the Tathagata's precious knowledge,
they may thereby obtain the three attainments.[3] Consider a 22
huge fire that blazes up and is then extinguished. Does that
massive fire then intentionally accept straw and kindling as
fuel?

"Even while it was burning that huge mass of fire did not accept straw and kindling as fuel, so why, once it is tamed and extinguished, would it, a thing lacking intention, receive them?

"But when the fire is tamed and put out, great king, is the world then devoid of fire?"

"No, sir. Kindling is the fuel that is the basis of fire, and people who want a fire can, with their own exertion and strength and for their own purposes, take a churning stick to the kindling and make fire. And then they can use the fire as they see fit."

23 tena hi mahārāja titthiyānaṃ vacanaṃ micchā bhavati: asādiyantassa kato adhikāro vañjho bhavati aphalo ti. yathā mahārāja mahatimahāaggikkhandho pajjali, evam-eva bhagavā dasasahassimhi lokadhātuyā buddhasiriyā pajjali; yathā mahārāja mahatimahāaggikkhandho pajjalitvā nibbuto, evam-eva bhagavā dasasahassimhi lokadhātuyā buddhasiriyā pajjalitvā anupādisesāya nibbānadhātuyā parinibbuto; yathā mahārāja nibbuto aggikkhandho tiṇakaṭṭhupādānaṃ na sādiyati, evam-eva kho lokahitassa sādiyanā pahīnā upasantā; yathā mahārāja manussā nibbute aggikkhandhe anupādāne attano thāmabalaviriyena paccattapurisakārena kaṭṭhaṃ manthayitvā aggiṃ nibbattetvā tena agginā aggikaraṇīyāni kammāni karonti, evam-eva devamanussā tathāgatassa parinibbutassa asādiyantass' eva dhāturatanaṃ vatthuṃ karitvā tathāgatassa ñāṇaratanārammaṇena sammāpaṭipattiṃ sevantā tisso sampattiyo paṭilabhanti. iminā pi mahārāja kāraṇena tathāgatassa parinibbutassa asādiyantass' eva kato adhikāro avañjho bhavati saphalo ti.

24 aparam-pi mahārāja uttariṃ kāraṇaṃ suṇohi yena kāraṇena tathāgatassa parinibbutassa asādiyantass' eva kato adhikāro avañjho bhavati saphalo: yathā mahārāja mahatimahāvāto vāyitvā uparameyya, api nu kho so mahārāja uparato vāto sādiyati puna nibbattāpanan-ti. na hi bhante

"Then teachers of other sects are wrong, great king, when 23
they say that a service done for one who does not receive it is barren and fruitless. For the Bhagavan blazed up with the splendor of a buddha in the ten-thousand-world system just as that huge fire blazed up. And just as the massive fire blazes up and then is extinguished, the Bhagavan blazes up with the splendor of a buddha in the ten-thousand-world system and then achieves final nibbana, the domain of nibbana where there is no remaining material support. And just as the massive fire, once put out, does not receive straw and kindling as fuel, so too he, for the benefit of the world, gave up receiving anything. Yet, great king, even where the huge fire has gone out, people will start other fires with their own exertion and strength and for their own purposes, taking a churning stick to kindling. And they will make use of that fire as they need to. In much the same way, gods and humans can build a site for a precious relic of the Tathagata even though he has attained final nibbana and does not receive anything. They may practice with the proper method, using the site as a basis for meditating on the Tathagata's precious knowledge, and reach the three attainments. It is for this reason, great king, that service done to the Tathagata, who has attained final nibbana and does not receive anything, can become fruitful and not be barren.

"Great king, please listen to another reason why service 24
done for the Tathagata, who has attained final nibbana and does not receive anything, is fruitful and not barren. Think of a massive windstorm that first rages but then dies down. Would that wind, once died down, decide to pick up again?"

"No, sir. There is no thought or attention in wind that is

uparatassa vātassa ābhogo vā manasikāro vā puna nibbattāpanāya, kiṅkāraṇaṃ: acetanā sā vāyodhātūti.

25 api nu tassa mahārāja uparatassa vātassa vāto ti samaññā upagacchatīti. na hi bhante, tālavaṇṭa-vidhūpanāni vātassa uppattiyā paccayā, ye keci manussā uṇhābhitattā pariḷāhaparipīḷitā te tālavaṇṭena vā vidhūpanena vā attano thāmabalaviriyena paccattapurisakārena vātaṃ nibbattetvā tena vātena uṇhaṃ nibbāpenti pariḷāhaṃ vūpasamentīti.

26 tena hi mahārāja titthiyānaṃ vacanaṃ micchā bhavati: asādiyantassa kato adhikāro vañjho bhavati aphalo ti. yathā mahārāja mahatimahāvāto vāyi, evam-eva bhagavā dasasahassimhi lokadhātuyā sītala-madhura-santa-sukhuma-mettāvātena upavāyi; yathā mahārāja mahatimahāvāto vāyitvā uparato, evam-eva bhagavā sītala-madhura-santa-sukhuma-mettāvātena upavāyitvā anupādisesāya nibbānadhātuyā parinibbuto; yathā mahārāja uparato vāto puna nibbattā panaṃ na sādiyati, evam-eva lokahitassa sādiyanā pahīnā upasantā; yathā mahārāja te manussā uṇhābhitattā pariḷāhaparipīḷitā, evam-eva devamanussā tividhaggi-santāpa-pariḷāha-paripīḷitā; yathā tālāvaṇṭa-vidhūpanāni vātassa nibbattiyā paccayā honti, evam-eva tathāgatassa dhātu ca ñāṇaratanañ-ca paccayo hoti tissannaṃ sampattīnaṃ paṭilābhāya; yathā manussā uṇhābhitattā pariḷāhaparipīḷitā

calmed, for the very reason that the element of wind is without intention."

"Moreover, great king, does the word 'wind' even continue 25
to apply to wind that has died down?"

"No, sir. But wind can be generated by a palm leaf or a fan, and people who are hot or are suffering from a fever can generate a breeze by fanning a palm leaf or a fan with their own exertion and strength and for their own purposes. And with this wind they cool off their heat and relieve their fevers."

"And so, great king, the teachers of other sects are wrong 26
when they say service done to one who does not receive it is barren and fruitless. For just like a huge windstorm that blows, the Bhagavan wafted through the ten-thousand-world system with the breeze of loving-kindness, cool, sweet, calm, and subtle. And just as the great wind blows but then ceases, so too the Bhagavan wafted with the cool, sweet, calm, and subtle breeze of loving-kindness, and then achieved final nibbana, the domain of nibbana where there is no further material support. That breeze is stilled and does not consent to being regenerated since, for the sake of the world, he gave up receiving everything. Gods and humans who are scorched by the burning and torment of the three fires* are like people who are hot or feverish. And generating a breeze with a palm leaf or a fan is much like meditating on the precious knowledge with the support of a relic of the Tathagata and thereby obtaining the three attainments. For just as those who are hot and feverish generate a breeze with a palm leaf or a fan

* Greed, hatred, and delusion.

tālavaṇṭena vā vidhūpanena vā vātaṃ nibbattetvā uṇhaṃ nibbāpenti pariḷāhaṃ vūpasamenti, evam-eva devamanussā tathāgatassa parinibbutassa asādiyantass' eva dhātuñ-ca ñāṇaratanañ-ca pūjetvā kusalaṃ nibbattetvā tena kusalena tividhaggi-santāpa-pariḷāhaṃ nibbāpenti vūpasamenti. iminā pi mahārāja kāraṇena tathāgatassa parinibbutassa asādiyantass' eva kato adhikāro avañjho bhavati saphalo ti.

27 aparam-pi mahārāja uttariṃ kāraṇaṃ suṇohi paravādānaṃ niggahāya: yathā mahārāja puriso bheriṃ ākoṭetvā saddaṃ nibbatteyya, yo so bherisaddo purisena nibbattito so saddo antaradhāyeyya, api nu kho so mahārāja saddo sādiyati puna nibbattāpanan-ti. na hi bhante, antarahito so saddo, na-tthi tassa puna uppādāya ābhogo vā manasikāro vā, sakiṃ nibbatte bherisadde antarahite so bherisaddo samucchinno hoti, bheri pana bhante paccayo hoti saddassa nibbattiyā, atha puriso paccaye sati attajena vāyāmena bheriṃ ākoṭetvā saddaṃ nibbattetīti.

28 evam-eva kho mahārāja bhagavā sīla-samādhi-paññā-vimutti-vimuttiñāṇadassana-paribhāvitaṃ dhāturatanañ-ca dhammañ-ca vinayañ-ca anusatthiñ-ca satthāraṃ ṭhapayitvā sayaṃ anupādisesāya nibbānadhātuyā parinibbuto, na ca parinibbute bhagavati sampattilābho upacchinno hoti, bhavadukkhapatipīḷitā sattā dhāturatanañ-ca dhammavinayañ-ca anusatthiñ-ca paccayaṃ karitvā sampattikāmā sampattiyo paṭilabhanti. iminā pi mahārāja kāraṇena tathā-

and thereby cool their heat or relieve their fever, gods and humans worship the precious knowledge by means of the Tathagata's relic, though he has achieved final nibbana and does not receive anything. They generate something good, and with it they cool the fever and torment of the three fires. In this way, great king, service done to the Tathagata, who has achieved final nibbana and does not receive it, is fruitful and not barren.

"Please hear further reasoning, great king, that may refute 27
the views of opponents. When a person beats a drum and generates a sound, the sound that he makes must eventually vanish. Does that sound agree to be produced again?"

"No, sir. Sound is something that once vanished is not reproduced. And it is without thought and attention, so that once a sound produced by a drum has disappeared, it is cut off. But another sound can be generated with the drum, and a person can put his own effort into striking the drum and produce sound by these means."

"Likewise, great king, the Bhagavan appointed as a 28
teacher his precious relics, the Dhamma, the *vinaya,* and the instruction, enhanced by moral discipline, concentration, understanding, freedom, and liberated knowing and seeing. Although he himself has attained the final nibbana where there is no further material support, and although the Bhagavan himself is extinguished, achieving the attainments is not cut off. Beings crushed by the suffering of life and seeking attainments make use of the precious relics, the Dhamma, the *vinaya,* and the instruction, and then reach the attainments. By this reasoning too, great king, service done

gatassa parinibbutassa asādiyantass' eva kato adhikāro avañjho bhavati saphaloti.

29 diṭṭhañ-c' etaṃ mahārāja bhagavatā anāgatam addhānaṃ kathitañ-ca bhaṇitañ-ca ācikkhitañ-ca. siyā kho pan' ānanda tumhākaṃ evam-assa: atīta-satthukaṃ pāvacanaṃ, na-tthi no satthā ti; na kho pan' etaṃ ānanda evaṃ daṭṭhabbaṃ, yo vo ānanda mayā dhammo ca vinayo ca desito paññatto so vo mam' accayena satthā ti. parinibbutassa tathāgatassa asādiyantassa kato adhikāro vañjho bhavati aphalo ti taṃ tesaṃ titthiyānaṃ vacanaṃ micchā abhūtaṃ vitathaṃ alikaṃ viruddhaṃ viparītaṃ, dukkhadāyakaṃ dukkhavipākaṃ apāyagamanīyan-ti.

30 aparam-pi mahārāja uttariṃ kāraṇaṃ suṇohi yena kāraṇena tathāgatassa parinibbutassa asādiyantass'eva kato adhikāro avañjho bhavati saphalo: sādiyati nu kho mahārāja ayaṃ mahāpaṭhavī: sabbabījāni mayi saṃvirūhantūti. na hi bhante ti. kissa pana tāni mahārāja bījāni asādiyantiyā mahāpaṭhaviyā saṃvirūhitvā daḷhamūlajaṭā-patiṭṭhitā khandhasārasākhā-parivitthiṇṇā pupphaphaladharā hontīti.

31 asādiyantī pi bhante mahāpaṭhavī tesaṃ bījānaṃ vatthu hoti paccayaṃ deti virūhanāya, tāni bījāni taṃ vatthuṃ nissāya tena paccayena saṃvirūhitvā daḷhamūlajaṭā-patiṭṭhitā khandhasārasākhāparivitthiṇṇā pupphaphaladharā hontīti.

to the Tathagata, who has attained final nibbana and does not receive it, is still fruitful and not barren.

“Moreover, great king, the Bhagavan foresaw the future, 29
and he described, explained, and spoke of it in this way: ‘It may be, Ananda, that you might think: “In the past we had the Teacher’s words, but now our Teacher is gone.” Do not see it this way, Ananda. The Dhamma and the *vinaya* have been taught and made known by me, and they are your teacher after my passing.’ So when teachers of other sects claim that service done for the Tathagata, who has attained final nibbana and does not receive it, is barren and fruitless, their words are wrong, false, untrue, unreal, disturbed, and perverse. Such claims give pain, result in suffering, and lead to hell.

“And please listen, great king, to yet another reason service 30
done for the Tathagata, who has attained final nibbana and does not receive it, is still fruitful and not barren. Does the great earth agree to receive seeds, saying, ‘May all these seeds germinate in me’?” “Of course not, sir.” “But then, great king, how do the seeds germinate in the earth if it does not agree to this? How do they manage to grow into a tangle of strong roots and develop a trunk, heartwood, and branches bearing fruit and flowers?”

“Although the earth does not give assent, sir, it becomes 31
the field for the seeds and it provides the conditions for them to grow. The seeds depend on the field and the conditions to grow and they develop into a tangle of strong roots with a trunk, heartwood, and branches bearing fruit and flowers.”

32 tena hi mahārāja titthiyā sake vāde naṭṭhā honti hatā viruddhā, sace te bhaṇanti: asādiyantassa kato adhikāro vañjho bhavati aphalo ti. yathā mahārāja mahāpaṭhavī evaṃ tathāgato arahaṃ sammāsambuddho, yathā mahārāja mahāpaṭhavī na kiñci sādiyati evaṃ tathāgato na kiñci sādiyati, yathā mahārāja tāni bījāni paṭhaviṃ nissāya saṃvirūhitvā daḷhamūlajaṭā-patiṭṭhitā khandhasārasākhā-parivitthiṇṇā pupphaphaladharā honti evaṃ devamanussā tathāgatassa parinibbutassa asādiyantass' eva dhātuñ-ca ñāṇaratanañ-ca nissāya daḷhakusalamūla-patiṭṭhitā samādhikkhandha-dhammasāra-sīlasākhā-parivitthiṇṇā vimuttipuppha-sāmaññaphaladharā honti. iminā pi mahārāja kāraṇena tathāgatassa parinibbutassa asādiyantass' eva kato adhikāro avañjho bhavati saphalo ti.

33 aparam-pi mahārāja uttariṃ kāraṇaṃ suṇohi yena kāraṇena tathāgatassa parinibbutassa asādiyantass' eva kato adhikāro avañjho bhavati saphalo: sādiyanti nu kho mahārāja ime oṭṭhā goṇā gadrabhā ajā pasū manussā antokucchismiṃ kimikulānaṃ sambhavan-ti. na hi bhante ti. kissa pana te mahārāja kimayo tesaṃ asādiyantānaṃ antokucchismiṃ sambhavitvā bahuputtanattā vepullataṃ pāpuṇantīti. pāpassa bhante kammassa balavatāya asādiyantānaṃ yeva tesaṃ sattānaṃ antokucchiṃ kimayo sambhavitvā bahuputtanattā vepullataṃ pāpuṇantīti.

“By this, great king, teachers of other sects will be checked, dismantled, and even demolished if they should say that service done to one who does not receive it is barren and fruitless. For the Perfectly Awakened Enlightened Tathagata is like the earth. Like the Tathagata, the earth does not agree to receive anything, and yet seeds depend on the earth to develop a tangle of strong roots, a trunk, heartwood, and branches that bear fruit and flowers. And gods and humans depend on relics and the precious knowledge of the Tathagata, though he has attained final nibbana and does not receive anything, to grow the strong roots of goodness and develop the trunk of concentration, the heartwood of the Dhamma, the branches of moral discipline, the flowers of freedom, and the fruits of renunciation. By this reasoning, great king, service done to the Tathagata, who has attained final nibbana and does not receive it, is fruitful and not barren. 32

“Great king, please listen to yet another reason service 33
done to the Tathagata, who has attained final nibbana and does not receive it, is fruitful and not barren. Camels, oxen, donkeys, goats, cattle, and people have various kinds of worms in their bellies. Have they actually agreed to host them?” “Of course not, sir.” “And yet how is it that these worms grow in the bellies of those who do not accept them? What is more, they flourish and multiply!” “It is due to the power of bad karma that worms can appear in the bellies of creatures who do not agree to them, and then flourish and multiply.”

34 evam-eva kho mahārāja tathāgatassa parinibbutassa
asādiyantass' eva dhātussa ca ñāṇārammaṇassa ca balavatāya tathāgate kato adhikāro avañjho bhavati saphalo ti.
aparam-pi mahārāja uttariṃ kāraṇaṃ suṇohi yena kāraṇena
tathāgatassa parinibbutassa asādiyantass' eva kato adhikāro
avañjho bhavati saphalo: sādiyanti nu kho mahārāja ime
manussā: ime aṭṭhanavuti rogā kāye nibbattantūti. na hi
bhante ti. kissa pana te mahārāja rogā asādiyantānaṃ kāye
nipatantīti. Pubbe katena bhante duccaritenāti.
35 yadi mahārāja pubbe kataṃ akusalaṃ idha vedanīyaṃ
hoti, tena hi mahārāja pubbe katam-pi idha katam-pi kusalākusalaṃ kammaṃ avañjhaṃ bhavati saphalan-ti. iminā pi
mahārāja kāraṇena tathāgatassa parinibbutassa asādiyantass'evakato adhikāro avañjho bhavati saphalo ti. sutapubbaṃ pana tayā mahārāja nandako nāma yakkho theraṃ
sāriputtaṃ āsādayitvā paṭhaviṃ paviṭṭho ti. āma bhante,
sūyati, loke pākaṭo eso ti. api nu kho mahārāja thero sāriputto sādiyi nandakassa yakkhassa mahāpaṭhavīgilanan-ti.
36 ubbattiyante pi bhante sadevake loke, patamāne pi
chamāyaṃ candimasuriye, vikirante pi sinerupabbatarāje,
thero sāriputto na parassa dukkhaṃ sādiyeyya, taṃ kissa
hetu: yena hetunā thero sāriputto kujjheyya vā dusseyya
vā so hetu therassa sāriputtassa samūhato samucchinno,
hetuno samugghātitattā bhante thero sāriputto jīvita-

"There is this similarity, great king: it is due to the strength of a relic and the support it offers for meditation on the knowledge of the Tathagata that a service done to him is fruitful and not barren, despite the fact that he has attained final nibbana and does not receive it. 34

"Please listen to yet another line of reasoning about this, great king. There are some ninety-eight diseases that can occur in the human body. Do people actually agree to have them?" "No, sir." "But then how do they afflict a body that does not agree to have them?" "Because of bad conduct done previously, sir."

"If a bad action done previously is to be experienced here, 35
then good and bad karma, whether done previously or done now, will be fruitful and not barren. By this reasoning, great king, service done to the Tathagata, who has attained final nibbana and does not receive it, is fruitful and not barren.

"Have you ever heard, great king, about the *yakkha* named Nandaka who struck the Elder Sariputta? The earth swallowed him up." "Yes, sir, I have heard this, for the story is well known in the world." "Did Elder Sariputta agree to the earth devouring the *yakkha* Nandaka?"

"Even if the world with its deities were being torn up, 36
sir, and the sun and the moon were falling to the ground, and the king of mountains, Mount Sineru, were crumbling, Elder Sariputta would not have consented to anyone suffering. What is the reason for this? Any source of getting angry or being offended had been removed and cut off in Elder Sariputta. Because of extirpating all such conditions, Elder Sariputta could not get angry even if his own life were threatened."

hārake pi kopaṃ na kareyyāti. yadi mahārāja thero sāriputto nandakassa yakkhassa paṭhavīgilanaṃ na sādiyi kissa pana nandako yakkho paṭhaviṃ paviṭṭho ti.

37 akusalassa bhante kammassa balavatāyāti. yadi mahārāja akusalassa kammassa balavatāya nandako yakkho paṭhaviṃ paviṭṭho, asādiyantassāpi kato aparādho avañjho bhavati saphalo, tena hi mahārāja kusalassa pi kammassa balavatāya asādiyantassa kato adhikāro avañjho bhavati saphalo ti. iminā pi mahārāja kāraṇena tathāgatassa parinibbutassa asādiyantass' eva kato adhikāro avañjho bhavati saphalo ti.

38 kati nu kho te mahārāja manussā ye etarahi mahāpaṭhaviṃ paviṭṭhā, atthi te tattha savanan-ti. āma bhante, sūyatīti. iṅgha tvaṃ mahārāja sāvehīti. ciñcamāṇavikā bhante, suppabuddho ca sakko, devadatto ca thero, nandako ca yakkho, nando ca māṇavako ti, sutaṃ metaṃ bhante: ime pañca janā mahāpaṭhaviṃ paviṭṭhā ti. kismiṃ te mahārāja aparaddhā ti. bhagavati ca bhante sāvakesu cāti. api nu kho mahārāja bhagavā vā sāvakā vā sādiyiṃsu imesaṃ mahāpaṭhaviṃ pavisanan-ti. na hi bhante ti. tena hi mahārāja tathāgatassa parinibbutassa asādiyantass' eva kato adhikāro avañjho bhavati saphalo ti.

39 suviññāpito bhante nāgasena pañho gambhīro uttānīkato[1], guyhaṃ vidaṃsitaṃ, gaṇṭhi bhinnā, gahanaṃ agaha-

"But how did the *yakkha* Nandaka enter the earth if the Elder Sariputta did not consent to the earth devouring him, great king?" "It was due to the strength of his bad karma that the *yakkha* Nandaka was swallowed by the earth, sir."

"So, great king, if the *yakkha* Nandaka entered the earth 37
due to the strength of his bad karma, then an offense committed even against someone who does not receive it is fruitful and not barren. Then it must also be the case that a service done to someone who does not receive it is fruitful and not barren, due to the strength of good karma. By this reasoning also, a service done to the Tathagata, who has attained final nibbana and does not receive it, is fruitful and not barren.

"Great king, have you ever heard anything about how 38
many people in our own time have been swallowed up by the earth?" "Sure, I have heard of such things." "Come, great king, tell what you've heard." "I have heard that there have been five people who have entered the earth: the young Brahman woman Chincha, the Sakyan Suppabuddha, the Elder Devadatta, the *yakkha* Nandaka, and the young Brahman Nanda."[4]

"Whom did they offend?" "The Bhagavan and his disciples, sir." "Did the Bhagavan or his disciples agree to their entering the earth, great king?" "No, sir." "By this also, a service done to the Tathagata, who has attained final nibbana and does not receive it, is fruitful and not barren."

"Revered Nagasena, you have thoroughly explained and 39
clarified this deep question, revealing what was obscure, cutting the knot, and clearing the thicket. The opposing view is demolished, false belief is broken up, and rival teachers

naṃ kataṃ, naṭṭhā paravādā, bhaggā kudiṭṭhi, nippabhā jātā kutitthiyā, tvaṃ gaṇivarapavaram-āsajjāti.

40 bhante nāgasena, buddho sabbaññū ti. āma mahārāja, bhagavā sabbaññū, na ca bhagavato satataṃ samitaṃ ñāṇadassanaṃ paccupaṭṭhitaṃ, āvajjanapaṭibaddhaṃ bhagavato sabbaññutañāṇaṃ, āvajjitvā yadicchakaṃ jānātīti. tena hi bhante nāgasena buddho asabbaññū, yadi tassa pariyesanāya sabbaññutañāṇaṃ hotīti.

41 vāhasataṃ kho mahārāja vīhīnaṃ aḍḍhacūḷañ-ca vāhā vīhisatt' ammaṇāni dve ca tumbā ekaccharakkhaṇe pavattacittassa ettakā vīhi lakkhaṃ ṭhapiyamāne parikkhayaṃ pariyādānaṃ gaccheyyuṃ. tatr' ime sattavidhā cittā pavattanti: ye te mahārāja sarāgā sadosā samohā sakkilesā abhāvitakāyā abhāvitasīlā abhāvitacittā abhāvitapaññā tesaṃ taṃ cittaṃ garukaṃ uppajjati dandhaṃ pavattati, kiṅkāraṇaṃ: abhāvitattā cittassa. yathā mahārāja vaṃsanāḷassa vitatassa visālassa vitthiṇṇassa saṃsibbita-visibbitassa sākhājaṭājaṭitassa ākaḍḍhiyantassa garukaṃ hoti āgamanaṃ dandhaṃ, kiṅkāraṇaṃ: saṃsibbita-visibbitattā sākhānaṃ, evam-eva kho mahārāja ye te sarāgā sadosā samohā sakkilesā abhāvitakāyā abhāvitasīlā abhāvitacittā abhāvitapaññā tesam taṃ

have lost their shine. You have joined the ranks of the most excellent and distinguished teachers.

“Nagasena, sir, is the Buddha omniscient?” 40

“Yes, great king, the Bhagavan is omniscient, but the Bhagavan’s knowledge and vision are not fully present at all times. The Bhagavan’s omniscient knowledge is connected to turning his attention to something. He comes to know whatever he wishes when he turns his attention to it.”

“But, Nagasena, the Buddha cannot be omniscient if his omniscient knowledge involves inquiry.”

“Suppose there were a hundred cartloads of rice, great 41
king, with two bushels and seven measures of rice per cart. Could someone arrive at the number of lakhs of rice grains, down to the very last one, while putting their mind to it for only as long as it takes to snap one’s fingers?

“With respect to this, there are seven kinds of awareness, great king. There are people with passion, delusion, and the defilements, who have not developed their bodies, their moral discipline, their awareness, or their understanding. When a serious thought occurs to them, they proceed sluggishly. For what reason? Because their awareness is not developed. Bamboo stalks that are long, wide, spread out, overgrown, and entangled with jumbled and interwoven branches are a serious matter to pull out, and the going is sluggish. Why? Because the branches are jumbled and interwoven. It is similar for those with passion, delusion, and the defilements, who have not developed their bodies, their moral discipline, their awareness, or their understanding. When a serious thought occurs to them, they proceed

cittaṃ garukaṃ uppajjati dandhaṃ pavattati, kiṅkāraṇaṃ: saṃsibbita-visibbitattā kilesehi. idaṃ paṭhamaṃ cittaṃ.

42 tatr' idaṃ dutiyaṃ cittaṃ vibhattim-āpajjati: ye te mahārāja sotāpannā pihitāpāyā diṭṭhippattā viññātasatthusāsanā tesaṃ taṃ cittaṃ tīsu ṭhānesu lahukaṃ uppajjati lahukaṃ pavattati, uparibhūmisu garukaṃ uppajjati dandhaṃ pavattati, kiṅkāraṇaṃ: tīsu ṭhānesu cittassa parisuddhattā, upari kilesānaṃ appahīnattā. Yathā mahārāja vaṃsanāḷassa tipabbagaṇṭhiparisuddhassa upari sākhājaṭājaṭitassa ākaḍḍhiyantassa yāva tipabbaṃ tāva lahukaṃ eti, tato upari thaddhaṃ, kiṅkāraṇaṃ: heṭṭhā parisuddhattā, upari sākhājaṭājaṭitattā, evam-eva kho mahārāja ye te sotāpannā pihitāpāyā diṭṭhippattā viññātasatthusāsanā tesaṃ taṃ cittaṃ tīsu ṭhānesu lahukaṃ uppajjati lahukaṃ pavattati, uparibhūmisu garukaṃ uppajjati dandhaṃ pavattati, kiṅkāraṇaṃ: tīsu ṭhānesu parisuddhattā, upari kilesānaṃ appahīnattā. idaṃ dutiyaṃ cittaṃ.

43 tatr' idaṃ tatiyaṃ cittaṃ vibhattim-āpajjati: ye te mahārāja sakadāgāmino, yesaṃ rāga-dosa-mohā tanubhūtā, tesaṃ taṃ cittaṃ pañcasu ṭhānesu lahukaṃ uppajjati lahukaṃ pavattati, uparibhūmisu garukaṃ uppajjati dandhaṃ pavattati, kiṅkāraṇaṃ: pañcasu ṭhānesu parisuddhattā,

sluggishly. Why? Because of the jumbling and interweaving of their defilements. This is the first kind of awareness.

"The second kind of awareness is analyzed in this way. 42
Stream winners, great king, are closed off from the realms of misery. They have achieved right view and have understood the dispensation of the Teacher. Their awareness concerning the first three states is nimble, and it proceeds lightly; it is only when it approaches a serious matter at the higher planes that it become sluggish.[5] Why? Because of the complete clarity of their awareness concerning the three states, and not having eliminated the defilements in the case of the higher ones. For those pulling out bamboo stalks that are cleared completely up to the first three nodes but jumbled and interwoven at the branches higher up, it is easy for the first three sections but difficult higher up. Why? Because of the clearing below and the interwoven jumble of branches above. Similarly, great king, stream winners are closed off from the realms of misery, have attained right view, and have understood the dispensation of the Teacher, so their awareness of the first three states is nimble, and the going is easy. But on a serious matter at the higher planes, it becomes sluggish. Why? Because of the complete clarity about the first three states, and not having eliminated the defilements higher up. This is the second kind of awareness.

"Now, the third kind of awareness is analyzed in this way. 43
Once returners are those with passion, hatred, and delusion diminished. Their awareness concerning the first five states is nimble and it proceeds lightly, but when it approaches a serious matter at the higher planes it become sluggish.[6] Why? Because of the complete clarity of their awareness

upari kilesānaṃ appahīnattā. yathā mahārāja vaṃsanāḷassa pañcapabbagaṇṭhiparisuddhassa upari sākhājaṭājaṭitassa ākaḍḍhiyantassa yāva pañcapabbaṃ tāva lahukaṃ eti, tato upari thaddhaṃ, kiṅkāraṇaṃ: heṭṭhā parisuddhattā, upari sākhājaṭājaṭitattā, evam-eva kho mahārāja ye te sakadāgāmino, yesaṃ rāga-dosa-mohā tanubhūtā, tesaṃ taṃ cittaṃ pañcasu ṭhānesu lahukaṃ uppajjati lahukaṃ pavattati, uparibhūmisu garukaṃ uppajjati dandhaṃ pavattati, kiṅkāraṇaṃ: pañcasu ṭhānesu cittassa parisuddhattā, upari kilesānaṃ appahīnattā. idaṃ tatiyaṃ cittaṃ.

44 tatr'idaṃ catutthaṃ cittaṃ vibhattim-āpajjati: ye te mahārāja anāgāmino, yesaṃ pañc' orambhāgiyāni saṃyojanāni pahīnāni, tesaṃ taṃ cittaṃ dasasu ṭhānesu lahukaṃ uppajjati lahukaṃ pavattati, uparibhūmisu garukaṃ uppajjati dandhaṃ pavattati, kiṅkāraṇaṃ: dasasu ṭhānesu cittassa parisuddhattā, upari kilesānaṃ appahīnattā. yathā mahārāja vaṃsanāḷassa dasapabbagaṇṭhiparisuddhassa upari sākhājaṭājaṭitassa ākaḍḍhiyantassa yāva dasapabbaṃ tāva lahukaṃ eti, tato upari thaddhaṃ, kiṅkāraṇaṃ: heṭṭhā parisuddhattā, upari sākhājaṭājaṭitattā, evam-eva kho mahārāja ye te

concerning the five states, and not having eliminated the defilements in the case of the higher ones. Great king, for those pulling out bamboo stalks that are cleared completely up to the first five nodes but jumbled and interwoven at the branches higher up, it is easy for the first five sections but difficult higher up. Why? Because of the clearing below and the interwoven jumble of branches above. Similarly, once returners are those who have decreased passion, hatred, and delusion, so their awareness of the first five states* is nimble, and the going is easy. But on a serious matter at the higher planes, it becomes sluggish. Why? Because of the complete clarity about the first five states, and not having eliminated the defilements higher up. This is the third kind of awareness.

"Now, the fourth kind of awareness is analyzed in this 44
way. Nonreturners are those who have eliminated the five bonds in the realm of desire. Their awareness concerning the ten states is nimble and it proceeds lightly, but when it approaches a serious matter at the higher planes it becomes sluggish.[7] Why? Because of the complete clarity of their awareness concerning the ten states, and not having eliminated the defilements in the case of the higher ones. For those pulling out bamboo stalks that are cleared completely up to the first ten nodes but jumbled and interwoven at the branches higher up, it is easy for the first ten sections, but difficult higher up. Why? Because of the clearing below and the interwoven jumble of branches above. Similarly, nonreturners are those who have eliminated the five bonds in the

* These states are also called bonds.

anāgāmino, yesaṃ pañc' orambhāgiyāni saṃyojanāni pahīnāni, tesaṃ taṃ cittaṃ dasasu ṭhānesu lahukaṃ uppajjati lahukaṃ pavattati, uparibhūmisu garukaṃ uppajjati dandhaṃ pavattati, kiṅkāraṇaṃ: dasasu ṭhānesu cittassa parisuddhattā, upari kilesānaṃ appahīnattā. idaṃ catutthaṃ cittaṃ.

45 tatr' idaṃ pañcamaṃ cittaṃ vibhattim-āpajjati: ye te mahārāja arahanto khīṇāsavā dhotamalā vantakilesā vusitavanto katakaraṇīyā ohitabhārā anuppattasadatthā parikkhīṇabhavasaṃyojanā pattapaṭisambhidā sāvakabhūmisu parisuddhā, tesaṃ taṃ cittaṃ sāvakavisaye lahukaṃ uppajjati lahukaṃ pavattati, paccekabuddhabhūmisu garukaṃ uppajjati dandhaṃ pavattati, kiṅkāraṇaṃ: parisuddhattā sāvakavisaye, aparisuddhattā paccekabuddhavisaye. yathā mahārāja vaṃsanāḷassa sabbapabbagaṇṭhiparisuddhassa ākaḍḍhiyantassa lahukaṃ hoti āgamanaṃ adandhaṃ, kiṅkāraṇaṃ: sabbapabbagaṇṭhiparisuddhattā, agahanattā vaṃsassa; evam-eva kho mahārāja ye te arahanto khīṇāsavā dhotamalā vantakilesā vusitavanto katakaraṇīya ohitabhārā anuppattasadatthā parikkhīṇabhavasaṃyojanā pattapaṭisambhidā sāvakabhūmisu parisuddhā, tesaṃ taṃ cittaṃ

realm of desire so their awareness of the first ten states is nimble, and the going is easy. But on a serious matter at the higher planes, it becomes sluggish. Why? Because of the complete clarity about the ten states, and not having eliminated the defilements higher up. This is the fourth kind of awareness.

"Now, the fifth kind of awareness is analyzed in this way. 45
Great king, arhats are those whose flaws are destroyed, stains washed away, and defilements purged.[8] They have lived the holy life, done what had to be done, laid down the burden, reached the highest ideal, destroyed the bonds of becoming, and achieved analytical insight, and are completely purified in the planes attainable by a disciple. Their awareness of anything within a disciple's ken approaches nimbly and proceeds lightly, but in the case of a serious matter on the plane of a solitary buddha, it gets sluggish. [9] Why? Because they have complete clarity within a disciple's ken but lack the complete clarity of things that fall within the range of a solitary buddha. Great king, for those pulling out bamboo stalks that are cleared completely in all sections, the going is easy and not sluggish. Why? With all the nodes cleared, the bamboo has no obstructions. Similarly, arhats have flaws destroyed, stains washed away, and defilements purged. They have lived the life, done what had to be done, laid down the burden, reached the highest ideal, destroyed the bonds of becoming, and achieved analytical insight, and are completely purified at the plane attainable by a disciple. Their awareness within the ken of disciples approaches nimbly and proceeds lightly, but on a serious matter at the

sāvakavisaye lahukaṃ uppajjati lahukaṃ pavattati, paccekabuddhabhūmisu garukam uppajjati dandhaṃ pavattati, kiṅkāraṇaṃ: parisuddhattā sāvakavisaye, aparisuddhattā paccekabuddha-visaye. idaṃ pañcamaṃ cittaṃ.

46 tatr' idaṃ chaṭṭhaṃ cittaṃ vibhattim-āpajjati: ye te mahārāja paccekabuddhā, sayambhuno anācariyakā, ekacārino khaggavisāṇakappā, sakavisaye parisuddhavimalacittā, tesaṃ taṃ cittaṃ sakavisaye lahukaṃ uppajjati lahukaṃ pavattati, sabbaññūbuddhabhūmisu garukaṃ uppajjati dandhaṃ pavattati, kiṅkāraṇaṃ: parisuddhattā sakavisaye, mahantattā sabbaññūbuddhavisayassa. yathā mahārāja puriso sakavisayaṃ parittaṃ nadiṃ rattim-pi divā pi yadicchakaṃ asambhīto otareyya, athāparato mahāsamuddaṃ gambhīraṃ vitthataṃ agādham-apāraṃ disvā bhāyeyya dandhāyeyya na visaheyya otarituṃ, kiṅkāraṇaṃ: ciṇṇattā sakavisayassa, mahantattā ca mahāsamuddassa; evam-eva kho mahārāja ye te paccekabuddhā, sayambhuno anācariyakā, ekacārino khaggavisāṇakappā, sakavisaye parisuddhavimala cittā, tesaṃ taṃ cittaṃ sakavisaye lahukaṃ uppajjati lahukaṃ pavattati, sabbaññūbuddhabhūmisu garukaṃ uppajjati dandhaṃ pavattati, kiṅkāraṇaṃ: parisuddhattā sakavisayassa, mahantattā sabbaññūbuddhavisayassa. idaṃ chaṭṭhaṃ cittaṃ.

47 tatr' idaṃ sattamaṃ cittaṃ vibhattim-āpajjati: ye te mahārāja sammāsambuddhā sabbaññuno dasabaladharā

plane of a solitary buddha, it grows sluggish. Why? Because of complete clarity in the ken of a disciple, but not complete clarity in the ken of a solitary buddha. This is the fifth kind of awareness.

"Now, the sixth kind of awareness is analyzed in this way. Solitary buddhas are those without teachers, self-arisen, wandering solitary and alone like a rhinoceros, with awareness completely stainless within their own range. Their awareness of anything within their ken is nimble and proceeds lightly, but in the case of a serious matter on the plane of an omniscient buddha, it gets sluggish. Why? Because of complete clarity within their own ken, and because of the sheer magnitude of the ken of omniscient buddhas. It is just like a person who can cross a small creek in his own locality either at night or day whenever desired, but then, upon seeing the vast ocean deep and wide, unfordable, and no shore at the other side, becomes fearful and sluggish and dares not cross it. Why? Because of traveling through his own range and because of the sheer magnitude of the great ocean. Just like this, great king, are those solitary buddhas, without teachers, self-arisen, wandering solitary like a rhinoceros, with awareness completely stainless within their own range. Their awareness within their ken is nimble and proceeds lightly, but on a serious matter at the plane of an omniscient buddha, it gets sluggish. Why? Because of the complete clarity within their own ken, and because of the sheer magnitude of the ken of omniscient buddhas. This is the sixth kind of awareness. 46

"Now, the seventh kind of awareness is analyzed in this way. Perfectly awakened buddhas, omniscient, bearing the 47

catuvesārajja-visāradā, aṭṭhārasahi buddhadhammehi samannāgatā, anantajinā anāvaraṇañāṇā, tesaṃ taṃ cittaṃ sabbattha lahukaṃ uppajjati lahukaṃ pavattati, kiṅkāraṇaṃ: sabbattha parisuddhattā. api nu kho mahārāja nārācassa sudhotassa vimalassa nigganthissa sukhumadhārassa ajimhassa avaṅkassa akuṭilassa daḷhacāpa-samārūḷhassa khomasukhume vā kappāsasukhume vā kambalasukhume vā balavanipātitassa dandhāyitattaṃ vā lagganaṃ vā hotīti.

48 na hi bhante, kiṅkāraṇaṃ: sukhumattā vatthānaṃ, sudhotattā nārācassa, nipātassa ca balavattā ti. evam-eva kho mahārāja ye te sammāsambuddhā sabbaññuno dasabaladharā catuvesārajja-visāradā, aṭṭhārasahi buddhadhammehi samannāgatā, anantajinā anāvaraṇañāṇā, tesaṃ taṃ cittaṃ sabbattha lahukaṃ uppajjati lahukaṃ pavattati, kiṅkāraṇaṃ: sabbattha parisuddhattā. idaṃ sattamaṃ cittaṃ.

49 tatra mahārāja yam-idaṃ sabbaññūbuddhānaṃ cittaṃ taṃ channam-pi cittānaṃ gaṇanaṃ atikkamitvā asaṅkheyyena guṇena parisuddhañ-ca lahukañ-ca. yasmā ca bhagavato cittaṃ parisuddhañca lahukañ-ca, tasmā mahārāja bhagavā yamakapāṭihīraṃ dasseti, yamakapāṭihīre mahārāja ñātabbaṃ: buddhānaṃ bhagavantānaṃ cittaṃ evaṃ lahuparivattan-ti, na tattha sakkā uttariṃ kāraṇaṃ vattuṃ. te pi mahārāja pāṭihīrā sabbaññūbuddhānaṃ cittaṃ upādāya gaṇanam-pi sankham-pi kalam-pi kalabhāgam-pi na upenti, āvajjanapaṭibaddhaṃ mahārāja bhagavato sabbaññutañāṇaṃ, āvajjitvā yadicchakaṃ jānāti. yathā mahārāja

ten powers,[10] poised with the four confidences,[11] enjoying the eighteen attributes of a buddha,[12] and victors of the infinite, have knowledge without obstruction. Their awareness approaches everything nimbly and proceeds lightly. Why? Because of complete clarity about everything. Moreover, great king, would an arrow, clean, stainless, sharp, finely edged, perfectly straight, uncrooked, unbent, fitted in a strong bow, and shot by a strong man into fine linen, fine cotton, or fine wool, be slow or hindered?"

"Of course not, sir. And why not? Because of the fineness 48
of the cloth, the cleanness of the arrow, and the strength of the shot."

"It is similar, great king, for perfectly awakened buddhas, omniscient, bearing the ten powers, poised with the four confidences, enjoying the eighteen attributes of a buddha, conquerors of the infinite, whose knowledge is unobstructed. Their awareness approaches everything nimbly and proceeds lightly. Why? Because of complete clarity about everything. This is the seventh kind of awareness.

"Now, the awareness of omniscient buddhas surpasses the 49
reckoning of the awareness of the other six, and is clear and light with innumerable qualities. And since the Bhagavan's awareness is clear and light, he presented the Twin Miracle.[13] The Twin Miracle should be understood as an example of the quickly changing awareness of blessed buddhas, for it is not possible to explain it any other way. Furthermore, great king, miracles cannot be reckoned or calculated as even a sixteenth part or a fraction of the awareness of omniscient buddhas. The omniscience of the Bhagavan relies on turning his attention to something, and when he attends to it, he

puriso hatthe ṭhapitaṃ yaṃ kiñci dutiye hatthe ṭhapeyya, vivaṭena mukhena vācaṃ nicchāreyya, mukhagataṃ bhojanaṃ gileyya, ummīletvā vā nimīleyya nimīletvā vā ummīleyya, sammiñjitaṃ vā bāhaṃ pasāreyya pasāritaṃ vā bāhaṃ sammiñjeyya, ciratarаṃ etaṃ mahārāja, lahutaraṃ bhagavato sabbaññutañāṇaṃ, lahutaraṃ āvajjanaṃ, āvajjitvā yadicchakaṃ jānāti, āvajjanavikalamattakena na tāvatā buddhā bhagavanto asabbaññuno nāma hontīti.

50 āvajjanam-pi bhante nāgasena pariyesanāya kātabbaṃ, iṅgha maṃ tattha kāraṇena saññāpehīti. yathā mahārāja purisassa aḍḍhassa mahaddhanassa mahābhogassa pahūta-jātarūpa-rajata-vittūpakaraṇassa pahūtadhana-dhaññassa sāli-vīhi-yava-taṇḍula-tila-mugga-māsa-pubbaṇṇāparaṇṇa-sappi-tela-navanīta-khīra-dadhi-madhu-guḷa-phāṇitā ca khaḷopi-kumbhi-pīṭhara-koṭṭha-bhājana-gatā bhaveyyuṃ, tassa ca purisassa pāhunako āgaccheyya bhattāraho bhattābhikaṅkhī, tassa ca gehe yaṃ randhaṃ bhojanaṃ taṃ pariniṭṭhitaṃ bhaveyya, kumbhito taṇḍule nīharitvā bhojanaṃ randheyya; api nu kho so mahārāja puriso tāvatakena bhojanavekallamattakena adhano nāma kapaṇo nāma bhaveyyāti.

51 na hi bhante, cakkavattirañño ghare pi bhante akāle bhojanavekallaṃ hoti, kiṃ pana gahapatikassāti. evam-eva kho mahārāja tathāgatassa āvajjanavikalamattakaṃ sabbaññu-

knows it in whatever way he wishes. And further, great king, the omniscience of the Bhagavan, his turning his attention to something, and his attending and coming to know whatever he wants are all quicker than the time it takes for a person to move something from one hand to the other, utter a word by opening the mouth, swallow food placed in the mouth, open closed eyes or close opened eyes, stretch out a bent arm, or flex an outstretched one. And even when they are not turning their attention to something, blessed buddhas are not to be considered as lacking omniscience."

"But, Nagasena, the turning of attention still has to be 50
done with an inquiry. Come, convince me with another explanation regarding this matter."

"Suppose, great king, there was a rich, affluent, and wealthy man with abundant gold, silver, luxuries, and possessions, lavish wealth and crops, including rice, paddy, barley, husked rice, sesame, black gram, mung bean, grain, vegetables, ghee, oil, fresh butter, milk, curds, honey, molasses, and sugar stocked in pots, jars, baskets, containers, and earthenware bowls.[14] Suppose a guest of this man arrives who deserves a meal and is eager for food. But the cooked food in the house has been used up, so they must take husked rice from a jar and cook a meal. Would you call the man poor or a beggar, great king, for that short period in which he did not have food ready?"

"No, sir. Meals are not available at all times even in the 51
house of a wheel-turning emperor, to say nothing of a householder."

"Then the Tathagata has omniscience even in the small intervals between attending to something. But once atten-

tañāṇaṃ, āvajjitvā yadicchakaṃ jānāti. yathā vā pana mahārāja rukkho assa phalito oṇata-vinato piṇḍibhārabharito, na kiñci tattha patitaṃ phalaṃ bhaveyya; api nu kho so mahārāja rukkho tāvatakena patitaphalavekallamattakena aphalo nāma bhaveyyāti.

52 na hi bhante, patanapaṭibaddhāni[2] tāni rukkhaphalāni, patite yadicchakaṃ labhatīti. evam-eva kho mahārāja tathāgatassa āvajjanapaṭibaddhaṃ sabbaññutañāṇaṃ, āvajjitvā yadicchakaṃ jānātīti. bhante nāgasena, āvajjitvā āvajjitvā buddho yadicchakaṃ jānātīti. āma mahārāja, bhagavā āvajjitvā āvajjitvā yadicchakaṃ jānāti; yathā mahārāja cakkavattirājā yadā cakkaratanaṃ sarati: upetu me cakkaratanan-ti, sarite cakkaratanaṃ upeti; evam-eva kho mahārāja tathāgato āvajjitvā āvajjitvā yadicchakaṃ jānātīti. daḷhaṃ bhante nāgasena kāraṇaṃ, buddho sabbaññū, sampaṭicchāma: buddho sabbaññū ti.

53 bhante nāgasena, devadatto kena pabbājito ti. cha-y-ime mahārāja khattiyakumārā: bhaddiyo ca anuruddho ca ānando ca bhagu ca kimbilo ca devadatto ca, upāli kappako sattamo, abhisambuddhe satthari sakyakulānandajanane bhagavantaṃ anupabbajantā nikkhamiṃsu; te bhagavā pabbājesīti.

tive, he knows it as he wishes. It is much like a tree so laden with fruit and heavy with the weight of the clusters that it bends low. But suppose that none of the fruit has fallen yet. Would you say the tree is barren of fruit in the short interval in which the fruit has not yet dropped, great king?"

"No, sir. The fruits of a tree are bound to fall, and when 52
they drop one can take them as one wishes."

"It is similar for the omniscience of the Tathagata, which relies on attending to something. Once attending, he knows whatever he wishes."

"Is it by attending in each case that the Buddha knows whatever he wants?"

"Yes, great king. The Bhagavan attends case by case and so knows whatever he wants, much as a wheel-turning emperor recalls the treasure of the wheel: "Let my wheel treasure appear!"[15] When it is remembered, the wheel treasure appears. Just like this, the Tathagata attends in each case and so knows whatever he wants."

"This explanation is sound, Nagasena. The Buddha is omniscient. I accept that the Buddha is omniscient.

"Nagasena, sir, by whom was Devadatta ordained?" 53

"Great king, there were six young Kshatriyas: Bhaddiya, Anuruddha, Ananda, Bhagu, Kimbila, and Devadatta, with the barber Upali as the seventh. When the Teacher was fully awakened, the Sakya family became joyful, and these men followed the Bhagavan and renounced the world. The Bhagavan ordained them."

54 nanu bhante devadattena pabbajitvā saṅgho bhinno ti. āma mahārāja, devadattena pabbajitvā saṅgho bhinno. na gihī saṅghaṃ bhindati, na bhikkhunī na sikkhamānā na sāmaṇero na sāmaṇerī saṅghaṃ bhindati, bhikkhu pakatatto samānasaṃvāsako samānasīmāyaṃ ṭhito saṅghaṃ bhindatīti. saṅghabhedako bhante puggalo kiṃ kammaṃ phusatīti. kappaṭṭhitikaṃ mahārāja kammaṃ phusa-tīti.

55 kim-pana bhante nāgasena buddho jānāti: devadatto pabbajitvā saṅghaṃ bhindissati, saṅghaṃ bhinditvā kappaṃ niraye paccissatīti. āma mahārāja, tathāgato jānāti: devadatto pabbajitvā saṅghaṃ bhindissati, saṅghaṃ bhinditvā kappaṃ niraye paccissatīti. yadi bhante nāgasena buddho jānāti: devadatto pabbajitvā saṅghaṃ bhindissati, saṅghaṃ bhinditvā kappaṃ niraye paccissatīti, tena hi bhante nāgasena: buddho kāruṇiko anukampako hitesī, sabbasattānaṃ ahitam-apanetvā hitam upadahatīti yaṃ vacanaṃ taṃ micchā. yadi taṃ ajānitvā pabbājesi, tena hi buddho asabbaññū. ayam-pi ubhatokoṭiko pañho tavānuppatto, vijaṭehi etaṃ mahājaṭaṃ, bhinda parappavādaṃ, anāgate addhāne tayā sadisā buddhimanto bhikkhū dullabhā bhavissanti, ettha tava balaṃ pakāsehīti.

56 kāruṇiko mahārāja bhagavā sabbaññū ca. kāruññena mahārāja bhagavā sabbaññutañāṇena devadattassa gatiṃ

"But, sir, is it not the case that once Devadatta was 54
ordained, the community was split?"

"Yes, great king, Devadatta was ordained and then the community split. A householder cannot split the community. Nor can a nun, probationer, male novice, or female novice split the community. Only a regular monk living in the same group and in the same boundary can split the community."

"Sir, what sort of karma does a person who splits the community acquire?" "He acquires karma that endures for an eon, great king." "But, Nagasena, didn't the Buddha know that Devadatta, once ordained, would split the community? And having split the community, that he would roast in hell for an eon?" "Yes, great king, the Tathagata did know that Devadatta, once ordained, would split the community, and having split the community, would roast in hell for an eon."

"But, Nagasena, if the Tathagata knew that Devadatta, 55
once ordained, would split the community, and by splitting the community would roast in hell for an eon, then the claim that the Buddha is compassionate, sympathetic, and well wishing, and that he removes harm and supplies welfare, must surely be false. On the other hand, if the Buddha ordained him not knowing this, then the Buddha was not omniscient. This two-pronged dilemma has reached you, and you should disentangle this big tangle and break up opponents' contentions. Intelligent monks like you will be hard to come by in the distant future, so show your power now."

"Great king, the Bhagavan was both compassionate and 56
omniscient. With his compassion and his omniscient knowl-

olokento addasa devadattaṃ aparāpariyakammaṃ āyūhitvā anekāni kappakoṭisatasahassāni nirayena nirayaṃ vinipātena vinipātaṃ gacchantaṃ. taṃ bhagavā sabbaññutañāṇena jānitvā: imassa apariyantakataṃ kammaṃ mama sāsane pabbajitassa pariyantakataṃ bhavissati, purimaṃ upādāya pariyantakataṃ dukkhaṃ bhavissati, apabbajito pi ayaṃ moghapuriso kappaṭṭhiyam eva kammaṃ āyūhissatīti kāruññena devadattaṃ pabbājesīti.

57 tena hi bhante nāgasena buddho vadhitvā telena makkheti, papāte pātetvā hatthaṃ deti, māretvā jīvitaṃ pariyesati, yaṃ so paṭhamaṃ dukkhaṃ datvā pacchā sukhaṃ upadahatīti.

58 vadheti pi mahārāja tathāgato sattānaṃ hitavasena, pāteti pi sattānaṃ hitavasena, māreti pi sattānaṃ hitavasena, vadhitvā pi mahārāja tathāgato sattānaṃ hitam-eva upadahati, pātetvā pi sattānaṃ hitam-eva upadahati, māretvā pi sattānaṃ hitam-eva upadahati. yathā mahārāja mātāpitaro nāma vadhitvā pi pātayitvā pi puttānaṃ hitam-eva upadah-anti, evam-eva kho mahārāja tathāgato vadheti pi sattānaṃ hitavasena, pāteti pi sattānaṃ hitavasena, māreti pi satt-ānaṃ hitavasena, vadhitvā pi mahārāja tathāgato sattānaṃ hitam-eva upadahati, pātetvā pi sattānaṃ hitam-eva upadahati, māretvā pi sattānaṃ hitam-eva upadahati. yena yena yogena sattānaṃ guṇavaḍḍhi hoti tena tena yogena sabbasattānaṃ hitam-eva upadahati. sace mahārāja devadatto na pabbajeyya gihibhūto samāno nirayasaṃvattanikaṃ

edge, the Bhagavan looked at Devadatta's destiny. He saw that Devadatta was pursuing karma with continuous results and was going from one hell to another, from one tormenting place to another, for many thousands and millions of eons. Knowing this with his omniscient knowledge, the Bhagavan reflected: *Karma with continuous results will become limited for someone who ordains in my dispensation, and so the suffering generated by the earlier karma will become limited. But if this foolish person does not ordain, he will rack up karma that lasts eons.* And so out of compassion, he ordained Devadatta."

"Then by this, Nagasena, the Buddha injures him but then 57
soothes him with oil; knocks him down a cliff but then lends him a hand; kills him and then revives him. First he causes pain and later provides happiness."

"Great king, even if the Tathagata injures someone, it is 58
for the benefit of beings. And if he knocks them down or even kills them, it is also for the benefit of beings. Should the Tathagata injure others, he then supplies beings with even more benefit; should he knock them down, he then supplies beings with even more benefit; should he take a life, he supplies beings with even more benefit. Just as when parents injure or knock down their children, they supply them with even more benefit, so does the Tathagata. Even if he injures, knocks down, or kills beings, he does so for the sake of providing them more benefit. He will use whatever means to increase beings' virtues in order to bring about the most benefit for all beings. Great king, if Devadatta had not been ordained and had remained a householder making more evil karma leading to hell, he would undergo much suffering, going from hell to hell and from one tormenting

bahuṃ pāpakammaṃ katvā anekāni kappakoṭisatasahassāni nirayena nirayaṃ vinipātena vinipātaṃ gacchanto bahuṃ dukkhaṃ vedayissati. taṃ bhagavā jānamāno kāruññena devadattaṃ pabbājesi: mama sāsane pabbajitassa dukkhaṃ pariyantakataṃ bhavissatīti kāruññena garukaṃ dukkhaṃ lahukaṃ akāsi.

59 Yathā mahārāja dhana-yasa-siri-ñātibalena balavā puriso attano ñātiṃ vā mittaṃ vā raññā garudaṇḍaṃ dhārentaṃ attano bahuvissatthabhāvena samatthatāya garukaṃ daṇḍaṃ lahukaṃ kāreti, evam-eva kho mahārāja bhagavā bahūni kappakoṭisatasahassāni dukkhaṃ vediyamānaṃ devadattaṃ pabbājetvā sīla-samādhi-paññā-vimutti-bala-samattha-bhāvena garukaṃ dukkhaṃ lahukaṃ akāsi. yathā vā pana mahārāja kusalo bhisakko sallakatto garukaṃ byādhiṃ balavosadhabalena lahukaṃ karoti, evam-eva kho mahārāja bahūni kappakoṭisatasahassāni dukkhaṃ vediyamānaṃ devadattaṃ bhagavā yogaññutāya pabbājetvā kāruññabalopatthaddha-dhammosadhabalena garukaṃ dukkhaṃ lahukaṃ akāsi. api nu kho so mahārāja bhagavā bahuvedanīyaṃ devadattaṃ appavedanīyaṃ karonto kiñci apuññaṃ āpajjeyyāti.

60 na kiñci bhante apuññaṃ āpajjeyya, antamaso gaddūhanamattam-pīti. imam-pi kho tvaṃ mahārāja kāraṇaṃ atthato sampaṭiccha yena kāranena bhagavā devadattaṃ pabbājesi. aparam-pi mahārāja uttariṃ kāraṇaṃ suṇohi yena kāraṇena bhagavā devadattaṃ pabbājesi. yathā mahārāja coraṃ āgucāriṃ gahetvā rañño dasseyyuṃ: ayaṃ te deva coro āgucārī, imassa yaṃ icchasi taṃ daṇḍaṃ paṇehīti, tam enaṃ rājā evaṃ vadeyya: tena hi bhaṇe imaṃ coraṃ bahinagaraṃ nīharitvā āghātane sīsaṃ chindathāti; evaṃ devāti

place to another for thousands and millions of eons. Knowing this, the Bhagavan ordained Devadatta out of compassion, reflecting: *The suffering of one ordained in my dispensation will become limited.* With his compassion he made heavy suffering lighter.

"Great king, consider a powerful man enjoying the influ- 59
ence of wealth, fame, good fortune, and relations. When his own kinsman or friend is subjected to a severe punishment by the king, he is able to make the severe punishment lighter by the strength of his being well trusted. In just this way, great king, the Bhagavan ordained Devadatta, who was facing suffering for many thousands and millions of eons, and made his heavy suffering light by the strength and power of moral discipline, concentration, wisdom, and freedom. Or consider a skilled physician, a surgeon, who makes a grave illness light with the power of strong medicine. Much like this, the Bhagavan, with his knowledge of means, ordained Devadatta, who was facing suffering for many thousands and millions of eons, and made his heavy suffering light by the strength of the medicine of the Dhamma supported by compassion. Moreover, great king, would the Bhagavan, in making Devadatta's great sufferings smaller, incur any demerit?"

"No, sir, in no way would he incur even an iota of demerit." 60

"Then, great king, you yourself should accept this reason why the Bhagavan ordained Devadatta. It is much like when a criminal thief is captured and shown to the king: 'This criminal is robbing you, Your Majesty, so inflict whatever punishment you want.' And so the king orders, 'Then drive the thief out of the city to the place of execution and chop off

kho te rañño paṭissutvā taṃ bahinagaraṃ nīharitvā āghātanaṃ nayeyyuṃ, tam-enaṃ passeyya kocid-eva puriso rañño santikā laddhavaro laddha-yasa-dhana-bhogo ādeyyavacano balavicchitakārī, so tassa kāruññaṃ katvā te purise evaṃ vadeyya: alaṃ bho, kiṃ tumhākaṃ imassa sīsacchedanena, tena hi bho imassa hatthaṃ vā pādaṃ vā chinditvā jīvitaṃ rakkhatha, aham-etassa kāraṇā rañño santike paṭivacanaṃ karissāmīti; te tassa balavato vacanena tassa corassa hatthaṃ vā pādaṃ vā chinditvā jīvitaṃ rakkheyyuṃ; api nu kho so mahārāja puriso evaṃkārī tassa corassa kiccakārī assāti.

61 jīvitadāyako so bhante puriso tassa corassa, jīvite dinne kiṃ tassa akataṃ nāma atthīti. yā pana tassa hatthapādacchedane vedanā so tāya vedanāya kiñci apuññaṃ āpajjeyyāti. attanā katena so bhante coro dukkhaṃ vedanaṃ vediyati, jīvitadāyako pana puriso na kiñci apuññaṃ āpajjeyyāti. evam-eva kho mahārāja bhagavā kāruññena devadattaṃ pabbājesi: mama sāsane pabbajitassa dukkhaṃ pariyantakataṃ bhavissatīti. pariyantakatañ-ca mahārāja devadattassa dukkhaṃ. devadatto mahārāja maraṇakāle:

his head.' Upon hearing the king, the men reply, 'Yes, Your Majesty,' and drive him outside the city and lead him to the execution grounds. But then he is seen by a certain man, a man who happens to be close to the king and a noble person of influence and well-heeded words, secure in fame, wealth, and prosperity. This man does the compassionate thing and says to the men: 'Refrain, sirs, from chopping off his head, and instead chop off a hand or a foot, and thus save his life. I am close to the king and will answer for this action.' And from the power of his words, they chop off the thief's hand or a foot and so save his life. Do you not think, great king, that in so doing, the man did rightly by the thief?"

"The man gave life to the thief, sir, and when life itself is 61
given, could there be anything that has not been done for him?"

"And surely, whatever may be the pain experienced from the chopping of the hand or foot, it was not something that would generate demerit for him."

"The thief underwent the painful experience because of what he himself had done, and the man who gave him life in no way incurs demerit from this."

"Just so, great king, the Bhagavan ordained Devadatta out of compassion, reflecting, *The suffering of one ordained in my dispensation will become limited.* And in fact, great king, Devadatta's suffering was limited. Devadatta took refuge with his last breath at the time of his death:

62 imehi aṭṭhīhi tam-aggapuggalaṃ devātidevaṃ
naradammasārathiṃ samantacakkhuṃ
satapuññalakkhaṇaṃ pāṇehi buddhaṃ saraṇaṃ
upemīti pāṇupetaṃ saraṇam-agamāsi.

63 devadatto mahārāja, chakoṭṭhāse kate kappe, atikkante
paṭhamakoṭṭhāse saṅghaṃ bhindi, pañcakoṭṭhāsaṃ niraye
paccitvā tato muccitvā aṭṭhissaro nāma paccekabuddho
bhavissati. api nu kho so mahārāja bhagavā evaṃkārī
devadattassa kiccakārī assāti. sabbadado bhante nāgasena
tathāgato devadattassa, yaṃ tathāgato devadattaṃ pacceka-
bodhiṃ pāpessati, kiṃ tathāgatena devadattassa akataṃ
nāma atthīti.

64 yaṃ pana mahārāja devadatto saṅghaṃ bhinditvā niraye
dukkhaṃ vedanaṃ vediyati, api nu kho bhagavā tatonidānaṃ kiñci apuññaṃ āpajjeyyāti. na hi bhante, attanā katena
bhante devadatto kappaṃ niraye paccati, dukkhapariyanta-
kārako satthā na kiñci apuññaṃ āpajjatīti.

65 imaṃ-pi kho tvaṃ mahārāja kāraṇaṃ atthato sampaṭiccha
yena kāraṇena bhagavā devadattaṃ pabbājesi. aparam-pi
mahārāja uttariṃ kāraṇaṃ suṇohi yena kāraṇena
bhagavā devadattaṃ pabbājesi. yathā mahārāja kusalo
bhisakko sallakatto vāta-pitta-semhasannipāta-utu-
pariṇāma-visamaparihāra-opakkamikopakkantaṃ pūti-

> With my living breaths and with these bones I take 62
> refuge in the Buddha, the supreme person, god above gods, charioteer of men to be tamed, all-seeing, who bears the marks of a hundred merits.

"Great king, an eon is divided into six parts. Devadatta split 63
the community after the first part had passed. He will roast in hell for the remaining five parts, and upon being released from it will become a solitary buddha called Atthissara. Do you not think, great king, that in so doing the Bhagavan did rightly by Devadatta?"

"Nagasena, the Tathagata gave everything to Devadatta, for when the Tathagata brought Devadatta to the awakening of a solitary buddha, what did he not do for him?"

"Of course, great king, having split the community, Deva- 64
datta did experience painful feelings in hell. But did the Bhagavan incur any demerit from this occasion?"

"No, sir. Devadatta is roasting in hell for an eon because of his own actions. In making that suffering limited, the Teacher has not incurred any demerit."

"Then, great king, it is in this respect that you should 65
accept the reason the Bhagavan ordained Devadatta. Moreover, please listen to yet another reason the Bhagavan ordained Devadatta. Consider a wound in which an arrow is still embedded, filled with caked blood, emitting a festering, putrid, and foul odor, and taking a sudden turn for the worse due to wind, bile, phlegm, the combination of them, a change of seasons, carelessness, or assault. A skilled physician, a surgeon, smears it with a harsh, acrid, caustic, and sharp medicine to heal it, and when it is healing and becomes

kuṇapa-duggandhābhisannaṃ antosallaṃ susiragataṃ pubba-ruhira-sampuṇṇaṃ vaṇaṃ vūpasamento vaṇamukhaṃ kakkhaḷa-tikhiṇa-khāra-kaṭukena bhesajjena anulimpati paripaccanāya, paripaccitvā mudubhāvam-upagataṃ satthena vikantayitva dahati salākāya, daḍḍhe khāralavaṇaṃ deti bhesajjenānulimpati vaṇarūhanāya byādhitassa sotthibhāvam-anuppattiyā; api nu kho so mahārāja bhisakko sallakatto ahitacitto bhesajjenānulimpati, satthena vikanteti, dahati salākāya, khāralavaṇaṃ detīti.

66 na hi bhante, hitacitto sotthikāmo tāni kiriyāni karotīti. yā pan' assa bhesajjakiriyākaraṇena uppannā dukkhavedanā, tatonidānam so bhisakko sallakatto kiñci apuññaṃ āpajjeyyāti. hitacitto bhante sotthikāmo bhisakko sallakatto tāni kiriyāni karoti, kiṃ so tatonidānaṃ apuññaṃ āpajjeyya, saggagāmī so bhante bhisakko sallakatto ti. evam-eva kho mahārāja bhagavā kāruññena devadattaṃ pabbājesi, dukkhaparimuttiyā. aparam-pi mahārāja uttariṃ kāraṇaṃ suṇohi yena kāraṇena bhagavā devadattaṃ pabbājesi. yathā mahārāja puriso kaṇṭakena viddho assa, ath' aññataro puriso tassa hitakāmo sotthikāmo tiṇhena kaṇṭakena vā satthamukhena vā samantā chinditvā paggharantena lohitena taṃ kaṇṭakaṃ nīhareyya; api nu kho so mahārāja puriso ahitakāmo taṃ kaṇṭakaṃ nīharatīti.

67 na hi bhante, hitakāmo so bhante puriso sotthikāmo taṃ kaṇṭakaṃ nīharati, sace so bhante puriso taṃ kaṇṭakaṃ na nīhareyya maraṇaṃ vā so tena pāpuṇeyya maraṇamattaṃ

softer, he cuts the infection out with a knife and cauterizes the wound with a surgical tool. At the cauterized site he administers a caustic solution and then applies medicine to close the wound, to bring about the well-being of the patient. Do you think, great king, that this physician, the surgeon, meant harm as he smeared the medicine, cut the wound with the knife, cauterized it with the tool, and administered the caustic solution?"

"No, sir, he meant well and sought to heal as he did what 66
had to be done."

"But did the physician, the surgeon, incur any demerit by occasioning the painful feeling generated by his doing what had to be done with these remedies?"

"Sir, the physician, the surgeon, meant well and wanted to heal as he did what had to be done, so how could he incur demerit from this cause? This surgeon is surely going to heaven."

"Great king, this is much like the Bhagavan ordaining Devadatta out of compassion and to free him from suffering. Please hear yet another reason it was out of compassion that the Bhagavan ordained Devadatta. Suppose a man was pierced by a thorn, and another man, wanting to help and seeking to heal him, cut all around it with a sharp thorn or with the tip of knife. With this effort he removed the thorn, though there was blood. Do you think, great king, that this man meant harm in removing the thorn?"

"No, sir, the man meant well, and wanting to heal him, 67
he removed the thorn. For if the man had not removed the thorn, the fellow would have perhaps died because of it, or had pain similar to death."

vā dukkhan-ti. evam-eva kho mahārāja tathāgato kāruññena devadattaṃ pabbājesi, dukkhaparimuttiyā; sace mahārāja bhagavā devadattaṃ na pabbājeyya kappakoṭisatasahassam-pi devadatto bhavaparamparāya niraye pacceyyāti.

68 anusotagāmiṃ bhante nāgasena devadattaṃ tathāgato paṭisotaṃ pāpesi, vipanthapaṭipannaṃ devadattaṃ panthe paṭipādesi, papāte patitassa devadattassa patiṭṭhaṃ adāsi, visamagataṃ devadattaṃ tathāgato samaṃ āropesi. ime ca bhante nāgasena hetū imāni ca kāraṇāni na sakkā aññena sandassetuṃ aññatra tavādisena buddhimatā ti.

69 bhante nāgasena, bhāsitam-p' etaṃ bhagavatā: aṭṭh' ime bhikkhave hetū aṭṭha paccayā mahato bhūmicālassa pātubhāvāyāti. asesavacanaṃ idaṃ, nissesavacanaṃ idaṃ, nippariyāyavacanaṃ idaṃ, natth' añño navamo hetu mahato bhūmicālassa pātubhāvāya; yadi bhante nāgasena añño navamo hetu bhaveyya mahato bhūmicālassa pātubhāvāya, tam-pi bhagavā hetuṃ katheyya, yasmā ca kho bhante nāgasena na-tth' añño navamo hetu mahato bhūmicālassa pātubhāvāya, tasmā anācikkhito bhagavatā. ayañ-ca navamo hetu dissati mahato bhūmicālassa pātubhāvāya, yaṃ vessantarena raññā mahādāne dīyamāne sattakkhattuṃ mahāpaṭhavī kampitā. yadi bhante nāgasena aṭṭh' eva hetū aṭṭha paccayā mahato bhūmicālassa pātubhāvāya, tena hi: vessantarena raññā mahādāne dīyamāne sattakkhattuṃ mahāpaṭhavī kampitā ti yaṃ vacanaṃ taṃ micchā. yadi vessantarena raññā mahādāne dīyamāne sattakkhattuṃ mahāpaṭhavī kampitā, tena hi: aṭṭh' eva hetū aṭṭha paccayā mahato bhūmicālassa pātubhāvāyāti tam-pi vacanaṃ micchā. ayam-pi ubhatokoṭiko pañho sukhumo dunniveṭhiyo andhakaraṇo

"Even so, great king, the Tathagata ordained Devadatta out of compassion by making his suffering limited. For if the Bhagavan had not ordained Devadatta, Devadatta would have roasted in hell for a long series of lives for thousands and millions of eons."

"Nagasena, as Devadatta was being carried away by 68
the current, the Tathagata made him go against the stream. As Devadatta was headed down the wrong road, the Tathagata set him on the right path; as he was sliding down a cliff, he gave him a foothold; and when he was shaky, he made him stable. Those who are not as intelligent as you are, Nagasena, are not able to explain these reasons and grounds."

"Nagasena, sir, the Bhagavan said: 'Monks, there are eight 69
causes, that is, eight conditions, that trigger massive earthquakes.' This was the entire, complete, and categorical utterance. And so there is no ninth cause of massive earthquakes. For had there been a ninth cause of massive earthquakes, the Bhagavan would have mentioned it. Since no ninth cause was noted by the Bhagavan, there cannot be a ninth cause of massive earthquakes. And yet, a ninth cause of a massive quake was evident when Prince Vessantara gave a great gift and the earth trembled seven times.[16] If, sir, there are only eight causes, eight conditions, triggering massive earthquakes, then the claim that when Prince Vessantara gave a great gift the earth trembled seven times must be false. Or, alternatively, if the claim about Vessantara is true, the claim about there being only eight causes must be false. This subtle two-pronged dilemma is bewildering, profound, and difficult to solve, and so I put it to you. Those of lesser under-

ca gambhīro ca, so tavānuppatto, n'eso aññena ittarapaññena sakkā vissajjetuṃ aññatra tavādisena buddhimatā ti.

70 bhāsitam-p' etaṃ mahārāja bhagavatā: aṭṭh' ime bhikkhave hetū aṭṭha paccayā mahato bhūmicālassa pātubhāvāyāti. vessantarena pi raññā mahādāne dīyamāne sattakkhattuṃ mahāpaṭhavī kampitā. tañ-ca pana akālikaṃ kadācuppattikaṃ, aṭṭhahi hetūhi vippamuttaṃ, tasmā agaṇitaṃ aṭṭhahi hetūhi. yathā mahārāja loke tayo yeva meghā gaṇīyanti: vassiko hemantiko pāvussako ti, yadi te muñcitvā añño megho pavassati na so megho gaṇīyati sammatehi meghehi, akālamegho t' eva saṅkhaṃ gacchati; evam-eva kho mahārāja vessantarena raññā mahādāne dīyamāne yaṃ sattakkhattuṃ mahāpaṭhavī kampitā, akālikaṃ etaṃ kadācuppattikaṃ, aṭṭhahi hetūhi vippamuttaṃ, na taṃ gaṇīyati aṭṭhahi hetūhi.

71 yathā vā pana mahārāja himavantā pabbatā pañca nadīsatāni sandanti, tesaṃ mahārāja pañcannaṃ nadīsatānaṃ das' eva nadiyo nadīgaṇanāya gaṇīyanti, seyyathīdaṃ: gaṅgā yamunā aciravatī sarabhū mahī sindhu sarassatī vetravatī vītaṃsā candabhāgā, avasesā nadiyo nadīgaṇanāya agaṇitā, kiṅkāraṇaṃ: na tā nadiyo dhuvasalilā; evam-eva kho mahārāja vessantarena raññā mahādāne dīyamāne yaṃ sattakkhattuṃ mahāpaṭhavī kampitā, akālikaṃ etaṃ kadācuppattikaṃ, aṭṭhahi hetūhi vippamuttaṃ, na taṃ gaṇīyati aṭṭhahi hetūhi.

72 yathā vā pana mahārāja rañño satam-pi dvisatam-pi amaccā honti, tesaṃ cha yeva janā amaccagaṇanāya

standing are not able to resolve it, and only one as intelligent as you are can do so."

"Great king, the Bhagavan did say that there are eight 70
causes, that is, eight conditions, that trigger massive earthquakes. And the earth did tremble seven times when Prince Vessantara gave his great gift. But that was an unusual incident, and as something that happened once it is separate from the eight, and not counted among the eight causes. It is similar to how there are thought to be three kinds of showering clouds—monsoon rains, winter rains, and rainstorms. Should another cloud roll in and burst, it is not counted among the usual clouds and is just considered an unseasonal cloud. Similarly, great king, when Prince Vessantara gave his great gift and the earth trembled seven times, it was an unusual incident, happening just once, separate from the eight, and not counted among the eight causes.

"It is similar, great king, to the five hundred rivers that flow 71
from the Himalaya mountains. Of these five hundred rivers only ten are properly considered rivers, namely, the Ganga, Yamuna, Achiravati, Sarabhu, Mahi, Sindhu, Saraswati, Vetravati, Vitamsa, and Chandabhaga, and the remaining rivers are not counted among the number of rivers. Why not? Because those rivers have water only seasonally. Similarly, when the earth trembled seven times as Prince Vessantara gave the great gift, it was an unusual incident, happening only once, separate from the eight and not counted among the eight causes.

"Consider also that of the one or two hundred ministers 72
of a king, only six people are actually counted as ministers, namely, the army general, the royal priest, the judge, the

gaṇīyanti, seyyathīdaṃ: senāpati purohito akkhadasso bhaṇḍāgāriko chattagāhako khaggagāhako, ete yeva amaccagaṇanāya gaṇīyanti, kiṅkāraṇaṃ: yuttattā rājaguṇehi, avasesā agaṇitā, sabbe amaccā t'eva saṅkhaṃ gacchanti; evam-eva kho mahārāja vessantarena raññā mahādāne dīyamāne yaṃ sattakkhattuṃ mahāpaṭhavī kampitā, akālikaṃ etaṃ kadācuppattikaṃ, aṭṭhahi hetūhi vippamuttaṃ, na taṃ gaṇīyati aṭṭhahi hetūhi.

73 sūyati nu kho mahārāja etarahi jinasāsane katādhikārānaṃ diṭṭhadhammasukhavedanīyaṃ kammaṃ, kitti ca yesaṃ abbhuggatā devamanussesūti. āma bhante, sūyati etarahi jinasāsane katādhikārānaṃ diṭṭhadhammasukhavedanīyaṃ kammaṃ, kitti ca yesaṃ abbhuggatā devamanussesu, satta te janā ti. ko ca ko ca mahārājāti. sumano ca bhante mālākāro ekasāṭako ca brāhmaṇo puṇṇo ca bhatako mallikā ca devī gopālamātā ca devī suppiyā ca upāsikā puṇṇā ca dāsī ti ime satta diṭṭhadhammasukhavedanīyā sattā, kitti ca imesaṃ abbhuggatā devamanussesūti.

74 apare pi sūyanti nu kho atīte mānusaken' eva sarīradehena tidasabhavanaṃ gatā ti. āma bhante, sūyantīti. ko ca ko ca mahārājāti. guttilo ca gandhabbo sādhīno ca rājā nimī ca rājā mandhātā ca rājā ti ime caturo janā sūyanti: ten' eva mānusakena sarīradehena tidasabhavanaṃ gatā ti, suciram-pi kataṃ

treasurer, the bearer of the royal parasol, and the royal sword bearer. The others are not counted in the number of ministers. Why is this? Because these are associated with royal prerogatives, while the others, while all called ministers, are not counted among them. In just this way, great king, when the earth trembled seven times as Prince Vessantara gave the great gift, it was an unusual incident, happening only once, separate from the eight and not counted among the eight causes.

“Great king, have you ever heard of a deed that was done 73
in this dispensation of the Victor that involved karma that was experienced in this very world? One that was famous among gods and humans?”

“Yes, I have heard of deeds done in this time in the Victor’s dispensation, famous among gods and humans, and involving karma experienced in this very world. These concerned seven people.” “And who are they, great king?” “Sumana the garland maker, the Brahman Ekasataka, the servant Punna, Queen Mallika, Queen Gopalamata, the laywoman Suppiya, and the female slave Punna.[17] These seven people are experiencing happiness in this world, and their fame has spread out among gods and humans.”

“And have you also heard that in the past, there were those 74
who went to the Heaven of the Thirty Gods with their human bodies?” “I have heard that, sir.” “Who were they, great king?” “The musician Guttila, King Sadhina, King Nimi, and King Mandhata are the four people I have heard of who went to the Heaven of the Thirty Gods with their human bodies.[18] I have also heard that their good and bad deeds were done a long time ago.”

sūyati sukata-dukkatan-ti. sutapubbaṃ pana tayā mahārāja: atīte vā addhāne vattamāne vā addhāne itthannāmassa dāne dīyamāne sakiṃ vā dvikkhattuṃ vā tikkhattuṃ vā mahāpaṭhavī kampitā ti. na hi bhante ti.

75 atthi me mahārāja āgamo adhigamo pariyatti savanaṃ sikkhābalaṃ sussūsā paripucchā ācariyupāsanaṃ, mayā pi na-ssutapubbaṃ: itthannāmassa dāne dīyamāne sakiṃ vā dvikkhattuṃ vā tikkhattuṃ vā mahāpaṭhavī kampitā ti, ṭhapetvā vessantarassa rājavasabhassa dānavaraṃ. bhagavato ca mahārāja kassapassa bhagavato ca sakyamunino ti dvinnaṃ buddhānaṃ antare gaṇanapathaṃ vītivattā vassakoṭiyo atikkantā, tattha pi me savanaṃ na-tthi: itthannāmassa dāne dīyamāne sakiṃ vā dvikkhattuṃ vā tikkhattuṃ vā mahāpaṭhavī kampitā ti. na mahārāja tāvatakena viriyena tāvatakena parakkamena mahāpaṭhavī kampati, guṇabhārabharitā mahārāja sabbasoceyyakiriyaguṇabhārabharitā dhāretuṃ na visahantī mahāpaṭhavī calati kampati pavedhati.

76 yathā mahārāja sakaṭassa atibhārabharitassa nābhiyo ca nemiyo ca phalanti akkho bhijjati, evam-eva kho mahārāja sabbasoceyyakiriyaguṇabhārabharitā mahāpaṭhavī dhāretuṃ na visahantī calati kampati pavedhati. yathā vā pana mahārāja gaganaṃ anilajalavegasañchāditaṃ ussannajalabhārabharitaṃ ativātena phuṭitattā nadati ravati gaḷagaḷāyati, evam-eva kho mahārāja mahāpaṭhavī rañño vessantarassa dānabala-vipulaussannabhārabharitā dhāretuṃ na visahantī calati kampati pavedhati.

"Have you ever heard before, great king, that perhaps in the distant past or in the current time the earth trembled once, twice, or even three times when gifts of these named persons were given?" "No, sir."

"For all of my learning of the scriptures, understanding, 75
study, listening, strength of training, obedience, questioning, and practice with teachers, I too have never heard of an
instance in which the earth trembled once, twice, or three
times when a gift was given, except for the excellent gift of
Vessantara, bull among kings. What is more, great king, in
the era between two buddhas, that is, between the Blessed
Kassapa and Sakyamuni, a period of hundreds of thousands
of years passed. I have never heard of any occasion on which
the earth trembled once, twice, or three times at the giving of
a gift in this period either. Nor does the great earth tremble
at just any effort or exertion. Only when weighed down by
a load of good qualities, that is, when buckling under the
weight of the good qualities of a completely pure action, is
the earth unable to hold up, and it shudders, trembles, and
quakes. Great king, it is just like how, on a wagon overloaded 76
with heavy cargo, the wheel rim and hub split and the axle
breaks. So too the earth is unable to bear up when buckling
under the weight of the good qualities of a completely pure
action, and it shudders, trembles, and quakes. Or it is like
the sky covered with stormy rain and wind, heavy and full
to bursting with water, roaring, howling, and splitting with
crashing storm winds. So too the earth, heavy and full to
bursting with the greatness and power of Prince Vessantara's
gift, was unable to bear up, and it shuddered, trembled, and
quaked.

77 na hi mahārāja rañño vessantarassa cittaṃ rāgavasena pavattati, na dosavasena pavattati, na mohavasena pavattati, na mānavasena pavattati, na diṭṭhivasena pavattati, na kilesavasena pavattati, na vitakkavasena pavattati, na arativasena pavattati, atha kho dānavasena bahulaṃ pavattati: kin-ti anāgatā yācakā mama santike āgaccheyyuṃ āgatā ca yācakā yathākāmaṃ labhitvā attamanā bhaveyyun-ti satataṃ samitaṃ dānam-pati mānasaṃ ṭhapitaṃ hoti. rañño mahārāja vessantarassa satataṃ samitaṃ dasasu ṭhānesu mānasaṃ ṭhapitaṃ hoti: dame same khantiyaṃ saṃvare yame niyame akkodhe avihiṃsāyaṃ sacce soceyye. rañño mahārāja vessantarassa kāmesanā pahīnā, bhavesanā paṭippassaddhā, brahmacariyesanāy' eva ussukkaṃ āpanno.

78 rañño mahārāja vessantarassa attarakkhā pahīnā, pararakkhāya ussukkaṃ āpanno: kin-ti ime sattā samaggā assu arogā sadhanā dīghāyukā ti bahulaṃ yeva mānasaṃ pavattati. dadamāno ca mahārāja vessantaro rājā taṃ dānaṃ na bhavasampattihetu deti, na dhanahetu deti, na paṭidānahetu deti, na upalāpanahetu deti, na āyuhetu deti, na vaṇṇahetu deti, na sukhahetu deti, na balahetu deti, na yasahetu deti, na puttahetu deti, na dhītuhetu deti, atha kho sabbaññutañāṇassa hetu sabbaññutañāṇaratanassa kāraṇā evarūpe atula-vipulānuttare dānavare adāsi. sabbaññu-taṃ patto ca imaṃ gāthaṃ abhāsi.

79 jāliṃ kaṇhājinaṃ dhītaṃ maddideviṃ patibbataṃ
cajamāno na cintesiṃ, bodhiyā yeva kāraṇā ti.

"And of course, great king, Prince Vessantara's mind did 77
not act out of passion, nor from hatred, delusion, pride, wrong view, the defilements, an impulsive thought, or aversion. Rather he acted out of an abundance of generosity, set solely upon being a lord of giving, and constantly and continually thinking, *May those who approach me get whatever they want and be pleased, and may future people come and ask.* Prince Vessantara constantly and continually developed the ten states of mind, making it tame, even, patient, restrained, quieted, disciplined, free of anger, free of harm, truthful, and pure. Prince Vessantara utterly lacked craving for sensual pleasure and had dispelled all craving for existence; he had zeal only for pursuing the religious life.
Prince Vessantara had stopped protecting himself and was 78
zealous only for protecting others. He put his mind entirely to thoughts of how others could become harmonious, healthy, prosperous, and long-lived. In giving his gift, great king, Prince Vessantara did not give in order to achieve a good rebirth or to be reciprocated, and he gave no consideration to such things as winning people over or gaining longevity, beauty, happiness, power, fame, sons, or daughters. He gave such an incomparable, lavish, and excellent gift for the sake of omniscience, for the jewel that is omniscience. And when he had won omniscience, he spoke this verse:

> I gave up Jali; my daughter, Kanhajina; and my 79
> devoted wife, Queen Maddi,
> without a thought, solely for the sake of awakening.

80 vessantaro mahārāja rājā akkodhena kodhaṃ jināti, asādhuṃ sādhunā jināti, kadariyaṃ dānena jināti, alikavādinaṃ saccena jināti, sabbaṃ akusalaṃ kusalena jināti. tassa evaṃ dadamānassa dhammānugatassa dhammasīsakassa dānanissanda-balaviriyavipulavihārena heṭṭhā mahāvātā sañcalanti, saṇikaṃ saṇikaṃ sakiṃ sakiṃ ākulākulā vāyanti, oṇamanti unnamanti vinamanti, sīnapattā pādapā papatanti, gumbagumbaṃ valāhakā gagane sandhāvanti, rajosañcitā vātā dāruṇā honti, gaganaṃ uppīḷitaṃ, vātā vāyanti sahasā dhamadhamāyanti, mahatimahā bhīmo saddo niccharati, tesu vātesu kupitesu udakaṃ saṇikaṃ saṇikaṃ calati, udake calite khubbhanti macchakacchapā, jāyanti yamaka-yamakā ūmiyo, tasanti jalacarā sattā, jalavīci yuganaddho vattati, vīcinādo pavattati, ghorā bubbuḷā uṭṭhahanti, pheṇamālā bhavanti, uttarati mahāsamuddo, disāvidisaṃ dhāvati udakaṃ, ussota-paṭisota-mukhā sandanti saliladhārā, tasanti asurā garuḷā nāgā yakkhā, ubbijjanti: kin-nu kho kathan-nu kho sāgaro viparivattatīti gamanapatham-esanti bhītacittā, khubhite luḷite jaladhare pakampati mahāpaṭhavī sanagāsasāgarā, parivattati sinerugiri kūṭaselasikharo vinamamāno hoti, vimanā honti ahi-nakula-biḷāra-kotthuka-sūkara-miga-pakkhino, rudanti

"Great king, Prince Vessantara conquered the angry man 80
without anger; he conquered the wicked without wickedness, the miserly with generosity, the liar with truth, and all bad things with good. Moreover, while he was giving, following the Dhamma and putting the Dhamma first, huge winds were stirred up from below with the full power, energy, and greatness issuing from the gift. They came on softly and gently at first, and then began to blow again and again in wild confusion, sweeping down, then up, and all around. Trees were stripped of their leaves and felled, thunderclouds rolled together in great masses in the heavens, fierce dust storms obscured the sky, and the winds blew violently and incessantly. A terrible and massive noise sounded. And while these winds raged, the waters began slowly and gently to stir, and as the water stirred, fish and turtles grew agitated. Swells, coming in pairs, then rose up, and the water creatures became terrified. Waves converged and advanced, there was a sound from the swells, and a dreadful spume foamed up until there were wreaths of froth. The seas boiled, the water surged in every direction, and cascading torrents from the mouths of rivers surged upstream and back. *Asuras, garuḷas, nāgas,* and *yakkhas** grew alarmed and frightened: 'What is this? How could the ocean turn upside down?' And, terrified, they sought some way of escape. While the sea was raging and tossing, the great earth with its mountains and oceans trembled. The rocky summit at the peak of Mount Sineru twisted and turned, and snakes, mongooses, cats, jackals, pigs, deer, and birds grew distraught. The *yakkhas* of little

* Various mythical beings.

yakkhā appesakkhā, hasanti yakkhā mahesakkhā, kampamānāya mahāpaṭhaviyā.

81 yathā mahārāja mahatimahāpariyoge uddhanagate udakasampuṇṇe ākiṇṇataṇḍule heṭṭhato aggi jalamāno paṭhamaṃ tāva pariyogaṃ santāpeti, pariyogo santatto udakaṃ santāpeti, udakaṃ santattaṃ taṇḍulaṃ santāpeti, taṇḍulaṃ santattaṃ ummujjati nimujjati, bubbuḷakajātaṃ hoti, pheṇamāli uttarati; evam-eva kho mahārāja vessantaro rājā yaṃ loke duccajaṃ taṃ caji, tassa taṃ duccajaṃ cajantassa dānassa sabhāvanissandena heṭṭhā mahāvātā dhāretuṃ na visahantā parikuppiṃsu, mahāvātesu parikupitesu udakaṃ kampi, udake kampite mahāpaṭhavī kampi, iti tadā mahāvātā ca udakañ-ca paṭhavī cāti ime tayo ekamanā viya ahesuṃ, mahādānanissandena vipulabalaviriyena, na-tth' ediso mahārāja aññassa dānānubhāvo yathā vessantarassa rañño mahādānānubhāvo.

82 yathā mahārāja mahiyā bahuvidhā maṇayo vijjanti, seyyathīdaṃ: indanīlo mahānīlo jotiraso veḷuriyo ummāpuppho sirīsapuppho manoharo suriyakanto candakanto vajiro kajjopakkamako phussarāgo lohitanko masāragallo, ete sabbe atikkamma cakkavattimaṇi aggam-akkhāyati, cakkavattimaṇi mahārāja samantā yojanaṃ obhāseti, evam-eva kho mahārāja yaṃ kiñci mahiyā dānaṃ vijjati api asadisadānaṃ paramaṃ, taṃ sabbaṃ atikkamma vessantarassa rañño mahādānaṃ aggam-akkhāyati. vessanta-

power cried and the *yakkhas* of great power laughed. All the while, the great earth quaked.

“Great king, it is just like when a big cauldron filled with 81
water and heaped with rice is placed in a hearth, and the fire burning underneath heats up the cauldron first. When the cauldron is hot it heats the water, and when the water is hot it heats the rice. When the rice is hot it surges up and plunges down, forms bubbles, and boils over in wreaths of foam. Great king, it was like this when Prince Vessantara gave up what is hardest to give in this world. For it was due to the nature of this gift—given by one who relinquished what is hardest to give—that great winds from below grew agitated and were simply unable to support it. Agitated, those great winds shook the waters. And when the waters were shaken, the great earth quaked. These three—wind, water, and earth—became as one due to the abundant power and energy issuing from that great gift. There is no other gift whose magnificence equals the magnificence of the great gift of Prince Vessantara.

“There are, great king, many kinds of gems found in 82
the earth, such as sapphire, great sapphire, *jotirasa,* lapis lazuli, the flax flower jewel, the siris tree blossom jewel, the captivating gem, sunstone, moonstone, diamond, the *kajjopakkamaka,* topaz, ruby, and cat’s eye. Yet the jewel of a wheel-turning emperor surpasses all of these and is spoken of first, for the jewel of a wheel-turning emperor shines for a league all around. Just like this, great king, the great gift of Prince Vessantara surpasses all other gifts found on the earth, even the most unequaled and supreme, and so it is

rassa mahārāja rañño mahādāne dīyamāne sattakkhattuṃ mahāpaṭhavī kampitā ti.

83 acchariyaṃ bhante nāgasena buddhānaṃ, abbhutaṃ bhante nāgasena buddhānaṃ, yaṃ tathāgato bodhisatto samāno asamo lokena evaṃ-khanti evaṃ-citto evaṃadhimutti evaṃ-adhippāyo. bodhisattānaṃ bhante nāgasena parakkamo dakkhāpito, pāramī ca jinānaṃ bhiyyo obhāsitā, cariyaṃ carato pi tāva tathāgatassa sadevake loke seṭṭhabhāvo anudassito; sādhu bhante nāgasena, thomitaṃ jinasāsanaṃ, jotitā jinapāramī, chinnā titthiyānaṃ vādaganṭhi, bhinnā parappavādakumbhā, pañho gambhīro uttānīkato, gahanaṃ agahanaṃ kataṃ, sammā laddhaṃ jinaputtānaṃ nibbāhanaṃ, evam-etaṃ gaṇivarapavara, tathā sampaṭicchāmīti.

84 bhante nāgasena, tumhe evaṃ bhaṇatha: sirirājena yācakassa cakkhūni dinnāni, andhassa sato puna dibbacakkhūni uppannānīti. etam-pi vacanaṃ sakasaṭaṃ saniggahaṃ sadosaṃ. hetusamugghāte ahetusmiṃ avatthumhi na-tthi dibbacakkhussa uppādo ti sutte vuttaṃ. yadi bhante nāgasena sivirājena yācakassa cakkhūni dinnāni, tena hi: puna dibbacakkhūni uppannānīti yaṃ vacanaṃ taṃ micchā. yadi dibbacakkhūni uppannāni, tena hi: sivirājena yācakassa cakkhūni dinnānīti yaṃ vacanaṃ tam-pi micchā. ayam-pi ubhatokoṭiko pañho, gaṇṭhito pi gaṇṭhitaro, vedhato pi vedhataro, gahanato pi gahanataro, so tavānuppatto, tattha chandam-abhijanehi nibbāhanāya paravādānaṃ niggahāyāti.

spoken of first. And so, great king, the earth quaked seven times when Prince Vessantara gave his great gift."

"It is a wonder of buddhas and it is a marvel of buddhas, 83
revered Nagasena, that when the Tathagata was a bodhisatta, he was unequaled in the world with respect to forbearance, awareness, resolve, and aspiration. The striving of bodhisattas has been shown, and even more has the perfection of the Victors shone forth. As long as there is a Tathagata practicing such conduct in the world along with its gods, the best conditions prevail. Well done, Nagasena! The dispensation of the Victor has been praised, the perfections of the Victor have been illuminated, the tangles of disputation have been cut through, the water pots of others' cavil have been smashed, a deep question has been explained, a thicket has been cleared, and a refuge for those in the lineage of the Victor has been rightly achieved. It is as you say, best of teachers, and I accept it."

"Revered Nagasena, you claim that 'when King Sivi 84
gave his eyes to a supplicant and became blind, divine eyes then appeared.' But this assertion is hard to swallow, easily refuted, and faulty. It is said in a *sutta* that with the removal of a cause—when there is no remaining cause and basis—there can be no arising of a divine eye. Nagasena, if King Sivi gave his eyes to a supplicant, then the claim that divine eyes appeared must be false. And if divine eyes appeared, then the claim that King Sivi gave his eyes to a supplicant must be false. This is another two-pronged dilemma, knottier than a knot, pricklier than a prickle, and more tangled than a tangle. Since it has now reached you, please work up the resolve to clear it away and refute the claims of opponents."

85 dinnāni mahārāja sivirājena yācakassa cakkhūm. tattha mā vimatiṃ uppādehi; puna dibbāni ca cakkhūni uppannāni, tatthāpi mā vimatiṃ janehīti. api nu kho bhante nāgasena hetusamugghāte ahetusmiṃ avatthumhi dibbacakkhu uppajjatīti. na hi mahārājāti. kim-pana bhante ettha kāraṇaṃ yena kāraṇena hetusamugghāte ahetusmiṃ avatthumhi dibbacakkhu uppajjati, iṅgha tāva kāraṇena maṃ saññāpehīti.

86 kim-pana mahārāja atthi loke saccaṃ nāma yena saccavādino saccakiriyaṃ karontīti. āma bhante, atthi loke saccaṃ nāma, saccena bhante nāgasena saccavādino saccakiriyaṃ katvā devaṃ vassāpenti, aggiṃ nibbāpenti, visaṃ paṭihananti, aññam-pi vividhaṃ kattabbaṃ karontīti.

87 tena hi mahārāja yujjati sameti: sivirājassa saccabalena dibbacakkhūni uppannānīti, saccabalena mahārāja avatthumhi dibbacakkhu uppajjati, saccaṃ yeva tattha vatthu bhavati dibbacakkhussa uppādāya. yathā mahārāja ye keci siddhā saccam anugāyanti: mahāmegho pavassatūti, tesaṃ saha saccam-anugītena mahāmegho pavassati; api nu kho mahārāja atthi ākāse vassahetu sannicito yena hetunā mahāmegho pavassatīti. na hi bhante, saccaṃ yeva tattha hetu bhavati mahato meghassa pavassanāyāti.

"King Sivi gave his eyes to a supplicant, great king. Do not foster doubt about this. And divine eyes then appeared. Do not harbor doubt on this matter either." 85

"But, Nagasena, sir, can a divine eye arise when there is the removal of the cause of sight, when there is no remaining cause and basis?" "Of course not, great king." "But then what, sir, is the reason whereby, when the cause of sight is removed and there is no remaining cause and basis, a divine eye could then appear? Come now, please convince me of the reasoning."

"Great king, is there actually truth in this world whereby 86
those speaking truly may perform an act of truth?"[19]

"Yes, sir, there really is truth in this world. And with the truth, Nagasena, those speaking truly may perform an act of truth that can make the sky rain, cause fire to die back, counter poison, and bring about various other desired ends."

"So then, great king, this fits and applies here. Divine eyes 87
then appeared for King Sivi by the power of truth, and it is by the power of truth, great king, that divine eyes appear where there is no remaining basis for them, because it is the truth itself that becomes the basis for the divine eyes. It is similar to when certain wizards recite a truth, saying, 'Let a great cloud shed rain,' and with their recitation of a truth, a great cloud does shower rain. But do the causes of rain actually come together in the sky whereby the great cloud sheds rain?"

"No, sir, but rather the truth itself becomes the cause whereby the great cloud showers rain."

88 evam-eva kho mahārāja na-tthi tassa pakatihetu, saccaṃ yev' ettha vatthu bhavati dibbacakkhussa uppādāyāti. yathā vā pana mahārāja ye keci siddhā saccam anugāyanti: jalita-pajjalita mahāaggikkhandho paṭinivattatūti, tesaṃ saha saccam-anugītena jalita-pajjalita-mahā-aggikkhandho khaṇena paṭinivattati, api nu kho mahārāja atthi tasmiṃ jalita-pajjalite mahāaggikkhandhe hetu sannicito yena hetunā jalita-pajjalita-mahāaggikkhandho khaṇena paṭinivattatīti. na hi bhante, saccaṃ yeva tattha vatthu hoti tassa jalita-pajjalitassa mahāaggikkhandhassa khaṇena paṭinivattanāyāti.

89 evam-eva kho mahārāja na-tthi tassa pakatihetu, saccaṃ yev' ettha vatthu bhavati dibbacakkhussa uppādāyāti. yathā vā pana mahārāja ye keci siddhā saccam anugāyanti: visaṃ halāhalaṃ agadaṃ bhavatūti, tesaṃ saha saccam-anugītena visaṃ halāhalaṃ khaṇena agadaṃ bhavati, api nu kho mahārāja atthi tasmiṃ halāhalavise hetu sannicito yena hetunā visaṃ halāhalaṃ khaṇena agadaṃ bhavatīti. na hi bhante, saccaṃ yeva tattha hetu bhavati visassa halāhalassa khaṇena paṭighātāyāti.

90 evam-eva kho mahārāja vinā pakatihetuṃ saccaṃ yev' ettha vatthu bhavati dibbacakkhussa uppādāyāti. catunnam-pi mahārāja ariyasaccānaṃ paṭivedhāya na-tth' aññaṃ vatthu, saccaṃ vatthuṃ karitvā cattāri ariyasaccāni paṭivijjhantīti. atthi mahārāja cīnavisaye cīnarājā, so mahāsamudde baliṃ kātukāmo catumāse catumāse saccakiriyaṃ katvā sīharathena antomahāsamudde yojanaṃ pavisati,

“Just so, great king, it is the truth itself that becomes the basis on which the divine eye appears, for there is no natural cause of it. 88

“Alternatively, it is similar to how certain wizards declare a truth, saying, ‘May this huge burning and blazing fire instantly die back,’ and with their recitation of a truth, the huge blazing and burning fire does instantly die back. But, great king, do the causes actually come together whereby the huge blazing and burning fire is instantly extinguished?” “Of course not, sir. It is the truth itself that becomes the basis whereby the huge blazing fire instantly dies back.”

“Just so, great king, it is the truth itself that becomes the 89
basis on which the divine eye appears, for there is no natural
cause of it. Alternatively, it is similar to how certain wizards recite a truth, saying, ‘May this lethal poison become a healing medicine,’ and with their recitation of a truth, the lethal poison instantly becomes a healing medicine. But, great king, is it that the causes are present in that lethal poison whereby it instantly becomes a healing medicine?”

“No, sir. It is the truth itself that becomes the cause that brings about the immediate removal of the lethal poison.”

“Just so, great king, it must be the truth itself, without 90
any natural cause, that became the basis that caused the divine eye to appear. What is more, there is no other basis for comprehending the Four Noble Truths. The truth creates the basis and then the Four Noble Truths pierce through.

“At one time in the Chinese realms, the king of China wanted to make an offering to the great ocean. Every four months he would perform an act of truth and then, in a lion

tassa rathasīsassa purato mahāvārikkhandho paṭikkamati, nikkhantassa puna ottharati, api nu kho mahārāja so mahāsamuddo sadevamanussena pi lokena pakatikāyabalena sakkā paṭikkamāpetun-ti.

91 atiparittake pi bhante taḷāke udakaṃ na sakkā sadeva-
manussena pi lokena pakatikāyabalena paṭikkamāpetuṃ, kiṃ pana mahāsamudde udakan-ti. iminā pi mahārāja kāraṇena saccabalaṃ ñātabbaṃ, na-tthi taṃ ṭhānaṃ yaṃ saccena na pattabban-ti. nagare mahārāja pāṭaliputte asoko dhammarājā sanegama-jānapada-amacca-bhaṭabala-mahāmattehi parivuto gaṅgaṃ nadiṃ navasalilasampuṇṇaṃ samatittikaṃ samabharitaṃ pañcayojanasatāyāmaṃ yojanaputhulaṃ sandamānaṃ disvā amacce evam-āha: atthi koci bhaṇe samattho imaṃ mahāgaṅgaṃ paṭisotaṃ sandāpetun-ti. amaccā āhaṃsu: dukkaraṃ devāti.

92 tasmiṃ yeva gaṅgākūle ṭhitā bindumatī nāma gaṇikā
assosi: raññā kira evaṃ vuttaṃ: sakkā nu kho imaṃ mahāgaṅgaṃ paṭisotaṃ sandāpetun-ti. sā evam-āha: ahaṃ hi nagare pāṭaliputte gaṇikā rūpūpajīvinī antimajīvikā, mama tāva rājā saccakiriyaṃ passatūti. atha sā saccakiriyaṃ akāsi. saha tassā saccakiriyāya khaṇena sā mahāgaṅgā galagalantī paṭisotaṃ sandittha, mahato janakāyassa passato.

93 atha rājā mahāgaṅgāya āvaṭṭaūmivegajanitaṃ halāhala-
saddaṃ sutvā vimhito acchariyabbhutajāto amacce evam āha: kissāyaṃ bhaṇe mahāgangā paṭisotaṃ sandatīti. bindu-

chariot, he would drive into the ocean as far as a league. The huge mass of water would retreat right in front his chariot and fill in again after it passed through. Great king, do you suppose that the great ocean was forced back by the natural physical power of gods and humans in this world?"

"The natural physical power of gods and humans in this 91
world is not able to force back even the water in a small pond, sir, let alone the water of the ocean."

"By this reasoning, great king, the power of truth should be known, and there is no place that cannot be reached by the truth. Once, in the city of Pataliputta, the righteous king Ashoka, while surrounded by townsmen, country people, his ministers, hired soldiers, troops, and courtiers, saw the Ganga river as wide as a league flowing along for five hundred leagues, brimming with fresh water, and swelling its banks. He asked his ministers: 'Look here, is there anyone capable of making the Great Ganga reverse course?' The ministers replied: 'That would be difficult, Your Majesty.'

"However, a courtesan known as Bindumati was standing 92
there on the banks of the Ganga, and she heard that the king had asked whether there was anyone able to make the Great Ganga reverse course. She stated: 'As a courtesan in the city of Pataliputta I live by my beauty and practice the lowest form of livelihood. May the king observe my act of truth.' Then she performed an act of truth. At the very instant of her act of truth, and as the huge crowd watched, the Great Ganga fell back and reversed course.

"At this the king, hearing the din produced by the speed 93
at which the waves of the Ganga whipped around, was

matī mahārāja gaṇikā tava vacanaṃ sutvā saccakiriyaṃ akāsi, tassā saccakiriyāya mahāgaṅgā ubbhamukhā sandatīti. atha saṃviggahadayo rājā turitaturito sayaṃ gantvā taṃ gaṇikaṃ pucchi: saccaṃ kira je tayā saccakiriyāya ayaṃ gaṅgā paṭisotaṃ sandāpitā ti.

94 āma devāti. rājā āha: kin-te tattha balaṃ atthi, ko vā te vacanaṃ ādiyati anummatto, kena tvaṃ balena imaṃ mahāgaṅgaṃ patisotaṃ sandāpesīti. sā āha: saccabalenāhaṃ mahārāja imaṃ mahāgaṅgaṃ paṭisotaṃ sandāpesin-ti. rājā āha: kin-te saccabalaṃ atthi coriyā dhuttiyā asatiyā chinnikāya pāpiyā bhinnasīmāya atikkantikāya andhajanavilopikāyāti.

95 saccaṃ mahārāja tādisikā ahaṃ, tādisikāya pi me mahārāja saccakiriyā atthi yāyāhaṃ iccha-mānā sadevakam-pi lokaṃ parivatteyyan-ti. rājā āha: katamā pana sā hoti saccakiriyā, iṅgha maṃ sāvehīti.

96 yo me mahārāja dhanaṃ deti khattiyo vā brāhmaṇo vā vesso vā suddo vā añño vā koci tesaṃ samakaṃ yeva upaṭṭhahāmi, khattiyo ti viseso na-tthi, suddo ti atimaññanā na-tthi, anunayapaṭighavippamuttā dhanasāmikaṃ paricarāmi, esā me deva saccakiriyā yāyāhaṃ imaṃ mahāgaṅgaṃ paṭisotaṃ sandāpesin-ti.

astonished and struck with awe and wonder. He asked his ministers: 'For whom, sirs, is the Great Ganga reversing course?'

"'Bindumati the courtesan heard your words and performed an act of truth, Your Majesty. It is because of her act of truth that the Great Ganga is flowing upstream.'

"Now the king's heart was agitated, and he hastened to the courtesan to ask for himself, 'Can it really be true, madam, that the Ganga reversed course because of your act of truth?'

"'Yes, Your Majesty.' 94

"The king replied: 'But how do you have such power? And who of sound mind would accept your claim? With what force could you make the Great Ganga reverse course?'

"'By the power of truth, Your Majesty, I made the Great Ganga reverse course,' she responded.

"'But you are a thief, wanton, wicked, and deceitful, who breaches and transgresses boundaries with evil deeds, and lives by plundering fools.'

"'It is true, Your Majesty, that I am such a person. But an 95
act of truth, even of a person like me who so wishes, can turn the world and its gods upside down.'

"'What is this act of truth? Come now, do tell me.'

"'Your Majesty, I attend equally to whoever gives me 96
money, whether Kshatriya, Brahman, Vaishya, Shudra, or anyone else, without noting the eminence of the Kshatriya and without despising the Shudra. Free of both attraction and repugnance, I serve any wealthy man. It was with this act of truth, Your Majesty, that I made the Great Ganga reverse course.'

97 iti pi mahārāja sacce thitā na kañci atthaṃ na vindanti. dinnāni ca mahārāja sivirājena yācakassa cakkhūni, dibbacakkhūni ca uppannāni, tañ-ca saccakiriyāya. yaṃ pana sutte vuttaṃ: maṃsacakkhusmiṃ naṭṭhe ahetusmiṃ avatthumhi na-tthi dibbacakkhussa uppādo ti, taṃ bhāvanāmayaṃ cakkhuṃ sandhāya vuttan-ti evam-etaṃ mahārāja dhārehīti. sādhu bhante nāgasena, sunibbeṭhito pañho, suniddiṭṭho niggaho, sumadditā parappavādā, evam-etaṃ, tathā sampaṭicchāmīti.

98 bhante nāgasena, bhāsitam-p' etaṃ bhagavatā: tiṇṇaṃ kho pana bhikkhave sannipātā gabbhassa avakkanti hoti: idha mātāpitaro ca sannipatitā honti, mātā ca utunī hoti, gandhabbo ca paccupaṭṭhito hoti; imesaṃ kho bhikkhave tiṇṇaṃ sannipātā gabbhassa avakkanti hotīti. asesavacanam-etaṃ, nissesavacanam-etaṃ, nippariyāyavacanam-etaṃ, arahassavacanam-etaṃ, sadeva-manussānaṃ majjhe nisīditvā bhaṇitaṃ.

99 ayañ-ca dvinnaṃ sannipātā gabbhassa avakkanti dissati: dukūlena tāpasena pārikāya tāpasyā utunīkāle dakkhiṇena hatthanguṭṭhena nābhi parāmaṭṭhā, tassa tena nābhiparāmasanena sāmo kumāro nibbatto. mātaṅgenāpi isinā brāhmaṇakaññāya utunīkāle dakkhiṇena hatthaṅguṭṭhena nābhi parāmaṭṭhā, tassa tena parāmasanena maṇḍabyo māṇavako nibbatto ti. yadi bhante nāgasena bhagavatā bhaṇitaṃ: tiṇṇaṃ kho pana bhikkhave sannipātā gabbhassa avakkanti hotīti, tena hi: sāmo ca kumāro maṇḍabyo ca māṇavako

“Therefore, great king, there is nothing that those firm in 97
the truth may not acquire. And so it is, great king, that King Sivi gave his eyes to a supplicant, and divine eyes appeared by virtue of an act of truth. When it is stated in a *sutta* that ‘When the physical eyes are destroyed there is no remaining cause and basis for a divine eye to arise,’ this should be understood as said only in reference to the eye achieved in meditation, great king.”

“Excellent, Nagasena! The question is unraveled, the refutation is well explained, and the view of the opponents is thoroughly crushed. Therefore, I accept it.

“Revered Nagasena, the Bhagavan said: ‘Monks, concep- 98
tion occurs from the coming together of three factors: the mother and father have united, the mother is in her fertile season, and a *gandhabba* is ready.[20] Monks, it is from the coming together of these three factors that conception occurs.’ This was the full statement, the complete statement, and the unqualified statement. And it was not a secret statement, for it was made while he was seated surrounded by
gods and humans. And yet, conception has been witnessed 99
at the coming together of just two of these. The child Sama was conceived by the touching of a navel when the ascetic Dukula, with the thumb of his right hand, touched the navel of the ascetic Parika in her fertile season. And the Brahman youth Mandabya was conceived also by touching when the sage Matanga touched, with the thumb of his right hand, the navel of a Brahman girl in her fertile season. Nagasena, if it was said by the Bhagavan, ‘Monks, conception occurs from the coming together of three factors,’ then the claim that the child Sama and the youth Mandabya were both conceived

ubho pi te nābhiparāmasanena nibbattā ti yaṃ vacanaṃ taṃ micchā. yadi tathāgatena bhaṇitaṃ: sāmo ca kumāro maṇḍabyo ca māṇavako nābhiparāmasanena nibbattā ti, tena hi: tiṇṇaṃ kho pana bhikkhave sannipātā gabbhassa avakkanti hotīti yaṃ vacanaṃ tam-pi micchā. ayam-pi ubhatokoṭiko pañho sugambhīro sunipuṇo visayo buddhimantānaṃ, so tavānuppatto, chinda vimatipathaṃ, dhārehi ñāṇavarapajjotan-ti.

100 bhāsitam-p' etaṃ mahārāja bhagavatā: tiṇṇaṃ kho pana bhikkhave sannipātā gabbhassa avakkanti hoti: idha mātāpitaro ca sannipatitā honti, mātā ca utunī hoti, gandhabbo ca paccupaṭṭhito hoti, evaṃ tiṇṇaṃ sannipātā gabbhassa avakkanti hotīti. bhaṇitañ-ca: sāmo ca kumāro maṇḍabyo ca māṇavako nābhiparāmasananibbattā ti.

101 tena hi bhante nāgasena yena kāraṇena pañho suvinicchito hoti tena kāraṇena maṃ saññāpehīti. sutapubbaṃ pana tayā mahārāja: saṅkicco ca kumāro isisiṅgo ca tāpaso thero ca kumārakassapo iminā nāma te nibbattā ti.

102 āma bhante, sūyati, abbhuggatā tesaṃ jāti: dve migadhenuyo tāva utunīkāle dvinnaṃ tāpasānaṃ passāvaṭṭhānaṃ āgantvā sasambhavaṃ passāvaṃ piviṃsu, tena passāvasambhavena saṅkicco ca kumāro isisiṅgo ca tāpaso nibbattā. therassa udāyissa bhikkhunupassayaṃ upagatassa rattacittena bhikkhuniyā aṅgajātaṃ upanijjhāyantassa sambhavaṃ kāsāve mucci; atha kho āyasmā udāyi taṃ bhikkhuniṃ

merely by touching a navel is false. But if the Tathagata said, 'The child Sama and the youth Madabhya were conceived by touching a navel,' then the statement 'Monks, conception occurs from the coming together of three things' is false. This very deep and subtle two-pronged dilemma is within the scope of intelligent persons, and it has now reached you. Please cut off the path of perplexity and hold up the supreme lamp of knowledge."

"Great king, the Bhagavan did say, 'Monks, concep- 100
tion occurs from the coming together of three factors—the mother and father are united, the mother is in her fertile season, and a *gandhabba* is ready. Monks, it is from the coming together of these three factors that conception occurs.' He also said: 'The child Sama and the youth Mandabya were conceived by the touching of a navel.'"

"Then, Nagasena, please teach me the reasoning whereby 101
this question has been properly decided."

"Have you ever heard, great king, of how the child Sankicca, the ascetic Isisinga, and Elder Kumara Kassapa were conceived?"

"Yes, sir, I have heard, as the circumstances of their 102
births have spread far and wide. It seems that two does in their fertile period came to a spot where two ascetics had urinated, and they drank the urine mixed with semen. With that semen the child Sankicca and the ascetic Isisinga were conceived. And then there was the case of Elder Udayi, who came to the nuns' quarters and, looking at a nun's private parts with lustful thoughts, shed semen on his robe. Then that revered Udayi told the nun: 'Go, sister, and fetch water,

etad-avoca: gaccha bhagini udakaṃ āhara, antaravāsakaṃ dhovissāmīti. re ‘yya, aham-eva dhovissāmīti. tato sā bhikkhunī utunīsamaye taṃ sambhavaṃ ekadesaṃ mukhena aggahesi, ekadesaṃ aṅgajāte pakkhipi, tena thero kumārakassapo nibbatto ti evam-etaṃ jano āhāti.

103 api nu kho tvaṃ mahārāja saddahasi taṃ vacanan-ti. āma bhante, balavaṃ tattha mayaṃ kāraṇaṃ upalabhāma yena mayaṃ kāraṇena saddahāma: iminā kāraṇena nibbattā ti. kim-pan’ ettha mahārāja kāraṇan-ti. suparikammakate bhante kalale bījaṃ nipatitvā khippaṃ saṃvirūhatīti. āma mahārājāti.

104 evam-eva kho bhante sā bhikkhunī utunī samānā saṇṭhite kalale ruhire pacchinnavege ṭhapitāya dhātuyā taṃ sambhavaṃ gahetvā tasmiṃ kalale pakkhipi, tena tassā gabbho saṇṭhāsi; evaṃ tattha kāraṇaṃ paccema tesaṃ nibbattiyā ti. evam etaṃ mahārāja, tathā sampaṭicchāmi: yonippavesena gabbho sambhavatīti. sampaṭicchasi pana tvaṃ mahārāja kumārakassapassa gabbhāvakkamanan-ti. āma bhante ti.

105 sādhu mahārāja, paccāgatosi mama visayaṃ, ekavidhena pi gabbhassāvakkantiṃ kathayanto mamānubalaṃ bhavissasi; atha yā pana tā dve migadhenuyo passāvaṃ pivitvā gabbhaṃ paṭilabhiṃsu tāsaṃ tvaṃ saddahasi gabbhassāvakkamanan-ti. āma bhante, yaṃ kiñci bhuttaṃ pītaṃ khāyitaṃ lehitaṃ sabban-taṃ kalalaṃ osarati, ṭhānagataṃ vuddhim-āpajjati. yathā bhante nāgasena yā kāci saritā nāma

and I will wash my inner robe.' But she said, 'Oh no, sir. I will wash it myself.' Further, it happened to be the nun's fertile period, and she took part of the robe with the semen in her mouth and applied part of it to her private parts, and by this Elder Kumara Kassapa was conceived. Or so people say."

"But do you believe this talk, great king?" 103

"Yes, sir, for we get strong reasons in this case, and with strong reasons we can believe that they were conceived by such means."

"But what, great king, exactly was the means in this case?"

"Sir, when a seed has fallen into well-prepared wet soil, does it germinate quickly?" "Yes, great king."

"Similarly, that nun in her fertile season inserted the 104
semen into her womb, putting it together with her fluids, which were readied when the menstrual blood that had settled in the womb stopped flowing. By this the embryo was established, and we arrive at the means of conception for this case." "I understand, great king, that with such entry into a womb an embryo is produced. And do you, great king, accept that there was such a conception in the case of Kumara Kassapa as well?" "I do, sir."

"Very good, great king. We have arrived at my position, for 105
you will follow me in saying that there is conception by this one method. But what of the case of the two does drinking urine who became pregnant? Do you believe in their conceptions?"

"I do, sir, because anything eaten, drunk, consumed, or licked travels down to the womb, and it generates growth where it arrives. Revered Nagasena, all sorts of rivers flow into the ocean and generate growth where they enter. Like-

sabbā tā mahāsamuddaṃ osaranti, ṭhānagatā vuddhim-āpajjanti, evam eva kho bhante nāgasena yaṃ kiñci bhuttaṃ pītaṃ khāyitaṃ lehitaṃ sabban-taṃ kalalaṃ osarati, ṭhānagataṃ vuddhim-āpajjati. tenāhaṃ kāraṇena saddahāmi: mukhagatena pi gabbhassāvakkanti hotīti.

106 sādhu mahārāja, bāḷhataraṃ upagatosi mama visayaṃ, mukhapānena pi dvayasannipāto bhavati, saṅkiccassa kumārassa isisiṅgassa tāpasassa therassa ca kumārakassapassa gabbhāvakkamanaṃ sampaṭicchasīti. āma bhante, sannipāto osaratīti.

107 sāmo pi mahārāja kumāro maṇḍabyo pi māṇavako tīsu sannipātesu antogadhā ekarasā ya purimena; tattha kāraṇaṃ vakkhāmi. dukūlo ca mahārāja tāpaso pārikā ca tāpasī ubho pi te araññavāsā ahesuṃ pavivekādhimuttā uttamatthagavesakā, tapatejena yāva brahmalokaṃ santāpesuṃ. tesaṃ tadā sakko devānam-indo sāyapātaṃ upaṭṭhānaṃ āgacchati. so tesaṃ garugatamettatāya upadhārento addasa anāgatamaddhāne dvinnam-pi tesaṃ cakkhūnaṃ antaradhānaṃ, disva te evam-āha: ekam-me bhonto vacanaṃ karotha, sādhu, ekaṃ puttaṃ janeyyātha, so tumhākaṃ upaṭṭhāko bhavissati ālambano cāti.

108 alaṃ kosiya, mā evaṃ bhaṇīti te tassa taṃ vacanaṃ na sampaṭicchiṃsu. anukampako atthakāmo sakko devānam-indo dutiyam-pi tatiyam-pi te evam āha: ekam-me bhonto vacanaṃ karotha, sādhu, ekaṃ puttaṃ janeyyātha, so tumhākaṃ upaṭṭhāko bhavissati ālambano cāti. tatiyam-pi

wise, Nagasena, whatever is eaten, drunk, consumed, or licked travels down to the womb where it generates growth. With this reasoning I do believe that conception can occur even by way of the mouth."

"Excellent, great king. We have undeniably arrived at my 106
position, for there can be the union of the two also by means of the mouth. So you now accept the conceptions of the child Sankicca, the ascetic Isisinga, and Elder Kumara Kassapa?"

"Yes, sir, there is union since it enters."

"Great king, the child Sama and the Brahman youth 107
Mandabya are considered to be essentially alike with respect to the first of the three factors that come together. Let me describe the means in their case. Two ascetics, Dukula and Parika, seeking seclusion and intent upon the highest goal, lived as forest hermits. By the brilliance of their asceticism they spread heat as far as the Brahma realm. As a consequence, Sakka, the king of the gods, came one morning to serve them. As he contemplated them with loving-kindness full of respect, he saw that in the distant future both would lose their sight. Foreseeing this, he told them: 'Good people, please do one thing that I suggest, and that is produce a son
who will become your attendant and support.' They did not 108
assent to his plea: 'Enough, Kosiya,* do not speak in such a way!' But Sakka was compassionate and well wishing, so he urged them a second time, and then a third: 'Good people, please do one thing that I suggest, and that is produce a son who will become your attendant and support.' On the third

* A name for Sakka.

te āhaṃsu: alaṃ kosiya, mā tvaṃ amhe anatthe niyojehi, kadā 'yaṃ kāyo na bhijjissati, bhijjatu ayaṃ kayo bhedanadhammo, bhijjantiyā pi dharaṇiyā, patante pi selasikhare, phalante pi ākāse, patante pi candimasuriye n'eva mayaṃ lokadhammehi missayissāma, mā tvaṃ amhākaṃ sammukhabhāvaṃ upagaccha, upagatassa te eso vissāso: anatthacaro tvaṃ maññe ti.

109 tato sakko devānam-indo tesaṃ manaṃ alabhamāno garugato pañjaliko puna yāci: yadi me vacanaṃ na ussahatha kātuṃ, yadā tāpasī utunī hoti pupphavatī tadā tvaṃ bhante dakkhiṇena hatthaṅguṭṭhena nābhiṃ parāmaseyyāsi, tena sā gabbhaṃ lacchati, sannipāto yev' esa gabbhāvakkantiyā ti. sakkom' ahaṃ kosiya taṃ vacanaṃ kātuṃ, na tāvatakena amhākaṃ tapo bhijjati, hotūti sampaṭicchiṃsu.

110 tāya ca pana velāya devabhavane atthi devaputto ussannakusalamūlo khīṇāyuko, āyukkhayaṃ patto yadicchakaṃ samattho okkamituṃ, api cakkavattikule pi. atha sakko devānam-indo taṃ devaputtaṃ upasaṅkamitvā evam-āha: ehi kho mārisa, suppabhāto te divaso, atthasiddhi upagatā, yam ahaṃ te upaṭṭhānam-āgamiṃ, ramaṇīye te okāse vāso bhavissati, patirūpe kule paṭisandhi bhavissati, sundarehi mātāpitūhi vaḍḍhetabbo bhavissasi, ehi me vacanaṃ karohīti yāci. dutiyam-pi tatiyam-pi yāci sirasi pañjalikato.

time, they replied, 'Enough, Kosiya, do not prevail upon us in regard to something against our aim. At some point, this body will not fail to break down. Let this body, subject to breaking down, break down. But though the earth may split, the rocky peaks tumble, the sky burst, and the sun and the moon fall, we will not become entangled with worldly things. Please do not come into our presence, for there should be trust toward a guest. And yet, surely you would lead us astray.'

"At this, Sakka, king of the gods, although not able to 109
change their minds, was still filled with respect. He placed his hands together in reverence and once again entreated them: 'If you are not able to do my bidding, then when the ascetic is in her season and is menstruating, then you, sir, are to touch her navel with the thumb of your right hand. By this, she will conceive a child, for this is itself a union leading to conception.' 'I can do as you say, Kosiya, for our asceticism will not be broken by such a thing. So be it,' and they consented.

"Now, at this time there was a god whose sources of merit 110
were abundant and whose life span in the divine world was exhausted. When his life span ran out, he was able to descend anywhere he wished, even into a dynasty of wheel-turning emperors. Now Sakka, king of the gods, approached this god and said: 'My good fellow, a fine day dawns for you and a great benefit has arrived, for I have come to render you a service. You will have a life in a delightful place. You will take rebirth in a suitable family and be raised by handsome parents. But,' he entreated, 'you must do as I tell you.' And a second and a third time he solicited him, cupping his hands

tato so devaputto evam-āha: katamaṃ taṃ mārisa kulaṃ yaṃ tvaṃ abhikkhaṇaṃ kittayasi punappunan-ti. dukūlo ca tāpaso pārikā ca tāpasī ti. so tassa vacanaṃ sutvā tuṭṭho sampaṭicchi: sādhu mārisa, yo tava chando so hotu; ākaṅkhamāno ahaṃ mārisa patthite kule uppajjeyyaṃ, kimhi kule uppajjāmi, aṇḍaje vā jalābuje vā saṃedaje vā opapātike vā ti.

111 jalābujāya mārisa yoniyā uppajjāhīti. atha sakko devānam-indo uppattidivasaṃ vigaṇetvā dukūlassa tāpasassa ārocesi: asukasmiṃ nāma divase tāpasī utunī bhavissati pupphavatī, tadā tvaṃ bhante dakkhiṇena hatthaṅguṭṭhena nābhiṃ parāmaseyyāsīti. tasmiṃ mahārāja divase tāpasī ca utunī pupphavatī ahosi, devaputto ca tatthūpago paccupaṭṭhito ahosi, tāpaso ca dakkhiṇena hatthaṅguṭṭhena tāpasiyā nābhiṃ parāmasi. iti te tayo sannipātā ahesuṃ.

112 nābhiparāmasanena tāpasiyā rāgo udapādi; so pan' assā rāgo nābhiparāmasanaṃ paṭicca, mā tvaṃ sannipātaṃ ajjhācāram-eva maññi. ūhasanam-pi sannipāto, ullapanam-pi sannipāto, upanijjhāyanam-pi sannipāto, pubbabhāgabhāvato rāgassa uppādāya āmasanena sannipāto jāyati, sannipātā okkamanaṃ hotīti anajjhācāre pi mahārāja parāmasanena gabbhāvakkanti hoti. yathā mahārāja aggi jalamāno aparāmasanena pi upagatassa sītaṃ byapahanti, evam-eva kho

reverently at his forehead. At this, the god replied: 'Which family is it, good sir, that you praise repeatedly, again and again?' 'The ascetic Dukula and the ascetic Parika.' Hearing this, he was pleased and agreed to it. 'Very well, good sir, let what you wish be done, for I myself have been hoping to be reborn in just the sort of family you request. But how am I to be born—through an egg, viviparously, in water, or spontaneously?'

"'You are to be born viviparously, my good fellow, by way 111
of a womb.'

"Then Sakka, king of the gods, calculated the day of his rebirth and addressed the ascetic Dukula: 'On a certain day, the ascetic will be in her season, having menstruated, and then, sir, you should touch her navel with the thumb of your right hand.' On this day, great king, the ascetic was in her season and had menstruated, the god had arrived there and was ready, and the male ascetic touched the female ascetic's navel with the thumb of his right hand. And so there was the coming together of the three factors.

"By the touch of her navel, passion arose for the female 112
ascetic. And since the passion was produced only by his touching her navel, you are not to suppose that the union in this case was actually misconduct, conjecturing, 'This union was produced by touch along with the arousal of a previously generated passion, for union is also a matter of smiling, coaxing, and gazing lustfully, and it was from such a union that there was conception.' Great king, the conception was by means of touch, and there was no misconduct whatsoever. Just as a blazing fire dispels even without contact the cold of one who draws near, so too, great king, there

mahārāja anajjhācāre pi parāmasanena gabbhassāvakkanti hoti.

113 catunnaṃ vasena mahārāja sattānaṃ gabbhāvakkanti hoti: kammavasena yonivasena kulavasena āyācanavasena; api ca sabbe p' ete sattā kammasambhavā kammasamuṭṭhānā. kathaṃ mahārāja kammavasena sattānaṃ gabbhāvakkanti hoti: ussannakusalamūlā mahārāja sattā yadicchakaṃ uppajjanti, khattiyamahāsālakule vā brāhmaṇamahāsālakule vā gahapatimahāsālakule vā devesu vā aṇḍajāya vā yoniyā jalābujāya vā yoniyā saṃsedajāya vā yoniyā opapātikāya vā yoniyā.

114 yathā mahārāja puriso aḍḍho mahaddhano mahābhogo pahūta-jātarūpa-rajato pahūta-vittūpakaraṇo pahūta-dhana-dhañño pahūta-ñātipakkho dāsiṃ vā dāsaṃ vā khettaṃ vā vatthuṃ vā gāmaṃ vā nigamaṃ vā janapadaṃ vā yaṃ kiñci manasā abhipatthitaṃ yadicchakaṃ dviguṇa-tiguṇam-pi dhanaṃ datvā kiṇāti, evam-eva kho mahārāja ussannakusalamūlā sattā yadicchakaṃ uppajjanti, khattiyamahāsālakule vā brāhmaṇamahāsālakule vā gahapatimahāsālakule vā devesu vā aṇḍajāya vā yoniyā jalābujāya vā yoniyā saṃsedajāya vā yoniyā opapātikāya vā yoniyā. evaṃ kammavasena sattānaṃ gabbhāvakkanti hoti.

115 kathaṃ yonivasena sattānaṃ gabbhāvakkanti hoti: kukkuṭānaṃ mahārāja vātena gabbhāvakkanti hoti, balākānaṃ meghasaddena gabbhāvakkanti hoti, sabbe pi deva agabbhaseyyakā sattā yeva, tesaṃ nānāvaṇṇena gabbhāvakkanti hoti. yathā mahārāja manussā nānāvaṇṇena mahiyā caranti, keci purato paṭicchādenti, keci pacchato paṭicchād-

can be conception by means of touch even when there is no misconduct.

"Conception of living beings occurs in four ways: by way 113
of karma, by way of origin, by way of kind, and by way of a request, though all beings are of course originated and generated by karma. How, great king, is there conception of beings according to karma? Beings whose sources of merit are abundant are born according to their wishes, whether into the lineages and great halls of Kshatriyas, Brahmans, or householders or among gods, or taking birth by egg,
viviparously, by water, or spontaneously. Great king, just 114
as a rich, wealthy, and prosperous man with lavish gold and silver, ample wealth and possessions, abundant grain and crops, and plenty of relations and adherents gives money, even twice or triple the amount, and buys whatever he wants, wishes, or fancies, whether female or male slave, field, property, village, market town, or countryside, so too beings with abundant sources of merit are born wherever they wish, whether into the lineages and great halls of Kshatriyas, Brahmans, or householders or among gods, or taking birth by egg, viviparously, by water, or spontaneously. In this way, beings are conceived according to karma.

"Now, how are beings conceived by way of origin? Great 115
king, conception occurs by means of wind for cocks and by the sound of storm clouds for cranes. And gods are beings that always avoid birth in a womb. Conception happens variously in these cases. And just as people roam the earth with various appearances—some covering themselves in front, some covering their backs, some naked, some close-shaven and wearing white, some wearing white and a topknot,

enti, keci naggā honti, keci bhaṇḍū honti setapaṭadharā, keci molibaddhā honti, keci bhaṇḍū kāsāvavasanā honti, keci kāsāvavasanā molibaddhā honti, keci jaṭino vākacīradharā honti, keci cammavasanā honti, keci rasmiyo nivāsenti, sabbe p' ete manussā nānāvaṇṇena mahiyā caranti; evam-eva kho mahārāja sattā yeva te sabbe, tesaṃ nānāvaṇṇena gabbhāvakkanti hoti. evaṃ yonivasena sattānaṃ gabbhāvakkanti hoti.

116 kathaṃ kulavasena sattānaṃ gabbhāvakkanti hoti: kulaṃ nāma mahārāja cattāri kulāni: aṇḍajaṃ jalābujaṃ saṃsedajaṃ opapātikaṃ; yadi tattha gandhabbo yato kutoci āgantvā aṇḍaje kule uppajjati so tattha aṇḍajo hoti -pe- jalābuje kule, saṃsedaje kule, opapātike kule uppajjati so tattha opapātiko hoti, tesu tesu kulesu tādisā yeva sattā sambhavanti. yathā mahārāja himavati nerupabbataṃ ye keci migapakkhino upenti sabbe te sakavaṇṇaṃ vijahitvā suvaṇṇavaṇṇā honti, evam-eva kho mahārāja yo koci gandhabbo yato kutoci āgantvā aṇḍajaṃ yoniṃ upagantvā sabhāvavaṇṇaṃ vijahitvā aṇḍajo hoti-pe-jalābujaṃ, saṃsedajaṃ, opapātikaṃ yoniṃ upagantvā sabhāvavaṇṇaṃ vijahitvā opapātiko hoti. evaṃ kulavasena sattānaṃ gabbhāvakkanti hoti.

117 kathaṃ āyācanavasena sattānaṃ gabbhāvakkanti hoti: idha mahārāja kulaṃ hoti aputtakaṃ bahusāpateyyaṃ saddhaṃ pasannaṃ sīlavantaṃ kalyāṇadhammaṃ tapanissitaṃ, devaputto ca ussannakusalamūlo cavanadhammo hoti, atha sakko devānam-indo tassa kulassa anukampāya

some close-shaven and wearing brown robes, some wearing brown robes and a topknot, some wearing the bast clothing of ascetics, some wearing hides, and some donning rays of light—as in fact all these people do roam the earth with various appearances, so too, great king, these beings are all conceived variously. In this way, beings are conceived by way of origin.

"How are beings conceived by way of kind? Great king, 116
'kind' here means four kinds: egg-born, viviparous, moisture-born, and spontaneous. If a *gandhabba* arrives from somewhere and is born in the egg-born way, then it is egg-born. And similarly for the viviparous, moisture-born, and spontaneous kinds, so that one born in the spontaneous way is born spontaneously. Beings such as these are born among these different kinds. Just as, great king, whatever beasts and birds go to the Himalayan mountain Neru abandon their own color and take on a golden hue, so too any *gandhabba* arriving from anywhere that takes the egg-born way of birth abandons its particular appearance and becomes egg-born. So too in the cases of viviparous, moisture, and spontaneous births, so that one taking a spontaneous birth abandons its particular appearance and is generated spontaneously. In this way, beings are conceived by way of kind.

"And finally, how are beings conceived by way of a request? 117
Great king, in this case there is a family that is very wealthy, faithful, believing, moral, virtuous, and austere, but childless. And there is also a god with abundant sources of merit whose time has run out. Now Sakka, king of the gods, out of compassion for the family entreats the god: 'Good sir, please direct yourself to the womb of the woman of this family.'

taṃ devaputtaṃ āyācati: paṇidhehi mārisa amukassa kulassa mahesiyā kucchin-ti, so tassa āyāca-nahetu taṃ kulaṃ paṇidheti. yathā mahārāja manussā puññakāmā samaṇaṃ manobhāvanīyaṃ āyācitvā gehaṃ upanenti: ayaṃ upagantvā sabbassa kulassa sukhāvaho bhavissatīti, evam-eva kho mahārāja sakko devānam indo taṃ devaputtaṃ āyācitvā taṃ kulaṃ upaneti. evaṃ āyācanavasena sattānaṃ gabbhāvakkanti hoti.

118 sāmo mahārāja kumāro sakkena devānam-indena āyācito pārikāya tāpasiyā kucchiṃ okkanto. sāmo mahārāja kumāro katapuñño, mātāpitaro sīlavanto kalyāṇadhammā, āyācako samattho, tiṇṇaṃ cetopaṇidhiyā sāmo kumāro nibbatto idha mahārāja nayakusalo puriso sukaṭṭhe anūpakhette bījaṃ ropeyya, api nu tassa bījassa antarāyaṃ vivajjentassa vuddhiyā koci antarāyo bhaveyyāti. na hi bhante, nirupaghātaṃ bhante bījaṃ khippaṃ saṃvirūheyyāti.

119 evam-eva kho mahārāja sāmo kumāro mutto uppannantarāyehi tiṇṇaṃ cetopaṇidhiyā nibbatto. api nu kho mahārāja sutapubbaṃ tayā isīnaṃ manopadosena iddho phīto mahājanapado sajano samucchinno ti. āma bhante, sūyati mahiyā: daṇḍakāraññaṃ mejjhāraññaṃ kāliṅgāraññaṃ mātaṅgāraññaṃ sabbantaṃ araññaṃ araññabhūtaṃ, sabbe p' ete janapadā isīnaṃ manopadosena khayaṃ gatā ti.

120 yadi mahārāja tesaṃ manopadosena susamiddhā janapadā ucchijjanti, api nu kho tesaṃ manopasādena kiñci nibbatteyyāti. āma bhante ti. tena hi mahārāja sāmo kumāro tiṇṇaṃ

Because of this request he is directed to this family. It is similar to how people desiring merit approach a renouncer with a well-cultivated mind and direct him to their house, thinking, *When he visits, there will be happiness for the whole family!* Similarly, great king, Sakka, king of the gods, entreats this god and directs him to the family. In this way, beings are conceived by way of request.

"Great king, the child Sama was requested by Sakka, king 118
of gods, and appeared in the ascetic Parika's womb. The child Sama had made merit and had virtuous and moral parents, and his supplicant was capable. By an earnest request made three times, the child Sama was born. In this connection, a man skilled in the appropriate methods might plant a seed in a well-tilled and irrigated field. Supposing that seed had every impediment removed, would there then be any obstacle to its growth?"

"No, sir, an unharmed seed would germinate quickly."

"Similarly, great king, the child Sama was free of any 119
impediments that could have arisen and was born by an earnest request made three times. Have you ever heard of a case where a rich, prosperous, and well-populated country was destroyed by the wrath of a sage?"

"Yes, sir, it is heard around the world that the forests of Dandaka Wood, the forests of Kalinga, Mejjha Wilderness, and the forests of Matanga were all desolated. These countries were destroyed by the wrath of sages."

"And if such magnificent countries could be destroyed by 120
their wrath, then surely anything might result from their graciousness."

"Indeed, sir."

balavantānaṃ cetopasādena nibbatto: isinimmito devanimmito puññanimmito ti evam-etaṃ mahārāja dhārehi. tayo 'me mahārāja devaputtā sakkena devānam-indena āyācitaṃ kulaṃ uppannā, katame tayo: sāmo kumāro, mahāpanādo, kusarājā, tayo p' ete bodhisattā ti. suniddiṭṭhā bhante nāgasena gabbhāvakkanti, sukathitaṃ kāraṇaṃ, andhakāro āloko kato, jaṭā vijaṭitā, nicchuddhā parappavādā, evam-etaṃ, tathā sampaṭicchāmīti.

121 bhante nāgasena, bhāsitam-p' etaṃ bhagavatā: pañc' eva dāni ānanda vassasatāni saddhammo ṭhassatīti. puna ca parinibbānasamaye subhaddena paribbājakena pañhaṃ puṭṭhena bhagavatā bhaṇitaṃ: ime ca subhadda bhikkhū sammā vihareyyuṃ, asuñño loko arahantehi assāti; asesavacanam-etaṃ, nissesavacanam-etaṃ, nippariyāyavacanam-etaṃ. yadi bhante nāgasena tathāgatena bhaṇitaṃ: pañc'eva dāni ānanda vassasatāni saddhammo ṭhassatīti, tena hi: asuñño loko arahantehi assāti yaṃ vacanaṃ taṃ micchā. yadi tathāgatena bhaṇitamasuñño loko arahantehi assāti, tena hi: pañc' eva dāni ānanda vassasatāni saddhammo ṭhassaṭīti tam-pi vacanaṃ micchā. ayam-pi ubhatokoṭiko pañho, gahanato pi gahanataro, balavato pi balavataro, gaṇṭhito pi gaṇṭhitaro, so tavānuppatto, tattha te ñāṇabalavipphāraṃ dassehi, makaro viya sāgarabbhantaragato ti.

122 bhāsitam-p' etaṃ mahārāja bhagavatā: pañc' eva dāni ānanda vassasatāni saddhammo ṭhassatīti. parinbbānasamaye ca subhaddassa paribbājakassa bhaṇitaṃ: ime

"Then, great king, please understand that the child Sama was produced by the graciousness of three forces: he was created by a sage, by a god, and by merit. There were three gods, great king, who were induced by Sakka, king of gods, to be born in particular families. Who are these three? The child Sama, Mahapanada, and the king of Kusa.[21] As a matter of fact, these three were all bodhisattas."[22]

"The conceptions are explained convincingly, revered Nagasena, and the reasoning is well stated. Darkness is made light, the tangle is unraveled, and opposing views are tossed out. And so I accept this."

"Revered Nagasena, the Bhagavan said: 'Ananda, the true 121
Dhamma will last five hundred years.' Yet at the time of the final nibbana when a question was asked by the renouncer Subhadda, the Bhagavan said: 'Subhadda, if these monks live rightly, the world will never be empty of arhats.' This was the full statement, the complete statement, and the unqualified statement. But, Nagasena, if the Tathagata said: 'Ananda, the true Dhamma will last five hundred years,' then his statement that 'the world will never be empty of arhats' is false. But if the Tathagata said, 'The world will never be empty of arhats,' then the assertion that 'Ananda, the true Dhamma will last five hundred years' is false. This is a two-pronged dilemma, more tangled than a tangle, stronger than the strong, knottier than a knot. It is put to you that you might display your pervading force of knowledge on the matter, like a leviathan in the middle of the ocean."

"Great king, the Bhagavan did say, 'Ananda, the true 122
Dhamma will last five hundred years.' And at the time of his final nibbana, he also said, 'Subhadda, if these monks live

ca subhadda bhikkhū sammā vihareyyuṃ, asuñño loko arahantehi assāti. tañ-ca pana mahārāja bhagavato vacanaṃ nānatthañ-c' eva hoti nānābyañjanañ-ca. ayaṃ sāsanaparicchedo, ayaṃ paṭipattiparidīpanā ti dūraṃ vivajjitā te ubho aññamaññaṃ. yathā mahārāja nabhaṃ paṭhavito dūraṃ vivajjitaṃ, nirayaṃ saggato dūraṃ vivajjitaṃ, kusalaṃ akusalato dūraṃ vivajjitaṃ, sukhaṃ dukkhato dūraṃ vivajjitaṃ, evam-eva kho mahārāja te ubho aññamaññaṃ dūraṃ vivajjitā. api ca mahārāja, mā te pucchā moghā assa, rasato te saṃsandetvā kathayissāmi.

123 pañc' eva dāni ānanda vassasatāni saddhammo ṭhassatīti yaṃ bhagavā āha, taṃ khayaṃ paridīpayanto sesakaṃ paricchindi: vassasahassaṃ ānanda saddhammo tiṭṭheyya sace bhikkhuniyo na pabbajeyyuṃ, pañc' eva dāni ānanda vassasatāni saddhammo ṭhassatīti. api nu kho mahārāja bhagavā evaṃ vadanto saddhammassa antaradhānaṃ vā vadeti abhisamayaṃ vā paṭikkosatīti. na hi bhante ti.

124 naṭṭhaṃ mahārāja parikittayanto sesakaṃ paridīpayanto paricchindi. yathā mahārāja puriso naṭṭhāyiko sabbasesakaṃ gahetvā janassa paridīpeyya: ettakaṃ me bhaṇḍaṃ naṭṭhaṃ, idaṃ sesakan-ti, evam-eva kho mahārāja bhagavā naṭṭhaṃ paridīpayanto sesakaṃ devamanussānaṃ kathesi: pañc' eva dāni ānanda vassasatāni saddhammo ṭhassatīti. yaṃ pana mahārāja bhagavatā bhaṇitaṃ: pañc'eva dāni ānanda vassasatāni saddhammo ṭhassatīti, sāsanaparicchedo eso; yaṃ pana parinibbānasamaye subhaddassa paribbāja-

rightly, the world will never be empty of arhats.' However, these words of the Bhagavan are different in meaning and different in phrasing. As the one refers to the end of the dispensation and the other to an illustration of its practice, the two are far distant from each other. Just as the sky is far distant from the earth, as hell is far distant from heaven, good is far distant from bad, and pleasure is far distant from pain, so too, great king, these two are far distant from each other. But so that your question is not asked in vain, I will explain, bringing these assertions together with reference to their functions.

"When the Bhagavan said, 'Ananda, the true Dhamma 123
will last five hundred years,' he was indicating that it would pass away, and he specified the time left: 'Ananda, if there had been no ordination for nuns, the true Dhamma would have lasted for a thousand years. But now it will last only five hundred years.' Now, great king, in speaking thus was the Bhagavan referring to the disappearance of the true Dhamma? Or was he speaking about the full realization of it?"

"Not the latter, sir."

"Making known and indicating what was lost, great king, 124
he specified the time left. Just as a bankrupt man collects what remains and indicates publicly, 'This much of my wealth is lost, this much is left,' so too the Bhagavan, indicating what was lost, told gods and humans what was left: 'Ananda, the true Dhamma will last five hundred years.'

"And so, great king, when the Bhagavan said, 'Ananda, the true Dhamma will last five hundred years,' this referred to the end of the dispensation. But at the time of his final

kassa samaṇe parikittayanto āha: ime ca subhadda bhikkhū sammā vihareyyuṃ, asuñño loko arahantehi assāti, paṭipattiparidīpanā esā. tvaṃ pana taṃ paricchedañ-ca paridīpanañ-ca ekarasaṃ karosi. yadi pana te chando ekarasaṃ katvā kathayissāmi, sādhukaṃ suṇohi manasikarohi avimanamānaso.

125 idha mahārāja taḷāko bhaveyya navasalilasampuṇṇo samukham-uttariyamāno paricchinno parivaṭumakato, apariyādinne yeva tasmiṃ taḷāke udakūpari mahāmegho aparāparaṃ anuppabandhanto abhivasseyya, api nu kho mahārāja tasmiṃ taḷāke udakaṃ parikkhayaṃ pariyādānaṃ gaccheyyāti. na hi bhante ti. kena kāraṇena mahārājāti. meghassa bhante anuppabandhanatāyāti.

126 evam-eva kho mahārāja jinasāsanavara-saddhamma-taḷāko ācārasīlaguṇavattapaṭipatti-vimalana-vasalilasampuṇṇo uttariyamāno bhavaggam-abhibhavitvā ṭhito. yadi tattha buddhaputtā ācārasīlaguṇavattapaṭipatti-meghavassaṃ aparāparaṃ anuppabandhāpeyyuṃ abhivassāpeyyuṃ, evam idaṃ jinasāsanavara-saddhamma-taḷāko ciraṃ dīgham-addhānaṃ tiṭṭheyya, arahantehi ca loko asuñño bhaveyya. imam-atthaṃ bhagavatā sandhāya bhāsitaṃ: ime ca subhadda bhikkhū sammā vihareyyuṃ, asuñño loko arahantehi assāti.

127 idha pana mahārāja mahatimahāaggikkhandhe jalamāne aparāparaṃ sukkha-tiṇa-kaṭṭha-gomayāni upasaṃhareyyuṃ, api nu kho so mahārāja aggikkhandho nibbāyeyyāti.

nibbana, addressing the renouncer Subhadda, he said to the monks: 'Subhadda, if these monks live rightly, the world will never be empty of arhats.' This was an explanation of practice. You are conflating the time limit and the explanation into a single function. But if you desire it, I will put them together and explain, so listen well and pay attention, with your mind at ease.

"Great king, suppose there were a reservoir full of fresh 125
water brimming at its mouth but held back and reinforced. As long as that reservoir is not dried up and if a great storm cloud overflowing with water were to rain unceasingly and continuously, would the water in the reservoir get dried up and exhausted?" "No, sir." "For what reason, great king?" "Because of the continuous rain from the cloud, sir."

"Similarly, the reservoir of the true Dhamma of the 126
Victor's excellent dispensation, supreme, brimming with the fresh and pure water that is good conduct, moral discipline, virtue, vows, and practice, and reaching up to the highest plane of existence, remains. If the lineage of the Buddha unceasingly and continuously rains down showers from the clouds of good conduct, moral discipline, virtue, vows, and practice, then the reservoir of the true Dhamma of the Victor's excellent dispensation will endure a long time, and the world will not be empty of arhats. This is the meaning referred to by the Bhagavan when he said: 'Subhadda, if these monks live rightly, the world will never be empty of arhats.'

"Great king, suppose there were a huge blazing and 127
massive fire and people continuously heaped dry grass, tinder, and cow dung on it. Do you think that the massive

na hi bhante, bhiyyo bhiyyo so aggikkhandho jaleyya, bhiyyo bhiyyo pabhāseyyāti.

128 evam-eva kho mahārāja dasasahassimhi lokadhātuyā jina-
sāsanavaraṃ ācārasīlaguṇavattapaṭipattiyā jalati pabhāsati. yadi pana mahārāja taduttariṃ buddhaputtā pañcahi padhāniyaṅgehi samannāgatā satatam-appamattā padaheyyuṃ, tīsu sikkhāsu chandajātā sikkheyyuṃ, cārittañ-ca vārittañ-ca sīlaṃ samattaṃ paripūreyyuṃ, evam-idaṃ jinasāsana-varaṃ bhiyyo bhiyyo ciraṃ dīgham-addhānaṃ tiṭṭheyya, asuñño loko arahantehi assāti imam-atthaṃ bhagavatā sandhāya bhāsitaṃ: ime ca subhadda bhikkhū sammā vihareyyuṃ, asuñño loko arahantehi assāti.

129 idha pana mahārāja siniddha-sama-sumajjita-sappa-bhāsa-
vimalādāsaṃ saṇhasukhuma-gerukacuṇṇena aparā- paraṃ majjeyyuṃ, api nu kho mahārāja tasmiṃ ādāse mala-kaddama-rajojallaṃ jāyeyyāti. na hi bhante, aññadatthu vimalataraṃ yeva bhaveyyāti.

130 evam-eva kho mahārāja jinasāsanavaraṃ pakatinimmal-
aṃ byapagata-kilesamalarajojallaṃ; yadi taṃ buddhaputtā ācārasīla-guṇa-vattapaṭipatti-sallekhadhutaguṇena jinasāsanavaraṃ sallikheyyuṃ, evam-idaṃ jinasāsanavaraṃ

fire would be extinguished?" "No, sir. The massive fire would burn even more and blaze even further."

"So too, great king, the Victor's excellent dispensation burns and blazes throughout the ten-thousandfold world system by good conduct, moral discipline, virtues, vows, and practice. And if, great king, those in the lineage of the Buddha endowed with the five factors that assist striving* were to exert themselves with constant vigilance, train zealously in the three trainings,† and fulfill perfectly the moral discipline with respect to what should be done and what should be avoided, then the Victor's excellent dispensation would endure longer and longer into the future, and the world will not be empty of arhats. This is the meaning referred to by the Bhagavan when he said: 'Subhadda, if these monks live rightly, the world will never be empty of arhats.' 128

"And suppose, great king, someone were to polish continuously with a powder of soft and fine red ochre a smooth, even, well-polished, shining, and stainless mirror. Would stains, mud, dust, or dirt appear on that mirror?" "No, sir. On the contrary, it would become even more clean." 129

"Similarly, great king, the Victor's excellent dispensation is naturally pure, with all stains, dust, and dirt of the defilements removed. But if the lineage of the Buddha were to observe the Victor's excellent dispensation with good conduct, moral discipline, virtues, vows, and practice, as well as the specific quality of austerities and ascetic practices, then the Victor's excellent dispensation would 130

* Faith, health, honesty, energy, and understanding.
† Higher moral precepts, awareness, and understanding.

ciraṃ dīgham-addhānaṃ tiṭṭheyya asuñño ca loko arahantehi assāti imam atthaṃ bhagavatā sandhāya bhāsitaṃ: ime ca subhadda bhikkhū sammā vihareyyuṃ, asuñño loko arahantehi assāti. paṭipattimūlakaṃ mahārāja satthusāsanaṃ paṭipattisārakaṃ, paṭipattiyā anantarahitāya tiṭṭhatīti.

131 bhante nāgasena, saddhammantaradhānan-ti yaṃ vadesi, katamaṃ taṃ saddhammantaradhānan-ti. tīṇ' imāni mahārāja sāsanantaradhānāni, katamāni tīṇi: adhigamantaradhānaṃ, paṭipattantaradhānaṃ, liṅgantaradhānaṃ. adhigame mahārāja antarahite suppaṭipannassāpi dhammābhisamayo na hoti, paṭipattiyā antarahitāya sikkhāpadapaññatti antaradhāyati, liṅgaṃ yeva tiṭṭhati, liṅge antarahite paveṇupacchedo hoti. imāni kho mahārāja tīṇi antaradhānānīti. suviññāpito bhante nāgasena pañho gambhīro uttānīkato, gaṇṭhi bhinno, naṭṭhā parappavādā bhaggā nippabhā katā, tvaṃ gaṇivaravasabhamāsajjāti.

132 bhante nāgasena, tathāgato sabbaṃ akusalaṃ jhāpetvā sabbaññutaṃ patto, udāhu sāvasese akusale sabbaññutaṃ patto ti. sabbaṃ mahārāja akusalaṃ jhāpetvā bhagavā sabbaññutaṃ patto, na-tthi bhagavato sesakaṃ akusalan-ti.

endure longer and longer into the future, and the world would not be empty of arhats. This is the meaning referred to by the Bhagavan when he said: 'Subhadda, if these monks live rightly, the world will never be empty of arhats.' Great king, the Teacher's dispensation has practice at its foundation and practice as its essence, and it is by means of practice that it will endure without disappearing."

"Revered Nagasena, when you speak of the disappearance 131
of the true Dhamma, what exactly is this disappearance of the true Dhamma?"

"Great king, there are actually three disappearances of the true Dhamma. What are the three? The disappearance of the knowledge, the disappearance of the practice, and the disappearance of the sign.* When the knowledge disappears, then even for one with good practice there is no comprehension of the Dhamma. When the practice disappears, then even the notion of training rules vanishes, and only the sign remains. And when the sign disappears, the tradition is broken. These, great king, are the three disappearances."

"This deep question has been taught well and made clear, revered Nagasena, for the knot is cut and the doctrines of opponents, destroyed and shattered, have lost all luster. You are the most excellent bull among teachers!

"Revered Nagasena, did the Tathagata attain omniscience 132
having burned off all bad karma, or did he attain omniscience when bad karma still remained?"[23]

"Great king, the Bhagavan attained omniscience having burned off all bad karma, and no bad remained."

* Monastic robes are the sign of Buddhism.

133 kim-pana bhante dukkhā vedanā tathāgatassa kāye uppannapubbā ti. āma mahārāja, rājagahe bhagavato pādo sakalikāya khato, lohitapakkhandikābādho uppanno, kāye abhisanne jīvakena vireko kārito, vātābādhe uppanne upaṭṭhākena therena uṇhodakaṃ pariyiṭṭhan-ti.

134 yadi bhante nāgasena tathāgato sabbaṃ akusalaṃ jhāpetvā sabbaññutaṃ patto, tena hi: bhagavato pādo sakalikāya khato lohitapakkhandikā ca ābādho uppanno ti yaṃ vacanaṃ taṃ micchā. yadi tathāgatassa pādo sakalikāya khato lohitapakkhandikā ca ābādho uppanno, tena hi: tathāgato sabbaṃ akusalaṃ jhāpetvā sabbaññutaṃ patto ti tam-pi vacanaṃ micchā, na-tthi bhante vinā kammena vedayitaṃ, sabban-taṃ vedayitaṃ kammamūlakaṃ, kammen' eva vediyati. ayam-pi ubhatokoṭiko pañho tavānuppatto, so tayā nibbāhitabbo ti.

135 na hi mahārāja sabban-taṃ vedayitaṃ kammamūlakaṃ. aṭṭhahi mahārāja kāraṇehi vedayitāni uppajjanti, yehi kāraṇehi puthusattā vedanā vediyanti, katamehi aṭṭhahi: vātasamuṭṭhānāni pi kho mahārāja idh' ekaccāni vedayitāni uppajjanti, pittasamuṭṭhānāni pi kho mahārāja -pe-semhasamuṭṭhānāni pi kho mahārāja-pe-sannipātikāni pi kho mahārāja-pe-utupariṇāmajāni pi kho mahārāja-pe-visamaparihārajāni pi kho mahārāja-pe-opakkamikāni pi kho mahārāja-pe kammavipākajāni pi kho mahārāja idh' ekaccāni vedayitāni uppajjanti. imehi kho mahārāja aṭṭhahi kāraṇehi puthusattā vedanā vediyanti. tattha ye te satte kam-maṃ vibādhati[3] te ime sattā kāraṇaṃ paṭibāhanti, tesaṃ taṃ vacanaṃ micchā ti.

"All right then, sir. But did painful feelings persist in the Tathagata's body?" 133

"Yes, great king, the Tathagata's foot was pierced by a splinter at Rajagaha. And once he was afflicted by bloody dysentery, and when his body was overflowing, a purgative was administered by Jivaka. Then there was the wind disease, when the elder who nursed him sought hot water."

"But, Nagasena, if the Tathagata attained omniscience 134
having burned off all bad karma, then the claims that the Tathagata had his foot pierced with a splinter, that he suffered bloody dysentery, and that he became ill must be false. Alternatively, if it is the case that the Tathagata had his foot pierced with a splinter, that he had bloody dysentery, and that he became ill, then the claim that when he attained omniscience he had burned off all bad karma must be false. For nothing that is experienced is free of karma, and everything experienced has its roots in karma and is experienced by the workings of karma. This two-pronged dilemma has reached you, and you must solve it."

"Great king, not every feeling has its roots in karma. What 135
is felt occurs due to eight kinds of causes. What are the eight causes by which ordinary people experience feelings? Some of what is felt arises from the humors of wind, bile, or phlegm, or from the combination of them; other feelings are due to a change in the seasons, carelessness, assault, or karma. Ordinary people, great king, experience feelings due to these eight causes. It is wrong to say that it is just karma that causes beings harm, and that beings might evade all causes of painful feeling."

136 bhante nāgasena, yañ-ca vātikaṃ yañ-ca pittikaṃ yañ-ca semhikaṃ yañ-ca sannipātikaṃ yañ-ca utupariṇāmajaṃ yañ-ca visamaparihārajaṃ yañ-ca opakkamikaṃ, sabbe te kammasamuṭṭhānā yeva, kammen' eva te sabbe sambhavantīti.

137 yadi mahārāja te pi sabbe kammasamuṭṭhānāva ābādhā bhaveyyuṃ, na tesaṃ koṭṭhāsato lakkhaṇāni bhaveyyuṃ. vāto kho mahārāja kuppamāno dasavidhena kuppati: sītena uṇhena jighacchāya pipāsāya atibhuttena ṭhānena padhānena ādhāvanena upakkamena kammavipākena; tatra ye te nava vidhā, na te atīte na anāgate, vattamānake bhave uppajjanti, tasmā na vattabbā: kammasambhavā sabbā vedanā ti. pittaṃ mahārāja kuppamānaṃ tividhena kuppati: sītena uṇhena visamabhojanena. semhaṃ mahārāja kuppamānaṃ tividhena kuppati: sītena uṇhena annapānena. yo ca mahārāja vāto yañ-ca pittaṃ yañ-ca semhaṃ tehi tehi kopehi kuppitvā missīhutvā sakaṃ sakaṃ vedanaṃ ākaḍḍhati. utupariṇāmajā mahārāja vedanā utupariṇāmena uppajjati, visamaparihārajā vedanā visamaparihārena uppajjati, opakkamikā mahārāja vedanā atthi kiriyā atthi kammavipākā, kammavipākajā vedanā pubbe katena kammena uppajjati. iti kho mahārāja appaṃ kammavipākajaṃ, bahutaraṃ avasesaṃ. tattha bālā: sabbaṃ kammavipākajaṃ yevāti atidhāvanti, taṃ kammaṃ na sakkā vinā buddhañāṇena vavatthānaṃ kātuṃ.

138 yaṃ pana mahārāja bhagavato pādo sakalikāya khato, taṃ vedayitaṃ n' eva vātasamuṭṭhānaṃ na pittasamuṭṭhānaṃ na

"But, Nagasena, surely whatever is generated by the humors wind, bile, phlegm, or their combination, or is due to a change of seasons, carelessness, or assault, is itself originated by karma, and everything is ultimately produced by karma." 136

"Great king, if all afflictions were produced by karma, they would have no characteristics distinguishing them. When the wind humor is disturbed, it disturbs in ten ways: by cold, heat, hunger, thirst, overeating, resting, exertion, running about, violence, and the effects of karma. The first nine of these occur not in the past or the future but in the process of the condition itself. Therefore, it cannot be said that all feelings are produced by karma. When bile is disturbed it disturbs in three ways: by cold, heat, and unbalanced eating. When phlegm is disturbed it disturbs in three ways: by cold, heat, and food and drink. And when wind, bile, and phlegm are each disturbed by their own irritations, and then combined, then each draws out its own feeling. Great king, a feeling arising from a change of seasons occurs because of the change of seasons; a feeling due to carelessness occurs because of carelessness; and a feeling from an assault is either from neutral activity or a result of karma. And a feeling produced from karma occurs by karma made previously. In fact, much more feeling is generated by these other causes than the little produced by karma. And so when fools claim that everything is produced by karma, they go too far. No one without the knowledge of the Buddha can make a determination concerning karma. 137

"Great king, when the Bhagavan's foot was pierced by a splinter, the feeling was not produced by wind, bile, phlegm, 138

semhasamuṭṭhānaṃ na sannipātikaṃ na utupariṇāmajaṃ na visamaparihārajaṃ na kammavipākajaṃ, opakkamikaṃ yeva. devadatto hi mahārāja bahūni jātisatasahassāni tathāgate āghātaṃ bandhi. so tena āghātena mahatiṃ garuṃ silaṃ gahetvā: matthake pātessāmīti muñci. ath' aññe dve selā āgantvā taṃ silaṃ tathāgataṃ asampattaṃ yeva sampaṭicchiṃsu, tāyaṃ pahārena papaṭikā bhijjitvā bhagavato pāde patitvā ruhiraṃ uppādesi.

139 kammavipākato vā mahārāja bhagavato esā vedaṇā nibbattā kiriyato vā, tat' uddhaṃ na-tth' aññā vedanā. yathā mahārāja khettaduṭṭhatāya vā bījaṃ na sambhavati bījaduṭṭhatāya vā, evam-eva kho mahārāja kammavipākato vā bhagavato esā vedanā nibbattā kiriyato vā, tat' uddhaṃ na-tth' aññā vedanā. yathā vā pana mahārāja koṭṭhaduṭṭhatāya vā bhojanaṃ visamaṃ pariṇamati āhāraduṭṭhatāya vā, evam-eva kho mahārāja kammavipākato vā bhagavato esā vedanā nibbattā kiri- yato vā, tat' uddhaṃ na-tth' aññā vedanā.

140 api ca mahārāja na-tthi bhagavato kammavipākajā vedanā, na-tthi visamaparihārajā vedanā, avasesehi samuṭṭhānehi bhagavato vedanā uppajjati. tāya ca pana vedanāya na sakkā bhagavantaṃ jīvitā voropetuṃ. nipatanti mahārāja imasmiṃ catumahābhūtike kāye iṭṭhā-niṭṭhā subhāsubhā vedanā. idha mahārāja ākāse khitto leḍḍu mahāpaṭhaviyā nipatati, api nu kho so mahārāja leḍḍu pubbe katena mahāpaṭhaviyā nipatatīti.

a combination of these, a change in seasons, carelessness, or as an effect of karma; rather it was due to an assault. Devadatta had borne malice against the Tathagata for many hundreds of thousands of births. Because of this malice he took a heavy boulder and, thinking, *I will make this fall on his head*, released it. But two other rocks came along and intercepted that boulder so that it did not reach the Tathagata. However, a fragment broke off from their impact and struck the Bhagavan's foot, drawing blood.

“Now, the feeling felt by the Bhagavan either must have 139
occurred as the result of karma or been just neutral activity, since there is no other feeling besides these. Just like when a seed does not germinate, it is due either to the poor quality of the field or to the poor quality of the seed, here too, great king, the feeling that occurred in the Bhagavan was either an effect of karma or neutral activity, since there is no other feeling besides these. Just as a meal turns bad either because something is wrong with the stomach or because something is wrong with the food, here too, the feeling that occurred in the Bhagavan was either an effect of karma or neutral activity, since there is no feeling besides these.

“Now, great king, the painful feeling was not generated in 140
the Bhagavan as a result of karma, nor was the feeling due to carelessness. Nor was the feeling produced in the Bhagavan by the other causes. And it was not able to deprive the Bhagavan of his life, despite the pain. Agreeable and disagreeable and pleasant and painful feelings befall the body with its four elements. Suppose a clod of earth were thrown up in the sky and then fell down to the earth. Does the clod fall because of something the earth did previously?”

141 na hi bhante, na-tthi so bhante hetu mahāpaṭhaviyā yeva hetunā mahāpaṭhavī kusalākusalaṃ vipākaṃ paṭisaṃvedeyya, paccuppannena bhante akammakena hetunā so leḍḍu mahāpaṭhaviyaṃ nipatatīti. yathā mahārāja mahāpaṭhavī evaṃ tathāgato daṭṭhabbo, yathā leḍḍu pubbe akatena mahāpaṭhaviyaṃ nipatati evam-eva kho mahārāja tathāgatassa pubbe akatena sā sakalikā pāde nipatitā. idha pana mahārāja manussā mahāpaṭhaviṃ bhindanti ca khaṇanti ca; api nu kho te mahārāja manussā pubbe katena mahāpaṭhaviṃ bhindanti ca khaṇanti cāti. na hi bhante ti.

142 evam-eva kho mahārāja yā sā sakalikā bhagavato pāde nipatitā na sā sakalikā pubbe katena bhagavato pāde nipatitā. yo pi mahārāja bhagavato lohitapakkhandikābādho uppanno so pi ābādho na pubbe katena uppanno, sannipātiken' eva uppanno. ye keci mahārāja bhagavato kāyikā ābādhā uppannā na te kammābhinibbattā, channaṃ etesaṃ samuṭṭhānānaṃ aññatarato nibbattā. bhāsitam-p' etaṃ mahārāja bhagavatā devātidevena saṃyuttanikāyavaralañjake[4] moliyasīvake veyyākaraṇe:

> 143 pittasamuṭṭhānāni pi kho sīvaka idh'ekaccāni vedayitāni uppajjanti; sāmam-pi kho etaṃ sīvaka veditabbaṃ yathā pittasamuṭṭhānāni pi idh' ekaccāni vedayitāni uppajjanti, lokassa pi kho etaṃ sīvaka saccasammataṃ yathā pittasamuṭṭhānāni pi idh'ekaccāni vedayitāni uppajjanti. tatra sīvaka ye te samaṇabrāhmaṇā evaṃvādino evaṃdiṭṭhino : yaṃ kiñcāyaṃ purisapuggalo paṭisaṃvedeti sukhaṃ vā dukkhaṃ vā adukkhamasukhaṃ vā sabban-taṃ pubbe katahetūti, yañ-ca sāmañ-ñātaṃ tañ-ca atidhāvanti, yañ-ca loke saccasammataṃ tañ-ca

"No, sir. There is no cause by which the great earth would undergo a good or bad karmic result, since the clod falls on the earth because of a cause in the present that is not connected to karma." 141

"Here the Tathagata should be seen as similar to the earth in that, like the clod falling on it without the earth's having done anything previously, the Tathagata was struck on the foot by a splinter without his having done anything previously. People break up the earth and dig it. Do people break up the earth and dig it because of what it did previously?"

"No, sir."

"Just so, great king, the splinter that struck the Bhagavan's 142
foot did not pierce it because of anything the Bhagavan did previously. Further, the Bhagavan's bloody dysentery and his other illness were not occasioned by his previous actions but rather by a combination of the humors. In fact, none of the Bhagavan's bodily afflictions was the result of karma; rather, they were produced by the remaining six causes. This was said also by the Bhagavan, god above gods, in the explanation to Moliyasivaka in the excellent declaration that is the *Saṃyuttanikāya:*

> Sivaka, in this world, some feelings that occur are 143
> caused by bile. One can know for oneself, Sivaka, that some feelings that occur are caused by bile, and that they are caused by bile is a truth generally held in the world. So when recluses and Brahmans hold a view or a position that claims that whatever a person undergoes, whether pleasant, painful, or neither

atidhāvanti, tasmā tesaṃ samaṇabrāhmaṇānaṃ micchā ti vadāmi. semhasamuṭṭhānāni pi kho sīvaka idh' ekaccāni vedayitāni uppajjanti, vātasamuṭṭhānāni pi kho sīvaka sannipātikāni pi kho sīvaka utupariṇāmajāni pi kho sīvaka visamaparihārajāni pi kho sīvaka - opakkamikāni pi kho sīvaka-kammavipākajāni pi kho sīvaka idh' ekaccāni vedayitāni uppajjanti; sāmam-pi kho etaṃ sīvaka veditabbaṃ yathā kammavipākajāni pi idh' ekaccāni vedayitāni uppajjanti, lokassa pi kho etaṃ sīvaka saccasammataṃ yathā kammavipākajāni pi idh' ekaccāni vedayitāni uppajjanti. Tatra sīvaka ye te samaṇabrāhmaṇā evaṃvādino evaṃdiṭṭhino: yaṃ kiñcāyaṃ purisapuggalo paṭisaṃvedeti sukhaṃ vā dukkhaṃ vā adukkhamasukhaṃ vā sabban-taṃ pubbe katheṭūti, yañ-ca sāmañ-ñātaṃ tañ-ca atidhāvanti, yañ-ca loke saccasammataṃ tañ-ca atidhāvanti, tasmā tesaṃ samaṇabrāhmaṇānaṃ micchā ti vadāmīti.

144 iti pi mahārāja na sabbā vedanā kammavipākajā. sabbaṃ mahārāja akusalaṃ jhāpetvā bhagavā sabbaññutaṃ patto ti evam-etaṃ dhārehīti. sādhu bhante nāgasena, evam-etaṃ, tathā sampaṭicchāmīti.

145 bhante nāgasena, tumhe bhaṇatha: yaṃ kiñci karaṇīyaṃ tathāgatassa sabban-taṃ bodhiyā yeva mūle pariniṭṭhitaṃ, na-tthi tathāgatassa uttariṃ karaṇīyam katassa vā paticayo ti. idañ-ca temāsaṃ paṭisallāṇaṃ dissati. yadi bhante nāga-

> pleasant nor painful, it is entirely caused by what was done previously, they go further than what is actually known to oneself and further than what is generally accepted as true in the world. Therefore, I say that these recluses and Brahmans are wrong. And, Sivaka, some feelings that occur are caused by phlegm, some are caused by wind, and some by a combination of the humors. Some feelings are due to a change in the seasons, some are due to carelessness, some are due to assault, and some are the effects of karma. That some feelings that occur are caused by karma can be known by oneself and is also a truth generally held. So, Sivaka, when recluses and Brahmans hold a view or position that claims that whatever a person undergoes, whether pleasant, painful, or neither pleasant nor painful, it is entirely caused by what was done previously, they go further than what is actually known by oneself, and they go further than what is generally accepted as true in the world. Therefore, I say that these recluses and Brahmans are wrong.

"And so, great king, not all feelings are due to the effects 144
of karma. Having burned up all bad karma, the Bhagavan attained omniscience. Please remember this."

"Very well, revered Nagasena, I accept what you say.

"Revered Nagasena, you say that whatever needed to be 145
done by the Tathagata was entirely accomplished at the root of the Bodhi Tree, and that there was nothing further or additional that the Tathagata needed to do. And yet, he was later observed in secluded meditation for three months.

sena yaṃ kiñci karaṇīyaṃ tathāgatassa sabban-taṃ bodhiyā yeva mūle pariniṭṭhitaṃ, na-tthi tathāgatassa uttariṃ karaṇīyam katassa vā paticayo; tena hi: temāsaṃ paṭisallīno ti yaṃ vacanaṃ taṃ micchā. yadi temāsaṃ paṭisallīno, tena hi: yaṃ kiñci karaṇīyaṃ tathāgatassa sabban-taṃ bodhiyā yeva mūle pariniṭṭhitan-ti tam-pi vacanaṃ micchā. na-tthi katakaraṇīyassa paṭisallāṇaṃ, sakaraṇīyass'eva paṭisallāṇaṃ. yathā nāma byādhitasseva;[5] bhesajjena karaṇīyaṃ hoti, abyādhitassa kiṃ bhesajjena, chātass' eva bhojanena karaṇīyaṃ hoti, achātassa kiṃ bhojanena; evam-eva kho bhante nāgasena na-tthi katakaraṇīyassa paṭisallāṇaṃ, sakaraṇīyass' eva paṭisallāṇaṃ. ayam-pi ubhatokoṭiko pañho tavānuppatto, so tayā nibbāhitabbo ti.

146 yaṃ kiñci mahārāja karaṇīyaṃ tathāgatassa sabbantaṃ bodhiyā yeva mūle pariniṭṭhitaṃ, na-tthi tathāgatassa uttariṃ karaṇīyaṃ katassa vā paticayo. bhagavā ca temāsaṃ paṭisallīno. paṭisallāṇaṃ kho mahārāja bahuguṇaṃ, sabbe pi tathāgatā paṭisallīyitvā sabbaññutaṃ pattā, taṃ te sukataguṇam-anussarantā paṭisallāṇaṃ sevanti. yathā mahārāja puriso rañño santikā laddhavaro paṭiladdhasabhogo taṃ sukataguṇam-anussaranto aparāparaṃ rañño upaṭṭhānaṃ eti, evam-eva kho mahārāja sabbe pi tathāgatā paṭisallīyitvā sabbaññutaṃ pattā, taṃ te sukataguṇam-anussarantā paṭisallāṇaṃ sevanti.

Nagasena, if everything that was to be done by the Tathagata was accomplished at the root of the Bodhi Tree, and there was nothing further or additional that he needed to do, then the claim about the three months in seclusion must be false. But if there were three months in seclusion, then the claim about the Tathagata accomplishing everything at the root of the Bodhi Tree with nothing further or additional to do must be false. There is no need for secluded meditation for one who has accomplished what needed to be done, since secluded meditation is for one who has more to do. Medicine is to be administered to the sick, not the healthy; food is to be provisioned for the hungry, not the sated. Nagasena, there is no need for secluded meditation for one who has accomplished what needed to be done, since secluded meditation is for one who has more to do. This two-pronged dilemma has reached you, and it is by you that it must solved."

"Great king, everything that was to be done by the Tatha- 146
gata was accomplished at the root of the Bodhi Tree, and there was nothing further or additional that the Tathagata needed to do. And the Bhagavan was in secluded meditation for three months. Secluded meditation has many special qualities, and all tathagatas attain omniscience having meditated in seclusion. Later, recalling the special qualities of what they have accomplished, they again practice secluded meditation. It is just like a man who has obtained favor in the presence of the king and been given property; he later recalls the special qualities of what was accomplished and comes again and again to wait on the king. So too all tathagatas attain omniscience having meditated in seclusion. Later, recalling the special qualities of what they have

147 yathā vā pana mahārāja puriso āturo dukkhito bāḷhagilāno bhisakkam-upasevitvā sotthim anuppatto taṃ sukataguṇam-anussaranto aparāparaṃ bhisakkam-upasevati, evam-eva kho mahārāja sabbe pi tathāgatā paṭisallīyitvā sabbaññutaṃ pattā, taṃ te sukataguṇam-anussarantā paṭisallāṇaṃ sevanti.

148 aṭṭhavīsati kho pan' ime mahārāja paṭisallāṇaguṇā ye guṇe samanupassantā tathāgatā paṭisallāṇaṃ sevanti, katame aṭṭhavīsati: idha mahārāja paṭisallāṇaṃ paṭisallīyamānaṃ rakkhati, āyuṃ vaḍḍheti, balaṃ deti, vajjaṃ pidahati, ayasam-apaneti, yasam-upaneti, aratiṃ vinodeti, ratim-upadahati, bhayam-apaneti, vesārajjaṃ karoti, kosajjam-apaneti, viriyam-abhijaneti, rāgam-apaneti, dosam-apaneti, moham-apaneti, mānaṃ nihanti, vitakkaṃ bhañjati, cittaṃ ekaggaṃ karoti, mānasaṃ snehayati, hāsaṃ janeti, garukaṃ karoti, lābham-uppādayati, na massiyaṃ karoti, pītiṃ pāpeti, pāmojjaṃ karoti, saṅkhā-rānaṃ sabhāvaṃ dassayati, bhavapaṭisandhiṃ ugghāṭeti, sabbasāmaññaṃ deti. ime kho mahārāja aṭṭhavīsati paṭisallāṇaguṇā ye guṇe samanupassantā tathāgatā paṭisallāṇaṃ sevanti.

149 api ca kho mahārāja tathāgatā santaṃ sukhaṃ samāpattiratim-anubhavitukāmā paṭisallāṇaṃ sevanti pariyositasankappā. catuhi kho mahārāja kāraṇehi tathāgatā paṭisallāṇaṃ sevanti, katamehi catuhi: vihāraphāsutāya pi mahārāja tathāgatā paṭisallāṇaṃ sevanti, anavajjaguṇabahulatāya pi tathāgatā paṭisallāṇaṃ sevanti, asesāriyavīthito pi tathāgatā paṭisallāṇaṃ sevanti, sabbabuddhānaṃ thuta-thomi-

accomplished, they again practice seclusion. Or consider 147
a man, grievously ill, miserable, and suffering, who visits a physician and regains his health. Recalling the special qualities of what was done, he again and again waits upon the physician. So too all tathagatas attain omniscience having meditated in seclusion; then, recalling the special qualities of what they have accomplished, they again practice seclusion.

"Moreover, great king, there are twenty-eight special 148
qualities of secluded meditation, and it is these qualities the tathagatas consider as they practice seclusion. What are the twenty-eight? Here they are: secluded meditation protects one who is meditating; increases longevity; gives power; closes down faults; removes obscurity; conduces to fame; dispels discontent; furnishes contentment; removes fear; creates self-confidence; removes idleness; generates exertion; removes passion; removes hatred; removes delusion; puts down pride; breaks down initial thoughts; focuses awareness; softens the mind; produces a smile; makes one serious; produces gains; makes one venerated; brings joy; creates delight; shows the real nature of the clusters; puts an end to rebirth; and makes one fully a renouncer. These, great king, are the twenty-eight special qualities of seclusion, and when the tathagatas consider these qualities they practice secluded meditation.

"Furthermore, great king, tathagatas longing to expe- 149
rience the contentment of their attainments and peaceful happiness practice secluded meditation with purposeful intention. Tathagatas practice seclusion for four reasons, great king: for the sake of living comfortably, for the sake of an abundance of blameless virtues, for the sake of the

ta-vaṇṇita-pasatthato pi tathāgatā paṭisallāṇaṃ sevanti. imehi kho mahārāja catuhi kāraṇehi tathāgatā paṭisallāṇaṃ sevanti.

150 iti kho mahārāja paṭisallāṇaṃ sevanti, na sakaraṇīyatāya, na katassa paticayāya, atha kho guṇavisesadassāvitāya tathāgatā paṭisallāṇaṃ sevantīti. sādhu bhante nāgasena, evam-etaṃ, tathā sampaṭicchāmīti.

151 bhante nāgasena, bhāsitam-p' etaṃ bhagavatā: tathāgatassa kho ānanda cattāro iddhipādā bhāvitā bahulīkatā yānikatā vatthukatā anuṭṭhitā paricitā susamāraddhā; ākaṅkhamāno ānanda tathāgato kappaṃ vā tiṭṭheyya kappāvasesaṃ vā ti. puna ca bhaṇitaṃ: ito tiṇṇaṃ māsānaṃ accayena tathāgato parinibbāyissatīti.

152 yadi bhante nāgasena bhagavatā bhaṇitaṃ: tathāgatassa kho ānanda cattāro iddhipādā bhāvitā-pe-kappā-vasesaṃ vā ti, tena hi temāsaparicchedo micchā. yadi tathāgatena bhaṇitaṃ: ito tiṇṇaṃ māsānaṃ accayena tathāgato parinibbāyissatīti, tena hi: tathāgatassa kho ānanda cattāro iddhipādā bhāvitā-pe-kappāvase-saṃ vā ti tam-pi vacanaṃ micchā. na-tthi tathāgatānaṃ aṭṭhāne gajjitaṃ, amoghavacanā buddhā bhagavanto tathavacanā advejjhavacanā. ayam-pi ubhatokoṭiko pañho gambhīro sunipuṇo dunnijjhāpayo, so tavānuppatto, bhind' etaṃ diṭṭhijālaṃ, ekaṃse ṭhapaya, bhinda parappavādan-ti.

complete Noble Path, and because it has been praised, extolled, exalted, and commended for all buddhas. It is for these four reasons that tathagatas practice seclusion.

"And therefore, great king, they practice seclusion not 150
because something remains to be done or because there is something additional to be done. Rather, they practice it because they can see the particular advantages of its special qualities."

"Very good, revered Nagasena. I am convinced.

"Revered Nagasena, the Bhagavan also said this: 'Ananda, 151
the Tathagata has developed, continually practiced, made use of, established, maintained, increased, and mastered the four bases of supernatural power. Ananda, if the Tathagata so wished, he could live an eon or the remainder of an eon.' But then he said, 'The Tathagata will attain final nibbana in three months' time.'

"Nagasena, if the Bhagavan said that the Tathagata had 152
developed the four bases of supernatural power and that he could live the rest of an eon, then the limitation of three months must be false. If the Tathagata said that he would attain final nibbana in three months' time, then the Tathagata's claim to Ananda that he had developed the four bases of supernatural power and could live the rest of an eon is false. For tathagatas do not thunder for no reason. Buddhas' words are not vain, and blessed ones are those whose words are true and without contradiction. This deep, extremely subtle, and difficult two-pronged dilemma is put to you. Please cut through the web of wrong views, establish certainty, and break down the arguments of opponents."

153 bhāsitam-p’ etaṃ mahārāja bhagavatā: tathāgatassa kho ānanda cattāro iddhipādā bhāvitā-pe-kappā-vasesaṃ vā ti. temāsaparicchedo ca bhaṇito. so ca pana kappo āyukappo vuccati. na mahārāja bhagavā attano balaṃ kittayamāno evam-āha, iddhibalaṃ pana mahārāja bhagavā parikittayamāno evam-āha: tathāgatassa kho ānanda cattāro iddhipādā bhāvitā-pe-kappāvasesaṃ vā ti. yathā mahārāja rañño assājāniyyo bhaveyya sīghagati anilajavo, tassa rājā javabalaṃ parikittayanto sanegama-jānapada-bhaṭa-balattha-brāhmaṇa-gaha-patika-amaccajanamajjhe evaṃ vadeyya: ākaṅkhamāno me bho ayaṃ hayavaro sāgarajalapariyantaṃ mahiṃ anuvicaritvā khaṇena idh’ āgaccheyyāti, na ca taṃ javagatiṃ tassaṃ parisāyaṃ dasseyya, vijjati ca so javo tassa, samattho ca so khaṇena sāgarajalapariyantaṃ mahiṃ anuvicarituṃ; evam-eva kho mahārāja bhagavā attano iddhibalaṃ parikittayamāno evam-āha, tam-pi tevijjānaṃ chaḷabhiññānaṃ arahantānaṃ vimalakhīṇāsavānaṃ devamanussānañ-ca majjhe nisīditvā bhaṇitaṃ: tathāgatassa kho ānanda cattāro iddhipādā bhāvitā bahulīkatā yānikatā vatthukatā anuṭṭhitā paricitā susamāraddhā; ākaṅkhamāno ānanda tathāgato kappaṃ vā tiṭṭheyya kappāvasesaṃ vā ti; vijjati ca taṃ mahārāja iddhibalaṃ bhagavato, samattho ca bhagavā iddhibalena kappaṃ vā ṭhātuṃ kappāvasesaṃva, na ca bhagavātaṃ iddhibalaṃ tassaṃ parisāyaṃ dasseti.

"Great king, the Bhagavan did say, 'Ananda, the Tathagata 153
has developed the four bases of supernatural power and could live the remainder of an eon.' And he did mention the limitation of three months. But 'eon' was said in the sense of 'life span.' Great king, when the Bhagavan told Ananda that the Tathagata had developed the four bases of supernatural power and could live the remainder of an eon, he was praising the supernatural powers, not declaring his own power. Suppose a king's thoroughbred horse were swift as the speed of the wind, and that the king were to declare before all the people, including townsmen, country people, soldiers, palace guards, Brahmans, householders, and ministers: 'Should my excellent horse wish to, while out roaming the earth bordered by the waters of the oceans, he could return here in a moment.' Though he does not demonstrate this speed to the assembly, the horse does possess it and is capable of racing from across the earth bordered by the waters of the ocean in a moment. Similarly, when the Bhagavan was seated among gods, humans, and arhats—that is, those stainless ones with the three knowledges, the six higher knowledges, and flaws destroyed—he made known his own supernatural powers when he said, 'Ananda, the Tathagata has developed, continually practiced, made use of, established, maintained, increased, and mastered the four bases of supernatural power.[24] Ananda, if the Tathagata so wished, he could live an eon or the remainder of an eon.' Great king, even though the Bhagavan did not display this supernatural power to the assembly, the Bhagavan does possess supernatural powers and is able to remain for an eon or the rest of an eon.

154 anatthiko mahārāja bhagavā sabbabhavehi, garahitā ca tathāgatassa sabbabhavā. bhāsitam-p' etaṃ mahārāja bhagavatā: seyyathā pi bhikkhave appamattako pi gūtho duggandho hoti, evam-eva kho ahaṃ bhikkhave appamattakam-pi bhavaṃ na vaṇṇemi, antamaso accharāsaṅghātamattampīti. api nu kho mahārāja bhagavā sabbabhavagatiyoniyo gūthasamaṃ disvā iddhibalaṃ nissāya bhavesu chandarāgaṃ kareyyāti.

155 na hi bhante ti. tena hi mahārāja bhagavā iddhibalaṃ parikittayamāno evarūpaṃ buddhasīhanādam-abhinadīti. sādhu bhante nāgasena, evam-etaṃ, tathā sampaṭicchāmīti.

paṭhamo vaggo.

"In fact, the Bhagavan had no desire for any realm of rebirth, and all realms of rebirth were rejected by the Tathagata. Great king, the Bhagavan also said this: 'I do not praise rebirth even for the second it takes to snap one's fingers. Even a tiny bit of dung is foul smelling.' Do you think that, having seen that every kind of rebirth, destiny, and womb is like dung, the Bhagavan would foster excitement and passion for existences that depend on supernatural power?" 154

"No, sir." 155

"Therefore, great king, when the Bhagavan was praising the supernatural powers, he roared the lion's roar of a buddha."

"Very well, revered Nagasena, it is so, and I accept it."

End of Part 1.

PART 2

156 bhante nāgasena, bhāsitam p' etaṃ bhagavatā: abhiññāyāham-bhikkhave dhammaṃ desemi, no anabhiññāyāti. puna ca vinayapaṇṇattiyā evaṃ bhaṇitaṃ: ākaṅkhamāno ānanda saṅgho mam' accayena khuddānukhuddakāni sikkhāpadāni samūhanatūti. kin-nu kho bhante nāgasena khuddānukhuddakāni sikkhāpadāni duppaññattāni udāhu avatthusmiṃ ajānitvā paññattāni, yaṃ bhagavā attano accayena khuddānukhuddakāni sikkhāpadāni samūhanāpeti. yadi bhante nāgasena bhagavatā bhaṇitaṃ: abhiññāyāham-bhikkhave dhammaṃ desemi, no anabhiññāyāti, tena hi: ākaṅkhamāno ānanda saṅgho mam' accayena khuddānukhuddakāni sikkhāpadāni samūhanatūti yaṃ vacanaṃ taṃ micchā. yadi tathāgatena vinayapaṇṇattiyā evaṃ bhaṇitaṃ: ākaṅkhamāno ānanda saṅgho mam' accayena khuddānukhuddakāni sikkhāpadāni samūhanatūti, tena hi: abhiññāyāham-bhikkhave dhammaṃ desemi, no anabhiññāyāti tam-pi vacanaṃ micchā. ayam-pi ubhatokoṭiko pañho saṇho sukhumo sunipuṇo gambhīro sugambhīro dunnijjhāpayo, so tavānuppatto, tattha te ñāṇabalavipphāraṃ dassehīti.

157 bhāsitam-p' etaṃ mahārāja bhagavatā: abhiññāyāham-bhikkhave dhammaṃ desemi, no anabhiññāyāti. vinayapaṇṇattiyā pi evaṃ bhaṇitaṃ: ākaṅkhamāno ānanda saṅgho mam' accayena khuddānukhuddakāni sikkhāpadāni samūhanatūti. taṃ pana mahārāja tathāgato bhikkhū vīmaṃsamāno āha: ukkalissanti nu kho mama sāvakā

PART 2

"Revered Nagasena, the Bhagavan also said this: 'I teach the 156
Dhamma through higher knowledge, not without higher knowledge.' But he also said of the rules of the *vinaya,* 'If the community wishes, Ananda, it may abolish the lesser and minor rules after I pass away.' Nagasena, is it that the lesser and minor rules were badly laid down and without grounds? Or were they laid down in ignorance, since the Bhagavan allowed for them to be abolished after he was gone? If, Nagasena, the Bhagavan said, 'I teach the Dhamma through higher knowledge, not without higher knowledge,' then his saying, 'If the community wishes, Ananda, it may abolish the lesser and minor rules after I pass away,' must be false. Or if the Tathagata did say of the *vinaya* that the lessor and minor rules could be abolished after he was gone, then the claim that he teaches the Dhamma through higher knowledge and not without it must be false. This two-pronged dilemma is abstruse, subtle, very clever, deep, profound, and hard to grasp. It has reached you, and so you must show the extent of your power and knowledge."

"Great king, the Bhagavan did say, 'I teach the Dhamma 157
through higher knowledge, not without higher knowledge.' And he also said with respect to the *vinaya* rules, 'If the community wishes, Ananda, it may abolish the lesser and minor rules after I pass away.' But, great king, the Tathagata once said this when he was testing the monks: 'Will my disciples, granted permission to do so by me, loosen the lesser and minor rules at my passing away, or will they hold on to

mayā vissajjāpiyamānā mam' accayena khuddānukhuddakāni sikkhāpadāni udāhu ādiyissantīti. yathā mahārāja cakkavattirājā putte evaṃ vadeyya: ayaṃ kho tātā mahājanapado sabbadisāsu sāgarapariyanto, dukkaro tātā tāvatakena balena dhāretuṃ, etha tumhe tātā mam' accayena paccante paccante dese pajahathāti; api nu kho te mahārāja kumārā pitu accayena hatthagate janapade sabbe te paccante paccante dese muñceyyun-ti.

158 na hi bhante, rājāno bhante luddhatarā, kumārā rajjalobhena taduttariṃ diguṇa-tiguṇaṃ janapadaṃ parikaḍḍheyyuṃ, kim-pana te hatthagataṃ janapadaṃ muñceyyun-ti. evam-eva kho mahārāja tathāgato bhikkhū vīmaṃsamāno evam-āha: ākaṅkhamāno ānanda saṅgho mam' accayena khuddānukhuddakāni sikkhāpadāni samūhanatūti. dukkhaparimuttiyā mahārāja buddhaputtā dhammalobhena aññam-pi uttariṃ diyaḍḍhaṃ sikkhāpadasataṃ gopeyyuṃ, kim-pana pakatipaññattaṃ sikkhāpadaṃ muñceyyun-ti.

159 bhante nāgasena, yaṃ bhagavā āha: khuddānukhuddakāni sikkhāpadānīti, etthāyaṃ jano sammūḷho vimatijāto adhikato saṃsayapakkhanno: katamāni tāni khuddakāni sikkhāpadāni, katamāni anukhuddakāni sikkhāpadānīti. dukkaṭaṃ mahārāja khuddakaṃ sikkhāpadaṃ, dubbhāsitaṃ anukhuddakaṃ sikkhāpadaṃ, imāni dve khuddānukhuddakāni sikkhāpadāni. pubbakehi pi mahārāja mahāttherehi ettha vimati uppāditā, tehi pi ekajjhaṃ na kato dhammasaṇṭhitipariyāye bhagavatā eso pañho upadiṭṭho ti.

them?' Great king, suppose a wheel-turning emperor were to tell his sons, 'This great country, bounded by the ocean in every direction, is difficult to maintain with this much force. After my death, sons, you should give up the regions on various borders.' Do you think that when the father dies and the princes come into possession of the country, they would release all of the bordering regions?"

"No, sir. Kings are greedier than that. With their greed for 158
rule, the princes would seek to win countries two or three times beyond theirs. So why would they let go of any of the country handed down to them?"

"Great king, this is much like the Tathagata testing the monks when he said, 'If the community wishes, Ananda, it may abolish the lesser and minor rules after I pass away.' With their greed for the Dhamma and for the sake of release from suffering, the Buddha's descendants would safeguard more than two hundred and fifty rules. So how could they give up the original rules?"

"Nagasena, the Bhagavan mentioned 'lesser and minor 159
rules.' People have grown confused, perplexed, puzzled, and doubtful concerning which rules are lesser and which rules are minor."

"Great king, there are two kinds of lesser and minor rules: rules concerning bad action are the lesser rules, and rules concerning bad speech are the minor ones.[25] But the great elders of old evinced perplexity on this matter as well. They did not achieve consensus, though the question was explained by the Bhagavan in his instruction on establishing the Dhamma."[26]

160 ciranikkhittaṃ bhante nāgasena jinarahassaṃ ajj' etarahi loke vivaṭaṃ pākaṭaṃ katan-ti.

161 bhante nāgasena, bhāsitam-p' etaṃ bhagavatā: na-tth' ānanda tathāgatassa dhammesu ācariyamuṭṭhīti. puna ca therena māluṅkyāputtena pañhaṃ puṭṭho na byākāsi. eso kho bhante nāgasena pañho dvayanto ekantanissito bhavissati ajānanena vā guyhakaranena vā. yadi bhante nāgasena bhagavatā bhaṇitaṃ: na-tth' ānanda tathāgatassa dhammesu ācariyamuṭṭhīti, tena hi therassa māluṅkyāputtassa ajānantena na byākataṃ. yadi jānantena na byākataṃ, tena hi atthi tathāgatassa dhammesu ācariyamuṭṭhi. ayam-pi ubhatokoṭiko[6] pañho tavānuppatto, so tayā nibbāhitabbo ti.

162 bhāsitam-p' etaṃ mahārāja bhagavatā: na-tth' ānanda tathāgatassa dhammesu ācariyamuṭṭhīti. abyākato ca therena māluṅkyāputtena pucchito pañho, tañ-ca pana na ajānanena na guyhakaraṇena. cattār'imāni mahārāja pañhabyākaraṇāni, katamāni cattāri: ekaṃsa-byākaraṇīyo pañho, vibhajja byākaraṇīyo pañho, paṭipucchābyākaraṇīyo pañho, ṭhapanīyo pañho.

163 katamo ca mahārāja ekaṃsabyākaraṇīyo pañho: rūpaṃ aniccan-ti ekaṃsabyākaraṇīyo pañho, vedanā aniccā ti, saññā aniccā ti, saṅkhārā aniccā ti, viññāṇaṃ aniccan-ti ekaṃsa-byākaraṇīyo pañho; ayaṃ ekaṃsabyākaraṇīyo

"Revered Nagasena, this secret of the Victor, so long buried, is today revealed and made known in the world. 160

"Revered Nagasena, the Bhagavan also said: 'Ananda, when it comes to the teachings, the Tathagata does not have a teacher's closed fist.' And yet, he did not answer a question asked by Elder Malunkyaputta.[27] This dilemma, Nagasena, will come to rest on one of two conclusions. Either it was due to ignorance or it was due to secrecy. If the Bhagavan said that he does not have a teacher's closed fist when it comes to the teachings, then his failure to reply to Elder Malunkyaputta is because of ignorance. Alternatively, if he knew but did not reply, then the Tathagata does in fact have a teacher's closed fist. This two-pronged dilemma has reached you, and you must solve it." 161

"Great king, the Bhagavan did say, 'Ananda, when it comes to the teachings, the Tathagata does not have a teacher's closed fist.' And the question asked by Elder Malunkyaputta did go unexplained, but not out of either ignorance or secrecy. Great king, there are four ways of answering questions. What are the four? There is the question that is answered definitively, the question that is answered with analysis, the question that is answered with a counter-question, and the question that is answered by setting it aside. 162

"Great king, what is a question best answered definitively? A question to be answered definitively would be, Is form impermanent? Other questions with definitive answers are: Is feeling impermanent? Is perception impermanent? Are the habitual patterns impermanent? Is awareness impermanent? This type of question has a definitive answer. 163

pañho. katamo vibhajja byākaraṇīyo pañho: aniccaṃ pana rūpan-ti vibhajja byākaraṇīyo pañho, aniccā pana vedanā ti, aniccā pana saññā ti, aniccā pana saṅkhārā ti, aniccaṃ pana viññāṇan-ti vibhajjabyākaraṇīyo pañho; ayaṃ vibhajja byākaraṇīyo pañho.

164 katamo paṭipucchābyākaraṇīyo pañho: kin-nu kho cakkhunā sabbaṃ vijānātīti, ayaṃ paṭipucchābyākaraṇīyo pañho. katamo ṭhapanīyo pañho: sassato loko ti ṭhapanīyo pañho, asassato loko ti, antavā loko ti, anantavā loko ti, antavā ca anantavā ca loko ti, na ev' antavā nānantavā loko ti, taṃ jīvaṃ taṃ sarīran-ti, aññaṃ jīvaṃ aññaṃ sarīran-ti, hoti tathāgato param-maraṇā ti, na hoti tathāgato param-maraṇā ti, hoti ca na ca hoti tathāgato param-maraṇā ti, n' eva hoti na na hoti tathāgato param-maraṇā ti ṭhapanīyo pañho; ayaṃ ṭhapanīyo pañho.

165 bhagavā mahārāja therassa māluṅkyāputtassa taṃ ṭhapanīyaṃ pañhaṃ na byākāsi. so pana pañho kiṅkāraṇā ṭhapanīyo: na tassa dīpanāya hetu vā kāraṇaṃ vā atthi, tasmā so pañho ṭhapanīyo, na-tthi buddhānaṃ bhagavantānaṃ akāraṇam-ahetukaṃ giram-udīraṇan-ti. sādhu bhante nāgasena, evam-etaṃ, tathā sampaṭicchāmīti.

166 bhante nāgasena, bhāsitam-p' etaṃ bhagavatā: sabbe tasanti daṇḍassa, sabbe bhāyanti maccuno ti. puna ca bhaṇi-

"What is a question best answered with analysis? A question to be answered with analysis would be, How is form impermanent? Other questions to be answered with analysis are: How is feeling impermanent? How is perception impermanent? How are the habitual patterns impermanent? How is awareness impermanent? This type of question is to be answered with analysis.

"What is a question best answered with a counter- 164
question? Is it the case that everything is known by means of the eye? is an example of a question to be answered with a counterquestion.

"What is a question best answered by setting it aside? Is the world eternal? This is a question to be set aside. Other questions to be answered by setting them aside are: Is the world not eternal? Is the world finite? Is the world infinite? Is the world both finite and infinite? Is the world neither finite nor infinite? Is the soul the body? Is the soul one thing and the body another? Does the Tathagata exist after death? Does the Tathagata not exist after death? Does he both exist and not exist after death? Does he neither exist nor not exist after death? These are the types of questions to be set aside.

"Great king, Elder Malunkyaputta's question was the type 165
to be set aside, and so the Bhagavan did not reply. For what reason was the question to be set aside? Because there was no cause or reason for explaining it, it was a question to be set aside. There are no sayings or utterances of blessed buddhas without reason or cause."

"Very well, then, Nagasena, it is so, and I accept it.

"Revered Nagasena, the Bhagavan said: 'All beings trem- 166
ble before the rod and all beings fear death.' But he also said:

taṃ: arahā sabbabhayam-atikkanto ti. kin-nu kho bhante nāgasena arahā daṇḍabhayā tasati, niraye vā nerayikā sattā jalitā kaṭhitā tattā santattā tamhā jalitaggijālakā mahā-nirayā cavamānā maccuno bhāyanti. yadi bhante nāgasena bhagavatā bhaṇitam: sabbe tasanti daṇḍassa, sabbe bhāyanti maccuno ti, tena hi: arahā sabbabhayam-atikkanto ti yaṃ vacanaṃ taṃ micchā. yadi bhagavatā bhaṇitaṃ: arahā sabbabhayam-atikkanto ti, tena hi: sabbe tasanti daṇḍassa, sabbe bhāyanti maccuno ti tam-pi vacanaṃ micchā. ayam-pi ubhatokoṭiko pañho tavānuppatto, so tayā nibbāhitabbo ti.

167 n' etaṃ mahārāja vacanaṃ bhagavatā arahante upādāya bhaṇitaṃ: sabbe tasanti daṇḍassa, sabbe bhāyanti maccuno ti, ṭhapito arahā tasmiṃ vatthusmiṃ, samūhato bhayahetu arahato; ye te mahārāja sattā sakilesā yesañ-ca adhimattā attānudiṭṭhi ye ca sukhadukkhesu unnatāvanatā, te upādāya bhagavatā bhaṇitaṃ: sabbe tasanti daṇḍassa, sabbe bhāyanti maccuno ti. arahato mahārāja sabbagati upacchinnā, yoni viddhaṃ-sitā, paṭisandhi upahatā, bhaggā phāsū, samūhatā sabbabhavālayā, samucchinnā sabbasaṅkhārā, hataṃ kusalākusalaṃ, vihatā avijjā, abījaṃ viññāṇaṃ kataṃ, daḍḍhā sabbakilesā, atiyattā lokadhammā, tasmā arahā na santasati sabbabhayehi.

168 idha mahārāja rañño cattāro mahāmattā bhaveyyuṃ, anurattā laddhayasā vissāsikā, ṭhapitā mahati issariye ṭhāne, atha rājā kismici karaṇīye samuppanne yāvatā sakavijite sabbajanassa āṇāpeyya: sabbeva me baliṃ karontu,

'An arhat has overcome all fear.' Nagasena, surely an arhat trembles from fear of the rod? And hell beings who are burning, boiling, melting, and scorching in hell fear death even as they fall from that great hell that blazes with hot fire. If, Nagasena, the Bhagavan said, 'All beings tremble before the rod and all beings fear death,' then the claim that 'an arhat has overcome all fear' is false. Alternatively, if the Bhagavan said, 'An arhat has overcome all fear,' then the claim that 'all beings tremble before the rod and all beings fear death' is false. This two-pronged dilemma has reached you, and you must solve it."

"Great king, when the Bhagavan said, 'All beings tremble 167
before the rod and all beings fear death,' he did not make this claim with respect to arhats. On this subject an arhat is an exception, for the arhat has removed the condition of fear. It was concerning beings with the defilements, who remain extremely dogmatic about the self and are raised high and dashed low by pleasure and pain, that the Bhagavan said, 'All beings tremble before the rod and all beings fear death.' Since an arhat has cut off all wanderings, shattered birth, destroyed rebirth, broken the snares, abolished all clinging to existence, extirpated all clusters, removed good and bad, demolished ignorance, made awareness stop proliferating, burned up all defilements, and fully subdued all worldly conditions, the arhat does not tremble with any fear whatsoever.

"Suppose a king had four chief ministers who were faith- 168
ful, renowned, trustworthy, and highly placed in government. Suppose a certain exigency came about whereby the king needed to make a command to the people in his realm:

sādhetha tumhe cattāro mahāmattā taṃ karaṇīyan-ti; api nu kho mahārāja tesaṃ catunnaṃ mahāmattānaṃ balibhayā santāso uppajjeyyāti.

169 na hi bhante ti. kena kāraṇena mahārājāti. ṭhapitā te bhante raññā uttame ṭhāne, na-tthi tesaṃ bali, samatikkantabalino te, avasese upādāya raññā āṇāpitaṃ: sabbeva me baliṃ karontūti. evam-eva kho mahārāja n' etaṃ vacanaṃ bhagavatā arahante upādāya bhaṇitaṃ, ṭhapito arahā tasmiṃ vatthusmiṃ, samūhato bhayahetu arahato; ye te mahārāja sattā sakilesā yesañ-ca adhimattā attānudiṭṭhi ye ca sukhadukkhesu unnatāvanatā, te upādāya bhagavatā bhaṇitaṃ: sabbe tasanti daṇḍassa, sabbe bhāyanti maccuno ti. tasmā arahā na tasati sabbabhayehīti.

170 n' etaṃ bhante nāgasena vacanaṃ sāvasesaṃ, niravasesavacanam-etaṃ: sabbe ti, tattha me uttariṃ kāraṇaṃ brūhi taṃ vacanaṃ patiṭṭhāpetun-ti. idha mahārāja gāme gāmasāmiko āṇāpakaṃ āṇāpeyya: ehi bho āṇāpaka, yāvatā gāme gāmikā te sabbe sīghaṃ mama santike sannipātehīti; so: sādhu sāmīti sampaṭicchitvā gāmamajjhe ṭhatvā tikkhattuṃ saddam-anussāveyya: yāvatā gāme gāmikā te sabbe sīghasīghaṃ sāmino santike sannipatantūti; tato te gāmikā āṇāpakassa vacanena turitaturitā sannipatitvā gāmasāmikassa ārocenti: sannipatitā sāmi sabbe gāmikā, yan-te karaṇīyaṃ taṃ karohīti.

171 iti so mahārāja gāmasāmiko kuṭipurise sannipātento sabbe gāmike āṇāpeti, te ca āṇattā na sabbe sannipatanti,

'Everyone must pay me a tax, and you four chief ministers are to arrange the business.' Do you think, great king, that the four chief ministers would feel fear and terror of the tax?"

"No, sir." 169

"For what reason, great king?"

"For those placed in high positions by the king, sir, there is no tax since they are beyond taxation. It was with respect to everyone else that the king commanded: 'Everyone must pay me a tax.' Similarly, great king, the Bhagavan's words were not said with respect to arhats. On this subject, arhats are an exception, as they have removed the condition of fear. When the Bhagavan said, 'All beings tremble before the rod and all beings fear death,' he was speaking of beings with the defilements, who remain extremely dogmatic about the self and are raised high and dashed low by pleasure and pain. Therefore, the arhat does not tremble with any fear whatsoever."

"But Nagasena, the original word was 'all,' which is inclu- 170
sive and a word that leaves nothing out. Give me a further reason to shore up the claim."

"Great king, suppose in a village the headman were to order the town crier: 'Come, town crier, quickly assemble all the villagers and bring them to me.' Replying, 'Very well, headman,' he stands in the center of the village and proclaims three times the words, 'All villagers in the village are to assemble immediately before the headman!' At this command, the villagers hasten and rush, and having assembled, say to the village headman: 'All the villagers are assembled, headman, so please do what is necessary.'

"Great king, when the village headman made an order 171
to all the villagers he was in fact assembling the heads of

kuṭipurisā yeva sannipatanti, ettakā yeva me gāmikā ti gāmasāmiko ca tathā sampaṭicchati; aññe bahutarā anāgatā, itthi-purisā dāsi-dāsā bhatakā kammakarā gāmikā gilānā gomahisā aj-eḷakā supāṇā, ye anāgatā sabbe te agaṇitā, kuṭipurise yeva upādāya āṇāpitattā: sabbe sannipatantūti. evam-eva kho mahārāja n' etaṃ vacanaṃ bhagavatā arahante upādāya bhaṇitaṃ, ṭhapito arahā tasmiṃ vatthusmiṃ, samūhato bhayahetu arahato; ye te mahārāja sattā sakilesā yesañ-ca adhimattā attānudiṭṭhi ye ca sukhadukkhesu unnatāvanatā, te upādāya bhagavatā bhaṇitaṃ: sabbe tasanti daṇḍassa, sabbe bhāyanti maccuno ti. tasmā arahā na tasati sabbabhayehi.

172 atthi mahārāja sāvasesaṃ vacanaṃ sāvaseso attho, atthi sāvasesaṃ vacanaṃ niravaseso attho, atthi niravasesaṃ vacanaṃ sāvaseso attho, atthi niravasesaṃ vacanaṃ niravaseso attho, tena tena attho sampaṭicchitabbo. pañcavidhena mahārāja attho sampaṭicchitabbo, āhaccapadena kho mahārāja, rasena, ācariyavaṃsatāya, adhippāyā, kāraṇuttariyatāya. ettha hi: āhaccapadan-ti suttaṃ adhippetaṃ, raso ti suttānulomaṃ, ācariyavaṃso ti ācariyavādo, adhippāyo ti attano mati, kāraṇuttariyatā ti imehi catuhi

households. Only the heads of households assemble following the command; not everyone comes. Yet the headman accepts that this many are his villagers. Many others do not come, including women and men, female and male slaves, servants, workmen, villagers who are ill, cows, buffalo, goats, rams, and dogs. And all of those who do not come are not counted since the command—'All villagers are to assemble'—was directed only to the heads of households.

"It is the same in this case, great king. The Bhagavan's words were not said with respect to arhats. On this subject, arhats are an exception, as they have removed the condition of fear. When the Bhagavan said, 'All beings tremble before the rod and all beings fear death,' he was speaking of beings with the defilements who are dogmatic about the self and raised high and dashed low by pleasure and pain. Therefore, the arhat does not tremble with any fear whatsoever.

"Great king, there can be restricted words with a restricted 172
meaning, restricted words with an inclusive meaning, inclusive words with a restricted meaning, and inclusive words with an inclusive meaning. In every case, it is the meaning that is to be accepted. And the meaning accepted is known by five kinds of considerations: because it is canonical, because of its essential substance, because it has been handed down by the lineage of teachers, because of its intention, and because of supplementary argumentation. Here, 'canonical' refers to the *suttas;* 'essential substance' means in keeping with the *suttas;* 'handed down by the lineage of teachers' means taught by the teachers; 'intention' refers to what is in one's mind; and 'supplementary argumentation' refers to reasons connected to these other four ways. The meaning

samentaṃ kāraṇaṃ. imehi kho mahārāja pañcahi kāraṇehi attho sampaṭicchitabbo. evam-eso pañho suvinicchito hotīti.

173 hotu bhante nāgasena, tathā taṃ sampaṭicchāmi, ṭhapito hotu arahā tasmiṃ vatthusmiṃ, tasantu avasesā sattā. niraye pana nerayikā sattā, dukkhā tippā kaṭukā vedanā vediyamānā, jalitapajjalita-sabbaṅgapaccaṅgā ruṇṇa-kāruñña-kandita-paridevita-lālappita-mukhā asayha-tibba-dukkhābhibhūtā attāṇā asaraṇā asaraṇībhūtā anappasokāturā antima-pacchima-gatikā ekantasoka-parāyanā, uṇha-tikhiṇa-caṇḍa-khara-tapana-tejavantā bhīmabhaya-janaka-ninnāda-mahāsaddā saṃsibbita-chabbidha-jālāmālā-kulā samantā satayojanānupharaṇaccivegā kadariyā tapanā mahānirayā cavamānā maccuno bhāyantīti.

174 āma mahārājāti. nanu bhante nāgasena nirayo ekanta-dukkhavedaniyo, kissa pana te nerayikā sattā ekantadukkhavedaniyā nirayā cavamānā maccuno bhāyanti, kissa niraye ramantīti. na te mahārāja nerayikā sattā niraye ramanti, muccitukāmāva te nirayā; maraṇass' eso mahārāja ānubhāvo yena tesaṃ santāso uppajjatīti. etaṃ kho bhante nāgasena na saddahissāmi yaṃ muccitukāmānaṃ cutiyā santāso uppajjati; hāsaniyaṃ bhante nāgasena taṃ ṭhānaṃ yaṃ te patthitaṃ labhanti. kāraṇena maṃ saññāpehīti.

to be accepted, great king, is in accordance with these five reasons. And so the dilemma is thoroughly decided."

"Let it be so, then, Nagasena. I am convinced that the arhat 173
is an exception when it comes to this subject, while all other beings do tremble. However, hell beings experience painful, piercing, and severe pain in hell as their bodies and limbs burn and blaze all over, and their mouths emit pitiful crying, wailing, bemoaning, and lamenting. They are overwhelmed with sharp and insuperable pain and find no shelter, no refuge, and no help. Afflicted with immeasurable misery, they roam from start to finish in destinies of supreme grief. They burn with hot, acute, fierce, and keen tortures, and their great cries, born of terror and fear, ring out. Stunned from being entangled with the six wreaths of fire that flame with blazing speed through a hundred leagues in every direction, they are tormented and tortured. And yet, as they fall from that great hell, they fear death."

"Yes, great king." 174

"But surely, revered Nagasena, hell is an entirely painful experience. So why would hell beings, feeling only pain, fear death as they fall out of hell? Is it that they take pleasure in hell?"

"No, great king, hell beings take no pleasure in hell and long to be released from it. It is the enormity of death, great king, that prompts their terror."

"Nagasena, I simply do not believe that fear of dying is generated in those longing for such release, for surely, sir, they attain the very state they have wished for. You must convince me with further reasoning."

175 maraṇan-ti kho mahārāja etaṃ adiṭṭhasaccānaṃ tāsaniyaṃ ṭhānaṃ, etthāyaṃ jano tasati ca ubbijjati ca. yo ca mahārāja kaṇhasappassa bhāyati so maraṇassa bhāyanto kaṇhasappassa bhāyati, yo ca hatthissa bhāyati-pe-sīhassa byagghassa dīpissa acchassa taracchassa mahisassa gavayassa aggissa udakassa khāṇukassa kaṇṭakassa bhāyati, yo ca sattiyā bhāyati so maraṇassa bhāyanto sattiyā bhāyati. maraṇass' eso mahārāja sarasabhāvatejo, tassa sarasabhāvatejena sakilesā sattā maraṇassa tasanti bhāyanti, muccitukāmā pi mahārāja nerayikā sattā maraṇassa tasanti bhāyanti.

176 idha mahārāja purisassa kāye medogaṇṭhi uppajjeyya, so tena rogena dukkhito upaddavā parimuccitukāmo bhisakkaṃ sallakattaṃ āmantāpeyya, tassa so bhisakko sallakatto sampaṭicchitvā tassa rogassa uddharaṇāya upakaraṇaṃ upaṭṭhāpeyya: satthakaṃ tikhiṇaṃ kareyya, dahanasalākā aggimhi pakkhipeyya, khāralavaṇaṃ nisadāya piṃsāpeyya; api nu kho mahārāja tassa āturassa tikhiṇasatthakacchedanena yamakasalākādahanena khāraloṇappavesanena tāso uppajjeyyāti.

177 āma bhante ti. iti mahārāja tassa āturassa rogā muccitukāmassāpi vedanābhayā santāso uppajjati, evam-eva kho mahārāja nirayā muccitukāmānam-pi nerayikānaṃ sattānaṃ maraṇabhayā santāso uppajjati. idha mahārāja puriso issarāparādhiko baddho saṅkhalikabandhanena gabbhe pakkhitto parimuccitukāmo assa, tam-enaṃ so issaro mocetukāmo pakkosāpeyya; api nu kho mahārāja tassa

"Great king, death is a state to be feared for those who 175
have not seen the truth, and on account of this they are afraid and terrified.[28] Someone afraid of a black snake actually fears death while fearing the black snake. Those afraid of elephants, lions, tigers, panthers, bears, hyenas, buffalo, bulls, fire, flood, spikes, and robbers are really fearing death when they are afraid of such things. For this, great king, is the power that is the essential nature of death: beings with the defilements fear and tremble at death because of the power of its essential nature, and though longing for release, hell beings also fear and tremble at death.

"Great king, suppose a fatty tumor were to appear on 176
a man's body, and he became pained and distressed by the disease. Longing to be free of it, he would consult a physician who is a surgeon. The surgical physician, having agreed to treat him, would procure the means of removing it by readying a sharp knife, placing cauterizing tools in the fire, and grinding lye and salt with a grindstone. Great king, would cutting with the sharp knife, cauterizing with a pair of tools, and applying lye and salt produce fear in the afflicted man?"

"Yes, sir." 177

"Despite longing to be rid of the disease, the afflicted man trembles from fear of pain. Great king, it is like this for the hell beings who tremble from fear of death despite longing to be released from hell.

"Consider too the case of a man who offends his master and is captured, bound with chains, and thrown in a cell. He longs to be free. Suppose the master were to send for him, wishing to release him. But wouldn't the man who had

issarāparādhikassa purisassa: katadoso ahan-ti jānantassa issaradassanena santāso uppajjeyyāti.

178 āma bhante ti. iti mahārāja tassa issarāparādhikassa purisassa muccitukāmassāpi issarabhayā santāso uppajjati, evam-eva kho mahārāja nirayā muccitukāmānam-pi nerayikānaṃ sattānaṃ maraṇabhayā santāso uppajjatīti. aparam-pi bhante uttariṃ kāraṇaṃ brūhi yenāhaṃ kāraṇena okappeyyan-ti.

179 idha mahārāja puriso daṭṭhavisena āsīvisena daṭṭho bhaveyya, so tena visavikārena pateyya uppateyya, vaṭṭeyya pavaṭṭeyya, ath' aññataro puriso balavantena mantapadena taṃ daṭṭhavisaṃ āsīvisaṃ ānetvā taṃ daṭṭhavisaṃ paccācamāpeyya; api nu kho mahārāja tassa visagatassa purisassa tasmiṃ daṭṭhavise sappe sotthihetu upagacchante santāso uppajjeyyāti. āma bhante ti.

180 iti mahārāja tathārūpe ahimhi sotthihetu pi upagacchante tassa santāso uppajjati, evam-eva kho mahārāja nirayā parimuccitukāmānam-pi nerayikānaṃ sattānaṃ maraṇabhayā santāso uppajjati. aniṭṭhaṃ mahārāja sabbasattānaṃ maraṇaṃ, tasmā nerayikā sattā nirayā parimuccitukāmā pi maccuno bhāyantīti. sādhu bhante nāgasena, evam-etaṃ, tathā sampaṭicchāmīti.

offended the master, knowing that he had committed a fault, tremble on seeing him?"

"Indeed, sir." 178

"So despite longing to be free, the man who offended against the master trembles from fear of the master. Great king, it is like this for the hell beings who tremble from fear of death despite longing to be released from hell."

"I may come to feel confident about this with more reasoning, sir, so please give a further reason."

"Suppose there was a man bitten by the poisonous fangs 179
of a snake. Because of the action of the venom he would fall down and start up, twisting and writhing. And suppose another man with the powerful words of a mantra could bring back the snake with the poisonous fangs and make it reabsorb the venom. Great king, do you think that the man who had been poisoned would tremble as the snake with its poisonous fangs approached, despite its being the means to save him?"

"Yes, sir."

"Great king, just as he trembles at the advance of the snake 180
even though it is the means to save him, so too do hell beings tremble from fear of death despite longing to be released from hell. No being desires death, great king, and therefore, hell beings fear death even though they long to be released from hell."

"Very good, revered Nagasena. I am convinced that this is so.

181 bhante nāgasena, bhāsitam-p' etaṃ bhagavatā:

na antalikkhe, na samuddamajjhe, na pabbatānaṃ vivaraṃ
pavissa,
na vijjatī so jagatippadeso yattha-ṭṭhito muñceyya
maccupāsā ti.

182 puna bhagavatā parittā ca uddiṭṭhā, seyyathīdaṃ: ratanasuttaṃ khandhaparittaṃ moraparittaṃ dhajaggaparittaṃ āṭānāṭiyaparittaṃ angulimālaparittaṃ. yadi bhante nāgasena ākāsagato pi samuddamajjhagato pi pāsāda-kuṭi-leṇa-guhā-pabbhāra-darī-bila-vivara-pabba-tantaragato pi na muccati maccupāsā, tena hi parittakammaṃ micchā. yadi parittakaraṇena maccupāsā parimutti bhavati, tena hi: na antalikkhe-pe-maccu-pāsā ti tam-pi vacanaṃ micchā. ayam-pi ubhato-koṭiko pañho gaṇṭhito pi gaṇṭhitaro tavānuppatto, so tayānibbāhitabbo ti.

183 bhāsitam-p' etaṃ mahārāja bhagavatā:

na antalikkhe, na samuddamajjhe, na pabbatānaṃ vivaraṃ
pavissa,
na vijjatī so jagatippadeso yattha-ṭṭhito muñceyya
maccupāsā ti.

184 parittā ca bhagavatā uddiṭṭhā. tañ-ca pana sāvasesāyukassa vayasampannassa apetakammāvaraṇassa, natthi mahārāja khīṇāyukassa ṭhitiyā kiriyā vā upakkamo vā. yathā mahārāja matassa rukkhassa sukkhassa koḷāpassa nisnehassa uparuddhajīvitassa gatāyusaṅkhārassa kumbhasahassena pi udake ākirante allattaṃ vā pallavitaharitabhāvo vā na

"Revered Nagasena, the Bhagavan also said this: 181

Nowhere can be found a place in the world—
whether between earth and sky, in the middle of the
sea, or tucked inside a cleft in the mountains— where
one may stand clear of the snares of Death.

"At the same time, the Bhagavan proposed protective 182
charms, for instance the *Jewel Sutta*, the Cluster Charm, the Mora Charm, the Top of the Banner Charm, the Atanatiya Charm, and the Angulimala Charm.[29] Nagasena, if one is not free from the snares of Death in the atmosphere, in the middle of the ocean, or tucked inside a mountain in a palace, hut, cave, cavern, hollow, den, or cleft, then the action of protective charms must be false. Alternatively, if one may elude the snares of Death by means of a protective charm, then the verse about the snares of Death must be false. This two-pronged dilemma is knottier than a knot. It has reached you, and you must solve it."

"Great king, the Bhagavan did say: 183

Nowhere can be found a place in the world—
whether between earth and sky, in the middle of the
sea, or tucked inside a cleft in the mountains— where
one may stand clear of the snares of Death.

"And the Bhagavan did propose protective charms. But 184
they are for one who still has life remaining, in the prime of life, and who is freed of obstructions related to karma. There is no expedient or action for maintaining a life span that is exhausted, great king. Even if a thousand jars of water were poured on a dead, dried-up, sapless, and

bhaveyya, evam-eva kho mahārāja bhesajjaparittakammena na-tthi khīṇāyukassa ṭhitiyā kiriyā vā upakkamo vā. yāni tāni mahārāja mahiyā osadhāni bhesajjāni tāni pi khīṇāyukassa akiccakarāni bhavanti, sāvasesāyukaṃ mahārāja vayasampannaṃ apetakammāvaraṇaṃ parittaṃ rakkhati gopeti, tass' atthāya bhagavatā parittā uddiṭṭhā.

185 yathā mahārāja kassako paripakke dhaññe mate sassanāḷe udakappavesaṃ vāreyya, yaṃ pana sassaṃ taruṇaṃ meghasannibhaṃ vayasampannaṃ taṃ udakavaḍḍhiyā vaḍḍhati, evam-eva kho mahārāja khīṇāyukassa bhesajjaparittakiriyā ṭhapitā paṭikkhittā, ye pana te manussā sāvasesāyukā vayasampannā tesaṃ atthāya parittabhesajjāni bhaṇitāni, te parittabhesajjehi vaḍḍhantīti.

186 yadi bhante nāgasena khīṇāyuko marati sāvasesāyuko jīvati, tena hi parittabhesajjāni niratthakāni hontīti. diṭṭhapubbo pana tayā mahārāja koci rogo bhesajjehi patinivattito ti. āma bhante, anekasatāni diṭṭhānīti. tena hi mahārāja: parittabhesajjakiriyā niratthikā ti yaṃ vacanaṃ taṃ micchā

desiccated tree, whose life had ceased and whose life element had gone, it would not become fresh and sprouting again. There is no expedient or action for maintaining a life span that is exhausted, even with the action of medicine or a protective charm. All the medicines and remedies on earth are ineffective for one whose life span is exhausted, great king. Yet the Bhagavan did propose protective charms for the sake of protecting and saving those with life remaining, in the prime of life, and who are free of karmic obstructions.

"Great king, just as a farmer prevents water from penetrat- 185
ing the hollow stalks of the crops once the grain has ripened and died, but cultivates them with increasing water when the crops, like clouds, are young and in the prime of life, so too the action of medicine and protective charms is an exception, and precluded for one whose life span is exhausted.[30] But protective charms and medicines are mentioned for the sake of people who still have life remaining and are in the prime of their lives, and they can flourish with protective charms and medicines."

"And yet, revered Nagasena, if one whose life span is 186
exhausted dies anyway and one who still has life remaining lives anyway, then protective charms and medicines are pointless."

"But have you never seen a disease reverse course because of a medicine, great king?"

"Yes, this has been observed in hundreds of cases, sir."

"Then saying that the action of protective charms and medicines is pointless is false, great king."

bhavatīti. dissanti bhante nāgasena vejjānaṃ upakkame bhesajjapānānulepā, tena tesaṃ upakkamena rogo patinivattatīti.

187 parittāni pi mahārāja pavattayamānānaṃ saddo sūyati, jivhā sukkhati, hadayaṃ byāvaṭṭati, kaṇṭho ākurati; tena tesaṃ pavattena[7] sabbabyādhayo vūpasamanti, sabbā ītiyo apagacchanti. diṭṭhapubbo pana tayā mahārāja koci ahinā daṭṭho mantapadena visaṃ pātiyamāno visaṃ cikkhassanto uddham-adho ācamayamāno ti. āma bhante, ajj' etarahi pi taṃ loke vattatīti.

188 tena hi mahārāja: parittabhesajjakiriyā niratthikā ti yaṃ vacanaṃ taṃ micchā bhavati. kataparittaṃ hi mahārāja purisaṃ ḍasitukāmo ahi na ḍasati, vivaṭaṃ mukhaṃ pidahati, corānaṃ ukkhittalaguḷam-pi na sambhavati, te laguḷaṃ muñcitvā pemaṃ karonti, kupito pi hatthināgo samāgantvā uparamati, pajjalitamahāaggikkhandho pi upagantvā nibbāyati, visaṃ halāhalam-pi khāyitaṃ agadaṃ sampajjati āhāratthaṃ vā pharati, vadhakā hantukāmā upagantvā dāsabhūtā sampajjanti, akkanto pi pāso na saṃvarati. sutapubbaṃ pana tayā mahārāja morassa kataparittassa satta vassasatāni luddako nāsakkhi pāsaṃ upanetuṃ, akataparittassa taṃ yeva divasaṃ pāsaṃ upanesīti.

189 āma bhante, sūyati, abbhuggato so saddo sadevake loke ti. tena hi mahārāja: parittabhesajjakiriyā niratthikā ti yaṃ vacanaṃ taṃ micchā bhavati. sutapubbaṃ pana tayā mahārāja: dānavo bhariyaṃ parirakkhanto samugge pakkh-

"Nagasena, doctors' medicines, tonics, and ointments have been observed to be efficacious, and by their efficacy disease reverses course."

"Similarly, great king, when the sound is heard from those 187
performing protective charms, all illnesses are relieved by the procedure, even a parched tongue, a heart beating irregularly, or a throat rasping. All calamities vanish. Great king, have you ever seen, in the case of a person bitten by a snake, the venom removed with the words of a mantra and coaxed from above and below to flow until it can be sucked out?"

"Yes, sir, this still takes place in the world even now."

"Therefore, the claim that the action of protective charms 188
and medicines is pointless is false. For when a protective charm has been performed, a snake wishing to bite a man does not bite and closes its gaping mouth. The raised club of robbers is of no avail, and they drop the club and behave with kindness. The rampaging, raging elephant suddenly stops; the massive blazing fire approaches but then is extinguished; deadly poison swallowed turns to its antidote or serves instead as food; murderous assassins advance but then become slaves; and the snare stepped on does not stay clasped. Great king, have you ever heard of the hunter who was not able for seven hundred years to trap a peacock who performed a protective charm? But on the one day the peacock did not perform the charm, it was caught in the snare."

"Yes, I have heard of this, sir, for word of it has spread 189
through the world up to the heavens."

"Therefore, great king, the claim that the action of protective charms and medicines is pointless is false. Have you ever

ipitvā gilitvā kucchinā pariharati, ath' eko vijjādharo tassa dānavassa mukhena pavisitvā tāya saddhiṃ abhiramati, yadā so dānavo aññāsi atha samuggaṃ vamitvā vivari, saha samugge vivaṭe vijjādharo yenakāmamaṃ pakkamīti.

190 āma bhante, sūyati, abbhuggato so pi saddo sadevake loke ti. nanu so mahārāja vijjādharo parittabalena gahaṇā mutto ti. āma bhante ti. tena hi mahārāja atthi paritta-balaṃ. sutapubbaṃ tayā mahārāja: aparo vijjādharo bārāṇa-siraññoantepure mahesiyā saddhiṃ sampaduṭṭho gahaṇaṃ patto samāno khaṇena adassanaṃ gato mantabalenāti. āma bhante, sūyatīti. nanu so mahārāja vijjādharo parittabalena gahaṇā mutto ti. āma bhante ti. tena hi mahārāja atthi parit-tabalan-ti.

191 bhante nāgasena, kiṃ sabbe yeva parittaṃ rakkhatīti. ekacce mahārāja rakkhati, ekacce na rakkhatīti. tena hi bhante nāgasena parittaṃ na sabbatthikan-ti. api nu kho mahārāja bhojanaṃ sabbesaṃ jīvitaṃ rakkhatīti. ekacce bhante rakkhati, ekacce na rakkhatīti. kiṅkāraṇā ti. yato bhante ekacce taṃ yeva bhojanaṃ atibhuñjitvā visūcikāya marantīti. tena hi mahārāja bhojanaṃ na sabbesaṃ jīvitaṃ rakkhatīti. dvīhi bhante nāgasena kāraṇehi bhojanaṃ jīvi-taṃ harati: atibhuttena vā usmādubbalatāya vā; āyudadaṃ bhante nāgasena bhojanaṃ durupacārena jīvitaṃ haratīti.

heard of the Danava demon who, in guarding his wife, put her in a box, swallowed her, and carried her about in his belly? But a magician went into his mouth and took pleasure with her. When the demon realized this, he vomited up the box and opened it. But just as the box was opened, the magician took off as he wished."[31]

"I have heard of this as well, sir, as word of it has spread 190
through the world up to the heavens."

"Surely the magician escaped capture by the power of protective charms, great king." "Of course, sir." "Therefore, great king, there is power in protective charms. Have you heard of the case of another magician who, committing adultery in the inner quarters of the king of Baranasi with the chief queen, was captured, but just at that moment became invisible by the power of a mantra?" "Yes, I have heard this, sir." "Surely the magician escaped capture by the power of protective charms." "Yes, sir." "Therefore, there is power in protective charms, great king."

"Nagasena, sir, does a protective charm protect every- 191
one?" "It protects some, great king, but it does not protect others." "Then a protective charm is not always useful, Nagasena." "But does food save the life of everyone, great king?" "Some it saves and some it does not save, sir." "Why is this?" "Because some, due to cholera, die having eaten too much food. And so, great king, food does not save the life of everyone." "Nagasena, food can take life for two reasons: either overeating or because one's heat is depleted. So even healthy food, Nagasena, can take life by improper application."

192 evam-eva kho mahārāja parittaṃ ekacce rakkhati, ekacce na rakkhati. tīhi mahārāja kāraṇehi parittaṃ na rakkhati: kammāvaraṇena kilesāvaraṇena asaddahanatāya. sattānurakkhanaṃ mahārāja parittaṃ attanā katena ārakkhaṃ jahati. yathā mahārāja mātā puttaṃ kucchigataṃ poseti hitena upacārena janeti, janayitvā asuci-mala-siṅghāṇikam-apanetvā uttamavarasugandhaṃ upalimpati, pare akkosante vā paharante vā ākampitahadayā ākaḍḍhitvā sāmino upaneti, yadi pana tassā putto aparaddho hoti velātivatto atha naṃ sā daṇḍa-muggara-jāṇu-muṭṭhīhi hanati potheti; api nu kho mahārāja tassa mātā labhati ākaḍḍhana-parikaḍḍhanaṃ gāhaṃ sāmino upanayanaṃ kātun-ti.

193 na hi bhante ti. kena kāraṇena mahārājāti. attano bhante aparādhenāti. evam-eva kho mahārāja sattānaṃ ārakkhaṃ parittaṃ attano aparādhena vañjhaṃ karotīti. sādhu bhante nāgasena, suvinicchito pañho, gahanaṃ agahanaṃ kataṃ, andhakāro āloko kato, viniveṭhitaṃ diṭṭhijālaṃ, tvaṃ gaṇivarapavaram-āsajjāti.

194 bhante nāgasena, tumhe bhaṇatha: lābhī tathāgato cīvara-piṇḍapāta-senāsana gilānapaccayabhesajja-parikkhārānan-ti. puna ca: tathāgato pañcasālaṃ brāhmaṇagāmaṃ piṇḍāya pavisitvā kiñcid-eva alabhitvā yathā-dhotena pattena nikkhanto ti. yadi bhante nāgasena tathāgato lābhī cīvara-piṇḍapāta-senāsana-gilānapaccaya-bhesajja-parikkhār-

"And so it is with a protective charm. It protects some but fails to protect others. There are three reasons a protective charm would fail to protect: an obstruction of karma, an obstruction of the defilements, or lack of faith. A protective charm that saves beings could fail because of something one did. Consider the mother who nourishes a son in her womb, gives birth to him with careful attendance, and having given birth, cleans him of impurities, stains, and mucus, and rubs him with highest quality perfumes. Should anyone scold or strike the child, her heart thumps and she drags the offender before her husband. But if her son is naughty or tardy, she strikes and spanks him with a rod or club over her knee, or with her hands. Great king, should this mother then be grabbed, dragged, and hauled up before her husband? 192

"No, sir." 193

"For what reason, great king?"

"Because it was his own fault, sir."

"So too, great king, it is because of one's own fault that a protective charm that saves beings fails."

"Excellent, Revered Nagasena. The dilemma is well decided, the thicket is cleared, the darkness made light, and the net of wrong views unraveled. You have joined the ranks of the finest and most distinguished teachers.

"Revered Nagasena, you say: 'The Tathagata received the requisites of a robe, alms bowl, lodging, and medicines for sickness.' But there is also this: 'The Tathagata entered the Brahman village Five Sal Trees for alms, but he received nothing. He left with bowl still clean.' Nagasena, if the Tathagata received the requisites of robe, alms bowl, lodging, and medicine for sickness, then it is false to claim that he 194

ānaṃ, tena hi: pañcasālaṃ brāhmaṇa-gāmaṃ piṇḍāya pavisitvā kiñcid-eva alabhitvā yathā-dhotena pattena nikkhanto ti yaṃ vacanaṃ taṃ micchā. yadi pañcasālaṃ brāhmaṇagāmaṃ piṇḍāya pavisitvā kiñcid-eva alabhitvā yathādhotena pattena nikkhanto, tena hi: lābhī tathāgato cīvara-piṇḍapāta-senāsana-gilānapaccayabhesajja-parikkhārānan-ti tam-pi vacanaṃ micchā. ayam-pi ubhatokoṭiko pañho sumahanto dunnibbedho tavānuppatto, so tayā nibbāhitabbo ti.

195 lābhī mahārāja tathāgato cīvara-piṇḍapāta-senāsana-gilānapaccayabhesajja-parikkhārānaṃ. pañcasālañ-ca brāhmaṇagāmaṃ piṇḍāya pavisitvā kiñcid-eva alabhitvā yathādhotena pattena nikkhanto. tañ-ca pana mārassa pāpimato kāraṇā ti. tena hi bhante nāgasena bhagavato gaṇanapathaṃ vītivattakappe abhisaṅkhataṃ kusalaṃ kin-ti niṭṭhitaṃ, adhunuṭṭhitena mārena pāpimatā taṃ kusalaṃ balavegavihāraṃ kin-ti pihitaṃ. tena hi bhante nāgasena tasmiṃ vatthusmiṃ dvīsu ṭhānesu upavādo āgacchati: kusalato pi akusalaṃ balavataraṃ hoti, buddhabalato pi mārabalaṃ balavataraṃ hotīti. tena hi rukkhassa mūlato pi aggaṃ bhārataraṃ hoti, guṇasamparikiṇṇato pi pāpiyaṃ balavataṃ hotīti.

196 na mahārāja tāvatakena kusalato pi akusalaṃ balavataraṃ nāma hoti buddhabalato ca mārabalaṃ balavataraṃ nāma hoti. api c' ettha kāraṇaṃ icchitabbaṃ. yathā mahārāja puriso rañño cakkavattissa madhuṃ vā madhupiṇḍikaṃ vā aññaṃ vā upāyanaṃ abhihareyya, tamenaṃ rañño dvārapālo evaṃ vadeyya: akālo bho ayaṃ rañño dassanāya, tena hi bho

sought alms in the Brahman village Five Sal Trees, received nothing, and left with bowl still clean. Alternatively, if he entered the Brahman village Five Sal Trees for alms, received nothing, and left with bowl still clean, then it is false to claim that the Tathagata received the requisites of robe, alms bowl, lodging, and medicine for sickness. This too is a very important and difficult two-pronged dilemma that has now reached you, and you must solve it."

"Great king, the Tathagata did receive the requisites of 195
robe, alms bowl, lodging, and medicine for sickness. And he did enter the Brahman village Five Sal Trees for alms, received nothing, and left with bowl still clean. But the cause of this was Mara, the wicked one."

"But then how was it that the merit made by the Bhagavan for eons of time came to an end? Nagasena, how could merit enduring with such force and power be obstructed by the wicked Mara suddenly rearing up? Therefore, a fault arises with regard to both positions on this matter. Either demerit is stronger than merit, or the power of Mara is stronger than the power of the Buddha. Then the crown of a tree is heavier than the base, and wickedness is stronger than a pile of virtues."

"Great king, it is not enough to claim that demerit is stron- 196
ger than merit and that the power of Mara is stronger than the power of the Buddha. Yet further reasoning is wanted here. Great king, consider a man taking honey, a delicacy made with honey, or some other tribute to a wheel-turning emperor. But suppose the king's doorkeeper were to tell him, 'This is a bad time to see the king, and you should take your tribute and turn back quickly before the king inflicts

tava upāyanaṃ gahetvā sīghasīghaṃ paṭinivatta pure tava rājā daṇḍaṃ dhāressatīti, tato so puriso daṇḍabhayā tasito ubbiggo taṃ upāyanaṃ ādāya sīghasīghaṃ paṭinivatteyya; api nu kho so mahārāja cakkavattī tāvatakena upāyanavikalamattakena dvārapālato dubbalataro nāma hoti, aññaṃ vā pana kiñci upāyanaṃ na labheyyāti.

197 na hi bhante, issāpakato so bhante dvārapālo upāyanaṃ nivāresi, aññena pana dvārena satasahassaguṇam-pi rañño upāyanaṃ upetīti. evam-eva kho mahārāja issāpakato māro pāpimā pañcasālake brāhmaṇagahapatike anvāvisi, aññāni pana anekāni devatāsatasahassāni amataṃ dibbaṃ ojaṃ gahetvā upagatāni: bhagavato kāye ojaṃ odahissāmāti bhagavantaṃ namassamānā pañjalikā ṭhitānīti.

198 hotu bhante nāgasena, sulabhā bhagavato cattāro paccayā loke uttamapurisassa, yācitova bhagavā devamanussehi cattāro paccaye paribhuñjati; api ca kho pana mārassa yo adhippāyo so tāvatakena siddho yaṃ so bhagavato bhojanassa antarāyam-akāsi. ettha me bhante kaṅkhā na chijjati, vimatijātohaṃ tattha saṃsayapakkhanno, na me tattha mānasaṃ pakkhandati yaṃ tathāgatassa arahato sammāsambuddhassa sadevake loke aggapuggalavarassa kusalavarapuññasambhavassa asamassa anupamassa appaṭisamassa chavakaṃ lāmakaṃ parittaṃ pāpam-anariyaṃ māro lābhantarāyam-akāsīti.

a punishment on you.' The man would be anxious and terrified of the threat of punishment, and would take the tribute and turn back with great haste. Does this mean that the wheel-turning emperor is weaker than the doorkeeper merely because he was deprived of this trifling tribute? And that he would never receive further tribute?"

"No, sir. Because the doorkeeper was envious, he sent 197
away the tribute, but a tribute to the king that is a hundred thousand times better may arrive by another door."

"It is the same, great king, for the wicked Mara, who, out of envy, took possession of the Brahman householders at Five Sal Trees. But then many hundred thousand other gods bearing divine and nourishing ambrosia arrived. Thinking, *We will provide nourishment for the Bhagavan's body,* they stood before the Bhagavan with hands placed together, honoring him."

"It may be then, Nagasena, that the four requisites of the 198
Bhagavan, supreme person in the world, were easily acquired. Entreated by gods and humans, the Bhagavan enjoyed the four requisites. Still, Mara's intention was successful to the extent that he created an obstacle to the Bhagavan's meal. My hesitation has not been removed on this point, sir, and, skeptical, I remain in doubt on the matter. Indeed, my mind does not take to the notion that wicked Mara, wretched, insignificant, and inferior, obstructed the receiving of alms by someone not his equal, his match, or his equivalent, that is, the Tathagata, an arhat, perfectly awakened, the best of best persons in the world with its gods, and the origin of the most excellent merit and goodness."

199 cattāro kho mahārāja antarāyā: adiṭṭhantarāyo uddissakatantarāyo upakkhaṭantarāyo paribhogantarāyo ti. tattha adiṭṭhantarāyo nāma: anodissa adassanena abhisaṅkhaṭaṃ koci antarāyaṃ karoti: kiṃ parassa dinnenāti, ayaṃ adiṭṭhantarāyo nāma. katamo uddissakatantarāyo: idh' ekaccaṃ puggalaṃ upadisitvā uddissa bhojanaṃ paṭiyattaṃ hoti, taṃ koci antarāyaṃ karoti, ayaṃ uddissakatantarāyo nāma. katamo upakkhaṭantarāyo: idha yaṃ kiñci upakkhaṭaṃ hoti appaṭiggahītaṃ tattha koci antarāyaṃ karoti, ayaṃ upakkhaṭantarāyo nāma. katamo paribhogantarāyo: idha yaṃ kiñci paribhogaṃ tattha koci antarāyaṃ karoti, ayaṃ paribhogantarāyo nāma. ime kho mahārāja cattāro antarāyā.

200 yaṃ pana māro pāpimā pañcasālake brāhmaṇagahapatike anvāvisi, taṃ n'eva bhagavato paribhogaṃ na upakkhaṭaṃ na uddissakataṃ, anāgataṃ asampattaṃ adassanena antarāyaṃ kataṃ; taṃ pana n' ekassa bhagavato yeva, atha kho ye tena samayena nikkhantā abbhāgatā sabbe pi te taṃ divasaṃ bhojanaṃ na labhiṃsu. nāhan-taṃ mahārāja passāmi sadevake loke samārake sabrahmake sassamaṇabrāhmaṇiyā pajāya sadevamanussāya yo tassa bhagavato uddissakataṃ upakkhataṃ paribhogaṃ antarāyaṃ kareyya; sace koci

"Great king, there are four situations when obstacles occur in giving:[32] there is an obstacle when the recipient is unspecified, an obstacle when the recipient is specified, an obstacle when the gift has been prepared, and an obstacle to the enjoyment of the gift. In the case of an obstacle occurring when the recipient is unspecified, someone creates an obstacle to giving in general, even when there is no particular recipient visible, saying, 'Why give to anyone?' This is an obstacle when the recipient is unspecified. What about an obstacle when the recipient is specified? Here a particular person is specified and food is made ready, but someone creates an obstacle. What about an obstacle when the gift has been prepared? In this case, something is prepared but before it is received someone creates an obstacle. What is an obstacle to the enjoyment of the gift? Just when something is to be enjoyed, someone creates an obstacle. This is called an obstacle to the enjoyment. These are the four obstacles, great king. 199

"When the wicked Mara took possession of the Brahman householders at Five Sal Trees, food had neither been prepared nor specified for the Bhagavan. The obstacle was created invisibly for those not yet arrived or present. For it was not just the Bhagavan. Every guest who set out there on that day failed to receive a meal. In the world and the heavens, among the generations of gods and humans, and among Maras, Brahmas, renouncers, and Brahmans, I do not see anyone who could create an obstacle to a meal prepared and specified for the Bhagavan. Should someone, out of envy, create an obstacle to a meal prepared and specified 200

issāya uddissakaṭaṃ upakkhaṭaṃ paribhogaṃ antarāyaṃ kareyya phaleyya tassa muddhā satadhā vā sahassadhā vā.

201 cattārome mahārāja tathāgatassa kenaci anāvaraṇīyā guṇā, katame cattāro: lābho mahārāja bhagavato uddissakato upakkhaṭo na sakkā kenaci antarāyaṃ kātuṃ, sarīrānugatā mahārāja bhagavato byāmappabhā na sakkā kenaci antarāyaṃ kātuṃ, sabbaññutaṃ mahārāja bhagavato ñāṇaratanaṃ na sakkā kenaci antarāyaṃ kātuṃ, jīvitaṃ mahārāja bhagavato na sakkā kenaci antarāyaṃ kātuṃ. ime kho mahārāja cattāro tathāgatassa kenaci anāvaraṇīyā guṇā. sabbe p' ete mahārāja guṇā ekarasā arogā akuppā aparūpakkamā, aphusāni kiriyāni. adassanena mahārāja māro pāpimā nilīyitvā pañcasālake brāhmaṇagahapatike anvāvisi. yathā mahārāja rañño paccante dese visame adassanena nilīyitvā corā panthaṃ dūsenti, yadi pana rājā te core passeyya api nu kho te corā sotthiṃ labheyyun-ti.

202 na hi bhante, pharasunā phālāpeyya satadhā vā sahassadhā vā ti. evam-eva kho mahārāja adassanena māro pāpimā nilīyitvā pañcasālake brāhmaṇagahapatike anvāvisi. yathā vā pana mahārāja itthī sapatikā adassanena nilīyitvā parapurisaṃ sevati, evam-eva kho mahārāja adassanena māro pāpimā nilīyitvā pañcasālake brāhmaṇagahapatike anāvisi; yadi mahārāja itthī sāmikassa sammukhā parapurisaṃ sevati, api nu kho sā itthī sotthiṃ labheyyāti.

for him, that person's head would split into a hundred or a thousand pieces.

"Great king, the Tathagata has four special qualities that 201
are impossible for anyone to obstruct. What are the four? It is not possible for anyone to create an obstacle to the Bhagavan's receiving something prepared and specified for him. No one can obstruct the Bhagavan's fathom-long halo radiating from his body. No one can obstruct the jewel of knowledge that is the Bhagavan's omniscience. And it is not possible for anyone to obstruct his life. Great king, these are the four qualities of the Tathagata that no one can obstruct. All of these qualities have the same function in that they are salubrious, steadfast, and unassailable, and their activities are invulnerable. Great king, it was the wicked Mara, lurking unseen, who took possession of the Brahman householders at Five Sal Trees. It is just like how robbers lurk unseen in a dangerous place at the outskirts of the kingdom and then ambush those on the road. But should the king see the robbers, do you think the robbers would be safe?"

"No, sir. He would take a hatchet and hack them into a 202
hundred or a thousand pieces."

"So too with the wicked Mara lurking unseen and taking possession of the Brahman householders at Five Sal Trees. It is just like how a married woman lurks unseen and embraces another man. In much the same way the wicked Mara lurked unseen and took possession of the Brahman householders at Five Sal Trees. Great king, if that woman while embracing another man encountered her husband, do you think the woman would be safe?"

203 na hi bhante, haneyyāpi taṃ bhante sāmiko, vadheyyāpi bandheyyāpi, dāsittaṃ vā upaneyyāti. evam-eva kho mahārāja adassanena māro pāpimā nilīyitvā pañcasālake brāhmaṇagahapatike anvāvisi. yadi mahārāja māro pāpimā bhagavato uddissakataṃ upakkhataṃ paribhogaṃ antarāyaṃ kareyya phaleyya tassa muddhā satadhā vā sahassadhā vā ti.

204 evam-etaṃ bhante nāgasena, corikāya kataṃ mārena pāpimatā, nilīyitvā māro pāpimā pañcasālake brāhmaṇagahapatike anvāvisi. sace so bhante māro pāpimā bhagavato uddissakataṃ upakkhataṃ paribhogaṃ antarāyaṃ kareyya, muddhā vā 'ssa phaleyya satadhā vā sahassadhā vā, kāyo vā 'ssa bhusamuṭṭhi viya vikireyya. sādhu bhante nāgasena, evam-etaṃ, tathā sampaṭicchāmīti.

205 bhante nāgasena, tumhe bhaṇatha: yo ajānanto pāṇātipataṃ karoti so balavataraṃ apuññaṃ pasavatīti. puna ca bhagavatā vinayapaṇṇattiyā bhaṇitaṃ: anāpatti ajānantassāti. yadi bhante nāgasena ajānitvā pāṇātipātaṃ karonto balavataraṃ apuññaṃ pasavati, tena hi: anāpatti ajānantassāti yaṃ vacanaṃ taṃ micchā. yadi anāpatti ajānantassa, tena hi: ajānitvā pāṇātipātaṃ karonto balavataraṃ apuññaṃ pasavatīti tam-pi vacanaṃ micchā. ayam-pi ubhatokoṭiko pañho duruttaro duratikkamo tavānuppatto, so tayā nibbāhitabbo ti.

206 bhāsitam-p' etaṃ mahārāja bhagavatā: yo ajānanto pāṇātipātaṃ karoti so balavataraṃ apuññaṃ pasavatīti. puna ca vinayapaṇṇattiyā pi bhagavatā bhaṇitaṃ: anāpatti ajānantas-

"No, sir, the husband might strike her, kill her, tie her up, 203
or force her into slavery."

"So too with the wicked Mara, great king. He lurked unseen and possessed the Brahman householders at Five Sal Trees. And in fact, had the wicked Mara obstructed a meal prepared and designated for the Bhagavan, his head would have split into a hundred or a thousand pieces."

"Revered Nagasena, when the wicked Mara lurked 204
and took possession of the Brahman householders at Five Sal Trees, he acted much like the robbers. And if the wicked Mara had obstructed a meal prepared and specified for the Bhagavan, his head would have split into a hundred or a thousand pieces, or else his body would have been scattered about like a handful of chaff. Very well, sir, I accept this.

"Revered Nagasena, you say: 'Whoever takes life unknow- 205
ingly produces stronger demerit.' But the Bhagavan also said this when laying down the *vinaya:* 'There is no offense for one who does not know.' Nagasena, if it is the case that one who destroys life unknowingly makes stronger demerit, then saying that there is no offense for one who does not know is false. And if there is no offense for one who does not know, then the claim that one who destroys life unknowingly produces stronger demerit must be false. This two-pronged dilemma is hard to get out of and hard to overcome. It has reached you, and you must solve it."

"Great king, the Bhagavan did say, 'Whoever takes life 206
unknowingly produces stronger demerit.' And when laying down the *vinaya,* the Bhagavan did say, 'There is no offense for one who does not know.' There is a difference in meaning

sāti. tattha atthantaraṃ atthi, katamaṃ atthantaraṃ: atthi mahārāja āpatti saññāvimokkhā, atthi āpatti no saññāvimokkhā; yā 'yaṃ mahārāja āpatti saññāvimokkhā taṃ āpattiṃ ārabbha bhagavatā bhaṇitaṃ: anāpatti ajānantassāti. sādhu bhante nāgasena, evam-etaṃ, tathā sampaṭicchāmīti.

207 bhante nāgasena, bhāsitam-p' etaṃ bhagavatā: tathāgatassa kho ānanda na evaṃ hoti: ahaṃ bhikkhusaṅghaṃ pariharissāmīti vā, mamuddesiko bhikkhusaṅgho ti vā ti. puna ca metteyyassa bhagavato sabhāvaguṇaṃ paridīpayamānena evaṃ bhaṇitaṃ: so anekasahassaṃ bhikkhusaṅghaṃ pariharissati seyyathā pi ahaṃ etarahi anekasataṃ bhikkhusaṅghaṃ pariharāmīti. yadi bhante nāgasena bhagavatā bhaṇitaṃ: tathāgatassa kho ānanda na evaṃ hoti: ahaṃ bhikkhusaṅghaṃ pariharāmīti vā, mamuddesiko bhikkhusaṅgho ti vā ti, tena hi: anekasataṃ bhikkhusaṅghaṃ pariharāmīti yaṃ vacanaṃ taṃ micchā. yadi tathāgatena bhaṇitaṃ: seyyathā pi ahaṃ etarahi anekasataṃ bhikkhusaṅghaṃ pariharāmīti, tena hi: tathāgatassa kho ānanda na evaṃ hoti: ahaṃ bhikkhusaṅghaṃ pariharāmīti vā, mamuddesiko bhikkhusaṅgho ti vā ti tam-pi vacanaṃ micchā. ayam-pi ubhatokoṭiko pañho tavānuppatto, so tayā nibbāhitabbo ti.

208 bhāsitam-p' etaṃ mahārāja bhagavatā: tathāgatassa kho ānanda na evaṃ hoti: ahaṃ bhikkhusaṅghaṃ pariharāmīti vā, mamuddesiko bhikkhusaṅgho ti vā ti. metteyyassāpi bhagavato sabhāvaguṇaṃ paridīpayamānena bhagavatā

in the cases. What is the difference in meaning? Great king, there is a kind of offense that has perception as a ground for acquittal, and there is a kind of offense that does not have perception as a ground for acquittal.[33] It was with respect to the offense that has perception as a ground for acquittal that the Bhagavan spoke when he said, 'There is no offense for one who does not know.'"

"Very well, Nagasena. I accept this.

"Revered Nagasena, the Bhagavan also said: 'Ananda, 207
it does not occur to the Tathagata to say, "I will lead the community of monks," and "The community of monks should defer to me."' But once when he was explaining the nature and qualities of the Bhagavan Metteyya, he said, 'He will lead a community of several thousand monks, just as I am now leading a community of several hundred monks.' Nagasena, if the Bhagavan said, 'Ananda, it does not occur to the Tathagata to say, "I will lead the community of monks," and "The community of monks should defer to me,"' then the claim 'I am leading a community of several hundred monks' is false. Alternatively, if the Bhagavan said, 'Just as I am now leading a community of several hundred monks,' then the claim about not leading the community of monks, and that the community should not defer to him, is false. This two-pronged dilemma has reached you, and you must solve it."

"Great king, the Bhagavan did say, 'Ananda, it does not 208
occur to the Tathagata to say, "I will lead the community of monks," and "The community of monks should defer to me."' And when he was explaining the nature and qualities of the Bhagavan Metteyya, he did say, 'He will lead a commu-

bhaṇitaṃ: so anekasahassaṃ bhikkhusaṅghaṃ pariharissati seyyathā pi ahaṃ etarahi anekasataṃ bhikkhusaṅghaṃ pariharāmīti. etasmiñ-ca mahārāja pañhe eko attho sāvaseso, eko attho niravaseso. na mahārāja tathāgato parisāya anugāmiko, parisā pana tathāgatassa anugāmikā. sammuti mahārāja esā: ahan-ti, mamāti, na paramattho eso. vigataṃ mahārāja tathāgatassa pemaṃ, vigato sineho, mayhan-ti pi tathāgatassa gahaṇaṃ natthi, upādāya pana avassayo hoti. yathā mahārāja paṭhavī bhummaṭṭhānaṃ sattānaṃ patiṭṭhā hoti upassayaṃ hoti, paṭhaviṭṭhā c' ete sattā, na ca mahāpaṭhaviyā: mayh' ete ti apekkhā hoti; evam-eva kho mahārāja tathāgato sabbasattānaṃ patiṭṭhā hoti upassayaṃ, tathāgataṭṭhā c' ete sattā, na ca tathāgatassa: mayh'ete ti apekkhā hoti.

209 yathā vā pana mahatimahāmegho abhivassanto tiṇarukkha-pasu-manussānaṃ vuddhiṃ deti santatim-anupāleti, vuṭṭhūpajīvino c' ete sattā sabbe, na ca mahāmeghassa: mayh' ete ti apekkhā hoti; evam-eva kho mahārāja tathāgato sabbasattānaṃ kusaladhamme janeti anupāleti, satthūpajīvino c' ete sattā sabbe, na ca tathāgatassa: mayh' ete ti apekkhā hoti; taṃ kissa hetu: attānudiṭṭhiyā pahīnattā ti.

210 sādhu bhante nāgasena, sunibbeṭhito pañho bahuvidhehi kāraṇehi, gambhīro uttānīkato, gaṇṭhi bhinno, gahanaṃ agahanaṃ kataṃ, andhakāro āloko kato, bhaggā parappavādā, jinaputtānaṃ cakkhuṃ uppāditan-ti.

nity of several thousand monks, just as I am now leading a community of several hundred monks.' But in this dilemma, one meaning is incomplete and one meaning is complete. Great king, the Tathagata does not seek a following; rather the following seeks him. Additionally, 'I' and 'me' are conventional and do not have an absolute sense. In the case of the Tathagata, affection has ended and love has ceased, and the Tathagata does not grasp onto anything as 'mine.' Yet although he does not grasp, he is a support. The earth is a foundation and home for terrestrial creatures, and these beings live on the earth. Still, the great earth does not long for them, saying, 'They are mine.' Similarly, great king, the Tathagata is a foundation and home for all beings. Beings stay with the Tathagata even though the Tathagata does not long for them, saying, 'They are mine.'

"Consider a massive and huge cloud raining and causing 209
grasses, trees, animals, and humans to grow, providing their sustenance. While all beings subsist on the rain, the massive cloud does not long for them, saying, 'They are mine.' Similarly, great king, the Tathagata provides for and causes all beings to generate good phenomenal states. Although all beings may subsist on the Teacher, the Tathagata does not long for them, saying, 'They are mine.' Why is this? It is because he has abandoned a false view of self."

"Excellent, revered Nagasena. The dilemma has been 210
unraveled with many reasons. Though profound, it has been made clear, and the knot broken, the thicket cleared, the darkness illuminated, and the views of opponents smashed. Vision has arisen for the descendants of the Victor.

211 bhante nāgasena, tumhe bhaṇatha: tathāgato abhejjapariso ti. puna ca bhaṇatha: devadattena ekappahāraṃ pañca bhikkhusatāni bhinnānīti. yadi bhante nāgasena tathāgato abhejjapariso, tena hi: devadattena ekappahāraṃ pañca bhikkhusatāni bhinnānīti yaṃ vacanaṃ taṃ micchā. yadi devadattena ekappahāraṃ pañcabhikkhusatāni bhinnāni, tena hi: tathāgato abhejjapariso ti tam-pi vacanaṃ micchā. ayam-pi ubhatokoṭiko pañho tavānuppatto gambhīro dunniveṭhiyo, gaṇṭhito pi gaṇṭhitaro, etthāyaṃ jano āvaṭo nivuto ovuto pihito pariyonaddho, ettha tava ñāṇabalaṃ dassehi paravādesūti.

212 abhejjapariso mahārāja tathāgato, devadattena ca ekappahāraṃ pañca bhikkhusatāni bhinnāni. tañ-ca pana bhedakassa balena, bhedake vijjamāne na-tthi mahārāja abhejjaṃ nāma. bhedake sati mātā pi puttena bhijjati, putto pi mātarā bhijjati, pitā pi puttena bhijjati, putto pi pitarā bhijjati, bhātā pi bhaginiyā bhijjati, bhaginī pi bhātarā bhijjati, sahāyo pi sahāyena bhijjati, nāvā pi nānādārusanghaṭitā ūmivegasampahārena bhijjati, rukkho pi madhukappasampannaphalo anilabalavegābhihato bhijjati, suvaṇṇam-pi jātivantaṃ lohena bhijjati. api ca mahārāja n' eso adhippāyo viññūnaṃ, n' esā buddhānaṃ adhimutti, n' eso paṇḍitānaṃ chando: tathāgato bhejjapariso ti.

213 api c' ettha kāraṇaṃ atthi yena kāraṇena tathāgato vuccati abhejjapariso ti. katamaṃ ettha kāraṇaṃ: tathāgatassa

"Revered Nagasena, you say: 'The Tathagata has a following that cannot be divided.' But then you say, 'Five hundred monks split off at one stroke of Devadatta.' Nagasena, if the Tathagata has a following that cannot be divided, then the claim that at one stroke Devadatta split off five hundred monks is false. Alternatively, if five hundred monks split off at one stroke of Devadatta, then it is false to say that the Tathagata's following cannot be divided. This deep and difficult two-pronged dilemma has reached you, and it is knottier than a knot. People nowadays are sealed off, veiled, hemmed in, obstructed, closed off, and hidden from it. Please demonstrate the power of your knowledge about the views of opponents." 211

"Great king, the Tathagata has a following that cannot be divided, and five hundred monks did split off at one stroke of Devadatta. However, this is because of the power of the schismatic. It is only when there is no schismatic present that it truly cannot be divided. When there is a schismatic, a mother can be divided from her son, a son from his mother, a father from his son, a son from his father, a brother from his sister, a sister from her brother, and a friend from a friend. A ship held together by various pieces of wood is broken up by the pounding and force of waves, a tree with fruit full of juice and sweetness is split by the power and velocity of wind, and even high-grade gold is broken by metal. Still, it is not the intention of wise people, the aspiration of buddhas, or the wish of the learned that the Tathagata have a following that can be split. 212

In addition, great king, there was a reason that the Tathagata said his following could not be split. What was 213

mahārāja katena ādānena vā appiyavacanena vā anatthacariyāya vā asamānattatāya vā yato kutoci cariyaṃ carantassa pi parisā bhinnā ti na sutapubbaṃ, tena kāraṇena tathāgato vuccati abhejjapariso ti. tayā p' etaṃ mahārāja ñātabbaṃ: atthi kiñci navaṅge buddhavacane suttāgataṃ: iminā nāma kāraṇena bodhisattassa katena tathāgatassa parisā bhinnā ti. na-tthi bhante, no c' etaṃ loke dissati no pi sūyati, sādhu bhante nāgasena, evam-etaṃ, tathā sampaṭicchāmīti.

dutiyo vaggo.

the reason? No one ever heard that the Tathagata had attachment, spoke an unkind word, behaved badly, or lacked impartiality, so how could the following of someone who behaved in such a way have been split? It was for this reason that the Tathagata said that his following could not be split. Therefore, great king, let it be understood: is there anything in the Buddha's ninefold words handed down in the *suttas* that says that the Tathagata's following was split because of something the Bodhisatta did?"

"No sir, no such thing has been seen or heard of. Well done, revered Nagasena. I am convinced."

End of Part 2.

PART 3

214 bhante nāgasena, bhāsitam-p' etaṃ bhagavatā: dhammo hi vāseṭṭha 'seṭṭho jane tasmiṃ'; diṭṭhe c' eva dhamme abhisamparāyañ-cāti. puna ca upāsako gihī sotāpanno pihitāpāyo diṭṭhippatto viññātasāsano bhikkhuṃ vā sāmaṇeraṃ vā puthujjanaṃ abhivādeti paccuṭṭheti. yadi bhante nāgasena bhagavatā bhaṇitaṃ: dhammo hi vāseṭṭha 'seṭṭho jane tasmiṃ'; diṭṭhe c' eva dhamme abhisamparāyañcāti, tena hi: upāsako gihī sotāpanno pihitāpāyo diṭṭhippatto viññātasāsano bhikkhuṃ vā sāmaṇeraṃ vā puthujjanaṃ abhivādeti paccuṭṭhetīti yaṃ vacanaṃ taṃ micchā. yadi upāsako gihī sotāpanno pihitāpāyo diṭṭhippatto viññātasāsano bhikkhuṃ vā sāmaṇeraṃ vā puthujjanaṃ abhivādeti paccuṭṭheti, tena hi: dhammo hi vāseṭṭha seṭṭho jane tasmiṃ; diṭṭhe c' eva dhamme abhisamparāyañcāti, tam-pi vacanaṃ micchā. ayam-pi ubhatokoṭiko pañho tavānuppatto, so tayā nibbāhitabbo ti.

215 bhāsitam-p' etaṃ mahārāja bhagavatā: dhammo hi vāseṭṭha 'seṭṭho jane tasmiṃ'; diṭthe c' eva dhamme abhisamparāyañ-cāti. upāsako ca gihī sotāpanno pihitāpāyo diṭṭhippatto viññātasāsano bhikkhuṃ vā sāmaṇeraṃ vā puthujjanaṃ abhivādeti paccuṭṭheti. tattha pana kāraṇaṃ atthi, katamaṃ taṃ kāraṇaṃ: vīsati kho pan' ime mahārāja

PART 3

"Revered Nagasena, the Bhagavan said this: 'Vasettha, the 214
Dhamma is the best thing for people both here and in the next life.' And yet, a layman householder who is a stream winner, who has closed off the realms of misery, attained right view, and understood the dispensation, still rises and greets respectfully a monk, even if he is just a novice or an ordinary fellow. If the Bhagavan said, 'Vasettha, the Dhamma is the best thing for people both here and in the next life,' then it is surely false to claim that a layman householder who is a stream winner, who has closed off the realms of misery, attained right view and understood the dispensation, still rises and greets respectfully a monk, even a novice or an ordinary fellow. Or if a layman householder who is a stream winner is to greet respectfully a monk, then the claim that the Dhamma is the best thing for people both here and in the next life is false.[34] This two-pronged dilemma has reached you, and it is by you that it must be solved."

"Great king, the Bhagavan did say, 'Vasettha, the Dhamma 215
is the best thing for people both here and in the next life.' And yes, a layman householder who is a stream winner, who has closed off the realms of misery, attained right view, and understood the dispensation, still rises and greets respectfully a monk, even a novice or an ordinary fellow. There is a reason for this. What is the reason? A renouncer is worthy of worship and honor such as rising and greeting with respect because of twenty virtues that make a renouncer a renouncer, as well as two signs. What are these twenty

samaṇassa samaṇakaraṇā dhammā dve ca liṅgāni yehi samaṇo abhivādana-paccuṭṭhāna-sammānana-pūjanāraho hoti. katame vīsati samāṇassa samaṇakaraṇā dhammā dve ca liṅgāni: seṭṭho yamo, aggo niyamo, cāro vihāro saṃyamo saṃvaro khanti soraccaṃ ekattacariyā ekattābhirati paṭisallāṇaṃ hiriottappaṃ viriyaṃ appamādo sikkhāsamādānaṃ uddeso paripucchā sīlādiabhirati nirālayatā sikkhāpadapāripūritā, kāsāvadhāraṇaṃ bhaṇḍubhāvo; ime kho mahārāja vīsati samaṇassa samaṇakaraṇā dhammā dve ca liṅgāni.

216 ete guṇe bhikkhu samādāya vattati, so tesaṃ dhammānaṃ anūnattā paripuṇṇattā sampannattā samannāgatattā asekhabhūmiṃ arahantabhūmiṃ okkamati, seṭṭhaṃ bhummantaraṃ okkamati, arahattāsannagato ti arahati upāsako sotāpanno bhikkhuṃ puthujjanaṃ abhivādetuṃ paccuṭṭhātuṃ. khīṇāsavehi so sāmaññaṃ upagato, na-tthi me so samayo ti arahati upāsako sotāpanno bhikkhuṃ puthujjanaṃ abhivādetuṃ paccuṭṭhātuṃ. aggaparisaṃ so upagato, nāhan-taṃ ṭhānaṃ upagato ti arahati upāsako sotāpanno bhikkhuṃ puthujjanaṃ abhivādetuṃ paccuṭṭhātuṃ.

217 labhati so pātimokkhuddesaṃ sotuṃ, nāhan-taṃ labhāmi sotun-ti arahati upāsako sotāpanno bhikkhuṃ puthujjanaṃ abhivādetuṃ paccuṭṭhātuṃ. so aññe pabbājeti upasampādeti, jinasāsanaṃ vaḍḍheti, aham-etaṃ na labhāmi kātun-ti arahati upāsako sotāpanno bhikkhuṃ puthujjanaṃ abhivādetuṃ paccuṭṭhātuṃ. appamāṇesu so sikkhāpadesu samattakārī, nāhaṃ tesu vattāmīti arahati upāsako sot-

virtues that make a renouncer a renouncer, and the two signs? The best restraint, the highest self-control, behavior, way of living, command, discipline, forbearance, gentleness, wandering in solitude, delight in solitude, seclusion, shame and apprehension, exertion, diligence, taking of the precepts, recitation, questioning, delighting in such things as moral discipline, homelessness, and fulfilling the monastic training; the signs are wearing the saffron robe and being shaved. These, great king, are the twenty virtues that make a renouncer a renouncer, and the two signs.

"A monk lives having taken up these qualities. By possess- 216
ing these virtues entirely, completely, and successfully, he approaches the perfect level, the level of an arhat. He reaches the best level of existence and becomes an arhat. Thinking this, a layman stream winner finds the monk worth rising for and greeting with respect, even if he is just an ordinary fellow.[35] Thinking, *It is he who has approached the company of those who have destroyed the flaws, while this crowd is not mine,* a lay stream winner finds even the ordinary monk worth
rising for and greeting with respect. Thinking, *It is he who* 217
has joined the assembly of the best, while I have not reached this position, a lay stream winner finds even the ordinary monk worth rising for and greeting with respect. Thinking, *It is he who is able to hear the recitation of the Patimokkha rules, while I am not able to hear it,* a lay stream winner finds even the ordinary monk worth rising for and greeting with respect. Thinking, *It is he who admits and ordains others, growing the dispensation of the Victor, while I am not able to do this,* a lay stream winner finds even the ordinary monk worth rising for and greeting with respect. Thinking, *It is he who fully*

āpanno bhikkhuṃ puthujjanaṃ abhivādetuṃ paccuṭṭhātuṃ. upagato so samaṇaliṅgaṃ, buddhādhippāye ṭhito, tenāhaṃ liṅgena dūram-apagato ti arahati upāsako sotāpanno bhikkhuṃ puthujjanaṃ abhivādetuṃ paccuṭṭhātuṃ. 'parūḷhakacchalomo so anañjita-amaṇḍito, 'anulittasīlagandho, ahaṃ pana maṇḍana-vibhūsanābhirato ti arahati upāsako sotāpanno bhikkhuṃ puthujjanaṃ abhivādetuṃ paccuṭṭhātuṃ.

218 api ca mahārāja: ye te vīsati samaṇakaraṇā dhammā dve ca liṅgāni sabbe p' ete dhammā bhikkhussa saṃvijjanti, so yeva te dhamme dhāreti aññe pi tattha sikkhāpeti, so me āgamo sikkhāpanañ-ca na-tthīti arahati upāsako sotāpanno bhikkhuṃ puthujjanaṃ abhivādetuṃ paccuṭṭhātuṃ. api ca yathā mahārāja rājakumāro purohitassa santike vijjaṃ adhīyati khattadhammaṃ sikkhati, so aparena samayena abhisitto ācariyaṃ abhivādeti paccuṭṭheti: sikkhāpako me ayan-ti; evam-eva kho mahārāja: sikkhāpako vaṃsadharo ti arahati upāsako sotāpanno bhikkhuṃ puthujjanaṃ abhivādetuṃ paccuṭṭhātuṃ.

219 api ca mahārāja iminā p' etaṃ pariyāyena jānāhi bhikkhubhūmiyā mahantataṃ asamavipulabhāvaṃ: yadi mahārāja upāsako sotāpanno arahattaṃ sacchikaroti, dveva tassa gatiyo bhavanti, anaññā: tasmiṃ yeva divase parinibbāyeyya

practices endless rules, not I, a lay stream winner finds even the ordinary monk worth rising for and greeting with respect. Thinking, *It is he who has achieved the sign of a recluse and is established within the Buddha's intentions, while I am far removed from the sign,* a lay stream winner finds even the ordinary monk worth rising for and greeting with respect. Thinking, *He may have long armpit hair, nails, and body hair, and is neither perfumed nor ornamented; yet he is fragrant with the anointing of moral discipline, while I am fond of ornaments and adornments,* a layman who is a stream winner finds the monk, even just an ordinary fellow, worth rising for and greeting with respect.

"And furthermore, great king, the lay stream winner 218
considers that *the twenty virtues that make a recluse and the two signs are all found in a monk. It is he who possesses these virtues and trains others in them; this practice and rule are not for me,* and so he finds even an ordinary monk worth rising for and greeting respectfully. Great king, it is like a royal prince who studies the knowledge of the Brahman priest and trains in statecraft. Later he is instated as king, but he still rises and greets his teacher respectfully, thinking, *He is my instructor.* In the same way, great king, the lay stream winner should rise and greet respectfully even the ordinary monk, thinking, *He is an instructor upholding a lineage.*

"Great king, by a further method of teaching you should 219
realize the greatness and unequaled magnitude of the level of a monk. If a layman who is a stream winner becomes an arhat, there are only two possible destinies for him. Either he will attain final nibbana on that very day, or he will ordain

vā bhikkhubhāvaṃ vā upagaccheyya; acalā hi sā mahārāja pabbajjā mahatī accuggatā, yad-idaṃ bhikkhubhūmīti.

220 ñāṇagato bhante nāgasena pañho sunibbeṭhito balavatā atibuddhinā tayā, na-y-imaṃ pañhaṃ samattho añño evaṃ viniveṭhetuṃ aññatra tavādisena buddhimatā ti.

221 bhante nāgasena, tumhe bhaṇatha: tathāgato sabbasattānaṃ ahitam-apanetvā hitam-upadahatīti. puna ca bhaṇatha: aggikkhandhūpame dhammapariyāye bhaññamāne saṭṭhimattānaṃ bhikkhūnaṃ uṇhalohitaṃ mukhato uggatan-ti. aggikkhandhūpamaṃ bhante dhammapariyāyaṃ desentena tathāgatena saṭṭhimattānaṃ bhikkhūnaṃ hitam-apanetvā ahitam-upadahitaṃ. yadi bhante nāgasena tathāgato sabbasattānaṃ ahitam-apanetvā hitam-upadahati, tena hi: aggikkhandhūpame dhammapariyāye bhaññamāne saṭṭhimattānaṃ bhikkhūnaṃ uṇhalohitaṃ mukhato uggatan-ti yaṃ vacanaṃ taṃ micchā. yadi aggikkhandhūpame dhammapariyāye bhaññamāne saṭṭhimattānaṃ bhikkhūnaṃ uṇhalohitaṃ mukhato uggataṃ, tena hi: tathāgato sabbasattānaṃ ahitam-apanetvā hitam-upadahatīti tam-pi vacanaṃ micchā. ayam pi ubhatokoṭiko pañho tavānuppatto, so tayā nibbāhitabbo ti.

222 tathāgato mahārāja sabbasattānaṃ ahitam-apanetvā hitam-upadahati. aggikkhandhūpame ca dhammapariyāye bhaññamāne saṭṭhimattānaṃ bhikkhūnaṃ uṇhalohitaṃ mukhato uggataṃ. tañ-ca pana na tathāgatassa katena, tesaṃ yeva attano katenāti. yadi bhante nāgasena tathāgato aggikkhandhūpamaṃ dhammapariyāyaṃ na bhāseyya, api nu tesaṃ uṇhalohitaṃ mukhato uggaccheyyāti.

as a monk. Ordination is truly steady, great, and lofty, and it is the level of the monk."

"The dilemma has been approached with knowledge, Nagasena, and unraveled superbly by the power of your intellect. Without an intellect such as yours, no one else but you could resolve it. 220

"Revered Nagasena, you say: 'The Tathagata removes harm and provides welfare for all beings.' Yet you also say, 'While he was preaching the simile of the mass of fire, a teaching on the Dhamma, hot blood gushed from the mouths of as many as sixty monks.'[36] By preaching this teaching of the Dhamma, the simile of the mass of fire, sir, the Tathagata surely removed benefit and caused harm to those sixty monks. If it is the case that the Tathagata removes harm and provides welfare for all beings, then it must be false to say that while he was preaching the simile of the mass of fire, a teaching on the Dhamma, hot blood gushed from the mouths of as many as sixty monks. Alternatively, if, while he was teaching the simile of the mass fire, hot blood gushed from the mouths of sixty monks, then it is false to say that he removes harm and provides benefit. This two-pronged dilemma has reached you, and you must solve it." 221

"Great king, the Tathagata does remove harm and provide benefit for all beings. And it is true that when he was teaching the mass of fire simile, a teaching on the Dhamma, hot blood gushed from the mouths of sixty monks. But the Tathagata did not do this. They themselves did it." 222

"Still, Nagasena, if the Tathagata had not taught the mass of fire simile in the teaching on the Dhamma, hot blood would not have gushed from their mouths."

223 na hi mahārāja, micchā paṭipannānaṃ tesaṃ bhagavato dhammapariyāyaṃ sutvā pariḷāho kāye uppajji, tena tesaṃ pariḷāhena uṇhalohitaṃ mukhato uggatan-ti. tena hi bhante nāgasena tathāgatass' eva katena tesaṃ uṇhalohitaṃ mukhato uggataṃ, tathāgato yeva tattha adhikāro tesaṃ nāsanāya. yathā nāma bhante nāgasena ahi vammīkaṃ paviseyya, ath' aññataro paṃsukāmo puriso vammīkaṃ bhinditvā paṃsuṃ hareyya, tassa paṃsuharaṇena vammīkassa susiraṃ pidaheyya, atha tatth' eva so assāsaṃ alabhamāno mareyya; nanu so bhante ahi tassa purisassa katena maraṇam-patto ti.

224 āma mahārājāti. evam-eva kho bhante nāgasena tathāgato yeva tattha adhikāro tesaṃ nāsanāyāti. tathāgato mahārāja dhammaṃ desayamāno anunayapaṭighaṃ na karoti, anunaya-paṭighavippamutto dhammaṃ deseti, evaṃ dhamme desiyamāne ye tattha sammā paṭipannā te bujjhanti, ye pana micchā paṭipannā te patanti. yathā mahārāja purisassa ambaṃva jambuṃ vā madhukaṃ vā cālayamānassa yāni tattha phalāni sārāni daḷhabandhanāni tāni tatth' eva accutāni tiṭṭhanti, yāni pana tattha phalāni pūtivaṇṭamūlāni dubbalabandhanāni tāni patanti; evam-eva kho mahārāja tathāgato dhammaṃ desayamāno anunayapaṭighaṃ na karoti, anunayapaṭighavippamutto dhammaṃ deseti, evaṃ dhamme desiyamāne ye tattha sammā paṭipannā te bujjhanti; ye pana micchā paṭipannā te patanti.

225 yathā vā pana mahārāja kassako dhaññaṃ ropetukāmo khettaṃ kasati, tassa kasantassa anekasatasahassāni tiṇāni

"No, great king. A fever arises in the body of those who 223
are practicing wrongly who hear the Bhagavan's Dhamma teaching. It is due to this fever that hot blood gushes from their mouths."

"Well then, Nagasena, hot blood gushed from their mouths because of something the Tathagata did. The Tathagata was the agent in this case leading to their destruction. Revered Nagasena, suppose a snake goes inside an anthill, but then a certain man wanting soil breaks up the anthill and takes the soil. By taking the soil he covers the hole of the anthill so that the snake can't breathe and so dies. Surely, sir, the snake died owing to what the man did."

"Yes, great king." 224

"Similarly, Nagasena, in this case the Tathagata was the agent of their destruction."

"Great king, when teaching the Dhamma the Tathagata does so free of attraction and repulsion. Free of both attraction and repulsion, he teaches the Dhamma, and those who practice rightly awaken as he teaches the Dhamma, while those practicing wrongly fall. Suppose, great king, a man shakes a mango, jambu, or honey tree. The fruits that are strong and firmly attached stay fixed, while the fruits that are weakly attached with rotting stems fall. Just like this, great king, the Tathagata teaches the Dhamma, harboring neither attraction nor repulsion. Free of attraction and repulsion, he teaches the Dhamma, and those who practice rightly awaken as he teaches the Dhamma while those practicing wrongly fall.

"Alternatively, suppose a farmer wishing to plant grain 225
plows a field. Many hundreds and thousands of grasses die

maranti; evam eva kho mahārāja tathāgato paripakkamānase satte bodhento anunaya-paṭighavippamutto dhammaṃ deseti, evaṃ dhamme desiyamāne ye tattha sammā paṭipannā te bujjhanti, ye pana micchā paṭipannā te tiṇāni viya maranti. yathā vā pana mahārāja manussā rasahetu yante ucchuṃ pīḷayanti, tesaṃ ucchuṃ pīḷayamānānaṃ ye tattha yantamukhagatā kimayo te pīḷiyanti; evam-eva kho mahārāja tathāgato paripakkamānase satte bodhento dhammayantam-abhipīḷayati, ye tattha micchā paṭipannā te kimī viya marantīti.

226 nanu bhante nāgasena te bhikkhū tāya dhammadesanāya patitā ti. api nu kho mahārāja tacchako rukkhaṃ rakkhanto ujukaṃ parisuddhaṃ karotīti. na hi bhante, vajjanīyaṃ bhante apanetvā evam-idaṃ tacchako rukkhaṃ ujukaṃ parisuddhaṃ karotīti.

227 evam-eva kho mahārāja tathāgato parisaṃ rakkhanto na sakkoti bodhaneyye satte bodhetuṃ, micchā paṭipanne pana satte apanetvā evam-ete bodhaneyye satte bodheti. attakatena pana te mahārāja micchā paṭipannā patanti. yathā mahārāja kadalī veḷu assatarī attajena haññati, evam-eva kho mahārāja ye te micchā paṭipannā te attakatena haññanti patanti. yathā mahārāja corā attakatena cakkhuppāṭanaṃ sūlāropanaṃ sīsacchedanaṃ pāpuṇanti, evam-eva kho mahārāja ye te micchā paṭipannā te attakatena haññanti jinasāsanā patanti.

from his plowing. In the same way, the Tathagata, freed of both flattery and hostility, taught the Dhamma, awakening those beings whose minds were matured. When he was teaching the Dhamma in this way those practicing rightly were awakened, while those practicing wrongly perished like the grasses. Or consider people who crush sugarcane in a mill. While they are crushing the sugarcane they also crush worms fed into the mouth of the sugar mill. In the same way, great king, while he is awakening beings whose minds are matured, the Tathagata causes crushing in the mill of the Dhamma, and those who are practicing wrongly perish, much like the worms."

"Yes, but Nagasena, sir, did not those monks fall because 226
of that teaching of the Dhamma?"

"Great king, can a carpenter make a log straight and clean just by observing it?"

"No, sir, the carpenter makes the log straight and clean by removing uneven parts."

"In the same way, great king, the Tathagata is not able, 227
just by observing the assembly, to awaken beings who are capable of awakening. Having removed those practicing wrongly, he awakens those capable of awakening. However, those practicing wrongly fall by their own doing, great king. Just as a plantain tree, a bamboo, and a mule destroy that which produces them, so too do those practicing wrongly fall, destroyed by their own doing.[37] Just as thieves have their eyes plucked out, get impaled on a stake, or are decapitated by their own doing, so too, great king, those practicing wrongly are destroyed by their own doing and fall from the dispensation of the Victor.

228 yesaṃ mahārāja saṭṭhimattānaṃ bhikkhūnaṃ uṇhalohitaṃ mukhato uggataṃ tesaṃ taṃ n' eva bhagavato katena na paresaṃ katena, atha kho attano yeva katena. yathā mahārāja puriso sabbajanassa amataṃ dadeyya, te taṃ amataṃ asitvā arogā dīghāyukā sabbītito parimucceyyuṃ, ath' aññataro puriso durupacārena taṃ asitvā maraṇaṃ pāpuṇeyya; api nu kho so mahārāja amatadāyako puriso tatonidānaṃ kiñci apuññaṃ āpajjeyyāti.

229 na hi bhante ti. evam-eva kho mahārāja tathāgato dasasahassimhi lokadhātuyā devamanussānaṃ amataṃ dhammadānaṃ deti, ye te sattā bhabbā te dhammāmatena bujjhanti, ye pana te sattā abhabbā te dhammāmatena haññanti patanti. bhojanaṃ mahārāja sabbasattānaṃ jīvitaṃ rakkhati, tam-ekacce bhuñjitvā visūcikāya maranti, api nu kho so mahārāja bhojanadāyako puriso tatonidānaṃ kiñci apuññaṃ āpajjeyyāti.

230 na hi bhante ti. evam-eva kho mahārāja tathāgato dasasahassimhi lokadhātuyā devamanussānaṃ amataṃ dhammadānaṃ deti, ye te sattā bhabbā te dhammāmatena bujjhanti, ye pana te sattā abhabbā te dhammāmatena haññanti patantīti. sādhu bhante nāgasena, evam-etaṃ, tathā sampaṭicchāmīti.

231 bhante nāgasena, bhāsitam-p' etaṃ tathāgatena: kāyena saṃvaro sādhu, sādhu vācāya saṃvaro, manasā saṃvaro sādhu, sādhu sabbattha saṃvaro ti. puna ca tathāgato catunnaṃ parisānaṃ majjhe nisīditvā purato devamanussā-

“Hot blood gushed from the mouths of those sixty monks 228
because of what they themselves did, and not by anything done by the Bhagavan or anyone else. Great king, suppose a man were to give ambrosia to all the people and they, having eaten it, were healthy, long-lived, and free of all illness. But one man, because of taking it improperly, eats it and dies. Is the person who gave the ambrosia the source of this? Would he generate demerit?”

“No, sir.” 229

“In much the same way, great king, the Tathagata gave the gift of the Dhamma, the ambrosia for gods and humans in the ten-thousand-world system. Those beings who are able, awaken by the ambrosia of the Dhamma, while those beings who are not able are destroyed by the ambrosia of the Dhamma, and they fall. Great king, food saves the lives of all creatures, but some still die due to cholera, and so would the person who gave the food generate demerit?”

“No, sir.” 230

“In much the same way, great king, the Tathagata gave the gift of the Dhamma, the ambrosia for gods and humans in the ten-thousand-world system. Those beings who are able, awaken by the ambrosia of the Dhamma, while those beings who are not able are destroyed by the ambrosia of the Dhamma, and they fall.”

“Very well, revered Nagasena. This is so, and I am convinced.

“Revered Nagasena, this was also said by the Tathagata: 231
‘Restraint of the body is excellent, restraint with speech is excellent, and restraint of the mind is excellent; restraint everywhere is excellent.’ And yet, once, while seated in the

naṃ selassa brāhmaṇassa kosohitaṃ vatthaguyhaṃ dassesi. yadi bhante nāgasena bhagavatā bhaṇitaṃ: kāyena saṃvaro sādhūti, tena hi: selassa brāhmaṇassa kosohitaṃ vatthaguyhaṃ dassesīti yaṃ vacanaṃ taṃ micchā. yadi selassa brāhmaṇassa kosohitaṃ vatthaguyhaṃ dassesi, tena hi: kāyena saṃvaro sādhūti tam-pi vacanaṃ micchā. ayam-pi ubhatokoṭiko pañho tavānuppatto, so tayā nibbāhitabbo ti.

232 bhāsitam-p' etaṃ mahārāja bhagavatā: kāyena saṃvaro sādhūti. selassa ca brāhmaṇassa kosohitaṃ vatthaguyhaṃ dassitaṃ. yassa kho mahārāja tathāgate kaṅkhā uppannā tassa bodhanatthāya bhagavā iddhiyā tappaṭibhāgaṃ kāyaṃ dasseti, so yeva taṃ pāṭihāriyaṃ passatīti.

233 ko pan' etaṃ bhante nāgasena saddahissati yaṃ parisagato eko yeva taṃ guyhaṃ passati, avasesā tatth' eva santā na passanti. iṅgha me tvaṃ tattha kāraṇaṃ upadisa, kāraṇena maṃ saññāpehīti. diṭṭhapubbo pana tayā mahārāja koci byādhito puriso parikiṇṇo ñātimittehīti. āma bhante ti. api nu kho mahārāja parisā passat' etaṃ vedanaṃ yāya so puriso vedanāya vediyatīti. na hi bhante, attanā yeva so bhante puriso vediyatīti.

234 evam-eva kho mahārāja yass' eva tathāgate kaṅkhā uppannā tass' eva tathāgato bodhanāya iddhiyā tappaṭibhāgaṃ kāyaṃ dasseti, so yeva taṃ pāṭihāriyaṃ passati. yathā vā pana mahārāja kañcid-eva purisaṃ bhūto āviseyya, api nu kho sā mahārāja parisā passati taṃ bhūtagāhan-ti. na

middle of the fourfold assembly, the Tathagata showed the Brahman Sela his sheathed private parts.[38] Revered Nagasena, if the Bhagavan said that restraint of the body is excellent, then the claim that he showed the Brahman Sela his sheathed private parts is false. Alternatively, if he showed the Brahman Sela his sheathed private parts, then his saying that restraint of the body is excellent is false. This two-pronged dilemma has reached you, and you must solve it."

"Great king, the Bhagavan did say that restraint of the 232
body is excellent. And he did show the Brahman Sela his sheathed private parts. Great king, for the sake of providing knowledge to those in whom doubt has arisen, the Bhagavan shows a body resembling his by means of his psychic power. In this way, Sela saw the miraculous feature."

"Nagasena, who can believe that only one person in the 233
assembly saw the hidden part and all the others present there did not see? Come now, specify a reason in this case that will convince me."

"Great king, have you ever seen a man afflicted by an illness, surrounded by friends and relatives?"

"Certainly, sir."

"Does the crowd see the feeling, that is, the feeling that the man is experiencing?"

"No, sir, only the man himself experiences it."

"Similarly, great king, the Tathagata shows a body 234
resembling his by means of his psychic power for the sake of providing knowledge to someone who has doubt about the Tathagata. In this way he sees the miraculous feature. Suppose a ghost enters a person. Would the crowd see that possession by the ghost?"

hi bhante, so yeva āturo tassa bhūtassa āgamanaṃ passatīti.

235 evam eva kho mahārāja yass' eva tathāgate kaṅkhā uppannā so yeva taṃ pāṭihāriyaṃ passatīti. dukkaraṃ bhante nāgasena bhagavatā kataṃ yaṃ ekassa pi adassanīyaṃ taṃ dassentenāti. na mahārāja bhagavā guyhaṃ dassesi, iddhiyā pana chāyaṃ dassesīti. chāyāya pi bhante diṭṭhāya diṭṭhaṃ yeva hoti guyhaṃ yaṃ disvā niṭṭhaṃ gato ti.

236 dukkarañ-cāpi mahārāja tathāgato karoti bodhaneyye satte bodhetuṃ. yadi mahārāja tathāgato kiriyaṃ kiriyaṃ hāpeyya, bodhaneyyā sattā na bujjheyyuṃ; yasmā ca kho mahārāja yogaññū tathāgato bodhaneyye bodhetuṃ, tasmā tathāgato yena yena yogena bodhaneyyā bujjhanti tena tena yogena bodhaneyye bodheti. yathā mahārāja bhisakko sallakatto yena yena bhesajjena āturo arogo hoti tena tena bhesajjena āturaṃ upasaṅkamati: vamanīyaṃ vameti, virecanīyaṃ vireceti, anulepanīyaṃ anulimpeti, anuvāsanīyaṃ anuvāseti; evam eva kho mahārāja tathāgato yena yena yogena bodhaneyyā sattā bujjhanti tena tena yogena bodheti.

237 yathā vā pana mahārāja itthī mūḷhagabbhā bhisakkassa adassanīyaṃ guyhaṃ dasseti, evam-eva kho mahārāja tathāgato bodhaneyye bodhetuṃ adassanīyaṃ guyhaṃ iddhiyā chāyaṃ dassesi. na-tthi mahārāja adassanīyo nāma okāso puggalaṃ upādāya. yadi mahārāja kaci bhagavato hadayaṃ

"No, sir, only the affected person sees the ghost enter."

"Similarly, great king, only the person in whom doubt 235
had occurred regarding the Tathagata sees the miraculous feature."

"Nagasena, what the Bhagavan did was quite difficult, in showing what should not be seen to just one person."

"Great king, the Bhagavan did not actually show the hidden part; he showed a shadow of it with his psychic power."

"So what was seen was really just a shadow, sir. Still, having shown the hidden part, he achieved the goal."

"And yes, great king, the Tathagata did do what was 236
difficult in order to awaken beings capable of awakening. If the Tathagata were to neglect this action or that, beings capable of awakening would not be awakened. But since the Tathagata knows the right means to awaken beings capable of being awakened, he awakens them with these means. A surgical physician approaches a sick person with whatever medicine will make the illness better. He helps one who needs an emetic to vomit, one who needs a purgative to purge, one who needs an ointment to apply one, and one needing oleation to take oil. Similarly, the Tathagata awakens beings capable of being awakened with whatever means will bring about awakening.

"Just as a woman having a difficult delivery shows to a 237
doctor what is hidden and should not be seen, so too, great king, does the Tathagata, with his psychic power, show a shadow of something hidden and not to be seen in order to awaken someone capable of awakening. 'Not to be seen' means that no opportunity occurs for a person. If someone were to become awakened by seeing the Bhagavan's heart,

disvā bujjheyya, tassa pi bhagavā yogena hadayaṃ dasseyya. yogaññū mahārāja tathāgato desanākusalo.

238 nanu mahārāja tathāgato therassa nandassa adhimuttiṃ jānitvā taṃ devabhavanaṃ netvā devakaññāyo dassesi: iminā 'yaṃ kulaputto bujjhissatīti, tena ca so kulaputto bujjhi. iti kho mahārāja tathāgato anekapariyāyena subhanimittaṃ hīḷento garahanto jigucchanto tassa bodhanahetu kakuṭapādiniyo accharāyo dassesi. evam-pi tathāgato yogaññū desanākusalo. puna ca paraṃ mahārāja tathāgato therassa cullapanthakassa bhātarā nikkaḍḍhitassa dukkhitassa dummanassa upagantvā sukhumaṃ coḷakhaṇḍaṃ adāsi: iminā 'yaṃ kulaputto bujjhissatīti, so ca kulaputto tena kāraṇena jinasāsane vasībhāvaṃ pāpuṇi. evam-pi tathāgato yogaññū desanākusalo.

239 puna ca paraṃ mahārāja tathāgato brāhmaṇassa mogharājassa yāvatatiyaṃ pañhaṃ puṭṭho na byākāsi: evam-imassa kulaputtassa māno upasamissati, mānūpasamā abhisamayo bhavissatīti, tena ca tassa kulaputtassa māno upasami, mānūpasamā so brāhmaṇo chasu abhiññāsu vasībhāvaṃ pāpuṇi. evam-pi tathāgato yogaññū desanākusalo ti.

then by some means the Bhagavan would show his heart. To say that the Tathagata 'knows the right means' means that he is skillful in teaching.

"Great king, did not the Tathagata produce resolve in 238
Elder Nanda by taking him to the realm of the gods and showing him the *apsarases,* thinking that this young man from a good family would be awakened by this?[39] And indeed, the young man of good family was awakened. With many modes of teaching the Tathagata brought about his contempt, disapproval, and disgust for beautiful things, and so to bring about his awakening, he showed him the dove-footed celestial *apsarases.* In this way the Tathagata knows the right means and is skillful in teaching.

"Furthermore, great king, the Tathagata once approached the monk Panthaka the Younger, who was distressed and upset at being thrown out by his brother.[40] He gave him a piece of cloth, thinking, *This son of a good family will become awakened with this.* And indeed, this son of a good family did attain mastery in the dispensation of the Victor by this means. Here too the Tathagata knows the right means and is skillful in teaching.

"And more. Once the Tathagata did not answer a question 239
until the third time it was asked by the Brahman Mogharaja, thinking to quiet the pride of this son from a good family. And indeed, his pride was quieted, and he achieved insight. By this means the pride of a son of a good family was quieted, and with pride calmed, the Brahman achieved mastery in the six higher knowledges. Here too the Tathagata knows the right means and is skillful in teaching."

240 sādhu bhante nāgasena, sunibbeṭhito pañho bahuvidhehi kāraṇehi, gahanaṃ agahanaṃ kataṃ, andhakāro āloko kato, gaṇṭhi bhinno, bhaggā parappavādā, jinaputtānaṃ cakkhuṃ tayā uppāditaṃ, nippaṭibhānā titthiyā, tvaṃ gaṇivara-pavaraṃ āsajjāti.

241 bhante nāgasena, bhāsitam-p' etaṃ therena sāriputtena dhammasenāpatinā: parisuddhavacīsamācāro āvuso tathāgato, na-tthi tathāgatassa vacīduccaritaṃ yaṃ tathāgato rakkheyya: mā me idaṃ paro aññāsīti. puna ca tathāgato therassa sudinnassa kalandaputtassa aparādhe pārājikaṃ paññāpento pharusāhi vācāhi moghapurisavādena samudācari, tena ca so thero moghapurisavādena garuttāsena tāsito vippaṭisārī nāsakkhi ariyamaggaṃ paṭivijjhituṃ. yadi bhante nāgasena parisuddhavacīsamācaro tathāgatho, na-tthi tathāgatassa vacīduccaritaṃ, tena hi: tathāgatena therassa sudinnassa kalandaputtassa aparādhe mogha-purisavādena samudāciṇṇan-ti yaṃ vacanaṃ taṃ micchā. yadi bhagavata therassa sudinnassa kalandaputtassa aparādhe moghapurisavādena samudāciṇṇaṃ, tena hi: parisuddhavacīsamācāro tathāgato, na-tthi tathāgatassa vacīduccaritan-ti tam-pi vacanaṃ micchā. ayam-pi ubhatokoṭiko pañho tavānuppatto, so tayā nibbāhitabbo ti.

242 bhāsitam-p' etaṃ mahārāja therena sāriputtena dhamma-

"Excellent, revered Nagasena. The dilemma has been resolved with many kinds of reasons. The thicket has been cleared, the darkness made light, the knot broken, and the views of opponents smashed. Because of you, vision has risen for the Victor's descendants. Those from opposing schools are at a loss for words, while you have joined the ranks of the best teachers. 240

"Revered Nagasena, Elder Sariputta, the General of the Dhamma, said: 'Friend, the Tathagata is perfectly pure in verbal conduct. And the Tathagata has no verbal misdeed that he must protect, whereby he would have to worry, "May no one come to know this about me."' Yet, when declaring the rule of defeat at the offense of Elder Sudinna, son of Kalanda, the Tathagata used harsh speech with the words 'Foolish man.'[41] At being called a foolish man, the elder was so regretful and terrified with fear of the teacher that he was not able to master the Noble Path. Nagasena, if the Tathagata is perfectly pure in verbal conduct and has no verbal misdeeds, then the report must be false that says that at the time of the offense of Elder Sudinna, son of Kalanda, the Tathagata addressed him with the words, 'Foolish man.' Alternatively, if the Bhagavan addressed Elder Sudinna, son of Kalanda, at the time of the offense with the words, 'Foolish man,' then the claim that the Tathagata is perfectly pure in verbal conduct and has no verbal misdeeds is false. This two-pronged dilemma has reached you, and you must solve it." 241

"Great king, Elder Sariputta, the General of the Dhamma, did say that the Tathagata is perfectly pure in verbal conduct and that the Tathagata had no verbal misdeeds that he had 242

senāpatinā: parisuddhavacīsamācāro āvuso tathāgato, na-tthi tathāgatassa vacīduccaritaṃ yaṃ tathāgato rakkheyya: mā me idaṃ paro aññāsīti. āyasmato ca sudinnassa kalandaputtassa aparādhe pārājikaṃ paññāpentena bhagavatā moghapurisavādena samudāciṇṇaṃ. tañ-ca pana na duṭṭhacittena, asārambhena yāthāvalakkhaṇena. kiñ-ca tattha yāthāvalakkhaṇaṃ. yassa mahārāja puggalassa imasmiṃ attabhāve catusaccābhisamayo na hoti, tassa purisattanaṃ moghaṃ, aññaṃ kayiramānaṃ aññena sambhavati, tena vuccati moghapuriso ti. iti pi mahārāja bhagavatā āyasmato sudinnassa kalandaputtassa sabhāvavacanena samudāciṇṇaṃ, no abhūtavādenāti.

243 sabhāvam-pi bhante nāgasena yo akkosanto bhaṇati, tassa mayaṃ kahāpaṇaṃ daṇḍaṃ dhārema, aparādho yeva so, vatthuṃ nissāya visuṃ vohāraṃ ācaranto akkosatīti. atthi pana mahārāja sutapubbaṃ tayā khalitassa abhivādanaṃ vā paccuṭṭhānaṃ vā sakkāraṃ vā upāyanānuppadānaṃ vā ti.

244 na hi bhante, yato kutoci yattha katthaci khalito paribhāsanāraho hoti tajjanāraho, uttamaṅgam-pi 'ssa chindanti, hananti pi bandhanti pi ghātenti pi jhāpenti[8] pīti. tena hi mahārāja bhagavatā kiriyā yeva katā no akiriyā ti. kiriyam-pi bhante nāgasena kurumānena patirūpena kātabbaṃ anucchavikena, savanena pi bhante nāgasena tathāgatassa sadevako loko ottapati hiriyati, bhiyyo dassanena, tat' uttariṃ upasaṅkamanena payirupāsanenāti.

to protect, worrying, 'May no one come to know this about me.' And while laying down the rule of defeat at the offense of the respected Sudinna, son of Kalanda, the Bhagavan did address him with the words 'Foolish man.' But this was not due to a bad thought or anger; rather it was due to characterizing the matter truly. What is the true characterization in this case? Great king, if there is no grasp of the Noble Truths by a person in this life, then there is folly in his being a human. If he is doing one thing but is capable of something else, then he is called a foolish man. Such was the case, great king, when the Bhagavan addressed the respected Sudinna, son of Kalanda, with true words rather than false."

"And yet, Nagasena, we impose a punishment of the fine 243
of a copper coin on someone who reviles someone, even if he speaks truly. When someone departs from acting in a customary way on some issue and instead reviles someone, it is considered an offense."

"Great king, have you ever heard of anyone rising and greeting respectfully, honoring, and giving tribute to a wicked person?"

"No, sir, whatever sort of wicked person he is, insofar as 244
he deserves censure and blame, they beat him, tie him up, cut off his head, and ruin him."

"Then, great king, the Bhagavan did what was to be done, without shirking it."

"Nagasena, by doing what had to be done, he acted properly and correctly. Upon hearing of the Tathagata, Nagasena, people and gods feel shame and apprehension, even more so when seeing him; and they feel it most when approaching to pay homage."[42]

245 api nu kho mahārāja tikicchako abhisanne kāye kupite dose sinehaniyāni bhesajjāni detīti. na hi bhante, tiṇhāni lekhaniyāni bhesajjāni arogakāmo detīti.

246 evam eva kho mahārāja tathāgato sabbakilesabyādhivūpasamanāya anusatthiṃ deti. pharusā pi mahārāja tathāgatassa vācā satte sinehayati, muduke karoti. yathā mahārāja uṇham-pi udakaṃ yaṃ kiñci sinehaniyaṃ sinehayati, muduṃ karoti, evam-eva kho mahārāja pharusā pi tathāgatassa vācā atthavatī hoti karuṇāsahagatā. yathā mahārāja pitu vacanaṃ puttānaṃ atthavantaṃ hoti karuṇāsahagataṃ, evam-eva kho mahārāja pharusā pi tathāgatassa vācā atthavatī hoti karuṇāsahagatā. pharusā pi mahārāja tathāgatassa vācā sattānaṃ kilesappahānā hoti. yathā mahārāja duggandham-pi gomuttaṃ pītaṃ, virasam-pi agadaṃ khāyitaṃ sattānaṃ byādhiṃ hanti, evam-eva kho mahārāja pharusā pi tathāgatassa vācā atthavatī hoti karuṇāsahagatā. yathā mahārāja mahanto pi tūlapuñjo parassa kāye nipatitvā rujaṃ na karoti, evam-eva kho mahārāja pharusā pi tathāgatassa vācā na kassaci dukkhaṃ uppādetīti. suvinicchito bhante nāgasena pañho bahūhi kāraṇehi, sādhu bhante nāgasena, evam-etaṃ, tathā sampaṭicchāmīti.

247 bhante nāgasena, bhāsitam p'etaṃ tathāgatena:

248 acetanaṃ brāhmaṇa assuṇantaṃ
jāno[9] ajānantam-imaṃ palāsaṃ
āraddhaviriyo dhuvaṃ appamatto
sukhaseyyaṃ pucchasi kissa hetūti.

249 puna ca bhaṇitaṃ:

"Furthermore, great king, would a doctor give gentle oils as medicines when the body is full of disordered humors?" 245

"No, sir, one wanting to bring about health gives sharp and scarifying medicines."

"In just this way, great king, for the sake of allaying all the diseases that are the defilements, the Tathagata gives admonishment. The words of the Tathagata, even if harsh, soften beings and make them pliable. Just as hot water softens something and makes it pliable, so too the words of the Tathagata are full of compassion and purpose. Just as a father's words to his children are full of compassion and purpose, so too the Tathagata's words, though harsh, are full of compassion and purpose. The Tathagata's harsh words eliminate beings' defilements. Drinking foul-smelling cow's urine and taking disagreeable medicine destroys disease. So too the words of the Tathagata, though harsh, are full of compassion and purpose. Just as a pile of cotton, even if large, can fall on someone's body without causing pain, so too the harsh words of the Tathagata do not actually cause anyone pain." 246

"Well done, revered Nagasena, this dilemma has been explained well with many reasons. I am convinced.

"Revered Nagasena, the Tathagata said this: 247

> Brahman, why do you, with your steady diligence, 248
> exertion, and understanding, ask an incognizant dhak
> tree, which lacks thought and cannot hear, about its
> welfare and happiness?[43]

"But then he also said: 249

250 iti phandanarukkho pi tāvade ajjhabhāsatha:
mayham-pi vacanaṃ atthi, bhāradvāja, suṇohi me ti.

251 yadi bhante nāgasena rukkho acetano, tena hi: phandanena rukkhena bhāradvājena saha sallapitan-ti yaṃ vacanaṃ taṃ micchā. yadi phandanena rukkhena bhāradvājena saddhiṃ sallapitaṃ, tena hi: rukkho acetano ti tam-pi vacanaṃ micchā. ayam-pi ubhatokoṭiko pañho tavānuppatto, so tayā nibbāhitabbo ti.

252 bhāsitam-p'etaṃ mahārāja bhagavatā: rukkho acetano ti. phandanena ca rukkhena bhāradvājena saddhiṃ sallapitaṃ. tañ-ca pana vacanaṃ lokasamaññāya bhaṇitaṃ, na-tthi mahārāja acetanassa rukkhassa sallāpo nāma, api ca mahārāja tasmiṃ rukkhe adhivatthāya devatāy'etaṃ adhivacanaṃ rukkho ti, rukkho sallapatīti c' esā lokapaṇṇatti.

253 yathā mahārāja sakaṭaṃ dhaññassa paripūritaṃ dhaññasakaṭan-ti jano voharati, na ca taṃ dhaññamayaṃ sakaṭaṃ, rukkhamayaṃ sakaṭaṃ, tasmiṃ sakaṭe dhaññassa pana ākiritattā dhaññasakaṭan-ti jano voharati; evam-eva kho mahārāja na rukkho sallapati, rukkho acetano, yā pana tasmiṃ rukkhe adhivatthā devatā tassāy' etaṃ adhivacanaṃ rukkho ti, rukkho sallapatīti c' esā lokapaṇṇatti.

254 yathā vā pana mahārāja dadhiṃ manthayamāno takkaṃ manthemīti voharati, na taṃ takkaṃ yaṃ so mantheti, dadhiṃ yeva so manthento takkaṃ manthemīti voharati; evam-eva kho mahārāja na rukkho sallapati, rukkho acetano,

Just then the quaking tree spoke: 250
'I have words, Bharadvaja, and you must listen to
me.'[44]

"Nagasena, if a tree is without thought then it is false to say 251
that a quaking tree had a conversation with Bharadvaja. Alternatively, if there was a conversation between a quaking tree and Bharadvaja, then it is false to say that a tree lacks thought. This two-pronged dilemma has reached you, and you must solve it."

"Great king, the Bhagavan did say that a tree lacks thought. 252
And a quaking tree did converse with Bharadvaja. But the wording spoken in this case was a popular idiom. It is not that there was actually a conversation with a tree, which lacks thought, but rather with the deity inhabiting the tree. 'Tree' is used metaphorically in the popular expression 'a tree converses.'

"It is just like when people say that a wagon full of grain is 253
a 'grain wagon,' it is not that the wagon is made of grain. The wagon is made of wood. People call it a grain wagon because of the wagon being heaped with grain. In the same way, great king, a tree does not converse since a tree lacks thought. But there is a deity living in the tree, and so the popular expression that a tree converses uses 'tree' metaphorically.

"Great king, it is just like when someone churning curds 254
says, 'I am churning buttermilk.' It isn't buttermilk that is being churned, but rather just the curds. One who says, 'I am churning buttermilk' is actually churning curds. In the same way, great king, a tree does not converse, since a tree lacks thought. But there is a deity living in the tree, and so

yā pana tasmiṃ rukkhe adhivatthā devatā tassāy' etaṃ adhivacanaṃ rukkho ti, rukkho sallapatīti c' esā lokapaṇṇatti.

255 yathā vā pana mahārāja asantaṃ sādhetukāmo asantaṃ sādhemīti voharati, asiddhaṃ siddhan-ti voharati, evam-esā lokasamaññā; evam-eva kho mahārāja na rukkho sallapati, rukkho acetano, yā pana tasmiṃ rukkhe adhivatthā devatā tassāy' etaṃ adhivacanaṃ rukkho ti, rukkho sallapatīti c' esā lokapaṇṇatti. yāya mahārāja lokasamaññāya jano voharati, tathāgato pi tāy' eva lokasamaññāya sattānaṃ dhammaṃ desetīti. sādhu bhante nāgasena, evam-etaṃ, tathā sampaṭicchāmīti.

256 bhante nāgasena, bhāsitam-p' etaṃ dhammasaṅgītikārakehi therehi: cundassa bhattaṃ bhuñjitvā kammārassāti me sutaṃ ābādhaṃ samphusī buddho pabāḷhaṃ māraṇantikan-ti. puna ca bhagavatā bhaṇitaṃ: dve 'me ānanda piṇḍapātā samā samaphalā samavipākā, ativiya aññehi piṇḍapātehi mahapphalatarā c' eva mahānisaṃsatarā cāti. yadi bhante nāgasena bhagavato cundassa bhattaṃ bhuttāvissa kharo ābādho uppanno, pabāḷhā vedanā pavattā māraṇantikā, tena hi: dve 'me ānanda piṇḍapātā samā samaphalā samavipākā, ativiya aññehi piṇḍapātehi mahapphalatarā c' eva mahānisaṃsatarā cāti yaṃ vacanaṃ taṃ micchā. yadi dve p' ete piṇḍapātā samā samaphalā samavipākā, ativiya aññehi piṇḍapātehi mahapphalatarā c' eva mahānisaṃsatarā ca, tena hi: bhagavato cundassa bhattaṃ bhuttāvissa kharo ābādho uppanno, pabāḷhā vedanā pavattā māraṇantikā ti tam-pi vacanaṃ micchā.

the popular expression that a tree converses uses 'tree' metaphorically.

"Great king, it is just like when someone who wants to 255
make something that does not exist says, 'I am making something that does not exist.' In this popular idiom one speaks of something that is not accomplished as if it were accomplished. In the same way, great king, a tree does not converse, since a tree lacks thought. But there is a deity living in the tree, and so the popular expression that the tree converses uses 'tree' metaphorically. The Tathagata teaches the Dhamma to beings with whatever popular expressions people use."

"Very well, Nagasena, I am convinced that this is so.

"Revered Nagasena, this was said by the elders performing 256
the Recitation of the Dhamma: 'I have heard that the Buddha, having eaten the alms of the smith Cunda, contracted a sharp and deadly illness.'[45] And yet, the Bhagavan said, 'These two almsgivings, Ananda, equally, with the same fruits and same results, are much more fruitful and beneficial than all other alms.'[46] Nagasena, sir, if the severe disease occurred after the Bhagavan had eaten Cunda's alms, occurring as a sharp and deadly pain, then it is surely false to claim: 'These two almsgivings, Ananda, equally, with the same fruits and same results, are much more fruitful and beneficial than all other alms.' Alternatively, if these two almsgivings are equally more fruitful and beneficial than all other alms, then it is false to claim that after he had eaten Cunda's alms, a severe illness, occurring as a sharp and deadly pain, arose in the

257 kin-nu kho bhante nāgasena so piṇḍapāto visagatatāya mahapphalo, roguppādakatāya mahapphalo, āyuvināsakatāya mahapphalo, bhagavato jīvitaharaṇatāya mahapphalo. tattha me kāraṇaṃ brūhi, parappavādānaṃ niggahāya. etthāyaṃ jano sammūḷho: lobhavasena, atibahuṃ khāyitena lohitapakkhandikā uppannā ti. ayam-pi ubhatokoṭiko pañho tavānuppatto, so tayā nibbāhitabbo ti.

258 bhāsitam-p' etaṃ mahārāja dhammasaṅgītikārakehi therehi: cundassa bhattaṃ bhuñjitvā kammārassāti me sutaṃ ābādhaṃ samphusī buddho pabāḷhaṃ māraṇantikan-ti. bhagavatā ca bhaṇitaṃ: dve 'me ānanda piṇḍapātā samā samaphalā samavipākā, ativiya aññehi piṇḍapātehi mahapphalatarā c' eva mahānisaṃsatarā ca; katame dve: yañ-ca piṇḍapātaṃ paribhuñjitvā tathāgato anuttaraṃ sammāsambodhiṃ abhisambujjhi, yañ-ca piṇḍapātaṃ paribhuñjitvā anupādisesāya nibbānadhātuyā parinibbāyati, ime dve piṇḍapātā samā samaphalā samavipākā, ativiya aññehi piṇḍapātehi mahapphalatarā c' eva mahānisaṃsatarā cāti.

259 so ca pana piṇḍapāto bahuguṇo anekānisaṃso. devatā mahārāja haṭṭhā pasannamānasā: ayaṃ bhagavato pacchimo piṇḍapāto ti dibbaṃ ojaṃ sūkaramaddave ākiriṃsu. tañ-ca pana sammāpākaṃ lahupākaṃ manuññaṃ bahurasaṃ jaṭharaggitejassa hitaṃ, na mahārāja tatonidānaṃ bhagavato koci anuppanno rogo uppanno, api ca mahārāja bhagavato pakatidubbale sarīre khīṇe āyusaṅkhāre uppanno rogo bhiyyo abhivaḍḍhi. yathā mahārāja pakatiyā jalamāno aggi aññasmiṃ upādāne dinne bhiyyo pajjalati, evam-eva kho

Bhagavan. Nagasena, how could this alms food be so fruitful 257
if it turned to poison and prompted illness? How could it be fruitful if it ruined his remaining life span and took his life? Tell me the reasoning here, for the sake of refuting the opponent's view. People are confused on this matter, thinking that the dysentery occurred due to eating too much out of greed. This two-pronged dilemma has reached you, and you must solve it.

"Great king, this was said by the elders performing the 258
Recitation of the Dhamma: 'I have heard that the Buddha, having eaten the alms of the smith Cunda, contracted a sharp and deadly illness.' And the Bhagavan did say, 'These two almsgivings, Ananda, equally, with the same fruits and same results, are much more fruitful and beneficial than all other alms.' Which two? The alms that the Tathagata ate before attaining the highest perfect awakening and the alms that he ate at the final nibbana, the domain where no further material support remains. These two alms are equal, with the same fruits and same results, and are much more fruitful and much more beneficial than all other alms.

"This almsgiving has many qualities and many bene- 259
fits. The gods were thrilled, and with minds full of happy devotion, they sprinkled divine nourishment onto the pig's delight, saying, 'This is the Bhagavan's last alms.'[47] Indeed, it had been prepared properly and cooked lightly, and was delightful, very tasty, and beneficial for the digestive fire. But, great king, a disease arose in the Bhagavan, and though it was not from that source and not previously present, once arisen, it greatly increased when the Bhagavan's body became naturally weak and his vital principle exhausted. Much as a

mahārāja bhagavato pakatidubbale sarīre khīṇe āyusaṅkhāre uppanno rogo bhiyyo abhivaḍḍhi.

260 yathā vā pana mahārāja soto pakatiyā sandamāno abhivaṭṭe mahāmeghe bhiyyo mahogho udakavāhako hoti, evam-eva kho mahārāja bhagavato pakatidubbale sarīre khīṇe āyusaṅkhāre uppanno rogo bhiyyo abhivaḍḍhi. yathā vā pana mahārāja pakatiyā 'bhisandamānadhātuko kucchi[10] aññasmiṃ ajjhohāre bhiyyo āyameyya, evam-eva kho mahārāja bhagavato pakatidubbale sarīre khīṇe āyusaṅkhāre uppanno rogo bhiyyo abhivaḍḍhi. na-tthi mahārāja tasmiṃ piṇḍapāte doso, na ca tassa sakkā doso āropetun-ti.

261 bhante nāgasena, kena kāraṇena te dve piṇḍapātā samā samaphalā samavipākā, ativiya aññehi piṇḍapātehi mahapphalatarā c' eva mahānisaṃsatarā cāti. dhammānumajjana-samāpattivasena mahārāja te dve piṇḍapātā samā samaphalā samavipākā, ativiya aññehi piṇḍapātehi mahapphalatarā c' eva mahānisaṃsatarā cāti.

262 bhante nāgasena, katamesaṃ dhammānaṃ anumajjana-samāpattivasena te dve piṇḍapātā samā samaphalā samavipākā, ativiya aññehi piṇḍapātehi mahapphalatarā c'eva mahānisaṃsatarā cāti. navannaṃ mahārāja anupubbavihārasamāpattīnaṃ anuloma-paṭiloma-samāpajjana-vasena te dve piṇḍapātā samā samaphalā samavipākā, ativiya aññehi piṇḍapātehi mahapphalatarā c' eva mahānisaṃsatarā cāti.

fire burning naturally burns even more when given fuel, so
too, great king, did the disease greatly increase when the
Bhagavan's body became naturally weak and his vital principle exhausted. Much as a stream flowing naturally turns 260
into a flood—a huge torrent of water—when rained upon by
a massive cloud, so too, great king, did the disease greatly
increase with the Bhagavan's body naturally weak and his
vital principle exhausted. Much as a belly naturally fills up
in one person's constitution but can bloat in someone else
when there is a lot of food, so too, great king, did the disease
greatly increase when the Bhagavan's body was naturally
weak and his vital principle exhausted. Great king, there was
no fault in that alms food, and no one can assign a fault to it."

"Nagasena, sir, what is the reason that these two almsgiv- 261
ings are equal, with the same fruits and same results, and
much more fruitful and beneficial than all other alms?"

"These two almsgivings, great king, equally, with the same fruits and same results, are much more fruitful and beneficial than all other alms because of his attainment of pondering phenomenal states continuously."

"Nagasena, which phenomenal states were they that, 262
because he pondered them continuously, made these two
almsgivings more fruitful and beneficial?"

"Great king, it was by his entering into the nine states of gradually ascending stages, first in one direction and then backward, that these two almsgivings equally, with the same fruits and same results, are much more fruitful and beneficial than all other alms."[48]

263 bhante nāgasena, dvīsu yeva divasesu adhimattaṃ tathāgato navānupubbavihārasamāpattiyo anuloma-paṭilomaṃ samāpajjīti. āma mahārājāti. acchariyaṃ bhante nāgasena, abbhutaṃ bhante nāgasena, yaṃ imasmiṃ buddhakkhette asadisa-parama-dānaṃ tam-pi imehi dvīhi piṇḍapātehi agaṇitaṃ. acchariyaṃ bhante nāgasena, abbhutaṃ bhante nāgasena, yāva mahantā navānupubbavihārasamāpattiyo, yatra hi nāma navānupubbavihārasamāpattivasena dānaṃ mahapphalataraṃ hoti mahānisaṃsatarañ-ca. sādhu bhante nāgasena, evam-etaṃ, tathā sampaṭicchāmīti.

264 bhante nāgasena, bhāsitam-p' etaṃ tathāgatena: abyāvaṭā tumhe ānanda hotha tathāgatassa sarīrapūjāyāti. puna ca bhaṇitaṃ: pūjetha naṃ pūjaniyassa dhātuṃ, evaṃkarā saggam-ito gamissathāti. yadi bhante nāgasena tathāgatena bhaṇitaṃ: abyāvaṭā tumhe ānanda hotha tathāgatassa sarīrapūjāyāti, tena hi: pūjetha naṃ pūjaniyassa dhātuṃ, evaṃkarā saggam-ito gamissathāti yaṃ vacanaṃ taṃ micchā. yadi tathāgatena bhaṇitaṃ: pūjetha naṃ pūjaniyassa dhātuṃ, evaṃkarā saggam-ito gamissathāti, tena hi: abyāvaṭā tumhe ānanda hotha tathāgatassa sarīrapūjāyāti tam-pi vacanaṃ micchā. ayam-pi ubhatokoṭiko pañho tavānuppatto, so tayā nibbāhitabbo ti.

265 bhāsitam-p' etaṃ mahārāja bhagavatā: abyāvaṭā tumhe ānanda hotha tathāgatassa sarīrapūjāyāti. puna ca bhaṇitaṃ: pūjetha naṃ pūjaniyassa dhātuṃ, evaṃkarā saggam-ito

"Nagasena, was it not truly extraordinary that he entered 263
into the nine states, gradually ascending the stages in one direction and then back, in just two days?" "Certainly, great king."

"It is a wonder and a marvel, revered Nagasena, that of the highest and unequaled giving to the fertile field of the Buddha, nothing compares to these two almsgivings. And it is also a wonder and a marvel, Nagasena, that inasmuch as there is greatness in attaining the nine gradual stages, this almsgiving is so much more fruitful and beneficial because of his attaining the gradual stages. Very good, Nagasena. I am persuaded that this is so.

"Revered Nagasena, the Tathagata said this: 'Ananda, do 264
not be occupied with worshiping the bodily remains of the Tathagata.'[49] But this also was said: 'Worship the relic worthy of worship. Doing so, one will go from here to heaven.' If, Nagasena, the Tathagata said, 'Ananda, do not be occupied with worshiping the bodily remains of the Tathagata,' then it is false to claim, 'Worship the relic worthy of worship; doing so, one will go from here to heaven.' Alternatively, if the Tathagata said that one worshiping a relic worthy of worship will go to heaven, then his telling Ananda not to be occupied with worshiping the remains of the Tathagata is false. This two-pronged dilemma has reached you, and you must solve it."

"Great king, the Bhagavan did say, 'Ananda, do not be occu- 265
pied with worshiping the bodily remains of the Tathagata,' and he also said, 'Worship the relic worthy of worship; doing so, one will go from here to heaven.' However, this assertion to Ananda to not be occupied with worshiping the remains

gamissathāti. tañ-ca pana na sabbesaṃ, jinaputtānaṃ yeva ārabbha bhaṇitaṃ: abyāvaṭā tumhe ānanda hotha tathāgatassa sarīrapūjāyāti. akammaṃ h'etaṃ mahārāja jinaputtānaṃ yad-idaṃ pūjā; sammasanaṃ saṅkhārānaṃ, yoniso manasikāro, saṭipaṭṭhānānupassanā, ārammaṇasāraggāho, kilesayuddhaṃ, sadatthamanuyuñjanā, etaṃ jinaputtānaṃ karaṇīyaṃ; avasesānaṃ devamanussānaṃ pūjā karaṇīyā.

266 yathā mahārāja mahiyā rājaputtānaṃ hatthi-assa-ratha-dhanu-tharu-lekha-muddā-sikkhā khattamanta-suti-muti-yuddha-yujjhāpana-kiriyā karaṇīyā, avasesānaṃ puthuvessasuddānaṃ kasi vaṇijjā gorakkhā karaṇīyā, evam-eva kho mahārāja akammaṃ h' etaṃ jinaputtānaṃ yad-idaṃ pūjā, sammasanaṃ saṅkhārānaṃ, yoniso manasikāro, satipaṭṭhānānupassanā, ārammaṇasāraggāho, kilesayuddhaṃ, sadatthamanuyuñjanā, etaṃ jinaputtānaṃ karaṇīyaṃ, avasesānaṃ devamanussānaṃ pūjākaraṇīyā.

267 yathā vā pana mahārāja brāhmaṇamāṇavakānaṃ irubbedaṃ yajubbedaṃ sāmavedaṃ athabbaṇavedaṃ lakkhaṇaṃ itihāsaṃ purāṇaṃ nighaṇḍu keṭubhaṃ akkharappabhedaṃ padaṃ veyyākaraṇaṃ bhāsamaggaṃ uppādaṃ supinaṃ nimittaṃ chaḷaṅgaṃ candaggāhaṃ suriyaggāhaṃ sukka-rāhu-caritaṃ uḷuggahayuddhaṃ devadundubhi-

of the Tathagata was addressed to the Victor's descendants,* not to everyone. Great king, worship is not the right action for the Victor's descendants. But what should be done by the Victor's descendants is mastering the clusters, careful attention, contemplating the four foundations of mindfulness, taking up the essential meditation subjects, doing battle with the defilements, and pursuing the highest good. Worship is to be done by everyone else, including gods and humans.

"This is similar, great king, to the duties of princes of the 266
earth, which include training with elephants, horses, chariots, bows, swords, writing, calculation, and hand gestures, and the work of war, including inciting to battle, gathering intelligence, and the learning associated with statecraft, while the duties of everyone else, that is, ordinary Vaishyas and Shudras, are farming, trade, and cattle raising. In much the same way, worship is not the right action for the Victor's descendants. The duties of the Victor's descendants include mastering the clusters, careful attention, contemplating the four foundations of mindfulness, taking up the essential meditation subjects, doing battle with the defilements, and pursuing the highest good. Worship is to be done by everyone else, including gods and humans.

"This is similar, great king, to the work of Brahman youths 267
in training in the *Ṛg Veda*, the *Yajur Veda*, the *Sāma Veda*, the *Atharva Veda*, interpreting auspicious marks, history, the Puranas, lexicography, ritual science, phonology, etymology, words, grammar, language styles, portents, dreams, omens, the six ancillary Vedic sciences, lunar eclipses, solar eclipses,

* Monks and nuns.

ssaraṃ okkanti ukkāpātaṃ bhūmikampaṃ disādāhaṃ bhummantalikkhaṃ jotisaṃ lokāyatikaṃ sācakkaṃ migacakkaṃ antaracakkaṃ missakuppādaṃ sakuṇarutaravitaṃ sikkhā karaṇīyā, avasesānaṃ puthuvessasuddānaṃ kasi vaṇijjā gorakkhā karaṇīyā, evam-eva kho mahārāja akammaṃ h' etaṃ jinaputtānaṃ yad-idaṃ pūjā, sammasanaṃ saṅkhārānaṃ, yoniso manasikāro, satipaṭṭhānānupassanā, ārammaṇasāraggāho, kilesayuddhaṃ, sadatthamanuyuñjanā, etaṃ jinaputtānaṃ karaṇīyaṃ, avasesānaṃ devamanussānaṃ pūjā karaṇīyā.

268 tasmā mahārāja tathāgato: mā ime akamme yuñjantu, kamme ime yuñjantūti āha: abyāvaṭā tumhe ānanda hotha tathāgatassa sarīrapūjāyāti. yad' etaṃ mahārāja tathāgato na bhaṇeyya, pattacīvaram-pi attano pariyādāpetvā bhikkhū buddhapūjaṃ yeva kareyyun-ti. sādhu bhante nāgasena, evam-etaṃ, tathā sampaṭicthāmīti.

269 bhante nāgasena, tumhe bhaṇatha: bhagavato gacchantassa ayaṃ acetanā mahāpaṭhavī ninnaṃ unnamati unnataṃ oṇamatīti. puna ca bhaṇatha: bhagavato pādo sakalikāya khato ti. yā sā sakalikā bhagavato pāde patitā kissa pana sā sakalikā bhagavato pādā na nivattā. yadi bhante nāgasena bhagavato gacchantassa ayaṃ acetanā mahāpaṭhavī ninnaṃ

the movements of the planets and Rahu, the occultation of stars and planets, the sounds of thunder, conception, meteor showers, earthquakes, glowing phenomena in the sky, knowledge about the earth and the atmosphere, astral science, materialist philosophy, dog augury, deer augury, augury concerning the intermediate compass points, mixed portents, and the sounds and cries of birds.[50] The duties of everyone else, that is, ordinary Vaishyas and Shudras, are farming, trade, and cattle raising. In much the same way, worship is not the right action for those in the lineage of the Victor. The duties of the Victor's descendants include mastering the clusters, careful attention, contemplating the four foundations of mindfulness, taking up the essential meditation subjects, doing battle with the defilements, and pursuing the highest good. Worship is to be done by everyone else, including gods and humans.

"This is why the Tathagata said, 'These people should not 268
engage in inappropriate action, and they should engage in the right action.' For had he not said this, great king, the monks would have become completely caught up with his bowl and robe and become occupied with worship of the Buddha."

"Very well, then, revered Nagasena. I am convinced of this.

"Revered Nagasena, you say, 'The great earth, though 269
lacking cognition, raised up low places and lowered high places when the Bhagavan went walking.' But you also say that the Bhagavan's foot was pierced by a splinter. But why did the splinter falling on the Bhagavan's foot not turn aside? For, Nagasena, sir, if the great earth, though lacking cogni-

unnamati unnataṃ oṇamati, tena hi: bhagavato pādo sakalikāya khato ti yam vacanataṃ micchā. yadi bhagavato pādo sakalikāya khato, tena hi: bhagavato gacchantassa ayaṃ acetanā mahāpaṭhavī ninnam unnamati unnataṃ oṇamatīti tam-pi vacanaṃ micchā. ayam-pi ubhatokoṭiko pañho tavānuppatto, so tayā nibbāhitabbo ti.

270 saccaṃ mahārāja atth' etam: bhagavato gacchantassa ayaṃ acetanā mahāpaṭhavī ninnaṃ unnamati unnataṃ oṇamati. bhagavato ca pādo sakalikāya khato. na ca pana sā sakalikā attano dhammatāya patitā, devadattassa upakkamena patitā. devadatto mahārāja bahūni jātisatasahassāni bhagavati āghātaṃ bandhi, so tena āghātena mahantaṃ kūṭāgārappamāṇaṃ pāsāṇaṃ: bhagavato upari pātessāmīti muñci. atha dve selā paṭhavito uṭṭhahitvā taṃ pāsāṇaṃ sampaṭicchiṃsu, atha nesaṃ sampahārena pāsāṇato papaṭikā bhijjitvā yena vā tena vā patantī bhagavato pāde patitā ti.

271 yathā ca bhante nāgasena dve selā pāsāṇaṃ sampaṭicchiṃsu, tath'eva papaṭikā pi sampaṭicchitabbā ti. sampaṭicchitam-pi mahārāja idh' ekaccaṃ paggharati passavati naṭṭhānaṃupagacchati. yathā mahārāja udakaṃ pāṇinā gahitaṃ angulantarikāhi paggharati passavati naṭṭhānam-upagacchati, khīraṃ takkaṃ madhuṃ sappi telaṃ maccharasaṃ maṃsarasaṃ pāṇinā gahitaṃ aṅgulantarikāhi paggharati passavati naṭṭhānam-upagacchati, evam-eva kho mahārāja sampaṭicchanatthaṃ upagatānaṃ dvinnaṃ selānaṃ sampahārena pāsāṇato papaṭikā bhijjitvā yena vā tena

tion, raised up low places and lowered high places when the Bhagavan went walking, then it is false to claim that the Bhagavan's foot was pierced with a splinter. Or if in fact the Bhagavan's foot was pierced with a splinter, then the claim that the earth raised up low places and lowered high places when he went walking is false. This two-pronged dilemma has reached you, and you must solve it."

"It is true, great king, that when the Bhagavan went walk- 270
ing, the great earth, though lacking cognition, raised the low places and lowered the high places. And the Bhagavan's foot was pierced with a splinter. But the splinter did not fall by its own condition; rather it fell because of an assault by Devadatta. Great king, Devadatta bore malice toward the Bhagavan for many hundreds and thousands of births, and it was because of this malice that he released a boulder the size of a huge several-story house, thinking, *I will make this fall on the Bhagavan.* Of course, two other rocks popped out of the earth and intercepted that boulder, and from their impact with the boulder, a fragment broke off, striking the Bhagavan's foot and drawing blood."

"You do realize, sir, that if the two rocks could intercept 271
the boulder, the fragment too could have been intercepted."

"Great king, when something is intercepted, some small bit slips away, spills, and gets lost. Consider how water scooped into the hand slips through, spills, and gets lost through the fingers. Similarly, milk, buttermilk, honey, ghee, oil, fish oil, and the juices from meat, when scooped into the hand, slip through, spill, and get lost through the fingers. In the same way, great king, as the two rocks came together to intercept the boulder, a fragment broke off from the impact, and it

vā patantī bhagavato pāde patitā. yathā vā pana mahārāja saṇha-sukhuma-aṇu-raja-samaṃ puḷinaṃ muṭṭhinā gahitaṃ aṅgulantarikāhi paggharati passavati naṭṭhānam-upagacchati, evam-eva kho mahārāja sampaṭicchanatthaṃ samāgacchantānaṃ dvinnaṃ selānaṃ sampahārena pāsāṇato papaṭikā bhijjitvā yena vā tena vā patantī bhagavato pāde patitā. yathā vā pana mahārāja kabaḷo mukhena gahito idh' ekaccassa mukhato muccitvā paggharati passavati naṭṭhānam-upagacchati, evam-eva kho mahārāja sampaṭicchanatthaṃ samāgacchantānaṃ dvinnaṃ selānaṃ sampahārena pāsāṇato papaṭikā bhijjitvā yena vā tena vā patantī bhagavato pāde patitā ti.

272 hotu bhante nāgasena, selehi pāsāṇo sampaṭicchito hotu, atha papaṭikāya pi apaciti kātabbā yath'eva mahāpaṭhaviyā ti. dvādas' ime mahārāja apacitiṃ na karonti, katame dvādasa: ratto rāgavasena apacitiṃ na karoti, duṭṭho dosavasena, mūḷho mohavasena, uddhato mānavasena, nigguṇo avisesatāya, atithaddho anisedhanatāya, hīno hīnasabhāvatāya, vacanakaro anissaratāya, pāpo kadariyatāya, dukkhāpito paṭidukkhāpanatāya, luddho lobhābhibhūtatāya, āyūhito atthasādhanena apacitiṃ na karoti. ime kho mahārāja dvādasa apacitiṃ na karonti.

273 sā ca pana papaṭikā pāsāṇasampahārena bhijjitvā animittakatadisā yena vā tena vā patamānā bhagavato pāde patitā. yathā mahārāja saṇha-sukhuma-aṇu-rajo anilabalasamāhato animittakatadiso yena vā tena vā abhikirati, evam-eva kho mahārāja sā papaṭikā pāsāṇasampahārena bhijjitvā animit-

was this that fell and struck the Bhagavan's foot. Consider also the way fine, subtle, minute, and dusty sand grabbed in a fist slips away, spills, and gets lost through the fingers. In the same way, great king, as the two rocks were intercepting the boulder, a fragment broke off from the impact, and it was this that struck the Bhagavan's foot. Even when a morsel of food is taken into the mouth, great king, a small bit escapes from the mouth and slips out, spills, and gets lost. So too did the two rocks intercept the boulder and shear off a fragment that then struck the Bhagavan's foot."

"Let it be so, then, Nagasena. Let it be that the boulder 272
was intercepted by the rocks. But surely the fragment would show as much reverence as the great earth, sir."

"There are twelve kinds of people who fail to show reverence. What are the twelve? The lustful because of passion do not show reverence; the hateful because of hate; the stupid because of delusion; the arrogant because of pride; those lacking qualities because of not being discriminating; the obdurate because of being obstructionist; the despicable because of being despicable; servants because of not having power; the wicked because of being selfish; those afflicted with pain because of lashing out with pain; the greedy because of being overcome with greed; and, finally, the ambitious striver does not show reverence because of pursuing wealth. These twelve do not show reverence, great king.

"But the fragment that broke off from impact with the 273
boulder fell in a random direction and struck the foot of the Bhagavan. Fine, subtle, and minute dust when swept up by the force of the wind goes in random directions and scatters. So too, great king, the fragment that broke off from the

takatadisā yena vā tena vā patamānā bhagavato pāde patitā. yadi pana mahārāja sā papaṭikā pāsāṇato visuṃ na bhaveyya, tam-pi te selā pāsāṇapapaṭikaṃ uppatitvā gaṇheyyuṃ. esā pana mahārāja papaṭikā na bhummaṭṭhā na ākāsaṭṭhā, pāsāṇasampahāravegena bhijjitvā animittakatadisā yena vā tena vā patamānā bhagavato pāde patitā. yathā vā pana mahārāja vātamaṇḍalikāya ukkhittaṃ purāṇapaṇṇaṃ animittakatadisaṃ yena vā tena vā patati, evam-eva kho mahārāja esā papaṭikā pāsāṇasampahāravegena animittakatadisā yena vā tena vā patamānā bhagavato pāde patitā. api ca mahārāja akataññussa kadariyassa devadattassa dukkhānubhavanāya sā papaṭikā bhagavato pāde patitā ti. sādhu bhante nāgasena, evam-etaṃ, tathā sampaṭicchāmīti.

274 bhante nāgasena, bhāsitam-p' etaṃ bhagavatā: āsavānaṃ khayā samaṇo hotīti. puna ca bhaṇitaṃ: catubbhi dhammehi samaṅgibhūtaṃ, taṃ ve naraṃ samaṇaṃ āhu loke ti. tatr' ime cattāro dhammā: khanti appāhāratā rativippahānaṃ ākiñcaññaṃ. sabbāni pan' etāni aparikkhīṇāsavassa sakilesass' eva honti. yadi bhante nāgasena āsavānaṃ khayā samaṇo hoti, tena hi: catubbhi dhammehi samaṅgibhūtaṃ taṃ ve naraṃ samaṇaṃ āhu loke ti yaṃ vacanaṃ taṃ micchā. yadi 'catubbhi dhammehi samaṅgibhūto'; samaṇo hoti, tena hi: āsavānaṃ khayā samaṇo hotīti tam-pi vacanaṃ micchā. ayam-pi ubhatokoṭiko pañho tavānuppatto, so tayā nibbāhitabbo ti.

275 bhāsitam-p' etaṃ mahārāja bhagavatā: āsavānaṃ khayā samaṇo hotīti. bhaṇitañ-ca: catubbhi dhammehi samaṅgibhūtaṃ taṃ ve naraṃ samaṇaṃ āhu loke ti. tad-idaṃ

impact with the boulder fell in a random direction and struck the Bhagavan's foot. If the fragment from the boulder had not separated from the boulder, then the two rocks would have carried along the fragment with the boulder. But this fragment did not stay in the air, nor did it stay on the earth. Rather, because of the force of the impact with the boulder it broke off and randomly fell and struck the Bhagavan's foot. Great king, old leaves picked up in a whirlwind have no determined direction and so fall wherever. This fragment had no determined direction because of the force of the impact with the boulder, and so it fell randomly, striking the foot of the Bhagavan. And of course, the fragment struck the Bhagavan's foot because of the painful suffering of the selfish and ungrateful Devadatta."

"Very well, revered Nagasena. This is so, and I accept it.

"Revered Nagasena, the Bhagavan said this: 'One is a 274
renouncer owing to destroying the flaws.'[51] But then he said: 'A man who practices four things is considered a renouncer by the world.' And these four things are forbearance, eating little, abandoning passion, and owning nothing. But all of these can be found in someone who has not destroyed the flaws and still has the defilements. Nagasena, if one is a renouncer due to destroying the flaws, then saying that 'a man who practices four things is considered a renouncer by the world' is false. Alternatively, if one who possesses the four things is a renouncer, then it is false to say, 'One is a renouncer due to destroying the flaws.' This two-pronged dilemma has reached you, and you must solve it."

"Great king, the Bhagavan did say, 'One is a renouncer due 275
to destroying the flaws.' And he also said that 'a man who

mahārāja vacanaṃ tesaṃ tesaṃ puggalānaṃ guṇavasena bhaṇitaṃ: catubbhi dhammehi samaṅgibhūtaṃ taṃ ve naraṃ samaṇaṃ āhu loke ti. idaṃ pana niravasesavacanaṃ: āsavānaṃ khayā samaṇo hotīti. api ca mahārāja ye keci kilesūpasamāya paṭipannā te sabbe upādāy' upādāya samaṇo khīṇāsavo aggam-akkhāyati.

276 yathā mahārāja yāni kānici jalajathalajapupphāni vassikaṃ tesaṃ aggam-akkhāyati, avasesāni yāni kānici vividhāni pupphajātāni sabbāni tāni pupphāni yeva, upādāy' upādāya pana vassikaṃ yeva pupphaṃ janassa patthitaṃ pihayitaṃ, evam-eva kho mahārāja ye keci kilesūpasamāya paṭipannā te sabbe upādāy' upādāya samaṇo khīṇāsavo aggam-akkhāyati. yathā vā pana mahārāja sabbadhaññānaṃ sāli aggam-akkhāyati, yā kāci avasesā vividhā dhaññajātiyo tā sabbā upādāy'upādāya bhojanāni sarīrayāpanāya, sāli yeva tesaṃ aggam-akkhāyati, evam-eva kho mahārāja ye keci kilesūpasamāya paṭipannā te sabbe upādāy' upādāya samaṇo khīṇāsavo aggam-akkhāyatīti. sādhu bhante nāgasena, evam-etaṃ, tathā sampaṭicchāmīti.

277 bhante nāgasena, bhāsitam-p' etaṃ bhagavatā: mamaṃ vā bhikkhave pare vaṇṇaṃ bhāseyyuṃ dhammassa vā saṅghassa vā vaṇṇaṃ bhāseyyuṃ, tatra tumhehi na ānando na somanassaṃ na cetaso ubbillāvitattaṃ karaṇīyan-ti. puna ca tathāgato selassa brāhmaṇassa yathābhucce vaṇṇe bhaññamāne ānandito sumano ubbillāvito bhiyyo uttariṃ sakaguṇaṃ pakittesi: rājāhamasmi sela dhammarājā anuttaro, dhammena cakkaṃ vattemi, cakkaṃ appativattiyan-ti.

practices four things is considered a renouncer by the world.' But this latter point was made specifically with respect to the special qualities of such people, while 'One is a renouncer due to destroying the flaws' is a comprehensive statement. Moreover, compared to all of those who are practicing for the sake of allaying the defilements, the renouncer who has
destroyed the flaws is considered to be the best. Great king, 276
whatever flowers grow on water or land, jasmine is considered the best of them. Compared to the many other kinds of flowers, jasmine is the flower most desired and most loved by people. Similarly, compared to all of those practicing for the sake of allaying the defilements, the renouncer who has destroyed the flaws is considered to be the best. And further, great king, rice is considered to be the best of all grains; compared to all the many other types of grains that are foods for nourishing the body, rice is deemed the best. Similarly, compared to all of those practicing for the sake of allaying the defilements, the renouncer who has destroyed the flaws is considered to be the best."

"Excellent, revered Nagasena, it is so, and I am convinced.

"Revered Nagasena, the Bhagavan also said this: 'Should 277
others speak in praise of the monks or of me, or should they speak in praise of the Dhamma or the community, then, Ananda, you should not take delight in this, nor should your mind become elated.' But on another occasion the Tathagata was so pleased, happy, and elated at the well-deserved praise spoken by the Brahman Sela that he proclaimed even further his own qualities: 'Sela, I am a king, the unequaled king of the Dhamma. I turn the wheel of the Dhamma, the wheel that never turns back.'

278 yadi bhante nāgasena bhagavatā bhaṇitaṃ: mamaṃ vā bhikkhave pare vaṇṇaṃ bhāseyyuṃ dhammassa vā saṅghassa vā vaṇṇaṃ bhāseyyuṃ, tatra tumhehi na ānando na somanassaṃ na cetaso ubbillāvitattaṃ karaṇīyan-ti, tena hi: selassa brāhmaṇassa yathābhucce vaṇṇe bhaññamāne ānandito sumano ubbillāvito bhiyyo uttariṃ sakaguṇaṃ pakittesīti yaṃ vacanaṃ taṃ micchā. yadi selassa brāhmanassa yathābhucce vaṇṇe bhaññamāne ānandito sumano ubbillāvito bhiyyo uttariṃ sakaguṇaṃ pakittesi, tena hi: mamaṃ vā bhikkhave pare vaṇṇaṃ bhāseyyuṃ dhammassa vā saṅghassa vā vaṇṇaṃ bhāseyyuṃ, tatra tumhehi na ānando na somanassaṃ na cetaso ubbillāvitattaṃ karaṇīyan-ti tam-pi vacanaṃ micchā. ayam-pi ubhatokoṭiko pañho tavānuppatto, so tayā nibbāhitabbo ti.

279 bhāsitam-p' etaṃ mahārāja bhagavatā: mamaṃ vā bhikkhave pare vaṇṇaṃ bhāseyyuṃ dhammassa vā saṅghassa vā vaṇṇaṃ bhāseyyuṃ, tatra tumhehi na ānando na somanassaṃ na cetaso ubbillāvitattaṃ karaṇīyan-ti. selassa ca brāhmaṇassa yathābhucce vaṇṇe bhaññamāne bhiyyo uttariṃ sakaguṇaṃ pakittitaṃ: rājā ham-asmi sela dhammarājā anuttaro, dhammena cakkaṃ vattemi, cakkaṃ appativattiyan-ti. paṭhamaṃ mahārāja bhagavatā dhammassa sabhāva-sarasa-lakkhaṇaṃ sabhāvaṃ avitathaṃ bhūtaṃ tacchaṃ tathatthaṃ paridīpayamānena bhaṇitaṃ: mamaṃ vā bhikkhave pare vaṇṇaṃ bhāseyyuṃ dhammassa vā saṅghassa vā vaṇṇaṃ bhāseyyuṃ, tatra tumhehi na ānando na somanassaṃ na cetaso ubbillāvitattaṃ karaṇīyan-ti.

"Nagasena, if the Bhagavan said, 'Should others speak in 278
praise of the monks or of me, or should they speak in praise of the Dhamma or the community, then, Ananda, you should not take delight in this nor should your mind become elated,' then this claim is false, namely, that 'the Tathagata was so pleased, happy, and elated at the well-deserved praise spoken by the Brahman Sela that he proclaimed even further his own qualities.' Alternatively, if the Tathagata was so pleased at the praise spoken by the Brahman Sela that he further proclaimed his own qualities, then saying that Ananda should not take delight or become elated when the monks, the Dhamma, the community, or he himself are praised, is false. This two-pronged dilemma has reached you, and you must solve it."

"Great king, the Bhagavan did say, 'Should others speak in 279
praise of the monks or of me, or should they speak in praise of the Dhamma or the community, then, Ananda, you should not take delight in this, nor should your mind become elated.' And at the well-deserved praise spoken by the Brahman Sela, he did proclaim even further his own qualities, saying, 'Sela, I am a king, the unequaled king of the Dhamma. I turn the wheel of the Dhamma, the wheel that never turns back.' The first was spoken by the Bhagavan because he was illuminating the actual, true, real, just, and right characteristic, function, and nature of the Dhamma. So he said: 'Should others speak in praise of the monks or of me, or should they speak in praise of the Dhamma or the community, then, Ananda, you should not take delight in this, nor should your mind become elated.'

280 yaṃ pana bhagavatā selassa brāhmaṇassa yathābhucce vaṇṇe bhaññamāne bhiyyo uttariṃ sakaguṇaṃ pakittitaṃ: rājā 'ham-asmi sela dhammarājā anuttaro ti, taṃ na lābhahetu na yasahetu na pakkhahetu na antevāsikamyatāya, atha kho anukampāya kāruññena hitavasena: evaṃ imassa dhammābhisamayo bhavissati tiṇṇañ-ca māṇava kasatānan-ti, evaṃ bhiyyo uttariṃ sakaguṇaṃ bhaṇitaṃ: rājā 'ham-asmi sela dhammarājā anuttaro ti. sādhu bhante nāgasena, evam-etaṃ, tathā sampaṭicchāmīti.

281 bhante nāgasena, bhāsitam-p' etaṃ bhagavatā: ahiṃsayaṃ paraṃ loke piyo hohisi māmako ti. puna ca bhaṇitaṃ: niggaṇhe niggahārahaṃ, paggaṇhe paggahārahan-ti. niggaho nāma bhante nāgasena hatthacchedo pādacchedo vadho bandhanaṃ kāraṇā māraṇaṃ santativikopanaṃ. na etaṃ vacanaṃ bhagavato yuttaṃ, na ca bhagavā arahati etaṃ vacanaṃ vattuṃ. yadi bhante nāgasena bhagavatā bhaṇitaṃ: ahiṃsayaṃ paraṃ loke piyo hohisi māmako ti, tena hi: niggaṇhe niggahārahaṃ, paggaṇhe paggahārahan-ti yaṃ vacanaṃ taṃ micchā. yadi tathāgatena bhaṇitaṃ: niggaṇhe niggahārahaṃ, paggaṇhe paggahārahan-ti, tena hi: ahiṃsayaṃ paraṃ loke piyo hohisi māmako ti tam-pi vacanaṃ micchā. ayam-pi ubhatokoṭiko pañho tavānuppatto, so tayā nibbāhitabbo ti.

282 bhāsitam-p' etaṃ mahārāja bhagavatā: ahiṃsayaṃ paraṃ loke piyo hohisi māmako ti. bhaṇitañ-ca: niggaṇhe niggahārahaṃ, paggaṇhe paggahārahan-ti. ahiṃsayaṃ paraṃ

"And when the Bhagavan was being deservedly praised by the Brahman Sela and then proclaimed further his own qualities, 'Sela, I am a king, the unequaled king of the Dhamma,' this was not for sake of gain, fame, or adherents, or out of a desire for disciples. Rather, it was out of compassion, care, and welfare, thinking that this would promote insight into the Dhamma for three hundred Brahman youths. So he declared further his own qualities, saying, 'Sela, I am a king, the unequaled king of the Dhamma.'" 280

"Very well, revered Nagasena, I am convinced that this is so.

"Revered Nagasena, the Bhagavan said, 'You should be loving and devoted to the world, never harming others.' But he also said, 'Censure those deserving censure, and show favor to those deserving favor.' Nagasena, censure means cutting off hands and feet, flogging, imprisoning, torturing, executing, and disrupting subsistence. Such a statement of the Bhagavan is not appropriate, and the Bhagavan should not have said these words. Sir, if the Bhagavan said, 'You should be loving and devoted to the world, never harming others,' then it is wrong to say, 'Censure those deserving censure, and show favor to those deserving favor.' Alternatively, if he said this about censuring those deserving censure and favoring those deserving favor, then it is false to say that one should be loving and devoted to the world, never harming others. This two-pronged dilemma has reached you, and you must solve it." 281

"Great king, the Bhagavan said both of these statements: 'You should be loving and devoted to the world, never harming others' and 'Censure those deserving censure, and show 282

loke piyo hohisi māmako ti, sabbesaṃ mahārāja tathāgatānaṃ anumataṃ etaṃ, esā anusatthi, esā dhammadesanā, dhammo hi mahārāja ahiṃsālakkhaṇo, sabhāvavacanaṃ etaṃ. yaṃ pana mahārāja tathāgato āha: niggaṇhe niggahārahaṃ, paggaṇhe paggahārahan-ti, bhāsā esā. uddhataṃ mahārāja cittaṃ niggahetabbaṃ, līnaṃ cittaṃ paggahetabbaṃ; akusalaṃ cittaṃ niggahetabbaṃ, kusalaṃ cittaṃ paggahetabbaṃ; ayoniso manasikāro niggahetabbo, yoniso manasikāro paggahetabbo; micchā paṭipanno niggahetabbo, sammā paṭipanno paggahetabbo; anariyo niggahetabbo, ariyo paggahetabbo; coro niggahetabbo, acoro paggahetabbo ti.

283 hotu bhante nāgasena, idāni tvaṃ paccāgatosi mama visayaṃ, yam-ahaṃ pucchāmi so me attho upagato; coro pana bhante nāgasena niggaṇhantena kathaṃ niggahetabbo ti. coro mahārāja niggaṇhantena evaṃ niggahetabbo paribhāsaniyo paribhāsitabbo, daṇḍaniyo daṇḍetabbo, pabbājaniyo pabbājetabbo, bandhaniyo bandhitabbo, ghātaniyo ghātetabbo ti.

284 yaṃ pana bhante nāgasena corānaṃ ghātanaṃ taṃ tathāgatānaṃ anumatan-ti. na hi mahārājāti. kissa pana coro anusāsaniyo anumato tathāgatānan-ti. yo so mahārāja ghātīyati na so tathāgatānaṃ anumatiyā ghātīyati, sayaṃkatena so ghātīyati, api ca dhammānusatthiṃ anusāsīyati, sakkā pana mahārāja purisaṃ akārakaṃ anaparādhaṃ

favor to those deserving favor.' The first claim about being loving and devoted to the world and not harming others was an instruction, a teaching on the Dhamma approved by all tathagatas, for the Dhamma has nonharming as its defining characteristic, so this was a statement about its very nature. But when the Tathagata said that about censuring those deserving censure and favoring those deserving favor, it was to say that an agitated mind should be censured and a good mind should be favored, and that a lack of careful attention should be censured and careful attention should be favored. Practicing wrongly should be censured while practicing rightly should be favored. The ignoble should be censured while the noble ones are favored, and the thief censured and the one who is not a thief favored."

"Let it be so, Nagasena. But come back into my domain, 283
as I am asking about the meaning as it concerns me. Sir, how should a thief be censured by one who has to do the censuring?"

"Great king, a thief should be censured by one doing the censuring in these ways: rebuke those who should be rebuked, punish those who should be punished, banish those who should be banished, imprison those who should be imprisoned, and kill those who should be killed."

"But Nagasena, sir, do the tathagatas approve of killing 284
thieves?" "No, great king." "Then why do the tathagatas approve that a thief is to be governed in this way?"

"Great king, whoever is killed is not killed at the approval of the tathagatas, but rather is killed by what he himself did. At the same time, is it possible for a wise person who is in conformity with the instruction of the Dhamma to seize an

vīthiyaṃ, carantaṃ gahetvā matimatā ghātayitun-ti. na hi bhante ti. kena kāraṇena mahārājāti. akārakattā bhante ti.

285 evam-eva kho mahārāja na coro tathāgatānaṃ anumatiyā haññati, sayaṃkatena so haññati, kim pan' ettha anusāsako kañci dosaṃ āpajjatīti. na hi bhante ti. tena hi mahārāja tathāgatānaṃ anusatthi samā anusatthi hotīti. sādhu bhante nāgasena, evam-etaṃ, tathā sampaṭicchāmīti.

286 bhante nāgasena, bhāsitam-p' etaṃ bhagavatā: akkodhano vigatakhilo 'ham-asmīti. puna ca tathāgato there sāriputta-moggallāne saparise paṇāmesi. kin-nu kho bhante nāgasena tathāgato kupito parisaṃ paṇāmesi udāhu tuṭṭho paṇāmesi: etaṃ tāva jānāhi imaṃ nāmāti. yadi bhante nāgasena kupito parisaṃ paṇāmesi, tena hi tathāgatassa kodho appativattito. yadi tuṭṭho paṇāmesi, tena hi avatthusmiṃ ajānantena paṇāmitā. ayam-pi ubhatokoṭiko pañho tavānuppatto, so tayā nibbāhitabbo ti.

287 bhāsitam-p' etaṃ mahārājā bhagavatā. akkodhano vigatakhilo 'ham-asmīti. paṇāmitā ca therā sāriputta-moggallānā saparisā, tañ-ca pana na kopena. idha mahārāja kocid eva puriso mahāpaṭhaviyā mūle vā khāṇuke vā pāsāṇe vā kaṭhale vā visame vā bhūmibhāge khalitvā patati, api nu kho mahārāja mahāpaṭhavī kupitā taṃ pātetīti. na hi bhante, na-tthi mahāpaṭhaviyā kopo vā pasādo vā. anunaya-paṭighavippamuttā mahāpaṭhavī, sayam-eva so alaso khalitvā patito ti.

innocent and guiltless man walking down the road and put him to death?" "No, sir." "Why not, great king?" "Because of his innocence, sir."

"In the same way, great king, a thief is not slain at the 285
approval of the tathagatas but is slain by what he did. Does the adviser in such a case commit a fault?" "No, sir." "Therefore, great king, the tathagatas' advice is advice that is just." "Very good, revered Nagasena. This is so, and I am convinced.

"Revered Nagasena, the Bhagavan once asserted: 'I 286
have no anger and am free of the rigidities.'[52] And yet, the Tathagata once dismissed Elders Sariputta and Moggallana with their assembly.[53] Nagasena, was the Tathagata angry when he dismissed that assembly or was he pleased as he dismissed it? You must make this understood. If he was angry when he dismissed the assembly, then the Tathagata had not turned away from anger. But if he dismissed it while pleased, then the dismissal was groundless and done out of ignorance. This two-pronged dilemma has reached you, and you must solve it."

"Great king, the Bhagavan did say, 'I have no anger and am 287
free of the rigidities.' And Elders Sariputta and Moggallana were dismissed with their assembly, though not out of anger. Consider someone who stumbles over a root, stump, stone, gravel, or some uneven piece of ground and falls on the great earth. Was the earth actually angry, great king, that it caused the person to fall?"

"No, sir. The earth has neither anger nor delight, and the earth is quite free of both affection and hostility. The klutz just tripped and fell."

288 evam-eva kho mahārāja na-tthi tathāgatānaṃ kopo vā pasādo vā, anunaya-paṭighavippamuttā tathāgatā arahanto sammāsambuddhā, atha kho sayaṃkaten' eva te attano aparādhena paṇāmitā. idha pana mahārāja mahāsamuddo na matena kuṇapena saṃvasati, yaṃ hoti mahāsamudde mataṃ kuṇapaṃ taṃ khippam-eva nicchubhati, thalaṃ ussādeti; api nu kho mahārāja mahāsamuddo kupito taṃ kuṇapaṃ nicchubhatīti. na hi bhante, na-tthi mahāsamuddassa kopo vā pasādo vā, anunaya-paṭighavippamutto mahāsamuddo ti.

289 evam-eva kho mahārāja na-tthi tathāgatānaṃ kopo vā pasādo vā, anunaya-paṭighavippamuttā tathāgatā arahanto sammāsambuddhā, atha kho sayaṃkaten' eva te attano aparādhena paṇāmitā. Yathā mahārāja paṭhaviyā khalito patīyati, evaṃ jinasāsanavare khalito paṇāmīyati; yathā mahāsamudde mataṃ kuṇapaṃ nicchubhīyati, evaṃ jinasāsanavare khalito paṇāmīyati. yaṃ pana te mahārāja tathāgato paṇāmesi, tesaṃ atthakāmo hitakāmo sukhakāmo visuddhikāmo: evaṃ ime jāti-jarā-byādhi-maraṇena parimuccissantīti paṇāmesīti. sādhu bhante nāgasena, evam-etaṃ, tathā sampaṭicchāmīti.

tatiyo vaggo.

"So too, great king. Tathagatas have no anger or delight. 288
Tathagatas are arhats and perfectly awakened buddhas, free of affection and hostility. Those dismissed did this themselves through their own fault. Consider how the great ocean does not keep a dead carcass and how a corpse in the ocean is quickly cast out and tossed up on dry land. Surely it is not because the great ocean is angry that it casts the corpse out?"

"No, sir. The great ocean has neither anger nor delight, and the ocean is free of affection and hostility."

"Similarly, great king, tathagatas have no anger or delight. 289
Tathagatas are arhats and perfectly awakened buddhas, free of affection and hostility. Those dismissed did this themselves through their own fault. Just as someone stumbles and falls on the earth, great king, one can stumble in the excellent dispensation of the Victor and be dismissed. Just as a corpse in the ocean is cast out, so too one stumbling in the excellent dispensation of the Victor is dismissed. And yet, great king, although the Tathagata dismissed them, he longed for their benefit, welfare, happiness, and purification. He dismissed them while thinking, *In this way, they will be freed from birth, old age, illness, and death.*"

"Very well, Nagasena, I am convinced of this."

End of Part 3.

PART 4

290 bhante nāgasena, bhāsitam-p' etaṃ bhagavatā etad-aggaṃ bhikkhave mama sāvakānaṃ bhikkhūnaṃ iddhimantānaṃ, yad-idaṃ mahāmoggallāno ti. puna ca kira so laguḷehi paripothito bhinnasīso sañcuṇṇitaṭṭhi maṃsa-dhamani-majja-parikatto[11] parinibbuto. yadi bhante nāgasena thero mahāmoggallāno iddhiyā koṭiṃ gato, tena hi: laguḷehi paripothito parinibbuto ti yaṃ vacanaṃ taṃ micchā. yadi laguḷehi paripothito parinibbuto, tena hi: iddhiyā koṭiṃ gato ti tam-pi vacanaṃ micchā. kinna samattho iddhiyā attano upaghātaṃ apanayituṃ, sadevakassa pi lokassa paṭisaraṇaṃ bhavituṃ araho ti. ayam-pi ubhatokoṭiko pañho tavānuppatto, so tayā nibbāhitabbo ti.

291 bhāsitam-p'etaṃ mahārāja bhagavatā: etad-aggaṃ bhikkhave mama sāvakānaṃ bhikkhūnaṃ iddhimantānaṃ, yad-idaṃ mahāmoggallāno ti. āyasmā ca mahāmoggallāno laguḷahato parinibbuto, tañ-ca pana kammādhiggahitenāti. nanu bhante nāgasena iddhimato iddhivisayo pi kammavipāko pi dve acintiyā, acintiyena acintiyaṃ apanayitabbaṃ. yathā nāma bhante keci phalakāmā kapitthena kapitthaṃ pothenti, ambena ambaṃ pothenti, evam-eva kho bhante nāgasena acintiyena acintiyaṃ pothayitvā apanetabban-ti.

PART 4

"Revered Nagasena, the Bhagavan once said: 'Monks, Moggallana the Great is chief among all of my monastic disciples possessing magical powers.' And yet it is said that he attained final nibbana after being seized and beaten with clubs; his head was smashed, his bones were crushed, and his veins and flesh cut up.[54] Nagasena, if Elder Moggallana the Great had attained supremacy among those with magical powers, then saying that he had attained final nibbana having been beaten with clubs is false. Or if he did attain final nibbana having been beaten with clubs, then claiming that he had attained supremacy in magical powers is false. And if he was not able to prevent his own murder with his powers, then why does he deserve to be a refuge for the world with its gods? This two-pronged dilemma has reached you, and you must solve it." 290

"Great king, the Bhagavan did say, 'Monks, Moggallana the Great is chief among all of my monastic disciples possessing magical powers.' And, yes, the revered Moggallana the Great was beaten to death with clubs, though this was because he was overpowered by karma." 291

"But revered Nagasena, there are two things that are unfathomable: the extent of magical powers for one proficient in them and the effects of karma. And what is unfathomable should be able to counter the unfathomable. Someone wanting fruit knocks a wood apple down with a wood apple or knocks a mango down with a mango. So what is unfathomable should be able to counter the unfathomable."

292 acintiyānam-pi mahārāja ekaṃ adhimattaṃ balavataraṃ. yathā mahārāja mahiyā rājāno honti samajaccā, samajaccānam-pi tesaṃ eko sabbe abhibhavitvā āṇaṃ pavatteti, evam-eva kho mahārāja tesaṃ acintiyānaṃ kammavipākaṃ yeva adhimattaṃ balavataraṃ, kammavipākaṃ yeva sabbe abhibhaviya āṇaṃ pavatteti, kammādhiggahitassa avasesā kiriyā okāsaṃ na labhanti. idha pana mahārāja koci puriso kismicid-eva pakaraṇe aparajjhati, na tassa mātā vā pitā vā bhagini-bhātaro vā sakhi-sahāyakā vā tāyanti, atha kho rājā yeva tattha abhibhaviya āṇaṃ pavatteti, kiṃ tattha kāraṇaṃ: aparādhikatā; evam-eva kho, mahārāja tesaṃ acintiyānaṃ kammavipākaṃ yeva adhimattaṃ balavataraṃ, kammavipākaṃ yeva sabbe abhibhaviya āṇaṃ pavatteti, kammādhiggahitassa avasesā kiriyā okāsaṃ na labhanti.

293 yathā vā pana mahārāja mahiyā davaḍāhe samuṭṭhite ghaṭasahassam-pi udakaṃ na sakkoti nibbāpetuṃ, atha kho aggi yeva tattha abhibhaviya āṇaṃ pavatteti, kiṃ tattha kāraṇaṃ: balavatā tejassa; evam-eva kho mahārāja tesaṃ acintiyānaṃ kammavipākaṃ yeva adhimattaṃ balavataraṃ, kammavipākaṃ yeva sabbe abhibhaviya āṇaṃ pavatteti, kammādhiggahitassa avasesā kiriyā okāsaṃ na labhanti. tasmā mahārāja āyasmato mahāmoggallānassa kammādhiggahitassa laguḷehi pothiyamānassa iddhiyā samannāhāro nāhosīti. sādhu bhante nāgasena, evam-etaṃ, tathā sampaṭicchāmīti.

"But one of the unfathomables is greater and more powerful, great king. The kings of the world are of the same class, but even within the same class one surpasses all the others and his rule prevails. Similarly, of the two, the unfathomable effects of karma are greater and more powerful. The effects of karma surpass everything else and their rule prevails. For one overpowered by karma, other kinds of agency do not stand a chance. 292

"Great king, consider the man who commits an offense in a certain undertaking. No one can protect him—not his mother, father, sister, brother, friend, or companion—no one except the king, who surpasses them and whose rule prevails. Why is this? Because of his offense. Similarly, great king, the unfathomable effects of karma are the greater and more powerful of the two, and the effects of karma surpass everything else, and their rule prevails. For one overpowered by karma, other kinds of agency do not stand a chance.

"Great king, consider a forest fire starting on the earth, 293
such that even a thousand jars of water are not able to extinguish it. The fire surpasses it and its rule prevails. Why is this? Because of the strength of its energy. And so it is with the unfathomable effects of karma. They are the greater and more powerful of the two, and the effects of karma surpass everything else and their rule prevails. For one overpowered by karma, other kinds of agency do not stand a chance. And so, great king, the revered Moggallana the Great was overpowered by karma, and could not concentrate on magical powers as he was being beaten with clubs."

"Very well, then, Nagasena. I am convinced.

294 bhante nāgasena, bhāsitam-p' etaṃ bhagavatā: tathāgatappavedito bhikkhave dhammavinayo vivaṭo virocati no paṭicchanno ti. puna ca pātimokkhuddeso kevalañ-ca vinayapiṭakaṃ pihitaṃ paṭicchannaṃ. yadi bhante nāgasena jinasāsane yuttaṃ vā pattaṃ vā samayaṃ vā labhetha, vinayapaṇṇatti vivaṭā sobheyya, kena kāraṇena: kevalaṃ tattha sikkhā saṃyamo niyamo sīla-guṇa-ācāra-paṇṇatti attharaso dhammaraso vimuttiraso. yadi bhante nāgasena bhagavatā bhaṇitaṃ: tathāgatappavedito bhikkhave dhammavinayo vivaṭo virocati no paṭicchanno ti, tena hi: pātimokkhuddeso kevalañ-ca vinayapiṭakaṃ pihitaṃ paṭicchannan-ti yaṃ vacanaṃ taṃ micchā. yadi pātimokkhuddeso kevalañ-ca vinaya-piṭakaṃ pihitaṃ paṭicchannaṃ, tena hi: tathāgatappavedito bhikkhave dhammavinayo vivaṭo virocati no paṭicchanno ti tam-pi vacanaṃ micchā. ayam-pi ubhato-koṭiko pañho tavānuppatto, so tayā nibbāhitabbo ti.

295 bhāsitam-p' etaṃ mahārāja bhagavatā: tathāgatappavedito bhikkhave dhammavinayo vivaṭo virocati no paṭicchanno ti. puna ca pātimokkhuddeso kevalañ-ca vinayapiṭakaṃ pihitaṃ paṭicchannaṃ. tañ-ca pana na sabbesaṃ, sīmaṃ katvā pihitaṃ. tividhena mahārāja bhagavatā pātimokkhuddeso

"Revered Nagasena, the Bhagavan also said this: 'The Dhamma and the *vinaya* taught by the Tathagata shine forth when uncovered, but not when they are hidden.' And yet, the Recitation of the Rules, in fact, the entire *vinaya*, is concealed and hidden.[55] Nagasena, if you follow the proper and fitting custom with respect to the dispensation of the Victor, then the regulations of the *vinaya* should shine forth uncovered. For what reason? Because in it the entire training—that is, restraint, self-control, and the regulations for moral discipline, virtue, and conduct—have the taste of the goal, the taste of the Dhamma, and the taste of freedom. Nagasena, if the Bhagavan said, 'The Dhamma and the *vinaya* taught by the Tathagata shine forth when uncovered, but not when they are hidden,' then the assertion that 'the Recitation of the Rules, in fact, the entire *vinaya*, is concealed and hidden' is false. Alternatively, if the Recitation of the Rules, and in fact, the entire *vinaya*, is concealed and hidden, then the claim that 'the Dhamma and the *vinaya* taught by the Tathagata shine forth when uncovered, but not when they are hidden' is false. This two-pronged dilemma has reached you, and you must solve it." 294

"Great king, the Bhagavan did say: 'The Dhamma and the *vinaya* taught by the Tathagata shine forth when uncovered, but not when they are hidden.' And the Recitation of the Rules, in fact, the entire *vinaya*, is concealed and hidden—though not for everyone. Rather, it is concealed once a monastic boundary is established.[56] Great king, once a boundary is established, the Recitation of the Rules is concealed by the Bhagavan on three grounds: because of the lineage of previous tathagatas; because of the 295

sīmaṃ katvā pihito: pubbakānaṃ tathāgatānaṃ vaṃsavasena pihito, dhammassa garukattā pihito, bhikkhubhūmiyā garukattā pihito.

296 kathaṃ pubbakānaṃ tathāgatānaṃ vaṃsavasena pātimokkhuddeso sīmaṃ katvā pihito: vaṃso eso mahārāja sabbesaṃ pubbakānaṃ tathāgatānaṃ, yad-idaṃ bhikkhumajjhe pātimokkhuddeso, avasesānaṃ pihito. yathā mahārāja khattiyānaṃ khattiyamāyā khattiyesu yeva carati, evam-etaṃ khattiyānaṃ lokassa paveṇi avasesānaṃ pihitā; evam-eva kho mahārāja vaṃso eso sabbesaṃ pubbakānaṃ tathāgatānaṃ, yad-idaṃ bhikkhumajjhe pāṭimokkhuddeso. avasesānaṃ pihito. yathā vā pana mahārāja mahiyā gaṇā vattanti, seyyathidaṃ: mallā atoṇā pabbatā dhammagiriyā brahmagiriyā natakā naccakā laṅghakā pisācā maṇibhaddā puṇṇabaddha candima-suriyā siridevatā kalidevatā sivā vasudevā ghanikā asipāsā bhaddiputtā, tesaṃ tesaṃ rahassaṃ tesu tesu gaṇesu yeva carati, avasesānaṃ pihitaṃ; evam-eva kho mahārāja vaṃso eso sabbesaṃ pubbakānaṃ tathāgatānaṃ, yad-idaṃ bhikkhumajjhe pātimokkhuddeso, avasesānaṃ pihito. evaṃ pubbakānaṃ tathāgatānaṃ vaṃsavasena pātimokkhuddeso sīmaṃ katvā pihito.

297 kathaṃ dhammassa garukattā pātimokkhuddeso sīmaṃ katvā pihito: dhammo mahārāja garuko bhāriyo, tattha sammattakārī aññaṃ ārādheti, taṃ tattha paramparā-

seriousness of the Dhamma; and because of the seriousness of the level of being a monastic.

"Why is it that once a boundary is established, the Recita- 296
tion of the Rules is concealed because of the lineage of previous tathagatas? Great king, it is in keeping with the lineage of all previous tathagatas that the Recitation of the Rules occurs only among monks and is concealed from everyone else. There are Kshatriya magical formulas that are for Kshatriyas and circulate only among Kshatriyas. These are customs common to the Kshatriyas and concealed from everyone else. So too it is in keeping with the lineage of all previous tathagatas that the Recitation of the Rules occurs only among monks and is concealed from everyone else. Great king, there are certain groups in the world, such as wrestlers, jugglers, mountaineers, performers, entertainers, acrobats, dancers, gymnasts, demon acrobats, Manibhadda troupes, Punnabaddha troupes, worshipers of the moon or the sun, devotees of the goddess Shri, devotees of Kali, Shiva, and Vasudeva, Ghanikas, Asipasas, and sons of Bhaddi.[57] There are secrets that circulate among each of these groups that remain concealed from others. So too it is in keeping with the lineage of all previous tathagatas that the Recitation of the Rules occurs only among monks and is concealed from everyone else. In this way, when a boundary is established, the Recitation of the Rules is concealed because of the lineage of previous tathagatas.

"Why is it that once a boundary is established, the Recita- 297
tion of the Rules is concealed because of the seriousness of the Dhamma? Great king, the Dhamma is serious and weighty. One who has attained proficiency in it wins the

sammattakāritāya pāpuṇāti, na taṃ tattha paramparāsammattakāritāya pāpuṇāti; mā cāyaṃ sāradhammo varadhammo asammattakārīnaṃ hatthagato oñāto avañāto hīḷito khīḷito garahito bhavatu, mā cāyaṃ sāradhammo varadhammo dujjanagato oñāto avañāto hīḷito khīḷito garahito bhavatūti evaṃ dhammassa garukattā pātimokkhuddeso sīmaṃ katvā pihito.

298 yathā mahārāja sāra-vara-pavara-abhijāta-jātimanta-rattalohitacandanaṃ nāma savarapuram-anugataṃ oñātaṃ avañātaṃ hīḷitaṃ khīḷitaṃ garahitaṃ bhavati, evam-eva kho mahārāja: mā 'yaṃ sāradhammo varadhammo paramparāasammattakārīnaṃ hatthagato oñāto avañāto hīḷito khīḷito garahito bhavatu, mā cāyaṃ sāradhammo varadhammo dujjanagato oñāto avañāto hīḷito khīḷito garahito bhavatūti evaṃ dhammassa garukattā pātimokkhuddeso sīmaṃ katvā pihito.

299 kathaṃ bhikkhubhūmiyā garukattā pātimokkhuddeso sīmaṃ katvā pihito: bhikkhubhāvo kho mahārāja atuliyo appamāṇo anagghaniyo, na sakkā kenaci agghāpetuṃ tuletuṃ parimetuṃ, mā 'yaṃ evarūpe bhikkhubhāve ṭhito lokena samasamo bhavatūti bhikkhūnaṃ yeva antare pātimokkhuddeso carati. yathā mahārāja loke varapavarabhaṇḍaṃ,

favor of another, who then either attains proficiency in the tradition or does not attain proficiency in the tradition.* May the excellent Dhamma, the best Dhamma, not come into the hands of those who do not have proficiency and thereby become degraded, despised, scorned, derided, and rejected. And may the excellent Dhamma, the best Dhamma, not reach bad people and thereby become degraded, despised, scorned, derided, and rejected. In this way, once a boundary is established, the Recitation of the Rules is concealed
because of the seriousness of the Dhamma. Great king, the 298
best and most excellent, fine, well-sourced, genuine, bright red sandalwood brought to the city known as Savage becomes degraded, despised, scorned, derided, and rejected.[58] May the best and most excellent Dhamma not come into the hands of someone not proficient in the tradition and thereby become degraded, despised, scorned, derided, and rejected, and may the best and most excellent Dhamma not reach bad people and thereby become degraded, despised, scorned, derided, and rejected. In this way, once a boundary is established, the Recitation of the Rules is concealed because of the seriousness of the Dhamma.

"Why is it that once a boundary is established, the Recita- 299
tion of the Rules is concealed because of the seriousness of the level of being a monastic? Great king, the status of a monastic cannot be weighed, measured, or reckoned. No one can calculate, weigh, or measure it. Let no one established in such monastic status become equivalent to worldly people. And so the Recitation of the Rules circulates only among

* The unbroken lineage of teachers.

vatthaṃ vā attharaṇaṃ vā gaja-turaṅga-ratha-suvaṇṇa-rajata-maṇi-muttā-itthiratanādīni vā nijjitakammasūrā vā, sabbe te rājānam-upagacchanti, evam-eva kho mahārāja yāvatā loke sikkhā-sugatāgamapariyatti-ācārasaṃyama-sīlasaṃvaraguṇā sabbe te bhikkhusaṅgham upagatā bhavanti. evaṃ bhikkhubhūmiyā garukattā pātimokkhuddeso sīmaṃ katvā pihito ti. sādhu bhante nāgasena, evam-etaṃ, tathā sampaṭicchāmīti.

300 bhante nāgasena, bhāsitam-p' etaṃ bhagavatā: sampajānamusāvāde pārājiko hotīti. puna ca bhaṇitaṃ: sampajānamusāvāde lahukaṃ āpattiṃ āpajjati ekassa santike desanāvatthukan-ti. bhante nāgasena, ko pan' ettha viseso, kiṃ kāraṇaṃ yañ-c' ekena musāvādena ucchijjati, yañ-c' ekena musāvādena satekiccho hoti. yadi bhante nāgasena bhagavatā bhaṇitaṃ: sampajānamusāvāde pārājiko hotīti, tena hi: sampajānamusāvāde lahukaṃ āpattiṃ āpajjati ekassa santike desanāvatthukan-ti yaṃ vacanaṃ taṃ micchā. yadi tathāgatena bhaṇitaṃ: sampajānamusāvāde lahukaṃ āpattiṃ āpajjati ekassa santike desanāvatthukan-ti, tena hi: sampajānamusāvāde pārājiko hotīti tam-pi vacanaṃ micchā. ayam-pi ubhatokoṭiko pañho tavānuppatto, so tayā nibbāhitabbo ti.

301 bhāsitam-p' etaṃ mahārāja bhagavatā: sampajānamusāvāde pārājiko hotīti. bhaṇitañ-ca: sampajānamusā-

monastics. Consider how the best and finest property in the world, be it clothing, carpets, elephants, horses, chariots, gold, silver, jewels, pearls, gem-like women, or heroes with unvanquished deeds, all goes to kings. So too, great king, as long as there is the training, the study of the scriptures of the Happy One,* and the qualities of good conduct, self-control, moral discipline, and restraint in the world, then all of these enter the community of monastics. And so, it is because of the seriousness of the level of being a monastic that the Recitation of the Rules is concealed once a boundary is established."

"Very well, revered Nagasena. It is so, and I accept it.

"Revered Nagasena, the Bhagavan said this: 'There is a 300
defeat in telling a deliberate lie.'[59] But he also said, 'In telling a deliberate lie one commits a light offense that requires disclosing in the presence of one other person.'[60] Nagasena, what is the distinction here? Why does one lie cut one off, while another lie may be remedied? If the Bhagavan said, 'There is a defeat in telling a deliberate lie,' then this claim must be false: 'In telling a deliberate lie one commits a light offense that requires disclosing in the presence of one other person.' Or, if the Bhagavan said, 'In telling a deliberate lie one commits a light offense that requires disclosing in the presence of one other person,' then this claim must be false: 'There is a defeat in telling a deliberate lie.' This two-pronged dilemma has reached you, and you must solve it."

"Great king, the Bhagavan did say, 'There is a defeat 301
in telling a deliberate lie.' And he also said, 'In telling a

* The Buddha.

vāde lahukaṃ āpattiṃ āpajjati ekassa santike desanāvatthukan-ti. tañ-ca pana vatthuvasena garuka-lahukaṃ hoti. taṃ kim-maññasi mahārāja: idha koci puriso parassa pāṇinā pahāraṃ dadeyya, tassa tumhe kiṃ daṇḍaṃ dhārethāti.

302 yadi so bhante āha: nakkhamāmīti, tassa mayaṃ akkhamamāne kahāpaṇaṃ harāpemāti. idha pana mahārāja so yeva puriso tava pāṇinā pahāraṃ dadeyya, tassa pana ko daṇḍo ti. hattham-pi 'ssa bhante chedāpeyyāma, pādam-pi chedāpeyyāma, yāva sīsaṃ kaḷīracchejjaṃ chedāpeyyāma, sabbam-pi taṃ gehaṃ vilumpāpeyyāma, ubhatopasse yāva sattamaṃ kulaṃ samugghātāpeyyāmāti.

303 ko pan' ettha mahārāja viseso, kiṃ kāraṇaṃ yaṃ ekassa pāṇippahāre sukhumo kahāpaṇo daṇḍo, yaṃ tava pāṇippahāre hatthacchejjaṃ pādacchejjaṃ yāva kaḷīracchejjaṃ sabbagehādānaṃ ubhatopasse yāva sattamakulā samugghāto ti. manussantarena bhante ti. evam-eva kho mahārāja sampajānamusāvādo vatthuvasena garuka-lahuko hotīti. sādhu bhante nāgasena, evam-etaṃ, tathā sampaṭicchāmīti.

304 bhante nāgasena, bhāsitam-p' etaṃ bhagavatā dhammatādhammapariyāye: pubbeva bodhisattānaṃ mātāpitaro niyatā honti, bodhi niyatā hoti, aggasāvakā niyatā honti, putto niyato hoti, upaṭṭhāko niyato hotīti. puna ca tumhe

deliberate lie one commits a light offense that requires disclosing in the presence of one other person.' But it is serious or light according to the subject. What do you think, great king? Suppose a certain man gave a blow to another with his hand. How would you have him punished?"

"If the victim says, 'I do not pardon him,' then, not pardon- 302
ing him either, I would have him fined a *kahapana* coin."*

"But, great king, suppose the man gave *you* a blow with his hand. What would his punishment be then?"

"Revered sir, I would have his hand chopped off, his foot chopped off, and his head, split like a bamboo, cut off. I would have his entire house plundered and his family seized to the seventh generation on both sides."

"Great king, what is the distinction here? For what reason 303
is the punishment a mere *kahapana* in the case of a blow by the hand to the one, while it entails cutting off a hand, cutting off a foot, cutting off a head split like a bamboo, taking an entire house, and seizing a family to the seventh generation on both sides, in the case of a blow by the hand to you?"

"Because of the difference in the persons, sir."

"So too, great king, a deliberate lie is serious or light according to the subject."

"Very well, Nagasena, so it is, and I am convinced.

"Revered Nagasena, the Bhagavan said in the Dhamma 304
discourse on the nature of things that for bodhisattas the parents are previously determined, the awakening tree is determined, the chief disciples are determined, the son is determined, and the attendant is determined.[61] But then you

* A nominal sum.

bhaṇatha: tusite kāye ṭhito bodhisatto aṭṭha mahāvilokanāni viloketi: kālaṃ viloketi, dīpaṃ viloketi, desaṃ viloketi, kulaṃ viloketi, janettiṃ viloketi, āyuṃ viloketi, māsaṃ viloketi, nekkhammaṃ viloketīti. bhante nāgasena, aparipakke ñāṇe bujjhanaṃ na-tthi, paripakke ñāṇe na sakkā nimesantaram-pi āgametuṃ, anatikkamanīyaṃ paripakkamānasaṃ.

305 kasmā bodhisatto kālaṃ viloketi: kamhi kāle uppajjāmīti. aparipakke ñāṇe bujjhanaṃ na-tthi, paripakke ñāṇe na sakkā nimesantaram-pi āgametuṃ; kasmā bodhisatto kulaṃ viloketi: kamhi kule uppajjāmīti. yadi bhante nāgasena pubbeva bodhisattassa mātāpitaro niyatā, tena hi: kulaṃ viloketīti yaṃ vacanaṃ taṃ micchā; yadi kulaṃ viloketi, tena hi: pubbeva bodhisattassa mātāpitaro niyatā ti tam-pi vacanaṃ micchā. ayam-pi ubhatokoṭiko pañho tavānuppatto, so tayā nibbāhitabbo ti.

306 niyatā mahārāja pubbeva bodhisattassa mātāpitaro, kulañ-ca bodhisatto viloketi. kin-ti pana kulaṃ viloketi: ye me mātāpitaro te khattiyā udāhu brāhmaṇā ti, evaṃ kulaṃ viloketi. aṭṭhannaṃ mahārāja pubbeva anāgataṃ oloketabbaṃ hoti, katamesaṃ aṭṭhannaṃ: vāṇijassa mahārāja pubbeva vikkayabhaṇḍaṃ oloketabbaṃ hoti, hatthināgassa pubbeva soṇḍāya anāgato maggo oloketabbo hoti, sākaṭikassa pubbeva anāgataṃ titthaṃ oloketabbaṃ hoti, niyyāmakassa pubbeva anāgataṃ tīraṃ oloketvā nāvā pesetabbā

say that when the Bodhisatta was present in the assembly in Tusita heaven, he reflected on the eight great investigations into the circumstances of his final birth. That is, he investigated the time, continent, place, family, mother, life span, month, and renunciation. Nagasena, when knowledge has not ripened there is no awakening, and when knowledge has ripened, it is not possible to linger even for the time it takes to blink. For a ripened mind cannot be overcome.

"Why then did the Bodhisatta reflect on the time, asking, 305
'At what time shall I be reborn?' When knowledge has not ripened, there is no awakening, and when knowledge has ripened, it is not possible to linger even for the time it takes to blink. And why did the Bodhisatta reflect on the family, asking, 'Which family shall I be born into?' If the mother and father of the Bodhisatta were already determined, then the claim that he reflected on the family is false. Or if he did reflect on the family, then the claim that the Bodhisatta's mother and father were already determined is false. This two-pronged dilemma has reached you, and you must solve it."

"Great king, the Bodhisatta's mother and father were 306
previously determined, and yet the Bodhisatta reflected on the family. But how did he reflect on the family? He reflected on the family thus, 'Are my mother and father to be Kshatriyas or Brahmans?' Great king, there are eight future matters that should be investigated in advance. What are the eight? A trader's merchandise should be investigated in advance; an unknown path for a bull elephant should be investigated in advance by its trunk; a future fording place should be investigated in advance by one driving a cart; an unknown

hoti, bhisakkassa pubbeva āyuṃ oloketvā āturo upasaṅkamitabbo hoti, uttarasetussa pubbeva thirāthirabhāvaṃ jānitvā abhirūhitabbaṃ hoti, bhikkhussa pubbeva anāgataṃ kālaṃ paccavekkhitvā bhojanaṃ bhuñjitabbaṃ hoti, bodhisattānaṃ pubbeva kulaṃ oloketabbaṃ hoti: khattiyakulaṃ vā brāhmaṇakulaṃ vā ti. imesaṃ kho mahārāja aṭṭhannaṃ pubbeva anāgataṃ oloketabbaṃ hotīti. sādhu bhante nāgasena, evam etaṃ, tathā sampaṭicchāmīti.

307 bhante nāgasena, bhāsitam-p' etaṃ bhagavatā: na bhikkhave attānaṃ pātetabbaṃ, yo pāteyya yathādhammo kāretabbo ti. puna ca tumhe bhaṇatha: yattha katthaci bhagavā sāvakānaṃ dhammaṃ desayamāno anekapariyāyena jātiyā jarāya byādhino maraṇassa samucchedāya dhammaṃ deseti, yo hi koci jāti-jarā-byādhi-maraṇaṃ samatikkamati taṃ paramāya pasaṃsāya pasaṃsatīti. yadi bhante nāgasena bhagavatā bhaṇitaṃ: na bhikkhave attānaṃ pātetabbaṃ, yo pāteyya yathādhammo kāretabbo ti, tena hi: jātiyā jarāya byādhino maraṇassa samucchedāya dhammaṃ desetīti yaṃ vacanaṃ taṃ micchā. yadi jātiyā jarāya byādhino maraṇassa samucchedāya dhammaṃ deseti, tena hi: na bhikkhave attānaṃ pātetabbaṃ, yo pāteyya yathādhammo kāretabbo ti tam-pi vacanaṃ micchā. ayam-pi ubhatokoṭiko pañho tavānuppatto, so tayā nibbāhitabbo ti.

shore should be investigated by a navigator before sending out the ship; a patient's vital power should be investigated by a physician before attending to the disease; the strength or weakness of a bridge should be known in advance by those seeking to cross it, and only then should it be mounted; the time remaining for a monk to eat should be considered before the meal is consumed;[62] and the family of a bodhisatta is to be investigated in advance as to whether it is a Kshatriya or Brahman family.[63] These, great king, are the eight future matters that should be investigated in advance."

"Very well then, revered Nagasena, it is so, and I am convinced.

"Revered Nagasena, the Bhagavan also said this: 'Monks, 307
one should not hurl oneself to one's death, and whoever does so will be dealt with according to the Dhamma.'[64] But you also say, 'Whenever the Bhagavan is teaching the Dhamma to the disciples, he teaches the Dhamma in various ways for the purpose of cutting off birth, old age, sickness, and death. And he extols with the highest praise anyone who transcends birth, old age, sickness, and death.' Nagasena, if the Bhagavan said, 'Monks, one should not hurl oneself to one's death, and whoever does so will be dealt with according to the Dhamma,' then saying that he teaches the Dhamma for the purpose of cutting off birth, old age, sickness, and death is false. Or if he does teach the Dhamma for the sake of cutting off birth, old age, sickness, and death, then this claim is false: 'Monks, one should not hurl oneself to one's death, and whoever does so will be dealt with according to the Dhamma.' This two-pronged dilemma has reached you, and you must solve it."

308 bhāsitam-p' etaṃ mahārāja bhagavatā: na bhikkhave attānaṃ pātetabbaṃ, yo pāteyya yathādhammo kāretabbo ti. yattha katthaci bhagavatā sāvakānaṃ dhammaṃ desayamānena ca anekapariyāyena jātiyā jarāya byādhino maraṇassa samucchedāya dhammo desito. tattha pana kāraṇaṃ atthi yena bhagavā kāraṇena paṭikkhipi samādapesi cāti. kim-pan' ettha bhante nāgasena kāraṇaṃ yena bhagavā kāraṇena paṭikkhipi samādapesi cāti.

309 sīlavā mahārāja sīlasampanno agadasamo sattānaṃ kilesavisavināsane, osadhasamo sattānaṃ kilesabyādhivūpasame, udakasamo sattānaṃ kilesarajojallāpaharaṇe, maṇiratanasamo sattānaṃ sabbasampattidāne, nāvāsamo sattānaṃ caturoghapāragamane, satthavāhasamo sattānaṃ jātikantāratāraṇe, vātasamo sattānaṃ tividhaggisantāpanibbāpane, mahāmeghasamo sattānaṃ mānasaparipūraṇe, ācariyasamo sattānaṃ kusalasikkhāpane, sudesikasamo sattānaṃ khemapatham-ācikkhane. evarūpo mahārāja bahuguṇo anekaguṇo appamāṇaguṇo guṇarāsi guṇapuñjo sattānaṃ vaḍḍhikaro sīlavā mā vinassīti sattānaṃ anukampāya mahārāja bhagavā sikkhāpadaṃ paññāpesi: na bhikkhave attānaṃ pātetabbaṃ, yo pāteyya yathādhammo kāretabbo ti. idam ettha mahārāja kāraṇaṃ yena kāraṇena bhagavā paṭikkhipi.

"Great king, the Bhagavan did say, 'Monks, one should not hurl oneself to one's death, and whoever does so will be dealt with according to the Dhamma.' And whenever the Bhagavan was teaching the Dhamma to the disciples, he taught the Dhamma in various ways for the purpose of cutting off birth, old age, sickness, and death. There is a reason the Bhagavan rejected the one and urged the other." 308

"What then is the reason the Bhagavan rejected the one and urged the other, Nagasena?"

"A virtuous person possessing moral discipline is like medicine for destroying the poison of beings' defilements, like a healing herb for relieving the illness of beings' defilements, like water washing away the dust and mud of beings' defilements, like the jewel treasure for giving every success to beings, like a boat conveying beings across the four floods,* like a caravan leader for bringing beings across the wilderness of births, like a wind putting out beings' burning with the three fires,† like a great cloud filling beings with purpose, like a teacher training beings in what is good, and like a skillful guide pointing beings to the path of peace.[65] May there not be the destruction of such a virtuous person, one with many virtues, numerous virtues, immeasurable virtues, a mass of virtues, a heap of virtues, one who brings about the welfare of beings. It was out of compassion for beings that the Bhagavan laid down this rule, 'Monks, one should not hurl oneself to one's death, and whoever does so will be dealt with according to the Dhamma.' This is the reason the Bhagavan rejected this in the first instance. 309

* Sensuality, becoming, views, and ignorance.

† Greed, hatred, and delusion.

310 bhāsitam-p' etaṃ mahārāja therena kumārakassapena vicitrakathikena pāyāsirājaññassa paralokaṃ dīpayamānena: yathā yathā kho rājañña samaṇabrāhmaṇā sīlavanto kalyāṇadhammā ciraṃ dīgham-addhānaṃ tiṭṭhanti, tathā tathā bahujanahitāya paṭipajjanti bahujanasukhāya lokānukampāya atthāya hitāya sukhāya devamanussānan-ti.

311 kena pana kāraṇena bhagavā samādapesi: jāti pi mahārāja dukkhā, jarā pi dukkhā, byādhi pi dukkhā, maraṇam-pi dukkhaṃ, soko pi dukkho, paridevo pi dukkho, dukkham-pi dukkhaṃ, domanassam-pi dukkhaṃ, upāyāso pi dukkho, appiyehi sampayogo pi dukkho, piyehi vippayogo pi dukkho, mātumaraṇam-pi dukkhaṃ, pitumaraṇam-pi dukkhaṃ, bhātumaraṇam-pi dukkhaṃ, bhaginimaraṇam-pi dukkhaṃ, puttamaranam-pi dukkhaṃ, dāramaraṇam-pi dukkhaṃ, ñātimaraṇam-pi dukkhaṃ, ñātibyasanam-pi dukkhaṃ, rogabyasanam-pi dukkhaṃ, bhogabyasanam-pi dukkhaṃ, sīlabyasanam-pi dukkhaṃ, diṭṭhibyasanam-pi dukkhaṃ, rājabhayam-pi dukkhaṃ, corabhayam-pi dukkhaṃ, veribhayam-pi dukkhaṃ, dubbhikkhabhayam-pi dukkhaṃ, aggibhayam-pi dukkhaṃ, udakabhayam-pi dukkhaṃ, ūmibhayam-pi dukkhaṃ, āvaṭṭabhayam-pi dukkhaṃ, kumbhīlabhayam-pi dukkhaṃ, susukābhayam-pi dukkhaṃ, attānuvādabhayam-pi dukkhaṃ, parānuvādabhayam-pi dukkhaṃ, daṇḍabhayam-pi dukkhaṃ, duggatibhayam-pi dukkhaṃ, parisasārajjabhayam-pi dukkhaṃ, ājīvikabha-yam-pi dukkhaṃ, maraṇabhayam-pi dukkhaṃ, vettehi tāḷanam-pi dukkhaṃ, kasāhi tāḷanam-pi dukkhaṃ, addhadaṇḍakehi tāḷanam-pi dukkhaṃ, hatthacchedanam-pi

"Moreover, great king, the eloquent Elder Kumara Kassapa, while illustrating the world beyond to Prince Payasi, said: 'Prince, as long as ascetics and Brahmans who are virtuous and committed to beautiful teachings continue to be present, then for that long they will be intent upon the benefit of many people, the happiness of many people, compassion for the world, and the well-being, benefit, and happiness of gods and humans.' 310

"Why then did the Bhagavan urge that old age is suffering, sickness is suffering, death is suffering, sorrow is suffering, grieving is suffering, pain is suffering, distress is suffering, trouble is suffering, association with what is disliked is suffering, separation from what is liked is suffering, the death of a mother is suffering, the death of a father is suffering, the death of a brother is suffering, the death of a sister is suffering, the death of one's child is suffering, the death of a wife is suffering, the death of a relative is suffering, the ruin of relatives is suffering, the ruin of health is suffering, the ruin of wealth is suffering, the ruin of virtue is suffering, the ruin of view is suffering, fear of kings is suffering, fear of thieves is suffering, fear of enemies is suffering, fear of famine is suffering, fear of fire is suffering, fear of water is suffering, fear of tidal waves is suffering, fear of whirlpools is suffering, fear of crocodiles is suffering, fear of alligators is suffering, fear of self-blame is suffering, fear of others' blame is suffering, fear of punishment is suffering, fear of bad future states is suffering, fear of nervousness in assemblies is suffering, fear about making a living is suffering, fear of death is suffering, being flogged with canes is suffering, being whipped is suffering, being beaten with 311

dukkhaṃ, pādacchedanam-pi dukkhaṃ, hatthapādacchedanam-pi dukkhaṃ, kaṇṇacchedanam-pi dukkhaṃ, nāsacchedanam-pi dukkhaṃ, kaṇṇanāsacchedanam-pi dukkhaṃ, bilaṅgathālikam-pi dukkhaṃ, saṅkhamuṇḍikam-pi dukkhaṃ, rāhumukham-pi dukkhaṃ, jotimālakam-pi dukkhaṃ, hatthapajjotikam-pi dukkhaṃ, erakavattikam-pi dukkhaṃ, cīrakavāsikam-pi dukkhaṃ, eṇeyyakam-pi dukkhaṃ, baḷisamaṃsikam-pi dukkhaṃ, kahāpaṇakam-pi dukkhaṃ, khārāpatacchikam-pi dukkhaṃ, palighaparivattikam-pi dukkhaṃ, palālapīṭhakam-pi dukkhaṃ, tattenapi telena osiñcanam-pi dukkhaṃ, sunakhehi khādāpanam-pi dukkhaṃ, jīvasūlāropanam-pi dukkhaṃ, asinā sīsacchedanam-pi dukkhaṃ, evarūpāni evarūpāni mahārāja bahuvidhāni anekavidhāni dukkhāni saṃsāragato anubhavati.

312 yathā mahārāja himavante pabbate abhivaṭṭaṃ udakaṃ gaṅgāya nadiyā pāsāṇa-sakkhara-khara-marumba-āvaṭṭa-gaggalaka-ūmikavankacadika-āvaraṇa-nīvarana-mūlaka-sākhāsu pariyottharati, evam-eva kho mahārāja evarūpāni evarūpāni bahuvidhāni anekavidhāni dukkhāni saṃsāragato anubhavati. pavattaṃ mahārāja dukkhaṃ, appavattaṃ sukhaṃ, appavattassa guṇaṃ pavatte ca bhayaṃ dīpayamāno mahārāja bhagavā appavattassa sacchikiriyāya jāti-jarā-byādhi-maraṇasamatikkamāya samādapesi. idam-ettha mahārāja kāraṇaṃ yena kāraṇena bhagavā

split rods is suffering, having one's hand cut off is suffering, having one's foot cut off is suffering, having both hand and foot cut off is suffering, having one's ear cut off is suffering, having one's nose cut off is suffering, having both ear and nose cut off is suffering, the 'gruel pot' torture is suffering, the 'polished shell shave' torture is suffering, the 'Rahu's mouth' torture is suffering, the 'fire wreath' torture is suffering, the 'flaming hand' torture is suffering, the 'grass torture' is suffering, the 'bark dress' torture is suffering, the 'black antelope' torture is suffering, the 'meat hook' torture is suffering, the 'coin' torture is suffering, the 'lye pickling' torture is suffering, the 'turning around the bar' torture is suffering, the 'straw bench' torture is suffering, dousing with burning oil is suffering, being eaten by dogs is suffering, being impaled alive on stakes is suffering, and having one's head cut off by a sword is suffering.[66] Such are the many and numerous kinds of suffering one experiences wandering through samsara, great king.

"Just as water rained on the Himalayan mountain flows 312
through the Ganga and then over rocks, gravel, rough sand, eddies, and whirlpools, over such obstacles and blockages made by branches and roots, with waves curving into the nooks, so too, great king, are the many and numerous sufferings one experiences wandering through samsara.[67] The whirl of rebirths is suffering, and freedom from the whirl is happiness. And so the Bhagavan, illuminating both the virtue of freedom from the whirl and the fear within it, urged the crossing over the stream of birth, old age, sickness, and death, and realizing for oneself freedom from the whirl. Such is the reason the Bhagavan urged it in this instance."

samādapesīti. sādhu bhante nāgasena, sunibbeṭhito pañho, sukathitaṃ kāraṇaṃ, evam-etaṃ, tathā sampaṭicchāmīti.

313 bhante nāgasena, bhāsitam-p' etaṃ bhagavatā: mettāya bhikkhave cetovimuttiyā āsevitāya bhāvitāya bahulīkatāya yānikatāya vatthukatāya anuṭṭhitāya paricitāya susamāraddhāya ekādas' ānisaṃsā pāṭikaṅkhā, katame ekādasa: sukhaṃ supati, sukhaṃ paṭibujjhati, na pāpakaṃ supinaṃ passati, manussānaṃ piyo hoti, amanussānaṃ piyo hoti, devatā rakkhanti, nāssa aggi vā visaṃ vā satthaṃ vā kamati, tuvaṭaṃ cittaṃ samādhiyati, mukhavaṇṇo vippasīdati, asammūḷho kālaṃ karoti, uttariṃ appaṭivijjhanto brahmalokūpago hotīti.

314 puna ca tumhe bhaṇatha: sāmo kumāro mettāvihārī migasaṅghena parivuto pavane vicaranto piliyakkhena raññā viddho visapītena sallena tatth' eva mucchito patito ti. yadi bhante nāgasena bhagavatā bhaṇitaṃ: mettāya bhikkhave-pe-brahmalokūpago hotīti, tena hi: sāmo kumāro mettāvihārī migasaṅghena parivuto pavane vicaranto piliyakkhena raññā viddho visapītena sallena tatth' eva mucchito patito ti yaṃ vacanaṃ taṃ micchā. yadi sāmo kumāro mettāvihārī migasaṅghena parivuto pavane vicaranto piliyakkhena raññā viddho visapītena sallena tatth' eva mucchito patito, tena hi: mettāya bhikkhave-pe-nāssa aggi vā visaṃ vā satthaṃ vā kamatīti tam-pi vacanaṃ micchā. ayam-pi ubhatokoṭiko pañho sunipuṇo parisaṇho sukhumo gambhīro, api sunipuṇānaṃ manujānaṃ gatte sedaṃ moceyya, so tav-

"Very well, revered Nagasena. The dilemma has been thoroughly unraveled and explained. This is so, and I accept it.

"Revered Nagasena, the Bhagavan also said this: 'Monks, 313
when freedom of the loving heart is practiced, cultivated,
frequented, mastered, made into one's foundation, established,
consolidated, and thoroughly undertaken, then
eleven benefits are anticipated. What are the eleven? One
sleeps well, wakes easily, and is free of nightmares; one
becomes dear to humans, dear to nonhumans, and protected
by the gods. One is unaffected by fire, poison, and weapons.
Concentrating the mind comes quickly, the expression on
one's face becomes serene, there is no confusion at death, and,
if not advancing higher, one will reach at least the Brahma
world.' But you also say this: 'The youth Sama dwelled in 314
loving-kindness while living in the forest surrounded by wild animals. Yet he was shot with a poison arrow by King Piliyakkha and collapsed on the spot.' Nagasena, if the Bhagavan told the monks of all the benefits of loving-kindness, including how it leads to the Brahma world, then it is false to claim that the youth Sama, dwelling in loving-kindness while he lived in the forest surrounded by wild animals, was shot with a poison arrow by King Piliyakkha and collapsed on the spot. Or if the youth Sama was dwelling in loving-kindness while living in the forest surrounded by wild animals when he was shot by a poison arrow by King Piliyakkha and collapsed on the spot, then it is false to claim that because of loving-kindness one is unaffected by fire, poison, and weapons. This two-pronged dilemma is so very clever, smooth, subtle, and deep that it would cause sweat to flow on the bodies of even the cleverest people, and it has reached you. Disentangle

ānuppatto, vijaṭehi taṃ mahājaṭājaṭitaṃ, anāgatānaṃ jinaputtānaṃ cakkhuṃ dehi nibbāhanāyāti.

315 bhāsitam-p' etaṃ mahārāja bhagavatā: mettāya bhikkhave-pe-nāssa aggi vā visaṃ vā satthaṃ vā kamatīti. sāmo ca kumāro mettāvihārī migasaṅghena parivuto pavane vicaranto piliyakkhena raññā viddho visapītena sallena tatth' eva mucchito patito. tattha pana mahārāja kāraṇaṃ atthi. katamaṃ tattha kāraṇaṃ: n' ete mahārāja guṇā puggalassa, mettābhāvanāy' ete guṇā. sāmo mahārāja kumāro ghaṭaṃ ukkhipanto tasmiṃ khaṇe mettābhāvanāya pamatto ahosi. yasmiṃ mahārāja khaṇe puggalo mettaṃ samāpanno hoti, na tassa puggalassa tasmiṃ khaṇe aggi vā visaṃ vā satthaṃ vā kamati, tassa ye keci ahitakāmā upagantvā taṃ na passanti, na tasmiṃ okāsaṃ labhanti; n' ete mahārāja guṇā puggalassa, mettābhāvanāy' ete guṇā.

316 idha mahārāja puriso saṅgāmasūro abhejjakavacajālikaṃ sannayhitvā saṅgāmaṃ otareyya, tassa sarā khittā upagantvā patanti vikiranti, na tasmiṃ okāsaṃ labhanti; n' eso mahārāja guṇo saṅgāmasūrassa, abhejjakavacajālikāy' eso guṇo, yassa sarā khittā upagantvā patanti vikiranti. evameva kho mahārāja n' ete guṇā puggalassa, mettābhāvanāy'ete guṇā; yasmiṃ mahārāja khaṇe puggalo mettaṃ samāpanno hoti na tassa puggalassa tasmiṃ khaṇe aggi vā visaṃ vā satthaṃ vā kamati, tassa ye keci ahitakāmā upagantvā taṃ

this great tangle of knots and, clearing it away, give vision to those the Victor's descendants yet to come."

"Great king, the Bhagavan did say, 'Monks, because of 315
loving-kindness one is unaffected by fire, poison, and weapons.' And the youth Sama was dwelling in loving-kindness as he lived in the forest surrounded by wild animals when he was shot with a poison arrow by King Piliyakkha and collapsed on the spot. But there is a reason for this. What is the reason? Great king, these special qualities do not belong to a person, but rather are due to the cultivation of loving-kindness. The youth Sama was picking up a pitcher and was careless about cultivating loving-kindness in that moment. In whatever moment a person attains loving-kindness, in that moment fire, poison, and weapons do not affect him, and those wishing him harm may approach but do not see him or get a chance. So these are not special qualities of the person, but rather qualities brought about by the cultivation of loving-kindness.

"Suppose a war hero were to put on impenetrable armor 316
and join a battle. Arrows hurled at him reach him, but then scatter and fall, and do not get their chance at that time. This is not a special quality of the war hero, but rather a quality due to the impenetrable armor that when hurled arrows reach him, they scatter and fall. In just this way, great king, these are not the special qualities of the person, but are qualities due to the cultivation of loving-kindness. When a person attains loving-kindness, great king, in that moment fire, poison, and weapons do not affect him, and those wishing him harm may approach but do not see him or get a chance. These

na passanti, tasmiṃ okāsaṃ na labhanti; n' ete mahārāja guṇā puggalassa, mettābhāvanāy' ete guṇā.

317 idha pana mahārāja puriso dibbaṃ antaradhānaṃ mūlaṃ hatthe kareyya, yāva taṃ mūlaṃ tassa hatthagataṃ hoti tāva na añño koci pakatimanusso taṃ purisaṃ passati, n'eso mahārāja guṇo purisassa, mūlass' eso guṇo antaradhānassa, yaṃ so pakatimanussānaṃ cakkhu-pathe na dissati. evam-eva kho mahārāja n'ete guṇāpuggalassa, mettābhāvanāy' ete guṇā; yasmiṃ mahārāja khaṇe puggalo mettaṃ samāpanno hoti na tassa puggalassa tasmiṃ khaṇe aggi vā visaṃ vā satthaṃ vā kamati, tassa ye keci ahitakāmā upagantvā taṃ na passanti, na tasmiṃ okāsaṃ labhanti; n' ete mahārāja guṇā puggalassa, mettābhāvanāy' ete guṇā.

318 yathā vā pana mahārāja purisaṃ sukataṃ mahatimahā-leṇam-anupaviṭṭhaṃ mahatimahāmegho abhivassanto na sakkoti temayituṃ, n' eso mahārāja guṇo purisassa, mahā-leṇassa so guṇo, yaṃ mahatimahāmegho abhivassamāno na taṃ temeti; evam eva kho mahārāja n' ete guṇā puggalassa, mettābhāvanāy' ete guṇā, yasmiṃ mahārāja khaṇe puggalo mettaṃ samāpanno hoti na tassa puggalassa tasmiṃ khaṇe aggi vā visaṃ vā satthaṃ vā kamati, tassa ye keci ahitakāmā upagantvā taṃ na passanti, na tassa sakkonti ahitaṃ kātuṃ, n' ete mahārāja guṇā puggalassa, mettābhāvanāy' ete guṇā ti.

319 acchariyaṃ bhante nāgasena, abbhutaṃ bhante nāgasena, sabbapāpanivāraṇā mettābhāvanā ti. sabbakusalaguṇāvahā

are not special qualities of the person, but rather qualities brought about by the cultivation of loving-kindness.

“Suppose a man were to take a magical disappearing root 317
into his hand and as long as the root is in his hand ordinary people cannot see him. This is not a quality of the person, but rather a quality of the disappearing root whereby he is not visible in the visual field of ordinary people. In just this way, great king, these are not the special qualities of the person but qualities due to the cultivation of loving-kindness. When a person attains loving-kindness, great king, in that moment fire, poison, and weapons do not affect him, and those wishing him harm may approach but do not see him or get a chance. These are not special qualities of the person, but rather qualities brought about by the cultivation of loving-kindness.

“Great king, it is just like how a huge thundercloud may 318
pour but cannot drench a man who has entered a large and well-formed cave. This is not a special quality of the man but rather of the large cave, whereby a huge thundercloud may pour but cannot drench him. In just this way, great king, these are not the special qualities of the person but are qualities due to the cultivation of loving-kindness. When a person attains loving-kindness, great king, in that moment fire, poison, and weapons do not affect him, and those wishing him harm may approach but do not see him or get a chance. These are not special qualities of the person but rather qualities brought about by the cultivation of loving-kindness.”

“Wonderful, revered Nagasena! Marvelous, revered 319
Nagasena! The cultivation of loving-kindness is the obstacle of every evil.”

mahārāja mettābhāvanā hitānam-pi ahitānam -pi, ye te sattā viññāṇabaddhā sabbesaṃ mahānisaṃsā mettābhāvanā saṃvibhajitabbā ti.

320 bhante nāgasena, kusalakārissa pi akusalakārissa pi vipāko samasamo udāhu koci viseso atthīti. atthi mahārāja kusalassa ca akusalassa ca viseso, kusalaṃ mahārāja sukhavipākaṃ saggasaṃvattanikaṃ, akusalaṃ dukkhavipākaṃ nirayasaṃvattanikan-ti.

321 bhante nāgasena, tumhe bhaṇatha: devadatto ekantakaṇho ekantakaṇhehi dhammehi samannāgato, bodhisatto ekantasukko ekantasukkehi dhammehi samannāgato ti. puna ca devadatto bhave bhave yasena ca pakkhena ca bodhisattena samasamo hoti, kadāci adhikataro vā. yadā devadatto nagare bārāṇasiyaṃ brahmadattassa rañño purohitaputto ahosi, tadā bodhisatto chavakacaṇḍālo ahosi vijjādharo, vijjaṃ parijapitvā akāle ambaphalāni nibbattesi; ettha tāva bodhisatto devadattato jātiyā nihīno yasasā ca nihīno.

322 puna ca paraṃ yadā devadatto rājā ahosi mahāmahīpati sabbakāmasamaṅgī, tadā bodhisatto tassūpabhogo ahosi hatthināgo sabbalakkhaṇasampanno, tassa cārugativilāsaṃ asahamāno rājā vadham-icchanto hatthācariyaṃ evam-avoca: asikkhito te ācariya hatthināgo, tassa ākāsagamanaṃ nāma kāraṇaṃ karohīti; tattha pi tāva bodhisatto devadattato jātiyā nihīno, lāmako tiracchānagato. puna ca paraṃ yadā devadatto manusso ahosi pavane naṭṭhāyiko, tadā bodhisatto mahāpaṭhavī nāma makkaṭo ahosi; ettha pi tāva dissati viseso manussassa ca tiracchānagatassa ca, ettha pi tāva bodhisatto devadattato jātiyā nihīno. puna ca paraṃ yadā devadatto manusso ahosi, soṇuttaro nāma nesādo balavā balavataro nāgabalo, tadā bodhisatto chad-

"The cultivation of loving-kindness carries every good quality for the friendly and the unfriendly alike, great king. And for those fixing their awareness on it, the cultivation of loving-kindness is very beneficial and should be everywhere shared.

"Revered Nagasena, is the result the same for one who 320
does good as for the one who does bad, or is there a difference?"

"Great king, there is a difference between good and bad. The good has happiness as its result and is conducive to heaven while the bad has suffering as its result and is conducive to hell."

"But Nagasena, you say that Devadatta is thoroughly 321
dark and possessed of every dark phenomenal state, while the Bodhisatta is thoroughly bright and possessed of every bright phenomenal state. And yet, in birth after birth Devadatta was equal to the Bodhisatta with respect to reputation and adherents, and sometimes even superior to him. When Devadatta was the son of King Brahmadatta's chaplain in Baranasi, the Bodhisatta was a wretched outcaste, a sorcerer who muttered spells and produced mango fruits out of season.[68] This is a case where the Bodhisatta was inferior to Devadatta by birth and inferior in reputation.

"And when Devadatta was a king, a great ruler of the earth 322
enjoying every pleasure, one of his luxuries was his bull elephant, that is, the Bodhisatta, who possessed every auspicious mark. With his pride not enduring the charm of the elephant's beautiful bearing, the king wished for his death and told the elephant trainer: 'Trainer, the bull elephant is poorly trained. Make him perform the Sky Walk.' This is a

danto nāma nāgarājā ahosi, tadā so luddako taṃ hatthināgaṃ ghātesi; tattha pi tāva devadattova adhikataro.

323 puna ca paraṃ yadā devadatto manusso ahosi vanacāraṇo aniketavāsī, tadā bodhisatto sakuṇo ahosi tittiro mantajjhāyī, tadāpi so vanacāraṇo taṃ sakuṇaṃ ghātesi; tattha pi tāva devadattova jātiyā adhikataro. puna ca paraṃ yadā devadatto kalābu nāma kāsirājā ahosi, tadā bodhisatto tāpaso ahosi khantivādī, tadā so rājā tassa tāpasassa kuddho hatthapāde vaṃsakaḷīre viya chedāpesi; tattha pi tāva devadatto yeva adhikataro jātiyā ca yasena ca. puna ca paraṃ yadā devadatto manusso ahosi vanacaro, tadā bodhisatto nandiyo nāma vānarindo ahosi, tadā pi so vanacaro taṃ vanarindaṃ ghātesi saddhiṃ mātarā kaniṭṭhabhātikena ca; tattha pi tāva devadatto yeva adhikataro jātiyā. puna ca paraṃ yadā devadatto manusso ahosi acelako kārambhiyo nāma, tadā bodhisatto paṇḍarako nāma nāgarājā ahosi; tattha pi tāva devadatto yeva adhikataro jātiyā.

324 puna ca paraṃ yadā devadatto manusso ahosi pavane jaṭilako, tadā bodhisatto tacchako nāma mahāsūkaro ahosi; tattha pi tāva devadatto yeva jātiyā adhikataro. puna ca paraṃ yadā devadatto cetīsu suraparicaro nāma rājā ahosi uparipurisamatte gagane vehāsaṅgamo, tadā bodhisatto kapilo nāma brāhmaṇo ahosi; tattha pi tāva devadatto yeva

case where the Bodhisatta was a lower being, an animal, and thus inferior to Devadatta by birth.

"And more. Once Devadatta was a man who became ruined in the woods while the Bodhisatta was a monkey called Great Earth. In this case too there is the distinction between human and animal, and the Bodhisatta was inferior to Devadatta by birth. And once Devadatta was a man named Sonuttara, a powerful hunter, with strength greater than that of an elephant, while the Bodhisatta was an elephant king called Chaddanta. The hunter killed the bull elephant and
so there too, Devadatta was the superior. And once Deva- 323
datta was a man, a homeless wanderer in the forest, while the Bodhisatta was a bird, a partridge who knew mantras. The forest wanderer killed this bird, and so there too Devadatta was superior. And once Devadatta was the king of Kasi named Kalabu, while the Bodhisatta was an ascetic preaching forbearance. The king grew enraged and had the ascetic's hands and feet cut off, much as the top of bamboo is split. In this case too, Devadatta was superior in birth and reputation.

"There is more. Once Devadatta was a woodsman and the Bodhisatta was a monkey king named Nandiya. The woodsman killed the monkey king together with his mother and youngest brother. There too Devadatta was superior by birth. And once Devadatta was a naked ascetic named Karambhiya while the Bodhisatta was a *nāga* king named
Pandaraka. There too, Devadatta was superior by birth. And 324
once Devadatta was a man who was a matted-hair ascetic in the forest while the Bodhisatta was a huge boar called Tacchaka. There too, Devadatta was superior by birth. And once Devadatta was Suraparicara by name, a king of

adhikataro jātiyā ca yasena ca. puna ca paraṃ yadā devadatto manusso ahosi sāmo nāma, tadā bodhisatto ruru nāma migarājā ahosi; tattha pi tāva devadatto yeva jātiyā adhikataro.

325 puna ca paraṃ yadā devadatto manusso ahosi luddako pavanacaro, tadā bodhisatto hatthināgo ahosi, so luddako tassa hatthināgassa sattakkhattuṃ dante chinditvā hari; tattha pi tāva devadatto yeva yoniyā adhikataro. puna ca paraṃ yadā devadatto sigālo ahosi khattiyadhammo, so yāvatā jambudīpe padesarājāno te sabbe anuyutte akāsi, tadā bodhisatto vidhuro nāma paṇḍito ahosi; tattha pi tāva devadatto yeva yasena adhikataro. puna ca paraṃ yadā devadatto hatthināgo hutvā laṭukikāya sakuṇikāya puttake ghātesi, tadā bodhisatto pi hatthināgo ahosi yūthapati; tattha tāva ubho pi te samasamā ahesuṃ.

326 puna ca paraṃ yadā devadatto yakkho ahosi adhammo nāma, tadā bodhisatto pi yakkho[12] ahosi dhammo nāma, tattha pi tāva ubho pi samasamā ahesuṃ. puna ca paraṃ yadā devadatto nāviko ahosi pañcannaṃ kulasatānaṃ issaro, tadā bodhisatto pi nāviko ahosi pañcannaṃ kulasatānaṃ issaro; tattha pi tāva ubho pi samasamāva ahesuṃ. puna ca paraṃ yadā devadatto satthavāho ahosi pañcannaṃ sakaṭasatānaṃ issaro, tadā bodhisatto pi satthavāho ahosi pañcannaṃ sakaṭasatānaṃ issaro; tattha pi tāva ubho pi samasamā ahesuṃ.

327 puna ca paraṃ yadā devadatto sākho nāma migarājā ahosi, tadā bodhisatto pi nigrodho nāma migarājā ahosi; tattha pi tāva ubho pi samasamā ahesuṃ. puna ca paraṃ yadā devadatto sākho nāma senāpati ahosi, tadā bodhisatto

the Ceti kingdom who could travel by air through the sky above people. The Bodhisatta was a Brahman called Kapila. There too Devadatta was superior by birth and reputation. And once Devadatta was a man called Sama while the Bodhisatta was the deer king called Ruru. There too Devadatta was superior by birth.

"Further, Devadatta was once a hunter wandering in the 325
forest and the Bodhisatta was a bull elephant. The hunter cut off and stole the bull elephant's tusks seven times. There too Devadatta was superior by birth. And once Devadatta was a jackal who lived according to the duties of Kshatriyas and made all the regional kings throughout Jambudipa his vassals. The Bodhisatta was a learned man named Vidhura. In this case, Devadatta was his superior in reputation.

"And once Devadatta was a bull elephant who destroyed the offspring of a quail. The Bodhisatta was also a bull elephant, the leader of a herd. In this case, they were equals.
And once Devadatta was a *yakkha* named Anti-Dhamma 326
while the Bodhisatta was a *yakkha* called Dhamma. There too, they were equals. And once Devadatta was a sailor and the chief of five hundred families. The Bodhisatta was also a sailor, chief of five hundred families, so there too, they were equals. And once Devadatta was a caravan leader, head of five hundred wagons, and the Bodhisatta was also a caravan leader heading five hundred wagons. In this case
also they were equals. And once Devadatta was a deer king 327
named Sakha and the Bodhisatta was a deer king also, named Nigrodha. In this case also they were equals. And similarly, Devadatta was once a general called Sakha while the Bodhi-

nigrodho nāma rājā ahosi; tattha pi tāva ubho pi samasamā ahesuṃ. puna ca paraṃ yadā devadatto khaṇḍahālo nāma brāhmaṇo ahosi, tadā bodhisatto cando nāma rājakumāro ahosi; tadā ayaṃ khaṇḍahālo yeva adhikataro.

328 puna ca paraṃ yadā devadatto brahmadatto nāma rājā ahosi, tadā bodhisatto tassa putto mahāpadumo nāma kumāro ahosi, tadā so rājā sakaputtaṃ corappapāte khipāpesi; yato kutoci pitāva puttānaṃ adhikataro hoti visiṭṭho ti tattha pi tāva devadatto yeva adhikataro. puna ca paraṃ yadā devadatto mahāpatāpo nāma rājā ahosi, tadā bodhisatto tassa putto dhammapālo nāma kumāro ahosi, tadā so rājā sakaputtassa hatthapāde sīsañ-ca chedāpesi; tattha pi tāva devadatto yeva uttaro adhikataro. ajj' etarahi ubho pi sakyakule jāyiṃsu, bodhisatto buddho ahosi sabbaññū lokanāyako, devadatto tassa atidevadevassa sāsane pabbajitvā iddhiṃ nibbattetvā buddhālayaṃ akāsi. kin-nu kho bhante nāgasena yaṃ mayā bhaṇitaṃ taṃ sabbaṃ tathaṃ udāhu vitathan-ti.

329 yan-tvaṃ mahārāja bahuvidhaṃ kāraṇaṃ osāresi, sabbantaṃ tath' eva no aññathā ti. yadi bhante nāgasena kaṇho pi sukko pi samasamagatikā honti, tena hi kusalam-pi akusalam-pi samasamavipākaṃ hotīti. na hi mahārāja kusalam-pi akusalam-pi samasamavipākaṃ hoti, na hi mahārāja, devadatto sabbajanehi paṭiviruddho, bodhisatteneva[13] paṭiviruddho, yo tassa bodhisatte paṭivirodho so tasmiṃ tasmiṃ yeva bhave paccati phalaṃ deti. devadatto pi mahārāja issariye ṭhito janapadesu ārakkhaṃ deti, setuṃ sabhaṃ

satta was a general called Nigrodha, where they were once again equals.

"And then Devadatta was once a Brahman known as Khandahala and the Bodhisatta was a prince known as Canda, and there Khandahala was superior. And once Devadatta 328
was a king named Brahmadatta and the Bodhisatta was his son, a prince called Mahapaduma. The king had his own son thrown down a robbers' cliff. Inasmuch as fathers are greater than their sons, Devadatta was his superior. And once Devadatta was a king called Mahapatapa and the Bodhisatta was his son, a prince called Dhammapala. The king had his own son's hands, feet, and head cut off. In that case Devadatta was much superior.

"Finally, in this time too, both were born in the Sakya family, and the Bodhisatta became the omniscient Buddha, leader of the world, while Devadatta, ordained in the dispensation of that god above gods, performed magical powers, and made a pretense of being a buddha. Nagasena, is everything that I have said true or untrue?"

"The many cases you have related are all true, great king, 329
and not otherwise."

"Then dark and bright lead to the same fate, Nagasena, and so good and bad lead to the same results."

"No, great king, good and bad do not lead to the same results. Devadatta was not opposed by all the people, but he was opposed by the Bodhisatta, and whatever hostility he had toward the Bodhisatta ripened over this and that existence and yielded fruit. And yet, when Devadatta ascended to rule, he provided protection to the country; had bridges, public rest houses, and merit-making halls built; and gave

puññasālaṃ kāreti, samaṇa-brāhmaṇānaṃ kapaṇiddhika-va-nibbakānaṃ nāthānāthānaṃ yathāpaṇihitaṃ dānaṃ deti; tassa so vipākena bhave bhave sampattiyo paṭilabhati. kass' etaṃ mahārāja sakkā vattuṃ: vinā dānena damena saṃyamena uposathakammena sampattiṃ anubhavissatīti.

330 yaṃ pana tvaṃ mahārāja evaṃ vadesi: devadatto ca bodhisatto ca ekato anuparivattantīti, so na jātisatassa accayena samāgamo ahosi, na jātisahassassa accayena, na jātisatasahassassa accayena, kadāci karahaci bahunnaṃ ahorattānaṃ accayena samāgamo ahosi. yaṃ pan' etaṃ mahārāja bhagavatā kāṇakacchapopamaṃ upadassitaṃ manussattapaṭilābhāya, tathūpamaṃ mahārāja imesaṃ samāgamaṃ dhārehi. na mahārāja bodhisattassa devadatten' eva saddhiṃ samāgamo ahosi, thero pi mahārāja sāriputto anekesu jātisatasahassesu bodhisattassa pitā ahosi, mahāpitā ahosi, cullapitā ahosi, bhātā ahosi, putto ahosi, bhāgineyyo ahosi, mitto ahosi. bodhisatto pi mahārāja anekesu jātisatasahassesu therassa sāriputtassa pitā ahosi, mahāpitā ahosi, cullapitā ahosi, bhātā ahosi, putto ahosi, bhāgineyyo ahosi, mitto ahosi.

331 sabbe pi mahārāja sattakāyapariyāpannā saṃsārasotam anugatā saṃsārasotena vuyhantā appiyehi pi piyehi pi samāgacchanti. yathā mahārāja udakaṃ sotena vuyhamānaṃ suci-asuci-kalyāṇa-pāpakena samāgacchati, evam eva kho mahārāja sabbe pi sattakayapariyāpannā saṃsārasotam-anugatā saṃsārasotena vuyhantā appiyehi pi piyehi pi samāgacchanti.

alms to renouncers, Brahmans, poor people, travelers, and wayfarers whether they had patrons or not, according to his resolutions. And so he achieved success in existence after existence by way of result. For whom is it possible to say that without giving, self-control, restraint, and the Uposatha Observance, one may achieve success?

"Furthermore, great king, you say that Devadatta and 330
the Bodhisatta journeyed together through samsara. But
although they often did not meet after a lapse of a hundred
births, nor after a lapse of a thousand births, nor after a
hundred thousand births, at certain times there was an
association as often as every few days and nights. Great
king, please bear in mind the simile taught by the Bhagavan
about the blind turtle, and that obtaining a human birth is
like this.[69] And the Bodhisatta did not have an association
only with Devadatta. In fact, Elder Sariputta was the father
of the Bodhisatta in numerous hundreds and thousands
of births, as well as his grandfather, uncle, brother, son,
nephew, and friend. And the Bodhisatta was also the father
of Elder Sariputta in numerous hundreds and thousands
of births, and his grandfather, uncle, brother, son, nephew,
and friend. All of those among the various forms of beings 331
flowing along the stream of samsara and carried along by
the stream of samsara encounter those who are loved and
those who are not loved. Much as the water carried along
by a stream encounters the pure and the impure and the
beautiful and the evil, so too, great king, all those among the
various forms of beings flowing along the stream of samsara
and carried along by the stream of samsara encounter the
loved and the unloved.

332 devadatto mahārāja yakkho samāno attanā adhammo pare adhamme niyojetvā sattapaññāsa vassakoṭiyo saṭṭhiñ-ca vassasatasahassāni mahāniraye pacci. bodhisatto pi mahārāja yakkho samāno attanā dhammo pare dhamme niyojetvā sattapaññāsa vassakoṭiyo saṭṭhiñ-ca vassasatasahassāni sagge modi sabbakāmasamaṅgī. api ca mahārāja devadatto imasmiṃ bhave buddhaṃ anāsādaniyam āsādayitvā samaggañ-ca saṅghaṃ bhinditvā paṭhaviṃ pāvisi; tathāgato bujjhitvā sabbadhamme parinibbuto upadhisaṅkhaye ti. sādhu bhante nāgasena, evam-etaṃ, tathā sampaṭicchāmīti.

333 bhante nāgasena, bhāsitam-p'etaṃ bhagavatā: sace labhetha khaṇaṃ vā raho vā, nimantakaṃ vā pi labhetha tādisaṃ, sabbā pi itthiyo kareyyu pāpaṃ, aññaṃ aladdhā pīṭhasappinā saddhin-ti. puna ca kathīyati: mahosadhassa bhariyā amarā nāma itthī gāmake ṭhapitā pavutthapatikā raho nisinnā vivittā rājapaṭisamaṃ sāmikaṃ karitvā sahassena nimantiyamānā pāpaṃ nākāsīti. yadi bhante nāgasena bhagavatā bhaṇitaṃ: sace labhetha khaṇaṃ vā raho vā, nimantakaṃ vā pi labhetha tādisaṃ, sabbā pi itthiyo kareyyu pāpaṃ, aññaṃ aladdhā pīṭhasappinā saddhin-ti, tena hi: mahosadhassa bhariyā amarā nāma itthī gāmake ṭhapitā pavutthapatikā raho nisinnā vivittā rājapaṭisamaṃ sāmikaṃ karitvā sahassena nimantiyamānā pāpaṃ nākāsīti yaṃ vacanaṃ taṃ micchā.

"Once Devadatta, as a *yakkha,* was 'Anti-Dhamma' 332
himself and incited others against the Dhamma; he then roasted in the Great Hell for fifty-seven crore and one hundred sixty thousand years. And the Bodhisatta, also as a *yakkha,* was 'Dhamma' himself, and incited others to the Dhamma; he then rejoiced in heaven for fifty-seven crore and one hundred sixty thousand years, lavished with every pleasure. Moreover, great king, in this existence, Devadatta attacked the Buddha, who is never to be attacked, and he split the community, so he was swallowed by the earth. The Tathagata became awakened in all things and achieved final awakening in the destruction of clinging to rebirth."

"Very well, Nagasena. It is so and I accept this.

"Revered Nagasena, the Bhagavan said: 'All women would 333
do evil if given the opportunity, could do so in secret, or were invited to; and not finding anyone else, they would do so with a lame man.'[70] And yet it is said that a woman named Amara, the wife of Mahosadha, stayed in the village while her husband was away and sat hidden and alone, having made her husband the equal of a king. Though offered a thousand, she did not commit evil.

"Nagasena, if the Bhagavan said that 'All women would do evil if given the opportunity, could do so in secret, or were invited to; and not finding anyone else, they would do so with a lame man,' then it is false to claim that a woman named Amara, the wife of Mahosadha, stayed in the village while her husband was away, sat hidden and alone, having made her husband the equal of a king, and though offered a thousand, did not commit evil.

334 yadi mahosadhassa bhariyā amarā nāma itthī gāmake ṭhapitā pavutthapatikā raho nisinnā vivittā rājapaṭisamaṃ sāmikaṃ karitvā sahassena nimantiyamānā pāpaṃ nākāsi, tena hi: sace labhetha khaṇaṃ vā raho vā, nimantakaṃ vā pi labhetha tādisaṃ, sabbā pi itthiyo kareyyu pāpaṃ, aññaṃ aladdhā pīṭhasappinā saddhin-ti tam-pi vacanaṃ micchā. ayam-pi ubhatokoṭiko pañho tavānuppatto, so tayā nibbāhitabbo ti.

335 bhāsitam-p'etaṃ mahārāja bhagavatā: sace labhetha khaṇaṃ vā raho vā, nimantakaṃ vā pi labhetha tādisaṃ, sabbā pi itthiyo kareyyu pāpaṃ, aññaṃ aladdhā pīṭhasappinā saddhin-ti. kathīyati ca: mahosadhassa bhariyā amarā nāma itthī gāmake ṭhapitā pavutthapatikā raho nisinnā vivittā rājapaṭisamaṃ sāmikaṃ karitvā sahassena nimantiyamānā pāpaṃ nākāsīti. kareyya sā mahārāja itthī sahassaṃ labhamānā tādisena purisena saddhiṃ pāpakammaṃ, na sā kareyya, sace khaṇaṃ vā raho vā nimantakaṃ vā pi tādisaṃ labheyya.

336 vicinantī sā mahārāja amarā itthī na addasa khaṇaṃ vā raho vā nimantakaṃ vā pi tādisaṃ. idhaloke garahabhayā khaṇaṃ na passi, paraloke nirayabhayā khaṇaṃ na passi, kaṭukavipākaṃ pāpan-ti khaṇaṃ na passi, piyaṃ na muñcitukāmā khaṇaṃ na passi, sāmikassa garukatāya khaṇaṃ na passi, dhammaṃ apacāyantī khaṇaṃ na passi, anariyaṃ garahantī

"Or if it is the case that the woman named Amara, the wife 334
of Mahosadha, stayed in the village while her husband was away, sitting hidden and alone, having made her husband the equal of a king, and though offered a thousand, did not commit evil, then it is false to claim that 'All women would do evil if given the opportunity, could do so in secret, or were invited to; and not finding anyone else, they would do so with a lame man.' This two-pronged dilemma has reached you, and you must solve it."

"Great king, the Bhagavan did say that 'all women would 335
do evil if given the opportunity, could do so in secret, or were invited to; and not finding anyone else, they would do so with a lame man.' And it is said that the woman named Amara, the wife of Mahosadha, stayed in the village while her husband was away, sitting hidden and alone, having made her husband the equal of a king, and though offered a thousand, did not commit evil. Would this woman do evil upon getting a thousand with any available man, or would she not do so even if there was an opportunity, secrecy, or an invitation?

"Great king, the woman Amara considered whether there 336
was an opportunity, secrecy, or an invitation, but did not see any. Out of fear of blame in this world, she did not see an opportunity, and out of fear of hell in the hereafter, she did not see an opportunity. Thinking that evil has severe results, she did not see an opportunity, and not wishing to lose one she loved, she did not see an opportunity. Due to respect for her husband, she did not see an opportunity, and reverencing the Dhamma, she did not see an opportunity. Despising the dishonorable, she did not see an opportunity, and not

khaṇaṃ na passi, kiriyaṃ na bhinditukāmā khaṇaṃ na passi. evarūpehi bahukehi kāraṇehi khaṇaṃ na passi.

337 raho pi sā loke vicinitvā na passantī pāpaṃ nākāsi. sace sā manussehi raho labheyya, atha amanussehi raho na labheyya; sace amanussehi raho labheyya, atha paracittavidūhi pabbajitehi raho na labheyya; sace paracittavidūhi pabbajitehi raho labheyya, atha paracittavidūnīhi devatāhi raho na labheyya; sace paracittavidūnīhi devatāhi raho labheyya, atha attanāva pāpehi raho na labheyya; sace attanāva pāpehi raho labheyya, atha adhammena raho na labheyya. evarūpehi bahuvidhehi kāraṇehi raho na labhitvā pāpaṃ nākāsi.

338 nimantakam-pi sā loke vicinitvā tādisaṃ alabhaṇtī pāpaṃ nākāsi. mahosadho mahārāja paṇḍito aṭṭhavīsatiyā aṅgehi samannāgato, katamehi aṭṭhavīsatiyā aṅgehi samannāgato: mahosadho mahārāja sūro, hirimā, ottāpī, sapakkho, mittasampanno, khamo, sīlavā, saccavādī, soceyyasampanno, akkodhano, anatimānī, anusuyyako, viriyavā, āyūhako, saṅgāhako, saṃvibhāgī, sakhilo, nivātavutti, saṇho,[14] asaṭho, amāyāvī, atibuddhi-sampanno, kittimā, vijjāsampanno, hitesī upanissitānaṃ, patthito sabbajanassa, dhanavā, yasavā. mahosadho mahārāja paṇḍito imehi aṭṭha-

wanting to break her vow, she did not see an opportunity. She did not see an opportunity for many such reasons as these.

“Having considered the matter of secrecy in this world, 337
she saw none and so did not commit evil. For if she had found secrecy among humans, she would not have found secrecy among nonhumans. If she had found secrecy among nonhumans, she would not have found secrecy among those renouncers who know the minds of others. If she had found secrecy among renouncers who know the minds of others, she would not have found secrecy among gods who know the minds of others. If she had found secrecy among gods who know the minds of others, she would not have found secrecy from herself with respect to evil things. And if she had found secrecy from herself with respect to evil things, she still would not have found secrecy because of the unrighteousness. Not finding secrecy for many such reasons as these, she did not commit evil.

“Having considered the matter of an invitation, she found 338
none in the world, and so did not commit evil. For Mahosadha was learned and possessed twenty-eight features. What are the twenty-eight features? Great king, Mahosadha was courageous, conscientious, and scrupulous; he had followers and friends; he was forbearing, virtuous, truthful, and pure. Lacking anger, conceit, and envy, he was full of exertion and striving; he was kind, generous, congenial, mild, gentle, guileless, and free of all deceit. He possessed great intelligence, cleverness, and knowledge. He sought the welfare of his dependents, was sought after by everyone, and was wealthy and famous. Mahosadha was learned and possessed these twenty-eight features. Not

vīsatiyā aṅgehi samannāgato. sā aññaṃ tādisaṃ nimantakaṃ alabhitvā pāpaṃ nākāsīti. sādhu bhante nāgasena, evam-etaṃ, tathā sampaṭicchāmīti.

339 bhante nāgasena, bhāsitam-p' etaṃ bhagavatā: vigatabhayasantāsā arahanto ti. puna ca nagare rājagahe dhanapālakaṃ hatthiṃ bhagavati opatantaṃ disvā pañca khīṇāsavasatāni pariccajitvā jinavaraṃ pakkantāni disāvidisaṃ, ekaṃ ṭhapetvā theraṃ ānandaṃ. kin-nu kho bhante nāgasena te arahanto bhayā pakkantā, paññāyissati sakena kammenāti dasabalaṃ pātetukāmā pakkantā, udāhu tathāgatassa atulaṃ vipulam-asamaṃ pāṭihāriyaṃ daṭṭhukāmā pakkantā. yadi bhante nāgasena bhagavatā bhaṇitaṃ: vigatabhayasantāsā arahanto ti, tena hi: nagare rājagahe dhanapālakaṃ hatthiṃ bhagavati opatantaṃ disvā pañca khīṇāsavasatāni pariccajitvā jinavaraṃ pakkantāni disāvidisaṃ ekaṃ ṭhapetvā theraṃ ānandan-ti yaṃ vacanaṃ taṃ micchā. yadi nagare rājagahe dhanapālakaṃ hatthiṃ bhagavati opatantaṃ disvā pañca khīṇāsavasatāni pariccajitvā jinavaraṃ pakkantāni disāvidisaṃ ekaṃ ṭhapetvā theraṃ ānandaṃ, tena hi: vigatabhayasantāsā arahanto ti tam pi vacanaṃ micchā. ayam-pi ubhatokoṭiko pañho tavānuppatto, so tayā nibbāhitabbo ti.

340 bhāsitam-p' etaṃ mahārāja bhagavatā: vigatabhayasantāsā arahanto ti. nagare ca rājagahe dhanapālakaṃ hatthiṃ bhagavati opatantaṃ disvā pañca khīṇāsavasatāni pariccajitvā jinavaraṃ pakkantāni disāvidisaṃ ekaṃ ṭhapetvā theraṃ ānandaṃ. tañ-ca pana na bhayā, nāpi bhagavant-

receiving an invitation by one equal to him, she did not commit evil."

"Very well, revered Nagasena. This is so, and I am convinced.

"Revered Nagasena, the Bhagavan also said that 'arhats 339
are free of fear and trembling.' And yet, once in the city of Rajagaha, seeing the elephant Dhanapalaka bearing down on the Bhagavan, five hundred arhats abandoned the Best of Victors and scattered in every direction.[71] All except for Elder Ananda. Can it be, Nagasena, that the arhats scattered out of fear? Did they scatter because they wanted the Ten-Powered One to fall, thinking that he would reveal his own karma? Or did they scatter hoping to watch the Tathagata's great, incomparable, and unmatched miracle? Nagasena, if the Bhagavan said, 'Arhats are free of fear and trembling,' then it is false to claim that in the city of Rajagaha five hundred arhats, seeing the elephant Dhanapalaka bearing down on the Bhagavan, abandoned the Best of Victors and scattered in every direction. All except for Elder Ananda. But if it did happen that seeing the elephant Dhanapalaka bearing down on the Bhagavan in Rajagaha City, five hundred arhats abandoned the Best of Victors and scattered in every direction, save for Elder Ananda, then the claim that arhats are free of fear and trembling is false. This two-pronged dilemma has reached you, and you must solve it."

"Great king, the Bhagavan did say, 'Arhats are free of fear 340
and trembling.' And in the city of Rajagaha five hundred arhats, upon seeing the elephant Dhanapalaka bear down on the Bhagavan, did abandon the Best of Victors and scatter in every direction. All except for Elder Ananda. But this was

aṃ pātetukāmatāya. yena pana mahārāja hetunā arahanto bhāyeyyuṃ vā taseyyuṃ vā so hetu arahantānaṃ samucchinno, tasmā vigatabhayasantāsā arahanto. bhāyati nu mahārāja mahāpaṭhavī khaṇante pi bhindante pi dhārente pi samudda-pabbata-girisikhare ti.

341 na hi bhante ti. kena kāraṇena mahārājāti. na-tthi bhante mahāpaṭhaviyā so hetu yena hetunā mahāpaṭhavī bhāyeyya vā taseyya vā ti. evam-eva kho mahārāja na-tthi arahantānaṃ so hetu yena hetunā arahanto bhāyeyyuṃ vā taseyyuṃ vā. bhāyati nu mahārāja girisikharaṃ chindante vā bhindante vā patante vā agginā dahante vā ti. na hi bhante ti. kena kāraṇena mahārājāti.

342 na-tthi bhante girisikharassa so hetu yena hetunā girisikharaṃ bhāyeyya vā taseyya vā ti. evam-eva kho mahārāja na-tthi arahantānaṃ so hetu yena hetunā arahanto bhāyeyyuṃ vā taseyyuṃ vā. yadi pi mahārāja lokadhātusatasahassesu ye keci sattakāyapariyāpannā sabbe pi te sattihatthā ekaṃ arahantaṃ upadhāvitvā tāseyyuṃ, na bhaveyya arahato cittassa kiñci aññathattaṃ, kiṅkāraṇaṃ: aṭṭhānam-anavakāsatāya. api ca mahārāja tesaṃ khīṇāsavānaṃ evaṃ cetoparivitakko ahosi: ajja naravarapavare jinavaravasabhe nagaravaram-anupaviṭṭhe vīthiyā dhanapālako hatthī āpatissati, asaṃsayam-atidevadevaṃ upaṭṭhāko na pariccajissati, yadi mayaṃ sabbe pi bhagavantaṃ na pariccajissāma, ānandassa guṇo pākaṭo na bhavissati, na h'eva ca tathāgataṃ samupagamissati hatthināgo, handa mayaṃ apagacchāma, evam-idaṃ mahato janakāyassa kilesabandhanamokkho bhavissati, ānandassa ca guṇo pākaṭo bhavissatīti.

not out of fear, nor because they wanted to see the Bhagavan fall. Since whatever might cause arhats to tremble or become afraid has been cut off, arhats are free of fear and trembling. Do you suppose, great king, that the great earth fears being dug or split, or having to hold up the oceans and the peaked
mountain ranges?" "No, sir. "Why is this, great king?" 341

"Because the great earth has nothing that would cause it to tremble or become afraid." "Similarly, arhats have nothing that would cause them to tremble or become afraid." "Do the mountain ranges fear being destroyed or split? Or falling or being burned by fire?" "No, sir." "Why is this, great king?"

"Because mountain ranges have nothing that would cause 342
them to tremble or become afraid."

"Similarly, arhats have nothing that would cause them to tremble or become afraid. Great king, if everyone among the various kinds of beings in the hundred-thousand-world system were to surround a single arhat with swords in hand to make him tremble, it would make no difference in the mind of the arhat. Why is this? Because there is no place or opportunity for fear. Moreover, great king, this was the thought in the mind of the arhats: *Today when the best and most excellent of men, the finest bull of Victors, enters the best of cities, the elephant Dhanapalaka will race down the street. But the attendant of the supreme god among gods will certainly not forsake him. If we do not all abandon the Bhagavan, then the bull elephant will not approach the Tathagata and Ananda's excellence will not be visible. Come, let us flee so that the great crowd of people will be freed from the snares of the defilements,*

343 evaṃ te arahanto ānisaṃsaṃ disvā disāvidisaṃ pakkantā ti. suvibhatto bhante nāgasena pañho, evam-etaṃ, na-tthi arahantānaṃ bhayaṃ vā santāso vā, ānisaṃsaṃ disvā te arahanto pakkantā disāvidisan-ti.

344 bhante nāgasena, tumhe bhaṇatha: tathāgato sabbaññū ti. puna ca bhaṇatha: tathāgatena sāriputtamoggallānapamukhe bhikkhusaṅghe paṇāmite cātumeyyakā ca sakyā brahmā ca sahampati bījūpamañ-ca vacchataruṇūpamañ-ca upadassetvā bhagavantaṃ pasādesuṃ khamāpesuṃ nijjhattaṃ akaṃsūti. kin-nu kho bhante nāgasena aññātā tā upamā tathāgatassa yāhi tathāgato upamāhi orato khamito upasanto nijjhattiṃ gato. yadi bhante nāgasena tathāgatassa tā upamā aññātā, tena hi buddho asabbaññū; yadi ñātā, tena hi okassa pasayha vīmaṃsāpekho paṇāmesi, tena hi tassa akāruññatā sambhavati. ayam-pi ubhatokoṭiko pañho tavānuppatto, so tayā nibbāhitabbo ti.

345 sabbaññū mahārāja tathāgato, tāhi ca upamāhi bhagavā pasanno orato khamito upasanto nijjhattiṃ gato. dhammasāmī mahārāja tathāgato, tathāgatappavediteh' eva te opammehi tathāgataṃ ārādhesuṃ tosesuṃ pasādesuṃ, tesañ-ca tathāgato pasanno sādhūti abbhanumodi. yathā mahārāja itthī sāmikassa santaken' eva dhanena sāmikaṃ ārādheti toseti pasādeti, tañ-ca sāmiko sādhūti abbhanumodati, evam-eva kho mahārāja cātumeyyakā ca sakyā brahmā ca

and the excellence of Ananda will be revealed. And so, seeing 343
this benefit, the arhats scattered in every direction."

"Revered Nagasena, the dilemma is well analyzed. And so it is that these arhats did not have fear and trembling, for they saw the benefit and so scattered in every direction.

"Revered Nagasena, you say that the Tathagata is omni- 344
scient. And yet you also say that once, when the Tathagata had dismissed a community of monks headed by Sariputta and Moggallana, the Catuma Sakyas and Brahma Sahampati told the Bhagavan the simile of the seeds and the simile of the weaned calf.[72] They appeased him and restored his patience and composure. Nagasena, were the similes that made the Tathagata become satisfied, patient, composed, and appeased not known previously to the Tathagata? If the Tathagata did not know these similes, then the Buddha is not omniscient. Or if he did know them, then he, wanting to test the monks, dismissed them forcibly, and this appears to be due to a lack of compassion in him. This two-pronged dilemma has reached you, and you must solve it."

"Great king, the Tathagata is omniscient and the Bhaga- 345
van became confident, satisfied, patient, composed, and appeased by the two similes. The Tathagata is the Lord of the Dhamma, and so the Tathagata was conciliated, satisfied, and pleased by similes taught by the Tathagata himself. Pleased with them, the Tathagata expressed his appreciation, saying, 'Well done!'

"Great king, suppose a woman satisfies, pleases, and wins the favor of her husband with her husband's own wealth, and he expresses his appreciation, saying, 'Well done!' Similarly, the Catuma Sakyas and Brahma Sahampati satis-

sahampati tathāgatappaveditehʼ eva opammehi tathāgataṃ ārādhesuṃ tosesuṃ pasādesuṃ, tesañ-ca tathāgato pasanno sādhūti abbhanumodi.

346 yathā vā pana mahārāja kappako rañño santakenʼ eva suvaṇṇapaṇakena rañño uttamaṅgaṃ pasādhayamāno rājānaṃ ārādheti toseti pasādeti, tassa ca rājā pasanno sādhūti abbhanumodati yathicchitam-anuppadeti; evam-eva kho mahārāja cātumeyyakā ca sakyā brahma ca sahampati tathāgatappaveditehʼ eva opammehi tathāgataṃ ārādhesuṃ tosesuṃ pasādesuṃ, tesañ-ca tathāgato pasanno sādhūti abbhanumodi. yathā vā pana mahārāja saddhivihāriko upajjhāyābhataṃ piṇḍapātaṃ gahetvā upajjhāyassa upanāmento upajjhāyaṃ ārādheti toseti pasādeti, tañ-ca upajjhāyo pasanno sādhūti abbhanumodati; evam-eva kho mahārāja cātumeyyakā ca sakyā brahmā ca sahampati tathāgatappaveditehʼ eva opammehi tathāgataṃ ārādhesuṃ tosesuṃ pasādesuṃ, tesañ-ca tathāgato pasanno sādhūti abbhanumoditvā sabbadukkhaparimuttiyā dhammaṃ desesīti. sādhu bhante nāgasena, evam-etaṃ, tathā sampaṭicchāmīti.

catuttho vaggo.

fied, pleased, and won the favor of the Tathagata with the very similes taught by the Tathagata himself. Pleased with them, the Tathagata expressed his appreciation, saying,
'Well done!' Or suppose the king's barber satisfies, pleases, 346
and wins the favor of the king by adorning the king's head with the king's own golden comb shaped like a cobra. Pleased with him, the king gives him a present according to his fancy and expresses his appreciation, 'Well done!' Similarly, the Catuma Sakyas and Brahma Sahampati satisfied, pleased, and won the favor of the Tathagata with the very similes taught by the Tathagata himself. Pleased with them, the Tathagata expressed his appreciation, saying, 'Well done!' Or suppose a fellow monk takes the very alms food brought by his teacher and satisfies, pleases, and wins the favor of the teacher by serving it to him, so that, pleased with him, the teacher expresses his appreciation, saying, 'Well done!' Similarly, great king, the Catuma Sakyas and Brahma Sahampati satisfied, pleased, and won the favor of the Tathagata with the very similes taught by the Tathagata himself. Pleased with them, the Tathagata expressed his appreciation, saying, 'Well done!' and then taught the Dhamma for the sake of releasing them from all suffering."

"Well done, revered Nagasena! This is so, and I am convinced."

End of Part 4.

PART 5

347 bhante nāgasena, bhāsitam-p' etaṃ bhagavatā:

348 santhavāto bhayaṃ jātaṃ, niketā jāyatī rajo, aniketam-asanthavaṃ, etaṃ ve munidassanan-ti.

349 puna ca bhaṇitaṃ: vihāre kāraye ramme, vāsay' ettha bahussute ti. yadi bhante nāgasena tathāgatena bhaṇitaṃ: santhavāto bhayaṃ jātaṃ, niketā jāyatī rajo, aniketam-asanthavaṃ, etaṃ ve munidassanan-ti, tena hi: vihāre kāraye ramme, vāsay' ettha bahussute ti yaṃ vacanaṃ taṃ micchā. yadi tathatena bhaṇitaṃ: vihāre kāraye ramme, vāsay' ettha bahussute ti, tena hi: santhavāto bhayaṃ jātaṃ-pe-dassanan-ti tam-pi vacanaṃ micchā. ayam-pi ubhatokoṭiko pañho tavānuppatto, so tayā nibbāhitabbo ti.

350 bhāsitam-p' etaṃ mahārāja bhagavatā santhavāto bhayaṃ jātaṃ, niketā jāyatī rajo, aniketam-asanthavaṃ, etaṃ ve munidassanan-ti. bhaṇitañ-ca: vihāre kāraye ramme, vāsay' ettha bahussute ti. yaṃ mahārāja bhagavatā bhaṇitaṃ: santhavāto pe-dassanan-ti, taṃ sabhāvavacanaṃ asesavacanaṃ nissesavacanaṃ nippariyāyavacanaṃ samaṇānucchavaṃ samaṇasāruppaṃ samaṇapatirūpaṃ samaṇārahaṃ samaṇagocaraṃ samaṇapaṭipadā samaṇapaṭipatti.

PART 5

"Revered Nagasena, the Bhagavan also said: 347

From intimacy, fear is born; from home life, 348
dust arises.
Free of home and free of intimacy— this is the vision
of the sage.

But he also said: 'One should have beautiful houses built to 349
house those who have heard much scripture.'[73] Nagasena, if the Tathagata said: 'From intimacy, fear is born; from home life, dust arises. Free of home and free of intimacy—this is the vision of the sage,' then the claim that 'One should have beautiful houses built to house those who have heard much scripture' is false. Or if the Tathagata said, 'One should have beautiful houses built to house those who have heard much scripture,' then the verse about fear in intimacy, and so on, is false. This two-pronged dilemma has reached you, and you must solve it."

"Great king, the Bhagavan did say, 'From intimacy, fear 350
is born; from home life, dust arises. Free of home and free of intimacy—this is the vision of the sage.' And he also said, 'One should have beautiful houses built to house those who have heard much scripture.' But, great king, when the Bhagavan said that about intimacy, it was a claim about something particular, a statement leaving nothing out, a complete assertion, and an unqualified claim regarding what is proper for renouncers, suitable for renouncers, correct for renouncers, fitting for renouncers, and appropriate for the scope, prac-

yathā mahārāja āraññako migo araññe pavane caramāno nirālayo aniketo yathicchakaṃ sayati, evam-eva kho mahārāja bhikkhunā: santhavāto bhayaṃ jātaṃ, niketā jāyatī rajo, aniketam-asanthavaṃ, etaṃ ve munidassanan-ti cintetabbaṃ.

351 yaṃ pana mahārāja bhagavatā bhaṇitaṃ: vihāre kāraye ramme, vāsay' ettha bahussute ti, taṃ dve atthavase sampassamānena bhagavatā bhaṇitaṃ, katame dve: vihāradānaṃ nāma sabbabuddhehi vaṇṇitaṃ anumataṃ thomitaṃ pasatthaṃ, taṃ te vihāradānaṃ datvā jāti-jarā-maraṇā parimuccissantīti; ayaṃ tāva paṭhamo ānisaṃso vihāradāne. puna ca paraṃ: vihāre vijjamāne bhikkhuniyo byattasanketā bhavissanti, sulabhaṃ dassanaṃ dassanakāmānaṃ, anikete duddassanā bhavissantīti; ayaṃ dutiyo ānisaṃso vihāradāne. ime dve atthavase sampassamānena bhagavatā bhaṇitaṃ: vihāre kāraye ramme, vāsay' ettha bahussute ti; na tattha buddhaputtena ālayo karaṇīyo nikete ti. sādhu bhante nāgasena, evam-etaṃ, tathā sampaṭicchāmīti.

352 bhante nāgasena, bhāsitam-p' etaṃ bhagavatā: uttiṭṭhe na-ppamajjeyya, udare saṃyato siyā ti. puna ca bhagavatā bhaṇitaṃ: ahaṃ kho pan' udāyi app-ekadā iminā pattena samatittikam-pi bhuñjāmi bhiyyo pi bhuñjāmīti. yadi bhante nāgasena bhagavatā bhaṇitaṃ: uttiṭṭhe na-ppamajjeyya, udare saṃyato siyā ti, tena hi: ahaṃ kho pan' udāyi app-ekadā iminā pattena samatittikam-pi bhuñjāmi bhiyyo pi bhuñjāmīti yaṃ vacanaṃ taṃ micchā. yadi tathāgatena

tice, and conduct of renouncers. A wild deer in the forest wanders homeless in the woods, has no dwelling, and sleeps wherever it likes. And so, great king, this statement is to be considered with respect to monastics: 'From intimacy, fear is born; from home life, dust arises. Free of home and free of intimacy—this is the vision of the sage.'

"When the Bhagavan said, 'One should have beautiful 351
houses built to house those who have heard much scripture,' he said this regarding only two reasons. What are the two? A gift of a residence is praised, approved, extolled, and esteemed by all buddhas, for those giving a gift of a residence are released from birth, old age, and death. This is the first benefit of giving a residence. Further, when nuns are staying in a residence, they will have meetings with accomplished people. Seeing such people will be easy for those who wish it, but if they were to be homeless, seeing them would be difficult. This is the second benefit of giving a residence. These are the two reasons recognized by the Bhagavan when he said, 'One should have beautiful houses built to house those who have heard much scripture.' Even so, a descendant of the Buddha should not accommodate attachment to a home."

"Very good, revered Nagasena! This is so, and I am convinced.

"Revered Nagasena, the Bhagavan also said this: 'Stand 352
up, do not be careless, for there should be restraint in filling the belly.' But the Bhagavan also once said, 'Udayin, I sometimes eat the full contents of my alms bowl, and sometimes I eat even more.' Nagasena, if the Bhagavan said, 'Stand up, do not be careless, for there should be restraint in filling

bhaṇitaṃ: ahaṃ kho pan' udāyi app-ekadā iminā pattena samatittikam-pi bhuñjāmi bhiyyo pi bhuñjāmīti, tena hi: uttiṭṭhe na-ppamajjeyya, udare saṃyato siyā ti tam-pi vacanaṃ micchā. ayam-pi ubhatokoṭiko pañho tavānuppatto, so tayā nibbāhitabbo ti.

353 bhāsitam-p' etaṃ mahārāja bhagavatā: uttiṭṭhe na-ppamajjeyya, udare saṃyato siyā ti. bhaṇitañ-ca: ahaṃ kho pan' udāyi app-ekadā iminā pattena samatittikam-pi bhuñjāmi bhiyyo pi bhuñjāmīti. yaṃ mahārāja bhagavatā bhaṇitaṃ: uttiṭṭhe na-ppamajjeyya, udare saṃyato siyā ti, taṃ sabhāvavacanaṃ asesavacanaṃ nissesavacanaṃ nippariyāyavacanaṃ bhūtavacanaṃ tacchavacanaṃ yāthāvavacanaṃ aviparītavacanaṃ isivacanaṃ munivacanaṃ bhagavantavacanaṃ arahantavacanaṃ paccekabuddhavacanaṃ jinavacanaṃ sabbaññūvacanaṃ, tathāgatassa arahato sammāsambuddhassa vacanaṃ.

354 udare asaṃyato mahārāja pāṇam-pi hanti, adinnam-pi ādiyati, paradāram-pi gacchati, musā pi bhaṇati, majjam-pi pivati, mātaram pi jīvitā voropeti, pitaram-pi jīvitā voropeti, arahantam-pi jīvitā voropeti, sangham-pi bhindati, duṭṭhena cittena tathāgatassa lohitam-pi uppādeti. nanu mahārāja devadatto udare asaṃyato saṅghaṃ bhinditvā kappaṭṭhiyaṃ kammaṃ āyūhi. evarūpāni mahārāja aññāni pi bahuvidhāni

the belly,' then his claim, 'Udayin, I sometimes eat the full contents of my alms bowl, and sometimes I eat even more,' is surely false. Or if the Tathagata did say, 'Udayin, I sometimes eat the full contents of my alms bowl, and sometimes I eat even more,' then it is false that he said, 'Stand up, do not be careless, for there should be restraint in filling the belly.' This two-pronged dilemma has reached you, and you must solve it."

"Great king, the Bhagavan said, 'Stand up, do not be care- 353
less, for there should be restraint in filling the belly.' And he also said, 'Udayin, I sometimes eat the full contents of my alms bowl, and sometimes I eat even more.' But when the Bhagavan said, 'Stand up, do not be careless, for there should be restraint in filling the belly,' it was a claim about something particular, a statement leaving nothing out, a complete assertion, an unqualified claim, an utterance about what is real, a true utterance, a definitive utterance, an unequivocal utterance, and a statement of sages, holy men, bhagavans, arhats, solitary buddhas, victors, and the omniscient ones. These are the words of the Tathagata, the Enlightened One, the
Perfectly Awakened One. Great king, one lacking restraint 354
in filling the belly kills living beings, takes what is not given, chases others' wives, tells lies, drinks alcohol, deprives his mother of life, deprives his father of life, deprives arhats of life, splits the community, and, with malicious intent, even causes the Tathagata's blood to spill. Did not Devadatta, splitting the community because he lacked restraint with respect to his belly, earn karma lasting an eon? Great king, seeing many other examples as well, the Bhagavan

kāraṇāni disvā bhagavatā bhaṇitaṃ: uttiṭṭhe na-ppamajjeyya, udare saṃyato siyā ti.

355 udare saṃyato mahārāja catusaccābhisamayaṃ abhisameti, cattāri sāmaññaphalāni sacchikaroti, catusu paṭisambhidāsu aṭṭhasu samāpattisu chasu ca abhiññāsu vasībhāvaṃ pāpuṇāti, kevalañ-ca samaṇadhammaṃ pūreti. nanu mahārāja sukapotako udare saṃyato hutvā yāva tāvatiṃsabhavanaṃ kampetvā sakkaṃ devānam-indaṃ upaṭṭhānam-upanesi. evarūpāni mahārāja aññāni pi bahuvidhāni kāraṇāni disvā bhagavatā bhaṇitaṃ: uttiṭṭhe na-ppamajjeyya, udare saṃyato siyā ti.

356 yaṃ pana mahārāja bhagavatā bhaṇitaṃ: ahaṃ kho pan' udāyi app-ekadā iminā pattena samatittikam-pi bhuñjāmi bhiyyo pi bhuñjāmīti, taṃ katakiccena niṭṭhitakiriyena siddhatthena vusitavosānena nirāvaraṇena sabbaññunā sayambhunā tathāgatena attānaṃ upādāya bhaṇitaṃ. yathā mahārāja vantassa virittassa anuvāsitassa āturassa sappāyakiriyā icchitabbā hoti, evam-eva kho mahārāja sakilesassa adiṭṭhasaccassa udare saṃyamo karaṇīyo hoti. yathā mahārāja maṇiratanassa sappabhāsassa jātimantassa abhijātiparisuddhassa majjana-nighaṃsana-parisodhanena karaṇīyaṃ na hoti, evam-eva kho mahārāja tathāgatassa buddhavisaye pāramiṃ gatassa kiriyākaraṇesu āvaraṇaṃ na hotīti. sādhu bhante nāgasena, evam-etaṃ, tathā sampaṭicchāmīti.

said, 'Stand up, do not be careless, for there should be restraint in filling the belly.'

"Great king, one restrained in filling the belly realizes 355
the knowledge of the Four Truths, sees with one's own eyes the four fruits of renunciation, achieves mastery in the four analytical insights, the eight attainments, and the six higher knowledges, and fulfills the complete teaching of renouncers.[74] Did not that young parrot, becoming restrained with respect to his belly, cause Tavatimsa heaven to quake and Sakka, king of gods, to come and serve him? Great king, seeing many other examples as well, the Bhagavan said, 'Stand up, do not be careless, for there should be restraint in filling the belly.'

"But, great king, when the Bhagavan said, 'Udayin, I some- 356
times eat the full contents of my alms bowl, and sometimes eat even more,' this was said by the omniscient and self-arisen Tathagata in reference to himself, for he is one whose work is done, whose activity is accomplished, whose aim has succeeded, whose achievement is fulfilled, and who is free of hindrances. Great king, just as the actions of an emetic, purgative, or enema are desirable and beneficial for the sick, so too restraint with respect to the belly should be practiced by one who has defilements and has not seen the truths. And just as nothing needs to be done to clean, polish, and shine the jewel treasure that is brilliant, genuine, and naturally perfect, there are no hindrances in the doings and activities of the Tathagata who has reached perfection in the realm of the buddhas."

"Very good, Revered Nagasena. It is so and I am convinced.

357 bhante nāgasena, bhāsitam-p' etaṃ bhagavatā: aham-asmi bhikkhave brāhmaṇo yācayogo sadā payatapāṇi antimadehadharo anuttaro bhisakko sallakatto ti. puna ca bhaṇitaṃ bhagavatā: etad-aggaṃ bhikkhave mama sāvakānaṃ bhikkhūnaṃ appābādhānaṃ yad-idaṃ bakkulo ti. bhagavato ca sarīre bahukkhattuṃ ābādho uppanno dissati. yadi bhante nāgasena tathāgato anuttaro, tena hi: etad-aggaṃ bhikkhave mama sāvakānaṃ bhikkhūnaṃ appābādhānaṃ yad-idaṃ bakkulo ti yaṃ vacanaṃ taṃ micchā. yadi thero bakkulo appābādhānaṃ aggo, tena hi: aham-asmi bhikkhave brāhmaṇo yācayogo sadā payatapāṇi antimadehadharo anuttaro bhisakko sallakatto ti tam-pi vacanaṃ micchā. ayam-pi ubhatokoṭiko pañho tavānuppatto, so tayā nibbāhitabbo ti.

358 bhāsitam-p' etaṃ mahārāja bhagavatā: aham-asmi bhikkhave brāhmaṇo yācayogo sadā payatapāṇi antimadehadharo anuttaro bhisakko sallakatto ti. bhaṇitañ-ca: etad-aggaṃ bhikkhave mama sāvakānaṃ bhikkhūnaṃ appābādhānaṃ yad-idaṃ bakkulo ti. tañ-ca pana bāhirānaṃ āgamānaṃ adhigamānaṃ pariyattīnaṃ yadidaṃ vijjamānataṃ sandhāya bhāsitaṃ. santi kho pana mahārāja bhagavato sāvakā ṭhānacaṅkamikā, te ṭhānena caṅkamena divārattiṃ vītināmenti, bhagavā pana mahārāja ṭhānena caṅkamena nisajjāya sayan-ena divārattiṃ vītināmeti; ye te mahārāja bhikkhū ṭhānacaṅkamikā te tena aṅgena atirekā.

359 santi kho pana mahārāja bhagavato sāvakā ekāsanikā, te jīvitahetu pi dutiyaṃ bhojanaṃ na bhuñjanti, bhagavā pana mahārāja dutiyam-pi yāva tatiyam-pi bhojanaṃ bhuñjati; ye te mahārāja bhikkhu ekāsanikā te tena aṅgena atirekā.

"Revered Nagasena, the Bhagavan also said this: 'Monks, 357
I am a Brahman, always responsive to requests, open-handed, living in my last body, an incomparable physician and surgeon.'[75] But the Bhagavan also said: 'Monks, Bakkula is chief among my monastic disciples who are seldom sick.' And it was evident that illness occurred many times in the Bhagavan's body. Nagasena, if the Tathagata was incomparable, then false is the assertion, 'Monks, Bakkula is chief among my monastic disciples who are seldom sick.' If Elder Bakkula was chief among those seldom sick, then the claim, 'Monks, I am a Brahman, always responsive to requests, open-handed, living in my last body, an incomparable physician and surgeon' is false. This two-pronged dilemma has reached you, and you must solve it."

"Great king, the Bhagavan did say, 'Monks, I am a Brah- 358
man, always responsive to requests, open-handed, living in my last body, an incomparable physician and surgeon.' And he also said, 'Monks, Bakkula is chief among my monastic disciples who are seldom sick.' But the first was said in reference to finding in himself study and knowledge of outside scriptures.[76] Great king, there are disciples who practice standing and walking, who spend the entire night and day standing and walking. But the Bhagavan would spend the entire night and day standing, walking, sitting, and lying down. The monks who practice standing and walking surpass
him in this respect. There are also disciples of the Bhagavan 359
who eat only at one sitting and do not eat a second meal even to save their lives. But the Bhagavan ate a second or even third meal. The monks who eat only at one sitting surpass him in this respect. Great king, there are many such examples

anekavidhāni mahārāja tāni kāraṇāni tesaṃ tesaṃ taṃ taṃ sandhāya bhaṇitāni. bhagavā pana mahārāja anuttaro sīlena samādhinā paññāya vimuttiyā vimuttiñāṇadassanena, dasahi ca balehi catuhi vesārajjehi aṭṭhārasahi buddhadhamm-ehi chahi asādhāraṇehi ñāṇehi. kevale ca buddhavisaye taṃ sandhāya bhaṇitaṃ: aham-asmi bhikkhave brāhmaṇo yācayogo sadā payatapāṇi antimadehadharo anuttaro bhisakko sallakatto ti.

360 idha mahārāja manussesu eko jātimā hoti, eko dhanavā, eko vijjavā, eko sippavā, eko sūro, eko vicakkhaṇo, sabbe p' ete abhibhaviya rājā yeva tesaṃ uttamo hoti; evam-eva kho mahārāja bhagavā sabbasattānaṃ aggo jeṭṭho seṭṭho. yaṃ pan' āyasmā bakkulo appābādho ahosi, taṃ abhinī-hāravasena. so hi mahārāja anomadassissa bhagavato udara-vātābādhe uppanne vipassissa ca bhagavato aṭṭhasaṭṭhiyā ca bhikkhusatasahassānaṃ tiṇapupphakaroge uppanne sayaṃ tāpaso samāno nānābhesajjehi taṃ byādhiṃ apanetvā app-ābādhataṃ patto, bhaṇito ca: etad-aggaṃ bhikkhave mama sāvakānaṃ bhikkhūnaṃ appābādhānaṃ yad-idaṃ bakkulo ti. bhagavato mahārāja byādhimhi uppajjante pi anuppajj-ante pi, dhutaṅgaṃ ādiyante pi anādiyante pi, na-tthi bhaga-vatā sadiso koci satto.

361 bhāsitam-p' etaṃ mahārāja bhagavatā devātidevena saṃyuttanikāyavaralañcake: yāvatā bhikkhave sattā apadā vā dipadā vā catuppadā vā bahuppadā vā rūpino vā arūpino

of this one or that one doing this or that. But the Bhagavan is incomparable with respect to morality, concentration, understanding, freedom, liberated knowing and seeing, the ten powers, the four confidences, the eighteen qualities of buddhas, and the six exclusive knowledges, all of which are only within the scope of a buddha.[77] It was regarding this that he said: 'Monks, I am a Brahman, always responsive to requests, open-handed, living in my last body, an incomparable physician and surgeon.'

"Great king, among people here, one has high birth, 360
another is rich, one is educated, another excels at the crafts, one is courageous, and another is sharp, but the king surpasses them all and is the best among them. So too the Bhagavan is the chief, best, and foremost of all beings.

"Now, the revered Bakkula was seldom sick, due to an earlier aspiration. For he was living as an ascetic when the Bhagavan Anomadassi suffered illness from winds in his belly and again when the Bhagavan Vipassi, along with sixty-eight hundred thousand of his monks, were afflicted with hay fever. Having cured their illnesses with various medicines, he became free of illness. And so this is said: "Monks, Bakkula is chief among my monastic disciples who are seldom sick.' Great king, whether illnesses were or were not afflicting the Bhagavan, and whether he was or was not undertaking the forest practices, there is no being like the Bhagavan.

"This is said by the Bhagavan, that god above gods, in the 361
excellent declaration that is the *Saṃyuttanikāya:* 'Whatever beings there are—whether lacking feet, having two feet, four feet, or many feet; whether possessing form or not possessing form; whether perceiving, not perceiving, or neither

vā saññino vā asaññino vā nevasaññi-nāsaññino vā tathāgato tesaṃ aggam-akkhāyati arahaṃ sammāsambuddho ti. sādhu bhante nāgasena, evam-etaṃ, tathā sampaṭicchāmīti.

362 bhante nāgasena, bhāsitam-p' etaṃ bhagavatā: tathāgato bhikkhave arahaṃ sammāsambuddho anuppannassa maggassa uppādetā ti. puna ca bhaṇitaṃ: addasā kho 'haṃ bhikkhave purāṇaṃ maggaṃ purāṇaṃ añjasam pubbakehi sammāsambuddhehi anuyātan-ti. yadi bhante nāgasena tathāgato anuppannassa maggassa uppādetā, tena hi: addasā kho 'haṃ bhikkhave purāṇaṃ maggaṃ purāṇaṃ añjasaṃ pubbakehi sammāsambuddhehi anuyātan-ti yaṃ vacanaṃ taṃ micchā. yadi tathāgatena bhaṇitaṃ: addasā kho 'haṃ bhikkhave purāṇaṃ maggaṃ purāṇaṃ añjasaṃ pubbakehi sammāsambuddhehi anuyātan-ti, tena hi: tathāgato bhikkhave arahaṃ sammāsambuddho anuppannassa maggassa uppādetā ti. tam-pi vacanaṃ micchā. ayam-pi ubhatokoṭiko pañho tavānuppatto, so tayā nibbāhitabbo ti.

363 bhāsitam-p' etaṃ mahārāja bhagavatā: tathāgato bhikkhave arahaṃ sammāsambuddho anuppannassa maggassa uppādetā ti. bhaṇitañ-ca: addasā kho 'haṃ bhikkhave purāṇaṃ maggaṃ purāṇaṃ añjasaṃ pubbakehi sammāsambuddhehi anuyātan-ti. taṃ dvayam-pi sabhāvavacanam eva. pubbakānaṃ mahārāja tathāgatānaṃ antaradhānena asati anusāsake maggo antaradhāyi, so taṃ tathāgato maggam luggaṃ paluggaṃ rūḷhaṃ pihitaṃ paṭicchannaṃ asañ-

perceiving nor not perceiving—the Tathagata, the Enlightened One, the Perfectly Awakened Buddha is declared the chief of them all."

"Excellent, revered Nagasena. This is so, and I am convinced.

"Revered Nagasena, the Bhagavan also said: 'Monks, the 362
Tathagata, the Enlightened One, the Perfectly Awakened Buddha brought into being a path not previously available.' But he also said, 'Monks, I saw an ancient path, an ancient road followed by perfectly awakened buddhas.' Nagasena, if the Tathagata brought into being a path not previously available, then it was false to claim, 'Monks, I saw an ancient path, an ancient road followed by perfectly awakened buddhas.' Or if the Tathagata said, 'Monks, I saw an ancient path, an ancient road, followed by perfectly awakened buddhas,' then false is the claim that 'the Tathagata, the Enlightened One, the Perfectly Awakened Buddha brought into being a path not previously available.' This two-pronged dilemma has reached you, and you must solve it."

"Great king, the Bhagavan did say, 'Monks, the Tathagata, 363
the Enlightened One, the Perfectly Awakened Buddha brought into being a path not previously available.' And he also said: "Monks, I saw an ancient path, an ancient road followed by perfectly awakened buddhas.' Both assertions are true. Great king, because of the disappearance of the previous tathagatas, the path also disappeared, since there was no longer a teacher. The path was ragged, broken, overgrown, concealed, covered, and impassable when the Tathagata, grasping it with his eye of understanding, recognized it as the path followed by previous perfectly awakened buddhas.

caraṇaṃ paññācakkhunā sammasamāno addasa pubbakehi sammāsambuddhehi anuyātaṃ, taṅkāraṇā āha: addasā kho 'haṃ bhikkhave purāṇaṃ maggaṃ purāṇaṃ añjasaṃ pubbakehi sammāsambuddhehi anuyātan-ti. pubbakānaṃ mahārāja tathāgatānaṃ antaradhānena asati anusāsake luggaṃ paluggaṃ rūḷhaṃ pihitaṃ paṭicchannaṃ maggaṃ yaṃ dāni tathāgato sañcaraṇaṃ akāsi, taṅkāraṇā āha: tathāgato bhikkhave arahaṃ sammāsambuddho anuppannassa maggassa uppādetā ti.

364 idha mahārāja rañño cakkavattissa antaradhānena maṇiratanaṃ girisikharantare nilīyati, aparassa cakkavattissa sammāpaṭipattiyā upagacchati; api nu kho taṃ mahārāja maṇiratanaṃ tassa pakatan-ti. na hi bhante, pākatikaṃ yeva taṃ bhante maṇiratanaṃ, tena pana nibbattan-ti. evam-eva kho mahārāja pākatikaṃ pubbakehi tathāgatehi anuciṇṇaṃ aṭṭhaṅgikaṃ sivaṃ maggaṃ asati anusāsake luggaṃ paluggaṃ rūḷhaṃ pihitaṃ paṭicchannaṃ asañcaraṇaṃ bhagavā paññācakkhunā sammasamāno uppādesi sañcaraṇaṃ akāsi, taṅkāraṇā āha: tathāgato bhikkhave arahaṃ sammāsambuddho anuppannassa maggassa uppādetā ti.

365 yathā vā pana mahārāja santaṃ yeva puttaṃ yoniyā janayitvā mātā janikā ti vuccati, evam-eva kho mahārāja tathāgato santaṃ yeva maggaṃ luggaṃ paluggaṃ rūḷhaṃ pihitaṃ paṭicchannaṃ asañcaraṇaṃ paññācakkhunā sammasamāno uppādesi sañcaraṇaṃ akāsi, taṅkāraṇā āha:

And for this reason he said, 'Monks, I saw an ancient path, an ancient road followed by perfectly awakened buddhas.' The Tathagata made that path—ragged, broken, overgrown, concealed, covered, and impassable without a teacher due to the disappearance of the previous tathagatas—passable again. And for this reason he said, 'Monks, the Tathagata, the Enlightened One, the Perfectly Awakened Buddha brought into being a path not previously available.'

"Great king, here in this world the jewel treasure hides 364
in a mountain peak when a wheel-turning emperor disappears. It comes again due to the right conduct of another wheel-turning emperor. But would you say that the jewel treasure was created by him?"

"No, sir. The jewel treasure is just restored and brought forth by him."

"Even so, great king, though the blessed Eightfold Path followed by previous tathagatas had become ragged, broken, overgrown, concealed, covered, and impassable without a teacher, it was restored by the Bhagavan. Recognizing it with his eye of understanding, he brought it forth and made it passable once more. It is for this reason that he said, 'Monks, the Tathagata, the Enlightened One, the Perfectly Awakened Buddha brought into being a path not previously available.'

"Great king, consider how a mother gives birth to a child 365
present in her womb, and so is said to produce it. So too does the Tathagata, recognizing it with his eye of understanding, bring forth and make passable again the existing path that had become ragged, broken, overgrown, concealed, covered, and impassable. It is for this reason that he said, 'Monks, the

tathāgato bhikkhave arahaṃ sammāsambuddho anuppannassa maggassa uppādetā ti. yathā vā pana mahārāja koci puriso yaṃ kiñci naṭṭhaṃ passati, tena taṃ bhaṇḍaṃ nibbattitan-ti jano voharati, evam-eva kho mahārāja tathāgato santaṃ yeva maggaṃ luggaṃ paluggaṃ rūḷhaṃ pihitaṃ paṭicchannaṃ asañcaraṇaṃ sammasamāno uppādesi sañcaraṇaṃ akāsi, taṅkāraṇā āha: tathāgato bhikkhave arahaṃ sammāsambuddho anuppannassa maggassa uppādetā ti.

366 yathā vā pana mahārāja koci puriso vanaṃ sodhetvā bhūmiṃ nīharati, tassa sā bhūmīti jano voharati, na c' esā bhūmi tena pavattitā, taṃ bhūmiṃ kāraṇaṃ katvā bhūmisāmiko nāma hoti; evam-eva kho mahārāja tathāgato santaṃ yeva maggaṃ luggaṃ paluggaṃ rūḷhaṃ pihitaṃ paṭicchannaṃ asañcaraṇaṃ paññāya sammasamāno uppādesi sañcaraṇaṃ akāsi, taṅkāraṇā āha: tathāgato bhikkhave arahaṃ sammāsambuddho anuppannassa maggassa uppādetā ti. sādhu bhante nāgasena, evam-etaṃ, tathā sampaṭicchāmīti.

367 bhante nāgasena, bhāsitam-p' etaṃ bhagavatā: pubbeva 'haṃ manussabhūto samāno sattānaṃ aviheṭhakajātiko ahosin-ti. puna ca bhaṇitaṃ: lomasakassapo nāma isi samāno anekasate pāṇe ghātayitvā vājapeyyaṃ mahāyaññaṃ yajīti. yadi bhante nāgasena bhagavata bhaṇitaṃ: pubbeva 'haṃ manussabhūto samāno sattānaṃ aviheṭhakajātiko

Tathagata, the Enlightened One, the Perfectly Awakened Buddha brought into being a path not previously available.'

"And, great king, it is much like a man who spots something that had been lost. People say that he has produced this property. Likewise, the Tathagata recognizes, brings forth, and makes passable again the existing path that had become ragged, broken, overgrown, concealed, covered, and impassable. It is for this reason that he said, 'Monks, the Tathagata, the Enlightened One, the Perfectly Awakened Buddha brought into being a path not previously available.'

"Furthermore, great king, it is like a man who clears the 366
forest and removes the soil. People then say that this is his soil. Even though he did not produce it, having worked on the soil, he is considered its owner. So too, recognizing it with his understanding, the Tathagata brings forth and makes passable again the existing path that had become ragged, broken, overgrown, concealed, covered, and impassable. It is for this reason that he said, 'Monks, the Tathagata, the Enlightened One, the Perfectly Awakened Buddha brought into being a path not previously available.'

"Very well, Nagasena. This is so, and I accept it.

"Revered Nagasena, the Bhagavan also said, 'In the former 367
existences I spent as a human, I was not in the habit of harming creatures.' But it is also said that while he was living as the sage known as Hairy Kassapa he performed the great *vājapeyya* sacrifice and had several hundred creatures put to death.[78] Nagasena, if the Bhagavan said, 'In the former existences I spent as a human, I was not in the habit of harming creatures,' then it is false to claim that while he was living as the sage known as Hairy Kassapa he performed the great

ahosin-ti, tena hi: lomasakassapena isinā anekasate pāṇe ghātayitvā vājapeyyaṃ mahāyaññaṃ yajitan-ti yaṃ vacanaṃ taṃ micchā. yadi lomasakassapena isinā anekasate pāṇe ghātayitvā vājapeyyaṃ mahāyaññaṃ yajitaṃ, tena hi: pubbeva 'haṃ manussabhūto samāno sattānaṃ aviheṭhakajātiko ahosin-ti tam-pi vacanaṃ micchā. ayam-pi ubhatokoṭiko pañho tavānuppatto, so tayā nibbāhitabbo ti.

368 bhāsitam-p' etaṃ mahārāja bhagavatā: pubbeva 'haṃ manussabhūto samāno sattānaṃ aviheṭhakajātiko ahosin-ti. lomasakassapena ca isinā anekasate pāṇe ghātayitvā vājapeyyaṃ mahāyaññaṃ yajitaṃ; tañ-ca pana rāgavasena visaññinā, no sacetanenāti. aṭṭh' ime bhante nāgasena puggalā pāṇaṃ hananti, katame aṭṭha: ratto rāgavasena pāṇaṃ hanati, duṭṭho dosavasena pāṇaṃ hanati, mūḷho mohavasena pāṇaṃ hanati, mānī mānavasena pāṇaṃ hanati, luddho lobhavasena pāṇaṃ hanati, akiñcano jīvikatthāya pāṇaṃ hanati, bālo hassavasena pāṇaṃ hanati, rājā vinayanavasena pāṇaṃ hanati. ime kho bhante nāgasena aṭṭha puggalā pāṇaṃ hananti. pākatikaṃ yeva bhante nāgasena bodhisattena katan-ti.

369 na mahārāja pakatikaṃ bodhisattena kataṃ. yadi mahārāja bodhisatto pakatibhāvena oṇameyya mahāyaññaṃ yajituṃ, na-y-imaṃ gāthaṃ bhaṇeyya:

vājapeyya sacrifice and had several hundred creatures put to death. If the great *vājapeyya* sacrifice was performed by Hairy Kassapa, putting several hundred creatures to death, then it is false to claim, 'In the former existences I spent as a human, I was not in the habit of harming creatures.' This two-pronged dilemma has reached you, and you must solve it."

"Great king, the Bhagavan did say, 'In the former exis- 368
tences I spent as a human, I was not in the habit of harming creatures.' And Hairy Kassapa put several hundred creatures to death as he performed the great *vājapeyya* sacrifice. This was not done intentionally, but was rather due to being unhinged by passion."

"Nagasena, there are eight people who kill creatures. Who are they? One impassioned kills creatures because of passion, one who is malignant kills creatures because of hatred, one deluded kills them because of delusion, one prideful kills out of pride, one greedy kills out of greed, one destitute kills for the sake of subsistence, a fool for the sake of a laugh, and a king for the sake of discipline. These, Nagasena, are the eight people who kill creatures. What was done by the Bodhisatta was in keeping with his nature."

"Great king, what was done by the Bodhisatta was not in 369
keeping with his nature. If the Bodhisatta was inclined by his natural state to perform a great sacrifice, then he would not have said this verse:

370 sasamuddapariyāyaṃ mahiṃ sāgarakuṇḍalaṃ na
icche saha nindāya, evaṃ sayha vijānahīti.

371 evaṃvādī mahārāja bodhisatto saha dassanena candavatiyā rājakaññāya visaññī ahosi khittacitto ratto, visaññībhūto ākulākulo turitaturito tena vikkhitta-bhanta-luḷita-cittena mahatimahā-pasughāta-galaruhira-sañcayaṃ vājapeyyaṃ mahāyaññaṃ yaji. yathā mahārāja ummattako khittacitto jalitam-pi jātavedaṃ akkamati, kupitam-pi āsīvisaṃ gaṇhāti, mattam-pi hatthiṃ upeti, samuddam-pi atīradassī pakkhandati, candanikam-pi oḷigallam-pi omaddati, kaṇṭakādhānam-pi abhirūhati, papāte pi patati, asucim-pi bhakkheti, naggo pi ratiyā carati, aññam-pi bahuvidhaṃ akiriyaṃ karoti; evam eva kho mahārāja bodhisatto saha dassanena candavatiyā rājakaññāya visaññī ahosi khittacitto, visaññībhūto ākulākulo turitaturito tena vikkhitta-bhanta-luḷita-cittena mahatimahā-pasughāta-galaruhira-sañcayaṃ vājapeyyaṃ mahāyaññaṃ yaji. khittacittena mahārāja kataṃ pāpaṃ diṭṭhadhamme pi na mahāsāvajjaṃ hoti, samparāye vipākena pi no tathā. idha mahārāja koci ummattako vajjham-āpajjeyya, tassa tumhe kiṃ daṇḍaṃ dhārethāti.

Know this, Sayha— 370
I would not wish for the earth bordered by the sea and
encircled by the oceans,
were it to come with disgrace.

"Though speaking in this way, the Bodhisatta became 371
unhinged at the sight of the king's daughter, Moonlight. He was impassioned and his mind was disturbed. He became unhinged, terribly perplexed, and much harried. Because his mind was agitated, awhirl, and deranged, he performed the great *vājapeyya* sacrifice in which a large quantity of blood flowed from killing so many large beasts.

"Great king, consider the madman with mind disturbed who enters fire even as it blazes, picks up a venomous snake even when it is angry, mounts an elephant when it is in rut, plunges into the ocean without seeing the shore, wades into dirty puddles and cesspools, climbs a thorny hedge, falls off a cliff, eats something filthy, wanders naked at night, and does even more things that are not to be done. Even so did the Bodhisatta become unhinged by Moonlight, the king's daughter, and his mind disturbed. Being unhinged, terribly perplexed, and much harried, with his mind agitated, awhirl, and deranged, he performed the great *vājapeyya* sacrifice in which a large quantity of blood flowed from killing so many large beasts. Great king, evil done by one with a disturbed mind is not greatly culpable either in this world or in the world to come, even with respect to its karmic effects. If a madman here were to commit an offense meriting death, how would you have him punished?"

372 ko bhante ummattakassa daṇḍo bhavissati, taṃ mayaṃ pothāpetvā nīharāpema, esova tassa daṇḍo ti. iti kho mahārāja ummattakassa aparādhe daṇḍo pi na bhavati, tasmā ummattakassa káte pi na doso bhavati, satekiccho. evam-eva kho mahārāja lomasakassapo isi saha dassanena candavatiyā rājakaññāya visaññī ahosi khittacitto ratto, visaññībhūto visaṭapayāto ākulākulo turitaturito tena vikkhitta-bhanta-luḷita-cittena mahatimahā-pasughāta-galaruhira-sañcayaṃ vājapeyyaṃ mahāyaññaṃ yaji. yadā ca pana pakaticitto ahosi paṭiladdhasati, tadā puna-d-eva pabbajitvā pañcābhiññāyo nibbattetvā brahmalokūpago ahosīti. sādhu bhante nāgasena, evam etaṃ, tathā sampaṭicchāmīti.

373 bhante nāgasena, bhāsitam-p' etaṃ bhagavatā: chaddanto nāgarājā:

374 vadhissam-etan-ti parāmasanto kāsāvam-addakkhi
dhajaṃ isīnaṃ;
dukkhena phuṭṭhass' udapādi saññā: arahaddhajo sabbhi
avajjharūpo ti.

375 puna ca bhaṇitaṃ: jotipālamāṇavo samāno kassapaṃ bhagavantaṃ arahantaṃ sammāsambuddhaṃ muṇḍakavādena samaṇakavādena asabbhāhi pharusāhi vācāhi akkosi paribhāsīti. yadi bhante nāgasena bodhisatto tiracchānagato samāno kāsāvaṃ abhipūjayi, tena hi: jotipālena māṇavena

"What punishment will there be for a madman? We would 372
have him beaten and expelled. Just this is his punishment."

"Therefore, great king, there is no punishment in the case of the offense of a madman. From this, even in the case of a madman's deed, there is no fault and it can be remedied. Similarly, the sage Hairy Kassapa became unhinged at seeing Moonlight, the king's daughter; his mind was disturbed and he was impassioned. Being unhinged, terribly perplexed, and much harried, with his mind agitated, awhirl, and deranged, he performed the great *vājapeyya* sacrifice in which a large quantity of blood flowed from killing so many large beasts. But once he returned to his natural mind and regained his mindfulness, he again renounced the world, produced the five higher knowledges, and went to the Brahma world."

"Very good, revered Nagasena. This is so, and I am convinced.

"Revered Nagasena, this was also said by the Bhagavan 373
concerning Six Tusks, the elephant king:

> Thinking, *If only I might kill him,* he then saw the 374
> saffron robe, the banner of sages.
> Though racked with pain, he perceived that the
> banner of noble ones is inviolable by the good.[79]

But it is also said that in his birth as the Brahman youth, 375
Jotipala, he insulted and reviled the Blessed Kassapa, the Enlightened and Perfectly Awakened Buddha, with harsh and rude speech, calling him 'a little ascetic' and 'bald-pated.'[80] Nagasena, if the Bodhisatta respected the robe while living as an animal, then it is false to claim that as the

kassapo bhagavā arahaṃ sammāsambuddho muṇḍakavādena samaṇakavādena asabbhāhi pharusāhi vācāhi akkuṭṭho paribhāsito ti yaṃ vacanaṃ taṃ micchā.

376 yadi jotipālena māṇavena kassapo bhagavā arahaṃ sammāsambuddho muṇḍakavādena samaṇakavādena asabbhāhi pharusāhi vācāhi akkuṭṭho paribhāsito, tena hi: chaddantena nāgarājena kāsāvaṃ pūjitan-ti tam-pi vacanaṃ micchā. yadi tiracchānagatena bodhisattena kakkhala-khara-kaṭuka-vedanaṃ vediyamānena luddakena nivatthaṃ kāsāvaṃ pūjitaṃ, kiṃ manussabhūto samāno paripakkañāṇo paripakkāya bodhiyā kassapaṃ bhagavantaṃ arahantaṃ sammāsambuddhaṃ dasabalaṃ lokanāyakaṃ uditoditaṃ jalitabyāmobhāsaṃ pavaruttamaṃ pavara-rucira-kāsikakāsāvam abhipārutaṃ disvā na pūjayi. ayam-pi ubhatokoṭiko pañho tavānuppatto, so tayā nibbāhitabbo ti.

377 bhāsitam-p' etaṃ mahārāja bhagavatā: chaddanto
nāgarājā:

378 vadhissam-etan-ti parāmasanto kāsāvam-addakkhi
dhajaṃ isīnaṃ;
dukkhena phuṭṭhass' udapādi saññā: arahaddhajo sabbhi
avajjharūpo ti.

379 jotipālena ca māṇavena kassapo bhagavā arahaṃ sammāsambuddho muṇḍakavādena samaṇakavādena asabbhāhi pharusāhi vācāhi akkuṭṭho paribhāsito. tañ-ca pana jātivasena kulavasena. jotipālo mahārāja māṇavo assaddhe

youth Jotipala he insulted and reviled the Blessed Kassapa, the Enlightened and Perfectly Awakened Buddha, with harsh and rude speech, calling him 'little ascetic' and 'bald-
pated.' But if Jotipala did insult and revile the Blessed Kass- 376
apa, the Enlightened and Perfectly Awakened Buddha, with harsh and rude speech, calling him 'a little ascetic' and 'bald-pated,' then the claim that the robe was respected by Six Tusks, the elephant king, is false. For if the Bodhisatta, even as an animal feeling harsh, sharp, and bitter pain, respected the robe worn by a hunter, then how could he as a human, with mature knowledge and mature discernment, see the Blessed Kassapa—the Enlightened and Perfectly Awakened Buddha, Ten-Powered One, Leader of the World, Highest of the High, whose radiance spread out for a fathom of flashing brilliance, splendid and excellent, and who was clad in a splendid and beautiful robe of Kasi cloth—and not respect him? This two-pronged dilemma has reached you, and you must solve it."

"Great king, the Bhagavan did say, concerning Six Tusks, 377
the elephant king:

> Thinking, *If only I might kill him,* he then saw the 378
> saffron robe, the banner of sages.
> Though racked with pain, he perceived that the
> banner of noble ones is inviolable by the good.'

And as the Brahman youth Jotipala, he insulted and reviled 379
the Blessed Kassapa, the Enlightened and Perfectly Awakened Buddha, with harsh and rude speech, calling him 'a little ascetic' and 'bald-pated.' But this was because of his birth and his family. Great king, the Brahman youth

appasanne kule paccājāto, tassa mātāpitaro bhagini-bhātaro dāsi dāsa-ceṭaka-parivāraka-manussā brahmadevatā brahmagarukā, te: brāhmaṇā eva uttamā pavarā ti avasese pabbajite garahanti jigucchanti, tesaṃ taṃ vacanaṃ sutvā jotipālo māṇavo ghaṭīkārena kumbhakārena satthāraṃ dassanāya pakkosito evam-āha: kiṃ pana tena[15] muṇḍakena samaṇakena diṭṭhenāti.

380 yathā mahārāja amataṃ visam-āsajja tittakaṃ hoti, yathā ca sītūdakaṃ aggim-āsajja uṇhaṃ hoti, evam-eva kho mahārāja jotipālo māṇavo assaddhe appasanne kule paccājāto, so kulavasena tathāgataṃ akkosi paribhāsi. yathā mahārāja jalita-pajjalito mahāaggikkhandho sappabhāso udakam-āsajja upahata-ppabhā-tejo sītalo kāḷako bhavati paripakka-nigguṇḍiphala-sadiso, evam-eva kho mahārāja jotipālo māṇavo puññavā saddho ñāṇa-vipula-sappabhāso assaddhe appasanne kule paccājāto, so kulavasena andho hutvā tathāgataṃ akkosi paribhāsi, upagantvā ca buddhaguṇam-aññāya ceṭakabhūto viya ahosi, jinasāsane pabbajitvā abhiññā ca samāpattiyo ca nibbattetvā brahmalokūpago ahosīti. sādhu bhante nāgasena, evam-etaṃ, tathā sampaṭicchāmīti.

381 bhante nāgasena, bhāsitam-p' etaṃ bhagavatā: ghaṭīkārassa kumbhakārassa āvesanaṃ sabbaṃ temāsaṃ ākāsacchadanaṃ aṭṭhāsi na cābhivassīti. puna ca bhaṇitaṃ: kassapassa tathāgatassa kuṭi ovassatīti. kissa pana bhante

Jotipala was born into an impious and unbelieving family. His parents, sisters, brothers, male and female slaves, servants, and people around him worshiped and reverenced Brahma. They thought only Brahmans were high and splendid, and disparaged and had contempt for other renouncers. Having heard their words, the Brahman youth Jotipala said when he was summoned to see the Teacher by the potter Ghatikara, 'What is the point of seeing this little bald-pated ascetic?'

"Just as, great king, ambrosia put in contact with poison 380
becomes bitter, and cool water placed near fire becomes warm, so too did the Brahman youth Jotipala, when born into an unbelieving and impious family, insult and revile the Tathagata due to his family. Consider how a huge and massive fire, blazing, burning, and full of brilliance, encounters water. Its light and flames get quenched and it becomes cool and blackened like a ripe chaste tree berry. Similarly, though the Brahman youth Jotipala was virtuous, faithful, and full of brilliance from his extensive knowledge, he was born into an unbelieving and impious family. Because of this family he became blind, and so insulted and reviled the Tathagata. But then he drew near and came to know the qualities of the Buddha. He became, as it were, his servant. Having renounced the world in the dispensation of the Victor, he generated the higher knowledges and the attainments, and then went to the Brahma realm."

"Very good, revered Nagasena. It is so and I am convinced.

"Revered Nagasena, the Bhagavan also said: 'The potter 381
Ghatikara's house stood open to the sky for three whole months, and it did not rain.' But he also said, 'The Tathagata Kassapa's hut was rained on.'[81] Nagasena, how could rain fall

nāgasena tathāgatassa evam-ussannakusalamūlassa kuṭi ovassati; tathāgatassa nāma so ānubhāvo icchitabbo. yadi bhante nāgasena ghaṭīkārassa kumbhakārassa āvesanaṃ anovassaṃ ākāsacchadanaṃ ahosi, tena hi: tathāgatassa kuṭi ovassatīti yaṃ vacanaṃ taṃ micchā. yadi tathāgatassa kuṭi ovassati, tena hi: ghaṭīkārassa kumbhakārassa āvesanaṃ anovassakaṃ ahosi ākāsacchadanan-ti tam-pi vacanaṃ micchā. ayam-pi ubhatokoṭiko pañho tavānuppatto, so tayā nibbāhitabbo ti.

382 bhāsitam-p' etaṃ mahārāja bhagavatā: ghaṭīkārassa kumbhakārassa āvesanaṃ sabbaṃ temāsaṃ ākāsacchadanaṃ aṭṭhāsi na cābhivassīti. bhaṇitañ-ca: kassapassa tathāgatassa kuṭi ovassatīti. ghaṭīkāro mahārāja kumbhakāro sīlavā kalyāṇadhammo ussannakusalamūlo andhe jiṇṇe mātāpitaro poseti, tassa asammukhā anāpucchā yev' assa ghare tiṇaṃ haritvā bhagavato kuṭiṃ chādesuṃ, so tena tiṇaharaṇena akampitaṃ asañcalitaṃ susaṇṭhitaṃ vipulam-asamaṃ pītiṃ paṭilabhi, bhiyyo somanassañ-ca atulaṃ uppādesi: aho vata me bhagavā lokuttamo suvissattho ti, tena tassa diṭṭhadhammiko vipāko nibbatto.

383 na hi mahārāja tathāgato tāvatakena vikārena calati. yathā mahārāja sineru girirājā anekasatasahassavātasampahārena pi na kampati na calati, mahodadhi varapavarasāgaro anekasatanahuta-mahāgaṅgā-satasahassehi pi na pūrati na vikāram-āpajjati; evam-eva kho mahārāja tathāgato na

on the hut of the Tathagata whose roots of goodness were so extensive? *This* is the desired power of a Tathagata? If the potter Ghatikara's house was free of rain as it stood open to the sky, then it is false to say that it rained on the hut of the Tathagata. Or if it did rain on the Tathagata's hut, then it is false to claim that it did not rain while the potter Ghatikara's house stood open to the sky. This two-pronged dilemma has reached you, and you must solve it."

"Great king, the Bhagavan did say, 'The potter Ghatikara's 382
house stood open to the sky for three whole months, and it did not rain.' And he also said, 'The Tathagata Kassapa's hut was rained on.' Great king, the potter Ghatikara was virtuous and beautiful in character, and his sources of merit were abundant. He supported his aged and blind parents. When he was absent, and without his permission, the thatch on his house was taken to cover the Bhagavan's hut. Yet he felt a surge of joy, great peace, and an untroubled, unrattled composure because of this theft of his thatch. And further immeasurable delight welled up: 'Oh, the Bhagavan, the highest in the world, has great confidence in me!' Because of this, its karmic result occurred right then.

"And what is more, great king, the Tathagata was not trou- 383
bled by such a trifling inconvenience. Just as Sineru, the king of mountains, does not shake or tremble from the impact of many hundred thousand winds, and just as the vast water that is the best and most splendid ocean does not fill up even with a hundred thousand great Ganga Rivers and countless hundred myriads more and is not troubled with any inconvenience, the Tathagata was not troubled by such a trifling inconvenience.

tāvatakena vikārena calati. yaṃ pana mahārāja tathāgatassa kuṭi ovassati, taṃ mahato janakāyassa anukampāya. dve 'me mahārāja atthavase sampassamānā tathāgatā sayaṃnimmitaṃ paccayaṃ na paṭisevanti: ayaṃ aggadakkhiṇeyyo satthā ti bhagavato paccayaṃ datvā devamanussā sabbaduggatito parimuccissantīti; pāṭihīraṃ dassetvā vuttiṃ pariyesantīti mā aññe upavadeyyun-ti.

384 ime dve atthavase sampassamānā tathāgatā sayaṃnimmitaṃ paccayaṃ na paṭisevanti. yadi mahārāja sakko vā taṃ kuṭiṃ anovassaṃ kareyya brahmā vā sayaṃ vā, sāvajjaṃ bhaveyya taṃ yeva kāraṇaṃ sadosaṃ saniggahaṃ: ime vibhūtaṃ[16] katvā lokaṃ sammohenti adhikataṃ karontīti, tasmā taṃ kāraṇaṃ vajjanīyaṃ. na mahārāja tathāgatā vatthuṃ yācanti, tāya avatthuyācanāya aparibhāsiyā bhavantīti. sādhu bhante nāgasena, evam-etaṃ, tathā sampaṭicchāmīti.

385 bhante nāgasena, bhāsitam-p' etaṃ tathāgatena: aham-asmi bhikkhave brāhmaṇo yācayogo ti. puna ca bhaṇitaṃ: rājā 'ham-asmi selāti. yadi bhante nāgasena bhagavatā bhaṇitaṃ: aham-asmi bhikkhave brāhmaṇo yācayogo ti, tena hi: rājā 'ham-asmi selāti yaṃ vacanaṃ taṃ micchā. yadi tathāgatena bhaṇitaṃ: rājā 'ham-asmi selāti, tena hi: aham-asmi bhikkhave brāhmaṇo yācayogo ti tam pi vacanaṃ micchā. khattiyo vā hi bhaveyya brāhmaṇo vā, na-tthi ekaya jātiyā dve vaṇṇā nāma. ayam-pi ubhatokoṭiko pañho tavānuppatto, so tayā nibbāhitabbo ti.

"Great king, if the Tathagata's hut was rained on, then it was for the sake of his compassion for the great multitude. Tathagatas take into consideration two reasons for not making use of requisites created by their own magical display. They consider how gods and humans will give requisites to the Bhagavan, thinking, *This teacher is worthy of the best,* and thereby will be released from every bad birth. And they would not have others find fault with buddhas, saying,
'They seek their livelihoods by displaying miracles.' Taking 384
into consideration these two reasons, tathagatas do not make use of requisites created by their own magical display. Great king, if Sakka or Brahma had kept rain from falling on the hut, or if he did so himself, then it would be blameworthy, for such an act is faulted and censured. By making rain vanish they bewilder people and sow confusion, and so this practice is to be avoided. Great king, tathagatas do not ask for things, and because they do not ask for things, they are not blameworthy."

"Very good, Nagasena. This is so, and I am convinced.

"Revered Nagasena, the Bhagavan also said: 'Monks, I am 385
a Brahman, responsive to requests.' But then he said, 'Sela, I am a king.'[82] Nagasena, if the Bhagavan said, 'Monks, I am a Brahman, responsive to requests,' then it is false to claim that he said, 'Sela, I am a king.' Or if the Tathagata said, 'Sela, I am a king,' then to say that he said, 'Monks, I am a Brahman, responsive to requests' is false. He must have been either a Kshatriya or a Brahman, as the two classes are not present in one birth. This two-pronged dilemma has reached you, and you must solve it."

386 bhāsitam-p' etaṃ mahārāja bhagavatā: aham-asmi bhikkhave brāhmaṇo yācayogo ti. puna ca bhaṇitaṃ: rājā 'ham-asmi selāti. tattha kāraṇaṃ atthi yena kāraṇena tathāgato brāhmaṇo ca rājā ca hotīti. kiṃ pana taṃ bhante nāgasena kāraṇaṃ yena kāraṇena tathāgato brāhmaṇo ca rājā ca hotīti.

387 sabbe mahārāja pāpakā akusalā dhammā tathāgatassa bāhitā pahīnā apagatā byapagatā ucchinnā khīṇā khayaṃ pattā nibbutā upasantā, tasmā tathāgato brāhmaṇo ti vuccati. brāhmaṇo nāma saṃsayam-anekaṃsaṃ vimatipathaṃ vītivatto, bhagavā pi mahārāja saṃsayam-anekaṃsaṃ vimatipathaṃ vītivatto, tena kāraṇena tathāgato brāhmaṇo ti vuccati. brāhmaṇo nāma sabbabhavagatiyoninissaṭo malarajagatavippamutto asahāyo, bhagavā pi mahārāja sabbabhavagatiyoninissaṭo malarajagatavippamutto asahāyo, tena kāraṇena tathāgato brāhmaṇo ti vuccati.

388 brāhmaṇo nāma agga-seṭṭha-vara-pavara-dibbavihārabahulo, bhagavā pi mahārāja agga-seṭṭha-vara-pavara-dibbavihārabahulo, tenāpi kāraṇena tathāgato brāhmaṇo ti vuccati. brāhmaṇo nāma ajjhayana-ajjhāpana-dāna-paṭiggahaṇa-dama-saṃyama-niyama-pubbamā nusatthi-pa-veṇi-vaṃsa-dharaṇo, bhagavā pi mahārāja ajjhayana-ajjhāpana-dānapaṭiggahaṇa-dama-saṃyama-niyama-pubba-jinācinnamānusatthi-paveṇi-vaṃsa-dharaṇo, tenāpi kāraṇena tathāgato brāhmaṇo ti vuccati.

"Great king, the Bhagavan did say, 'Monks, I am a Brahman, responsive to requests.' And he also said, 'Sela, I am a king.' There is a reason the Tathagata is both a Brahman and a king." 386

"What is the reason the Tathagata is both a Brahman and a king, Nagasena?"

"Great king, for the Tathagata all evils and bad phenom- 387
ena are taken away, eliminated, removed, eradicated, cut
off, destroyed, demolished, exhausted, extinguished, and
allayed. In this respect, he is called a Brahman. For a Brahman is one who has overcome the ways of doubt, perplexity,
and consternation, and the Bhagavan has also overcome the
ways of doubt, perplexity, and consternation; in this respect
the Tathagata is called a Brahman. A Brahman has escaped
birth in all states and conditions of life, is free from conditions of impurity and defilement, and is independent. The
Bhagavan too has escaped birth in all states and conditions
of life, is free from conditions of impurity and defilement,
and is independent; in this respect also the Tathagata is
called a Brahman. A Brahman is devoted to the best, supe- 388
rior, excellent, splendid, and divine ways of living, and the
Bhagavan too is devoted to the best, superior, excellent,
splendid, and divine ways of living; in this respect also the
Tathagata is called a Brahman. A Brahman continues an
ancient instruction, lineage, and tradition requiring study,
learning, giving, receiving, self-control, restraint, and absti-
nence. The Bhagavan continues an instruction, lineage, and
tradition practiced by previous victors, requiring study,
learning, giving, receiving, self-control, restraint, and absti-
nence; in this respect also the Tathagata is called a Brahman.

brāhmaṇo nāma brahāsukhavihāra-jjhānajhāyī, bhagavā pi mahārāja brahāsukhavihāra-jjhānajhāyī, tenāpi kāraṇena tathāgato brāhmaṇo ti vuccati. brāhmaṇo nāma sabbabhavābhavagatisu abhijātivattitam-anucaritaṃ jānāti, bhagavā pi mahārāja sabbabhavābhavagatisu abhijātivattitam-anucaritaṃ jānāti, tenāpi kāraṇena tathāgato brāhmaṇo ti vuccati.

389 brāhmaṇo ti mahārāja bhagavato n' etaṃ nāmaṃ mātarā kataṃ, na pitarā kataṃ, na bhātarā kataṃ, na bhaginiyā kataṃ, na mittāmaccehi kataṃ, na ñātisālohitehi kataṃ, na samaṇabrāhmaṇehi kataṃ, na devatāhi kataṃ. vimokkhantikam-etaṃ buddhānaṃ bhagavantānaṃ nāmaṃ, bodhiyā yeva mūle mārasenaṃ vidhamitvā atītānāgata-paccuppanne pāpake akusale dhamme bāhetvā saha sabbaññutañāṇassa paṭilābhā paṭiladdha-pātubhūta-samuppannamatte saccikā paññatti, yad-idaṃ brāhmaṇo ti. tena kāraṇena tathāgato vuccati brāhmaṇo ti.

390 kena pana bhante nāgasena kāraṇena tathāgato vuccati rājā ti. rājā nāma mahārāja yo koci rajjaṃ kāreti lokam-anusāsati, bhagavā pi mahārāja dasasahassimhi lokadhātuyā dhammena rajjaṃ kāreti, sadevakaṃ lokaṃ samārakaṃ sabrahmakaṃ sassamaṇabrāhmaṇiṃ pajaṃ anusāsati, tenāpi kāraṇena tathāgato vuccati rājā ti. rājā nāma mahārāja sabbajanamanusse abhibhavitvā nandayanto ñātisaṅghaṃ socayanto amittasaṅghaṃ mahatimahāyasasiriharaṃ thirasāradaṇḍaṃ anūnasatasalākālaṅkataṃ ussāpeti paṇḍara-

A Brahman contemplates the *jhānas* that are ways of living in immense happiness, and the Bhagavan too contemplates the *jhānas* that are ways of living in immense happiness; in this respect too the Tathagata is called a Brahman. A Brahman has gained knowledge of the occurrences and movements of his previous births in all the various walks of life, and the Bhagavan too has gained knowledge of the occurrences and movements of his previous births in all the various walks of life; in this respect also the Tathagata is called a Brahman.

"Great king, the designation 'Brahman' was not given to 389
the Bhagavan by a mother, father, brother, sister, friend, official, relative, kinsman, renouncer, Brahman, or god. This designation for the bhagavans, the buddhas, signifies final freedom. The designation is the achievement of the knowledge of omniscience that accompanies the routing of the armies of Mara at the root of the Bodhi Tree and eradicating past, present, and future evils and bad phenomenal states. This sense of Brahman is true only where it arises, appears, and has been won. The Tathagata is called a Brahman in this respect."

"But why was the Tathagata called a king, Nagasena?" 390

"Great king, a king is someone who rules a kingdom and governs people. The Bhagavan rules a kingdom in the ten thousand worlds with the Dhamma, and he governs the divine realm with its *maras* and *brahmas,* and the people with their renouncers and Brahmans. The Tathagata is called a king in this respect. Great king, the designation 'king' refers to one who has surpassed all other people, bringing joy to his circle of relatives and sorrow to his foes. He hoists the spotlessly white royal parasol fitted completely with a

vimala-setacchattaṃ, bhagavā pi mahārāja socayanto mārasenaṃ micchā paṭipannaṃ nandayanto devamanusse sammā paṭipanne dasasahassimhi lokadhātuyā mahatimahāyasasiriharaṃ khanti-thirasāradaṇḍaṃ ñāṇavara-satasalākālaṅkataṃ ussāpeti aggavaravimuttipaṇḍaravimalasetacchattaṃ, tenāpi kāraṇena tathāgato vuccati rājā ti.

391 rājā nāma upagata-sampattajanānaṃ bahunnam-abhivandanīyo bhavati, bhagavā pi mahārāja upagata-sampatta-devamanussānaṃ bahunnam abhivandanīyo, tenāpi kāraṇena tathāgato vuccati rājā ti. rājā nāma yassa kassaci ārādhakassa pasīditvā varitaṃ varaṃ datvā kāmena tappayati, bhagavā pi mahārāja yassa kassaci kāyena vācāya manasā ārādhakassa pasīditvā varitaṃ varam-anuttaraṃ sabbadukkhaparimuttiṃ datvā asesakāmavarena tappayati, tenāpi kāraṇena tathāgato vuccati rājā ti.

392 rājā nāma āṇaṃ vītikkamantaṃ vigarahati jāpeti dhaṃseti, bhagavato pi mahārāja sāsanavare āṇaṃ atikkamanto alajjī maṅkubhāvena oñāto hīḷito garahito bhavitvā vajjati jinasāsanavaramhā, tenāpi kāraṇena tathāgato vuccati rājā ti. rājā nāma pubbakānaṃ dhammikānaṃ rājūnaṃ paveṇim-anusatthiyā dhammādhammam-anudīpayitvā dhammena rajjaṃ kārayamāno pihayito piyo patthito bhavati janamanussānaṃ, ciraṃ rājakulavaṃsaṃ ṭhapayati dhamma-

hundred ribs and a solid and strong shaft that symbolizes his great and magnificent glory and majesty. The Bhagavan brings sorrow to the armies of Mara behaving wrongly, and joy to the gods and humans behaving well. He hoists the spotlessly white parasol of highest and excellent freedom fitted with a hundred ribs of knowledge and the solid and strong shaft of forbearance that symbolizes his great and magnificent glory and majesty in the ten thousand worlds. In this respect also, the Tathagata is called a king.

“A king is someone to be honored by the multitudes of 391
people who approach and present themselves. Great king,
the Bhagavan also is to be honored by the multitudes of
gods and humans who approach and present themselves;
in this respect also the Tathagata is called a king. A king is
gracious to anyone who propitiates him, granting a desired
boon and giving satisfaction according to his pleasure. The
Bhagavan is also gracious to anyone who propitiates him
with body, speech, or mind, granting the highest desired
boon that is freedom from all suffering, and giving satisfaction according to his wholly sublime pleasure. In this
respect also the Tathagata is called a king. A king censures, 392
fines, and punishes those who transgress his command. A
shameless person who out of moral weakness transgresses
the commands found in the best teaching and becomes
contemptible, despised, and reproached is excluded from
the favor of the Victor’s dispensation. In this respect also
the Tathagata is called a king.

“Great king, one called a king explains what is righteous and unrighteous with instruction in the tradition of the ancient and righteous kings, and since he rules the kingdom

guṇabalena, bhagavā pi mahārāja pubbakānaṃ sayambhūnaṃ paveṇimanusatthiyā dhammādhammam-anudīpayitvā dhammena lokam-anusāsamāno pihayito piyo patthito devamanussānaṃ ciraṃ sāsanaṃ pavatteti dhammaguṇabalena; tenāpi kāraṇena tathāgato vuccati rājā ti. evam-anekavidhaṃ mahārāja kāraṇaṃ yena kāraṇena tathāgato brāhmaṇo pi bhaveyya rājā pi bhaveyya, sunipuṇo bhikkhu kappam-pi no naṃ sampādeyya, kiṃ atibahuṃ bhaṇitena, saṅkhittaṃ sampaṭicchitabban-ti. sādhu bhante nāgasena, evam-etaṃ, tathā sampaṭicchāmīti.

393 bhante nāgasena, bhāsitam-p' etaṃ bhagavatā:

394 gāthābhigītam-me abhojanīyaṃ, sampassataṃ brāhmaṇa
n' esa dhammo,
gāthābhigītam-panudanti buddhā, dhamme sati
brāhmaṇa vuttir-esāti.

395 puna ca bhagavā parisāya dhammaṃ desento kathento ānupubbikathaṃ paṭhamaṃ tāva dānakathaṃ katheti, pacchā sīlakathaṃ, tassa bhagavato sabbalokissarassa bhāsitaṃ sutvā devamanussā abhisaṅkharitvā dānaṃ denti, tassa

righteously, he becomes favored, beloved, and adored by the people. Because of the strength of his righteous virtues, he establishes the dynasty of his royal family for a long time. The Bhagavan too explains what is righteous and unrighteous with instruction in the tradition of the ancient, self-arisen ones, and since he teaches the world righteously he becomes favored, beloved, and adored by gods and humans. Because of the strength of his righteous virtues his dispensation lasts a long time. In this respect also, the Tathagata is said to be a king.

"There are so many different reasons, great king, that the Tathagata may be a Brahman or a king, that even in an eon a clever monk could not arrive at them all. Why speak further? A brief account should be accepted."

"Very well, revered Nagasena. It is so, and I am convinced.

"Revered Nagasena, the Bhagavan also said this: 393

> I do not partake of gifts gained by chanting verses, 394
> for this is not the conduct observed by those who see,
> Brahman.
> Buddhas reject that which is gained by chanting
> verses.
> Since such a principle exists, Brahman, this is their
> practice.

However, once the Bhagavan was imparting the Dhamma to 395
an assembly and taught a graduated sermon. He gave first a teaching on giving and then a teaching on morality. When gods and humans heard what had been said by the Bhagavan, who is the lord of the entire world, they got up and gave a gift. The disciples enjoyed the gift that had been set out for

taṃ uyyojitaṃ dānaṃ sāvakā paribhuñjanti. yadi bhante nāgasena bhagavatā bhaṇitaṃ: gāthābhigītam-me abhojanīyan-ti, tena hi: bhagavā dānakathaṃ paṭhamaṃ kathetīti yaṃ vacanaṃ taṃ micchā. yadi dānakathaṃ paṭhamaṃ katheti, tena hi: gāthābhigītam me abhojanīyan-ti tam-pi vacanaṃ micchā. kiṅkāraṇaṃ: yo so bhante dakkhiṇeyyo gihīnaṃ piṇḍapātadānassa vipākaṃ katheti tassa te dhammakathaṃ sutvā pasannacittā aparāparaṃ dānam denti, ye taṃ dānaṃ paribhuñjanti sabbe te gāthābhigītaṃ paribhuñjanti. ayam-pi ubhatokoṭiko pañho nipuṇo gambhīro tavānuppatto, so tayā nibbāhitabbo ti.

396 bhāsitam-p' etaṃ mahārāja bhagavatā:

397 gāthābhigītam-me abhojanīyaṃ, sampassataṃ brāhmaṇa
n' esa dhammo,
gāthābhigītam-panudanti buddhā, dhamme sati
brāhmaṇa vuttir-esāti.

398 katheti ca bhagavā paṭhamaṃ dānakathaṃ. tañ-ca pana kiriyaṃ sabbesaṃ tathāgatānaṃ: paṭhamaṃ dānakathāya tattha cittaṃ abhiramāpetvā pacchā sīle niyojenti. yathā mahārāja manussā taruṇadārakānaṃ paṭhamaṃ tāva kīḷābhaṇḍakāni denti, seyyathīdaṃ: vaṃkakaṃ ghaṭikaṃ ciṅgulakaṃ pattāḷhakaṃ rathakaṃ dhanukaṃ, pacchā te sake sake kamme niyojenti; evam-eva kho mahārāja tathāgato paṭhamaṃ tāva dānakathāya cittaṃ abhiramāpetvā pacchā sīle niyojeti. yathā vā pana ma-hārāja bhisakko nāma āturānaṃ paṭhamaṃ tāva catuhapañcāhaṃ telaṃ pāyeti balakaraṇāya sinehanāya, pacchā vireceti, evam-eva kho

him. Nagasena, if the Bhagavan said, ' I do not partake of gifts gained by chanting verses,' then it is false to say that the Bhagavan gave a teaching on giving first. If he did give a teaching on giving first, then it is false to say that he said, 'I do not partake of gifts gained by chanting verses.' How can this be so? Someone worthy of gifts teaches householders the benefits of giving alms. They hear the teachings on giving and, with minds full of faith, give gifts again and again. Surely everyone who enjoys such gifts is in fact enjoying gifts gained by chanting verses. This subtle and profound two-pronged dilemma has reached you, and you must solve it."

"Great king, the Bhagavan did say: 396

I do not partake of gifts gained by chanting verses, 397
for this is not the conduct observed by those who see,
Brahman.
Buddhas reject that which is gained by chanting
verses.
Since such a principle exists, Brahman, this is their
practice.

And the Bhagavan did give the teaching on giving first. In 398
fact, this is what all tathagatas do: having first delighted the audience's mind by a teaching on giving, they then urge morality. Great king, people first give toys to young children, such as a toy plow, a game of sticks, a toy windmill, a pretend measure, a little chariot, or a play bow, so that later they can urge them to do each of their chores. Similarly, the Tathagata first delights the mind with a teaching on giving and then urges morality. Just as a physician first has a patient take oil for four or five days for strengthening and soothing

mahārāja tathāgato paṭhamaṃ dānakathāya cittaṃ abhiramāpetvā pacchā sīle niyojeti. dāyakānaṃ mahārāja dānapatīnaṃ cittaṃ mudukaṃ hoti maddavaṃ siniddhaṃ, tena te dānasetusaṅkamena dānanāvāya saṃsārasāgarapāram-anugacchanti, tasmā tesaṃ paṭhamaṃ kammabhūmim-anusāsati, na ca tena viññattiṃ āpajjatīti.

399 bhante nāgasena, viññattin-ti yaṃ vadesi, kati pana tā viññattiyo ti. dve 'mā mahārāja viññattiyo: kāyaviññatti vacīviññatti cāti. tattha atthi kāyaviññatti sāvajjā, atthi anavajjā; atthi vacīviññatti sāvajjā, atthi anavajjā. katamā kāyaviññatti sāvajjā: idh' ekacco bhikkhu kulāni upagantvā anokāse ṭhito ṭhānaṃ bhajati, ayaṃ kāyaviññatti sāvajjā, tāya ca viññāpitaṃ ariyā na paribhuñjanti, so ca puggalo ariyānaṃ samaye oñāto hoti hīḷito khīḷito garahito paribhūto acittikato, bhinnājīvo t'eva saṅkhaṃ gacchati. puna ca paraṃ mahārāja: idh' ekacco bhikkhu kulāni upagantvā anokāse ṭhito galaṃ paṇāmetvā morapekkhitaṃ pekkhati: evaṃ ime passantīti, tena ca te passanti, ayam-pi kāyaviññatti sāvajjā, tāya ca viññāpitaṃ ariyā na paribhuñjanti, so ca puggalo ariyānaṃ samaye oñāto hoti hīḷito khīḷito garahito paribhūto acittikato, bhinnājīvo t' eva saṅkhaṃ gacchati.

400 puna ca paraṃ mahārāja: idh' ekacco bhikkhu hanukāya vā bhamukāya vā aṅguṭṭhena vā viññāpeti, ayam-pi kāyaviññ-

and then administers a purgative, so too the Tathagata first delights the mind with a teaching on giving and then urges morality. Great king, the minds of benefactors and major donors become soft, mild, and smooth, and they cross over the ocean of samsara with the bridge, causeway, and ship of giving. Therefore, he instructed them in this way first on karmic grounds, even while he rejected hinting."

"Revered Nagasena, you mention 'hinting.' What kinds 399
of hinting are there?'

"Great king, there are two kinds of hinting: hinting with the body and verbal hinting. Some bodily hinting is blameworthy, and some is blameless; some verbal hinting is blameworthy, and some is blameless. What sort of hinting with the body is blameworthy? A certain monk approaches families and determines to stand in an obtrusive spot. This is blameworthy bodily hinting, because noble people do not eat food hinted for in this way, and such a person becomes degraded, scorned, derided, rejected, treated with contempt, and reviled in the opinion of noble people. He is regarded as one whose livelihood is compromised. And here is a further example: a certain monk approaches families, stands in an obtrusive spot, and sticks out his neck like a peacock trying to attract attention, hoping that they notice him. And because of this, they do notice him. This is blameworthy bodily hinting, because noble people do not eat food hinted for in this way, and such a person becomes degraded, scorned, derided, rejected, treated with contempt, and reviled in the opinion of noble people. He is regarded as one whose livelihood is
compromised. And here is a further example: a certain monk 400
hints with his jaw, eyebrow, or thumb. This too is blame-

atti sāvajjā, tāya ca viññāpitaṃ ariyā na paribhuñjanti, so ca puggalo ariyānaṃ samaye oñāto hoti hīḷito khīḷito garahito paribhūto acittikato, bhinnājīvo t' eva saṅkhaṃ gacchati. katamā kāyaviññatti anavajjā: idha bhikkhu kulāni upagantvā sato samāhito sampajāno ṭhāne pi aṭṭhāne pi yathānusatthiṃ gantvā ṭhāne tiṭṭhati, dātukāmesu tiṭṭhati, adātukāmesu pakkamati; ayaṃ kāyaviññatti anavajjā, tāya ca viññāpitaṃ ariyā paribhuñjanti, so ca puggalo ariyānaṃ samaye vaṇṇito hoti thuto pasattho, sallekhitācāro parisuddhājīvo t' eva saṅkhaṃ gacchati.

401 bhāsitam-p' etaṃ mahārāja bhagavatā devātidevena:

402 na ve yācanti sappaññā, ariyā garahanti yācanaṃ,
uddissa ariyā tiṭṭhanti, esā ariyāna' yācanā ti.

403 vacīviññatti sāvajjā: idha mahārāja bhikkhu vācāya bahuvidhaṃ viññāpeti cīvara-piṇḍapāta-senāsanagilānapaccaya-bhesajja-parikkhāraṃ, ayaṃ vacīviññatti sāvajjā, tāya ca viññāpitaṃ ariyā na paribhuñjanti, so ca puggalo ariyānaṃ samaye oñāto hoti hīḷito khīḷito garahito paribhūto acittikato, bhinnājīvo t' eva saṅkhaṃ gacchati.

404 puna ca paraṃ mahārāja: idh' ekacco bhikkhu paresaṃ sāvento evaṃ bhaṇati: iminā me attho ti, tāya ca vācāya paresaṃ sāvitāya tassa lābho uppajjati; ayam-pi vacīviññatti sāva-

worthy bodily hinting, because noble people do not eat food hinted for in this way; such a person becomes degraded, scorned, derided, rejected, treated with contempt, and reviled in the opinion of noble people. He is regarded as one whose livelihood is compromised.

"What sort of bodily hinting is blameless? In this case, a certain monk approaches families and is mindful, composed, and circumspect. He stands in this place or that place, having gone where he was told, and stands there. He remains in the presence of those who wish to give but departs from those who do not wish to give. This is blameless bodily hinting, and because noble people eat food hinted for in this way, such a person becomes praised, extolled, and commended in the opinion of noble people. He is regarded as one whose
practice is austere and whose livelihood is pure. Great king, 401
the Bhagavan, god above gods, also said this:

> The wise do not beg, for noble people reject begging. 402
> Noble persons are seen simply standing, for this is the
> 'begging' of the noble.

"What sort of verbal hinting is blameworthy? In this case, 403
great king, a monk verbally hints for the various requisites of robe, alms bowl, lodging, and medicine for sickness. This is blameworthy verbal hinting, and because noble people do not use things hinted for in this way, such a person becomes degraded, scorned, derided, rejected, treated with contempt, and reviled in the opinion of noble people. He is regarded as one whose livelihood is compromised.

"Here is another example, great king: a certain monk 404
mentions, in the hearing of others, 'I am in need of this,'

jjā, tāya ca viññāpitaṃ ariya na paribhuñjanti, so ca puggalo ariyānaṃ samaye oñāto hoti hīḷito khīḷito garahito paribhūto acittikato, bhinnājīvo t'eva saṅkhaṃ gacchati. puna ca paraṃ mahārāja: idh' ekacco bhikkhu vacīvipphārena parisāya sāveti: evañ-ca evañ-ca bhikkhūnaṃ dātabban-ti, tañ-ca te vacanaṃ sutvā parikittitaṃ abhiharanti; ayam-pi vacīviññatti sāvajjā, tāya ca viññāpitaṃ ariyā na paribhuñjanti, so ca puggalo ariyānaṃ samaye oñāto hoti hīḷito khīḷito garahito paribhūto acittikato, bhinnājīvo t' eva saṅkhaṃ gacchati.

405 nanu mahārāja thero pi sāriputto atthaṃgate suriye rattibhāge gilāno samāno therena mahāmoggallānena bhesajjaṃ pucchiyamāno vācaṃ bhindi, tassa tena vacībhedena bhesajjaṃ uppajji; atha thero sāriputto: vacībhedena me imaṃ bhesajjaṃ uppannaṃ, mā me ājīvo bhijjīti ājīvabhedabhayā taṃ bhesajjaṃ pajahi, na upajīvi. evam-pi vacīviññatti sāvajjā, tāya ca viññāpitaṃ ariyā na paribhuñjanti, so ca puggalo ariyānaṃ samaye oñāto hoti hīḷito khīḷito garahito paribhūto acittikato, bhinnājīvo t' eva saṅkhaṃ gacchati.

and then he comes to acquire it because of others hearing what he said. This also is blameworthy verbal hinting, and because noble people do not use things hinted for in this way, such a person becomes degraded, scorned, derided, rejected, treated with contempt, and reviled in the opinion of noble people. He is regarded as one whose livelihood is compromised. And another example, great king: a certain monk makes sure that others hear him verbally expounding on how this or that should be given to the monks; hearing this, they offer what was mentioned. This also is blameworthy verbal hinting, and because noble people do not use things hinted for in this way, such a person becomes degraded, scorned, derided, rejected, treated with contempt, and reviled in the opinion of noble people. He is regarded as one whose livelihood is compromised.

"Great king, is it not the case that once Elder Sariputta did 405
speak up when he was sick at nighttime, after the sun had set, and was asked by Elder Moggallana the Great about medicine for his benefit? Because he did speak up, medicine was procured for him. But then Elder Sariputta said, 'May my livelihood not be compromised with respect to the procuring of this medicine due to my speaking up,' and out of fear of compromising his livelihood, he rejected the medicine and did not use it for support. For this too is blameworthy verbal hinting, and because noble people do not use things hinted for in this way, such a person becomes degraded, scorned, derided, rejected, treated with contempt, and reviled in the opinion of noble people; he is regarded as one whose livelihood is compromised.

406 katamā vacīviññatti anavajjā: idha mahārāja bhikkhu sati paccaye bhesajjaṃ viññāpeti ñātipavāritesu kulesu, ayaṃ vacīviññatti anavajjā, tāya ca viññāpitaṃ ariyā paribhuñjanti, so ca puggalo ariyānaṃ samaye vaṇṇito hoti thomito pasattho, parisuddhājīvo t' eva saṅkhaṃ gacchati, anumato tathāgatehi arahantehi sammāsambuddhehi. yaṃ pana mahārāja tathāgato kasibhāradvājassa brāhmaṇassa bhojanaṃ pajahi, taṃ āveṭhana-viniveṭhana-kaḍḍhana-niggaha-paṭikammena nibbattaṃ, tasmā tathāgato taṃ piṇḍapātaṃ paṭikkhipi, na upajīvīti.

407 sabbakālaṃ bhante nāgasena tathāgate bhuñjamāne devatā dibbaṃ ojaṃ patte ākiranti, udāhu sūkaramaddave ca madhupāyāse cāti dvīsu yeva piṇḍapātesu ākiriṃsūti. sabbakālaṃ mahārāja tathāgate bhuñjamāne devatā dibbaṃ ojaṃ gahetvā upatiṭṭhitvā uddhaṭuddhaṭe ālope ākiranti. yathā mahārāja rañño sūdo rañño bhuñjantassa sūpaṃ gahetvā upatiṭṭhitvā kabaḷe kabaḷe sūpaṃ ākirati, evam-eva kho mahārāja sabbakālaṃ tathāgate bhuñjamāne devatā dibbaṃ ojaṃ gahetvā upatiṭṭhitvā uddhaṭuddhaṭe ālope dibbaṃ ojaṃ ākiranti. verañjāyam-pi mahārāja tathāgatassa sukkhayavapulake bhuñjamānassa devatā dibbena ojena temayitvā temayitvā upasaṃhariṃsu, tena tathā-

"What sort of verbal hinting is blameless? Here a monk hints for medicine when there is appropriate cause, but only among families where he has been invited to ask for something by his relatives. This is blameless verbal hinting, and because noble people use things hinted for in this way, such a person becomes praised, extolled, and commended in the opinion of noble people. He is regarded as one whose livelihood is pure and approved by the enlightened, perfectly awakened tathagatas. Great king, once the Tathagata rejected food from the Brahman Bharadvaja, who worked the plow, food that had been offered along with a counter-argument for entangling, unraveling, refuting, and debating. The Tathagata threw away those alms and did not make use of them."[83] 406

"Revered Nagasena, do the gods sprinkle divine nourishment into the Tathagata's bowl every time he eats, or do they sprinkle it on only two of his alms, namely, the pig's delight and the honeyed milk-rice?"[84] 407

"Great king, every time the Tathagata eats, the gods bring divine nourishment and stand by to sprinkle it on each mouthful as he lifts it up. It is just like how the royal cook brings the sauce when the king is eating and stands by to sprinkle it on each bite. So too the gods bring divine nourishment every time the Tathagata is eating, and they stand by to sprinkle it on each mouthful as it is lifted up. And at Veranja also, great king, they provided for him, having moistened with divine nourishment again and again the dried and shriveled barley that the Tathagata was eating. The Tathagata's body was strengthened by that."

gatassa kāyo upacito ahosīti. lābhā vata bhante nāgasena tāsaṃ devatānaṃ yā tathāgatassa sarīrapaṭijaggane satataṃ samitaṃ ussukkam-āpannā. sādhu bhante nāgasena, evam-etaṃ, tathā sampaṭicchāmīti.

408 bhante nāgasena, tumhe bhaṇatha: tathāgatena catuhi ca asaṅkheyyehi kappānaṃ kappasatasahassena ca etth' antare sabbaññutañāṇaṃ paripācitaṃ mahato janakāyassa samuddharaṇāyāti. puna ca: sabbaññutaṃ pattassa appossukkatāya cittaṃ nami, no dhammadesanāyāti. yathā nāma bhante nāgasena issāso vā issāsantevāsī vā bahuke divase saṅgāmatthāya upāsanaṃ sikkhitvā sampatte mahāyuddhe osakkeyya, evam-eva kho bhante nāgasena tathāgatena catuhi ca asaṅkheyyehi kappānaṃ kappasatasahassena ca etth' antare sabbaññutañāṇaṃ paripācetvā mahato janakāyassa samuddharaṇāya sabbaññutaṃ pattena dhammadesanāya osakkitaṃ.

409 yathā vā pana bhante nāgasena mallo vā mallantevāsī vā bahuke divase nibbuddhaṃ sikkhitvā sampatte mallayuddhe osakkeyya, evam-eva kho bhante nāgasena tathāgatena catuhi ca asaṅkheyyehi kappānaṃ kappasatasahassena ca etth' antare sabbaññutañāṇaṃ paripācetvā mahato janakāyassa samuddharaṇāya sabbaññutaṃ pattena dhammadesanāya osakkitaṃ.

410 kin-nu kho bhante nāgasena tathāgatena bhayā osakkitaṃ, udāhu apākaṭatāya osakkitaṃ, udāhu dubbalatāya osakkitaṃ, udāhu asabbaññutāya osakkitaṃ. kiṃ tattha kāraṇaṃ, iṅgha me tvaṃ kāraṇaṃ brūhi kaṅkhāvitaraṇāya. yadi bhante nāgasena tathāgatena catuhi ca asaṅkheyyehi kappānaṃ kappasatasahassena ca etth' antare sabbaññutañāṇaṃ paripācitaṃ mahato janakāyassa samuddharaṇāya,

"Nagasena, making such effort constantly and continuously in looking after the Tathagata's body was a great gain for those gods. Very well, revered Nagasena. It is as you say, and I am convinced.

"Revered Nagasena, you say: 'Omniscience was fully 408
developed over four incalculables and a hundred thousand eons by the Tathagata to save the great multitude of beings.' And yet, after he had achieved omniscience, his mind inclined to living in ease and not teaching the Dhamma. Just like the archer or archery student who studies archery for many days for the sake of going to war but then retreats when the great battle is joined, so too did the Tathagata retreat from teaching the Dhamma, though he had achieved omniscience for the sake of saving the great multitude of beings, the very omniscience that he had fully developed over four
incalculables and a hundred thousand eons. Or just like the 409
wrestler or wrestling student who studies wrestling for many days but then retreats when the big match occurs, so too did the Tathagata retreat from teaching the Dhamma, though he had achieved omniscience for the sake of saving the great multitude of beings, the very omniscience that he had fully developed over four incalculables and a hundred thousand eons.

"Nagasena, did the Tathagata retreat out of fear, or did 410
he retreat because of things not being clear? Or was it due to weakness? Or because of not being omniscient? What was the reason in this case? Come now, tell me the reason in order to dispel my doubts. Nagasena, if the Tathagata fully developed omniscience over four incalculables and a hundred thousand eons for the sake of saving the great

tena hi: sabbaññutaṃ pattassa appossukkatāya cittaṃ nami, no dhammadesanāyāti yaṃ vacanaṃ taṃ micchā. yadi sabbaññutaṃ pattassa appossukkatāya cittaṃ nami, no dhammadesanāya, tena hi: tathāgatena catuhi ca asaṅkheyyehi kappānaṃ kappasatasahassena ca etth' antare sabbaññutañāṇaṃ paripācitaṃ mahato janakāyassa samuddharaṇāyāti tam-pi vacanaṃ micchā. ayam-pi ubhatokoṭiko pañho gambhīro dunnibbedho tavānuppatto, so tayā nibbāhitabbo ti.

411 aripācitañ-ca mahārāja tathāgatena catuhi ca asaṅkheyyehi kappānaṃ kappasatasahassena ca etth' antare sabbaññutañāṇaṃ mahato janakāyassa samuddharaṇāya; pattasabbaññutassa ca appossukkatāya cittaṃ nami, no dhammadesanāya. tañ-ca pana dhammassa gambhīra-nipuṇa-duddasa-duranubodha-sukhuma-duppaṭivedhataṃ sattānañ-ca ālayārāmataṃ sakkāyadiṭṭhiyā daḷhasuggahitatañ-ca disvā: kin-nu kho kathan-nu kho ti appossukkatāya cittaṃ nami, no dhammadesanāya; sattānaṃ paṭivedhacintanamānasaṃ yev' etaṃ.

412 yathā mahārāja bhisakko sallakatto anekabyādhiparipīḷitaṃ naraṃ upasaṅkamitvā evaṃ cintayati: kena nu kho upakkamena katamena vā bhesajjena imassa byādhi vūpasameyyāti; evam-eva kho mahārāja tathāgatassa sabbakilesabyādhiparipīḷitaṃ janaṃ dhammassa ca gambhīra-nipuṇa-duddasa-duranubodha-sukhuma-duppaṭivedhataṃ disvā: kin-nu kho kathan-nu kho ti appossukkatāya cittaṃ nami, no dhammadesanāya; sattānaṃ paṭivedhacintanamānasaṃ yev' etaṃ. yathā mahārāja rañño khattiyassa muddhāvasittassa dovārika-anīkaṭṭha-pārisajja-negama-bhaṭa-balattha-amacca-rājañña-rājūpajīvine jane

multitude of beings, then it is surely false to claim that after he had achieved omniscience his mind inclined to living in ease and not teaching the Dhamma. Conversely, if after he had achieved omniscience the Tathagata's mind inclined to living in ease and not teaching the Dhamma, then it is false to claim that he fully developed omniscience over four incalculables and a hundred thousand eons for the sake of saving the great multitude of beings. This profound and difficult two-pronged dilemma has reached you, and you must solve it."

"Great king, the Tathagata fully developed omniscience 411
over four incalculables and a hundred thousand eons for the sake of saving the great multitude of beings. And yes, after he had achieved omniscience, his mind did incline to living in ease and not teaching the Dhamma. But this was because he saw that for beings caught up in desire and pleasure and held fast by false views of individuality, the Dhamma is deep, recondite, imperceptible, hard to understand, subtle, and difficult to penetrate. He wondered *Who?* and *How?* as he considered whether beings might comprehend it, and his mind inclined to living in ease and not teaching the Dhamma.

"Great king, a physician who is a surgeon approaches a 412
man afflicted with various illnesses thinking, *Which remedies and medicines will cure his illness?* Similarly, the Tathagata saw that people are afflicted with the illness of all the defilements and that the Dhamma is deep, recondite, imperceptible, hard to understand, subtle, and difficult to penetrate. He wondered *Who?* and *How?* as he considered whether beings might comprehend it, and his mind inclined to living in ease and not teaching the Dhamma. Great king, a Kshatriya

disvā evaṃ cittam-uppajjeyya: kin-nu kho kathan-nu kho ime saṅgaṇhissāmīti; evam-eva kho mahārāja tathāgatassa dhammassa gambhīra-nipuṇa-duddasa-duranubodha-sukhuma-duppaṭivedhataṃ sattānañ-ca ālayārāmataṃ sakkāyadiṭṭhiyā daḷhasuggahitatañ-ca disvā: kin-nu kho kathan-nu kho ti appossukkatāya cittaṃ nami, no dhammadesanāya; sattānaṃ paṭivedhacintanamānasaṃ yev' etaṃ.

413 api ca mahārāja sabbesaṃ tathāgatānaṃ dhammatā esā yaṃ brahmunā āyācitā dhammaṃ desenti. tattha pana kiṃ kāraṇaṃ. ye tena samayena manussā tāpasaparibbājakā samaṇabrāhmanā sabbe te brahmadevatā honti brahmagarukā brahmaparāyanā; tasmā tassa balavato yasavato ñātassa paññātassa uttarassa accuggatassa oṇamanena sadevako loko oṇamissati okappessati adhimuccissatīti imināva mahārāja kāraṇena tathāgatā brahmunā āyācitā dhammaṃ desenti. yathā mahārāja koci rājā vā rājamahāmatto vā yassa oṇamati apacitiṃ karoti, balavatarassa tassa oṇamanena avasesā janatā oṇamati apacitiṃ karoti; evam-eva kho mahārāja brahme onamite tathāgatānaṃ sadevako loko oṇamissati. pūjitapūjako mahārāja loko, tasmā so brahmā sabbesaṃ tathāgatānaṃ āyācati dhammadesanāya, tena ca kāraṇena tathāgatā brahmunā āyācitā dhammaṃ desentīti.

who has been crowned monarch looks upon the people in the king's employ—the gatekeepers, bodyguards, retainers, traders, mercenaries, soldiers, ministers, and courtiers—and the thought occurs to him, *I must protect them. But who? How?* Similarly, the Tathagata saw that the Dhamma is deep, recondite, imperceptible, hard to understand, subtle, and difficult to penetrate, and that beings are caught up in desire and pleasure and held fast by false views of individuality. He wondered *Who?* and *How?* as he considered whether beings might comprehend it, and his mind inclined to living in ease and not teaching the Dhamma.

"Moreover, great king, it is in the nature of things that 413
all tathagatas are beseeched by Brahma before teaching the Dhamma. What is the reason for this? At that time all people who were ascetics, wanderers, renouncers, and Brahmans worshiped and reverenced Brahma, and took Brahma as their refuge. Therefore, the tathagatas, thinking that the world with its gods will believe, have confidence in, and bow down owing to their prostration of one so powerful, famous, knowledgeable, wise, high, and lofty, were implored by Brahma before teaching the Dhamma. Just as whomever a king or a prime minister bows down to and worships, the rest of the people will also bow down to and worship, owing to the prostration of the very powerful, when Brahma bows to the tathagatas, the world with its gods will bow also. The world worships those who are worshiped, great king, and so Brahma implores all tathagatas to teach the Dhamma. This is the reason the tathagatas are implored by Brahma before teaching the Dhamma."

sādhu bhante nāgasena, sunibbeṭhito pañho, atibhadrakaṃ veyyākaraṇam, evam etaṃ, tathā sampaṭicchāmīti.

pañcamo vaggo.

"Very well, revered Nagasena. The dilemma has been unraveled and the exposition is auspicious. It is so, and I am convinced."

End of Part 5.

PART 6

414 bhante nāgasena, bhāsitam-p' etaṃ bhagavatā: na me ācariyo atthi, sadiso me na vijjati, sadevakasmiṃ lokasmiṃ na-tthi me paṭipuggalo ti. puna ca bhaṇitaṃ: iti kho bhikkhave āḷāro kālāmo ācariyo me samāno antevāsiṃ maṃ samānaṃ attanā samasamaṃ ṭhapesi uḷārāya ca maṃ pūjāya pūjesīti. yadi bhante nāgasena tathāgatena bhaṇitaṃ: na me ācariyo atthi, sadiso me na vijjatīti tena hi: iti kho bhikkhave āḷāro kālāmo ācariyo me samāno antevāsiṃ maṃ samānaṃ attanā samasamaṃ ṭhapesīti yaṃ vacanaṃ taṃ micchā. yadi tathāgatena bhaṇitaṃ: iti kho bhikkhave āḷāro kālāmo ācariyo me samāno antevāsiṃ maṃ samānaṃ attanā samasamaṃ ṭhapesīti, tena hi: na me ācariyo atthi, sadiso me na vijjatīti tam-pi vacanaṃ micchā. ayam-pi ubhatokoṭiko pañho tavānuppatto, sa tayā nibbāhitabbo ti.

415 bhāsitam-p' etaṃ mahārāja bhagavatā: na me ācariyo atthi, sadiso me na vijjati, sadevakasmiṃ lokasmiṃ na-tthi me paṭipuggalo ti. bhaṇitañ-ca: iti kho bhikkhave āḷāro kālāmo ācariyo me samāno antevāsiṃ maṃ samānaṃ attanā samasamaṃ ṭhapesi uḷārāya ca maṃ pūjāya pūjesīti. tañ-ca pana vacanaṃ pubbeva sambodhā anabhisambuddhassa bodhisattass' eva sato ācariyabhāvaṃ sandhāya bhāsitaṃ. pañc' ime mahārāja pubbeva sambodhā anabhisambuddhassa bodhisattassa sato ācariyā, yehi anusiṭṭho bodhisatto tattha tattha divasaṃ vītināmesi. katame pañca.

416 ye te mahārāja aṭṭha brāhmaṇā jātamatte bodhisatte lakkhaṇāni parigaṇhiṃsu, seyyathīdaṃ: rāmo, dhajo, lakkhaṇo, mantī, yañño, suyāmo, subhojo, sudatto, te tassa sotthiṃ

PART 6

"Revered Nagasena, the Bhagavan also said this: 'I have no teacher, for there is no one like me; in the world with its gods I have no rival.' But he also said, 'Monks, while he was my teacher, Alara Kalama placed me, his student, at exactly the same level as himself, and he honored me with the utmost reverence.'[85] Nagasena, if the Tathagata said, 'I have no teacher, for there is no one like me,' then it is false to claim, 'Monks, while he was my teacher, Alara Kalama placed me, his student, at exactly the same level as himself.' Alternatively, if the Tathagata did say, 'Monks, while he was my teacher, Alara Kalama placed me, his student, at exactly the same level as himself,' then it is false to claim, 'I have no teacher, for there is no one like me.' This two-pronged dilemma has reached you, and you must solve it." 414

"Great king, the Bhagavan did say, 'I have no teacher, for there is no one like me; in the world with its gods I have no rival.' And he also said, 'Monks, while he was my teacher, Alara Kalama placed me, his student, at exactly the same level as himself, and he honored me with the utmost reverence.' But the claim about having a teacher was made by the Bodhisatta prior to the awakening, when he had not yet attained perfect awakening. Great king, prior to the awakening, when he was not yet perfectly awakened, the Bodhisatta had five teachers. The Bodhisatta spent his days in various places being instructed by them. Who are the five? 415

"Great king, the first teachers were the eight Brahmans who examined the auspicious marks at the time of the Bodhi- 416

pavedayitvā rakkhākammaṃ akaṃsu, te ca paṭhamaṃ ācariyā. puna ca paraṃ mahārāja: bodhisattassa pitā suddhodano rājā yaṃ tena samayena abhijātaṃ udiccaṃ jātivantaṃ padakaṃ veyyākaraṇaṃ chaḷaṅgavantaṃ sabbamittaṃ nāma brāhmaṇaṃ upanetvā sovaṇṇena bhiṅkārena udakaṃ oṇojetvā: imaṃ kumāraṃ sikkhāpehīti adāsi, ayaṃ dutiyo ācariyo. puna ca paraṃ mahārāja: yā sā devatā bodhisattaṃ saṃvejesi, yassā vacanaṃ sutvā bodhisatto saṃviggo ubbiggo tasmiṃ yeva khaṇe nekkhammaṃ nikkhamitvā[17] pabbaji, ayaṃ tatiyo ācariyo. puna ca paraṃ mahārāja: āḷāro kālāmo ayaṃ catuttho ācariyo. puna ca paraṃ mahārāja: uddako rāmaputto, ayaṃ pañcamo ācariyo. ime kho mahārāja pubbeva sambodhā anabhisambuddhassa bodhisattassa sato pañca ācariyā. te ca pana ācariyā lokiye dhamme.

417 imasmiñ-ca pana mahārāja lokuttare dhamme sabbaññutañāṇapaṭivedhāya na-tthi tathāgatassa anuttaro anusāsako. sayambhū mahārāja tathāgato anācariyako, tasmā kāraṇā tathāgatena bhaṇitaṃ: na me ācariyo atthi, sadiso me na vijjati, sadevakasmiṃ lokasmiṃ na-tthi me paṭipuggalo ti. sādhu bhante nāgasena, evam-etaṃ, tathā sampaṭicchāmīti.

418 bhante nāgasena, bhāsitam-p'etaṃ bhagavatā: aṭṭhānam-etaṃ bhikkhave anavakāso yaṃ ekissā lokadhātuyā dve arahanto sammāsambuddhā apubbaṃ acarimaṃ

satta's birth, namely, Rama, Dhaja, Lakkhana, Manti, Yanna, Suyama, Subhoja, and Sudatta. They declared his blessings and undertook the duty of guarding him. And then King Suddhodana, the Bodhisatta's father, summoned a Brahman named Sabbamitta, who was highborn, well bred, highly ranked, and skilled with words, grammar, and the six ancillary sciences. He poured the ceremonial water with the golden vessel and gave the prince to him, asking that he instruct him. This was the second teacher. And then, a god prompted urgency in the Bodhisatta. Hearing his words, the Bodhisatta became agitated and urgent, and he renounced the world right then and there and took up the ascetic life. This was the third teacher. And then there was Alara Kalama, who was the fourth teacher, and Uddaka Ramaputta, the fifth teacher. Great king, these were the Bodhisatta's five teachers before he was awakened and prior to his perfect awakening. Moreover, they were teachers in worldly matters.

"But with respect to transcendent matters, great king, 417
there is no instructor higher than the Tathagata for penetrating the knowledge of omniscience. The Tathagata is self-arisen and without a teacher, and for this reason the Tathagata said: 'I have no teacher, for there is no one like me; in the world with its gods I have no rival.'"

"Very well, revered Nagasena. This is so, and I am convinced.

"Revered Nagasena, the Bhagavan also said, 'Monks, on no 418
occasion and in no place can two enlightened and perfectly awakened buddhas occur in one world system at the same time. This is impossible.' When teaching, all tathagatas teach the thirty-seven awakening factors; when talking, they talk

uppajjeyyuṃ, n' etaṃ ṭhānaṃ vijjatīti. desentā pi bhante nāgasena sabbe pi tathāgatā sattatiṃsa bodhapakkhiye dhamme desenti, kathayamānā ca cattāri ariyasaccāni kathenti, sikkhāpentā ca tisu sikkhāsu sikkhāpenti, anusāsamānā ca appamādapaṭipattiyā anusāsanti. yadi bhante nāgasena sabbesam-pi tathāgatānaṃ ekā desanā ekā kathā ekā sikkhā ekā 'nusatthi, kena kāraṇena dve tathāgatā ekakkhaṇe na uppajjanti. ekena pi tāva buddhuppādena ayaṃ loko obhāsajāto, yadi dutiyo buddho bhaveyya dvinnaṃ pabhāya ayaṃ loko bhiyyosomattāya obhāsajāto bhaveyya, ovadamānā ca dve tathāgatā sukhaṃ ovadeyyuṃ, anusāsamānā ca sukhaṃ anusāseyyuṃ. tattha me kāraṇaṃ brūhi, yathā 'haṃ nissaṃsayo bhaveyyan-ti.

419 ayaṃ mahārāja dasasahassī lokadhātu ekabuddhadhāraṇī, ekass' eva tathāgatassa guṇaṃ dhāreti; yadi dutiyo buddho uppajjeyya nāyaṃ dasasahassī lokadhātu dhāreyya, caleyya kampeyya nameyya oṇameyya vinameyya vikireyya vidhameyya viddhaṃseyya, naṭṭhānam upagaccheyya. yathā mahārāja nāvā ekapurisasantāraṇī bhaveyya, ekasmiṃ purise abhirūḷhe samupādikā bhaveyya, atha dutiyo puriso āgaccheyya tādiso āyunā vaṇṇena vayena pamāṇena kisa-thūlena sabbaṅgapaccaṅgena, so taṃ nāvaṃ abhirūheyya, api nu sā mahārāja nāvā dvinnam-pi dhāreyyāti.

420 na hi bhante, caleyya kampeyya nameyya oṇameyya vinameyya vikireyya vidhameyya viddhaṃseyya, naṭṭhānam-upagaccheyya, osīdeyya udake ti. evam-eva kho mahārāja ayaṃ dasasahassī lokadhātu ekabuddhadhāraṇī, ekass' eva tathāgatassa guṇaṃ dhāreti; yadi dutiyo buddho

about the Four Noble Truths; when instructing, they give instructions on the three trainings; and when advising, they advise the practice of diligence. Nagasena, if there is just one teaching, just one preaching, just one instruction, and just one point of advice of all tathagatas, then why is it that two tathagatas cannot occur at the same time? Since the world is filled with radiance by the arising of one buddha, then surely the world would become even more radiant with twice the light, should two buddhas arise. And with two tathagatas doing the admonishing and advising, they would admonish and advise easily. Tell me the reasoning, whereby I may be rid of perplexity."

"Great king, this ten-thousand-world system sustains 419
only one buddha and supports the special qualities of only the Tathagata. Should a second buddha arise, the ten-thousand-world system would not bear up and would shake, tremble, bend, buckle, crumple, collapse, fall to ruin, disintegrate, and disappear. Great king, consider a boat made to convey a single person. When one person climbs aboard, it sinks to the level of the water, but then a second person, similar in age, appearance, vitality, measure, leanness, and strength in body and limb, arrives and climbs into the boat. Would the boat hold both of them?"

"No, sir, it would shake, tremble, bend, buckle, crumple, 420
collapse, fall to ruin, disintegrate, and disappear. It would sink under the water."

"Similarly, great king, this ten-thousand-world system sustains only one buddha and supports the special qualities of only the Tathagata. Should a second buddha arise, the ten-thousand-world system would not bear up and would

uppajjeyya, nāyaṃ dasasahassī lokadhātu dhāreyya, caleyya kampeyya nameyya oṇameyya vinameyya vikireyya vidhameyya viddhaṃseyya, naṭṭhānam-upagaccheyya. yathā vā pana mahārāja puriso yāvadatthaṃ bhojanaṃ bhuñjeyya chādentaṃ yāva kaṇṭham-abhipūrayitvā, so dhāto pīṇito paripuṇṇo nirantaro tandikato anoṇamidaṇḍajāto puna-d-eva tattakaṃ bhojanaṃ bhuñjeyya; api nu kho so mahārāja puriso sukhito bhaveyyāti.

421 na hi bhante, sakiṃ bhuttova mareyyāti. evam-eva kho mahārāja ayaṃ dasasahassī lokadhātu ekabuddhadhāraṇī, ekass' eva tathāgatassa guṇaṃ dhāreti; yadi dutiyo buddho uppajjeyya, nāyaṃ dasasahassī lokadhātu dhāreyya, caleyya kampeyya nameyya oṇameyya vinameyya vikireyya vidhameyya viddhaṃseyya, naṭṭhānam-upagaccheyyāti. kin-nu kho bhante nāgasena atidhammabhārena paṭhavī calatīti.

422 idha mahārāja dve sakaṭā ratanaparipūritā bhaveyyuṃ yāva mukhasmā, ekasmā sakaṭato ratanaṃ gahetvā ekasmiṃ sakaṭe ākireyyuṃ, api nu taṃ mahārāja sakaṭaṃ dvinnam-pi sakaṭānaṃ ratanaṃ dhāreyyāti. na hi bhante, nābhi pi tassa phaleyya, arā pi tassa bhijjeyyuṃ, nemī pi tassa opateyya, akkho pi tassa bhijjeyyāti. kin-nu kho mahārāja atiratanabhārena sakaṭaṃ bhijjatīti. āma bhante ti.

423 evam eva kho mahārāja atidhammabhārena paṭhavī calati. api ca mahārāja imaṃ kāraṇaṃ buddhabalaparidīpanāya osāritaṃ. aññam-pi tattha abhirūpaṃ kāraṇaṃ suṇohi yena

shake, tremble, bend, buckle, crumple, collapse, fall to ruin, disintegrate, and disappear. Great king, suppose further that a man were to eat as much food as he wanted and become filled up to the neck with something delectable. Would he—satiated, bloated, overfull, stuffed, drowsy, and like an inflexible log—enjoy eating more food? Would the man be comfortable?"

"No, sir. Eating even once more might kill him." 421

"Similarly, great king, this ten-thousand-world system sustains only one buddha and supports the special qualities of only the Tathagata. Should a second buddha arise, the ten-thousand-world system would not bear up and would shake, tremble, bend, buckle, crumple, collapse, fall to ruin, disintegrate, and disappear."

"And yet, Nagasena, does the earth shake because of bearing too much righteousness?"

"Great king, suppose there were two carts filled to the top 422
with jewels, and someone were to take the jewels from one cart and heap them on the other cart. Would the second cart be able to hold the jewels of both carts?"

"No, sir, its hub would split, the spokes would snap, the wheel rim collapse, and the axle break."

"So the cart would break because of bearing too many jewels?"

"Yes, sir."

"In much the same way, great king, the earth shakes because 423
of too much righteousness. Of course, this reasoning has been recounted for illuminating the power of the buddhas. But listen to another lovely reason two perfectly awakened buddhas do not occur at the same time. Great king, if two

kāraṇena dve sammāsambuddhā ekakkhaṇe n' uppajjanti. yadi mahārāja dve sammāsambuddhā ekakkhaṇe uppajjeyyuṃ, tesaṃ parisāya vivādo uppajjeyya: tumhākaṃ buddho, amhākaṃ buddho ti ubhatopakkhajātā bhaveyyuṃ. yathā mahārāja dvinnaṃ balavāmaccānaṃ parisāya vivādo uppajjeyya: tumhākaṃ amacco, amhākaṃ amacco ti ubhatopakkhajātā honti; evam-eva kho mahārāja yadi dve sammāsambuddhā ekakkhaṇe uppajjeyyuṃ, tesaṃ parisāya vivādo uppajjeyya: tumhākaṃ buddho, amhākaṃ buddho ti ubhatopakkhajātā bhaveyyuṃ. idaṃ tāva mahārāja ekaṃ kāraṇaṃ yena kāraṇena dve sammāsambuddhā ekakkhaṇe na uppajjanti.

424 aparam-pi mahārāja uttariṃ kāraṇaṃ suṇohi yena kāraṇena dve sammāsambuddhā ekakkhaṇe na uppajjanti. yadi mahārāja dve sammāsambuddhā ekakkhaṇe uppajjeyyuṃ, aggo buddho ti yaṃ vacanaṃ taṃ micchā bhaveyya, jeṭṭho buddho ti yaṃ vacanaṃ taṃ micchā bhaveyya, seṭṭho buddho ti yaṃ vacanaṃ taṃ micchā bhaveyya, visiṭṭho buddho ti uttamo buddho ti pavaro buddho ti asamo buddho ti-asamasamo buddho ti appaṭimo buddho ti appaṭibhāgo buddho ti appaṭipuggalo buddho ti yaṃ vacanaṃ taṃ micchā bhaveyya. idam-pi kho tvaṃ mahārāja kāraṇaṃ atthato sampaṭiccha yena kāraṇena dve sammāsambuddhā ekakkhaṇe na uppajjanti.

425 api ca kho mahārāja buddhānaṃ bhagavantānaṃ sabhāvapakati esā yaṃ eko yeva buddho loke uppajjati, kasmā kāraṇā: mahantatāya sabbaññūbuddhaguṇānaṃ. aññam-pi mahārāja yaṃ loke mahantaṃ taṃ ekaṃ yeva hoti: paṭhavī

perfectly awakened buddhas were to arise at the same time, contention would occur between the two followings, and two factions would emerge in relation to 'your Buddha' and 'our Buddha.' It would be similar, great king, to the contention that would arise between the followings of powerful ministers, where two factions would emerge in relation to 'your minister' and 'our minister.' It would be much the same if two perfectly awakened buddha*s* were to occur at the same time, in that contention and factions would emerge. 'Great king, this is one reason two perfectly awakened buddhas do not occur at the same time.

"But listen to an additional reason two perfectly awak- 424
ened buddhas do not occur at the same time. Great king, if two perfectly awakened buddhas were to arise at the same time, the claim that 'the Buddha is foremost' would be false. So too would all these statements be false: 'The Buddha is the best,' 'the Buddha is supreme,' 'the Buddha is superior,' 'the Buddha is the highest,' 'the Buddha is preeminent,' 'the Buddha is without equal,' 'the Buddha is equal to the unequaled,' 'the Buddha is matchless,' and 'the Buddha is without counterpart.' Great king, because of this entailment, you must accept this reasoning whereby two perfectly awakened buddhas do not occur at the same time.

"Furthermore, great king, it is the particular nature of 425
blessed buddhas that only one buddha arises in the world. For what reason? The vastness of the qualities of the omniscient Buddha. There are other vast things in this world that are singular: the earth is vast, and it is singular; the ocean is vast, and it is singular; Sineru, king of mountains, is vast, and

mahārāja mahantā, sā ekā yeva; sāgaro mahanto, so eko yeva; sineru girirājā mahanto, so eko yeva; ākāso mahanto, so eko yeva; sakko mahanto, so eko yeva; māro mahanto, so eko yeva; mahābrahmā mahanto, so eko yeva; tathāgato arahaṃ sammāsambuddho mahanto, so eko yeva lokasmiṃ. yatth' ete uppajjanti tattha aññassa okāso na hoti. tasmā mahārāja tathāgato arahaṃ sammāsambuddho eko yeva lokasmiṃ uppajjatīti.

426 sukathito bhante nāgasena pañho opammehi kāraṇehi, anipuṇo p' etaṃ sutvā attamano bhaveyya, kim-pana mādiso mahāpañño; sādhu bhante nāgasena, evam-etaṃ, tathā sampaṭicchāmīti.

427 bhante nāgasena, bhāsitam-p' etaṃ bhagavatā mātucchāya mahāpajāpatiyā gotamiyā vassikasāṭikāya dīyamānāya: saṅghe gotami dehi, saṅghe te dinne ahañ-c' eva pūjito bhavissāmi saṅgho cāti. kin-nu kho bhante nāgasena tathāgato saṅgharatanato na bhāriko na garuko na dakkhiṇeyyo, yaṃ tathāgato sakāya mātucchāya sayampiñjitaṃ sayaṃluñcitaṃ sayaṃpoṭhitaṃ sayaṃkantitaṃ sayaṃvāyitaṃ vassikasāṭikaṃ attano dīyamānaṃ saṅghassa dāpesi. yadi bhante nāgasena tathāgato saṅgharatanato uttaro bhaveyya adhiko vā visiṭṭho vā: mayi dinne mahapphalaṃ bhavissatīti na tathāgato mātucchāya sayampiñjitaṃ sayaṃluñcitaṃ sayaṃpoṭhitaṃ taṃ vassikasāṭikaṃ saṅghe dāpeyya. yasmā ca kho bhante nāgasena tathāgato attānaṃ na pattīyati na upanissayati, tasmā tathāgato mātucchāya taṃ vassikasāṭikaṃ saṅghassa dāpesīti.

it is singular; space is vast, and it is singular; Sakka is vast, and he is singular; Mara is vast, and he is singular; Great Brahma is vast, and he is singular; and the Tathagata, the Enlightened and Perfectly Awakened Buddha, is vast, and he is singular in the world. Where these occur there is just no room for another. Therefore, great king, the Tathagata, the Enlightened and Perfectly Awakened Buddha, arises in the world alone."

"The dilemma is well explained with analogies and reasons. 426
Even a blundering dolt would be pleased upon hearing this, to say nothing of a very wise person like me. Well done, revered Nagasena. This is so, and I am persuaded.

"Revered Nagasena, when Mahapajapati Gotami, the 427
Bhagavan's maternal aunt, was gifting cloth in the rainy season, he said, 'Give to the community, Gotami, for when something is given to the community I will be honored along with the community.' But Nagasena, sir, is not the Tathagata as important, serious, and worthy of gifts as the jewel that is the community?[86] And yet, when his own maternal aunt was gifting her rainy season cloth that she herself had carded, combed, worked, spun, and woven, he made her give it to the community. If the Tathagata were higher or more eminent than, or superior to the community, he would have said, 'When something is given to me, it will become very fruitful,' and the Tathagata would not have made his maternal aunt give to the community a rainy season cloth that she had herself carded, combed, and worked. Revered Nagasena, it would seem that because the Tathagata does not himself benefit from or depend on such things, he made his maternal aunt gift the rainy season cloth to the community."

428 bhāsitam-p' etaṃ mahārāja bhagavatā mātucchāya mahāpajāpatiyā gotamiyā vassikasāṭikāya dīyamānāya: saṅghe gotami dehi, saṅghe dinne ahañ-c' eva pūjito bhavissāmi saṅgho cāti. taṃ pana na attano patimānanassa avipākatāya na adakkhiṇeyyatāya, api ca kho hitatthāya anukampāya: anāgatam-addhānaṃ saṅgho mam' accayena cittikato bhavissatīti vijjamāne yeva guṇe parikittayanto evam-āha: saṅghe gotami dehi, saṅghe dinne ahañ-c' eva pūjito bhavissāmi saṅgho cāti.

429 yathā mahārāja pitā dharamāno yeva amacca-bhaṭabalattha-dovārika-anīkaṭṭha-pārisajja janamajjhe rañño santike puttassa vijjamānaṃ yeva guṇaṃ pakitteti: idha ṭhapito anāgatam-addhānaṃ janamajjhe pūjito bhavissatīti; evam eva kho mahārāja tathāgato hitatthāya anukampāya: anāgatam-addhānaṃ saṅgho mama accayena cittikato bhavissatīti vijjamāne yeva guṇe pakittayanto evam-āha: saṅghe gotami dehi, saṅghe dinne ahañ-c' eva pūjito bhavissāmi saṅgho cāti.

430 na kho mahārāja tāvatakena vassikasāṭikānuppadānamattakena saṅgho tathāgatato adhiko nāma hoti visiṭṭho vā. yathā mahārāja mātāpitaro puttānaṃ ucchādenti parimaddanti nahāpenti sambāhenti, api nu kho mahārāja tāvatakena ucchādanaparimaddana-nahāpana-sambāhanamattakena putto mātāpitūhi adhiko nāma hoti visiṭṭho vā ti.

"Great king, when his maternal aunt Mahapajapati 428
Gotami was gifting a cloth for the rainy season, the Bhagavan did say, 'Give to the community, Gotami, for when something is given to the community I will be honored along with the community.' But this was not due to any lack of fruitfulness in her serving him, nor due to his being unworthy of gifts. Rather, it was for the sake of welfare and out of compassion. He considered, *In the distant future after my death, the community will be highly regarded,* and so he praised its present virtues, saying, 'Give to the community, Gotami, for when something is given to the community
I will be honored along with the community.' Great king, 429
while he is still living, a father praises his son's existing qualities in the presence of the king and before such people as his ministers, mercenaries, soldiers, gatekeepers, bodyguards, and retainers, thinking, *If he is established here, then in the future he will be honored among the people.* Similarly, for the sake of welfare and out of compassion, the Tathagata thinks, *In the distant future after my death, the community will be highly regarded,* and so praises its present virtues, saying, 'Give to the community, Gotami, for when something is given to the community I will be honored along with the community.'

"And surely the community does not come to be more 430
eminent than or superior to the Tathagata merely by being presented a rainy season cloth, great king. Parents massage, shampoo, bathe, and scrub their children, but does this mean that the child comes to be more eminent than or superior to the parents merely by being massaged, shampooed, bathed, and scrubbed?"

431 na hi bhante, akāmakaraṇīyā bhante puttā mātāpitunnaṃ, tasmā mātāpitaro puttānaṃ ucchādana-parimaddana-nahāpana-sambāhanaṃ karontīti. evam-eva kho mahārāja na tāvatakena vassikasāṭikānuppadānamattakena saṅgho tathāgatato adhiko nāma hoti visiṭṭho vā. api ca tathāgato akāmakaraṇīyaṃ karonto mātucchāya taṃ vassikasāṭikaṃ saṅghassa dāpesi. yathā vā pana mahārāja kocid-eva puriso rañño upāyanaṃ āhareyya, taṃ rājā upāyanaṃ aññatarassa bhaṭassa vā balatthassa vā senāpatissa vā purohitassa vā dadeyya, api nu kho so mahārāja puriso tāvatakena upāyanapaṭilābhamattakena raññā adhiko nāma hoti visiṭṭho vā ti.

432 na hi bhante, rājabhattiko bhante so puriso rājūpajīvī, taṃ ṭhāne ṭhapento rājā upāyanaṃ detīti. evam-eva kho mahārāja na tāvatakena vassikasāṭikānuppadānamattakena saṅgho tathāgatato adhiko nāma hoti visiṭṭho vā, atha kho tathāga tabhattiko tathāgatopajīvī, taṃ ṭhāne ṭhapento tathāgato saṅghassa vassikasāṭikaṃ dāpesi. api ca mahārāja tathāgatassa evaṃ ahosi: sabhāvapatipūjanīyo saṅgho, mama santakena saṅghaṃ patipūjessāmīti saṅghassa vassikasāṭikaṃ dāpesi. na mahārāja tathāgato attano yeva patipūjanaṃ vaṇṇeti, atha kho ye loke patipūjanārahā tesam-pi tathāgato patipūjanaṃ vaṇṇeti.

"No, sir. Children must be handled by their parents even 431
when they don't wish to be. Therefore, the children's parents do the massaging, shampooing, bathing, and scrubbing."

"So too, great king, the community does not come to be more eminent than or superior to the Tathagata merely by being presented a rainy season cloth. Furthermore, the Tathagata made her do something she did not wish to do when he made his maternal aunt give the rainy season cloth to the community. Suppose a certain man takes a tribute to the king, but the king gives it to someone else, either a mercenary, soldier, general, or palace priest. Surely the person does not come to be more eminent than or superior to the king merely by receiving a tribute in this way."

"No, sir, a person serving the king depends on the king. 432
The king gives him the tribute as he places him in that position."

"So too, great king, the community does not come to be more eminent than or superior to the Tathagata merely by being presented a rainy season cloth. And one serving the Tathagata depends on the Tathagata. The Tathagata gave the community the rainy season cloth as he placed it in that position. Furthermore, this occurred to the Tathagata: *By its very nature the community is worthy of worship, so I will worship the community with my property.* And so he had the rainy season cloth gifted to the community. Great king, the Tathagata does not praise the worship of only himself. There are those in this world who are worthy of worship, and the Tathagata praises the worship of them also.

433 bhāsitam-p' etaṃ mahārāja bhagavatā devātidevena majjhimanikāyavaralañcake dhammadāyādadhammapariyāye appicchapaṭipattiṃ pakittayamānena: asu yeva me purimo bhikkhu pujjataro ca pāsaṃsataro cāti. na-tthi mahārāja bhavesu koci satto tathāgatato dakkhiṇeyyo vā uttaro vā adhiko vā visiṭṭho vā, tathāgatova uttaro adhiko visiṭṭho. bhāsitam-p' etaṃ mahārāja saṃyuttanikāyavare māṇavagāmikena devaputtena bhagavato purato ṭhatvā devamanussamajjhe:

434 vipulo rājagahikānaṃ giri seṭṭho pavuccati, seto
himavataṃ seṭṭho, ādicco aghagāminaṃ,
samuddo udadhīnaṃ seṭṭho, nakkhattānañ-ca candimā;
sadevakassa lokassa buddho aggaṃ pavuccatīti.

435 tā kho pan' etā mahārāja māṇavagāmikena devaputtena gāthā sugītā na duggītā, subhāsitā na dubbhāsitā, anumatā ca bhagavatā. nanu mahārāja therena pi sāriputtena dhammasenāpatinā bhaṇitaṃ: eko manopasādo saraṇāgamanaṃ añjalippaṇāmo vā ussahate tārayituṃ mārabalanisūdane buddhe ti. bhagavatā ca bhaṇitaṃ devātidevena: ekapuggalo bhikkhave loke uppajjamāno uppajjati bahujanahitāya bahujanasukhāya lokānukampāya atthāya hitāya sukhāya

"Further, great king, the Bhagavan, god above gods, 433
also spoke to this point in the excellent declaration that is the *Majjhimanikāya,* in the Dhamma teaching known as 'Inheritors of the Dhamma.' While commending the practice of being content with little, he said, 'The first monk is more praised and respected by me.'[87] There is no being in any existence that is more worthy of gifts, higher or more eminent than, or superior to the Tathagata, great king. And in the excellent *Saṃyuttanikāya,* this was declared by the god Manavagamika as he stood before the Bhagavan in the midst of gods and humans:

> Of the Rajagaha hills, Mount Vipula is the best. 434
> Of the Himalayas, White Mountain is the best.
> Of celestial bodies, the sun; of bodies of water, the
> ocean;
> of heavenly bodies at night, the moon;
> and of the world with its gods, the Buddha is
> proclaimed the chief.

"These verses by the god Manavagamika were not sung 435
badly or spoken wrongly; they were well sung, rightly spoken, and approved by the Bhagavan. Great king, did not Elder Sariputta, General of the Dhamma, also say: 'There is but a single serene confidence of the heart, a single taking refuge, and a single raising of hands together in praise that can take us across—that directed to the Buddha, destroyer of Mara's power'? And finally, the Bhagavan, god above gods, said: 'Monks, there is one person arising in the world who arises for the benefit of the many, for the happiness of the many, out of compassion for the world, for the welfare,

devamanussānaṃ; katamo ekapuggalo: tathāgato arahaṃ sammāsambuddho-pe-devamanussānan-ti. sādhu bhante nāgasena, evam-etaṃ, tathā sampaṭicchāmīti.

436 bhante nāgasena, bhāsitam-p' etaṃ bhagavatā: gihino vā 'haṃ bhikkhave pabbajitassa vā sammāpaṭipattiṃ vaṇṇemi, gihī vā bhikkhave pabbajito vā sammā paṭipanno sammāpaṭipattādhikaraṇaṃ ārādhako hoti ñāyaṃ dhammaṃ kusalan-ti. yadi bhante nāgasena gihī odātavasano kāmabhogī puttadārasambādhasayanaṃ ajjhāvasanto kāsikacandanaṃ paccanubhonto mālā-gandha-vilepanaṃ dhārento jātarūpa-rajataṃ sādiyanto maṇikanaka-vicitta-molibaddho sammā paṭipanno ārādhako hoti ñāyaṃ dhammaṃ kusalaṃ, pabbajito pi bhaṇḍu kāsāvavatthavasano parapiṇḍamajjhupagato catusu sīlakkhandhesu sammā paripūrakārī diyaḍḍhesu sikkhāpadasatesu samādāya vattanto terasasu dhutaguṇesu anavasesaṃ vattanto sammā paṭipanno ārādhako hoti ñāyaṃ dhammaṃ kusalaṃ; tattha bhante ko viseso gihino vā pabbajitassa vā, aphalaṃ hoti tapokammaṃ, niratthikā pabbajjā, vañjhā sikkhāpadagopanā, moghaṃ dhutaguṇasamādānaṃ, kiṃ tattha dukkham-anuciṇṇena, nanu nāma sukhen' eva sukhaṃ adhigantabban-ti.

437 bhāsitam-p' etaṃ mahārāja bhagavatā: gihino vā 'haṃ bhikkhave pabbajitassa vā sammāpaṭipattiṃ vaṇṇemi, gihī vā bhikkhave pabbajito vā sammā paṭipanno sammāpaṭipattādhikaraṇaṃ ārādhako hoti ñāyaṃ dhammaṃ kusalan-

benefit, and happiness of gods and humans. Who is that one person? The Tathagata, the Enlightened and Perfectly Awakened Buddha."

"Very well, then, revered Nagasena. This is so, and I am convinced.

"Revered Nagasena, the Bhagavan also said, 'Monks, I 436
commend the right conduct of both the householder and the renouncer. Monks, one practicing rightly, whether householder or renouncer, accomplishes the method that is the good Dhamma because of that right conduct.' Nagasena, if the householder practicing rightly—while dressed in white, enjoying pleasures, living among couches crowded with wife and children, enjoying sandalwood from Kasi, wearing garlands, scents, and perfumes, handling gold and silver, and sporting a turban studded with gold and gems—accomplishes the method that is the good Dhamma, and if a renouncer practicing rightly—with head shaved, wearing the saffron robe, getting by with alms given by others, completing properly the four branches of morality, undertaking one hundred and fifty precepts, proceeding fully with the thirteen ascetic practices—also accomplishes the method that is the good Dhamma, then what distinguishes the householder from the renouncer?[88] Practicing austerities is fruitless, renunciation is useless, protecting the training precepts is fruitless, and undertaking the ascetic practices is folly. Why pursue pain when one can achieve happiness with pleasure?"

"Great king, the Bhagavan did say, 'Monks, I commend the 437
right conduct of both the householder and the renouncer. Monks, one practicing rightly, whether householder or renouncer, accomplishes the method that is the good

ti. evam-etaṃ mahārāja, sammā paṭipannova seṭṭho. pabbajito pi mahārāja: pabbajito' mhīti na sammā paṭipajjeyya, atha kho so ārakāva sāmaññā, ārakāva brahmaññā; pag-eva gihī odātavasano. gihī pi mahārāja sammā paṭipanno ārādhako hoti ñāyaṃ dhammaṃ kusalaṃ, pabbajito pi mahārāja sammā paṭipanno ārādhako hoti ñāyaṃ dhammaṃ kusalaṃ. api ca mahārāja pabbajitova sāmaññassa issaro adhipati, pabbajjā mahārāja bahuguṇā anekaguṇā appamāṇaguṇā, na sakkā pabbajjāya guṇā parimāṇaṃ kātuṃ.

438 yathā mahārāja kāmadadassa maṇiratanassa na sakkā dhanena aggho parimāṇaṃ kātuṃ: ettakaṃ maṇiratanassa mūlanti; evam-eva kho mahārāja pabbajjā bahuguṇā anekaguṇā appamāṇaguṇā, na sakkā pabbajjāya guṇā parimāṇaṃ kātuṃ. yathā vā pana mahārāja mahāsamudde ūmiyo na sakkā parimāṇaṃ kātuṃ: ettakā mahāsamudde ūmiyo ti; evam-eva kho mahārāja pabbajjā bahuguṇā anekaguṇā appamāṇaguṇā, na sakkā pabbajjāya guṇā parimāṇaṃ kātuṃ.

439 pabbajitassa mahārāja yaṃ kiñci karaṇīyaṃ sabban-taṃ khippam-eva samijjhati no cirarattāya; kiṅkāraṇaṃ: pabbajito mahārāja appiccho hoti santuṭṭho pavivitto asaṃsaṭṭho āraddhaviriyo nirālayo aniketo paripuṇṇasīlo sallekhitācāro dhutapaṭipattikusalo hoti; taṅkāraṇā pabbajitassa yaṃ kiñci karaṇīyaṃ sabban-taṃ khippam-eva samijjhati no cirarattāya. yathā mahārāja nigganṭhi-sama-sudhota-uju-vimala-nārāco susajjito sammā vahati, evam-eva kho mahārāja pabbajitassa yaṃ kiñci karaṇīyaṃ sabban-taṃ khippam-eva

Dhamma because of that right conduct.' And it is so that one practicing rightly is the best. And should a renouncer call himself a renouncer but not practice rightly, then he is far from renunciation and far from being a Brahman. Much more so for the householder wearing white. The householder practicing rightly accomplishes the method that is the good Dhamma, and the renouncer practicing rightly also accomplishes the method that is the good Dhamma. Nevertheless, it is the renouncer who is the lord and master of renunciation. Renouncers have so many numerous and immeasurable virtues that it is not possible to gauge the virtues of those
renouncing the world. Great king, just as it is not possible 438
to calculate the monetary value of the wish-granting jewel treasure, saying, 'This is the price of the wish-granting jewel treasure,' renouncers have so many numerous and immeasurable virtues that it is not possible to gauge the virtues of those renouncing the world. Just as it is not possible to count the waves in the great ocean, saying, 'This is the number of waves,' renouncers have so many numerous and immeasurable virtues that it is not possible to gauge the virtues of those renouncing the world.

"Great king, whatever is achieved by a renouncer takes 439
effect completely and quickly, without delay. Why is this? A renouncer is content, satisfied, secluded, aloof from society, full of energy, without desires, homeless, keeping moral precepts, practicing the penances, and skilled in the practice of asceticism. For this reason, whatever is achieved by a renouncer takes effect completely and quickly, without delay. Great king, just as a sharp, even, clean, straight, and stainless arrow well shot flies properly, so too whatever is

samijjhati no cirarattāyāti. sādhu bhante nāgasena, evametaṃ, tathā sampaṭicchāmīti.

440 bhante nāgasena, yadā bodhisatto dukkarakārikaṃ akāsi, n' etādiso aññatra ārambho ahosi nikkamo kilesayuddhaṃ maccusenavidhamanaṃ āhārapariggaho dukkarakārikā, evarūpe parakkame kañci assādaṃ alabhitvā tam-eva cittaṃ parihāpetvā evam-avoca: na kho panāhaṃ imāya kaṭukāya dukkarakārikāya adhigacchāmi uttarimanussadhammam[18] alamariyañāṇadassanavisesaṃ, siyā nu kho añño maggo bodhāyāti. tato nibbinditvā aññena maggena sabbaññutaṃ patto puna tāya paṭipadāya sāvake anusāsati samādapeti:

441 ārabhatha, nikkamatha, yuñjatha buddhasāsane,
dhunātha maccuno senaṃ, naḷāgāraṃva kuñjaro ti.

442 kena nu kho bhante nāgasena kāraṇena tathāgato yāya paṭipadāya attanā nibbiṇṇo virattarūpo tattha sāvake anusāsati samādapetīti. tadā pi mahārāja etarahi pi sā yeva paṭipadā, taṃ yeva paṭipadaṃ paṭipajjitvā bodhisatto sabbaññutaṃ patto. api ca mahārāja bodhisatto ativiriyaṃ karonto niravasesato āhāraṃ uparundhi, tassa āhārūparodhena cittadubbalyaṃ uppajji, so tena dubbalyena nāsakkhi sabbaññutaṃ pāpuṇituṃ, so mattamattaṃ kabaḷiṅkārāhāraṃ sevanto tāy' eva paṭipadāya nacirass' eva sabbaññutaṃ pāpuṇi. sā

achieved by a renouncer takes effect completely and quickly, without delay."

"Very good, revered Nagasena, this is so, and I am persuaded.

"Revered Nagasena, when the Bodhisatta was practicing 440
the austerities, there was no other endeavor, no exertion, no battle with the defilements, no dispelling the armies of Mara, no abstention from food, and no practice of austerities like it. But he took no relish in such efforts and abandoned the thought of them, saying, 'With these harsh austerities, I have not reached a state beyond being human or any distinction in knowledge and vision worthy of the noble ones. Could there be another path to awakening?' Turning away from this, he attained omniscience by another path. Yet he taught and roused his disciples by this method, saying:

> Arouse your energy and strive on! Become disciplined 441
> in the Buddha's dispensation.
> Mow down Mara's army, like an elephant mows down
> a grass hut.

"Nagasena, why did the Tathagata turn away from this 442
method himself, repelled, and yet teach and encourage his disciples in it?"

"At that time, great king, as nowadays, this was the method, and it was by following this method that the Bodhisatta attained omniscience. To be sure, the Bodhisatta practiced too much exertion and stopped taking food altogether. Because of his stopping food, a weakness in his

yeva mahārāja paṭipadā sabbesaṃ tathāgatānaṃ sabbaññutañāṇapaṭilābhāya. yathā mahārāja sabbasattānaṃ āhāro upatthambho, āhārūpanissitā sabbe sattā sukhaṃ anubhavanti; evam-eva kho mahārāja sā yeva paṭipadā sabbesaṃ tathāgatānaṃ sabbaññutañāṇapaṭilābhāya.

443 n' eso mahārāja doso ārambhassa, na nikkamassa, na kilesayuddhassa, yena tathāgato tasmiṃ samaye na pāpuṇi sabbaññutañāṇaṃ, atha kho āhārūparodhass' ev' eso doso, sadā paṭiyattā yeva sā paṭipadā. yathā mahārāja puriso addhānaṃ ativegena gaccheyya, tena so pakkhahato vā bhaveyya pīṭhasappī vā asañcaro paṭhavitale, api nu kho mahārāja mahāpaṭhaviyā doso atthi yena so puriso pakkhahato ahosīti. na hi bhante, sadā paṭiyattā bhante mahāpaṭhavī, kuto tassā doso, vāyāmass' ev' eso doso yena so puriso pakkhahato ahosīti.

444 evam-eva kho mahārāja n' eso doso ārambhassa, na nikkamassa, na kilesayuddhassa yena tathāgato tasmiṃ samaye na pāpuṇi sabbaññutañāṇaṃ, atha kho āhārūparodhass' ev' eso doso, sadā paṭiyattā yeva sā paṭipadā. yathā vā pana mahārāja puriso kiliṭṭhaṃ sāṭakaṃ nivāseyya, na so taṃ dhovāpeyya, n' eso doso udakassa, sadā paṭiyattaṃ udakaṃ, purisass' ev'eso doso; evam-eva kho mahārāja n'eso doso ārambhassa, na nikkamassa, na kilesayuddhassa, yena tathāgato tasmiṃ samaye na pāpuṇi sabbaññutañāṇaṃ, atha kho āhārūpa-

mind occurred, and because of that weakness he was not able to attain omniscience. Returning little by little to taking solid food, he attained omniscience after a short time. This is the method, great king, used by all tathagatas to attain omniscience. Just as food is a support for all beings and all beings relying on food experience ease, so too this method conduces to the attainment of omniscience of all tathagatas.
There was no fault in his endeavoring, his exertion, or his 443
battle with the defilements by which the Tathagata failed to attain omniscience at that time. Rather, the fault was just the abstaining from food, while the method itself is always ready for use. Suppose a man were to travel too rapidly on a long journey, and because of this become paralyzed on one side or fall lame and unmoving to the ground. Would you say, great king, that it is the fault of the great earth that the man is paralyzed?"

"No, sir. The great earth is always ready for use, so how could it be its fault? The fault whereby the man became paralyzed lies entirely in his overexerting himself."

"So too the Tathagata did not fail to attain omniscience at 444
that time due to a fault in his endeavoring, his exertion, or his battle with the defilements. Rather, the fault was entirely abstaining from food, while the method itself is always ready for use. Great king, suppose a man were to wear a soiled cloak and not have it washed. It is not the fault of the water, for water is always ready for use. It is entirely the man's fault. So too the Tathagata did not fail to attain omniscience at that time due to a fault in his endeavoring, his exertion, or his battle with the defilements. Rather, the fault was entirely the abstaining from food, while the method itself is always ready

rodhass' ev' eso doso, sadā paṭiyattā yeva sā paṭipadā. tasmā tathāgato tāy' eva paṭipadāya sāvake anusāsati samādapeti. evaṃ kho mahārāja sadā paṭiyattā anavajjā sā paṭipadā ti. sādhu bhante nāgasena, evam-etaṃ, tathā sampaṭicchāmīti.

445 bhante nāgasena, mahantaṃ idaṃ tathāgatasāsanaṃ sāraṃ varaṃ seṭṭhaṃ pavaraṃ anupamaṃ parisuddhaṃ vimalaṃ paṇḍaraṃ anavajjaṃ, na yuttaṃ gihiṃ tāvatakaṃ pabbājetuṃ, gihiṃ yeva ekasmiṃ phale vinetvā yadā apunarāvattī hoti tadā so pabbājetabbo; kiṅkāraṇaṃ: ime dujjanā tāva tattha sāsane visuddhe pabbajitvā paṭinivattitvā hīnāy' āvattanti, tesaṃ paccāgamanena ayaṃ mahājano evaṃ vicinteti: tucchakaṃ vata bho etaṃ samaṇassa gotamassa sāsanaṃ bhavissati, yaṃ ime paṭinivattantīti. idam-ettha kāraṇan-ti.

446 yathā mahārāja taḷākaṃ bhaveyya sampuṇṇa-suci-vimala-sītala-salilaṃ, atha yo koci kiliṭṭho mala-kaddama-gato taṃ taḷākaṃ gantvā anahāyitvā kiliṭṭhova paṭinivatteyya, tattha mahārāja katamaṃ jano garaheyya, kiliṭṭhaṃ vā taḷākaṃ vā ti. kiliṭṭhaṃ bhante jano garaheyya: ayaṃ taḷākaṃ gantvā anahāyitvā kiliṭṭhova paṭinivatto, kiṃ imaṃ anahāyitukāmaṃ taḷāko sayaṃ nahāpessati, ko doso taḷākassāti.

447 evam-eva kho mahārāja tathāgato vimuttivara-salilasampuṇṇaṃ saddhammavara-taḷākaṃ māpesi: ye keci kilesamalakiliṭṭhā sacetanā budhā te idha nahāyitvā sabbakilese

for use. For this reason, the Tathagata roused and taught his disciples with this method. And so, great king, this method is always ready for use and blameless."

"Very well, revered Nagasena. This is so, and I am convinced.

"Revered Nagasena, the dispensation of the Tathagata 445
is vast, substantial, excellent, supreme, distinguished, unequaled, pure, stainless, clear, and blameless. It is not right for someone to ordain while merely a householder. It is only when the householder is led to the fruit of the first path* and does not revert that he should be ordained. Why is this? When bad people ordain in the pure dispensation, they lapse and return to household life. Because of their backsliding, people think, *The ascetic Gotama's dispensation will most certainly amount to nothing, since these people have lapsed in it.* This is the reasoning here."

"Great king, think of a bathing tank full of clean, pure, 446
and cool water. But then someone soiled, dirty, and caked with mud arrives at the tank, and without bathing turns back while still dirty. Whom would people blame in this case, the dirty fellow or the tank?"

"People would blame the dirty fellow, sir. He went to the tank, did not bathe, and turned back while still dirty. How can a tank by itself wash someone who does not wish to bathe? What fault is there in the tank?"

"Similarly, great king, the Tathagata built the bathing tank 447
of the excellent true Dhamma full of the waters of highest freedom, thinking, *Whoever is wise and thoughtful but soiled*

* Stream entry.

pavāhayissantīti; yadi koci taṃ saddhammavara-taḷākaṃ gantvā anahāyitvā sakilesova paṭinivattitvā hīnāy' āvattati, taṃ yeva jano garahissati: ayaṃ jinasāsane pabbajitvā tattha patiṭṭhaṃ alabhitvā hīnāy' āvatto, kiṃ imaṃ appaṭipajjantaṃ jinasāsanaṃ sayaṃ sodhessati, ko doso jinasāsanassāti.

448 yathā vā pana mahārāja puriso paramabyādhito roguppattikusalaṃ amoghadhuvasiddhakammaṃ bhisakkaṃ sallakattaṃ disvā na tikicchāpetvā sabyādhikova paṭinivatteyya, tattha katamaṃ jano garaheyya, āturaṃ vā bhisakkaṃ vā ti. āturaṃ bhante jano garaheyya: ayaṃ roguppattikusalaṃ amoghadhuvasiddhakammaṃ bhisakkaṃ sallakattaṃ disvā na tikicchāpetvā sabyādhikova paṭinivatto, kiṃ imaṃ atikicchāpentaṃ bhisakko sayaṃ tikicchissati, ko doso bhisakkassāti.

449 evam-eva kho mahārāja tathāgato antosāsanasamugge kevalaṃ sakalakilesabyādhi vūpasamanasamatthaṃ amatosadhaṃ pakkhipi: ye keci kilesabyādhipīḷitā sacetanā budhā te imaṃ amatosadhaṃ pivitvā sabbakilesabyādhiṃ vūpasamessantīti; yadi koci taṃ amatosadhaṃ apivitvā sakilesova paṭinivattitvā hīnāy' āvattati, taṃ yeva jano garahis-

with the stains of the defilements will bathe here and wash away all the defilements. Should someone arrive at the tank that is the excellent true Dhamma but turn back without bathing and while still defiled, and then lapse and return to the household life, people will blame only him, saying, 'He ordained in the dispensation of the Victor but found no support in it and returned to the household life. Yet how can the Victor's dispensation on its own cleanse someone who doesn't follow it? What fault is there in the Victor's dispensation?'

"Great king, consider also a person who is severely ill who 448
sees a physician, a surgeon skilled in knowing the cause of disease and whose remedies are unerring, lasting, and successful. But he does not permit medical treatment and turns back while still ill. Whom would people blame in this case, the sick man or the physician?"

"People would blame the sick man, sir, saying, 'He saw a physician, a surgeon skilled in knowing the cause of disease and whose remedies are unerring, lasting, and successful, but he did not permit medical treatment and turned back while still ill. How could the physician by himself cure someone refusing treatment? What fault is there in the physician?"

"Similarly, great king, the Tathagata placed the healing 449
ambrosial medicine able to allay the illness of all the defilements into his medicine chest that is the dispensation. Whoever is wise and thoughtful but oppressed by the illness of the defilements and takes the ambrosial healing medicine will allay the illness of all the defilements. But if someone does not take the ambrosial medicine and turns back while still full of defilements, lapses, and returns to the house-

sati: ayaṃ jinasāsane pabbajitvā tattha patiṭṭhaṃ alabhitvā hīnāy' āvatto, kiṃ imaṃ appaṭipajjantaṃ jinasāsanaṃ sayaṃ bodhessati,[19] ko doso jinasāsanassāti.

450 yathā vā pana mahārāja chāto puriso mahatimahāpuññabhattaparivesanaṃ gantvā taṃ bhattaṃ abhuñjitvā chātova paṭinivatteyya, tattha katamaṃ jano garaheyya, chātaṃ vā puññabhattaṃ vā ti. chātaṃ bhante jano garaheyya: ayaṃ khudāpīḷito puññabhattaṃ paṭilabhitvā abhuñjitvā chātova paṭinivatto, kiṃ imassa abhuñjantassa bhojanaṃ sayaṃ mukhaṃ pavisissati, ko doso bhojanassāti.

451 evam-eva kho mahārāja tathāgato antosāsanasamugge paramapavaraṃ santaṃ sivaṃ paṇītaṃ amataṃ paramamadhuraṃ kāyagatāsatibhojanaṃ ṭhapesi: ye keci kilesachātajjhattā[20] taṇhāparetamānasā sacetanā budhā te imaṃ bhojanaṃ bhuñjitvā kāma-rūpārūpabhavesu sabbaṃ taṇham-apanessantīti; yadi koci taṃ bhojanaṃ abhuñjitvā taṇhāsitova paṭinivattitvā hīnāy' āvattati, taṃ yeva jano garahissati: ayaṃ jinasāsane pabbajitvā tattha patiṭṭhaṃ alabhitvā hīnāy' āvatto, kiṃ imaṃ appaṭipajjantaṃ jinasāsanaṃ sayaṃ sodhessati, ko doso jinasāsanassāti.

452 yadi mahārāja tathāgato gihiṃ yeva ekasmiṃ phale vinītaṃ pabbājeyya, na nāmāyaṃ pabbajjā kilesappahānāya

hold life, then people will blame only him: 'He ordained in the dispensation of the Victor but found no support in it and returned to the household life. Yet how can the Victor's dispensation on its own awaken someone who doesn't follow it? What fault is there in the Victor's dispensation?'

"Great king, suppose a famished person came to a great 450
merit-making and bountiful distribution of food, and yet declined the meal. Though famished, he turned back. Whom would people blame, the famished person or those giving alms?"

"The people would blame the famished man, sir. Though ravaged by hunger and offered alms food, he declines it and goes away famished. Can food by itself enter the mouth of someone refusing it? What fault is there in the food?"

"Similarly, great king, the Tathagata placed in his chest 451
the highest, most excellent, peaceful, auspicious, plentiful, ambrosial, and deliciously sweet meal of mindfulness of the body. Anyone wise and thoughtful, though famished inside from the defilements and having a mind overcome with thirst, will take this food and be rid of all thirst in the realms of desire, form, and formlessness.[89] But should someone decline this food while still attached to thirst, lapse, and return to household life, then people will blame only him, saying, 'He ordained in the dispensation of the Victor but found no support in it and returned to the household life. Yet how can the Victor's dispensation on its own cleanse someone who doesn't follow it? What fault is there in the Victor's dispensation?'

"Great king, if the Tathagata were to ordain only the 452
householder who had reached the first fruit, then renun-

visuddhiyā vā, na-tthi pabbajjāya karaṇīyaṃ. yathā mahārāja puriso anekasatena kammena taḷākaṃ khaṇāpetvā parisāya evam-anusāveyya: mā me bhonto keci saṅkiliṭṭhā imaṃ taḷākaṃ otaratha, pavāhitarajojallā parisuddhā vimalamaṭṭā imaṃ taḷākaṃ otarathāti; api nu kho mahārāja tesaṃ pavāhitarajojallānaṃ parisuddhānaṃ vimalamaṭṭānaṃ tena tāḷākena karaṇīyaṃ bhaveyyāti.

453 na hi bhante, yass' atthāya te taṃ taḷākaṃ upagaccheyyuṃ taṃ aññatr' eva tesaṃ kataṃ karaṇīyaṃ, kiṃ tesaṃ tena taḷākenāti. evam-eva kho mahārāja yadi tathāgato gihiṃ yeva ekasmiṃ phale vinītaṃ pabbājeyya, tatth' eva tesaṃ kataṃ karaṇīyaṃ, kiṃ tesaṃ pabbajjāya. yathā vā pana mahārāja sabhāva-isibhattiko sutamantapadadharo atakkiko roguppattikusalo amoghadhuva-siddhakammo bhisakko sallakatto sabbarogūpasamabhesajjaṃ sannipātetvā parisāya evam-anusāveyya: mā kho bhonto keci sabyādhikā mama santike upagacchatha, abyādhikā arogā mama santike upagacchathāti, api nu kho mahārāja tesaṃ abyādhikānaṃ arogānaṃ paripuṇṇānaṃ udaggānaṃ tena bhisakkena karaṇīyaṃ bhaveyyāti.

454 na hi bhante, yass' atthāya te taṃ bhisakkaṃ sallakattaṃ upagaccheyyuṃ taṃ aññatr' eva tesaṃ kataṃ karaṇīyaṃ, kiṃ tesaṃ tena bhisakkenāti. evam-eva kho mahārāja yadi tathāgato gihiṃ yeva ekasmiṃ phale vinītaṃ pabbājeyya,

ciation would be of no use, given that renunciation is for the sake of purification and getting rid of the defilements. It would be like a man who had a bathing tank dug by the work of many hundreds of people and then announced to the crowd, 'Let no one who is dirty enter the tank. Only those with dirt and dust washed off, clean and spotless, may enter the tank.' Would the tank be of any use, great king, for those with dirt and dust already washed off, who are clean and spotless?"

"No, sir. They would have already done elsewhere what 453
they had come to this tank to do. So of what use is the tank to them?"

"It would be much the same, great king, if the Tathagata were to ordain only the householder who had reached the first fruit. What would be the point of renouncing if one had already done what was to be done? Consider a clever physician, a surgeon skilled in knowing the cause of disease, with unerring, lasting, and successful remedies, a follower of the true sages, learned in the words and mantras of his sacred lore. Suppose he were to prepare medicine for allaying all disease, and then were to announce to the crowd, 'Let no one with disease approach me. Only those healthy and free of disease may come into my presence.' Would that physician be of any use to those who are completely free of disease, healthy and happy?"

"No, sir. They would have already done elsewhere what 454
they had come to this surgical physician for. What would be the use of such a physician to them?"

"It would be much the same, great king, if the Tathagata were to ordain only the householder who had reached the

tatth' eva tesaṃ kataṃ karaṇīyaṃ, kiṃ tesaṃ pabbajjāya. yathā vā pana mahārāja koci puriso anekathālipākasataṃ bhojanaṃ paṭiyādāpetvā parisāya evam-anusāveyya: mā me bhonto keci chātā imaṃ parivesanaṃ upagacchatha, subhuttā tittā suhitā dhātā pīṇitā paripuṇṇā imaṃ parivesanaṃ upagacchathāti, api nu kho mahārāja tesaṃ bhuttāvīnaṃ tittānaṃ suhitānaṃ dhātānaṃ pīṇitānaṃ paripuṇṇānaṃ tena bhojanena karaṇīyaṃ bhaveyyāti.

455 na hi bhante, yass'atthāya te taṃ parivesanaṃ upagaccheyyuṃ taṃ aññatr' eva tesaṃ kataṃ karaṇīyaṃ, kiṃ tesaṃ tāya parivesanāyāti. evam-eva kho mahārāja yadi tathāgato gihiṃ yeva ekasmiṃ phale vinītaṃ pabbājeyya, tatth' eva tesaṃ kataṃ karaṇīyaṃ, kiṃ tesaṃ pabbajjāya. api ca mahārāja ye hīnāy' āvattanti te jinasāsanassa pañca atuliye guṇe dassenti; katame pañca: bhūmimahantabhāvaṃ dassenti, parisuddhavimalabhāvaṃ dassenti, pāpehi asaṃvāsiyabhāvaṃ dassenti, duppaṭivedhabhāvaṃ dassenti, bahusaṃvararakkhiyabhāvaṃ dassenti.

456 kathaṃ bhūmimahantabhāvaṃ dassenti: yathā mahārāja puriso adhano hīnajacco nibbiseso buddhiparihīno mahatimahārajjaṃ paṭilabhitvā na cirass eva paripaṭati paridhaṃsati parihāyati yasato, na sakkoti issariyaṃ sandhāretuṃ,

first fruit. What would be the point of renouncing if one had already done what was to be done?"

"Suppose, great king, someone were to prepare many hundreds of plates of food to give away and then announced to the crowd, 'Let no one who is hungry come to this distribution of food. Only the well-fed, sated, satisfied, well-nourished, and completely stuffed should come for the distribution.' Would that distribution of food be of any use for those who are well-fed, sated, satisfied, well-nourished, and completely stuffed?"

"No, sir. They would have already done elsewhere what 455
they had come to this distribution to do. What would be the use of distributing food to them?"

"It would be much the same, great king, if the Tathagata were to ordain only the householder who had reached the first fruit. What would be the point of renouncing if one had already done what was to be done? Moreover, great king, those who return to the household life demonstrate five incomparable qualities of the Victor's dispensation. What are the five? They demonstrate the nature of its high level; its pure and stainless nature; its incompatibility with wicked things; its hard-to-penetrate nature; and how it must be defended with many restraints.

"In what way do they demonstrate the nature of its 456
high level? Great king, suppose a poor man of low birth, lacking any distinction, and deficient in intellect were to receive a magnificent kingdom. He would soon fall from glory, collapse, and go to ruin, unable to support kingship. Why is this? Because of the magnificence of kingship. It is the same for those lacking any distinction, having accom-

kiṅkāraṇaṃ: mahantattā issariyassa; evam-eva kho mahārāja ye keci nibbisesā akatapuññā buddhiparihīnā jinasāsane pabbajanti te taṃ pabbajjaṃ pavaruttamaṃ san-dhāretuṃ na visahantā na cirass' eva jinasāsanā paripatitvā paridhaṃsitvā parihāyitvā hīnāy' āvattanti, na sakkonti jinasāsanaṃ sandhāretuṃ, kiṅkāraṇaṃ: mahantattā jinasāsanabhūmiyā. evaṃ bhūmimahantabhāvaṃ dassenti.

457 kathaṃ parisuddhavimalabhāvaṃ dassenti. yathā mahārāja vāri pokkharapatte vikirati vidhamati viddhaṃs-ati, naṭṭhānam-upagacchati, nūpalippati, kiṅkāraṇaṃ: parisuddhavimalattā padumassa; evam-eva kho mahārāja ye keci saṭhā kūṭā vaṅkā kuṭilā visamadiṭṭhino jinasāsane pabbajanti te parisuddha-vimala-nikkaṇṭaka-paṇḍara-vara-pavara-sāsanato na cirass eva vikiritvā vidhamitvā viddhaṃsitvā na saṇṭhahitvā nūpalippitvā hīnāy' āvattanti, kiṅkāraṇaṃ: parisuddhavimalattā jinasāsanassa. evaṃ parisuddhavimalabhāvaṃ dassenti.

458 kathaṃ pāpehi asaṃvāsiyabhāvaṃ dassenti. yathā mahārāja mahāsamuddo na matena kuṇapena saṃvasati, yaṃ hoti mahāsamudde mataṃ kuṇapaṃ taṃ khippam eva tīraṃ upaneti thalaṃ vā ussādeti, kiṅkāraṇaṃ: mahābhūtānaṃ bhavanattā mahāsamuddassa; evam-eva kho mahārāja ye keci pāpā akiriyā osannaviriyā kuthitā kiliṭṭhā dujjanā manussā jinasāsane pabbajanti te na cirass eva jinasāsanato

plished no merit, and deficient in intellect, who ordain in the Victor's dispensation. They are not able to support the splendid and excellent renunciation and soon fall from the Victor's dispensation, collapsing and going to ruin. Not able to support the Victor's dispensation, they return to householder life. Why is this? Because of the magnificence of the level of the Victor's dispensation. In this way they demonstrate the nature of its high level.

"In what way do they demonstrate its pure and stainless 457
nature? It is similar, great king, to how water on a lotus leaf scatters, disperses, and falls away, unable to land anywhere and adhere. Why is this? Because of the purity and stainlessness of the lotus. It is the same for those charlatans, crooked, shifty, and cunning with wicked views, who ordain in the Victor's dispensation. They soon scatter, disperse, and fall away from the pure, stainless, smooth, bright, excellent, and splendid dispensation; unable to continue and adhere to it, they return to household life. Why is this? Because of the purity and stainlessness of the Victor's dispensation. In this way, they demonstrate its pure and stainless nature.

"In what way do they demonstrate its incompatibility 458
with wicked things? It is similar, great king, to how the great ocean does not accept a dead body, a corpse. Whenever a dead body, a corpse, is thrown into the ocean, it is quickly carried to the shore and tossed out on dry land. Why is this? Because the great ocean is the abode of great beings. It is the same for those evil people who do nothing, strive only feebly, and are rotten, dirty, and bad. They ordain in the Victor's dispensation but soon turn back from that abode of great beings who are the stainless arhats with flaws destroyed.

arahantavimala-khīṇāsavamahābhūta-bhavanato nikkhamitvā na saṃvasitvā hīnāy' āvattanti, kiṅkāraṇaṃ: pāpehi asaṃvāsiyattā jinasāsanassa. evaṃ pāpehi asaṃvāsiyabhāvaṃ dassenti.

459 kathaṃ duppaṭivedhabhāvaṃ dassenti. yathā mahārāja ye keci acchekā asikkhitā asippino matippahīnā issatthā vālaggavedhaṃ na visahantā vigaḷanti pakkamanti, kiṅkāranaṃ: saṇha-sukhuma-duppaṭivedhattā vālaggassa; evam-eva kho mahārāja ye keci duppaññā jaḷā eḷamūgā mūḷhā dandhagatikā janā jinasāsane pabbajanti te taṃ parama-saṇhasukhuma-catusacca-paṭivedhaṃ paṭivijjhituṃ na visahantā jinasāsanā vigaḷitvā pakkamitvā na cirass eva hīnāy' āvattanti, kiṅkāraṇaṃ: parama-saṇha-sukhuma-duppaṭivedhatāya saccānaṃ. evaṃ duppaṭivedhabhāvaṃ dassenti.

460 kathaṃ bahusaṃvararakkhiyabhāvaṃ dassenti. yathā mahārāja kocid-eva puriso mahatimahāyuddhabhūmim upagato parasenāya disāvidisāhi samantā parivārito sattihatthaṃ janam-upentaṃ disvā bhīto osakkati paṭinivattati palāyati, kiṅkāraṇāṃ: bahuvidhayuddhamukharakkhanabhayā; evam-eva kho mahārāja ye keci pākatā asaṃvutā ahirikā akiriyā akkhantī capalā calitā ittarā bālajanā jinasāsane pabbajanti te bahuvidhaṃ sikkhāpadaṃ parirakkhituṃ na visahantā okkamitvā paṭinivattitvā palāyitvā na

Incompatible with it, they return to household life. Why is this? Because the Victor's dispensation is incompatible with wicked things. In this way, they demonstrate its incompatibility with wicked things.

"In what way do they demonstrate its hard-to-penetrate 459
nature? It is similar, great king, to unskilled, untrained, untaught, and scatterbrained archers who are not able to pierce a hair but rather drop the arrow, missing the mark. Why is this? Because of the difficulty in piercing something as fine and subtle as a hair. It is the same for those idlers of poor understanding, dull, deaf, dumb, and foolish. They ordain in the Victor's dispensation but are not able to penetrate the understanding of the Four Truths due to their utmost fineness and subtlety, and they soon drop from the Victor's dispensation, missing the mark, and return to household life. Why is this? Because of the Truths being difficult to penetrate due to their utmost fineness and subtlety. In this way, they demonstrate its hard-to-penetrate nature.

"In what way do they demonstrate how it must be defended 460
with many restraints? It is similar, great king, to a certain man who arrives at the scene of a great and momentous battle. He finds himself completely surrounded by the enemy army, with people advancing from all directions bearing swords. Terrified, he falls back, turns around, and flees. Why is this? Because he fears defending himself in the face of a battle on many fronts. It is the same when foolish people who are undisciplined, intemperate, shameless, useless, impatient, unsteady, and unreliable ordain in the Victor's dispensation. They are not able to defend the monastic rules on many fronts, and they fall back, turn around, and flee. They soon

cirass eva hīnāy' āvattanti, kiṅkāraṇaṃ: bahuvidhasaṃvararakkhiyabhāvattā jinasāsanassa. evaṃ bahuvidhasaṃvararakkhiyabhāvaṃ dassenti.

461 thalajuttame pi mahārāja vassikāgumbe kimividdhāni pupphāni honti, tāni aṅkurāni sankuṭitāni antarā yeva paripaṭanti, na ca tesu paripaṭitesu vassikāgumbo hīḷito nāma hoti, yāni tattha ṭhitāni pupphāni tāni sammā gandhena disāvidisaṃ abhibyāpenti, evam-eva kho mahārāja ye te jinasāsane pabbajitvā hīnāy' āvattanti te jinasāsane kimividdhāni vassikāpupphāni viya vaṇṇagandharahitāni nibbaṇṇākārasīlā abhabbā vepullāya, na ca tesaṃ hīnāy' āvattanena jinasāsanaṃ hīḷitaṃ nāma hoti, ye tattha ṭhitā bhikkhū te sadevakaṃ lokaṃ sīlavaragandhena abhibyāpenti.

462 sālīnam-pi mahārāja nirātaṅkānaṃ lohitakānaṃ antare karumbhakaṃ nāma sālijāti uppajjitvā antarā yeva vinassati, na ca tassā vinaṭṭhattā lohitakasālī hiḷitā nāma honti, ye tattha ṭhitā sālī te rājūpabhogā honti; evam-eva kho mahārāja ye te jinasāsane pabbajitvā hīnāy' āvattanti te lohitakasālīnam-antare karumbhakā viya jinasāsane na vaḍḍhitvā vepullataṃ pāpuṇitvā antarā yeva hīnāy' āvattanti, na ca tesaṃ hīnāy' āvattanena jinasāsanaṃ hīḷitaṃ nāma hoti, ye tattha ṭhitā bhikkhū te arahattassa anucchavikā honti.

return to household life. Why is this? Because it is the nature of the Victor's dispensation that it is to be defended with many restraints. In this way, they demonstrate how it must be defended with many restraints.

"Great king, flowers on even the best jasmine bushes 461
growing on dry land are sometimes eaten by insects, so that even the inner shoots shrivel and fall off. But even though these have fallen, the jasmine bush is not despised, since the remaining blossoms pervade every direction with their true fragrance. Similarly, great king, those who ordain in the dispensation of the Victor and return to household life are like jasmine flowers eaten by insects and deprived of their color and scent; their moral precepts and appearance have become colorless and they are incapable of development in the Victor's dispensation. But the dispensation of the Victor is not despised because of their return to household life. The monks who remain pervade the world with its gods with the exquisite fragrance of morality.

"Great king, even among healthy red rice, there is a kind 462
of red rice called *karumbhaka* that grows around it and then dies off. But the red rice is not despised because of its dying off. Rather, the remaining red rice is considered food fit for kings. Similarly, great king, those who ordain in the Victor's dispensation and return to household life are like the *karumbhaka* growing between the red rice. Not growing in the Victor's dispensation, they do not reach maturity, and they return to household life. But the dispensation of the Victor is not despised because of their return to household life, and the monks who remain in it are fit to become arhats.

463 kāmadadassāpi mahārāja maṇiratanassa ekadesaṃ kakkasaṃ uppajjati, na ca tattha kakkasuppannattā maṇiratanaṃ hīḷitaṃ nāma hoti, yaṃ tattha parisuddhaṃ maṇiratanassa taṃ janassa hāsakaraṃ hoti; evam-eva kho mahārāja ye te jinasāsane pabbajitvā hīnāy' āvattanti kakkasā te jinasāsane papaṭikā, na ca tesaṃ hīnāy' āvattanena jinasāsanaṃ hīḷitaṃ nāma hoti, ye tattha ṭhitā bhikkhū te devamanussānaṃ hāsajanakā honti.

464 jātisampannassa pi mahārāja lohitacandanassa ekadesaṃ pūtikaṃ hoti appagandhaṃ, na tena lohitacandanaṃ hīḷitaṃ nāma hoti, yaṃ tattha apūtikaṃ sugandhaṃ taṃ samantā vidhūpeti abhibyāpeti; evam-eva kho mahārāja ye te jinasāsane pabbajitvā hīnāy' āvattanti te lohitacandana-sārantare pūtikadesam-iva chaḍḍanīyā jinasāsane, na ca tesaṃ hīnāy' āvattanena jinasāsanaṃ hīḷitaṃ nāma hoti, ye tattha ṭhitā bhikkhū te sadevakaṃ lokaṃ sīlavaracandanagandhena anulimpayantīti.

465 sādhu bhante nāgasena, tena tena anucchavikena tena tena sadisena kāraṇena niravajjam-anupāpitaṃ jinasāsanaṃ seṭṭhabhāvena paridīpitaṃ, hīnāy' āvattamānā pi te jinasāsanassa seṭṭhabhāvaṃ yeva paridīpentīti.

466 bhante nāgasena, tumhe bhaṇatha: arahā ekaṃ vedanaṃ vediyati kāyikaṃ na cetasikan-ti. kin-nu kho bhante nāgasena arahato cittaṃ yaṃ kāyaṃ nissāya pavattati tattha arahā anissaro assāmī avasavattī ti. āma mahārājāti. na kho

"Great king, there may be a rough spot on the precious wish-granting jewel treasure. But the jewel treasure is not despised because of the presence of that roughness. For it is the purity of the jewel treasure that makes people joyful. Similarly, those who ordain in the Victor's dispensation and return to household life are the rough pieces in the dispensation. But the Victor's dispensation is not despised because of their leaving it, for the monks who remain generate joy for gods and humans. 463

"Great king, even on the finest-quality red sandalwood there may be one part that is rotten and lacking fragrance. Still, the red sandalwood is not despised because of this since the healthy part diffuses and pervades the fragrance everywhere. Similarly, great king, those who ordain in the Victor's dispensation and return to household life are like the rotten bit around the heartwood of the red sandalwood that must be cut out. The Victor's dispensation is not despised because of it, since the remaining monks anoint the world and the gods with the exquisite sandal incense that is morality." 464

"Very well, revered Nagasena. With one pleasing simile after another the Victor's dispensation has been shown to be faultless because of its supreme nature. The very instances of people returning to the household life themselves illustrate the dispensation's supreme nature. 465

"Revered Nagasena, you say, 'An arhat experiences only bodily feeling, not mental feeling. Is this because the arhat's mind exists in reliance on the body, and so the arhat does not control, master, or rule it?" 466

"Yes, great king."

bhante nāgasena yuttam etaṃ yaṃ so sakacittassa pavattamāne kāye anissaro hoti assāmī avasavattī, sakuṇo pi tāva bhante yasmiṃ kulāvake paṭivasati tattha so issaro hoti sāmī vasavattī ti.

467 das' ime mahārāja kāyānugatā dhammā bhave bhave kāyaṃ anudhāvanti anuparivattanti. katame dasa. sītaṃ uṇhaṃ jighacchā pipāsā uccāro passāvo thīnamiddhaṃ jarā byādhi maraṇaṃ. ime kho mahārāja dasa kāyānugatā dhammā bhave bhave kāyaṃ anudhāvanti anuparivattanti; tattha arahā anissaro assāmī avasavattī ti. bhante nāgasena, kena kāraṇena arahato kāye āṇā na-ppavattati issariyaṃ vā, tattha me kāraṇaṃ brūhīti.

468 yathā mahārāja ye keci paṭhavinissitā sattā sabbe te paṭhaviṃ nissāya caranti viharanti vuttiṃ kappenti, api nu mahārāja tesaṃ paṭhaviyā āṇā pavattati issariyaṃ vā ti. na hi bhante ti. evam eva kho mahārāja ara-hato cittaṃ kāyaṃ nissāya pavattati, na ca pana arahato kāye āṇā pavattati issariyaṃ vā ti. bhante nāgasena, kena kāraṇena puthujjano kāyikam-pi cetasikam-pi vedanaṃ vediyatīti.

469 abhāvitattā mahārāja cittassa puthujjano kāyikaṃ-pi cetasikam-pi vedanaṃ vediyati. yathā mahārāja goṇo chāto paritasito abala-dubbala-parittaka-tiṇesu vā latāya vā upanibaddho assa, yadā so goṇo parikupito hoti tadā saha upanibandhanena pakkamati; evam-eva kho mahārāja abhāvitacittassa vedanā uppajjitvā cittaṃ parikopeti, cittaṃ parikupitaṃ kāyaṃ ābhujati nibbhujati, samparivattakaṃ

"It cannot be correct, Nagasena, that one's own mind does not control, master, and rule the body as long as it lasts. Even a bird controls, masters, and rules its nest as long as it lives in it, sir."

"Great king, there are ten phenomena that accompany the 467
body in birth after birth, and they pursue and follow the body. What are the ten? Cold, heat, hunger, thirst, defecation, urination, exhaustion and drowsiness, aging, illness, and death.[90] These ten phenomena accompanying the body in birth after birth, and pursue and follow the body. An arhat does not control, master, or rule them."

"Nagasena, for what reason does an arhat exert neither command nor authority over the body? Give me a reason for this."

"Great king, all terrestrial creatures move, dwell, and 468
make their living relying on the earth. But do they exert command or authority over the earth?" "No, sir." "It is the same, great king, in that an arhat's mind exists in reliance on the body, and yet the arhat does not exert command or authority over the body."

"Nagasena, why does an ordinary person experience both bodily and mental feeling?"

"Great king, it is owing to an uncultivated mind that an 469
ordinary person experiences both bodily and mental feeling. A hungry and thirsty ox may be tied up with a creeper or a weak and feeble thin reed, but when the ox gets agitated, it makes off with such bindings. Similarly, a feeling arises for one with an uncultivated mind, and it agitates the mind. The agitated mind contracts and contorts the body, and makes it roll around. At this, the one with the uncultivated

karoti, atha so abhāvitacitto tasati ravati, bheravarāvam-abhiravati. idam-ettha mahārāja kāraṇaṃ yena kāraṇena puthujjano kāyikam-pi cetasikam-pi vedanaṃ vediyatīti.

470 kiṃ pana taṃ kāraṇaṃ yena kāraṇena arahā ekaṃ vedanaṃ vediyati, kāyikaṃ na cetasikan-ti. arahato mahārāja cittaṃ bhāvitaṃ hoti subhāvitaṃ dantaṃ sudantaṃ assavaṃ vacanakaraṃ, so dukkhāya vedanāya phuṭṭho samāno aniccan-ti daḷhaṃ gaṇhāti, samādhitthambhe cittaṃ upanibandhati, tassa taṃ cittaṃ samādhitthambhe upanibaddhaṃ na vedhati na calati, ṭhitaṃ hoti avikkhittaṃ, tassa vedanāvikāravipphārena kāyo pana ābhujati nibbhujati samparivattati. idam-ettha mahārāja kāraṇaṃ yena kāraṇena arahā ekaṃ vedanaṃ vediyati, kāyikaṃ na cetasikan-ti.

471 bhante nāgasena, taṃ nāma loke acchariyaṃ yaṃ kāye calamāne cittaṃ na calati, tattha me kāranaṃ brūhīti. yathā mahārāja mahatimahārukkhe khandhasākhā-palāsasampanne anilabalasamāhate sākhā calati, api nu tassa khandho pi calatīti. na hi bhante ti. evam-eva kho mahārāja arahā dukkhāya vedanāya phuṭṭho samāno aniccan-ti daḷhaṃ gaṇhāti, samādhitthambhe cittaṃ upanibandhati, tassa taṃ cittaṃ samādhitthambhe upanibaddhaṃ na vedhati na calati, ṭhitaṃ hoti avikkhittaṃ, tassa vedanāvikāravipphārena kayo ābhujati nibbhujati samparivattati, cittaṃ pana tassa na vedhati na calati, khandho viya mahārukk-

mind trembles, wails, and cries a scream of terror. This is the reason, great king, that an ordinary person experiences both bodily and mental feeling."

"But what is the reason why an arhat feels only one feeling, 470
the bodily and not the mental?"

"Great king, the mind of an arhat is developed, well cultivated, tamed, restrained, compliant, and obedient. When coming into contact with a painful feeling, one holds steady, thinking, 'This is impermanent,' and fastens the mind to the post of concentration. One's mind, fastened to the post of concentration, does not wobble or shake but is firm and unrattled. However, the body contracts, gets contorted, and rolls around because of disturbances and perturbations of feeling. This is the reason the arhat experiences only one feeling, the bodily, but not the mental, great king."

"Revered Nagasena, it is a wonder in this world that when 471
the body is shaking, the mind does not shake. Give me a reason for this."

"Great king, when a huge tree with a great trunk, branches, and leaves is struck by a strong wind, the branches shake. But does the trunk shake also?" "No, sir." "In much the same way, great king, an arhat coming into contact with a painful feeling holds steady, thinking, 'This is impermanent,' and fastens the mind to the post of concentration. One's mind, fastened to the post of concentration, does not wobble or shake but is firm and unrattled. But though one's body contracts, gets contorted, and rolls around because of disturbances and perturbations of feeling, the mind, like the trunk of a huge tree, does not wobble or shake."

"This is a wonder and a marvel, revered Nagasena. Never

hassāti. acchariyaṃ bhante nāgasena, abbhutaṃ bhante nāgasena, na me evarūpo sabbakāliko dhammappadīpo diṭṭhapubbo ti.

472 bhante nāgasena, idha yo koci gihī pārājikaṃ ajjhāpanno bhaveyya, so aparena samayena pabbajeyya, attanā pi so na jāneyya: gihī pārājikaṃ ajjhāpanno 'smīti, na pi tassa añño koci ācikkheyya: gihī pārājikaṃ ajjhāpannosīti, so ca tathattāya patipajjeyya, api nu tassa dhammābhisamayo bhaveyyāti. na hi mahārājāti. kena bhante kāraṇenāti. yo tassa hetu dhammābhisamayāya so tassa samucchinno, tasmā dhammābhisamayo na bhavatīti.

473 bhante nāgasena, tumhe bhaṇatha: jānantassa kukkuccaṃ hoti, kukkucce sati āvaraṇaṃ hoti, āvaṭe citte dhammābhisamayo na hotīti. imassa pana ajānantassa akukkuccajātassa santacittassa viharato kena kāraṇena dhammābhisamayo na hoti; visamena visamen' eso pañho gacchati, cintetvā vissajjethāti.

474 rūhati mahārāja sukaṭṭhe sukalale maṇḍakhette sāradaṃ sukhasayitaṃ bījan-ti. āma bhante ti. api nu mahārāja taṃ yeva bījaṃ ghanaselasilātale rūheyyāti. na hi bhante ti. kissa pana mahārāja taṃ yeva bījaṃ kalale rūhati, kissa ghanasele na rūhatīti. natthi bhante tassa bījassa rūhanāya ghanasele hetu, ahetunā bījaṃ na rūhatīti.

before have I seen such a lamp of the Dhamma lit for all time."

"Revered Nagasena, suppose a householder here were to 472
commit a 'defeat,' and then at a later time were to ordain without comprehending, 'As a householder, I was guilty of committing a defeat.'[91] And suppose that no one else explained to him, 'As a householder, you were guilty of a defeat.' Would he achieve the sublime state? Or even be able to realize fully the Dhamma?"[92]

"No, great king."

"For what reason, sir?"

"For him the causal condition for realizing the Dhamma has been eradicated, so realizing the Dhamma does not occur."

"And yet, Nagasena, you say, 'For one who comprehends 473
what one has done, there is remorse; for one with remorse, there is a hindrance; and for one whose mind is hindered, there is no realizing the Dhamma.'[93] Why then does one who does not comprehend—and so has no remorse and lives with a peaceful mind—not realize the Dhamma? This dilemma goes to the discrepancy on these points. Please consider this, and reply."

"Great king, does a seed capable of sprouting and well 474
placed in properly tilled, moist, and fertile ground sprout?" "Yes, sir." "But would that seed sprout when placed on the surface of solid rock or stone?" "No, sir." "Why, great king, does the seed sprout in moist soil but not on solid rock?" "On solid rock, sir, there is no causal condition for a seed to sprout, and without such a condition, the seed does not sprout."

475 evam-eva kho mahārāja yena hetunā tassa dhammābhisamayo bhaveyya so tassa hetu samucchinno, ahetunā dhammābhisamayo na hoti. yatthā vā pana mahārāja daṇḍa-leḍḍu-lakuṭamuggarā paṭhaviyāṭhānam-upagacchanti, api nu mahārāja te yeva ḍaṇḍa-leḍḍu-lakuṭa-muggarā gagane ṭhānam-upagacchantīti. na hi bhante ti. kiṃ pan' ettha mahārāja kāraṇaṃ yena kāraṇena te yeva daṇḍa-leḍḍu-lakuṭa-muggarā paṭhaviyā ṭhānam-upagacchanti, kena kāraṇena gagane na tiṭṭhantīti. na-tthi bhante tesaṃ daṇḍa-leḍḍu-lakuṭa-muggarānaṃ patiṭṭhānāya ākāse hetu, ahetunā na tiṭṭhantīti.

476 evam-eva kho mahārāja tassa tena dosena abhisamayahetu samucchinno, hetusamugghāte ahetunā abhisamayo na hoti. yathā vā pana mahārāja thale aggi jalati, api nu kho mahārāja so yeva aggi udake jalatīti. na hi bhante ti. kiṃ pan' ettha mahārāja kāraṇaṃ yena kāraṇena so yeva aggi thale jalati, kena kāraṇena udake na jalatīti. na-tthi bhante aggissa jalanāya udake hetu, ahetunā na jalatīti. evam-eva kho mahārāja tassa tena dosena abhisamayahetu samucchinno, hetusamugghāte ahetunā dhammābhisamayo na hotīti.

477 bhante nāgasena, puna p' etaṃ atthaṃ cintehi, na me tattha cittasaññatti bhavati: ajānantassa asati kukkucce āvaraṇaṃ hotīti; kāraṇena maṃ saññāpehīti. api nu mahārāja visaṃ halāhalaṃ ajānantena pi khāyitaṃ jīvitaṃ haratīti. āma bhante ti. evam eva kho mahārāja ajānantena pi kataṃ

"It is the same, great king, for one whose causal condition 475
for realizing the Dhamma has been eradicated. Without this condition, there is no realizing the Dhamma. Alternatively, great king, sticks, clods of earth, clubs, and cudgels find a resting spot on the earth, but do the same sticks, clods of earth, clubs, and cudgels find a resting spot in the sky?" "No, sir." "But what is the reason that the sticks, clods of earth, clubs, and cudgels find a resting spot on the earth but do not stay up in the sky?" "Sir, there is no causal condition in the sky for fixing sticks, clods, clubs, and cudgels, and without a causal condition, they won't stay up."

"It is the same, great king, for one whose causal condition 476
for realization has been eradicated because of a fault. When the causal condition has been uprooted, there is no realization owing to the lack of the condition. It is similar to how fire burns on dry land. But does fire burn on water as well?" "No, sir." "What is the reasoning here, great king, whereby fire burns on dry land but does not burn on water?" "There is no causal condition on water for the burning of fire, sir, and without the condition, it does not burn."

"It is much the same, great king, for one whose causal condition for realization has been eradicated by a fault. When the condition has been uprooted, there is no realizing the Dhamma because the condition is lacking."

"Revered Nagasena, please consider further this matter, 477
for I have no conviction concerning this point, namely, that for one who does not comprehend what one has done and so is free of remorse, there could be a hindrance. Persuade me with a reason."

"Great king, does a deadly poison destroy the life of

pāpaṃ abhisamayantarāyakaraṃ hoti. api nu mahārāja aggi ajānitvā akkamantaṃ ḍahatīti. āma bhante ti. evam-eva kho mahārāja ajānantena pi kataṃ pāpaṃ abhisamayantarāyakaraṃ hoti.

478 api nu mahārāja ajānantaṃ āsīviso ḍasitvā jīvitaṃ haratīti. āma bhante ti. evam-eva kho mahārāja ajānantena pi kataṃ pāpaṃ abhisamayantarāyakaraṃ hoti. nanu mahārāja kāliṅgarājā samaṇakolañño sattaratanaparikiṇṇo hatthiratanam-abhiruyha kuladassanāya gacchanto ajānanto pi nāsakkhi bodhimaṇḍassa uparito gantuṃ. idam-ettha mahārāja kāraṇaṃ yena kāraṇena ajānantena pi kataṃ pāpaṃ abhisamayantarāyakaraṃ hotīti. jinabhāsitaṃ bhante nāgasena kāraṇaṃ na sakkā paṭikkosituṃ, esov' etassa attho, tathā sampaṭicchāmīti.

479 bhante nāgasena, gihidussīlassa ca samaṇadussīlassa ca ko viseso kiṃ nānākaraṇaṃ; ubho p' ete samasamagatikā, ubhinnam-pi samasamo vipāko hoti, udāhu kiñci nānākaraṇaṃ atthīti.

480 dasa ime mahārāja guṇā samaṇadussīlassa gihidussīlato visesena atirekā, dasahi ca kāraṇehi uttariṃ dakkhiṇaṃ visodheti. katame dasa guṇā samaṇadussīlassa gihidussīlato visesena atirekā. idha mahārāja samaṇadussīlo buddhe sagāravo hoti, dhamme sagāravo hoti, saṅghe sagāravo hoti, sabrahmacārisu sagāravo hoti, uddesa-paripucchāya vāyamati, savanabahulo hoti, bhinnasīlo pi mahārāja dussīlo parisagato ākappaṃ upaṭṭhapeti, garahabhayā kāyikaṃ vācasikaṃ rakkhati, padhānābhimukham-assa

one who takes it, even if unknowingly?" "Yes, sir." "Similarly, great king, evil done, even unknowingly, prevents
realization. Does a fire burn someone who unwittingly treads
on it?" "It does, sir." "Similarly, great king, evil done, even
unknowingly, prevents realization. Does a venomous snake 478
that bites someone who is not aware of it still take that one's
life?" "It does, sir." "Similarly, great king, evil done, even
unknowingly, prevents realization. Consider how Samana-
kolanna, the king of Kalinga, flanked by his seven royal treasures, mounted on his elephant treasure, and while traveling
to see his family was unable to pass over, even unwittingly,
the base of the Bodhi Tree.[94] This is the reasoning whereby
evil done even unknowingly prevents realization."

"It is not possible, revered Nagasena, to scorn the reasoning spoken by the Victor. This is the meaning of it, and I am
convinced.

"Revered Nagasena, what is the difference between a 479
householder with moral lapses and a renouncer with moral
lapses? What is the distinction between them? Do both have
exactly the same future birth? Is the fruit the same for both?
Or is there a difference?"

"Great king, there are ten qualities that are enough to 480
distinguish a renouncer with moral lapses from a householder with moral lapses; and furthermore, by ten ways
he purifies an offering. What are the ten qualities that
are enough to distinguish a renouncer with moral lapses
from a householder with moral lapses? Here, great king, a
renouncer with moral lapses still has respect for the Buddha,
respect for the Dhamma, respect for the community,
and respect for those living the religious life; he strives in

hoti cittaṃ, bhikkhusāmaññaṃ upagato hoti. karonto pi mahārāja samaṇadussīlo pāpaṃ paṭicchannaṃ ācarati. yathā mahārāja itthī sapatikā nilīyitvā rahassen' eva pāpam-ācarati, evam-eva kho mahārāja karonto pi samaṇadussīlo pāpaṃ paṭicchannaṃ ācarati. ime kho mahārāja dasa guṇā samaṇadussīlassa gihidussīlato visesena atirekā.

481 katamehi dasahi kāraṇehi uttariṃ dakkhiṇaṃ visodheti. avajjha-kavaca-dhāraṇatāya pi dakkhiṇaṃ visodheti, isisāmañña-bhaṇḍuliṅga-dhāraṇato pi dakkhiṇaṃ visodheti, saṅghasamayam-anupaviṭṭhatāya pi dakkhiṇaṃ visodheti, buddha-dhamma-saṅgha-saraṇagatatāya pi dakkhiṇaṃ visodheti, padhānāsayaniketavāsitāya pi dakkhiṇaṃ visodheti, jinasāsanadhanapariyesanato pi dakkhiṇaṃ visodheti, pavaradhammadesanato pi dakkhiṇaṃ visodheti, dhammadīpagatiparāyanatāya pi dakkhinaṃ visodheti, aggo buddho ti ekantaujudiṭṭhitāya pi dakkhiṇaṃ visodheti, uposathasamādānato pi dakkhiṇaṃ visodheti. imehi kho mahārāja dasahi kāraṇehi uttariṃ dakkhiṇaṃ visodheti.

482 suvipanno pi hi mahārāja samaṇaḍussīlo dāyakānaṃ dakkhiṇaṃ visodheti. yathā mahārāja udakaṃ subahalam-pi kalala-kaddama-rajojallaṃ apaneti, evam eva kho mahārāja suvipanno pi samaṇadussīlo dāyakānaṃ dakkhiṇaṃ visodheti. yathā vā pana mahārāja uṇhodakam sukaṭhitam-pi pajjalan-

recitation and questioning and has heard much. Though his moral precepts are broken and he has moral lapses, when he enters an assembly he comports himself well and guards his bodily and verbal behavior out of fear of rebuke. His mind inclines toward striving, and he has achieved the company of monks. Even though a renouncer with moral lapses does evil, he behaves secretly. Much as a married woman behaves clandestinely as she does secret evil, so too, great king, the renouncer with moral lapses behaves secretly when doing evil. These ten qualities of the renouncer with moral lapses are enough to distinguish him from a householder with moral lapses.

"And what are the ten ways that he further purifies an 481
offering? He makes an offering pure by wearing inviolable armor; he makes an offering pure by wearing the sign of a shaved head associated with sages; he makes it pure by entering the congregation of the community; by taking refuge in the Buddha, the Dhamma, and the community; by living in the company of those intent on striving; by seeking the treasure of the Victor's dispensation; by teaching the excellent Dhamma; by aiming at a birth where there is sanctuary in the Dhamma; by his absolute and upright conviction that the Buddha is the best; and, finally, he makes an offering pure by undertaking the Uposatha. In these ten ways, great king, he further purifies an offering.

"Great king, a renouncer whose morals have lapsed, even 482
one truly depraved, purifies the offering of donors. Just as ample amounts of water carry away mud, muck, grime, and dirt, so too even a truly depraved renouncer whose morals have lapsed purifies the offering of donors. Just as hot or

taṃ mahantaṃ aggikkhandhaṃ nibbāpeti, evam-eva kho mahārāja suvipanno pi samaṇadussīlo dāyakānaṃ dakkhiṇaṃ visodheti. yathā vā pana mahārāja bhojanaṃ virasampi khudādubbalyaṃ apaneti, evam-eva kho mahārāja suvipanno pi samaṇadussīlo dāyakānaṃ dakkhiṇaṃ visodheti. bhāsitam-p' etaṃ mahārāja devātidevena majjhimanikāyavaralañcake dakkhiṇāvibhaṅge veyyākaraṇe:

483 yo sīlavā dussīlesu dadāti dānaṃ dhammena laddhā
supasannacitto,
abhisaddahaṃ kammaphalaṃ uḷāraṃ, sā dakkhiṇā
dāyakato visujjhatīti.

484 acchariyaṃ bhante nāgasena, abbhutaṃ bhante nāgasena, tāvatakaṃ mayaṃ pañhaṃ apucchimha, taṃ tvaṃ opammehi kāraṇehi vibhāvento amatamadhuraṃ savanūpagaṃ akāsi. yathā nāma bhante sūdo vā sūdantevāsī vā tāvatakaṃ maṃsaṃ labhitvā nānāvidhehi sambhārehi sampādetvā rājūpabhogaṃ karoti, evam-eva kho bhante nāgasena tāvatakaṃ mayaṃ pañhaṃ apucchimha, taṃ tvaṃ opammehi kāraṇehi vibhāvetvā amatamadhuraṃ savanūpagaṃ akāsīti.

485 bhante nāgasena, imaṃ udakaṃ aggimhi tappamānaṃ ciccitāyati ciṭiciṭāyati saddāyati bahuvidhaṃ; kin-nu kho bhante nāgasena udakaṃ jīvati, kiṃ kīlamānaṃ saddāyati, udāhu aññena paṭipīḷitaṃ saddāyatīti. na hi mahārāja udakaṃ jīvati, na-tthi udake jīvo vā satto vā api ca mahārāja

even boiling water extinguishes a huge blazing mass of fire, so too does even a truly depraved renouncer whose morals have lapsed purify the offering of donors. Just as food, even if tasteless, takes away the weakness of hunger, so too does even a truly depraved renouncer whose morals have lapsed purify the offering of donors. Moreover, great king, the god above gods spoke to this in the explanation of the Analysis of Offerings in the excellent declaration that is the *Majjhimanikāya:*

When a virtuous person gives a gift to the unvirtuous 483
with composed confidence and righteously
acquired means,
fully trusting in the superb fruits of karma, the
offering is purified by the donor."

"It is a wonder and a marvel, revered Nagasena, that I asked 484
such a question, and that you, explaining with analogies and reasoning, made the sweetness of ambrosia reach this listener. Just as a chef or chef's apprentice takes such meat as is available and procures various kinds of ingredients to make it a dish for a king, I asked you, revered Nagasena, such a question, and you, explaining with analogies and reasoning, made the sweetness of ambrosia reach this listener.

"Revered Nagasena, when this water is heated over fire 485
it hisses and sizzles and makes many kinds of noises. Nagasena, is the water alive? Is it playing when it makes this noise? Or is it in pain when it makes this sound?"

"No, great king, the water is not alive, nor is there a soul or a living being present in water. Water hisses and sizzles

aggisantāpavegassa mahantatāya udakaṃ cicciṭāyati ciṭiciṭāyati saddāyati bahuvidhan-ti.

486 bhante nāgasena, idh' ekacce titthiyā: udakaṃ jīvatīti sītūdakaṃ paṭikkhipitvā udakaṃ tāpetvā vekaṭikavekaṭikaṃ paribhuñjanti, te tumhe garahanti paribhavanti: ekindriyaṃ samaṇā sakyaputtiyā jīvaṃ viheṭhentīti; taṃ tesaṃ garahaṃ paribhavaṃ vinodehi apanehi nicchārehīti.

487 na hi mahārāja udakaṃ jīvati, na-tthi mahārāja udake jīvo vā satto vā; api ca mahārāja aggisantāpavegassa mahantatāya udakaṃ cicciṭāyatī ciṭiciṭāyati saddāyati bahuvidhaṃ. yathā mahārāja udakaṃ sobbha-sara-sarita-daha-taḷāka-kandara-padara-udapāna-ninna-pokkharaṇigataṃ vātāta-pavegassa mahantatāya pariyādiyati parikkhayaṃ gacchati, api nu tattha udakaṃ cicciṭāyati ciṭiciṭāyati saddāyati bahuvidhan-ti. na hi bhante ti.

488 yadi mahārāja udakaṃ jīveyya, tatthāpi udakaṃ saddāyeyya. iminā pi mahārāja kāraṇena jānāhi: na-tthi udake jīvo vā satto vā, aggisantāpavegassa mahantatāya udakaṃ cicciṭāyati ciṭiciṭāyati saddāyati bahuvidhan-ti. aparam-pi mahārāja uttariṃ kāraṇaṃ suṇohi: natthi udake jīvo vā satto vā, aggisantāpavegassa mahantatāya udakaṃ saddāyatīti. yadā pana mahārāja udakaṃ taṇḍulehi sammissitaṃ bhājanagataṃ hoti pihitaṃ uddhane aṭṭhapitaṃ, api nu tattha udakaṃ saddāyatīti. na hi bhante, acalaṃ hoti santasantan-ti.

and makes many noises due to the tremendous agitation of the fire's heat."

"Nagasena, sir, there are some teachers of other sects 486
around here who say that water is alive. Refusing cold water, they boil water, and subsist on various kinds of unclean food.[95] They revile and impugn you, saying, 'These renouncers in the lineage of the Sakya destroy single-faculty life forms.' Please dispel, drive off, and get rid of their reviling and impugning."

"Great king, water is not alive, and there is no soul or living 487
being in water. Water hisses and sizzles and makes many noises due to the tremendous agitation of the fire's heat. Water in puddles, ponds, rivers, lakes, tanks, gorges, mountain crevices, wells, floodplains, and lotus pools dries up and disappears because of the sheer force of wind and heat. But does the water hiss and sizzle and make many noises at this time?"

"It does not, sir."

"Great king, if water were alive, then water would make 488
a sound in these cases also. Please know by this reasoning, great king, that there is no soul or living being present in water. Water hisses and sizzles and makes many noises due to the tremendous agitation of the fire's heat. And please listen to another reason there is no soul or living being in water, and that makes noise due to the tremendous agitation of the fire's heat. When water is mixed with rice grains and placed in a pot, covered, but not put in an oven, does the water then make a sound?"

"No, sir, it is still and quiet."

489 taṃ yeva pana mahārāja udakaṃ bhājanagataṃ aggiṃ ujjāletvā uddhane ṭhapitaṃ hoti, api nu tattha udakaṃ acalaṃ hoti santasantan-ti. na hi bhante, calati khubbhati luḷati āvilati ūmijātaṃ hoti uddham-adho disāvidisaṃ gacchati uttarati patarati, pheṇamāli hotīti. kissa pana taṃ mahārāja pākatikaṃ udakaṃ na calati, santasantaṃ hoti, kissa pana aggigataṃ calati khubbhati luḷati āvilati ūmi-jātaṃ hoti uddham-adho disāvidisaṃ gacchati pheṇamāli hotīti. pākatikaṃ bhante udakaṃ na calati, aggigataṃ pana udakaṃ aggisantāpavegassa mahantatāya cicciṭāyati ciṭiciṭāyati saddāyati bahuvidhan-ti.

490 iminā pi mahārāja kāraṇena jānāhi: na-tthi udake jīvo vā satto vā, aggisantāpavegassa mahantatāya udakaṃ saddāyatīti. aparam-pi mahārāja uttariṃ kāraṇaṃ suṇohi: natthi udake jīvo vā satto vā, aggisantāpavegassa mahantatāya udakaṃ saddāyatīti. hoti taṃ mahārāja udakaṃ ghare ghare udakavārakagataṃ pihitan-ti. āma bhante ti. api nu taṃ mahārāja udakaṃ calati khubbhati luḷati āvilati ūmijātaṃ hoti uddham-adho disāvidisaṃ gacchati uttarati patarati pheṇamāli hotīti. na hi bhante, acalaṃ taṃ hoti pākatikaṃ udakavāragataṃ udakan-ti. sutapubbaṃ pana tayā mahārāja: mahāsamudde udakaṃ calati khubbhati luḷati āvilati ūmijātaṃ hoti uddham-adho disāvidisaṃ gacchati uttarati patarati pheṇamāli hoti ussakkitvā velāya paharati saddāyati bahuvidhan-ti.

491 āma bhante, sutapubbaṃ etaṃ mayā diṭṭhapubbañ-ca, mahāsamudde udakam hatthasatam-pi dve pi hatthasatāni gagane ussakkatīti. kissa mahārāja udakavāragataṃ udakaṃ na calati na saddāyati, kissa pana mahāsamudde udakaṃ

“Yet, great king, when water is placed in a pot and put 489
in an oven where a fire has been kindled, does it remain still and quiet then?” “No, sir. It simmers, jiggles, seethes, churns, becomes waves, swirls up and down and side to side, boils over, and becomes a ring of foam.” “Why then, great king, does water naturally stay still and quiet, but when put over fire it simmers, jiggles, seethes, churns, becomes waves, swirls up and down and side to side, and becomes a ring of foam?” “Water does not naturally simmer, sir, but when placed on fire it hisses, sizzles, and makes many noises because of the tremendous agitation of the fire’s heat.”

“With this reasoning, great king, you may know that there 490
is no soul or living being in water, and that water makes sound because of the tremendous agitation of the fire’s heat. Please listen to another reason that there is no soul or living being in water, and that water makes sound because of the tremendous agitation of the fire’s heat. Is it the case that in every house water is placed in a water jar and covered?” “It is, sir.” “Does that water simmer, jiggle, seethe, churn, become waves, swirl up and down and side to side, boil over, and become a ring of foam, great king?” “No, sir, water in a water jar is naturally still.” “And yet, have you ever heard, great king, that water in the great ocean simmers, jiggles, seethes, churns, becomes waves, swirls up and down and side to side, boils over, becomes a ring of foam, swells up, and breaks on the shore?”

“Indeed, sir. Not only have I heard this, but I have seen 491
water swell up a hundred or two hundred cubits into the sky.” “Then why does the water in a water jar not simmer or make noise, while water in the great ocean does so?” “Sir, it

calati saddāyatīti. vātavegassa mahantatāya bhante mahāsamudde udakaṃ calati saddāyati, udakavāragataṃ udakaṃ aghaṭṭitaṃ kehici na calati na saddāyatīti.

492 yathā mahārāja vātavegassa mahantatāya mahāsamudde udakaṃ calati saddāyati, evam-evaṃ aggisantāpavegassa mahantatāya udakaṃ saddāyati. nanu mahārāja bheripokkharaṃ sukkhaṃ sukkhena gocammena onandhantīti. āma bhante ti. api nu mahārāja bheriyā jīvo vā satto vā atthīti. na hi bhante ti. kissa pana mahārāja bheri saddāyatīti. itthiyā vā bhante purisassa vā tajjena vāyāmenāti.

493 yathā mahārāja itthiyā vā purisassa vā tajjena vāyāmena bheri saddāyati, evam-evaṃ aggisantāpavegassa mahantatāya udakaṃ saddāyati. iminā pi mahārāja kāraṇena jānāhi: na-tthi udake jīvo vā satto vā, aggisantāpavegassa mahantatāya udakaṃ saddāyatīti. mayham-pi tāva mahārāja tava pucchitabbaṃ atthi, evam-eso pañho suvinicchito hoti. kin-nu kho mahārāja sabbehi pi bhājanehi udakaṃ tappamānaṃ saddāyati, udāhu ekaccehi yeva bhājanehi tappamānaṃ saddāyatīti. na hi bhante sabbehi pi bhājanehi udakaṃ tappamānaṃ saddāyati, ekaccehi yeva bhājanehi udakaṃ tappamānaṃ saddāyatīti.

494 tena hi mahārāja jahitosi sakasamayaṃ, paccāgatosi mama visayaṃ, na-tthi udake jīvo vā satto vā; yadi mahārāja sabbehi pi bhājanehi udakaṃ tappamānaṃ saddāyeyya, yuttam-idaṃ: udakaṃ jīvatīti vattuṃ. na hi mahārāja udakaṃ dvayaṃ hoti: yaṃ saddāyati taṃ jīvati, yaṃ na saddāyati taṃ

is due to the tremendous force of the wind that water in the great ocean simmers and makes noise while water in a water jar does not move or make noise as long as it is not shaken by someone."

"Great king, just as it is due to the tremendous force of 492
the wind that water in the great ocean moves and makes noise, so too does water make noise due to the tremendous force of fire's heat. Do not people cover the dried body of a kettledrum with dried cowhide?" "They do indeed, sir." "And yet there is no soul or living being in the drum, great king?" "No, sir." "Then why does the drum make sound, great king?" "By the proper efforts of a woman or man, sir."

"If, great king, a drum sounds by the proper efforts of a 493
woman or a man, then similarly, water sounds by the tremendous force of the heat of fire. And so you may know by this reason also that there is no soul or living being in water, and that water makes noise because of the tremendous force of fire's heat. Now that this dilemma has been thoroughly settled in this way, let me ask a question of you, great king. Does water that is heated in every kind of vessel make noise, or does it make noise only when heated in certain types of vessels?"

"Water does not make sound when heated in every kind of vessel, sir, only when heated in certain vessels."

"By this you have abandoned your own view and crossed 494
over to my side that in water there is no soul or living being. Great king, if water made noise when heated in every type of vessel, then it would it be correct to say that water is alive. There are not two types of water—water that makes sound and is alive, and water that does not make sound and is not

na jīvatīti. yadi mahārāja udakaṃ jīveyya, mahantānaṃ hatthināgānaṃ ussannakāyānaṃ pabhinnānaṃ soṇḍāya ussiñcitvā mukhe pakkhipitvā kucchiṃ pavesayantānaṃ tam pi udakaṃ tesaṃ dantantare cippiyamānaṃ saddāyeyya. hatthasatikā pi mahānāvā garukā bhārikā anekasatasahassabhāraparipūrā mahāsamudde vicaranti, tāhi pi cippiyamānaṃ udakaṃ saddāyeyya. mahatimahantā pi macchā anekasatayojanikakāyā, timī timiṅgalā timirapiṅgalā, abbhantare nimuggā mahāsamudde nivāsaṭṭhānatāya paṭivasantā mahā-udakadhārā ācamanti dhamanti ca, tesam-pi taṃ dantantare pi udarantare pi cippiyamānaṃ udakaṃ saddāyeyya. yasmā ca kho mahārāja evarūpehi evarūpehi mahantehi patipīḷanehi patipīḷitaṃ udakaṃ na saddāyati, tasmā pi na-tthi udake jīvo vā satto vā ti evam etaṃ mahārāja dhārehīti.

495 sādhu bhante nāgasena, desāgato pañho anucchavikāya vibhattiyā vibhatto. yathā nāma bhante nāgasena mahatimahagghaṃ maṇiratanaṃ chekaṃ ācariyaṃ kusalaṃ sikkhitaṃ maṇikāraṃ pāpuṇitvā kittiṃ labheyya thomanaṃ pasaṃsaṃ, muttāratanaṃ vā muttikaṃ, dussaratanaṃ vā dussikaṃ, lohitacandanaṃ vā gandhikaṃ pāpuṇitvā kittiṃ labheyya thomanaṃ pasaṃsaṃ, evam-eva kho bhante nāgasena desāgato pañho anucchavikāya vibhattiyā vibhatto, evam-etaṃ, tathā sampaṭicchāmīti.

chaṭṭho vaggo.

alive. If water were alive, it would make noise when it gets drawn up by the trunks of huge rutting bull elephants and poured into their mouths where is pressed between their teeth and enters their bellies. And consider a huge ship a hundred cubits long, heavily laden and filled with many hundreds and thousands of goods, traveling in the ocean. Water pressed down by such ships would make a noise also. And enormous fish with bodies many hundreds of leagues long, massive fish, giants and leviathans, take in and blow out great quantities of water as they live in their dwelling places submerged in the deep ocean. The water pressed under their teeth and in their bellies would make a sound. And yet, even water pressed by such great pressures as these does not make a sound. Therefore, please understand, great king, that there is no soul or living being in water."

"Very well, then, revered Nagasena. The question has 495
arrived at a place where it is settled with appropriate detail. Much as a large and very costly jewel treasure that has reached a skilled, accomplished, and clever master jeweler would acquire fame, acclaim, and praise, and much as a precious pearl that has reached a dealer in pearls, or fine cloth reaching a cloth merchant, or red sandalwood reaching a perfumer would in every case acquire fame, acclaim, and praise, so too, revered Nagasena, this question has arrived at a place where it is settled with appropriate detail. It is so, and I accept it."

End of Part 6.

PART 7

496 bhante nāgasena, bhāsitam-p' etaṃ bhagavatā: nippapañcā-
rāmā bhikkhave viharatha nippapañcaratino ti. kataman-taṃ nippapañcan-ti. sotāpattiphalaṃ mahārāja nippapañcaṃ, sakadāgāmiphalaṃ nippapañcaṃ, anāgāmiphalaṃ
nippapañcaṃ, arahattaphalaṃ nippapañcan-ti.
497 yadi bhante nāgasena sotāpattiphalaṃ nippapañcaṃ, saka-
dāgāmi-anāgāmi-arahattaphalaṃ nippapañcaṃ, kissa pana
ime bhikkhū uddisanti paripucchanti suttaṃ geyyaṃ veyyākaraṇaṃ gāthaṃ udānaṃ itivuttakaṃ jātakaṃ abbhutadhammaṃ vedallaṃ, navakammena palibujjhanti dānena
ca pūjāya ca; nanu te jinapaṭikkhittaṃ kammaṃ karontīti.
498 ye te mahārāja bhikkhū uddisanti paripucchanti suttaṃ
geyyam veyyākaraṇaṃ gāthaṃ udānaṃ itivuttakaṃ jātakaṃ
abbhutadhammaṃ vedallaṃ, navakammena palibujjhanti
dānena ca pūjāya ca, sabbe te nippapañcassa pattiyā karonti.
ye te mahārāja sabhāvaparisuddhā pubbe vāsitavāsanā te
ekacittakkhaṇena nippapañcā honti; ye pana te bhikkhū
mahārajakkhā[21] te imehi payogehi nippapañcā honti. yathā

PART 7

"Revered Nagasena, the Bhagavan said, 'Monks, live your 496
lives delighting in being free of proliferating thoughts and taking pleasure in being free of proliferating thoughts. What is this 'being free of proliferating thoughts?'"[96]

"Great king, being free of proliferating thoughts is the fruit of stream entry, the fruit of once return, the fruit of nonreturn, and the fruit of arhatship."[97]

"Nagasena, if being free of proliferating thoughts is the 497
fruit of stream entry, and the fruit of once return, nonreturn, and arhatship, then how do these monks instruct and query the *suttas,* recitations, expositions, verses, inspired utterances, quotations, birth stories, teachings of wonders, and questions-and-answers?* How do they get caught up in making building repairs, offerings, and worship? Are they not doing work rejected by the Victor?"

"Great king, the monks who instruct and query the 498
suttas, recitations, expositions, verses, inspired utterances, quotations, birth stories, teachings of wonders, and questions-and-answers, as well as get caught up in building repairs, offerings, and worship, are all doing these things for the sake of attaining freedom from proliferating thoughts. Those whose impressions from previous lives are purified by their very nature can become free of proliferating thoughts in a moment of single-minded focus. But those monks with much dust in their eyes become free of proliferating thoughts

* The ninefold division of the genres of the Buddha's words.

mahārāja eko puriso khette bījaṃ ropetvā attano yathābalaviriyena vinā pākāravatiyā dhaññaṃ uddhareyya, eko puriso khette bījaṃ ropetvā vanaṃ pavisitvā kaṭṭhañ-ca sākhañ-ca chinditvā vatipākāraṃ katvā dhaññaṃ uddhareyya, yā tattha tassa vatipākārapariyesanā sā dhaññatthāya; evam-eva kho mahārāja ye te sabhāvaparisuddhā pubbe vāsitavāsanā te ekacittakkhaṇena nippapañcā honti, vinā vatipākāraṃ puriso viya dhaññuddhāro; ye pana te bhikkhū mahārajakkhā te imehi payogehi nippapañcā honti, vatipākāraṃ katvā puriso viya dhaññuddhāro.

499 yathā vā pana mahārāja mahatimahante ambarukkhamatthake phalapiṇḍi bhaveyya, atha tattha yo koci iddhimā āgantvā tassa phalaṃ hareyya, yo pana tattha aniddhimā so kaṭṭhañ-ca valliñca chinditvā nisseṇiṃ bandhitvā tāya taṃ rukkhaṃ abhirūhitvā phalaṃ hareyya, yā tattha tassa nisseṇipariyesanā sā phalatthāya; evam-eva kho mahārāja ye te sabhāvaparisuddhā pubbe vāsitavāsanā te ekacittakkhaṇena nippapañcā honti, iddhimā viya rukkhaphalaṃ haranto; ye pana te bhikkhū maharājakkhā te iminā payogena saccāni abhisamenti, nisseṇiyā viya puriso rukkhaphalaṃ haranto.

500 yathā vā pana mahārāja eko puriso atthakaraṇiko ekako yeva sāmikaṃ upagantvā atthaṃ sādheti, eko dhanavā dhanavasena parisaṃ vaḍḍhetvā parisāya atthaṃ sādheti,

only with such means. Great king, this is similar to the person who plants seed in a field and then reaps grain with his own strength and exertion without putting up a fence; another person plants seed in a field, goes into the woods, cuts twigs and branches, and builds an encircling fence before reaping the grain. In his case, looking for an encircling fence was for the sake of the grain. Those whose impressions from previous lives are purified by their very nature, and who become free of proliferating thoughts in a moment of single-minded focus, are like the person reaping grain without the encircling fence. But monks with much dust in their eyes who become free of proliferating thoughts only with such means are like the person who reaps grain having built a fence.

"Great king, suppose there were a cluster of fruit at the 499
very top of a huge mango tree and someone were to come along with magical powers and gather the fruit. But someone without magical powers cuts twigs and creepers and builds a ladder, climbs up the tree with it, and gathers the fruit. In his case, seeking the ladder is for the sake of the fruit. Those whose impressions from previous lives are purified by their very nature and who become free of proliferating thoughts in a moment of single-minded focus are like the one gathering the tree's fruit by means of magical powers. But monks with much dust in their eyes who become free of proliferating thoughts and grasp the truths only by these means are like the person gathering the tree's fruit with a ladder.

"Great king, it is similar to a person in service who 500
approaches the master alone and earns a profit, while a wealthy person uses his wealth to increase the size of his company and then, by means of the company, earns a profit.

yā tattha tassa parisapariyesanā sā atthatthāya; evam-eva kho mahārāja ye te sabhāvaparisuddhā pubbe vāsitavāsanā te ekacittakkhaṇena chasu abhiññāsu vasībhāvaṃ pāpuṇanti, puriso viya ekako atthasiddhiṃ karonto; ye pana te bhikkhū mahārajakkhā te imehi payogehi sāmaññattham-abhisādhenti, parisāya viya puriso atthasiddhiṃ karonto.

501 uddeso pi mahārāja bahukāro, paripucchā pi bahukārā, navakammam-pi bahukāraṃ, dānam-pi bahukāraṃ, pūjā pi bahukārā tesu tesu karaṇīyesu. yathā mahārāja puriso rājūpasevī katāvī amaccabhaṭa-balattha-dovārika-anīkaṭṭha-pārisajjajanehi, te tassa karaṇīye anuppatte sabbe pi upakārā honti; evam-eva kho mahārāja uddeso pi bahukāro, paripucchā pi bahukārā, navakammam-pi bahukāraṃ, dānam-pi bahukāraṃ, pūjā pi bahukārā tesu tesu karaṇīyesu. yadi mahārāja sabbe pi abhijātiparisuddhā bhaveyyuṃ, anusāsakena karaṇīyaṃ na bhaveyya; yasmā ca kho mahārāja savanena karaṇīyaṃ hoti.

502 thero mahārāja sāriputto aparimitamasankheyyakappaṃ upādāya upacitakusalamūlo paññāya koṭiṃ gato, so pi vinā savanena nāsakkhi āsavakkhayam pāpuṇituṃ. tasmā mahārāja bahukāraṃ savanaṃ, tathā uddeso pi paripucchā pi, tasmā uddesa-paripucchā pi nippapañcā asaṅkhatā ti. sunijjhāpito bhante nāgasena pañho, evametaṃ, tathā sampaṭicchāmīti.

In his case, searching for a company is for the sake of the profit. Those whose impressions from previous lives are purified by their very nature, and who attain mastery in the six higher knowledges in a moment of single-minded focus, are like the person who earns the profit alone. But monks with much dust in their eyes attain the profit of renunciation only by these means, like the person making profit by means of a company.

"Instructing is very helpful and querying is very help- 501
ful, great king. And among the various things that must be done, building repairs, offerings, and worship are also very helpful. It is similar to one serving the king who gets things done by means of such people as ministers, mercenaries, soldiers, gatekeepers, bodyguards, and retainers; all of these become useful when they accomplish his work. Similarly, great king, instructing is very helpful, querying is very helpful, and among the various things that must be done, building repairs, offerings, and worship are also very helpful. If everyone were purified from birth, there would be no work to be done by a teacher. But there is something
to be accomplished by learning, great king. Elder Sariputta, 502
whose roots of merit had accumulated for innumerable and incalculable eons, had reached the peak of understanding. But even he was not able to achieve the destruction of the flaws without learning. Therefore, learning is very helpful, great king, and so too are instructing and querying. And thus, even instructing and querying are conducive to being free of proliferating thoughts, the unconditioned."[98]

"The dilemma has been thoroughly treated, revered Nagasena. It is so, and I am persuaded."

503 bhante nāgasena, tumhe bhaṇathā: yo gihī arahattaṃ patto dvev' assa gatiyo bhavanti, anaññā: tasmiṃ yeva divase pabbajati vā parinibbāyati vā, na so divaso sakkā atikkametun-ti. sace so bhante nāgasena tasmiṃ divase ācariyaṃ vā upajjhāyaṃ vā pattacīvaraṃ vā na labhetha, api nu so arahā sayaṃ vā pabbajeyya, divasaṃ vā atikkameyya, añño vā koci arahā iddhimā āgantvā taṃ pabbājeyya, parinibbāyeyya vā ti.

504 na so mahārāja arahā sayaṃ pabbajeyya, sayaṃ pabbajanto theyyaṃ āpajjati; na ca divasaṃ atikkameyya; aññassa arahantassa āgamanaṃ bhaveyya vā na vā bhaveyya, tasmiṃ yeva divase parinibbāyeyyāti. tena hi bhante nāgasena arahattassa santabhāvo vijahito hoti, yena adhigatassa jīvita-hāro bhavatīti.

505 visamaṃ mahārāja gihiliṅgaṃ, visame liṅge liṅgadubbalatāya arahattaṃ patto gihī tasmiṃ yeva divase pabbajati vā parinibbāyati vā; n' eso mahārāja doso arahattassa, gihiliṅgass' eso doso, yad-idaṃ liṅgadubbalatā. yathā mahārāja bhojanaṃ sabbasattānaṃ āyupālakaṃ jīvitarakkhakaṃ visamakoṭṭhassa mandadubbalagahaṇikassa avipākena jīvitaṃ harati, n' eso mahārāja doso bhojanassa, koṭṭhass' eso doso, yad-idaṃ aggidubbalatā; evam-eva kho mahārāja visame

"Revered Nagasena, you say, 'There are only two destinies 503
for a householder who attains arhatship—on that very day
he either ordains or attains final nibbana.* The day cannot
pass otherwise.' Nagasena, if on that day he does not have
a teacher, master, or robe and bowl available, then could he
ordain himself? Would the day still pass? Or would someone
else with magical powers come and ordain him? Or would
he attain final nibbana?"

"Great king, an arhat cannot become ordained by himself; 504
one ordaining oneself commits a theft.[99] Nor could the day
pass. Whether another arhat came or not, on that very day,
he would attain final nibbana."

"Because of this, Nagasena, the peaceful state of the arhat
is forfeited, since the life is taken of one who reaches it."

"Great king, the distinctive attribute of household life is 505
that it is incompatible with nibbana; since its attribute is
incompatible, then the householder who attains arhatship
ordains or attains final nibbana that very day because of the
deficiency in this attribute. This is not the fault of arhatship but the fault of the household life, because it has this
deficiency.[100] It is like food that safeguards longevity and
protects the life of all beings, yet takes the life of one with
an imbalanced belly and slow and weak digestion owing to
not having that effect. Great king, this is not the fault of the
food but the fault of the belly, because there is a deficiency of
digestive fire in it. In much the same way, since the distinctive attribute is incompatible, the householder who attains
arhatship either ordains or attains final nibbana that very

* Final nibbana means that he dies.

liṅge liṅgadubbalatāya arahattaṃ patto gihī tasmiṃ yeva divase pabbajati vā parinibbāyati vā; n' eso mahārāja doso arahattassa, gihiliṅgass' eso doso, yad-idaṃ liṅgadubbalatā.

506 yathā vā pana mahārāja parittaṃ tiṇasalākaṃ upari garuke pāsāṇe ṭhapite dubbalatāya bhijjitvā patati, evam-eva kho mahārāja arahattaṃ patto gihī tena liṅgena arahattaṃ dhāretuṃ asakkonto tasmiṃ yeva divase pabbajati vā parinibbāyati vā. yathā vā pana mahārāja puriso abalo dubbalo nihīnajacco parittapuñño mahatimahārajjaṃ labhitvā khaṇena paripaṭati paridhaṃsati osakkati, na sakkoti issariyaṃ dhāretuṃ; evam-eva kho mahārāja arahattaṃ patto gihī tena liṅgena arahattaṃ dhāretuṃ na sakkoti, tena kāraṇena tasmiṃ yeva divase pabbajati vā parinibbāyati vā ti. sādhu bhante nāgasena, evam-etaṃ, tathā sampaṭicchāmīti.

507 bhante nāgasena, atthi arahato satisammoso ti. vigatasatisammosā kho mahārāja arahanto, na-tthi arahantānaṃ satisammoso ti. āpajjeyya pana bhante arahā āpattin-ti. āma mahārājāti. kismiṃ vatthusmin-ti. kuṭikāre mahārāja, sañcaritte, vikāle kālasaññāya, pavārite appavāritasaññāya, anatiritte atirittasaññāyāti.

508 bhante nāgasena, tumhe bhaṇatha: ye āpattiṃ āpajjanti te dvīhi kāraṇehi āpajjanti, anādariyena vā ajānanena vā

day, owing to the deficiency in its attribute. This is not the fault of arhatship, great king, but the fault of the attribute of household life that it has this deficiency.

"Much as a heavy rock placed on a thin stalk of grass 506
breaks it due to its weakness, and falls, so too, great king, one living the household life who attains arhatship is not able to support it because of this distinctive attribute, and so on that very day ordains or attains final nibbana. It is also like a weak and ineffectual man with low status and little merit getting a magnificent kingdom, who instantly collapses, goes to ruin, and retreats. He is unable to support kingship. In the same way, great king, because of this attribute, one living the household life who attains arhatship is not able to support it, and for this reason ordains or attains final nibbana that very day."

"Very well, revered Nagasena, this is so, and I am convinced.

"Revered Nagasena, can an arhat have a lapse of mind- 507
fulness?"

"Great king, arhats are free of lapses of mindfulness, and there can be no lapse of mindfulness of arhats."

"But can an arhat commit a monastic offense, sir?" "Yes, great king." "Concerning what sort of matters?" "In building a hut, great king, and in acting as a go-between, in thinking it is time to eat when it is not time, in thinking one has not been invited to eat when one has been invited, and in thinking food is left over when it is not."

"Nagasena, you say that those who commit offenses do 508
so because of two reasons: disrespect or ignorance. Sir,

ti. api nu kho bhante arahato anādariyaṃ hoti, yaṃ arahā āpattiṃ āpajjatīti. na hi mahārājāti. yadi bhante nāgasena arahā āpattiṃ āpajjati na-tthi ca arahato anādariyaṃ, tena hi atthi arahato satisammoso ti.

509 na-tthi mahārāja arahato satisammoso, āpattiñ-ca arahā āpajjatīti. tena hi bhante kāraṇena maṃ saññāpehi, kiṃ tattha kāraṇan-ti. dve 'me mahārāja kilesā: lokavajjaṃ paṇṇattivajjañ-cāti. katamaṃ mahārāja lokavajjaṃ. dasa akusalakammapathā, idaṃ vuccati lokavajjaṃ. katamaṃ paṇṇattivajjaṃ. yaṃ loke atthi samaṇānaṃ ananucchavikaṃ ananulomikaṃ, gihīnaṃ anavajjaṃ, tattha bhagavā sāvakānaṃ sikkhāpadaṃ paññāpeti yāvajīvaṃ anatikkamanīyaṃ: vikālabhojanaṃ mahārāja lokassa anavajjaṃ, taṃ jinasāsane vajjaṃ; bhūtagāmavikopanaṃ mahārāja lokassa anavajjaṃ, taṃ jinasāsane vajjaṃ; udake hassadhammaṃ mahārāja lokassa anavajjaṃ, taṃ jinasāsane vajjaṃ; iti evarūpāni evarūpāni mahārāja jinasāsane vajjāni; idaṃ vuccati paṇṇattivajjaṃ. yaṃ kilesaṃ lokavajjaṃ abhabbo khīṇāsavo taṃ ajjhācarituṃ, yaṃ kilesaṃ paṇṇattivajjaṃ taṃ ajānanto āpajjeyya.

510 avisayo mahārāja ekaccassa arahato sabbaṃ jānituṃ, na hi tassa balaṃ atthi sabbaṃ jānituṃ. anaññātaṃ mahārāja arahato itthipurisānaṃ nāmam-pi gottam-pi, maggo pi tassa mahiyā anaññāto; vimuttiṃ yeva mahārāja ekacco arahā

when an arhat commits an offense, is it because the arhat is disrespectful?" "No, great king." "Well then, Nagasena, if the arhat commits an offense but does not do so out of disrespect, then the arhat does have a lapse of mindfulness."

"Great king, an arhat does not have a lapse of mindfulness, 509
yet an arhat can commit an offense." "Convince me, sir, with reasoning. What is the reason in this case?"

"Great king, there are two kinds of defilement: ordinary wrongdoing and transgressing the rules. What is ordinary wrongdoing? The ten bad courses of action are said to be ordinary wrongdoing.[101] What is transgressing the rules? That which is improper and unsuitable for renouncers in the world but not blameworthy for householders. It was regarding this that the Bhagavan laid down the monastic rules for the disciples that are not to be transgressed for as long as they live. Eating at the wrong time, great king, is not a matter of ordinary wrongdoing, but it is a transgression in the Victor's dispensation. Injuring plants is not an ordinary wrongdoing, but it is a transgression in the Victor's dispensation. Playing in water is not an ordinary wrongdoing, but it is a transgression in the Victor's dispensation. These are the sort of things that are transgressions in the Victor's dispensation, and so are called transgressions of the rules. One with flaws destroyed is incapable of committing a defilement that is an ordinary wrongdoing, but may unwittingly commit a
defilement that is a transgression of the rules. It is not the 510
ken of every arhat to know everything, great king, for one does not have the power to know everything. The name or family of a woman or a man may be unknown to the arhat, or one may be ignorant about a road on the earth. Yet every

jāneyya, chaḷabhiñño arahā sakavisayaṃ jāneyya. sabbaññū mahārāja tathāgatova sabbaṃ jānātīti. sādhu bhante nāgasena, evam-etaṃ, tathā sampaṭicchāmīti.

511 bhante nāgasena, dissanti loke buddhā, dissanti paccekabuddhā, dissanti tathāgatasāvakā, dissanti cakkavattirājāno, dissanti padesarājāno, dissanti devamanussā, dissanti sadhanā, dissanti adhanā, dissanti sugatā, dissanti duggatā, dissati purisassa itthiliṅgaṃ pātubhūtaṃ, dissati itthiyā purisaliṅgaṃ pātubhūtaṃ, dissati sukataṃ dukkataṃ kammaṃ, dissanti kalyāṇapāpakānaṃ kammānaṃ vipākūpabhogino sattā, atthi loke sattā aṇḍajā jalābujā saṃsedajā opapātikā, atthi sattā apadā dipadā catuppadā bahuppadā, atthi loke yakkhā rakkhasā kumbhaṇḍā asurā dānavā gandhabbā petā pisācā, atthi kinnarā mahoragā nāgā supaṇṇā siddhā vijjādharā, atthi hatthī assā gāvo mahisā oṭṭhā gadrabhā ajā eḷākā migā sūkarā sīhā byagghā dīpī acchā kokā taracchā soṇā sigālā atthi bahuvidhā sakuṇā, atthi suvaṇṇaṃ rajataṃ muttā maṇi saṅkho silā pavāḷaṃ lohitaṅko masāragallaṃ veḷuriyo vajiraṃ phaḷikaṃ kāḷalohaṃ tambalohaṃ vaṭṭalohaṃ kaṃsalohaṃ, atthi khomaṃ koseyyaṃ kappāsikaṃ sāṇaṃ bhaṅgaṃ kambalaṃ, atthi sāli vīhi yavo kaṅgu kudrūso varako godhūmo muggo māso tilaṃ kulatthaṃ, atthi mūlagandho sāragandho pheggugandho tacagandho

arhat would know about freedom, and an arhat with the six higher knowledges would know their own ken. Only the omniscient Tathagata knows everything, great king."

"Very well, revered Nagasena. This is so, and I am convinced.

"Revered Nagasena, buddhas are seen in the world, soli- 511
tary buddhas are seen, disciples of the Tathagata are seen, and wheel-turning emperors are seen. There are found regional kings, gods, humans, rich people, poor people, people doing well, and people doing poorly. There can be found the features of women appearing on a man and the features of men appearing on a woman. There is karma that is either done well or done badly, and there are beings that experience the fruits of both beautiful and wicked karma. In this world there are creatures born of eggs, in water, viviparously, and spontaneously; and creatures with no feet, two feet, four feet, and many feet. There are *yakkhas, rakkhasas, kumbhaṇḍas, asuras, dānavas, gandhabbas,** hungry ghosts, and goblins; there are *kinnaras,* great snakes, *nāga* serpents, winged creatures, wizards, and magicians. There are elephants, horses, oxen, buffalo, camels, donkeys, goats, rams, deer, pigs, lions, tigers, panthers, bears, wolves, hyenas, dogs, jackals, and many varieties of birds. There are gold, silver, pearls, gems, mother-of-pearl, quartz, coral, rubies, cat's eye, beryl, diamond, crystal, iron, copper, alloyed metal, and bronze. There are linen, silk, cotton, hemp, canvas, and wool. There are rice, paddy, barley, millet, vetch, beans, wheat, black gram, mung beans, sesame, and horse gram.

* Various demons, monsters, ogres, and demigods.

pattagandho pupphagandho phalagandho sabbagandho, atthi tiṇa-latā-gaccha-rukkha-osadhi-vanaspati-nadī-pabbata-samudda-maccha-kacchapā, sabbaṃ loke atthi. yaṃ bhante loke na-tthi taṃ me kathehīti.

512 tīṇ' imāni mahārāja loke na-tthi, katamāni tīṇi. sacetanā vā acetanā vā ajarāmarā loke na-tthi, saṅkhārānaṃ niccatā na-tthi, paramatthena sattūpaladdhi na-tthi. imāni kho mahārāja tīṇi loke na-tthīti. sādhu bhante nāgasena, evam-etaṃ, tathā sampaṭicchāmīti.

513 bhante nāgasena, dissanti loke kammanibbattā, dissanti hetunibbattā, dissanti utunibbattā; yaṃ loke akammajaṃ ahetujaṃ anutujaṃ taṃ me kathehīti. dve 'me mahārāja lokasmiṃ akammajā ahetujā anutujā, katame dve. ākāso mahārāja akammajo ahetujo anutujo, nibbānaṃ mahārāja akammajaṃ ahetujaṃ anutujaṃ. ime kho mahārāja dve akammajā ahetujā anutujā ti.

514 mā bhante nāgasena jinavacanaṃ makkhehi, mā ajānitvā pañhaṃ byākarohīti. kiṃ kho mahārāja ahaṃ vadāmi, yaṃ maṃ tvaṃ evaṃ vadesi: mā bhante nāgasena jinavacanaṃ makkhehi, mā ajānitvā pañhaṃ byākarohīti. bhante nāgasena, yuttam-idaṃ tāva vattuṃ: ākāso akammajo ahetujo

There are perfumes from roots, perfumes from heartwood, from sapwood, bark, leaves, flowers, fruits, and perfumes made with all of these. There are grasses, creepers, shrubs, trees, herbs, champion trees of the forest, rivers, mountains, seas, fish, and turtles. All of this is present in the world. Tell me, sir, what is not in the world?"

"Great king, these three things are not in the world. What 512
three? There is nothing in the world, whether cognizant or not, that does not grow old and die. There is no permanence in habitual patterns. And there is found no 'being' in the absolute sense. These three things are not found in the world, great king."

"Excellent, Nagasena. This is so, and I am convinced.

"Revered Nagasena, things generated by karma, things 513
generated by causes, and things generated by the seasons are seen in the world. Tell me, is there anything in the world not born of karma, of causes, or of the seasons?"

"There are two things in the world that are not born from karma, causes, or the seasons. What are the two? Space is not born of karma, causes, or the seasons, and nibbana is not born of karma, causes, or the seasons. These are the two things not born of karma, causes, or the seasons."

"Revered Nagasena, please do not smear the words of 514
the Victor, and do not answer the question without knowing."

"But what, great king, have I said whereby you say to this to me: 'Revered Nagasena, please do not smear the words of the Victor, and do not answer the question without knowing?'"

"What you said about space—that space is not born of karma, causes, or the seasons—is correct, sir. But,

anutujo ti. anekasatehi pana bhante nāgasena kāraṇehi bhagavatā sāvakānaṃ nibbānassa sacchikiriyāya maggo akkhāto, atha ca pana tvaṃ evaṃ vadesi: ahetujaṃ nibbānan-ti.

515 saccaṃ mahārāja bhagavatā anekasatehi kāraṇehi sāvakānaṃ nibbānassa sacchikiriyāya maggo akkhāto, na ca pana nibbānassa uppādāya hetu akkhāto ti. ettha mayaṃ bhante nāgasena andhakārato andhakārataraṃ pavisāma, vanato vanataraṃ pavisāma, gahanato gahanataraṃ pavisāma, yatra hi nāma nibbānassa sacchikiriyāya hetu atthi, tassa pana dhammassa uppādāya hetu na-tthi. yadi bhante nāgasena nibbānassa sacchikiriyāya hetu atthi, tena hi nibbānassa uppādāya pi hetu icchitabbo. yathā bhante nāgasena puttassa pitā atthi, tena kāraṇena pituno pi pitā icchitabbo; yathā antevāsikassa ācariyo atthi, tena kāraṇena ācariyassa pi ācariyo icchitabbo; yathā aṅkurassa bījaṃ atthi, tena kāraṇena bījassa pi bījaṃ icchitabbaṃ; evam-eva kho bhante nāgasena yadi nibbānassa sacchikiriyāya hetu atthi, tena kāraṇena nibbānassa uppādāya pi hetu icchitabbo. yathā rukkhassa vā latāya vā agge sati tena kāraṇena majjham-pi atthi mūlam-pi atthi, evam-eva kho bhante nāgasena yadi nibbānassa sacchikiriyāya hetu atthi, tena kāraṇena nibbānassa uppādāya pi hetu icchitabbo ti.

516 anuppādaniyaṃ mahārāja nibbānaṃ, tasmā na nibbānassa uppādāya hetu akkhāto ti. iṅgha bhante nāgasena kāraṇaṃ dassetvā kāraṇena maṃ saññāpehi, yathā 'haṃ jāneyyaṃ: nibbānassa sacchikiriyāya hetu atthi, nibbānassa uppādāya

Nagasena, the Bhagavan pointed the disciples to the path to experiencing nibbana by hundreds of means. And yet you say that nibbana is not born of causes."

"Great king, it is true that the Bhagavan pointed the disciples to the path of experiencing nibbana by hundreds of means. But he did not point to a cause for the arising of nibbana." 515

"Here we are entering a blindness darker than blindness, Nagasena. Inasmuch as you say there is a cause for experiencing nibbana but no cause for the arising of the phenomenal state of it, we are entering a jungle thicker than a jungle and a thicket denser than a thicket. If there is a cause for experiencing nibbana, then we would also expect a cause for the arising of nibbana. Sir, just as there is a father of a son, then by this reasoning we would also expect a father of the father. As there is a teacher of a student, then by this reasoning we would also expect a teacher of the teacher. As there is a seed of a sprout, by this reasoning we would also expect a seed of the seed. Similarly, Nagasena, if there is a cause for the experience of nibbana, then by this reasoning, we would also expect a cause for the arising of nibbana. Just as there is a top of a tree or a creeper, then we reason that there is also a middle and a root. Similarly, if there is a cause for the experience of nibbana, then by this reasoning we would also expect a cause for the arising of nibbana."

"Great king, nibbana is not something to be produced, and therefore no cause for the arising of nibbana is indicated." 516

"Look here, Nagasena, give me a reason whereby I may be convinced and may know for myself that though there is a

hetu na-tthīti. tena hi mahārāja sakkaccaṃ sotaṃ odaha, sādhukaṃ suṇohi, vakkhāmi tattha kāraṇaṃ. sakkuṇeyya mahārāja puriso pākatikena balena ito himavantaṃ pabbatarājaṃ upagantun-ti. āma bhante ti. sakkuṇeyya pana so mahārāja puriso pākatikena balena himavantaṃ pabbatarājaṃ idha-m-āharitun-ti. na hi bhante ti.

517 evam-eva kho mahārāja sakkā nibbānassa sacchikiriyāya maggo akkhātuṃ, na sakkā nibbānassa uppādāya hetu dassetuṃ. sakkuṇeyya mahārāja puriso pākatikena balena mahāsamuddaṃ nāvāya uttaritvā pārimatīraṃ gantun-ti. āma bhante ti. sakkuṇeyya pana so mahārāja puriso pākatikena balena mahāsamuddassa pārimatīraṃ idha-m-āharitun-ti. na hi bhante ti.

518 evam-eva kho mahārāja sakkā nibbānassa sacchikiriyāya maggo akkhātuṃ, na sakkā nibbānassa uppādāya hetu dassetuṃ; kiṅkāraṇaṃ: asaṅkhatattā dhammassāti. asaṅkhataṃ bhante nāgasena nibbānan-ti. āma mahārāja, asaṅkhataṃ nibbānaṃ, na kehici kataṃ; nibbānaṃ mahārāja na vattabbaṃ: uppannan-ti vā anuppannan-ti vā uppādaniyan-ti vā atītan-ti vā anāgatan-ti vā paccuppannan-ti vā cakkhuviññeyyan-ti vā sotaviññeyyan-ti vā ghānaviññeyyan-ti vā jivhāviññeyyan-ti vā kāyaviññeyyan-ti vā ti.

519 yadi bhante nāgasena nibbānaṃ na uppannaṃ na anuppannaṃ na uppādaniyaṃ na atītaṃ na anāgataṃ na paccuppannaṃ na cakkhuviññeyyaṃ na sotaviññeyyaṃ na ghānaviññeyyaṃ na jivhāviññeyyaṃ na kāyaviññeyyaṃ, tena hi bhante nāgasena tumhe natthidhammaṃ nibbānaṃ

cause for the experiencing of nibbana, there is no cause for the arising of nibbana."

"Then lend an attentive ear, great king, and listen well as I explain the reasoning in this case. Is it possible for a man with his natural strength to go from here to Himalaya, the king of mountains?" "Yes, sir." "Then is it possible for a man with his natural strength to bring Himalaya, king of mountains, here?" "Of course not, sir."

"In much the same way, great king, it is possible to point 517
to the path for experiencing nibbana, but it is not possible to indicate a cause for the arising of nibbana. Is it possible for a man with his natural strength to board a ship and cross the great ocean to reach the far shore?" "Certainly, sir." Then is it possible for a man with his natural strength to bring the far shore of the great ocean here?" "No, sir."

"Similarly, great king, it is possible to point to the path 518
for experiencing nibbana, but it is not possible to indicate a cause for the arising of nibbana. Why is this? Because this phenomenal state is unconditioned."

"Nagasena, is it that nibbana is not conditioned?"

"Precisely. Nibbana is not conditioned, great king. It is created by no one. Of nibbana, one cannot say that it is arisen, that it is unarisen, or that it may be produced; that it is past, future, or present; or that it is perceivable by the eye, ear, nose, tongue, or body."

"Nagasena, if nibbana is not arisen, not unarisen, and 519
not able to be produced; nor past, future, or present; nor perceivable by the eye, ear, nose, tongue, or body, then you are referring to nibbana as a phenomenon that does not exist, and so there is no nibbana."

apadisatha, natthi nibbānan-ti. atthi mahārāja nibbānaṃ, manoviññeyyaṃ nibbānaṃ, visuddhena mānasena paṇītena ujukena anāvaraṇena nirāmisena sammā paṭipanno ariyasāvako nibbānaṃ passatīti.

520 kīdisaṃ pana taṃ bhante nibbānaṃ, yan-taṃ opammehi ādīpanīyaṃ kāraṇehi maṃ saññāpehi yathā yathā atthidhammaṃ opammehi ādīpanīyan-ti. atthi mahārāja vāto nāmāti. āma bhante ti. iṅgha mahārāja vātaṃ dassehi vaṇṇato vā saṇṭhānato vā aṇuṃ vā thūlaṃ vā dīghaṃ vā rassaṃ vā ti. na sakkā bhante nāgasena vāto upadassayituṃ, na so vāto hatthagahaṇaṃ vā nimmaddanaṃ vā upeti, api ca atthi so vāto ti.

521 yadi mahārāja na sakkā vāto upadassayituṃ, tena hi na-tthi vāto ti. jānām' ahaṃ bhante nāgasena, vāto atthīti me hadaye anupaviṭṭhaṃ, na cāhaṃ sakkomi vātaṃ upadassayitun-ti. evam-eva kho mahārāja atthi nibbānaṃ, na ca sakkā nibbānaṃ upadassayituṃ vaṇṇena vā saṇṭhānena vā ti. sādhu bhante nāgasena, sūpadassitaṃ opammaṃ, suniddiṭṭhaṃ kāraṇaṃ, evam-etaṃ, tathā sampaṭicchāmi: atthi nibbānan-ti.

522 bhante nāgasena, katame ettha kammajā, katame hetujā, katame utujā, katame na kammajā na hetujā na utujā ti. ye keci mahārāja sattā sacetanā sabbe te kammajā, aggi ca sabbāni ca bījajātāni hetujāni, paṭhavī ca pabbatā ca udakañ-ca vāto ca sabbe te utujā, ākāso ca nibbānañ-ca ime dve akammajā ahetujā anutujā. nibbānaṃ pana mahārāja na vattabbaṃ: kammajan-ti vā hetujan-ti vā utujan-ti vā uppannan-ti vā anuppannan-ti vā uppādaniyan-ti vā atītan-ti vā anāgatan-ti vā paccuppannan-ti vā cakkhuviññeyyan-ti vā sotaviññeyyan-ti vā ghānaviññeyyan-ti vā jivhāviññeyyan-ti

"Great king, nibbana does exist. Nibbana is perceivable by the mind. A noble disciple practicing rightly with a pure mind, accomplished, upright, without hindrances, and free of material desires sees nibbana."

"Then what is nibbana like, sir? Surely it can be explained 520
with analogies. Convince me with reasons and explain with
analogies just how such a phenomenon can exist."

"Is there such a thing as wind, great king?" "Of course,
sir." "Then show the wind, great king, by its color or shape,
and whether it is small or large, long or short." "It is not
possible, Nagasena, to point to the wind, because wind does
not lend itself to touching or taking by the hand. Still, wind
does exist." "Great king, if it is not possible to point to the 521
wind, then wind does not exist." "I know in my heart that
wind exists, sir, even if I am not able to point to it."

"It is the same with nibbana, great king. Nibbana exists even if one is unable to point to it by its color or shape."

"Excellent, revered Nagasena. The analogy has been well demonstrated and the reasoning well expressed. And so I am convinced that nibbana exists.

"Revered Nagasena, what are the things in this world born 522
of karma, born of causes, and born of the seasons, and what is
not born of karma, born of causes, and born of the seasons?"

"Great king, whatever beings are cognizant are all born of karma. Fire and whatever is produced by a seed are born of causes, and the earth, mountains, water, and wind are born of the seasons. And two things—space and nibbana—are not born of karma, causes, or the seasons. This may not be said of nibbana, that it is born of karma, causes, or the seasons; that it is produced, unproduced, or able to be produced; that

vā kāyaviññeyyan-ti vā. api ca mahārāja manoviññeyyaṃ nibbānaṃ yaṃ so sammā paṭipanno ariyasāvako visuddhena ñāṇena passatīti.

523 ramaṇīyo bhante nāgasena pañho suvinicchito nissaṃsayo ekantagato, vimati upacchinnā, tvaṃ gaṇivarapavaram-āsajjāti.

524 bhante nāgasena, atthi loke yakkhā nāmāti. āma mahārāja, atthi loke yakkhā nāmāti. cavanti pana te bhante yakkhā tamhā yoniyā ti. āma mahārāja, cavanti te yakkhā tamhā yoniyā ti. kissa pana bhante nāgasena tesaṃ matānaṃ yakkhānaṃ sarīraṃ na dissati, kuṇapagandho pi na vāyatīti.

525 dissati mahārāja matānaṃ yakkhānaṃ sarīraṃ, kuṇapagandho pi tesaṃ vāyati. matānaṃ mahārāja yakkhānaṃ sarīraṃ kīṭavaṇṇena vā dissati, kimivaṇṇena vā dissati, kipillikavaṇṇena vā dissati, paṭaṅgavaṇṇena vā dissati, ahivaṇṇena vā dissati, vicchikavaṇnena vā dissati, satapadivaṇṇena vā dissati, dijavaṇṇena vā dissati, migavaṇṇena vā dissatīti. ko hi bhante nāgasena añño imaṃ pañhaṃ puṭṭho vissajjeyya aññatra tavādisena buddhimatā ti.

526 bhante nāgasena, ye te ahesuṃ tikicchakānaṃ pubbakā ācariyā, seyyathīdaṃ: nārado dhammantarī aṅgīraso kapilo kaṇḍaraggisāmo atulo pubbakaccāyano, sabbe p' ete ācariyā sakiṃ yeva roguppattiñ-ca nidānañ-ca sabhāvañ-ca samuṭṭhānañ-ca tikicchañ-ca kiriyañ-ca siddhāsiddhañ-ca sabban-taṃ niravasesaṃ jānitvā: imasmiṃ kāye ettakā rogā uppajjissantīti ekappahārena kalāpaggāhaṃ karitvā suttaṃ bandhiṃsu. asabbaññuno ete sabbe. kissa pana tathāgato

it is past, future, or present; and that it is perceivable by the eye, ear, nose, tongue, or body. However, great king, nibbana is perceivable by the mind, and a noble disciple practicing rightly sees it with purified knowledge."

"This delightful question has been undoubtedly and completely explained, revered Nagasena, and my perplexity is removed. You have joined the ranks of the most excellent and distinguished teachers. 523

"Revered Nagasena, are there beings in this world known as *yakkhas?*" "Yes, great king, there are *yakkhas* in this world." "Do these *yakkhas* move on at death from this state of birth?" "Yes, great king, *yakkhas* do move on from this state." "Why then do we never see the bodies of dead *yakkhas,* Nagasena, or catch the stench of their corpses?" 524

"In fact one does see the bodies of dead *yakkhas,* and the stench of their corpses is emitted. Great king, the bodies of dead *yakkhas* are seen in the form of insects, or in the form of worms, ants, moths, snakes, scorpions, centipedes, birds, or wild animals." 525

"Revered Nagasena, who else when asked this question would reply with such wisdom?

"Revered Nagasena, these were the former teachers of doctors: Narada, Dhammantarin, Angirasa, Kapila, Kandaraggisama, Atula, and Kaccayana of the East. Fully knowing everything concerning the origins of diseases, their source, nature, causes, cure, progression, and what is proven and unproven, all of these teachers could spot at once that 'such are the diseases that will arise in this body.' [102] They composed their treatises having constructed the entire collection all at once. And none of them was omniscient. 526

sabbaññū samāno anāgataṃ kiriyaṃ buddhañāṇena jānitvā: ettake nāma vatthusmiṃ ettakaṃ nāma sikkhāpadaṃ paññāpetabbaṃ bhavissatīti paricchinditvā anavasesato sikkhāpadaṃ na paññāpesi; uppannuppanne vatthusmiṃ, ayase pākaṭe, dose vitthārike puthugate, ujjhāyantesu manussesu, tasmiṃ tasmiṃ kale sāvakānaṃ sikkhāpadaṃ paññāpesīti.

527 ñātam-etaṃ mahārāja tathāgatassa: imasmiṃ samaye imesu manussesu sādhikaṃ diyaḍḍhaṃ sikkhāpadasataṃ paññāpetabbaṃ bhavissatīti. api ca tathāgatassa evaṃ ahosi: sace kho ahaṃ sādhikaṃ diyaḍḍhaṃ sikkhāpadasataṃ ekappahāraṃ paññāpessāmi, mahājano santāsamāpajjissati: bahukaṃ idha rakkhitabbaṃ, dukkaraṃ vata bho samaṇassa gotamassa sāsane pabbajitun-ti pabbajitukāmā pi na pabbajissanti, vacanañ-ca me na saddahissanti, asaddahantā te manussā apāyagāmino bhavissanti; uppannuppanne vatthusmiṃ dhammadesanāya viññāpetvā pākaṭe dose sikkhāpadaṃ paññāpessāmīti.

528 acchariyaṃ bhante nāgasena buddhānaṃ, abbhutaṃ bhante nāgasena buddhānaṃ, yāva mahantaṃ tathāgatassa sabbaññutañāṇaṃ; evam-etaṃ bhante nāgasena, suniddiṭṭho eso attho tathāgatena, bahukaṃ idha rakkhitabban-ti sutvā sattānaṃ santāso uppajjeyya, eko pi jinasāsane na pabbajeyya, evam-etaṃ, tathā sampaṭicchāmīti.

529 bhante nāgasena, ayaṃ suriyo sabbakālaṃ kaṭhinaṃ tapati, udāhu kañci kālaṃ mandaṃ tapatīti. sabbakālaṃ

Why then did the Tathagata—who was omniscient and who did know with his buddha knowledge that there would be future incidents where such and such a rule would need to be laid down concerning certain matters—why did he not determine the rules from the start and declare them? Instead, he laid down the rules to his disciples over time as each matter occurred and when the disgrace was already well known, the fault was broadcast widely, and people were offended."

"Great king, the Tathagata did know that more than 527
one hundred and fifty rules would need to be laid down at some point to these people. However, this occurred to the Tathagata: *If I declare more than one hundred and fifty rules all at once, the people will take fright, thinking that there is so much to be guarded against here that ordaining in the dispensation of the renouncer Gotama is too difficult. Though wanting to ordain, they will not do so. And they will not have faith in my words, and without faith, these people will have an unfortunate destiny. Let me instead lay down the rules when a fault is already well known, instructing them with a teaching on the Dhamma as each matter arises.*"

"Revered Nagasena, it is a wonder and a marvel of buddhas 528
that the magnitude of the Tathagata's omniscience is so great. The meaning has been well explained by the Tathagata in this case, that beings would take fright upon hearing how much must be guarded against, and not even one would ordain in the Victor's dispensation. I am convinced that this is how it is.

"Revered Nagasena, does the sun burn fiercely all the time, 529
or does it sometimes burn dimly?"

mahārāja suriyo kaṭhinaṃ tapati, na kañci kālaṃ mandaṃ tapatīti. yadi bhante nāgasena suriyo sabbakālaṃ kaṭhinaṃ tapati, kissa pana app-ekadā suriyo kaṭhinaṃ tapati app-ekadā mandaṃ tapatīti.

530 cattāro 'me mahārāja suriyassa rogā yesaṃ aññatarena rogena patipīḷito suriyo mandaṃ tapati. katame cattāro. abbhaṃ mahārāja suriyassa rogo, tena rogena patipīḷito suriyo mandaṃ tapati; mahikā mahārāja suriyassa rogo, tena rogena patipīḷito suriyo mandaṃ tapati; megho mahārāja suriyassa rogo, tena rogena patipīḷito suriyo mandaṃ tapati; rāhu mahārāja suriyassa rogo, tena rogena pati-pīḷito suriyo mandaṃ tapati. ime kho mahārāja cattāro suriyassa rogā, tesaṃ aññatarena patipīḷito suriyo mandaṃ tapatīti. acchariyaṃ bhante nāgasena, abbhutaṃ bhante nāgasena, suriyassa pi tāva tejosampannassa rogo uppajjissati, kimaṅga pana aññesaṃ sattānaṃ; na-tthi bhante esā vibhatti aññassa aññatra tavādisena buddhimatā ti.

531 bhante nāgasena, kissa hemante suriyo kaṭhinaṃ tapati, no tathā gimhe ti. gimhe mahārāja anupahataṃ hoti rajojallaṃ, vātakkhubhitā reṇū gaganānugatā honti, ākāse pi abbhā subahalā honti, mahāvāto ca adhimattaṃ vāyati; te sabbe nānākulā samāyutā suriyaraṃsiyo pidahanti; tena gimhe suriyo mandaṃ tapati. hemante pana mahārāja heṭṭhā paṭhavī nibbutā hoti, upari mahāmegho upaṭṭhito hoti, upasantaṃ hoti rajojallaṃ, reṇu ca santasantaṃ gagane carati, vigatavalāhako ca hoti ākāso, vāto ca mandamandaṃ vāyati; etesaṃ uparatiyā visadā honti suriyaraṃsiyo, upaghātavimuttassa suriyassa tāpo ativiya tapati. idam-ettha

"Great king, the sun always burns fiercely, and it never burns dimly."

"If the sun always burns fiercely, then why does it sometimes seem to burn fiercely and sometimes to burn dimly?"

"Great king, the sun has four afflictions, any one of which 530
can obscure it and make it burn dimly. What are the four? A thundercloud is an affliction of the sun, and when obscured by it, the sun burns dimly. Fog is an affliction of the sun, and when obscured by it, the sun burns dimly. Mist and the eclipse god Rahu are also the sun's afflictions, and it burns dimly when obscured by them. These are the four afflictions of the sun, any one of which can obscure it and make it burn dimly."

"It is a wonder and a marvel, Nagasena, that an affliction can arise for even the sun—which possesses so much fiery energy—to say nothing of other beings. These matters could be detailed by no one else unless as wise as you are, sir.

"Revered Nagasena, why does the sun burn fiercely in the 531
winter but not as much in the summer?"

"Great king, in the summer dirt and dust get tossed up and pollen gets stirred up and taken into the sky by the wind. There are dense clouds in the sky, and strong winds blow hard. And all of these various disturbances combined obscure the sun's rays so that the sun burns dimly in the summer. But in the winter, the earth below is at rest, and above, the great clouds stand by; dirt and dust settle, and pollen moves about peacefully in the sky. The sky is cloudless and winds blow gently. Due to the ceasing of all of this, the sun's rays are clear. When free of impairment, the heat of the sun burns excessively. Great king, this is the reason

mahārāja kāraṇaṃ yena kāraṇena suriyo hemante kaṭhinaṃ tapati, no tathā gimhe ti. sabbītimutto bhante suriyo kaṭhinaṃ tapati, meghādisahagato kaṭhinaṃ na tapatīti.

sattamo vaggo.

that the sun burns fiercely in the winter, but not as much in the summer."

"So it is, sir, that when free of all of this, the sun burns fiercely, but when accompanied by clouds and so on, it does not burn fiercely."

End of Part 7.

PART 8

532 bhante nāgasena, sabbeva bodhisattā puttadāraṃ denti, udāhu vessantaren' eva raññā puttadāraṃ dinnan-ti. sabbe pi mahārāja bodhisattā puttadāraṃ denti, na vessantaren' eva raññā puttadāraṃ dinnan-ti. api nu kho bhante te tesaṃ anumatena dentīti. bhariyā mahārāja anumatā, dārakā pana bālatāya lālappiṃsu; yadi te atthato jāneyyuṃ, te pi anumodeyyuṃ, na te vilapeyyun-ti.

533 dukkaraṃ bhante nāgasena bodhisattena kataṃ, yaṃ so attano orase piye putte brāhmaṇassa dāsatthāya adāsi. idam-pi dutiyaṃ dukkarato dukkarataraṃ, yaṃ so attano orase piye putte bālake taruṇake latāya bandhitvā tena brāhmaṇena latāya anumajjiyante disvā ajjhupekkhi. idam-pi tatiyaṃ dukkarato dukkarataraṃ, yaṃ so sakena balena bandhanā muccitvā āgate dārake sārajjam-upagate punad-eva latāya bandhitvā adāsi. idam-pi catutthaṃ dukkarato dukkarataraṃ, yaṃ so dārake: ayaṃ kho tāta yakkho khādituṃ neti amhe ti vilapante: mā bhāyitthāti na assāsesi.

534 idam-pi pañcamaṃ dukkarato dukkarataraṃ, yaṃ so jālissa kumārassa rudamānassa pādesu nipatitvā: alaṃ tāta, kaṇhājinaṃ nivattehi, aham-eva gacchāmi yakkhena saha, khādatu maṃ yakkho ti yācamānassa eva na sampaṭicchi. idam-pi chaṭṭhaṃ dukkarato dukkarataraṃ, yaṃ so jālikumārassa: pāsāṇasamaṃ nūna te tāta hadayaṃ, yaṃ tvaṃ amhākaṃ dukkhitānaṃ pekkhamāno nimmanussake brahāraññe yakkhena nīyamāne na nivāresīti vilapamānassa

PART 8

"Revered Nagasena, do all bodhisattas give away their wife 532
and children, or did only Prince Vessantara give away his wife and children?"

"Not just Prince Vessantara, great king, but all bodhisattas give away their wife and children."

"But do they give them with their consent, sir?"

"Great king, the wives consented, but the children cried and cried because of being young. Had they understood the purpose, they too would have rejoiced and not lamented."

"The Bodhisatta did what was difficult, Nagasena, when 533
he gave away the beloved children from his own breast to the Brahman as slaves. And then he did a second, even more difficult thing: with a vine he tied up his young and tender children from his own breast, whom he loved, and remained looking on even as he watched that Brahman flog them with the vine. Then he did a third, even more difficult thing: when his son freed himself with his own strength from the bonds and ran back frightened, the Bodhisatta again bound him with the vine and gave him away. Then he did a fourth, even more difficult thing: when the children cried out, 'Daddy, this *yakkha* is taking us away to eat us!' he did
not comfort them and tell them not to be afraid. Then he 534
did a fifth, even more difficult thing: he still did not relent when Prince Jali threw himself down at his feet, wailing, and begged, 'Enough, Daddy, please release Kanhajina, and I will go with the *yakkha!* Let the *yakkha* eat me.' Then he did a sixth, even more difficult thing: he had no pity as Prince Jali

kāruññaṃ nākāsi. idam-pana sattamaṃ dukkarato dukkarataraṃ, yaṃ tassa rūḷarūḷassa bhīmabhīmassa nīte dārake adassanaṃ gamite na phali hadayaṃ satadhā vā sahassadhā vā; puññakāmena manujena kiṃ paradukkhāpanena, nanu nāma sakadānaṃ dātabbaṃ hotīti.

535 dukkarassa mahārāja katattā bodhisattassa kittisaddo dasasahassimhi lokadhātuyā sadevamanussesu abbhuggato, devā devabhavane pakittenti, asurā asurabhavane pakittenti, garuḷā garuḷabhavane pakittenti, nāgā nāgabhavane pakittenti, yakkhā yakkhabhavane pakittenti; anupubbena tassa kittisaddo paramparāya ajj' etarahi idha amhākaṃ samayaṃ anuppatto, taṃ mayaṃ dānaṃ vikittentā vikopentā nisinnā: sudinnaṃ udāhu duddinnan-ti. so kho panāyaṃ mahārāja kittisaddo nipuṇānaṃ viññūnaṃ vidūnaṃ vibhāvīnaṃ bodhisattānaṃ dasa guṇe anudassati, katame dasa agedhatā nirālayatā cāgo pahānaṃ apunarāvattitā sukhumatā mahantatā duranubodhatā dullabhatā asadisatā buddhadhammassa; so kho panāyaṃ mahārāja kittisaddo nipuṇānaṃ viññūnaṃ vidūnaṃ vibhāvīnaṃ bodhisattānaṃ ime dasa guṇe anudassatīti.

536 bhante nāgasena, yo paraṃ dukkhāpetvā dānaṃ deti, api nu taṃ dānaṃ sukhavipākaṃ hoti saggasaṃvattanikan-ti. āma mahārāja, kiṃ vattabban-ti. iṅgha bhante nāgasena kāraṇaṃ upadassehīti. idha mahārāja koci samaṇo vā brāhmaṇo vā sīlavā hoti kalyāṇadhammo, so bhaveyya pakkhahato vā pīṭhasappī vā aññataraṃ vā byādhiṃ āpanno; tam-enaṃ

lamented, 'Daddy, your heart must be made of stone, that while we are being dragged off by this *yakkha* into a huge and desolate forest, you watch our misery and do not forbid it.' Then he did a seventh, even more difficult thing: his heart did not split into a hundred or a thousand pieces as the children were led to harsh, cruel, and dreadful horrors and went out of sight.[103] How can a person desiring merit inflict pain on others? Shouldn't he have given away himself instead?"

"Great king, the Bodhisatta's renown went forth among 535
gods and humans across the ten-thousand-world system because he did what was so difficult to do. The gods proclaim it in the divine realm, the *asuras* proclaim it in the *asura* realm, the *garuḷa* eagles proclaim it in the *garuḷa* realm, the *nāga* serpents proclaim it in the *nāga* realm, and the *yakkhas* proclaim it in the *yakkha* realm. And his renown has gradually and successively reached our meeting here today so that we may sit here defaming and disparaging the gift, asking whether it was given rightly or wrongly. Now, the renown demonstrates ten virtues of clever, wise, learned, and intelligent bodhisattas. What are the ten? Their lack of greed, freedom from desire, generosity, giving things up, not turning back, subtlety, magnitude, incomprehensibility, rarity, and the sheer incomparability of the state of being a buddha. And so, great king, the renown demonstrates these ten virtues of clever, wise, learned, and intelligent bodhisattas."

"Nagasena, when one gives a gift that causes pain to 536
another, can the gift result in happiness and be conducive to heaven?"

"Of course, great king. What more should be said?"

yo koci puññakāmo yānaṃ āropetvā patthitaṃ desam-anupāpeyya; api nu kho mahārāja tassa purisassa tatonidānaṃ kiñci sukhaṃ nibbatteyya, saggasaṃvattanikaṃ taṃ kamman-ti.

537 āma bhante, kiṃ vattabbaṃ, hatthiyānaṃ vā so bhante puriso labheyya assayānaṃ vā rathayānaṃ vā thale thalayānaṃ jale jalayānaṃ devesu devayānaṃ manussesu manussayānaṃ, tadanucchavikaṃ tadanulomikaṃ bhave bhave nibbatteyya, tadanucchavikāni c' assa sukhāni nibbatteyyuṃ, sugatito sugatiṃ gaccheyya, ten'eva kammābhisandena iddhiyānam-abhiruyha patthitaṃ nibbānanagaraṃ pāpuṇeyyāti.

538 tena hi mahārāja paradukkhāpanena dinnadānaṃ sukhavipākaṃ hoti saggasaṃvattanikaṃ, yaṃ so puriso balivadde dukkhāpetvā evarūpaṃ sukhaṃ anubhavati. aparam-pi mahārāja uttariṃ kāraṇaṃ suṇohi, yathā paradukkhāpanena dinnadānaṃ sukhavipākaṃ hoti saggasaṃvattanikaṃ. idha mahārāja yo koci rājā janapadato dhammikaṃ baliṃ uddharāpetvā āṇāpavattanena dānaṃ dadeyya, api nu kho so mahārāja rājā tatonidānaṃ kiñci sukhaṃ anubhaveyya, saggasaṃvattanikaṃ taṃ dānan-ti.

"Look here, Nagasena, you need to provide a reason for this."

"Great king, suppose there were a renouncer or a Brahman here of beautiful character and virtue. But he is paralyzed, lame, or afflicted with some other malady. And suppose someone desiring merit were to place him in a vehicle and take him where he wanted to go. Would this result in any happiness for this man? Would there be karma conducive to heaven?"

"Of course, sir. What more should be said? In birth after 537
birth the man would receive, as would be fitting and appropriate, an elephant vehicle, a horse vehicle, a chariot, a land vehicle for land travel, a water vessel for water, a divine vehicle among gods, or a human vehicle among humans. It would generate pleasures for him, and he would go from one good birth to the next because of it. And as a result of just this karma, he would ride the vehicle of magical powers and reach the sought-after City of Nibbana."

"Therefore, great king, a gift given that causes pain to 538
others results in happiness and is conducive to heaven, much as the man experiences such happiness despite causing pain to the oxen.[104] Great king, please listen to further reasoning whereby giving a gift that causes pain to others could result in happiness and be conducive to heaven. Suppose a king were to raise a lawful tax from the country and give a gift by issuing an order. Would the king experience any happiness as a result of this cause, and would the gift be conducive to heaven?"

539 āma bhante, kiṃ vattabbaṃ, tatonidānaṃ so bhante rājā uttariṃ anekasatasahassaṃ guṇaṃ labheyya, rājūnaṃ atirājā bhaveyya, devānaṃ atidevo bhaveyya, brahmānaṃ atibrahmā bhaveyya, samaṇānaṃ atisamaṇo bhaveyya, brāhmaṇānaṃ atibrāhmaṇo bhaveyya, arahantānaṃ atiarahā bhaveyyāti. tena hi mahārāja paradukkhāpanena dinnadānaṃ sukhavipākaṃ hoti saggasaṃvattanikaṃ, yaṃ so rājā balinā janaṃ pīḷetvā dinnadānena evarūpaṃ uttariṃ yasasukhaṃ anubhavatīti.

540 atidānaṃ bhante nāgasena vessantarena raññā dinnaṃ, yaṃ so sakaṃ bhariyaṃ parassa bhariyatthāya adāsi, sake orase putte brāhmaṇassa dāsatthāya adāsi. atidānaṃ nāma bhante nāgasena loke vidūhi ninditaṃ garahitaṃ. yathā nāma bhante nāgasena atibhārena sakaṭassa akkho bhijjati, atibhārena nāvā osīdati, atibhuttena bhojanaṃ visamaṃ pariṇamati, ativassena dhaññaṃ vinassati, atidānena bhogakkhayaṃ upeti, atitāpena upaḍayhati, atirāgena ummattako hoti, atidosena vajjho hoti, atimohena anayaṃ āpajjati, atilobhena coragahaṇam-upagacchati, atibhayena nirujjhati, atipūrena nadī uttarati, ativātena asani patati, atiagginā odanaṃ uttarati, atisañcarena na ciraṃ jīvati; evam-eva kho bhante nāgasena atidānaṃ nāma loke vidūhi ninditaṃ garahitaṃ. atidānaṃ bhante nāgasena vessantarena raññā dinnaṃ, na tattha kiñci phalaṃ icchitabban-ti.

541 atidānaṃ mahārāja loke vidūhi vaṇṇitaṃ thutaṃ pasatthaṃ, ye keci yādisaṃ kīdisaṃ dānaṃ denti, atidāna-

"Of course, sir. What more should be said? The king would 539
acquire many hundreds and thousands of further qualities as a result of that. The king would be become a king above kings, a god above gods, a Brahma above brahma gods, a renouncer above renouncers, a Brahman above Brahmans, or an arhat above arhats."

"Therefore, great king, a gift given by one causing pain to others results in happiness and is conducive to heaven, much as the king experiences the further happiness of such fame by giving a gift despite oppressing people with a tax."

"Nagasena, Prince Vessantara gave an extreme gift when 540
he gave his own wife to become the wife of another and when he gave the children from his own breast to become slaves of the Brahman.[105] And, sir, extreme giving is condemned and censured by those who are wise in the world. Consider how an overloaded cart breaks an axle, overburdened cargo sinks a ship, excessive food causes indigestion, too much rain destroys crops, extreme giving ruins wealth, extreme heat burns, excessive passion makes one go mad, too much hatred gets one killed, extreme delusion brings destruction, extreme greed gets one seized by thieves, extreme fright causes death, being overfull causes a river to flood, intense wind causes lightning to strike, too much fire makes rice boil over, and too much roaming shortens life. It is surely the same, revered Nagasena, with extreme giving, which is condemned and censured by those who are wise in the world. As the gift given by Prince Vessantara was extreme, sir, there could be no desirable reward in it."

"Great king, extreme giving is praised, extolled, and 541
commended by those wise in the world, for whoever gives

dāyī loke kittiṃ pāpuṇāti. yathā mahārāja atipavaratāya dibbaṃ vanamūlaṃ gahitaṃ api hatthapāse ṭhitānaṃ parajanānaṃ na dassayati, agado atijaccatāya pīḷāya samugghātako rogānaṃ antakaro, aggi atijotitāya ḍahati, udakaṃ atisītatāya nibbāpeti, padumaṃ atiparisuddhatāya na upalippati vārikaddamena, maṇi atiguṇatāya kāmadado, vajiraṃ atitikhiṇatāya vijjhati maṇi-muttā-phaḷikaṃ, paṭhavī atimahantatāya naroraga-miga-pakkhī jala-sela-pabbata-dume dhāreti, samuddo atimahantatāya aparipūraṇo, sineru atibhārikatāya acalo, ākāso ativitthāratāya ananto, suriyo atippabhatāya timiraṃ ghāteti, sīho atijātitāya vigatabhayo, mallo atibalavatāya paṭimallaṃ khippaṃ ukkhipati, rājā atipuññatāya adhipati, bhikkhu atisīlavantatāya nāga-yakkha-nara-marūhi namassaniyo, buddho atiaggatāya anupamo. evam-eva kho mahārāja atidānaṃ nāma loke vidūhi vaṇṇitaṃ thutaṃ pasatthaṃ, ye keci yādisaṃ kīdisaṃ dānaṃ denti, atidānadāyī loke kittiṃ pāpuṇāti. atidānena vessantaro rājā dasasahassimhi lokadhātuyā vaṇṇito thuto pasattho mahito kittito, ten' eva atidānena vessantaro rājā ajj' etarahi buddho jāto aggo sadevake loke.

such a gift achieves fame as a giver of extreme gifts. It is much like someone who, though standing within arm's reach, becomes invisible to other people by holding a magical wild root; this is by means of its extreme excellence. And it is similar to a medicine that removes pain and eliminates disease by means of its extremely powerful nature; or fire that burns by its excessive heat; water that extinguishes by its extreme coolness; a lotus not defiled by muddy water because of its extreme purity; a jewel capable of granting wishes by means of its extreme qualities; a diamond that pierces jewels, pearls, and quartz by its extreme sharpness; the earth that holds up humans, snakes, wild animals, birds, water, stone, mountains, and trees by its sheer magnitude; the ocean that never overflows by its sheer size; Mount Sineru that is immovable because of its extreme weight; space that is endless because of its extreme vastness; the sun that dispels darkness by its extreme brilliance; a lion that is free of fear because of its highest lineage; a wrestler who immediately throws his opponent by his extreme strength; a king who rules because of the greatness of his merit; a monk who is revered among *nāga* serpents, *yakkhas,* humans, and gods because of his extreme virtue; and the Buddha, who is unequaled because of his being at the very top. Similarly, great king, extreme giving is praised, extolled, and commended by those wise in the world, for whoever gives such a gift achieves fame as a giver of extreme gifts. Prince Vessantara is praised, extolled, commended, honored, and celebrated in the ten-thousand-world system. And it is because of his extreme gift that Prince Vessantara became the Buddha, foremost in the world with its gods, in our own time.

542 atthi pana mahārāja loke ṭhapanīyaṃ dānaṃ yaṃ dakkhiṇeyye anuppatte na dātabban-ti. dasa kho pan' imāni bhante nāgasena dānāni loke adānasammatāni, yo tāni dānāni deti so apāyagāmī hoti; katamāni dasa. majjadānaṃ bhante nāgasena loke adānasammataṃ, yo taṃ dānaṃ deti so apāyagāmī hoti; samajjadānaṃ pe itthidānaṃ pe usabhadānaṃ pe cittakammadānaṃ pe satthadānaṃ pe visadānaṃ-sankhalikadānam-kukkuṭa-sūkaradānaṃ pe tulākūṭa-mānakūṭadānaṃ bhante nāgasena loke adānasammataṃ, yo taṃ dānaṃ deti so apāyagāmī hoti. imāni kho bhante nāgasena dasa dānāni loke adānasammatāni, yo tāni dānāni deti so apāyagāmī hotīti.

543 nāhaṃ taṃ mahārāja adānasammataṃ pucchāmi. imaṃ kho 'haṃ mahārāja taṃ pucchāmi: atthi pana mahārāja loke ṭhapanīyaṃ dānaṃ yaṃ dakkhiṇeyye anuppatte na dātabban-ti. na-tthi bhante nāgasena loke ṭhapanīyaṃ dānaṃ yaṃ dakkhiṇeyye anuppatte na dātabbaṃ; cittappasāde uppanne keci dakkhiṇeyyānaṃ bhojanaṃ denti, keci acchādanaṃ, keci sayanaṃ, keci āvasathaṃ, keci attharaṇapāpuraṇaṃ, keci dāsidāsaṃ, keci khettavatthuṃ, keci dipadacatuppadaṃ, keci satam sahassaṃ satasahassaṃ, keci mahārājjaṃ, keci jīvitam-pi dentīti.

544 yadi pana mahārāja keci jīvitam pi denti, kiṅkāraṇā vessantaraṃ dānapatiṃ atibāḷhaṃ paripātesi sudinne putte ca dāre ca. api nu kho mahārāja atthi lokapakati lokāciṇṇaṃ:

"Now then, great king, is there any gift in the world that should be withheld and not given even when a worthy recipient is present?" 542

"Nagasena, there are ten kinds of giving that are conventionally considered improper gifts. Whoever gives these gifts goes to ruin. What are the ten? Giving alcohol, Nagasena, is considered an improper gift, and whoever gives this gift goes to ruin. Gifts of festivals, women, bulls, paintings, weapons, poisons, chains, chickens and pigs, and false weights and measures, sir, are conventionally considered improper gifts, and whoever gives them goes to ruin. These are the ten gifts conventionally considered to be improper, and whoever gives them goes to ruin."

"Great king, I am not asking about what is considered an 543
improper gift. Rather, what I am asking is this: Is there any gift in the world that should be withheld and not given even when a worthy recipient is present?"

"No, Nagasena, there is no gift in the world that should be withheld and not given when a worthy recipient is available. When serene confidence arises in their minds, some give food to worthy recipients, some give clothing, some give bedding, some give housing, some give covering cloaks, some give male and female slaves, some give plots of land, some give two- or four-footed animals, some give a hundred, a thousand, or a hundred thousand, some give a great kingdom, and some give even their lives."

"But, great king, if some give even their lives, then why 544
do you so violently attack Vessantara, a lord of giving, with respect to his proper gift of wife and children? Furthermore, great king, is it not a common occurrence and conventional

labhati pitā puttaṃ iṇaṭṭo vā ājīvikapakato vā āvapituṃ vā vikkiṇituṃ vā ti. āma bhante, labhati pitā puttaṃ iṇaṭṭo vā ājīvikapakato vā āvapituṃ vā vikkiṇituṃ vā ti.

545 yadi mahārāja labhati pitā puttaṃ iṇaṭṭo vā ājīvikapakato vā āvapituṃ vā vikkiṇituṃ vā, vessantaro pi mahārāja rājā alabhamāno sabbaññutañāṇaṃ upadduto dukkhito tassa dhammadhanassa paṭilābhāya puttadāraṃ āvapesi ca vikkiṇi ca. iti mahārāja vessantarena raññā aññesaṃ dinnaṃ yeva dinnaṃ, katam yeva kataṃ. kissa pana tvaṃ mahārāja tena dānena vessantaraṃ dānapatiṃ atibāḷhaṃ apasādesīti.

546 nāhaṃ bhante nāgasena vessantarassa dānapatino dānaṃ garahāmi, api ca puttadāraṃ yācanena niminitvā attānaṃ dātabban-ti. etaṃ kho mahārāja asabbhi kāraṇaṃ, yaṃ puttadāraṃ yācante attānaṃ dadeyya; yaṃ yaṃ hi yācante taṃ tad-eva dātabbaṃ, etaṃ sappurisānaṃ kammaṃ. yathā mahārāja koci puriso pānīyaṃ āharāpeyya, tassa yo bhojanaṃ dadeyya api nu so mahārāja puriso tassa kiccakārī assāti. na hi bhante, yaṃ so āharāpeti tam-eva tassa dento kiccakārī assāti.

547 evam-eva kho mahārāja vessantaro rājā brāhmaṇe puttadāraṃ yācante puttadāraṃ yeva adāsi. sace mahārāja brāhmaṇo vessantarassa sarīraṃ yāceyya, na so mahārāja attānaṃ rakkheyya, na kampeyya, na rajjeyya, tassa dinnaṃ pariccattaṃ yeva sarīraṃ bhaveyya. sace mahārāja koci vessant-

practice that a father who has come into debt or lost his livelihood may sell or put his child up as a deposit?"

"Yes, sir, it is the case that a father who has come into debt or lost his livelihood may sell or put his child up as a deposit."

"Great king, if a father in debt or without his livelihood 545
may sell or pledge his child, then did not Prince Vessantara, distressed and anguished at not attaining the knowledge of omniscience, also sell and put up for deposit his wife and children for the sake of his acquiring the treasure of the Dhamma? Great king, Prince Vessantara just gave what others have given and did what others have done. Why then do you so violently disparage Vessantara, lord of giving, because of this gift?"

"Sir, I do not blame the gift of Vessantara, lord of giving, 546
but still, he should have bartered with the supplicant over his wife and children, and given himself instead."

"It would be a contemptible deed, great king, to give himself when asked for his wife and children. For whatever is asked for should be given, and this is the action of good people. Suppose, great king, a certain man were to ask that water be brought, but someone were to bring him food instead. Would that person be rendering him a service?"

"No, sir. Only by giving what one has been asked to bring does one render him a service."

"It is the same here, great king. Prince Vessantara was 547
asked by the Brahman for his wife and children, and so he gave his wife and children.[106] If the Brahman had asked for the body of Vessantara, he would not have defended himself, nor trembled, nor been attached; he would have even given up and abandoned his body. If someone had approached

araṃ dānapatiṃ upagantvā yāceyya: dāsattaṃ me upehīti, dinnaṃ pariccattaṃ yev' assa sarīraṃ bhaveyya, na so datvā tapeyya. rañño mahārāja vessantarassa kāyo bahusādhāraṇo. yathā mahārāja pakkā maṃsapesi bahusādhāraṇā, evam-eva kho mahārāja rañño vessantarassa kayo bahusādhāraṇo. yathā vā pana mahārāja phalito rukkho nānādijagaṇasādhāraṇo, evam-eva kho mahārāja rañño vessantarassa kāyo bahusādhāraṇo. kiṅkāraṇā: evāhaṃ patipajjanto sammāsambodhiṃ pāpuṇissāmīti.

548 yathā mahārāja puriso adhano dhanatthiko dhanapariyesanaṃ caramāno ajapathaṃ saṅkupathaṃ vettapathaṃ gacchati, jalathalavaṇijjaṃ karoti, kāyena vācāya manasā dhanaṃ ārādheti, dhanapaṭilābhāya vāyamati; evam-eva kho mahārāja vessantaro dānapati adhano buddhadhanena sabbaññutaratanapaṭilābhāya yācakānaṃ dhanadhaññaṃ dāsidāsaṃ yānavāhanaṃ sakalaṃ sāpateyyaṃ sakaṃ puttadāraṃ attānañ-ca cajitvā sammāsambodhiṃ yeva pariyesati. yathā vā pana mahārāja amacco muddakāmo muddādhikaraṇaṃ yaṃ kiñci gehe dhanadhaññaṃ hiraññasu vaṇṇaṃ taṃ sabbaṃ datvā pi muddapaṭilābhāya vāyamati. evam-eva kho mahārāja vessantaro dānapati sabban-taṃ bāhirabbhantaraṃ dhanaṃ datvā jīvitam-pi paresaṃ datvā sammāsambodhiṃ yeva pariyesati.

549 api ca mahārāja vessantarassa dānapatino evaṃ ahosi: yaṃ so brāhmaṇo yācati tam-evāhaṃ tassa dento kiccakārī nāma homīti, evaṃ so tassa puttadāram-adāsi. na kho mahārāja vessantaro dānapati dessatāya brāhmaṇassa puttadāram-adāsi, na adassanakāmatāya puttadāram-adāsi, na:

Vessantara, lord of giving, and told him, 'Become my slave,' he would have even given up and abandoned his body, and having given it, would have felt no pain. Prince Vessantara's body was shared by many, great king. Just as a piece of cooked meat is shared by many, Prince Vessantara's body was shared by many. Just as a fruiting tree is shared by many flocks of birds, Prince Vessantara's body was shared by many. Why was this? Because he said, 'Only by practicing this will I attain perfect awakening.'

"Great king, consider how a poor man seeking wealth and 548
wandering in search of riches travels through goat tracks, paths full of sticks, and overgrown jungle paths; he trades on water and dry land, wins wealth with body, speech, and mind, and strives for the sake of gaining wealth. So too, great king, Vessantara, lord of giving and lacking wealth with respect to the riches of a buddha, gave up wealth, grain, male slaves, female slaves, vehicles, mounts, his entire property, his own wife and children, and himself to supplicants for the sake of gaining the jewel of omniscience as he sought perfect awakening. Or consider a minister wanting the state seal, that is, the chancellorship, as he gives away all the wealth, grain, gold, and money in his house. Vessantara, lord of giving, also gave external and internal wealth, great king, giving even his own life to others as he sought perfect awakening.

"Furthermore, great king, this occurred to Vessantara, 549
lord of giving: 'I will give the Brahman whatever he asks for, and thereby be of service to him.' And so he gave his wife and children. It was not that Vessantara, lord of giving, gave his wife and children to the Brahman because of detesting them, or because he no longer wished to see them. Nor did

atibahukā me puttadārā, na sakkomi te posetun-ti puttadāram-adāsi, na ukkaṇṭhito: appiyā me ti nīharitukāmatāya puttadāram-adāsi; atha kho sabbaññutaratanass eva piyattā sabbaññutañāṇassa kāraṇā vessantaro rājā evarūpaṃ atulaṃ vipulam-anuttaraṃ piyaṃ manāpaṃ dayitaṃ pāṇasamaṃ puttadāradānavaraṃ brāhmaṇassa adāsi. bhāsitam-p'etaṃ mahārāja bhagavatā devātidevena cariyāpiṭake:

550 na me dessā ubho puttā, maddī devī na dessiyā;
sabbaññutaṃ piyaṃ mayhaṃ, tasmā piye adās'
ahan-ti.

551 tatra mahārāja vessantaro rājā puttadānaṃ datvā paṇṇasālaṃ pavisitvā nipajji, tassa atipemena dukkhitassa balavasoko uppajji, hadayavatthuṃ uṇham-ahosi, nāsikāya appahontiyā mukhena uṇhe assāsa-passāse vissajjesi, assūni parivattitvā lohitabindūni hutvā nettehi nikkhamiṃsu. evaṃ kho mahārāja dukkhena vessantaro rājā brāhmaṇassa puttadānam-adāsi: mā me dānapatho parihāyīti. api ca mahārāja vessantaro rājā dve atthavase paṭicca brāhmaṇassa dve dārake adāsi, katame dve. dānapatho ca me aparihīno bhavissati, dukkhite ca me puttake vanamūlaphalehi itonidānaṃ ayyako mocessatīti. jānāti hi mahārāja vessantaro rājā: na me dārakā sakkā kenaci dāsabhogena bhuñjituṃ, ime ca dārake ayyako nikkhiṇissati, evaṃ amhākam-pi gamanaṃ bhavissatīti. ime kho mahārāja dve atthavase paṭicca brāhmaṇassa dve dārake adāsi.

552 api ca mahārāja vessantaro rājā jānāti: ayaṃ kho brāhmaṇo jiṇṇo vuddho mahallako dubbalo bhaggo daṇḍaparāyano khīṇāyuko parittapuñño, n' eso samattho ime dārake dāsa-

he give away his wife and children while thinking, *A wife and children are too much for me, and I cannot look after them.* Nor did he, dissatisfied, give away his wife and children out of a wish to throw them out, thinking that he did not love them. Rather, the reason that Prince Vessantara gave the Brahman such an excellent, vast, immeasurable, and incomparable gift as his wife and children—who were beloved, delightful, and as cherished as his own life—was only his love for the jewel of omniscience and for the sake of omniscient knowledge. The Bhagavan, god above gods, also said this in the *Cariyāpiṭaka:*

I did not despise my two children, nor did I despise Princess Maddi. 550
But omniscience is dear to me, and so I gave away those I loved.

"Great king, after Prince Vessantara gave away his wife and 551
children he went into the grass hut and lay down. Because of his acute affection he was afflicted with intense grief and his heart grew hot. Hot gasps and sighs emitted from his mouth since he was unable to breathe through his nose. Tears flowed and became drops of blood issuing from his eyes. It was with such anguish, great king, that Prince Vessantara gave away his wife and children as he thought, *May my path of giving not be lacking.*[107]

"Moreover, great king, Prince Vessantara counted on two considerations when he gave his children to the Brahman. What are the two? *My path of giving will not be lacking and, as a consequence of this, their grandfather will free the children suffering from living in the forest on fruits and roots.*[108] For Prince Vessantara knew this: *No one is able to make use of my*

bhogena bhuñjitun-ti. sakkuṇeyya pana mahārāja puriso pākatikena balena ime candimasuriye evaṃ mahiddhike evaṃ mahānubhāve gahetvā peḷāya vā samugge vā pakkhipitvā nippabhe katvā thālakaparibhogena paribhuñjitun-ti. na hi bhante ti.

553 evam-eva kho mahārāja imasmiṃ loke candimasuriyapaṭibhāgassa vessantarassa dārakā na sakkā kenaci dāsabhogena bhuñjituṃ. aparam-pi mahārāja uttariṃ kāraṇaṃ suṇohi yena kāraṇena vessantarassa dārakā na sakkā kenaci dāsabhogena bhuñjituṃ. yathā mahārāja rañño cakkavattissa maṇiratanaṃ subhaṃ jātimantaṃ aṭṭhaṃsaṃ suparikammakataṃ catuhatthāyāmaṃ sakaṭanābhipariṇāhaṃ na sakkā kenaci pilotikāya veṭhetvā peḷāya pakkhipitvā satthakanisānaparibhogena paribhuñjituṃ; evam-eva kho mahārāja loke cakkavattirañño maṇiratanapaṭibhāgassa vessantarassa dārakā na sakkā kenaci dāsabhogena bhuñjituṃ. aparam-pi mahārāja uttariṃ kāraṇaṃ suṇohi yena kāraṇena vessantarassa dārakā na sakkā kenaci dāsabhogena bhuñjituṃ. yathā mahārāja tidhāppabhinno sabbaseto sattappatiṭṭhito aṭṭharatanubbedho navaratanāyāmapariṇāho pāsādiko dassanīyo uposatho nāgarājā na sakkā kenaci suppena vā sarāvena vā pidahituṃ, govacchako viya

children as slaves. Their grandfather will redeem the children so that they will come back to us. Great king, these were the two considerations he relied upon as he gave the two children to the Brahman.

"Furthermore, great king, Prince Vessantara knew this: 552
This Brahman is old, decrepit, aged, feeble, and broken. He leans on a staff, his life is nearly extinguished, and he has little merit. He is unable to make use of my children as slaves. Would a man with his own natural strength be able to grasp the moon and the sun in their high position and majesty, put them in a basket or a box, stop them from shining, and make use of them as plates?"

"Of course not, sir."

"Similarly, great king, Vessantara resembled the moon 553
and the sun, and no one in this world could make use of his children as slaves. Please hear another reason no one could make use of Vessantara's children as slaves. Consider the jewel treasure of a wheel-turning emperor, brilliant, genuine, cut expertly into eight facets, in circumference like the hub of a wheel four cubits wide. No one is able to wrap it in a cloth, stuff it in a box, and make use of it for sharpening knives. Great king, Vessantara resembled the jewel treasure of a wheel-turning emperor, and no one in this world could make use of his children as slaves. Please hear yet another reason no one could make use of Vessantara's children as slaves. Consider the bull elephant Uposatha showing signs of rut in three ways, pure white, with sevenfold strength, eight measures in height and nine in girth and length, beautiful and attractive.[109] No one would be able to cover him with a cup or a winnowing basket and put him in a cowshed for

vacchakasālāya pakkhipitvā pariharituṃ vā, evam-eva kho mahārāja loke uposathanāgarājapaṭibhāgassa vessantarassa dārakā na sakkā kenaci dāsabhogena bhuñjituṃ.

554 aparam-pi mahārāja uttariṃ kāraṇaṃ suṇohi yena kāraṇena vessantarassa dārakā na sakkā kenaci dāsabhogena bhuñjituṃ. yathā mahārāja mahāsamuddo dīgha-puthula-vitthiṇṇo gambhīro appameyyo duruttaro apariyogāḷho anāvaṭo na sakkā kenaci sabbattha pidahitvā ekatitthena paribhogaṃ kātuṃ, evam-eva kho mahārāja loke mahāsamuddapaṭibhāgassa vessantarassa dārakā na sakkā kenaci dāsabhogena bhuñjituṃ. aparam-pi mahārāja uttariṃ kāraṇaṃ suṇohi yena kāraṇena vessantarassa dārakā na sakkā kenaci dāsabhogena bhuñjituṃ. yathā mahārāja himavanto pabbatarājā pañcayojanasataṃ accuggato nabhe tisahassayojanāyāmavitthāro caturāsītikūṭasahassapatimaṇḍito pañcannaṃ mahānadīsatānaṃ pabhavo mahābhūtagaṇālayo nānāvidhagandhadharo dibbosadhasatasamalaṅkato nabhe valāhako viya accuggato dissati; evam-eva kho mahārāja loke himavantapabbatarājapaṭibhāgassa vessantarassa dārakā na sakkā kenaci dāsabhogena bhuñjituṃ.

555 aparam-pi mahārāja uttariṃ kāraṇaṃ suṇohi yena kāraṇena vessantarassa dārakā na sakkā kenaci dāsabhogena bhuñjituṃ. yathā mahāja rattandhakāratimisāyaṃ uparipabbatagge jalamāno mahā aggikkhandho suvidūre pi paññāyati, evam-eva kho mahārāja vessantaro rājā pabbatagge jalamāno mahā aggikkandho viya suvidūre pi pākaṭo paññāyati, tassa dārakā na sakkā kenaci dāsabhogena bhuñjituṃ. aparam-pi mahārāja uttariṃ kāraṇaṃ suṇohi yena

little calves to keep him. It is like this for Vessantara, who resembled the bull elephant Uposatha; no one in the world could make use of his children as slaves.

“Listen to yet another reason, great king, why no one 554
could make use of Vessantara’s children as slaves. Consider the great ocean, which is vast in length and breadth, deep, immeasurable, hard to cross, unfathomable, and unable to be closed off. No one could close it off and turn it into a single ford. It is like this for Vessantara, who resembled the great ocean; no one in the world could make use of his children as slaves. Listen to still another reason, great king, why no one could make use of Vessantara’s children as slaves. Consider Himalaya, king of mountains, towering five hundred leagues high in the sky, extending three thousand leagues wide, adorned with eighty-four thousand peaks, the source of five hundred great rivers, the abode of multitudes of great beings, bearing many kinds of fragrances, splendidly decorated with hundreds of divine herbs, and seen like a cloud high in the sky. It is like this for Vessantara, who resembled Himalaya, king of mountains; no one in the world could make use of his children as slaves.

“Listen further, great king, for another reason why no one 555
could make use of Vessantara’s children as slaves. Consider how a massive fire burning high on a mountaintop in the dense dark of the night can be seen even far away. Prince Vessantara was like the massive fire burning on a mountaintop—so well known that he could be seen even far away. No one could make use of his children as slaves. Please hear a final reason no one could make use of Vessantara’s children as slaves, great king. In the season of the blossoming of a

kāraṇena vessantarassa dārakā na sakkā kenaci dāsabhogena bhuñjituṃ. yathā mahārāja himavante pabbate nāgapupphasamaye ujuvāte vāyante dasa dvādasa yojanāni pupphagandho vāyati, evam-eva kho mahārāja vessantarassa rañño api yojanasahassehi pi yāva akaniṭṭhabhavanaṃ etth' antare surāsura-garuḷa-gandhabba-yakkha-rakkhasa-mahoraga-kinnara-indabha-vanesu kittisaddo abbhuggato sīlavaragandho c' assa sampavāyati, tena tassa dārakā na sakkā kenaci dāsabhogena bhuñjituṃ.

556 anusiṭṭho mahārāja jālikumāro pitarā vessantarena raññā: ayyako te tāta tumhe brāhmaṇassa dhanaṃ datvā nikkiṇanto taṃ nikkhasahassaṃ datvā nikkiṇātu, kaṇhājinaṃ nikkiṇanto dāsasataṃ dāsisataṃ hatthisataṃ assasataṃ dhenusataṃ usabhasataṃ nikkhasatan-ti sabbasataṃ datvā nikkiṇātu; yadi te tāta ayyako tumhe brāhmaṇassa hatthato āṇāya balasā mudhā gaṇhāti, mā tumhe ayyakassa vacanaṃ karittha, brāhmaṇass' eva anuyāyino hothāti, evam-anusāsitvā pesesi. tato jālikumāro gantvā ayyakena puṭṭho kathesi:

557 sahassagghaṃ hi maṃ tāta brāhmaṇassa pitā adā, atho kaṇhājinaṃ kaññaṃ hatthinañ-ca satena cāti.

558 sunibbeṭhito bhante nāgasena pañho, subhinnaṃ diṭṭhijālaṃ, sumadditā parappavādā, sakasamayo sudīpito,

nāga tree on Mount Himalaya, a soft wind blows and the fragrance of the flowers wafts ten or twelve leagues. Similarly, Prince Vessantara's fame had spread, and the fragrance of his virtue had perfumed thousands of leagues throughout the realms of the gods, *asuras, garuḷa* eagles, *gandhabbas, yakkhas, rakkhasas,* great snakes, *kinnaras,* and Indra all the way up to the Akanittha realm.* No one could make use of his children as slaves.

"Great king, Prince Jali was instructed by his father, Prince 556
Vessantara: 'Son, when your grandfather is giving wealth to the Brahman to ransom you, you may be redeemed when he gives a thousand pieces of gold. But when he is ransoming Kanhajina, let him redeem her by giving a hundred male slaves, a hundred female slaves, a hundred elephants, a hundred horses, a hundred cows, a hundred bulls, and a hundred pieces of gold. But son, if your grandfather takes you in hand from the Brahman by his command, by force, and for free, then do not obey the words of your grandfather, and instead remain subject to the Brahman only.' Instructing him thus, he sent him away. And so, when Prince Jali went and was questioned by his grandfather, he reported this:

> Grandpa, my father gave me to the Brahman, at the price of a thousand; 557
> but the girl Kanhajina is worth a hundred elephants, and all the rest."

"Revered Nagasena, the question has been unraveled, 558
the net of false views has been broken, the contentions of

* One of the highest heavens.

byañjanaṃ suparisodhitaṃ, suvibhatto attho, evam-etaṃ, tathā sampaṭicchāmīti.

559 bhante nāgasena, sabbeva bodhisattā dukkarakārikaṃ karonti, udāhu gotamen' eva bodhisattena dukkarakārikā katā ti. na-tthi mahārāja sabbesaṃ bodhisattānaṃ dukkarakārikā, gotamen' eva bodhisattena dukkarakārikā katā ti. bhante nāgasena, yadi evaṃ ayuttaṃ yaṃ bodhisattānaṃ bodhisattehi vemattatā hotīti.

560 catuhi mahārāja ṭhānehi bodhisattānaṃ bodhisattehi vemattatā hoti, katamehi catuhi: kulavemattatā addhānavemattatā āyuvemattatā pamāṇavemattatā. imehi kho mahārāja catuhi ṭhānehi bodhisattānaṃ bodhisattehi vemattatā hoti. sabbesam-pi mahārāja buddhānaṃ rūpe sīle samādhimhi paññāya vimuttiyā vimuttiñāṇadassane catuvesārajje dasatathāgatabale chāsādhāraṇañāṇe cuddasabuddhañāṇe aṭṭhārasabuddhadhamme kevale ca buddhadhamme na-tthi vemattatā, sabbe pi buddhā buddhadhammehi samasamā ti.

561 yadi bhante nāgasena sabbe pi buddhā buddhadhammehi samasamā, kena kāraṇena gotamen' eva bodhisattena dukkarakārikā katā ti. aparipakke mahārāja ñāṇe aparipakkāya bodhiyā gotamo bodhisatto nekkhammam-abhinikkhanto, aparipakkaṃ ñāṇaṃ paripācayamānena dukkarakārikā

adversaries have been thoroughly crushed, your own views have been well illuminated, the details have been thoroughly refined, and the meaning well analyzed. This is so, and I am convinced.

“Revered Nagasena, do all bodhisattas practice austerities, 559
or was it only Gotama who practiced austerities when he was a bodhisatta?”

“Great king, austerities are not for all bodhisattas, and they were practiced only by Gotama as a bodhisatta.”

“If that is so, sir, then it is not right that there would be differences among bodhisattas.”

“Great king, there are differences among bodhisattas with 560
respect to four conditions. What are the four? The difference in family, in the length of time of their journeys, in life span, and in stature. In reference to these four conditions, there are differences among bodhisattas. However, there are no differences in the qualities of buddhas in beauty, morality, concentration, understanding, freedom, liberated knowing and seeing, the four confidences, the ten powers of a tathagata, the six exclusive knowledges, the fourteen buddha knowledges, and the eighteen characteristics of buddhas.[110] All buddhas are the same with respect to the qualities of buddhas, great king.”

“If all buddhas are the same with respect to the qualities 561
of buddhas, Nagasena, then why did only Gotama practice austerities as a bodhisatta?”

“Great king, the Bodhisatta Gotama renounced the household life when his knowledge had not ripened and his awakening was not ripe. He practiced austerities as he worked to ripen the knowledge not yet ripened.”

katā ti. bhante nāgasena, kena kāraṇena bodhisatto aparipakke ñāṇe aparipakkāya bodhiyā mahābhinikkhamanaṃ nikkhanto, nanu nāma ñāṇaṃ paripācetvā paripakke ñāṇe nikkhamitabban-ti.

562 bodhisatto mahārāja viparītaṃ itthāgāraṃ disvā vippaṭisārī ahosi, tassa vippaṭisārissa arati uppajji, araticittaṃ uppannaṃ disvā aññataro mārakāyiko devaputto: ayaṃ kho kālo araticittassa vinodanāyāti vehāsaṃ ṭhatvā idaṃ vacanam-abravi:

563 mārisa mārisa, mā kho tvaṃ ukkaṇṭhito ahosi,
ito te sattame divase dibbaṃ cakkaratanaṃ
pātubhavissati sahassāraṃ sanemikaṃ sanābhikaṃ
sabbākāraparipūraṃ, paṭhavigatāni ca te ratanāni
ākāsaṭṭhāni ca sayam-eva upagacchissanti,
dvisahassa-parittadīpa-parivāresu catusu
mahādīpesu ekamukhena āṇāpanaṃ vattissati,
parosahassañ-ca te puttā bhavissanti sūrā vīraṅgarūpā
parasenappamaddanā, tehi puttehi parikiṇṇo
sattaratanasamannāgato catudīpam-anusāsissasīti.

564 yathā nāma divasasantattaṃ ayosūlaṃ sabbattha ḍahantaṃ kaṇṇasotaṃ paviseyya, evam-eva kho mahārāja bodhisattassa taṃ vacanaṃ kaṇṇasotaṃ pavisittha, iti so pakatiyāva ukkaṇṭhito tassā devatāya vacanena bhiyyosomattāya ubbiji saṃviji saṃvegam āpajji. yathā vā pana mahārāja mahatimahāaggikkhandho jalamāno aññena kaṭṭhena upadahito bhiyyosomattāya jaleyya, evam-eva kho mahārāja bodhisatto pakatiyāva ukkaṇṭhito tassā devatāya vacanena bhiyyo-

"But why then did the Bodhisatta make the great renunciation when his knowledge was not yet ripened and his awakening was not yet ripe? Surely he should have ripened his knowledge, and then, when the knowledge was ripened, renounced."

"Great king, having seen the women's quarters in disarray, 562
the Bodhisatta felt regret. Regretful, he became dispassionate. Seeing that his mind had become dispassionate, a god in Mara's retinue considered: *Now is the time for dispelling his dispassion.* Stationing himself in the air, he spoke these words:

> Good sir, good sir, do not be distressed. Seven days 563
> from now a divine wheel treasure will appear to you with a thousand spokes, a rim, a hub, and complete in all its parts. And all other treasures found on the earth and fixed in the sky will also arrive of their own accord; orders will be given by your mouth alone on the four great continents surrounded by their two thousand small islands; and you will have more than a thousand sons who are valiant heroes crushing enemy armies. Flanked by these sons, you will possess the seven treasures and rule the four continents.

"But these words entered the ear of the Bodhisatta much 564
as a burning iron stake heated all day long would enter one's ear. Distressed as he naturally was, great king, by the god's words, he grew still more agitated, urgent, and beset with angst. Much as a huge and massive fire already burning would blaze even more when given additional wood, the Bodhisatta, distressed as he naturally was, grew still more

somattāya ubbiji saṃviji saṃvegam-āpajji. yathā vā pana mahārāja mahāpaṭhavī pakatitintā nibbattaharitasaddalā āsittodakā cikkhallajātā puna-d-eva mahāmeghe abhivaṭṭe bhiyyosomattāya cikkhallatarā assa, evam-eva kho mahārāja bodhisatto pakatiyāva ukkaṇṭhito tassā devatāya vacanena bhiyyosomattāya ubbiji saṃviji saṃvegam āpajjīti.

565 api nu kho bhante nāgasena bodhisattassa yadi sattame divase dibbaṃ cakkaratanaṃ nibbatteyya, patinivatteyya bodhisatto dibbe cakkaratane nibbatte ti. na hi mahārāja sattame divase bodhisattassa dibbaṃ cakkaratanaṃ nibbatteyya, api ca palobhanatthāya tāya devatāya musā bhaṇitaṃ. yadi pi mahārāja sattame divase dibbaṃ cakkaratanaṃ nibbatteyya, bodhisatto na nivatteyya. kiṅkāraṇaṃ. aniccanti mahārāja bodhisatto daḷhaṃ aggahesi, dukkhaṃ, anattā ti daḷhaṃ aggahesi upādānakkhayaṃ patto. yathā mahārāja anotattadahato udakaṃ gaṅgaṃ nadiṃ pavisati, gaṅgāya nadiyā mahāsamuddaṃ pavisati, mahāsamuddato pātālamukhaṃ pavisati, api nu taṃ udakaṃ pātālamukhagataṃ paṭinivattitvā mahāsamuddaṃ paviseyya, mahāsamuddato gaṅgaṃ nadiṃ paviseyya, gaṅgāya nadiyā puna anotattaṃ paviseyyāti.

566 na hi bhante ti. evam-eva kho mahārāja bodhisattena kappānaṃ satasahassaṃ caturo ca asaṅkheyye kusalaṃ paripācitaṃ imassa bhavassa kāraṇā, so 'yaṃ antimabhavo

agitated, urgent, and beset with angst at the words of this god. Great king, much as the great earth, naturally moist, green, and grassy, gets swampy when sprinkled with water and becomes still more swampy at the downpour of a great cloud, the Bodhisatta, distressed as he naturally was, grew still more agitated, urgent, and beset with angst at the words of the god."

"But, Nagasena, suppose that on the seventh day the divine 565
wheel treasure had appeared to the Bodhisatta. Would he have turned back if the divine wheel treasure were actually present?"

"Great king, the divine wheel treasure would not have appeared to the Bodhisatta on the seventh day, because the god had spoken a falsehood for the sake of tempting him. But even if the divine wheel treasure had appeared on the seventh day, the Bodhisatta would not have turned back. Why is this? The Bodhisatta had firmly understood impermanence; he had firmly understood suffering and nonself, and attained the withering away of attachment. Great king, the water from Lake Anotatta flows into the Ganga River, and from the Ganga flows into the great ocean, and from the great ocean flows into the mouth of the great chasm under the sea. Do you think that the water in the mouth of the great chasm would turn back, flow into the great ocean, flow from the great ocean into the river Ganga, and then flow from the Ganga back into Anotatta?"

"Certainly not, sir." 566

"It is much the same, great king, for the Bodhisatta, who had ripened his merit for the sake of this birth for four immeasurables and a hundred thousand eons. He had reached his

anuppatto, paripakkaṃ bodhiñāṇaṃ, chahi vassehi buddho bhavissati sabbaññū loke aggapuggalo, api nu kho mahārāja bodhisatto cakkaratanassa kāraṇā paṭinivatteyyāti. na hi bhante ti.

567 api ca mahārāja mahāpaṭhavī parivatteyya sakānana-sapabbatā, na tv-eva bodhisatto paṭinivatteyya apatvā sammāsambodhiṃ. āroheyya pi ce mahārāja gaṅgāya udakaṃ paṭisotaṃ, na tv-eva bodhisatto paṭinivatteyya apatvā sammāsambodhiṃ. visusseyya pi ce mahārāja mahāsamuddo aparimitajaladharo gopade udakaṃ viya, na tv-eva bodhisatto paṭinivatteyya apatvā sammā-sambodhiṃ. phaleyya pi ce mahārāja sineru pabbatarājā satadhā vā sahassadhā vā, na tv-eva bodhisatto paṭinivatteyya apatvā sammāsambodhiṃ. pateyyum-pi ce mahārāja candimasuriyā satārakā leḍḍu viya chamāyaṃ, na tv-eva bodhisatto paṭinivatteyya apatvā sammāsambodhiṃ. saṃvaṭṭeyya pi ce mahārāja ākāso kilañjam-iva, na tv-eva bodhisatto paṭinivatteyya apatvā sammāsambodhiṃ. kiṅkā-raṇā. padālitattā sabbabandhanā-nan-ti.

568 bhante nāgasena, kati loke bandhanānīti. dasa kho pan' imāni mahārāja loke bandhanāni, yehi bandhanehi baddhā sattā na nikkhamanti, nikkhamitvā pi paṭinivattanti. katamāni dasa. mātā mahārāja loke bandhanaṃ, pitā mahārāja loke bandhanaṃ, bhariyā mahārāja loke bandha-naṃ, puttā mahārāja loke bandhanaṃ, ñātī mahārāja loke

last birth and ripened his knowledge of awakening. In six years he would become the omniscient Buddha and the foremost person in the world. Would the Bodhisatta have turned back, great king, for the sake of the wheel treasure?"

"Of course not, sir."

"Great king, even if the world with its forests and moun- 567
tains were flipped over, the Bodhisatta would not have turned back without reaching perfect awakening. Even if the waters of the Ganga were to flow against the current, the Bodhisatta would not have turned back without reaching perfect awakening. Even if the great ocean holding incalculable water were to dry up completely like the water in a hoofprint, the Bodhisatta would not have turned back without reaching perfect awakening. Even if Sineru, king of mountains, were to split into a hundred or a thousand pieces, the Bodhisatta would not have turned back without reaching perfect awakening. Even if the moon, the sun, and the stars were to drop to the ground like clods of earth, the Bodhisatta would not have turned back without reaching perfect awakening. And, great king, even if space itself were to collapse like a reed screen, the Bodhisatta would not have turned back without reaching perfect awakening. Why is this? Because of his having broken every bond."

"Nagasena, how many ties are there binding us to the 568
world?"

"Great king, there are ten ties to the world that bind beings so that they do not renounce, or if they do renounce, they turn back. What are the ten? Mothers are a tie to the world, fathers are a tie to the world, wives are a tie to the world, children are a tie to the world, relatives are a tie to the world,

bandhanaṃ, mittā mahārāja loke bandhanaṃ, dhanaṃ mahārāja loke bandhanaṃ, lābhasakkāro mahārāja loke bandhanaṃ, issariyaṃ mahārāja loke bandhanaṃ, pañca kāmaguṇā mahārāja loke bandhanaṃ. imāni kho mahārāja dasa loke bandhanāni, yehi bandhanehi baddhā sattā na nikkhamanti, nikkhamitvā pi paṭinivattanti. tāni dasa pi bandhanāni bodhisattassa chinnāni dālitāni padālitāni. tasmā mahārāja bodhisatto na paṭinivattīti.

569 bhante nāgasena, yadi bodhisatto uppanne araticitte devatāya vacanena aparipakke ñāṇe aparipakkāya bodhiyā nekkhammam-abhinikkhanto, kiṃ tassa dukkarakārikāya katāya, nanu nāma sabbabhakkhena bhavitabbaṃ ñāṇa-paripākaṃ āgamayamānenāti.

570 dasa kho pan' ime mahārāja puggalā lokasmiṃ oñātā avañātā hīḷitā khīḷitā garahitā paribhūtā acittikatā. katame dasa. itthī mahārāja vidhavā lokasmiṃ oñātā avañātā hīḷitā khīḷitā garahitā paribhūtā acittikatā, dubbalo mahārāja puggalo, amittañāti mahārāja puggalo, mahagghaso mahārāja puggalo, agarukulavāsiko mahārāja puggalo, pāpamitto mahārāja puggalo, dhanahīno mahārāja puggalo, ācārahīno mahārāja puggalo, kammahīno mahārāja puggalo, payogahīno mahārāja puggalo lokasmiṃ oñāto avañāto hīḷito khīḷito garahito paribhūto acittikato. ime kho mahārāja dasa puggalā lokasmiṃ oñātā avañātā hīḷitā khīḷitā garahitā

friends are a tie to the world, wealth is a tie to the world, gain and honor are a tie to the world, kingship is a tie to the world, and, finally, great king, the five sense pleasures are a tie to the world. These are the ten ties binding us to the world, binding beings so that they do not renounce, or if they do renounce, they turn back. They are the ten ties that the Bodhisatta cut off, ruptured, and broke. Therefore, great king, the Bodhisatta did not turn back."

"Nagasena, if, when his mind became dispassionate 569
because of the god's words, the Bodhisatta renounced household life even though his knowledge and awakening were not yet ripened, then why did he practice austerities? Surely the ripening of knowledge would occur by one approaching it while taking all kinds of food."

"Great king, there are ten kinds of people who are degraded, 570
despised, scorned, derided, rejected, treated with contempt, and reviled in the world. Who are the ten? A woman who is a widow is degraded, despised, scorned, derided, rejected, treated with contempt, and reviled. A weak person, a person lacking friends and relatives, a person who overeats, a person who has not been a student in a teacher's home, a person who is a wicked friend, a person lacking wealth, a person lacking proper conduct, a person lacking action, and a person without any occupation are degraded, despised, scorned, derided, rejected, treated with contempt, and reviled in the world. These ten people are degraded, despised, scorned, derided, rejected, treated with contempt, and reviled in the world, great king. This perception occurred to the Bodhisatta as he was bearing in mind these ten conditions: *Let me not be found wanting in action and occupation and so rejected*

paribhūtā acittikatā. imāni kho mahārāja dasa ṭhānāni anussaramānassa bodhisattassa evaṃ saññā uppajji: mā 'haṃ kammahīno assaṃ payogahīno garahito devamanussānaṃ, yan-nūnāhaṃ kammasāmī assaṃ kammagaru kammādhipateyyo kammasīlo kammadhoreyyo kammaniketavā appamatto vihareyyan-ti. evaṃ kho mahārāja bodhisatto ñāṇaṃ paripācento dukkarakārikaṃ akāsīti.

571 bhante nāgasena, bodhisatto dukkarakārikaṃ karonto evam-āha: na kho panāhaṃ imāya kaṭukāya dukkarakārikāya adhigacchāmi uttariṃ manussadhammā alamariyañāṇadassanavisesaṃ, siyā nu kho añño maggo bodhāyāti. api nu tasmiṃ samaye bodhisattassa maggaṃ ārabbha satisammoso ahosīti.

572 pañcavīsati kho pan' ime mahārāja cittadubbalīkaraṇā dhammā yehi dubbalīkataṃ cittaṃ na sammā samādhiyati āsavānaṃ khayāya. katame pañcavīsati. kodho mahārāja citassa dubbalīkaraṇo dhammo yena dubbalīkataṃ cittaṃ na sammā samādhiyati āsavānaṃ khayāya; upanāho makkho paḷāso issā macchariyaṃ māyā sāṭheyyaṃ thambho sārambho māno atimāno mado pamādo thīnamiddhaṃ tandī ālasyaṃ pāpamittatā rūpā saddā gandhā rasā phoṭṭhabbā khudāpipāsā arati mahārāja cittadubbalikaraṇo dhammo yena dubbalīkataṃ cittaṃ na sammā samādhiyati āsavānaṃ khayāya. ime kho mahārāja pañcavīsati cittadubbalīkaraṇā dhammā yehi dubbalīkataṃ cittaṃ na sammā samādhiyati āsavānaṃ khayāya

573 bodhisattassa kho mahārāja khudāpipāsā kāyaṃ pariyādiyiṃsu, kāye pariyādiṇṇe cittaṃ na sammā samādhiyati āsavānaṃ khayāya. satasahassaṃ mahārāja kappānaṃ caturo ca asaṅkheyye kappe bodhisatto catunnaṃ yeva

by gods and humans. Let me then live diligently as a lord of action, honored for action, master of action, virtuous in action, harnessed to action, and associated with action. And so, great king, as the Bodhisatta was ripening his knowledge, he practiced austerities."

"Nagasena, as the Bodhisatta was practicing austerities 571
he said this: 'I am not reaching the highest state of being human, the excellent knowing and seeing worthy of the noble ones, by practicing these severe austerities. Could there be another path to awakening?' Is it that the Bodhisatta became confused with respect to the path?"

"Great king, there are twenty-five things that weaken the 572
mind. When weakened by them the mind does not properly concentrate on destroying the flaws. What are the twenty-five? Anger weakens the mind so that, weakened by it, the mind does not properly concentrate on destroying the flaws. Holding a grudge, hypocrisy, spite, envy, avarice, deceit, treachery, obstinacy, impetuosity, pride, arrogance, conceit, indolence, dullness and lethargy, sloth, idleness, having wicked friends, visible forms, sounds, smells, tastes, tangible objects, hunger and thirst, and aversion are things that weaken the mind, great king, and a mind weakened by them does not properly concentrate on destroying the flaws. These are the twenty-five things causing a weakened mind, and a mind weakened by them does not properly concentrate on destroying the flaws.

"Great king, the Bodhisatta's body was exhausted by 573
hunger and thirst, and when one's body is exhausted, the mind does not properly concentrate on destroying the flaws. In birth after birth for four incalculables and a hundred

ariyasaccānaṃ abhisamayaṃ anvesi tāsu tāsu jātisu, kiṃ pan' assa pacchime bhave abhisamayajātiyaṃ maggaṃ ārabbha satisammoso hessati. api ca mahārāja bodhisattassa saññāmattaṃ uppajji: siyā nu kho añño maggo bodhāyāti. pubbe kho mahārāja bodhisatto ekamāsiko samāno pitu sakkassa kammante sītāya jambucchāyāya sirisayane pallankaṃ ābhujitvā nisinno vivicc' eva kāmehi vivicca akusalehi dhammehi savitakkaṃ savicāraṃ vivekajaṃ pītisukhaṃ paṭhamajjhānaṃ upasampajja vihāsi-pe-catutthajjhānaṃ upasampajja vihāsīti. sādhu bhante nāgasena, evam-etaṃ, tathā sampaṭicchāmi: ñāṇaṃ paripācento bodhisatto dukkarakārikaṃ akāsīti.

574 bhante nāgasena, katamaṃ adhimattaṃ balavataraṃ, kusalaṃ vā akusalaṃ vā ti. kusalaṃ mahārāja adhimattaṃ balavataraṃ, no tathā akusalan-ti. nāhaṃ bhante nāgasena taṃ vacanaṃ sampaṭicchāmi: kusalaṃ adhimattaṃ balavataraṃ, no tathā akusalan-ti. dissanti bhante nāgasena idha pāṇātipātino adinnādāyino kāmesu micchācārino musāvādino gāmaghātakā panthadūsakā nekatikā vañcanikā, sabbe te tāvatakena pāpena labhanti hatthacchedaṃ pādacchedaṃ hatthapādacchedaṃ kaṇṇacchedaṃ nāsacchedaṃ kaṇṇanāsacchedaṃ bilaṅgathālikaṃ saṅkhamuṇḍikaṃ rāhumukhaṃ jotimālikaṃ hatthapajjotikaṃ erakavattikaṃ cīrakavāsikaṃ

thousand eons, the Bodhisatta sought to realize the Noble Truths. How could he possibly become confused about the path in his last life, the very birth in which realization occurred? Still, great king, the thought merely occurred to him that there might be another path to awakening. And previously, great king, when the Bodhisatta was only a month old and his father, the Sakya, was busy with the plowing, he sat up cross-legged in his royal bed in the cool shade of a rose apple tree. Sitting there secluded from sense desires and bad mental phenomena, he reached the first *jhāna,* which is accompanied by thought, deliberation, and the joy and happiness born of seclusion, and remained in it. He reached and remained in the other *jhānas* up to the fourth, as well."

"Excellent, revered Nagasena. This is so, and I am convinced that while ripening his knowledge, the Bodhisatta practiced austerities.

"Revered Nagasena, which is more powerful, goodness 574
or immorality?"

"Goodness is much more powerful, great king, for immorality is not like it."

"I find I cannot agree with this claim, sir, that goodness is much more powerful and that immorality is not like it. Nagasena, in this world we see those who kill, steal, behave wrongly in relation to sensual pleasures, tell lies, sack villages, rob highways, cheat, and swindle. In accordance with their wicked deeds, they get their hands cut off, feet cut off, or both hands and feet cut off; or they get their ears, nose, or both ears and nose cut off; or they are subjected to the gruel pot torture, polished shell shave torture, or Rahu's mouth torture; or to the fire-wreath, flaming-hand, grass,

eṇeyyakaṃ baḷisamaṃsikaṃ kahāpaṇakaṃ khārāpatacchikam palighaparivattikaṃ palālapīṭhakaṃ, tattena pi telena osiñcanaṃ, sunakhehi pi khādāpanaṃ, sūlāropanaṃ, asinā pi sīsacchedaṃ; keci rattiṃ pāpaṃ katvā rattiṃ yeva vipākaṃ anubhavanti, keci rattiṃ katvā divā yeva anubhavanti, keci divā katvā divā yeva anubhavanti, keci divā katvā rattiṃ yeva anubhavanti, keci dve tayo divase vītivatte anubhavanti; sabbe pi te diṭṭheva dhamme vipākaṃ anubhavanti.

575 atthi pana bhante nāgasena koci ekassa vā dvinnaṃ vā tiṇṇaṃ vā catunnaṃ vā pañcannaṃ vā dasannaṃ vā satassa vā sahassassa vā satasahassassa vā saparivāraṃ dānaṃ datvā diṭṭhadhammikaṃ bhogaṃ vā yasaṃ vā sukhaṃ vā anubhavitā, sīlena vā uposathakammena vā ti. atthi mahārāja cattāro purisā dānaṃ datvā sīlaṃ samādiyitvā uposathakammaṃ katvā diṭṭheva dhamme ten' eva sarīradehena tidasapure yasam-anuppattā ti.

576 ko ca ko ca bhante ti. mandhātā mahārāja rājā, nimi rājā, sādhīno rājā, guttilo ca gandhabbo ti. bhante nāgasena, anekehi taṃ bhavasahassehi antaritaṃ, dvinnam-p' etaṃ amhākaṃ parokkhaṃ; yadi samatthosi, vattamānake bhave bhagavato dharamānakāle kathehīti.

577 vattamānake pi mahārāja bhave puṇṇako dāso therassa sāriputtassa bhojanaṃ datvā tadah' eva seṭṭhiṭṭhānaṃ ajjhupagato, so etarahi puṇṇako seṭṭhīti paññāyi. gopālamātā devī attano kese vikkiṇitvā laddhehi aṭṭhahi kahāpaṇehi therassa

bark-dress, black-antelope, meat-hook, coin, lye-pickling, bar-turning, straw-bench, or oil-dousing tortures; or they are eaten by dogs, impaled on stakes while alive, or beheaded with a sword. Some do evil at night and experience its fruits that very night. Some do evil at night and experience the fruit the very next day. Some act by day and experience the effects that day, while others, that very night. Some experience the effects two or three days later. But all experience the fruit in their present life.

"But is there anyone, Nagasena, who gives a gift with great 575
ceremony to one, two, three, four, five, ten, a hundred, a thousand, a hundred thousand, who then, in that very life, comes to enjoy prosperity, glory, or pleasure owing to their morality or to their practice of the Uposatha Observance?"

"Great king, there were four people who gave gifts, took the moral precepts, and practiced the Uposatha Observance, and then attained glory in the Heaven of the Thirty Gods while still in their present lives and bodies."

"And who were they, sir?" 576

"King Mandhata, King Nimi, King Sadhina, and the musician Guttila, great king."[111]

"Nagasena, we are separated from them by many thousands of lifetimes, and they are hidden from our sight. If you can, sir, please speak of what occurred in the present existence at the time when the Bhagavan was living."

"In the present period, the slave Punnaka gave food to 577
Elder Sariputta and on that very day was promoted to the position of a merchant. From then on he was known as Punnaka the Merchant. Queen Gopalamata sold her own hair for eight *kahāpaṇa* coins, which she used to give alms to

mahākaccāyanassa attaṭṭhamakassa piṇḍapātaṃ datvā tadah' eva rañño udenassa aggamahesittaṃ pattā. suppiyā upāsikā aññatarassa gilānabhikkhuno attano ūrumaṃsena paṭicchādaniyaṃ datvā dutiyadivase ye rūḷhavaṇā sacchavi arogā jātā. mallikā devī bhagavato ābhidosikaṃ kummāsapiṇḍaṃ datvā tadah' eva rañño kosalassa aggamahesī jātā. sumano mālākāro aṭṭhahi sumanapupphamuṭṭhīhi bhagavantaṃ pūjetvā taṃ divasaṃ yeva mahāsampattiṃ patto. ekasāṭako brāhmaṇo uttarasāṭakena bhagavantaṃ pūjetvā taṃ divasam yeva sabbaṭṭhakaṃ labhi. sabbe p' ete mahārāja diṭṭhadhammikaṃ bhogañ-ca yasañ-ca anubhaviṃsūti.

578 bhante nāgasena, vicinitvā pariyesitvā cha jane yeva addasāsīti. āma mahārājāti. tena hi bhante nāgasena akusalaṃ yeva adhimattaṃ balavataraṃ, no tathā kusalaṃ. ahaṃ hi bhante nāgasena ekadivasaṃ yeva dasa pi purise passāmi pāpassa kammassa vipākena sūlesu āropente, vīsatim-pi tiṃsam-pi cattālīsam-pi paññāsam-pi purise purisasatam-pi purisasahassam-pi passāmi pāpassa kammassa vipākena sūlesu āropente. nandakulassa bhante nāgasena bhaddasālo nāma senāpatiputto ahosi, tena ca raññā candaguttena saṅgāmo samupabbūḷho ahosi. tasmiṃ kho pana bhante nāgasena saṅgāme ubhatobalakāye asīti kavandharūpāni ahesuṃ, ekasmiṃ kira sīsakalande paripuṇṇe ekaṃ kavandharūpaṃ uṭṭhahati, sabbe p' ete pāpass' eva kammassa vipākena anayabyasanaṃ āpannā. iminā pi bhante nāgasena kāraṇena bhaṇāmi: akusalaṃ yeva adhimattaṃ balavataraṃ, no tathā

Elder Kassapa the Great and seven others. On that very day she became the chief consort of King Udena. The laywoman Suppiya gave a certain sick monk meat broth with flesh from her own thigh. The very next day her wound was healed, her skin had grown back, and she was restored to health. Queen Mallika gave a lump of leftover boiled rice to the Bhagavan, and became the chief queen of King Kosala that very day. Sumana the garland maker worshiped the Bhagavan with eight handfuls of jasmine blossoms and came into great prosperity that day. And the Brahman Ekasataka worshiped the Bhagavan with his outer cloak and received 'all the eights' that same day.[112] All of these, great king, experienced prosperity and glory in their present lives."

"Still, Nagasena, having looked for and examined the 578
matter, you have found only six such people?"

"Yes, great king."

"Well then, immorality is much more powerful, sir, and it is not like goodness. For I have seen on one day alone ten men impaled on a stake because of a wicked deed, or even twenty, thirty, forty, or fifty men impaled on a stake because of their wicked deeds; or even a hundred or a thousand men. The son of a general named Bhaddasala, of Nanda's royal family, engaged a raging battle with Candagutta. In that battle, Nagasena, there were eighty headless bodies among both armies. They say that in one basket filled with heads, a headless body actually reared up. All of the others also came to misfortune and devastation by the fruit of their evil karma. For this reason, I say that immorality is much more powerful and goodness is not like it, Nagasena. And have

kusalan-ti. sūyati bhante nāgasena imasmiṃ buddhasāsane kosalena raññā asadisadānaṃ dinnan-ti.

579 āma mahārāja, sūyatīti. api nu kho bhante nāgasena kosalarājā taṃ asadisadānaṃ datvā tatonidānaṃ kañci diṭṭhadhammikaṃ bhogaṃ vā yasaṃ vā sukhaṃ vā paṭilabhīti. na hi mahārājāti. yadi bhante nāgasena kosalarājā evarūpaṃ anuttaraṃ dānaṃ datvā pi na labhi tatonidānaṃ diṭṭhadhammikaṃ bhogaṃ vā yasaṃ vā sukhaṃ vā, tena hi bhante nāgasena akusalaṃ yeva adhimattaṃ balavataraṃ, no tathā kusalan-ti. parittattā mahārāja akusalaṃ khippaṃ pariṇamati, vipulattā kusalaṃ dīghena kālena pariṇamati. upamāya pi mahārāja etaṃ upaparikkhitabbaṃ. yathā mahārāja aparante janapade kumudabhaṇḍikā nāma dhaññajāti māsalunā antogehagatā hoti, sāliyo chappañcamāsehi pariṇamanti; kiṃ pan' ettha mahārāja antaraṃ ko viseso kumudabhaṇḍikāya ca sālīnañ-cāti.

580 parittatā bhante kumudabhaṇḍikāya, vipulatā ca sālīnaṃ. sāliyo bhante nāgasena rājārahā rājabhojanaṃ, kumudabhaṇḍikā dāsakammakarānaṃ bhojanan-ti. evam-eva kho mahārāja parittattā akusalaṃ khippaṃ pariṇamati, vipulattā kusalaṃ dīghena kālena pariṇamatīti.

581 yaṃ tattha bhante nāgasena khippaṃ pariṇamati taṃ nāma loke adhimattaṃ balavataraṃ, tasmā akusalaṃ adhimattaṃ balavataraṃ, no tathā kusalaṃ. yathā nāma bhante nāgasena yo koci yodho mahatimahāyuddhaṃ pavisitvā paṭisattuṃ upakacchake gahetvā ākaḍḍhitvā khippata-

you heard, sir, that in this dispensation of the Buddha, King Kosala gave an incomparable gift?"

"Yes, great king, I have heard that." 579

"Well then, Nagasena, having given an incomparable gift, did King Kosala receive prosperity, glory, or pleasure from that source at any time in his present life?"

"No, great king."

"Nagasena, if King Kosala gave such a supreme gift and did not receive prosperity, glory, or pleasure from that source in his present life, then immorality is much more powerful, and goodness is not like it."

"Great king, because of its being inferior, immorality develops quickly, while because of its greatness, goodness develops over a long time. This should also be investigated with an analogy. In the Aparanta country there is a kind of grain called *kumudabhaṇḍika* that is reaped and harvested within a month. Rice takes five or six months to ripen. What is the difference, great king, between *kumudabhaṇḍika* grain and rice?"

"The difference lies in *kumudabhaṇḍika* being inferior and 580
rice being great, sir. Nagasena, rice is the food fit for kings, while *kumudabhaṇḍika* is the food of slaves and workers."

"Similarly, great king, immorality develops quickly because of its being inferior, while goodness develops over a long time because of its greatness."

"Be that as it may, Nagasena, whatever develops quickly is 581
much more powerful in this world, and so immorality is more powerful, and it is not like goodness. Suppose a soldier were to join a great battle and seize his enemy by the armpit. Dragging him off, he takes him quickly to his lord. The soldier

raṃ sāmino upaneyya so yodho loke samattho sūro nāma, yo ca bhisakko khippaṃ sallaṃ uddharati rogam-apaneti so bhisakko cheko nāma, yo gaṇako sīghasīghaṃ gaṇetvā khippaṃ dassayati so gaṇako cheko nāma, yo mallo khippaṃ paṭimallaṃ ukkhipitvā uttānakaṃ pāteti so mallo samattho sūro nāma; evam-eva kho bhante nāgasena yaṃ khippaṃ pariṇamati kusalaṃ vā akusalaṃ vā taṃ loke adhimattaṃ balavataran-ti.

582 ubhayam-pi taṃ mahārāja kammaṃ samparāyavedaniyaṃ yeva, api ca akusalaṃ sāvajjatāya khaṇena diṭṭhadhamma-vedaniyaṃ hoti. pubbakehi mahārāja khattiyehi ṭhapito eso niyamo: yo pāṇaṃ hanati so daṇḍāraho, yo adinnaṃ ādiyati, yo paradāraṃ gacchati, yo musā bhaṇati, yo gāmaṃ ghāteti, yo panthaṃ dūseti, yo nikativañcanaṃ karoti so daṇḍāraho vadhitabbo chettabbo bhettabbo hantabbo ti. taṃ te upādāya vicinitvā vicinitvā daṇḍenti vadhenti chindanti bhindanti hananti ca. api nu mahārāja atthi kehici ṭhapito niyamo: yo dānaṃ vā deti sīlaṃ vā rakkhati uposathakammaṃ vā karoti tassa dhanaṃ vā yasaṃ vā dātabban-ti. api nu taṃ vicinitvā vicinitvā dhanaṃ vā yasaṃ vā denti, corassa katakammassa vadhabandhanaṃ viyāti.

583 na hi bhante ti. yadi mahārāja dāyakānaṃ vicinitvā vicinitvā dhanaṃ vā yasaṃ vā dadeyyuṃ, kusalam-pi diṭṭhadhammavedaniyaṃ bhaveyya. yasmā ca kho mahārāja dāyake na vicinanti: dhanaṃ vā yasaṃ vā dassāmāti, tasmā kusalaṃ na

comes to be known in the world as competent and valiant. Consider how a physician who quickly extracts arrows and removes illness is called a proficient doctor. Consider how an accountant who counts very rapidly and quickly shows the figures is called a skillful accountant. Consider too how a wrestler who quickly throws his opponent and flattens him on his back is called competent and valiant. Similarly, Nagasena, whichever one develops quickly, be it goodness or immorality, is much more powerful in this world."

"Great king, the karma of both will be experienced in the 582
future. However, because of its blameworthiness, immorality is experienced immediately in one's present life. Great king, this rule was established by the ancient Kshatriyas: 'Whoever kills living beings deserves punishment. Whoever takes what is not given, goes to the wife of another, tells lies, sacks villages, robs highways, cheats, or swindles deserves punishment and should be put to death, maimed, tortured, or flogged.' According to this, they carefully investigate and then bring about punishment, whether putting to death, maiming, torturing, or flogging. On the other hand, great king, did anyone ever establish a rule to the effect that whoever gives gifts, guards virtue, and practices the Uposatha Observance should be given prosperity and glory? Do they carefully investigate and then bestow prosperity and glory, much as they bind and kill a robber for the deed he has done?"

"Of course not, sir." 583

"Great king, if having carefully investigated a giver, they were to give prosperity and glory, then goodness would be experienced in the present life. But since they do not inves-

diṭṭhadhammavedaniyaṃ. iminā mahārāja kāraṇena akusalaṃ diṭṭhadhammavedaniyaṃ, samparāyeva so adhimattaṃ balavataraṃ vedanaṃ vediyatīti. sādhu bhante nāgasena, tavādisena buddhimantena vinā n' eso pañho sunibbedhiyo; lokikam-bhante nāgasena lokuttarena viññāpitan-ti.

584 bhante nāgasena, ime dāyakā dānaṃ datvā pubbapetānaṃ ādisanti: imaṃ tesaṃ pāpuṇātūti. api nu te kañci tatonidānaṃ vipākaṃ paṭilabhantīti. keci mahārāja paṭilabhanti, keci na paṭilabhantīti. ke bhante paṭilabhanti, ke na paṭilabhantīti. nirayūpapannā mahārāja na paṭilabhanti, saggagatā na paṭilabhanti, tiracchānayonigatā na paṭilabhanti; catunnaṃ petānaṃ tayo petā na paṭilabhanti: vantāsikā khuppipāsino nijjhāmataṇhikā; labhanti petā paradattūpajīvino, te pi saramānā yeva labhantīti.

585 tena hi bhante nāgasena dāyakānaṃ dānaṃ vissotaṃ hoti aphalaṃ, yesaṃ uddissa kataṃ yadi te na paṭilabhantīti. na hi taṃ mahārāja dānaṃ aphalaṃ hoti avipākaṃ, dāyakā yeva tassa phalaṃ anubhavantīti. tena hi bhante kāraṇena maṃ saññāpehīti. idha mahārāja keci manussā maccha-maṃsa-surā-bhatta-khajjakāni paṭiyādetvā ñātikuṃ gacchanti;

tigate givers, thinking, *Let us bestow prosperity and glory,* then goodness is not experienced in the present life. By this reasoning, great king, its feeling is much more powerful and is experienced in the future, while immorality is experienced in this present life."

"Very good, Nagasena. The dilemma could not be so thoroughly resolved except by someone as wise as you. Nagasena, while it was a worldly question, it has been explained in a transcendent way.

"Revered Nagasena, these givers give a gift and dedicate 584
it to the previously departed, thinking, *May they receive this.* But do they actually receive merit from this source?"

"Some receive it, others do not, great king."

"Who receives it, and who does not receive it, sir?"

"Those born in hell do not receive it, great king, nor do those who have gone to heaven or been born as animals. Three of the four classes of ghosts do not receive it: those eating vomit, those tormented by hunger and thirst, and those consumed by craving. But ghosts who live on the gifts of others and those bearing them in memory do receive it."

"Well then, a gift given by donors is wasted and fruitless, 585
Nagasena, if it is made specifying someone who does not receive it."

"Great king, the gift is not fruitless and without merit, for givers themselves will experience the fruit of it."

"Then convince me with reasoning, sir."

"Suppose some people were to prepare a meal of solid food with fish, meat, and alcohol, and go to visit their relatives. If the relatives do not accept the present, does the present then go to waste and get lost?" "Of course not, sir, as

yadi te ñātakā taṃ upāyanaṃ na sampaṭiccheyyuṃ, api nu taṃ upāyanaṃ vissotaṃ gaccheyya vinasseyya vā ti. na hi bhante, sāmikānaṃ yeva taṃ hotīti. evam-eva kho mahārāja dāyakā yeva tassa phalaṃ anubhavanti.

586 yathā vā pana mahārāja puriso gabbhaṃ paviṭṭho asati purato nikkhamanamukhe kena nikkhameyyāti. paviṭṭhen' eva bhante ti. evam-eva kho mahārāja dāyakā yeva tassa phalaṃ anubhavantīti. hotu bhante nāgasena, evam-etaṃ, tathā sampaṭicchāma: dāyakā yeva tassa phalaṃ anubhavanti, na mayaṃ taṃ kāraṇaṃ vilomemāti. bhante nāgasena, yadi imesaṃ dāyakānaṃ dinnaṃ dānaṃ pubbapetānaṃ pāpuṇāti te ca tassa vipākaṃ anubhavanti, tena hi yo pāṇātipātī luddo lohitapāṇi paduṭṭhamanasaṅkappo manusse ghātetvā dāruṇaṃ kammaṃ katvā pubbapetānaṃ ādiseyya: imassa me kammassa vipāko pubbapetānaṃ pāpuṇātūti, api nu tassa vipāko pubbapetānaṃ pāpuṇātīti.

587 na hi mahārājāti. bhante nāgasena, ko tattha hetu kiṃ kāraṇaṃ yena kusalaṃ pāpuṇāti akusalaṃ na pāpuṇātīti. n' eso mahārāja pañho pucchitabbo, mā ca tvaṃ mahārāja: vissajjako atthīti apucchitabbaṃ pucchi; kissa ākāso nirālambo, kissa gaṅgā uddhamukhā na sandati, kissa ime manussā ca dijā ca dipadā, migā catuppadā ti tam-pi maṃ tvaṃ pucchissasīti.

588 nāhan-taṃ bhante nāgasena vihesāpekkho pucchāmi, api ca nibbāhanatthāya sandehassa pucchāmi. bahumanussā loke vāmagāhino vicakkhukā; kin-ti te otāraṃ na labheyyun ti evāhan-taṃ pucchāmīti. na sakkā mahārāja saha akatena ananumatena saha pāpaṃ kammaṃ saṃvibhajituṃ. yathā

it is still the owners'." "In much the same way, great king,
givers still experience the fruit of it. Suppose a man enters 586
an inner chamber but finds before him no door for exiting.
How would he leave?" "In the same way he entered, sir." "So
too, great king, givers themselves experience the fruits of it."

"Let it be so then, Nagasena, and I am convinced: givers themselves experience the fruit. We don't dispute this reasoning. But, Nagasena, if a gift given by these donors does reach the previously departed and they experience the fruit of it, then would it also be the case that a vicious person—someone who kills creatures, is bloody-handed, has a wicked mind and intentions, and has killed people—could dedicate the fruit of the cruel deed he did to the previously departed?"

"Certainly not, great king." 587

"But why, sir, can merit transfer but not demerit?"

"This is not a question that should be asked, great king. Please do not think that just because there is someone present who answers questions that you should ask me what should not be asked, else soon you will be asking me why space is unsupported, why the Ganga does not flow back up to its source, and why humans and birds are two-footed while wild animals are four-footed."

"Revered Nagasena, I am not trying to exasperate you 588
when I ask this. Rather, I ask in order to remove doubt. There are many people in the world who are left-handed or partly blind. Why should they not get an opportunity?[113] And so I ask this."

"Great king, it is not possible to share an evil deed with someone who has neither performed nor assented to it. People convey water even a long way with an aqueduct, but

mahārāja manussā udakanibbāhanena udakaṃ suvidūram-pi haranti, api nu mahārāja sakkā ghanamahāselapabbato nibbāhanena yathicchitaṃ haritun-ti. na hi bhante ti. evam-eva kho mahārāja sakkā kusalaṃ saṃvibhajituṃ, na sakkā akusalaṃ saṃvibhajituṃ. yathā vā pana mahārāja sakkā telena padīpo jaletuṃ, api nu mahārāja sakkā udakena padīpo jaletun-ti. na hi bhante ti.

589 evam-eva kho mahārāja sakkā kusalaṃ saṃvibhajituṃ, na sakkā akusalaṃ saṃvibhajituṃ. yathā vā pana mahārāja kassakā taḷākato udakaṃ nīharitvā dhaññaṃ paripācenti, api nu kho mahārāja sakkā mahāsamuddato udakaṃ nīharitvā dhaññaṃ paripācetun-ti. na hi bhante ti. evam- eva kho mahārāja sakkā kusalaṃ saṃvibhajituṃ, na sakkā akusalaṃ saṃvibhajitun-ti.

590 bhante nāgasena, kena kāraṇena sakkā kusalaṃ saṃvibhajituṃ, na sakkā akusalaṃ saṃvibhajituṃ; kāraṇena maṃ saññāpehi, nāhaṃ andho anāloko, sutvā vedissāmīti. akusalaṃ mahārāja thokaṃ, kusalaṃ bahukaṃ, thokattā akusalaṃ kattāraṃ yeva pariyādiyati, bahukattā kusalaṃ sadevakaṃ lokaṃ ajjhottharatīti. opammaṃ karohīti. yathā mahārāja parittaṃ ekaṃ udabindu paṭhaviyaṃ nipateyya, api nu kho taṃ mahārāja udabindu dasa pi dvādasa pi yojanāni ajjhotthareyyāti. na hi bhante, yattha taṃ udabindu nipatitaṃ tatth' eva pariyādiyatīti. kena kāraṇena mahārājāti. parittattā bhante udabindussāti.

591 evam-eva kho mahārāja parittaṃ akusalaṃ, parittattā kattāraṃ yeva pariyādiyati, na sakkā saṃvibhajituṃ. yathā vā pana mahārāja mahatimahāmegho abhivasseyya tappayanto dharaṇitalaṃ, api nu kho so mahārāja mahāmegho samantato otthareyyāti. āma bhante, pūrayitvā so

can they also move a massive stone mountain by this conveyance wherever they want?" "Of course not, sir." "In the same way, it is possible to share merit, but it is not possible to share demerit. Great king, one can light a lamp with oil, but can one also light a lamp with water?" "No, sir."

"Even so, great king, one can share merit, but one cannot 589
share demerit. A farmer can take water from a tank and ripen his grain, but can he also take water from the great ocean and ripen grain?" "Of course not, sir." "Even so, great king, one can share merit, but one cannot share demerit."

"Well then, great king, why is it that one can share merit 590
but not demerit? Convince me with a reason. I am not blind or without light. Hearing it, I will understand."

"Great king, demerit is limited, while merit is vast. Because of its limited extent, demerit affects only the agent, and because of its vastness, merit spreads across the world with its gods."

"Make an analogy."

"A single small drop of water might fall on the earth, but would that drop of water spread ten or twelve leagues, great king?" "Of course not, sir, the drop of water would only affect the spot where it fell." "Why is this, great king?" "Because of the smallness of the drop of water, sir."

"In the same way, great king, demerit is small, and because 591
of its smallness demerit affects only the agent and cannot be shared. Alternatively, great king, suppose a massive rain cloud would pour down and quench the surface of the earth; does that huge cloud cover everything?" "Yes, sir, having filled up puddles, ponds, rivers, tributaries, gorges, mountain crevices, lakes, tanks, wells, and lotus pools, the

mahāmegho sobbha-sara-sarita-sākhā-kandara-padara-daha-taḷāka-udapāna-pokkharaṇiyo dasa pi dvādasa pi yojanāni ajjhotthareyyāti. kena kāraṇena mahārājāti. mahantattā bhante meghassāti. evam-eva kho mahārāja kusalaṃ bahukaṃ, bahukattā sakkā devamanussehi pi saṃvibhajitun-ti.

592 bhante nāgasena, kena kāraṇena akusalaṃ thokaṃ, kusalaṃ bahutaran-ti. idha mahārāja yo koci dānaṃ deti sīlaṃ samādiyati uposathakammaṃ karoti, so haṭṭho pahaṭṭho hasito pahasito pamudito pasannamānaso vedajāto hoti; tassa aparāparaṃ pīti uppajjati, pītimanassa bhiyyo bhiyyo kusalaṃ pavaḍḍhati. yathā mahārāja udapāne bahusalilasampuṇṇe ekena desena udakaṃ paviseyya ekena nikkhameyya, nikkhamante pi aparāparaṃ uppajjati, na sakkā hoti khayaṃ pāpetuṃ; evam-eva kho mahārāja kusalaṃ bhiyyo bhiyyo pavaḍḍhati. vassasate pi ce mahārāja puriso kataṃ kusalaṃ āvajjeyya, āvajjite āvajjite bhiyyo bhiyyo kusalaṃ pavaḍḍhati, tassa taṃ kusalaṃ sakkā hoti yathicchakehi saddhiṃ saṃvibhajituṃ. idam ettha mahārāja kāraṇaṃ yena kāraṇena kusalaṃ bahutaraṃ.

593 akusalaṃ pana mahārāja karonto pacchā vippaṭisārī hoti, vippaṭisārino cittaṃ patilīyati patikuṭati pativaṭṭati, na sampasārīyati, socati tappati hāyati khīyati, na parivaḍḍhati, tatth' eva pariyādiyati. yathā mahārāja sukkhāya nadiyā mahāpuḷināya unnatāvanatāya kuṭila-saṅkuṭilāya uparito parittaṃ udakaṃ āgacchantaṃ hāyati khīyati, na parivaḍḍhati, tatth' eva pariyādiyati; evam-eva kho mahārāja akusalaṃ karontassa cittaṃ patilīyati patikuṭati pativaṭṭati, na sampasārīyati, socati tappati hāyati khīyati, na parivaḍḍhati, tatth' eva pariyādiyati. idam-ettha mahārāja

huge rain cloud would cover ten or twelve leagues." "Why is this, great king?" "Because of the vastness of the rain cloud, sir." "Just so, great king, merit is vast and because of its vastness, merit can be shared with gods and humans."

"But why is it that demerit is limited, Nagasena, and merit 592
vast?"

"Great king, consider the case of someone who gives gifts, takes the moral precepts, and practices the Uposatha Observance, and becomes excited, happy, smiling, laughing, delighted, pleased, and filled with enthusiasm. Joy occurs again and again and merit increases more and more for one with a joyful mind. Water may enter a cistern already full of water through one spot and flow out through another; but where it flows out, it fills up again and cannot diminish. Similarly, great king, merit grows greater and greater. Suppose a man would turn his attention to merit made, even over a hundred years, and each time he attends to it, the merit increases more and more. His merit can be shared with whomever he wants. In this way and for this reason, great king, merit is more powerful.

"However, great king, someone who does something 593
immoral later regrets it; the mind of a remorseful person recoils, shrinks back, and turns away rather than reaching out, and it grieves, burns, dries up, wastes away, and is exhausted then and there. When a small amount of water lands on a dry riverbed with large sandy banks rising and falling and twisting and turning, it shrivels and wastes away; it does not increase, but becomes exhausted then and there. Similarly, great king, the mind of someone who has done something immoral recoils, shrinks back, and turns away

kāraṇaṃ yena kāraṇena akusalaṃ thokan-ti. sādhu bhante nāgasena, evametaṃ, tathā sampaṭicchāmīti.

594 bhante nāgasena, imasmiṃ loke naranāriyo supinaṃ passanti kalyāṇam-pi pāpakam-pi, diṭṭhapubbam-pi adiṭṭhapubbam-pi, katapubbam-pi akatapubbam-pi, khemam-pi sabhayam-pi, dūre pi santike pi, bahuvidhāni pi anekavaṇṇasahassāni dissanti. kiñ-c' etaṃ supinaṃ nāma, ko c' etaṃ passatīti.

595 nimittam-etaṃ mahārāja supinaṃ nāma yaṃ cittassa āpātham-upagacchati. cha-y-ime mahārāja supinaṃ passanti: vātiko supinaṃ passati, pittiko supinaṃ passati, semhiko supinaṃ passati, devatūpasaṃhārato supinaṃ passati, samudāciṇṇato supinaṃ passati, pubbanimittato supinaṃ passati. tatra mahārāja yaṃ pubbanimittato supinaṃ passati taṃ yeva saccaṃ, avasesaṃ micchā ti. bhante nāgasena, yo pubbanimittato supinaṃ passati, kiṃ tassa cittaṃ sayaṃ gantvā taṃ nimittaṃ vicināti, taṃ vā nimittaṃ cittassa āpātham-upagacchati, añño vā āgantvā tassa ārocetīti.

596 na mahārāja tassa cittaṃ sayaṃ gantvā taṃ nimittaṃ vicināti, nāpi añño koci āgantvā tassa āroceti, atha kho taṃ yeva nimittaṃ cittassa āpātham-upagacchati. yathā mahārāja ādāso na sayaṃ kuhiñci gantvā chāyaṃ vicināti, nāpi añño koci chāyaṃ ānetvā ādāsaṃ āropeti, atha kho yato kutoci chāyā āgantvā ādāsassa āpātham-upagacchati; evam-eva kho mahārāja na tassa cittaṃ sayaṃ gantvā taṃ nimittaṃ

rather than reaching out, and it grieves, burns, dries up, wastes away, and becomes exhausted then and there. This is the reasoning, great king, for why demerit is limited."

"Very well, revered Nagasena, this is so, and I am convinced.

"Revered Nagasena, in this world men and women see 594
dreams that are beautiful and wicked, that are about things seen before and things never before seen, about things they have done and things they have not done, that are peaceful and frightening, remote and close up, and in which many forms and thousands of colors appear. What is this thing we call a 'dream'? And who sees it?"

"Great king, a dream is a sign that appears in the mind's 595
field of perception. There are six people who see dreams, great king: one with a preponderance of the windy humor sees dreams, as well as one with the bilious humor and one with the phlegmatic humor; one sees dreams because of being possessed by a god, because of usual habits, and because of receiving a prophetic sign. Among these, great king, only the dream of receiving a prophetic sign is true, and the rest are false."

"Nagasena, if someone receiving a prophetic sign sees a dream, does the mind itself go and seek out the sign, does the sign appear in the mind's field of perception, or does something come and inform the mind of it?"

"Great king, one's mind does not itself go and seek out the 596
sign, nor does something else arrive and inform it. Rather, the sign just appears in the mind's field of perception. It is like a mirror that does not go anywhere seeking out a reflection; nor does someone else bring a reflection and inform the mirror. Rather, from wherever a reflection might

vicināti, nāpi añño koci āgantvā āroceti, atha kho yato kutoci nimittaṃ āgantvā cittassa āpātham-upagacchatīti.

597 bhante nāgasena, yan-taṃ cittaṃ supinaṃ passati, api nu taṃ cittaṃ jānāti: evaṃ nāma vipāko bhavissati khemaṃ vā bhayaṃ vā ti. na hi mahārāja taṃ cittaṃ jānāti: evaṃ vipāko bhavissati khemaṃ vā bhayaṃ vā ti; nimitte pana uppanne aññesaṃ katheti, tato te atthaṃ kathentīti. iṅgha bhante nāgasena kāraṇaṃ dassehīti.

598 yathā mahārāja sarīre tilakā piḷakā daddūni uṭṭhahanti lābhāya vā alābhāya vā yasāya vā ayasāya vā nindāya vā pasaṃsāya vā sukhāya vā dukkhāya vā, api nu tā mahārāja tilakā piḷakā jānitvā uppajjanti: imaṃ nāma mayaṃ atthaṃ nipphādessāmāti. na hi bhante, yādise tā okāse piḷakā sambhavanti, tattha tā piḷakā disvā nemittakā byākaronti: evaṃ nāma vipāko bhavissatīti. evam-eva kho mahārāja yan-taṃ cittaṃ supinaṃ passati na taṃ cittaṃ jānāti: evaṃ nāma vipāko bhavissati khemaṃ vā bhayaṃ vā ti; nimitte pana uppanne aññesaṃ katheti, tato te atthaṃ kathentīti.

599 bhante nāgasena, yo supinaṃ passati so niddāyanto passati udāhu jagganto passatīti. yo so mahārāja supinaṃ passati na so niddāyanto passati nāpi jagganto passati, api ca okkante middhe asampatte bhavaṅge etth' antare supinaṃ passati. middhasamārūḷhassa mahārāja cittaṃ bhavaṅgagataṃ hoti, bhavaṅgagataṃ cittaṃ nappavattati, appavattaṃ cittaṃ sukhadukkhaṃ na-ppajānāti, appaṭivijānantassa supino

come, it just appears in the mirror's range. Similarly, great king, the mind does not itself go and seek out the sign, nor does someone arrive and inform it. Rather, from wherever the sign comes, it just appears in the mind's field of perception."

"Nagasena, when the mind sees a dream, does the mind 597
also know, *Such and such a result, whether peaceful or frightening, will occur?*"

"No, sir, the mind does not know that such and such a result, peaceful or frightening, will occur. But when the sign has appeared and one reports it to others, they explain the meaning of it."

"Come now, sir, please explain the reasoning."

"Great king, consider how moles, boils, and skin pigmen- 598
tation may appear on the body, whether for gain or loss, glory or obscurity, blame or praise, happiness or suffering. Do the moles and boils know as they appear, *We will bring about this object?*"

"Of course not, sir. But fortune tellers will see where these boils occur and explain that such and such will be the result."

"Similarly, great king, a mind that sees a dream does not know that such and such peaceful or frightening thing will occur. But when the sign has appeared and is reported to others, they explain the meaning of it."

"Nagasena, does one see a dream while asleep or awake?" 599

"Great king, one who sees a dream is neither asleep nor awake but rather in between, as one falls asleep but before reaching the life-continuum consciousness.[114] It is here in this interval that one sees the dream. The mind of one fallen asleep enters the life-continuum consciousness, and

na hoti, pavattamāne cite supinaṃ passati. yathā mahārāja timire andhakāre appabhāse suparisuddhe pi ādāse chāyā na dissati, evam-eva kho mahārāja middhasamārūḷhe citte bhavaṅgagate tiṭṭhamāne pi sarīre cittaṃ appavattaṃ hoti, appavatte citte supinaṃ na passati.

600 yathā mahārāja ādāso evaṃ sarīraṃ daṭṭhabbaṃ, yathā andhakāro evaṃ middhaṃ daṭṭhabbaṃ, yathā āloko evaṃ cittaṃ daṭṭhabbaṃ. yathā vā pana mahārāja mahikotthaṭassa suriyassa pabhā na dissati, santā yeva suriyarasmi appavattā hoti, appavattāya suriyarasmiyā āloko na hoti; evam-eva kho mahārāja middhasamārūḷhassa cittaṃ bhavaṅgagataṃ hoti, bhavaṅgagataṃ cittaṃ nappavattati, appavatte citte supinaṃ na passati. yathā mahārāja suriyo evaṃ sarīraṃ daṭṭhabbaṃ, yathā mahikottharaṇaṃ evaṃ middhaṃ daṭṭhabbaṃ, yathā suriyarasmi evaṃ cittaṃ daṭṭhabbaṃ.

601 dvinnaṃ mahārāja sante pi sarīre cittaṃ appavattaṃ hoti: middhasamārūḷhassa bhavaṅgagatassa sante pi sarīre cittaṃ appavattaṃ hoti, nirodhasamāpannassa sante pi sarīre cittaṃ appavattaṃ hoti. jāgarantassa mahārāja cittaṃ lolaṃ hoti vivaṭaṃ pākaṭaṃ anibaddhaṃ, evarūpassa citte nimittaṃ āpāthaṃ na upeti. yathā mahārāja purisaṃ vivaṭaṃ pākaṭaṃ akiriyaṃ arahassaṃ rahassakāmā parivajjenti, evam-eva kho mahārāja jāgarantassa dibbo attho āpāthaṃ na upeti, tasmā

the mind in the life-continuum consciousness is not active; the inactive mind does not know pleasure or pain. There is no dreaming for one who does not recognize it, for it is while the mind is active that one sees a dream. One does not see a reflection even in a well-polished mirror, great king, in utter darkness where there is no light. So too one does not see a dream while the mind is inactive, at the time when the mind of one fallen asleep has entered the life-
continuum consciousness, even if the body is resting. The 600
body should be understood as similar to the mirror, great king, sleep should be understood as the darkness, and the mind should be understood as that which sees. Light from the sun enveloped by fog cannot be seen. Though the sun's rays are present, they are not active, and there is no light when the sun's rays are inactive. Similarly, the mind of one who has fallen asleep enters the life-continuum consciousness, and the mind in the life-continuum consciousness is not active; while the mind is inactive one does not see dreams. The body should be understood as similar to the sun, great king, sleep should be understood to be like the enveloping fog, and the mind should be understood to be like the rays of the sun.

"Great king, there are two circumstances in which, though 601
the body is present, the mind is inactive. In the first, the mind is inactive while the body is present for one who has fallen asleep and entered the life-continuum consciousness. In the second, the mind is inactive while the body is still present for one who has attained 'stopping.' For someone who is awake, the mind is wavering, open, uncontrolled, and unstable. For such a person, a sign does not appear in the mind's field of

jāgaranto supinaṃ na passati. yathā vā pana mahārāja bhikkhuṃ bhinnājīvaṃ anācāraṃ pāpamittaṃ dussīlaṃ kusītaṃ hīnaviriyaṃ kusalā bodhapakkhiyā dhammā āpāthaṃ na upenti, evam-eva kho mahārāja jāgarantassa dibbo attho āpāthaṃ na upeti, tasmā jāgaranto supinaṃ na passatīti.

602 bhante nāgasena, atthi middhassa ādi-majjha-pari-yosānan-ti. āma mahārāja, atthi middhassa ādi, atthi majjhaṃ, atthi pariyosānan-ti. katamaṃ ādi, katamaṃ majjhaṃ, katamaṃ pariyosānan-ti. yo mahārāja kāyassa onāho pariyonāho dubbalyaṃ mandatā akammaññatā kāyassa, ayaṃ middhassa ādi; yo mahārāja kapiniddāpareto vokiṇṇakaṃ jaggati, idaṃ middhassa majjhaṃ; bhavaṅgagati pariyosānaṃ. majjhūpagato mahārāja kapiniddāpareto supinam passati. yathā mahārāja koci yatacārī samāhitacitto ṭhitadhammo acalabuddhi pahīnakotūhalasaddaṃ vanam-ajjhogāhitvā sukhumaṃ atthaṃ cintayati, na ca so tattha middhaṃ okkamati, so tattha samāhito ekaggacitto sukhumaṃ atthaṃ paṭivijjhati; evam-eva kho mahārāja jāgaro na middhasamāpanno ajjhupagato kapiniddaṃ kapiniddāpareto supinaṃ passati. yathā mahārāja kotūhalasaddo evaṃ jāgaraṇaṃ daṭṭhabbaṃ, yathā vivittaṃ vanaṃ evaṃ kapiniddāpareto daṭṭhabbo, yathā so kotūhalasaddaṃ ohāya middhaṃ

perception. Great king, just as people who want to keep secrets avoid a person who is open, uncontrolled, useless, and indiscreet, so too divine purpose does not appear in the field of perception for someone awake, and so one does not see dreams while awake. Just as good phenomenal states conducive to awakening do not appear in the field of perception of a monk whose livelihood is compromised, who lacks proper conduct, who is a friend of the wicked, who is immoral, indolent, and lacking any exertion, divine purpose does not appear in the field of perception of someone who is awake, and so one does not see dreams while awake."

"Nagasena, is there a beginning, middle, and end of sleep?" 602

"Yes, great king, there is a beginning, a middle, and an end of sleep."

"What are the beginning, middle, and end?"

"The beginning of sleep, great king, is a covering and enveloping of the body, and a weakness, dullness, and inertness of the body. The middle of sleep is a mixed stage when one is overcome with 'monkey sleep.'[115] The end is when one has entered the life-continuum consciousness. One sees a dream in the middle stage, when one is overcome with monkey sleep, great king. It is much like someone whose conduct is restrained, mind is composed, mental phenomena are steadfast, and intellect is unruffled, who has plunged into the woods away from all the noise and commotion to ponder a subtle matter. He does not fall fully asleep there, but it is there that he comprehends the subtle matter while composed and focused. Similarly, someone awake and not fully asleep who enters monkey sleep sees a dream when overcome by monkey sleep. The waking state should be

vivajjetvā majjhattabhūto sukhumaṃ atthaṃ paṭivijjhati, evaṃ jāgaro na middhasamāpanno kapiniddāpareto supinaṃ passatīti. sādhu bhante nāgasena, evam-etaṃ, tathā sampaṭicchāmīti.

603 bhante nāgasena, ye te sattā maranti, sabbe te kāle yeva maranti, udāhu akāle pi marantīti. atthi mahārāja kāle pi maraṇaṃ, atthi akāle pi maraṇan-ti. ke te bhante nāgasena kāle maranti, ke akāle marantīti. diṭṭhapubbā pana mahārāja tayā ambarukkhā vā jamburukkhā vā aññasmā vā pana phalarukkhā phalāni patantāni āmāni ca pakkāni cāti. āma bhante ti. yāni tāni mahārāja phalāni rukkhato patanti sabbāni tāni kāle yeva patanti udāhu akāle pīti. yāni tāni bhante nāgasena phalāni paripakkāni vilīnāni patanti sabbāni tāni kāle patanti; yāni pana tāni avasesāni phalāni tesu kānici kimividdhāni patanti, kānici lakuṭahatāni patanti, kānici vātapahaṭāni patanti, kānici antopūtikāni hutvā patanti, sabbāni tāni akāle patantīti.

604 evam eva kho mahārāja ye te jarāvegahatā maranti te yeva kāle maranti; avasesā keci kammapatibāḷhā maranti, keci gatipatibāḷhā, keci kiriyapatibāḷhā marantīti. bhante nāgasena, ye te kammapatibāḷhā maranti, ye pi te gatipatibāḷhā maranti, ye pi te kiriyapatibāḷhā maranti, ye pi te jarāvegapatibāḷhā maranti, sabbe te kāle yeva maranti; yo

understood as the noise and commotion, and the monkey sleep should be understood as the private woods. The person overcome with monkey sleep—still partly awake and not fully asleep—sees a dream much as the person who leaves the noise and commotion but doesn't fall asleep can comprehend a subtle matter while staying in between."

"Very good, revered Nagasena. This is so, and I am persuaded.

"Revered Nagasena, when beings die, do they die only at 603
the proper time, or do they also die in an untimely way?"

"There are timely deaths and untimely deaths, great king."

"Nagasena, who dies at the proper time, and whose deaths are untimely?'

"Great king, have you ever noticed how both ripe and unripe fruit falls from your mango trees, rose apple trees, or other kinds of trees?" "Of course, sir." "When these fruits fall from the trees, do they all fall at the proper time, or do some fall at the wrong time?" "When fully ripe and mature fruit falls, all of it falls at the proper time, sir, but all the rest of the fruit falls in an untimely way, with some due to being infested with worms, some by being struck with a club, some by the force of the wind, and some because of being rotten inside."

"Similarly, great king, only those slain from the effects 604
of old age die at the proper time. The rest die obstructed by their karma, obstructed by their destined birth, and obstructed by their actions."

"Nagasena, those obstructed by their karma, by their destined birth, and by their actions all die at the proper time, just like those slain by the effects of old age. Even those who

pi mātukucchigato marati, so tassa kālo, kāle yeva so marati; yo pi vijātaghare marati, so tassa kālo, so pi kāle yeva marati; yo pi māsiko marati pe yo pi vassasatike marati, so tassa kālo, kāle yeva so marati. tena hi bhante nāgasena akāle maraṇaṃ nāma na hoti; ye keci maranti sabbe te kāle yeva marantīti.

605 satt' ime mahārāja vijjamāne pi uttariṃ āyusmiṃ akāle
maranti. katame satta. jighacchito mahārāja bhojanaṃ alabhamāno upahatabbhantaro vijjamāne pi uttariṃ āyusmiṃ akāle marati; pipāsito mahārāja pānīyaṃ alabhamāno parisukkhahadayo vijjamāne pi uttariṃ āyusmiṃ akāle marati; ahinā daṭṭho mahārāja visavegābhihato tikicchakaṃ alabhamāno vijjamāne pi uttariṃ āyusmiṃ akāle marati; visam-āsito mahārāja ḍayhantesu aṅgapaccaṅgesu agadaṃ alabhamāno vijjamāne pi uttariṃ āyusmiṃ akāle marati; aggigato mahārāja jhāyamāno nibbāpanaṃ alabhamāno vijjamāne pi uttariṃ āyusmiṃ akāle marati; udakagato mahārāja patiṭṭhaṃ alabhamāno vijjamāne pi uttariṃ āyusmiṃ akāle marati; sattihato mahārāja ābādhiko bhisakkaṃ alabhamāno vijjamāne pi uttariṃ āyusmiṃ akāle marati. ime kho mahārāja satta vijjamāne pi uttariṃ āyusmiṃ akāle maranti. tatra pāhaṃ mahārāja ekaṃsena vadāmi.

606 aṭṭhavidhena mahārāja sattānaṃ kālakiriyā hoti: vātasamuṭṭhānena pittasamuṭṭhānena semhasamuṭṭhānena sannipātikena utupariṇāmena visamaparihārena opakka-

die while still in their mothers' wombs have their time, and they die at the proper time. And even those who die in the birth chamber have their time, and they too die at the proper time. Whether someone dies when only a month old or dies after a hundred years, that is their time, and one dies just at the proper time. Because of this, Nagasena, there really is no untimely death, for everyone who dies, dies at the proper time."

"Great king, there are seven who have additional life to 605
live yet die in an untimely way. Which seven? Someone starving, great king, who can't get food and whose insides are destroyed, dies while still having additional life to live. Someone parched, who can't get anything to drink and whose heart is dried up, dies while still having additional life to live. Someone bitten by a snake and struck by the force of the venom who can't get medicine dies while still having additional life to live. Someone who has taken poison and cannot get a cure while the limbs and extremities are burning dies while still having additional life to live. Someone fallen into fire who is on fire and unable to get doused dies while still having additional life to live. Someone fallen into water who can't reach firm ground dies while still having additional life to live. And someone cut by a knife and seriously injured who is unable to get to a physician dies while still having additional life to live. These are the seven who die while still having additional life to live, great king. There you have it, great king, for I speak definitively.

"Great king, death occurs to living beings in eight ways. 606
Death comes to beings because of a preponderance of the windy humor, the bilious humor, the phlegmatic humor, or

mikena kammavipākena mahārāja sattānaṃ kālakiriyā hoti. tatra mahārāja yad-idaṃ kammavipākena kālakiriyā sā yeva tattha sāmāyikā kālakiriyā, avasesā asāmāyikā kālakiriyā. bhavati ca:

607 jighacchāya pipāsāya ahinā daṭṭho visena ca aggi-udaka-
sattīhi akāle tattha mīyati.
vāta-pittena semhena sannipāten' utūhi ca
visamopakkamakammehi akāle tattha mīyatīti.

608 keci mahārāja sattā pubbe katena tena tena akusalakamma-
vipākena maranti. idha mahārāja yo pubbe pare jighacchāya māreti so bahūni vassasatasahassāni jighacchāya paripīḷito chāto parikilanto sukkha-pamilāta-hadayo sukkhito visukkhito jhāyanto abbhantaraṃ paridayhanto jighacchāya yeva marati daharo pi majjhimo pi mahallako pi; idam-pi tassa sāmāyikaṃ maraṇaṃ. yo pubbe pare pipāsāya māreti so bahūni vassasatasahassāni peto hutvā nijjhāmataṇhiko samāno lūkho kiso parisukkhitahadayo pipāsāya yeva marati daharo pi majjhimo pi mahallako pi; idam-pi tassa sāmāyikaṃ maraṇaṃ.

609 yo pubbe pare ahinā dasāpetvā māreti so bahūni vassa-
satasahassāni ajagaramukhen' eva ajagaramukhaṃ kaṇhasappamukhen' eva kaṇhasappamukhaṃ parivattitvā tehi khāyitakhāyito ahīhi daṭṭho yeva marati daharo pi majjhimo pi mahallako pi; idam-pi tassa sāmāyikaṃ maraṇaṃ. yo pubbe pare visaṃ datvā māreti so bahūni vassasatasahassāni ḍayhantehi aṅgapaccaṅgehi bhijjamānena sarīrena kuṇapagandhaṃ vāyanto visen' eva marati daharo pi majjhimo pi mahallako pi; idam-pi tassa sāmāyikaṃ maraṇaṃ.

the combination of them; a change in the seasons; carelessness; assault; and as a result of karma. Among these, great king, death as a result of karma happens at the right time, while all of the other deaths are untimely. For it is said:

> Death by starvation, thirst, snakebite, poison fire, 607
> water, or knife is untimely.
> And death by wind, bile, phlegm, or their
> combination, by the seasons, or by the action of
> carelessness or assault is also untimely.[116]

Great king, some beings die by the fruits of bad karma 608
because of what they did previously. In this case, someone who caused others to die by starvation in the past will also die by starvation over many hundreds and thousands of years, whether in youth, midlife, or old age, starving, famished, hungry, exhausted, with a dried-up and withered heart, desiccated, emaciated, wasted, and scorched inside. This one's death happens at the proper time. Someone who previously caused others to die of thirst also dies in youth, midlife, or old age by thirst, and becomes a hungry ghost for many hundreds and thousands of years, scorched by thirst, wretched, emaciated, and with heart parched. This one's death also happens at the proper time.
And someone who previously caused others to be bitten by 609
snakes dies in youth, midlife, or old age by snakebite, and gets eaten again and again for many hundreds and thousands of years, turning from the mouth of one goat-swallowing snake to the mouth of another goat-swallowing snake, from the mouth of one black snake to the mouth of another black snake. This one's death also happens at the proper time.

yo pubbe pare agginā māreti so bahūni vassasatasahassāni aṅgārapabbaten' eva aṅgārapabbataṃ yamavisayen' eva yamavisayaṃ parivattitvā daḍḍhavidaḍḍhagatto agginā yeva marati daharo pi majjhimo pi mahallako pi; idam-pi tassa sāmāyikaṃ maraṇaṃ. yo pubbe pare udakena māreti so bahūni vassasatasahassāni hata-vilutta-bhagga-dubbalagatto khubhitacitto udake yeva marati daharo pi majjhimo pi mahallako pi; idam-pi tassa sāmāyikaṃ maraṇaṃ. yo pubbe pare sattiyā māreti so bahūni vassasatasahassāni chinna-bhinna-koṭṭita-vikoṭṭito sattimukhasamāhato sattiyā yeva marati daharo pi majjhimo pi mahallako pi; idam-pi tassa sāmāyikaṃ maraṇan-ti.

610 bhante nāgasena, akāle maraṇaṃ atthīti yaṃ vadesi, iṅgha me tvaṃ tattha kāraṇaṃ atidisāti. yathā mahārāja mahatimahāaggikkhandho ādiṇṇa-tiṇa-kaṭṭha-sākhā-palāso pariyādiṇṇabhakkho upādānasaṅkhayā nibbāyati, so aggi vuccati anītiko anupaddavo samaye nibbuto nāmāti, evameva kho mahārāja yo koci bahūni divasasahassāni jīvitvā jarājiṇṇo āyukkhayā anītiko anupaddavo marati so vuccati samaye maraṇam-upagato ti. yathā vā pana mahārāja maha-

"Someone who previously killed others by giving them poison dies by poison in youth, midlife, or old age for many hundreds and thousands of years, with burning limbs and extremities, body splitting open, and emitting the stench of a corpse. This one's death also happens at the proper time. Someone who previously caused others to die by fire dies in youth, midlife, or old age, body burned and charred by fire, and turning from one mountain of burning embers to the next and one realm of Yama to the next for many hundreds and thousands of years. This one's death also happens at the proper time. Someone who previously killed others with water dies in water in youth, midlife, or old age for many hundreds and thousands of years with body injured, plundered, broken, and weak, and mind in turmoil. This one's death also happens at the proper time. And someone who previously killed others with a knife dies by knife in youth, midlife, or old age for many hundreds and thousands of years, cut, hacked, beaten, flogged, and struck in the face with a knife. This one's death happens at the proper time as well."

"Nagasena, you insist that there is untimely death. Come 610
now, please give me further reasoning on this matter."

"Great king, suppose a huge and massive fire consuming grass, sticks, branches, and leaves goes out when its sustenance runs out and its fuel is exhausted. The fire is said to be free of calamity and accident when it is extinguished at that time. Similarly, great king, whoever lives thousands of days and dies old and decrepit, life span exhausted, and free of calamity and accident is said to reach death at the proper time. But then consider the huge and massive fire consum-

timahāaggikkhandho ādiṇṇa-tiṇa-kaṭṭha-sākhā-palāso assa, taṃ apariyādiṇṇe yeva tiṇa-kaṭṭha-sākhā-palāse mahatimahāmegho abhippavassitvā nibbāpeyya, api nu kho so mahārāja mahāaggikkhandho samaye nibbuto nāma hotīti.

611 na hi bhante ti. kissa pana so mahārāja pacchimo aggikkhandho purimakena aggikkhandhena samasamagatiko nāhosīti. āgantukena bhante meghena patipīḷito so aggikkhandho asamayanibbuto ti. evam-eva kho mahārāja yo koci akāle marati so āgantukena rogena patipīḷito vātasamuṭṭhānena vā pittasamuṭṭhānena vā semhasamuṭṭhānena vā sannipātikena vā utupariṇāmajena vā visamaparihārajena vā opakkamikena vā jighacchāya vā pipāsāya vā sappadaṭṭhena vā visam-āsitena vā agginā vā udakena vā sattiyā vā patipīḷito akāle marati. idam-ettha mahārāja kāraṇaṃ yena kāraṇena akāle maraṇaṃ atthi.

612 yathā vā pana mahārāja gagane mahatimahāvalāhako uṭṭhahitvā ninnañ-ca thalañ-ca paripūrayanto abhivassati, so vuccati megho anītiko anupaddavo vassatīti, evam-eva kho mahārāja yo koci ciraṃ jīvitvā jarājiṇṇo āyukkhayā anītiko anupaddavo marati so vuccati samaye maraṇam-upagato ti. yathā vā pana mahārāja gagane mahatimahāvalāhako uṭṭhahitvā antarā yeva mahatā vātena abbhatthaṃ gaccheyya, api nu kho so mahārāja valāhako samaye vigato nāma hotīti.

613 na hi bhante ti. kissa pana so mahārāja pacchimo valāhako purimakena valāhakena samasamagatiko nāhosīti. āgantukena bhante vātena patipīḷito so valāhako asamayappatto

ing grass, sticks, branches, and leaves onto which an enormous rain cloud showers, extinguishing it before the grass, sticks, branches, and leaves are exhausted. Would you say that the massive fire was extinguished at the proper time, great king?"

"No, sir." 611

"But why is the later massive fire not the same as the first fire, great king?"

"The later fire was not extinguished at the proper time, sir, because of being doused by an incidental cloud."

"Similarly, great king, one who dies in an untimely manner oppressed by incidental illness or afflicted by a preponderance of wind, bile, phlegm, or their combination; by the change of seasons; by carelessness, assault, starvation, thirst, snakebite, poison, fire, water, or knife dies an untimely death. This is the reasoning here, great king, why death may be untimely.

"Consider also, great king, a great and enormous thunder- 612
cloud that rises up in the sky and rains, filling up the valleys and plains. Such a cloud is said to rain while free of calamity and accident. In much the same way, someone who lives a long time and dies old and decrepit, life span exhausted, and free of calamity and accident is said to reach death at the proper time. But then suppose another great and enormous thundercloud rises up in the sky but gets driven off by a great wind. Can this thundercloud be said to disappear at the proper time, great king?"

"No, sir." 613

"But why is the later thundercloud not like the first one, great king?"

yeva vigato ti. evam-eva kho mahārāja yo koci akāle marati so āgantukena rogena patipīḷito vātasamuṭṭhānena vā-pe-sattivegapatipīḷito vā akāle marati. idam-ettha mahārāja kāraṇaṃ yena kāraṇena akāle maraṇaṃ atthi.

614 yathā vā pana mahārāja balavā āsīviso kupito kañcid-eva purisaṃ ḍaseyya, tassa taṃ visaṃ anītikam anupaddavaṃ maraṇaṃ pāpeyya, taṃ visaṃ vuccati anītikam-anupaddavaṃ koṭigatan-ti; evam-eva kho mahārāja yo koci ciraṃ jīvitvā jarājiṇṇo āyukkhayā anītiko anupaddavo marati so vuccati anītiko anupaddavo jīvitakoṭigato sāmāyikaṃ maraṇam-upagato ti. yathā vā pana mahārāja balavatā āsīvisena daṭṭhassa antarā yeva ahiguṇṭhiko agadaṃ datvā avisaṃ kareyya, api nu kho taṃ mahārāja visaṃ samaye vigataṃ nāma hotīti.

615 na hi bhante ti. kissa pana taṃ mahārāja pacchimaṃ visaṃ purimakena visena samasamagatikaṃ nāhosīti. āgantukena bhante agadena patipīḷitaṃ visaṃ akoṭigataṃ yeva vigatan-ti. evam-eva kho mahārāja yo koci akāle marati so āgantukena rogena patipīḷito vātasamuṭṭhānena vā-pe sattivegapatipīḷito vā akāle marati. idam-ettha mahārāja kāraṇaṃ yena kāraṇena akāle maraṇaṃ atthi. yathā vā pana mahārāja issattho saraṃ pāteyya, sace so saro yathāgati-gamanapatha-matthakaṃ gacchati, so saro vuccati anītiko anupaddavo yathāgati-gamana-patha-matthakaṃ

"Beset with that incidental wind, this cloud disappeared at the wrong time, sir."

"In much the same way, great king, someone who dies in an untimely manner, oppressed by incidental disease or afflicted by a preponderance of wind, and all the rest, up to being overcome by the force of a knife, dies an untimely death. This is the reasoning, great king, why death may be untimely.

"You may also consider, great king, a powerful venomous 614
snake that is provoked and bites someone. The venom would cause death without calamity or accident, for it could be said that the venom—without calamity or accident—achieved its purpose. Similarly, someone who lives a long time and dies old and decrepit, life span exhausted, and free of calamity and accident is said to be one whose life has achieved its purpose and so reaches death at the proper time. Meanwhile, suppose the snake trainer were to give an antidote to the person bitten by the powerful and venomous snake, and it were to counteract the venom. Does the venom then disappear at the proper time, great king?"

"No, sir." 615

"What is the difference between the first and the second venom, great king?"

"Blocked by the incidental antidote, the venom has disappeared without achieving its purpose, sir."

"In much the same way, great king, someone who dies an untimely death oppressed by incidental illness owing to anything from the arising of the wind humor to a knife attack has met an untimely death. This is the reasoning here, great king, why death may be untimely. Consider also an archer

gato nāmāti; evam-eva kho mahārāja yo koci ciraṃ jīvitvā jarājiṇṇo āyukkhayā anītiko anupaddavo marati so vuccati anītiko anupaddavo samaye maraṇam-upagato ti. yathā vā pana mahārāja issattho saraṃ pāteyya, tassa taṃ saraṃ tasmiṃ yeva khaṇe koci gaṇheyya, api nu kho so mahārāja saro yathāgatigamanapatha-matthakaṃ gato nāma hotīti. na hi bhante ti. kissa pana so mahārāja pacchimo saro purimakena sarena samasamagatiko nāhosīti. āgantukena bhante gahaṇena tassa sarassa gamanaṃ upacchinnan-ti.

616 evam-eva kho mahārāja yo koci akāle marati so āgantukena rogena patipīḷito vātasamuṭṭhānena vā-pe-sattivegapatipīḷito vā akāle marati. idam ettha mahārāja kāraṇaṃ yena kāraṇena akāle mara-ṇaṃ atthi. yathā vā pana mahārāja yo koci lohamayaṃ bhājanaṃ ākoṭeyya, tassa ākoṭanena saddo nibbattitvā yathā-gati-gamanapatha-matthakaṃ gacchati, so saddo vuccati anītiko anupaddavo yathāgati-gamanapatha-matthakaṃ gato nāmāti; evam-eva kho mahārāja yo koci bahūni divasasahassāni jīvitvā jarājiṇṇo āyukkhayā anītiko anupaddavo marati so vuccati anītiko anupaddavo samaye maraṇam-upagato ti. yathā vā pana mahārāja yo koci lohamayaṃ bhājanaṃ ākoṭeyya, tassa ākoṭanena saddo nibbatteyya, nibbatte sadde adūragate koci āmaseyya, sah' āmasanena saddo nirujjheyya, api nu kho so mahārāja saddo yathāgati-gamanapatha-matthakaṃ gato nāma hotīti.

617 na hi bhante ti. kissa pana mahārāja pacchimo saddo purimakena saddena samasamagatiko nāhosīti. āgantukena bhante āmasanena so saddo uparato ti. evam-eva kho

who lets an arrow fly. If the arrow reaches the distance of the course aimed at, then the arrow is said to be free of calamity and accident. Similarly, great king, someone who has lived long and dies old and decrepit, life span exhausted, and free of calamity and accident is said to die at the proper time. But suppose the archer let an arrow fly but at that very instant someone were to grab it. Would the arrow go the distance of the course aimed at?" "Of course not, sir." "What is the difference between the first and the second arrow, great king?" "The arrow's course was interrupted by the incidental grabbing, sir."

"In much the same way, great king, someone who meets 616
an untimely death oppressed by incidental illness due to anything from the arising of the wind humor to a knife attack has died an untimely death. This is the reasoning here why death may be untimely. Suppose someone were to strike a brass bowl, and the sound produced by its being struck would ring the full length of its course. The sound could be said to be without calamity and accident and so rings the full length of its course. In much the same way, great king, someone who has lived thousands of days, who dies old and decrepit, life span exhausted, and free of calamity and accident is said to die at the proper time. But suppose someone struck a brass bowl and the striking produced a sound. But then someone touches it before the sound travels far and stops the sound with the touch. Great king, would the sound ring the full length of its course?"

"Of course not, sir." "But what is the difference between 617
the first and the second sound, great king?" "The sound stopped because of the incidental touch, sir." "In much the

mahārāja yo koci akāle marati so āgantukena rogena patipīḷito vātasamuṭṭhānena vā-pe-sattivegapatipīḷito vā akāle marati. idam-ettha mahārāja kāraṇaṃ yena kāraṇena akāle maraṇaṃ atthi. yathā vā pana mahārāja khette suvirūḷhaṃ dhaññabījaṃ sammā pavattamānena vassena otatavitata-ākiṇṇa-bahu-phalaṃ hutvā sassuṭṭhānasamayaṃ pāpuṇāti, taṃ dhaññaṃ vuccati anītikam-anupaddavaṃ samayasampattaṃ nāma hotīti; evam-eva kho mahārāja yo koci bahūni divasasahassāni jīvitvā jarājiṇṇo āyukkhayā anītiko anupaddavo marati so vuccati anītiko anupaddavo samaye maraṇam-upagato ti. yathā vā pana mahārāja khette suvirūḷhaṃ dhaññabījaṃ udakena vikalaṃ mareyya, api nu kho taṃ mahārāja dhaññaṃ samayasampattaṃ nāma hotīti.

618 na hi bhante ti. kissa pana taṃ mahārāja pacchimaṃ dhaññaṃ purimakena dhaññena samasamagatikaṃ nāhosīti. āgantukena bhante uṇhena patipīḷitaṃ taṃ dhaññaṃ matan-ti. evam-eva kho mahārāja yo koci akāle marati so āgantukena rogena patipīḷito vātasamuṭṭhānena vā-pe sattivegapatipīḷito vā akāle marati. idam-ettha mahārāja kāraṇaṃ yena kāraṇena akāle maraṇaṃ atthi. sutapubbaṃ pana tayā mahārāja sampannaṃ taruṇasassaṃ kimayo uṭṭhahitvā samūlaṃ nāsentīti.

619 sutapubbañ-c' eva taṃ bhante amhehi diṭṭhapubbañ-cāti. kin-nu kho taṃ mahārāja sassaṃ kāle naṭṭhaṃ, udāhu akāle naṭṭhan-ti. akāle bhante; yadi kho taṃ bhante sassaṃ kimayo na khādeyyuṃ, sassuddharaṇasamayaṃ

same way, great king, someone who dies an untimely death, oppressed by incidental illness due to anything from the arising of the wind humor to a knife attack, has died an untimely death. This is the reasoning here why death may be untimely. You may also wish to consider how seeds of grain growing well on a field become covered, spread out, and dense with many fruits with the arrival of suitable rain, and produce a seasonal yield of grain. The grain could be said to have reached its proper time, without calamity or accident. In much the same way, someone who has lived thousands of days who dies old and decrepit, life span exhausted, and free of calamity and accident is said to die at the proper time. But then consider grain seeds growing well on a field that then die owing to the lack of water. Does the grain reach its proper time, great king?"

"Of course not, sir." 618

"What is the difference between the first grain and the second, great king?" "The grain died afflicted by incidental heat, sir." "Similarly, great king, someone who dies an untimely death oppressed by incidental illness due to anything from the arising of the wind humor to a knife attack has met an untimely death. This is the reasoning here why death may be untimely. But have you ever heard, great king, of successful crops that worms come up and destroy down to the roots?"

"We have not only heard of this, sir, we have actually seen 619
it."

"Is the loss of the crops timely or untimely, great king?"

"Untimely, sir. If the worms had not eaten the crops, a timely harvest of the crops would have occurred." "Is it the

pāpuṇeyyāti. kim-pana mahārāja āgantukena upaghātena sassaṃ vinassati, nirupaghātaṃ sassaṃ sassuddharaṇasamayaṃ pāpuṇātīti. āma bhante ti.

620 evam-eva kho mahārāja yo koci akāle marati so āgantukena rogena patipīḷito vātasamuṭṭhānena vā-pe-sattivegapatipīḷito vā akāle marati. idam-ettha mahārāja kāraṇaṃ yena kāraṇena akāle maraṇaṃ atthi. sutapubbaṃ pana tayā mahārāja sampanne sasse phalabhāranamite mañjaritapatte karakavassaṃ nāma vassajāti nipatitvā vināseti aphalaṃ karotīti. suttapubbañ-c' eva taṃ bhante amhehi diṭṭhapubbañcāti.

621 api nu kho taṃ mahārāja sassaṃ kāle naṭṭhaṃ udāhu akāle naṭṭhan-ti. akāle bhante; yadi kho taṃ bhante karakavassaṃ na vasseyya, sassuddharaṇasamayaṃ pāpuṇeyyāti. kim-pana mahārāja āgantukena upaghātena sassaṃ vinassati, nirupaghātaṃ sassaṃ sassuddharaṇasamayaṃ pāpuṇātīti. āma bhante ti. evam-eva kho mahārāja yo koci akāle marati so āgantukena rogena patipīḷito vātasamuṭṭhānena vā pittasamuṭṭhānena vā semhasamuṭṭhānena vā sannipātikena vā utupariṇāmajena vā visamaparihārajena vā opakkamikena vā jighacchāya vā pipāsāya vā sappadaṭṭhena vā visam āsitena vā agginā vā udakena vā sattivegapatipīḷito vā akāle marati; yadi pana āgantukena rogena patipīḷito na bhaveyya, samayeva maraṇaṃ pāpuṇeyya. idam-ettha mahārāja kāraṇaṃ yena kāraṇena akāle maraṇaṃ atthīti.

622 acchariyaṃ bhante nāgasena, abbhutaṃ bhante nāgasena, sudassitaṃ kāraṇaṃ, suddassitaṃ opammaṃ akāle maraṇassa paridīpanāya; atthi akāle maraṇan-ti uttānīka-

case, great king, that the crops were destroyed by an incidental injury, and that without this injury they would have produced a timely harvest?" "Yes, sir."

"It is the same, great king, for someone who dies an 620
untimely death oppressed by incidental illness owing to anything from the arising of the wind humor to a knife attack; that one has died an untimely death. This is the reasoning here why death may be untimely. Have you ever heard, great king, of successful crops bending low from the weight of their fruit and bursting open, and then a kind of rain called a hailstorm crashes down, destroying and wasting them?"

"Again, sir, we have not only heard of this but have actually seen it."

"Are the crops lost in a timely or untimely way, great 621
king?" "Untimely, sir, for if the hailstorm had not hailed, then a timely harvest of the crops would have occurred." "Is it that the crops were destroyed by an incidental injury, but without that injury the crops would have produced a timely harvest?" "Exactly, sir."

"And so it is, great king, that one who dies in an untimely manner, oppressed by incidental illness or afflicted by a preponderance of wind, bile, phlegm, or their combination; by the change of seasons; by carelessness, assault, starvation, thirst, snakebite, poison, fire, water, or knife attack, dies an untimely death. This is the reasoning here, great king, why death may be untimely."

"This is a marvel and a wonder, revered Nagasena. To 622
illuminate how death may be untimely, the reasoning and analogies are thoroughly demonstrated. The ways death is untimely have been made evident, manifest, and clear. Any

taṃ pākaṭaṃ kataṃ vibhūtaṃ kataṃ. acittavikkhittako pi bhante nāgasena manujo ekamekena pi tāva opammena niṭṭhaṃ gaccheyya: atthi akāle maraṇan-ti; kim-pana manujo sacetano. paṭhamopammen' evāhaṃ bhante saññatto. atthi akāle maraṇan-ti, api ca aparāparaṃ nibbāhanaṃ sotukāmo na sampaṭicchin-ti.

623 bhante nāgasena, sabbesaṃ parinibbutānaṃ cetiye pāṭihīraṃ hoti, udāhu ekaccānaṃ yeva hotīti. ekaccānaṃ mahārāja hoti, ekaccānaṃ na hotīti. katamesaṃ bhante hoti, katamesaṃ na hotīti.

624 tiṇṇannaṃ mahārāja aññatarassa adhiṭṭhānā parinibbutassa cetiye pāṭihīraṃ hoti. katamesaṃ tiṇṇannaṃ. idha mahārāja arahā devamanussānaṃ anukampāya tiṭṭhantova adhiṭṭhāti: evaṃnāmacetiye pāṭihīraṃ hotūti, tassa adhiṭṭhānavasena cetiye pāṭihīraṃ hoti; evaṃ arahato adhiṭṭhānavasena parinibbutassa cetiye pāṭihīraṃ hoti. puna ca paraṃ mahāraja devatā manussānaṃ anukampāya parinibbutassa cetiye pāṭihīraṃ dassenti: iminā pāṭihīrena saddhammo niccasampaggahīto bhavissati, manussā ca pasannā kusalena abhivaḍḍhissantīti; evaṃ devatānaṃ adhiṭṭhānena parinibbutassa cetiye pāṭihīraṃ hoti. puna ca paraṃ mahārāja itthī vā puriso vā saddho pasanno paṇḍito byatto medhāvī buddhisampanno yoniso cintayitvā gandhaṃ vā mālaṃ vā dussaṃ vā aññataraṃ vā kiñci adhiṭṭhahitvā cetiye ukkhipati: evaṃ nāma hotūti, tassa pi adhiṭṭhānavasena parinibbutassa cetiye pāṭihīraṃ hoti; evaṃ manussānaṃ adhiṭṭhānavasena parinibbutassa cetiye pāṭihīraṃ hoti. imesaṃ kho mahārāja

reasonably balanced person could reach the conclusion that death may be untimely with even one of your analogies, to say nothing of the thinking person. I perceived with the first analogy that there is untimely death, but wanting to hear further elaboration, I did not agree right away.

“Revered Nagasena, does a miracle occur at every final 623
nibbana shrine, or only at some?”[117]

“It happens at some but not at others, great king.”

“In which cases may it occur and in which cases does it not occur, sir?”

“A miracle occurs at a final nibbana shrine because of an 624
aspiration of one of three types of people. Which three? In the first case, an arhat stands there and makes an aspiration out of compassion for gods and humans, ‘May there be a miracle at such and such a shrine,’ and because of this aspiration, a miracle occurs at that shrine. In this way, a miracle can occur at a final nibbana shrine by means of an arhat’s aspiration. In the second case, great king, the gods display a miracle at a final nibbana shrine out of compassion for humans, thinking, *The True Dhamma will be forever supported because of this miracle, and people will be pleased and increase in merit.* In this way, a miracle can occur at a final nibbana shrine by means of the aspiration of gods. In the last case, great king, a faithful, believing, learned, experienced, intelligent, and wise woman or man carefully considers and concentrates on a fragrance, garland, cloth, or other such thing and places it upon a shrine, thinking, *May such and such happen.* In this way, a miracle can occur at a final nibbana shrine by means of a human aspiration. By the aspiration of one of these three

tiṇṇannaṃ aññatarassa adhiṭṭhānavasena parinibbutassa cetiye pāṭihīraṃ hoti.

625 yadi maharaja tesaṃ adhiṭṭhānaṃ na hoti, khīṇāsavassa pi chaḷabhiññassa cetovasippattassa cetiye pāṭihīraṃ na hoti. asati pi mahārāja pāṭihīre caritaṃ disvā suparisuddhaṃ okappetabbaṃ niṭṭhaṃ gantabbaṃ saddahitabbaṃ: suparinibbuto ayaṃ buddhaputto ti. sādhu bhante nāgasena, evam-etaṃ, tathā sampaṭicchāmīti.

626 bhante nāgasena, ye te sammā paṭipajjanti tesaṃ sabbesaṃ yeva dhammābhisamayo hoti, udāhu kassaci na hotīti. kassaci mahārāja hoti, kassaci na hotīti. kassa bhante hoti, kassa na hotīti. tiracchānagatassa mahārāja supaṭipannassāpi dhammābhisamayo na hoti, pettivisayūpapannassa micchādiṭṭhikassa kuhakassa mātughātakassa pitughātakassa arahantaghātakassa saṅghabhedakassa lohituppādakassa theyyasaṃvāsakassa titthiyapakkantakassa bhikkhunidūsakassa terasannaṃ garukāpattīnaṃ aññataraṃ āpajjitvā avuṭṭhitassa paṇḍakassa ubhatobyañjanakassa supaṭipannassāpi dhammābhisamayo na hoti, yo pi manussadaharako ūnakasattavassiko tassa supatipannassāpi dhammābhisamayo na hoti. imesaṃ kho mahārāja soḷasannaṃ puggalānaṃ supaṭipannānam-pi dhammābhisamayo na hotīti.

types of people, great king, a miracle may occur at a final nibbana shrine.

If there were no aspirations by them, then there would be 625
no miracles at the shrine of even someone who had destroyed the flaws and achieved mastery of the six higher knowledges, great king. But even if there is no miracle, seeing pure conduct should inspire confidence and faith and lead to the conclusion, 'This descendant of the Buddha has completely attained final nibbana.'"

"Very well, then, Nagasena. This is so, and I am convinced.

"Revered Nagasena, is there realization of the Dhamma 626
for everyone who practices rightly or only for some?"

"There is for some but not for others, great king."

"For whom is there realization, and for whom is there not, sir?"

"There is no realization of the Dhamma for an animal, even one practicing correctly. And there is no realization of the Dhamma for one born in the realm of the departed, for one holding wrong view, a charlatan, a matricide, a patricide, the killer of an arhat, a schismatic dividing the community, someone spilling the Buddha's blood, one living dishonestly in the community, one who has joined a non-Buddhist sect, one who violates a nun, one who has committed any of the thirteen serious offenses and not come back into the fold, a eunuch, and an intersex person—even if they practice correctly. Nor may a human child under seven years old realize the Dhamma, despite practicing correctly. There is no realization of the Dhamma for these sixteen persons, even if they practice correctly, great king."

627 bhante nāgasena, ye te pannarasa puggalā viruddhā yeva tesaṃ dhammābhisamayo hotu vā mā vā hotu, atha kena kāraṇena manussadaharakassa ūnakasattavassikassa supaṭipannassāpi dhammābhisamayo na hoti, ettha tāva pañho bhavati. nanu nāma daharakassa na rāgo hoti, na doso hoti, na moho hoti, na māno hoti, na micchādiṭṭhi hoti, na arati hoti, na kāmavitakko hoti. amissito kilesehi so nāma daharako yutto ca patto ca arahati ca cattāri saccāni ekapaṭivedhena paṭivijjhitun-ti.

628 tañ-ñev' ettha mahārāja kāraṇaṃ yenāhaṃ kāraṇena bhaṇāmi: ūnakasattavassikassa supaṭipannassāpi dhammābhisamayo na hotīti. yadi mahārāja ūnakasattavassiko rajanīye rajjeyya, dussanīye dusseyya, mohanīye muyheyya, madanīye majjeyya, diṭṭhiṃ vijāneyya, ratiñ-ca aratiñ-ca vijāneyya, kusalākusalaṃ vitakkeyya, bhaveyya tassa dhammābhisamayo. api ca mahārāja ūnakasattavassikassa cittaṃ abalaṃ dubbalaṃ parittaṃ appaṃ thokaṃ mandaṃ avibhūtaṃ, asaṅkhatā nibbānadhātu garukā bhārikā vipulā mahatī; ūnakasattavassiko mahārāja tena dubbalena cittena parittakena mandena avibhūtena na sakkoti garukaṃ bhārikaṃ vipulaṃ mahatiṃ asaṅkhataṃ nibbānadhātuṃ paṭivijjhituṃ. yathā mahārāja sinerupabbatarājā garuko bhāriko vipulo mahanto, api nu kho taṃ mahārāja puriso attano pākatikena thāma-bala-viriyena sakkuṇeyya sinerupabbatarājānaṃ uddharitun-ti.

629 na hi bhante ti. kena kāraṇena mahārājāti. dubbalattā bhante purisassa, mahantattā sinerupabbatarājassāti.

"It may or may not be the case, Nagasena, that fifteen of these persons are obstructed with respect to realizing the Dhamma. But why would a human child under seven years old not realize the Dhamma when practicing correctly? Here is a dilemma for you. Surely there is no passion, hatred, delusion, pride, wrong view, aversion, or sensual thought in a young child. Not mixed up with the defilements, a young child is fit, ready, and worthy to penetrate the Four Truths with a single comprehension." 627

"I speak to this very point, great king, with the following reasoning. There is no realization of the Dhamma for someone under seven years despite practicing correctly. If a child under seven could be passionate about something inspiring passion, be hateful about something inspiring hate, be deluded about something causing delusion, be intoxicated about something arousing arrogance, ascertain wrong views, discriminate between what is attractive and what is repugnant, and reflect on good and bad, then there could be realization of the Dhamma for them. But the mind of a child under seven is weak, powerless, limited, small, trifling, dim, and unclear, while the unconditioned domain of nibbana is heavy, serious, extensive, and vast. A child younger than seven is not able to penetrate the heavy, serious, extensive, vast, and unconditioned domain of nibbana with this weak, limited, dim, and unclear mind. Great king, Sineru, king of mountains, is heavy, serious, extensive, and vast. Could a man with his ordinary strength, power, and exertion by himself lift up Sineru, king of mountains?" 628

"Of course not, sir." 629

"For what reason, great king?"

evam-eva kho mahārāja ūnakasattavassikassa cittaṃ abalaṃ dubbalaṃ parittaṃ appaṃ thokaṃ mandaṃ avibhūtaṃ, asaṅkhatā nibbānadhātu garukā bhārikā vipulā mahatī, ūnakasattavassiko tena dubbalena cittena parittakena mandena avibhūtena na sakkoti garukaṃ bhārikaṃ vipulaṃ mahatiṃ asaṅkhataṃ nibbānadhātuṃ paṭivijjhituṃ, tena kāraṇena ūnakasatta-vassikassa supaṭipannassāpi dhammābhisamayo na hoti. yathā vā pana mahārāja ayaṃ mahāpaṭhavī dīghā āyatā puthulā vitthatā visālā vitthiṇṇā vipulā mahantā, api nu kho taṃ mahārāja mahāpaṭhaviṃ sakkā parittakena udakabindukena temetvā udakacikkhallaṃ kātun-ti.

630 na hi bhante ti. kena kāraṇena mahārājāti. parittattā bhante udakabindussa, mahantattā mahāpaṭhaviyā ti. evam-eva kho mahārāja ūnakasattavassikassa cittaṃ abalaṃ dubbalaṃ parittaṃ appaṃ thokaṃ mandaṃ avibhūtaṃ, asaṅkhatā nibbānadhātu dīghā āyatā puthulā vitthatā visālā vitthiṇṇā vipulā mahantā, ūnakasattavassiko tena dubbalena cittena parittakena mandena avibhūtena na sakkoti mahatiṃ asaṅkhataṃ nibbānadhātuṃ pativijjhituṃ, tena kāraṇena ūnakasattavassikassa supaṭipannassāpi dhammābhisamayo na hoti. yathā vā pana mahārāja abala-dubbala-paritta-appa-thoka-mandaggibhaveyya, api nu kho mahārāja tāvatakena mandena agginā sakkā sadevake loke andhakāraṃ vidhametvā ālokaṃ dassetun-ti.

"Because of the weakness of the man and the vastness of Sineru, the king of mountains, sir."

"Similarly, great king, since the mind of a child under seven is weak, powerless, limited, small, trifling, dim, and unclear, while the unconditioned domain of nibbana is heavy, serious, extensive, and vast, the child under seven is not able to penetrate the heavy, serious, extensive, vast, and unconditioned domain of nibbana with this weak, limited, dim, and unclear mind. There is no realization of the Dhamma for a child under seven, even if practicing correctly, for this reason. The great earth is long, spread out, broad, wide, roomy, massive, extensive, and vast, great king. Can the great earth be moistened by a tiny drop of water and turned into a swamp?"

"Of course not, sir." 630

"For what reason, great king?"

"Because of the smallness of the drop of water and the vastness of the great earth, sir."

"Similarly, great king, since the mind of a child under seven is weak, powerless, limited, small, trifling, dim, and unclear, while the unconditioned domain of nibbana is long, spread out, broad, wide, roomy, massive, extensive, and vast, a child under seven is not able to penetrate the vast and unconditioned domain of nibbana with this weak, limited, dim, and unclear mind. For this reason, there is no realization of the Dhamma for a child younger than seven, even if practicing correctly. Consider a weak, powerless, limited, small, trifling, and dim fire, great king. Could such a dim fire dispel the darkness of the world with its gods and light it up?"

631 na hi bhante ti. kena kāraṇena mahārājāti. mandattā bhante aggissa, lokassa mahantattā ti. evam-eva kho mahārāja ūnakasattavassikassa cittaṃ abalaṃ dubbalaṃ parittaṃ appaṃ thokaṃ mandaṃ avibhūtaṃ, mahatā ca avijjandhakārena pihitaṃ, tasmā dukkaraṃ ñāṇālokaṃ dassayituṃ, tena kāraṇena ūnakasattavassikassa supaṭipannassāpi dhammābhisamayo na hoti. yathā vā pana mahārāja āturo kiso aṇu-parimita-kāyo sālakakimi hatthināgaṃ tidhāppabhinnaṃ navāyataṃ tivitthataṃ dasapariṇāhaṃ aṭṭharatanikaṃ ṭhānam upagataṃ disvā gilituṃ parikaḍḍheyya, api nu kho so mahārāja sālakakimi sakkuṇeyya taṃ hatthināgaṃ gilitun-ti.

632 na hi bhante ti. kena kāraṇena mahārājāti. parittattā bhante sālakasarīrassa, mahantattā hatthināgassāti. evam-eva kho mahārāja ūnakasattavassikassa cittaṃ abalaṃ dubbalaṃ parittaṃ appaṃ thokaṃ mandaṃ avibhūtaṃ, mahatī asaṅkhatā nibbānadhātu, so tena dubbalena cittena parittakena mandena avibhūtena na sakkoti mahatiṃ asaṅkhataṃ nibbānadhātuṃ paṭivijjhituṃ, tena kāraṇena ūnakasattavassikassa supaṭipannassāpi dhammābhisamayo na hotīti. sādhu bhante nāgasena, evam-etaṃ, tathā sampaṭicchāmīti.

"Of course not, sir." 631

"For what reason, great king?"

"Because of the dimness of the fire and the vastness of the world, sir."

"Similarly, great king, since the mind of a child under seven is weak, powerless, limited, small, trifling, dim, unclear, and covered by the darkness of ignorance, it is hard to reveal the light of knowledge. And for this reason there is no realization of the Dhamma for a child under seven, even if practicing correctly. Suppose a sick and emaciated *sālaka* worm, with its tiny and limited body, were to see, charging its lair, a bull elephant—nine measures in length, three in breadth, ten in girth, eight in height, and exhibiting rutting on three places of its body—and were to rear up to swallow it. Great king, would the *sālaka* worm be able to swallow the bull elephant?"

"Of course not, sir." 632

"For what reason, great king?"

"Because of the smallness of the *sālaka*'s body and the vastness of the bull elephant, sir."

"Similarly, great king, the mind of a child under seven is weak, powerless, limited, small, trifling, dim, and unclear, while the unconditioned domain of nibbana is vast. It is not possible for the vast and unconditioned domain of nibbana to be penetrated by this weak, limited, dim, and unclear mind. For this reason also there is no realization of the Dhamma for a child younger than seven years, despite practicing correctly."

"Excellent, revered Nagasena. This is so, and I am convinced.

633 bhante nāgasena, kiṃ ekantasukhaṃ nibbānaṃ, udāhu dukkhena missan-ti. ekantasukhaṃ mahārāja nibbānaṃ dukkhena amissan ti. na mayan-taṃ bhante nāgasena vacanaṃ saddahāma: ekantasukhaṃ nibbānan-ti. evam-ettha mayaṃ bhante nāgasena paccema: nibbānaṃ dukkhena missan-ti; kāraṇañ-c' ettha upalabhāma: nibbānaṃ dukkhena missan-ti, katamaṃ ettha kāraṇaṃ: ye te bhante nāgasena nibbānaṃ pariyesanti tesaṃ dissati kāyassa ca cittassa ca ātāpo paritāpo, ṭhāna-caṅkama-nisajjā-sayana-āhāra-pariggaho, middhassa ca uparodho, āyatanānañ-ca patipīḷanaṃ, dhanadhañña-piyañātimitta-pajahanaṃ; ye keci loke sukhitā sukhasamappitā te sabbe pi pañcahi kāmaguṇehi āyatane ramenti brūhenti, manāpika-manāpika-bahuvidha-subhanimittena rūpena cakkhuṃ ramenti brūhenti, manāpika-manāpika-gītavādita-bahuvidha-subhanimittena saddena sotaṃramenti brūhenti, manāpika-manāpika-puppha-phala-patta-taca-mūla-sāra-bahuvidha-subhanimittena gandhena ghānaṃ ramenti brūhenti, manāpikamanāpika-khajja-bhojja-leyya-peyya-sāyaniya-bahuvidha-subhanimittena rasena jivhaṃ ramenti brūhenti, manāpika-manāpika-saṇhasukhuma-mudumaddava-bahuvidha-subha-nimittena phassena kāyaṃ ramenti brūhenti,

"Revered Nagasena, is nibbana entirely happy or is it mixed with pain?" 633

"Nibbana is entirely happy and is not mixed with pain, great king."

"We don't believe you, sir, when you say that nibbana is entirely happy, and we counter with this: nibbana is mixed with pain. And we have reasons for claiming that nibbana is mixed with pain. Torment and mortification of body and mind are observed in those seeking nibbana, whether abstaining from standing, pacing, sitting, lying down, or food; curtailing sleep; suppressing the senses; or forsaking wealth, grain, loved ones, relatives, and friends. And yet those who are pleased and enjoy happiness all cultivate and are delighted by the senses through the five sense pleasures. That is, they cultivate the eye and are delighted by visible forms and the many ways their beautiful attributes are pleasant and charming; they cultivate the ear and are delighted by sound and the many ways the beautiful attributes of songs and music may be pleasant and charming; they cultivate the nose and are delighted by fragrance and the many ways the beautiful attributes of flowers, fruits, leaves, bark, roots, and heartwood may be pleasant and charming; they cultivate the tongue and are delighted by taste and the many ways the beautiful attributes of what is tasted, eaten, licked, drunk, and savored may be pleasant and charming; they cultivate the body and are delighted by touch and the many ways the beautiful attributes of delicacy, softness, tenderness, and smoothness may be pleasant and charming; and they cultivate the mind and are delighted by the many kinds of thought and

manāpikāmanāpika-kalyāṇapāpaka-subhāsubha bahuvidha-vitakka-manasikārena manaṃ ramenti brūhenti.

634 tumhe taṃ cakkhu-sota-ghāna-jivhā-kāya-mano-brūhanaṃ hanatha upahanatha chindatha upacchindatha rundhatha uparundhatha, tena kāyo pi paritappati cittam-pi paritappati, kāye paritatte kāyikaṃ dukkhaṃ vedanaṃ vediyati, citte paritatte cetasikaṃ dukkhaṃ vedanaṃ vediyati. nanu māgandiyo pi paribbājako bhagavantaṃ garahamāno evam-āha: bhūtahacco[22] samaṇo gotamo ti. idam-ettha kāraṇaṃ yenāhaṃ kāraṇena brūmi: nibbānaṃ dukkhena missan-ti.

635 na hi mahārāja nibbānaṃ dukkhena missaṃ, ekantasukhaṃ nibbānaṃ. yaṃ pana tvaṃ mahārāja brūsi: nibbānaṃ dukkhan-ti, n' etaṃ dukkhaṃ nibbānaṃ nāma, nibbānassa pana sacchikiriyāya pubbabhāgo eso, nibbānapariyesanaṃ etaṃ. ekantasukhaṃ yeva mahārāja nibbānaṃ, na dukkhena missaṃ. tattha kāraṇaṃ vadāmi. atthi mahārāja rājūnaṃ rajjasukhaṃ nāmāti. āma bhante, atthi rājūnaṃ rajjasukhan-ti.

636 api nu kho taṃ mahārāja rajjasukhaṃ dukkhena missan-ti. na hi bhante ti. kissa pana te mahārāja rājāno paccante kupite tesaṃ paccantanissitānaṃ paṭisedhāya amaccehi pariṇāyakehi bhaṭehi balatthehi parivutā pavāsaṃ gantvā ḍaṃsamakasa-vātātapa-patipīḷitā samavisame paridhāvanti mahāyuddhañ-ca karonti jīvitasaṃsayañ-ca pāpuṇantīti.

attention, whether pleasant or not, auspicious or wicked, beautiful or ugly.

"But those of you seeking nibbana destroy, kill off, cut 634
down, break up, restrain, and check the cultivation of the eye, ear, nose, tongue, body, and mind. And because of this, the body is tormented and the mind is tormented. When the body is distressed, one feels painful bodily feeling, and when the mind is distressed, one feels painful mental feeling. Is it not the case that the wanderer Magandiya reviled the Bhagavan in this way: 'The renouncer Gotama is a destroyer of being.'[118] This is the reason I say that nibbana is mixed with pain."

"Great king, nibbana is certainly not mixed with pain, for 635
nibbana is entirely happy. You are asserting, great king, that nibbana is painful. But this pain is not nibbana; rather it is the preliminary stage to experiencing nibbana. It is the quest for nibbana. Nibbana itself is entirely happy and not mixed with pain. I shall state the reasoning in the matter. Great king, do kings have a happiness associated with kingship?"

"Yes, sir, there is a happiness of kingship for kings."

"And is this happiness of kingship mixed with pain?" 636

"Not at all, sir."

"But what about when kings have a disturbance at the border and in order to subjugate the frontier subjects, they set out on an expedition surrounded by ministers, advisers, soldiers, and guards? They journey over both level and rugged ground oppressed by gadflies, mosquitoes, wind, and heat and join a great battle, casting their very lives into doubt."

637 n' etaṃ bhante nāgasena rajjasukhaṃ nāma, rajjasukhassa pariyesanāya pubbabhāgo eso. dukkhena bhante nāgasena rājāno rajjaṃ pariyesitvā rajjasukhaṃ anubhavanti. evaṃ bhante nāgasena rajjasukhaṃ dukkhena amissaṃ, aññaṃ taṃ rajjasukhaṃ, aññaṃ dukkhan-ti. evam-eva kho mahārāja ekantasukhaṃ nibbānaṃ na dukkhena missaṃ, ye pana taṃ nibbānaṃ pariyesanti te kāyañ-ca cittañ-ca ātāpetvā ṭhāna-caṅkama-nisajjā-sayanāhāraṃ pariggahetvā middhaṃ uparundhitvā āyatanāni patipīḷetvā kāyañ-ca jīvitañ-ca pariccajitvā dukkhena nibbānaṃ pariyesitvā ekantasukhaṃ nibbānaṃ anubhavanti, nihatapaccāmittāva rājāno rajjasukhaṃ. evaṃ mahārāja ekantasukhaṃ nibbānaṃ na dukkhena missaṃ, aññaṃ nibbānaṃ, aññaṃ dukkhaṃ.

638 aparam-pi mahārāja uttariṃ kāraṇaṃ suṇohi: ekantasukhaṃ nibbānaṃ na dukkhena missaṃ, aññaṃ dukkhaṃ, aññaṃ nibbānan-ti. atthi mahārājā ācariyānaṃ sippavantānaṃ sippasukhaṃ nāmāti. āma bhante, atthi ācariyānaṃ sippavantānaṃ sippasukhan-ti. api nu kho taṃ mahārāja sippasukhaṃ dukkhena missan-ti. na hi bhante ti. kissa pana te mahārāja ācariyānaṃ abhivādana-paccupaṭṭhānena udakāharaṇa-ghara-sammajjana-dantakaṭṭhamukhodakānuppadānena ucchiṭṭha-paṭiggahaṇa-ucchādana-nahāpana-pādaparikammena sakacittaṃ

"But this is not what we call the happiness associated with kingship, Nagasena. This is the preliminary stage of the quest for the happiness of kingship. Having sought kingship with pain, Nagasena, kings experience the happiness of kingship. And so the happiness of kingship is not mixed with pain, but rather the happiness of kingship is one thing, and pain is something else." 637

"In the same way, great king, nibbana is entirely happy and not mixed with pain. Those seeking nibbana mortify body and mind; abstain from standing, pacing, sitting, lying down, or food; curtail sleep; suppress the senses; and give up body and life. Seeking nibbana by means of pain, they experience nibbana as entirely happy, much as kings experience the happiness of kingship once their adversaries are put down. And so, great king, nibbana is entirely happy and not mixed with pain. Nibbana is one thing, and pain is something else.

"Please listen to another reason, great king, why nibbana 638
is entirely happy and not mixed with pain, and nibbana is one thing and pain is something else. Is there a happiness associated with craftsmanship for those teachers who have mastery in the crafts?"

"Yes, sir, for teachers with mastery in the crafts, there is a happiness associated with craftsmanship."

"Is this happiness of craftsmanship mixed with pain, great king?"

"No, sir."

"But how is it that they mortify their bodies with bad food and uncomfortable bedding, show respect and wait on their teacher, bring water, sweep his house, provide him tooth sticks and water for rinsing the mouth, receive his leftovers,

nikkhipitvā paracittānuvattanena dukkhaseyyāya visamabhojanena kāyaṃ ātāpentīti.

639 n' etaṃ bhante nāgasena sippasukhaṃ nāma, sippapariyesanāya pubbabhāgo eso. dukkhena bhante nāgasena ācariyā sippaṃ pariyesitvā sippasukhaṃ anubhavanti. evaṃ bhante nāgasena sippasukhaṃ dukkhena amissaṃ, aññaṃ taṃ sippasukhaṃ, aññaṃ dukkhan-ti. evam-eva kho mahārāja ekantasukhaṃ nibbānaṃ na dukkhena missaṃ, ye pana taṃ nibbānaṃ pariyesanti te kāyañ-ca cittañ-ca ātāpetvā ṭhāna-caṅkama-nisajjā-sayanāhāraṃ pariggahetvā middhaṃ uparundhitvā āyatanāni patipīḷetvā kāyañ-ca jīvitañ-ca pariccajitvā dukkhena nibbānaṃ pariyesitvā ekantasukhaṃ nibbānaṃ anubhavanti, ācariyā viya sippasukhaṃ. evaṃ mahārāja ekantasukhaṃ nibbānaṃ na dukkhena missaṃ, aññaṃ dukkhaṃ, aññaṃ nibbānan-ti. sādhu bhante nāgasena, evam-etaṃ, tathā sampaṭicchāmīti.

640 bhante nāgasena, nibbānaṃ nibbānan-ti yaṃ vadesi, sakkā pana tassa nibbānassa rūpaṃ vā saṇṭhānaṃ vā vayaṃ vā pamāṇaṃ vā opammena vā kāraṇena vā hetunā vā nayena vā upadassayitun-ti. appaṭibhāgaṃ mahārāja nibbānaṃ, na sakkā nibbānassa rūpaṃ vā saṇṭhānaṃ vā vayaṃ vā pamāṇaṃ vā opammena vā kāraṇena vā hetunā vā nayena vā upadassayitun-ti.

641 etam-p' ahaṃ bhante nāgasena na sampaṭicchāmi yaṃ atthidhammassa nibbānassa rūpaṃ vā saṇṭhānaṃ vā vayaṃ vā pamāṇaṃ vā opammena vā kāraṇena vā hetunā

wash his feet, prepare his bath, massage him, and are obedient to another's mind while setting aside their own minds?"

"But Nagasena, this is not the happiness associated with 639
craftsmanship; rather it is the preliminary part of the quest for craftsmanship. Having sought the craft painfully, masters experience the happiness of craftsmanship. And in this way, Nagasena, the happiness of craftsmanship is not mixed with pain. The happiness of craftsmanship is one thing, and pain is something else."

"In the same way, great king, nibbana is entirely happy and not mixed with pain. Those seeking nibbana mortify body and mind; abstain from standing, pacing, sitting, lying down, or food; curtail sleep; suppress the senses; and give up body and life. Seeking nibbana by means of pain, they experience nibbana as entirely happy, much as masters enjoy the happiness associated with craftsmanship. And so, great king, nibbana is entirely happy and not mixed with pain. Nibbana is one thing, and pain is something else."

"Excellent, revered Nagasena. This is so, and I am convinced.

"Revered Nagasena, you speak often of nibbana—'nibbana 640
this and nibbana that'—but can you point out the form of nibbana with an analogy, argument, reasoning, or method? Or its composition, age, or measure?"

"Nibbana resembles nothing else, great king, so it is impossible to point out its form, composition, age, or measure with an analogy, argument, reasoning, or method."

"But I am not convinced that the form, composition, age, 641
or measure of nibbana cannot be understood by means of an analogy, argument, reasoning, or method, for it is, after

vā nayena vā apaññāpanaṃ, kāraṇena maṃ saññāpehīti. hotu mahārāja, kāraṇena taṃ saññāpessāmi. atthi mahārāja mahāsamuddo nāmāti. āma bhante, atth' eso mahāsamuddo ti.

642 sace taṃ mahārāja koci evaṃ puccheyya: kittakaṃ mahārāja mahāsamudde udakaṃ, kati pana te sattā ye mahāsamudde paṭivasantīti; evaṃ puṭṭho tvaṃ mahārāja kin-ti tassa byākareyyāsīti. sace maṃ bhante koci evaṃ puccheyya: kittakaṃ mahārāja mahāsamudde udakaṃ, kati pana te sattā ye mahāsamudde paṭivasantīti, tam-ahaṃ bhante evaṃ vadeyyaṃ: apucchaṃ maṃ tvaṃ ambho purisa pucchasi, n' esā pucchā kenaci pucchitabbā, ṭhapanīyo eso pañho, avibhatto lokakkhāyikehi mahāsamuddo, na sakkā mahāsamudde udakaṃ pariminituṃ sattā vā ye tattha vāsamupagatā ti. evāhaṃ bhante tassa paṭivacanaṃ dadeyyan-ti.

643 kissa pana tvaṃ mahārāja atthidhamme mahāsamudde evaṃ paṭivacanaṃ dadeyyāsi, nanu vigaṇetvā tassa ācikkhitabbaṃ: ettakaṃ mahāsamudde udakaṃ ettakā ca sattā mahāsamudde paṭivasantīti. na sakkā bhante, avisayo eso pañho ti. yathā mahārāja atthi dhamme yeva mahāsamudde na sakkā udakaṃ parigaṇetuṃ sattā vā ye tattha vāsam-upagatā, evam-eva kho mahārāja atthidhammass' eva nibbānassa na sakkā rūpaṃ vā saṇṭhānaṃ vā vayaṃ vā pamāṇaṃ vā opammena vā kāraṇena vā hetunā vā nayena vā upadassayituṃ. vigaṇeyya mahārāja iddhimā cetovasippatto mahā-

all, a phenomenon that exists. Convince me with reasoning."

"Let it be so, great king. I will persuade you with reasoning. Is there such a thing as the great ocean?"

"Yes, sir, the great ocean does exist."

"What if someone were to ask you this: 'Great king, how 642
much water is in the great ocean? And how many creatures live in the ocean?' If you were asked this, how would you respond?"

"If someone were to ask me how much water is in the great ocean and how many creatures live in it, then I would reply: 'Look here, man. You are asking something that should not be asked. No one should ask such a thing. The question should be set aside, for the great ocean has not been analyzed by those who speculate about the world. It is impossible to estimate the water or the creatures who live there.' I would give this response to him."

"But why would you give this reply concerning the great 643
ocean, great king, which is, after all, a phenomenon that exists? Why not estimate and then inform him: 'There is this much water in the great ocean, and this many creatures live in the ocean.'"

"Impossible, sir. The question is beyond our scope."

"Just as it is impossible to estimate the water in the great ocean—which, after all, does exist—and the number of creatures living in it, so too, great king, it is not possible to point out the form, composition, age, or measure of nibbana, by an analogy, argument, reasoning, or method. Even if someone who had mastered the mind were to reckon with magical powers the water in the great ocean and the creatures living there, this mastermind, even with magical powers,

samudde udakaṃ tatrāsaye ca satte, na tv eva so iddhimā cetovasippatto sakkuṇeyya nibbānassa rūpaṃ vā saṇṭhānaṃ vā vayaṃ vā pamāṇaṃ vā opammena vā kāraṇena vā hetunā vā nayena vā upadassayituṃ. aparam-pi mahārāja uttariṃ kāraṇaṃ sunohi: atthi-dhammass' eva nibbānassa na sakkā rūpaṃ vā saṇṭhānaṃ vā vayaṃ vā pamāṇaṃ vā opammena vā kāraṇena vā hetunā vā nayena vā upadassayitun-ti. atthi mahārāja devesu arūpakāyikā nāma devā ti.

644 āma bhante, sūyati: atthi devesu arūpakāyikā nāma devā ti. sakkā pana mahārāja tesaṃ arūpakāyikānaṃ devānaṃ rūpaṃ vā saṇṭhānaṃ vā vayaṃ vā pamāṇaṃ vā opammena vā kāraṇena vā hetunā vā nayena vā upadassayitun-ti. na hi bhante ti. tena hi mahārāja na-tthi arūpakāyikā devā ti. atthi bhante arūpakāyikā devā, na ca sakkā tesaṃ rūpaṃ vā saṇṭhānaṃ vā vayaṃ vā pamāṇaṃ vā opammena vā kāraṇena vā hetunā vā nayena vā upadassayitun-ti.

645 yathā mahārāja atthisattānaṃ yeva arūpakāyikānaṃ devānaṃ na sakkā rūpaṃ vā saṇṭhānaṃ vā vayaṃ vā pamāṇaṃ vā opammena vā kāraṇena vā hetunā vā nayena vā upadassayituṃ, evam-eva kho mahārāja atthidhammass' eva nibbānassa na sakkā rūpaṃ vā saṇṭhānaṃ vā vayaṃ vā pamāṇaṃ vā opammena vā kāraṇena vā hetunā vā nayena vā upadassayitun-ti.

646 bhante nāgasena, hotu ekantasukhaṃ nibbānaṃ na ca sakkā tassa rūpaṃ vā saṇṭhānaṃ vā vayaṃ vā pamāṇaṃ vā opammena vā kāraṇena vā hetunā vā nayena vā upadassayituṃ. atthi pana bhante nibbānassa guṇaṃ aññehi anupaviṭṭhaṃ, kiñci opammanidassanamattan ti. sarū-

would not be able to point out the form, composition, age, or measure of nibbana with an analogy, argument, reasoning, or method. Please listen to a further reason it is not possible to point out the form, composition, age, or measure of nibbana, although it does exist, with an analogy, argument, reasoning, or method. Great king, among the gods, is there a class of gods that lack form?"

"Yes, sir, I have heard that among the gods there is a class 644
of formless gods."

"But then can you, great king, point out the form, composition, age, or measure of these formless gods with an analogy, argument, reasoning, or method?"

"No, sir."

"Therefore, great king, gods without form do not exist."

"Sir, the class of formless gods does exist even though it is not possible to point out their form, composition, age, or measure with an analogy, argument, reasoning, or method."

"Great king, just as it is not possible to point out with an 645
analogy, argument, reasoning, or method the form, composition, age, or measure of the formless gods—though such beings do exist—it is also not possible to point out with an analogy, argument, reasoning, or method the form, composition, age, or measure of nibbana, though it is a phenomenon that does exist."

"Let it be so, revered Nagasena, that nibbana is entirely 646
happy, though it is not possible to point out its form, composition, age, or measure with an analogy, argument, reasoning, or method. But is there a special quality of nibbana shared with other things that might just illustrate it by analogy?"

pato mahārāja na-tthi, guṇato pana sakkā kiñci opammanidassanamattaṃ upadassayitun-ti.

647 sādhu bhante nāgasena, yathā 'haṃ labhāmi nibbānassa guṇato pi ekadesaparidīpanamattaṃ tathā sīghaṃ brūhi, nibbāpehi me hadayapariḷāhaṃ, vinaya sītala-madhura-vacana-mālutenāti. padumassa mahārāja eko guṇo nibbānaṃ anupaviṭṭho, udakassa dve guṇā, agadassa tayo guṇā, mahāsamuddassa cattāro guṇā, bhojanassa pañca guṇā, ākāsassa dasa guṇā, maṇiratanassa tayo guṇā, lohitacandanassa tayo guṇā, sappimaṇḍassa tayo guṇā, girisikharassa pañca guṇā nibbānaṃ anupaviṭṭhā ti.

648 bhante nāgasena, padumassa eko guṇo nibbānaṃ anupaviṭṭho ti yaṃ vadesi, katamo padumassa eko guṇo nibbānaṃ anupaviṭṭho ti. yathā mahārāja padumaṃ anupalittaṃ udakena, evam-eva kho mahārāja nibbānaṃ sabbakilesehi anupalittaṃ. ayaṃ mahārāja padumassa eko guṇo nibbānaṃ anupaviṭṭho ti. bhante nāgasena, udakassa dve guṇā nibbānaṃ anupaviṭṭhā ti yaṃ vadesi, katame udakassa dve guṇā nibbānaṃ anupaviṭṭhā ti. yathā mahārāja udakaṃ sītalaṃ pariḷāhanibbāpanaṃ, evam-eva kho mahārāja nibbānaṃ sītālam sabbakilesa-pariḷāha-nibbāpanaṃ. ayaṃ mahārāja udakassa paṭhamo guṇo nibbānaṃ anupaviṭṭho. puna ca paraṃ mahārāja udakaṃ kilanta-tasita-pipāsita-ghammābhitattānaṃ jana-pasu-pajānaṃ pipāsāvinayanaṃ, evameva kho mahārāja nibbānaṃ kāma-taṇhā-bhavataṇhā-vibhavataṇhā-pipāsā-vinayanaṃ. ayaṃ mahārāja udakassa dutiyo guṇo nibbānaṃ anupaviṭṭho. ime kho mahārāja udakassa dve guṇā nibbānaṃ anupaviṭṭhā ti.

"There is nothing similar in form, great king, and one can only point out an illustration by way of analogy with a special quality."

"Very well, then, Nagasena, I'll take it. Speak swiftly to 647
even one point that would shed a little light on a special quality of nibbana, sir. Quench the burning in my heart, dispelling it with the cool and sweet breezes of your words."

"Great king, there is one quality of a lotus that is shared with nibbana, and two qualities of water, three qualities of an antidote, four qualities of the great ocean, five qualities of food, ten qualities of space, three qualities of the jewel treasure, three qualities of red sandalwood, three qualities of the finest part of ghee, and five qualities of a mountain peak that are shared with nibbana."

"Nagasena, you say that there is one quality of a lotus 648
shared with nibbana. What is the quality of a lotus that is shared with nibbana?"

"Just as a lotus is unsullied by water, great king, nibbana is unsullied by any of the defilements. This is the quality of the lotus that is shared with nibbana."

"Nagasena, you say that there are two qualities of water shared with nibbana. What are the two qualities of water that are shared with nibbana?"

"Just as cool water quenches burning, great king, so too does cool nibbana quench the burning of all of the defilements. This is the first quality of water shared with nibbana. And just as water dispels the thirst of humans and beasts that are scorched by the heat, exhausted, parched, and thirsty, so too does nibbana dispel the thirst that is the craving for desires, craving for being, and craving for life to end. This is

649 bhante nāgasena, agadassa tayo guṇā nibbānaṃ anupaviṭṭhā ti yaṃ vadesi, katame agadassa tayo guṇā nibbānaṃ anupaviṭṭhā ti. yathā mahārāja agado visapīḷitānaṃ sattānaṃ paṭisaraṇaṃ, evam-eva kho mahārāja nibbānaṃ kilesavisa-pīḷitānaṃ sattānaṃ paṭisaraṇaṃ. ayaṃ mahārāja agadassa paṭhamo guṇo nibbānaṃ anupaviṭṭho. puna ca paraṃ mahārāja agado rogānaṃ antakaro, evam-eva kho mahārāja nibbānaṃ sabbadukkhānaṃ antakaraṃ. ayaṃ mahārāja agadassa dutiyo guṇo nibbānaṃ anupaviṭṭho. puna ca paraṃ mahārāja agado amataṃ, evam-eva kho mahārāja nibbānaṃ amataṃ. ayaṃ mahārāja agadassa tatiyo guṇo nibbānaṃ anupaviṭṭho. ime kho mahārāja agadassa tayo guṇā nibbānaṃ anupaviṭṭhā ti.

650 bhante nāgasena, mahāsamuddassa cattāro guṇā nibbānaṃ anupaviṭṭhā ti yaṃ vadesi, katame mahāsamuddassa cattāro guṇā nibbānaṃ anupaviṭṭhā ti. yathā mahārāja mahāsamuddo suñño sabbakuṇapehi, evam-eva kho mahārāja nibbānaṃ suññaṃ sabbakilesakuṇapehi. ayaṃ mahārāja mahāsamuddassa paṭhamo guṇo nibbānaṃ anupaviṭṭho. puna ca paraṃ mahārāja mahāsamuddo mahanto anorapāro, na pūrati sabbasavantīhi, evam-eva kho mahārāja nibbānaṃ mahantaṃ anorapāraṃ, na pūrati sabbasattehi. ayaṃ mahārāja mahāsamuddassa dutiyo guṇo nibbānaṃ anupaviṭṭho. puna ca paraṃ mahārāja mahāsamuddo mahantānaṃ bhūtānaṃ āvāso, evam-eva kho mahārāja nibbānaṃ mahantānaṃ arahantānaṃ vimalakhīṇāsava-balappatta-vasībhūta-mahā- bhūtānaṃ āvāso. ayaṃ mahārāja mahāsamuddassa tatiyo guṇo nibbānaṃ anupaviṭṭho. puna ca paraṃ mahārāja

the second quality of water shared with nibbana, and these two are the qualities water shares with nibbana."

"Nagasena, you say that there are three qualities of an antidote shared with nibbana. What are the three qualities of an antidote that are shared with nibbana?" 649

"Just as an antidote is a remedy for beings stricken with poison, great king, so too nibbana is a remedy for beings stricken with the poison of the defilements. This is the first quality of an antidote shared with nibbana. And just as an antidote puts an end to illness, so too nibbana puts an end to all suffering. This is the second quality of an antidote shared with nibbana. And further, just as an antidote is ambrosia, so too, great king, nibbana is ambrosia. This is the third quality of an antidote shared with nibbana, and so these three are the qualities that an antidote shares with nibbana."

"Nagasena, you say that there are four qualities of the great ocean shared with nibbana. What are the four qualities of the ocean that are shared with nibbana?" 650

"Just as the great ocean is devoid of all corpses, so too, great king, nibbana is devoid of all corpses—that is, the corpses that are the defilements. This is the first quality of the great ocean shared with nibbana. And just as the great ocean is vast and boundless and does not spill over with all the rivers flowing into it, so too nibbana is vast and boundless and does not spill over with all beings. This is the second quality of the great ocean shared with nibbana. And just as the great ocean is a home for great beings, so too nibbana is a home for the great arhats—that is, those great beings who are stainless and have destroyed the flaws, achieved power, and become masters. This is the third quality of the ocean

mahāsamuddo aparimita-vividha-vipula-vīcipuppha-saṅkusumito, evam-eva kho mahārāja nibbānaṃ aparimita-vividha-vipula-parisuddha-vijjāvimuttipuppha-saṅkusumitaṃ. ayaṃ mahārāja mahāsamuddassa catuttho guṇo nibbānaṃ anupaviṭṭho. ime kho mahārāja mahāsamuddassa cattāro guṇā nibbānaṃ anupaviṭṭhā ti.

651 bhante nāgasena, bhojanassa pañca guṇā nibbānaṃ anupaviṭṭhā ti yaṃ vadesi, katame bhojanassa pañca guṇā nibbānaṃ anupaviṭṭhā ti. yathā mahārāja bhojanaṃ sabbasattānaṃ āyudhāraṇaṃ, evam eva kho mahārāja nibbānaṃ sacchikataṃ jarā-maraṇa-nāsanato āyudhāraṇaṃ. ayaṃ mahārāja bhojanassa paṭhamo guṇo nibbānaṃ anupaviṭṭho. puna ca paraṃ mahārāja bhojanaṃ sabbasattānaṃ balavaḍḍhanaṃ, evam-eva kho mahārāja nibbānaṃ sacchikataṃ sabbasattānaṃ iddhibalavaḍḍhanaṃ. ayaṃ mahārāja bhojanassa dutiyo guṇo nibbānaṃ anupaviṭṭho. puna ca paraṃ mahārāja bhojanaṃ sabbasattānaṃ vaṇṇajananaṃ, evam-eva kho mahārāja nibbānaṃ sacchikataṃ sabbasattānaṃ guṇavaṇṇajananaṃ. ayaṃ mahārāja bhojanassa tatiyo guṇo nibbānaṃ anupaviṭṭho. puna ca paraṃ mahārāja bhojanaṃ sabbasattānaṃ darathavūpasamanaṃ, evam-eva kho mahārāja nibbānaṃ sacchikataṃ sabbasattānaṃ sabbakilesadarathavūpasamanaṃ. ayaṃ mahārāja bhojanassa catuttho guṇo nibbānaṃ anupaviṭṭho. puna ca paraṃ mahārāja bhojanaṃ sabbasattānaṃ jighacchādubbalya paṭivinodanaṃ, evam-eva kho mahārāja nibbānaṃ sacchikataṃ sabbasattānaṃ sabbadukkha-jighacchādubbalyapaṭivinodanaṃ. ayaṃ mahārāja bhojanassa pañcamo guṇo nibbānaṃ anupaviṭṭho. ime kho mahārāja bhojanassa pañca guṇā nibbānaṃ anupaviṭṭhā ti.

shared with nibbana. And finally, great king, just as the great ocean blooms with immeasurable, diverse, and abundant flowery waves, so too nibbana blooms with the immeasurable, diverse, abundant, and pure flowers of knowledge and freedom. This is the fourth quality of the ocean shared with nibbana, and these four are the qualities the ocean shares with nibbana."

"Nagasena, you say that there are five qualities of food 651
that are shared with nibbana. What are these five qualities of food shared with nibbana?"

"Just as food sustains the life of all beings, great king, so too nibbana, when it is experienced, sustains life by annihilating old age and death. This is the first quality of food shared with nibbana. And just as food increases the strength of all beings, so too nibbana, when it is experienced, increases the magical powers of all beings. This is the second quality of food shared with nibbana. And just as food produces beauty for all beings, so too nibbana, when it is experienced, produces the beauty of virtue for all beings. This is the third quality of food shared with nibbana. And just as food allays anxiety for all beings, so too nibbana, when it is experienced, allays the anxieties of each defilement for all beings. This is the fourth quality of food shared with nibbana. And finally, great king, just as food dispels the weakness of hunger for all beings, so too nibbana, when it is experienced, dispels the weakness of hunger and every suffering for all beings. This is the fifth quality of food shared with nibbana, great king, and these five are the qualities that food shares with nibbana."

652 bhante nāgasena, ākāsassa dasa guṇā nibbānaṃ anupaviṭṭhā ti yaṃ vadesi, katame ākāsassa dasa guṇā nibbānaṃ anupaviṭṭhā ti. yathā mahārāja ākāso na jāyati na jīyati na mīyati na cavati na uppajjati, duppasaho acorāharaṇo anissito vihagagamano nirāvaraṇo ananto, evam-eva kho mahārāja nibbānaṃ na jāyati na jīyati na mīyati na cavati na uppajjati, duppasahaṃ acorāharaṇaṃ anissitaṃ ariyagamanaṃ nirāvaraṇaṃ anantaṃ. ime kho mahārāja ākāsassa dasa guṇā nibbānaṃ anupaviṭṭhā ti.

653 bhante nāgasena, maṇiratanassa tayo guṇā nibbānaṃ anupaviṭṭhā ti yaṃ vadesi, katame maṇiratanassa tayo guṇā nibbānaṃ anupaviṭṭhā ti. yathā mahārāja maṇiratanaṃ kāmadadaṃ, evam eva kho mahārāja nibbānaṃ kāmadadaṃ. ayaṃ mahārāja maṇiratanassa paṭhamo guṇo nibbānaṃ anupaviṭṭho. puna ca paraṃ mahārāja maṇiratanaṃ hāsakaraṃ, evam-eva kho mahārāja nibbānaṃ hāsakaraṃ. ayaṃ mahārāja maṇiratanassa dutiyo guṇo nibbānaṃ anupaviṭṭho. puna ca paraṃ mahārāja maṇiratanaṃ ujjotatthakaraṃ, evam-eva kho mahārāja nibbānaṃ ujjotatthakaraṃ. ayaṃ mahārāja maṇiratanassa tatiyo guṇo nibbānaṃ anupaviṭṭho. ime kho mahārāja maṇiratanassa tayo guṇā nibbānaṃ anupaviṭṭhā ti.

654 bhante nāgasena, lohitacandanassa tayo guṇā nibbānaṃ anupaviṭṭhā ti yaṃ vadesi, katame lohitacandanassa tayo guṇā nibbānaṃ anupaviṭṭhā ti. yathā mahārāja lohitacandanaṃ dullabhaṃ, evam-eva kho mahārāja nibbānaṃ dullabhaṃ. ayaṃ mahārāja lohitacandanassa paṭhamo guṇo nibbānaṃ anupaviṭṭho. puna ca paraṃ mahārāja lohitacandanaṃ asamasugandhaṃ, evam-eva kho mahārāja

"Nagasena, you say that there are ten qualities of space shared with nibbana. What are these ten qualities of space that are shared with nibbana?" 652

"Just as space is not born, does not age, does not die, does not move, does not get reborn, is hard to overpower, cannot be carried off by thieves, rests on nothing, is the sphere of birds, is endless, and is without obstructions, nibbana is not born, does not die, does not move, and does not get reborn; it is hard to overpower, cannot be carried away by thieves, rests on nothing, is the sphere of arhats, and is endless and without obstructions.[119] These are the ten qualities that space shares with nibbana, great king."

"Nagasena, you say that there are three qualities of the jewel treasure shared with nibbana. What are these three qualities of the jewel treasure that are shared with nibbana?" 653

"Just as the jewel treasure is a giver of wishes, so too, great king, nibbana gives wishes. This is the first quality of the jewel treasure shared with nibbana. And just as the jewel treasure generates a smile, nibbana generates a smile. This is the second quality of the jewel treasure shared with nibbana. And just as the jewel treasure produces radiance, nibbana produces radiance. This is the third quality of the jewel treasure shared with nibbana, and these three are the qualities that the jewel treasure shares with nibbana, great king."

"Nagasena, you say that there are three qualities of red sandalwood shared with nibbana. What are the three qualities of red sandalwood that are shared with nibbana?" 654

"Just as red sandalwood is hard to find, great king, so too nibbana is hard to find. This is the first quality of red sandalwood shared with nibbana. And just as red sandalwood has a

nibbānaṃ asamasugandhaṃ. ayaṃ mahārāja lohitacandanassa dutiyo guṇo nibbānaṃ anu-paviṭṭho. puna ca paraṃ mahārāja lohitacandanaṃ sajjanapasatthaṃ, evam-eva kho mahārāja nibbānaṃ ariyajanapasatthaṃ. ayaṃ mahārāja lohitacandanassa tatiyo guṇo nibbānaṃ anupaviṭṭho. ime kho mahārāja lohitacandanassa tayo guṇā nibbānaṃ anupaviṭṭhā ti.

655 bhante nāgasena, sappimaṇḍassa tayo guṇā nibbānaṃ anupaviṭṭhā ti yaṃ vadesi, katame sappimaṇḍassa tayo guṇā nibbānaṃ anupaviṭṭhā ti. yathā mahārāja sappimaṇḍo vaṇṇasampanno, evam-eva kho mahārāja nibbānaṃ guṇavaṇṇasampannaṃ. ayaṃ mahārāja sappimaṇḍassa paṭhamo guṇo nibbānaṃ anupaviṭṭho. puna ca paraṃ mahārāja sappimaṇḍo gandhasampanno, evam- eva kho mahārāja nibbānaṃ sīlagandhasampannaṃ. ayaṃ mahārāja sappimaṇḍassa dutiyo guṇo nibbānaṃ anupaviṭṭho. puna ca paraṃ mahārāja sappimaṇḍo rasasampanno, evam-eva kho mahārāja nibbānaṃ rasasampannaṃ. ayaṃ mahārāja sappimaṇḍassa tatiyo guṇo nibbānaṃ anupaviṭṭho. ime kho mahārāja sappimaṇḍassa tayo guṇā nibbānaṃ anupaviṭṭhā ti.

656 bhante nāgasena, girisikharassa pañca guṇā nibbānaṃ anupaviṭṭhā ti yaṃ vadesi, katame girisikharassa pañca guṇā nibbānaṃ anupaviṭṭhā ti. yathā mahārāja girisikharaṃ accuggataṃ, evam-eva kho mahārāja nibbānaṃ accuggataṃ. ayaṃ mahārāja girisikharassa paṭhamo guṇo nibbānaṃ anupaviṭṭho. puna ca paraṃ mahārāja girisikharaṃ acalaṃ, evam-eva kho mahārāja nibbānaṃ acalaṃ. ayaṃ mahārāja girisikharassa dutiyo guṇo nibbānaṃ anupaviṭṭho. puna

fragrance that is unequaled, nibbana has a fragrance that is unequaled. This is the second quality of red sandalwood that is shared with nibbana. And just as red sandalwood is praised by good people, nibbana is praised by noble people. This is the third quality of red sandalwood shared with nibbana, and these three are the qualities that red sandalwood shares with nibbana, great king."

"Nagasena, you say that there are three qualities of the 655
finest part of ghee that are shared with nibbana. What are the three qualities of the finest part of ghee shared with nibbana?"

"Just as the finest part of ghee has luster, nibbana has the luster of virtue. This is the first quality of the finest part of ghee shared with nibbana. And just as the finest part of ghee is fragrant, nibbana is fragrant with the scent of morality. This is the second quality of the finest part of ghee shared with nibbana. And just as the finest part of ghee has flavor, nibbana has flavor. This is the third quality of the finest part of ghee shared with nibbana, and these three are the qualities that the finest part of ghee shares with nibbana."

"Nagasena, you say that there are five qualities of a moun- 656
tain peak shared with nibbana. What are the five qualities of a mountain peak that are shared with nibbana?"

"Just as a mountain peak is towering, great king, nibbana is also towering. This is the first quality of a mountain peak shared with nibbana. And just as a mountain peak is unshaken, nibbana does not shake. This is the second quality of a mountain peak shared with nibbana. And just as a mountain peak is difficult to scale, nibbana is difficult for any of the defilements to scale. This is the third quality of a mountain

ca paraṃ mahārāja girisikharaṃ duradhirohaṃ, evam-eva kho mahārāja nibbānaṃ duradhirohaṃ sabbakilesānaṃ. ayaṃ mahārāja girisikharassa tatiyo guṇo nibbānaṃ anupaviṭṭho. puna ca paraṃ mahārāja girisikharaṃ sabbabījānaṃ avirūhanaṃ, evam-eva kho mahārāja nibbānaṃ sabbakilesānaṃ avirūhanaṃ. ayaṃ mahārāja girisikharassa catuttho guṇo nibbānaṃ anupaviṭṭho. puna ca paraṃ mahārāja girisikharaṃ anunayapaṭighavippamuttaṃ, evam-eva kho mahārāja nibbānaṃ anunayapaṭighavippamuttaṃ. ayaṃ mahārāja girisikharassa pañcamo guṇo nibbānaṃ anupaviṭṭho. ime kho mahārāja girisikharassa pañca guṇā nibbānaṃ anupaviṭṭhā ti. sādhu bhante nāgasena, evam-etaṃ, tathā sampaṭicchāmīti.

657 bhante nāgasena, tumhe bhaṇatha: nibbānaṃ na atītaṃ na anāgataṃ na paccuppannaṃ, na uppannaṃ na anuppannaṃ na uppādaniyan-ti. idha bhante nāgasena yo koci sammā paṭipanno nibbānaṃ sacchikaroti so uppannaṃ sacchikaroti udāhu uppādetvā sacchikarotīti. yo koci mahārāja sammā paṭipanno nibbānaṃ sacchikaroti so na uppannaṃ sacchikaroti na uppādetvā sacchikaroti. api ca mahārāja atth' esā nibbānadhātu yaṃ so sammā paṭipanno sacchikarotīti.

658 mā bhante nāgasena imaṃ pañhaṃ paṭicchannaṃ katvā dīpehi, vivataṃ pākaṭaṃ katvā dīpehi, chandajāto ussāhajāto yaṃ te sikkhitaṃ taṃ sabbaṃ etth' ev' ākirāhi, etthāyaṃ jano sammūḷho vimatijāto saṃsayapakkhanno, bhind' etaṃ antodosasallan-ti. atth' esā mahārāja nibbānadhātu santā

peak shared with nibbana. And just a mountain peak does not allow any seeds to take root, so too nibbana does not allow any defilements to take root. This is the fourth quality of a mountain peak shared with nibbana. Finally, great king, a mountain peak is free of both attraction and repugnance, and nibbana is free of both attraction and repugnance. This is the fifth quality of a mountain peak shared with nibbana, and these five are the five special qualities that a mountain peak shares with nibbana."

"Very good, revered Nagasena. This is so, and I am persuaded.

"Revered Nagasena, you say that nibbana is not past, pres- 657
ent, or future, and that it is not arisen, not unarisen, and not something one can produce. Regarding this, Nagasena, suppose someone practices rightly and experiences nibbana. Does this person experience what has arisen, or does one first produce it and then experience it?"

"Someone practicing rightly who experiences nibbana neither experiences something arisen nor produces it first and then experiences it, great king. And yet, the domain of nibbana does exist, and it is what one practicing rightly experiences."

"Revered Nagasena, instead of illuminating this question 658
by first concealing it, illuminate it by making it open and clear. Generate zeal and effort and disseminate everything you have learned regarding this, for people are bewildered, perplexed, and thrust headlong into doubt on this matter. Please destroy this arrow of an inner fault."

"Great king, the domain of nibbana is peaceful, happy, and excellent, and it is what someone practicing rightly and

sukhā paṇītā, taṃ sammā paṭipanno jinānusatthiyā saṅkhāre sammasanto paññāya sacchikaroti. yathā mahārāja antevāsiko ācariyānusatthiyā vijjaṃ paññāya sacchikaroti, evam-eva kho mahārāja sammā paṭipanno jinānusatthiyā paññāya nibbānaṃ sacchikaroti.

659 katham-pana nibbānaṃ daṭṭhabban-ti: anītito nirupaddavato abhayato khemato santato sukhato sātato paṇītato sucito sītalato daṭṭhabbaṃ. yathā mahārāja puriso bahukaṭṭhapuñjena jalita-kaṭhitena agginā ḍayhamāno vāyāmena tato muñcitvā niraggikokāsaṃ pavisitvā tattha paramasukhaṃ labheyya, evam-eva kho mahārāja yo sammā paṭipanno so yoniso manasikārena byapagata-tividhaggisantāpaṃ paramasukhaṃ nibbānaṃ sacchikaroti. yathā mahārāja aggi evaṃ tividhaggi daṭṭhabbo, yathā aggigato puriso evaṃ sammā paṭipanno daṭṭhabbo, yathā niraggikokāso evaṃ nibbānaṃ daṭṭhabbaṃ. yathā vā pana mahārāja puriso ahi-kukkura-manussa kuṇapa-sarīravaḷañja-koṭṭhāsarāsigato kuṇapa-jaṭājaṭitantaram-anupaviṭṭho vāyāmena tato muñcitvā nikkuṇapokāsaṃ pavisitvā tattha paramasukhaṃ labheyya, evam-eva kho mahārāja yo sammā paṭipanno so yoniso manasikārena byapagata-kilesakuṇapaṃ paramasukhaṃ nibbānaṃ sacchikaroti. yathā mahārāja kuṇapaṃ evaṃ pañca kāmaguṇā daṭṭhabbā, yathā kuṇapagato puriso evaṃ sammā paṭipanno daṭṭhabbo, yathā nikkuṇapokāso evaṃ nibbānaṃ daṭṭhabbaṃ.

660 yathā vā pana mahārāja puriso bhīto tasito kampito viparīta-vibbhanta-citto vāyāmena tato muñcitvā daḷhaṃ thiram

who knows thoroughly the habitual patterns according to the Victor's instructions experiences by means of understanding. Just as a student experiences knowledge according to the teacher's instruction by means of understanding, one practicing rightly according to the Victor's instructions experiences nibbana by understanding.

"But how should nibbana be understood? It should be 659
understood in terms of being free of calamity, affliction, and fear, and in terms of peace, tranquility, happiness, joy, excellence, purity, and coolness. Great king, just a man scorched by a blazing hot fire heaped with lots of wood who manages with effort to break free of it and move to a place away from the fire finds the highest happiness there, someone practicing rightly with careful attention experiences nibbana as the highest happiness, far removed from the burning of the three fires. Fire here should be understood as the three fires, the person in the fire as the person practicing rightly, and the place away from the fire as nibbana. Or consider a man flung into a cesspool or onto a heap of snake, dog, and human corpses and entangled in the matted hair of the dead bodies, who manages with effort to break free and move to a place away from the corpses. He would find the highest happiness there. Similarly, great king, someone practicing rightly with careful attention experiences nibbana as the highest happiness, far removed from the corpses of the defilements. The corpses should be understood as the sense pleasures, great king, the person flung on the corpses as the person practicing rightly, and the place away from the corpses as nibbana.

"Or consider a frightened, terrified, and trembling man, 660
with mind upset and confused, who manages with effort to

acalam abhayaṭṭhānaṃ pavisitvā tattha paramasukhaṃ labheyya, evam-eva kho mahārāja yo sammā paṭipanno so yoniso manasikārena byapagata-bhayasantāsaṃ paramasukhaṃ nibbānaṃ sacchikaroti. yathā mahārāja bhayaṃ evaṃ jāti-jarā-byādhi-maraṇaṃ paṭicca aparāparaṃ pavatta-bhayaṃ daṭṭhabbaṃ, yathā bhīto puriso evaṃ sammā paṭipanno daṭṭhabbo, yathā abhayaṭṭhānaṃ evaṃ nibbānaṃ daṭṭhabbaṃ. yathā vā pana mahārāja puriso kiliṭṭha-malina-kalala-kaddamadese patito vāyāmena taṃ kalala-kaddamaṃ apavāhetvā parisuddhavimaladesamupagantvā tattha paramasukhaṃ labheyya, evam-eva kho mahārāja yo sammā paṭipanno so yoniso manasikārena byapagata-kilesa-mala-kaddamaṃ paramasukhaṃ nibbānaṃ sacchikaroti. yathā mahārāja kalalaṃ evaṃ lābha-sakkāra-siloko daṭṭhabbo, yathā kalalagato puriso evaṃ sammā paṭipanno daṭṭhabbo, yathā parisuddhavimaladeso evaṃ nibbānaṃ daṭṭhabbaṃ.
661 tañ-ca pana nibbānaṃ sammā paṭipanno kin-ti sacchikaroti: yo so mahārāja sammā paṭipanno so saṅkhārānaṃ pavattaṃ sammasati, pavattaṃ sammasamāno tattha jātiṃ passati jaraṃ passati byādhiṃ passati maraṇaṃ passati, na tattha kiñci sukhaṃ sātaṃ passati, ādito pi majjhato pi pariyosānato pi so tattha na kiñci gayhūpagaṃ passati. yathā mahārāja puriso divasasantatte ayoguḷe jalite tatte kaṭhite ādito pi majjhato pi pariyosānato pi na kañci gayhūpagaṃ padesaṃ passati, evam-eva kho mahārāja yo saṅkhārānaṃ pavattaṃ sammasati so pavattaṃ sammasamāno tattha jātiṃ passati jaraṃ passati byādhiṃ passati maraṇaṃ passati, na tattha kiñci sukhaṃ sātaṃ passati, ādito pi majjhato pi pariyosānato pi na kiñci gayhūpagaṃ passati. tassa gayhū-

break free of this and go to a place without fear, steady, firm, and secure. He would find the highest happiness there. Similarly, great king, one practicing rightly with careful attention experiences nibbana as the highest happiness, with fear and terror gone. The fear should be understood as the fear of continuing existence again and again conditioned by birth, old age, sickness, and death, and the place without fear should be understood as nibbana. Or consider a man fallen into a place with foul, grimy, and slimy mud who manages with effort to extract himself from the slime and the mud and go to a clean and spotless place. He would find the highest happiness there. Similarly, great king, one practicing rightly with careful attention experiences nibbana as the highest happiness, free of the dirt and mud of the defilements. The slime should be understood as gain, honor, and fame; the person fallen into the slime should be understood as the person practicing rightly, and the clean and spotless place as nibbana.

"But how does one who practices rightly experience 661
nibbana? Great king, someone practicing rightly knows thoroughly the continuing existence of the habitual patterns, and knowing thoroughly this continuing existence, sees birth there, sees old age there, sees sickness there, and sees death there. But one does not see any happiness and joy there, nor does one see anything there, from beginning, middle, or end, that may be held on to. As a man does not see any place in the beginning, middle, or end to grab on a glowing, burning, and scorching iron ball that has been heated all day, someone who knows thoroughly the continuing existence of the habitual patterns knows thoroughly continuing existence

pagaṃ apassantassa citte arati saṇṭhāti, kāyasmiṃ ḍāho okkamati, so attāṇo asaraṇo asaraṇībhūto bhavesu nibbindati. yathā mahārāja puriso jalitajālaṃ mahantaṃ aggikkhandhaṃ paviseyya, so tattha attāṇo asaraṇo asaraṇībhūto aggimhi nibbindeyya, evam-eva kho mahārāja tassa gayhūpagaṃ apassantassa cite arati saṇṭhāti, kāyasmiṃ ḍāho okkamati, so attāṇo asaraṇo asaraṇībhūto bhavesu nibbindati.

662 tassa pavatte bhayadassāvissa evaṃ cittaṃ uppajjati: santattaṃ kho pan' etaṃ pavattaṃ ādittaṃ sampajjalitaṃ bahudukkhaṃ bahupāyāsaṃ; yadi koci labhetha appavattaṃ, etaṃ santaṃ etaṃ paṇītaṃ, yad-idaṃ sabbasaṅkhārasamatho sabbūpadhipaṭinissaggo taṇhakkhayo virāgo nirodho nibbānan-ti. iti h' idaṃ tassa appavatte cittaṃ pakkhandati pasīdati pahaṃsīyati kuhīyati: paṭiladdhaṃ kho me nissaraṇan-ti. yathā mahārāja puriso vippanaṭṭho videsapakkhanno nibbāhanamaggaṃ disvā tattha pakkhandati pasīdati pahaṃsīyati kuhīyati: paṭiladdho me nibbāhanamaggo ti, evam-eva kho mahārāja pavatte bhayadassāvissa appavatte cittaṃ pakkhandati pasīdati pahaṃsīyati kuhīyati: paṭiladdhaṃ kho me nissaraṇan-ti. so appavattāya maggaṃ āyūhati gavesati bhāveti bahulīkaroti, tassa tadatthaṃ sati santiṭṭhati, tadatthaṃ viriyaṃ

and sees only birth, old age, sickness, and death there. One does not see any happiness and joy there, nor anything, from beginning, middle, or end, that may be held on to. When one sees that there is nothing that can be held on to, one's mind sinks into disenchantment, and fever arises in the body. One wearies of being without help, without refuge, and without shelter through endless rebirths. Great king, a person entering a massive burning and blazing fire grows weary of being in the fire without help, without refuge, and without shelter. Similarly, when one sees that there is nothing that can be held on to, one's mind sinks into disenchantment, a fever arises in the body, and one wearies of being without help, refuge, or shelter through endless rebirths.

"Now, for one who sees with fear this continuing existence, 662
the thought occurs: *This continuing existence is on fire, burning, blazing, with much suffering and many troubles. If only one could find the end of continuing existence—this would be peace, this would be excellent! This would be nibbana!—the calming of all the habitual patterns, the forsaking of all attachments, the destruction of craving, dispassion, that is, stopping*. One's mind leaps to the end of continued existence and delights, rejoices, and exults: *I have found an escape!* Great king, someone lost while traveling in a foreign land who comes to see a road out leaps upon it, and delights, rejoices, and exults: *I have found an escape!* Similarly, the mind of someone who sees this continuing existence with fear leaps to its ending and delights, rejoices, and exults: *I have found an escape!* One applies oneself to striving, developing, and practicing the path; one's mindfulness becomes established for this purpose; exertion becomes established for this purpose; and

santiṭṭhati, tadatthaṃ pīti santiṭṭhati, tassa taṃ cittaṃ aparāparaṃ manasikaroto pavattaṃ samatikkamitvā appavattaṃ okkamati; appavattam-anuppatto mahārāja sammā paṭipanno nibbānaṃ sacchikarotīti vuccatīti. sādhu bhante nāgasena, evam-etaṃ, tathā sampaṭicchāmīti.

663 bhante nāgasena, atthi so padeso puratthimāya vā disāya dakkhiṇāya vā disāya pacchimāya vā disāya uttarāya vā disāya, uddhaṃ vā adho vā tiriyaṃ vā, yattha nibbānaṃ sannihitan-ti. na-tthi mahārāja so padeso puratthimāya vā disāya dakkhiṇāya vā disāya pacchimāya vā disāya uttarāya vā disāya, uddhaṃ vā adho vā tiriyaṃ vā, yattha nibbānaṃ sannihitan-ti. yadi bhante nā-gasena na-tthi nibbānassa sannihitokāso, tena hi na-tthi nibbānaṃ, yesañ-ca taṃ nibbānaṃ sacchikataṃ tesam pi sacchikiriyā micchā. kāraṇaṃ tattha vakkhāmi: yathā bhante nāgasena mahiyā dhaññuṭṭhānaṃ khettaṃ atthi, gandhuṭṭhānaṃ pupphaṃ atthi, pupphuṭṭhānaṃ gumbo atthi, phaluṭṭhānaṃ rukkho atthi, ratanuṭṭhānaṃ ākaro atthi, tattha yo koci yaṃ yaṃ icchati so tattha gantvā taṃ taṃ harati; evam-eva kho bhante nāgasena yadi nibbānaṃ atthi, tassa nibbānassa uṭṭhānokāso pi icchitabbo. yasmā ca kho bhante nāgasena nibbānassa uṭṭhānokāso na-tthi, tasmā na-tthi nibbānan-ti brūmi, yesañ-ca nibbānaṃ sacchikataṃ tesam-pi sacchikiriyā micchā ti.

664 na-tthi mahārāja nibbānassa sannihitokāso, atthi c' etaṃ nibbānam, sammā paṭipanno yoniso manasikārena nibbānaṃ sacchikaroti. yathā pana mahārāja atthi aggi nāma, na-tthi tassa sannihitokāso, dve kaṭṭhāni sanghaṭṭento aggiṃ adhigacchati, evam-eva kho mahārāja atthi nibbānaṃ, na-tthi

joy becomes established for this purpose. The mind attends to it again and again, transcending continuing existence, until one reaches the end of continued existence. Great king, the person practicing rightly who reaches the end of continuing existence is said to experience nibbana."

"Excellent, revered Nagasena. This is so, and I am convinced.

"Revered Nagasena, is there any place in any direction— 663
east, south, west, north, above, below, or across—where nibbana is stored?"

"No, great king. There is nowhere in any direction—east, south, west, north, above, below, or across—where nibbana is stored."

"Well then, Nagasena, if there is no place where nibbana is stored, then nibbana does not exist. And those who have experienced nibbana have had a bogus experience. I will explain the reasoning on this. Nagasena, on this earth there are fields yielding grain, flowers yielding fragrance, bushes yielding flowers, trees yielding fruits, and mines yielding gems, so that anyone who wants such things may go there and take them. In the same way, Nagasena, if nibbana exists, then we expect that there is a place yielding nibbana. Since there is no place yielding nibbana, sir, I say that nibbana does not exist. Those who have experienced nibbana have had a bogus experience."

"Great king, there is no place where nibbana is stored, 664
and yet nibbana does exist. Those who practice rightly experience nibbana by means of careful attention. Fire exists, great king, even though there is no place where it is stored. One rubs two sticks together and gets fire. Similarly, nibbana

tassa sannihitokāso, sammā paṭipanno yoniso manasikārena nibbānaṃ sacchikaroti. yathā vā pana mahārāja atthi satta ratanāni nāma, seyyathīdaṃ: cakkaratanaṃ hatthiratanaṃ assaratanaṃ maṇiratanaṃ itthiratanaṃ gahapatiratanaṃ pariṇāyakaratanaṃ, na ca tesaṃ ratanānaṃ sannihitokāso atthi, khattiyassa pana sammā paṭipannassa paṭipattibalena tāni ratanāni upagacchanti; evam-eva kho mahārāja atthi nibbānaṃ, na-tthi tassa sannihitokāso, sammā paṭipanno yoniso manasikārena nibbānaṃ sacchikarotīti.

665 bhante nāgasena, nibbānassa sannihitokāso mā hotu, atthi pana taṃ ṭhānaṃ yattha ṭhito sammā paṭipanno nibbānaṃ sacchikarotīti. āma mahārāja, atthi taṃ ṭhānaṃ yattha ṭhito sammā paṭipanno nibbānaṃ sacchikarotīti. katamaṃ pana bhante taṃ ṭhānaṃ yattha ṭhito sammā paṭipanno nibbānaṃ sacchikarotīti.

666 sīlaṃ mahārāja ṭhānaṃ, sīle patiṭṭhito yoniso manasikaronto saka-yavane pi cīna-vilāte pi alasande pi nikumbe pi kāsi-kosale pi kasmīre pi gandhāre pi nagamuddhani pi brahmaloke pi yattha katthaci pi ṭhito sammā paṭipanno nibbānaṃ sacchikaroti. yathā mahārāja yo koci cakkhumā puriso saka-yavane pi cīna-vilāte pi alasande pi nikumbe pi kāsi-kosale pi kasmīre pi gandhāre pi nagamuddhani pi brahmaloke pi yattha katthaci pi ṭhito ākāsaṃ passati, evam-eva kho mahārāja sīle patiṭṭhito yoniso manasikaronto saka-yavane pi-pe-yattha katthaci pi ṭhito sammā paṭipanno nibbānaṃ sacchikaroti. yathā vā pana mahārāja saka-yavane pi-pe-

exists even though there is no place where it is stored, and one who practices rightly experiences nibbana by careful attention. The seven treasures do exist—that is, the wheel treasure, the elephant treasure, the horse treasure, the jewel treasure, the woman treasure, the householder treasure, and the chief minister treasure—though there is no place where the treasures are stored. However, these treasures come to a Kshatriya practicing rightly by the power of his conduct. In much the same way, great king, nibbana exists though there is no place where it is stored. One practicing rightly experiences nibbana by careful attention."

"All right then, Nagasena, let it be so that there is no place 665
where nibbana is stored. But is there a place where one practicing rightly can stand and experience nibbana?"

"Yes, great king, there is a place where someone practicing rightly may stand and experience nibbana."

"Well, then, what place is it that one practicing rightly may stand and experience nibbana, sir?"

"The place is morality, great king. Taking one's stand 666
on morality and carefully attending—whether standing in Scythia, Bactria, China, Vilata, Alexandria, Nikumba, Kasi, Kosala, Kashmir, Gandhara, on the summit of Mount Sineru, in the Brahma world, or anywhere else—one practicing rightly may experience nibbana. Great king, anyone with eyes can see the sky, whether standing in Scythia, Bactria, China, Vilata, Alexandria, Nikumba, Kasi, Kosala, Kashmir, Gandhara, on the summit of Mount Sineru, in the Brahma world, or anywhere else. In the same way, great king, one taking one's stand on morality may practice rightly, attend carefully, and experience nibbana whether standing in

yattha katthaci pi ṭhitassa pubbadisā atthi, evam-eva kho mahārāja sīle patiṭṭhitassa yoniso manasikarontassa saka-yavane pi-pe-yattha katthaci pi ṭhitassa sammā paṭipannassa atthi nibbānasacchikiriyā ti.

667 sādhu bhante nāgasena, desitaṃ tayā nibbānaṃ, desitā nibbānasacchikiriyā, parikkhatā sīlaguṇā, dassitā sammā-paṭipatti, ussāpito dhammaddhajo, saṇṭhāpitā dhamma-netti, avañjho suppayuttānaṃ sammāpayogo, evam-etaṃ gaṇivarapavara, tathā sampaṭicchāmīti.

aṭṭhamo vaggo

Scythia, Bactria, or anywhere else. There will be the eastern direction for anyone whether standing in Scythia, Bactria, or anywhere else, great king. Similarly, one taking one's stand on morality and carefully attending may practice rightly and experience nibbana whether standing in Scythia, Bactria, or anywhere else."

"Excellent, revered Nagasena. You have taught nibbana, 667
explained the experience of nibbana, set forth the virtues of morality, shown right practice, raised the banner of the Dhamma, and composed a guide to the Dhamma. Correct practice will not be fruitless for those applying themselves fully. Best of the best teachers, this is so, and I am convinced."

End of Part 8.

CHAPTER 4

A Question Resolved by Inference

1 atha kho milindo rājā yen' āyasmā nāgaseno ten' upasaṅkami, upasaṅkamitvā āyasmantaṃ nāgasenaṃ abhivādetvā ekamantaṃ nisīdi. ekamantaṃ nisinno kho milindo rājā ñātukāmo sotukāmo dhāretukāmo, ñāṇālokaṃ daṭṭhukāmo aññāṇaṃ bhinditukāmo, ñāṇālokaṃ uppādetukāmo avijj-andhakāraṃ nāsetukāmo, adhimattaṃ dhitiñca ussāhañ-ca satiñ-ca sampajaññañ-ca upaṭṭhapetvā āyasmantaṃ nāgasenaṃ etad-avoca:

2 bhante nāgasena, kim-pana buddho tayā diṭṭho ti. na hi mahārājāti. kim-pana te ācariyehi buddho diṭṭho ti. na hi mahārājāti. bhante nāgasena, na kira tayā buddho diṭṭho, nāpi kira te ācariyehi buddho diṭṭho. tena hi bhante nāgasena na-tthi buddho, na h' ettha buddho paññāyatīti. atthi pana te mahārāja pubbakā khattiyā ye te tava khattiyavaṃsassa pubbaṅgamā ti.

3 āma bhante, ko saṃsayo, atthi pubbakā khattiyā ye mama khattiyavaṃsassa pubbaṅgamā ti. diṭṭhapubbā tayā mahārāja pubbakā khattiyā ti. na hi bhante ti. ye pana taṃ mahārāja anusāsanti, purohitā senāpatino akkhadassā mahāmattā, tehi pubbakā khattiyā diṭṭhapubbā ti. na hi bhante ti. yadi pana te mahārāja pubbakā khattiyā na diṭṭhā, nāpi kira te anusāsakehi pubbakā khattiyā diṭṭhā, kattha pubbakā khattiyā, na h' ettha pubbakā khattiyā paññāyantīti.

Then King Milinda approached the revered Nagasena, and 1
drawing near, greeted him and sat down to one side. While seated to the side, King Milinda longed to know, hear, understand, and see the light of knowledge. Yearning to remove his lack of understanding, generate the light of knowledge, and dispel the darkness of ignorance, he aroused utmost resolution, determination, mindfulness, and deliberation. He spoke to the revered Nagasena:

"Revered Nagasena, have you ever seen the Buddha?" 2

"Oh no, great king."

"But have your teachers seen the Buddha?"

"No, great king."

"Revered Nagasena, if you haven't seen the Buddha and your teachers haven't seen the Buddha, then surely the Buddha does not exist, for the Buddha has not been seen in our time."

"But, great king, were there past Kshatriyas who were the precursors of your lineage of Kshatriyas?"

"Yes, of course, sir. What doubt could there be that there 3
were past Kshatriyas who were the precursors of my Kshatriya lineage?" "Have you ever seen those past Kshatriyas?" "Of course not, sir." "What about those who have taught you, great king—the palace priests, generals, judges, and chief ministers? Have they seen those past Kshatriyas?" "Oh no, sir." "If you have not seen those past Kshatriyas, and your instructors have not seen them, then where are those past Kshatriyas? For those past Kshatriyas have not been seen in our time."

4 dissanti bhante nāgasena pubbakānaṃ khattiyānaṃ anubhūtāni paribhogabhaṇḍāni, seyyathīdaṃ: setacchattaṃ uṇhīsaṃ pādukā vālavījani khaggaratanaṃ mahārahāni ca sayanāni, yehi mayaṃ jāneyyāma saddaheyyāma: atthi pubbakā khattiyā ti. evam-eva kho mahārāja mayam-p' etaṃ bhagavantaṃ jāneyyāma saddaheyyāma atthi taṃ kāraṇaṃ yena mayaṃ kāraṇena jāneyyāma saddaheyyāma: atthi so bhagavā ti. katamaṃ taṃ kāraṇaṃ: atthi kho mahārāja tena bhagavatā jānatā passatā arahatā sammāsambuddhena anubhūtāni paribhogabhaṇḍāni, seyyathīdaṃ: cattāro satipaṭṭhānā cattāro sammappadhānā, cattāro iddhipādā, pañc' indriyāni pañca balāni, sattā bojjhaṅgā, ariyo aṭṭhaṅgiko maggo, yehi sadevako loko jānāti saddahati: atthi so bhagavā ti. iminā mahārāja kāraṇena, iminā hetunā, iminā nayena, iminā anumānena ñātabbaṃ: atthi so bhagavā ti.

5 bahū jane tārayitvā nibbuto upadhikkhaye, anumānena ñātabbaṃ: atthi so dipaduttamo ti.

6 bhante nāgasena, opammaṃ karohīti. yathā mahārāja nagaravaḍḍhakī nagaraṃ māpetukāmo paṭhamaṃ tāva samaṃ anunnatam-anoṇataṃ asakkharapāsāṇaṃ nirupaddavam-anavajjaṃ ramaṇīyaṃ bhūmibhāgaṃ anuviloketvā yaṃ tattha visamaṃ taṃ samaṃ kārāpetvā khāṇukaṇṭakaṃ visodhāpetvā tattha nagaraṃ māpeyya sobhanaṃ vibhattaṃ

"Revered Nagasena, the things that past Kshatriyas used 4
and enjoyed have been seen, namely, the white parasol, turban, slippers, yak-tail fans, sword treasure, and precious couches. These we can witness, and so we believe that the former Kshatriyas did exist."

"It is the same with us, great king, for we can know and believe that the Bhagavan exists. And there is evidence whereby we can know and believe that the Bhagavan exists. What is this evidence? Great king, there are things that the Perfectly Awakened Enlightened Bhagavan, who knows and sees, used and enjoyed, namely, the four foundations of mindfulness, the four right strivings, the four bases of supernatural power, the five faculties, the five powers, the seven awakening factors, and the Noble Eightfold Path factors. It is by these that the world with its gods knows and believes that the Bhagavan exists. By this evidence, reasoning, method, and inference, great king, it should be known that 'the Bhagavan exists.'

"Having rescued so many, he is serene in the 5
destruction of attachments.
"This should be known by inference: 'He is the best
of those who walk on two feet.'"

"Revered Nagasena, please make an analogy." 6

"Great king, consider an urban architect who wants to build a city. First he would look for a stretch of land that is even, neither elevated nor low-lying, free of rocks and gravel, and secure, blameless, and attractive. He would then have the hilly places leveled and the stumps and thorny plants removed. There he would build the city, a city beautiful, well

bhāgaso mitaṃ ukkiṇṇa-parikha-pākāraṃ daḷha-gopuraṭṭāla-koṭṭakaṃ puthu-caccara-catukka-sandhi-siṅghāṭakaṃ suci-samatala-rājamaggaṃ su-vibhatta-antarāpaṇaṃ ārām-uyyāna-taḷāka-pokkharaṇī-udapāna-sampannaṃ bahuvidha-devaṭṭhāna-patimaṇḍitaṃ sabbadosavirahitaṃ, so tasmiṃ nagare sabbathā vepullataṃ patte aññaṃ desaṃ upagaccheyya.

7 atha taṃ nagaraṃ aparena samayena iddhaṃ bhaveyya phītaṃ subhikkhaṃ khemaṃ samiddhaṃ sivaṃ anītikaṃ nirupaddavaṃ nānājanasamākulaṃ, puthū khattiyā brāhmaṇā vessā suddā hatthārohā assārohā rathikā pattikā dhanuggahā tharuggahā celakā calakā piṇḍadāvikā uggā rājaputtā pakkhandino mahānāgā sūrā vammino yodhino dāsaputtā bhaṭṭiputtā mallagaṇā āḷārikā sūdā kappakā nahāpakā cundā mālākārā suvaṇṇakārā sajjhakārā sīsakārā tipukārā lohakārā vaṭṭakārā ayakārā maṇikārā pesakārā kumbhakārā loṇakārā cammakārā rathakārā dantakārā rajjukārā kocchakārā suttakārā vilivakārā dhanukārā jiyakārā usukārā cittakārā raṅgakārā rajakā tantavāyā tunnavāyā heraññikā dussikā gandhikā tiṇahārakā kaṭṭhahārakā bhatakā paṇṇikā phalikā mūlikā odanikā pūvikā macchikā maṃsikā majjikā naṭakā naccakā laṅghakā indajālikā vetālikā mallā chavaḍāhakā pupphachaḍḍakā venā nesādā gaṇikā lāsikā kumbhadāsiyo

planned, apportioned, and measured. It would have moats and ramparts dug, sturdy town gates, watchtowers, gatehouses, wide crossroads, intersections, squares, and plazas, clean and level royal boulevards, well-planned bazaars, and ample gardens, parks, reservoirs, lotus ponds, and wells. It would be embellished with many kinds of shrines and would be flawless in every way. Suppose that when the city was fully completed, he departed for another country.

“As time passed, the city would become rich and pros- 7
perous, with plentiful food, peaceful, successful, blessed, free of calamity, secure, and filled with many different kinds of people. Many Kshatriyas, Brahmans, Vaishyas, and Shudras would come to live in that city. So too would mahouts, horsemen, chariot drivers, foot soldiers, archers, swordsmen, standard bearers, military officers, officials in charge of supplies, noble princes, brave fighters, men like great elephants, heroes, and warriors clad in armor. There would arrive slaves, servants, wrestling troops, chefs, cooks, barbers, bath attendants, carvers, florists, goldsmiths, silversmiths, lead workers, tinsmiths, coppersmiths, brass workers, blacksmiths, jewelers, weavers, potters, salt makers, tanners, cartwrights, ivory artisans, rope makers, comb makers, cotton spinners, basket makers, bowyers, bow-string makers, fletchers, painters, dye makers, dyers, workers on looms, tailors, money changers, cloth merchants, and perfume blenders. There would be grass cutters, sellers of firewood, hired workers, vegetable sellers, fruit sellers, root venders, rice venders, confectioners, fish mongers, meat sellers, actors, dancers, acrobats, jugglers, bards, boxers, cremators, removers of night soil, reed workers, hunters,

saka-yavana-cīna-vilātā ujjenakā bhārukacchakā kāsi-kosalāparantakā māgadhakā sāketakā soraṭṭhakā pāṭheyyakā koṭumbara-mādhurakā alasanda-kasmīra-gandhārā taṃ nagaraṃ vāsāya upagatā nānā-visayino janā navaṃ suvibhattaṃ adosam-anavajjaṃ ramaṇīyaṃ taṃ nagaraṃ passitvā anumānena jānanti: cheko vata bho so nagaravaḍḍhakī yo imassa nagarassa māpetā ti.

8 evam-eva kho mahārāja so bhagavā asamo asamasamo appaṭisamo asadiso atulo asaṅkheyyo appameyyo aparimeyyo amitaguṇo guṇapāramippatto anantadhiti anantatejo anantaviriyo anantabalo buddhabalapāramiṃ gato sasenaṃ māraṃ parājetvā diṭṭhijālaṃ padāletvā avijjaṃ khepetvā vijjaṃ uppādetvā dhammukkaṃ dhārayitvā sabbaññutaṃ pāpuṇitvā nijjita-vijita-saṅgāmo dhammanagaraṃ māpesi.

9 bhagavato kho mahārāja dhammanagaraṃ sīla-pākāraṃ hiri-parikhaṃ ñāṇa-dvārakoṭṭhakaṃ viriya-aṭṭālakaṃ saddhā-esikaṃ sati-dovārikaṃ paññā-pāsādaṃ suttanta-caccaraṃ abhidhamma-siṅghāṭakaṃ vinaya-vinicchayaṃ satipaṭṭhāna-vīthikaṃ. tassa kho pana mahārāja satipaṭṭhānavīthiyaṃ evarūpā āpaṇā pasāritā honti, seyyathīdaṃ: pupphāpaṇaṃ gandhāpaṇaṃ phalāpaṇaṃ agadāpaṇaṃ osadhāpaṇaṃ amatāpaṇaṃ ratanāpaṇaṃ sabbāpaṇan-ti.

courtesans, female dancers, and slave women carrying water pots.[1] They would hail from Scythia, Bactria, China, Vilata, Ujjain, Bharukaccha, Kasi, Kosala, the west coast of Konkan, Magadha, Saketa, Surattha, Pava, Kotumbara, Mathura, Alexandria, Kashmir, and Gandhara.[2] People from many places would see the attractive new city so well planned, flawless, and impeccable, and would know by inference that the architect who built this city was truly skilled.

"In much the same way, great king, the Bhagavan is with- 8
out equal, equal to the unequaled, incomparable, peerless, measureless, inestimable, infinite, and boundless. His qualities cannot be measured and have reached perfection. His steadfastness, energy, exertion, and powers are endless. Having won perfection in the powers of a buddha, he defeated Mara and his armies, destroyed the net of wrong view, cast aside ignorance, gave rise to knowledge, bore the torch of the Dhamma, and achieved omniscience. Unvanquished and victorious in battle, he built the City of the Dhamma.

"What is more, great king, the Bhagavan's Dhamma City 9
has the moral precepts as its moats, a sense of shame as its ramparts, knowledge as its gates and gatehouses, exertion as its watchtower, faith as its pillars, mindfulness as its gatekeepers, understanding as its palace, the *suttas* as its crossroads, the *abhidhamma* as its plazas, the *vinaya* as its law court, and the foundations of mindfulness as its city streets. And on its streets—that is, the foundations of mindfulness—there are laid out bazaars with shops selling flowers, shops selling perfumes, and shops for fruits, antidotes, medicinal herbs, ambrosia, and jewels; and general stores as well."

bhante nāgasena, katamaṃ buddhassa bhagavato pupphāpaṇan-ti.

atthi kho pana mahārāja tena bhagavatā jānatā passatā arahatā sammāsambuddhena ārammaṇavibhattiyo akkhātā, seyyathīdaṃ: aniccasaññā anattasaññā asubhasaññā ādīnavasaññā pahānasaññā virāgasaññā nirodhasaññā sabbaloke anabhiratasaññā sabbasaṅkhāresu aniccasaññā ānāpānasati uddhumātakasaññā vinīlakasaññā vipubbakasaññā vicchiddakasaññā vikkhāyitakasaññā vikkhittakasaññā hatavikkhittakasaññā lohitakasaññā puḷavakasaññā aṭṭhikasaññā mettāsaññā karuṇāsaññā muditāsaññā upekkhāsaññā maraṇānussati kāyagatāsati. imā kho mahārāja buddhena bhagavatā ārammaṇavibhattiyo akkhātā. tattha yo koci jarāmaraṇā muccitukāmo so tesu aññataraṃ ārammaṇaṃ gaṇhāti, tena ārammaṇena rāgā vimuccati, dosā vimuccati, mohā vimuccati, mānato vimuccati, diṭṭhito vimuccati, saṃsāraṃ tarati, taṇhāsotaṃ nivāreti, tividhaṃ malaṃ visodheti, sabbakilese upahantvā amalaṃ virajaṃ suddhaṃ paṇḍaraṃ ajātiṃ ajaraṃ amaraṃ sukhaṃ sītibhūtaṃ abhayaṃ nagaruttamaṃ nibbānanagaraṃ pavisitvā arahatte cittaṃ vimoceti. idaṃ vuccati mahārāja bhagavato pupphāpaṇan-ti.

"Revered Nagasena, what is the Blessed Buddha's flower shop?"

"Great king, there are various objects of meditation 10
that were taught by the Bhagavan, the Perfectly Awakened Enlightened One who knows and sees. These are: the perception of impermanence, the perception of nonself, the perception of the impure, the perception of the disadvantages, the perception of what is to be abandoned, the perception of dispassion, and the perception of stopping. There are the perceptions of not taking delight in anything in the world and of the impermanence of all of the habitual patterns. There are also mindfulness of breathing and the perceptions of the ten kinds of corpses, namely, the bloated, discolored, festering, cut up, gnawed, dismembered, killed and dismembered, bleeding, worm-infested, and the bones.[3] And the perceptions of loving-kindness, compassion, sympathetic joy, and equanimity. There are also mindfulness of death and mindfulness of the body. These are the objects of meditation taught by the Blessed Buddha. Anyone wishing to become free of old age and death takes up one or another of these and by means of this object of meditation is liberated from passion, liberated from hatred, liberated from delusion, liberated from pride, liberated from views; one crosses over samsara, cuts off the stream of craving, and washes away the three types of stains. Having destroyed all of the defilements and entered the City of Nibbana, the best of cities, stainless, dustless, pure, fair, free of birth, ageless, deathless, blissful, cooling, and free of fear, one's mind is set free in arhatship. This, great king, is called the flower shop of the Bhagavan.

11 kammamūlaṃ gahetvāna āpaṇaṃ upagacchatha, ārammaṇaṃ kiṇitvāna tato muccatha muttiyā ti.

12 bhante nāgasena, katamaṃ buddhassa bhagavato gandhāpaṇan-ti. atthi kho mahārāja tena bhagavatā sīlavibhattiyo akkhātā, yena sīlagandhena anulittā bhagavato puttā sadevakaṃ lokaṃ sīlagandhena dhūpenti sampadhūpenti, disam-pi anudisam-pi anuvātam-pi paṭivātam-pi vāyanti ativāyanti pharitvā tiṭṭhanti. katamā tā sīlavibhattiyo: saraṇasīlaṃ pañcasīlaṃ aṭṭhaṅgasīlaṃ dasaṅgasīlaṃ pañcuddesapariyāpannaṃ pātimokkhasaṃvarasīlaṃ. idaṃ vuccati mahārāja bhagavato gandhāpaṇan-ti. bhāsitam-p’ etaṃ mahārāja bhagavatā devātidevena:

13 na pupphagandho paṭivātam-eti, na candanaṃ, tagaramallikā vā; satañ-ca gandho paṭivātam-eti, sabbā disā sappuriso pavāti.

candanaṃ, tagaraṃ vā pi, uppalaṃ, atha vassikī, etesaṃ gandhajātānaṃ sīlagandho anuttaro.

"Taking the price of karma, enter a shop and purchase 11
an object of meditation. With this become
liberated in freedom!"

"Revered Nagasena, what is the Blessed Buddha's perfume 12
shop?"

"Great king, there are various precepts of morality taught by the Bhagavan. When the descendants of the Buddha are anointed with them, they perfume and pervade the world and its gods with the fragrance of morality, as they waft, drift, and suffuse the directions, the intermediate points, the breezes, and the countercurrents, and then linger. What are these various precepts of morality? The precepts of taking refuge, the five precepts, the eight precepts, the ten precepts, and the precept of restraint of the monastic rules included in the five recitations.[4] This, great king, is called the Bhagavan's perfume shop, for this was said by the Bhagavan, god above gods:

The fragrance of flowers does not travel against the 13
wind, nor does sandalwood, butterfly gardenia, or
jasmine.
But the fragrance of the virtuous travels even against
the wind, as a good person infuses all directions
with scent.

Sandalwood, butterfly gardenia, lotus, and jasmine—
the fragrance of the moral precepts surpasses even
these kinds of perfumes.

appamatto ayaṃ gandho yāyaṃ tagara-candanī; yo ca
sīlavataṃ gandho vāti devesu uttamo ti.

14 bhante nāgasena, katamaṃ buddhassa bhagavato phalāpaṇan-ti. phalāni kho mahārāja bhagavatā akkhātāni, seyyathīdaṃ: sotāpattiphalaṃ sakadāgāmiphalaṃ anāgāmiphalaṃ arahattaphalaṃ suññataphalasamāpatti animittaphalasamāpatti appaṇihitaphalasamāpatti. tattha yo koci yaṃ phalaṃ icchati so kammamūlaṃ datvā patthitaṃ phalaṃ kiṇāti, yadi sotāpattiphalaṃ, yadi sakadāgāmiphalaṃ, yadi anāgāmiphalaṃ, yadi arahattaphalaṃ, yadi suññataphalasamāpattiṃ, yadi animittaphalasamāpattiṃ, yadi appaṇihitaphalasamāpattiṃ.

15 yathā mahārāja kassaci purisassa dhuvaphalo ambo bhaveyya, so na tāva tato phalāni pāteti yāva kayikā na āgacchanti, anuppatte pana kayike mūlaṃ gahetvā evaṃ ācikkhati: ambho purisa, eso kho dhuvaphalo ambo, tato yaṃ icchasi ettakaṃ phalaṃ gaṇhāhi, salāṭukaṃ vā dovilaṃ vā kesikaṃ vā āmaṃ vā pakkaṃ vā ti, so tena attanā dinnamūlena yadi salāṭukaṃ icchati salāṭukaṃ gaṇhāti, yadi dovilaṃ icchati dovilaṃ gaṇhāti, yadi kesikaṃ icchati kesikaṃ gaṇhāti, yadi āmakaṃ icchati āmakaṃ gaṇhāti, yadi pakkaṃ icchati pakkaṃ gaṇhāti; evam-eva kho mahārāja yo yaṃ phalaṃ icchati so kammamūlaṃ datvā patthitaṃ phalaṃ gaṇhāti, yadi sotāpattiphalaṃ-pe-yadi appaṇihitaphalasamāpattiṃ. idaṃ vuccati mahārāja bhagavato phalāpaṇan-ti.

The fragrance of butterfly gardenia and sandalwood
is slight, while the fragrance of the virtuous is
supreme, and drifts among the gods."

"Revered Nagasena, what is the Blessed Buddha's fruit 14
shop?"

"Great king, the Bhagavan spoke of certain fruits, namely, the fruit of stream entry, the fruit of once return, the fruit of nonreturn, the fruit of arhatship, and the attainments that are the fruits of emptiness, signlessness, and desirelessness.[5] Whoever yearns for such fruits as these gives the price of karma and purchases the preferred fruit, whether the fruit of stream entry, once return, nonreturn, arhatship, or the attainments of the fruits of emptiness, signlessness, and desirelessness.

"Suppose, great king, a man had a mango tree that 15
constantly bore fruit. He would not pick the fruit until a customer came along. But when a customer arrived, he would accept his money and explain: 'My good man, this mango tree is always fruiting, so please take such fruit as you prefer—unripe, immature, fibrous, partially ripe, or ripe.' Then with the price paid, if the fellow wants unripe fruit, he takes the unripe; if he prefers immature fruit, he takes the immature; and likewise with the fibrous, partially ripe, and ripe fruit. In just the same way, great king, one pays the price for whichever fruit one prefers and takes the fruit, whether it be the fruit of stream entry or any of the rest, up to the fruit of desirelessness. This, great king, is called the Bhagavan's fruit shop.

16 kammamūlaṃ janā datvā gaṇhanti amatapphalaṃ, tena te sukhitā honti ye kītā amatapphalan-ti.

17 bhante nāgasena, katamaṃ buddhassa bhagavato agadāpaṇan-ti. agadāni kho mahārāja bhagavatā akkhātāni, yehi agadehi so bhagavā sadevakaṃ lokaṃ kilesavisato parimoceti. katamāni pana tāni agadāni: yān' imāni mahārāja bhagavatā cattāri ariyasaccāni akkhātāni, seyyathīdaṃ: dukkhaṃ ariyasaccaṃ, dukkhasamudayaṃ ariyasaccaṃ, dukkhanirodhaṃ ariyasaccaṃ, dukkhanirodhagāminī paṭipadā ariyasaccaṃ. tattha ye keci aññāpekkhā catusaccaṃ dhammaṃ suṇanti, te jātiyā parimuccanti, jarāya parimuccanti, maraṇā parimuccanti, soka-parideva-dukkha-domanass-upāyāsehi parimuccanti. idaṃ vuccati mahārāja bhagavato agadāpaṇan-ti.

18 ye keci loke agadā visānaṃ paṭibāhakā, dhammāgada-samaṃ na-tthi; etaṃ pivatha bhikkhavo ti.

19 bhante nāgasena, katamaṃ buddhassa bhagavato osadhāpaṇan-ti. osadhāni kho mahārāja bhagavatā akkhātāni, yehi osadhehi so bhagavā devamanusse tikicchati, seyyathīdaṃ: cattāro satipaṭṭhānā, cattāro sammappadhānā, cattāro iddhipādā, pañc' indriyāni, pañca balāni, satta bojjhaṅgā, ariyo aṭṭhaṅgiko maggo. etehi osadhehi bhagavā micchādiṭṭhiṃ vireceti, micchāsaṅkappaṃ vireceti, micchāvācaṃ vireceti, micchākammantaṃ vireceti, micchāājīvaṃ vireceti, micchāvāyāmaṃ vireceti, micchāsatiṃ vireceti, micchāsamādhiṃ vireceti, lobhavamanaṃ kāreti, dosavamanaṃ kāreti, mohavamanaṃ kāreti, mānavamanaṃ kāreti, diṭṭhivama-

"People give the price of karma and take the fruit of ambrosia. Those who have purchased the fruit of ambrosia become delighted by it." 16

"Revered Nagasena, what is Blessed Buddha's antidote shop?" 17

"Great king, the Bhagavan spoke of certain antidotes by which he releases the world and its gods from the poison of the defilements. What are these antidotes? The Bhagavan spoke of the Four Noble Truths, namely, the truth of suffering, the truth of the cause of suffering, the truth of stopping suffering, and the truth of the path leading to the stopping of suffering. Anyone seeking knowledge who listens to the Dhamma of these Noble Truths is released from future rebirths, released from old age and death, and released from sorrow, grieving, suffering, distress, and trouble. This, great king, is called the Bhagavan's antidote shop.

"Whatever antidotes may be found in this world that counteract poisons, none is equal to the antidote that is the Dhamma. Monks, do take it!" 18

"Revered Nagasena, what is the Blessed Buddha's medicinal herb shop?" 19

"Great king, the Bhagavan spoke of certain medicinal herbs by which he cures humans and gods, namely, the four foundations of mindfulness, the four right strivings, the four bases of supernatural power, the five faculties, the five powers, the seven awakening factors, and the Noble Eightfold Path factors. With these herbs, the Bhagavan purges wrong view, and he purges wrong intention, wrong

naṃ kāreti, vicikicchāvamanaṃ kāreti, uddhaccavamanaṃ kāreti, thīnamiddhavamanaṃ kāreti, ahirikānottappavamanaṃ kāreti, sabbakilesavamanaṃ kāreti. idaṃ vuccati mahārāja bhagavato osadhāpaṇan-ti.

20 ye keci osadhā loke vijjanti vividhā bahū, dhammosadhasamaṃ na-tthi; etaṃ pivatha bhikkhavo.

dhammosadhaṃ pivitvāna ajarāmaraṇā siyuṃ, bhāvayitvā ca passitvā nibbutā upadhikkhaye ti.

21 bhante nāgasena, katamaṃ buddhassa bhagavato amatāpaṇan-ti. amataṃ kho mahārāja bhagavatā akkhātaṃ, yena amatena so bhagavā sadevakaṃ lokaṃ abhisiñci, yena amatena abhisittā devamanussā jāti-jarā-byādhi-maraṇa-soka-parideva-dukkha-domanass-upāyā-sehi parimucciṃsu: katamaṃ taṃ amataṃ: yad-idaṃ kāyagatāsati. bhāsitam-p' etaṃ mahārāja bhagavatā devātidevena: amatan-te bhikkhave paribhuñjanti ye kāyagatāsatiṃ paribhuñjantīti. idaṃ vuccati mahārāja bhagavato amatāpaṇan-ti.

22 byādhitaṃ janataṃ disvā amatāpaṇaṃ pasārayi; kammena taṃ kiṇitvāna amataṃ ādetha bhikkhavo ti.

speech, wrong action, wrong livelihood, wrong effort, wrong mindfulness, and wrong concentration. And he causes the expelling of greed and the expelling of hatred, delusion, pride, views, perplexity, agitation, lethargy, listlessness, shamelessness, the lack of moral sense, and all the defilements. This, great king, is called the Bhagavan's herb shop.

"Whatever the many and various medicinal herbs that 20
may be found in this world, none is equal to the
herb of the Dhamma. Monks, do take it!
"Taking the medicinal herb of the Dhamma, they
would become be free of old age and death, and
meditating on it and realizing it, they become
serene in the destruction of attachments."

"Revered Nagasena, what is the Blessed Buddha's ambro- 21
sia shop?"

"Great king, the Bhagavan spoke of an ambrosia that may be sprinkled on the world with its gods. And when sprinkled with this ambrosia, humans and gods are released from birth, aging, illness, death, sorrow, grieving, suffering, distress, and trouble. What is this ambrosia? It is mindfulness of the body. The Bhagavan, god above gods, said: 'Monks, those who make use of mindfulness of the body are making use of ambrosia.' This, great king, is called the Bhagavan's ambrosia shop.

"Seeing people afflicted with illness, he set up the 22
shop of ambrosia. Buying this ambrosia with
karma, take it, monks!"

23 bhante nāgasena, katamaṃ buddhassa bhagavato ratan-
āpaṇan-ti. ratanāni kho mahārāja bhagavatā akkhātāni, yehi ratanehi bhūsitā bhagavato puttā sadevakaṃ lokaṃ virocenti obhāsenti pabhāsenti jalanti pajjalanti uddhaṃ adho tiriyaṃ ālokaṃ dassenti. katamāni tāni ratanāni: sīlaratanaṃ samādhiratanaṃ paññāratanaṃ vimuttiratanaṃ vimuttiñāṇadassanaratanaṃ paṭisambhidāratanaṃ bojjhaṅgaratanaṃ.

24 katamaṃ mahārāja bhagavato sīlaratanaṃ: pātimokkha-
saṃvarasīlaṃ indriyasaṃ-varasīlaṃ ājīvapārisuddhisīlaṃ paccayasannissitasīlaṃ cullasīlaṃ majjhimasīlaṃ mahāsīlaṃ maggasīlaṃ phalasīlaṃ. sīlaratanena kho mahārāja vibhūsitassa puggalassa sadevako loko samārako sabrahmako sassamaṇa-brāhmaṇī pajā pihayati pattheti. sīlaratanapilandho kho mahārāja bhikkhu disam-pi anudisam-pi uddham-pi adho pi tiriyam-pi virocati atirocati; heṭṭhato avīciṃ, uparito bhavaggaṃ upādāya etth' antare sabbaratanāni atikkamitvā atisayitvā ajjhottharitvā tiṭṭhati. evarūpāni kho mahārāja sīlaratanāni bhagavato ratanā-paṇe pasāritāni. idaṃ vuccati mahārāja bhagavato sīlaratanan-ti.

"Revered Nagasena, what is the Blessed Buddha's shop 23
of jewels?"

"Great king, the Bhagavan spoke of certain jewels. When those in the lineage of the Buddha are adorned with them, they light up the world with its gods. They cast light above, below, and across, gleaming, sparkling, and radiating luster and brilliance. What are these jewels? The jewel of morality, the jewel of concentration, the jewel of understanding, the jewel of freedom, the jewel of liberated knowing and seeing, the jewel of analytical insight, and the jewel of the awakening factors.

"What are the Bhagavan's jewels of morality, great king? 24
The moral precepts of restraint in the monastic rules, the moral precepts curbing the faculties, the moral precepts of purifying one's livelihood, the moral precepts of relying only on the monastic requisites, the precepts described in the short, medium, and long sections on morality, the morality of the path, and the morality of its fruits.[6] Moreover, the world with its gods, Maras, Brahmas, and people, including Brahmans and renouncers, yearn and long for a person adorned with the jewel of morality. And more: a monk decked out with the jewel of morality lights up and illuminates the cardinal and intermediate directions, and above, below, and across. He stands here surpassing, outshining, and overwhelming all jewels from Avici Hell below to the highest realm above and everywhere in between. Such are the jewels of morality displayed in the Bhagavan's jewel shop. This, great king, is called the Bhagavan's jewel of morality.

25 evarūpāni sīlāni santi buddhassa āpaṇe; kammena taṃ kiṇitvāna ratanaṃ vo pilandhathāti.

26 katamaṃ mahārāja bhagavato samādhiraṭanaṃ: savitakka-savicāro samādhi, avitakka-vicāramatto samādhi, avitakka- avicāro samādhi, suññato samādhi, animitto samādhi, appaṇihito samādhi. samādhiratanaṃ kho mahārāja pilandhassa bhikkhuno ye te kāmavitakkā byāpādavitakkā vihiṃsāvitakkā mān-uddhacca-diṭṭhi-vicikicchā-kilesavatthūni vividhāni ca kuvitakkāni te sabbe samādhiṃ āsajja vikiranti vidhamanti viddhaṃsanti na saṇthanti na upalippanti. yathā mahārāja vāri pokkharapatte vikirati vidhamati viddhaṃsati na saṇṭhāti na upalippati, taṃ kissa hetu: parisuddhattā padumassa; evam-eva kho mahārāja samādhiratanaṃ pilandhassa bhikkhuno ye te kāmavitakka-byāpādavitakka-vihiṃsā-vitakka-mān-uddhacca-diṭṭhi-vicikicchā-kilesavatthūni vividhāni ca kuvitakkāni te sabbe samādhiṃ āsajja vikiranti vidhamanti viddhaṃsanti na saṇṭhanti na upalippanti, taṃ kissa hetu: parisuddhattā samādhissa. idaṃ vuccati mahārāja bhagavato samādhiratanan-ti. evarūpāni kho mahārāja samādhiratanāni bhagavato ratanāpaṇe pasāritāni.

"Such are the moral precepts in the Buddha's shop. 25
Buying this jewel with karma, adorn yourselves!

"And what, great king, is the Bhagavan's jewel of concen- 26
tration? Concentration with initial thought and deliberation, concentration without initial thought but with deliberation, concentration with neither initial thought nor deliberation, concentration on emptiness, concentration on signlessness, and concentration on desirelessness. When a monk is adorned with the jewel of concentration, initial thoughts directed to desire, malice, and violence, and all bad initial thoughts that have as their basis the defilements of pride, agitation, views, and perplexity come into contact with this concentration and are shattered, scattered, and dispersed. They do not settle and they do not stick around. It is just like how water on a lotus leaf shatters, scatters, and disperses; it does not settle and it does not stick around. Why is this? Because of the purity of the lotus. It is the same, great king, for the monk adorned with the jewel of concentration. Initial thoughts directed to desire, malice, and violence, and all bad initial thoughts that have as their basis the defilements of pride, agitation, views, and perplexity come into contact with this concentration and are shattered, scattered, and dispersed, and are not able to settle or stick around. This, great king, is said to be the Bhagavan's jewel of concentration, and such are the jewels of concentration displayed in the Bhagavan's jewel shop.

27 samādhiratanamālassa kuvitakkā na jāyare, na ca vikkhippate cittaṃ; etaṃ tumhe pilandhathāti.

28 katamaṃ mahārāja bhagavato paññāratanaṃ: yāya mahārāja paññāya ariyasāvako idaṃ kusalan-ti yathābhūtaṃ pajānāti, idaṃ akusalan-ti yathābhūtaṃ pajānāti, idaṃ sāvajjaṃ idaṃ anavajjaṃ, idaṃ sevitabbaṃ idaṃ na sevitabbaṃ, idaṃ hīnaṃ idaṃ paṇītaṃ, idaṃ kaṇhaṃ idaṃ sukkaṃ idaṃ kaṇha-sukka-sappaṭibhāgan-ti yathābhūtaṃ pajānāti, idaṃ dukkhan-ti yathābhūtaṃ pajānāti, ayaṃ dukkhasamudayo ti yathābhūtaṃ pajānāti, ayaṃ dukkhanirodho ti yathābhūtaṃ pajānāti, ayaṃ dukkhanirodhagāminī paṭipadā ti yathābhūtaṃ pajānāti, idaṃ vuccati mahārāja bhagavato paññāratanan-ti.

29 paññāratanamālassa na ciraṃ vattate bhavo, khippaṃ phasseti amataṃ, na ca so rocate bhave ti.

30 katamaṃ mahārāja bhagavato vimuttiratanaṃ: vimuttiratanan-ti kho mahārāja arahattaṃ vuccati, arahattaṃ patto kho mahārāja bhikkhu vimuttiratanaṃ pilandho ti vuccati. yathā mahārāja puriso muttākalāpa-maṇi-kanaka-pavāḷābharaṇa-patimaṇḍito akalu-tagara-tālī-

"Bad initial thoughts do not arise for one wearing a 27
necklace in which the jewels are concentration.
So they do not trouble the mind. And so, adorn
yourselves with them!

"And what, great king, is the jewel of understanding? It 28
is the understanding by which a noble disciple understands phenomenal states as they arise, noting that 'this one is good.'[7] He understands as it arises that 'this one is bad,' and 'this one is blameworthy, this one is blameless, this one is useful, this one is useless, this one is base, this one is exalted, this one is a mix of dark and bright.' He understands as it arises that 'this is suffering,' and he understands as it arises that 'this is the origin of suffering.' He understands as it arises that 'this is the stopping of suffering,' and he understands as it arises that 'this is the path leading to the stopping of suffering.' This is said to be the Bhagavan's jewel of understanding.

"Existence in samsara does not last long for 29
one wearing a necklace with the jewel of
understanding. Attain the deathless quickly,
and take no delight in existence!

"What, great king, is the Bhagavan's jewel of freedom? 30
The jewel of freedom is said to be arhatship, great king, and a monk who has become an arhat is described as adorned with the jewel of freedom. Consider a man adorned with a string of pearls and ornaments made of gems, gold, and coral, anointed with fragrant aloe, crape jasmine, *tālīsaka,* and red sandalwood on his limbs, and festooned

saka-lohitacandanānulitta-gatto nāga-punnāga-sāla-salaḷa-campaka-yūthikātimuttaka-pāṭal-uppala-vassika-mallikā-vicitto sesajane atikkamitvā virocati atirocati obhāsati pabhāsati sampabhāsati jalati pajjalati abhibhavati ajjhottharati mālā-gandha-ratanābharaṇehi, evam-eva kho mahārāja arahattaṃ patto khīṇāsavo vimutti-ratanapilandho upādāy' upādāya vimuttānaṃ bhikkhūnaṃ atikkamitvā samatikkamitvā virocati atirocati obhāsati pabhāsati sampabhāsati jalati pajjalati abhibhavati ajjhottharati vimuttiyā; taṃ kissa hetu: aggaṃ mahārāja etaṃ pilandhanaṃ sabbapilandhanānaṃ, yad-idaṃ vimuttipilan-dhanaṃ. idaṃ vuccati mahārāja bhagavato vimuttiratanan-ti.

31 maṇimālādharaṃ gehajano sāmiṃ udikkhati, vimutti-
ratanamālan-tu udikkhanti sadevakā ti

32 katamaṃ mahārāja bhagavato vimuttiñāṇadassana-
ratanaṃ: paccavekkhanañāṇaṃ mahārāja bhavato vimuttiñāṇadassanaratanan-ti vuccati, yena ñāṇena ariyasāvako magga-phala-nibbānāni pahīnakilesāvasiṭṭhakilese ca paccavekkhati.

with ironwood flowers, beautyleaf, sal, *salaḷa,* campak, *yūthika* jasmine, hiptage, trumpet flower, water lilies, great-flowered jasmine, and Arabian jasmine. Outshining everyone else, he lights up, illuminates, brightens, gleams, glows, sparkles, blazes, surpasses, and overwhelms them with his garlands, fragrances, and jewels. In the same way, great king, compared to other monks liberated with this or that, one with flaws fully destroyed who has become an arhat is adorned with the jewel of freedom, outshining and outdoing them. He lights up, illuminates, brightens, gleams, glows, sparkles, blazes, surpasses, and overwhelms them with his freedom. Why is this? Great king, among all adornments, the best adornment is the adornment of freedom. This is said to be the Bhagavan's jewel of freedom.

> "Servants look up to the master wearing gems and 31
> garlands, but the world with its gods looks up
> to one wearing a garland made of the jewels of
> freedom.

"What, great king, is the Bhagavan's jewel of liberated 32
knowing and seeing? The Bhagavan's jewel of liberated knowing and seeing is said to be the understanding that comes with reviewing. With this understanding the noble disciple reviews the path, the fruits, and nibbana with respect to which defilements have been abandoned and which still remain.

33 yena ñāṇena bujjhanti ariyā katakiccataṃ, taṃ ñāṇaratanaṃ laddhuṃ vāyametha jinorasā ti.

34 katamaṃ mahārāja bhagavato paṭisambhidāratanaṃ: catasso kho mahārāja paṭisambhidāyo: atthapaṭisambhidā dhammapaṭisambhidā niruttipaṭisambhidā paṭibhānapaṭisambhidā ti. imehi kho mahārāja catuhi paṭisambhidāratanehi samalaṅkato bhikkhu yaṃ yaṃ parisaṃ upasaṅkamati, yadi khattiyaparisaṃ yadi brāhmaṇaparisaṃ yadi gahapatiparisaṃ yadi samaṇaparisaṃ, visārado upasaṅkamati, amankubhūto abhīru acchambhī anutrāsī vigatalomahaṃso parisaṃ upasaṅkamati. yathā mahārāja yodho saṅgāmasūro sannaddhapañcāvudho asambhīto saṅgāmaṃ otarati: sace amittā dūre bhavissanti usunā pātayissāmi, tato orato bhavissanti sattiya paharissāmi, tato orato bhavissanti kaṇayena paharissāmi, upagataṃ santaṃ maṇḍalaggena dvidhā chindissāmi, kāyūpagataṃ churikāya vinivijjhissāmīti.

35 evam-eva kho mahārāja catupaṭisambhidāratanamaṇḍito bhikkhu asambhīto parisaṃ upasaṅkamati: yo koci maṃ atthapaṭisambhide pañhaṃ pucchissati, tassa atthena atthaṃ kathayissāmi, kāraṇena kāraṇaṃ kathayissāmi, hetunā hetuṃ kathayissāmi, nayena nayaṃ kathayissāmi, nissaṃsayaṃ karissāmi, vimatiṃ vivecessāmi, tosayissāmi pañhaveyyākaraṇena; yo koci maṃ dhammapaṭisambhide pañhaṃ pucchissati, tassa dhammena dhammaṃ kathayissāmi, amatena amataṃ kathayissāmi, asaṅkhatena asaṅ-

"With this understanding noble disciples recognize 33
tasks still to be done, and so, children of
the Victor, strive to obtain this jewel of
understanding.

"What, great king, is the Bhagavan's jewel of analytical 34
insight? There are four types of analytical insight: analysis of meanings, analysis of phenomenal states, analysis of language, and analysis of comprehension . A monk adorned with these four jewels of analytical insight approaches any assembly—be it an assembly of Kshatriyas, Brahmans, householders, or renouncers—with confidence and composure, unabashed, undaunted, unafraid, and unbothered. A warrior, a hero in battle, armed with five weapons, goes to battle without fear, thinking, *If the enemies are far away I will drop them with my arrows. If they are close by I will slay them with javelins. If they come closer I will kill them with spears. If they approach I will slice them in two with my circular saber. And if they make physical contact I will stab them with my dagger.*

"In just this way, great king, a monk adorned with the four 35
types of analytical insight enters any assembly without fear, thinking, *Should anyone ask me a question concerning the analysis of meanings, I will explain to that person meaning by meaning, explaining reason by reason, cause by cause, and method by method. I will remove doubt, dispel perplexity, and cause delight with answers to the question. And should anyone ask me a question concerning the analysis of phenomenal states, I will explain to that person phenomenal state by phenomenal state, explaining the deathless by the deathless, the unconditioned*

khataṃ kathayissāmi, nibbānena nibbānaṃ kathayissāmi, suññatāya suññataṃ kathayissāmi, animittena animittaṃ kathayissāmi, appaṇihitena appaṇihitaṃ kathayissāmi, anejena anejaṃ kathayissāmi, nissaṃsayaṃ karissāmi, vimatiṃ vivecessāmi, tosayissāmi pañhaveyyākaraṇena.

36 yo koci maṃ niruttipaṭisambhide pañhaṃ pucchissati, tassa niruttiyā niruttiṃ kathayissāmi, padena padaṃ kathayissāmi, anupadena anupadaṃ kathayissāmi, akkharena akkharaṃ kathayissāmi, sandhiyā sandhiṃ kathayissāmi, byañjanena byañjanaṃ kathayissāmi, anubyañjanena anubyañjanaṃ kathayissāmi, vaṇṇena vaṇṇaṃ kathayissāmi, sarena saraṃ kathayissāmi, paññattiyā paññattiṃ kathayissāmi, vohārena vohāraṃ kathayissāmi, nissaṃsayaṃ karissāmi, vimatiṃ vivecessāmi, tosayissāmi pañhaveyyākaraṇena; yo koci maṃ paṭibhānapaṭisambhide pañhaṃ pucchissati, tassa paṭibhānena paṭibhānaṃ kathayissāmi, opammena opammaṃ kathayissāmi, lakkhaṇena lakkhaṇaṃ kathayissāmi, rasena rasaṃ kathayissāmi, nissaṃsayaṃ karissāmi, vimatiṃ vivecessāmi, tosayissāmi pañhaveyyākaraṇenāti. idaṃ vuccati mahārāja bhagavato paṭisambhidāratanan-ti.

37 paṭisambhidā kiṇitvāna ñāṇena phassayeyya yo, asambhīto anubbiggo atirocati sadevake ti.

38 katamaṃ mahārāja bhagavato bojjhaṅgaratanaṃ: satt' ime mahārāja bojjhaṅgā: satisambojjhaṅgo dhammavicayasambojjhaṅgo viriyasambojjhaṅgo pītisambojjhaṅgo passaddhisambojjhaṅgo samādhisambojjhaṅgo upekhāsambojjhaṅgo. imehi kho mahārāja sattahi bojjhaṅgaratanehi patimaṇḍito

by what is unconditioned, nibbana by nibbana, what is empty
by emptiness, the signless by the signless, the desireless by the
desireless, and the imperturbable by the imperturbable. I will
remove doubt, dispel perplexity, and cause delight with answers
to the question. Should someone ask me a question concerning 36
the analysis of language, I will explain to that person language
by means of language, explaining line by line, word by word,
letter by letter, euphonic combination by euphonic combination,
consonant by consonant, phrasing by phrasing, tone by tone,
vowel by vowel, definition by definition, and common usage by
common usage. I will remove doubt, dispel perplexity, and cause
delight with answers to the question. And should someone ask me
a question concerning the analysis of knowledge, I will explain
to that person knowledge by knowledge, explaining analogy by
analogy, characteristic by characteristic, and function by func-
tion. I will remove doubt, dispel perplexity, and cause delight
with answers to the question. This, great king, is said to be the
Bhagavan's jewel of the analytical insights.

"Whoever purchases the analytical insights takes 37
hold of knowledge, and confident and undaunted,
outshines the world with its gods.

"And what, great king, is the Bhagavan's jewel of awak- 38
ening factors? There are seven awakening factors: the awakening factor of mindfulness, the awakening factor of discriminating phenomenal states, the awakening factor of exertion, the awakening factor of joy, the awakening factor of calmness, the awakening factor of concentration, and the awakening factor of equanimity. Adorned with these seven awakening factors, great king, a monk dispels all darkness,

bhikkhu sabbaṃ tamaṃ abhibhuyya sadevakaṃ lokaṃ obhāseti pabhāseti ālokaṃ janeti. idaṃ vuccati mahārāja bhagavato bojjhaṅgaratanan-ti.

39 bojjhaṅgaratanamālassa uṭṭhahanti sadevakā; kammena taṃ kiṇitvāna ratanaṃ vo pilandhathāti.

40 bhante nāgasena, katamaṃ buddhassa bhagavato sabbāpaṇan-ti. sabbāpaṇaṃ kho mahārāja bhagavato navaṅgaṃ buddhavacanaṃ, sārīrikāni pāribhogikāni cetiyāni, saṅgharatanañ-ca. sabbāpaṇe mahārāja bhagavatā jātisampatti pasāritā, bhogasampatti pasāritā, āyusampatti pasāritā, ārogyasampatti pasāritā, vaṇṇasampatti pasāritā, paññāsampatti pasāritā, mānusikasampatti pasāritā, dibbasampatti pasāritā, nibbānasampatti pasāritā. tattha ye taṃ taṃ sampattiṃ icchanti te kammamūlaṃ datvā patthitapatthitaṃ sampattiṃ kiṇanti, keci sīlasamādānena kinanti, keci uposathakammena kiṇanti; appamattakena pi kammamūlena upādāy' upādāya sampattiyo paṭilabhanti. yathā mahārāja āpaṇikassa āpaṇe tila-mugga-māse parittakena pi taṇḍula-mugga-māsena appakena pi mūlena upādāy' upādāya gaṇhanti; evam-eva kho mahārāja bhagavato sabb-

generates radiance, shines, and lights up the world with its gods. This is said to be the Bhagavan's jewel of the awakening factors.

> "The world with its gods rises before one wearing a 39
> necklace made up of the jewels of the awakening
> factors. Purchase this jewel with karma and deck
> yourself out."

"And finally, revered Nagasena, what is the Blessed 40
Buddha's general store?"

"The Bhagavan's general store, great king, is the Buddha's ninefold words, the bodily relics, things he used, shrines, and the jewel that is the community. And in the general store, success in rebirth is laid out for sale. Also set out for sale are success in wealth, success in longevity, success in health, success in beauty, success in understanding, human success, divine success, and success in nibbana. There, those seeking these kinds of success give the price of karma and purchase the requested success. Some make their purchase by taking the precepts and some make their purchase with the Uposatha Observance. They receive success according to the price of karma, even a trifling amount. Great king, it is much like how in a shopkeeper's shop selling sesame, beans, and lentils, people buy small amounts of rice grains, beans, and lentils according to the price, even a trifling amount. Similarly, in the Bhagavan's general store, they receive success according to the price of karma, even if trifling. This, great king, is called the Bhagavan's general store.

āpaṇe appamattakena pi kammamūlena upādāy' upādāya sampattiyo paṭilabhanti. idaṃ vuccati mahārāja bhagavato sabbā- paṇan-ti.

41 āyu ārogatā vaṇṇaṃ saggaṃ uccākulīnatā asaṅkhatañ-ca amataṃ atthi sabbāpaṇe jine.

appena bahukenāpi kammamūlena gayhati; kiṇitvā saddhāmūlena samiddhā hotha bhikkhavo ti.

42 bhagavato kho mahārāja dhammanagare evarūpā janā paṭivasanti: suttantikā venayikā ābhidhammikā dhammakathikā jātakabhāṇakā dīghabhāṇakā majjhimabhāṇakā saṃyuttabhāṇakā aṅguttarabhāṇakā khuddakabhāṇakā sīlasampannā samādhisampannā paññāsampannā bojjhaṅgabhāvanāratā vipassakā sadattham-anuyuttā āraññikā rukkhamūlikā abbhokāsikā palālapuñjakā sosānikā nesajjikā paṭipannakā phalaṭṭhā sekhā phalasamaṅgino sotāpannā sakadāgāmino anāgāmino arahanto tevijjā chaḷabhiññā iddhimanto paññāya pāramiṃ gatā satipaṭṭhāna-sammappadhāna-iddhipāda-indriyabala-bojjhaṅga-magga-vara-

"In the Victor's general store there are long life, 41
health, beauty, heaven, birth in a high-ranking
family, and what is unconditioned and deathless.
"These are acquired with the price of karma, whether
a little or a lot.
"Purchase them with the price of faith, monks, and
become prosperous.

"Great king, these are the kinds of people who live in the 42
Bhagavan's Dhamma City: experts in the *suttas*, *vinaya* specialists, *abhidhamma* masters, Dhamma preachers, *jātaka* reciters, and reciters specializing in the *Dīgha*, *Majjhima*, *Saṃyutta*, *Aṅguttara*, and *Khuddaka* collections. There are those successful with morality, those successful with concentration, and those successful with understanding. There are those delighting in cultivating the awakening factors, insight meditators, and forest dwellers intent upon the highest goal, including those living at the roots of trees, those dwelling in the open air, those sleeping on piles of straw, those staying near cremation grounds, and those sleeping in a sitting posture. There are those in training who have started the path of progress to the fruits, and those endowed with the fruits, namely stream winners, once returners, nonreturners, and arhats. There are those possessing the three knowledges, those with the six higher knowledges, those possessing supernatural powers, and those who have reached the perfection of understanding. There are people skillful in the foundations of mindfulness, the right strivings, the bases of supernatural power, the faculties, the powers, the awakening factors, the excellent

jhāna-vimokkha-rūpārūpa-santasukhasamāpatti[1]-ku-salā, tehi arahantehi ākulaṃ samākulaṃ ākiṇṇaṃ samākiṇṇaṃ naḷavana-saravanam-iva dhammanagaraṃ ahosi. bhavatīha:

43 vītarāgā vītadosā vītamohā anāsavā vītataṇhā anādānā
dhammanagare vasanti te.
āraññakā dhutadharā jhāyino lūkhacīvarā vivekābhiratā
dhīrā dhammanagare vasanti te.
nesajjikā santhatikā atho pi ṭhānacaṅkamā
paṃsukūladharā sabbe dhammanagare vasanti te.
ticīvaradharā santā cammakhaṇḍacatutthakā ratā ekāsane
viññū dhammanagare vasanti te.
44 appicchā nipakā dhīrā appāhārā alolupā lābhālābhena
santuṭṭhā dhammanagare vasanti te.
jhāyī jhānaratā dhīrā santacittā samāhitā ākiñcaññaṃ
patthayānā dhammanagare vasanti te.
paṭipannā phalaṭṭhā ca sekhā phalasamaṅgino āsiṃsakā
uttamatthaṃ dhammanagare vasanti te.

path, the *jhānas,* freedom, the form and formless worlds, and the attainment of peace and happiness. Dhamma City is full, crammed, crowded, and bursting with arhats like a thicket of reeds and rushes. For this has been said:

> In Dhamma City there live those rid of passion, those 43
> rid of hate, those rid of delusion, those free of
> the flaws, those rid of craving, and those beyond
> attachment.
> In Dhamma City live forest dwellers practicing
> the ascetic practices, meditators in thin robes,
> delighting in their seclusion, and resolute.
> Those staying in a seated posture, those sleeping on a
> mat, and even those who practice only standing
> and walking and wearing cast-off robes all live in
> Dhamma City.
> Wise ones peacefully wearing the three robes with a
> hide for a fourth, delighted with but a single meal
> a day, also live in Dhamma City.
> Those satisfied with little, prudent, resolute, 44
> abstemious, temperate, and content whether
> receiving alms or not also live in Dhamma City.
> Contemplatives delighting in the *jhānas,* resolute,
> minds at peace, composed, and yearning to be free
> of possessions also live in Dhamma City.
> Those practicing, those who have attained the fruits
> of practice, and those learners possessing the
> fruits and aiming at the highest goal also live in
> Dhamma City.

sotāpannā ca vimalā sakadāgāmino ca ye anāgāmī ca
arahanto dhammanagare vasanti te.
45 satipaṭṭhānakusalā bojjhaṅgabhāvanāratā vipassakā
dhammadharā dhammanagare vasanti te.
iddhipādesu kusalā samādhibhāvanāratā
sammappadhānam-anuyuttā dhammanagare vasanti te.
abhiññāpāramippattā pettike gocare ratā antalikkhamhi
caraṇā dhammanagare vasanti te.
okkhittacakkhū mitabhāṇī guttadvārā susaṃvutā sudantā
uttame dhamme dhammanagare vasanti te.

46 tevijjā chaḷabhiññā ca iddhiyā pāramīgatā paññāya pāramippattā dhammanagare vasanti te ti.

47 ye kho te mahārāja bhikkhū aparimita-ñāṇavara-dharā asaṅgā atuliyaguṇā atulayasā atulabalā atulatejā dhammacakkānuppavattakā paññāpāramiṃ gatā, evarūpā kho mahārāja bhikkhū bhagavato dhammanagare dhammasenā-

Stream winners, pure ones who are once-returners,
nonreturners, and arhats dwell in Dhamma City.
Those skilled in the foundations of mindfulness, those 45
delighting in cultivating the awakening factors,
insight practitioners, and experts in the Dhamma
live in Dhamma City.
Those skilled in the bases of supernatural
power, those delighting in the cultivation of
concentration, and those intent on the right
strivings live in Dhamma City.
Those who have reached perfection in the higher
knowledges, delighting in their ancestral range,
and who can fly through the air live in Dhamma
City.
Those with eyes downcast, speech measured, sense
doors guarded, self-controlled, and disciplined
properly in the highest Dhamma also live in
Dhamma City.

Those possessed of the three knowledges, those 46
possessed of the six higher knowledges, those who
have reached perfection in the magical powers,
and those who have attained the perfection of
understanding also live in Dhamma City.

"Moreover, great king, monks who are the excellent bear- 47
ers of the unlimited knowledge, who remain free of attachment, with qualities unequaled, and with fame, strength,
and energy beyond measure, turn the wheel of the Dhamma
and reach the perfection of understanding. Such monks

patino ti vuccanti. ye pana te mahārāja bhikkhu iddhimanto adhigatapaṭisambhidā pattavesārajjā gaganacarā durāsadā duppasahā anālambacarā sasāgara-mahī-dhara-paṭhavikampakā canda-suriya-parimajjakā vikubbana-m-adhiṭṭhānābhinīhāra-kusalā iddhiyā pāramiṃ gatā, evarūpā kho mahārāja bhikkhū bhagavato dham-managare purohitā ti vuccanti.

48 ye pana te mahārāja bhikkhū dhutaṅgam-anugatā appicchā santuṭṭhā viññatti-m-anesana-jigucchakā piṇḍāya sapadānacārino bhamarāva gandham-anughāyitvā pavisanti vivittakānanaṃ kāye ca jīvite ca nirapekkhā arahattam-anuppattā dhutaṅgaguṇe agganikkhittā, evarūpā kho mahārāja bhikkhū bhagavato dhammanagare akkhadassā ti vuccanti. ye pana te mahārāja bhikkhū parisuddhā vimalā nikkilesā cutūpapātakusalā dibbacakkhumhi pāramiṃ gatā, evarūpā kho mahārāja bhikkhū bhagavato dhammanagare nagarajotakā ti vuccanti. ye pana te mahārāja bhikkhu bahussutā āgatāgamā dhammadharā vinayadharā mātikādharā sithila-dhanita-dīgha-rassa-garuka-lahukakkhara-paricchedakusalā navaṅgasāsanadharā, evarūpā kho mahārāja bhikkhū bhagavato dhammanagare dhammarakkhā ti vuccanti.

are called the generals of the Dhamma in the Bhagavan's Dhamma City. Furthermore, monks who possess supernatural powers, who have comprehended the analytical insights and have reached the confidences, are difficult to approach and hard to overcome, and can travel through the sky, move without support, shake the earth with its seas and mountains, and touch the sun and the moon. Skilled in mental resolve in producing miracles, they have reached perfection in magical power. Such monks are called the palace priests in the Bhagavan's Dhamma City.

"Great king, those monks who have followed the ascetic 48
practices, content and satisfied with little, repelled by improprieties in gathering alms by hinting, and who seek alms without skipping any houses, are like bees who taste the flowers' perfume and then enter secluded woods. Heedless of the body and its vitality, they have become arhats and are considered supreme in the qualities of forest asceticism. Such monks are called the judges in Dhamma City. And those monks who are pure, stainless, without defilements, and skilled in knowing about death and rebirth have reached perfection in divine vision. Such monks are called illuminators of the Bhagavan's Dhamma City. And those monks who have heard many texts and passed them down, experts in the Dhamma, experts in the *vinaya,* experts in the matrices,* skilled in determining the phonetics of soft, aspirated, long, short, heavy, and light sounds, and experts in the nine parts of the dispensation are called the guardians of the Dhamma in the Bhagavan's Dhamma City.

---

* The *abhidhamma.*

49 ye pana te mahārāja bhikkhū vinayaññū vinayakovidā nidāna-paṭhana-kusalā āpatti-anāpatti-garuka-lahuka-sa-tekiccha-atekiccha-vuṭṭhāna-desanā-niggaha-paṭikamma-osāraṇa-nissāraṇa-paṭisāraṇa-kusalā vinaye pāramiṃ gatā, evarūpā kho mahārāja bhikkhū bhagavato dhammanagare rūpadakkhā ti vuccanti. ye pana te mahārāja bhikkhū vimuttivara-kusumamāla-baddhā vara-pavara-mahaggha-seṭṭha-bhāvam anuppattā bahujanakantam-abhipatthitā, evarūpā kho mahārāja bhikkhū bhagavato dhammanagare pupphāpaṇikā ti vuccanti. ye pana te mahārāja bhikkhū catusaccābhisamaya-paṭividdhā diṭṭhasaccā viññātasāsanā catusu sāmaññaphalesu tiṇṇavicikicchā paṭiladdhaphalasukhā aññesam-pi paṭipannānaṃ te phale saṃvibhajanti, evarūpā kho mahārāja bhikkhū bhagavato dhammanagare phalāpanikā ti vuccanti. ye pana te mahārāja bhikkhū sīlavarasugandham anulittā anekavidhabahuguṇadharā kilesamaladuggandha-vidhamakā, evarūpā kho mahārāja bhikkhū bhagavato dhammanagare gandhāpaṇikā ti vuccanti.

50 ye pana te mahārāja bhikkhū dhammakāmā piyasamudāhārā abhidhamme abhivinaye uḷārapāmojjā araññagatā pi rukkhamūlagatā pi suññāgāragatā pi dhammavararasaṃ pivanti, kāyena vācāya manasā dhammavararasam-ogāḷhā adhimattapaṭibhānā dhammesu dhammesanapaṭipannā ito vā tato vā yattha yattha appicchakathā santuṭṭhikathā pavivekakathā asaṃsaggakathā viriyārambhakathā sīla-

"Moreover, great king, those monks who know the *vinaya,* 49
have experience with the *vinaya,* are skilled in reading the original contexts, and are skilled in what is and what is not an offense, what is serious and what is inconsequential, what can be remedied and what cannot be, what should occasion rehabilitation, confession, reprimand, redress, readmission, suspension, and the formal act of seeking forgiveness have reached perfection in the *vinaya.* Such monks are called the money changers in the Bhagavan's Dhamma City. The monks on whom are tied the flower garlands of highest freedom, who have attained the best, excellent, and most precious supreme state, and who are favored and approved by many people—these monks are called the flower sellers in the Bhagavan's Dhamma City. The monks who have realized the Four Truths, have seen the truths, understood the dispensation, overcome doubts about the four fruits of renunciation, found the bliss of the fruits, and shared the fruits with others on the path—these monks are called the fruit sellers in the Bhagavan's Dhamma City. The monks who are scented with the perfume of highest moral discipline and bearing numerous and various virtues dispel the stench and stains of the defilements. These monks, great king, are called the perfume sellers in the Bhagavan's Dhamma City.

"Further, great king, monks seeking the Dhamma, 50
who cherish conversation, take supreme delight in the *abhidhamma* and higher *vinaya,* head to the forest, retreat to the base of trees, and frequent empty huts, drink the essence of the excellent Dhamma. Immersed in the essence of the excellent Dhamma with body, speech, and mind, extremely intelligent, following and yearning for the teaching among

kathā samādhikathā paññākathā vimuttikathā vimuttiñāṇadassanakathā tattha tattha gantvā taṃ taṃ kathārasaṃ pivanti, evarūpā kho mahārāja bhikkhū bhagavato dhammanagare soṇḍā pipāsā ti vuccanti. ye pana te mahārāja bhikkhū pubbarattāpararattaṃ jāgariyānuyogam-anuyuttā nisajja-ṭṭhāna-caṅkamehi rattindivaṃ atināmenti, bhāvanānuyogam-anuyuttā kilesapaṭibāhanāya sadatthapasutā, evarūpā kho mahārāja bhikkhū bhagavato dhammanagare nagaraguttikā ti vuccanti.

51 ye pana te mahārāja bhikkhū navaṅgaṃ buddhavacanaṃ
atthato ca byañjanato ca nayato ca kāraṇato ca hetuto ca
udāharaṇato ca vācenti anuvācenti bhāsanti anubhāsanti,
evarūpā kho mahārāja bhikkhū bhagavato dhammanagare
dhammāpaṇikā ti vuccanti. ye pana te mahārāja bhikkhū
dhammaratanabhogena āgama-pariyatti-sutabhogena
bhogino dhanino niddiṭṭha-sara-byañjana-lakkhaṇa-
paṭivedhā viññū pharaṇā, evarūpā kho mahārāja bhikkhū
bhagavato dhammanagare dhammaseṭṭhino ti vuccanti.
ye pana te mahārāja bhikkhū uḷāradesanāpaṭivedhā pari-
ciṇṇārammaṇa-vibhatti-niddesā sikkhāguṇapāramippattā,
evarūpā kho mahārāja bhikkhū bhagavato dhammanagare
vissutadhammikā ti vuccanti.

teachings, they repair to here, there, or wherever there are teachings of frugality or talk of contentment, seclusion, solitude, embarking on exertions, moral discipline, concentration, understanding, freedom, and liberated knowing and seeing. And they drink in the essence of each of these teachings. Such monks are called the town drunks, thirsty for their next drink, in the Bhagavan's Dhamma City. And those monks who devote the early and late parts of the night to the practice of wakefulness, who spend day and night in seated, standing, and walking meditation, devoted to the practices of cultivation, are, by driving off the defilements, intent upon the highest good. These, great king, are the city watchmen in the Bhagavan's Dhamma City.

"What is more, great king, there are monks who teach, 51
recite, speak to, and repeat the nine parts of the Buddha's words in terms of meaning, phrasing, methods, reasons, causes, and examples. These monks are called the Dhamma shopkeepers in the Bhagavan's Dhamma City. And there are wise and prosperous monks teeming with the wealth of the jewels of the Dhamma and the riches of having heard and mastered the scriptures. Wealthy, they have comprehended the sounds, phrasing, and defining characteristics as they were proclaimed. These monks are called the wealthy merchants of the Dhamma in the Blessed One's Dhamma City. And there are monks who have comprehended the highest teachings, performed the detailed exposition and classification of the meditation subjects, and achieved perfection in the qualities of the training. These monks, great king, are called the renowned Dhamma masters in the Bhagavan's Dhamma City.

52 evaṃ suvibhattaṃ kho mahārāja bhagavato dhammanagaraṃ, evaṃ sumāpitaṃ, evaṃ suvihitaṃ, evaṃ suparipūritaṃ, evaṃ suvavatthāpitaṃ, evaṃ surakkhitaṃ, evaṃ sugopitaṃ, evaṃ duppasayhaṃ paccatthikehi paccāmittehi. iminā mahārāja kāraṇena iminā hetunā iminā nayena iminā anumānena ñātabbaṃ: atthi so bhagavā ti.

53 yathā pi nagaraṃ disvā suvibhattaṃ manoramaṃ anumānena jānanti vaḍḍhakissa mahattanaṃ,

tath' eva lokanāthassa disvā dhammapuraṃ varaṃ anumānena jānanti: atthi so bhagavā iti.

54 anumanena jānanti ummī disvāna sāgare: yathā 'yaṃ dissate ummī mahanto so bhavissati;

tathā buddhaṃ sokanudaṃ sabbattha-m-aparājitaṃ taṇhakkhayam anuppattaṃ

bhavasaṃsāramocanaṃ anumānena ñātabbaṃ ummī disvā sadevake:

yathā dhammummivipphāro aggo buddho bhavissati.

55 anumānena jānanti disvā accuggataṃ giriṃ: yathā accuggato eso himavā so bhavissati; tathā disvā

dhammagiriṃ sītibhūtaṃ nirūpadhiṃ accuggataṃ bhagavato acalaṃ suppatiṭṭhitaṃ anumānena

ñātabbaṃ disvāna dhammapabbataṃ: tathā hi so mahāvīro aggo buddho bhavissati.

"Thus, great king, the Bhagavan's Dhamma City is well planned. And in these ways it is well built, well appointed, well stocked, well settled, well protected, and well guarded. And thus it is hard to subdue by adversaries and foes. And it is by this evidence, reasoning, method, and inference that it can be known that 'the Bhagavan exists.' 52

"Just as when people see a delightful and well-planned 53
city, and know by inference the greatness of the
city architect, when people see the excellent City
of the Dhamma of the lord of the world, they
know by inference that 'the Bhagavan exists.'
"Seeing the waves in the ocean, people know by 54
inference that if these are the waves that are seen,
the ocean will be huge.
"Likewise, the Buddha has expelled all sorrow, is
unvanquished anywhere, has destroyed craving,
and brings deliverance from the round of rebirth.
"Seeing his waves, the world with its gods should
know by inference that the one spreading the
waves of the Dhamma is the best, the Buddha.
"When people see a towering mountain, they know 55
by inference that the Himalayas must be also
colossal.
"Likewise, seeing the Dhamma mountain of
the Bhagavan, towering, bringing coolness,
passionless, unmoving, and well established,
they should know by inference, glimpsing the
Dhamma mountain, that likewise there is a great
hero, the best, the Buddha.

56 yathā pi gajarājassa padaṃ disvāna mānusā anumānena jānanti: mahā eso gajo iti,
tath' eva buddhanāgassa padaṃ disvā vibhāvino anumānena jānanti: uḷāro so bhavissati.

57 anumānena jānanti bhīte disvāna kummige: migarājassa saddena bhītā 'me kummigā iti;
tath' eva titthiye disvā vitthate bhītamānase anumānena ñātabbaṃ: dhammarājena gajjitaṃ.

58 nibbutaṃ paṭhaviṃ disvā haritapattaṃ mahodikaṃ anumānena jānanti: mahāmeghena nibbutaṃ; tath' ev' imaṃ janaṃ disvā āmoditapamoditaṃ anumānena ñātabbaṃ: dhammameghena tappitaṃ.

59 laggaṃ disvā bhusaṃpaṅkaṃ kalaladdagataṃ mahiṃ anumānena jānanti: vārikkhandho mahāgato;
tath' ev' imaṃ janaṃ disvā rajapaṅkasamohitaṃ vahitaṃ dhammanadiyā vissaṭṭhaṃ dhammasāgare,
dhammāmatagataṃ disvā sadevakam-imaṃ mahiṃ, anumānena ñātabbaṃ: dhammakkhandho mahāgato.

60 anumānena jānanti ghāyitvā gandham-uttamaṃ: yathā 'yaṃ vāyatī gandho hessanti pupphitā dumā;

"People seeing the footprint of an elephant king know 56
by inference that this elephant is huge.
"Likewise, seeing the footprint of the great elephant
that is the Buddha, the wise know by inference
that this one is superb.
"Seeing lesser animals terrified, people know by 57
inference that these little creatures are frightened
by the sound of the king of beasts.
"Likewise, seeing other sects scared and perplexed,
they should know by inference the roaring of the
king of the Dhamma.
"Seeing the earth cooled, verdant, and flowing with 58
water, people know by inference that it has been
cooled by a great cloud.
"Likewise, seeing people happy and rejoicing, they
should know by inference that they have been
pleased by the cloud of the Dhamma.
"Seeing the earth awash with mire and sticky wet 59
mud, people should know by inference that a
great amount of water has fallen.
"Likewise, seeing people covered with dust and mud
get carried by the river of the Dhamma and
released into the ocean of the Dhamma, and
seeing the earth with its gods plunged into the
ambrosia of the Dhamma, they should know by
inference that the corpus of the Dhamma is great.
"And getting a whiff of a truly fine fragrance, they 60
know by inference that if there is a scent here
there must be trees in blossom.

tath' evāyaṃ sīlagandho pavāyati sadevake, anumānena ñātabbaṃ: atthi buddho anuttaro ti.

61 evarūpena kho mahārāja kāraṇasatena kāraṇasahassena hetusatena hetusahassena nayasatena nayasahassena opammasatena opammasahassena sakkā buddhabalaṃ upadassayituṃ. yathā mahārāja dakkho mālākāro nānā-puppharāsimhā ācariyānusatthiyā paccattapurisakārena vicittaṃ mālāguṇarāsiṃ kareyya, evam-eva kho mahārāja so bhagavā vicittapuppharāsi viya anantaguṇo appameyyaguṇo, aham-etarahi jinasāsane mālākāro viya pupphaganthako pubbakānaṃ ācariyānaṃ maggena pi mayhaṃ buddhibalena pi asaṅkheyyena pi kāraṇena anumānena buddhabalaṃ dīpayissāmi, tvaṃ pan' ettha chandaṃ janehi savanāyāti.

62 dukkaraṃ bhante nāgasena aññesaṃ evarūpena kāraṇena anumānena buddhabalaṃ upadassayituṃ, nibbuto 'smi bhante nāgasena tumhākaṃ paramavicittena pañhaveyyākaraṇenāti.

anumānapañhaṃ.

"Likewise, when the perfume of moral discipline wafts
by the world with its gods, they should know by
inference that the supreme Buddha exists.

"And so it is possible, great king, to demonstrate the 61
power of the Buddha by hundreds and thousands of forms of evidence, reasoning, methods, and analogies. Great king, consider a talented garland maker who can make a pile or a whole line of many kinds of garlands from a mound of various flowers by following what he learned from his teacher and by working as a single person. The Bhagavan has endless and immeasurable qualities, like the pile of many kinds of flowers. And I am like a garland maker in the present dispensation of the Victor, stringing together flowers. I will illuminate the power of the Buddha by way of the path of the former teachers, by the strength of my own wits, by countless reasons, and by using inference. But it is you who must generate the desire to listen."

"It is difficult for others to demonstrate the power of the 62
Buddha by such evidence and inference. I am happy, revered Nagasena, with your excellent and varied explanation of the question."

So concludes the Question Resolved by Inference.

CHAPTER 5

Ram Horn Dilemmas II
Questions and Discussions About Yogis

1 passat' āraññake bhikkhū ajjhogāḷhe dhute guṇe, puna passati gihī rājā anāgāmiphale ṭhite. ubho pi te viloketvā uppajji saṃsayo mahā: bujjheyya ce gihī dhamme dhutaṅgaṃ nipphalaṃ siyā; paravādivādamathanaṃ nipuṇaṃ piṭakattaye handa pucche kathiseṭṭhaṃ, so me kaṅkhaṃ vi-nessatīti.

2 atha kho milindo rājā yen' āyasmā nāgaseno ten' upasaṅkami, upasaṅkamitvā āyasmantaṃ nāgasenaṃ abhivādetvā ekamantaṃ nisīdi. ekamantaṃ nisinno kho milindo rājā āyasmantaṃ nāgasenaṃ etad-avoca: bhante nāgasena, atthi koci gihī agāriko kāmabhogī puttadārasambādhasayanaṃ ajjhāvasanto kāsikacandanaṃ paccanubhonto mālā-gandha-vilepanaṃ dhārayanto jātarūparajataṃ sādiyanto maṇi-muttā-kañcana-vicittamolibaddho, yena santaṃ paramatthaṃ nibbānaṃ sacchikatan-ti.

3 na mahārāja ekañ-ñeva sataṃ na dve satāni na tīṇi catu-pañca satāni na sahassaṃ na satasahassaṃ na koṭisataṃ na koṭisahassaṃ na koṭisatasahassaṃ; tiṭṭhatu mahārāja dasannaṃ vīsatiyā satassa sahassassa abhisamayo, katamena te pariyāyena anuyogaṃ dammīti. tvam-ev' etaṃ brūhīti.

4 tena hi te mahārāja kathayissāmi, satena vā sahassena vā satasahassena vā koṭiyā vā koṭisatena vā koṭisahassena vā koṭisatasahassena vā. yā kāci navaṅge buddhavacane sallekhitācārapaṭipatti-dhutaguṇavaraṅga-nissitā kathā, tā sabbā idha samosarissanti. yathā mahārāja ninnunnata-samavisama-athalathala-desabhāge abhivaṭṭaṃ udakaṃ sabban-taṃ

The king saw monks in the forest intent on the ascetic practices, but he also saw householders steady in the fruits of nonreturn.[1] As he reflected on both of them, a great doubt emerged: *If householders awaken to the Dhamma, then the ascetic practices must be futile. Come, let me ask the best of speakers practiced in crushing opponents' talk, and he will dispel my perplexity.* 1

Then King Milinda approached the revered Nagasena, 2
and drawing near, greeted him and sat down to one side. While seated to the side, King Milinda said to the revered Nagasena: "Nagasena, sir, is there any householder who, as a layperson enjoying pleasures, living with couches crowded with wife and children, enjoying Kasi sandalwood, wearing garlands, scents, and perfumes, handling gold and silver, and sporting a turban studded with gold and gems, has experienced the highest and peaceful goal that is nibbana?"

"Oh, not just one, great king, nor even a hundred, two 3
hundred, three, four, or five hundred, a thousand, a hundred thousand, ten million, a hundred times ten million, a hundred thousand times ten million—let alone realization by ten, twenty, a hundred, or a thousand. But by what way of teaching can I manage the question?"

"You tell me, sir."

"Great king, I will speak of a hundred, a thousand, a 4
hundred thousand, ten million, a hundred times ten million, or a hundred thousand times ten million. And I will gather here all further discussion in the Buddha's ninefold words related to the practice of the penances and the excellent kinds of ascetic practice. Just as everywhere water falls, whether in a region with low land or high, even or uneven,

tato vinigaḷitvā mahodadhiṃ sāgaraṃ samosarati; evam-eva kho mahārāja sampādake sati yā kāci navaṅge buddhavacaṇe sallekhitācārapaṭipatti-dhutaguṇavaraṅga-nissitā kathā tā sabbā idha samosarissanti. mayham-p' ettha mahārāja paribyattatāya buddhiyā kāraṇaparidīpanaṃ samosarissati, ten' eso attho suvibhatto vicitto paripuṇṇo samānīto bhavissati. yathā mahārāja kusalo lekhācariyo anusiṭṭho lekhaṃ osārento attano byattatāya buddhiyā kāraṇaparidīpanena lekhaṃ paripūreti, evaṃ sā lekhā samattā paripuṇṇā anūnikā bhavissati; evam-eva mayham-p' ettha paribyattatāya buddhiyā kāraṇaparidīpanaṃ samosarissati, ten' eso attho suvibhatto vicitto paripuṇṇo parisuddho samānīto bhavissati.

5 nagare mahārāja sāvatthiyā pañcakoṭimattā ariyasāvakā bhagavato upāsaka-upāsikāyo sattapaṇṇāsa sahassāni tīṇi satasahassāni anāgāmiphale patiṭṭhitā, te sabbe pi gihī yeva na pabbajitā. puna tatth' eva gaṇḍambamūle yamakapāṭihāriye vīsati pāṇakoṭiyo abhisamiṃsu. puna mahārāhulovāde mahāmaṅgalasuttante samacittapariyāye parābhavasuttante purābhedasuttante kalahavivādasuttante cūḷabyūhasuttante mahābyūhasuttante tuvaṭakasuttante sāriputtasuttante gaṇanapatham-atītānaṃ devatānaṃ dhammābhisamayo ahosi.

or dry land or wet, it flows down from there and collects in the great sea that is the ocean, so too, great king, when there is someone who is receptive, all discussion in the Buddha's ninefold words related to the practices of the penances and the excellent kinds of ascetic practice may be collected. With my wide experience and intelligence, I can gather illustrations of the evidence and analyze thoroughly, ornament, fill out, and settle the meaning. Great king, it is much as a skilled writing teacher instructed to display his writing completes a piece with his own experience, intelligence, and illustrations of the evidence. Thus the writing becomes filled in, complete, and lacking nothing. In the same way, I will gather an explanation of the evidence with my wide experience and intelligence and analyze, ornament, fill out, and settle the meaning.

"Great king, in the city of Savatthi, the Bhagavan had fifty 5
million noble disciples who were laymen and laywomen. Of these, 357 achieved the fruits of nonreturn, and they were all householders, not renouncers. And right there at the base of the Ganda's mango tree where the Twin Miracle took place, two hundred million living beings grasped the teachings. And beyond all reckoning is the number of gods who grasped the Dhamma as recounted in the *Great Teachings to Rahula,* the *Greater Sutta on Auspicious Things,* the *Teaching About an Even Mind,* the *Sutta on Ways to Fail,* the *sutta* called *Before the Breakup,* the *Sutta on Quarrels and Disputes,* the *Smaller Sutta on Deployment,* the *Greater Sutta on Deployment,* the *Sutta on Being Quick About It,* and *Sariputta's Sutta.*[2]

6 nagare rājagahe paññāsa sahassāni tīṇi satasahassāni ariyasāvakā bhagavato upāsika-upāsikayo, puna tatth' eva dhanapālahatthināgadamane navuti pāṇakoṭiyo, pārāyanasamāgame pāsāṇake cetiye cuddasa pāṇakoṭiyo, puna indasālaguhāyaṃ asīti devatākoṭiyo, puna bārāṇasiyaṃ isipatane migadāye paṭhame dhammadesane aṭṭhārasa brahmakoṭiyo aparimāṇā ca devatāyo, puna tāvatiṃsabhavane paṇḍukambalasilāyaṃ abhidhammadesanāya asīti devatākoṭiyo, devorohaṇe saṅkassanagaradvāre lokavivaraṇapāṭihāriye pasannānaṃ nara-marūnaṃ tiṃsa koṭiyo abhisamiṃsu.

7 puna sakkesu kapilavatthusmiṃ nigrodhārāme buddhavaṃsadesanāya mahāsamayasuttantadesanāya ca gaṇanapatham-atītānaṃ devatānaṃ dhammābhisamayo ahosi. puna sumanamālākārasamāgame garahadinnasamāgame ānandaseṭṭhisamāgame jambukājīvakasamāgame maṇḍūkadevaputtasamāgame maṭṭakuṇḍalidevaputtasamāgame sulasānagarasobhanisamāgame sirimānagarasobhanisamāgame pesakāradhītusamāgame cūḷasubhaddāsamāgame sāketabrāhmaṇassa āḷāhanadassanasamāgame sūnāparantakasamāgame sakkapañhasamāgame tirokuḍḍasamāgame ratanasuttasamāgame paccekaṃ caturāsītiyā pāṇasahassānaṃ dhammābhisamayo ahosi.

"And in the city of Rajagaha, three hundred and fifty thou- 6
sand noble disciples were laymen and laywomen. Near there,
present at the taming of the bull elephant Dhanapala, were
nine hundred living beings; at the Pasanaka shrine, where
the Parayana *suttas* were assembled, were a hundred and
forty million living beings; and at Indasala Cave there were
eight hundred million gods. Moreover, at the deer park at
Sarnath near Baranasi at the time of the first teaching of the
Dhamma, there were eighty million Brahma gods and countless other gods. And in the Heaven of the Thirty-Three at
Pandukambala Rock, there were eight hundred million gods
present when the *abhidhamma* was taught. And at the gates
of Sankassa City where the Buddha descended from the gods
and performed the miracle of revealing the worlds to the
faithful, three hundred million humans and gods grasped
the teachings.

"Furthermore, among the Sakyas in Kapilavatthu in 7
Banyan Grove where the *Chronicle of the Buddhas* and the
Mighty Gathering Sutta were taught, gods beyond all reckoning grasped the Dhamma. And at each of the following
occasions eighty-four thousand living beings grasped the
Dhamma: at the assembly of Sumana the Garland Maker,
at the assembly of Garahadinna, and at those of Ananda the
merchant, Jambuka the Ajivaka, the god Manduka, the god
Mattakundali, the courtesan Sulasa, the courtesan Sirima,
the weaver's daughter Culasubhadda, and the assembly at
the spectacle of the cremation of the Brahman Saketa. And
also at the assembly at Sunaparantaka, the assembly where
Sakka put his questions, the assembly of the Without-the-
Walls teaching, and the assembly of the *Jewel Sutta*.

8 yāvatā mahārāja bhagavā loke aṭṭhāsi tāva tīsu maṇḍalesu soḷasasu mahājanapadesu yattha yattha bhagavā vihāsi tattha tattha yebhuyyena dve tayo catu pañca sataṃ sahassaṃ satasahassaṃ devā ca manussā ca santaṃ paramatthaṃ nibbānaṃ sacchikariṃsu. ye te mahārāja devā gihī yeva te, na te pabbajitā. etāni c' eva mahārāja aññāni ca anekāni devatākoṭisatasahassāni gihī agārikā kāmabhogino santaṃ paramatthaṃ nibbānaṃ sacchikariṃsūti.

9 yadi bhante nāgasena gihī agārikā kāmabhogino santaṃ paramatthaṃ nibbānaṃ sacchikaronti, atha imāni dhutaṅgāni kam-atthaṃ sādhenti; tena kāraṇena dhutaṅgāni akiccakarāni honti. yadi bhante nāgasena vinā mantosadhehi byādhayo vūpasamanti, kiṃ vamanavirecanādinā sarīradubbalakaraṇena; yadi muṭṭhīhi paṭisattuniggaho bhavati, kiṃ asi-satti-sara-dhanu-kodaṇḍa-laguḷa-muggarehi; yadi gaṇṭhi-kuṭila-susira-kaṇṭa-latā-sākhā ālambitvā rukkhamabhirūhanaṃ bhavati, kiṃ dīgha-daḷha-nisseṇipariyesanena; yadi thaṇḍilaseyyāya dhātusamatā bhavati, kiṃ sukhasamphassa mahatimahāsirisayana-pariyesanena; yadi ekako sāsaṅka-sabhaya-visama-kantāra-taraṇasamattho bhavati, kiṃ sannaddha-sajja-mahatimahā-sattha-pariyesanena; yadi nadī-saraṃ bāhunā tarituṃ samattho bhavati, kiṃ dhuvasetu-nāvā-pariyesanena; yadi sakasantakena ghāsacchādanaṃ kātuṃ pahoti, kiṃ parūpasevanā-piyasamullāpa-pacchāpuredhāvanena; yadi akhātataḷāke

"As long as the Bhagavan was present in the world, great king, and wherever he stayed in the three central zones or in the sixteen great regions, it usually happened that two, three, four, five, a hundred, a thousand, or a hundred thousand gods and humans experienced the highest and peaceful goal that is nibbana. And of course the gods were householders, not renouncers, great king. These and so many other hundreds, thousands, and millions of gods were householders, laypeople enjoying pleasures, who experienced the highest and peaceful goal that is nibbana." 8

"But, Nagasena, if householders as laypeople enjoying 9
pleasures experience the highest and peaceful goal that is nibbana, then what purpose do the ascetic practices serve? By this reasoning, the ascetic practices need not be observed. For if illnesses are cured without mantras or medicinal herbs, then why bring about the weakening of the body with things like emetics and purgatives? If enemies are restrained with fists, what is the point of swords, knives, arrows, bows, crossbows, clubs, and cudgels? Why look for a tall and sturdy ladder when a tree may be climbed by hoisting oneself up on knots, bends, holes, thorns, vines, and branches? If sleeping on the bare ground supports a balance of the humors, then why bother to seek fine and large beds soft to the touch? If it is possible to cross through dangerous, frightening, and lawless highways alone, then why look for armed, equipped, impressive, and large caravans? Why look for ferries or permanent bridges if one can cross a lake or a river with one's own arms? If one can provide food and shelter with one's own property, then why run back and forth flattering and serving others? And why dig wells, tanks, and reservoirs

udakaṃ labhati, kiṃ udapāna-tāḷāka-pokkharaṇi-khaṇanena. evam-eva kho bhante nāgasena yadi gihī agārikā kāmabhogino santaṃ paramatthaṃ nibbānaṃ sacchikaronti, kiṃ dhutaguṇavarasamādiyanenāti.

10 aṭṭhavīsati kho pan' ime mahārāja dhutaṅgaguṇā yathābhuccaguṇā yehi guṇehi dhutaṅgāni sabbabuddhānaṃ pihayitāni patthitāni; katame aṭṭhavīsati: idha mahārāja dhutaṅgaṃ suddhājīvaṃ sukhaphalaṃ anavajjaṃ na paradukkhāpanaṃ abhayaṃ asampīḷaṃ ekantavaḍḍhikaṃ aparihāniyaṃ amāyaṃ ārakkhā patthitadadaṃ sabbasattadamanaṃ saṃvarahitaṃ patirūpaṃ anissitaṃ vippamuttaṃ rāgakkhayaṃ dosakkhayaṃ mohakkhayaṃ mānappahānaṃ kuvitakkacchedanaṃ kaṅkhāvitaraṇaṃ kosajjaviddhaṃsanaṃ aratippahānaṃ khamanaṃ atulaṃ appamāṇaṃ sabbadukkhakkhayagamanaṃ. ime kho mahārāja aṭṭhavīsati dhutaṅgaguṇā yathābhuccaguṇā yehi guṇehi dhutaṅgāni sabbabuddhānaṃ pihayitāni patthitāni.

11 ye kho te mahārāja dhutaguṇe sammā upasevanti te aṭṭhārasahi guṇehi samupetā bhavanti; katamehi aṭṭhārasahi: cāro tesaṃ suvisuddho hoti, paṭipadā supūritā hoti, kāyikaṃ vācasikaṃ surakkhitaṃ hoti, manosamācāro suvisuddho hoti, viriyaṃ supaggahitaṃ hoti, bhayaṃ vūpasammati, attānudiṭṭhi byapagatā hoti, āghāto uparato hoti,

if you can get water from a lake? And so, Nagasena, if householders as laypeople enjoying pleasures can experience the highest and peaceful goal that is nibbana, what is the point of taking up the excellent ascetic practices?”

“Great king, there are twenty-eight special qualities 10
of the ascetic practices, special qualities that are real. And it is because of these special qualities that all buddhas long for and seek out the ascetic practices. What are the twenty-eight? Now an ascetic practice is a pure livelihood, it results in happiness, is blameless, does not cause suffering for others, is without danger, is free of trouble, leads only to progress, cannot be lost, is free of deception, is protective, grants wishes, disciplines all beings, benefits self-control, is proper, is free, is emancipated, destroys passion, destroys hatred, destroys delusion, rids one of pride, cuts off bad thoughts, removes doubt, terminates laziness, removes discontent, is forbearance, is matchless, is immeasurable, and leads to the destruction of all suffering. Great king, it is because of these twenty-eight special qualities—special qualities that are real—that all buddhas long for and seek the ascetic practices.

“And those who observe the ascetic practices properly 11
are awarded with eighteen special qualities. What are the eighteen? Their behavior becomes thoroughly purified, their progress fulfilled, their physical and verbal conduct well guarded, and their mental behavior thoroughly purified. Their exertions become well energized, their fears are allayed, their false views of self vanish, and their malice ceases. Their loving-kindess becomes established, their sustenance is understood, and they attract the respect of

mettā upaṭṭhitā hoti, āhāro pariññāto hoti, sabbasattānaṃ garukato hoti, bhojane mattaññū hoti, jāgariyaṃ anuyutto hoti, aniketo hoti, yattha phāsu tatthavihārī hoti, pāpajegucchī hoti, vivekārāmo hoti, satataṃ appamatto hoti. ye te mahārāja dhutaguṇe sammā upasevanti te imehi aṭṭhārasahi guṇehi samupetā bhavanti.

12 dasa ime mahārāja puggalā dhutaguṇārahā; katame dasa: saddho hoti hirimā dhitimā akuho atthavasī alolo sikkhākāmo daḷhasamādāno anujjhānabahulo mettāvihārī. ime kho mahārāja dasa puggalā dhutaguṇārahā.

13 ye te mahārāja gihī agārikā kāmabhogino santaṃ paramatthaṃ nibbānaṃ sacchikaronti sabbe te purimāsu jātisu terasasu dhutaguṇesu katupāsanā katabhūmikammā; te tattha cārañ-ca paṭipattiñ-ca sodhayitvā ajj' etarahi gihīva santā santaṃ paramatthaṃ nibbānaṃ sacchikaronti. yathā mahārāja kusalo issattho antevāsike paṭhamaṃ tāva upāsanasālāyaṃ cāpabheda-cāpāropana-gahaṇa-muṭṭhi-patipīḷana-aṅgulivināmana-pādaṭhapana-saragahaṇa-sandahana-ākaḍḍhana-sandhāraṇa-lakkhaniyamana-khipane tiṇapurisaka-chaṇaka-tiṇa-palāla-mattikā-puñja-phalaka-lakkha-vedhe anusikkhāpetvā rañño santike upāsanaṃ ārādhayitvā ājaññaratha-gaja-turaṅga-dhanadhañña-hiraññasuvaṇṇa-dāsidāsa-bhariya-gāmavaraṃ labhati; evam-

all creatures. They become moderate in eating, take pleasure in waking, are free of a house, are agreeable wherever they live, are repelled by wickedness, delight in seclusion, and are constantly vigilant. Great king, those who observe the ascetic practices properly are awarded with these eighteen special qualities.

"And there are ten kinds of people who are fit for the 12
ascetic practices. Who are the ten? Those who are faithful, possessed of shame, resolute, and not faking it. Those who have a sense of purpose, are stable, are seeking training, are steadfast in their undertakings, are not easily offended, and who live full of loving-kindess. Great king, these are the ten people fit for the ascetic practices.

"Great king, those householders who, as laypeople enjoy- 13
ing pleasures, experience the highest and peaceful aim that is nibbana in their previous lives all practiced the thirteen ascetic practices and by stages completed these actions. Having purified their conduct and progress then, they, as householders now, experience the highest and peaceful aim that is nibbana. Consider the skilled archer who first lines up his students in the archery hall and then trains them in taking up, breaking down, and raising the bow, clenching the fist, bending the fingers, planting the feet, taking an arrow, arranging it, drawing it back, restraining it, aiming at a mark, releasing it, and piercing the target, whether a straw man, a pile of chickpeas, grass, straw, mud, or a shield. His archery attracts the favor of the king and he receives thoroughbreds, chariots, elephants, horses, wealth, grain, gold, money, male and female slaves, a wife, and the finest villages. In much the same way, householders who,

eva kho mahārāja ye te gihī agārikā kāmabhogino santaṃ paramatthaṃ nibbānaṃ sacchikaronti, te sabbe purimāsu jātisu terasasu dhutaguṇesu katupāsanā katabhūmikammā; te tatth' eva cārañ-ca paṭipattiñ-ca sodhayitvā ajj' etarahi gihī yeva santā santaṃ paramatthaṃ nibbānaṃ sacchikaronti. na mahārāja dhutaguṇesu pubbāsevanaṃ vinā ekissā yeva jātiyā arahattaṃ sacchikiriyā hoti, uttamena pana viriyena uttamāya paṭipattiyā tathārūpena ācariyena kalyāṇamittena arahattaṃ sacchikiriyā hoti.

14 yathā vā pana mahārāja bhisakko sallakatto ācariyaṃ dhanena vā vattapaṭipattiyā vā ārādhetvā sattha-gahaṇa-chedana-lekhana-vedhana-salluddharaṇa-vaṇa-dhovana-sosana-bhesajjānulimpana-vamana-virecanānuvāsana-kiriyam-anusikkhitvā vijjāsu katasikkho katupāsano katahattho āture upasaṅkamati tikicchāya; evam-eva kho mahārāja ye te gihī agārikā kāmabhogino santaṃ paramatthaṃ nibbānaṃ sacchikaronti, te sabbe purimāsu jātisu terasasu dhutaguṇesu katupāsanā katabhūmikammā; te tatth' eva cārañ-ca paṭipattiñ-ca sodhayitvā ajj' etarahi gihī yeva santā santaṃ paramatthaṃ nibbānaṃ sacchikaronti. na mahārāja dhutaguṇehi avisuddhānaṃ dhammābhisamayo hoti. yathā mahārāja udakassa asecanena bījānaṃ avirūhanaṃ hoti, evam-eva kho mahārāja dhutaguṇehi avisuddhānaṃ dhammābhisamayo na hoti. yathā vā pana mahārāja akatakusalānaṃ akatakalyāṇānaṃ sugatigamanaṃ na hoti,

as laypeople enjoying pleasures, experience the highest and peaceful aim that is nibbana do so because they all practiced the thirteen ascetic practices and by stages completed these actions in their previous lives. Having cleansed their conduct and progress then, they, as householders now, experience the highest and peaceful aim that is nibbana. Great king, without previously observing the ascetic practices there is no experiencing arhatship in just one birth. For it is only with utmost exertion, utmost practice, and a good friend and teacher such as the archer that one may become an arhat.

"Consider, great king, a skilled physician, a surgeon, 14
who acquires a teacher either with money or by rendering him a service and learns how to hold a knife, cut, mark, pierce, and remove an arrow, and then wash the wound, dry it out, apply medicine, and administer a purgative, emetic, or oil. Only when his training and service are complete and he has become a practiced hand in the art of healing does he approach patients. In much the same way, householders who, as laypeople enjoying pleasures, experience the highest and peaceful aim that is nibbana do so because they all practiced the thirteen ascetic practices and by stages completed these actions in their previous lives. Having cleansed their conduct and progress then, they, as householders now, experience the highest and peaceful aim that is nibbana. There is no realizing the Dhamma for those not purified by the ascetic practices. Just as seeds do not grow without being sprinkled with water, there is no realizing the Dhamma for those not purified by the ascetic practices. Just as there is no going to heavenly realms for those who have failed to make merit or do beautiful things, great king, there

evam-evakhomahārājadhutaguṇehiavisuddhānaṃdhammābhisamayo na hoti.

15 paṭhavisamaṃ mahārāja dhutaguṇaṃ visuddhikāmānaṃ patiṭṭhaṭṭhena. āposamaṃ mahārāja dhutaguṇaṃ visuddhikāmānaṃ sabbakilesamala-dhovanaṭṭhena. tejosamaṃ mahārāja dhutaguṇaṃ visuddhikāmānaṃ sabbakilesavana-jjhāpanaṭṭhena. vāyosamaṃ mahāraja dhutaguṇaṃ visuddhikāmānaṃ sabbakilesamalarajo-pavāhanaṭṭhena. agadasamaṃ mahārāja dhutaguṇaṃ visuddhi-kāmānaṃ sabbakilesabyādhi-vūpasamanaṭṭhena. amatasamaṃ mahārāja dhutaguṇaṃ visuddhikāmānaṃ sabbakilesavisa-nāsanaṭṭhena. khettasamaṃ mahārāja dhutaguṇaṃ visuddhikāmānaṃ sabbasāmaññaguṇasassa-virūhanaṭṭhena. manoharasamaṃ mahārāja dhutaguṇaṃ visuddhikāmānaṃ patthiticchita-sabbasampattivara-dadaṭṭhena. nāvāsamaṃ mahārāja dhutaguṇaṃ visuddhikāmānaṃ saṃsāramahaṇṇava-pāragamanaṭṭhena. bhīruttāṇasamaṃ mahārāja dhutaguṇaṃ visuddhikāmānaṃ jarāmaraṇabhītānaṃ assāsakaraṇaṭṭhena.

16 mātusamaṃ mahārāja dhutaguṇaṃ visuddhikāmānaṃ kilesadukkha-patipīḷitānaṃ anuggāhakaṭṭhena. pitusamaṃ mahārāja dhutaguṇaṃ visuddhikāmānaṃ kusalavaḍḍhikāmānaṃ sabbasāmaññaguṇa-janakaṭṭhena. mittasamaṃ mahārāja dhutaguṇaṃ visuddhikāmānaṃ sabbasāmaññaguṇapariyesana-avisaṃvādakaṭṭhena. padumasamaṃ mahārāja dhutaguṇaṃ visuddhikāmānaṃ

is no realizing the Dhamma for those not purified by the ascetic practices.

“Great king, just like the earth, the ascetic practices are the 15
foundation for those seeking purification. Just like water, the ascetic practices rinse away the stains of all defilements for those seeking purification. Just like fire, the ascetic practices burn down the jungle of all defilements for those seeking purification. Just like the wind, the ascetic practices blow away the dirt and the dust of all defilements for those seeking purification. Just like an antidote, the ascetic practices allay the illness of all defilements for those seeking purification. Just like ambrosia, the ascetic practices destroy the poison of all defilements for those seeking purification. Just like a field, the ascetic practices grow the crops of all the special qualities of renunciation for those seeking purification. Just like a magical wishing gem, the ascetic practices give excellent good fortune in everything requested and desired for those seeking purification. Just like a ship, the ascetic practices make crossing the great ocean of samsara possible for those seeking purification. Just like safe refuge for the fearful, great king, the ascetic practices bring comfort to those afraid of old age and death and seeking purification.

“Just like a mother, great king, the ascetic practices provide 16
loving care for those tormented by the suffering of the defilements and seeking purification. Just like a father, the ascetic practices generate all the special qualities of renunciation for those desiring to increase merit and seeking purification. Just like a friend, the ascetic practices are trustworthy in the quest for all the special qualities of renunciation for those seeking purification. Just like a lotus, the ascetic

sabbakilesamalehi anupalittaṭṭhena. catujātiyavaragandhasamaṃ mahārāja dhutaguṇaṃ visuddhikāmānaṃ kilesaduggandha-paṭivinodanaṭṭhena. girirājavarasamaṃ mahārāja dhutaguṇaṃ visuddhikāmānaṃ aṭṭhalokadhammavātehi akampiyaṭṭhena. ākāsasamaṃ mahārāja dhutaguṇaṃ visuddhikāmānaṃ sabbattha-gahaṇāpagata-uru-visaṭa-vitthata-mahantaṭṭhena. nadīsamaṃ mahārāja dhutaguṇaṃ visuddhikāmānaṃ kilesamalapavāhanaṭṭhena.

17 sudesikasamaṃ mahārāja dhutaguṇaṃ visuddhikāmānaṃ jātikantāra-kilesavanagahana-nittharaṇ-aṭṭhena. mahāsatthavāhasamaṃ mahārāja dhutaguṇaṃ visuddhikāmānaṃ sabbabhayasuñña-khema-abhaya-vara-pavara-nibbānanagara-sampāpanaṭṭhena. sumajjitavimalādāsasamaṃ mahārāja dhutaguṇaṃ visuddhikāmānaṃ saṅkhārānaṃ sabhāvadassanaṭṭhena. phalakasamaṃ mahārāja dhutaguṇaṃ visuddhikāmānaṃ kilesa-laguḷasara-satti-paṭibāhanaṭṭhena. chattasamaṃ mahārāja dhutaguṇaṃ visuddhikāmānaṃ kilesavassa-tividhaggisantāpātapa-paṭibāhanaṭṭhena. candasamaṃ mahārāja dhutaguṇaṃ visuddhikāmānaṃ pihayita-patthitaṭṭhena. suriyasamaṃ mahārāja dhutaguṇaṃ visuddhikāmānaṃ moha-tamatimira-

practices are unblemished by the stains of all the defilements for those seeking purification. Just like a blend of the four finest perfumes, the ascetic practices drive off the stench of the defilements for those seeking purification. Just like the greatest king of the mountains, the ascetic practices are unshaken by the winds of the eight worldly conditions* for those seeking purification. Just like space, the ascetic practices have magnitude, and are capacious, expansive, and spread out from one's reach everywhere for those seeking purification. Just like a river, great king, the ascetic practices carry away the stains of the defilements for those seeking purification.

"Just like a skillful guide, great king, the ascetic practices 17
lead one through the dense jungle of the defilements that are the wilderness of rebirth for those seeking purification. Just like a master caravan leader, the ascetic practices aid one in reaching the excellent and supreme City of Nibbana, peaceful and free of every fear and danger for those seeking purification. Just like a spotless and well-polished mirror, the ascetic practices reflect the distinctive nature of the habitual patterns for those seeking purification. Just like a shield, the ascetic practices deflect the clubs, knives, and arrows of the defilements for those seeking purification. Just like an umbrella, the ascetic practices deflect the burning heat of the three fires and the rains of the defilements for those seeking purification. Like the moon, the ascetic practices are longed for and desired by those seeking purification. Like the sun, the ascetic practices dispel the dank darkness of delusion

* Gain, loss, fame, disrepute, praise, blame, pleasure, and pain.

nāsanaṭṭhena. sāgarasamaṃ mahārāja dhutaguṇaṃ visuddhikāmānaṃ anekavidha-sāmaññaguṇa-vararatanuṭṭhānaṭṭhena aparimita-m-asaṅkhya-m appameyyaṭṭhena ca.

18 evaṃ kho mahārāja dhutaguṇaṃ visuddhikāmānaṃ bahūpakāraṃ sabbadarathapariḷāhanudaṃ aratinudaṃ bhayanudaṃ bhavanudaṃ khilanudaṃ malanudaṃ sokanudaṃ dukkhanudaṃ rāganudaṃ dosanudaṃ mohanudaṃ mānanudaṃ diṭṭhinudaṃ sabbākusaladhammanudaṃ yasāvahaṃ hitāvahaṃ sukhāvahaṃ phāsukaraṃ pītikaraṃ yogakkhemakaraṃ anavajjaṃ iṭṭhasukhavipākaṃ guṇarāsi guṇapuñjaṃ aparimita-m-appameyya-guṇaṃ varaṃ pavaraṃ aggaṃ.

19 yathā mahārāja manussā upatthambhavasena bhojanaṃ upasevanti, hitavasena bhesajjaṃ upasevanti, upakāravasena mittaṃ upasevanti, tāraṇavasena nāvaṃ upasevanti, sugandhavasena mālāgandhaṃ upasevanti, abhayavasena bhīruttāṇaṃ upasevanti, patiṭṭhāvasena paṭhaviṃ upasevanti, sippavasena ācariyaṃ upasevanti, yasavasena rājānaṃ upasevanti, kāmadadavasena maṇiratanaṃ upasevanti; evam-eva kho mahārāja sabbasāmaññaguṇadadavasena ariyā dhutaguṇaṃ upasevanti.

20 yathā vā pana mahārāja udakaṃ bījavirūhanāya, aggi jhāpanāya, āhāro balāharaṇāya, latā bandhanāya, satthaṃ chedanāya, pānīyaṃ pipāsāvinayanāya, nidhi assāsakaraṇāya, nāvā tīrasampāpanāya, bhesajjaṃ byādhivūpasamanāya, yānaṃ

for those seeking purification. And finally, great king, like the ocean, the ascetic practices are unlimited, incalculable, and immeasurable, and produce the finest treasures that are the many special qualities of renunciation for those seeking purification.

"Thus, great king, for those seeking purification the ascetic practices are of great service for dispelling all anxiety and pain, dispelling discontent, and dispelling fear, becoming, harshness, impurities, sorrow, suffering, passion, hatred, delusion, pride, wrong view, and all bad phenomenal states. And for bringing honor, bringing benefit, bringing happiness, making one comfortable, making one joyful, and bringing about the calm of yoga, they are the best, the most excellent, and supreme. They are blameless, their results are agreeable and pleasant, they are a heap and pile of special qualities, and their special qualities are unlimited and immeasurable. 18

"Just as, great king, people pursue food for the sake of sustenance, seek medicine for the sake of its benefits, go to a friend to get help, find a boat to cross over, seek a fragrant garland for the appealing scent, look for safe refuge to be rid of fear, look to the earth for support, find a teacher for the arts, serve the king to acquire fame, and look for the jewel treasure for the sake of its granting wishes, noble ones look to the ascetic practices for the sake of their granting every special quality of renunciation. 19

"And just as, great king, water is for growing seeds; fire is for burning; food is for giving power; vines for binding; a knife for cutting; a drink for alleviating thirst; stored goods for bringing relief; a boat for reaching the shore; medicine for 20

sukhagamanāya, bhīruttāṇaṃ bhayavinodanāya, rājā ārakkhatthāya, phalakaṃ daṇḍa-leḍḍu-laguḷa-sara-sattipaṭibāhanāya, ācariyo anusāsanāya, mātā posanāya, ādāso olokanāya, alaṅkāro sobhanāya, vatthaṃ paṭicchādanāya, nisseṇi ārohaṇāya, tulā nikkhepanāya, mantaṃ parijapanāya, āvudhaṃ tajjaniyapaṭibāhanāya, padīpo andhakāravidhamanāya, vāto pariḷāhanibbāpanāya, sippaṃ vuttinipphādanāya, agadaṃ jīvitarakkhanāya, ākaro ratanuppādāya, ratanaṃ alankārāya, āṇā anatikkamanāya, issariyaṃ vasavattanāya,

21 evam-eva kho mahārāja dhutaguṇaṃ sāmaññabījavirūhanāya kilesamalajhāpanāya iddhibalāharaṇāya satisaṃvara-nibandhanāya vimativicikicchā-samucchedanāya taṇhāpipāsā-vinayanāya abhisamay-assāsakaraṇāya caturogha-nittharaṇāya kilesa-byādhi-vūpasamāya nibbānasukha-paṭilābhāya jāti-jarā-byādhi-maraṇa-soka-prideva-dukkha-domanass-upāyāsa bhayavinodanāya sāmaññaguṇa-parirakkhanāya aratikuvitakka-paṭibāhanāya sakalasāmaññatthānusāsanāya sabbasāmaññaguṇa-posanāya samatha-vipassanā-magga-phala-nibbāna-dassanāya sakalalokathutathomita-mahatimahā-sobhākaraṇāya sabbāpāya-pidahanāya sāmaññattha-sela-sikharamuddhani-abhirūhanāya vaṅka-kuṭila-visama-citta-nikkhepanāya

alleviating illness; a vehicle for easy traveling; safe refuge for alleviating fear; a king for protecting; a shield for deflecting rods, stones, clubs, knives, and arrows; a teacher for brilliance; a mother for nurturance; a mirror for looking into; an ornament for making one beautiful; clothes for covering; a ladder for climbing; a measure for settling accounts; a mantra for repeating; a weapon for heading off threats; a lamp for dispelling darkness; a breeze for quenching a fever; the arts for acquiring a livelihood; an antidote for protecting life; a mine for producing gems; a gem for adornment; a command for preventing transgression; and authority for wielding power, so too are the ascetic practices.

“Great king, the ascetic practices are for the sake of grow- 21
ing the seeds of renunciation; for burning away the stains of the defilements; for bringing one supernatural power; for binding with the restraints of mindfulness; for cutting off doubt and perplexity; for alleviating the thirst that is craving; for bringing the relief of realization; for ferrying one across the four floods;* for alleviating the illness of the defilements; for obtaining easy travel to nibbana; for alleviating fear of birth, old age, sickness, death, sorrow, grieving, pain, distress, and trouble; for protecting the qualities of renunciation; for deflecting bad thoughts and discontent; for learning the entire purpose of renunciation; for nurturing all the special qualities of renunciation; for looking into calm meditation, insight meditation, the path, the fruits, and nibbana; for making one so fabulously beautiful that one is praised and admired throughout the whole world;

* Sense desire, being drawn to rebirth, holding wrong views, and ignorance.

sevitabbāsevitabbadhamme sādhu sajjhāyakaraṇāya sabbakilesapaṭisattu-tajjanāya avijjandhakāra-vidhamanāya tividhaggi-santāpa-pariḷāha-nibbāpa-nāya saṇha-sukhuma-santa-samāpatti-nipphādanāya sakalasāmaññaguṇaparirakkhanāya bojjhaṅga-vararatan-uppādāya yogijaṅālankaraṇāya anavajja-nipuṇa-sukhuma-santisukha-m-anatikkamanāya sakala-sāmañña-ariyadhamma-vasavattanāya. iti mahārāja imesaṃ guṇānaṃ adhigamāya yad-idaṃ ekamekaṃ dhutaguṇaṃ. evaṃ mahārāja atuliyaṃ dhutaguṇaṃ appameyyaṃ asamaṃ appaṭibhāgaṃ appaṭiseṭṭhaṃ uttaraṃ seṭṭhaṃ visiṭṭhaṃ adhikaṃ āyataṃ puthulaṃ visaṭaṃ vitthataṃ garukaṃ bhāriyaṃ mahantaṃ.

22 yo kho mahārāja puggalo pāpiccho icchāpakato kuhako luddho odariko lābhakāmo yasakāmo kittikāmo ayutto appatto ananucchaviko anaraho appatirūpo dhutaṅgaṃ samādiyati, so diguṇaṃ daṇḍam-āpajjati, sabbaguṇaghātam-āpajjati, diṭṭhadhammikaṃ hīḷanaṃ khīḷanaṃ garahanaṃ uppaṇḍanaṃ khipanaṃ asambhogaṃ nissāraṇaṃ nicchubhanaṃ pavāhanaṃ pabbājanaṃ paṭilabhati, samparāye pi satayojanike avīcimahāniraye uṇha-kaṭhita-tatta-santatta-accijālāmālake anekavassakoṭisatasahassāni uddham-adho tiriyaṃ pheṇuddeha kaṃsamparivattakaṃ

for covering all losses; for mounting the rocky heights and peaks of renunciation; for settling a mind that is crooked, shifty, and lawless; for bringing about the repetition of "well done" concerning things to be observed and not observed; for heading off the enemies that are the defilements; for dispelling the darkness of ignorance; for quenching the fever and burning of the three fires; for acquiring subtle, delicate, and peaceful attainments; for protecting all the special qualities of renunciation; for producing the finest gems that are the awakening factors; for adorning people who are yoga practitioners; for preventing transgression of the peaceful happiness that is blameless, fine, and subtle; and for wielding the power of the noble Dhamma over all renunciation. This is to say, great king, that each of the ascetic practices is for the sake of acquiring these qualities just listed. And in this way, the ascetic practices are matchless, immeasurable, without equal, resembling nothing, unsurpassed, highest, best, superior, extraordinary, extensive, broad, diffuse, serious, weighty, and huge.

"Great king, a person who is wicked, filled with desires, 22
deceitful, greedy, gluttonous, wanting gain, lusting for fame, desiring glory, and unworthy, who wrongly, problematically, unsuitably, and improperly undertakes the ascetic practices, incurs a double punishment and brings about the destruction of all the special qualities. In this very life the person receives scorn, contempt, blame, ridicule, mockery, exclusion, expulsion, being cast out, dismissal, and banishment. And in the next life, one boils in the great hell called Avici, a hundred leagues in size, hot, boiling, burning, scorching, blazing, and garlanded in flames, being rolled about in a swirl of froth,

paccati. tato muccitvā kisa-pharusa-kāḷaṅgapaccaṅgo sūn-uddhumāta-susir uttamaṅgo chāto pi- pāsito visama-bhīma-rūpavaṇṇo bhagga-kaṇṇasoto ummīlita-nimīlita-netta-nayano arugatta-pakkagatto puḷavākiṇṇa-sabbakāyo, vāta-mukhe jalamāno viya aggikkhandho anto jalamāno pajjalamāno, attāṇo asaraṇo āruṇṇaruṇṇa-kāruñña-ravaṃ paridevamāno nijjhāmataṇhiko samaṇamahāpeto hutvā āhiṇḍamāno mahiyā aṭṭassaraṃ karoti.

23 yathā mahārāja koci ayutto appatto ananucchaviko anaraho appatirūpo hīno kujātiko khattiyābhisekena abhisiñcati, so labhati hatthacchedaṃ pādacchedaṃ hatthapādacchedaṃ kaṇṇacchedaṃ nāsacchedaṃ kaṇṇanāsacchedaṃ bilaṅgathālikaṃ saṅkhamuṇḍikaṃ rāhumukhaṃ jotimālikaṃ hatthapajjotikaṃ erakavattikaṃ cīrakavāsikaṃ eṇeyyakaṃ baḷisamaṃsikaṃ kahāpaṇakaṃ khārāpatacchikaṃ palighaparivattikaṃ palālapīṭhakaṃ, tattena telena osiñcanaṃ, sunakhehi khādāpanaṃ, jīvasūlāropanaṃ, asinā sīsacchedaṃ, anekavihitam-pi kammakaraṇaṃ anubhavati. kiṅkāraṇaṃ. ayutto appatto ananucchaviko anaraho appatirūpo hīno kujātiko mahante issariye ṭhāne attānaṃ ṭhapesi, velaṃ ghātesi; evam-eva kho mahārāja yo koci puggalo pāpiccho-pe-mahiyā aṭṭassaraṃ karoti.

24 yo pana mahārāja puggalo yutto patto anucchaviko araho patirūpo appiccho santuṭṭho pavivitto asaṃsaṭṭho

up, down, and across, for many hundreds, thousands, and millions of years. Released from there, one becomes a hungry ghost in the guise of a renouncer, famished, parched, with body and limbs blackened, rough, and haggard, and head swollen, bloated, and perforated. One's color and shape are patchy and horrible, ears tattered, eyes blinking open and closed, limbs oozing and putrid, body riddled with maggots, belly like a mass of fire raging hotter in the wind, and one is crying and weeping for compassion but without shelter or refuge. One wanders the earth wailing pitifully.

"Great king, consider someone who is unworthy, base, 23
and low caste, who wrongly, problematically, unsuitably, and improperly gets consecrated with the consecration of a Kshatriya. He gets a hand cut off, a foot cut off, both hands and feet cut off, ears cut off, nose cut off, or both ears and nose cut off. Or he is subject to the gruel pot torture, the polished shell torture, Rahu's mouth torture, the fire wreath torture, the flaming hand torture, the grass torture, the bark dress torture, the black antelope torture, the meat hook torture, the coin torture, the lye pickling torture, the 'turning around the bar' torture, or the straw bench torture. Or he is doused with burning oil, eaten by dogs, impaled alive on stakes, or beheaded with a sword. Why is this? Someone unworthy, base, and low caste who wrongly, problematically, unsuitably, and improperly assumes the status of kingship for himself has destroyed boundaries. It is similar, great king, to the case of the wicked person just described who then winds up wandering the earth wailing pitifully.

"But then there is the person who is not wicked, and who is 24
content; detached; secluded; practicing exertions; resolute,

āraddhaviriyo pahitatto asaṭho amāyo na odariko na lābhakāmo na yasakāmo na kittikāmo saddho saddhāpabbajito jarāmaraṇā muccitukāmo sāsanaṃ paggaṇhissāmīti dhutaguṇaṃ samādiyati, so diguṇaṃ pūjaṃ arahati: devānañ-ca manussānañ-ca piyo hoti manāpo pihayito patthito, jātisumana-mallikādīnaṃ viya pupphaṃ nahātānulittassa, jighacchitassa viya paṇītabhojanaṃ, pipāsitassa viya sītala-vimala-surabhi-pānīyaṃ, visagatassa viya osadhavaraṃ, sīghagamanakāmassa viya ājaññarathava-ruttamaṃ, atthakāmassa viya manoharamaṇiratanaṃ, abhisiñcitukāmassa viya paṇḍara-vimala-setacchattaṃ, dhammakāmassa viya arahattaphalādhigamam-anuttaraṃ. tassa cattāro satipaṭṭhānā bhāvanāpāripūriṃ gacchanti, cattāro sammappadhānā cattāro iddhipādā panc' indriyāni pañca balāni satta bojjhaṅgā ariyo aṭṭhaṅgiko maggo bhāvanāpāripūriṃ gacchati, samatha-vipassanā adhigacchati, adhigamapaṭipatti pariṇamati, cattāri sāmaññaphalāni catasso paṭisambhidā tisso vijjā chaḷ-abhiññā kevalo ca samaṇadhammo sabbe tass' ādheyyā honti. vimuttipaṇḍaravimala-setacchattena abhisiñcati.

yathā mahārāja rañño khattiyassa abhijātakulakulīnassa khattiyābhisekena abhisittassa paricaranti saraṭṭha-negama-jānapada-bhaṭa-balatthā, aṭṭhatiṃsā ca rājaparisā

honest; true; abstemious; shunning gain, fame, and glory; and faithful, who ordained out of faith. Seeking release from old age and death, this one rightly, correctly, suitably, and properly observes the ascetic practices, thinking, *I will master the teaching.* He deserves two kinds of worship, for he is dear to both gods and humans, delightful, yearned for, and sought after, much as the blossoms of the great-flowered and Arabian jasmines are to someone freshly bathed and anointed. He is like a full meal to someone starving; a cool, pure, and fragrant drink to the parched; the finest medicinal herb to the poisoned; the most splendid thoroughbred horse to a person in a hurry; the magical jewel treasure to the person desiring property; the stainless white parasol to one desiring consecration; and the highest understanding of the fruits of arhatship for one seeking the Dhamma. In him the four foundations of mindfulness reach their full cultivation. And the four right strivings, the four bases of supernatural power, the five faculties, the five powers, the seven awakening factors, and the Eightfold Noble Path factors all reach their full cultivation. He reaches calm and insight and brings his understanding and practice to maturity. Indeed, the four fruits of renunciation, the four analytical insights, the three knowledges, the six higher knowledges, and the entire practice of the renouncer all come to be vested in him. He is consecrated with the stainless white parasol of freedom.

"Consider also, great king, those who serve a Kshatriya 25
king of high birth on both sides who has been consecrated
with the Kshatriya consecration. The townsmen, country
people, and hired soldiers of the kingdom, the thirty-eight

naṭa-naccakāmukha-maṅgalikāsotthivācakāsamaṇa-brāhmaṇasabbapāsaṇḍagaṇā abhigacchanti, yaṃ kiñci paṭhaviyā paṭṭana-ratanākara-nagara-suṅkaṭṭhāna-verajjaka-chejjabhejjajana-manusāsanaṃ sabbattha sāmiko bhavati; evam-eva kho mahārāja yo koci puggalo yutto patto-pe-vimutti-paṇḍaravimala-setacchattena abhisiñcati.

26 teras' ime mahārāja dhutaṅgāni yehi suddhikato nibbānamahāsamuddaṃ pavisitvā bahuvidhadhammakīḷaṃ abhikīḷati, rūpārūpa-aṭṭhasamāpattiyo vaḷañjeti, iddhividhaṃ dibbasotadhātuṃ paracittavijānanaṃ pubbenivāsānussatiṃ dibbacakkhuṃ sabbāsavakkhayañ-ca pāpuṇāti. katame terasa: paṃsukūlikaṅgaṃ tecīvarikaṅgaṃ piṇḍapātikaṅgaṃ sapadānacārikaṅgaṃ ekāsanikaṅgaṃ pattapiṇḍikaṅgaṃ khalupacchābhattikaṅgaṃ āraññakaṅgaṃ rukkhamūlikaṅgaṃ abbhokāsikaṅgaṃ sosānikaṅgaṃ yathasanthatikaṅgaṃ nesajjikaṅgaṃ. imehi kho mahārāja terasahi dhutaguṇehi pubbe āsevitehi nisevitehi ciṇṇehi pariciṇṇehi caritehi upacaritehi paripūritehi kevalaṃ sāmaññaṃ paṭilabhati, tass' ādheyyā honti kevalā santā sukhā samāpattiyo.

27 yathā mahārāja sadhano nāviko paṭṭane suṭṭhu katasuṅko mahāsamuddaṃ pavisitvā vaṅgaṃ takkolaṃ cīnaṃ sovīraṃ suraṭṭhaṃ alasandaṃ kolapaṭṭanaṃ suvaṇṇabhūmiṃ

who compose the royal retinue, and acrobats, dancers, fortune tellers, heralds, groups of renouncers, Brahmans, and all types of non-Buddhist thinkers approach him. He becomes the lord everywhere on earth with respect to instruction on seaports, gemstone mines, cities, customs houses, foreigners, and the punishment and maiming of people. It is similar, great king, in the case of the proper and correct person just described who is consecrated with the stainless white parasol of freedom.

"One purified by these thirteen ascetic practices, great 26
king, enters the great ocean of nibbana and sports there, celebrating the many aspects of the Dhamma, tracking the eight attainments of the form and formless realms, and winning the various forms of magical power, clairaudience, knowing the thoughts of others, remembering past lives, the divine eye, and the destruction of the flaws. What are the thirteen? Wearing thrown-out rags, wearing the three robes, the alms food eater's practice, seeking alms house to house without skipping any, eating at only one session, eating everything in just one bowl, refusing second helpings, living in the forest, living at the base of a tree, living in the open air, living in a charnel ground, sleeping wherever one is told, and staying only in a seated posture. Only by previously practicing, observing, living, fulfilling, making a habit of, enacting, and completing these thirteen ascetic practices, great king, does one attain renunciation. And on the basis of this, all the peaceful and happy attainments come into being.

"Great king, consider the wealthy sea captain who has 27
prospered collecting customs and then sets out to sea, going to Bengal, Takkola, China, Sauvira, Kathiawar, Alexandria,

gacchati aññam-pi yaṃ kiñci nāvāsañcaraṇaṃ, evam-eva kho mahārāja imehi terasahi dhutaguṇehi pubbe āsevitehi nisevitehi ciṇṇehi pariciṇṇehi caritehi upacaritehi paripūritehi kevalaṃ sāmaññaṃ paṭilabhati, tass' ādheyyā honti kevalā santā sukhā samāpattiyo.

28 yathā mahārāja kassako paṭhamaṃ khettadosaṃ tiṇakaṭṭha-pāsāṇaṃ apanetvā kasitvā vapitvā sammā udakaṃ pavesetvā rakkhitvā gopetvā lavana-maddanena bahudhaññako hoti, tass' ādheyyā bhavanti ye keci adhanā kapaṇā daḷiddā duggatajanā; evam-eva kho mahārāja imehi terasahi dhutaguṇehi pubbe āsevitehi nisevitehi-pe-kevalā santā sukhā samāpattiyo.

29 yathā vā pana mahārāja khattiyo muddhāvasitto abhijātakulakulīno chejja-bhejja-janam-anusāsane issaro hoti vasavattī sāmiko icchākaraṇo, kevalā ca mahāpaṭhavī tass' ādheyyā hoti; evam-eva kho mahārāja imehi terasahi dhutaguṇehi pubbe āsevitehi nisevitehi ciṇṇehi pariciṇṇehi caritehi upacaritehi paripūritehi jinasāsanavare issaro hoti vasavattī sāmiko icchākaraṇo, kevalā ca samaṇaguṇā tass' ādheyyā honti.

30 nanu mahārāja thero upaseno vaṅgantaputto sallekhadhutaguṇe paripūrakāritāya anādiyitvā sāvatthiyā saṅghassa katikaṃ sapariso naradammasārathiṃ paṭisallāṇagataṃ upasaṅkamitvā bhagavato pāde sirasā vanditvā ekamantaṃ nisīdi. bhagavā ca taṃ suvinītaṃ parisaṃ oloketvā haṭṭha-

Kolapattana, Suvannabhumi, and other seaports. Similarly, great king, only someone who has previously practiced, observed, lived, fulfilled, made a habit of, enacted, and completed these thirteen ascetic practices attains renunciation. And on the basis of this, all the peaceful and happy attainments come into being.

"Consider also a farmer who first clears the defects in 28
a field—grass, jungle, and stones—and then plows, sows, properly irrigates, fences, and guards it. With the reaping and threshing, much grain is produced, and whoever is poor, down-and-out, begging, unfortunate, and in a bad way comes to depend upon it. In the same way, great king, only someone who has previously practiced and observed these thirteen ascetic practices attains renunciation. And on the basis of this, all the peaceful and happy attainments come into being.

"Or consider a properly anointed Kshatriya of noble birth 29
on both sides, lord over punishing and maiming people, a ruler wielding authority who does as he pleases. The great earth entirely depends upon him, great king. Similarly, only someone who has previously practiced, observed, lived, fulfilled, made a habit of, enacted, and completed these thirteen ascetic practices becomes a lord with respect to the excellent dispensation of the Victor, a ruler wielding authority and doing as one pleases. And all of the qualities of being a renouncer depend on this.

"Is it not the case, great king, that once Elder Upasena, 30
son of Vanganta, having fulfilled the severe austerity of the ascetic practices, was able to breach the agreement made at Savatthi concerning the Buddha's seclusion when he, with his assembly, approached the Buddha?[3] Worshiping the

tuṭṭho pamudito udaggo parisāya saddhiṃ sallāpaṃ sallapitvā asambhinnena brahmassarena etad avoca: pāsādikā kho pana tyāyaṃ upasena parisā, kathaṃ tvaṃ upasena parisaṃ vinesīti.

31 so pi sabbaññunā dasabalena devātidevena puṭṭho yathābhūta-sabhāvaguṇa-vasena bhagavantaṃ etad-avoca: yo koci maṃ bhante upasaṅkamitvā pabbajjaṃ vā nissayaṃ vā yācati tam ahaṃ evaṃ vadāmi: ahaṃ kho āvuso āraññako piṇḍapātiko paṃsukūliko tecīvariko; sace tvam-pi āraññako bhavissasi piṇḍapātiko paṃsukūliko tecīvariko evāhantaṃ pabbājessāmi nissayaṃ dassāmīti; sace so me bhante paṭisuṇitvā nandati oramati, evāhan-taṃ pabbājemi nissayaṃ demi; sace na nandati na oramati, na taṃ pabbājemi na nissayaṃ demi; evāhaṃ bhante parisaṃ vinemīti. evam-pi mahārāja dhutaguṇavara-samādiṇṇo jinasāsanavare issaro hoti vasavattī sāmiko icchākaraṇo, tass' ādheyyā honti kevalā santā sukhā samāpattiyo.

32 yathā mahārāja padumaṃ abhivuddha-parisuddha-udiccajātippabhavaṃ siniddhaṃ muduṃ lobhaniyaṃ sugandhaṃ piyaṃ patthitaṃ pasatthaṃ jalakaddama-m-anu-palittaṃ aṇu-patta-kesara-kaṇṇikābhimaṇḍitaṃ bhamara-gaṇasevitaṃ sītalasalilasaṃvaddhaṃ, evam-eva kho mahārāja imehi terasahi dhutaguṇehi pubbe āsevitehi nisevitehi ciṇṇehi pariciṇṇehi caritehi upacaritehi paripūritehi ariyasāvako tiṃsa-guṇavarehi samupeto hoti. katamehi tiṃsa-guṇavarehi: siniddha-mudu-maddava-mettacitto hoti, ghātitahata-vihata-kileso hoti, hata-nihata-māna-dappo hoti,

Bhagavan's feet with his head, he sat down to one side. The Bhagavan observed his well-disciplined assembly and was pleased, satisfied, delighted, and charmed. He engaged the assembly in conversation and then declared in a clear and beautiful voice: 'Upasena, your assembly is delightful. How have you managed to discipline this assembly?'

"When asked by the omniscient ten-powered god above 31
gods, he replied in keeping with the particular nature of the special qualities as they really are: 'Sir, I say the following to whoever approaches me asking for ordination or guidance: "Friend, I live in the forest, eat alms, wear rags, and wear the three robes. If you also live in the forest, eat alms, wear rags, and wear the three robes, then I will ordain you or give you guidance." Sir, if he agrees, pleased and rejoicing, then I ordain him or give him guidance. This is how I discipline my assembly.' Thus, great king, someone who seriously observes the excellent ascetic practices becomes a lord with respect to the excellent dispensation of the Victor, a ruler wielding authority and doing as one pleases. And all of the qualities of being a renouncer depend on this.

"Great king, consider the lotus, a child of the cool waters. 32
When born it rises up pure, glossy, delicate, appealing, fragrant, beloved, desired, untainted by water and mud, adorned with tiny petals, stamens, and its pistil, and the resort of clusters of bees. It is similar to how the noble disciple who has previously practiced, observed, lived, fulfilled, made a habit of, enacted, and completed these thirteen ascetic practices comes to possess thirty excellent special qualities. What are the thirty qualities? One's heart becomes full of loving-kindess and affectionate, soft, and gentle; the

acala-daḷha-niviṭṭha-nibbematika-saddho hoti, paripuṇṇa-pīṇita-pahaṭṭha-lobhaniya-santa-sukha-samāpatti-lābhī hoti, sīla-varapavara-asama-sucigandha-paribhāvito hoti, devamanussānaṃ piyo hoti manāpo, khīṇāsava-ariya-varapuggala-patthito, devamanussānaṃ vandita-pūjito, budha-vibudha-paṇḍita-janānaṃ thuta-thavita-thomita-pasattho, idha vā huraṃ vā lokena anupalitto, appathokavajje pi bhayadassāvī, vipulavarasampattikāmānaṃ maggaphala-varatthasādhano, āyācita-vipula-paṇīta-paccaya-bhāgī, aniketasayano, jhānajjhāsita-tapavara-vihārī, vijaṭita-kilesa-jālavatthu, bhinna-bhagga-sankuṭita-sañchinna-gati-nīvaraṇo, akuppadhammo, abhinītavāso, anavajjabhogī,[1] gativimutto, uttiṇṇa-sabbavicikiccho, vimuttijjhāsitatto, diṭṭhadhammo, acala-daḷhabhīruttāṇam-upagato, samucchinnānusayo, sabbāsavakkhayaṃ patto, santa-sukha-samāpatti-vihāra-bahulo, sabbasamaṇaguṇa-samupeto. imehi tiṃsa-guṇavarehi samupeto hoti.

defilements are slain, destroyed, and decimated; pride and arrogance are struck down and defeated; faith becomes unwavering, fortified, settled, and integrated; and one obtains the perfect attainments of peace and happiness that are desired, gratifying, and appealing. One becomes infused with the clean scent equal to the best and most excellent moral discipline; one comes to be pleasing and beloved to gods and humans; sought out by fine and noble persons with flaws destroyed; worshiped and praised by gods and humans; admired, extolled, celebrated, and commended by wise, astute, and learned people; and untainted by the world in this or the next life. One becomes quick to see danger in even trifling or minor faults; accomplished in the best aims of the path and the fruits of those seeking ample and excellent prosperity; and the recipient of bounteous and plentiful requisites when requested. One remains without home or bed; lives intent upon the *jhānas* and the highest austerities; has disentangled the basis for the net of the defilements; and has seen to it that the hindrance of rebirth is broken, shattered, shriveled, and crumbled. One's character is steady, one's observances are excellent, one enjoys only blameless things, and one is freed from rebirth; this person has left behind all doubts, is intent upon freedom, has seen the Dhamma, and has arrived at a steady and fortified safe refuge. Finally, one's problematic tendencies are cut off; one has reached the destruction of every flaw, lives devoted to the attainment of peace and happiness, and is endowed with every special quality of a renouncer. These are the thirty excellent special qualities one comes to possess.

33 nanu mahārāja thero sāriputto dasasahassimhi lokadhātuyā aggapuriso, ṭhapetvā dasabalaṃ lokācariyaṃ. so pi aparimita-m-asaṅkheyya-kappe samācitakusalamūlo brāhmaṇakulakūlīno manāpikaṃ kāmaratiṃ anekasaṅkhadhanavarañ-ca ohāya jinasāsane pabbajitvā imehi terasahi dhutaguṇehi kāya-vacī-cittaṃ damayitvā ajj' etarahi anantaguṇasamannāgato gotamassa bhagavato sāsanavare dhammacakkam-anupavattako jāto. bhāsitam-p'etaṃ mahārāja bhagavatā devātidevena ekuttara-nikāyavaralañcake: nāham-bhikkhave aññaṃ ekapuggalam-pi samanupassāmi yo tathāgatena anuttaraṃ dhammacakkaṃ pavattitaṃ samma-d-eva anupavatteti yatha-y idaṃ sāriputto; sāriputto bhikkhave tathāgatena anuttaraṃ dhammacakkaṃ pavattitaṃ samma-d-eva anupavattetīti.

34 sādhu bhante nāgasena, yaṃ kiñci navaṅgaṃ buddhavacanaṃ, yā ca lokuttarā kiriyā, yā ca loke adhigamavipulavarasampattiyo, sabban-taṃ terasasu dhutaguṇesu samodhānopagatan-ti.

navamo vaggo.
[meṇḍakapañho samatto.]

“Is it not the case, great king, that Elder Sariputta is the best person in the ten-thousand-world system except for the world’s teacher, the ten-powered one? He had accumulated the roots of merit over immeasurable and incalculable eras. He then, as a Brahman on both sides of his family, renounced the tempting pleasures of the senses and wealth beyond calculation to ordain in the Victor’s dispensation. He tamed his body, speech, and mind with these thirteen ascetic practices, and now, in our time, came to possess endless qualities and turned the Wheel of the Dhamma in the excellent dispensation of Bhagavan Gotama. For this was said by the Bhagavan in the excellent declaration that is the *Aṅguttaranikāya:* ‘Monks, I do not see even one other person who properly continues to turn the supreme Wheel of the Dhamma set in motion by the Tathagata as does Sariputta. Monks, Sariputta continues to turn properly the supreme Wheel of the Dhamma turned by the Tathagata.’” 33

“Very good, Nagasena. The nine genres of the Buddha’s words, worldly moral activity, and the extensive and excellent attainments of knowledge in the world are all combined in the thirteen ascetic practices.” 34

End of Part 9 of the Ram Horn Dilemmas.

CHAPTER 6

Questions and Discussions of Analogies

PART 1

1 bhante nāgasena, katihi aṅgehi samannāgato bhikkhu arahattaṃ sacchikarotīti. idha mahārāja arahattaṃ sacchikātukāmena bhikkhunā ghorassarassa ekaṃ aṅgaṃ gahetabbaṃ. kukkuṭassa pañca aṅgāni gahetabbāni. kalandakassa ekaṃ aṅgaṃ gahetabbaṃ. dīpiniyā ekaṃ aṅgaṃ gahetabbaṃ. dīpikassa dve aṅgāni gahetabbāni. kummassa pañca aṅgāni gahetabbāni. vaṃsassa ekaṃ aṅgaṃ gahetabbaṃ. cāpassa ekaṃ aṅgaṃ gahetabbaṃ. vāyasassa dve aṅgāni gahetabbāni. makkaṭassa dve aṅgāni gahetabbāni. lāpulatāya ekaṃ aṅgaṃ gahetabbaṃ. padumassa tīṇi aṅgāni gahetabbāni. bījassa dve aṅgāni gahetabbāni. sālakalyāṇikāya ekaṃ aṅgaṃ gahetabbaṃ. nāvāya tīṇi aṅgāni gahetabbāni. nāvālakanakassa dve aṅgāni gahetabbāni. kūpassa ekaṃ aṅgaṃ gahetabbaṃ. niyyāmakassa tīṇi aṅgāni gahetabbāni. kammakarassa ekaṃ aṅgaṃ gahetabbaṃ. samuddassa pañca aṅgāni gahetabbāni. paṭhaviyā pañca aṅgāni gahetabbāni. āpassa pañca aṅgāni gahetabbāni. tejassa pañca aṅgāni gahetabbāni. vāyussa pañca aṅgāni gahetabbāni. pabbatassa pañca aṅgāni gahetabbāni. ākāsassa pañca aṅgāni gahetabbāni. candassa pañca aṅgāni gahetabbāni. suriyassa satta aṅgāni gahetabbāni. sakkassa tīṇi aṅgāni gahetabbāni. cakkavattissa cattāri aṅgāni gahetabbāni.

2 upacikāya ekaṃ aṅgaṃ gahetabbaṃ. biḷārassa dve aṅgāni gahetabbāni. undurassa ekaṃ aṅgaṃ gahetabbaṃ. vicchikassa ekaṃ aṅgaṃ gahetabbaṃ. nakulassa ekaṃ aṅgaṃ gahetabbaṃ. jarasigālassa dve aṅgāni gahetabbāni. migassa tīṇi aṅgāni gahetabbāni. gorūpassa cattāri aṅgāni gaheta-

PART 1

"Revered Nagasena, how many attributes must a monk possess to become an arhat?" 1

"Great king, a monk seeking to become an arhat must acquire one attribute of the braying ass. He must acquire five attributes of the cock, one attribute of the squirrel, one attribute of the female leopard, and two attributes of the male leopard. He must acquire five attributes of the turtle, one attribute of bamboo, one of the bow, two of the crow, and two of the monkey. He must also acquire one attribute of the vines of a gourd plant, three attributes of the lotus, two attributes of the seed, and one of the beautiful sal tree. He must acquire three attributes of a ship, two attributes of the ship's anchor, one of the mast, three of the sea captain, one of the dock worker, and five attributes of the ocean. He must acquire five attributes of the earth, five of water, and five attributes each of fire, wind, mountains, space, and the moon. He must acquire seven attributes of the sun, three attributes of Sakka, and four of the wheel-turning emperor.

"He must acquire one attribute of the termite, two attri- 2
butes of the cat, one of the rat, and one of the scorpion. He must acquire one attribute of the mongoose, two attributes of an old jackal, three of the deer, four of the ox, two of the boar, five of the elephant, seven of the lion, and three of

bbāni. varāhassa dve aṅgāni gahetabbāni. hatthissa pañca aṅgāni gahetabbāni. sīhassa satta aṅgāni gahetabbāni. cakkavākassa tīṇi aṅgāni gahetabbāni. peṇāhikāya dve aṅgāni gahetabbāni. gharakapoṭassa ekaṃ aṅgaṃ gahetabbaṃ. ulūkassa dve aṅgāni gahetabbāni. satapattassa ekaṃ aṅgaṃ gahetabbaṃ. vaggulissa dve aṅgāni gahetabbāni. jalūkāya ekaṃ aṅgaṃ gahetabbaṃ. sappassa tīṇi aṅgāni gahetabbāni. ajagarassa ekaṃ aṅgaṃ gahetabbaṃ. panthamakkaṭakassa ekaṃ aṅgaṃ gahetabbaṃ. thanasitadārakassa ekaṃ aṅgaṃ gahetabbaṃ. cittakadharakummassa ekaṃ aṅgaṃ gahetabbaṃ. pavanassa pañca aṅgāni gahetabbāni. rukkhassa tīṇi aṅgāni gahetabbāni. meghassa pañca aṅgāni gahetabbāni. maṇiratanassa tīṇi aṅgāni gahetabbāni. māgavikassa cattāri aṅgāni gahetabbāni. bāḷisikassa dve aṅgāni gahetabbāni. tacchakassa dve aṅgāni gahetabbāni. kumbhassa ekaṃ aṅgaṃ gahetabbaṃ. kāḷāyasassa dve aṅgāni gahetabbāni. chattassa tīṇi aṅgāni gahetabbāni. khettassa tīṇi aṅgāni gahetabbāni. agadassa dve aṅgāni gahetabbāni. bhojanassa tīṇi aṅgāni gahetabbāni. issatthassa cattāri aṅgāni gahetabbāni. rañño cattāri aṅgāni gahetabbāni. dovārikassa dve aṅgāni gahetabbāni. nisadāya ekaṃ aṅgaṃ gahetabbaṃ. padīpassa dve aṅgāni gahetabbāni. mayūrassa dve aṅgāni gahetabbāni. turaṅgassa dve aṅgāni gahetabbāni. soṇḍikassa dve aṅgāni gahetabbāni. indakhīlassa dve aṅgāni gahetabbāni. tulāya ekaṃ aṅgaṃ gahetabbaṃ. khaggassa dve aṅgāni gahetabbāni. macchassa dve aṅgāni gahetabbāni.

the ruddy shelduck. He must acquire two attributes of the *peṇāhika* bird, one of the house pigeon, two of the owl, one of the sarus crane, two of the bat, one of the leech, three of the serpent, one of the goat-swallowing snake, and one of the road spider. He must acquire one attribute of the child at the breast, one of the painted tortoise, five of the forest, three of a tree, five of a rain cloud, and three of the jewel treasure. He must acquire four attributes of the hunter, three attributes of the fisherman, two of the carpenter, one of the water pot, two of black iron, three of an umbrella, and three of a field. He must acquire two attributes of an antidote, three attributes of food, four of the archer, four of the king, two of the gatekeeper, one of the grindstone, and two of a lamp. He must acquire two attributes of the peacock, two attributes of the steed, two of the barkeep, two of the threshold, one of a balance, two of a sword, and two of a fish.

3 iṇagāhakassa ekaṃ aṅgaṃ gahetabbaṃ. byādhitassa dve aṅgāni gahetabbāni. matassa dve aṅgāni gahetabbāni. nadiyā dve aṅgāni gahetabbāni. usabhassa ekaṃ aṅgaṃ gahetabbaṃ. maggassa dve aṅgāni gahetabbāni. suṅkasāyikassa ekaṃ aṅgaṃ gahetabbaṃ. corassa tīṇi aṅgāni gahetabbāni. sakuṇagghiyā ekaṃ aṅgaṃ gahetabbaṃ. sunakhassa ekaṃ aṅgaṃ gahetabbaṃ. tikicchakassa tīṇi aṅgāni gahetabbāni. gabbhiniyā dve aṅgāni gahetabbāni. camariyā ekaṃ aṅgaṃ gahetabbaṃ. kikiyā dve aṅgāni gahetabbāni. kapotikāya tīṇi aṅgāni gahetabbāni. ekanayanassa dve aṅgāni gahetabbāni. kassakassa tīṇi aṅgāni gahetabbāni. jambukasigāliyā ekaṃ aṅgaṃ gahetabbaṃ. caṅgavārakassa dve aṅgāni gahetabbāni. dabbiyā ekaṃ aṅgaṃ gahetabbaṃ. iṇasādhakassa tīṇi aṅgāni gahetabbāni. anuvicinakassa ekaṃ aṅgaṃ gahetabbaṃ. sārathissa dve aṅgāni gahetabbāni. bhojakassa dve aṅgāni gahetabbāni. tunnavāyassa ekaṃ aṅgaṃ gahetabbaṃ. nāvāyikassa ekaṃ aṅgaṃ gahetabbaṃ. bhamarassa dve aṅgāni gahetabbānīti. mātikā samattā.

4 bhante nāgasena, ghorassarassa ekaṃ aṅgaṃ gahetabban-ti yaṃ vadesi, kataman-taṃ ekaṃ aṅgaṃ gahetabban-ti. yathā mahārāja gadrabho nāma saṅkārakūṭe pi catukke pi siṅghāṭake pi gāmadvāre pi thusarāsimhi pi yattha katthaci sayati, na sayanabahulo hoti, evam-eva kho mahārāja yoginā yogāvacarena tiṇasanthāre pi paṇṇasanthāre pi kaṭṭhamañcake pi chamāya pi yattha katthaci cammakhaṇḍaṃ pattharitvā yattha katthaci sayitabbaṃ, na sayanabahulena bhavitabbaṃ. idaṃ mahārāja ghorassarassa ekaṃ aṅgaṃ gahetabbaṃ. bhāsitam-p' etaṃ mahārāja bhagavatā devātidevena: kaḷiṅgarūpadhānā bhikkhave etarahi mama sāvakā viharanti appamattā ātāpino padhānasmin-ti.

"He must acquire one attribute of the borrower, two attributes of the invalid, two of the corpse, two of the river, one of the bull, and two attributes of the road. He must acquire one attribute of the customs officer, three attributes of the thief, one of the hawk, one of the dog, three of the physician, two of the pregnant woman, one of the female yak, two of the blue jay, three of the pigeon, and two of the one-eyed man. He must acquire three attributes of the farmer, one attribute of the female jackal, two of the sieve, one of a ladle, three of the debt collector, one of the examiner, and two of the charioteer. Finally, he must acquire two attributes of one who provides food, one attribute of the tailor, one of the sailor; and he must acquire two attributes of the bee. This is the complete outline." 3

"Revered Nagasena, you say that he must acquire one attribute of the braying ass. What is that one attribute that he must acquire?" 4

"Great king, consider how wherever the ass lies down to rest, whether on a pile of rubbish, in a square, at a crossroads, at the village gate, or on a heap of straw, it does not rest for long. Similarly, great king, wherever the yogi, an earnest disciple, spreads out his leather mat, whether it be a bed of grass, a bed of leaves, a wooden bed, or the bare ground, and lies down to sleep, he would not rest for long. Great king, this is the one attribute of the braying ass that he must acquire. For the Bhagavan, god above gods, said, 'Monks, nowadays my disciples are ardent, zealous,

bhāsitam-p' etaṃ mahārāja therena sāriputtena dhammasenāpatinā pi: pallaṅkena nisinnassa jaṇṇukenābhivassati; alam-phāsuvihārāya pahitattassa bhikkhuno ti.

bhante nāgasena, kukkuṭassa pañca aṅgāni gahetabbānīti yaṃ vadesi, katamāni tāni pañca aṅgāni gahetabbānīti. yathā mahārāja kukkuṭo kālena samayena patisallīyati, evam-eva kho mahārāja yoginā yogāvacarena kālena samayen'; eva cetiyaṅgaṇaṃ sammajjitvā pānīyaṃ paribhojanīyaṃ upaṭṭhapetvā sarīraṃ paṭijaggitvā nahāyitvā cetiyaṃ vanditvā buḍḍhānaṃ bhikkhūnaṃ dassanāya gantvā kālena samayena suññāgāraṃ pavisitabbaṃ. idaṃ mahārāja kukkuṭassa paṭhamaṃ aṅgaṃ gahetabbaṃ. puna ca paraṃ mahārāja kukkuṭo kālena samayen' eva vuṭṭhāti, evam-eva kho mahārāja yoginā yogāvacarena kālena samayen' eva vuṭṭhahitvā cetiyaṅgaṇaṃ sammajjitvā pānīyaṃ paribhojanīyaṃ upaṭṭhapetvā sarīraṃ paṭijaggitvā cetiyaṃ vanditvā puna-d-eva suññāgāraṃ pavisitabbaṃ. idaṃ mahārāja kukkuṭassa dutiyaṃ aṅgaṃ gahetabbaṃ. puna ca paraṃ mahārāja kukkuṭo paṭhaviṃ khaṇitvā khaṇitvā ajjhohāraṃ ajjhoharati, evam-eva kho mahārāja yoginā yogāvacarena paccavekkhitvā paccavekkhitvā ajjhohāraṃ ajjhoharitabbaṃ: n' eva davāya na madāya na maṇḍanāya na vibhūsanāya, yāvad-eva imassa kāyassa ṭhitiyā yāpanāya vihiṃsūparatiyā brahmacariyānuggahāya; iti purāṇañ-ca vedanaṃ paṭihaṅkhāmi navañ-ca vedanaṃ na uppādessāmi, yātrā ca me bhavissati anavajjatā ca phāsuvihāro cāti. idaṃ mahārāja kukkuṭassa tatiyaṃ aṅgaṃ gahetabbaṃ. bhāsitam-p' etaṃ mahārāja bhagavatā devātidevena: kantāre puttamaṃsaṃva, akkhass' abbhañjanaṃ yathā, evaṃ āhari āhāraṃ, yāpanatthāy' amucchito ti.

and striving, and live with a wooden block for a pillow.' And Elder Sariputta, General of the Dhamma, said this: 'So long as the rain does not fall on his knees as he sits cross-legged, the resolute monk lives in comfort.'"

"Revered Nagasena, you say that he must acquire five attributes of the cock. What are the five attributes that he must acquire?"

"Great king, just as the cock retreats at the right time, the yogi, an earnest disciple, should sweep the terrace of the shrine at just the right time, serve food and drink, take care of his body, bathe, worship the shrine, go to see elderly monks, and then repair to an empty hut. This is the first attribute of the cock to be acquired. Additionally, just as the cock rises at the right time, the yogi, an earnest disciple, should rise at exactly the right time, sweep the terrace of the shrine, serve food and drink, take care of his body, worship the shrine, and again enter the empty hut. This is the second attribute of the cock to be acquired. Additionally, just as the cock keeps scratching away at the ground seeking something to eat, the yogi, an earnest disciple, should eat each mouthful reflecting over and over: *This is not for sport, excess, beautification, or adornment, but merely for supporting and maintaining the body, easing harm, and assisting the religious life. Thus I shall banish old feelings and not give rise to new feelings; I will keep going, living blamelessly and comfortably.* This, great king, is the third attribute of the cock to be acquired. For the Bhagavan, god above gods, said: 'Take food only for the sake of subsistence without being obsessed, as with the flesh of the child in the wilderness and the greasing of the axle.'[1]

6 puna ca paraṃ mahārāja kukkuṭo sacakkhuko pi rattiṃ andho hoti, evam-eva kho mahārāja yoginā yogāvacarena anandhen'; eva andhena viya bhavitabbaṃ, araññe pi gocaragāme piṇḍāya carantena pi rajanīyesu rūpa-sadda-gandha-rasa-phoṭṭhabba-dhammesu andhena badhirena mūgena viya bhavitabbaṃ, na nimittaṃ gahetabbaṃ, nānubyañjanaṃ gahetabbaṃ. idaṃ mahārāja kukkuṭassa catutthaṃ aṅgaṃ gahetabbaṃ. bhāsitam-p' etaṃ mahārāja therena mahākaccāyanena:

7 cakkhum' assa yathā andho, sotavā badhiro yathā, jivhāv'
assa yathā mūgo, balavā dubbalo-r-iva, atha atthe
samuppanne sayetha matasāyikan-ti.

8 puna ca paraṃ mahārāja kukkuṭo leḍḍu-daṇḍa-lakuṭa-muggarehi paripātiyanto pi sakaṃ gehaṃ na vijahati, evam-eva kho mahārāja yoginā yogāvacarena cīvarakammaṃ karontena pi navakammaṃ karontena pi vattapaṭivattaṃ karontena pi uddisantena pi uddisāpentena pi yoniso manasikāro na vijahitabbo; sakaṃ kho pan' etaṃ mahārāja yogino gehaṃ yad-idaṃ yoniso manasi-kāro. idaṃ mahārāja kukkuṭassa pañcamaṃ aṅgaṃ gahetabbaṃ. bhāsitam-p' etaṃ mahārāja bhagavatā devātidevena: ko ca bhikkhave bhikkhuno gocaro sako pettiko visayo: yad-idaṃ cattāro satipaṭṭhānā ti. bhāsitam-p' etaṃ mahārāja therena sāriputtena dhammasenāpatinā pi: yathā sumanto mātaṅgo sakaṃ soṇḍaṃ na maddati bhakkhābhakkhaṃ vijānāti attano vuttikappanaṃ tath' eva buddhaputtena appamattena vā pana jinavacanaṃ na madditabbaṃ manasikāravarutta-man-ti.

"Additionally, great king, just as the cock has eyes to see 6
but is blind at night, the yogi, an earnest disciple, though not blind, should behave as if blind whether in the forest or wandering for alms in the village. One should be as though blind, deaf, and mute to pleasing visible forms, sounds, fragrances, tastes, textures, and phenomenal states, taking no notice of appearances and taking no notice of details. This, great king, is the fourth attribute of the cock that must be acquired. For this was said by Elder Kaccayana the Great:

> One with eyes should act as if blind; one with ears as if deaf; one with a tongue as if mute; and one who is strong as if weak. 7
> Then, when the goal has been reached, one should lie on the bed of death.

"Finally, great king, even when chased with clods, sticks, 8
clubs, and bats, the cock does not abandon its own nest. Similarly, the yogi, an earnest disciple, even when sewing a robe, making repairs, performing the usual duties, reciting, or leading others in recitation, does not abandon careful attention. For careful attention is the yogi's own home. This is the fifth attribute of the cock that must be acquired. For the Bhagavan, god above gods, said: 'Monks, what is a monk's own ancestral range? It is the four foundations of mindfulness.' And, great king, Elder Sariputta, General of the Dhamma, said: 'Just as a well-tamed elephant does not trample its own trunk and discerns what is edible and inedible from its own provisions, the vigilant child of the Buddha should not trample the Victor's words concerning the best and supreme attention.'"

9 bhante nāgasena, kalandakassa ekaṃ aṅgaṃ gahetabban-ti yaṃ vadesi, kataman-taṃ ekaṃ aṅgaṃ gahetabban ti. yathā mahārāja kalandako paṭisattumhi opatante naṅguṭṭhaṃ papphoṭetvā mahantaṃ katvā ten' eva nanguṭṭhalakuṭena paṭisattuṃ paṭibāhati, evam-eva kho mahārāja yoginā yogāvacarena kilesasattumhi opatante satipaṭṭhānalakuṭaṃ papphoṭetvā mahantaṃ katvā ten' eva satipaṭṭhānalakuṭena sabbe kilesā paṭibāhitabbā. idaṃ mahārāja kalandakassa ekaṃ aṅgaṃ gahetabbaṃ. bhāsitam-p' etaṃ mahārāja therena cullapanthakena: yadā kilesā opatanti sāmaññaguṇadhaṃsanā, satipaṭṭhānalakuṭena hantabbā te punappunan-ti.

10 bhante nāgasena, dīpiniyā ekaṃ aṅgaṃ gahetabban-ti yaṃ vadesi, kataman-taṃ ekaṃ aṅgaṃ gahetabban-ti. yathā mahārāja dīpinī sakiṃ yeva gabbhaṃ gaṇhāti, na punappunaṃ purisaṃ upeti, evam-eva kho mahārāja yoginā yogāvacarena āyati paṭisandhiṃ uppattiṃ gabbhaseyyaṃ cutiṃ bhedaṃ khayaṃ vināsaṃ saṃsārabhayaṃ duggatiṃ visamaṃ sampīḷitaṃ disvā: punabbhave na paṭisandahissāmīti yoniso manasikāro karaṇīyo. idaṃ mahārāja dīpiniyā ekaṃ aṅgaṃ gahetabbaṃ. bhāsitam-p' etaṃ mahārāja bhagavatā devātidevena suttanipāte dhaniyagopālakasutte:

"Revered Nagasena, you say that there is one attribute of 9
the squirrel that must be acquired. What is this one attribute that must be acquired?"

"Great king, a squirrel, when swooped down upon by an enemy, expands and brandishes its tail, and wards off the enemy with a tail like a cudgel. Similarly, the yogi, an earnest disciple, when swooped down upon by the enemies of the defilements, expands and brandishes the cudgel that is the foundations of mindfulness. With the foundations of mindfulness as a cudgel, all of the defilements are warded off. This, great king, is the single attribute of the squirrel that must be acquired. For Elder Culla Panthaka said: 'When the defilements swoop down, obliterating the special qualities of renunciation, beat them back again and again with the cudgel of the foundations of mindfulness.'"

"Revered Nagasena, you say that there is one attribute of 10
the female leopard that must be acquired. What is that one attribute that must be acquired?"

"Great king, the female leopard conceives only once and does not go again and again to the male. Similarly, the yogi, an earnest disciple, sees future conception, gestation, lying in the womb, perishing, the body giving out, destruction, the fear of samsara, and bad future states as disagreeable and troubling, and so applies himself to careful attention, thinking, *I will not be reborn again.* This is the one attribute of the female leopard that must be acquired, great king. For the Bhagavan, god above gods, said in the *Dhaniya the Herdsman Sutta* in the *Suttanipāta:*

11 usabho-r-iva chetvā bandhanāni, nāgo pūtilataṃva dālayitvā, nāhaṃ puna upessaṃ gabbhaseyyaṃ; atha ce patthayasi pavassa devāti.

12 bhante nāgasena, dīpikassa dve aṅgāni gahetabbānīti yaṃ vadesi, katamāni tāni dve aṅgāni gahetabbānīti. yathā mahārāja dīpiko arañño tiṇagahanaṃ vā vanagahanaṃ vā pabbatagahanaṃ vā nissāya nilīyitvā mige gaṇhāti, evam-eva kho mahārāja yoginā yogāvacarena vivekaṃ sevitabbaṃ, araññaṃ rukkhamūlaṃ pabbataṃ kandaraṃ giriguhaṃ susānaṃ vanapatthaṃ abbhokāsaṃ palālapuñjaṃ appasaddaṃ appanigghosaṃ vijanavātaṃ manussarāhaseyyakaṃ paṭisallāṇasāruppaṃ; vivekaṃ sevamāno hi mahārāja yogī yogāvacaro na cirass' eva chaḷabhiññāsu vasībhāvaṃ pāpuṇāti. idaṃ mahārāja dīpikassa paṭhamaṃ aṅgaṃ gahetabbaṃ. bhāsitam-p' etaṃ mahārāja therehi dhammasaṅgāhakehi: yathā pi dīpiko nāma nilīyitvā gaṇhatī mige, tath' evāyaṃ buddhaputto yuttayogo vipassako araññaṃ pavisitvāna gaṇhāti phalam-uttaman-ti.

13 puna ca paraṃ mahārāja dīpiko yaṃ kañci pasuṃ vadhitvā vāmena passena patitaṃ na bhakkheti, evam-eva kho mahārāja yoginā yogāvacarena veḷudānena vā pattadānena vā pupphadānena vā phaladānena vā sinānadānena vā mattikadānena vā cuṇṇadānena vā dantakaṭṭhadānena vā mukhodakadānena vā cāṭukammatāya vā muggasuppatāya vā pāribhaṭṭakatāya vā jaṅghapesaniyena vā vejjakammena

As a bull cuts through its bonds, as an elephant tears through rotting vine, 11
I will not come to lie in a womb again. So if you want, gods, let it rain!"

"Revered Nagasena, you say that there are two attributes 12
of the male leopard that must be acquired. What are the two attributes to be acquired?"

"Great king, a leopard in the forest lying in wait in dense grasses, a thick copse, or a mountain thicket seizes a deer. Similarly, the yogi, an earnest disciple, keeps to his own haunts in the forest, at the root of a tree, in the hills, grottoes, mountain caves, charnel grounds, remote woodlands, open air, or among haystacks, silent places away from the noise, deserted locales conducive to seclusion where one sleeps hidden away from people. Embracing solitude, the yogi, an earnest disciple, will quickly attain mastery of the six higher knowledges. This, great king, is the first attribute of the male leopard that must be acquired. For this was said by the elders at the Recitation of the Dhamma: 'Just as a leopard lying in wait seizes a deer, a Buddha's descendant, a meditator intent on discipline, enters the forest and seizes the highest fruit.'

"Additionally, great king, the male leopard does not eat 13
any beast that when killed collapses on its left side. Similarly, the yogi, an earnest disciple, does not partake of food acquired by offering bamboo; offering leaves, flowers, fruit, baths, clay, soap powder, tooth sticks, or water for rinsing the mouth; or by flattery, being like bean soup, entertaining people, running messages, acting as a doctor, acting as

vā dūtakammena vā pahiṇagamanena vā piṇḍapatipiṇḍena vā dānānuppadānena vā vatthuvijjāya vā nakkhattavijjāya vā aṅgavijjāya vā aññataraññatarena vā buddhapatikuṭṭhena micchājīvena nipphāditaṃ bhojanaṃ na paribhuñjitabbaṃ, vāmena passena patitaṃ pasuṃ viya dīpiko. idaṃ mahārāja dīpikassa dutiyaṃ aṅgaṃ gahetabbaṃ. bhāsitam-p' etaṃ mahārāja therena sāriputtena dhammasenāpatinā: vacīviññattivipphārā uppannaṃ madhupāyasaṃ sace bhutto bhaveyyāhaṃ s' ājīvo garahito mama. yadi pi me antaguṇaṃ nikkhamitvā bahī care n' eva bhindeyya' ājīvaṃ, cajamāno pi jīvitan-ti.

14 bhante nāgasena, kummassa pañca aṅgāni gahetabbānīti yaṃ vadesi, katamāni tāni pañca aṅgāni gahetabbānīti. yathā mahārāja kummo udakacaro udake yeva vāsaṃ kappeti, evam-eva kho mahārāja yoginā yogāvacarena sabbapāṇabhūtapuggalānaṃ hitānukampinā mettāsahagatena cetasā vipulena mahaggatena appamāṇena averena abyāpajjhena sabbāvantaṃ lokaṃ pharitvā viharitabbaṃ. idaṃ mahārāja kummassa paṭhamaṃ aṅgaṃ gahetabbaṃ. puna ca paraṃ kummo udake uppilavanto sīsaṃ ukkhipitvā yadi keci passati, tatth' eva nimujjati gāḷham-ogāhati: mā maṃ te puna passeyyunti, evam-eva kho mahārāja yoginā yogāvacarena kilesesu opatantesu ārammaṇasare nimujjitabbaṃ gāḷham-ogāhi-tabbaṃ: mā maṃ kilesā puna passeyyun-ti. idaṃ mahārāja kummassa dutiyaṃ aṅgaṃ gahetabbaṃ. puna ca paraṃ mahārāja kummo udakato nikkhamitvā kāyaṃ otāpeti, evam-eva kho mahārāja yoginā yogāvacarena nisajja-ṭṭhāna-sayana-caṅkamato mānasaṃ nīharitvā

a messenger, going on errands, exchanging alms, giving gifts, practicing the art of determining locations for buildings, engaging in astrology, reading omens on the limbs, or any of the other kinds of wrong livelihood deplored by the Buddha.[2] And in this he is like the leopard that does not eat a beast fallen on its left side. This, great king, is the second attribute of the male leopard. For Elder Sariputta, General of the Dhamma, said: 'My livelihood would be blameworthy were I to eat honey or rice milk acquired by casting around verbal hints. Even if my bowels obtrude and spill out and my life is sacrificed, I will not breach my livelihood.'"

"Great king, you say that there are five attributes of the 14
turtle that must be acquired. What are the five attributes to be acquired?"

"Great king, just as the turtle, a water creature, makes its home in the water, so too the yogi, an earnest disciple, should live pervading the whole world with a mind infused with loving-kindness, trembling for the welfare of all people and living creatures, expansive, enlarged, boundless, kind, and free of malice. This is the first attribute of the turtle to be acquired. Additionally, the turtle floating in the water pokes its head up and, if it sees anyone, dives in again and plunges deep, hoping, *May they not see me again.* Similarly, the yogi, an earnest disciple, should dive into the lake of his meditation subject when the defilements descend, and he should plunge deep, hoping, *May the defilements not see me again.* This is the second attribute of the turtle to be acquired. Additionally, as the turtle emerges from the water and warms its body, so too the yogi, an earnest disciple, should withdraw his mind from sitting, standing, lying down, and walking,

sammappadhāne mānasaṃ otāpetabbaṃ. idaṃ mahārāja kummassa tatiyaṃ aṅgaṃ gahetabbaṃ.

15 puna ca paraṃ mahārāja kummo paṭhaviṃ khaṇitvā vivitte vāsaṃ kappeti, evam-eva kho mahārāja yoginā yogāvacarena lābha-sakkāra-silokaṃ pajahitvā suññaṃ vivittaṃ kānanaṃ vanapatthaṃ pabbataṃ kandaraṃ giriguhaṃ appasaddaṃ appanigghosaṃ pavivittam-ogāhitvā vivitte yeva vāsam-upagantabbaṃ. idaṃ mahārāja kummassa catutthaṃ aṅgaṃ gahetabbaṃ. bhāsitam-p' etaṃ mahārāja therena upasenena vaṅgantaputtena: vivittaṃ appanigghosaṃ vāḷamiganisevitaṃ seve senāsanaṃ bhikkhu paṭisallāṇakāraṇā ti. puna ca paraṃ mahārāja kummo cārikaṃ caramāno yadi kañci passati vā saddaṃ suṇāti vā, soṇḍipañcamāni aṅgāni sake kapāle nidahitvā appossukko tuṇhībhūto tiṭṭhati kāyam-anurakkhanto, evam-eva kho mahārāja yoginā yogāvacarena sabbattha rūpa-sadda-gandha-rasa-phoṭṭhabba-dhammesu āpatantesu chasu dvāresu saṃvarakavāṭaṃ anugghāṭetvā mānasaṃ samodahitvā saṃvaraṃ katvā satena sampajānena vihātabbaṃ samanadhammaṃ anurakkhamānena. idaṃ mahārāja kummassa pañcamaṃ aṅgaṃ gahetabbaṃ. bhāsitam-p' etaṃ mahārāja bhagavatā devātidevena saṃyuttanikāyavare kummūpamasuttante: kummova aṅgāni sake kapāle samodahaṃ bhikkhu manovitakke anissito aññam-aheṭhayāno parinibbuto na upavadeyya kañcīti.

16 bhante nāgasena, vaṃsassa ekaṃ aṅgaṃ gahetabban-ti yaṃ vadesi, kataman-taṃ ekaṃ aṅgaṃ gahetabban-ti. yathā mahārāja vaṃso yattha vāto tattha anulometi nāññattha-m-anudhāvati, evam-eva kho mahārāja yoginā yogāvacarena yaṃ buddhena bhagavatā bhāsitaṃ navaṅgaṃ

and warm it in right striving. This, great king, is the third attribute of the turtle to be acquired.

“And, great king, just as the turtle digs the ground and 15
makes a secluded nest, the yogi, an earnest disciple, rejects wealth, honor, and glory, and should pass into seclusion in a deserted and solitary forest, a remote woodland, the hills, a grotto, a mountain cave—a silent place away from the noise—and there make his solitary home. This is the fourth attribute of the turtle to be acquired. For Elder Upasena, son of Vanganta, said: ‘For the sake of seclusion, a monk should make his solitary bed among the haunts of wild animals and far from the noise.’ Finally, just as the turtle walking about sees someone coming or hears a sound and draws its neck and legs into its shell, waiting silently and still, and so saves its life, the yogi, an earnest disciple, should latch the six doors of restraint when visible forms, sounds, smells, tastes, tangible things, and phenomenal states anywhere strike him; he should collect his mind, secure self-control, and dismiss them with the mindful deliberation that is the protection of the conduct of renouncers. This is the fifth attribute of the turtle to be acquired. For the Bhagavan, god above gods, said this in the *sutta* on the turtle simile in the excellent *Saṃyutta-nikāya:* ‘As the turtle pulls its limbs into its own shell, so too the monk pulls in his mind and thoughts, independent, injuring none, reviling nobody, and completely calm.’”

“Revered Nagasena, you say that there is one attribute of 16
bamboo that must be acquired. What is that one attribute to be acquired?”

“Great king, just as bamboo bends with the wind and does not go its own way, so too the yogi, an earnest disciple, should

satthusāsanaṃ taṃ anulomayitvā kappiye anavajje ṭhatvā samaṇadhammaṃ yeva pariyesitabbaṃ. idaṃ mahārāja vaṃsassa ekaṃ aṅgaṃ gahetabbaṃ. bhāsitam-p' etaṃ mahārāja therena rāhulena: navaṅgaṃ buddhavacanaṃ anulometvāna sabbadā kappiye anavajjasmiṃ ṭhatvā 'pāyaṃ samuttaran-ti.

17 bhante nāgasena, cāpassa ekaṃ aṅgaṃ gahetabban ti yaṃ vedesi, kataman-taṃ ekaṃ aṅgaṃ gahetabban-ti. yathā mahārāja cāpo sutacchito mito yāv' aggamūlaṃ samakam-eva anunamati na paṭitthambhati, evam-eva kho mahārāja yoginā yogāvacarena thera-nava-majjhima-samakesu anunamitabbaṃ na paṭippharitabbaṃ. idaṃ mahārāja cāpassa ekaṃ aṅgaṃ gahetabbaṃ. bhāsitam-p' etaṃ mahārāja bhagavatā devātidevena vidhura-puṇṇakajātake:

18 cāpo vānuname dhīro, vaṃsova anulomayaṃ paṭilomaṃ
na vatteyya, sa rājavasatiṃ vase ti.

19 bhante nāgasena, vāyasassa dve aṅgāni gahetabbānīti yaṃ vadesi, katamāni tāni dve aṅgāni gahetabbānīti. yathā mahārāja vāyaso āsaṅkitaparisaṅkito yattapayatto carati, evam-eva kho mahārāja yoginā yogāvacarena āsaṅkitaparisankitena yattapayattena upaṭṭhitāya satiyā saṃvutehi

pursue only the conduct of renouncers, conforming to the dispensation of the Teacher and the nine parts spoken by the Blessed Buddha, and staying with what is proper and blameless. This, great king, is the one attribute of bamboo that must be acquired. For this was said by Elder Rahula: 'Always conforming to the nine parts of the Buddha's words, staying with what is proper and blameless, they leave misery behind.'"

"Revered Nagasena, you say that there is one attribute of 17
the bow that must be acquired. What is that one attribute to be acquired?"

"Great king, just as a well-made and measured bow bends evenly from the top to the bottom and is not rigid, so too the yogi, an earnest disciple, should bend evenly toward elders, novices, and those of middle rank, and not be rigid. This, great king, is the one attribute of the bow to be acquired. For the Bhagavan, god above gods, said this in the *Vidhura Puṇṇaka Jātaka*:

> A strong person bends like a bow and yields like bamboo. 18
> Not going against the grain, he lives in the court of the king."

"Revered Nagasena, you say that there are two attributes 19
of the crow that must be acquired. What are the two attributes to be acquired?"

"Great king, just as the crow moves about suspicious, skeptical, guarded, and cautious, the yogi, an earnest disciple, should roam around suspicious, skeptical, guarded, and cautious, mindfulness aroused and faculties protected.

indriyehi caritabbaṃ. idaṃ mahārāja vāyasassa paṭhamaṃ aṅgaṃ gahetabbaṃ. puna ca paraṃ mahārāja vāyaso yaṃ kiñci bhojanaṃ disvā ñātīhi saṃvibhajitvā bhuñjati, evam-eva kho mahārāja yoginā yogāvacarena ye te lābhā dhammikā dhammaladdhā antamaso pattapariyāpannamattam-pi tathārūpehi lābhehi appaṭivibhattabhoginā bhavitabbaṃ sīlavantehi sabrahmacārīhi. idaṃ mahārāja vāyasassa dutiyaṃ aṅgaṃ gahetabbaṃ. bhāsitam-p' etaṃ mahārāja therena sāriputtena dhammasenāpatinā: sace me upanāmenti yathāladdhaṃ tapassino, sabbesaṃ vibhajitvāna tato bhuñjāmi bhojanan-ti.

bhante nāgasena, makaṭassa dve aṅgāni gahetabbānīti yaṃ vadesi, katamāni tāni dve aṅgāni gahetabbānīti. yathā mahārāja makkaṭo vāsam-upagacchanto tathārūpe okāse mahatimahārukkhe pavivitte sabbattha pasākhe[1] bhīruttāṇe vāsam-upagacchati, evam-eva kho mahārāja yoginā yogāvacarena lajjiṃ pesalaṃ sīlavantaṃ kalyāṇadhammaṃ bahussutaṃ dhammadharaṃ piyaṃ garuṃ bhāvaniyaṃ vattāraṃ vacanakkhamaṃ ovādakaṃ viññāpakaṃ sandass-akaṃ samādapakaṃ samuttejakaṃ sampahaṃsakaṃ, evarūpaṃ kalyāṇamittaṃ ācariyaṃ upanissāya viharitabbaṃ. idaṃ mahārāja makkaṭassa paṭhamaṃ aṅgaṃ gahetabbaṃ. puna ca paraṃ mahārāja makkaṭo rukkhe yeva carati tiṭṭhati nisīdati, yadi middhaṃ okkamati tatth' eva rattiṃ vāsam-anubhavati, evam-eva kho mahārāja yoginā yogāvacarena pavanābhimukhena bhavitabbaṃ, pavane yeva ṭhānacaṅkama-nisajja-sayanaṃ niddaṃ okkamitabbaṃ,

This, great king, is the first attribute of the crow that is to be acquired. And just as a crow shares whatever food it finds with its relatives before eating it, the yogi, an earnest disciple, should become someone who never fails to share as much food as he acquires with his virtuous fellows in the religious life, even if it is but a small portion appropriately placed in his bowl, as long as it is rightfully acquired. This, great king, is the second attribute of the crow that is to be acquired. For Elder Sariputta, General of the Dhamma, said: ‘If they present alms to me, an ascetic, then I share all that is received. And then I take my meal.’”

“Revered Nagasena, you say that there are two attributes 20
of the monkey that must be acquired. What are the two attributes to be acquired?”

“Great king, just as the monkey approaching its home makes its bed in a secluded place high up in the sky in a huge tree all covered with branches, the yogi, an earnest disciple, should live depending on a teacher, the good friend who is conscientious, lovable, and virtuous, and one whose practice is beautiful. Such a friend has heard much scripture; is an expert in the Dhamma; is beloved, esteemed, and cultivated; and speaks and endures speech, admonishing, instructing, showing, inspiring, encouraging, and approving. This, great king, is the first attribute of the monkey to be acquired. In addition, the monkey moves about in that very tree, standing and sitting; should it get sleepy, it stays the night right there. So too the yogi, an earnest disciple, should become cultivated in the presence of a forest, and only in that forest should he stand up, move around, take a seat, lie down, and fall asleep. For it is only there that the foundations of

tatth' eva satipaṭṭhānam-anubhavitabbaṃ. idaṃ mahārāja makkaṭassa dutiyaṃ aṅgaṃ gahetabbaṃ. bhāsitam-p' etaṃ mahārāja therena sāriputtena dhammasenāpatinā: caṅkamanto pi tiṭṭhanto, nisajjasayanena vā, pavane sobhate bhikkhu, pavanantaṃva vaṇṇitan-ti.

21 uddānaṃ: ghorassaro ca kukkuṭo kalando dīpini-dīpiko kummo vaṃso ca cāpo ca vāyaso atha makkaṭo ti.

paṭhamo vaggo.

mindfulness are to be experienced. This, great king, is the second attribute of the monkey to be acquired. For Elder Sariputta, General of the Dhamma, said: 'A monk comes to shine in the forest, whether moving, standing, sitting, or lying down; and so the forest is praised.'"

In summary, this is the braying ass, the cock, the squirrel, 21
the female leopard, the male leopard, the turtle, bamboo, bow, crow, and now, the monkey.

End of Part 1.

PART 2

22 bhante nāgasena, lāpulatāya ekaṃ aṅgaṃ gahetabban-ti yaṃ vadesi, katamam-taṃ ekaṃ aṅgaṃ gahetabban-ti. yathā mahārāja lāpulatā tiṇe vā kaṭṭhe vā latāya vā soṇḍikāhi ālambitvā tassūpari vaḍḍhati, evam eva kho mahārāja yoginā yogāvacarena arahatte abhivaḍḍhitukāmena manasā ārammaṇaṃ ālambitvā arahatte abhivaḍḍhitabbaṃ. idaṃ mahārāja lāpulatāya ekaṃ aṅgaṃ gahetabbaṃ. bhāsitam-p' etaṃ mahārāja therena sāriputtena dhammasenāpatinā: yathā lāpulatā nāma tiṇe kaṭṭhe latāya vā ālambitvā soṇḍikāhi tato vaḍḍhati uppari, tath' eva buddhaputtena arahattaphalakāminā ārammaṇaṃ ālambitvā vaḍḍhitabbaṃ asekhaphale ti.

23 bhante nāgasena, padumassa tīṇi aṅgāni gahetabbānīti yaṃ vadesi, katamāni tāni tīṇi aṅgāni gahetabbānīti. yathā mahārāja padumaṃ udake jātaṃ udake saṃvaddhaṃ anupalittaṃ udakena, evam-eva kho mahārāja yoginā yogāvacarena kule gaṇe lābhe yase sakkāre sammānanāya paribhogapaccayesu ca sabbattha anupalittena bhavitabbaṃ. idaṃ mahārāja padumassa paṭhamaṃ aṅgaṃ gahetabbaṃ. puna ca paraṃ mahārāja padumaṃ udakā accuggamma ṭhāti, evam-eva kho mahārāja yoginā yogāvacarena sabbalokaṃ abhibhavitvā accuggamma lokuttaradhamme ṭhātabbaṃ.

PART 2

"Revered Nagasena, you say that one must acquire one attribute of the vines of a gourd plant. What is that one attribute that is to be acquired?" 22

"Great king, just as the vines of the gourd fasten onto a reed, a piece of wood, or a creeper with their tendrils and grow over it, so too the yogi, an earnest disciple, should fasten onto a meditation subject with his mind seeking to grow into arhatship, and thereby grow into arhatship. This, great king, is the one attribute of the vines of the gourd plant to be acquired. For Elder Sariputta, General of the Dhamma, said: 'Just as the vines of a gourd fasten with their tendrils onto a reed, a piece of wood, or a creeper and grow over it, so too those in the Buddha's lineage seeking the fruits of arhatship should fasten onto a meditation subject and grow into perfection.'"

"Revered Nagasena, you say that there are three attributes 23
of the lotus that must be acquired. What are the three attributes to be acquired?"

"Great king, just as the lotus is born in the water and grows in the water but is untainted by the water, the yogi, an earnest disciple, should be untainted everywhere, whether near family, in company, or enjoying gain, fame, honor, and veneration, and in relying on the requisites. This is the first attribute of the lotus to be acquired. Additionally, great king, just as the lotus rises far up out of the water, the yogi, an earnest disciple, overcomes the entire world and should remain far up out of it in a transcendent state. This is the

idaṃ mahārāja padumassa dutiyaṃ aṅgaṃ gahetabbaṃ. puna ca paraṃ mahārāja pa-dumaṃ appamattakena pi anilena eritaṃ calati, evam eva kho mahārāja yoginā yogāvacarena appamattakesu pi kilesesu saññamo karaṇīyo, bhayadassāvinā viharitabbaṃ. idaṃ mahārāja padumassa tatiyaṃ aṅgaṃ gahetabbaṃ. bhāsitam-p' etaṃ mahārāja bhagavatā devātidevena: aṇumattesu vajjesu bhayadassāvī samādāya sikkhati sikkhāpadesūti.

24 bhante nāgasena, bījassa dve aṅgāni gahetabbānīti yaṃ vadesi, katamāni tāni dve aṅgāni gahetabbānīti. yathā mahārāja bījaṃ appakam-pi samānaṃ bhaddake khette vuttaṃ deve sammā dhāraṃ pavecchante subahūni phalāni anudassati, evam-eva kho mahārāja yoginā yogāvacarena yathā paṭipāditaṃ sīlaṃ kevalaṃ sāmaññaphalam-anudassati evaṃ sammā paṭipajjitabbaṃ. idaṃ mahārāja bījassa paṭhamaṃ aṅgaṃ gahetabbaṃ. puna ca paraṃ mahārāja bījaṃ suparisodhite khette ropitaṃ khippam-eva saṃvirūhati, evam-eva kho mahārāja yoginā yogāvacarena mānasaṃ supariggahītaṃ suññāgāre parisodhitaṃ satipaṭṭhāna-khettavare khittaṃ khippam eva virūhati. idaṃ mahārāja bījassa dutiyaṃ aṅgaṃ gahetabbaṃ. bhāsitam-p' etaṃ mahārāja therena anuruddhena: yathā pi khette parisuddhe bījaṃ c' assa patiṭṭhitaṃ, vipulaṃ tassa phalaṃ hoti, api toseti kassakaṃ; tath' eva yogino cittaṃ suññāgāre visodhitaṃ satipaṭṭhānakhettamhi khippam-eva virūhatīti.

25 bhante nāgasena, sālakalyāṇikāya ekaṃ aṅgaṃ gahetabban-ti yaṃ vadesi, kataman-taṃ ekaṃ aṅgaṃ gahetabban-ti.

second attribute of the lotus to be acquired. And then, just as the lotus quivers when stirred by even the slightest breeze, the yogi, an earnest disciple, should practice awareness with respect to even the slightest defilements and live seeing their perils. This is the third attribute of the lotus to be acquired, great king. For the Bhagavan, god above gods, said: 'Seeing peril in the slightest offense, one undertakes and learns the monastic rules.'"

"Revered Nagasena, you say that there are two attributes 24
of the seed that must be acquired. What are the two attributes to be acquired?"

"Great king, just as even a tiny seed sown on a good field yields abundant fruit when a god releases proper rain, when moral discipline is fully embraced by the yogi, an earnest disciple, it yields the fruit of renunciation; thus it must be followed properly. This is the first attribute of the seed that is to be acquired. In addition, just as a seed planted in a well-cleared field develops very quickly, a mind well mastered by the yogi, an earnest disciple, purified in solitude, and cast into the excellent field of the foundations of mindfulness develops very quickly. This is the second attribute of the seed to be acquired. For Elder Anuruddha said: 'When a field is cleared and a seed placed in it, its fruit will be plentiful and the farmer will be pleased. And so it is with the mind of a yogi: purified in the field of the foundations of mindfulness in solitude, it develops very quickly.'"

"Revered Nagasena, you say that there is one attribute 25
of the beautiful sal tree that must be acquired. What is that attribute to be acquired?"

"Great king, just as the beautiful sal tree grows into the

yathā mahārāja sālakalyāṇikā antopaṭhaviyaṃ yeva abhivaḍḍhati hatthasatam-pi bhiyyo pi, evam-eva kho mahārāja yoginā yogāvacarena cattāri sāmaññaphalāni catasso paṭisambhidā chaḷ-abhiññāyo kevalañ-ca samaṇadhammaṃ suññāgāre yeva paripūrayitabbaṃ. idaṃ mahārāja sālakalyāṇikāya ekaṃ aṅgaṃ gahetabbaṃ. bhāsitam-p' etaṃ mahārāja therena rāhulena: sālakalyāṇikā nāma pādapo dharaṇīruho antopaṭhaviyaṃ yeva satahattho pi vaḍḍhati. yathā kālamhi sampatte paripākena so dumo uggañchitvāna ekāhaṃ satahattho pi vaḍḍhati, evam evāhaṃ mahāvīra, sālakalyāṇikā viya, abbhantare suññāgāre dhammato abhivaḍḍhayin-ti.

26 bhante nāgasena, nāvāya tīṇi aṅgāni gahetabbānīti yaṃ vadesi, katamāni tāni tīṇi aṅgāni gahetabbānīti. yathā mahārāja nāvā bahuvidha-dāru-sanghāṭa-sama-vāyena bahum-pi janaṃ tārayati, evam-eva kho mahārāja yoginā yogāvacarena ācāra-sīla-guṇa-vattapaṭi-vatta-bahuvidhadhamma-saṅghāṭa-samavāyena sadevako loko tārayitabbo. idaṃ mahārāja nāvāya paṭhamaṃ aṅgaṃ gahetabbaṃ. puna ca paraṃ mahārāja nāvā bahuvidha-ūmi-tthanita-vega-visaṭa-m-āvaṭṭavegaṃ sahati, evam-eva kho mahārāja yoginā yogāvacarena bahuvidha-kiles-ūmi-vegaṃ lābhasakkāra-yasasiloka-pūjana-vandanā parakulesu nindāpasaṃsā sukhadukkha-sammā-nanavimānana-bahuvidha-

ground a hundred cubits or more, so too the yogi, an earnest disciple, should perfect the four fruits of renunciation, the four analytical insights, the six higher knowledges, and the entire renouncer's practice in solitude. This, great king, is the one attribute of the beautiful sal tree that is to be acquired. For Elder Rahula said: 'The tree growing in the earth known as the beautiful sal tree grows into the ground even as much as a hundred cubits. In the fullness of time when the tree reaches maturity, it shoots up and grows as much as a hundred cubits in one day. So too do I, great hero, like the beautiful sal tree, grow internally through the Dhamma while in seclusion.'"

"Revered Nagasena, you say that there are three attributes 26
of a ship that must be acquired. What are the three attributes to be acquired?"

"Great king, just as a ship transports many people because of being constructed out of a combination of many types of wood, the yogi, an earnest disciple, should transport the world with its gods because of being constructed by a combination of many practices, all kinds of observances, and the special qualities of conduct and moral discipline. This is the first attribute of a ship that is to be acquired. And further, as a ship withstands the force of many kinds of roiling waves and the impact of massive cyclones, the yogi, an earnest disciple, should withstand the force of the waves of the many defilements and the impact of the waves of the many kinds of faults that come from the pleasure, pain, respect, and contempt issuing from wealth, honor, fame, glory, worship, veneration, and the praise and blame of other families. This is the second attribute of a ship that is to be acquired. And finally,

dosa-ūmivegañ-ca sahitabbaṃ. idaṃ mahārāja nāvāya dutiyaṃ aṅgaṃ gahetabbaṃ. puna ca paraṃ mahārāja nāvā aparimita-m-ananta-m-apāra-m-akkhobhita-gambhīre mahatimahāghose timi-timiṅgala-makara-maccha-gaṇākule mahatimahāsamudde carati, evam-eva kho mahārāja yoginā yogāvacarena tiparivaṭṭa-dvādasākāra-catusaccābhisamaya-paṭivedhe mānasaṃ sañcārayitabbaṃ. idaṃ mahārāja nāvāya tatiyaṃ aṅgaṃ gahetabbaṃ. bhāsitam-p' etaṃ mahārāja bhagavata devātidevena saṃyuttanikāyavare saccasaṃyutte: vitakkentā ca kho tumhe bhikkhave: idaṃ dukkhan-ti vitakkeyyātha, ayaṃ dukkhasamudayo ti vitakkeyyātha, ayaṃ dukkhanirodho ti vitakkeyyātha, ayaṃ dukkhanirodhagāminī paṭipadā ti vitakkeyyāthāti.

27 bhante nāgasena, nāvālakanakassa dve aṅgāni gahetabbānīti yaṃ vadesi, katamāni tāni dve aṅgāni gahetabbānīti. yathā mahārāja nāvālakanakaṃ bahu-ūmijālākulavikkhobhita-salilatale mahatimahāsamudde nāvaṃ laketi ṭhapeti, na deti disāvidisaṃ harituṃ, evam-eva kho mahārāja yoginā yogāvacarena rāga-dosa-moh-ummijāle mahatimahāvitakka-sampahāre cittaṃ laketabbaṃ, na dātabbaṃ disāvidisaṃ harituṃ. idaṃ mahārāja nāvālakanakassa paṭhamaṃ aṅgaṃ gahetabbaṃ. puna ca paraṃ mahārāja nāvālakanakaṃ na pilavati, visīdati, hatthasate pi udake nāvaṃ laketi ṭhānaṃ-upaneti, evam-eva kho mahārāja yoginā yogāvacarena lābha-yasa-sakkāra-mānana-vandana-pūjana-apacitisu

just as a ship sails through the vast ocean, which is immeasurable, endless, shoreless, unperturbed, deep, given to great roaring, and home to giant fish, leviathans, sea monsters, and schools and families of other fish, the yogi, an earnest disciple, makes the mind sail through the comprehension and realization of the Four Truths in their three phases and twelve modes.[3] This, great king, is the third attribute of a ship to be acquired. For this was said by the Bhagavan, god above gods, in the excellent *Saṃyuttanikāya* in the section on the Truths: 'Monks, when you are reflecting, reflect in this way: "This is suffering." Then reflect: "This is the origin of suffering." Then reflect: "This is the stopping of suffering." And then reflect: "This is the path leading to the stopping of suffering."'"

"Revered Nagasena, you say that there are two attributes 27
of the ship's anchor that must be acquired. What are the two attributes to be acquired?"

"Great king, just as the ship's anchor holds fast and stabilizes the ship on the surface of the water of the great ocean tossing and made restless by many crosscurrents and waves, not permitting it to be carried off in any direction, the yogi, an earnest disciple, holds fast the mind in the great clashing of thoughts in the crossurrents and waves of greed, hatred, and delusion, and does not permit it to be carried off in any direction. This is the first attribute of the ship's anchor to be acquired. And just as the ship's anchor does not float but instead plunges into the water for a hundred cubits and so holds it fast and keeps it in place, the mind of the yogi, an earnest disciple, should not float even at the very pinnacle of prosperity and renown when one is honored with wealth,

lābhagga-yasagge pi na pilavitabbaṃ, sarīrayāpanamattake yeva cittaṃ ṭhapetabbaṃ. idaṃ mahārāja nāvālakanakassa dutiyaṃ aṅgaṃ gahetabbaṃ. bhāsitam-p' etaṃ mahārāja therena sāriputtena dhammasenāpatinā: yathā samudde lakanaṃ na plavati, visīdati, tath' eva lābhasakkāre mā plavatha, visīdathāti.

28 bhante nāgasena, kūpassa ekaṃ aṅgaṃ gahetabban-ti yaṃ vadesi, kataman-taṃ ekaṃ aṅgaṃ gahetabban-ti. yathā mahārāja kūpo rajjuñ-ca varattañ-ca lakārañ-ca dhāreti, evam-eva kho mahārāja yoginā yogāvacarena satisampajaññasamannāgatena bhavitabbaṃ, abhikkante paṭikkante ālokite vilokite sammiñjite pasārite sanghāṭi-patta-cīvara-dhāraṇe asite pīte khāyite sāyite uccāra-passāvakamme gate ṭhite nisinne sutte jāgarite bhāsite tuṇhībhāve sampajānakārinā bhavitabbaṃ. idaṃ mahārāja kūpassa ekaṃ aṅgaṃ gahetabbaṃ. bhāsitam-p' etaṃ mahārāja bhagavatā devātidevena: sato bhikkhave bhikkhu vihareyya sampajāno, ayaṃ vo amhākaṃ anusāsanī ti.

29 bhante nāgasena, niyyāmakassa tīṇi aṅgāni gahetabbānīti yaṃ vadesi, katamāni tāni tīṇi aṅgāni gahetabbānīti. yathā mahārāja niyyāmako rattindivaṃ satataṃ samitaṃ appamatto yattapayatto nāvaṃ sāreti, evam-eva kho mahārāja yoginā yogāvacarena cittaṃ niyāmayamānena rattindivaṃ satataṃ samitaṃ appamattena yoniso manasikārena cittaṃ niyāmetabbaṃ. idaṃ mahārāja niyyāmakassa

fame, honor, reverence, veneration, and worship, and instead stay fixed solely on sustaining the body. This is the second attribute of the ship's anchor to be acquired, great king. For Elder Sariputta, General of the Dhamma, said: 'Just as the anchor plunges rather than floating, so too you must not float in wealth and honor, and instead must plunge down.'"

"Revered Nagasena, you say that there is one attribute of 28
the mast that must be acquired. What is that one attribute to be acquired?"

"Great king, just as the mast holds up the ropes, stays, and sails, the yogi, an earnest disciple, should come to possess mindfulness and circumspection. He should act deliberately, whether approaching or departing; looking forward or away; bending or stretching; carrying his cloak, alms bowl, and robe; eating, drinking, chewing, tasting; obeying the calls of nature; moving; standing; sitting; sleeping; being awake; speaking or staying quiet. This, great king, is the one attribute of the mast to be acquired. For the Bhagavan, god above gods, said: 'Monks, stay mindful and deliberate—this is our teaching to you.'"

"Revered Nagasena, you say that there are three attributes 29
of the sea captain that must be acquired. What are the three attributes to be acquired?"

"Great king, just as the sea captain pilots the ship constantly and continuously, night and day, with diligence, effort, and caution, the yogi, an earnest disciple, should pilot the mind with careful attention by controlling it constantly and continuously, night and day, with diligence. This, great king, is the first attribute of the sea captain to be acquired.

paṭhamaṃ aṅgaṃ gahetabbaṃ. bhāsitam-p' etaṃ mahārāja bhagavatā devātidevena dhammapade:

30 appamādaratā hotha, sacittam-anurakkhatha, duggā
uddharath' attānaṃ, panke sannova kuñjaro ti.

31 puna ca paraṃ mahārāja niyyāmakassa yaṃ kiñci mahāsamudde kalyāṇaṃ vā pāpakaṃ vā sabban-taṃ viditaṃ hoti, evam-eva kho mahārāja yoginā yogāvacarena kusalākusalaṃ sāvajjānavajjaṃ hīna-ppaṇītaṃ kaṇha-sukka-sappaṭibhāgaṃ vijānitabbaṃ. idaṃ mahārāja niyyāmakassa dutiyaṃ aṅgaṃ gahetabbaṃ. puna ca paraṃ mahārāja niyyāmako yante muddikaṃ deti: mā koci yantaṃ āmasitthāti, evam-eva kho mahārāja yoginā yogāvacarena citte saṃvara-muddikā dātabbā: mā kañci pāpakaṃ akusalavitakkaṃ vitakkesīti. idaṃ mahārāja niyyāmakassa tatiyaṃ aṅgaṃ gahetabbaṃ. bhāsitam-p' etaṃ mahārāja bhagavatā devātidevena saṃyuttanikāyavare: mā bhikkhave pāpake akusale vitakke vitakkayittha seyyathīdaṃ: kāmavitakkaṃ byāpādavitakkaṃ vihiṃsāvitakkan-ti.

32 bhante nāgasena, kammakarassa ekaṃ aṅgaṃ gahetabban-ti yaṃ vadesi, kataman-taṃ ekaṃ aṅgaṃ gahetabban-ti. yathā mahārāja kammakaro evaṃ cintayati: bhatako ahaṃ, imāya nāvāya kammaṃ karomi, imāyāhaṃ nāvāya vāhasā bhattavetanaṃ labhāmi, na me pamādo karaṇīyo, appamādena me ayaṃ nāvā vāhetabbā ti, evam-eva kho mahārāja yoginā yogāvacarena evaṃ cintayitabbaṃ: imaṃ kho ahaṃ cātummahābhūtikaṃ kāyaṃ sammasanto satataṃ samitaṃ appamatto upaṭṭhitasati sato sampajāno samāhito ekagga-

For the Bhagavan, god above gods, said this in the *Dhammapada:*

> Delight in diligence and guard the mind; 30
> like an elephant sunk in the mud, raise yourself up out
> of your bad ways.

"Additionally, great king, just as the sea captain knows 31
the ocean fully, good and bad, the yogi, an earnest disciple,
should know what is good and bad, blameless and blameworthy, base and exalted, with their dark and bright counterparts. This is the second attribute of the sea captain to be
acquired. And just as the sea captain puts a seal on the ship's
machinery saying, 'No one may touch this machinery,' the
yogi, an earnest disciple, should put the seal of restraint on
the mind, saying, 'Think no evil or bad thoughts.' This, great
king, is the third attribute of the sea captain to be acquired.
For the Bhagavan, god above gods, said this in the excellent *Saṃyuttanikāya:* 'Monks, do not think evil and bad
thoughts, such as thoughts of sensual desire, thoughts of
malice, or thoughts of harm.'"

"Revered Nagasena, you say that there is one attribute of 32
the dock worker that must be acquired. What is this attribute
to be acquired?"

"Great king, the dock worker thinks: *I am a hired hand. I work for this ship, and it is because of this ship that I get my wages and my keep. Let me not be careless, for it is through my diligence that the ship may sail.* Similarly, the yogi, an earnest disciple, should think: *Meditating on the body as composed of the four elements, and being constantly and continuously diligent, attentive, mindful, deliberate, composed, and mentally*

citto jāti-jarā-byādhi-maraṇa-soka-parideva-dukkha-domanass-upāyā-sehi parimuccissāmīti appamādo me karaṇīyo ti. idaṃ mahārāja kammakarassa ekaṃ aṅgaṃ gahetabbaṃ. bhāsitam-p' etaṃ mahārāja therena sāriputtena dhammasenāpatinā: kāyaṃ imaṃ sammasatha, parijānātha punappunaṃ; kāye sabhāvaṃ disvāna dukkhass' antaṃ karissathāti.

33 bhante nāgasena, samuddassa pañca aṅgāni gahetabbānīti yaṃ vadesi, katamāni tāni pañca aṅgāni gahetabbānīti. yathā mahārāja mahāsamuddo matena kunapena saddhiṃ na saṃvasati, evam-eva kho mahārāja yoginā yogāvacarena rāga-dosa-moha-māna-diṭṭhi-makkha-paḷāsa-issā-macchariya-māyā-saṭha-kuṭila-visama-duccarita-kilesamalehi saddhiṃ na saṃvasitabbaṃ. idaṃ mahārāja samuddassa paṭhamaṃ aṅgaṃ gahetabbaṃ. puna ca paraṃ mahārāja samuddo muttā-maṇi-veḷuriya-sankha-silā-pavāḷa-phaḷikamaṇi-vividharatana-nicayaṃ dhārento pidahati, na bahi vikirati, evam-eva kho mahārāja yoginā yogāvacarena magga-phala-jhāna-vimokha-samādhi-samāpatti-vipassanā-'bhiññā-vividhaguṇaratanāni adhigantvā pidahitabbāni, na bahi nīharitabbāni. idaṃ mahārāja samuddassa dutiyaṃ aṅgaṃ gahetabbaṃ. puna ca paraṃ mahārāja samuddo mahatimahābhūtehi saddhiṃ saṃvasati, evam-eva kho mahārāja yoginā yogāvacarenā appicchaṃ santuṭṭhaṃ dhutavādaṃ sallekhavuttiṃ ācārasampannaṃ lajjiṃ pesalaṃ garuṃ bhāvaniyaṃ vattāraṃ vacanakkhamaṃ codakaṃ pāpagarahiṃ ovādakaṃ anusāsakaṃ viññāpakaṃ sandass-

focused, I will become liberated from birth, aging, illness, death, sorrow, grieving, pain, distress, and trouble. So let me be diligent. This, great king, is the one attribute of the dock worker to be acquired. For Elder Sariputta, General of the Dhamma, said: 'Meditate on this body and reflect again and again; seeing the nature of the body, you will bring about the end of suffering.'"

"Revered Nagasena, you say that there are five attributes 33
of the ocean that must be acquired. What are the five attributes to be acquired?"

"Great king, just as the ocean does not associate with a dead body, the yogi, an earnest disciple, should not associate with the stains of the defilements of passion, hatred, delusion, pride, wrong views, hypocrisy, spite, envy, meanness, deceit, treachery, dishonesty, disagreeableness, and bad behavior. This is the first attribute of the ocean to be acquired. And just as the ocean, though stocked with the manifold treasures and wealth of pearls, gems, lapis lazuli, mother of pearl, coral, and crystal, conceals them and does not toss them out, the yogi, an earnest disciple, who has attained the manifold treasures and special qualities of the path, the fruits, the *jhānas,* freedom, concentration, the attainments, insight meditation, and higher knowledge, should conceal them and not broadcast them. This is the second attribute of the ocean to be acquired. And just as the ocean harbors huge and magnificent creatures, the yogi, an earnest disciple, should live relying on a good friend in the religious life who is frugal, content, a proponent of asceticism, practicing austerity, possessing good conduct, conscientious, lovable, esteemed, and cultivated. Such a friend speaks and endures

akaṃ samādapakaṃ samuttejakaṃ sampahaṃsakaṃ kalyāṇamittaṃ sabrahmacāriṃ upanissāya vasitabbaṃ. idaṃ mahārāja samuddassa tatiyaṃ aṅgaṃ gahetabbaṃ.

34 puna ca paraṃ mahārāja samuddo navasalila-sampuṇṇa-gaṅgā-yamunā-aciravatī-sarabhū-mahī-ādīhi nadīsatasahassehi antalikkhe saliladhārāhi ca pūrito pi sakaṃ velaṃ nātivattati, evam-eva kho mahārāja yoginā yogāvacarena lābha-sakkāra-siloka-vandana-mānana-pūjanakāraṇā jīvitahetu pi sañcicca sikkhāpadavītikkamo na karaṇīyo. idaṃ mahārāja samuddassa catutthaṃ aṅgaṃ gahetabbaṃ. bhāsitam-p' etaṃ mahārāja bhagavatā devātidevena: seyyathā pi mahārāja mahāsamuddo ṭhitadhammo velaṃ nātikkamati, evam-eva kho mahārāja yaṃ mayā sāvakānaṃ sikkhāpadaṃ paññattaṃ taṃ mama sāvakā jīvitahetu pi nātikkamantīti. puna ca paraṃ mahārāja samuddo sabbasavantīhi gaṅgāyamunā-aciravatī-sarabhū-mahīhi antalikkhe udakadhārāhi pi na paripūrati, evam-eva kho mahārāja yoginā yogāvacarena uddesa-paripucchā-savana-dhāraṇa-vinicchaya-abhidhamma-vinaya-gāḷha-suttanta-viggaha-padanikkhepa-padasandhi-padavibhatti-navaṅga-jinasāsanavaraṃ suṇantenāpi na tappitabbaṃ. idaṃ mahārāja samuddassa pañcamaṃ aṅgaṃ gahetabbaṃ. bhāsitam-p' etaṃ mahārāja bhagavatā devātidevena sutasomajātake:

speech, exhorting, censuring evil, admonishing, teaching, instructing, showing, inspiring, encouraging, and approving. This, great king, is the third attribute of the ocean to be acquired.

“And further, great king, just as the ocean does not spill 34
over its own banks even as it is filled by a hundred thousand freshwater rivers such as the Ganga, Yamuna, Achiravati, Sarabhu, and Mahi, and is supplied also with rain water from the sky, the yogi, an earnest disciple, should never transgress the monastic rules on purpose, even for the sake of his livelihood, on account of gain, honor, glory, veneration, reverence, or worship. This is the fourth attribute of the ocean to be acquired. For the Bhagavan, god above gods, said: ‘Just as the great ocean is stable and does not spill over its banks, great king, my disciples do not transgress the monastic rule of disciples laid down by me, even for the sake of their livelihood.’ And finally, just as the ocean is not completely filled even by all the rivers, the Ganga, Yamuna, Achiravati, Sarabhu, and Mahi, and the water falling from the sky, the yogi, an earnest disciple, is never sated with recitation, questioning, listening, remembering, investigating, or even just hearing the excellent dispensation of the Victor in its nine parts, and the division of the words, the junctions between words, the composition of words, and the analysis of the *abhidhamma, vinaya,* and profound *suttanta.** This, great king, is the fifth attribute of the ocean to be acquired. For the Bhagavan, god above gods, said this in the *Sutasoma Jātaka:*

* The *sutta* collection.

35 aggi yathā tiṇakaṭṭhaṃ ḍahanto na tappati, sāgaro vā nadīhi, evaṃ h' ime paṇḍitā, rājaseṭṭha, sutvā na tappanti subhāsitenāti.

36 uddānaṃ: lāpūlatā ca padumaṃ bījaṃ sālakalyāṇikā nāvā ca nāvālakanaṃ kūpo niyyāmako tathā kammakaro samuddo ca vaggo tena pavuccatīti.

dutiyo vaggo.

As fire is never sated with burning grass and wood, nor 35
the ocean with rivers,
so too, best of kings, these learned people are never
sated with hearing well-spoken words.'"

In summary, with this, the section on the vines of the 36
gourd plant, the lotus, the seed, the beautiful sal tree, the
ship, the ship's anchor, the mast, the sea captain, the dock
worker, and the ocean has been stated.

End of Part 2.

PART 3

37 bhante nāgasena, paṭhaviyā pañca aṅgāni gahetabbānīti yam vadesi, katamāni tāni pañca aṅgāni gahetabbānīti. yathā mahārāja paṭhavī iṭṭhāniṭṭhāni kappūrāgaru-tagara-candana-kuṅkumādīni ākirante pi pitta-semha-pubba-ruhira-seda-meda-kheḷa-siṅghāṇika-lasika-mutta-karīsādīni ākirante pi tādisā yeva, evam-eva kho mahārāja yoginā yogāvacarena iṭṭhāniṭṭhe lābhālābhe yasāyase nindāpasaṃsāya sukhe dukkhe sabbattha tādinā yeva bhavitabbaṃ. idaṃ mahārāja paṭhaviyā paṭhamaṃ aṅgaṃ gahetabbaṃ. puna ca paraṃ mahārāja paṭhavī maṇḍaṇa-vibhūsanāpagatā sakagandha-paribhāvitā, evam eva kho mahārāja yoginā yogāvacarena vibhūsanāpagatena sakasīlagandha-paribhāvitena bhavitabbaṃ. idaṃ mahārāja paṭhaviyā dutiyaṃ aṅgaṃ gahetabbaṃ. puna ca paraṃ mahārāja paṭhavī nirantarā acchiddā asusirā bahalā ghanā vitthiṇṇā, evam-eva kho mahārāja yoginā yogāvacarena nirantara-m-akhaṇḍācchidda-m-asusira-bahala-ghana-vitthiṇṇa-sīlena bhavitabbaṃ. idaṃ mahārāja paṭhaviyā tatiyaṃ aṅgaṃ gahetabbaṃ.

38 puna ca paraṃ mahārāja paṭhavī gāma-nigama-nagara-janapada-rukkha-pabbata-nadī-taḷāka-pokkharaṇi-miga-pakkhi-manuja-nara-nārī-gaṇaṃ dhārentī pi akilāsu hoti, evam eva kho mahārāja yoginā yogāvacarena ovad-

PART 3

"Revered Nagasena, you say that there are five attributes of the earth that must be acquired. What are the five attributes to be acquired?" 37

"Great king, the earth stays as it is whether strewn with the pleasant or the disagreeable, whether strewn with such things as camphor, aloe, butterfly gardenia, sandal, and saffron, or with such things as bile, phlegm, pus, blood, sweat, fat, saliva, snot, synovial fluid, urine, and excrement. Similarly, the yogi, an earnest disciple, should be everywhere such as he is, through the pleasant and the disagreeable, gain and loss, fame and obscurity, blame and praise, and happiness and suffering. This is the first attribute of the earth to be acquired. And just as the earth has no need of finery or ornaments but is suffused with its own fragrance, the yogi, an earnest disciple, should be without ornaments and suffused with the fragrance of his own moral discipline. This is the second attribute of the earth to be acquired. And just as the earth is solid, unbroken, not porous, thick, massive, and vast, the yogi, an earnest disciple, should cultivate moral discipline that is solid, entirely unbroken, not porous, thick, massive, and vast. This is the third attribute of the earth to be acquired.

"Further, great king, the earth never gets weary despite 38
holding up villages, towns, cities, countries, trees, mountains, rivers, reservoirs, lotus ponds, deer, birds, humans, and hosts of men and women. Similarly, the yogi, an earnest disciple, should never weary of admonishing, teaching,

antena pi anusāsantena pi viññāpentena pi sandassentena pi samādapentena pi samuttejentena pi sampahaṃsentena pi dhammadesanāsu akilāsunā bhavitabbaṃ. idaṃ mahārāja paṭhaviyā catutthaṃ aṅgaṃ gahetabbaṃ. puna ca paraṃ mahārāja paṭhavī anunayapaṭighavippamuttā, evam-eva kho mahārāja yoginā yogāvacarena anunaya-paṭighavippamuttena paṭhavīsamena cetasā viharitabbaṃ. idaṃ mahārāja paṭhaviyā pañcamaṃ aṅgaṃ gahetabbaṃ. bhāsitam-p' etaṃ mahārāja upāsikāya cullasubhaddāya sakasamaṇe parikittayamānāya: ekañ-c' evāhaṃ vāsiyā taccheyya' kupitamānasā, ekañ-c' evāhaṃ gandhena ālimpeyya' pamoditā, amusmiṃ paṭigho na-tthi, rāgo asmiṃ na vijjati. paṭhavīsamacittā te, tādisā samaṇā mamāti.

39 bhante nāgasena, āpassa pañca aṅgāni gahetabbānīti yaṃ vadesi, katamāni tāni pañca aṅgāni gahetabbānīti. yathā mahārāja āpo susaṇṭhita-m-akampita-m-aluḷita-sabhāvaparisuddho, evam-eva kho mahārāja yoginā yogāvacarena kuhana-lapana-nemittaka-nippesikataṃ apanetvā susaṇṭhita m-akampita-m aluḷita-sabhāvaparisuddhācārena bhavitabbaṃ. idaṃ mahārāja āpassa paṭhamaṃ aṅgaṃ gahetabbaṃ. puna ca paraṃ mahārāja āpo sītalasabhāvasaṇṭhito, evam-eva kho mahārāja yoginā yogāvacarena sabbasattesu khanti-mettā-'nuddaya-sampannena hitesinā anukampakena bhavitabbaṃ. idaṃ mahārāja āpassa dutiyaṃ aṅgaṃ gahetabbaṃ. puna ca paraṃ mahārāja āpo asuciṃ suciṃ karoti, evam-eva kho mahārāja yoginā yogāvacarena gāme vā araññe vā upajjhāye ācariye ācariyamattesu sabbattha anadhikaraṇena bhavitabbaṃ anavakāsakārinā. idaṃ mahārāja āpassa tatiyaṃ aṅgaṃ gahetabbaṃ. puna ca paraṃ mahārāja āpo bahujanapatthito, evam-eva kho

instructing, showing, inspiring, encouraging, and approving the teachings of the Dhamma. This is the fourth attribute of the earth to be acquired. Finally, just as the earth is free of both attraction and repugnance, the yogi, an earnest disciple, should live with a mind like earth, free of attraction and repugnance. This is the fifth attribute of the earth to be acquired. For this was said by Culla Subhadda, a laywoman, when praising her own ascetics: 'Were I, with an angry mind, to strike one with an ax, or with a pleased mind, anoint another with fragrance, there would be no repugnance in the one or attraction in the other. Such are my ascetics, as their minds are like the earth.'"

"Revered Nagasena, you say that there are five attributes 39
of water that must be acquired. What are the five attributes to be acquired?"

"Great king, just as water is clear by nature, very still, and without agitation and turbulence, the yogi, an earnest disciple, should have conduct clear by nature, very still, and without agitation and turbulence, having set aside deceit, chatter, hinting, and belittling. This is the first attribute of water to be acquired. Additionally, just as water stays naturally cool, the yogi, an earnest disciple, should abound in patience, loving-kindness, and mercy for all beings, compassionate, and seeking their welfare. This is the second attribute of water to be acquired. And just as water makes what is dirty clean, the yogi, an earnest disciple, should, in everything he does everywhere, whether village or forest, avoid litigation with respect to a preceptor, teacher, or one having the status of a teacher. This is the third attribute of water to be acquired. And just as water is sought by many people,

mahārāja yoginā yogāvacarena appiccha-santuṭṭha-pavivitta-paṭisallāṇena satataṃ sabbalokamabhipatthitena bhavitabbaṃ. idaṃ mahārāja āpassa catutthaṃ aṅgaṃ gahetabbaṃ. puna ca paraṃ mahārāja āpo na kassaci ahitam-upadahati, evam-eva kho mahārāja yoginā yogāvacarena parabhaṇḍana-kalaha-viggaha-vivāda-rittajjhāna-arati-jananaṃ kāya-vacī-cittehi pāpakaṃ na karaṇīyaṃ. idaṃ mahārāja āpassa pañcamaṃ aṅgaṃ gahetabbaṃ. bhāsitam-p' etaṃ mahārāja bhagavatā devātidevena kaṇhajātake:

40 varañ ce me ado sakka, sabbabhūtānam-issara, na
mano vā sarīraṃ vā maṅkato sakka kassaci kudāci
upahaññetha, etaṃ sakka varaṃ vare ti.

41 bhante nāgasena, tejassa pañca aṅgāni gahetabbānīti yaṃ vadesi, katamāni tāni pañca aṅgāni gahetabbānīti. yathā mahārāja tejo tiṇa-kaṭṭha-sākhā-palāsaṃ ḍahati, evam-eva kho mahārāja yoginā yogāvacarena ye te abbhantarā vā bāhirā vā kilesā iṭṭhāniṭṭhārammaṇānubhavanā sabbe te ñāṇagginā ḍahitabbā. idaṃ mahārāja tejassa paṭhamaṃ aṅgaṃ gahetabbaṃ. puna ca paraṃ mahārāja tejo niddayo akāruṇiko, evam-eva kho mahārāja yoginā yogāvacarena sabbakilesesu kāruññam-anuddayā na kātabbā idaṃ mahārāja tejassa dutiyaṃ aṅgaṃ gahetabbaṃ. puna ca paraṃ mahārāja tejo sītaṃ paṭihanti, evam-eva kho mahārāja yoginā yogāvacarena viriya-santāpa-tejaṃ abhijanetvā kilesā paṭihantabbā. idaṃ mahārāja tejassa tatiyaṃ aṅgaṃ gahetabbaṃ puna ca paraṃ mahārāja tejo anunayapaṭighavippamutto uṇham-abhijaneti, evam eva kho mahārāja yoginā yogāvacarena

the yogi, an earnest disciple, should always be highly sought by the whole world because of his frugality, contentment, seclusion, and solitude. This is the fourth attribute of water to be acquired. And finally, just as water never causes anyone harm, the yogi, an earnest disciple, should never do evil with body, speech, or mind, as it would generate dislike, strife, quarreling, disputes, or contention with others, or make *jhāna* practice barren.This is the fifth attribute of water to be acquired. For, great king, this was said by the Bhagavan, god above gods, in the *Kaṇha Jātaka*:

> If you grant me a boon, Sakka, lord of all creatures, 40
> may it be that no one be harmed mentally or physically
> on my account. This, Sakka, is the best of boons."

"Revered Nagasena, you say that there are five attributes 41
of fire that must be acquired. What are the five attributes to be acquired?"

"Great king, just as fire burns grass, sticks, branches, and leaves, the yogi, an earnest disciple, should with the fire of knowledge burn all the defilements, whether inner or outer, or experienced from pleasant or unpleasant sense objects. This is the first attribute of fire to be acquired. And just as fire is cruel and merciless, the yogi, an earnest disciple, should show no compassion or mercy to any of the defilements. This is the second attribute of fire to be acquired. And just as fire wards off the cold, the yogi, an earnest disciple, should ward off the defilements by generating the fire and heat of exertion. This is the third attribute of fire to be acquired. And just as fire is free of attraction and repugnance as it generates warmth, the yogi, an earnest disciple, should live with

anunayapaṭighavippamuttena tejosamena cetasā viharitabbaṃ idaṃ mahārāja tejassa catutthaṃ aṅgaṃ gahetabbaṃ. puna ca paraṃ mahārāja tejo andhakāraṃ vidhamati ālokaṃ dassayati, evam-eva kho mahārāja yoginā yogāvacarena avijjandhakāraṃ vidhamitvā ñāṇālokaṃ dassayitabbaṃ. idaṃ mahārāja tejassa pañcamaṃ aṅgaṃ gahetabbaṃ. bhāsitam-p' etaṃ mahārāja bhagavatā devātidevena sakaputtaṃ rāhulaṃ ovadantena: tejosamaṃ rāhula bhāvanaṃ bhāvehi, tejosamaṃ hi te rāhula bhāvanaṃ bhāvayato anuppannā c' eva akusalā dhammā na uppajjanti uppannā ca akusalā dhammā cittaṃ na pariyādāya ṭhassantīti.

42 bhante nāgasena, vāyussa pañca aṅgāni gahetabbānīti yaṃ vadesi, katamāni tāni pañca aṅgāni gahetabbānīti. yathā mahārāja vāyu supupphitavanasaṇḍantaram abhivāyati, evam-eva kho mahārāja yoginā yogāvacarena vimutti-vara-kusuma-pupphitārammaṇa-vanantare ramitab-baṃ. idaṃ mahārāja vāyussa paṭhamaṃ aṅgaṃ gahetabbaṃ. puna ca paraṃ mahārāja vāyu dharaṇīruha-pādapa-gaṇe mathayati, evam-eva kho mahārāja yoginā yogāvacarena vanantaragatena saṅkhāre vicinantena kilesā mathayitabbā. idaṃ mahārāja vāyussa dutiyaṃ aṅgaṃ gahetabbaṃ. puna ca paraṃ mahārāja vāyu ākāse carati, evam-eva kho mahārāja yoginā yogāvacarena lokuttaradhammesu mānasaṃ sañcārayitabbaṃ. idaṃ mahārāja vāyussa tatiyaṃ aṅgaṃ gahetabbaṃ. puna ca paraṃ mahārāja vāyu gandham-anubhavati, evam-eva kho mahārāja yoginā yogāvacarena attano sīla-surabhigandho anubhavitabbo. idaṃ mahārāja vāyussa catutthaṃ aṅgaṃ gahetabbaṃ. puna ca paraṃ mahārāja vāyu nirālayo aniketavāsī, evam-eva kho mahārāja yoginā yogāvacarena nirālaya-m-aniketa-m-asanthavena sabbattha

a mind like fire, free of attraction and repugnance. This is the fourth attribute of fire to be acquired. And finally, just as fire dispels darkness and sheds light, the yogi, an earnest disciple, should dispel the darkness of ignorance and shed the light of knowledge. This, great king, is the fifth attribute of fire to be acquired. For the Bhagavan, god above gods, cautioned his own son, Rahula, thus: 'Cultivate meditation like fire, Rahula. From cultivating meditation like fire, Rahula, bad phenomenal states that have not already arisen will not arise, and those bad phenomena that have arisen in the mind will not persist.'"

"Revered Nagasena, you say that there are five attributes 42
of the wind that must be acquired. What are the five attributes to be acquired?"

"Great king, just as the wind blows through jungle thickets in full bloom, the yogi, an earnest disciple, should delight in the forests of meditation subjects blooming with the finest flower of all—freedom. This is the first attribute of the wind to be acquired. And just as the wind shakes copses of trees growing up from the earth, the yogi, an earnest disciple, having retreated into the woods, should shake off the defilements, having first examined the habitual patterns. This is the second attribute of the wind to be acquired. And just as the wind drifts through the sky, the yogi, an earnest disciple, should make the mind drift among transcendent things. This is the third attribute of the wind to be acquired. And just as the wind carries scent, the yogi, an earnest disciple, should carry the scent of the finest fragrance of one's own moral discipline. This is the fourth attribute of the wind to be acquired. And, finally, just as the wind has no home, no

vimuttena bhavitabbaṃ. idaṃ mahārāja vāyussa pañcamaṃ aṅgaṃ gahetabbaṃ. bhāsitam-p' etaṃ mahārāja bhagavatā devātidevena suttanipāte:

43 santhavāto bhayaṃ jātaṃ, niketā jāyatī rajo, aniketam-
asanthavaṃ, etaṃ ve munidassanan-ti.

44 bhante nāgasena, pabbatassa pañca aṅgāni gahetabbānīti yaṃ vadesi, katamāni tāni pañca aṅgāni gahetabbānīti. yathā mahārāja pabbato acalo akampiyo asampavedhī, evam-eva kho mahārāja yoginā yogāvacarena sammānane vimānane sakkāre asakkāre garukāre agarukāre yase ayase nindāya pasaṃsāya sukhe dukkha iṭṭhāniṭṭhesu sabbattha rūpa-sadda-gandha-rasa-phoṭṭhabba-dhammesu rajanīyesu na rajjitabbaṃ, dussanīyesu na dussitabbaṃ, muyhanīyesu na muyhitabbaṃ, na kampitabbaṃ, na calitabbaṃ, pabbatena viya acalena bhavitabbaṃ. idaṃ mahārāja pabbatassa paṭhamaṃ aṅgaṃ gahetabbaṃ. bhāsitam-p' etaṃ mahārāja bhagavatā devā-tidevena: selo yathā ekaghano vātena na samīrati, evaṃ nindāpasaṃsāsu na samiñjanti paṇḍitā ti. puna ca paraṃ mahārāja pabbato thaddho na kenaci saṃsaṭṭho, evam-eva kho mahārāja yoginā yogāvacarena thaddhena asaṃsaṭṭhena bhavitabbaṃ, na kenaci saṃsaggo karaṇīyo. idaṃ mahārāja pabbatassa dutiyaṃ aṅgaṃ gahe-

house to dwell in, the yogi, an earnest disciple, should be free everywhere, homeless, without a house, and independent. This, great king, is the fifth attribute of the wind to be acquired. For the Bhagavan, god above gods, said this in the *Suttanipāta:*

> From intimacy, fear is born; from home life, dust 43
> arises.
> Free of home and free of intimacy, this is the vision of
> the sage."

"Revered Nagasena, you say that there are five attributes 44
of a mountain that must be acquired. What are the five attributes to be acquired?"

"Great king, just as a mountain remains still, without trembling or quaking, the yogi, an earnest disciple, should everywhere be still like a mountain, without trembling or quaking, in the face of respect, contempt, honor, dishonor, esteem, disdain, fame, obscurity, blame, praise, pleasure, pain, the desirable, and the disagreeable; the yogi should take no delight in appealing visible forms, sounds, fragrances, tastes, tangible things, or mental objects, should not be sullied by hateful things, and should not get muddled in perplexities. This is the first attribute of a mountain to be acquired. For the Bhagavan, god above gods, said: 'As a solid rock is not stirred by the wind, the learned are not stirred by praise or blame.' And just as a mountain is unyielding and associates with no one, the yogi, an earnest disciple, should become unyielding and without associations, making contact with no one. This is the second attribute of a mountain to be acquired. For the Bhagavan, god above gods, said:

tabbaṃ. bhāsitam-p' etaṃ mahārāja bhagavatā devātidevena asaṃsaṭṭhaṃ gahaṭṭhehi anāgārehi cūbhayaṃ, anokasāriṃ appicchaṃ, tam-ahaṃ brūmi brāhmaṇan-ti.

45 puna ca paraṃ mahārāja pabbate bījaṃ na virūhati, evam-eva kho mahārāja yoginā yogāvacarena sakamānase kilesā na virūhāpetabbā. idaṃ mahārāja pabbatassa tatiyaṃ aṅgaṃ gahetabbaṃ. bhāsitam-p' etaṃ mahārāja therena subhūtinā:

46 rāgūpasaṃhitaṃ cittaṃ yadā uppajjate mama, sayam-
eva paccavekkhitvā ekako taṃ damem' ahaṃ:
rajjasi rajanīyesu, dussanīyesu dussasi, muyhase
mohanīyesu; nikkhamassu vanā tuvaṃ. visuddhānaṃ
ayaṃ vāso, nimmalānaṃ tapassinaṃ; mā kho
visuddhaṃ dūsesi, nikkhamassu vanā tuvan-ti.

47 puna ca paraṃ mahārāja pabbato accuggato, evam-eva kho mahārāja yoginā yogāvacarena ñāṇaccuggatena bhavitabbaṃ. idaṃ mahārāja pabbatassa catutthaṃ aṅgaṃ gahetabbaṃ. bhāsitam p' etaṃ mahārāja bhagavata devātidevena:

48 pamādaṃ appamādena yadā nudati paṇḍito,
paññāpāsādam-āruyha asoko sokinim-pajaṃ,
pabbataṭṭhova bhummaṭṭhe, dhīro bāle avekkhatīti.

49 puna ca paraṃ mahārāja pabbato anunnato anoṇato, evam-eva kho mahārāja yoginā yogāvacarena unnatāvanati na karaṇīyā. idaṃ mahārāja pabbatassa pañcamaṃ aṅgaṃ gahetabbaṃ. bhāsitam-p' etaṃ mahārāja upāsikāya cullasubhaddāya sakasamaṇe parikittayamānāya:

'Avoiding association with householders and recluses alike, wandering homeless and content with little—this is what I call a Brahman.'

"And just as a seed does not grow on a mountain, a yogi, 45
an earnest disciple, does not permit defilements to grow in the mind. This is the third attribute of a mountain to be acquired. For Elder Subhuti said this:

> If my mind turns to passion, I examine myself and 46
> then subdue it single-handedly:
> *You take pleasure in delightful things, are tarnished by hateful things, and get muddled in perplexities. You must leave the forest, for it is the home of pure and stainless ascetics. Do not sully the pure—you must leave the forest.*

"Additionally, great king, as a mountain is very lofty, the 47
yogi, an earnest disciple, should be very lofty with respect to knowledge. This is the fourth attribute of a mountain to be acquired. For the Bhagavan, god above gods, said:

> The learned person who dispels carelessness with 48
> diligence and climbs the tower of understanding is free of sorrow.
> One surveys beings much as a tenacious person on a mountaintop surveys fools on the plains below.

"Finally, great king, just as a mountain cannot be raised up 49
or brought low, the yogi, an earnest disciple, should not be raised up or brought low. This is the fifth attribute of a mountain to be acquired. For this was also said by the laywoman Culla Subhadda when praising her own ascetics:

lābhena unnato loko, alābhena ca oṇato;
lābhālābhena ekaṭṭhā, tādisā samaṇā mamāti.

50 bhante nāgasena, ākāsassa pañca aṅgāni gahetabbānīti yaṃ vadesi, katamāni tāni pañca aṅgāni gahetabbā-nīti. yathā mahārāja ākāso sabbaso agayho, evam eva kho mahārāja yoginā yogāvacarena sabbaso kilesehi agayhena bhavitabbaṃ. idaṃ mahārāja ākāsassa paṭhamaṃ aṅgaṃ gahetabbaṃ. puna ca paraṃ mahārāja ākāso isi-tāpasa-bhūta-dijagaṇānusañcarito, evam-eva kho mahārāja yoginā yogāvacarena: aniccaṃ dukkham anattā ti saṅkhāresu mānasaṃ sañcārayitabbaṃ. idaṃ mahārāja ākāsassa dutiyaṃ aṅgaṃ gahetabbaṃ. puna ca paraṃ mahārajā ākāso santāsaniyo, evam-eva kho mahārāja yoginā yogāvacarena sabbabhavapaṭisandhisu mānasaṃ ubbejayitabbaṃ, assādo na kātabbo. idaṃ mahārāja ākāsassa tatiyaṃ aṅgaṃ gahetabbaṃ. puna ca paraṃ mahārāja ākāso ananto appamāṇo aparimeyyo, evam-eva kho mahārāja yoginā yogāvacarena anantasīlena aparimitañāṇena bhavitabbaṃ. idaṃ mahārāja ākāsassa catutthaṃ aṅgaṃ gahetabbaṃ. puna ca paraṃ mahārāja ākāso alaggo asatto appatiṭṭhito apalibuddho, evam-eva kho mahārāja yoginā yogāvacarena kule gaṇe lābhe āvāse palibodhe paccaye sabbakilesesu ca sabbattha alaggena bhavitabbaṃ, anāsattena appatiṭṭhitena apalibuddhena bhavitabbaṃ. idaṃ mahārāja ākāsassa pañcamaṃ aṅgaṃ gahetabbaṃ. bhāsitam-p' etaṃ mahārāja bhagavatā devātidevena sakaputtaṃ rāhulaṃ ovadantena: seyyathā pi rāhula ākāso na katthaci patiṭṭhito, evam-eva kho tvaṃ rāhula ākāsasamaṃ bhāvanaṃ bhāvehi; ākāsasamaṃ

'The world is raised up by gain and brought low by
loss, while my ascetics stay the same through gain
or loss.'"

"Revered Nagasena, you say that there are five attributes of space that must be acquired. What are the five attributes to be acquired?"

"Great king, just as space wholly eludes one's grasp, the 50
yogi, an earnest disciple, should wholly elude the grasp of the defilements. This is the first attribute of space to be acquired. And just as space is frequented by sages, ascetics, ghosts, and flocks of birds, the mind of the yogi, an earnest disciple, should be frequented by thoughts of impermanence, suffering, and nonself with respect to all habitual patterns. This is the second attribute of space to be acquired. And just as space inspires terror, the mind of the yogi, an earnest disciple, should be terrified of all future lives and rebirths and find no contentment. This is the third attribute of space to be acquired. And just as space is endless, immeasurable, and incalculable, the yogi, an earnest disciple, should have endless moral discipline and incalculable knowledge. This is the fourth attribute of space to be acquired. And finally, just as space is detached, untethered, without foundation, and without constraints, the yogi, an earnest disciple, should always be detached from family, community, wealth, the drawbacks, the monastic requisites, and all defilements; he should be untethered, without foundation, and without constraints.[4] This is the fifth attribute of space to be acquired, great king. For this was said by the Bhagavan, god above gods, exhorting his own son, Rahula: 'You should develop

hi te rāhula bhāvanaṃ bhāvayato uppannuppannā manāpāmanāpā phassā cittaṃ na pariyādāya ṭhassantīti.

51 bhante nāgasena, candassa pañca aṅgāni gahetabbānīti yaṃ vadesi, katamāni tāni pañca aṅgāni gahetabbānīti. yathā mahārāja cando sukkapakkhe udayanto uttaruttariṃ vaḍḍhati, evam-eva kho mahārāja yoginā yogāvacarena ācāra-sīla-guṇa-vattapaṭipattiyā āgamādhigame paṭisallāṇe satipaṭṭhāne indriyesu guttadvāratāya bhojane mattaññutāya jāgariyānuyoge uttaruttariṃ vaḍḍhitabbaṃ. idaṃ mahārāja candassa paṭhamaṃ aṅgaṃ gahetabbaṃ. puna ca paraṃ mahārāja cando uḷārādhipati, evam eva kho mahārāja yoginā yogāvacarena uḷāracchandādhipatinā bhavitabbaṃ. idaṃ mahārāja candassa dutiyaṃ aṅgaṃ gahetabbaṃ. puna ca paraṃ mahārāja cando nisāya carati, evam-eva kho mahārāja yoginā yogāvacarena pavivittena bhavitabbaṃ. idaṃ mahārāja candassa tatiyaṃ aṅgaṃ gahetabbaṃ. puna ca paraṃ mahārāja cando vimānaketu, evam-eva kho mahārāja yoginā yogāvacarena sīlaketunā bhavitabbaṃ. idaṃ mahārāja candassa catutthaṃ aṅgaṃ gahetabbaṃ. puna ca paraṃ mahārāja cando āyācita-patthito udeti, evam-eva kho mahārāja yoginā yogāvacarena āyācita-patthitena kulāni upasaṅkamitabbāni. idaṃ mahārāja candassa pañcamaṃ aṅgaṃ gahetabbaṃ. bhāsitam-p' etaṃ mahārāja bhagavatā devātidevena saṃyuttanikāyavare: candūpamā

meditation that is similar to space, Rahula, for space has no foundation anywhere. From developing meditation similar to space, charming and disagreeable contacts come and go without gaining a foothold in the mind and remaining.'"

"Revered Nagasena, you say that there are five attributes 51
of the moon that must be acquired. What are the five attributes to be acquired?"

"Great king, just as the moon rising in the bright fortnight grows fuller and fuller, the yogi, an earnest disciple, should grow fuller and fuller in good conduct, moral discipline, virtue, vows, practice, scriptural study, solitary meditation, the foundations of mindfulness, guarding the doors of the faculties, eating moderately, and attentive watchfulness. This is the first attribute of the moon to be acquired. And just as the moon is an illustrious monarch, the yogi, an earnest disciple, should become an illustrious monarch over desire. This is the second attribute of the moon to be acquired. And just as the moon travels at night, the yogi, an earnest disciple, should be solitary. This is the third attribute of the moon to be acquired. And just as the moon presides over its heavenly mansion, the yogi, an earnest disciple, should preside over moral discipline. This is the fourth attribute of the moon to be acquired. And finally, great king, just as the moon rises when supplicated and entreated, the yogi, an earnest disciple, visits families when supplicated and entreated. This is the fifth attribute of the moon to be acquired. For this was said by the Bhagavan, god above gods, in the excellent *Saṃyuttanikāya:* 'Monks, you are to be like the moon when you visit families—drawing back the body and mind, always

bhikkhave kulāni upasaṅkamatha, apakass' eva kāyaṃ apakassa cittaṃ, niccaṃ naviyā kulesu appagabbhā ti.

52 bhante nāgasena, suriyassa satta aṅgāni gahetabbānīti yaṃ vadesi, katamāni tāni satta aṅgāni gahetabbānīti. yathā mahārāja suriyo sabbaṃ udakaṃ parisoseti, evam-eva kho mahārāja yoginā yogāvacarena sabbe kilesā anavasesaṃ parisosetabbā. idaṃ mahārāja suriyassa paṭhamaṃ aṅgaṃ gahetabbaṃ. puna ca paraṃ mahārāja suriyo tamandhakāraṃ vidhamati, evam-eva kho mahārāja yoginā yogāvacarena sabbaṃ rāgatamaṃ dosatamaṃ mohatamaṃ mānatamaṃ diṭṭhitamaṃ kilesatamaṃ sabbaṃ duccaritatamaṃ vidhamayitabbaṃ. idaṃ mahārāja suriyassa dutiyaṃ aṅgaṃ gahetabbaṃ. puna ca paraṃ mahārāja suriyo abhikkhaṇaṃ carati, evam eva kho mahārāja yoginā yogāvacarena abhikkhaṇaṃ yoniso manasikāro kātabbo. idaṃ mahārāja suriyassa tatiyaṃ aṅgaṃ gahetabbaṃ. puna ca paraṃ mahārāja suriyo raṃsimālī, evam-eva kho mahārāja yoginā yogāvacarena ārammaṇamālinā bhavitabbaṃ. idaṃ mahārāja suriyassa catutthaṃ aṅgaṃ gahetabbaṃ. puna ca paraṃ mahārāja suriyo mahājanakāyaṃ santāpento carati, evam-eva kho mahārāja yoginā yogāvacarena ācāra-sīla-guṇa-vattapaṭipattiyā jhāna-vimokha-samādhi-samāpatti-indriya-bala-bojjhaṅga-satipaṭṭhāna-sammappadhāna-iddhipādehi sadevako loko santāpayitabbo. idaṃ mahārāja suriyassa pañcamaṃ aṅgaṃ gahetabbaṃ.

53 puna ca paraṃ mahārāja suriyo rāhubhayā bhīto carati, evam-eva kho mahārāja yoginā yogāvacarena duccarita-duggati-visamakantāra-vipāka-vinipāta-kilesajālajaṭite

acting as though you were a newcomer to the families, and being without pretensions.'"

"Revered Nagasena, you say that there are seven attributes 52
of the sun that must be acquired. What are the seven attributes to be acquired?"

"Great king, just as the sun dries up all water, the yogi, an earnest disciple, should completely dry up all defilements. This is the first attribute of the sun to be acquired. And just as the sun dispels the darkness, the yogi, an earnest disciple, should dispel the darkness of passion, the darkness of hate, the darkness of delusion, the darkness of pride, the darkness of wrong view, the darkness of the defilements, and the darkness of all wrongdoing. This is the second attribute of the sun to be acquired. And just as the sun is constantly moving, the yogi, an earnest disciple, should constantly practice careful attention. This is the third attribute of the sun to be acquired. And just as the sun has a halo of rays, the yogi, an earnest disciple, should have a halo of meditation subjects. This is the fourth attribute of the sun to be acquired. And just as the sun warms great multitudes of people, the yogi, an earnest disciple, should warm the world and its gods with good conduct, moral discipline, virtue, vows, practices, the *jhānas,* the deliverances, concentration, the attainments, faculties, powers, awakening factors, foundations of mindfulness, right striving, and the bases of supernatural power. This is the fifth attribute of the sun to be acquired.

"Additionally, great king, just as the sun wanders fright- 53
ened of Rahu, the god of eclipses, the yogi, an earnest disciple, should stir up the mind with great fear and urgency, having seen beings entangled in the snares of the defilements

diṭṭhisaṅghāṭapaṭimukke kupathapakkhanne kummagga-paṭipanne satte disvā mahatā saṃvegabhayena mānasaṃ saṃvejetabbaṃ. idaṃ mahārāja suriyassa chaṭṭhaṃ aṅgaṃ gahetabbaṃ. puna ca paraṃ mahārāja suriyo kalyāṇapāpake dasseti, evam eva kho mahārāja yoginā yogāvacarena indriyabala-bojjhaṅga-satipaṭṭhāna-sammappadhāna-iddhipāda-lokiyalo-kuttaradhammā dassetabbā. idaṃ mahārāja suriyassa sattamaṃ aṅgaṃ gahetabbaṃ. bhāsitam-p' etaṃ mahārāja therena vaṅgīsena: yathā pi suriyo udayanto rūpaṃ dasseti pāṇinaṃ, suciñ-ca asuciñ-cāpi, kalyāṇañ-cāpi pāpakaṃ, tathā bhikkhu dhammadharo avijjāpihitaṃ janaṃ pathaṃ dasseti vividhaṃ, ādiccov' udayaṃ yathā ti.

54 bhante nāgasena, sakkassa tīṇi aṅgāni gahetabbānīti yaṃ vadesi, katamāni tāni tīṇi aṅgāni gahetabbānīti. yathā mahārāja sakko ekantasukhasamappito, evam eva kho mahārāja yoginā yogāvacarena ekantapavivekasukhābhiratena bhavitabbaṃ. idaṃ mahārāja sakkassa paṭhamaṃ aṅgaṃ gahetabbaṃ. puna ca paraṃ mahārāja sakko deve disvā paggaṇhāti hāsam-abhijaneti, evam eva kho mahārāja yoginā yogāvacarena kusalesu dhammesu alīnam-atanditaṃ santaṃ mānasaṃ paggahetabbaṃ, hāsam-abhijanetabbaṃ, uṭṭhahitabbaṃ ghaṭitabbaṃ vāyamitabbam. idaṃ mahārāja sakkassa dutiyaṃ aṅgaṃ gahetabbaṃ. puna ca paraṃ mahārāja sakkassa anabhirati na uppajjati, evam-eva kho mahārāja yoginā yogāvacarena suññāgāre anabhirati na uppādetabbā. idaṃ mahārāja sakkassa tatiyaṃ aṅgaṃ gahetabbaṃ. bhāsitam-p' etaṃ mahārāja therena subhū-

and the punishments resulting from the lawless highways of wrong action and bad ways, tied up in the tangle of wrong views, taking the wrong path, and going down a wicked road. This is the sixth attribute of the sun to be acquired. And lastly, just as the sun reveals both the beautiful and the wicked, the yogi, an earnest disciple, should reveal the faculties, powers, awakening factors, foundations of mindfulness, right strivings, the bases of supernatural power, and the worldly and transcendent phenomenal states. This is the seventh attribute of the sun to be acquired, great king. For Elder Vangisena said: 'As the rising sun reveals the forms—pure and impure, beautiful and wicked—of living creatures, the monk, expert in the Dhamma and rising like the sun, reveals the many parts of the path to people shrouded in ignorance.'"

"Revered Nagasena, you say that there are three attributes 54
of Sakka that must be acquired. What are the three attributes to be acquired?"

"Great king, just as Sakka enjoys utmost happiness, the yogi, an earnest disciple, should delight in the utmost happiness of seclusion. This is the first attribute of Sakka to be acquired. And when Sakka sees gods, he takes care of them and brings them joy. Similarly, the yogi, an earnest disciple, should exert and apply himself, striving, taking care of the good phenomenal states, making the mind open, active, and peaceful, and generating joy.This is the second attribute to be acquired. And just as discontent never arises for Sakka, so too discontent with his empty hut never arises for the yogi, an earnest disciple. This is the third attribute to be acquired, great king. For Elder Subhuti said: 'Since I became

tinā: sāsane te mahāvīra yato pabbajito ahaṃ, nābhijānāmi uppannaṃ mānasaṃ kāmasaṃhitan-ti.

55 bhante nāgasena, cakkavattissa cattāri aṅgāni gahetabbānīti yaṃ vadesi, katamāni tāni cattāri aṅgāni gahetabbānīti. yathā mahārāja cakkavattī catuhi saṅgahavatthūhi janaṃ saṅgaṇhāti, evam-eva kho mahārāja yoginā yogāvacarena catassannaṃ parisānaṃ mānasaṃ saṅgahetabbaṃ anuggahetabbaṃ sampahaṃsetabbaṃ. idaṃ mahārāja cakkavattissa paṭhamaṃ aṅgaṃ gahetabbaṃ. puna ca paraṃ mahārāja cakkavattissa vijite corā na uṭṭhahanti, evam-eva kho mahārāja yoginā yogāvacarena kāmarāga-byāpāda-vihiṃsāvitakkā na uppādetabbā. idaṃ mahārāja cakkavattissa dutiyaṃ aṅgaṃ gahetabbaṃ. bhāsitam-p' etaṃ mahārāja bhagavatā devātidevena:

56 vitakkūpasame ca yo rato asubhaṃ bhāvayatī sadā
sato, esa kho byantikāhiti, esa-cchecchati
mārabandhanan-ti.

57 puna ca paraṃ mahārāja cakkavattī divase divase samuddapariyantaṃ mahāpaṭhaviṃ anuyāyati kalyāṇapāpakāni vicinamāno, evam-eva kho mahārāja yoginā yogāvacarena kāyakammaṃ vacīkammaṃ manokammaṃ divase divase paccavekkhitabbaṃ: kin-nu kho me imehi tīhi ṭhānehi anupavajjassa divaso vītivattatīti. idaṃ mahārāja cakkavattissa tatiyaṃ aṅgaṃ gahetabbaṃ. bhāsitam-p' etaṃ mahārāja bhagavatā devātidevena ekuttarikanikāyavare: kathambhūtassa me rattindivā vītipatantīti pabbajitena abhiṇhaṃ paccavekkhitabban-ti. puna ca paraṃ mahārāja

a renouncer in your dispensation, great hero, I have never known a thought connected to sensual desire to arise.'"

"Revered Nagasena, you say that there are four attributes 55
of the wheel-turning emperor that must be acquired. What are the four attributes to be acquired?"

"Great king, just as the wheel-turning emperor helps the people by means of the four bases of sympathy, the yogi, an earnest disciple, should help, satisfy, and delight the minds of the fourfold assembly.[5] This is the first attribute of the wheel-turning emperor to be acquired. And just as thieves never appear in the dominions of the wheel-turning emperor, thoughts of sensual passion, malice, and violence do not occur to the yogi, an earnest disciple. This is the second attribute of the wheel-turning emperor. For the Bhagavan, god above gods, said:

> One who delights in calming one's thoughts, and is 56
> constantly mindful when meditating on the foul topics, severs and removes Mara's shackles.[6]

"Further, just as the wheel-turning emperor travels day 57
after day through the whole earth bordered by the oceans to investigate what is beautiful and what is wicked, the yogi, an earnest disciple, day after day reviews his bodily actions, verbal actions, and mental actions: *How might I spend the day blameless in these three domains?* This is the third attribute of the wheel-turning emperor to be acquired. For the Bhagavan, god above gods, said this in the excellent *Aṅguttaranikāya:* 'A renouncer should repeatedly reflect, *How am I spending my days and nights?*' And finally, just as the wheel-turning emperor has thoroughly arranged protec-

cakkavattissa abbhantarabāhirārakkhā susaṃvihitā hoti, evam-eva kho mahārāja yoginā yogāvacarena abbhantarānaṃ bāhirānaṃ kilesānaṃ ārakkhāya satidovāriko ṭhapetabbo. idaṃ mahārāja cakkavattissa catutthaṃ aṅgaṃ gahetabbaṃ. bhāsitam-p' etaṃ mahārāja bhagavatā devātidevena: satidovāriko bhikkhave ariyasāvako akusalaṃ pajahati kusalaṃ bhāveti, sāvajjaṃ pajahati anavajjaṃ bhāveti, suddham-attānaṃ pariharatīti.

58 uddānaṃ: paṭhavī āpo ca tejo ca vāyo ca pabbatena ca ākāso canda-suriyo ca sakko ca cakkavattinā ti.

tatiyo vaggo.

tion against internal and external threats, the yogi should post mindfulness as a gatekeeper guarding against internal and external defilements. This is the fourth attribute of the wheel-turning emperor to be acquired, great king. For this was said by the Bhagavan, god above gods: 'A noble disciple, monks, with mindfulness as a gatekeeper, turns away the bad and cultivates the good, turns away the blameworthy and cultivates the blameless, and makes himself pure.'"

In summary, this is the earth, water, fire, wind, mountain, 58
space, moon, sun, Sakka, and wheel-turning emperor.

End of Part 3.

PART 4

59 bhante nāgasena, upacikāya ekaṃ aṅgaṃ gahetabban-ti yaṃ vadesi, kataman-taṃ ekaṃ aṅgaṃ gahetabban-ti. yathā mahārāja upacikā uparicchadanaṃ katvā attānaṃ pidahitvā gocarāya carati, evam-eva kho mahārāja yoginā yogāvacarena sīlasaṃvarachadanaṃ katvā mānasaṃ pidahitvā piṇḍāya caritabbaṃ. sīlasaṃvarachadanena kho mahārāja yogī yogāvacaro sabbabhayasamatikkanto hoti. idaṃ mahārāja upacikāya ekaṃ aṅgaṃ gahetabbaṃ. bhāsitam-p' etaṃ mahārāja therena upasenena vaṅgantaputtena: sīlasaṃvarachadanaṃ yogī katvāna mānasaṃ anupalitto lokena bhayā ca parimuccatīti.

60 bhante nāgasena, biḷārassa dve aṅgāni gahetabbānīti yaṃ vadesi, katamāni tāni dve aṅgāni gahetabbānīti. yathā mahārāja biḷāro guhāgato pi susiragato pi hammiyantaragato pi unduraṃ yeva pariyesati, evam-eva kho mahārāja yoginā yogāvacarena gāmagatenāpi araññagatenāpi rukkhamūlagatenāpi suññāgāragatenāpi satataṃ samitaṃ appamattena kāyagatāsatibhojanaṃ yeva pariyesitabbaṃ. idaṃ mahārāja biḷārassa paṭhamaṃ aṅgaṃ gahetabbaṃ. puna ca paraṃ mahārāja biḷāro āsanne yeva gocaraṃ pariyesati, evam-eva kho mahārāja yoginā yogāvacarena imesu yeva pañcas' upādānakkhandhesu udayabbayānupassinā viharitabbaṃ: iti rūpaṃ, iti rūpassa samudayo, iti rūpassa atthagamo; iti vedanā, iti vedanāya samudayo, iti vedanāya

PART 4

"Revered Nagasena, you say that there is one attribute of the termite that must be acquired. What is that one attribute to be acquired?" 59

"Great king, just as the termite builds a casing overhead to cover itself and then goes looking for food, the yogi, an earnest disciple, should build a casing of moral discipline and self-control to cover the mind, and then go out seeking alms. Great king, it is with this casing of moral discipline and self-control that the yogi overcomes all fear. This is the one attribute of the termite to be acquired. For this was said by Elder Upasena, son of Vanganta: 'The yogi who builds a casing of moral discipline and self-control for the mind is untainted by the world and released from fear.'"

"Revered Nagasena, you say that there are two attributes of the cat that must be acquired. What are the two attributes to be acquired?" 60

"Great king, just as the cat goes into caves, burrows, and the interior recesses of houses only to chase rats, the yogi, an earnest disciple, should go into villages, forests, the roots of trees, and empty huts constantly, continuously, and carefully only to chase the nourishment that is mindfulness of the body. This is the first attribute of the cat to be acquired. And just as the cat pursues only feeding grounds that are nearby, the yogi, an earnest disciple, should live observing the rising and falling of the five clusters of clinging: 'This is form, this is the origin of form, this is the passing away of form; this is feeling, this is the origin of feeling, this is the passing away

atthagamo; iti saññā, iti saññāya samudayo, iti saññāya atthagamo; iti saṅkhārā, iti saṅkhārānaṃ samudayo, iti saṅkhārānaṃ atthagamo; iti viññāṇaṃ, iti viññāṇassa samudayo, iti viññāṇassa atthagamo ti. idaṃ mahārāja biḷārassa dutiyaṃ aṅgaṃ gahetabbaṃ. bhāsitam-p' etaṃ mahārāja bhagavatā devātidevena: na ito dūre bhavitabbaṃ, bhavaggaṃ kiṃ karissati, paccuppannamhi vohāre sake kāyamhi vindathāti.

61 bhante nāgasena, undurassa ekaṃ aṅgaṃ gahetabban-ti yaṃ vadesi, kataman-taṃ ekaṃ aṅgaṃ gahetabban-ti. yathā mahārāja unduro ito c' ito ca vicaranto āhārūpasiṃsako yeva carati, evam-eva kho mahārāja yoginā yogāvacarena ito c' ito ca vicarantena yoniso manasikārūpasiṃsaken' eva bhavitabbaṃ. idaṃ mahārāja undurassa ekaṃ aṅgaṃ gahetabbaṃ. bhāsitam-p' etaṃ mahārāja therena upasenena vaṅgantaputtena: dhammasīsaṃ karitvāna viharanto vipassako anolīno viharati upasanto sadā sato ti.

62 bhante nāgasena, vicchikassa ekaṃ aṅgaṃ gahetabban-ti yaṃ vadesi, kataman-taṃ ekaṃ aṅgaṃ gahetabban-ti. yathā mahārāja vicchiko naṅgulāvudho, naṅgulaṃ ussāpetvā carati, evam-eva kho mahārāja yoginā yogāvacarena ñāṇāvudhena bhavitabbaṃ, ñāṇaṃ ussāpetvā viharitabbaṃ. idaṃ mahārāja vicchikassa ekaṃ aṅgaṃ gahetabbaṃ. bhāsitam-p' etaṃ mahārāja therena upasenena vaṅgantaputtena:

of feeling; this is perception, this is the origin of perception, this is the passing away of perception; these are the habitual patterns, this is the origin of the habitual patterns, this is the passing away of the habitual patterns; this is awareness, this is the origin of awareness, this is the passing away of awareness.' This, great king, is the second attribute of the cat to be acquired. For the Bhagavan, god above gods, said: 'Do not be far away, for what have you to do with the top of the world? Rather, be present with what is happening here, and discover what is occurring in your own body.'"

"Revered Nagasena, you say that there is one attribute of 61
the rat that must be acquired. What is that one attribute to be acquired?"

"Great king, just as the rat wanders here and there, traveling around and hoping for food, the yogi, an earnest disciple, should wander, hoping only for careful attention. This is the one attribute of the rat to be acquired, great king. For Elder Upasena, son of Vanganta, also said: 'Having placed the Dhamma at the forefront, living while practicing insight, staying homeless, one is always peaceful and mindful.'"

"Revered Nagasena, you say that there is one attribute of 62
the scorpion that must be acquired. What is that one attribute to be acquired?"

"Great king, just as the scorpion has a weapon on its tail and moves around with its tail raised high, the yogi, an earnest disciple, should possess the weapon of knowledge and dwell with knowledge raised high. This is the one attribute of the scorpion to be acquired. For this too was said by Elder Upasena, son of Vanganta: 'Having seized the sword of knowledge, living while practicing insight,

ñāṇakhaggaṃ gahetvāna viharanto vipassako parimuccati sabbhayā, duppasaho ca so bhave ti.

63 bhante nāgasena, nakulassa ekaṃ aṅgaṃ gahetabban-ti yaṃ vadesi, kataman-taṃ ekaṃ aṅgaṃ gahetabban-ti. yathā mahārāja nakulo uragam-upagacchanto bhesajjena kāyaṃ paribhāvetvā uragam-upagacchati gahetuṃ, evam-eva kho mahārāja yoginā yogāvacarena kodhāghātabahulaṃ kalaha-viggaha-vivāda-virodhābhibhūtaṃ lokam-upagacchantena mettābhesajjena mānasaṃ anulimpitabbaṃ. idaṃ mahārāja nakulassa ekaṃ aṅgaṃ gahetabbaṃ. bhāsitam-p' etaṃ mahārāja therena sāriputtena dhammasenāpatinā: tasmā sakaṃ paresam-pi, kātabbā mettabhāvanā, mettacittena pharitabbaṃ, etaṃ buddhāna' sāsanan-ti.

64 bhante nāgasena, jarasigālassa dve aṅgāni gahetabbānīti yaṃ vadesi, katamāni tāni dve aṅgāni gahetabbānīti. yathā mahārāja jarasigālo bhojanaṃ paṭilabhitvā ajigucchamāno yāvadatthaṃ āharayati, evam-eva kho mahārāja yoginā yogāvacarena bhojanaṃ paṭilabhitvā ajigucchamānena sarīrayāpanamattam-eva paribhuñjitabbaṃ. idaṃ mahārāja jarasigālassa paṭhamaṃ aṅgaṃ gahetabbaṃ. bhāsitam-p' etaṃ mahārāja therena mahākassapena:

65 senāsanamhā oruyha gāmaṃ piṇḍāya pāvisiṃ;
bhuñjantaṃ purisaṃ kuṭṭhiṃ sakkacca naṃ
upaṭṭhahiṃ. so me pakkena hatthena ālopaṃ
upanāmayi, ālopaṃ pakkhipantassa aṅgulim-p'

one is released from fear and is hard to subdue in the next life.'"

"Revered Nagasena, you say that there is one attribute 63
of the mongoose that must be acquired. What is that one attribute?"

"Great king, just as a mongoose approaching a snake first infuses its body with a medicine and then advances on the snake and seizes it, the yogi, an earnest disciple, should anoint the mind with the medicine of loving-kindness when approaching the world, as it is overcome with quarrels, disputes, contention, and enmity and rife with anger and hostility. This, great king, is the one attribute of the mongoose to be acquired. For Elder Sariputta, General of the Dhamma, said: 'Therefore, the cultivation of loving-kindness should be practiced toward oneself and others, and one should be pervaded with loving-kindness. This is the teaching of the buddhas.'"

"Revered Nagasena, you say that there are two attributes 64
of an old jackal that must be acquired. What are the two attributes to be acquired?"

"Great king, whenever an old jackal gets food, it eats as much as it can without disgust. Similarly, the yogi, an earnest disciple, who receives food should enjoy it without disgust, simply for nourishing the body. This is the first attribute of an old jackal to be acquired. For Elder Mahakassapa said:

> Coming down from my lodging, I entered the village 65
> for alms.
> I stood respectfully by a leper who was eating.
> With his diseased hand he offered me a mouthful.

ettha chijjatha. kuḍḍamūlañ-ca nissāya ālopaṃ
paribhuñjisaṃ; bhuñjamāneva bhutte vā
jegucchaṃ-me na vijjatīti.

66 puna ca paraṃ mahārāja jarasigālo bhojanaṃ paṭilabhitvā na vicināti: lūkhaṃ vā paṇītaṃ vā ti, evam-eva kho mahārāja yoginā yogāvacarena bhojanaṃ paṭilabhitvā na vicinitabbaṃ: lūkhaṃ vā paṇītaṃ vā sampannaṃ vā asampannaṃ vā ti, yathāladdhena santussitabbaṃ. idaṃ mahārāja jarasigālassa dutiyaṃ aṅgaṃ gahetabbaṃ. bhāsitam-p' etaṃ mahārāja therena upasenena vaṅgantaputtena:

67 lūkhena pi ca santusse, nāññaṃ patthe rasaṃ bahuṃ,
rasesu anugiddhassa jhāne na ramatī mano, itarītarena
santuṭṭhe sāmaññaṃ paripūratīti.

68 bhante nāgasena, migassa tīṇi aṅgāni gahetabbānīti yaṃ vadesi, katamāni tāni tīṇi aṅgāni gahetabbānīti. yathā mahārāja migo divā araññe carati, rattiṃ abbhokāse, evam-eva kho mahārāja yoginā yogāvacarena diva araññe viharitabbaṃ, rattiṃ abbhokāse. idaṃ mahārāja migassa paṭhamaṃ aṅgaṃ gahetabbaṃ. bhāsitam-p' etaṃ mahārāja bhagavatā devātidevena lomahaṃsana-pariyāye: so kho ahaṃ

As he was offering the mouthful, his finger broke off
right there.
Resting against the base of the wall, I ate that
mouthful.
Neither while eating nor after was disgust found in
me.

"In addition, great king, whenever an old jackal gets 66
food, it does not discriminate, thinking 'disagreeable' or 'fine.' Similarly, the yogi, an earnest disciple, who receives food should be satisfied with whatever is received and not discriminate, thinking, 'disagreeable' or 'fine,' 'cooked well' or 'prepared badly.' This is the second attribute of an old jackal to be acquired. For Elder Upasena, son of Vanganta, also said:

One should be satisfied with even disagreeable fare 67
and not hanker for something tastier.
The mind of one craving for flavors does not delight in
the *jhānas*.
One content with anything at all perfects
renunciation."

"Revered Nagasena, you say that there are three attributes 68
of the deer that must be acquired. What are the three attributes to be acquired?"

"Great king, just as the deer wanders in the forest by day and in open spaces by night, the yogi, an earnest disciple, should stay in the forest by day and in open spaces by night. This is the first attribute of the deer to be acquired. For the Bhagavan said this in the "Hair-Raising Treatise":

sāriputta yā tā rattiyo sītā hemantikā antaraṭṭhake himapātasamaye tathārūpāsu rattisu rattiṃ abbhokāse viharāmi, divā vanasaṇḍe; gimhānaṃ pacchime māse divā abbhokāse viharāmi, rattiṃ vanasaṇḍe ti. puna ca paraṃ mahārāja migo sattimhi vā sare vā opatante vañceti palāyati, na kāyam-upaneti, evam-eva kho mahārāja yoginā yogāvacarena kilesesu opatantesu vañcayitabbaṃ palāyitabbaṃ, na cittam-upanetabbaṃ. idaṃ mahārāja migassa dutiyaṃ aṅgaṃ gahetabbaṃ. puna ca paraṃ mahārāja migo manusse disvā yena vā tena vā palāyati: mā maṃ te addasaṃsūti, evam-eva kho mahārāja yoginā yogāvacarena bhaṇḍana-kalaha-viggaha vivādasīle dussīle kusīte saṅgaṇikārāme disvā yena vā tena vā palāyitabbaṃ: mā maṃ te addasaṃsu ahañ-ca te mā addasan-ti. idaṃ mahārāja migassa tatiyaṃ aṅgaṃ gahetabbaṃ. bhāsitam-p' etaṃ mahārāja therena sāriputtena dhammasenāpatinā: mā me kadāci pāpiccho kusīto hīnavīriyo appassuto anācāro sameto katthacī ahū ti.

69 bhante nāgasena, gorūpassa cattāri aṅgāni gahetabbānīti yaṃ vadesi, katamāni tāni cattāri aṅgāni gahetabbānīti. yathā mahārāja gorūpo sakaṃ gehaṃ na vijahati, evam-eva kho mahārāja yoginā yogāvacarena sako kāyo na vijahitabbo: anicc-ucchādana-parimaddana-bhedana-vikiraṇa-viddhaṃsanadhammo ayaṃ kāyo ti. idaṃ mahārāja gorūpassa paṭhamaṃ aṅgaṃ gahetabbaṃ. puna ca paraṃ mahārāja gorūpo ādiṇṇadhuro sukhadukkhena dhuraṃ vahati, evam-eva kho mahārāja yoginā yogāvacarena ādiṇṇabrahmacariyena sukhadukkhena yāva jīvitapa-

'Sariputta, in the cold winter nights during the eight-day period of frost, I spent the nights in the open air and the days in the forest grove.[7] And in the last month of the hot season, I spent the days in the open spaces and the nights in the forest grove.' Further, great king, just as the deer dodges falling arrows and spears and dashes away, not offering its body, the yogi, an earnest disciple, should dodge falling defilements and dash away, not offering his mind. This is the second attribute of the deer to be acquired. And finally, just as the deer dashes this way or that upon seeing humans, thinking, *May they not see me!* the yogi, an earnest disciple, should dash away, having spotted those who are given to strife, quarreling, disputing, and contention, who are badly behaved, indolent, and fond of society, thinking, *May they not see me, and may I not see them!* This is the third attribute of the deer to be acquired, great king. For Elder Sariputta, General of the Dhamma, said: 'Let no one wicked, indolent, weak in exertion, ignorant, and badly behaved ever have anything to do with me.'"

"Revered Nagasena, you say that there are four attributes 69
of the ox that must be acquired. What are the four attributes to be acquired?"

"Great king, just as the ox does not forsake its own home, the yogi, an earnest disciple, should not forsake his own body, thinking, *This body is subject to impermanence, decay, wearing out, breaking apart, dissolving, and destruction.* This is the first attribute of the ox to be acquired. And just as the ox, having taken up the yoke, bears the yoke whether easily or painfully, the yogi, an earnest disciple, having taken up the religious life, should practice the religious life, whether

riyādānā āpāṇakoṭikaṃ brahmacariyaṃ caritabbaṃ. idaṃ mahārāja gorūpassa dutiyaṃ aṅgaṃ gahetabbaṃ. puna ca paraṃ mahārāja gorūpo chandena ghāyamāno pānīyaṃ pivati, evam-eva kho mahārāja yoginā yogāvacarena ācariyupajjhāyānaṃ anusatthi chandena pemena pasādena ghāyamānena paṭiggahetabbā. idaṃ mahārāja gorūpassa tatiyaṃ aṅgaṃ gahetabbaṃ. puna ca paraṃ mahārāja gorūpo yena kenaci vāhiyamāno vahati, evam-eva kho mahārāja yoginā yogāvacarena thera-nava-majjhimabhikkhūnam-pi gihiupāsakassāpi ovādānusāsanī sirasā sampaṭicchitabbā. idaṃ mahārāja gorūpassa catutthaṃ aṅgaṃ gahetabbaṃ. bhāsitam-p' etaṃ mahārāja therena sāriputtena dhammasenāpatinā: tadahu pabbajito santo, jātiyā sattavassiko, so pi maṃ anusāseyya, sampaṭicchāmi matthake. tibbaṃ chandañ-ca pemañ-ca tasmiṃ disvā upaṭṭhape, ṭhapeyy' ācariye ṭhāne, sakkacca naṃ punappunan-ti.

70 bhante nāgasena, varāhassa dve aṅgāni gahetabbānīti yaṃ vadesi, katamāni tāni dve aṅgāni gahetabbānīti. yathā mahārāja varāho santatta-kaṭhite gimhasamaye sampatte udakaṃ upagacchati, evam-eva kho mahārāja yoginā yogāvacarena dosena citte āluḷita-khalita-vibbhanta-santatte sītalāmatapaṇīta-mettābhāvanaṃ upagantabbaṃ. idaṃ mahārāja varāhassa paṭhamaṃ aṅgaṃ gahetabbaṃ. puna ca paraṃ mahārāja varāho cikkhallamudakam-upagantvā nāsikāya paṭhaviṃ khaṇitvā doṇiṃ katvā doṇikāya sayati, evam-eva kho mahārāja yoginā yogāvacarena mānase kāyaṃ nikkhipitvā ārammaṇantaragatena sayitabbaṃ. idaṃ mahārāja varāhassa dutiyaṃ aṅgaṃ gahetabbaṃ. bhāsi-

easily or painfully, for his whole life up to the very end. This is the second attribute of the ox to be acquired. And just as the ox, consumed with eagerness for water, drinks it, the yogi, an earnest disciple, consumed with eagerness, love, and composed confidence, should receive the instruction of teachers and preceptors. This is the third attribute of the ox to be acquired. And just as the ox proceeds, carrying its burden for anyone, the yogi, an earnest disciple, with head bowed, should accept admonishment and instruction by elders, novices, and middle-ranking monks, as well as householders and laypeople. This, great king, is the fourth attribute of the ox to be acquired. For Elder Sariputta, General of the Dhamma, said: 'Should someone seven years of age and ordained only today instruct me, I will accept it with my head bowed. Seeing keen eagerness and love there, I serve and place that one in the role of a teacher, respectfully, again and again.'"

"Revered Nagasena, you say that there are two attributes 70
of the boar that must be acquired. What are the two attributes to be acquired?"

"Great king, just as the boar heads for water in the scorching and boiling heat of the summer, the yogi, an earnest disciple, should head for the cool, sweet, and ambrosial meditation on loving-kindness whenever his mind is agitated, faltering, distraught, and scorched by anger. This is the first attribute of the boar to be acquired. And just as the boar, upon reaching the muddy water, digs into the earth with its snout, makes a trench, and lies in the trench, the yogi, an earnest disciple, entrusting his body to his mind, should rest inside the meditation subject. This, great king, is the second

tam-p' etaṃ mahārāja therena piṇḍolabhāradvājena: kāye sabhāvaṃ disvāna vicinitvā vipassako ekākiyo adutiyo seti ārammaṇantare ti.

71 bhante nāgasena, hatthissa pañca aṅgāni gahetabbānīti yaṃ vadesi, katamāni tāni pañca aṅgāni gahetabbānīti. yathā mahārāja hatthī nāma caranto yeva paṭhaviṃ dāleti, evam-eva kho mahārāja yoginā yogāvacarena kāyaṃ sammasamānen' eva sabbe kilesā dāletabbā. idaṃ mahārāja hatthissa paṭhamaṃ aṅgaṃ gahetabbaṃ. puna ca paraṃ mahārāja hatthī sabbakāyen' eva apaloketi, ujukaṃ yeva pekkhati, na disāvidisā viloketi, evam-eva kho mahārāja yoginā yogāvacarena sab-bakāyena apalokinā bhavitabbaṃ, na disāvidisā viloketabbā, na uddhaṃ ulloketabbaṃ, na adho oloketabbaṃ, yugamattaṃ pekkhinā bhavitabbaṃ. idaṃ mahārāja hatthissa dutiyaṃ aṅgaṃ gahetabbaṃ. puna ca paraṃ mahārāja hatthī anibaddhasayano gocarāya-m-anugantvā na tam-eva desaṃ vāsattham-upagacchati, na dhuvapatiṭṭhālayo, evam-eva kho mahārāja yoginā yogāvacarena anibaddhasayanena bhavitabbaṃ, nirālayena piṇḍāya gantabbaṃ; yadi passati vipassako manuññaṃ patirūpaṃ ruciradese bhavaṃ maṇḍapaṃ vā rukkhamūlaṃ vā guhaṃ vā pabbhāraṃ vā, tatth' eva vāsam-upagantabbaṃ, dhuvapatiṭṭhālayo na kātabbo. idaṃ mahārāja hatthissa tatiyaṃ aṅgaṃ gahetabbaṃ.

72 puna ca paraṃ mahārāja hatthī udakaṃ ogāhitvā suci-vimala-sītala-salilaparipuṇṇaṃ kumud-uppala-paduma-puṇḍarīkasañchannaṃ mahatimahantaṃ paduma-

attribute of the boar to be acquired. For Elder Pindola Bharadvaja said: 'Seeing and examining the nature of the body, the meditator rests solitary and alone inside the meditation subject.'"

"Revered Nagasena, you say that there are five attributes 71
of the elephant that must be acquired. What are the five attributes to be acquired?"

"Great king, when the elephant moves, it splits the ground. Similarly, the yogi, an earnest disciple, should split apart all defilements by mastering the body. This is the first attribute to be acquired. And when an elephant looks at something with its entire body, it gazes straight ahead and does not glance about in all directions. Similarly, the yogi, an earnest disciple, should cultivate looking with the entire body, not glancing around in all directions, not looking up, not looking down, and gazing only a short distance ahead. This is the second attribute of the elephant to be acquired. Additionally, the elephant has no permanent sleeping place; when moving through its range it calls no place home, and it has no stable or fixed dwelling. Similarly, the yogi, an earnest disciple, should lack a permanent sleeping place and should wander homeless for alms. Should the insight practitioner see a charming and proper situation in an agreeable place—a pavilion, the base of a tree, a cave, or a hollow—he must approach it only as a residence and not make it his stable or fixed dwelling. This is the third attribute of the elephant to be acquired.

"Further, just as the elephant plunges into water— 72
plunges, that is, into a large and magnificent lotus lake full of pure, clear, and cool water covered with lilies and blue,

saraṃ ogāhitvā kīḷati gajavarakīḷaṃ, evam-eva kho mahārāja yoginā yogāvacarena suci-vimala-vippasanna-m-anāvi-la-dhammavaravāri-puṇṇaṃ vimuttikusumasañchannaṃ mahāsatipaṭṭhānapokkharaṇiṃ ogāhitvā ñāṇena saṅkhārā odhunitabbā vidhunitabbā, yogāvacarakīḷā kīḷitabbā. idaṃ mahārāja hatthissa catutthaṃ aṅgaṃ gahetabbaṃ. puna ca paraṃ mahārāja hatthī sato pādaṃ uddharati sato pādaṃ nikkhipati, evam-eva kho mahārāja yoginā yogāvacarena satena sampajānena pādaṃ uddharitabbaṃ, satena sampajānena pādaṃ nikkhipitabbaṃ, abhikkama-paṭikkame sammiñjana-pasāraṇe sabbattha satena sampajānena bhavitabbaṃ. idaṃ mahārāja hatthissa pañcamaṃ aṅgaṃ gahetabbaṃ. bhāsitam-p' etaṃ mahārāja bhagavatā devātidevena saṃyuttanikāyavare: kāyena saṃvaro sādhu, sādhu vācāya saṃvaro, manasā saṃvaro sādhu, sādhu sabbattha saṃvaro; sabbattha saṃvuto lajjī rakkhito ti pavuccatīti.

73 uddānaṃ: upacikā biḷāro ca unduro vicchikena ca nakulo sigālo migo gorūpo varāho hatthinā dasāti.

catuttho vaggo.

red, and white lotuses—and plays wonderful elephant games, the yogi, an earnest disciple, should plunge into the lotus pond of the great foundations of mindfulness filled with the wonderful water of the flawless Dhamma, pure, clear, and limpid. There he should play the game of yogis, shaking and sloughing off of the habitual patterns by means of knowledge. This is the fourth attribute of the elephant to be acquired. And finally, great king, just as the elephant lifts its foot up and puts its foot down mindfully, the yogi, an earnest disciple, should lift his foot up and put his foot down mindfully and deliberately and be mindful and deliberate everywhere, whether advancing or retreating, bending down, or stretching out. This is the fifth attribute of the elephant to be acquired. For in the excellent *Saṃyuttanikāya* the Bhagavan, god above gods, said: 'Restraint over the body is excellent, restraint with speech is excellent, and restraint over the mind is excellent; restraint everywhere is excellent. One everywhere restrained and modest is called 'guarded.'"

In summary, these are the ten: the termite, the cat, the rat, 73
the scorpion, the mongoose, the jackal, the deer, the ox, the boar, and the elephant.

End of Part 4.

PART 5

74 bhante nāgasena, sīhassa satta aṅgāni gahetabbānīti yaṃ vadesi, katamāni tāni satta aṅgāni gahetabbānīti. yathā mahārāja sīho nāma seta-vimala-pari-suddha-paṇḍaro, evam-eva kho mahārāja yoginā yogāvacarena seta-vimala-parisuddha-paṇḍaracittena byapagatakukkuccena bhavitabbaṃ. idaṃ mahārāja sīhassa paṭhamaṃ aṅgaṃ gahetabbaṃ. puna ca paraṃ mahārāja sīho catucaraṇo vikkantacārī, evam-eva kho mahārāja yoginā yogāvacarena caturiddhipādacaraṇena bhavitabbaṃ. idaṃ mahārāja sīhassa dutiyaṃ aṅgaṃ gahetabbaṃ. puna ca paraṃ mahārāja sīho abhirūpa-rucira-kesarī, evam-eva kho mahārāja yoginā yogāvacarena abhirūparucira-sīla-kesarinā bhavitabbaṃ. idaṃ mahārāja sīhassa tatiyaṃ aṅgaṃ gahetabbaṃ. puna ca paraṃ mahārāja sīho jīvitapariyādāne pi na kassaci oṇamati, evam-eva kho mahārāja yoginā yogāvacarena cīvara-piṇḍapāta-senāsana-gilānapaccayabhesajja-parikkhāra-pariyādāne pi na kassaci oṇamitabbaṃ. idaṃ mahārāja sīhassa catutthaṃ aṅgaṃ gahetabbaṃ.

75 puna ca paraṃ mahārāja sīho sapadānabhakkho, yasmiṃ okāse nipatati tatth' eva yāvadatthaṃ bhakkhayati, na varamaṃsaṃ vicināti; evam-eva kho mahārāja yoginā yogāvacarena sapadānabhakkhena bhavitabbaṃ, na kulāni vicinitabbāni, na pubbagehaṃ hitvā kulāni upasaṅkamitabbāni, na bhojanaṃ vicinitabbaṃ, yasmiṃ okāse kabaḷaṃ

PART 5

"Revered Nagasena, you say that there are seven attributes 74
of the lion that must be acquired. What are the seven attributes to be acquired?"

"Great king, just as the lion is pale, spotless, bright, and fair, the yogi, an earnest disciple, should be one whose mind is pale, spotless, bright, and fair because of being free of regrets. This is the first attribute of the lion to be acquired. And just as the four-pawed lion walks heroically, the yogi, an earnest disciple, should walk with the four bases of supernatural power. This is the second attribute of the lion to be acquired. And just as the lion has a handsome and splendid mane, the yogi, an earnest disciple, should have a mane of handsome and splendid moral discipline. This is the third attribute of the lion to be acquired. And just as, even at the end of its days, the lion bows down to no one, the yogi, an earnest disciple, should bow down to no one, even at the end of his requisites of the robe, alms bowl, lodging, and medicine for sickness. This is the fourth attribute of the lion to be acquired.

"Additionally, great king, the lion feeds without inter- 75
ruption right then and there when the occasion permits, and eats as much as it likes without selecting the choicest meat. In a similar way, the yogi, an earnest disciple, should gather alms without interruption and not select families, refrain from skipping one house to arrive at another, or be discriminating about food. When an occasion presents him a mouthful, he should eat it right then and there, solely for

ādiyati tasmiṃ yeva okāse bhuñjitabbaṃ sarīrayāpanamattaṃ, na varabhojanaṃ vicinitabbaṃ. idaṃ mahārāja sīhassa pañcamaṃ aṅgaṃ gahetabbaṃ. puna ca paraṃ mahārāja sīho asannidhibhakkho, sakiṃ gocaraṃ bhakkhayitvā na puna taṃ upagacchati, evam-eva kho mahārāja yoginā yogāvacarena asannidhikāraparibhoginā bhavitabbaṃ. idaṃ mahārāja sīhassa chaṭṭhaṃ aṅgaṃ gahetabbaṃ. puna ca paraṃ mahārāja sīho bhojanaṃ aladdhā na paritassati, laddhā pi bhojanaṃ agadhito amucchito anajjhāpanno paribhuñjati, evam-eva kho mahārāja yoginā yogāvacarena bhojanaṃ aladdhā na paritassitabbaṃ, laddhā pi bhojanaṃ agadhitena amucchitena anajjhāpannena ādīnavadassāvinā nissaraṇapaññena paribhuñjitabbaṃ. idaṃ mahārāja sīhassa sattamaṃ aṅgaṃ gahetabbaṃ. bhāsitam-p' etaṃ mahārāja bhagavatā devātidevena saṃyuttanikāyavare theraṃ mahākassapaṃ parikittayamānena: santuṭṭho 'yaṃ bhikkhave kassapo itarītarena piṇḍapātena, itarītarapiṇḍapātasantuṭṭhiyā ca vaṇṇavādī, na ca piṇḍapātahetu anesanaṃ appatirūpaṃ āpajjati, aladdhā ca piṇḍapātaṃ na paritassati, laddhā ca piṇḍapātaṃ agadhito amucchito anajjhāpanno ādīnavadassāvī nissaraṇapañño paribhuñjatīti.

76 bhante nāgasena, cakkavākassa tīṇi aṅgāni gahetabbānīti yaṃ vadesi, katamāni tāni tīṇi aṅgāni gahetabbānīti. yathā mahārāja cakkavāko yāva jīvitapariyādānā dutiyikaṃ na vijahati, evam-eva kho mahārāja yoginā yogāvacarena yāva jīvitapariyādānā yoniso manasikāro na vijahitabbo. idaṃ mahārāja cakkavākassa paṭhamaṃ aṅgaṃ gahetabbaṃ. puna ca paraṃ mahārāja cakkavāko sevāla-paṇaka-bhakkho,

sustaining the body and without selecting the choicest food. This is the fifth attribute of the lion to be acquired. Further, the lion does not eat stored food, and once it has eaten in a feeding range, it does not go there again. The yogi, an earnest disciple, should not make use of stored food either. This is the sixth attribute of the lion to be acquired. And finally, the lion is not perturbed when not finding food, but when it does get a meal, enjoys it without ensnarement, infatuation, or offense. Similarly, the yogi, an earnest disciple, should not be perturbed when not getting food, but when he does get a meal, he should enjoy it without ensnarement, infatuation, or offense, while seeing the dangers in it and understanding the escape from it. This is the seventh attribute of the lion to be acquired, great king. For the Bhagavan, god above gods, said this in the excellent *Saṃyuttanikāya* when commending Elder Kassapa the Great: 'Monks, this Kassapa is content with any alms at all, and he praises contentment with any alms at all. He commits nothing improper or unseemly for the sake of alms. He is not perturbed when not receiving alms, but when he does get alms food, he enjoys it without ensnarement, infatuation, or offense, while seeing the dangers in it and understanding the escape from it.'"

"Revered Nagasena, you say that there are three attributes 76
of the ruddy shelduck that must be acquired. What are the three attributes to be acquired?"

"Great king, just as the ruddy shelduck never forsakes its mate as long as it lives, the yogi, an earnest disciple, should never forsake careful attention for as long as he lives. This is the first attribute to be acquired. And the ruddy shelduck feeds on aquatic mosses and leaves and is content with them.

tena ca santuṭṭhiṃ āpajjati, tāya ca santuṭṭhiyā balena ca vaṇṇena ca na parihāyati, evam-eva kho mahārāja yoginā yogāvacarena yathālābhasantoso karaṇīyo. yathālābhasantuṭṭho kho pana mahārāja yogī yogāvacaro na parihāyati sīlena, na parihāyati samādhinā, na parihāyati paññāya, na parihāyati vimuttiyā, na parihāyati vimuttiñāṇadassanena, na parihāyati sabbehi kusalehi dhammehi. idaṃ mahārāja cakkavākassa dutiyaṃ aṅgaṃ gahetabbaṃ. puna ca paraṃ mahārāja cakkavāko pāṇe na viheṭhayati, evam-eva kho mahārāja yoginā yogāvacarena nihitadaṇḍena nihitasatthena lajjinā dayāpannena sabbapāṇabhūta-hitānukampinā bhavitabbaṃ. idaṃ mahārāja cakkavākassa tatiyaṃ aṅgaṃ gahetabbaṃ. bhāsitam-p' etaṃ mahārāja bhagavatā devātidevena cakkavākajātake:

77 yo na hanti, na ghāteti, na jināti, na jāpaye, ahiṃsā'
sabbabhūtesu veraṃ tassa na kenacīti.

78 bhante nāgasena, peṇāhikāya dve aṅgāni gahetabbānīti yaṃ vadesi, katamāni tāni dve aṅgāni gahetabbānīti. yathā mahārāja peṇāhikā sakapatimhi usūyāya chāpake na posayati, evam-eva kho mahārāja yoginā yogāvacarena sakamane kilese uppanne usūyāyitabbaṃ, satipaṭṭhānena sammāsaṃvarasusire pakkhipitvā manodvāre kāyagatā sati bhāvetabbā. idaṃ mahārāja peṇāhikāya paṭhamaṃ aṅgaṃ gahetabbaṃ. puna ca paraṃ mahārāja peṇāhikā pavane

Because it is content with them, its strength and color do not decline. Similarly, the yogi, an earnest disciple, should foster contentment with whatever is received. For a yogi, an earnest disciple, who is content with whatever is received does not decline in moral discipline, concentration, understanding, freedom, liberated knowing and seeing, and all good phenomenal states. This is the second attribute of the ruddy shelduck to be acquired. Also, just as the ruddy shelduck does not harm living beings, the yogi, an earnest disciple, should put down rod and knife, be modest and merciful, and tremble for the welfare of all living creatures. This is the third attribute of the ruddy shelduck to be acquired. For the Bhagavan, god above gods, said this in the *Ruddy Shelduck Jātaka*:

> No one has enmity toward one not harming all beings, 77
> who neither kills and pillages nor causes others to kill
> and pillage."

"Revered Nagasena, you say that there are two attributes 78
of the *peṇāhika* bird that must be acquired. What are the two attributes to be acquired?"

"Great king, when she is discontented with her mate, the *peṇāhika* bird does not feed her young. Similarly, the yogi, an earnest disciple, should be discontented when defilements arise in himself and, having filled in the gaps of proper restraint by means of the foundations of mindfulness, should install mindfulness of the body at the gates of the mind.[8] This is the first attribute of the *peṇāhika* bird to be acquired. Also, although by day the *peṇāhika* bird moves about her range in the woods, at night she joins a flock of birds for her own

divasaṃ gocaraṃ caritvā sāyaṃ pakkhigaṇaṃ upeti attano guttiyā, evam-eva kho mahārāja yoginā yogāvacarena ekānikena pavivekaṃ sevitabbaṃ saṃyojanaparimuttiyā, tatra ratiṃ alabhamānena upavādabhayaparirakkhanāya saṅghaṃ osaritvā saṅgharakkhitena vasitabbaṃ. idaṃ mahārāja peṇāhikāya dutiyaṃ aṅgaṃ gahetabbaṃ. bhāsitam-p' etaṃ mahārāja brahmunā sahampatinā bhagavato santike:

79 sevetha pantāni senāsanāni, careyya
saṃyojanavippamokkhā;
sace ratiṃ nādhigaccheyya tattha, saṅghe vase rakkhitatto
satīmā ti.

80 bhante nāgasena, gharakapoṭassa ekaṃ aṅgaṃ gahetabban-ti yaṃ vadesi, kataman-taṃ ekaṃ aṅgaṃ gahetabban-ti. yathā mahārāja gharakapoṭo paragehe vasamāno na tesaṃ kiñci bhaṇḍassa nimittaṃ gaṇhāti, majjhatto vasati saññābahulo, evam-eva kho mahārāja yoginā yogāvacarena parakulaṃ upagatena tasmiṃ kule itthīnaṃ vā purisānaṃ vā mañce vā pīṭhe vā vatthe vā alaṅkāre vā upabhoge vā paribhoge vā bhojanavikatisu vā na nimittaṃ gahetabbaṃ, majjhattena bhavitabbaṃ, samaṇasaññā paccupaṭṭhapetabbā. idaṃ mahārāja gharakapoṭassa ekaṃ aṅgaṃ gahetabbaṃ. bhāsitam-p' etaṃ mahārāja bhagavatā devātidevena cullanāradajātake: pavisitvā parakulaṃ pānesu bhojanesu vā mitaṃ khāde, mitaṃ bhuñje, na ca rūpe manaṃ kare ti.

protection. Similarly, the yogi, an earnest disciple, should be alone and practice solitude to free himself from the ties that bind. But if he does not find delight there, he should resort to the community for the sake of protecting himself from blame or danger, and should live with the protection of the community. This, great king, is the second attribute of the *peṇāhika* bird to be acquired. For Brahma Sahampati said this in the presence of the Bhagavan:

> One should repair to remote lodgings and practice for 79
> the sake of release from the ties that bind.
> But should one find no delight there, guarded and
> mindful, live in the community."

"Revered Nagasena, you say that there is one attribute of 80
the house pigeon that must be acquired. What is that one attribute to be acquired?"

"Great king, the house pigeon living in others' dwellings does not take any notice of their property; while keenly perceptive, it stays indifferent. Similarly, when the yogi, an earnest disciple, visits another's household he should take no notice of the women or men in that family, nor of the bed, chair, clothing, ornaments, items for enjoyment, possessions, or types of food. He should stay indifferent and call forth the perception of a renouncer. This, great king, is the one attribute of the house pigeon to be acquired. For this was said by the Bhagavan, god above gods, in the *Culla Nārada Jātaka*: 'Entering another's house for food or drink, be measured in chewing, be measured in eating, and do not attend to visible objects.'"

81 bhante nāgasena, ulūkassa dve aṅgāni gahetabbānīti yaṃ vadesi, katamāni tāni dve aṅgāni gahetabbānīti. yathā mahārāja ulūko kākehi paṭiviruddho rattiṃ kākasaṅghaṃ gantvā bahū pi kāke hanati, evam-eva kho mahārāja yoginā yogāvacarena aññāṇena paṭivirodho kātabbo, ekena raho nisīditvā aññāṇaṃ sampamadditabbaṃ, mūlato chinditabbaṃ. idaṃ mahārāja ulūkassa paṭhamaṃ aṅgaṃ gahetabbaṃ. puna ca paraṃ mahārāja ulūko supaṭisallīno hoti, evam-eva kho mahārāja yoginā yogāvacarena paṭisallāṇārāmena bhavitabbaṃ paṭisallāṇaratena. idaṃ mahārāja ulūkassa dutiyaṃ aṅgaṃ gahetabbaṃ. bhāsitaṃ-p' etaṃ mahārāja bhagavatā devātidevena saṃyuttanikāyavare: idha bhikkhave bhikkhu paṭisallāṇārāmo paṭisallāṇarato: idaṃ dukkhan-ti yathābhūtaṃ pajānāti, ayaṃ dukkhasamudayo ti yathābhūtaṃ pajānāti, ayaṃ dukkhanirodho ti yathābhūtaṃ pajānāti, ayaṃ dukkhanirodhagāminī paṭipadā ti yathābhūtaṃ pajānātīti.

82 bhante nāgasena, satapattassa ekaṃ aṅgaṃ gahetabban-ti yaṃ vadesi, kataman-taṃ ekaṃ aṅgaṃ gahetabban-ti. yathā mahārāja satapatto ravitvā paresaṃ khemaṃ vā bhayaṃ vā ācikkhati, evam-eva kho mahārāja yoginā yogāvacarena paresaṃ dhammaṃ desayamānena vinipātaṃ bhayato dassayitabbaṃ, nibbānaṃ khemato dassayitabbaṃ. idaṃ mahārāja satapattassa ekaṃ aṅgaṃ gahetabbaṃ. bhāsitaṃ-p' etaṃ mahārāja therena piṇḍolabhāradvājena: niraye bhayasantāsaṃ, nibbāne vipulaṃ sukhaṃ, ubhayān' etāni atthāni dassetabbāni yoginā ti.

"Revered Nagasena, you say that there are two attributes 81
of the owl that must be acquired. What are the two attributes to be acquired?"

"Great king, just as the owl is hostile to crows, going at night to a flock of crows and killing many of them, the yogi, an earnest disciple, should foster hostility to ignorance and, sitting alone in private, should utterly crush ignorance and cut it off at the root. This is the first attribute of the owl to be acquired. And just as the owl is very solitary, the yogi, an earnest ascetic, should be devoted to solitude and take delight in solitude. This is the second attribute of the owl to be acquired. For the Bhagavan, god above gods, said this in the excellent *Saṃyuttanikāya:* 'Monks, the monk who is devoted to solitude and delights in solitude grasps as it really is, that 'this is suffering,' grasps as it really is, that 'this is the origin of suffering,' grasps as it really is, that 'this is the stopping of suffering,' and grasps as it really is, that 'this is the path leading to the stopping of suffering.'"

"Revered Nagasena, you say that there is one attribute 82
of the sarus crane that must be acquired. What is that one attribute to be acquired?"

"Great king, just as the sarus crane cries out to announce peril or security to others, so too the yogi, an earnest disciple, when teaching the Dhamma to others, should reveal hell as perilous and reveal nibbana as security. This is the one attribute of the sarus crane to be acquired, great king. For Elder Pindola Bharadvaja said: 'The yogi should reveal both cases: fearful trembling in hell and broad happiness in nibbana.'"

83 bhante nāgasena, vaggulissa dve aṅgāni gahetabbānīti yaṃ vadesi, katamāni tāni dve aṅgāni gahetabbānīti. yathā mahārāja vagguli gehaṃ pavisitvā vicaritvā nikkhamati, na tattha palibuddhati, evam-eva kho mahārāja yoginā yogāvacarena gāmaṃ piṇḍāya pavisitvā sapadānaṃ vicaritvā paṭiladdhalābhena khippam-eva nikkhamitabbaṃ, na tattha palibuddhena bhavitabbaṃ. idaṃ mahārāja vaggulissa paṭhamaṃ aṅgaṃ gahetabbaṃ. puna ca paraṃ mahārāja vagguli paragehe vasamāno na tesaṃ parihāniṃ karoti, evam-eva kho mahārāja yoginā yogāvaca-rena kulāni upasaṅkamitvā atiyācanāya vā viññattibahulatāya vā kāyadosabahulatāya vā atibhāṇitāya vā samāna-sukha-dukkhatāya vā na tesaṃ koci vippaṭisāro karaṇīyo, na pi tesaṃ mūlakammaṃ parihāpetabbaṃ, sabbathā vaḍḍhi yeva icchitabbā. idaṃ mahārāja vaggulissa dutiyaṃ aṅgaṃ gahetabbaṃ. bhāsitam-p' etaṃ mahārāja bhagavatā devātidevena dīghanikāyavare lakkhaṇa-suttante:

84 saddhāya sīlena sutena buddhiyā cāgena dhammena
bahūhi sādhuhi dhanena dhaññena ca khettavatthunā
puttehi dārehi catuppadehi ca ñātīhi mittehi ca
bandhavehi balena vaṇṇena sukhena cūbhayaṃ
kathaṃ na hāyeyyuṃ pare ti icchati, atthassa-m-
iddhiñ-ca panābhikaṅkhatīti.

85 bhante nāgasena, jalūkāya ekaṃ aṅgaṃ gahetabban-ti yaṃ vadesi, kataman-taṃ ekaṃ aṅgaṃ gahetabban-ti. yathā mahārāja jalūkā yattha allīyati tatth' eva daḷhaṃ allīyitvā

"Revered Nagasena, you say that there are two attributes 83
of the bat that must be acquired. What are the two attributes to be acquired?"

"Great king, just a bat enters a house, flies around, comes back out, and does not linger there, the yogi, an earnest disciple, upon entering a village for alms, should move around it without skipping houses, and then depart quickly with what he has received without lingering there. This is the first attribute of the bat to be acquired. Further, the bat does not cause harm when living in others' homes. Similarly, when the yogi, an earnest disciple, visits households, he should not cause them to regret it by requesting too much, by a lot of hinting, by engaging in a lot of bodily faults, by talking too much, or by being indifferent to their pleasure or pain; nor should he harm their main business, but instead he should wish for their prosperity in all things. This is the second attribute of the bat to be acquired. For the Bhagavan, god above gods, said this in the *Lakkhaṇa Sutta* in the excellent *Dīghanikāya:*

He wishes and longs for others' success in their aims: 84
How may they not decline with respect to faith, morality, learning, wisdom, generosity, Dhamma, and many other good things; and wealth, grain, arable fields, children, wives, and four-legged animals, relatives, friends, kin, strength, beauty, and happiness?

"Revered Nagasena, you say that there is one attribute of 85
the leech that must be acquired. What is that one attribute to be acquired?"

"Great king, just as the leech attaches somewhere

ruhiraṃ pivati, evam-eva kho mahārāja yoginā yogāvacarena yasmiṃ ārammaṇe cittaṃ allīyati taṃ ārammaṇaṃ vaṇṇato ca saṇṭhānato ca disato ca okāsato ca paricchedato ca liṅgato ca nimittato ca daḷhaṃ patiṭṭhāpetvā ten' ev' ārammaṇena vimuttirasam-asecanakaṃ pātabbaṃ. idaṃ mahārāja jalūkāya ekaṃ aṅgaṃ gahetabbaṃ. bhāsitam-p' etaṃ mahārāja therena anuruddhena:

86 parisuddhena cittena ārammaṇe patiṭṭhāya tena cittena
pātabbaṃ vimuttirasam-asecanan-ti.

87 bhante nāgasena, sappassa tīṇi aṅgāni gahetabbānīti yaṃ vadesi, katamāni tāni tīṇi aṅgāni gahetabbānīti. yathā mahārāja sappo urena gacchati, evam-eva kho mahārāja yoginā yogāvacarena paññāya caritabbaṃ; paññāya caramānassa kho mahārāja yogino cittaṃ ñāye carati, vilakkhaṇaṃ vivajjeti salakkhaṇaṃ bhāveti. idaṃ mahārāja sappassa pathamaṃ aṅgaṃ gahetabbaṃ. puna ca paraṃ mahārāja sappo caramāno osadhaṃ parivajjento carati, evam-eva kho mahārāja yoginā yogāvacarena duccaritaṃ parivajjentena caritabbaṃ. idaṃ mahārāja sappassa dutiyaṃ aṅgaṃ gahetabbaṃ. puna ca paraṃ mahārāja sappo manusse disvā tappati socati cintayati, evam-eva kho mahārāja yoginā yogāvacarena kuvitakke vitakketvā aratiṃ uppādayitvā tappitabbaṃ socitabbaṃ cintayitabbaṃ: pamādena me divaso vītināmito, na so puna sakkā laddhun-ti. idaṃ

and then, fastening firmly to that spot, drinks blood, the yogi, an earnest disciple, should attach the mind to a meditation object and, fastening it firmly on that object with respect to its color, position, direction, appearance, delimitation, mark, and sign, drink the captivating extract of freedom by means of that very object. This, great king, is the one attribute of the leech to be acquired. For Elder Anuruddha said:

> With a pure mind, fasten on a meditation object— 86
> with this mind, drink the captivating extract of
> freedom."

"Revered Nagasena, you say that there are three attributes 87
of the serpent that must be acquired. What are the three attributes to be acquired?"

"Great king, just as the serpent travels along by its belly, the yogi, an earnest disciple, should travel along with understanding. For the yogi traveling with understanding moves into the right method, avoids the wrong characteristics, and cultivates the right characteristics.[9] This is the first attribute of the serpent to be acquired. And just as the moving serpent avoids healing herbs, the yogi, an earnest disciple, should travel avoiding bad conduct. This is the second attribute of the serpent to be acquired. And just as the serpent is tormented, suffering, and worried upon seeing humans, the yogi, an earnest disciple, when producing aversion and ruminating on bad thoughts, should be tormented, suffering, and worried: *Having spent the day in idleness, I can never get it back.* This, great king, is the third attribute of the serpent to be acquired. For this was said in the *Bhallāṭiya Jātaka*

mahārāja sappassa tatiyaṃ aṅgaṃ gahetabbaṃ. bhāsitam-p' etaṃ mahārāja bhallāṭiyajātake dvinnaṃ kinnarānaṃ:

88 yam-ekarattiṃ vippavasimha ludda, akāmakā,
aññamaññaṃ sarantā, tam-ekarattiṃ anutappamānā
socāma, sā ratti punan-na hessatīti.

89 bhante nāgasena, ajagarassa ekaṃ aṅgaṃ gahetabban-ti yaṃ vadesi, kataman-taṃ ekaṃ aṅgaṃ gahetabban-ti. yathā mahārāja ajagaro mahatimahākāyo bahū pi divase ūnūdaro dīnataro kucchipūraṃ āhāraṃ na labhati, aparipuṇṇo yeva yāvad-eva sarīrayāpanamattakena yāpeti, evam-eva kho mahārāja yogino yogāvacarassa bhikkhācariyapasutassa parapiṇḍam-upagatassa paradinnapāṭikaṅkhissa sayaṃ-gāhapaṭiviratassa dullabhaṃ udaraparipūraṃ āhāraṃ, api ca atthavasikena kulaputtena cattāro pañca ālope abhuñjitvā avasesaṃ udakena paripūretabbaṃ. idaṃ mahārāja ajagarassa ekaṃ aṅgaṃ gahetabbaṃ. bhāsitam-p' etaṃ mahārāja therena sāriputtena dhammasenāpatinā:

90 allaṃ sukkhañ-ca bhuñjanto na bāḷhaṃ suhito siyā,
ūnūdaro mitāhāro sato bhikkhu paribbaje. cattāro pañca

concerning two *kinnaras:*[10]

Hunter, there was one night we were away from 88
home. Though without our love, we remembered
each other; it is for that one night that we grieve,
sorrowing—
'That night will never come again.'"

"Revered Nagasena, you say that there is one attribute of 89
the goat-swallowing snake that must be acquired. What is that one attribute of the goat-swallowing snake that must be acquired?"

"Great king, a goat-swallowing snake with a huge and mighty body, made miserable for many days by an empty belly and not finding food to fill it, depleted, keeps going with what little still sustains the body. Similarly, the yogi, an earnest disciple, intent on making the alms round, approaching others for their alms, hankering for anything given by another but shrinking from just grabbing something for himself, may find it very hard to get food to fill the belly. Still, the sensible person from a good family eats four or five mouthfuls and then should fill up with water. This is the one attribute of the goat-swallowing snake to be acquired. For Elder Sariputta, General of the Dhamma, said:

Whether eating moist food or dry, one should not be 90
overfed.
The monk should wander mindful, with an empty
belly and measured food.

ālope abhutvā udakaṃ pive, alam-phāsuvihārāya pahitattassa bhikkhuno ti.

91 uddānaṃ: kesarī cakkavāko ca peṇāhi gharakapoṭako ulūko satapatto ca vaggulī ca jalūpikā sappo ajagaro c' eva, vaggo tena pavuccatīti.

pañcamo vaggo.

Let him abstain from the last four or five mouthfuls
and drink water.
Enough with living in comfort for the persevering
monk!"

In summary, with this, the chapter has described the 91
maned lion, the ruddy shelduck, the *peṇāhika* bird, the house
pigeon, the owl, the crane, the bat, the leech, the serpent,
and the goat-swallowing snake.

End of Part 5.

PART 6

92 bhante nāgasena, panthamakkaṭakassa ekaṃ aṅgaṃ gahetabban-ti yaṃ vadesi, katamaṃ-taṃ ekaṃ aṅgaṃ gahetabban-ti. yathā mahārāja panthamakkaṭako panthe makkaṭajālavitānaṃ katvā yadi tattha jālake laggati kimi vā makkhikā vā paṭaṅgo vā, taṃ gahetvā bhakkhayati, evam-eva kho mahārāja yoginā yogāvacarena chasu dvāresu satipaṭṭhānajālavitānaṃ katvā yadi tattha kilesamakkhikā bajjhanti, tatth' eva ghātetabbā. idaṃ mahārāja panthamakkaṭakassa ekaṃ aṅgaṃ gahetabbaṃ. bhāsitam-p' etaṃ mahārāja therena anuruddhena: cittaṃ niyame chasu dvāresu satipaṭṭhānavaruttame, kilesā tattha laggā ce hantabbā te vipassinā ti.

93 bhante nāgasena, thanasitadārakassa ekaṃ aṅgaṃ gahetabban-ti yaṃ vadesi, katamaṃ-taṃ ekaṃ aṅgaṃ gahetabban-ti. yathā mahārāja thanasitadārako sakatthe laggati, khīratthiko rodati, evam-eva kho mahārāja yoginā yogāvacarena sadatthe laggitabbaṃ, sabbattha dhammañāṇena bhavitabbaṃ, uddese paripucchāya sammappayoge paviveke garusaṃvāse kalyāṇamittasevane. idaṃ mahārāja thanasitadārakassa ekaṃ aṅgaṃ gahetabbaṃ. bhāsitam-p' etaṃ mahārāja bhagavatā devātidevena dīghanikāyavare parinibbānasuttante: iṅgha tumhe ānanda sadatthe ghaṭatha,

PART 6

"Revered Nagasena, you say that there is one attribute of the 92
road spider that must be acquired. What is that one attribute to be acquired?"

"Great king, the road spider builds a web across the road. If a worm, fly, or grasshopper gets stuck in the web, the spider grabs it and eats it. Similarly, the yogi, an earnest disciple, should build a web of the foundations of mindfulness across the six sensory doorways. If the flies of the defilements get caught in it, he should slay them right there. This is the one attribute of the road spider to be acquired, great king. For Elder Anuruddha also said: 'Restrain the mind at the six doorways with the highest and excellent foundations of mindfulness. The defilements caught there should be slain by the insight practitioner.'"

"Revered Nagasena, you say that there is one attribute of 93
the child at the breast that must be acquired. What is that one attribute to be acquired?"

"Great king, just as the child at the breast cries for milk and latches on for its own sake, the yogi, an earnest disciple, should latch on for his own sake, and should in all things—recitation, asking questions, proper practice, seclusion, living with the teacher, and associating with good friends—become one with the knowledge of the Dhamma. This, great king, is the one attribute of the child at the breast to be acquired. For the Bhagavan, god above gods, said this in the *Final Nibbana Sutta* in the excellent *Dīghanikāya:* 'You must strive for the highest good, Ananda, practice for the

sadatthe anuyuñjatha, sadatthe appamattā ātāpino pahitattā viharathāti.

94 bhante nāgasena, cittakadharakummassa ekaṃ aṅgaṃ gahetabban-ti yaṃ vadesi, kataman-taṃ ekaṃ aṅgaṃ gahetabban-ti. yathā mahārāja cittakadharakummo udakabhayā udakaṃ parivajjetvā vicarati, tāya ca pana udakaṃ parivajjanāya āyunā na parihāyati, evam eva kho mahārāja yoginā yogāvacarena pamāde bhayadassāvinā bhavitabbaṃ, appamāde guṇavisesadassāvinā, tāya ca pana bhayadassāvitāya na parihāyati sāmaññā, nibbānassa santike upeti. idaṃ mahārāja cittakadharakummassa ekaṃ aṅgaṃ gahetabbaṃ. bhāsitam-p' etaṃ mahārāja bhagavatā devātidevena dhammapade:

95 appamādarato bhikkhu, pamāde bhayadassivā, abhabbo
parihānāya nibbānass' eva santike ti.

96 bhante nāgasena, pavanassa pañca aṅgāni gahetabbānīti yaṃ vadesi, katamāni tāni pañca aṅgāni gahetabbānīti. yathā mahārāja pavanaṃ nāma asucijanaṃ paṭicchādeti, evam-eva kho mahārāja yoginā yogāvacarena paresaṃ aparaddhaṃ khalitaṃ paṭicchādetabbaṃ, na vivaritabbaṃ. idaṃ mahārāja pavanassa paṭhamaṃ aṅgaṃ gahetabbaṃ. puna ca paraṃ mahārāja pavanaṃ suññaṃ pacurajanehi, evam-eva kho mahārāja yoginā yogāvacarena rāga-dosa-moha-māna-diṭṭhijālehi sabbehi ca kilesehi suññena bhavitabbaṃ. idaṃ mahārāja pavanassa dutiyaṃ aṅgaṃ gahetabbaṃ. puna ca paraṃ mahārāja pavanaṃ vivittaṃ janasambādharahitaṃ, evam-eva kho mahārāja yoginā yogāvacarena pāpa-

highest good, and live diligent, ardent, and intent on the highest good!'"

"Revered Nagasena, you say that there is one attribute of 94
the painted tortoise that must be acquired. What is the one attribute to be acquired?"

"Great king, the painted tortoise, out of fear of the water, avoids water as it moves around. Yet even as it avoids water, it does not shorten its life. Similarly, the yogi, an earnest disciple, should become one who sees danger in laziness and sees special qualities in diligence. And precisely because he sees danger in this way, his renunciation does not decline and he draws near to nibbana. This, great king, is the one quality of the painted tortoise to be acquired. For the Bhagavan, god above gods, said this in the *Dhammapada:*

> The monk who delights in diligence and sees danger in 95
> laziness
> is incapable of declining. He draws near to nibbana
> itself."

"Revered Nagasena, you say that there are five attributes 96
of the forest that must be acquired. What are the five attributes to be acquired?"

"Great king, just as the forest conceals impure people, the yogi, an earnest disciple, should conceal and not expose the faults and weaknesses of others. This is the first attribute to be acquired. And just as the forest lacks large numbers of people, the yogi, an earnest disciple, should lack passion, hatred, delusion, pride, the web of wrong views, and all defilements. This is the second attribute of the forest to be acquired. And just as the forest stands apart from the crush

kehi akusalehi dhammehi anariyehi pavivittena bhavitabbaṃ. idaṃ mahārāja pavanassa tatiyaṃ aṅgaṃ gahetabbaṃ. puna ca paraṃ maharāja pavanaṃ santaṃ parisuddhaṃ, evam-eva kho mahārāja yoginā yogāvacarena santena parisuddhena bhavitabbaṃ, nibbutena pahīnamānena pahīnamakkhena bhavitabbaṃ. idaṃ mahārāja pavanassa catutthaṃ aṅgaṃ gahetabbaṃ. puna ca paraṃ mahārāja pavanaṃ ariyajana-saṃsevitaṃ, evam-eva kho mahārāja yoginā yogāvacarena ariyajanasaṃsevitena bhavitabbaṃ. idaṃ mahārāja pava-nassa pañcamaṃ aṅgaṃ gahetabbaṃ. bhāsitam-p' etaṃ mahārāja bhagavatā devātidevena saṃyuttanikāyavare: pavivittehi ariyehi pahitattehi jhāyihi niccaṃ āraddha-viriyehi paṇḍitehi sahā vase ti.

97 bhante nāgasena, rukkhassa tīṇi aṅgāni gahetabbānīti yaṃ vadesi, katamāni tāni tīṇi aṅgāni gahetabbānīti. yathā mahārāja rukkho nāma pupphaphaladharo, evam-eva kho mahārāja yoginā yogāvacarena vimuttipuppha-sāmañña-phala-dhārinā bhavitabbaṃ. idaṃ mahārāja rukkhassa paṭhamaṃ aṅgaṃ gahetabbaṃ. puna ca paraṃ mahārāja rukkho upagatānam-anuppaviṭṭhānaṃ janānaṃ chāyaṃ deti, evam-eva kho mahārāja yoginā yogāvacarena upagat-ānam-anuppaviṭṭhānaṃ puggalānaṃ āmisapaṭisanthārena vā dhammapaṭisanthārena vā paṭisantharitabbaṃ. idaṃ mahārāja rukkhassa dutiyaṃ aṅgaṃ gahetabbaṃ. puna ca paraṃ mahārāja rukkho chāyāvemattaṃ na karoti, evam-eva kho mahārāja yoginā yogāvacarena sabbasattesu vemattatā na kātabbā, cora-vadhaka-paccatthikesu pi attani pi sama-samā mettābhāvanā kātabbā: kin-ti ime sattā averā abyā-pajjhā anīghā sukhī attānaṃ parihareyyun-ti. idaṃ mahārāja rukkhassa tatiyaṃ aṅgaṃ gahetabbaṃ. bhāsitam-p' etaṃ

of the crowd, the yogi, an earnest disciple, should be aloof from wicked and bad phenomenal states and anything base. This is the third attribute of the forest to be acquired. And just as the forest is peaceful and holy, the yogi, an earnest disciple, should become peaceful, holy, serene, and free of pride and anger. This is the fourth attribute of the forest to be acquired. And finally, great king, just as the forest is associated with noble people, the yogi, an earnest disciple, should be associated with noble people. This is the fifth attribute of the forest to be acquired. For the Bhagavan, god above gods, said this in the excellent *Saṃyuttanikāya:* 'Keep company with secluded noble persons, resolute meditators, and learned ones, as their exertions are constantly aroused.'"

"Revered Nagasena, you say that there are three attributes 97
of a tree that must be acquired. What are the three attributes to be acquired?"

"Great king, just as a tree bears flowers and fruit, the yogi, an earnest disciple, should bear the flowers of freedom and the fruit of renunciation. This is the first attribute of a tree to be acquired. And just as a tree gives shade to people who approach seeking its shelter, the yogi, an earnest disciple, should be hospitable to people who approach seeking shelter, hospitable in providing supplies, and hospitable in providing the Dhamma. This is the second attribute of a tree to be acquired. Additionally, just as a tree makes no distinction in the shade it offers, the yogi, an earnest disciple, should make no distinction among all beings, cultivating loving-kindness equally to himself as to robbers, killers, and adversaries, thinking, *How may these beings be free of enmity, free of malice, free of injury, and happy, and come to care for*

mahārāja therena sāriputtena dhammasenāpatinā: vadhake devadattamhi, core aṅgulimālake, dhanapāle, rāhule c' eva, sabbattha samako munīti.

98 bhante nāgasena, meghassa pañca aṅgāni gahetabbānīti yaṃ vadesi, katamāni tāni pañca aṅgāni gahetabbānīti. yathā mahārāja megho uppannaṃ rajojallaṃ vūpasameti, evam-eva kho mahārāja yoginā yogāvacarena uppannaṃ kilesarajojallaṃ vūpasametabbaṃ. idaṃ mahārāja meghassa paṭhamaṃ aṅgaṃ gahetabbaṃ. puna ca paraṃ mahārāja megho paṭhaviyā uṇhaṃ nibbāpeti, evam-eva kho mahārāja yoginā yogāvacarena mettābhāvanāya sadevako loko nibbāpetabbo. idaṃ mahārāja meghassa dutiyaṃ aṅgaṃ gahetabbaṃ. puna ca paraṃ mahārāja megho sabbabījāni virūhāpeti, evam-eva kho mahārāja yoginā yogāvacarena sabbasattānaṃ saddhaṃ uppādetvā taṃ saddhābījaṃ tīsu sampattisu ropetabbaṃ, dibbamānusikāsu sampattisu yāva paramatthanibbānasukhasampatti. idaṃ mahārāja meghassa tatiyaṃ aṅgaṃ gahetabbaṃ. puna ca paraṃ mahārāja megho ututo samuṭṭhahitvā dharaṇitalaruhe tiṇa-rukkha-latā-gumba-osadhi-vanaspatayo parirakkhati, evam-eva kho mahārāja yoginā yogāvacarena yoniso manasikāraṃ nibbattetvā tena yoniso manasikārena samaṇadhammo parirakkhitabbo, yoniso manasikāramūlakā sabbe kusalā dhammā. idaṃ mahārāja meghassa catutthaṃ aṅgaṃ gahetabbaṃ. puna ca paraṃ mahārāja megho vassamāno nadī-taḷāka-pokkharaṇiyo kandara-padara-sara-sobbha-udapānāni ca paripūreti udakadhārāhi, evam-eva kho mahārāja yoginā yogā-

themselves? This is the third attribute of a tree to be acquired, great king. For Elder Sariputta, General of the Dhamma, said: 'The Sage was the same to all—the killer Devadatta, the robber Angulimala, Dhanapala, and even Rahula.'"[11]

"Revered Nagasena, you say that there are five attributes 98
of the rain cloud that must be acquired. What are the five attributes to be acquired?"

"Great king, just as the rain cloud dispels stirred-up dust and dirt, the yogi, an earnest disciple, should dispel the dust and dirt of the defilements when they get stirred up. This is the first attribute of the rain cloud to be acquired. And just as the rain cloud cools the heat of the earth, the yogi, an earnest disciple, should cool the world and its gods with loving-kindness meditation. This is the second attribute of the rain cloud to be acquired. And just as the rain cloud causes all seeds to germinate, the yogi, an earnest disciple, should generate faith in all beings and make the seed of faith grow into the three attainments, that is, the divine and human attainments and the attainment of the bliss of nibbana, the highest purpose. This is the third attribute of the rain cloud to be acquired. And just as the rain cloud appearing in the proper season protects the grasses, trees, vines, jungles, herbs, and forest trees growing on the surface of the earth, the yogi, an earnest disciple, should generate careful attention, and with careful attention protect the practice of the renouncer, since all good phenomenal states are rooted in careful attention. This is the fourth attribute of the rain cloud to be acquired. And just as the pouring rain cloud fills up rivers, reservoirs, lotus ponds, valleys, gullies, lakes, pools, and wells with rainfall, the yogi, an earnest disciple,

vacarena āgamapariyattiyā dhammamegham-abhivassayitvā adhigamakāmānaṃ mānasaṃ paripūrayitabbaṃ. idaṃ mahārāja meghassa pañcamaṃ aṅgaṃ gahetabbaṃ. bhāsitam-p' etaṃ mahārāja therena sāriputtena dhammasenāpatinā: bodhaneyyaṃ janaṃ disvā satasahasse pi yojane khaṇena upagantvāna bodheti taṃ mahāmunīti.

99 bhante nāgasena, maṇiratanassa tīṇi aṅgāni gahetabbānīti yaṃ vadesi, katamāni tāni tīṇi aṅgāni gahetabbānīti. yathā mahārāja maṇiratanaṃ ekantaparisuddhaṃ, evam-eva kho mahārāja yoginā yogāvacarena ekantaparisuddhājīvena bhavitabbaṃ. idaṃ mahārāja maṇiratanassa paṭhamaṃ aṅgaṃ gahetabbaṃ. puna ca paraṃ mahārāja maṇiratanaṃ na kenaci saddhiṃ missīyati, evam-eva kho mahārāja yoginā yogāvacarena pāpehi pāpasahāyehi saddhiṃ na missitabbaṃ. idaṃ mahārāja maṇiratanassa dutiyaṃ aṅgaṃ gahetabbaṃ. puna ca paraṃ mahārāja maṇiratanaṃ jātiratanehi yojīyati, evam-eva kho mahārāja yoginā yogāvacarena uttamavarajātimantehi saddhiṃ saṃvasitabbaṃ, paṭipannaka-phalaṭṭha-sekhaphalasamaṅgīhi sotāpanna-sakadāgāmi-anāgāmi-arahanta-tevijjachaḷabhiñña-samaṇa-maṇiratanehi saddhiṃ saṃvasitabbaṃ. idaṃ mahārāja maṇiratanassa tatiyaṃ aṅgaṃ gahetabbaṃ. bhāsitam-p' etaṃ mahārāja bhagavatā devātidevena suttanipāte:

should, through study of the texts, pour down the cloud of the Dhamma and fill up the minds of those longing for understanding. This, great king, is the fifth attribute of the rain cloud to be acquired. For Elder Sariputta, General of the Dhamma, said: 'Seeing people ready to be awakened even a hundred thousand leagues away, the Great Sage arrives in an instant and wakes them up.'"

"Revered Nagasena, you say that there are three attributes 99
of the jewel treasure that must be acquired. What are the three attributes to be acquired?"

"Great king, just as the jewel treasure is completely pure, the yogi, an earnest disciple, should become completely pure in livelihood. This is the first attribute of the jewel treasure to be acquired. And just as the jewel treasure is not mixed with anything, the yogi, an earnest disciple, should not mix with anything evil or with wicked companions. This is the second attribute of the jewel treasure to be acquired. And just as the jewel treasure is set with natural gemstones, the yogi, an earnest disciple, should live with those of high, excellent, and genuine birth and should live with those precious gems who are starting the path, those established in the attainment of the fruits, those possessing the fruits of the trainer, stream winners, once returners, nonreturners, arhats, those with the three knowledges, those with the six higher knowledges, and renouncers. This is the third attribute of the jewel treasure to be acquired, great king. For the Bhagavan, god above gods, said this in the *Suttanipāta:*

100 suddhā suddhehi saṃvāsaṃ kappayavho patissatā, tato
samaggā nipakā dukkhass' antaṃ karissathāti.

111 bhante nāgasena, māgavikassa cattāri aṅgāni gahetabbānīti yaṃ vadesi, katamāni tāni cattāri aṅgāni gahetabbānīti. yathā mahārāja māgaviko appamiddho hoti, evam-eva kho mahārāja yoginā yogāvacarena appamiddhena bhavitabbaṃ. idaṃ mahārāja māgavikassa paṭhamaṃ aṅgaṃ gahetabbaṃ. puna ca paraṃ mahārāja māgaviko migesu yeva cittaṃ upanibandhati, evam-eva kho mahārāja yoginā yogāvacarena ārammaṇesu yeva cittaṃ upanibandhitabbaṃ. idaṃ mahārāja māgavikassa dutiyaṃ aṅgaṃ gahetabbaṃ. puna ca paraṃ mahārāja māgaviko kālaṃ kammassa jānāti, evam-eva kho mahārāja yoginā yogāvacarena paṭisallāṇassa kālo jānitabbo: ayaṃ kālo paṭisallāṇassa, ayaṃ kālo nikkhamanāyāti. idaṃ mahārāja māgavikassa tatiyaṃ aṅgaṃ gahetabbaṃ. puna ca paraṃ mahārāja māgaviko migaṃ disvā hāsam abhijaneti: imaṃ lacchāmīti, evam-eva kho mahārāja yoginā yogāvacarena ārammaṇe abhiramitabbaṃ, hāsam abhijanetabbaṃ: uttariṃ visesam-adhigacchissāmīti. idaṃ mahārāja māgavikassa catutthaṃ aṅgaṃ gahetabbaṃ. bhāsitam-p' etaṃ mahārāja therena mogharājena: ārammaṇe labhitvāna pahitattena bhikkhunā bhiyyo hāso janetabbo: adhigacchissāmi uttarin-ti.

112 bhante nāgasena, bāḷisikassa dve aṅgāni gahetabbānīti yaṃ vadesi, katamāni tāni dve aṅgāni gahetabbānīti. yathā mahārāja bāḷisiko baḷisena macche uddharati, evam-eva kho

May the pure dwell with the pure, heedful of what is 100
permitted.
From this, harmonious and wise, let them make an
end of suffering."

"Revered Nagasena, you say that there are four attributes 111
of the hunter that must be acquired. What are the four attributes to be acquired?"

"Great king, just as the hunter is alert, the yogi, an earnest disciple, should become alert. This is the first attribute of the hunter to be acquired. Also, just as the hunter fastens his mind only on the deer, the yogi, an earnest disciple, should fasten his mind only on the objects of meditation. This is the second attribute of the hunter to be acquired. And just as the hunter knows the timing of his work, the yogi, an earnest disciple, should know the time for withdrawing in meditation: *This is the time to withdraw, this is the time to emerge.* This is the third attribute of the hunter to be acquired. And just as the hunter feels delight at seeing a deer, thinking, *I will get it,* so too the yogi, an earnest disciple, should take pleasure in his meditation object and feel delight: *I will attain a higher distinction.* This is the fourth attribute of the hunter to be acquired, great king. For Elder Mogharaja said: 'Having acquired a meditation object, a resolute monk should produce more delight: *I will acquire something further.*'"

"Revered Nagasena, you say that there are two attributes 112
of the fisherman that must be acquired. What are the two attributes to be acquired?"

mahārāja yoginā yogāvacarena ñāṇena uttariṃ sāmaññaphalāni uddharitabbāni. idaṃ mahārāja bāḷisikassa paṭhamaṃ aṅgaṃ gahetabbaṃ. puna ca paraṃ mahārāja bāḷisiko parittakaṃ vadhitvā vipulaṃ lābham-adhigacchati, evam-eva kho mahārāja yoginā yogāvacarena parittalokāmisamattaṃ pariccajitabbaṃ; lokāmisamattaṃ mahārāja pariccajitvā yogī yogāvacaro vipulaṃ sāmaññaphalam-adhigacchati. idaṃ mahārāja bāḷisikassa dutiyaṃ aṅgaṃ gahetabbaṃ. bhāsitam-p' etaṃ mahārāja therena rāhulena: suññatañ-cānimittañ-ca vimokkhañ-cāppaṇihitaṃ caturo phale chaḷ-abhiññā, cajitvā lokāmisaṃ, labhe ti.

113 bhante nāgasena, tacchakassa dve aṅgāni gahetabbānīti yaṃ vadesi, katamāni tāni dve aṅgāni gahetabbānīti. yathā mahārāja tacchako kāḷasuttaṃ anulometvā rukkhaṃ tacchati, evam-eva kho mahārāja yoginā yogāvacarena jinasāsanam-anulomayitvā sīlapaṭhaviyaṃ patiṭṭhahitvā saddhāhatthena paññāvāsiṃ gahetvā kilesā tacchetabbā. idaṃ mahārāja tacchakassa paṭhamaṃ aṅgaṃ gahetabbaṃ. puna ca paraṃ mahārāja tacchako pheggumaṃ apaharitvā sāram-ādiyati, evam-eva kho mahārāja yoginā yogāvacarena sassataṃ, ucchedaṃ, taṃ jīvaṃ taṃ sarīraṃ, aññaṃ jīvaṃ aññaṃ sarīraṃ, tad uttamaṃ aññad-uttamaṃ, akaṭam-abhabbaṃ, apurisakāraṃ, abrahmacariyavāsaṃ, sattavināsaṃ navasattapātubhāvaṃ, saṅkhārasassatabhāvaṃ, yo karoti so paṭisamvedeti, añño karoti añño paṭisaṃvedeti, kamma-

"Great king, just as the fisherman hauls up fish with a fish-hook, so too the yogi, an earnest disciple, should haul up the fruits of renunciation with knowledge. This is the first attribute of the fisherman to be acquired. And just as the fisherman kills tiny bait so that he can get a large haul, the yogi, an earnest disciple, should sacrifice the trivial things of this world. Having sacrificed worldly things, the yogi, an earnest disciple, hauls up the abundant fruit of renunciation. This is the second attribute of the fisherman to be acquired. For Elder Rahula said: 'Having abandoned the things of this world, one should acquire the four fruits, the six higher knowledges, and the empty, signless, and desireless deliverances.'"[12]

"Revered Nagasena, you say that there are two attributes 113
of the carpenter that must be acquired. What are the two attributes to be acquired?"

"Great king, just as the carpenter saws through a tree marked with a black string, the yogi, an earnest disciple, should, tracing the Victor's dispensation, stand firmly on the ground of morality, take up the sword of wisdom with the hand of faith, and saw through the defilements. This is the first attribute of the carpenter to be acquired. Additionally, just as the carpenter removes the softwood and takes up the hardwood, the yogi, an earnest disciple, should remove such notions as eternalism, annihilationism, that the soul and the body are the same, that the soul and the body are different, that this or another is the best, that nothing is produced and no one is capable, that there is no human agency, that the religious life is pointless, that beings are totally destroyed and brand new beings appear, that habitual patterns are

phaladassanā ca kiriyaphaladiṭṭhi ca, iti evarūpāni c' eva aññāni ca vivādapathāni apanetvā saṅkhārānaṃ sabhāvaṃ paramasuññataṃ nirīha-nijjīvataṃ accantaṃ suññataṃ ādiyitabbaṃ. idaṃ mahārāja tacchakassa dutiyaṃ aṅgaṃ gahetabbaṃ. bhāsitam-p' etaṃ mahārāja bhagavatā devātidevena suttanipāte:

114 kāraṇḍavaṃ niddhamatha, kasambuñ-cāpakassatha, tato
palāpe vāhetha, assamaṇe samaṇamānine.
niddhamitvāna pāpicche pāpāacāragocare suddhā
suddhehi saṃvāsaṃ kappayavho patissatā ti.

115 uddānaṃ: makkaṭo dārako kummo vanaṃ rukkho ca
pañcamo, megho maṇi māgaviko bāḷisī tacchakena cāti.

chaṭṭho vaggo.

eternal, that whoever acts then experiences the effects, that one person acts and another experiences the effects, that the fruits of neutral activity should be seen as the fruits of karma, and other such views and avenues of contention. He should take up instead highest emptiness as the true nature of the habitual patterns, and complete emptiness as without activity or life. This is the second attribute of the carpenter to be acquired, great king. For the Bhagavan, god above gods, said this is in the *Suttanipāta:*

Sweep away the chaff, throw away the rubbish, 114
and toss out the idle, the pretenders fancying that they
are renouncers!
With the evil wishers and the evildoers swept away,
the pure may dwell with the pure, heedful of what is
permitted."

In summary, this is the spider, the child, the tortoise, the 115
forest, and, fifthly, the tree. And then the cloud, the jewel, the hunter, the fisherman, and the carpenter.

End of Part 6.

PART 7

116 bhante nāgasena, kumbhassa ekaṃ aṅgaṃ gahetabban-ti yaṃ vadesi, kataman-taṃ ekaṃ aṅgaṃ gahetabban-ti. yathā mahārāja kumbho sampuṇṇo na saṇati, evam-eva kho mahārāja yoginā yogāvacarena āgame adhigame pariyattiyaṃ sāmaññe pāramiṃ patvā na saṇitabbaṃ, na tena māno karaṇīyo, na dappo dassetabbo, nihatamānena nihatadappena bhavitabbaṃ ujukena amukharena avikatthinā. idaṃ mahārāja kumbhassa ekaṃ aṅgaṃ gahetabbaṃ. bhāsitam-p' etaṃ mahārāja bhagavatā devātidevena suttanipāte:

117 yad-ūnakaṃ taṃ saṇati, yaṃ pūraṃ santam eva taṃ;
rittakumbhūpamo bālo, rahado pūrova paṇḍito ti.

118 bhante nāgasena, kālāyasassa dve aṅgāni gahetabbānīti yaṃ vadesi, katamāni tāni dve aṅgāni gahetabbānīti. yathā mahārāja kāḷāyaso suthitova vahati, evam-eva kho mahārāja yogino yogāvacarassa mānasaṃ yoniso manasikāre appitaṃ vahati. idaṃ mahārāja kāḷāyasassa paṭhamaṃ aṅgaṃ gahetabbaṃ. puna ca paraṃ mahārāja kāḷāyaso sakiṃ pītaṃ udakaṃ na vamati, evam eva kho mahārāja yoginā yogāvacarena yo sakiṃ upanno pasādo na puna so vamitabbo: uḷāro so bhagavā sammāsambuddho, svākkhāto dhammo,

PART 7

"Revered Nagasena, you say that there is one attribute of the 116
water pot that must be acquired. What is that one attribute to be acquired?"

"Great king, just as a full water pot does not make a sound, the yogi, an earnest disciple, should not make a sound, having reached perfection in renunciation and mastery in grasping the texts. He should take no pride in this and display no arrogance. Striking down pride and arrogance, one should be honest but not noisy or boasting. This, great king, is the one attribute of the water pot to be acquired. For the Bhagavan, god above gods, said this in the *Suttanipāta:*

What is empty makes a sound, what is full is only quiet; 117
a fool is like an empty water pot, while the learned person is a full lake."

"Revered Nagasena, you say that there are two attributes 118
of black iron that must be acquired. What are the two attributes to be acquired?"

"Great king, just as even well-wrought iron carries weight, the yogi, an earnest disciple, concentrated on careful attention, carries weight. This is the first attribute of black iron to be acquired. And also, just as iron does not expel water once it has taken it in, once serene confidence that 'the Perfectly Awakened Buddha is eminent, the Dhamma is well taught, and the community is highly accomplished' has arisen, the yogi, an earnest disciple, should not expel it. And once the

supaṭipanno saṅgho ti; rūpaṃ aniccaṃ, vedanā aniccā, saññā aniccā, saṅkhārā aniccā, viññāṇaṃ aniccan-ti yaṃ sakiṃ uppannaṃ ñāṇaṃ na puna taṃ vamitabbaṃ. idaṃ mahārāja kāḷāyasassa dutiyaṃ aṅgaṃ gahetabbaṃ. bhāsitam-p' etaṃ mahārāja bhagavatā devātidevena: dassanamhi parisodhito naro ariyadhamme niyato visesagū na pavedhati anekabhāgaso, sabbato ca mukhabhāvānam-eva so ti.

119 bhante nāgasena, chattassa tīṇi aṅgāni gahetabbānīti yaṃ vadesi, katamāni tāni tīṇi aṅgāni gahetabbānīti. yathā mahārāja chattaṃ uparimuddhani carati, evam-eva kho mahārāja yoginā yogāvacarena kilesānaṃ uparimuddhani-carena bhavitabbaṃ. idaṃ mahārāja chattassa paṭhamaṃ aṅgaṃ gahetabbaṃ. puna ca paraṃ mahārāja chattaṃ muddhanupatthambhaṃ hoti, evam-eva kho mahārāja yoginā yogāvacarena yoniso manasikārupatthambhena bhavitabbaṃ. idaṃ mahārāja chattassa dutiyaṃ aṅgaṃ gahetabbaṃ. puna ca paraṃ mahārāja chattaṃ vātātapameghavuṭṭhiyo paṭihanti, evam-eva kho mahārāja yoginā yogāvacarena nānāvidhadiṭṭhi-puthusamaṇabrāhmaṇānaṃ matavāta-tividhaggisantāpa-kilesavuṭṭhiyo paṭihantabbā. idaṃ mahārāja chattassa tatiyaṃ aṅgaṃ gahetabbaṃ. bhāsitam-p' etaṃ mahārāja therena sāriputtena dhammasenāpatinā:

knowledge that 'form is impermanent, feeling is impermanent, perception is impermanent, habitual patterns are impermanent, and awareness is impermanent' has arisen, one should not expel it. This is the second attribute of black iron to be acquired, great king. For the Bhagavan, god above gods, said: 'There are few matters in which a person purified in view, restrained in the noble Dhamma, and reaching distinction trembles, and he arrives at the foremost state in every respect.'"

"Revered Nagasena, you say that there are three attributes 119
of an umbrella that must be acquired. What are the three attributes to be acquired?"

"Great king, just as an umbrella travels along above one's head, the yogi, an earnest disciple, should have conduct that rises above the defilements. This is the first attribute of an umbrella to be acquired. And just as an umbrella is supported over the head, so too the yogi, an earnest disciple, should be supported by careful attention. This is the second attribute of an umbrella to be acquired. And just as an umbrella wards off wind, heat, and cloudbursts, the yogi, an earnest disciple, should ward off the winds of opinion of the many renouncers and Brahmans with their various types of views, the heat of the threefold fire,* and the rain of the defilements. This, great king, is the third attribute of the umbrella to be acquired. For Elder Sariputta, General of the Dhamma, said:

* Greed, hatred, and delusion.

120 yathā pi chattaṃ vipulaṃ acchiddaṃ thirasaṃhataṃ
vātātapaṃ nivāreti, mahatī devavuṭṭhiyo, tath' eva
buddhaputto pi sīlacchattadharo suci kilesavuṭṭhiṃ
vāreti santāpatividhaggayo ti.

121 bhante nāgasena, khettassa tīṇi aṅgāni gahetabbānīti yaṃ vadesi, katamāni tāni tīṇi aṅgāni gahetabbānīti. yathā mahārāja khettaṃ mātikāsampannaṃ hoti, evam-eva kho mahārāja yoginā yogāvacarena sucaritavattapaṭivatta-mātikāsampannena bhavitabbaṃ. idaṃ mahārāja khettassa paṭhamaṃ aṅgaṃ gahetabbaṃ. puna ca paraṃ mahārāja khettaṃ mariyādāsampannaṃ hoti, tāya ca mariyādāya udakaṃ rakkhitvā dhaññaṃ paripācenti, evam-eva kho mahārāja yoginā yogāvacarena sīla-hiri-mariyādāsampannena bhavitabbaṃ, tāya ca sīla-hiri-mariyādāya sāmaññaṃ rakkhitvā cattāri sāmaññaphalāni gahetabbāni. idaṃ mahārāja khettassa dutiyaṃ aṅgaṃ gahetabbaṃ. puna ca paraṃ mahārāja khettaṃ uṭṭhānasampannaṃ hoti kassakassa hāsajanakaṃ, appam-pi bījaṃ vuttaṃ bahu hoti, bahu vuttaṃ bahutaraṃ hoti, evam-eva kho mahārāja yoginā yogāvacarena uṭṭhānasampannena vipulaphaladāyinā bhavitabbaṃ, dāyakānaṃ hāsajanakena bhavitabbaṃ, yathā appaṃ dinnaṃ bahu hoti, bahu dinnaṃ bahutaraṃ hoti. idaṃ mahārāja khettassa tatiyaṃ aṅgaṃ gahetabbaṃ.

Just as an umbrella, broad, untorn, and durably made, 120
wards off wind, heat, and the great rains sent by
the gods,
one in the Buddha's lineage, pure, and carrying the
umbrella of moral discipline, wards off the rain
of the defilements and the scorching heat of the
three fires."

"Revered Nagasena, you say that there are three attributes 121
of a field that must be acquired. What are the three attributes
to be acquired?"

"Great king, just as a field possesses irrigation canals, the yogi, an earnest disciple, should possess the canals that are the observances of proper behavior. This is the first attribute of the field to be acquired. And just as a field has embankments, that is, embankments that secure water so that the grain can ripen, the yogi, an earnest disciple, should possess the embankments of moral discipline and shame, since the embankments of moral discipline and shame secure renunciation so that he may grasp renunciation's four fruits.* This is the second attribute of the field to be acquired. And finally, when a field is productive it generates delight in the farmer that from sowing even a little seed there is so much, and from sowing a lot there is even more. Similarly, the yogi, an earnest disciple, should be productive and yield abundant fruit and so generate delight in his benefactors that from giving even a little there is so much, and from giving a lot there is even more. This is the third attribute of the field to be acquired,

* Stream entry, once return, nonreturn, and arhatship.

bhāsitam-p' etaṃ mahārāja therena upālinā vinayadharena: khettūpamena bhavitabbaṃ uṭṭhānavipuladāyinā; esa khettavaro nāma yo dadāti vipulaṃ phalan-ti.

122 bhante nāgasena, agadassa dve aṅgāni gahetabbānīti yaṃ vadesi, katamāni tāni dve aṅgāni gahetabbānīti. yathā mahārāja agade kimī na saṇṭhahanti, evam-eva kho mahārāja yoginā yogāvacarena mānase kilesā na saṇṭhapetabbā. idaṃ mahārāja agadassa paṭhamaṃ aṅgaṃ gahetabbaṃ. puna ca paraṃ mahārāja agado daṭṭha-phuṭṭha-diṭṭha-asita-pīta-khāyita-sāyitaṃ sabbaṃ visaṃ paṭihanti, evam-eva kho mahārāja yoginā yogāvacarena rāga-dosa-moha-māna-diṭṭhi-visaṃ sabbaṃ paṭihanitabbaṃ. idaṃ mahārāja agadassa dutiyaṃ aṅgaṃ gahetabbaṃ. bhāsitam-p' etaṃ mahārāja bhagavatā devātidevena: saṅkhārānaṃ sabhāvatthaṃ daṭṭhukāmena yoginā agadeneva hotabbaṃ kilesavisanāsane ti.

123 bhante nāgasena, bhojanassa tīṇi aṅgāni gahetabbānīti yaṃ vadesi, katamāni tāni tīṇi aṅgāni gahetabbānīti. yathā mahārāja bhojanaṃ sabbasattānaṃ upatthambho, evam-eva kho mahārāja yoginā yogāvacarena sabbasattānaṃ maggupatthambhena bhavitabbaṃ. idaṃ mahārāja bhojanassa paṭhamaṃ aṅgaṃ gahetabbaṃ. puna ca paraṃ mahārāja bhojanaṃ sattānaṃ balaṃ vaḍḍheti, evam-eva kho mahārāja yoginā yogāvacarena puññavaḍḍhiyā vaḍḍhitabbaṃ. idaṃ mahārāja bhojanassa dutiyaṃ aṅgaṃ gahetabbaṃ. puna ca paraṃ mahārāja bhojanaṃ sabbasattānaṃ abhipatthitaṃ, evam-eva kho mahārāja yoginā yogāvacarena sabbalokābhipatthitena bhavitabbaṃ. idaṃ mahārāja bhojanassa tatiyaṃ aṅgaṃ gahetabbaṃ. bhāsitam-p' etaṃ mahārāja therena

great king. For Elder Upali, master of the *vinaya*, said: 'One should be like a field yielding abundant produce, for the best fields give plentiful fruit.'"

"Revered Nagasena, you say that there are two attributes 122
of an antidote that must be acquired. What are the two attributes to be acquired?"

"Great king, just as bugs do not stay in an antidote, the yogi, an earnest disciple, does not permit defilements to stay in the mind. This is the first attribute of an antidote to be acquired. Additionally, as an antidote staves off every poison, whether from a bite, contact, poisoned food, or anything drunk, chewed, or tasted, the yogi, an earnest disciple, should ward off every poison, whether that of passion, hate, delusion, pride, or wrong view. For the Bhagavan, god above gods, said: 'The yogi wishing to see into the nature and purpose of the habitual patterns should become like an antidote in obliterating the poison of the defilements.'"

"Revered Nagasena, you say that there are three attributes 123
of food that must be acquired. What are the three attributes of food to be acquired?"

"Great king, just as food is the sustenance of all creatures, the yogi, an earnest disciple, should become the sustenance of all creatures with respect to the path. This is the first attribute of food to be acquired. And just as food increases creatures' strength, the yogi, an earnest disciple, should increase in the growth of merit. This is the second attribute of food to be acquired. And finally, just as food is sought by all creatures, the yogi, an earnest disciple, should become sought by the whole world. This is the third attribute of food to be acquired, great king. For Elder Moggallana the Great said:

mahāmoggallānena: saṃyamena niyamena sīlena paṭipattiyā patthitena bhavitabbaṃ sabbalokassa yoginā ti.

124 bhante nāgasena, issatthassa cattāri aṅgāni gahetabbānīti yaṃ vadesi, katamāni tāni cattāri aṅgāni gahetabbānīti. yathā mahārāja issattho sare pātayanto ubho pāde paṭhaviyaṃ daḷhaṃ patiṭṭhāpeti, jaṇṇū avekallaṃ karoti, sarakalāpaṃ kaṭisandhimhi ṭhapeti, kāyaṃ upatthaddhaṃ karoti, dve hatthe sandhiṭṭhānaṃ āropeti, muṭṭhiṃ pīḷayati, aṅguliyo nirantaraṃ karoti, gīvaṃ paggaṇhāti, cakkhūni mukhañ-ca pidahati, nimittaṃ ujuṃ karoti, hāsam uppādeti: vijjhissāmīti; evam-eva kho mahārāja yoginā yogāvacarena sīlapaṭhaviyaṃ viriyapāde patiṭṭhāpetabbaṃ, khantisoraccaṃ avekallaṃ kātabbaṃ, saṃvare cittaṃ ṭhapetabbaṃ, saṃyamaniyame attā upanetabbo, icchāmucchā pīḷayitabbā, yoniso manasikāre cittaṃ nirantaraṃ kātabbaṃ, viriyaṃ paggahetabbaṃ, cha dvārā pidahitabbā, sati upaṭṭhāpetabbā, hāsam-uppādetabbaṃ: sabbakilese ñāṇanārācena vijjhissāmīti. idaṃ mahārāja issatthassa paṭhamaṃ aṅgaṃ gahetabbaṃ. puna ca paraṃ mahārāja issattho āḷakaṃ pariharati vaṅka-jimha-kuṭila-nārācassa ujukaraṇāya, evam-eva kho mahārāja yoginā yogāvacarena imasmiṃ kāye satipaṭṭhāna-āḷakaṃ pariharitabbaṃ vaṅka-jimha-kuṭila-cittassa ujukaraṇāya. idaṃ mahārāja issatthassa dutiyaṃ aṅgaṃ gahetabbaṃ.

125 puna ca paraṃ mahārāja issattho lakkhe upāseti, evam-eva kho mahārāja yoginā yogāvacarena imasmiṃ kāye upāsitabbaṃ; kathaṃ mahārāja yoginā yogāvacarena imasmiṃ kāye upāsitabbaṃ; aniccato upāsitabbaṃ, dukkhato upāsi-

'May the yogi with self-control, restraint, moral discipline, and practice come to be sought by the whole world.'"

"Revered Nagasena, you say that there are four attributes 124
of the archer that must be acquired. What are the four attributes to be acquired?"

"Great king, with both feet planted firmly on the ground, the archer lets arrows fly. He straightens out the knees, fixes the quiver to his waist, holds the body rigid, puts both hands to the place of junction, clenches his fist, tightens the gaps between the fingers, stretches out the string to his neck, closes his mouth and eyes, takes aim straight at the mark, and feels joy: *I will pierce it.* Similarly, the yogi, an earnest disciple, should plant both feet of exertion on the ground of moral discipline, straighten out forbearance and gentleness, fix the mind on restraint, bring himself under control and restraint, clench his urges and desires, tighten the gaps in the mind with respect to careful attention, stretch out exertion, close the six doorways, engage mindfulness, and feel joy: *I will pierce all the defilements with the shaft of knowledge.* This is the first attribute of the archer to be acquired. Moreover, just as the archer carries an arrow straightener for straightening bent, curved, or crooked arrows, the yogi, an earnest disciple, should carry the arrow straightener consisting of the foundations of mindfulness directed to the body for straightening bent, curved, or crooked thoughts. This is the second attribute of the archer to be acquired.

"In addition, great king, just as the archer tracks a target, 125
the yogi, an earnest disciple, should track this body. But how should the yogi, an earnest disciple, track this body? He should track it with respect to its impermanence, with

tabbaṃ, anattato upāsitabbaṃ, rogato-pe-gaṇḍato sallato aghato ābādhato parato palokato ītito upaddavato bhayato upasaggato calato pabhaṅguto addhuvato attāṇato aleṇato asaraṇato asaraṇībhūtato rittato suññato ādīnavato asārato aghamūlato vadhakato sāsavato saṅkhatato jātidhammato jarādhammato byādhidhammato maraṇadhammato sokadhammato paridevadhammato upāyāsadhammato saṅkilesadhammato, evaṃ kho mahārāja yoginā yogāvacarena imasmiṃ kāye upāsitabbaṃ. idaṃ mahārāja issatthassa tatiyaṃ aṅgaṃ gahetabbaṃ. puna ca paraṃ mahārāja issattho sāyapātaṃ upāsati, evam-eva kho mahārāja yoginā yogāvacarena sāyapātaṃ ārammaṇe upāsitabbaṃ. idaṃ mahārāja issatthassa catutthaṃ aṅgaṃ gahetabbaṃ. bhāsitam-p' etaṃ mahārāja therena sāriputtena dhammasenāpa tinā:

126 yathā issatthako nāma sāyapātaṃ upāsati. upāsanaṃ na
riñcanto labhate bhattavetanaṃ:
tath' eva buddhaputto pi karoti kāyupāsanaṃ,
kāyupāsanaṃ na riñcanto arahattam-adhigacchatīti.
issatthassa pañhaṃ pañcamaṃ.

127 iti chasu kaṇḍesu bāvīsativaggapatimaṇḍitesu dvāsaṭṭhiadhikā dvesatā imasmiṃ potthake āgatā milindapañhā samattā. anāgatā ca pana dvācattālīsā honti. agatā ca anāgatā

respect to its suffering, with respect to its lack of self, and with respect to its diseases, boils, splinters, aches, illnesses, and further effects. He should track the body with respect to its decay, fragility, accidents, perils, misfortunes, mobility, fracturing, transience, vulnerability, lack of shelter, and lack of refuge. He should track its hollowness, vainness, emptiness, disadvantages, and insubstantiality, noting that it is the source of pain, the cause of destruction, and full of corruptions, and how it is conditioned, subject to birth, old age, illness, and death, and subject to sorrow, grieving, trouble, and the defilements. This is the third attribute of the archer to be acquired. And finally, just as the archer tracks the target morning and evening, the yogi, an earnest disciple, should track the meditation subject morning and evening. This is the fourth attribute of the archer to be acquired, great king. For Elder Sariputta, General of the Dhamma, said:

> Just as the archer shoots morning and night, 126
> since it is by never abandoning archery that he earns
> his wages and his keep,
> a descendant of the Buddha should practice tracking
> the body,
> as it is by never failing to track the body that one
> arrives at arhatship."

This is the fifth question of the archer.

And thus the 262 questions of Milinda, handed down in 127
this book in six chapters adorned with twenty-two parts, have come to an end. But forty-two have not been handed down.[13] Combining all together what has been handed down

ca sabbā samodhānetvā catuhi adhikā tisatapañhā honti. sabbāva milindapañhā ti saṅkhaṃ gacchanti.

128 rañño ca therassa ca pucchāvissajjanāvasāne caturāsītisatasahassa-yojana-bahalā udakapariyantaṃ katvā ayaṃ mahāpaṭhavī chadhā pakampittha, vijjullatā niccharimsu, devatā dibbapupphavassaṃ pavassiṃsu, mahābrahmā sādhukāram-adāsi, mahāsamuddakucchiyaṃ meghatthanitanigghoso viya mahāghoso ahosi. iti so milindo rājā ca orodhagaṇā ca sirasā añjalim-paṇāmetvā vandiṃsu.

129 milindo rājā ativiya pamuditahadayo sumathitamānahadayo buddhasāsane sāramatino ratanattaye sunikkaṅkho niggumbo nitthaddho hutvā therassa guṇesu pabbajjāsu paṭipadā-iriyāpathesu ca ativiya pasanno vissattho nirālayo nihatamānadappo uddhaṭadāṭho viya bhujagindo evam-āha: sādhu sādhu bhante nāgasena, buddhavisayo pañho tayā vissajjito; imasmiṃ buddhasāsane ṭhapetvā dhammasenāpati-sāriputtattheraṃ añño tayā sadiso pañhavissajjane natthi. khamatha me bhante nāgasena mama accayaṃ. upāsakaṃ maṃ bhante nāgasena dhāretha ajjatagge pāṇupetaṃ saraṇaṃ gatan-ti.

130 tadā rājā balakāyehi nāgasenatheraṃ payirupāsitvā milindaṃ nāma vihāraṃ kāretvā therassa niyyādetvā catuhi paccayehi koṭisatehi khīṇāsavehi bhikkhūhi nāgasena-

and what has not been handed down, there are 304 questions. All of it is considered the *Questions of Milinda.*

At the conclusion of the questions and answers of the king and the elder, this great earth, measuring eighty-four hundred thousand leagues up to the water, quaked six times. Lightning struck, the gods rained down a shower of celestial flowers, and Great Brahma gave a cry of "Well done!" And in the deep recesses of the ocean there was a great roar like the thundering of a storm cloud. At this, King Milinda and the hosts of palace women joined their hands at their foreheads and paid homage. 128

The pride that had been in his heart was routed, and King Milinda's heart was now extremely joyous. He grasped the essence of the Buddha's dispensation and became clear and completely free of doubt and obstinacy with respect to the Three Jewels. Wholly won over to the elder's special qualities and his monastic practices and deportment, he was confident and free of desires. His pride and arrogance humbled, he was like the king of snakes with fangs removed. He exclaimed, "Well done, well done, Revered Nagasena! You have answered questions that lie in the scope of the Buddha. No one else in this dispensation of the Buddha is your equal in answering questions, save Elder Sariputta, General of the Dhamma. Please pardon my transgression, revered Nagasena. Receive me as a layman, Nagasena, taking refuge from this day forward for the rest of my life." 129

Then the king and his troops honored Elder Nagasena. He built a monastery named Milinda and dedicated it to the elder. With the hundreds of millions of arhats, he worshiped Elder Nagasena with the four requisites. And later, won over 130

theraṃ paricari. puna pi therassa paññāya pasīditvā puttassa rajjaṃ niyyādetvā agārasmā anagāriyaṃ pabbajitvā vipassanaṃ vaḍḍhetvā arahattaṃ pāpuṇīti. tena vuttaṃ:

131 paññā pasatthā lokasmiṃ, kathā saddhammaṭṭhitiyā,
paññāya vimatiṃ hantvā santiṃ papponti paṇḍitā.
yasmiṃ khandhe ṭhitā paññā, sati yattha anūnakā,
pūjāvisesassa dharo aggo sova anuttaro.
tasmā hi paṇḍito poso sampassaṃ attham-attano
paññāvantābhipūjeyya, cetiyaṃ viya pūjiyan-ti.

132 milindassa c' eva nāgasenatherassa ca pañhā-veyyākaraṇa-pakaraṇaṃ samattaṃ.

by the elder's understanding, he bequeathed the kingdom to his son, went forth from home into homelessness, developed insight, and attained arhatship. Because of this, it is said:

Understanding is praised in the world, and preaching 131
continues the true Dhamma.
Slaying doubt with understanding, the learned
achieve peace.
One in whom understanding is firmly collected
and whose mindfulness is complete deserves
veneration, foremost, as though supreme.
Therefore, the learned person perceiving their
own aims should reverence the wise as though
worshiping at a shrine.

The composition on the questions and explanations of 132
Milinda and the elder Nagasena is complete.

ABBREVIATIONS

C	Chaṭṭha Saṅgāyana edition
Miln	*Milindapañha*
S	Sri Lanka Tripitaka Project edition, *Milindapanha*, 1994
T	Trenckner edition, *The Milindapanho*, 1890
Ṭīkā	*Milindaṭīkā*

NOTES TO THE TEXT

Chapter 1

1 manta] C; samanta T, S.
2 pajjhāyanto] C, S; pajihāyanto T.
3 vacanena] C, S; vanena T.

Chapter 2

1 andhakāre gehe] S; andhakāro gehe T; andhakāragehe C.
2 vayappattā] C, S; vavappattā T.
3 sabbā sati] S, C; sabbaṃ satiṃ T.

Chapter 3
Ram Horn Dilemmas I

1 uttānīkato] C; tānīkato T; uttanīkato S.
2 patanapaṭibaddhāni] C, S; patanapaṭibaddhām T.
3 vibādhati] S, C; vibhādati T.
4 lañjake] S; lañcake T; lañchake C.
5 byādhitasseva] C, S; āitasseva T.
6 ubhatokoṭiko] C, S; abhatokoṭiko T.
7 pavattena] C, S; pattena T.
8 jhāpenti] C; jāpenti T, S.
9 jāno] C; jānaṃ T, S.
10 abhissandamānadhātuko kucchi] S; abhisannadhātu kucchi T, C.
11 sañcuṇṇitaṭṭhimaṃsadhamanichinnaparigatto] S; saṃcuṇṇitaṭṭhimaṃsadhamanimajjāparigatto C; sañcuṇṇitaṭṭhimaṃsadhamanimajjaparikatto T.
12 yakkho] C; yakko T, S.
13 bodhisatteneva] C, S; bodhisatto n'eva T.
14 saṇho added by C, lacking in T and S.
15 tena] C; te T, S.
16 vibhūtaṃ] C, S; vibhūsaṃ T.
17 nekkhammaṃ nikkhamitvā] C, S; nekkhamnikkhamitvā T.
18 uttarimanussadhammam] C; uttariṃ manussadhammā T, S.
19 bodhessati] C; sodhessati T, S.
20 kilesachātajjhattā] C; kilesacchātajjhattā S; kilesakilantajjhattā T.

21 mahārajakkhā] C, S; mahārājakkhā T.
22 bhūtahacco] bhūnahu C; bhunahano S.

Chapter 4

1 santasukhasamāpatti] C, S; santasukhasamātti T.

Chapter 5
Ram Horn Dilemmas II

1 anavajjabhogī] C, S; anavajjhogī T.

Chapter 6

1 sabbattha pasākhe] S; sabbaṭṭhakasākhe T, C.

NOTES TO THE TRANSLATION

1 Former Connections

1 *Abhidhamma, vinaya,* and *suttas* are three genres and collections of Buddhist scriptures; see Glossary.

2 Uttarakuru is a mythical land of plenty to the north, with its capital at Alakamanda, a divine city ruled by Kubera, god of wealth.

3 Moral discipline can refer to specific moral precepts or morality in general. See *sīla* in Glossary.

4 In Buddhist stories people often make an aspiration about what they will be in a future life, on the strength of a noble, true, or good act of karma.

5 The elder Tissa was predicted by the Buddha to teach the *Kathāvatthu* (an *abhidhamma* text) 218 years after the Buddha's final nibbana, a prediction that extends canonical status to the text.

6 *Nīti* here is likely political philosophy or policy. Some scholars have taken it here to mean logic and possibly Nyāya philosophy, although the *Milindapañha* may precede this school of logic (for a discussion of the issues, see Schumann 2019; Ooi, Schumann, Sirisawad 2023).

7 "Stopping" (*nirodha*), as explained later in the text, is ceasing to crave pleasure and ceasing the suffering that follows such craving.

8 History (*itihāsa*) is the *Mahābhārata,* which is often referred to as the fifth Veda.

9 Phenomenal states (*dhamma*) are the constituents of experience analyzed by the *abhidhamma* texts. See this technical meaning of *dhamma* in Glossary.

10 The clusters are the five groupings of all of the phenomena in human experience (form, feeling, perception, habitual patterns, and awareness). See *khandhas* in Glossary.

11 The bases of sensory experience are the six sensory organs, their objects, and the operations between them. See *āyatana* in Glossary.

12 This epiphany is uttered upon grasping fully the Four Noble Truths (as in the *Turning of the Wheel of the Dhamma Sutta, Saṁyuttanikāya* 5.423, and elsewhere).

13 Insight meditation is the realization through advanced meditation

that all things are impermanent, suffering, and without essence. See *vipassanā* in Glossary.

14 Stream entry is an advanced attainment. See *sotapatti* in Glossary.

15 A league (*yojana*) is about seven miles.

16 The analytical insights are four advanced capacities of discrimination. See *paṭisambhidā* in Glossary.

17 Brahma is one of the highest gods and presides over various heavens.

18 Canonical sources commonly divide the Buddha's teachings into nine genres or styles: *suttas,* recitations, expositions, verses, inspired utterances, quotations, birth stories, teachings of wonders, and questions-and-answers (listed at *Miln* 3.498).

19 The Three Baskets of scripture are the *suttas,* the *vinaya,* and the *abhidhamma* (see Glossary). The *suttas'* five collections (*nikāyas*) are the four main books and a fifth collection of miscellaneous books.

20 Understanding, sometimes translated as wisdom, is a specific attainment of grasping the truth. See *paññā* in Glossary.

2 Questions of Milinda

1 These most evil acts are killing one's mother, father, or an arhat; spilling the blood of a buddha; and causing a schism in the monastic order.

2 The five categories of phenomenal states listed here—form (*rūpa*), feeling (*vedanā*), perception (*saññā*), habitual patterns (*saṅkhāra*), and awareness (*viññāṇa*)—constitute a standard Buddhist analysis of the human being according to the five "clusters" (*khandhas*) said to explain human experience without reference to a permanent, unchanging self. See Glossary for the Pali terms.

3 Vasil'kov (1993: 68–69) suggests that the detail that Milinda rides off on a horse rather than his chariot indicates his defeat in the contest with Nagasena.

4 Sabbadinna's name means "All is given," so this incident involves wordplay when King Milinda wonders whether Sabbadinna is resisting the order that he give (*deti*) to all (*sabba*). Perhaps also intended is play with the other minister's name, Mankura, when Sabbadinna becomes abashed (*maṅku*). Anantakaya and Devamantiya may be Indianized versions of Antiochus and Demetrious.

5 By these gestures of etiquette and taking a low seat, King Milinda is positioning himself as coming to Nagasena to learn, rather than continuing the public debate of the earlier discussion.

6 See *paññā* (understanding) and *dhamma* (phenomenal states) in Glossary.

7 What is translated here as "earnest disciple" is literally a "practitioner of yoga" in the broad sense of spiritual discipline.

8 See Glossary for *sīla* (moral discipline), *viriya* (exertion), *sati* (mindfulness), *samādhi* (concentration), and *dhamma* (phenomenal states). These experiences are good (*kusala*) in that they are blameless, healthy, and skillful.

9 See Glossary for these technical terms: *indriya* (faculty), *bala* (power), *bojjhaṅga* (awakening factors), *satipaṭṭhāna* (foundation of mindfulness), *sammappadhāna* (right striving), *iddhipāda* (basis of supernatural power), *jhāna* (meditative absorption), *vimokkha* (deliverances), *samādhi* (concentration). The attainments (*samāpatti*) are usually a list of meditative achievements that include the four *jhānas* and four (sometimes five) additional sublime states.

10 Hindrances are certain internal phenomena that block spiritual progress. See *nīvaraṇa* in Glossary.

11 Stream entry (*sotapatti*) is an advanced spiritual achievement whereby one will attain nibbana within seven lifetimes; once return (*sakadāgāma*) means one will achieve nibbana in one's next life. Nonreturn (*anāgāma*) means that one will attain nibbana in this life. See Glossary under these Pali terms.

12 Calm meditation is the use of the *jhānas* to bring about peace. See *samatha* in Glossary. Insight meditation is *vipassanā.*

13 In Indian lore, the wheel-turning emperor has seven marvelous "treasures," one of which is a prime minister.

14 The defilements are the *kilesas,* usually greed, hatred, and delusion. See Glossary.

15 One of the Buddha's close disciples, Sariputta was especially skilled in *abhidhamma* analysis and renowned for his wisdom.

16 This is an *abhidhamma*-style teaching in the *suttas.* In this teaching, feeling (*vedanā*) is variously analyzed and broken down to resist an essentialist understanding of feeling and emotion (*Saṃyuttanikāya* 4.231–233; *Majjhimanikāya* 1.396–400). See Glossary.

17 Name-and-form (*nāmarūpa*) is a shorthand way of describing and

classifying the constantly changing phenomena that constitute a person; form (*rūpa*) in this context refers to the experience of material phenomena, and name (*nāma*), to the experience of mental activities and awareness. See Glossary under *nāmarūpa.*

18 These twelve links starting with ignorance constitute the central teaching of dependent origination.Sensory contact is when one of the six sense organs touches the sense object. See *phassa* in Glossary.

19 Awareness (*viññāṇa*) is the act of being conscious of something; see Glossary.

20 In other words, salt, or perhaps better, saltiness, is perceived only with the tongue. But salt goes along with other features in a sensory field (it is seen to be brought in carts, it is felt to be heavy) that can be perceived by the other senses.

21 Milinda uses the second person plural here and often throughout the dialogues: "you Buddhists say."

22 This may refer to a monastic water pot that suspends the water over a filter before use. However, Vasil'kov (1993: 72–73) suggests that it is a Greek object, the clepsydra, or water clock, which also works well for the illustration; he notes a similar discussion with this same object by Empedocles.

23 This is a play on "the conduct of Brahma" (*brahmacariya*), usually translated as "celibacy," but here the literal meaning is queried.

24 "Island" can refer to a place between two bodies of water. It is not clear which Alexandria is being referred to here. There may have been as many as seventy newly founded cities called Alexandria after the Macedonian conqueror, though not all of them have been discovered (Halkias 2014: 67).

25 There is some ambiguity in the Pali here: the translation could also be "one is not awakened by the factor of the investigation into phenomenal states without the other six awakening factors," an interpretation more in keeping with Theravada orthodoxy (see Levman 2021: 122–124).

26 The question seems to involve a popular expression in which one can refer to water with the word for ocean. The answer makes use of a pun that works only in the Pali, because the word ocean, *samudda,* is constructed from *sama* (equal) and *udaka* (water).

27 This question comes from a frequent saying of the Buddha, that just as the ocean has one taste, the taste of salt, the Dhamma and the

vinaya have but one taste, the taste of freedom (at *Aṅguttaranikāya* 4.203, for example).

28 "Dhamma" can refer to the teaching and the truth, but it is also the word for phenomenal states. See *Miln* 2.20 and 2.37, where understanding has as one of its defining characteristics *cutting through,* which carries the sense of breaking down for analysis.

3 Ram Horn Dilemmas I: The Great Chapter

1 The "descendants of the Victor" (*jinaputta*) or those "in the lineage of the Victor" are the Buddha's sons or children, a term that uses kinship language for monastics.

2 The Bodhi Tree was the place the Buddha attained nibbana, according to legend, at age thirty-five. His passing away at age eighty is an event known as his "final nibbana" (*parinibbāna*).

3 The three attainments here are likely human happiness, divine happiness, and nibbana (see *Miln* 6.98).

4 All of these stories are from the commentary on the *Dhammapada.* Chincha belonged to a rival order. In an attempt to ruin the Buddha's reputation, she was involved in a plot to feign pregnancy and claim that the Buddha was the father of the child. The plot was exposed, and the earth swallowed her up (*Dhammapada-aṭṭhakathā* 3.178–182). Suppabuddha was the father-in-law of the Buddha and was angry at the Buddha for abandoning his daughter, Bhaddakaccana (also called Yashodhara), at the time of his renunciation. Suppabuddha was also the father of Devadatta and the uncle of the Buddha. Once he got drunk and menacingly blocked the Buddha's path. For this he entered the earth (3.44–47). Devadatta, the Buddha's cousin, was a monk in the order, yet is widely depicted as having become a hostile rival. Nanda was swallowed up by the earth for having raped the nun Uppalavanna (2.47–50).

5 The first three states are the view that humans have a fixed identity, the experience of doubt, and the misconception that morality and ritual are enough.

6 The five states are the first three states mentioned previously, plus ill will and sensual desire.

7 The ten stages are the previous five and five more: craving for material form, craving for nonmaterial existence, conceit, restlessness, and ignorance.

8 Flaws (*āsavas*) are corrupting dipositions that are fully eradicated by arhats, who are then known as "those with flaws destroyed." See *āsava* in Glossary.

9 A solitary buddha (*paccekabuddha*) is a buddha who discovers the Dhamma on his own but does not teach it to others; he is "solitary" in that he does not have a following. Solitary buddhas are present in eras between the dispensations of perfectly awakened buddhas.

10 The ten powers of a buddha are that he knows what is possible and what is not possible; the results of past, present, and future karma; the ways leading to all destinations; the world with all its elements; the various inclinations of beings; the different faculties of creatures and humans; the defilements as they emerge and as they are purified in the *jhānas,* the deliverances, concentrations, and attainments; his past lives; and the past and future lives and karma of all beings; and that he has directly realized perfect freedom of mind and of understanding (*Majjhimanikāya* 1.70–71).

11 The four confidences of a buddha are full confidence that he is fully awakened, has destroyed the flaws, has removed all obstacles, and can teach others (*Majjhimanikāya* 1.71–72).

12 The eighteen special attributes of a buddha are alluded to only at the commentarial level, not enumerated (see Endo 1990: 167 for a Sanskrit list).

13 To refute his opponents, the Buddha performed the Twin Miracle at Sāvatthī: parading on a jeweled walkway in the sky, he created pairs of opposing phenomena like fire and water streaming from his body, along with rays of colored light casting to the heavens.

14 *Pīṭhara* is unclear, and I follow Horner and Rhys Davids in guessing at "baskets."

15 In the myth of the wheel-turning emperor, the sovereignty and legitimacy of the universal emperor are symbolized by his possession of seven treasures (listed at *Miln* 3.654), including the treasure of a wheel, that appear at his bidding.

16 The great gift of Vessantara was when he gave away his beloved children, Jali and Kanhajina, and his wife, Maddi. For a translation, see Cone and Gombrich 1977.

17 Their stories are briefly told at *Miln* 3.567, except for that of the slave woman Punna; she was said to have succeeded in persuading the Buddha to stay longer in the company of the wealthy merchant Anathapindaka. For this she became Anathapindaka's daughter

before becoming a nun and an arhat (Malalasekera 1995: vol. 2, 228).

18 They are mentioned at *Miln* 3.565-566 for their moral discipline and gift giving, which allowed them to go to heaven in human form.

19 An "act of truth" in Indian lore is a public declaration of a truth that can have magical power to repair a situation or provide a boon to the speaker.

20 *Gandhabba* here refers to a being driven by karma to rebirth; it appears at conception (*Majjhimanikāya* 1.265–266). The term for conception means literally "entry or descent into the womb."

21 Mahāpanāda's story is told in *Suruci Jātaka,* #489, and King Kusa's is told in *Kusa Jātaka,* #531.

22 This is to say that the Bodhisatta was each of these three persons in his previous lives.

23 I have supplied "karma" here, as what follows makes it clear that residual bad karma is meant.

24 The three knowledges are the remembrance of one's past lives, the ability to see where and why others are reborn, and the knowledge of the destruction of the flaws. The six higher knowledges are recollection of past lives, the divine eye, knowledge of the destruction of the defilements, magical powers, knowing the minds of others, and the divine ear (see *abhiññā* in Glossary).

25 Bad action *(dukkaṭa)* is also a class of offense in the *vinaya.*

26 Although Dhamma is sometimes considered to be the doctrinal teachings of the *suttas* in distinction to the *vinaya,* the monastic rules, here Dhamma is much more widely conceived to include the *vinaya,* as suggested by the commentary. The suggestion is that the Buddha taught about the lesser and minor rules as he laid them down on the occasions of the first offenses (*Ṭīkā* 144).

27 In the *Cūḷa-Mālunkya Sutta* (*Majjhimanikāya* 1.426–432) the monk Malunkyaputta says he will not continue as a monk unless the Buddha answers questions about whether the world is eternal or not, about the body and the soul, and about whether or not buddhas exist after final nibbana. The Buddha remains silent on these questions.

28 Truth *(sacca)* here can also refer specifically to the Four Noble Truths.

29 Protective charms are powerful words that can safeguard people,

and as here, they include several standard *suttas* often used for their magical efficacy.

30 The young crops are like clouds presumably because they swell with water.

31 The story is told in *Jātaka* #436.

32 The Pali here is spare, and throughout this paragraph I have added language implied by context to the effect that these obstacles occur in the context of giving a gift or alms.

33 *Saññāvimokkha,* "having perception as a ground for acquittal," is a specific type of *vinaya* term (see Horner 2015: xlviii–l, in which she consulted Bhikkhu Ñāṇamoli).

34 This dilemma suggests a clash of hierarchies. If the Dhamma and the advanced stages it makes possible, such as stream entry, is the best thing, why would a stream winner who happens to be a layman have to greet an ordinary monk as his superior?

35 *Arhati,* worth or to be worthy of, repeated throughout here, is playing on "arhat," but it is impossible to work this wordplay into the English.

36 This is the *Aggikkhandhūpama Sutta* (*Aṅguttaranikāya* 4.128–135), one of the Buddha's hellfire sermons, in which he taught in vivid terms of the blazing fires and tortures of hell that await an immoral or hypocritical monk. Hearing the sermon, sixty of the monks vomited hot blood, sixty further monks left the monkhood, while sixty others were liberated.

37 Plantain and bamboo destroy the parent plant when they fruit. It was commonly believed that a female mule would die if she foaled.

38 The sheathed private parts or penis is said to be one of the thirty-two marks of the Buddha in the *Lakkhaṇa Sutta* in the *Dīghanikāya,* though scholars are unclear on exactly what it means.

39 The story of Nanda, the Buddha's half-brother, who was deeply in love with his wife and did not want to become a monk, describes the Buddha's intervention to change his mind. He took him to heaven to behold the celestial damsels (*apsarases*) with whom he would dally in the next life should he embrace monasticism in this life. Their heavenly beauty made Nanda disenchanted with his human wife.

40 The story of Culla Panthaka is found in several places. He was a bit of a dullard, so his brother made him leave the monastery.

The Buddha gave him a piece of cloth and an opportunity to concentrate, whereupon he became awakened.

41 This famous episode of the laying down of the first *vinaya* rule was prompted by the monk Sudinna's sexual infraction. The Buddha spoke to him harshly and identified the first rule as a "rule of defeat," a rule requiring monks to defrock.

42 Shame and apprehension are two highly valued moral sentiments that protect one from wrongdoing and act in some respects like a conscience; shame (*hiri*) is being abashed at the prospect of doing something wrong, and apprehension (*ottappa*) is fearing the effects of wrong action.

43 *Jātaka* #307.

44 *Jātaka* #475.

45 The Recitation of the Dhamma is the First Council, when the monks recited and codified the scriptures. This famous episode is in the *Mahāparinibbāna Sutta* (*Dīghanikāya* 2.128), where Cunda gave alms and the Buddha got sick.

46 The Buddha said this concerning the almsgiving of Sujata on the eve of his awakening and again at Cunda's almsgiving. He says this to comfort Cunda and so that Cunda will not be blamed for the Buddha's death (*Dīghanikāya* 2.136).

47 The almsfood given by Cunda was called "pig's delight." Scholars disagree about whether the meal was pork or something pigs enjoy, such as truffles.

48 Before his final nibbana, the Buddha entered nine meditative states: the first four *jhānas,* then the sphere of infinite space, the sphere of infinite consciousness, the sphere of nothingness, the sphere of neither perception nor nonperception, and then the cessation of feeling and perception (*Dīghanikāya* 2.156).

49 The Buddha told this to Ananda shortly before his final nibbana, but he went on to describe the preparation of the relics by Kshatriyas, Brahmans, and householders (*Dīghanikāya* 2.141).

50 "Language styles" (*bhāsamaggaṃ*) is a bit unclear, but following usage, a *mārga* (Pali, *magga*) can be a way or a path of literary composition, so perhaps here we have the translation "language styles."

51 Destroying the flaws (*khīnāsava*) means one is an arhat.

52 The "rigidities" (*khila*) are forms of mental "barrenness," and are said to be greed, hatred, and delusion at *Saṃyuttanikāya* 5.57.

53 This happened when five hundred monks, headed by Sariputta and Moggallana, came into a grove in which the Buddha was staying and were noisy, so the Buddha asked that they go away (*Majjhimanikāya* 1.456–462).

54 "Final nibbana" is the term for the passing away of an arhat or buddha. The *suttas* describe how Moggallana was horribly murdered by brigands.

55 The Recitation of the Rules (*pātimokkhuddesa*) is the fortnightly ritual recitation of the *vinaya* rules by monks or nuns. Laypeople are not permitted to be present.

56 The "boundary" (*sīmā*) marks the region or the parish in which all monastics living there gather to recite the rules.

57 The exact groups named by this list are in some instances unclear.

58 The *Ṭīkā* says that the city of Savara, or Savage, is a town of rustics.

59 A "defeat" is the most serious monastic violation and involves permanent expulsion from the order. Telling a deliberate lie about one's spiritual attainments is considered a defeat.

60 See *Vinaya* 4.1–4 and *Vinaya* 3.59, where a deliberate lie is considered a monastic offense that can be expiated (*pācittiya*). This does not include a deliberate lie about having reached advanced spiritual attainments, which is a special case. For ordinary lies, expiation involves disclosing or confessing the matter to just one other monk or nun.

61 We do not have a discourse called "on the nature of things," but it is likely that Milinda is referring to the *Mahāpadāna Sutta* in the *Dīghanikāya*, which describes some of the matters in this dilemma and often refers to them as the "nature of things" or matters of "universal rule" (*dhammatā*).

62 Monks and nuns are obliged to eat before noon.

63 In their final lives, bodhisattas must be born into one of these two top classes.

64 This refers to a *vinaya* case where a monk, intending to commit suicide, threw himself down a ravine but wound up hitting and killing someone. He survived and was subjected to a monastic penalty (*Vinaya* 3.82).

65 "The jewel treasure": a magical gemstone held by world-turning emperors, one of their seven treasures.

66 These many torments are given in the *Greater Discourse on the Mass of Suffering Sutta* (*sutta* 13 in the *Majjhimanikāya*).

67 I remain stumped by *cadika,* translated here as "with waves curving into the nooks," in *ūmikavankacadika,* as were Horner and Rhys Davids, and am guessing at the sense.

68 The many anecdotes that follow are from *Jātaka* stories of the Bodhisatta's previous births.

69 This simile likens the rarity of achieving birth as a human to the likelihood that a blind sea turtle in the ocean who surfaces for breath once a century would be likely to poke its head through a yoke floating on the surface (*Majjhimanikāya* 3.169).

70 This verse is said in the *Kuṇāḷa Jātaka* (#536). The ensuing story of Amara is told in the *Mahāummagga Jātaka* (#546).

71 This account differs in several respects from the way it is told in the *Cullahaṁsa Jātaka* (#533) and at *Vinaya* 2.194, not least in that in these tellings, the arhats and disciples around the Buddha did not flee (although in the *Vinaya* version they do request to turn back, which the Buddha denies). It was Devadatta who set this fierce elephant, then called Nalagiri, on the Buddha.

72 This story is the *Catumā Sutta* (*sutta* 67) in the *Majjhimanikāya.* It tells of how the Buddha dismissed a large group of noisy monks but then was appeased by being told that the monks were young, like seedlings and calves, and needed the care of the Buddha.

73 This is said in the *Vinaya* (*Cullavagga* 6.5) on the occasion when the Buddha began to permit houses to be built for the monks; prior to that he insisted that they live as homeless renouncers. In this context, the Buddha permits lodgings because of the shelter they provide; this makes the gift of a residence by laypeople highly praised. But the passage does not mention the benefit for nuns that Nagasena will bring up in this dilemma.

74 The four fruits of renunciation are stream entry (*sotapatti*), once return (*sakadāgāma*), nonreturn (*anāgāma*), and arhatship (*arahatta*); the eight attainments are the four *jhānas* and the four further planes of concentration: experiencing infinite space, infinite consciousness, nothingness, and neither perception nor nonperception.

75 Here "Brahman" is used to indicate, as Buddhist texts sometimes do, not a class distinction but a moral one.

76 The *Ṭīkā* says that "outside scriptures" refers to Ayurveda.

77 Some of these lists are mentioned at *Miln* 3.47. The six exclusive

knowledges are knowledge of: others' dispositions; others' temperaments, great compassion, how to do the twin miracle, how to remove obstacles, and omniscient knowledge (as listed at *Jātaka-aṭṭhakathā* 1.78).

78 The commentator on the *Suttanipāta* says that cattle are destroyed at this blood sacrifice in multiples of seventeen (Bodhi 2017). The story is *Jātaka* #433. In it the Bodhisatta performs a royal sacrifice in which many beasts are killed before he becomes filled with remorse, though the sacrifice is not mentioned as the "*vājapeyya*."

79 This is *Jātaka* #514, in which the Bodhisatta, as Six Tusks, is struck by the arrows of a man disguised in a monk's robe and utters this verse.

80 This story is told in the *Ghaṭīkāra Sutta* (*Majjhimanikāya* 2.45–54).

81 This story is told in the *Ghaṭīkāra Sutta* (*Majjhimanikāya* 2.45–54). Ghaṭīkāra is thrilled when his grass thatch roof is removed and given to Kassapa.

82 These statements occur at *Miln* 3.277 and 3.279-280.

83 The Brahman Bharadvaja worked in the fields and urged the Buddha to do likewise; the Buddha countered with verses about his religious work and was then offered food by the Brahman. The Buddha recited the verse mentioned in this discussion about not accepting alms for teachings and rejected the offering (*Kasibhāradvāja Sutta* in the *Suttanipāta*).

84 These two almsgivings refer to the two highly meritorious almsgivings discussed in the dilemma beginning on *Miln* 3.256.

85 Alara Kalama was a teacher with whom the Bodhisatta studied after his renunciation but before he struck out on his own and attained awakening. Another such teacher in this period was Uddaka Ramaputta, mentioned below.

86 Buddhists revere three jewels: the jewel of the Buddha, the jewel of the Dhamma, and the jewel of the community (*saṅgha*).

87 This story is in the third *sutta* of the *Majjhimanikāya*. In it the Buddha emphasizes that his disciples are inheritors of the Dhamma, not of material things. Taking this to heart, one monk refuses the Buddha's leftover food though he is hungry and weak, claiming that he is heir of the Dhamma, not of the Buddha's property, and the Buddha approves of this. A second monk takes the food and is said to be less praiseworthy

than the first monk.

88 The four branches of morality are listed at *Visuddhimagga* 1.42: following the monastic rules, practicing proper conduct and alms gathering, fearing the slightest fault, and undertaking the training precepts.

89 There are three realms in which beings are born in samsara: the realm of desire (hells, the worlds of animals, humans, and ghosts, and the lower heavens), heavenly worlds of form, and heavenly formless worlds.

90 Exhaustion and drowsiness *(thīnamiddham)* are two items treated as one. Usually they are together considered a hindrance ("lethargy and listlessness") that arhats are said to overcome. Here I take it to be the physical demand of needing rest.

91 A "defeat" (*pārājika*) is an offense that requires monks and nuns to be disrobed. It is not a term that applies to householders. The Sinhalese commentary cited by Rhys Davids says that a *pārājika* for householders would be matricide, patricide, injuring the Bodhi Tree, murdering an arhat, or raping a nun (Rhys Davids 1890: vol. 2, 78, n. 1).

92 "Realize fully the Dhamma" (*dhammābhisamaya*) means fully understanding the Dhamma, and thus being converted to it.

93 This specific assertion has not been traced in the sources, despite Milinda's claiming that Buddhists have said it. The Buddha did teach, however, that remorse (*kukkucca*), that is, agitation and restlessness over wrongdoing, is among the five hindrances to spiritual progress (as at *Dīghanikāya* 1.246, for example).

94 This story is from the *Kāliṅga Bodhi Jātaka* (#479). According to tradition, no one can pass over, whether by land or through the air, the circular base of the Bodhi Tree.

95 *Vekaṭikavekaṭikaṃ* as "various kinds of unclean food" is unclear.

96 Proliferating thoughts (*papañca*) are the tendency of the mind to construct, amplify, and multiply conceptions, distinctions, and mental commentary that overlay basic experience.

97 Arhatship is the state of having attained nibbana. See *arahatta* in Glossary. To achieve the "fruit" of each of these advanced states is to have completely fulfilled it.

98 The Pali implies "conducive to," which I have supplied.

99 That is, one has taken something—ordination—that has not been given.

100 I have supplied "with nibbana" here in the first statement, following "it is incompatible," as it is implicit in the claim.

101 The ten bad courses of action are killing, stealing, sexual misconduct, lying, malicious speech, harsh speech, idle chatter, covetousness, ill will, and holding wrong views.

102 I have gone with the translation "what is proven and unproven" for *siddhāsiddha*, in the sense of what medicine is successful and not. It may, however, be referring to the Siddha system of healing. Rhys Davids (1890: vol. 2, 109) takes it as "treatment and management," and Horner (2015: vol. 2, 91) as "the (various) diets," following *The Pali Text Society's Pali-English Dictionary* (Rhys Davids and Stede 1921–1925) on *siddha* as formed from *sijjati* in the meaning of cooking.

103 "Harsh, cruel, and dreadful horrors" *(rūḷarūḷassa)* is unclear; the *Ṭīkā* glosses it as *pharusātipharusassa,* "harsh and cruel." There is some ambiguity in the sentence, and the *Ṭīkā* says that *pharusātipharusassa bhīmabhīmassa* modifies Jujaka, though we would expect the instrumental. Horner (2015: vol. 2, 97) takes it to refer to the Bodhisatta ("in great distress and terror"). I follow Rhys Davids that this is the dative case and refers to the horrors to which the children are being led (1890: vol. 2, 115); see also Kachru 2023: 104.

104 Presumably the oxen pulling the vehicle.

105 This "extreme gift" (*atidāna*) is perhaps deliberately ambiguous in that the prefix *ati* can be both "great" and "excessive". On this ambiguity, see Collins 2016: 7–11.

106 In fact, the story has him giving his children to the Brahman Jujaka, but he gives his wife to Sakka, who is merely testing him. For the story, see Cone and Gombrich 1977.

107 The Bodhisatta had worked for countless lives to perfect giving, and the final and hardest perfection of giving—the giving away of those one loves—must be completed before perfection is reached.

108 The children had been living in the forest in hardship as a result of Vessantara's exile. This maneuver will allow the grandfather to ransom them from the Brahman and thereby restore them to the palace.

109 Uposatha is the elephant treasure of a great wheel-turning emperor in the *Mahāsudassana Sutta* (*Dīghanikāya, sutta* 17).

110 These listings are given at *Miln* 3.47 and 3.259.

111 They are mentioned at *Miln* 3.74 in the same context, as are the figures below.

112 A gift of "all the eights" consists of a series of eights: eight elephants, eight horses, eight male slaves, eight female slaves, and so on.

113 The sense of this seems to be that the king is likening himself to partly blind or left-handed people, who should be given a chance at things.

114 The "life-continuum consciousness" (*bhavaṅga*) is the inactive state of the mind resting in itself with no active conscious processes occurring, which here corresponds to deep sleep (Gethin 1994: 11–35).

115 Apparently, monkeys sleep lightly. Or it might be that the mind flits about in this dream sleep, much like a leaping monkey.

116 *Visamopakkamakammehi* ("by the action of carelessness or assault") more naturally this would be "by karma, carelessness, or assault," but that would contravene what Nagasena is relying on this passage to support, which is that karma does not issue in an untimely death.

117 A final nibbana shrine (*cetiya*) refers to a monument standing where a buddha attained final nibbana, that is, death.

118 This entire discussion is drawn from the *Māgandiya Sutta* (*sutta* 75 in *Majjhimanikāya*).

119 Though we expect a list of ten, eleven qualities are given.

4 *A Question Resolved by Inference*

1 Reed workers (*venā*) and hunters (*nesādā*) are terms for particular mixed castes; "slave women carrying water pots" (*kumbhadāsī*) may be a euphemism for harlots.

2 See Schmiedchen 2017 on the identification of these regions and the cosmopolitan conception of this city welcoming people from all over the Indian subcontinent and its borderlands.

3 These advanced meditation practices contemplating ten types of decaying bodies, useful for dismantling lust and vanity, are outlined in detail in the *Visuddhimagga*, ch. 6. Many of the other meditation subjects in this paragraph are also detailed in the *Visuddhimagga*.

4 The monastic rules (*pāṭimokkha*) are the rules for monks and nuns

as they are divided into five recitations according to different classes of rules.

5 The advanced attainments of seeing all things as empty of essence, lacking signs or distinguishing marks, and without any desire.

6 There is a standard sermon describing moral precepts on three different levels of detail repeated at *Dīghanikāya* 2.4–12. The "morality of the path" is probably the four paths: stream entry, once return, nonreturn, and arhatship; the "morality of its fruits" is the moral achievement when the four paths are traveled.

7 The practice of understanding is being able to identify and analyze the contents of experience as they occur. I have inserted "phenomenal states" to make this clear (*dhammas* as phenomena is implied). *Yathābhūta* is most literally "as it has arisen," but here I put it in present tense; *yathābhūta* can also be translated as "as it truly is."

5 *Ram Horn Dilemmas II: Questions and Discussions About Yogis*

1 The "Ram Horn Dilemmas" are divided into nine parts; the first eight constitute chapter 3, while the ninth is this chapter.

The thirteen specific forest ascetic practices discussed in this chapter are listed at *Miln* 5.26.

2 Most of these are in the *Suttanipāta,* and at their conclusions it is said in the *suttas* themselves or in their commentaries that very large numbers of gods became arhats.

3 In this story, the Buddha had made the community promise that he would not be disturbed during a period of seclusion. Upasena nevertheless approached him and was well received.

6 *Questions and Discussions of Analogies*

1 This refers to a story in which starving parents in the wilderness ate their only child. The greasing of the axle suggests just enough to keep going.

2 Someone with the character of bean soup is uneven.

3 That is to say, the Four Noble Truths have three phases: the knowledge of each truth, the knowledge of the task it requires, and the knowledge that the task has been completed. These three

phases applied to the Four Truths are the twelve modes in which they are experienced.

4 The "drawbacks" are having hair and beard (see *Miln* 1.29).

5 The four bases of sympathy of the wheel-turning emperor are generosity, kind speech, beneficial conduct, and impartiality (*Dīghanikāya* 3.152). The fourfold assembly in Buddhism consists of monks, nuns, laymen, and laywomen.

6 The foul topics of meditation are specific practices of studying corpses and the impurities of the body in order to cultivate detachment.

7 The "Hair-Raising Treatise" is how the Buddha referred to the *Great Lion's Roar Sutta* (*Majjhimanikāya, sutta* 12), due to the fierceness of his austerities described in it.

8 Rhys Davids mentions a Sinhala tradition holding that this bird puts her young in the crevice of a tree and guards them there while refusing to feed them, a detail relevant to understanding this analogy (Rhys Davids 1890: vol. 2, 343, n.1).

9 This refers to either practices of meditation in which one discerns the proper characteristic features of one's meditation subject (as suggested by *Vibhaṅga-aṭṭhakathā* 250) or the kinds of definitional practices identifying characteristics of phenomena seen in chapter 2, part 1.

10 A *kinnara* is a mythic bird with a human head. The story referred to describes two *kinnaras,* lovers, who were forced to spend a night apart by a terrible flood. The memory of that night filled them with sorrow for 697 years and caused them to weep whenever they thought of it.

11 Devadatta was the Buddha's chief adversary, Angulimala was a mass murderer, Dhanapala was an elephant who tried to kill the Buddha, and Rahula was the Buddha's son.

12 These are three contemplative gateways to freedom: the empty deliverance is seeing all things as lacking essence; the signless is seeing all things as free of any single definable mark; and the desireless is looking upon all things without craving.

13 That is, items were listed at the start of this chapter that have not been discussed, but the number of the neglected items is 38, not 42, in the manuscripts available to us. It is not clear how the divisions and counts in this paragraph are in evidence in Trenckner's edition and the other editions consulted.

GLOSSARY

abhidhamma one of the three collections of the Buddha's words, and as such, considered canonical scripture; its seven books analyze the components of experience, often by way of ramifying lists and classifications; also a style of technical analysis in keeping with these books

abhiññā (higher knowledges) usually in a list of six supernatural powers: the recollection of past lives, the divine eye, knowledge of the destruction of the defilements, magical powers, knowing the minds of others, and the divine ear

anāgāma (nonreturn) an advanced achievement whereby one will attain nibbana within this lifetime; "nonreturners" have achieved this

arahatta (*arhat*ship) the attainment of becoming an *arhat,* that is, someone who has achieved nibbana

āsava (flaw) one of the corrupting dispositions—sensual desire, being drawn to rebirth, wrong views, and ignorance—that must be destroyed to attain nibbana; "one who has destroyed the flaws" or is "free of the flaws" (*khīṇāsava*) is a common term for *arhat*

āyatana (base of sensory experience) both the sensory organs and their objects, and the operations between them: seeing; hearing; smelling; tasting; touching; and the mind sense, which apprehends the phenomenal states

bala (power) one of five aids in spiritual development: faith, exertion, mindfulness, concentration, and understanding

bojjhaṅga (awakening factor) one of seven main spiritual factors: mindfulness, discriminating phenomenal states, exertion, joy, tranquility, concentration, and equanimity; in the entire system there are thirty-seven awakening factors including the five powers, the five spiritual faculties, the seven main spiritual factors, the eightfold path practices, the four foundations of mindfulness, four right strivings, and the four bases of spiritual power

DHAMMA (1) the Buddha's teaching; also understood to describe the truth or the way things are; (2) (lowercase) "phenomenal state," a constituent of experience listed and analyzed in the *suttas* and to a further degree in the *abhidhamma*

EIGHTFOLD PATH the fourth of the Four Noble Truths, it is the way to achieve nibbana: through right view, right thought, right speech, right action, right livelihood, right effort, right mindfulness, and right concentration

iddhipāda (basis of supernatural power) one of four: that achieved by concentration due to zeal and determined striving, due to exertion and determined striving, due to purity of mind and determined striving, and due to investigation and determined striving; these give magical powers, such as flying through the air and becoming invisible

indriya (faculty) a governing operation of the mind; there are various lists, but the *Milindapañha* emphasizes the five spiritual faculties: faith, exertion, mindfulness, concentration, and understanding

jhāna meditative state of deep alertness in which the mind becomes absorbed in specific objects of attention; there is a sequence of four that are progressively more refined states of awareness

KARMA action; specifically, the morally relevant actions that both are caused by previous conditions and themselves bring about future effects in samsara

khandhas (the clusters) the five composites or groupings of all the phenomena constituting a person's experience: form, feeling, perception, habitual patterns, and awareness; the doctrine of the clusters is used to explain human experience without reference to a permanent, unchanging self or soul

kilesa (defilements) the impure and distressing patterns of thought and experience that must be eliminated to attain nibbana; various lists are given, but the main ones are greed, hatred, and delusion

nāmarūpa (name-and-form) a shorthand way of describing and classifying the constantly changing phenomena that constitute a person; "form" refers to the experience of material phenomena (the first *khandha*), and "name" refers to the experience of mental activities and awareness (the remaining four *khandhas*)

NIBBANA the Pali equivalent of nirvana, often translated as "awakening" or "enlightenment"; more literally, the "blowing out" of all desire, defilement, and suffering, as the ultimate aim of Buddhist practice, when one is free of samsara and will not be reborn

nīvaraṇa (hindrances) five phenomena blocking spiritual progress: desire, ill will, dullness and lethargy, restlessness and anxiety, and doubt

NOBLE TRUTHS the encapsulation of the Buddha's teaching in four basic ideas: (1) there is suffering; (2) there is a cause, or origin, of suffering, namely, craving; (3) there is an end to suffering, namely, nibbana; (4) the Eightfold Path is the way to nibbana

paññā (understanding) wisdom; the correct discernment of the truth; as a technical term, refers to a specific phenomenal state that results from analysis and investigation into phenomena

paṭisambhidā (the analytical insights) four advanced capacities of discrimination: analysis of ends or meaning, of phenomenal states, of language, and of comprehension

phassa (sensory contact) the phenomenal state of the sensory organ touching the sense object

rūpa (form) (1) one of the five *khandhas* that constitute a human being, namely, the category of phenomena that experience the material world; (2) the object of visual sense experience. See also *nāmarūpa*

sakadāgāma (once return) an advanced achievement whereby one will attain nibbana in one's next life; "once returners" have achieved this

samādhi (concentration) both a state and a practice of advanced attention constituting the eighth limb of the Eightfold Path

samatha (calm meditation) specific meditation practices using the *jhānas* and aimed at calming and focusing the mind

sammappadhāna (right striving) exerting oneself so that no bad phenomenal states arise, existing bad states are abandoned, good states arise, and existing good states endure

SAMSARA the world of constant rebirth that ends only when one attains nibbana

saṅkhārā (habitual patterns) conditioned and conditioning karmic activities of the mind that construct experience, including a range of phenomena like intentions, dispositions, patterns of thought, personality traits, processes of memory, and emotional constructs; a classification of phenomena that constitutes one of the five clusters that make up a person

saññā (perception) both the act of sensory intake and recognizing and naming what one perceives;

also one of the five basic clusters that constitute a person

sati (mindfulness) the capacity to bring something into one's awareness and attend to it; also memory

satipaṭṭhāna (foundation of mindfulness) one of four introspective practices: contemplating body in body, feeling in feeling, mind in mind, and phenomenal states in phenomenal states

sīla (moral discipline, morality, moral precepts) variously translated; when referring to the five precepts, the prohibiting of killing, stealing, lying, sexual misconduct, and taking intoxicants

sotapatti (stream entry) advanced spiritual attainment in which one will attain nibbana within seven lifetimes; a "stream winner" has attained this

sutta a teaching or sermon of the Buddha usually given in dialogic form; in the plural, the *suttas* comprise one of the three scriptural collections of the Buddha's word: there are four main books and a large collection of miscellaneous texts

UPOSATHA a formal act of the monastic community to gather and recite the *vinaya* rules and confess violations of them; can also refer to lay practices of undertaking the five moral precepts on Uposatha days

vedanā (feeling) phenomenal state, the hedonic tone or valence in which something is experienced or felt

vimokkha (the deliverances) the stages of release or liberation on the way to nibbana

vinaya one of the three collections or genres of the Buddha's words; its seven books contain the rules for monks and nuns, and exegesis on monastic discipline

viññāṇa (awareness) the act of being conscious or aware of something, often conceived as a momentary phenomenon

vipassanā (insight meditation) advanced meditation that involves an epiphany of understanding that all things are impermanent, suffering, and without essence

viriya (exertion) a spiritual faculty that involves steadfast effort and striving

BIBLIOGRAPHY

Editions and Translations

The Milindapañho: Being Dialogues between King Milinda and the Buddhist Sage Nāgasena. 1890. Edited by V. Trenckner. London: Pali Text Society. Digitized by the Dhammakaya Foundation, Khlong Song, Thailand, 2015.

Milindaṭīkā. 1961. Edited by P. S. Jaini. London: Pali Text Society.

Milindapañha. 1994. Edited by the Buddha Jayanti Tripitaka Series. Maharagama, Sri Lanka: Sri Lanka Tripitaka Project.

Suttantapiṭake Khuddakanikāye Milindapañha. 1998. Edited by the Chaṭṭha Saṅgāyana. Igatpuri: Vipassana Research Institute. http://www.tipitaka.org.

Milindapañha-aṭṭhakathā. 1999. Edited by Madhav Despande. Tokyo: International Institute for Buddhist Studies.

The Questions of King Milinda. 1890. Translated by T. W. Rhys Davids. 2 vols. Oxford: Clarendon Press.

Milinda's Questions. 2015. Translated by I. B. Horner. 2 vols. Bristol, U.K.: Pali Text Society. Originally published 1963.

Other Sources

Baums, Stefan. 2018. "Greek or Indian? The Questions of Menander and Onomastic Patterns in Early Gandhāra." In *Buddhism in Gandhāra: An Archaeology of Museum Collections,* ed. H. P. Ray. New York: Routledge, pp. 33–46.

Bodhi, Bhikkhu, trans. 2017. *The Suttanipāta.* Somerville, Mass.: Wisdom Publications.

Boisvert, Mathieu. 2000. "Conception and Intrauterine Life in the Pāli Canon." *Studies in Religion* 29, 3: 301–311.

Bopearachchi, Osmund. 2020. *When West Met East: Gandhāran Art Revisited.* 2 vols. New Delhi: Manohar Publishers & Distributors.

Collins, Steven, ed. 2016. *Readings of the Vessantara Jātaka.* New York: Columbia University Press.

Cone, Margaret. 2001. *A Dictionary of Pāli, Part I: A-Kh.*Oxford: Pali Text Society.

———. 2010. *A Dictionary of Pāli, Part II: G-N.* Bristol, U.K.: Pali Text Society.

———. 2020. *A Dictionary of Pāli, Part III: P-Bh.* Bristol, U.K.: Pali Text Society.

Cone, Margaret, and Richard Gombrich, trans. 1977. *The Perfect Generosity of Prince Vessantara.* Oxford: Clarendon Press.

Demiéville, Paul. 1924. "Les versions chinoises du *Milindapañha.*" *Bulletin de l'École française d'Extrême-Orient* 24: 1–258.

Endo, Toshiichi. 1990. "Some Significant Epithets and Qualities of the Buddha as Found in the *Milindapañha.*" In *Ānanda: Papers on Buddhism and Indology.* Columbo, Sri Lanka: State Printing Corporation, pp. 160–171.

Gerow, Edwin. 1977. *Indian Poetics.* Wiesbaden: Otto Harrassowitz.

Gethin, R. M. L. 1992. *The Buddhist Path to Awakening: A Study of the Bodhi-Pakkhiyā Dhammā.* Leiden: E. J. Brill.

———. 1994. "Bhavaṅga and Rebirth According to the Abhidhamma." *The Buddhist Forum,* Vol. 3. London: School of Oriental and African Studies, pp. 11–35.

Gonda, Jan. 1949a. *Remarks on Similes in Sanskrit Literature.* Leiden: E. J. Brill.

———. 1949b. "Tern's Hypothesis on the Origin of the *Milindapañha.*" *Mnemosyne* 2, 1: 44–62.

Halkias, Georgios T. 2014. "When the Greeks Converted the Buddha: Asymmetrical Transfers of Knowledge in Indo-Greek Cultures." In *Religions and Trade: Religious Formation, Transformation and Cross-Cultural Exchange between East and West,* ed. P. Wick and V. Rabens. Leiden: E. J. Brill, pp. 65–115.

Kachru, Sonam. 2023. "The *Milindapañha:* How to Use a Philosophical Resource and Find a Literary Gem." In *The Routledge Handbook of Indian Buddhist Philosophy,* ed. W. Edelglass, P. J. Harter, and S. McClintock. London: Routledge, pp. 97–112.

Kubica, Olga. 2014. "Beyond Influence: A Reflection on the History of Research on the *Milindapañha,* with a Comparison of the Text to the *Kitab al khazari.*" *Eos* 101: 187–206.

———. 2016. "Greek Literature and Cultural Life East of the Euphrates: The Greeks and Buddhism." *Eos* 103: 143–147.

———. 2021. "Reading the *Milindapañha:* Indian Historical Sources and the Greeks in Bactria." In *The Graeco-Bactrian and Indo-Greek World,* ed. Rachel Mairs. New York: Routledge, pp. 430–445.

Lamotte, Étienne. 1988. *History of Indian Buddhism from the Origins to the Śaka Era.* Translated by Sarah Webb-Boin. Publications de l'Institut orientaliste de Louvain 36. Louvain-la-Neuve: Université catholique de Louvain, Institut orientaliste.

Langenberg, Amy. 2017. *Birth in Buddhism: The Suffering Fetus and Female Freedom.* London: Routledge.

Levman, Bryan. 2021. "Revisiting *Milindapañha.*" *Journal Asiatique* 309, 1: 107–130.

Malalasekera, G. P. 1995. *Dictionary of Pāli Proper Names.* 2 vols. New Delhi: Munshiram Manoharlal Publishers.

McDermott, James P. 1977. "Kamma in the *Milindapañha.*" *Journal of the American Oriental Society* 97, 4: 460–468.

Mendis, N. K. G., ed. 2001. *The Questions of King Milinda: An Abridgement of the Milindapañha.* With an introduction by Bhikkhu Bodhi. Kandy, Sri Lanka: Buddhist Publication Society. Original edition, 1993.

Mori, Sodo. 1998–1999. "The *Milindapañha* and the Pāli *Aṭṭhakathā* Literature." *Indologica Taurinensia* 23–24: 291–312.

Murdoch, Iris. 2010. *The Sovereignty of Good.* London: Routledge. Original edition, 1971.

Narain, A. K. 1989. "The Greeks of Bactria and India." In *Cambridge Ancient History.* Vol. 8: *Rome and the Mediterranean to 133 BC.* 2nd ed. Ed. A. E. Astin et al. Cambridge: Cambridge University Press, pp. 388–421.

Obeyesekere, Ranjini., trans. 1991. *Jewels of the Doctrine: Stories of the Saddharma Ratnāvaliya.* Albany: State University of New York Press.

Ooi, Eng Jin. 2021. "Survey of the Pāli *Milindapañha* Manuscripts Kept at the National Library of Thailand: A Brief Catalog." *Journal of the Siam Society* 109, 1: 169–210.

Ooi, Eng Jin, Andrew Schumann, and Natchapol Sirisawad. 2023. "Defining a *Meṇḍaka* Question in the *Questions of Milinda* and Its Commentarial Texts." *Journal of Indian Philosophy,* 1–23.

Pesela, Bhikkhu, trans. 1991. *The Debate of King Milinda: An Abridgement of the Milindapañha.* Delhi: Motilal Banarsidass.

Potter, Karl. 1996. "*Milindapañha.*" In *Encyclopedia of Indian Philosophies.* Vol. 3: *Abhidharma Buddhism to 150 A.D.,* ed. K. Potter et al. Delhi: Motilal Banarsidass: 471–488.

Rhys Davids, T. W., and William Stede. 1921–1925. *The Pali Text Society's Pali-English Dictionary.* Oxford: Pali Text Society.

Salomon, Richard. 2018 *The Buddhist Literature of Ancient Gandhāra: An Introduction with Selected Translations.* Somerville, Mass.: Wisdom.

Schmiedchen, Annette. 2017. "The Description of Sāgala (Present-Day Sailkot) in an Ancient Buddhist Text." *Ancient Pakistan* 28: 61–68.

Schumann, Andrew. 2019. "On the Origin of Indian Logic from the Viewpoint of the Pali Canon." *Logica Universalis* 13: 347–393.

Sick, David. 2007. "When Socrates Met the Buddha: Greek and Indian Dialectic in Hellenistic Bactria and India." *Journal of the Royal Asiatic Society,* Series 3, 17, 3: 253–278.

Skilling, Peter. 1998. "A Note on King Milinda in the *Abhidharmakośabhāṣya.*" *Journal of the Pali Text Society* 24: 81–101.

———. 2010. "Problems with Milinda (1): The Opening Verses and Prose of the Printed Siamese *Milindapañha.*" *Journal for the Centre of Buddhist Studies, Sri Lanka* 8: 1–24.

Stoneman, Richard. 2019. *The Greek Experience of India: From Alexander to the Indo-Greeks.* Princeton, N.J.: Princeton University Press.

Tarn, W. W., 1938. *The Greeks in Bactria and India.* Cambridge: Cambridge University Press.

Thich, Minh Châu. 1964. *Milindapañha and Nāgasenabhikshusūtra: A Comparative Study through Pāli and Chinese Sources.* Calcutta: Firma K. L. Mukhopadhyay.

Vasil'kov, Yaroslav. 1993. "Did East and West Really Meet in Milinda's Questions?" *Kul'turologiia: The Petersburg Journal of Cultural Studies* 1, 1: 64–77.

von Hinüber, Oskar. 1987. "The Oldest Dated Manuscript of the *Milindapañha.*" *Journal of the Pali Text Society* 11: 111–118.

———. 1988. "An Additional Note on the Oldest Dated Manuscript of the *Milindapañha.*" *Journal of the Pali Text Society* 12: 173–174.

———. 1997. *A Handbook of Pali Literature.* New Delhi: Munshiram Manoharlal.

INDEX

ABOUT THE BOOK

Murty Classical Library of India volumes are designed by Rathna Ramanathan and Guglielmo Rossi. Informed by the history of the Indic book and drawing inspiration from polyphonic classical music, the series design is based on the idea of "unity in diversity," celebrating the individuality of each language while bringing them together within a cohesive visual identity.

The Pali and English texts are set in Antwerp, designed by Henrik Kubel from A2-TYPE and chosen for its versatility and balance with the Indic typography. The design is a free-spirited amalgamation and interpretation of the archives of type at the Museum Plantin-Moretus in Antwerp.

All the fonts commissioned for the Murty Classical Library of India will be made available, free of charge, for non-commercial use. For more information about the typography and design of the series, please visit *http://www.hup.harvard.edu/mcli.*

Printed on acid-free paper by Maple Press, York, Pennsylvania.